SAN JOAQUIN VALLEY LIBRARY
W9-AKJ-258

60984 81800

The Greenwood Encyclopedia of American Poets and Poetry

Advisory Board

The Greenwood Encyclopedia of AMERICAN POETS AND POETRY

Volume 5

S – Z

Jeffrey Gray, Editor
James McCorkle and Mary McAleer Balkun, Associate Editors

GREENWOOD PRESS
WESTPORT, CONNECTICUT • LONDON

Library of Congress Cataloging-in-Publication Data

The Greenwood encyclopedia of American poets and poetry / Jeffrey Gray, editor ; James McCorkle and Mary McAleer Balkun, associate editors.
p. cm.
Includes bibliographical references and index.
ISBN 0-313-32381-X (set : alk. paper) — ISBN 0-313-33009-3 (v. 1 : alk. paper) — ISBN 0-313-33010-7 (v. 2 : alk. paper) — ISBN 0-313-33011-5 (v. 3 : alk. paper) — ISBN 0-313-33012-3 (v. 4 : alk. paper) — ISBN 0-313-33013-1 (v. 5 : alk. paper)
1. American poetry—Encyclopedias. 2. Poets, American—Biography—Encyclopedias. I. Gray, Jeffrey, 1944- II. McCorkle, James. III. Balkun, Mary McAleer.
PS303.G74 2006
811.00903–dc22 2005025445

British Library Cataloguing in Publication Data is available.

Library of Congress Catalog Card Number: 2005025445
ISBN: 0-313-32381-X (set)
0-313-33009-3 (vol. 1)
0-313-33010-7 (vol. 2)
0-313-33011-5 (vol. 3)
0-313-33012-3 (vol. 4)
0-313-33013-1 (vol. 5)

First published in 2006

Greenwood Press, 88 Post Road West, Westport, CT 06881
An imprint of Greenwood Publishing Group, Inc.
www.greenwood.com

Printed in the United States of America

The paper used in this book complies with the Permanent Paper Standard issued by the National Information Standards Organization (Z39.48–1984).

10 9 8 7 6 5 4 3 2 1

Copyright Acknowledgments

The author and publisher gratefully acknowledge permission to use the following material:

"Four Motions for the Pea Vines," "Motion," "Small Songs," and "Still" from *Collected Poems 1951–1971* by A. R. Ammons. Copyright © 1972 by A. R. Ammons. Used by permission of W. W. Norton & Company, Inc. "Easter Morning," from *A Coast of Trees* by A. R. Ammons. Copyright © 1981 by A. R. Ammons. Used by permission of W. W. Norton & Company, Inc.

"Paradise and Method" from *Paradise and Method: Poetics and Praxis* by Bruce Andrews (Evanston, IL: Northwestern University Press, 1996). Reprinted by permission of Northwestern University Press.

"Anti-Short Story" from *Veil: New and Selected Poems* by Rae Armantrout. Copyright © 2001 by Rae Armantrout. Reprinted by permission of Wesleyan University Press.

"Spain 1937" (© 1940, renewed 1968 by W. H. Auden), "In Praise of Limestone" (© 1951 by W. H. Auden, William Meredith, and Monroe K. Spears, Executors of the Estate of W. H. Auden), and "Bucolics" (© 1976 by Edward Mendelson, William Meredith, and Monroe K. Spears, Executors of the Estate of W.H. Auden) from *Collected Poems* by W. H. Auden. Used by permission of Random House, Inc. and Faber & Faber, Ltd.

Excerpts from Charles Bernstein's *Republics of Reality: 1975–1995* (Los Angeles: Sun & Moon Books, 2000), *With Strings* (Chicago: University of Chicago Press, 2001), *Controlling Interests* (New York: Roof Books, 1980, rpt. 2004), *My Way: Speeches and Poems* (Chicago: University of Chicago Press, 1999) and *Dark City* (Los Angeles: Sun & Moon Press, 1992). Used by permission of Charles Bernstein.

Excerpts from Frank Bidart's *Desire: Collected Poems* (© 1997 by Frank Bidart), *In the Western Night: Collected Poems 1965–1990.* (© 1990 by Frank Bidart), and *Star Dust* (© 2004 by Frank Bidart). Reprinted by permission of Farrar, Strauss and Giroux, LLC. Excerpts from *Desire: Collected Poems* also used with the permission of Carcarnet Press Limited.

Excerpts from "Gerontion" from *Collected Poems 1909–1962* by T.S. Eliot. Reprinted by permission of Faber & Faber.

"Build Soil" from *The Poetry of Robert Frost*, edited by Edward Connery Lathem. Copyright 1969 by Henry Holt and Company, copyright 1936 by Robert Frost, copyright 1964 by Leslie Frost Ballantine. Published by Jonathan Cape. Reprinted by permission of the Random House Group Ltd.
"Coming" from *The Mill of Particulars* by Robert Kelly (Los Angeles: Black Sparrow Press, 1972). Copyright © 1973 by Robert Kelly. Reprinted by permission of Black Sparrow Books, an imprint of David R. Godine, Publisher, Boston.

"A Theory of Prosody" from *A Walk with Tom Jefferson* by Philip Levine. Copyright © 1988 by Philip Levine. Used by permission of Alfred A. Knopf, a division of Random House, Inc.

Excerpts from *Representative Works* by Jackson MacLow (New York: Roof Books). Reprinted with permission of Anne Tardos. Excerpts from "1st Dance-Making Things New..." Reprinted with permission of Anne Tardos and Barrytown/Station Hill Press.

Excerpts from Pablo Neruda, *Canto General*, 50th Anniversary Edition (The University of California Press and Pablo Neruda). Reprinted with permission.

Extracts from *Collected Poems* by Frank O'Hara. Copyright © 1971 by Maureen Granville-Smith, Administratrix of the Estate of Frank O'Hara. Used by permission of Alfred A. Knopf, a division of Random House, Inc.
Excerpts from *Selected Writings of Charles Olson* (© 1951, 1966 by Charles Olson). Reprinted by permission of New Directions Publishing Corp.

"1930s" from *New Collected Poems* by George Oppens. Copyright © 1934 by The Objectivist Press. Reprinted by permission of New Directions Publishing Corp.

Hannah Weiner texts used by permission of Charles Bernstein, for Hannah Weiner in trust, and by Mandeville Special Collections Library, University of California, San Diego.

"Sunday in the Park" from *Paterson* by William Carlos Williams. Copyright © 1948 by William Carlos Williams. Reprinted by permission of New Directions Publishing Corp. and Pollinger Limited.

Every reasonable effort has been made to trace the owners of copyright materials in this book, but in some instances this has proven impossible. The author and publisher will be glad to receive information leading to more complete acknowledgments in subsequent printings of the book and in the meantime extend their apologies for any omissions.

Contents

List of Entries

List of Poets

Pre–Twentieth-Century Poets

Abbey, Henry
Adams, Henry Brooks
Adams, John
Adams, John Quincy
Albee, John
Alcott, Amos Bronson
Alcott, Louisa May
Aldrich, Anne Reeve
Aldrich, Thomas Bailey
Allen, Elizabeth Akers
Allston, Washington
Alsop, George
Austin, Mary
Balbuena, Bernardo de
Bangs, John Kendrick
Barlow, Joel
Bates, Charlotte Fiske
Bates, Katharine Lee
Beers, Henry Augustin
Belknap, Jeremy
Bell, Robert Mowry
Bierce, Ambrose
Bleecker, Ann Eliza
Bloede, Gertrude
Blood, Benjamin
Bodman, Manoah
Boucher, Jonathan
Brackenridge, Hugh Henry
Bradford, William
Bradley, Mary Emily Neeley
Bradstreet, Anne Dudley
Braithwaite, William Stanley
Brooks, Charles Timothy
Brooks, Maria Gowen
Bryant, William Cullen
Byles, Mather
Byrd, William, II
Carleton, Will
Cary, Alice
Cary, Phoebe
Cawein, Madison
Chandler, Elizabeth Margaret
Channing, William Ellery
Channing, (William) Ellery
Child, Lydia Maria
Church, Benjamin
Cleghorn, Sarah Norcliffe
Colman, Benjamin
Cooke, Ebenezer
Cooke, Rose Terry
Coolbrith, Ina
Cotton, John
Cradock, Thomas
Cranch, Christopher Pearse
Crane, Stephen
Dana, Richard Henry
Dandridge, Danske
Danforth, Samuel
Davies, Samuel
De Vere, Mary Ainge
Deland, Margaret
Dickinson, Emily
Doane, George Washington
Dodge, Mary Mapes
Drake, Joseph Rodman
Dreiser, Theodore
Duché, Jacob
Dudley, Thomas
Dunbar, Paul Laurence
Dwight, Timothy
Eastman, Elaine Goodale
Emerson, Ralph Waldo
English, Thomas Dunn
Equiano, Olaudah
Evans, Nathaniel
Faugeres, Margaretta Bleecker
Fenollosa, Ernest
Fenollosa, Mary McNeil
Fergusson, Elizabeth Graeme
Field, Eugene
Fields, Annie
Fields, James Thomas
Fiske, John
Fordham, Mary Weston
Forten, Sarah Louisa
Freneau, Philip
French, Mary
Fuller, Margaret
Garland, Hamilin
Garrison, William Lloyd

Gilman, Charlotte Perkins
Godfrey, Thomas
Goodhue, Sarah Whipple
Gorton, Samuel
Gould, Hannah Flagg
Grainger, James
Green, Joseph
Griffits, Hannah
Grimké, Angelina Weld
Grimke, Charlotte L. Forten
Guiney, Louise Imogen
Hale, Sarah Josepha
Halleck, Fitz-Greene
Hammon, Jupiter
Harper, Frances Ellen Watkin
Harris, Joel Chandler
Harte, Francis Bret
Hartman, Sadakichi
Hawthorne, Nathaniel
Haynes, Lemuel
Higginson, Thomas Wentworth
Hoffman, Charles Fenno
Holmes, Oliver Wendell
Hopkins, Lemuel
Horton, George Moses
Howe, Julia Ward
Howells, William Dean
Humphreys, David
Jackson, Helen Hunt
Jewett, Sarah Orne
Johnson, Edward
Josselyn, John
Juana Inés de la Cruz, Sor
Kemble, Fanny (Francis Anne)
Key, Francis Scott
Knight, Sarah Kemble
Lanier, Sidney
Larcom, Lucy
Lathrop, Rose Hawthorne
Lazarus, Emma
Leland, Charles Godfrey
Lewis, Richard
Lili'uokalani, Queen (Lydia Kamaka'eha)
Lincoln, Abraham
Livingston, William
Lodge, George Cabot
Longfellow, Henry Wadsworth
Longfellow, Samuel
Lowell, James Russell
Lowell, Maria White
Manwell, Juana (Owl Woman)
Markham, Edwin
Martí, José
Mather, Cotton
Melville, Herman
Menken, Adah Isaacs
Miller, Alice Duer
Miller, Cincinnatus Heine (Joaquin Miller)
Mitchell, Jonathan
Monroe, Harriet
Moody, William Vaughn
Moore, Clement Clarke
Moore, Milcah Martha
Morton, Sarah Wentworth
Morton, Thomas
Murray, Judith Sargent
Norton, John, II
Noyes, Nicholas
Oakes, Urian
Odell, Jonathan
Odiorne, Thomas
O'Hara, Theodore
O'Reilly, John Boyle
Osgood, Frances Sargent Locke
Page, Thomas Nelson
Paine, Thomas
Parke, John
Parker, Theodore
Pastorius, Francis Daniel
Paulding James Kirke
Peabody, Josephine Preston
Peck, Samuel Minturn
Pérez de Villagra, Gaspar
Phelps, Charles Henry
Piatt, Sarah Morgan Bryant
Pierpont, John
Pike, Albert
Plato, Ann
Poe, Edgar Allan
Posey, Alexander Lawrence
Ray, Henrietta Cordelia
Realf, Richard
Reese, Lizette Woodworth
Ridge, John Rollin
Riley, James Whitcomb
Rose, Aquila
Saffin, John
Santayana, George
Sargent, Epes
Schoolcraft, Jane Johnson (Bame-wa-wa-ge-zhik-a-quay)
Sears, Edmund Hamilton
Seccombe, Joseph
Selyns, Henricus
Sewall, Samuel
Sigourney, Lydia Huntley
Sill, Edward Rowland
Simms, William Gilmore
Smith, Anna Young
Smith, Captain John
Smith, Elizabeth Oakes Prince
Smith, Samuel Joseph
Spofford, Harriet Prescott
Stansbury, Joseph
Stedman, Edmund Clarence
Steere, Richard
Sterling, James
Stickney, Trumbull
Stockton, Annis Boudinot
Stoddard, Elizabeth
Stuart, Ruth McEnery
Tabb, John Banister
Taylor, Bayard
Taylor, Edward
Terry, Lucy
Thaxter, Celia
Thayer, Ernest Lawrence
Thomas, Edith Matilda
Thoreau, Henry David
Tompson, Benjamin
Trask, Katrina
Trumbull, John
Tucker, St. George
Tuckerman, Frederick Goddard
Tyler, Royall
Very, Jones
Ward, Elizabeth Stuart Phelps
Ward, Nathaniel
Warren, Mercy Otis
Wells, Carolyn
Wharton, Edith
Wheatley, Phillis
Whitman, Sarah Helen Power
Whitman, Walt
Whittier, John Greenleaf
Wigglesworth, Michael
Wilcox, Carlos
Wilcox, Ella Wheeler

Williams, Roger
Willis, Nathaniel Parker
Wilson, John
Wolcott, Roger
Wood, William
Woodworth, Samuel
Woolsey, Sarah Chauncey (also Chauncy)
Woolson, Constance Fenimore
Work, Henry Clay
Wright, Susanna

Twentieth- and Twenty-first–Century Poets

Ackerman, Diane
Adair, Virginia Hamilton
Adams, Léonie
Addonizio, Kim
Ai
Aiken, Conrad Potter
Alexander, Elizabeth
Alexander, Meena
Alexander, Will
Alexie, Sherman
Algarín, Miguel
Ali, Agha Shahid
Alvarez, Julia
Ammons, A.R.
Anania, Michael
Andrews, Bruce (Errol)
Angelou, Maya
Antin, David
Arensberg, Walter Conrad
Armantrout, Rae
Ash, John
Ashbery, John
Atwood, Margaret (Eleanor)
Auden, W.H.
Baca, Jimmy Santiago
Baker, David
Bang, Mary Jo
Baraka, Amiri
Barnes, Djuna
Becker, Robin
Bell, Marvin
Benedikt, Michael
Benét, Stephen Vincent
Bennett-Coverly, Louise
Berg, Stephen
Bernard, April
Bernstein, Charles
Berrigan, Ted
Berry, Wendell
Berryman, John
Berssenbrugge, Mei-mei
Bidart, Frank
Bierds, Linda
Birney, Earle
Bishop, Elizabeth
Bishop, John Peale
Blackburn, Paul
Blackmur, R.P.
Blaser, Robin
Bly, Robert
Bogan, Louise
Bök, Christian
Boland, Eavan
Bontemps, Arna
Booth, Philip
Boyle, Kay
Brainard, Joe
Brathwaite, Edward Kamau
Brautigan, Richard
Brock-Broido Lucie
Brodsky, Joseph
Bromige, David
Bronk, William
Brooks, Gwendolyn
Brossard, Nicole
Broumas, Olga
Brown, Sterling A.
Bruchac, Joseph
Buckley, Christopher
Bukowski, Charles
Burkard, Michael
Byer, Kathryn Stripling
Bynner, Witter
Cage, John
Campo, Raphel
Carroll, Jim
Carroll, Paul
Carruth, Hayden
Carson, Anne
Carver, Raymond
Cassity, Turner
Castillo, Ana
Cather, Willa
Ceravolo, Joseph
Cervantes, Lorna Dee
Cha, Theresa Hak Kyung
Chandra, G.S. Sharat
Chappell, Fred
Chin, Marilyn
Chrystos
Ciardi, John
Clampitt, Amy
Clifton, Lucille
Codrescu, Andrei
Cofer, Judith Ortiz
Cole, Henri
Coleman, Wanda
Collier, Michael
Collins, Billy
Coolidge, Clark
Cooper, Jane
Corman, Cid
Corn, Alfred
Corso, Gregory
Cortez, Jayne
Coulette, Henri
Cowdery, Mae Virginia
Crane, Harold Hart
Crapsey, Adelaide
Crase, Douglas
Creeley, Robert
Crews, Judson
Cruz, Victor Hernández
Cullen, Countee
cummings, e.e.
Cunningham, J.V.
Dahlen, Beverly
Davidson, Michael
Davison, Peter
Delgado, Juan
Dennis, Carl
Dent, Tory
Derricotte, Toi
Deutsch, Babette
De Vries, Peter
Dewdney, Christopher

Di Prima, Diane
Dickey, James
Digges, Deborah
DiPalma, Ray
Disch, Tom
Dobyns, Stephen
Donaghy, Michael
Dorn, Edward
Doty, Mark
Dove, Rita
Dragonette, Ree
Drucker, Johanna
Dubie, Norman
DuBois, W.E.B.
Dugan, Alan
Duhamel, Denise
Dumas, Henry Lee
Dunbar-Nelson, Alice
Duncan, Robert
Dunn, Stephen
DuPlessis, Rachel Blau
Dylan, Bob
Eady, Cornelius
Eberhart, Richard
Economou, George
Edson, Russell
Eigner, Larry
Eliot, T.S.
Elmslie, Kenward
Emanuel, Lynn
Enslin, Theodore
Equi, Elaine
Erdrich, Louise
Eshleman, Clayton
Espada, Martín
Evans, Abbie Huston
Evans, Donald
Everson, William (Brother Antonious)
Everwine, Peter
Fairchild, B.H.
Fearing, Kenneth
Feldman, Irving
Ferlinghetti, Lawrence
Field, Edward
Finch, Annie
Finkel, Donald
Finkelstein, Norman
Fitzgerald, Robert
Forché, Carolyn
Foster, Edward Halsey
Francis, Robert
Fraser, Kathleen
Friebert, Stuart
Friend, Robert
Frost, Carol
Frost, Robert
Fulton, Alice
Galassi, Jonathon
Gallagher, Tess
Galvin, James
Gander, Forrest
Gardner, Isabella
Garrigue, Jean
Geisel, Theodore (Dr. Seuss)
Gerstler, Amy
Gibran, Kahlil
Gidlow, Elsa
Gilbert, Jack
Gilbert, Sandra
Ginsberg, Allen
Ginsberg, Louis
Gioia, Dana
Giovanni, Nikki
Giovannitti, Arturo
Gizzi, Michael
Gizzi, Peter
Glatt, Lisa
Glück, Louise
Goldbarth, Albert
Goldsmith, Kenneth
Gonzalez, Ray
Goodison, Lorna
Graham, Jorie
Grahn, Judy
Greger, Debora
Gregg, Linda
Gregor, Arthur
Grenier, Robert
Grimké, Angelina Weld
Grossman, Allen
Guest, Barbara
Guest, Edgar A.
Gunn, Thom
Gwynn, R.S.
H.D. (Hilda Doolittle)
Hacker, Marilyn
Hadas, Rachel
Hagedorn, Jessica
Hahn, Kimiko
Haines, John
Hall, Donald
Hamby, Barbara
Harjo, Joy
Harper, Michael S.
Harrison, Jim
Harryman, Carla
Hartman, Charles
Hass, Robert
Hayden, Robert
Heaney, Seamus
Hecht, Anthony
Hejinian, Lynn
Heller, Michael
Herrera, Juan Felipe
Heyen, William
Higgins, Dick
Hilbert, Donna
Hillman, Brenda
Hirsch, Edward
Hirschman, Jack
Hirshfield, Jane
Hoagland, Tony
Hogan, Linda
Hollander, John
Hollo, Anselm
Holman, Bob
Hongo, Garrett
Honig, Edwin
Howard, Richard
Howe, Fanny
Howe, Susan
Hudgins, Andrew
Hughes, Langston
Hugo, Richard
Ignatow, David
Inada, Lawson Fusao
Jackson, Richard
Jacobsen, Josephine
Jarrell, Randall
Jeffers, Robinson
Johnson, Fenton
Johnson, Georgia Douglas
Johnson, Helene
Johnson, James Weldon
Johnson, Ronald
Jones, Rodney
Jordan, June
Joris, Pierre
Joseph, Allison

Joseph, Lawrence
Justice, Donald
Kaufman, Bob
Kees, Weldon
Kelly, Robert
Kennedy, X.J.
Kenyon, Jane
Kerouac, Jack
Kilmer, Alfred Joyce
Kim, Myung Mi
Kinnell, Galway
Kinzie, Mary
Kirby, David
Kiyooka, Roy (Kenzie)
Kizer, Carolyn
Klein-Healy, Eloise
Kleinzahler, August
Klepfisz, Irena
Kloefkorn, William
Knight, Etheridge
Knott, Bill
Koch, Kenneth
Koertge, Ron
Komunyakaa, Yusef
Kooser, Ted
Kostelanetz, Richard
Kowit, Steve
Kramer, Aaron
Kroetsch, Robert
Kumin, Maxine
Kunitz, Stanley
Kyger, Joanne
Lansing, Gerrit
Laughlin, James
Lauterbach, Ann
Laux, Dorianne
Lax, Robert
Lea, Sydney
Lee, Li-Young
Lehman, David
Leib (Brahinsky), Mani
Leithauser, Brad
Levertov, Denise
Levin, Phillis
Levine, Philip
Levis, Larry
Lewis, Janet
Lieberman, Laurence
Lifshin, Lyn
Lindsay, Vachel
Locklin, Gerald
Loden, Rachel
Logan, John
Logan, William
Lorde, Audre
Louis, Adrian C.
Lowell, Amy
Lowell, Robert
Loy, Mina
Lummis, Suzanne
Lux, Thomas
Mac Cormack, Karen
Mac Low, Jackson
Mackey, Nathaniel
MacLeish, Archibald
Major, Clarence
Mariani, Paul
Martin, Charles
Masters, Edgar Lee
Mathews, Harry
Matthews, William
Matthias, John
Maxwell, Glyn
Mayer, Bernadette
McCaffery, Steve
McClatchy, J.D.
McClure, Michael
McGrath, Campbell
McGrath, Thomas
McHugh, Heather
McKay, Claude
McPherson, Sandra
Menashe, Samuel
Meredith, William
Merrill, James
Merton, Thomas
Merwin, W.S.
Messerli, Douglas
Mezey, Robert
Miles, Josephine
Millay, Edna St. Vincent
Miller, Vassar
Mills, Ralph J., Jr.
Miłosz, Czesław
Momaday, N. Scott
Montague, John
Moore, Marianne
Mora, Pat
Morgan, Robert
Morley, Hilda
Moss, Howard
Moss, Stanley
Moss, Thylias
Muldoon, Paul
Mullen, Harryette
Mura, David
Muske-Dukes, Carol
Myles, Eileen
Nash, Ogden
Nelson (Waniek), Marilyn
Nemerov, Howard
Nichol, b(arrie)p(hilip)
Niedecker, Lorine
Nims, John Frederick
Noguchi, Yone
Norse, Harold
North, Charles
Notley, Alice
Nye, Naomi Shihab
Oates, Joyce Carol
O'Hara, Frank
Olds, Sharon
Oliver, Mary
Olson, Charles
Oppen, George
Oppenheimer, Joel
Ortiz, Simon J.
Ostriker, Alicia
Padgett, Ron
Paley, Grace
Palmer, Michael
Pankey, Eric
Parini, Jay
Parker, Dorothy
Pastan, Linda
Patchen, Kenneth
Peacock, Molly
Perelman, Bob
Perillo, Lucia
Phillips, Carl
Phillips, Dennis
Piercy, Marge
Piñero, Miguel
Pinkerton, Helen
Pinsky, Robert
Plath, Sylvia
Plumly, Stanley
Ponsot, Marie
Pound, Ezra Loomis
Pratt, Minnie Bruce

List of Topics

African American Poetry
African American Slave Songs
Agrarian School (the Agrarians)
Almanac Poetry (Seventeenth-Century)
Angel Island Poetry
Anthologies
Anxiety of Influence
Asian American Poetry
Bay Psalm Book
Beat Poetry
Bible and American Poetry
Black Arts Movement
Black Mountain School
Blues
British Poetry
Canadian Poetry
Canon Formation
Caribbean Poetry
Chicano Poetry
Children's Poetry
Chinese Poetry
Closure
Commonplace Book
Concrete Poetry
Confessional Poetry
Contemporary African American Poetry Collectives
Corridos
Creative Writing Programs
Dada
Deep Image
Devotional Poetry
Digital Poetry
East European Poetry
Ecopoetics
Ekphrastic Poetry
Elegy
Epic
Ethnopoetics
Expatriates
Experimental Poetry and the Avant-Garde
Feminist Poetics
Fireside Poets
Fluxus
Free Verse
French Poetry
Fugitives
Gay and Lesbian Poetry
Genteel Versifiers
Graveyard Poetry
Harlem Renaissance
Hawai'ian Internment Camp Poetry of Japanese American Internees
Ideogram
Imagism
Intentional Fallacy
Irish Poetry
Japanese Poetry
Jazz
Language Poetry
Latin American Poetry
Latino Poetry
Light Verse
Line
Linear Fallacy
Literary Independence Poem
Literary Magazines
Long Poem
Lyric Essay
Lyric Poetry
Mail Art
Minimalism
Minstrelsy
Modernism
Modernismo
Narrative Poetry
Native American Poetry
Negritude
New Criticism
New England Primer
New Formalism
New York School
Objective Correlative
Objectivist Poetry
Open Form
Pastoral
Pastoral Elegy
Performance Poetry

Topical Entries Grouped by Subtopics

American Poetics
Closure
Deep Image
Intentional Fallacy
Line
Linear Fallacy
Objective Correlative
Open Form
Poetic Forms
Prosody and Versification
Sentimentality
Sublime
Symbolism
Variable Foot

Ethnic, Cultural, and Political Influences
African American Poetry
African American Poetry Collectives
African American Slave Songs
Angel Island Poetry
Asian American Poetry
Black Arts Movement
British Poetry
Canadian Poetry
Caribbean Poetry
Chicano Poetry
Chinese Poetry
Corridos
East European Poetry
Feminist Poetics
French Poetry
Gay and Lesbian Poetry
Harlem Renaissance
Hawai'ian Internment Camp Poetry of Japanese American Internees
Irish Poetry
Japanese Poetry
Latin American Poetry
Latino Poetry
Minstrelsy
Modernismo
Native American Poetry
Negritude
Poetry and Politics, including War and Anti-War Poetry
Puerto Rican Poetry
Yiddish Poetry

Genres, Movements, and Schools
Agrarian School (the Agrarians)
Almanac Poetry (Seventeenth-Century)
Beat Poetry
Black Arts Movement
Black Mountain School
Children's Poetry
Concrete Poetry
Confessional Poetry
Corridos
Dada
Devotional Poetry
Digital Poetry
Ecopoetics
Ekphrastic Poetry
Elegy
Epic
Ethnopoetics
Expatriates
Experimental Poetry and the Avant-Garde
Feminist Poetics
Fireside Poets
Fluxus
Free Verse
Fugitives
Genteel Versifiers
Graveyard Poetry
Ideogram
Imagism
Language Poetry
Light Verse
Literary Independence Poem

Long Poem
Lyric Essay
Lyric Poetry
Mail Art
Minimalism
Minstrelsy
Modernism
Modernismo
Narrative Poetry
New Formalism
New York School
Objectivist Poetry
Open Form
Pastoral
Pastoral Elegy
Performance Poetry
Phenomenological Poetics
Postmodern Poetics
Projective Verse
Prose Poem
San Francisco Renaissance
Slam Poetry
Sound Poetry
Stand-up Poetry
Verse Drama
Visual Poetry
Vorticism

Poetry, Art, and Music

Blues
Jazz

Publications

Anthologies
Commonplace Book
Literary Magazines
New England Primer
Periodicals, Pre–Twentieth Century
Post–World War II Avant-Garde Poetry Magazines
Small Press Book Publishing

Religion and Poetry

Bay Psalm Book
Bible and American Poetry
Devotional Poetry
Puritan Poetry
Religion and Poetry

The Study and Promotion of Poetry

Anxiety of Influence
Canon Formation
Creative Writing Programs
New Criticism
Poetics, Nineteenth-Century
Poetics, Seventeenth- and Eighteenth-Century
Poetics, Twentieth-Century
Poetry Manifestoes
Poetry Prizes
Translation

Preface

Content and Structure

The Greenwood Encyclopedia of American Poets and Poetry is the largest reference work on American poetry ever assembled. Its span extends from the earliest appearance of poetry in what was to become the United States (and to some extent the Americas at large) to poetry at the beginning of the twenty-first century. Within this compass we include more than nine hundred essays, not only on the most recognized names but also on hundreds of others: early poets whose work was significant but little-known at the time, and later poets who, in a world of poetry now unrecognizably expanded, are emerging into prominence, either regionally or nationally.

The reader will also find topical entries on key schools, movements, poetic theories, practices, and terms. Since the *Encyclopedia* is not a dictionary of general literary terms, literary terms are included only if they were coined in the New World, or if they apply to American poetic practice. Thus, the entry on **sublime** will address the American sublime rather than the general concept. Similarly, the reader may assume that an entry on **ekphrastic poetry** or the **long poem**, for example, will principally concern instances and practitioners of these genres or approaches within American poetry. This is also true of entries such as **British poetry**, **Irish poetry**, and the like, which do not address all poetry from Ireland but rather Irish poetry's influence on and relation to American poetry and poetics.

Access

Entries are presented alphabetically regardless of period or type. While this is the simplest and perhaps most convenient arrangement, we also offer a total of five lists of entries that give readers other ways to get their bearings within this large encyclopedia:

1. An alphabetical list of all entries
2. A list of pre–twentieth-century poets
3. A list of twentieth-century poets
4. A list of topics
5. A list of the topics grouped under sub-headings

In this way, readers who may be interested, for example, only in those poets writing before the twentieth century may scan the list of names featured. For readers interested in certain American poetry subjects, the topics list prevents those entries from escaping notice among the hundreds of poet entries, and the reader can thus easily locate information on **Native American poetry**, **negritude**, **New Criticism**, **New Formalism**, the **New York School**, and many more subjects.

Following the A–Z entries in the volumes is a comprehensive bibliography of general sources on American poetry. Each entry in the A–Z section also includes further reading resources.

As further navigational aids, words or names in **boldface** indicate cross-references to guide the reader to related entries, and an index provides extensive access to the encyclopedia's contents.

Scope

A canon becomes a canon by leaving something out. Although copiously inclusive (if not canon-averse), *The Greenwood Encyclopedia of American Poets and Poetry* is nevertheless not "complete." If our inclusions are greater than any reference work on the subject thus far, our exclusions are equally, and inevitably, legion.

The problem is not so much the past, which, precisely because it recedes, appears mappable, but the present, which is vast, vibrant, and uncontainable, perhaps particularly so in America where few constraints remain to limit voices that demand hearing. Even if the editors attempted to represent all of the several thousand living, English-writing poets listed in the current *Directory of American Poets*, the *Encyclopedia* would still not be complete, since many more thousands of poets—hardly mute or inglorious—are writing in little magazines and on the Internet, some of whom will eventually assume prominent places in the landscape of poetry.

As examples of this uncontainability, consider the two categories in our title—"American" and "poetry"—and their tempting but slippery slopes. First, we live in the "Americas," and while even the Anglophone world increasingly understands "America" to mean what José Martí called "Nuestra America"—that is, an entity much larger than the United States—our purpose has been to represent predominantly Anglophone poetry, poetry of the Northern Hemisphere and parts of the Caribbean. While we have also attempted to account for important inter- and intra-American influences in all directions, the *Encyclopedia* is designed for English-speaking readers, who would not expect to find full treatments of Brazilian and Peruvian poets, for example, in an encyclopedia of American poetry.

Constructions of the Americas aren't the only geographical/cultural problem. Most Americans are by definition immigrants, and to understand their writing is to examine their histories and ethnicities. Thus, we have included entries that attempt to account for influences from abroad—for example, **Irish poetry**, **French poetry**, **Chinese poetry**, **Japanese poetry**, and so forth. This too is a nearly limitless slope; our choice was to do some of it as well as we could and leave much undone, or not to do it at all. We chose the former path.

The second category of the title—poetry—is not geographical but literary and generic. What constitutes "poetry"? For an encyclopedia that, initially at least, will appear in print, we should begin by acknowledging a bias toward that medium. The problem is, again, not the past but the present: poets now emerging who present their work principally on sound recordings or who are principally performers, and whose audiences know their work largely through performance, are underrepresented here. Song and performance are not neglected, however, in such entries as **performance poetry**, **jazz**, **minstrelsy**, **slam poetry**, **sound poetry**, **African American slave songs**, and so on. While we may not agree with Whitman that "the singers do not beget, only the Poet begets," with some musical exceptions, our leaning has been toward the enormous tradition of *printed* poetry from America's beginnings to the present time.

The other area that a print bias may only obliquely acknowledge is not sonic but visual: the Internet. If there are tens of thousands writing poetry in print, there may be several times that number writing online. Among poets with a very large Internet presence, one would have to list, among many others, Richard Denner, Luis Garcia, John Oliver Simon, Belle Randall, Paul Hunter, Charles Potts, John Bennett, Mark Halperin, and Joe Powell. These poets, while not represented here, may be Googled readily. (And we do include an entry on **Digital Poetry**.)

A last comment is necessary on the most interesting problem of all: the synchronic leaning of the twenty-first–century world. Our sympathies as writers and editors may tend toward the diachronic, but the culture at large and literature studies in particular, as college class enrollments reveal, show a much greater interest in the present than in the past. The *Encyclopedia*'s imbalance in the number of twentieth-century and contemporary poets represented here vis-à-vis those of earlier periods reflects this interest–existing as much among established scholars as among students—along with several other factors:

The enormous growth in both population and in print technology and distribution over the past century

The pronounced flourishing of poetry following the upheavals of literary modernism early in the twentieth century, and the successive waves of poetry since then, particularly from the 1960s, often extending but sometimes challenging the precepts and practices of modernism

The burgeoning of poetic practice in the United States over the past forty years as a result of poetry workshops at universities across the nation, a situation earlier poets, for good or ill, could not avail themselves of

Because of this "excess" (as William Carlos Williams called poetry), our criteria for inclusion of twentieth-century poets have had to be different from those of earlier periods. Where now tens of thousands of writers publish books, formerly only a handful did. Some of our entries are on early poets who published only a few poems and never a book, a circumstance that seems quaint from today's perspective, suggesting either humility, a different set of priorities, or simply a level of economic and technological constraint difficult to comprehend in our own time.

Acknowledgments

In compiling the *Greenwood Encyclopedia of American Poets and Poetry*, we have often received counsel–from our advisory board but also from many colleagues and contributors, who offered suggestions about inclusions, exclusions, and lengths of entries. While we have not been able to accommodate all such suggestions, many suggested entries *have* been included to the greater benefit of the work as a whole.

Among our contributors are the most distinguished scholars, critics, and poets of the field. We owe thanks to our advisory board, some of whom are also contributors, for their many suggestions and helpful leads over the past couple of years, often connecting the right entry to the right writer. At Greenwood, we are much indebted to George Butler, who got the project off the ground, and to Mariah Gumpert and Anne Thompson for keeping this vast mission on track. For support from Seton Hall University's English Department, we thank former chair Martha Carpentier and secretary Rebecca Warren. We are particularly grateful for the work of our assistants from that department: Jocelyn Dumaresq, Sherry Chung, Peter Donahue, and Caitlin Womersley. We are indebted to our editorial staff, including colleagues such as Jeanne McNett, John Wargacki, and Robert Squillace, who helped in reading and editing entries; and Melissa Fabros, who was indispensable in creating and maintaining the EOAP website. We also wish to thank John A. Balkun, Lei Jun, and Cynthia Williams. There are far too many contributors to thank in this small space but among those who wrote a great many entries, helped critique entries, or matched writers with entries, we must mention Steven Gould Axelrod, Charles Bernstein, Burt Kimmelman, Don Marshall, Marjorie Perloff, Tad Richards, Linda Russo, and John Shields.

The Greenwood Encyclopedia of American Poets and Poetry

S

SAFFIN, JOHN (1626–1710)

John Saffin is perhaps best known to historians for a public disagreement with Samuel Sewall over a slave named Adam. In the context of early American literary aesthetics, however, Saffin clearly stands as a **Puritan poet** anxious to experiment in various poetic genres. This interest contradicts the perception that the Puritans were not interested in artistic endeavors, as it does also the idea of Puritan distrust of the senses and the imagination (Elliott, 71). Commenting on the specific genres with which Saffin experimented with, Harrison T. Meserole states, "The quantity of his verse ranks him seventh or eighth among colonial poets, but it is the quality of his work . . . that establishes his place among important poets of early America" (195).

Born in Somerset, England, to well-to-do parents, John Saffin moved with his family to Scituate, Massachusetts, in 1634 or 1635. Though Saffin did not enroll in college, a fact not typical of males in colonial America during the seventeenth century, he received an education through the tutelage of Charles Chauncy; this training, along with additional legal training (he "read the law" with the firm of Foster and Hoar), allowed Saffin to participate in various professions, including the law, land ownership, and the merchant industry (Shawcross, 1262). Saffin's reputation changed, however, with the publication in the early twentieth century of *The Notebook of John Saffin, 1665–1708* (1928), which contains about fifty poems in various styles and on various topics.

One genre that Saffin undertakes is the acrostic poem in which the first letter of each line spells out the individual's name being honored or praised within the poem itself. Although the acrostic can certainly be seen as a highly constrained poetic genre, Jeffrey Walker reminds readers that "the Puritan anagram and acrostic represent with few exceptions a form of Puritan gaudiness, a conscious attempt on the poets' part to show off, not only for their fellow New Englanders, but also for their God" (248). In "An Acrostick on Mrs. Elizabeth Hull," Saffin refers to the object of his admiration as "Elustrious Dame whose virtues rare doe shine" (Meserole, 195) and as, a few lines later, a "Beautious-Sweet-Smileing and Heart-moveing Creature" (195). This acrostic represents a case of Puritan poetry moving beyond what is usually thought to be a rigid, unemotional style.

The emotional and personal sides in Saffin's poetry come out even more fully in "A Lamentation on my Dear Son Simon who dyed of the Small pox on the 23 November 1678." Mirroring characteristics of the Puritan funeral elegy, particularly in its praise of the features of the departed and in its assurance to the reader that the departed has attained a better world with God, the poem beings with an agonizing first couplet: "Simon my son, son of my Nuptiall knot / Ah! Simon's gone, Simon my son is not" (Meserole, 197).

Saffin clearly saw his son's future as promising, for the speaker describes him as possessing "pregnant witt, quick Genius, parts sublime" (Messerole, 197). He envisions him climbing "Pernassus [sic]," home of the classical Muses and challenging "Apelles," a legendary Greek painter "Who best should . . . a Rarest piece contrive" (Messerole, 196). Such classical allusions permeate Saffin's poetry owing in large part to his Latin grammar school education (Shields, 25).

"Sweetly (my Dearest) I left thee asleep" stands as an example of Saffin's love poetry, the genre in which he departed most, as Kathryn Zabelle Derounian points out, from the Puritan mainstream (175). In *The Notebook of John Saffin, 1665–1708*, the author states that most of the poems in the book "are rather amorous, or Encomicastick" (2). Saffin then outlines his view of aesthetics, writing that "good verse ought to be concise and significant, plaine, elegant" (2). These characteristics of good verse, according to Saffin, are seen within the "Sweetly" poem, suggesting that his interest in love poems may stem from his idea of what constitutes "good" verse.

Written four years before the marriage of Saffin and Martha Willett, the poem opens with the speaker's predicament, specifically that he must temporarily part from his sleeping wife: "Faine would I wake her, but love did Reply / O wake her not, so sweetly let her lye" (Derounian, 198). The speaker resolves the internal predicament by deciding to depart, but not before kissing his sleeping wife: "Thus in sad silence I alone and mute, / My lips bad thee farewell, with a Salute" (Derounian, 198). But the one kiss makes him linger, hinders his going: "I thought one kiss to little then stole twaine / And then another" (Derounian, 198). Finally, the speaker moves to a more "rationale" tone (Derounium, 178), consoling himself in the fact that "yet the consummation will Repay / The Debt that's due many a happy day" (Derounian, 199).

Further Reading. ***Selected Primary Sources:*** Saffin, John, *American Poetry of the Seventeenth Century*, ed. Harrison T. Meserole (University Park: Pennsylvania State University Press, 1985); ———, *The Notebook of John Saffin, 1665–1708*, (New York: Harbor Press, 1928). ***Selected Secondary Sources:*** Derounian, Kathryn Zabelle, "'Mutual Sweet Content': The Love Poetry of John Saffin," in *Puritan Poets and Poetics: Seventeenth-Century American Poetry in Theory and Practice*, ed. Peter White (University Park: Pennsylvania State University Press, 1985, 175–184); Elliott, Emory, *The Cambridge Introduction to Early American Literature* (Cambridge: Cambridge University Press, 2002); Shawcross, John T., "John Saffin," in *American Writers before 1800: A Biographical and Critical Dictionary*, Vol. 3 (Westport, CT: Greenwood Press, 1983, 1262–1265); Shields, John, *The American Aeneas: Classical Origins of the American Self* (Knoxville: University of Tennessee Press, 2001); Walker, Jeffrey, "Anagrams and Acrostics; Purtian Poetic Wit," in *Puritan Poets and Poetics: Seventeenth-Century American Poetry in Theory and Practice*, ed. Peter White (University Park: Pennsylvania State University Press, 1985, 247–257).

Eric D. Lamore

SALINAS, LUIS OMAR (1937–)

Since 1967 Luis Omar Salinas has been an important voice in American poetry. Salinas's first book, *Crazy Gypsy*, (1970), is now a classic of **Chicano poetry**, reflecting the politics and self actualization of those highly charged and changing times. In the late 1960s and early 1970s, Salinas was one of a group associated with the prominent poets **Philip Levine**, **Peter Everwine**, and **Robert Mezey**, who were teaching at Fresno State College, as it was then known. With another professor in the English department, Lillian Faderman, Salinas co-edited a poetry anthology in 1973, *From the Barrio: A Chicano Anthology*. It would be ten years before Salinas published his second book, *Afternoon of the Unreal* (1980), which reflected the influences of his reading of Spanish poetry—the generation of '27 as it is called—including Lorca, Jimenez, Machado, Hernandez, and others—as well as South American poets Neruda and Vallejo. A deeper imagism, an element of the surreal, combined with his ability to target specific emotional states, characterize Salina's mature voice. A sense of melancholy, a romantic longing, and a wildness balanced by wit and irony, would surface in Salinas's subsequent books—*Prelude to Darkness* (1981) *and Darkness under the Trees / Walking behind the Spanish* (1982). In 1984 he received a rare General Electric Foundation Award to support his writing, and in 1985 he was invited to read at the Library of Congress with Sandra Cisneros.

Luis Omar Salinas was born in Robstown, Texas, on June 27, 1937, to Olivia and Rosendo Salinas. In 1941 Olivia Salinas grew weak with tuberculosis and died. Luis was adopted by his aunt and uncle, Oralia and Alfredo Salinas. Eventually the family moved to Fresno, where Luis attended elementary and high school, and then to Bakersfield, where he received an AA degree in history. In 1958 Salinas enrolled at California State University, Los Angeles, where he studied with the poet **Henri Coulette**, who became a strong influence on his poetry.

Salinas began attending classes at Fresno State College in 1967, and in Philip Levine's workshop he met fellow poets **Larry Levis**, B.H. Boston, DeWayne Rail, Greg Pape, **David St. John**, and others of that group that would emerge from Fresno in the 1960s and 1970s. There he also befriended Fresno poets **Gary Soto**,

Ernesto Trejo, and Jon Veinberg, all of whom would be significant in their support of his poetry.

Given his engagement with social and political subjects in his poetry, a number of faculty and staff members in La Raza Studies at Fresno State College collaborated to publish Salina's first book, *Crazy Gypsy*, which sold about four thousand copies in eight months in two editions. In the title poem we meet the lyric Salinas mourning the death of his mother, and we meet the angry and political Salinas of the times, throwing stones at policemen. Yet, although the first lines of this poem are forthright and lyrical, the stanza ends with an image from the subconscious that alerts us to the range of his voice and imagination and expands the emotional center of the poem—"and walk on seaweed / in my dreams."

In *Afternoon of the Unreal*, Salinas tries to understand the hardships and unjust turns of fate in his life. Completed not long after publication of *Afternoon of the Unreal*, *Prelude to Darkness* is book of struggle—personal, emotional, psychic, and psychological. The poems reveal an expansive soul, one that desires to be generous, righteous, and accepting, yet a soul that at almost every turn is confronted by the unmanageable particulars of the world—"And I've been smiling too long / to be overworked / and underpaid."

Although appearing under the same cover as *Darkness under the Trees* and written only a few months later, *Walking behind the Spanish* is a large step forward in Salinas's poetic accomplishment. With concentrated and inventive imagery, Salinas moves beyond the lyric impulse alone to eulogize the great generation of Spanish poets, empathizing with their dedication to poetry and humanity, which, in some instances, brought the poets to early deaths at the hands of Franco and the fascists. Salinas embraces the example of their lives and poetry in order to enlarge his own vision. One of the most moving poems is one to an unlikely hero, the poet's adoptive father. "My Father Is a Simple Man" is direct and simply spoken as befits its subject, a man who, the poem suggests, will depart life without "fanfare or applause," but from whom the poet "shall have learned what little / there is about greatness."

The year 1987 saw publication of *The Sadness of Days: Selected and New Poems* by Arte Publico Press at the University of Houston. Fourteen poems comprise the "new" section in *Sadness of Days*, selected from those Salinas thought the best of his writing between 1982 and 1986. This was a transitional period and not a particularly productive time.

Twenty-two new poems constitute *Follower of Dusk* (1991), which won the annual chapbook contest from Flume Press, Chico, California. Those poems also formed the core of *Sometimes Mysteriously*, which was selected as the Salmon Run Press's annual national book publication winner. By that point in his career—1997—Salinas had just entered his sixth decade, and his poems and his visions had developed and changed. In the new poems an element of hope and wistful resignation is evident.

Greatest Hits (2002) is remarkable not only for its selection of Salinas's twelve best-known poems from the last twenty-seven years but also for the narrative by the poet, offering the history of the poems, which is part of the format for the series. In the last paragraph, Salinas talks about the title poem, "Sometimes Mysteriously":

> This poem was a turning point in my life. . . . I was beginning to attain more authority in my life and in my work. Having survived, almost miraculously, so much of my life, having found my poetry, I began more often to take a positive outlook on the days I have left.

This tone of sober resignation is also found in a frequently anthologized poem from the book, "My Fifty-Plus Years Celebrate Spring." The occasion for the poet is the arrival of spring in the San Joaquin Valley, a cause for both observation and reflection, turning the poem toward political and social commentary. Even while the observation is imbued with surreal flights, the reflection considers the condition of workers and, finally, a spurious idea of heavenly reward that depends on hard labor. Recounting four decades in the valley, in which he has seen the sun "building its altars" and Mexican laborers working every day in the packing houses, the speaker notes that if hard labor is really ennobling as is so often claimed, then the road leading to heaven "must be crowded / beyond belief." Being a poet of wit and irony who is aware of the seriousness of wordplay, Salinas intends the last line of the poem—"beyond belief"—to suggest not only its usual meaning but also lack of faith and the need to get beyond faith. Salinas would like to believe in reward and redemption, but his experience and that of the workers he observes has him both doubting and hoping in a space ultimately "beyond belief."

Salina's work has always revealed a "romantic" proclivity, a desire for the magnanimous gesture, a desire to embrace the world as he walks through it. He would happily be the troubadour, a poet who has found contentment in surviving and in writing. The modern odes of his latest book, *Elegies for Desire* (2005), admit the possibility of hope, of life finally turning out for the better. He remains an active and vigorous poet, working daily in Sanger, California.

Further Reading. ***Selected Primary Sources:*** Salinas, Luis Omar, *Afternoon of the Unreal* (Fresno, CA: Abramas, 1980); ———, *Crazy Gypsy* (Fresno, CA: Origines, 1970); ———, *Darkness under the Trees / Walking Behind the*

Spanish (Berkeley: University of California Chicano Library Studies, 1982); ———, *Elegy for Desire* (Tucson: University of Arizona Press, 2005); ———, *Follower of Dusk* (Chico, CA: Flume Press, 1991); ———, *Greatest Hits 1969–1996* (Johnstown, OH: Pudding House, 2002); ———, *I Go Dreaming Serenades* (San Jose, CA: Mango, 1979); ———, *Prelude to Darkness* (San Jose, CA: Mango, 1981); ———, *The Sadness of Days: Selected and New Poems* (Houston: Arte Publico Press, 1987); ———, *Sometimes Mysteriously* (Anchorage, AK: Salmon Run Press, 1997). ***Selected Secondary Sources:*** Buckley, Christopher, "Any Good Fortune [An Interview with Luis Omar Salinas]" (*Quarterly West* 55 [Fall/Winter 2002–2003]: 149–157); ———, Review of *Prelude to Darkness*, in *Appreciations: Selected Reviews, Views, & Interviews, 1975–2000* (Santa Barbara, CA: Millie Grazie Press, 2001, 30–34); Lomeli, Francisco A., and Carl R. Shirley, eds., *Chicano Writers, First Series* (Detroit: Gale Research, 1989, 234–238); Magill, Frank N., ed., "The Poetry of Luis Omar Salinas," in *Masterpieces of Latino Literature* (New York: HarperCollins, 1994, 475–478); Ríos, Alberto, "Chicano Borderlands Literature and Poetry," in *Contemporary Latin American Culture Unity and Diversity* (Tempe, AZ: Center for Latin American Studies, 1984, 79–93); Soto, Gary, "Luis Omar Salinas: Chicano Poet" (*MELUS* 9.2 [Summer 1982]: 47–82); ———, "Voices of Sadness and Silence" (*Bloomsbury Review* [July 1988]: 21); Shirley, Carl R., and Paula W. Shirley, *Understanding Chicano Literature* (Columbia: University of South Carolina Press, 1988, 25); Wolff, Donald, "Strange Hours of the Day [Review of *Afternoon of the Unreal*]" (*Berkeley Poetry Review* 14.1 [1982]: 55–58); Wolff, Donald, "A Life Charmed and Haunted [Review of *Sometimes Mysteriously*]" (*SOLO* 3 [1999]: 156–159).

Christopher Buckley

SALTER, MARY JO (1954–)

Called "an exemplar of the **New Formalism**" by **Rita Dove** in 2002 and frequently featured in works devoted to that school, Mary Jo Salter nonetheless never sought to be identified as a New Formalist. A dedicated craftsman who knows how to use form like a jeweler's setting to display every facet of a word or phrase, she deftly reveals the universal in personal experiences and in objects and places. Often humorous and poignant at once, her poems have both an appealing humility and a sure-footed confidence.

Salter was born in Grand Rapids, Michigan, in 1954, raised in Detroit and Baltimore, and educated at Harvard, where she studied under **Elizabeth Bishop** and **Robert Fitzgerald** (she met husband **Brad Leithauser** in a workshop led by Bishop), and at Cambridge University. Another formative relationship began for Salter in 1979, when, working at the *Atlantic Monthly*, she impulsively wrote a "fan letter" in reply to an unsolicited manuscript from **Amy Clampitt**. Their correspondence and friendship lasted until Clampitt's death in 1994. Presently, Salter is **Emily Dickinson** Senior Lecturer in the Humanities at Mount Holyoke College.

Salter's five collections of poems to date are *Henry Purcell in Japan* (1985), *Unfinished Painting* (the 1989 Lamont Selection for the year's most distinguished second volume of poetry), *Sunday Skaters* (nominated in 1994 for the National Book Critics Circle Award), *A Kiss in Space* (1999), and *Open Shutters* (2003), as well as a children's book, *The Moon Comes Home* (1989). She is a co-editor of *The Norton Anthology of Poetry* and has received many awards, including a year in France on an **Amy Lowell** Poetry Traveling Scholarship. She is on the board of the Amy Clampitt Trust, the Bogliasco Foundation, and the *Kenyon Review*, and has been vice president of the Poetry Society of America since 1995. Her first play, *Falling Bodies*, was produced in 2004.

In reading Salter's poems one sees a genuine pleasure in the surprising "artful correspondences" between things and ideas that are brought to life by correlating sounds. Always sensitive to the nuances revealed when the observer's expectations are jarred, she delights in the imprecise rhyme, in the altered figure of speech, and in juxtapositions of words that create a provocative dissonance (like the painted-on Genovese shutters she describes in "Trompe l'Oeil" [2003]: "Paint hung out to dry— / shirttails flapping on a frieze"). Her love of puns and double meanings hints at the influence of the work of **James Merrill**, to whom she pays homage in the poem "Tanker" (2003), which is a tanka about a sudden understanding of Merrill's own tanker and tanka pun in his poem "Fort Lauderdale" ("No one but you would have made / a bonsai of a bonsai"). She surprises readers with "misheard" lines (a "lunging service" promised on a moving airplane in "Two Prayers") and mis-seen images (a homeless woman in "What Do Women Want?" [1994] whose "flask of vodka" is revealed to be dishwashing soap: "poor thing— her dirty secret nothing worse / than the dream of meals to wash up after"). Salter's fluency with traditional forms allows her to bend and reinvent formal poetry, with results that can be solemn or playful.

Salter's extensive travels in Iceland, Japan, and France have given rise to numerous poems in which travel and the experience of foreignness become metaphors for travel into different mentalities and perspectives. Craft and art are a strong presence in Salter's subject matter as well, and much of her work imagines the lives and preoccupations of artists and inventors, from a sidewalk chalk artist in "The Rebirth of Venus" (1989) to Emily Dickinson, **Robert Frost**, and Thomas Jefferson, to her own mother, a painter whose work and early death from cancer occasioned many of Salter's poems.

Salter exploits the familiar sounds and rhythms of formal poetry to evoke particular moods or to create expectations, which she then disturbs. She opens "Chernobyl" (1989) with a familiar, singsong convention from children's storytelling: "Once upon a time / The word alone was scary." The poem's plain vocabulary, regular *ABAB* rhymed lines, and use of feminine endings, reverberate surprisingly against the poem's grim subject matter to remind us of how quickly disasters become distant stories ("Fear is harder to retain / Than hope, or indifference"). In "Elegies for Etsuko," the suicide of a young friend is treated in a series of poems with structures from villanelle to free verse, creating a formal mirror of the many conflicting responses we have to loss. But whether the subject matter is large (the September 11 attacks) or small ("My Husband Has a Crush on Myrna Loy"), Salter's poems are consistent in their open-minded, delicately observed details—even when taking her own psychoanalysis as subject, she manages to avoid the **confessional poetry** trap of writing that is only personal. Her work, always self-aware, is never selfish.

Domestic objects—a refrigerator magnet, the Christmas tree, her father's home movies—are treated with the same care as a painting by Titian. Uniquely masterful in her exaltation of the daily and the domestic, Salter perceives and expresses the important correlations among the most mundane objects and experiences with a seemingly effortless interpolation of poetic resonance into everyday life, formalizing the day-to-day as if to hint that that a grand scheme does indeed underpin all human experience.

Further Reading. ***Selected Primary Sources:*** Finch, Annie, ed., *A Formal Feeling Comes* (Ashland, OR: Story Line Press, 1994); Salter, Mary Jo, *A Kiss in Space* (New York: Alfred A. Knopf, 1999); ———, *Open Shutters* (New York: Alfred A. Knopf, 2003); ———, *Sunday Skaters* (New York: Alfred A. Knopf, 1994); ———, *Unfinished Painting* (New York: Alfred A. Knopf, 1989). ***Selected Secondary Sources***: Taylor, Henry, "Faith and Practice: The Poems of Mary Jo Salter" (*Hollins Critic* XXXVII.1 [February 2000]: 1–6); Whited, Stephen, "Mary Jo Salter" (*Book* [March/April 1999], http://www.bookmagazine.com/archive/issue3/poetics.shtml).

Amy Glynn Greacen

SAN FRANCISCO RENAISSANCE

Closely associated with, and sometimes not distinguished from, the **Beat** movement, the San Francisco Renaissance was actually a consortium of different, and oftentimes differing, artistic communities. Though many credit **Allen Ginsberg**'s famous reading of "Howl" at Six Gallery in October 1955 with kicking off the movement, Ginsberg had in fact arrived on the scene of an already thriving and diverse poetry community based in San Francisco and Berkeley.

In April 1947 Madeline Gleason organized the First Festival of Modern Poetry at the Lucien Labaudt Gallery. Over the space of two evenings, twelve poets gave readings, including **Kenneth Rexroth**, **Robert Duncan**, and **Jack Spicer**. This event marked an early public recognition of the range of experimental poetic practice that was flowering in the city.

Rexroth had come to San Francisco from Chicago in 1927. The generally acknowledged father of the renaissance, Rexroth was himself a Renaissance man, who translated poetry from Greek, Latin, French, Spanish, Japanese, and Chinese, and who wrote a novel and books of criticism on an astounding range of subjects in addition to the poetry for which he is best known. A painter, labor activist, and music lover, Rexroth was integral in introducing San Francisco poets to one another, and his Friday night literary salons became the center of the city's increasingly vibrant and experimental poetry scene. A second-generation **Objectivist** with ties to **Pound** and **Williams**, his early work prefigures the **Language poetry** movement of the 1980s. He was among the first American poets to explore **Japanese** forms, such as haiku, as well as incorporating **jazz** concepts and rhythms into his work, which would become one of the most identifiable hallmarks of Beat poetry.

Robert Duncan had taught at **Black Mountain** College, forging a connection between that group and the San Francisco poets. As a student at Berkeley, he formed liaisons with **Jack Spicer** and **Robin Blaser**—the work of this "Berkeley Renaissance" subgroup shared themes of homosexuality, occultism, and an oppositional stance to the university's literature department (then headed by **Josephine Miles**). Spicer, who led the influential "Poetry as Magic" seminar at San Francisco State University, had an abiding interest in Lorca's *canto jondo* that forged a tie to the **Deep Image** poets.

Devotedly avant-garde and often subversive, the Rexroth group provided an important context for subsequent counter-culture developments. Duncan and Spicer's open exploration of homosexuality themes, and particularly Duncan's 1944 essay *The Homosexual in Society*, which compared the plight of gays to that of Jews and Blacks, enabled dialogue on a formerly taboo topic. Anarcho-pacifist Rexroth's vision of himself as standing in opposition to a monolithic mainstream was an important precursor to the New Left.

Their modes of expression ranged from **confessional** to **Imagist** to vatic, from surrealism to satire, but where there appear to be few thematic or stylistic similarities, this diverse group of writers were connected by a shared social and historical context—in particular, war. With its origins at the end of World War II and its ending around the beginning of the Vietnam war, war with Korea and the Cold War in between, the San Francisco renaissance was a movement galvanized by loss and an American self-perception that was rapidly shifting. Rexroth characterized the poetry of this period as "elegiac."

In many ways, though, the real unifying principle for the renaissance writers was the city itself. San Francisco's mythic physical beauty, its tolerance of alternative lifestyles, and its rich immigrant history have made it a magnet for those seeking galvanic change since the Gold Rush. The renaissance was a confluence of mostly immigrant writers, each of whom brought histories and aesthetic sensibilities informed by their places of origin, and San Francisco, in turn, informed and became a figure in their work. For Rexroth, San Francisco's landscapes were *paysages moralisés* with which he engaged in political commentary. For **Gary Snyder**, arguably one of America's most important "poets of place," landscape provides historical and social analogies. For **Lawrence Ferlinghetti** and Spicer, there were riches to be excavated in the sights and sounds of San Francisco's bars and streets.

By the 1950s there was a definite groundswell throughout the Bay Area arts communities, and the "renaissance" is probably best defined as the convergence and collaboration, often across genres and media, of these groups. Ruth Witt-Diamant founded the San Francisco State College Poetry Center in 1954, with a dedicatory reading by **W.H. Auden**. The center became a place in which representatives of the different poetry subcultures of the Bay Area could be introduced to one another's work. Meanwhile, the California School of Fine Arts, under the direction of Douglas MacAgy, brought to the city Abstract Expressionist painters such as Clyfford Still, whose exhibitions resulted in an explosion of new forms on the canvasses of local artists.

Underground and independent film was also thriving, with filmmakers James Broughton, Harry Smith, Kenneth Anger, and Jordan Belsen working in the Bay Area. The San Francisco Museum of Art housed a film showcase that brought Man Ray and Hans Richter to the city. Experimental composer Henry Partch drew students of composition to salons on his houseboat in Sausalito. There was a series of new-music concerts called "Vortex" at the planetarium. The Cellar hosted an exhibit of Joan Brown's paintings accompanied by the jazz of Brew Moore and Pony Poindexter, and students from the School of Fine Arts congregated at The Place for "**Dada** Night." Collaboration between artists of every discipline was flourishing.

Although the University of California–Berkeley, Stanford, and San Francisco State made their contributions to the burgeoning arts scene, and although several of the renaissance writers had impressive academic pedigrees, it is important to note that the nerve center of the San Francisco renaissance was not in its academic institutions but in its bars and galleries and coffeehouses. The movement was heavily oriented away from the structures and subject matter that characterized the mid-century academic mainstream. Following Pound's famous exhortation to "Make it new!" the renaissance writers brought forth works on historically taboo subject matter; they openly embraced homosexuality, experimentation with drugs, and withdrawal from mainstream society. They sought inspiration in the foggy, jazz-soaked streets of North Beach and the old underworld of the Barbary Coast, in the colorful nightlife of Chinatown, in the exploding art galleries, and the multilingual chatter of the sidewalks and parks and docks. At The Cellar bar, Rexroth read poems, while a jazz band riffed on "Things Ain't What They Used to Be." Jack Spicer hosted "Blabbermouth Nights" at The Place, where the likes of **Richard Brautigan** and **John Wieners**, performed extemporaneous poems that borrowed an improvisational energy from jazz and a "rap" colloquial style from Beat muse Neal Cassady. Dylan Thomas arrived for a series of readings in 1952, electrifying audiences with an alcohol-induced fervor that laid waste to the traditional academic gravitas of the poetry reading.

Small presses and literary magazines outside the area were awakening to the San Francisco scene—*Evergreen Review*'s second issue featured much of the San Francisco writing, including the complete text of "Howl." New Directions and Grove Press in New York and Olympia Press in Paris were also bringing increased attention to the San Francisco writers, publishing work by Kerouac, Ginsburg, Burroughs, and Duncan among many others. One of the most important elements of the renaissance was the founding of City Lights Books in 1953 at the intersection of Columbus and Broadway in the heart of North Beach. The first all paperback bookstore in the United States, City Lights was originally created by Peter Martin and Lawrence Ferlinghetti in order to fund Martin's magazine of the same name. They soon became book publishers, launching the "Pocket Poets" series in 1955, and publishing the surrealist poetry of Philip Lamantia and the first film criticism of Pauline Kael, as well as, more famously, *Howl*. The store rapidly became a resource for local artists, particularly those who had trouble getting attention from mainstream publishers. Next door at Café Vesuvio, proprietor Henri Lenoir created another important gathering space for experimental writers and artists, attracted, as Lenoir put it, "by the non-bourgeois atmosphere created by the avant-garde paintings I hung on the walls."

This prolific, diverse, and interconnected outpouring of artistic expression was the stage set for Ginsberg's arrival from New York in August 1953. **Jack Kerouac** and William Burroughs joined him, as did Cassady and **Gregory Corso**. Snyder, **Philip Whalen**, and Lew Welch, who had attended Reed College in Oregon around the same time Spicer, Duncan, and **Robin Blaser** were at Berkeley, joined the New Yorkers in San Francisco and formed the affiliation that would come to be known as the Beat movement.

The Beats shared some general aesthetic similarities, but also vast differences, and were bound more by social than by stylistic affiliation. Snyder especially stood out for his devotion to Zen and to wilderness landscapes over the more common Beat imagery of the urban and downtrodden. However, in the spirit of interconnection and convergence that characterized the San Francisco Renaissance, each writer influenced the others. Snyder inspired Whalen, Ginsberg, and Kerouac to convert to Zen, infusing Eastern philosophy into much Beat writing. Ginsberg wrote his seminal "Howl" in response to Kerouac's own spontaneous, automatic writing style. Spicer's belief that poetry was dictated to the poet infused the collective aesthetic as well; his spontaneous poetry nights, in which many of his colleagues competed for prizes, rejuvenated a sense of poetry as a public, participatory act.

The famous reading at Six Gallery in the fall of 1955 saw the fusion of the San Francisco renaissance with the originally bicoastal Beat movement. **Michael McClure** had come to San Francisco to paint but met Ginsberg at the opening of the Poetry Center and became one of the poets to read at the event, along with Ginsberg, Whalen, Lamantia, Snyder, and Rexroth as master of ceremonies. The reading drew over one hundred people to the gallery, a far larger crowd than the poets had expected. The climax of the evening was Ginsberg's impassioned recitation of "Howl." The poem's wild, vivid language and controversial subject matter, along with the fervid delivery, signaled to those present that a new literary power was emerging in San Francisco. Ferlinghetti immediately asked to publish the manuscript, an action that would lead him to defend himself in an obscenity trial soon afterward. The trial, in which both Ferlinghetti and Ginsberg were acquitted, secured nationwide fame for Ginsberg and City Lights. It also contributed to consciousness of the free speech movement and brought attention to the significant artistic energy that was at work in San Francisco. Each of the six poets did further readings at the Telegraph Hill Neighborhood Center and at the Town Hall Theater in Berkeley. The Beats went on to become some of the most widely read American poets.

"We had gone beyond a point of no return, and we were ready for it," McClure recalled in his memoir, *Scratching the Beat Surface.* "None of us wanted to go back to the gray, chill, militaristic silence, to the intellective void—to the land without poetry—to the spiritual drabness. We wanted to make it new and we wanted to invent it and the process of it as we went into it. We wanted voice and we wanted vision" (24).

The San Francisco renaissance was actually a relatively small, localized phenomenon and dissipated after a few years as the "Beatnik" hype drove scores of imitators to the city, and substance abuse and dissipating relationships forced some of the original writers apart. Snyder left for Japan, and Burroughs headed to Tangier. Spicer and Kerouac died of complications from alcohol abuse. Somewhat ironically, however, this small group of anti-establishment writers in their West Coast outpost shunned mainstream poetry only to become the mainstream. The San Francisco poets with their tenets of breath-based lines, spontaneous, often vatic poetry that fed on the energy of a live audience and an urban, bohemian aesthetic lifestyle have influenced generations of verse writing, just as they made San Francisco the permanent home of the counter-culture.

Further Reading. Davidson, Michael, *The San Francisco Renaissance: Poetics and Community at Mid-Century* (Cambridge: Cambridge University Press, 1989); Kerouac, Jack, *The Dharma Bums* (New York: Penguin, 1991); Kherdian, David, *Six Poets of the San Francisco Renaissance: Portraits and Checklists* (New York: Giglia, 1986); McClure, Michael, *Scratching the Beat Surface* (New York: Penguin, 1994).

Amy Glynn Greacen

SANCHEZ, SONIA (1934–)

One of the foremost poets of the **Black Arts Movement** (BAM), Sonia Sanchez continues to build on a nearly four-decade career in literature and activism that centers most visibly on her poetry. Her work has never settled into stasis but has consistently reflected her ongoing spiritual, political, and artistic development in both its content and form, while remaining recognizably and characteristically her own. Sanchez's poetry has influenced two generations of African American poets and spoken word artists. Her early interests in **jazz** and African chanting, like her current willingness to embrace aspects of hip-hop music and poetry, speak to her concurrent commitments to the written and oral aspects of multiple poetic traditions. Although her work is of increasing interest to a wider variety of critics and readers, to date the quality, quantity, and popularity of her writing are vastly out of proportion to the scant critical attention it has received.

Wilsonia Benita Driver, as Sanchez was first named, was born in Birmingham, Alabama. Her mother, Lena Driver (née Jones), died in childbirth when Sanchez was only one year old. The poet's father, Wilson L. Driver, left Sanchez and her sister, Patricia, with his mother, Elizabeth Driver, and headed north. The sisters did not rejoin their father until Sanchez was nine years old and he was living in Harlem with his third wife. In the meantime, their grandmother, whom they called "Mama," provided them with stability and loving support until her death, when Sanchez was six. This loss and, secondarily, the ensuing series of residences with relatives and family friends, pained Sanchez so deeply that she stuttered for years. During this period Sanchez began to write poetry, which she credits with keeping her alive. She earned her BA from Hunter College and did post-graduate study on poetry with **Louise Bogan** at New York University. Sanchez and others in that class subsequently formed a poetry workshop that met in Greenwich Village and drew such participants as **Amiri Baraka**, Haki Madhubuti (Don L. Lee), and Larry Neal, with whom Sanchez began working in BAM political activism. At this point Sanchez published the first of her seven plays, *The Bronx Is Next* (1968), and her first collection of poetry, *Homecoming* (1969), consciously placing her work with a black publisher **Dudley Randall**'s Broadside Press. She has gone on to publish twelve more poetry books, including a collection of poems for children titled *It's a New Day: Poems for Young Brothas and Sistuhs* (1971), in addition to other children's books. She also has made audio recordings of her poetry, most recently the compact disc *Full Moon of Sonia* (2004).

Among her numerous awards and fellowships are the Pennsylvania Governor's Award for Excellence in the Humanities, a National Endowment for the Arts Award, the Lucretia Mott Award, the Peace and Freedom Award from Women International League for Peace and Freedom (WILPF), a Pew Fellowship in the Arts, an American Book Award from the Before Columbus Foundation for *Homegirls & Handgrenades* (1984), nominations for the NAACP Image Award and the National Book Critics Circle Award for *Does Your House Have Lions?* (1997), the Langston Hughes Poetry Award, the Harper Lee Award, and the Poetry Society of America's Robert Frost Medal. Sanchez's academic career began in 1965 at the Downtown School in New York and subsequently took her to San Francisco State College, where she pioneered black studies courses; University of Pittsburgh, where she taught the nation's first course in black women's literature; Rutgers University; Manhattan Community College; Amherst College; University of Pennsylvania; and Temple University, where she was the first Presidential Scholar and held the Laura Carnell Chair in English until her retirement in 1999.

Her earliest books record her growing consciousness of American racism and reflect her perspective as a BAM artist and social activist. *Homecoming* and *We a BaddDDD People* (1970) capture her deliberate wielding of the black aesthetic espoused by BAM artists and critics. Her experimental typography forgoes capitalization, treats punctuation as optional, relies on slash marks and unconventional spacing to convey pace, and uses variant spellings to indicate emphasis and pronunciation. In these techniques, along with her expansive use of the page space, Sanchez draws upon the rhythms and structures of jazz and the sounds and syntax of urban black vernacular speech (though she mockingly notes parallels to **e.e. cummings**'s style, in "To Chuck"). For example, the title poem of her first book marks the speaker's return home by announcing "i have been a / way so long"; her enjambment between the unhyphenated syllables of a word ("away") typographically enacts the violence of her separation from the neighborhood where she grew up. She implies that "college," often presented as "a way" out of the so-called ghetto, has caused this separation by teaching her to look at her home "tourist / style," dispassionately and without understanding—a "freudian" way that she rejects. In *We a BaddDDD People*, Sanchez's experiments are more emphatic; in "rite on: wite america 3," she highlights the way this country's violent pioneer past continues into the present, evidenced by "the falling / gun / shells on our blk / tomorrows." These representative early poems show Sanchez's formal choices and her poetry's relentless critique of American racism, sexism, and elitism, in accordance with the insistence that black culture and struggle fundamentally inform the style and substance of BAM poetry.

These two books are represented along with her next two, *Love Poems* (1973) and *Blues Book for Blue Black Magical Women* (1973), in *I've Been a Woman: New and Selected Poems* (1978). Her writing from this period represents a second phase of Sanchez's career. The late 1960s saw her actively working to raise black consciousness and engender social revolution under a black nationalist ideological banner inspired by the teachings of Malcolm X. By 1971 Sanchez—who had earlier married and divorced Puerto Rican immigrant Albert Sanchez—had divorced her second husband, poet **Etheridge Knight**, and begun raising their three children alone. She joined the Nation of Islam, admiring its black institution-building work but primarily seeking the good education available to the Nation's children. By 1975 differences between her Pan-Africanist, socialist ideology and the Nation's black nationalism drove Sanchez out of that community. Her poetry takes on a notably lyrical quality during this period that is hinted at, but undeveloped, in her earlier work. Her images now encompass the natural world, as well as the urban landscape, resonating beyond—but not turning away from—the particularities of racial oppression, as when she sees her beloved "swaying like a lost flower / waiting to be plucked." *Love Poems* is full of untitled haiku and several sonnets, such as the oft-referenced "Father and Daughter," marking Sanchez's reconsideration of the possibilities of given forms. *Blues Book* is a single book-length poem that explores a black everywoman's life from girlhood to old age. The poem's five parts draw upon autobiographical details of Sanchez's experience and a mythologized Africa, locating her strength in "the ancient / black / woman" of "yesterday tribes," who sings as she goes: "womb ripe. walking. loud with mornings. walking. / making pilgrimage to herself." The new poems in *I've Been a Woman* continue to look back to African culture for images and formal strategies, notably the "praise poem," a Swahili form that uses hyperbole to celebrate the society's significant figures.

Sanchez's next and perhaps most acclaimed book, *Homegirls & Handgrenades*, might be considered a multi-genre collection; at times, Sanchez calls the long unlineated pieces **prose poems** and, at other times, short stories. In a well-known prose piece, "Norma," Sanchez's metaphors synecdochically depict the transformation of a young "mathematical genius" and "linguist" who had "ordained us all with her red clay Mississippi talk" into a drug-addicted high school dropout who spoke with a "voice . . . like stale music in barrooms." Bored and frustrated by her teachers' failure to challenge or even appreciate her intellectual abilities, Norma gets pregnant and loses the chance to exercise her potential. The ravages of drugs and government-sanctioned racist violence upon black families and futures are themes that run through the book. Its penultimate poem, "A Letter to Dr. Martin Luther King," is generally seen as a companion piece to the final poem, "MIA's." The former, a prose poem on the occasion of the assassinated leader's unrealized fifty-fourth birthday, examines the desolation of the present through what King's past promised for America's future; the latter mourns those who are "missing in action" in Atlanta, Johannesburg, and El Salvador, even as it calls for the men and women of the world to "summon the dead to life again" by "breathing hope and victory / into their unspoken questions." *Under the Soprano Sky* (1987), her next book, similarly juxtaposes themes of intimacy and political struggle—famously, her response to the Philadelphia police force's decision to bomb and burn down the residence of members of MOVE, a radical political group. Formally, Sanchez still features the black vernacular in these books, but she has dropped much of the more radical typography of the early poems.

The decade between 1995 and 2005 saw the publication of four more books of Sanchez's poetry, including another collection of new and selected poems, *Shake Loose My Skin* (2002). *Wounded in the House of a Friend* (1995) chronicles the supremely hurtful betrayals of our loved ones, featuring poems from a wide formal range: haiku, tanka, blues stanzas, long free-verse poems, and prose poems. She balances painful poems about infidelity and mothers who trade their little girls' virginity for drugs with praise poems for the a cappella ensemble Sweet Honey in the Rock and the women of Spelman College. This volume was followed by the book-length poem *Does Your House Have Lions?,* an **epic elegy** for Wilson, her brother from one of her father's subsequent marriages, who died of AIDS. The poem is notable for being composed entirely of rhyme royal stanzas and for its highly charged language, which blends elevated English with phrases from the West African language of Wolof: "my eyes say no requiem / *mangi dem, mangi dem, mangi dem.*" Sanchez weaves together the voices of sister (Sanchez), brother, father, and ancestors into a song of familial healing in preparation for the brother's transition. Her next book, *Like the Singing Coming Off the Drums: Love Poems* (1998), returns primarily to the haiku, the tanka, and her invented form, the sonku, to crystallize moments of sensual self-awareness, sexual attraction, celebration of particular lives, and mourning for losses: "i am a carnival of / stars a poem of blood." *Shake Loose My Skin* opens with "Homecoming" and pulls together many of the threads of Sanchez's entire oeuvre. Her love for black people has expanded to encompass all people; her denunciation of oppression is more wide-ranging and even more urgent, though less strident. The collection ends with Sanchez at her most visionary, in "Aaaayeee Babo (Praise God)": "We have become nightingales singing us out of fear / Splashing the failed places with light." Using words to create the world in which she wants to live, she invites us all, "black, brown, yellow, white": "Come praise our innocence / our decision to be human."

Further Reading. ***Selected Primary Sources:*** Sanchez, Sonia, *Does Your House Have Lions?* (Boston: Beacon Press, 1997); ———, *Homecoming* (Detroit: Broadside Press, 1969); ———, *Homegirls & Handgrenades* (New York: Thunder's Mouth Press, 1984); ———, *I've Been a Woman: New and Selected Poems* (Chicago: Third World Press, 1978); ———, *Shake Loose My Skin: New and Selected Poems* (Boston: Beacon Press, 1999); ———, *We a BaddDDD People* (Detroit: Broadside Press, 1970); ———, *Wounded in the House of a Friend* (Boston: Beacon Press, 1995). ***Selected Secondary Sources:*** Gabbin, Joanne V., "Sonia Sanchez" in *The History of Southern Women's Literature*, ed. Carolyn Perry and Mary Louise Weaks (Baton Rouge: Louisiana State University Press, 2002, 535–540); Joyce, Joyce A., *Ijala: Sonia Sanchez and the African Poetic Tradition* (Chicago: Third World Press, 1996); Kelly, Susan, "Discipline and Craft: An Interview with Sonia Sanchez" (*African American Review* 34.4 [2000]: 679–687); Rome, Danielle Alyce, "An Interview with Sonia Sanchez," in *Speaking of the Short Story: Interviews with Contemporary Writers* (Jackson: University Press of Mississippi, 1997, 229–236); Williams, David, "The Poetry of Sonia Sanchez" in *Black Women Writers (1950–1980): A Critical Evaluation*, ed. Mari Evans (Garden City, NY: Anchor Press, 1984, 433–448).

Evie Shockley

SANDBURG, CARL (1876–1967)

Poet for the people, Carl Sandburg is also well known for his six-volume biography of Lincoln. His gritty voice is still familiar, thanks to numerous recordings. Besides reading poetry, he was given to performing folk songs with guitar. When **Harriet Monroe** published his most anthologized poem, "Chicago," in *Poetry* in 1914, Carl Sandburg was already thirty-eight years old. At forty, his admiration of **Ezra Pound** reflected something of his own inquisitive background: "He has prowled in streets, taprooms, libraries and lexicons" ("The Work of Ezra Pound," 1916). Less remembered are stories written for his daughters and published early in his career (*Rootabaga Stories,* 1922; *Rootabaga Pigeons,* 1923; *Abe Lincoln Grows Up,* 1928; *Early Moon,* 1930). The literary elite did not approve of Sandburg's style, and his poetry fell into disfavor as early as the 1920s, but the major blow came from **William Carlos Williams** in *Poetry* (1951). Although Williams and others accused Sandburg of ideology, rhetoric, cataloguing, haphazard rhythms, and prose style, it now seems clear that there is "more to Sandburg's poetics than the contradictorily dismissive comments suggest" (Johansen, 2001). Or, as George and Willene Hendrick noted in their introduction to Sandburg's *Selected Poems* (1996), "While his racy and colloquial language never appealed to the academy, his poetry spoke to the masses and was accessible to all who could read." Indeed, because his poems captured the words people used, Sandburg was influential for a number of younger poets, including **Langston Hughes**. In his brief forward to the *Mark Twain Jest Book* (1957), Sandburg wrote some phrases about Twain that might be applied to himself. He mentioned "an American accent and lingo" and "America moving toward art of its own" in the range of Twain's work. Then he added: "His tolerance ran far and had its main difficulty with hypocrites."

Sandburg was born in Galesburg, Illinois, on January 6, 1878, to Swedish immigrant parents. His father worked ten-hour days, six days a week, as a blacksmith's helper for the Chicago, Burlington, and Quincy Railroad in Galesburg, Illinois. Witnessing the 1888 railroad engineers' strike on the CB&Q line, young Sandburg differed from his father and felt sympathy for the strikers. The struggles of the poor, which his parents confronted and which he felt personally, were to mark his poetry. In June 1892, he finished eighth grade and stopped school to go to work. A voracious reader, he delivered and read local and Chicago newspapers, to which he added a six-hour-a-day, seven-day-a-week milk delivery route. In October of that year two of his younger brothers died of diphtheria. The following year, aged fifteen, he was confirmed at Elim Lutheran Church in Galesburg. *Always the Young Strangers* (1953) vividly describes Sandburg's early years, notably his first three-day visit to Chicago in 1896. In June 1897 he took the train west to work in the Kansas wheat fields and began a private journal in which he took notes on vernacular speech (Niven). Joining the Sixth Infantry Regiment of the Illinois Volunteers two days after the Spanish-American War began, Sandburg went to battle in 1898 and chronicled his experiences in a pocket notebook, experiences that determined his pacifist stance at the beginning of the Great War. His veteran status enabled him to go to Lombard College on free tuition, and he supported himself with part-time work as a fireman. With Fred Dickinson, he began selling "views" (photographs) in 1899. Leaving college in his fourth year, without a degree, he explored different avenues from 1902 to 1907, including various speaking engagements, but had difficulty finding his path. Meanwhile, his college professor Philip Green Wright had been impressed enough with his student to print copies of Sandburg's poems "Complacency" and "Austerity" on a small Truddle-Gordon handpress in the basement of his home in February 1903 (Niven).

In December 1906 Sandburg began writing for newspapers, and he eventually settled into a job as editor of *The Opera House Guide* in Chicago in 1907. In December he met Lilian Steichen, an active Socialist with whom he was soon exchanging letters (Niven). After attending the national convention of the Socialist party, where Eugene Debs obtained the presidential nomination in May, they were married in June 1908 in Milwaukee, Wisconsin. The stability of their relationship (he would always call her Paula) provided him with a solid framework within which to write. They had three children, Margaret, Janet, and Helga. In 1912 they lived at 4646 North Hermitage Avenue in Chicago. Sandburg's employment was not as stable as his marriage, however, and soon he was working for several papers, including *Chicago Daily News,* where he met Ben Hecht. Some of Sandburg's articles were published as *The Chicago Race Riots, July 1919* (1919), in which he exposed the inequalities that existed, denouncing the lack of new housing in the Black Belt, although the population had more than doubled during the war. He effectively traced the escalation of violence that led to the riots ("Eight bombs or dynamite containers have been exploded within the last five months") (13). Such perceptive analysis would be put to good use in his poems.

Living in Chicago in the 1920s, Sandburg began researching the life of Lincoln, sometimes working at the bookshop run by his friend Ralph Newman, as well as collecting American folklore and ballads, which led to *The American Songbag* (1927). Prairie poet and part of the Chicago Renaissance, Sandburg received his first Pulitzer Prize for history in 1940, with *Abraham Lincoln, The War Years* (1939). He narrated Aaron Copland's "A Lincoln Portrait," which was commissioned after Pearl Harbor. In 1945 Sandburg and his wife moved to Connemara Farm in Flat Rock, North Carolina (their home is now open to the public as a National Park and Historic Site). In 1948 Sandburg published *Remembrance Rock,* a collection of prose pieces in commemoration of soldiers. His second Pulitzer Prize came for *The Complete*

Poems (1950). In the introduction to the revised and condensed one-volume *Abraham Lincoln* (1954), Sandburg wrote of **Whitman**'s admiration for Lincoln. Situating Lincoln "at the vortex of a vast dark human struggle," Sandburg perceived him as equally important to his creative poetics as both Whitman and Pound. Sandburg died at Connemara on July 22, 1967.

Influenced by Robert Browning, Walt Whitman, and by poems in **Edgar Lee Master**'s *The Spoon River Anthology* (1915), Carl Sandburg's poetry came of age at the beginning of the Great War, during the peak of the **Imagist** movement. Like **Amy Lowell** and **Ezra Pound**, he was published in *Poetry* and received the encouragement of Harriet Monroe and Alice Corbin. In January 1916, after mailing his manuscript of poems to Alfred Harcourt at Henry Holt, Sandburg was asked to remove delicate subject matter. Accordingly, *Chicago Poems* (1916) appeared with its already famous title poem and a censored version of "Billy Sunday," under the title "To a Contemporary Bunkshooter." But Sandburg's unexpurgated "Billy Sunday" (first published in 1915 in *The Masses* and the *International Socialist Review*) can be read in *Billy Sunday and Other Poems* (1993) and *Selected Poems* (1996). The opening question to "Billy Sunday" is repeated in various ways throughout the poem: "You come along—tearing your shirt—yelling about Jesus. I want / to know what the hell you know about Jesus?" Besides religious fraud, the plight of the working poor was Sandburg's concern in *Chicago Poems*. "Ready to Kill" is about the anger that a bronze statue of a general causes for the narrator, who wonders why "the real huskies"—the workers, who are busy "feeding people instead of butchering them"—do not have statues dedicated to them. The influence of Imagism is felt in poems such as "Fog" and "Pool," which may also be linked to **T.S. Eliot**'s feline metaphors for "the yellow fog" in "The Love Song of J. Alfred Prufrock," which had first appeared in *Poetry* magazine in 1915. Sandburg's second collection, *Cornhuskers* (1918), opens with the poem "Prairie," providing the agrarian theme. Imagism is an influence also in the lyrical "River Roads." The poem's third-person imperative "let" begins six of the lines, prefiguring later uses Sandburg will make of the imperative (for example, in "Lesson" in *Honey and Salt*). Birds, the moon, "Laughing Corn," "Autumn Movement," and the view of the prairie from a train fill this volume. In "Manitoba Childe Roland," the European classic becomes Americanized. Sandburg's socialist idealism considers the Great War, shifting in tone from criticism to support—from "Grass," "Flanders," "House," "John Ericsson Day Memorial, 1918," "Remembered Women," "Out of White Lips," "Memoire," and "A Million Young Workmen, 1915" to "The Four Brothers."

In *Smoke and Steel* (1920), the title poem shows the cost of industrial success. The charms of the prairie are contrasted to "Steel barbwire around The Works," where the steel mills take all: "Smoke into steel and blood into steel." "The Mayor of Gary" begins "I asked the Mayor of Gary about the 12-hour day and the 7-day week." Losing one's identity in banal routine is an issue in "The Sins of Kalamazoo," in which the song is "We don't know where we're going but we're on our way." *Slabs of the Sunburnt West* (1922) opens with "The Windy City," recalling the Indian heritage of Chicago and recommending: "listen while they jazz the classics." The poem proclaims, "It is wisdom to think the people are the city," (a message Langston Hughes repeats in "Chicago" published in 1964). The prose poem in admiration of "Brancusi" begins jocularly, "Brancusi is a galoot." Indeed, Sandburg seems relaxed in this volume, mixing high and low culture, using his slang easily. He consistently defended its use, as in "A Fly, a Flea and a Filchbim"—from *Fables, Foibles, and Foobles*, 1988—which describes a man at the New York Public Library with "slang dictionaries under his arm. What he is tired of is correct speech." Yet, "Primer Lesson" cautions "When you let proud words go, it is / not easy to call them back."

The title poem for *Good Morning America* (1928) was the Phi Beta Kappa poem at Harvard. "Good Morning America" evokes Lincoln metaphorically as "a living, arterial highway moving across state lines from coast to coast." The volume opens with thirty-eight "Tentative (First Model) Definitions of Poetry," many of which are playful, such as "Poetry is the achievement of the synthesis of hyacinths and biscuits." After almost a decade without a new poetry collection, Sandburg reached a high point with *The People, Yes* (1936). Composed primarily in 1934-1935, the darkest period of the Great Depression, the poem's 107 sections blend various genres, which are identified for the reader at the outset: "several stories and psalms," "memoranda variations," "sayings and yarns," invested with the music of "jig time and tap dancing" and the sounds of "street crowds, work gangs, sidewalk clamor," ending on "interludes of midnight cool blue" and "the phantom frames of skyscrapers." The poem recasts biblical themes into American idiom, giving "form and structure to the humanistic faith of the New World" (Arenstein). The question of origins is central from the opening's tower of Babel to the story of the "Howdeehow powpow" where the gatherers listened to the silence, which was interrupted by "a little old woman from Kalamazoo / Who gave out a long slow wail over what she was missing / because she was stone deaf." This American epic of the anonymous who shape ends with the questions: "Where to? what next?"

The first edition of the *Complete Poems* (1950) contains a number of new poems about World War II. "On a

Flimmering Floom You Shall Ride," says a note, is about **Archibald MacLeish** appearing before "a Congressional examining committee pressing him to divulge the portents and meanings of his poems." "Mr. Longfellow and His Boy" speaks of the son's deep wounds from a prior war. In "The Abracadabra Boys" and "Many Handles," Sandburg may be poking fun at those who consider themselves the poetic elite. Ten new poems appeared along with excerpts from previous works of poetry and prose in *The Sandburg Range* (1957). *Harvest Poems: 1910–1960* (1960) offers an elegy of sorts for the co-editor of *Poetry*, "Alice Corbin Is Gone." The poem "Now They Bury Her Again" begins "Poetry is dead? So they say." The question may relate to *Poetry* magazine but more likely is a rejoinder to Theodore Adorno's famous remark, "To write poetry after Auschwitz is barbaric." Published when Sandburg was eighty-seven, the collection *Honey and Salt* (1963) celebrates romantic love with two long poems. The title poem asks a series of questions about love and gives no real answers, apart from image, simile, personification, and metaphor. Love comes, says the poem, "Both bidden and unbidden, a sneak and a shadow."

While Sandburg's poetry is now usually absent from college literature syllabi and even from anthologies of **modernist** poetry, it has long enjoyed a large readership for its accessibility, its music, its sympathy for the oppressed, and its poetic grasp of American history.

Further Reading. ***Selected Primary Sources***: Sandburg, Carl, *The American Songbag* (New York: Harvest Books, 1990); ———, *Billy Sunday and Other Poems*, ed. George and Willene Hendrick (New York: Harcourt, Brace & Co, 1993); ———, *Breathing Tokens*, ed. Margaret Sandburg (New York: Harcourt, Brace, Jovanovich, 1978); ———, *The Chicago Race Riots 1919* (1919) (New York: Harcourt, Brace & Co, 1969); ———, *The Complete Poems of Carl Sandburg* (New York: Harcourt Brace & Co., 1970); ———, *Faibles, Foibles, and Foobles*, ed. George Hendrick (Urbana: University of Illinois Press, 1988); ———, *Selected Poems*, ed. George and Willene Hendrick (New York: Harcourt Brace & Co, 1996); ———, "The Work of Ezra Pound" (*Poetry* 7.5 [February 1916]: 249–257). ***Selected Secondary Sources:*** Arenstein, J.D., "Carl Sandburg's Biblical Roots" (*ANQ* 16.2 [Spring 2003]: 54–61); Botkin, B.A., ed., *A Treasury of American Folklore: Stories, Ballads, and Traditions of the People* (New York: Crown, 1944); Brumm, Anne-Marie, "The Cycle of Life: Motifs in the Chicago Poems of Carl Sandburg" (*Zeitschriftfür Anglistik und Amerikanistik* 31.3 [1983]: 237–255); Bryan, George B., "The Proverbial Carl Sandburg (1878–1967): An Index of Folk Speech in His American Poetry" (*Proverbium: Yearbook of International Proverb Scholarship* 20 [2003]: 15–49); Clemens, Cyril, *Mark Twain Jest Book* (Kirkwood Missouri: Mark Twain Journal, 1957); Fauchereau, Serge, *Lecture de la poésie américaine* (Paris: Somogy Editions d'Art, 1998); Johansen, J.G., "Sandburg's 'They Will Say'" (*Explicator* 59.3 [Spring 2001]: 134–135); Niven, Penelope, *Carl Sandburg: A Biography* (New York: Charles Scribner's Sons, 1991); Sandburg, Margaret, ed., *The Poet and the Dream Girl, The Love Letters of Lilian Steichen & Carl Sandburg* (Urbana: University of Illinois Press, 1987).

Jennifer Kilgore

SANDERS, ED (JAMES EDWARD) (1939–)

Ed Sanders is best known for his nonfiction account of the murderer Charles Manson and his cult followers of the late 1960s. His most ambitious undertaking is a history of the United States in poetry. But his most important influence on American poetry came earlier in his career, as a young neo-**Beat** arriving in New York in the late 1950s, where he studied the classics at New York University (BA 1964) and proceeded to make himself the poetic center of 1960s counter-culture. Even more than **Allen Ginsberg**, whose most important work was done earlier, Sanders epitomized the poet as hippie. A publisher, bookstore owner, and singer-songwriter as well as a poet, Sanders became a pop culture icon whose work and career stand alongside that of Phil Ochs and R. Crumb as much as they do Ginsberg and **Robert Lowell**.

Sanders was born August 17, 1939, in Kansas City, one of the great musical centers of America, where he listened to jazz great Jay McShann, studied with the drummer for the Kansas City Philharmonic, and belonged to the Society of Barbershop Quartet Singers. He credits reading *Howl* as a seventeen-year-old with changing his life. Within a few months, he had dropped out of the University of Missouri and hitchhiked to New York, where he attended every Beat reading he could find and was also drawn to political activism. Arrested in 1961 for a protest in which he attempted to board a nuclear-powered submarine, he wrote a thirty-page poem on toilet paper and the inside of cigarette packs. On his release, he smuggled the manuscript out in his shoes and sent it to **Lawrence Ferlinghetti**, who published it under the title *Poem from Jail*.

In 1962 he started a literary magazine, *Fuck You: A Magazine of the Arts*, dedicated to neo-Beat and political activist writing. The title was more scandalous then than it would become in later years, and it got Sanders arrested for obscenity. In 1964 he opened the Peace Eye Bookstore, which became a counter-culture center on the Lower East Side. Along with poet Tuli Kupferberg, whose work he had frequently published, he formed a satiric folk-rock group, The Fugs, in 1965. In addition to political satire and comic scatology, primarily written by Sanders, The Fugs also performed musical settings of William Blake poems, such as "How Sweet I Roamed from Field to Field."

In 1971 Sanders published *The Family*, a history of the Manson family, based largely on entrees to the group permitted by his anti-establishment reputation. It became his most successful book. Other significant prose works that followed include *Investigative Poetry*, which took **Charles Olson**'s work, particularly *The Maximus Poems*, as a starting point and argued for a resumption of poetry's responsibility for a theory of history; *The Party: A Chronological Perspective on a Confrontation at a Buddhist Seminary*, an account of a scandal involving the treatment of **W.S. Merwin** at the Naropa Instititute; and *Tales of Beatnik Glory*, a fictionalized memoir.

Sanders has won the **Frank O'Hara** Prize of the Modern Poetry Association (1967) and the American Book Award (1988) for *Thirsting for Peace in a Raging Century: Selected Poems 1961–1985*. He has received National Endowment for the Arts awards (1966 and 1970), a National Endowment for the Arts fellowship (1987–1988), and a Guggenheim fellowship (1983–1984).

Sanders's poetry is characterized by a base of colloquial, often obscene language, which can expand to accommodate a range of allusion, often to mythology (he has described *Poem from Jail* as being based on an ancient legend). It is often political and offers an apocalyptic and absurdist worldview, with jeremiads against the powerful and the hypocrisies of civilization. In his own words, his aesthetic was "total assault against the culture."

Sanders worked from the aesthetic principle described by **Kerouac** as "spontaneous bop prosody," which had very little to do with the rigorous technique of bop, but did value spontaneity above all. His work has been criticized for the kinds of excesses that come from spontaneity, such as repetition and settling for easy but flamboyant effects, but it has also been praised for its powerful use of vernacular language and its willingness to tackle large themes.

After *The Family*, which took him a year and a half to write, he began to gravitate toward longer poetic forms, which frequently involved research. Following his own advice in *Investigative Poetry*, he wrote book-length biographies in verse of Anton Chekhov (1995) and Allen Ginsberg (2000) and began a history of the United States in poetry, starting with one year, 1968 (1997), and continuing into a full-fledged history.

In 1977 Sanders and his wife, the painter and writer Miriam R. Sanders, moved to Woodstock, New York, where in 1995 they started a weekly newspaper, the *Woodstock Journal*, devoted to Sanders's twin interests of poetry and assault on mainstream politics and culture.

Further Reading. ***Selected Primary Sources:*** Sanders, Ed, *America: A History in Verse, Volume 1 (1900–1939)* (Santa Rosa, CA: Black Sparrow Press, 2000); ———, *America: A History in Verse, Volume 2 (1940–1961)* (Santa Rosa, CA: Black Sparrow Press, 2000); ———, *America: A History in Verse, Volume 3 (1962–1970)* (Santa Rosa, CA: Black Sparrow Press, 2002); ———, *Chekhov* (Santa Rosa, CA: Black Sparrow Press, 1995); ———, *1968: A History in Verse* (Santa Rosa, CA: Black Sparrow Press, 1997); ———, *Peace Eye* (Cleveland, OH: Frontier Press, 1967); ———, *Poem from Jail* (San Francisco: City Lights Books, 1963); ———, *The Poetry and Life of Allen Ginsberg* (New York: Overlook Press, 2000); ———, *Thirsting for Peace in a Raging Century: Selected Poems 1961–1985* (Minneapolis, MN: Coffee House Press, 1987). ***Selected Secondary Sources:*** Ed Sanders issue (*Review of Contemporary Fiction* 19.1 [1999], includes articles by Barry Miles, 14–22; Ann Charters, 47–49; Barry Wallenstein, 50–54; Tom Clark, 55–56; Regina Weinreich, 57; Robert Creeley, 58–60; Kasia Boddy, 61–80; Thomas Myers, 81–90; Lance Olsen, 91–100; Joseph Dewey, 101–111; David Herd, 122–37; Brooke Horvath, 138–143).

Tad Richards

SANER, REG (1930–)

Reg Saner's poetry reflects an impassioned appreciation for the natural world. His poems take readers through rough, inhospitable terrain to pure wilderness, a region of schist cairns, snow-fed lakes, and glacial residue. Writing in the **Whitmanic** tradition, Saner shows some literary kinship with **Gary Snyder**, but his voice is unique, his approach to nature all his own—dynamic, particular, personal.

Born and educated in Illinois, he has spent the bulk of his adult life in Colorado. He earned his BA (1952), MA (1956), and Ph.D. (1962) in English from the University of Illinois–Urbana, and subsequently joined the faculty of the University of Colorado–Boulder. Professor of English since 1973 (currently emeritus), he has taught courses in literature and creative writing. The climate, landscape, and history of the Four Corners region have exercised a significant influence upon his work, inspiring topics and themes that dominate much of his writing. His first book of poetry, *Climbing into the Roots*, won the Academy of American Poets Walt Whitman award in 1975 and was followed by two further books of poetry: *So This Is the Map* (1981), and *Essay on Air* (1984). Other honors include a National Endowment for the Arts fellowship in 1976, the Colorado Governor's award in 1983, and the *Quarterly Review of Literature* 45th Anniversary Award in 1989. He also has won recognition for his nonfiction studies of the American Southwest. *The Four-Cornered Falcon: Essays on the Interior West and the Natural Scene* was published in 1993; a second collection of essays, *Reaching Keet Seel: Ruin's Echo and the Anasazi*, garnered him the Wallace Stegner Award in 1998.

Saner's attention is riveted on a Colorado landscape of talus and tundra, cliffs and ravines. Consistently, poems take readers to elevations far beyond zones of ordinary human activity or habitation. In these all but inaccessible heights, the climber experiences exhilaration bordering upon the sublime, declaring "I come because / the useless is pure Greek" ("How the Laws of Physics Love Chocolate," *Climbing into the Roots*, 1976). Geology is transformed via metaphor from an abstract science into a set of forces palpitant with immediacy, and apparently insentient phenomena become vital: "Mountains blow out of the ground / millennial inch by inch" ("Cony Creek," *Climbing into the Roots*); spruce trees "improvise" ("Homing," *So This Is the Map*, 1981); "lichen mouths [are] sipping at stones" ("Four Cairns," *Climbing into the Roots*). Saner wields personification with abandon, bringing human and nonhuman into close conjunction. "The sky kept showing off," he exults in "The Day the Air was on Fire" (*So This Is the Map*); "granite / held me at gunpoint," he insists, "and wind was a thug" ("Return to Tundra at Bighorn Flats," *So This Is the Map*). This barrage of figurative description enables him to communicate a sense of connectedness with earth's seemingly least human features: "centuries off in my bones / a granite flute practices notes" ("Cony Creek," *Climbing into the Roots*).

Although he is best known for his vivid rendering of high desert country, Saner also sets poems in more populous environs, often returning to the rural Illinois of his own past, as in "Where I Come From" (*So This Is the Map*). Highway and driving experiences serve as a locus of interest that contrasts intriguingly with the poet's commitment to hiking and skiing: a "white / customized Merc tears ass" down an Illinois highway, while in Nebraska two cars pass each other at ninety miles per hour, generating a split-second moment of camaraderie ("Palmyra, Illinois in Bug-Time," "Smiling at 180," *Climbing into the Roots*). "U.S. 36 has always poured possibilities / through your hometown," he notes, remembering provincial youngsters "charging the horizon" on their way to a wider future ("Road Life," *Essay on Air*, 1984). In poems set in Europe, chiefly Italy, Saner finds himself drawn to artifacts from the past. Like the Anasazi cliff houses in his native land, Etruscan relics or the ruins of Pompeii stimulate his imagination: "the dead setting out their marvels / offhandedly" ("Waking to the Ceiling of an Italian Farmhouse," *Essay on Air*). Contemplating connections between human cultures past and present, he records, too, processes of deterioration that seem to bring human endeavor into increasing harmony with natural phenomena. His collections include, in addition, a few elegiac pieces, as well as love poems to his wife: "Anna Primavera" (*So This Is the Map*) or "Anne, Your Name's Mouth and Kiss" (*Essay on Air*).

Saner writes in **free verse** exclusively. Except for alliteration and some assonance, he makes no use of musical repitition. He generates clean, dynamic rhythms suited to convey the high-spirited energy characteristic of his poetry. Lines are short to medium in length and set flush left, with no distracting experiments in spacing or placement. The poems are dotted with allusion, most frequently to sources from the Greco-Roman world or the Old Testament rather than to English or American literature: Augustine, Sisyphus, Achilles, Aquinas, Pharoah, or Jonah. Occasionally Saner pays tribute to music or the visual arts. He compares the paintings of Hieronymus Bosch, for example, to the fantastical formations (shaped by wind and water) that he encounters on treks through high mountain country. Above all else, allusion helps to illustrate and support his persistent interest in the physics of motion, from its astronomical to its geological manifestations. He mentions Anaxagoras, Copernicus, and Pythagoras, for instance, invokes non-Euclidian reality, atomic structure, magnetic fields, and Zeno's paradox. Such references lend a note of scientific assurance to his extravagantly metaphoric apprehension of the universe.

Further Reading. ***Selected Primary Sources:*** Saner, Reg, *Climbing into the Roots* (New York: Harper, 1976); ———, *Essay on Air* (Athens: Ohio Review Books, 1984); ———, *The Four-Cornered Falcon: Essays on the Interior West and the Natural Scene* (Baltimore: Johns Hopkins University Press, 1993); ———, *Reaching Keet Seel: Ruin's Edge and the Anasazi* (Salt Lake City: University of Utah Press, 1998); ———, *So This Is the Map* (New York: Random House, 1981). ***Selected Secondary Sources:*** Dodd, Wayne, "Reg Saner: An Interview" (*Ohio Review* 32 [1984]: 46–63); Martz, Louis L., "Ammons, Warren, and the Tribe of Walt" (*Yale Review* 72 [1982]: 63–84); Oehring, Connie, "'Going in' to the Center Place" (*High Plains Literary Review* 14.2–3 [1999]: 173–180).

Judith P. Saunders

SANTAYANA, GEORGE (1863–1952)

George Santayana is better known for his philosophy than his poetry, but he recognized the importance and necessity of his early poetry as the initiation of his thought into a world of traditions, providing him the means to translate his emotions into ideas and thus to develop the poetic prose of his philosophy. He influenced poets such as **Conrad Aiken**, **T.S. Eliot**, **Wallace Stevens**, and **Robert Frost**, who were students in his philosophy courses at Harvard. As a true cosmopolitan, he reminded his American followers of their European heritage, and as with Tocqueville, his critical observations of the country helped shape their American identity at the turn of the century.

Although Santayana spent half his life in America (1872–1912), he never became a citizen. Instead, he retained the citizenship of his birthplace, Spain, where he lived with his parents, Agustín Ruiz de Santayana and

Josefina Borrás Sturgis, until their separation in 1869. His parents were older. Agustín was a retired diplomat, and Josefina was the daughter of a diplomat and the widow of George Sturgis, a member of an old New England family, with whom she had three children. Upon their separation, Santayana remained in Spain with his father after his mother returned to Boston and the Sturgis family with his two stepsisters and stepbrother. But in 1872 Agustín sent his son to Boston to live with his mother and attend the Boston Latin School and then Harvard. As an emigrant who never fully emigrated, Santayana developed the multilingual perspective of a child who communicated in Spanish with his parents, in English with his siblings, and in Latin and Greek at school. For this reason, he was never quite comfortable with common American idiom, which he thought was essential to producing pure, spontaneous poetry.

It was at Harvard during his years as a student that Santayana produced many of his verses as well as cartoons for the *Harvard Lampoon.* There he also met William James, one of his professors, who likened Santayana to **Emerson** for his style of writing and his brilliant leaps in thought, but James was never able to cultivate in Santayana the New England sense of duty that would have made him a devoted disciple. Upon completing his Harvard degree, Santayana shared a traveling fellowship and spent two years in Germany studying philosophy on his own terms to earn his advanced degree at Harvard. Upon his return and graduation, James offered him a position at Harvard teaching a course on empiricism. He would remain at Harvard for another twenty-three years.

His first philosophical publication was *The Sense of Beauty* (1896). It was followed by *Interpretations of Poetry and Religion* (1900). Both texts conceive a theory of aesthetics that involves every aspect of life from politics to religion, arguing that the aesthetic value of an activity or pursuit originates in the observer's appreciation and reaction, not in the pursuit or object itself. Opposed to the Romanticism of the period, Santayana wanted the poet to engage and apprehend the world through concrete images, avoiding the abstractions of the philosopher and scientist. For these reasons, the poet should prefer fact over fancy.

These earlier efforts laid the foundation for Santayana's developing philosophical system, which would be introduced a few years later in his masterwork, *The Life of Reason* (1905–1906). *The Life of Reason* included five volumes: *Reason in Common Sense, Reason in Society, Reason in Religion, Reason in Art,* and *Reason in Science.* This dense work resisted idealism and continued to promote his earlier pragmatic materialism.

Santayana resigned his professorship at Harvard and left America in 1912 to return to Europe, where he continued to wrestle with his philosophical system, writing *Scepticism and Animal Faith* (1923) and later the substantial work *Realms of Being* (1927–1940). Throughout this same period, Santayana continued to publish articles on a variety of subjects from government to art and published his only novel, *The Last Puritan* (1936), while he worked on a multivolume autobiography, *Persons and Places* (1944). During this productive period Santayana became acquainted with **Ezra Pound**, who initiated a correspondence with him in 1928. Pound courted Santayana's approval and collaboration on a book concerning educational reform, and Santayana tolerated his attention but never agreed to the collaboration. Pound's attentions demonstrate the extent to which Santayana and his philosophy influenced literary works and criticism during the period.

In September 1952, Santayana died in Rome, where he had spent his final years. Since his death, Santayana's work has suffered years of neglect. Only in the last two decades have some of his works returned to publication.

Further Reading. ***Selected Primary Sources:*** Santayana, George, *The Complete Poems of George Santayana* (Lewisburg, PA: Bucknell University Press, 1979); ———, *Santayana on America* (New York: Harcourt, Brace, & World, 1968); ———, *The Works of George Santayana,* 15 vols. (New York: Charles Scribner's Sons, 1936–1940). ***Selected Secondary Sources:*** Boynton, Robert, "A Poetic Approach to Politics: A Study in the Political Philosophy of George Santayana" (*Journal of Politics* 20.4 [November 1958]: 676–694); McCormick, John, *George Santayana* (New York: Alfred A. Knopf, 1987); McCormick, John, "George Santayana and Ezra Pound" (*American Literature* 54.3 [October 1982]: 413–433).

Jennifer Billingsley

SARGENT, EPES (1813–1880)

Epes Sargent was a poet, grammarian, playwright, journalist, editor, and general contributor to his milieu's literary life. Although his output was varied and prolific, Sargent's most commercially successful poem was the catchy "A Life on the Ocean Wave" (1938), which was set to music by Henry Russell and became the regimental march of the Royal Marines.

Sargent was born in Gloucester, Massachusetts, to the eponymous Epes Sargent, who descended from one of the wealthiest families in the Northeast, and Hannah Dane Coffin. Sargent graduated from the Boston Latin School in 1829, and his father took him to Russia, where Sargent stayed in Saint Petersburg for a few months, writing letters to his former school in Boston, which were published in the school's literary journal, the *Collegian,* a magazine founded in part by his brother, John Osborne, and future Supreme Court justice **Oliver Wendell Holmes**. Upon returning to America, Sargent took up residence in Boston, publishing poems in the

Atlantic Monthly, the *United States Democratic Review*, and *Harper's New Monthly Magazine*.

In 1827, two years after the inception of the *Atlantic Souvenir*, Samuel Griswold Goodrich began the *Token*, an annual that ran until 1843. Sargent served as editor during Goodrich's travels in Europe, seeing the issue to press. During his thirties, Sargent worked as a journalist for a number of important news publications, including the *Boston Daily Advertiser*, *Parley's Magazine*, the *Token*, and the *New England Magazine*. For a few years, he served as a political correspondent in Washington, D.C., for the *Boston Daily Atlas*, where he had worked as an editor since his early twenties. While working in the U.S. Capitol, he made political friends, especially in the Whig party, experiences that eventually led to his book "The Life and Public Services of Henry Clay" (1842).

In 1837 Sargent's first literary productions, "Bride of Genoa" and "Velasco," were staged at the Tremont Theater in Boston, followed by a subsequent run in New York and New Orleans. In 1839 he moved to New York to serve as an assistant editor of the *Mirror*; while in the city, he became a member of the Union club and founder of another club, and continued to write for the stage. He returned to Boston in 1846 to edit the *Evening Transcript*. In 1847 Sargent published "Songs of the Sea, with Other Poems," based on nautical adventures during a trip to Cuba and largely considered his masterwork. This collection received acclaim from such critics as **Edgar Allan Poe**, Edwin Percy Whipple, and Henry Theodore Tuckerman. Sargent also wrote "American Adventure by Land and Sea" (1847) describing his arctic voyages. On May 10, 1848, Sargent married Elizabeth W. Weld of Roxbury and labeled himself an "excursionist" in a local Minnesota paper.

In the educational field, Sargent's contribution was significant. Some of his works became the standard bearers in the field, such as "The Standard Speaker" (1852); "The First-Class Standard Reader, for the public and private schools" (1854); "The Standard Speller (1857); "A School Manual of English Etymology and Textbook of Derivatives, Prefixes, and Suffixes" (1873); and "Six Charts for Use Teaching, Reading, and Spelling in Primary Schools." During his editorial career Sargent had good relationships with Daniel Webster, John C. Calhoun, William C. Preston, and Henry Clay, who said that Sargent's "Memoir" of him was the best and most authentic in existence.

Sargent's poems are characterized by regularity of form and rhyme, an explicit engagement with his country's turbulent politics, and his own spiritual growth. Thus, a poem such as "Cabalistic Words" published in the *Atlantic* in 1862, begins with a note in brackets:

> Since the following poem was written, we have had from the President the pledge that the "cabalistic words" shall be uttered by him on the first of January, 1863, unless the rebellion is abandoned before that time. Thanks and honor to the President for the promise! But we shall not look for the magical operation of the words till they are uttered without reservation or qualifications.

The poem then begins by addressing "O Commander of the Faithful." Another poem "Pro Patria," perhaps a harbinger of Wilfred Owen's later poem "Dulce et Decorum Est" begins: "Drift, snows of winter, o'er the turf / That hides in death his cherished form! / And roar, ye pine-trees, like the surf / That breaks before this eastern storm!" yet ends with a bromide of sentimentality: "Oh, fallen in manhood's fairest noon,— / We will remember, 'mid our sighs, / He never yields his life too soon, / For country and for right who dies."

Sargent's ear for the dramatic is manifest in poems such as "The Moor's Revenge" (*Harper's*, 1852), which includes long runs of Shakespearean-influenced tragic soliloquy cast in unswerving tetrameter-trimeter stanzas:

> These limbs convulsed, these fiery pangs,
> These eyeballs hot and blear—
> Ha! know you not what they portend!
> The plague—the plague is hear!

At other times, Sargent could be Keatsian and mystical, as in these lines from his sonnet "The Planet Jupiter" (*Songs of the Sea, with Other Poems*, 1847):

> Bright planet! lustrous effluence! thou ray
> From the Eternal Source of life and light!
> Gleam on the track where Truth shall lead the way,
> And gild the inward as the outward night!

Although his output was varied and prolific, Sargent's most commercially successful poem was the catchy "A Life on the Ocean Wave" (1938), which was set to music by Henry Russell and became the regimental march of the Royal Marines:

> Like an eagle caged, I pine
> On this dull, unchanging shore:
> Oh! give me the flashing brine,
> The spray and the tempest's roar!
> ...
> And the song of our hearts shall be,
> While the winds and the waters rave,
> A home on the rolling sea!
> A life on the ocean wave!

In the last twenty to thirty years of his life, Sargent became interested in Theosophy and spiritism, writing many articles for newspapers that overtly embraced the subject. Williams James reviewed Sargent's book *Planchette: or the Despair of Science* (1869), initiating a fascination with mediums, the paranormal, and the untapped potentialities of human consciousness. Sargent wrote further books on these subjects, such as "The Palpable Proof of Immortality" (1875) and "The Scientific Basis of Spiritualism" (1880). Sargent visited Europe in 1872, spending some time in southern France. Back in the States he discovered that he had oral cancer; he passed away on December 30, 1880.

Further Reading. ***Selected Primary Sources:*** Sargent, Epes, *Songs of the Sea* (Boston, 1847); ———, *The Standard Speller* (Macon, GA: 1861); ———, "The Life and Services of Henry Clay" (Auburn, 1843; with additions by Horace Greeley, 1852); ———, "The Moor's Revenge" (*Harper's New Monthly Magazine* 4.23 [April 1852]); Sargent, Epes, "Pro Patria" (*Atlantic Monthly* 15.88 [February 1965]). ***Selected Secondary Sources:*** Adams, Oscar Fay, "A Dictionary of American Authors" (1901), UVA Library holdings, http://etext.lib.virginia .edu/eaf/authors/es.htm.

Ravi Shankar

SAROYAN, ARAM (1943–)

Aram Saroyan's 1960s poetry bears similarities to **minimalist** visual art. In emphasizing the materiality of language in his **visual poems**, in rejecting conventional attachments of meaning to words, and in the attempt to efface the poetic subject, Saroyan anticipates **Language poetry** in some of his writing. Saroyan's work appeared in several anthologies of **concrete poetry** in the 1960s. He was influenced by the **Black Mountain School** and the **Beat poets** and was active in the New York poetry scene in the 1960s. As the editor of the little magazine *Lines* (1964–1965) and founder of Lines Press (1964–1967), Saroyan published **Ted Berrigan**, **Clark Coolidge**, Ian Hamilton Finlay, **Robert Grenier**, **Robert Lax**, **Bernadette Mayer**, **bp nichol**, **Lorine Niedecker**, **Ron Padgett**, and **Gertrude Stein**. Saroyan may have achieved his widest fame—or notoriety—as the author of a one-word poem, which became a focus of controversy in the debate over funding for the arts. The poem, "lighght" (first published in the *Chicago Review*, 1966; also in *Aram Saroyan*, 1968), earned Saroyan a National Endowment for the Arts Award, and was later used by conservative politicians as an example of the frivolity of government-funded arts projects. In 1970 "lighght" was denounced in Congress as a waste of public money.

The son of playwright and short story writer William Saroyan, Aram Saroyan was born in New York and attended the University of Chicago, New York University, and Columbia University. He married Gailyn McClanahan in 1968; together they have three children. After a period in Cambridge, Massachusetts, where Saroyan worked as an editor for Telegraph Press, the family moved to the artistic community of Bolinas, California in 1972. Saroyan taught for the University of California in Los Angeles from 1988–1994 and has been a lecturer in the University of Southern California Masters of Professional Writing Program since 1996. He is a former president of the PEN Center USA West. In addition to poetry, Saroyan has published novels, short stories, a literary biography, a memoir, and true a crime account.

The visual element was an important one in much of Saroyan's early poetry, and this led to his publication in several anthologies of concrete poetry. Saroyan told Mary Ellen Solt, who published him in *Concrete Poetry: A World View*, that the typewriter with which he wrote had a major impact on the poems themselves. To highlight this effect, Solt included two versions of Saroyan's poem "Crickets" (1966), one typeset and the other reproducing the appearance of Saroyan's original typescript. The grainy, irregular appearance of the letters in the typescript version highlights their materiality and their status as shapes made of ink stamped on the surface of the page. This concern with the materiality of written language reaches its ultimate minimalist potential in a poem that consists solely of a chunky letter "m" with an extra hump and leg (1965–1966).

Saroyan attempts to prevent words from being resolved into meaning in the reading process and to allow them to be looked at rather than seen through. He deforms conventional spelling in some of his one-word poems in order to achieve this effect. "Lighght" is one such poem, the extra letters drawing attention to those elements of the word "light" that are solely visual and that are silent rather than pronounced. "Noom" (1966, *The Rest*) hints at the opposite of midday, with the reversed spelling of moon in what might be read too quickly as "noon." The pause of a yawn in the form of a comma interrupts the greeting "morni,ng" (1968, *Aram Saroyan*).

Repetition is common in Saroyan's work. Two instances of the word "coffee," one on top of the other, hint at caffeine-induced enthusiasm and rapidity of speech. But "silence," in a similar arrangement, with extra space at the beginning of the second line, creates a different effect. The implied pause of the space, combined with the subject named, imparts the gravity of a serious request for the cessation of noise. One of Saroyan's "Crickets" poems consists of the title word repeated numerous times in a column near the right-hand margin of the page, in a manner resembling Donald Judd's "stack" sculptures.

A number of Saroyan's poems are extremely brief descriptions of things heard. The most salient aspect is not the sound of the words but the statement of a sonic event. These are the aural equivalent of snapshots. They are poems with an objective focus. Ego and subjectivity are effaced, and the poet becomes a recording instrument. In one such poem, the proximity of a fly is juxtaposed with birds that are "near & / far" (1966, *Sled Hill Voices*) There is no intrusion here of the poet onto the material; he functions merely as the ear in relation to which the things named can be placed. Identifying the location of the sounds, as in "whistling in the street a car turning in the room ticking" (1966, *Sled Hill Voices*) demarcates an aural space.

Like **Robert Creeley**, whom he traveled cross-country to meet in 1964, Saroyan at times focuses on the circumstances of composition and emphasizes the personal and domestic. This is especially the case in his post-1970 work. By the late 1960s, Saroyan had abandoned his minimalist aesthetic; the change is reflected in the poems written in Bolinas from 1972 to 1981 and collected in *Day and Night: Bolinas Poems* (1998). This volume includes many poems written for and about family members and other poets, and a number of them reflect on personal memory and the day-to-day life of a husband and father. "O My Generation" (1976) lists details of life in America for Saroyan and his contemporaries in the manner of **Whitman** and **Ginsberg**. "Day and Night" (1981), with its very brief lines and three-line stanzas, structurally resembles a Creeley poem, as do others in the book. "How to Be an American Poet" (ca. 1980) opens with the advice "The secret of poetry is to start simple" and to stay simple, as Saroyan has done, although in varying modes.

Further Reading. ***Primary Sources:*** Saroyan, Aram, *Aram Saroyan* (New York: Random House, 1968); ———, *Day and Night: Bolinas Poems* (Santa Rosa, CA: Black Sparrow, 1998); ———, *Open Field Suite* (Ellsworth, ME: Blackwood Broadsides, 1998); ———, *Pages* (New York: Random House, 1969); ———, *The Rest* (New York: Telegraph Press, 1971); ———, *Sled Hill Voices: 13 Poems* (London: Goliard, 1966). ***Secondary Sources:*** Clay, Steven, and Rodney Phillips, *A Secret Location on the Lower East Side: Adventures in Writing, 1960–1980* (New York: New York Public Library; Astor, Lenox and Tilden Foundation; and Granary Books, 1998); Saroyan, Aram, *Friends in the World: The Education of a Writer* (Minneapolis, MN: Coffee House Press, 1992); Solt, Mary Ellen, ed., *Concrete Poetry: A World View* (Bloomington: Indiana University Press, 1970).

Karen Alexander

SARTON, MAY (1912–1995)

Although May Sarton is better known for her journals and novels, she considered herself a poet first. During her writing career, Sarton produced nineteen novels, three memoirs, nine journals, and several volumes of letters, yet it was the seventeen volumes of poetry that mattered most to her. For May Sarton, the writing of poetry was a way of life, one to which she dedicated herself for over sixty years. At the age of eighteen, four of Sarton's sonnets were published in the December 1930 issue of **Harriet Monroe**'s *Poetry, A Magazine of Verse*; her poetry would appear in that journal's pages many more times, the last being in 1992, when at eighty years of age, she was awarded the Levinson Prize for poetry.

Born an only child in Wondelgem, Belgium, in 1912 to George and Mabel Sarton, at the age of two May Sarton moved with her parents to Cambridge, Massachusetts. As a young girl Sarton learned from her parents the importance of a disciplined approach to learning and writing, coupled with the joy of reading poetry aloud. Raised as a precocious, free-thinking child, Sarton attended the progressive Shady Hill School from 1926 to 1929, where she met the founder and poetry teacher Agnes Hocking, who would become foundational in teaching her the importance of memorizing and reciting poetry. This experience would serve Sarton well not only during her brief association with the theater but also later with poetry readings and lectures.

May Sarton began to "seriously" write poetry as a young girl and by fifteen would say with certainty in her juvenile poem "Ego," "I shall be a poet."

After graduation from high school Sarton, although continuing to write poetry, turned her interest toward acting, having been infuenced by the performances of Eva le Gallienne. In spite of objections from her parents, Sarton declined a scholarship to Vassar to move to New York and become a member of Le Gallienne's Civic Repertory Theatre and later director of her own Associated Actors Theatre.

Beginning in 1931 at age nineteen, Sarton traveled to Europe to live in Paris for a year, while her parents were staying in Lebanon. This marked the beginning of a lifelong adventure of annually visiting Europe, where she would meet and befriend a series of extraordinary people, including Virginia Woolf, Elizabeth Bowen, Julian and Juliette Huxley, Basil de Selincourt, and S.S. Koteliansky. Sarton would also reconnect with the Belgian poet Marie Closset (pen name Jean Dominique), whom she originally met at age twelve. Closset remained one of the most influential women in Sarton's life, both as a poet and as an intimate friend. After the demise of her Associated Actors Theatre, a victim of the Great Depression, Sarton turned to writing as her life's profession and never looked back. The pattern of dual allegiance to Europe and the United States would continue until 1958, when she bought a house in Nelson, New Hampshire, and her sentiments began to turn more toward America. It was shortly after the purchase of this house that Sarton, while traveling in Europe, realized she was yearning for her house in America, no longer feeling like an exile with no home of her own. Many poems were written about her home in Nelson, including "Moving In," "Reflection by a Fire," and "Mud Season," which appeared in the volume *Cloud, Stone, Sun, Vine.*

Although Sarton published seventeen volumes of verse over the course of her lifetime, certain volumes stand out as significant in contributing to her poetic development, including *Encounter in April* (1937), *Inner Landscape* (1939), *In Time Like Air* (1958), *Cloud, Stone, Sun, Vine* (1961), A *Private Mythology* (1966), *Collected Poems* (1973, 1993), and *Coming into Eighty* (1994).

Sarton's first volume of poetry, *Encounter in April,* included the earlier sonnets published in *Poetry* magazine in 1930, as well as the much-lauded ten-part free-verse poem "She Shall Be Called Woman." According to Mark Fulk in *Understanding May Sarton,* this poem presents some of the themes that would become characteristic of Sarton's poetry: exploration of sexual love, the awakening of a woman to the potentials within her own body, and the recasting of mythology in feminist modes (20).

In her journal *Recovering*, Sarton referred to herself as a lyric poet; "the simple lyric is the rarest and most precious kind of poem" (143) and identified with lyric poets, such as **Elinor Wylie, H.D.** (Hilda Doolittle), and **Edna St. Vincent Millay**, whose poetry "communicated a vision of life." The strong influences of these poets can readily be seen in many of Sarton's poems in *Encounter in April.*

Sarton's first book of poetry met with mostly positive reviews. William Rose Benét, literary critic for the *Saturday Review of Literature,* singled out the poem "First Snow" as being filled with "aristocratic grace" and "She Shall Be Called Woman" as the most powerful poem in the book (1937). Conrad Sherman, critic for *Poetry* magazine, agreed with Benét's assessment but cautioned that too often Sarton's sonnets recalled the poetry of Edna St. Vincent Millay. This would be the prevailing criticism, an assessment Sarton would later come to agree with, noting she should not have imitated Millay but rather gone directly for inspiration to the Elizabethan poets themselves. Many years later, while selecting poems for her collected volume of verse, Sarton chose only three poems from *Encounter in April,* admitting that the remaining poems were too derivative.

Sarton's second book of poetry, *Inner Landscape,* (1939) was published simultaneously in the United States and in England. It contained a significant number of poems from *Encounter in April,* including the sonnets, as well as new poems, such as the assertive, epistolary "Letter to James Stephens" and "Prayer Before Work." Now her poems were beginning to be recognized by important publications such as the *Spectator,* the *Observer,* and the *Times Literary Supplement* in England and the *New York Times Book Review, Saturday Review of Literature,* and the *Christian Science Monitor* in the United States. In addition, the influential English literary critic Basil de Selincourt, in his review in the *Observer,* highly praised Sarton's poetic skills, noting that her "tool" for expression is "deep searching to the point of ruthlessness and very delicate" (1939). Sarton later credited de Selincourt's positive review as helping to launch her poetic career.

Over the next nineteen years, Sarton would produce three more volumes of poetry as well as five novels, including the influential and controversial novel *Faithful Are the Wounds.* Critical evaluation of Sarton's poetry during these years, although mixed, was mostly positive. Basil de Selincourt wrote of *Inner Landscape* in his review for the *Observer* that Sarton's universality was wholly personal. Her poems tell the story of "human passion, unique, holy and unforgettable." Moving from the influence of early **modernists** such as Millay and H.D., Sarton turned to the works of William Butler Yeats, **Louise Bogan**, and Rainier Maria Rilke. Honing her poetry skills during these middle years, Sarton demonstrated a greater maturity, most evident with the 1958 publication of *In Time Like Air,* in which the title poem as well as poems such as "On Being Given Time" and "At Muzot" showed Sarton at the height of her powers. Indeed, *In Time Like Air* was nominated for a National Book Award. Reviewers for both the *New York Times Book Review* and the *New Yorker* praised the strength, wit, music, and calm intensity of the poems in this book. This was especially significant for Sarton because these would be the last positive comments made by the *New York Times Book Review,* and the only review from the *New Yorker* that she would receive: **Louise Bogan**, poetry editor for the *New Yorker* and someone whom Sarton considered a friend and peer for over thirty years, failed to print any substantial review of Sarton's poetry in the pages of that publication.

In 1961 Sarton's seventh volume of verse, *Cloud, Stone, Sun, Vine,* was published. Its appearance marked a dramatic turning point in Sarton's poetry career and would change the direction of her life. This dramatic change was prompted by a review from **Karl Shapiro** for the December 24, 1961, issue of the *New York Times Book Review,* one that would change the critical reception of Sarton's poetry for the rest of her life. Calling her a "bad poet" whose poems are a "chamber of clichés," Shapiro set the tone for future critical evaluation of Sarton's verse. In a 1993 interview with Katie Davis for National Public Radio, Sarton commented that she believed this negative review contributed to the fact that her poetry does not appear in major college anthologies.

After Shapiro's scathing review, Sarton turned away from what she referred to as the "poetry circuit," moving into an old farmhouse in Nelson, New Hampshire, to seek the solace of solitude that this house in a small, isolated village provided. This move eventually proved to be the salve Sarton needed to heal emotionally, and it was during her years in Nelson that she wrote some of her most important works, including the memoir *Plant Dreaming Deep* (1968), *The Journal of a Solitude* (1973) and her powerful novel *Mrs. Stevens Hears the Mermaids Singing* (1965).

Although continuing to write poetry throughout this period, Sarton's next published volume, *A Private Mythology* (1966), would not appear for another six years. This important volume contains many poems in free verse, a change of style for Sarton, who had always championed the importance of form in poetry: "I love the freedom that comes from form, not just in art but in life as well," she told Michael Finley in a 1986 interview. Sarton had written free verse earlier, yet the significant number of free verse poems that appeared in *A Private Mythology* marked an important turning point as she describes in her essay "On Growth and Change"; free verse allowed her "to break through to below the level of reason" and to "explore the silences within" (1966). The critics, though, were harsh in their comments, echoing those of Helen Vendler, who, in the *Massachusetts Review*, described Sarton as a "derivative poet" whose poetry deals in all the "clichés of literate verse" (557).

In 1974 the first of two editions of collected poems would be published. The first edition, covering the years 1930 to 1973, included selected verse from all her published volumes up to 1973. It is significant that from her first volume of poetry, *Encounter in April*, she chose to include only three poems: "First Snow," "She Shall Be Called Woman," and "Strangers," believing still that the other poems in this volume were too imitative. The second edition of collected poems (1993) contained all of the selections from the first volume as well as selections from all of Sarton's later volumes of poetry, ending with *The Silence Now* (1988). The significance of these collected volumes lies in the fact that they made available poetry that had gone out of print as well as introducing a whole new generation of readers to Sarton's poetry.

Coming into Eighty (1994) was Sarton's last published volume of poetry. Drawing upon the example of W.B. Yeats, who changed his style radically in old age, Sarton experimented with new forms and new ways of writing poems. Because of physical limitations due to age, Sarton accepted the fact that her life had been reduced to essences, giving her time to explore the "innermost" with absolute attention. As she describes in the preface, the poems flowed from her in the middle of the night when all was quiet. They represented a radical change of routine for Sarton because for all of her writing life she had risen early in order to write at her desk all morning and then would spend afternoons gardening or doing some other physical activity. In the preface to this volume, Sarton describes herself as a "foreigner in the land of old age" admitting that at eighty years old she had to learn its language. It was a change, she welcomed (11).

Reviews were more positive than those written about previous volumes, as many critics welcomed Sarton's ability to celebrate life in spite of her advanced age and fragile health. **"Minimalism"** is the word most often applied to these poems' terse lines; and as Christine Stenstrom writes in *Library Journal*, these are "spare and delicately focused poems . . . inspired by the small blessings of life" (84).

Several of the poems in *Coming into Eighty* had previously been published in *Poetry* magazine, completing the circle, that had begun in 1930 and which ended in 1994. The sixty-four years of Sarton's writing life included seventeen books of verse and hundreds of individual poems, which were written with "clear intensity and technical variety," as Henry Taylor noted in his blurb for *Coming into Eighty.*

Since May Sarton's death in 1995, three volumes of selected letters have been edited by Susan Sherman. This is significant because Sarton frequently included poems in her letters, and Sherman has faithfully reproduced many of these poems, some of which do not appear in the published volumes of poetry. In addition, Sherman has edited a book of Sarton's juvenilia, *Catching Beauty: The Earliest Poems* (2002).

Such a large body of poetry invites a variety of critical opinions. For the most part, critics have been divided about the quality of Sarton's work, some faulting her for too many clichés, too much sentimentality, or trivial subject matter, and others, conversely, praising her lush imagery, her "personal" universality, and her deceptively clear lines. When there is such critical disparity, the truth surely lies somewhere in between. It would finally take the combined critical assessments of feminist scholars, such as Constance Hunting, Sandra Gilbert, and Susan Swartzlander, to identify the strengths in Sarton's poetry, crediting her with leading the way for future women poets who had moved beyond the male literary tradition. With such seminal poems as "She Shall Be Called Woman," "Letter from Chicago," Sarton's response to Virginia Woolf's suicide, and one of her most important poems "My Sisters, Oh My Sisters," an exploration of the greatness and the cost of women's art, Sarton persevered in her writing without a clear mandate from the literary establishment. Quoting her father's words in her journal *After the Stroke*, Sarton embraced his philosophy: "I do not need to hope in order to undertake nor to succeed in order to persevere" (147). In the end it was not for recognition, money, or praise that Sarton wrote poetry, but rather, as she explained in her essay "A Poet's Letter to a Beginner,"

"The only reason for writing poetry is because you have to, because it is what gives you joy" ("*The Writer*," 74).

Further Reading. ***Selected Primary Sources:*** Sarton, May, *Cloud, Stone, Sun, Vine* (New York: W.W. Norton, 1961); ———, *Collected Poems 1930–1993* (New York: W.W. Norton, 1993); ———, *Coming into Eighty* (New York: W.W. Norton, 1994); ———, *Encounter in April* (Boston: Houghton Mifflin, 1937); ———, *In Time Like Air* (New York: Rinehart, 1958); ———, *A Private Mythology* (New York: W.W. Norton, 1966); Sarton, May, "The Writing of a Poem" (*Scripps College Bulletin* 31 #2 [February 1957]: 1–17). ***Selected Secondary Sources:*** Blouin, Lenora P., "The Stern Growth of a Lyric Poet" (*Bulletin of Bibliography* 57.4 [December 2000]: 191–206); Fulk, Mark K., *Understanding May Sarton* (Columbia: University of South Carolina Press, 2001); Gilbert, Sandra, "'That Great Sanity, That Sun, the Feminine Power': May Sarton and the (New) Female Poetic Tradition," in *A Celebration of May Sarton*, ed. Constance Hunting (Orono, ME; Puckerbrush Press, 1994); Hunting, Constance, "May Sarton," in *American Poets 1880–1945, Dictionary of Literary Biography*, vol. 48 (Detroit: Gale Research, 1986, 376–386); Kallet, Marilyn, ed., *A House of Gathering Poets on May Sarton's Poetry* (Knoxville: University of Tennessee Press, 1993).

Lenora P. Blouin

SCALAPINO, LESLIE (1947–)

A significant figure in San Francisco poetry since the 1970s, Leslie Scalapino is often associated with the **Language** school, the West Coast contingent of which she belongs to, alongside poets such as **Robert Grenier** and **Lyn Hejinian**. She shares with the latter poets an interest in experimental writing and post-structuralist ideas about the perceptual surface of language, resisting what she sees as a tradition of poetry too entrenched in symbolism. In addition to poetry, Scalapino writes fiction, plays, and essays, though often she combines these genres or collaborates with other poets in her work. Since 1976, she has published over thirty volumes of poetry.

Scalapino was born in Santa Barbara, California. Her father was a political science professor and her mother a singer. She attended public schools in Berkeley and later went to Reed College in Oregon, where she was influenced by poets such as **Gary Snyder**, Lew Welch, and, most importantly, **Philip Whalen**, whose penchant for Asian religion and experimental writing she has cited as informing her work. Scalapino received her BA in 1966 in medieval and nineteenth-century French poetry, specifically Baudelaire and Rimbaud. She later attended an MA program at University of California–Berkeley, which she left in 1969, frustrated with the traditionalism of the program during a time of great social and political upheaval.

One of the abiding motivations of Scalapino's work is the tension between a male-dominated **canon** of Western literature and her passionate commitment to sounding women's and minority voices. For Scalapino, many of the semantic aspects of language are expressions for the institutions of power. She revises these, in part, by writing poetry that is anti-lyrical and grammatically subversive, again working with the perceptual or syntactic aspects of the language. Like the work of the Language poets, these experiments attempt to uncover how language participates in the social constructedness of subjectivity. As Marjorie Perloff argues, Scalapino's "decentering of the subject foregrounds the artifice of the verbal process" (49). At the same time, however, Scalapino attempts to relinquish the ego, resisting all assumptions that her critique will reveal a fully natural, psychological self.

Many of these themes are evident even in her first volume of poetry, *O and Other Poems* (1976), which is dedicated to Virginia Woolf and made up of meticulously descriptive, first-person poems. The final piece, "Water," muses on Woolf's suicide by reimagining her last day in the first person, when Woolf knew that her "I" had vanished, and that also "There was no audience. / No echo." This appropriation of the mute experience of death by Scalapino's distinctly feminine voice allows her to reflect on the state or fate of **modernism**, the fate of women in relation to the canon of literature, and her own identity. In the wake of such a poetic project, what there is of the self remains elusive; Tyrus Miller writes of Scalapino's work that "the detached yet anxious 'I' [slips] in and out of focus" (222).

In writing about herself, then, Scalapino reveals what is discovered of the self beneath her critical lens. Unsurprisingly, what she reveals is neither subject nor ego, but a process, an active self. Her *Autobiography* (2003) is accompanied by a commentary and poem, "Zither," which rewrites *King Lear* without characters, plot, or language, highlighting only the action of the characters. In an interview with Edward Foster, she states, "[The self] is the act of seeing, but you believe that you're seeing something which you take to be real . . . the only thing that the self is then is the seeing of it (33)." It is this active self that suffuses all of her writing. As a poetic idea, it is as much an expression of Eastern thought (an interest likely acquired on her many visits to Asia with her parents throughout her childhood) as it is of Western literary history and post-structuralism. Thus, much of her work exhibits, as Miller says, "the uncertain certainty of a relative path, a meandering way, a 'Tao of physics' in place of a dead God" (225). Scalapino takes up political situations in the East as topics for several of her books, such as *The Tango* (2001), a collaborative collection of paintings, photographs, and text about monks in formal debate at the Sera monastery in Tibet.

As Scalapino muses on structures of experience, she also plays visually with the conventions of versification and prosody to express this meandering and active self. Her playfulness has several sources. She describes her own writing as aelotropic, referring to the concept in physics of an entity that exhibits different characteristics as it turns in one direction or another. She also cites film, especially the work of Godard and Bergman, as having an important effect on her work. In fact, Edith Jarolim identifies Scalapino's poetry as "cinematic" or "videomatic." Her poetry is highly visual, with small sections of text, or moments of it, scattered across the pages, drawing the reader's attention visually away from the assumption of semantic wholeness. Her interest in the visual extends even further than the perceptual surface of the text itself. The volume *Crowd and Not Evening or Light* (1992), the second half of which is composed of a series of photographs with handwritten "captions" beside or below them, resembles a personal scrapbook. But the photographs are impersonal, almost dreary, and the captions are disjunctive, thus highlighting the artifice of the medium and foregrounding the intersection between the interior subject and the exterior world.

Leslie Scalapino has taught at the Naropa Institute in Boulder, Colorado; at Mills College in Oakland, California; at the San Francisco Art Institute; and at Bard College in the Milton Avery Graduate Program of the Arts. She is the editor of O Books, which publishes younger radical poets in the San Francisco Bay Area. Her writing has received the Lawrence Lipton Prize, the San Francisco State Poetry Center Award, the American Book Award of the Before Columbus Foundation, and two National Endowment for the Arts poetry fellowships.

Further Reading. ***Selected Primary Sources:*** Scalapino, Leslie, *Considering How Exaggerated Music Is* (San Francisco: North Point Press, 1982); ———, *Crowd and Not Evening or Light* (Oakland, CA: O Books, 1992); ———, *The Front Matter, Dead Souls* (Middletown, CT: Wesleyan University Press, 1996); ———, *How Phenomena Appear to Unfold* (Berkeley, CA: Potes & Poets Press, 1991); ———, *Instead of an Animal* (Oakland, CA: Cloud Marauder Press, 1978); ———, *O and Other Poems* (Berkeley, CA: Sand Dollar Press, 1976); ———, *Objects in the Terrifying Tense / Longing from Taking Place* (New York: Roof Books, 1994); ———, *The Tango* (text and photographs by Scalpino, collaboration with artist Marina Adams) (New York: Granary Press, 2001); ———, *way* (San Francisco: North Point Press, 1988); ———, *The Woman Who Could Read the Minds of Dogs* (Berkeley, CA: Sand Dollar Press, 1976); ———, *Zither & Autobiography* (Middletown, CT: Wesleyan University Press, 2003). ***Selected Secondary Sources:*** Foster, Edward, "An Interview with Leslie Scalapino" (*Talisman: A Journal of Contemporary Poetry & Poetics* 8 [Spring 1992]: 32–41); Jarolim, Edith, "No Satisfaction: The Poetry of Leslie Scalapino" (*North Dakota Quarterly* 55.4 [Fall 1987]: 268–275); Miller, Tyrus, "Leslie Scalapino's *Way*" (*Sulfur* 26 [Spring 1990]: 222–225); Perloff, Marjorie, *Radical Artifice: Writing Poetry in the Age of Media* (Chicago: University of Chicago Press, 1991; 49–51).

Stefanie E. Sobelle

SCARBROUGH, GEORGE (1915–)

Having earned a reputation early in his career as the "youngest of the **Fugitives**," George Scarbrough has worked in relative obscurity in the national arena, acquiring a long-standing cadre of admirers in the Southern region, including **James Dickey**, **Forrest Gander**, R.T. Smith, and **Fred Chappell**, each singing his praises in various venues, each hoping that the "rediscovery" will be permanent. Gander takes Scarbrough to be one of "the underrecognized, the unanthologized, the downright obstinate and hellbent species of Southern poet who, despite the lack of recognition and difficulty finding publishers, persevere in their efforts to create a musculature of a different order than that flexed by either the so-called mainstream Southern poets or the so-called vanguard urban ones" (13). Scarbrough's assiduous avoidance of literary circles has been often cited, but his poetry bears the marks of one wrestling with the very possibility of self-reliance.

The third of seven children, and the first, he claims, that his mother did not want, George Scarbrough was born on October 20, 1915, in Benton, Tennessee, "county-born and county-bred," as he describes himself (Gander, 13). His father, William Oscar Scarbrough, a half-Cherokee itinerant farmer, had little use for learning and openly scorned and abused his "sissy" son, whereas his mother, Louise Anabel Scarbrough (née McDowell) encouraged him to read. If his autobiographical novel, *A Summer Ago*, is to be believed, Scarbrough—like his young protagonist Alan McDowell—was forced to sell a beloved bull calf he had raised over a summer in order to pay for school books for the sixth grade; and what's more, the sum from the sale being enough, he bought half of his brother's eighth-grade texts and a dress for his mother, only to come home to indifference: "You'll wake the baby" was all his brother could say when Alan burst excited onto the porch. All the while, the novel traces the introverted boy's awe of the natural world, the tears that "unaccountably stung his eyes" at the sight of a sycamore grove, and his negotiation of the inexplicable adult world, rife with undue hostility, puzzling idioms (about gnats, in particular), abject obsessions (a snake-charming preacher's spectacle), and sage and sober advice ("the learning is always too late").

Scarbrough showed promise early in his career, being singled out of the dozen classmates who were studying literature at Sewanee, the University of the South. His diligence since age eleven, when he began to write poetry, yielded accolades and publications in local newspapers and in the *Sewanee Review.* Completing a BA at Lincoln Memorial University and an MA in creative writing at the University of Tennessee, he began work toward a Ph.D. but never finished. He attended the University of Iowa's Writers Workshop and then returned to Tennessee for good.

Scarbrough's most consistent visibility as a poet came with a trio of books published by Dutton in a span of seven years in the late 1940s and 1950s: *Tellico Blue, The Course Is Upward,* and *Summer So-Called.* These three books exhibit a poet perfecting a formal technique learned under the tutelage of Andrew Lytle, Tudor Long, and George Baker, with such poems as an elegiac sonnet for his father, "Death Is a Creek, Backward Flowing," and a lamentation for lost family connections in another sonnet, "For Five Brothers." The poems exhibit a more open lineation, but not without reservations: "My soul drew up or down to the minimal." With *Summer So-Called,* Scarbrough is clearly more comfortable in free verse, hammering out his own tangled verbal idiom, as when, referring to a dime held in his pocket as his father shoves him, he writes, "Astronomic in a facial universe, / Penumbral and off-side the shining."

After the mid-1950s Scarbrough's publishing ceased, until he was approached by Patricia Wilcox, then publisher of Iris Press in Binghamton, New York, who helped him to produce his *New and Selected Poems* in 1977. In the "new" poems selected, he shares an affinity with **Seamus Heaney** for the deep-rootedness of sound, the sense of speaking for the land and through the land, even as he is also "the interlocutor, man, who must have / his rattle, even in Eden." This perpetual sense of being in the "Eden" of Appalachia is always shot through with the sense of a figure out of place, as in "Pied Beauty," in which an effeminate boy smears on facial cream and frolics amid lush flora ("Don't upbraid, don't / offend him") or in the "The Private Papers of J.L. McDowell, M.D. [Mountain Doctor]," in which a distant relative (largely fictionalized) ruminates upon ailments and traditional medicine.

Invitation to Kim, Scarbrough's next book of poems, was the first in twelve years and was nominated for the Pulitzer Prize. It contains "fetched-together / Fragments" for the poet's absent brother. The humility and self-deprecation of these poems is gnarled up in lineation to the point of breaking into both tenderness and despondency, as when he says he is "freak" enough "To imagine the freak among us / Genius would have been." Scarbrough has, however, little patience for melodrama, as may be seen in an apparent potshot at **Sylvia Plath**: "Daddy, You Bastard" alternates between the banality (in Hannah Arendt's sense) of abuse, as when the father wears a hat when whipping the child, "as if to formalize the event," and its terrible beauty ("Your hands were golden, / bone-streaked cups of wrath").

Scarbrough's most recent work is a sequence of poems based on the reclusive fourth-century Chinese Buddhist monk Han-Shan and his friend Shi-Te. There are still echoes of Scarbrough's family experiences in these new poems; Han-Shan answers a rather oddly hostile stranger, with whom he is exchanging non sequiturs, saying "In a new country, one learns / To temper the wind to the shorn lamb," merely repeating without understanding words his grandmother had said. One can hear in Han-Shan's rejection of life in the capital Scarbrough's disdain for the "unctuous hypocrites" of university administrations. Most of the Han-Shan poems seem intent on a fierce defense of solitude, as well as the enriching beauty of an isolated garden set against the city life left behind: The memory of the scent of a lemon tree mixes with that of the harsh voices of the emperor's officials "and the cold seizure / of Manacles".

Further Reading. ***Selected Primary Sources:*** Scarbrough, George, "From the Han-Shan Sequence" (*Virginia Quarterly Review* [Fall 2004]: 196–209); ———, *The Course Is Upward* (New York: Dutton, 1951); ———, *Invitation to Kim* (Memphis, TN: Iris, 1989); ———, *New and Selected Poems* (Binghamton, NY: Iris, 1977); ———, *A Summer Ago* (Memphis, TN: St. Luke's, 1986); ———, *Summer So-Called* (New York: Dutton, 1956); ———, *Tellico Blue* (New York: Dutton, 1949). ***Selected Secondary Sources:*** Gander, Forrest, "The Inflorescence of Variety: An Iconoclastic Southern Poet" (*Shenandoah* [Spring 2001]: 12–16); Mackin, Randal Thomas, *Walking the Paths of His Own Premise: The Life and Literature of George Scarbrough* (D.A. diss., Middle Tennessee State University, 2002); Smith, R.T., "Lusher Materia Medica I Have Not Seen" (*Shenandoah* [Spring 2001]: 7–10).

Douglas Basford

SCHNACKENBERG, GJERTRUD (1953–)

Often claimed as a **New Formalist**, Gjertrud Schnackenberg's work goes far beyond this narrow category. Equally engaged with the distant vistas of history and the close bonds of love and family, equally at home with baroque intricacy and plainspoken diction, and equally comfortable with traditional forms and looser structures, Schnackenberg, judging from the four books she has published so far, is a poet with extensive skills and wide-ranging interests.

Schnackenberg was born in Tacoma, Washington, the daughter of second-generation Norwegian Lutherans: Walter Charles Schnackenberg, a professor of Russian and medieval history at Pacific Lutheran University, and Doris Ione Strom Schnackenberg. She graduated from

Mount Holyoke—from which she twice received the prestigious Glascock Award for Poetry—in 1975. Shortly after graduating, she married a former professor, Paul Smyth; after the marriage dissolved, she returned to Mount Holyoke to teach during the early 1980s. When Schnackenberg published her first collection, the chapbook *Portraits and Elegies*, in 1982, accolades followed quickly: She received the Lavan Younger Poets Award from the Academy of American Poets in 1983, a Rome fellowship in literature from the American Academy and Institute of Arts and Letters for 1983–1984, and an Amy Lowell fellowship for 1984–1985, which enabled her to prolong her stay in Italy for two more years. She was also awarded an honorary doctorate from Mount Holyoke in 1985. Her second collection, *The Lamplit Answer*, appeared in 1985 and solidified her reputation as a poet of great emotional power, immense formal skill, and formidable learning. When her third collection, *A Gilded Lapse of Time*, was published in 1992, poet and critic **William Logan** hailed her as "the best poet writing today under 40." The year 2000 saw the publication of a fourth collection, as well as *Supernatural Love: Poems 1997–1992*. In 1987 Schnackenberg married the philosopher Robert Nozick, who died in 2002. Her other honors include fellowships from the Bunting and Guggenheim institutes, a grant from the National Endowment for the Arts, and an award in literature from the American Academy of Arts and Letters. She has also been a visiting fellow at St. Catherine's College, Oxford, and a visiting scholar at the Getty Research Institute for the History of Art and the Humanities, and currently lives in Boston.

Portraits and Elegies, which is framed by two long sequences with a shorter poem in the middle, opens with "Laughing with One Eye," at once a portrait and an elegy for Schnackenberg's father, who died in 1973. Written primarily in rhyming quatrains embedded within longer stanzas, the poem's twelve sections describe family outings at home ("Nightfishing") and abroad ("Bavaria"), dreams in which Schnackenberg finds herself faced with an "Abyss where now I lay me down to sleep" ("Dream"), and memories of her father playing the piano, visiting an aunt in Norway, and defusing a traffic accident in Stratford-on-Avon through the sheer force of his "kindly and wry" demeanor ("The Bicyclist"). Schnackenberg steers the sequence away from abstraction not only though of the various locations of its sections but also as a result of the images on which she focuses her grief and contemplation: a "kitchen's old-fashioned planter's clock" ("Nightfishing"), the "*Steinway* in German script above the keys" of the family piano ("Intermezzo"), and the pair of reading glasses still lying on her father's desk ("'There Are No Dead'"). An elegiac tone informs the rest of the collection, as does the blend of intelligence and tenderness that distinguishes so much of Schnackenberg's work. In "Darwin in 1881" the aged naturalist—fused throughout with Shakespeare's Prospero—meditates, in the final year of his life, on "the ship-sunk emptiness / Of grownup children's rooms," the isolation that makes him feel "an island as he walks," and the melancholy truth that all he has learned from Nature is that "it will grow small, fade, disappear." The volume's final long poem, "19 Hadley Street," moves backward in time in order to portray two centuries in the life of a Massachusetts family.

Schnackenberg's next collection, *The Lamplit Answer*, confirmed the promise of her first book. In poems about exiled musicians and abandoned lovers, fairy tales and demonic dolls, and heartbroken husbands and precocious daughters, Schnackenberg again displays the formal and thematic power that inform her work overall, while also revealing new aesthetic, historical, spiritual, and personal concerns. Throughout the book's four sections, Chopin, living in Paris, broods on the fall of Warsaw to the Russians ("Kremlin of Smoke"); a lovesick speaker composes a witty mock-sonata while she waits for an absent lover to return (this section also features "Love Letter," the only poem not included in *Supernatural Love*); and a widowed painter poignantly "take(s) it up" with the God who stole his wife from him ("The Self-Portrait of Ivan Generalic"). Schnackenberg writes with equal dexterity of an unwitting Faustian pact between the Punch-and-Judy-inspired Clumsy and the satanic No-No ("Two Tales of Clumsy"), the final famished days of the mystical philosopher Simone Weil ("The Heavenly Feast"), and a speaker's failed attempts to find meaning in an advent calendar, through whose "Picture-boxes in the stars" "No one answers, no one comes" ("Advent Calendar"). In perhaps her finest poem to date, "Imaginary Prisons," she retells the story of Sleeping Beauty through the stark lens of Piranesi's "series of engravings of fantastical prisons" (*Supernatural Love*, 265n), showing overgrown brambles, doomed suitors, and a palace's gallery of inhabitants, frozen in time. And in the collection's final, shattering poem, "Supernatural Love," she recalls a shared moment between her four-year-old self and her father involving his study of the word *carnation*, her "habit of identifying them as "Christ's flowers," and the slowly dawning fact that she is right, since the word has at its "root" the Latin word for flesh (*carnatio*) and is a form of clove from the French *clou* (nail). Body and spirit, natural and supernatural love, and a father's affection and Christ's passion come together in this closely observed scene.

Schnackenberg's third and fourth volumes received mixed reviews, with some praising her ambition and even more passionate engagement with history while others criticized her increasingly abstract language and digressive style. In *A Gilded Lapse of Time*, the speaker, a latter-day Dante—a modified version of whose *terza rima* Schnackenberg uses in several sections—wanders through Italy meditating on the deterioration of culture as she explores the life and thought of a host of classical and Christian figures: Tacitus, Tiberius, Abraham, Isaac, Herod, and St. Augustine. As was evident from her earliest poems, Schnackenberg is at her best when she anchors grand themes—in this case, the vanished past—in local images: A workman in a church who "Touches a flake of gold leaf in the hem / Of His threadbare gown with tweezers woefully small"; the distant sound of "snowflakes gathering overhead / In the treasure vaults of snow from another age"; a font "Where fragments of lost names illegibly / Shiver behind an ancient grille"; and numerous paintings. Extensive and complex wordplay—cathedrals' "gilt" versus historical "guilt," splendid "apses" versus historical "lapses"—unifies and animates the collection as well. Certainly its final sequence; "A Monument in Utopia," a tribute to Osip Mandelstam, is as stirring and memorable as anything Schnackenberg has written. Looser lines and the panoramic cultural vistas of *A Gilded Lapse of Time* replace Schnackenberg's more formally exacting and emotionally accessible earlier work, but these poems continue to exhibit her learning and scope. **Rosanna Warren** writes that the book "manages to bind within the compass of its will a formidable range of diction, weaving 'crud' and 'Ostrogothic dusk' with quotations from St. Augustine, and never entirely losing sight of the small, modern person 'stranded in the aftermath.'"

In *The Throne of Labdacus*, a book-length sequence about the Oedipus myth, Schnackenberg again plunges into the distant past, but this time she is entirely absent from her narrative. In terse couplets which occasionally rhyme across stanzas, she does not so much retell the story of Oedipus as explode it, surveying the fragments of "gossip, folktale, rumor, dream" surrounding it, and asking what lies behind "the layers of stunned silence / at the heart of the text." Did the shepherd who rescued Oedipus from the hilltop give his own child to King Laius? Did Oedipus in fact do "what he did with open eyes"? Did the grisly story take place at all? Schnackenberg focuses these questions around the figure of Apollo, who, as the book unfolds, wonders how to set Sophocles's play to music. Although *The Throne of Labdacus*, like Schnackenberg's previous collection, put some critics off—Logan, noting its "musty, housebound air," complained that "this poem has her depths without her passion"—it also features some of her most memorable images: Tablets containing the story of Oedipus are "Like pieces broken from the moon / Above the citadel of Thebes"; Apollo's lyre hangs "limp, trapped, / As if it had hanged itself"; and in a bravura passage, the letters of the Greek alphabet are likened to the components of Sophocles' story—Lambda is "a lame man / Leaning on a stick"; Psi is a "slain Sphinx"; Eta is a "rock throne". *The Throne* is not merely a retelling of an ancient story but a haunting parable of the fragility of our myths and the limits of our knowledge.

Further Reading. ***Selected Primary Sources:*** Schnackenberg, Gjertrud, *Supernatural Love: Poems 1976–1992* (New York: Farrar, Straus and Giroux, 2000); ———, *The Throne of Labdacus* (New York: Farrar, Straus, and Giroux, 2000); ———, "The Epistle of Paul the Apostle to the Colossians," in *Incarnation: Contemporary Writers on the New Testament*, ed. Alfred Corn (New York: Viking, 1990, 189–211). ***Selected Secondary Sources:*** Logan, William, "Author! Author!" (*New Criterion* [December 2000]); McClatchy, J.D., "Three Senses of Self" (*New York Times Book Review* [26 May 1985]); Mendelsohn, Daniel, "Breaking Out" (*New York Review of Books* [29 March 2001]); Warren, Rosanna, "Visitations" (*New Republic* [13 September 1993]).

Rachel Wetzsteon

SCHOOLCRAFT, JANE JOHNSTON (BAME-WA-WAS-GE-ZHIK-A-QUAY) (1800–1841)

Jane Johnston Schoolcraft, born of an Irish fur trader and an Ojibway mother at the convergence of Lakes Superior and Huron, a spot called Saulte Saint Marie, spent her life combining her two cultures. With her husband, Henry Rowe Schoolcraft, she documented Ojibway stories, traditions, history, and songs in English. Fluent in both English and her mother's Ojibway, she was Henry Rowe's most important source for his treatise *Algic Researches, Comprising Inquires Respecting the Mental Characteristics of the North American Indians* (1939), and together the two published a literary magazine of Ojibway culture, *Literary Voyager* or *Muzzeniegun* (1826–1827).

Born in 1800, Schoolcraft was, with her seven brothers and sisters, educated in her early years at home in Ojibway by her mother and in English by her father. She read classics in English, and from her mother learned Ojibway legends and stories about her grandfather, Waub Ojeeg, an Ojibway chief about whom Schoolcraft later wrote in her verse history, "Otagamiad" (1827). In 1809 she finished her education in Ireland. In 1822 Henry Rowe Schoolcraft came to Saulte Sainte Marie as an Indian agent, and in 1823 the two married. Both feared the disappearance of elements of Ojibway culture, so they set about their project of translating the folk tales and myths that Schoolcraft and her family knew into the *Algic Researches.* In the winter of 1826–1827, the Schoolcrafts began a literary society, complete with a handwritten magazine; the *Literary*

Voyager began circulating not only in the little outpost but also in Detroit and New York. In addition to linguistic studies, essays, and biographies of Ojibway people and their speeches, the magazine also contained poems and stories by Jane Schoolcraft. That winter, their first son, William, died. The couple had two more children, although Jane never fully recovered from the loss. She died in 1841.

Although Jane Schoolcraft and Henry often wrote on the same subjects, their approaches sometimes differed, as in the case of Schoolcraft's grandfather, Ojeeg. In Henry's prose biography of the chief, a spirit of the vanishing Indian, whose weakening and disappearance are inevitable, pervades; Schoolcraft's version portrays historical characters who are considerably more defiant. Written in rhymed heroic couplets, Schoolcraft in her "Otagamiad" captures the lofty **epic** style common in classic works, as she regales the actions and speeches of brave warriors. She also uses vocabulary from conventional English poetry: words such as "oft" and "'twere." The figures in the poems, Ojeeg and the members of his gathering council, discuss their dire situation of being continually encroached upon by white men "Whose public faith, so often pledg'd in vain,/ 'Twere base for freemen e'er to trust again." Ojeeg calls forcibly for war, with no alternatives left them, lest they be slaves forever. One by one, other members of the council are given their turns to speak, including Camudwa, who begs for one more effort at peaceful diplomacy, and offers to bring a message of reasoned and passionate speech to the white men himself.

When writing for the *Literary Voyager*, Schoolcraft used several pen names: her Ojibway name, given to her by her mother (her father called her Jane), Bame-wa-was-ge-zhik-a-quay (Woman of the Stars Rushing through the Sky), or Leelinau for translations of Ojibway legends and tales; and, for her poetry, Rosa. Her writing style in prose was much like that of her contemporary American colleagues, and her poetic style, as has been said, is traditional. But in her prose pieces, often creation or origin myths such as "The Origin of the Robin: An Allegory" (1826–1827) or stories of the early ages such as "Mishosha, or the Magician and His Daughter" (1826–1827), Schoolcraft sometimes includes pieces of verse that are written in a more straightforward and yet also incantatory style: verse meant to perform an act as much as to describe one. In one of her most frequently anthologized prose pieces, "The Forsaken Brother, A Chippewa Tale" (1826–1827), a young boy, who has been abandoned by his older brother and sister, learns to live in the woods by scavenging off the kills of wolves. In time the wolves grow to pity him and take care always to leave him some meat. The boy lives with the wolves all winter, and when in the spring his brother hears the boy crying out, the older boy is filled with regret for what he has done. He calls for his little brother to come to him, but the only reply the younger boy makes is a chant, which Schoolcraft renders as verse or song: "*Neesya, neesya, shyegwuh gushuh!* / . . . My brother, my brother, / I am now turning into a wolf!" The boy's song is intermingled with a wolf's howling, until finally the transformation from boy to animal is complete. Schoolcraft's inclusion of the half-Ojibway and half-English verse serves as a testament to her own duality as a human and a writer, as well as to the slippery line that divides the worlds of human and animal, one that Schoolcraft often crosses with ease in the transcription of the tales of her mother.

Further Reading. ***Selected Primary Sources:*** Schoolcraft, Jane Johnston, "The Forsaken Brother: A Chippewa Tale," in *A Sweet, Separate Intimacy: Women Writers of the American Frontier, 1800–1922*, ed. Susan Cummins Miller (Salt Lake City: University of Utah Press, 2000, 13–15); "Otagamiad," in *The First West: Writing from the American—Frontier 1776–1860*, ed. Edward Watts and David Rachels (New York: Oxford University Press, 2002, 335–337). ***Selected Secondary Sources:*** Miller, Susan Cummins, ed., "Jane Johnston Schoolcraft," in *A Sweet, Separate Intimacy, Women Writers of the American Frontier, 1800–1922* (Salt Lake City: University of Utah Press, 2000: 9–10); Parins, James W., "Jane Johnston Schoolcraft (1800–1841)," in *The Heath Anthology of American Literature, Vol. 1*, ed. Paul Lauter (Lexington, MA: D.C. Heath & Co., 1990, 1216–1217); Watts, Edward, and David Rachels, eds., "Minor Native Voices," in *The First West: Writing from the American Frontier 1776–1860* (New York: Oxford University Press, 2002, 333).

Cheri Johnson

SCHULMAN, GRACE (1935–)

Grace Schulman's contribution to American poetry is threefold: her own poetry, her scholarly and academic work, and her continuing support of poetry in the public sphere. Schulman's poetry developed partly from the mentoring she received from **Marianne Moore** late in the elder poet's life, but early on she found her own voice—lyrical, knowing, sometimes wry, and always engaging. Very much a poet of New York, she fills her work with images of the city at its best and its worst, and, for her, beauty is always to be found on the sidewalks of New York. Starting with the publication of her first book of poetry, *Burn Down the Icons* (1976), Schulman established herself as a poet of precision and control, much as **Elizabeth Bishop** had a generation earlier. Even in these early poems, Schulman shows a firm mastery of her art, allowing concrete details to lead the reader to the emotions behind each poem. In this way, she was extending the **Imagist** doctrine (espoused by

Ezra Pound and best demonstrated in the early work of **H.D.**) of "show, don't tell;" yet she is not a mere follower of Imagism. Indeed, Schulman has brought together the meticulous observations of the Imagist poets, the personal details of **confessional** poets, such as **Robert Lowell**, and the more open and experimental use of language that came to the fore in American poetry during the last half of the twentieth century. Sonnets such as "The Abbess of Whitby" complemented the modern, even conversational style of poems such as "That Maple" and "Poetry Editor" in Schulman's first volume, signaling the emergence of a new voice in American poetry.

Born in Brooklyn, New York, Schulman received her BS from Bard College, American University, in 1954 and her MA (1960) and Ph.D. (1971) in English from New York University. Prior to 1962 she wrote for national newspapers and magazines such as *Harper's Bazaar* and *Glamour.* She married Jerome L. Schulman, a scientist, when she was twenty-four. Her first published poems, "Street Dance in Barcelona" and "Shango Sacrifice," appeared in the Autumn–Winter 1964–1965 issue of *Poetry Northwest.* Schulman has taught poetry at Princeton, Columbia, and Wesleyan, as well as at the City University of New York's Graduate Center. She is the recipient of a 2004–2005 Guggenheim Foundation Fellowship in Poetry and was awarded the Aiken Taylor Award for Modern Poetry (2002) and the Delmore Schwartz Award for Poetry (1996). In 2003 Viking Press published *The Poems of Marianne Moore,* an important and well-received chronological collection, edited by Schulman, which brought to light numerous versions of Moore's poetry that were uncollected or previously unpublished. Through her work as poetry editor at the *Nation,* Schulman has consistently published both new and established poets, providing national exposure for their poetry, and in 1973 founded "Discovery" / The *Nation,* a contest for new poets. Starting in 1974, two years after joining the *Nation,* she began a ten-year tenure as Director of the Unterberg Poetry Center at the 92nd Street YM-YWHA in New York City, where, under her guidance, the poetry programs flourished, established poets found their works nurtured and supported, and new poets found a place where their voices could be heard. In addition, the courses she teaches as Distinguished Professor at the City University of New York's Baruch College, as well as her lectures and media appearances, continue to provide a wide audience (and numerous students each semester) with insights into the beauty and joy of poetry.

In *Hemispheres* (1984), Schulman's second collection of verse, poems such as "Blessed Is the Light" and "Let There Be Translators!" heralded what would become a familiar style for the poet—ringing words of praise and incantation which echo, in rhythm and feeling, the writings of the Torah and the Bible. "Blessed is the light that turns to fire . . . / Blessed is the inexhaustible sun" writes Schulman, yet what begins as a celebration of natural forces becomes, in a turn at the poem's end, a marvelous prayer in praise of physical love: "Praised be the body, our bodies, that lie down and open and rise, falling in flame." Even in her early work, she wrote herself into her poems, fitting her bodily presence into the lines and meter of her verse, and this celebratory physicality is another hallmark of her work over the years. Indeed, it is often through physical action—especially walking—that the speakers of her poems experience the beauty to be found in the world around them.

There is also beauty in the joy and grief of everyday life, and one of her most famous poems, "The Present Perfect" (1994), is a good example of Schulman's ability to express that beauty poetically: "I hear your voice that calls me to see wildflowers / poking through gravel cracks in our neighbors' driveway, / slender but fortunate, built to last their day" are lines addressed to the poet's husband, for this is a love poem for him, but it is a love poem about infertility. "For us, there was no miracle of birth," she writes, but "we had each other's silences," and a life without children becomes, by the poem's end, a life lived with love and sadness and, perhaps, peace. "Psalm for an Anniversary" (2001) also celebrates the poet's marriage, both its past difficulties (its "ruptures healed") and its "second chances," and is a companion-piece to "The Present Perfect." In "One Year without Mother" (2001), she uses the highly formal structure of the sonnet sequence to chronicle her mother's death. It is a reconciliation of sorts with a mother who, even in dying, exhibits a bittersweet love for her daughter. "You held the living fast / and scorned memorials," writes Schulman in the first sonnet of the sequence ("What Can You Believe?"), and the reader cannot help but notice that, despite that scorn, she has constructed a moving monument to her mother's life and death. With the publication of *Days of Wonder: New and Selected Poems* (2002), Grace Schulman's contribution to contemporary American poetry was confirmed. She brings a clear-eyed gaze to the world around her, and through her poetry allows readers to see that world as she sees it, full of possibilities.

Further Reading. ***Selected Primary Sources***: Schulman, Grace, *Burn Down the Icons: Poems* (Princeton, NJ: Princeton University Press, 1976); ———, *Days of Wonder: New and Selected Poems* (Boston: Houghton Mifflin, 2002); ———, *For That Day Only: Poems* (New York: Sheep Meadow Press, 1994); ———, *Hemispheres* (New York: Sheep Meadow Press, 1984); ———, *The Paintings of Our Lives: Poems* (Boston: Houghton Mifflin, 2001). ***Selected Secondary Sources:*** Gilbert, Sandra M., Review of *Hemispheres* (*Poetry* [December 1985]: 161);

Rehak, Melanie, Review of *Paintings of Our Lives* (*New York Times Book Review* [15 April 2001]: 22); Shaw, Robert B., Review of *For That Day Only* (*Poetry* [May 1995]: 104).

Wendy Galgan

SCHULTZ, SUSAN M. (1958–)

Poet, scholar, critic, editor, publisher, and educator Susan M. Schultz is largely responsible for bringing innovative and experimental writing from the Pacific Rim to the attention of North American audiences through her press Tinfish and her journal of the same name started in 1995. Operating within what **Ron Silliman** has called "the new sentence," Schultz's poetry is often a prose-like exploration of personal history and language. Although not completely contemporary with the **Language poets** and Language poetry's heyday, her work has been usefully compared by Hank Lazer to the work of **Lyn Hejinian** and has many technical qualities in common with the work of writers like **Bruce Andrews**. Using a cut-up technique, she incorporates phrase- and sentence-level linguistic units from the media, her reading, memory, conversations, and surroundings to produce a poetry that grapples with the ways in which she sees life and the world and the ways in which personal writing might also be used to investigate formal and linguistic innovation.

Born in 1958 in Belleville, Illinois, Schultz soon moved to northern Virginia and spent most of her childhood in the suburbs of Alexandria and McLean. She studied history at Yale and received a BA in 1980. She received an MA and Ph.D. in English from the University of Virginia in 1984 and 1989, respectively. She taught briefly in the English Department of the College of William and Mary in Williamsburg, Virginia (1989–1990); she then moved to Hawai'i to begin teaching in the English Department at the University of Hawai'i - Manoa.

Her publications include the book-length collections of poetry *Aleatory Allegories* (2000), *Memory Cards & Adoption Papers* (2001), and *And Then Something Happened* (2004), as well as twelve chapbooks. Her poetry often explores personal themes through the form of the **prose poem**. For example, in *Memory Cards & Adoption Papers* Schultz explores her relationship with her mother and her quest to become a mother herself—eventually adopting a Cambodian boy, Sangha, with her husband Bryant. The poems move in and out of reflection, observation, and appropriation, folding it all together and problematizing syllogistic movement while providing a linguistic context for her examination of the forces at work within herself and in the world around her. "After my father wrote to Nixon to demand he fire Melvin Laird," she writes, "his taxes were audited for years. *The political is personal.* Sterilize bottle nipples and expect your baby to grieve (or not) for several days" (86, italics hers). Politics here, like everything else, is always personal. For Schultz her memories of her family are just as politically charged as adoption manuals and the rhetoric of governmental regulations: "*Parents wanting to adopt Cambodian children must be 210 years older than they are* (U.S. State Department)" (74, italics hers). It is through our work making the connections between the disparate elements of *Memory Cards & Adoption Papers* that Schultz tells us about herself even though she does not give us a coherent, sustained personal narrative. She piles sentence upon sentence, with little or no overt connective narrative; however, what we get in this language pile is a context through which an amalgam portrait of Schultz and her feelings about adoption and motherhood shines. Her next book, *And Then Something Happened*, continued in this vein, exploring, among other things, her relationship with her son Sangha and her feelings toward the processes of adoption and childrearing.

Unlike **Cid Corman,** whose Origin press published primarily North American innovators, even though he lived in Japan for nearly fifty years, Schultz has set out to publish Anglophone experimental and innovative writing from around the Pacific Rim, forging close relationships with both Pidgin and Islander practitioners in Hawai'i as well as with practitioners from Asia, Australia, New Zealand, and Oceana. Tinfish Press, which Schultz started in 1995, has published over twenty-two books, including the award-winning *Physics* (2001) by Lisa Asagi and Gaye Chan and two influential works on Hawai'ian Islander language and culture: *Sista Tongue* (2002) by Lisa Kana`e and *Living Pidgin: Contemplations on Pidgin Culture* (2002) by Lee Tonouchi. In addition to experimental writing, these books exhibit innovative design. For example, *Physics* and *Twelve Scenes from 12 a.m.* (2001), both collaborations between Lisa Asagi and Gaye Chan, are map folds reminiscent of European covered maps; Steve Carll's *Hamburger* (2002) comes in a foil hamburger wrapper; Normie Salvador's *philter* (2003) has a glued-together cover and must be torn apart—and in the process likely destroyed—in order to be read; and Schultz's own { *Material Lyrics* } (2001) nestles, left-handed, into a die-cut envelope. Schultz's magazine *Tinfish* has consistently showcased experimental work from around the Pacific Rim alongside work by more recognized contemporary practitioners such as Bruce Andrews, **Eileen Myles**, Ron Silliman, **Clark Coolidge**, and Randolph Healy. The issues themselves also stretch the conventions of design along with our notions of poetic form and language. Issue four, for instance, initiated a practice of using found paper for cover stock; it was covered with overprinted scrap from a commercial press with tipped-on titles and designs. Issue fourteen was covered with a recycled Hawai'i Annual Economic Report trimmed and die-cut with circles of various diameters both front and back. By placing such a heavy emphasis on design issues and by going to Pacific Rim artists for cover design, Schultz is suggesting that experiment and innovation in poetic form and language should be accompanied by a similar experiment in design and the visual and tactile quality of the work.

Further Reading. ***Selected Primary Sources:*** Shultz, Susan M., *Aleatory Allegories* (Cambridge, England: Salt Publishing, 2000); ———, *And Then Something Happened* (Cambridge, England: Salt Publishing, 2004); ———, "Local Vocals: Hawai'i's Pidgin Literature, Performance, and Postcoloniality," in *Close Listening: Poetry and the Performed Word*, ed. Charles Bernstein (Oxford, England: Oxford University Press, 1998); ———, { *Material Lyrics* } (Kane`ohe, HI: Tinfish Press, 2001); ———, *Memory Cards & Adoption Papers* (Bedford, MA: Potes & Poets Press, 2001); ———, "Towards a 'Haole' Poetics," in *A Poetics of Criticism*, eds. Juliana Spahr, et al. (Buffalo, NY: Leave Books, 1994); ———, ed., *The Tribe of John: Ashbery and Contemporary Poetry* (Tuscaloosa: University of Alabama Press, 1995). ***Selected Secondary Sources:*** Asagi, Lisa, and Gaye Chan, *Physics* (Kane`ohe, HI: Tinfish Press, 2001); ———, *Twelve Scenes from 12 a.m.* (Kane`ohe, HI: Tinfish Press, 2001); Carll, Steve, *Hamburger* (Kane`ohe, HI: Tinfish Press, 2002); Lazer, Hank, "*Memory Cards & Adoption Papers* by Susan M. Schultz" (Raintaxi Online Edition [Winter 2002/2003]); Kana'e, Lisa, *Sista Tongue* (Kane`ohe, HI: Tinfish Press, 2002); Salvador, Normie, *philter* (Kane`ohe, HI: Tinfish Press, 2003); Tonouchi, Lee, *Living Pidgin: Contemplations on Pidgin Culture* (Kane`ohe, HI: Tinfish Press, 2002).

William R. Howe

SCHWARTZ, DELMORE (1913–1966)

Delmore Schwartz wrote cerebral poems, and his philosophies were similar to those of other writers of the New York intellectual school to which he belonged. Living and working in New York City for most of his life, Schwartz was involved with such fellow intellectuals and writers as Irving Howe and **Wallace Stevens**. Among this set he was known for his extraordinary intelligence, and publication in several leftist journals established and edited by these Jewish American intellectuals gave Schwartz his start and his reputation. Like many poets in the middle decades of the twentieth century, Schwartz articulated leftist philosophies in his works, published widely but actually made his living from an itinerant academic career, and became one of a group of poets studied by eager English majors in the universities of the 1950s and 1960s.

Schwartz is preoccupied in his verse with the mechanics of human perception and the interplay of physical and mental life, particularly in the popular culture milieu of the twentieth century. Always at the center of this theme, of course, is Schwartz the poet lionizing the place of poetry in the construction of knowledge and love, the things that make life worth living because they accord it permanence and offer man entry into the world of knowledge and enlightenment. He sees this ideal world as largely unobtainable outside of art because it is compromised by time and mortality. It also became increasingly elusive in the twentieth century due to the unprecedented anxieties of modern life.

Delmore David Schwartz was born in Brooklyn to middle-class Jewish parents on December 8, 1913. His mother and father had a turbulent relationship, which had an effect on Schwartz's own ability to develop successful domestic and interpersonal relationships. By 1923, his father had left the family and moved to Chicago. Although he grew up in New York City, in 1931 Schwartz also went to the Midwest to attend the University of Wisconsin. However, after only one year, he returned to New York and enrolled at New York University, from which he graduated in 1935 with a BA in philosophy, thereafter immediately enrolling in graduate school at Harvard University in hopes of becoming an academician.

Schwartz was always a prolific writer. Besides poetry, he wrote philosophical essays, literary criticism, translations, fiction, and drama. Even as early as 1936, his writing began to receive accolades. His essay "Poetry as Imitation" won the Bowdoin Prize in the Humanities (Harvard's most prestigious writing award) that year. Shortly thereafter, his criticism, poetry, and fiction began to be accepted and printed in magazines. His first short story, "In Dreams Begin Responsibilities," was published in the *Partisan Review* in 1938, starting his long relationship with that magazine, culminating in his appointment as its poetry editor in 1943. This upturn in his writing career and his courtship of and marriage to Gertrude Buckman in 1938 apparently distracted his attention from his studies, and he never finished his doctorate.

In 1939 Schwartz began his association with New Directions publishing house, which brought out his first volume of prose and poetry that year, also entitled *In Dreams Begin Responsibilities*. The collection was well-reviewed and attracted positive attention from such established literary figures as **William Carlos Williams** and **T.S. Eliot**. Praise from the latter literary giant was particularly pleasing to Schwartz, who considered Eliot (according to Richard McDougall in his Twayne volume) "the epitome of the poet-intellectual," a model of the kind of thinker and writer that Schwartz wanted to be (26). Shortly thereafter, Schwartz was accepted as a resident at the Yaddo writing colony in Saratoga Springs, New York, where he stayed for a year. This was followed by the receipt of two consecutive Guggenheim fellowships and, despite the absence of a graduate degree, an appointment as an instructor of English at Harvard University. In 1944 his position was upgraded to assistant professor, and he taught courses in writing there from 1940 to 1947. He resigned in 1947, reportedly unhappy with academic life and the perceived anti-Semitism at Harvard.

He moved back to New York and later established residence for six years on a farm in New Jersey, but he traveled often, continuing to make a living by assuming various visiting professorships at universities throughout the country, including Princeton, Bennington College, Kenyon College, Indiana University, University of Chicago, and Syracuse University. Additionally, he served as poetry editor and movie critic for *The New Republic* between 1955 and 1957.

Throughout his life, Schwartz had problems with alcoholism, excessive drug use, and severe bipolar disorder. As a result of these problems' effect on his personality, making him simultaneously self-doubting and selfish, as well as to the legacy of his ill-matched parents, he was unable to sustain a successful relationship. He divorced Buckman in 1944, and in 1949 married fiction writer Elizabeth Pollet. They separated in 1952 and the marriage ended in 1957, dissolving allegedly because of Schwartz's increasingly paranoiac accusations of infidelity, none of which apparently had any basis in fact. As he grew older, even though he remained a popular writer, he drank more and became less collegial. During his last few years, his writing began to decline due to increasingly manic episodes and became, in the words of Douglas Dunn in his introduction to the posthumous collection of Schwartz's poetry *What Is To Be Given*, "more brittle [and] self-conscious in its cleverness (ix)." By 1966, at the age of 53, Schwartz was penniless and alone, living in a Manhattan hotel. On July 11 of that year, he suffered a heart attack in the hotel lobby and died. Perhaps the most moving testimonial to his life is his friend **Saul Bellow**'s fictionalized portrayal of Schwartz as Humboldt in the 1975 novel *Humboldt's Gift*.

Despite his peripatetic, busy lifestyle and increasing personal problems, Schwartz's poetic canon was prolific and continual. The publication of *In Dreams Begin Responsibilities* was followed by the **verse drama** *Shenandoah*, the eighth in a New Directions series "The Poet of the Month" (1941); *Genesis: Book I*, a single long **prose poem** (1943); *Vaudeville for a Princess and Other Poems* (1950); *6 Poems/6 Woodcuts*, of which only twenty copies were printed (1953); *Summer Knowledge*, a collection of poems written from 1938 to the time of publication, which won the Bollingen Prize in Poetry for that year (1959) published posthumously, *What Is To Be Given: Selected Poems* (1976); a reissue of *Shenandoah* with other verse plays (1979); and *Last and Lost Poems of Delmore Schwartz*, which includes poems written but not published during his lifetime (1979). The latter volume was a tribute from New Directions, edited by Robert Phillips. Additionally, the volume *Syracuse Poems* was published in 1965, being a collection from the creative writing class Schwartz taught at Syracuse.

Schwartz's early training in the language of philosophy characterizes much of his poetic oeuvre, and his intellectual background allows multiple allusions to literary and historical figures throughout his verse. He is particularly fond of allusions to Shakespeare and the Greek poets. Poems such as "Concerning the Synthetic Unity of Apperception" illustrate the rather obscure, highly allusive, and philosophical tone of much of his work. Despite this cerebral approach the poems, many of celebrate physical life and reality and several describe in detail the bustle of New York City. Most of his poems, including "Concerning the Synthetic Unity of Apperception," are commentaries on the negative impact that time and death have on the human capacity to love.

Several critics observe that Schwartz's six years living in the countryside of New Jersey added a strand of nature imagery to his poetry. Actually, both detailed accounts of New York City life, such as "Sonnet: O City, City," and nature poetry, such as "Summer Knowledge," use their disparate settings to deliver the same philosophy. The sonnet depicts death "in the subway ride, / Being amid six million souls." Automobiles and office buildings become objects that block man's mind from knowing truth. Yet even though summer knowledge is, to Schwartz, "green knowledge, country knowledge . . . bird knowledge and the knowing that trees possess," a knowledge that can be found only in country life, that life is also a depiction of death. Schwartz concludes this latter poem with the statement, "summer knowledge is not knowledge at all," but, like life on the subway, is "the consummation and the annihilation" all life must face. Other nature poems, however—like "A Small Score," "A Little Morning Music," and "Is It the Morning? Is It the Little Morning?"—offer simple pictures of the glory of nature unsullied by man. Unlike most of Schwartz's other poetry, the pieces in the "Morning Bells" section of *Summer Knowledge*, written during his time in New Jersey, are exclusively descriptive, without his usual intellectualizing.

His two most often anthologized poems, both originally published in *In Dreams Begin Responsibilities*, are "The Heavy Bear Who Goes with Me" and "In the Naked Bed in Plato's Cave," both of which express Schwartz's concerns about human perception, its encounter with the world of objective reality, and its ability to reach an enlightened and loving state.

"The Heavy Bear Who Goes with Me" embodies Schwartz's preoccupation with the disconnect between mental and biological reality, typified by a bearlike body—the persona's constant companion—that is "a stupid clown of the spirit's motive." In the poem, we see Schwartz's concern with the limitations of the physical to satisfy the soul. Although the bear is "in love with candy, anger, and sleep" and clumsily enjoys its own physicality, it is also terrified of "the darkness beneath," which points to the inevitable death and annihilation that it is not equipped to confront. Love enters later in the poem and becomes another focus of the mental and physical disconnect. The bear "Stretches to embrace the very dear / With whom [the persona] would walk without him near." The persona's attempts at love thus fail due to the bear that, at this point in the poem, symbolizes the throes of desire that can be fulfilled only through the grossness of physical contact.

"In the Naked Bed in Plato's Cave" features one of Schwartz's stylistic hallmarks: the juxtaposition of realistic New York scenes and abstract philosophy. Directly allusive to Plato's allegory of the cave in Book VII of *The Republic*, the poem represents Plato's world of shadows as the persona's New York bedroom. Plato's fire that creates the shadows becomes "reflected headlights" on the bedroom wall; the echoes from the shadowy world outside the cave in Plato's dialogue become "a fleet of trucks" grinding in the distance and "the milkman's chop" as he ascends the stairs and leaves his bottles outside the door. And like Socrates's imagined prisoners, when the persona looks out his window at the world of reality, it is too much for him and he is forced to return to bed "with exhausted eyes." But the last stanza of the poem departs from the idealistic philosophy of Socrates and Plato, whose persona successfully detaches himself from the world of shadows in order to ascend into the world of the Ideal. Within Schwartz's persona's room, when daylight gradually lifts objects from darkness and shadows, turning the world of "ignorant night" into the day, light presents not knowledge or enlightenment, but "travail" and mutability: "the mystery of beginning / Again and again." The last phrase of the poem, "while History is unforgiven," betrays Schwartz's message: man's imprisonment in the world of physical reality offers no release into pure truth. Man is diminished by his day-to-day existence and there is no escape.

The verse play *Shenandoah* is also of particular note because of its highly autobiographical nature. In it the infant Shenandoah Fish is obviously a representation of Schwartz himself; although he is given the name "Shenandoah" to assure that he will not kill his forebears (Jewish babies are never named after living relatives, lest they sign those people's death warrants), one name his parents toyed with earlier is "Delmore." The setting of the play is a Jewish American home in which the mother is preoccupied with but fairly clueless about social realities, and the father, much to her dismay, is often absent. The interplay between the characters echoes Schwartz's attitude about his own childhood. And the child's canny revelations voice Schwartz's pet theme of the passage of time and the reality of death. *Genesis: Book I* continues Schwartz's autobiographical theme in a poem of over 100 pages chronicling his development as a poet. Because its reviews were basically negative, Schwartz abandoned this project, allowing *Genesis: Book II* to remain in manuscript.

Ruminations on his own childhood, presented thematically as concerns for the passage of time and the differences in perspective between young and old, are present in his shorter poetry as well. The dialogue poem "Father and Son" is an example. The conflict between the generations focuses on their attitudes toward time: The son sees it as "full of promises," but the father insists that life should be lived with the full knowledge that "you are dying" and even insists that he knows his son must be afraid of time. The son maintains he is not, saying such an attitude is premature when one is as young as he: "I would be sudden now and rash in joy, / As if I lived forever, the future my toy." At the end of the poem, however, the father offers his son the solace of memory and the advice to live "as if death were now," still refusing to believe that youth is any excuse for ignoring life's realities.

One of Schwartz's longest and most successful later poems is "Seurat's Sunday Afternoon Along the Seine," written in the late 1950s and appearing for the first time in *Summer Knowledge.* It is an ode to sight, beginning with the poet's speculation about what the people in the painting are looking at as the poet himself looks at them and ending with the assertion, "If you can look at any thing for long enough, / You will rejoice in the miracle of love." What the poet sees in Seurat's French Impressionism is a static representation of hope in the permanence of things. Trees grip the ground "with a perfected tenacity"; a child holds her mother's arm "as if it were a permanent genuine certainty"; a middle-class couple is in the act of strolling "as if they were unaware or free of time, and the grave." The poem then continues to contrast the permanence of art with the mutability of reality or "time's fire which turns / Whatever is into another thing . . . Within the uncontrollable blaze of time and of history." This viewpoint casts Seurat as "at once painter, poet, architect, and alchemist," who has created an eternal Sunday of happiness free from the horror of human change or the consciousness of death. The creation is ironic, though, because, as Schwartz notes, Seurat "hardly suspects that in six years he will no longer be alive!" Schwartz's belief in art's ability to freeze time juxtaposes in the poem with a longing to transcend the trivialities of the same everyday existence pictured in the painting, and more importantly, to transcend time and death.

However, when Schwartz tries to claim the same exalted permanence for musical works of art in

"Vivaldi," a poem that attempts to mimic the movements of a classical concerto, he is less successful. Music, the poem says, is "The motion beyond emotion . . . the immortality of mortality." Although part of the poem describes the actual playing and singing of the concerto at Mass, unlike the Seurat poem, "Vivaldi" relies too heavily on abstractions and finally becomes merely effusive and obscure.

Cynthia Ozick, in her introduction to *Screeno*, a retrospective collection of Schwartz's works that New Directions published in 2004, calls Schwartz's poetry "earnest odes to beauty and despair" (12). Throughout his poetic canon, Schwartz articulates a yearning for idealized truth, enlightened knowledge, and love that is permanent—whether in the relation of husband and wife, parent and child, lover and lover, or man and knowledge—while fully realizing that the condition of man is to be caught in "time's fire" and to be subject to annihilation, a condition that places his desires always one step away from fruition. To add to his poetic frustration, life in the world of the twentieth century, particularly in the bustling complexity of New York City, distanced one even more from truth and love. There seems to be no answer, no way of ridding oneself of the heavy bear, present even in the beauty of countryside mornings, except through the one artifact of permanence for which Schwartz has the ultimate respect, the work of art. As he says in "The Kingdom of Poetry," poetry is more valuable, interesting, and charming

> Than Niagara Falls, the Grand Canyon, the Atlantic
> Ocean
> And other much admired natural phenomena.

Philosophically abstruse and sometimes meandering to the point of reader confusion, Schwartz's poetry nevertheless expresses the dilemma of man in the modern world and offers him salvation through a form of art that "heightens reality" and is "a history of joy."

Further Reading. ***Selected Primary Sources:*** Schwartz, Delmore, *Genesis: Book I* (New York: J. Laughlin, 1943); ———, *Last and Lost Poems*, ed. Robert Phillips (New York: Vanguard Press, 1979); ———, *Screeno: Stories and Poems* (New York: New Directions, 2004); ———, *Shenandoah* (Norfolk, CT: New Directions, 1941); ———, *Summer Knowledge: Selected Poems* (New York: New Directions, 1954); ———, *Syracuse Poems* (Syracuse, NY: Department of English, Syracuse University, 1965); ———, *Vaudeville for a Princess and Other Poems* (New York: New Directions, 1950); ———, *What Is To Be Given: Selected Poems* (Manchester, England: Carcanet New Press, 1976). ***Selected Secondary Sources:*** Atlas, James, *Delmore Schwartz: The Life of an American Poet* (New York: Farrar, Straus, Giroux, 1977); Bawer, Bruce, *The Middle Generation: The Lives and Poetry of Delmore Schwartz, Randall Jarrell, John Berryman, Robert Lowell* (Hamden, CT: Archon, 1986); McDougall, Richard, *Delmore Schwartz* (New York: Twayne, 1974); Pollet, Elizabeth, ed., *Portrait of Delmore: Journals and Notes of Delmore Schwartz, 1939–1959* (New York: Farrar, Straus, Giroux, 1986).

Rosemary Fithian Guruswamy

SCHWERNER, ARMAND (1927–1999)

Armand Schwerner's impressive, idiosyncratic life work, *The Tablets*, is a supposed "translation" of fictional half-legible Sumerian clay tablets. Released in installments over the course of thirty years, this was a work in progress, and indeterminacy—change, lapses of understanding, and attempts to reconnect—generates its energy. A seriocomic, philosophical work, it has been compared to **Pound**'s Cantos, **Olson**'s Maximus Poems, **Williams**'s Paterson, **Duncan**'s Passages, and **Zukofsky**'s "A." Though it draws on such late twentieth-century currents as **ethnopoetics**, Buddhism, deconstruction, and **postmodern** devices, *The Tablets* are so rooted in a defamiliarized, archaic vision that they seem to stand outside their time. Schwerner considered *The Tablets* "wisdom literature." His uncompromising, questioning aesthetic—influenced by Pascal and Montaigne as well as by Buddhist teachings—informs *The Tablets* as well as Schwerner's **avant-garde** work as a performance artist, musician (specializing in reeds), and translator of **Native American poetry**, Sophocles's *Philoctetes*, and Dante's *Inferno*.

Schwerner was born on May 11, 1927, in Antwerp, Belgium, to a working-class Jewish family that immigrated to New York in 1936. Distinguishing himself at William Howard Taft High School, he briefly attended Cornell University, publishing his first poems in the *Cornell Review*. He spent 1947–1948 at the Universite de Geneve and received a BA in 1950 and an MA in 1964 from Columbia University. For many years he was a professor of English at the College of Staten Island of the City University of New York. Though he resided in Staten Island, he frequently made the twenty-five-minute ferryboat trip to New York City, maintaining vital connections with musicians, dancers, and writers, including **Michael Heller**, **Jackson Mac Low**, Charles Stein, and Ellen Zweig. Schwerner's personal life was shadowed with tragedy. His marriage in 1961 ended in divorce, after which Schwerner raised his two sons, the younger of whom died in a train accident. Schwerner died at age seventy-one after several years' battle with cancer of the jaw.

Schwerner co-authored a prose satire, *The Domesday Dictionary*, in 1963; his poetic career began under the aegis of **Jerome Rothenberg**, whose Hawk's Well Press published his first volume, *The Lightfall* (1963). With

George Quasha, Rothenberg edited a best-selling anthology, *America a Prophecy: A New Reading of American Poetry from Pre-Colombian Times to the Present* (1973), featuring two of Schwerner's tablets. One of these, Tablet XV, became Schwerner's signature work. It imagines the *hieros gamos* (sacred marriage) between the Sumerian priestess (representing the great goddess) and her mortal consort whose annual union ensured fertility in the land. This frankly erotic tablet is well suited to collaborations with dancers and musicians, and Schwerner performed it with great expressiveness. The most memorable of the repeated lines envision ecstasy:

> that I slowly turn for you, high priestess
> that you do my body in oil, in glycerin, that you do me

The poem builds in passion and meaning, tempered by the refrain

> that you do me slowly almost not at all.

After this calming refrain, new levels of meaning emerge:

> my body becomes a sentence that never stops,
> driving . . .
> from one tablet to another.

Tablet XII, the other tablet reprinted in Quasha and Rothenberg's anthology, helped establish Schwerner as a sophisticated manipulator of **narrative** personae in the manner of Nabokov in *Pale Fire* (1962). Tablet XII consists of three parts. First is an introduction by the fussy scholar-translator. (The scholar-translator's words are "transmitted through" Armand Schwerner here as in other tablets.) Second is a fictive Sumerian creation myth with an unsettling and rather Freudian conclusion. After the creation, the creator gods ask, "what / would you have us do now?" and the rapacious "gods of the earth" (mortals) reply, with no emotion, "kill / the craftsmen-gods" and "from their blood make a man and more men." The third section consists of several pages of musical notation.

Tablet XII provides a glimpse of Schwerner's layered, ironic, collage-like modus operandi. The introduction parodies both the historical nineteenth-century philological tradition and the Eliotic anti-historical formalist **New Criticism** of the twentieth century that replaced it. The scholar-translator quotes "Sumeromusicologist" "F. W. Galpin, Litt. D., F.L.S., Canon Emeritus of Chelmsford Cathedral and Hon. Freeman of the Worshipful Company of Musicians." The titles poke fun at philology; the "Canon" may be a droll allusion to Eliot's canon-fixation and Anglicanism. Chelmsford cathedral, in North London, was the site of Marconi's first wireless telegraph broadcast, transmitted May 3, 1920—a technological leap like the advent of writing in Sumer. Canon Galpin has transcribed what may be music from a mysterious tablet in Berlin known as KAR 1, 4. He waxes fulsome imagining "strains of nearly 4,000 years ago," and ends with a sweetly silly rhetorical flourish, inviting his "friends" (readers) to judge whether his words and music are not "well wed." The open-ended request for reader response precludes any final reading. *The Tablets* as a whole are built like a nest of Chinese boxes. They invite, frustrate, and reenact an archaeological quest for origins.

Schwerner published *The Tablets* in **small-press** editions culminating in the fine posthumous edition of twenty-seven tablets including journal notes and divagations from the National Poetry Foundation (1999), which contains a CD of Schwerner reading. Some critics, such as Lazar, have found a measure of resolution, if not closure, in these divagations, in which Schwerner seems to speak directly. Portions of *The Tablets* were used in theatrical performances by the Living Theater (1989–1990) and the dance-drama *Dragon Bond Rite* (1995). His books of short poems reveal his intense practice of Buddhism. *The Work, the Joy & the Triumph of the Will* (1977) opens with a poem, "the teaching," that offers "an iron pin to guide and discipline that / amok elephant your mind." The harrowing *Bacchae Sonnets* 1–7 (1977) are dedicated to the Tibetan teacher Chogyam Trungpa, Rimpoche. Schwerner's poems in *Sounds of the River Naranjana* appeared in 1983, the year he received lay ordination after studying with sensei Glassman at the Zen Community of New York.

Further Reading. ***Selected Primary Sources:*** Schwerner, Armand, *Bacchae Sonnets 1–7* (Baltimore, MD: Pod, 1977); ———, trans., *Cantos from Dante's Inferno* (Jersey City, NJ: Talisman House, 2001); ———, *The Lightfall* (New York: Hawks Well Press, 1963); ———, *The Selected Shorter Poems* (San Diego, CA: Junction Press, 1999); ———, *The Sounds of the River Naranjana and Tablets I–XXIV* (Barrytown, NY: Station Hill, 1983); ———, *The Tablets.* (Orono, ME: National Poetry Foundation, 1999); ———, *The Work, the Joy & the Triumph of the Will, with a translation of Philoctetes* (Cathedral Station, NY: New Rivers, 1977); ———, and Donald M. Kaplan, *The Domesday Dictionary* (New York: Simon & Schuster, 1963). ***Selected Secondary Sources:*** Lazar, Hank, "Sacred Forgery and the Grounds of Poetic Archaeology: Armand Schwerner's *The Tablets*" (*Chicago Review* 46.1 [2000]: 142–154); McHale, Brian, "Archaeologies of Knowledge: Hill's Middens, Heaney's Boggs, Schwerner's Tablets" (*New Literary History* 30.1 [1999]: 239–262); *Talisman* 19 (1998–1999), Armand Schwerner Issue.

Kathryn VanSpanckeren

SEARS, EDMUND HAMILTON (1810–1876)

Along with many of his contemporaries, mostly other Unitarian ministers, Edmund Hamilton Sears wrote poetry, sermons, hymns, and essays for newspapers and journals. Sears was one of the Unitarians, along with **Ralph Waldo Emerson**, **John Pierpont**, and **Charles Timothy Brooks**, who recognized and participated in the Transcendentalist movement. But Sears is probably best known for his two Christmas hymns, or carols—"Calm, on the Listening Ear of Night" and "It Came upon a Midnight Clear."

Sears was born on April 6, 1810, in Sandisfield, Massachusetts, into a long line of Puritans. Sears, the youngest of three brothers, and his parents, Joseph and Lucy (Smith) Sears, all worked on the family farm. But time on the farm was hard on the young Sears; he was a fragile boy and prone to sickness, and between sickness and work on the farm, he had little time to spend on education. Yet even at that, he managed to enter Union College in Schenectady, New York, graduating in 1834—a short three years after enrollment. Following his graduation, Sears engaged in the study of law, but after just nine months, he quit and accepted a teaching position at Brattleboro Academy. At the same time, he began study for the ministry with Addison Brown.

Less than a year later, Sears entered Cambridge Theological School, where he encountered the writing of two prominent Unitarian theologians—Henry Ware and **William Ellery Channing**. After his graduation from Cambridge in 1837, Sears left the comfortable life of the East and traveled west to a settlement in Ohio, where he stayed for another year. In 1839 Sears married Ellen Bacon, and in 1840 he was installed as pastor of the Congregational Church in Lancaster, Massachusetts. Unfortunately, Sears was never a hearty man, and due to an illness in 1846, he found it necessary to resign as pastor in Lancaster. But his health returned enough the next year that he was able to return to the pulpit in Wayland, where he remained for the next seventeen years. During his time in Wayland, Sears published *Regeneration* in 1853 and *Athanasia; or, Foregleams of Immortality* in 1858. *Regeneration* and *Athanasia*, both in their own way, work as spaces for Sears to explicate in detail his personal relationships with the Unitarian and Transcendental doctrines and, through the doctrines, his personal relationships with God and Christ. Previous to *Athanasia*, Sears was asked by The American Unitarian Association to write a sermon, or essay, denouncing and exposing the ills of slavery. Sears agreed, and his *Revolution or Reform: A Discourse Occasioned by the Present Crisis* soon became a popular anti-slavery document.

Sears was proud of his Puritan origin, and in 1857 he published *Pictures of the Olden Time as Shown in the Fortunes of a Family of Pilgrims and Genealogies and Biographical Sketches of the Ancestry and Descendants of Richard Sears*, a book-length account of the Sears family, beginning in 1535. *Pictures* is no doubt of interest as a historical document, but the text is also a window into Sears's personal, civic, and spiritual background as it had come down through the centuries to him—it emphasizes economy, hard work, and the spiritual foregrounding of life.

The years between 1859 and 1871 found Sears not only in the pulpit but also working alongside Rufus Ellis as associate editor of the well-known Unitarian periodical the *Monthly Religious Magazine*. In 1866 Sears left Wayland for Weston, where he succeeded Joseph Field as pastor. Sears would continue with his pastoral duties in Weston until his death ten years later. He took his position as pastor and other civic duties seriously, but Sears always found time to write, and during his tenure in Weston he wrote what might have been his finest work: *The Forth Gospel: The Heart of Christ* (1857). Sears wrote two more books before he died, *Sermons and Songs of the Christian Life* (1875) and *Life in Christ*, published posthumously in 1877.

The publishing date for Sears's most famous Christmas hymn, "It Came upon a Midnight Clear," is cause for some confusion. Erik Routley, in *The English Carol*, cites "It Came Upon a Midnight Clear" as first published in 1850 (160), whereas John Hollander, in *American Poetry: The Nineteenth Century*, writes that the hymn was first published in the anthology *Five Christmas Hymns* in 1852 (1,022). Routley also notes that the last stanza of "It Came Upon a Midnight Clear" was changed in the *Hymnal Companion* of 1871. Apparently the editor(s) of the *Hymnal Companion* felt the book's readers might struggle, misinterpret, or take offense at Sears's using a non-direct approach to the hymn by *alluding* to the nativity and the first coming of Christ instead of being more direct. The *Hymnal Companion*'s version of the poem replaces Sears's original "Comes round the age of gold" with "Shall come the time foretold" and his "By prophet bards foretold" with "By prophets seen of old." The changes in the verse, while small, do point out the changes in the church with which Sears's generation of ministers were struggling.

"It Came Upon a Midnight Clear" also has much to say about Sears's poetry. While the hymn employs simple eight-line stanzas and an *abcbdefe* rhyme scheme, "Upon a Midnight Clear" also makes use of alternating eight- and then seven-beat lines—all of which, combined, create a poem that can be sung. Sears's poems can be read as hymns; his hymns can be read as poems; both the poems and hymns can be sung. If Sears's writing accomplishes anything extraordinary, that is his blurring of the lines normally drawn between genres of writing, between hymns and poetry or songs and poetry; even Sears's prose, especially his religious prose, benefits from his sense of an expanded poetics.

In 1873 he enjoyed a tour of Europe. Not long after his return, while working in his garden, Sears fell out of a tree. Even after he fell, Sears never retired from the pulpit, and although he never regained the slim hold he had on health, he continued to write and to preach. Finally, on January 16, 1876, as a new year began, Sears passed away quietly in his home.

Further Reading. ***Selected Primary Sources:*** Hollander, John, ed., *American Poetry: The Nineteenth Century*, vol. 1 (New York: Literary Classics-Penguin, 1993); Routley, Erik, *The English Carol* (London: Wyman and Sons Ltd., 1958); Lunt, William P., ed., *The Christian Psalter: A Collection of Psalms and Hymns for Social and Private Worship* (Boston: Charles C. Little and James Brown, 1841); Sears, Edmund H., *Athanasia: or, Foregleams of Immortality* (Boston: American Unitarian Association, 1870); ———, *Pictures of the Olden Times, Time as Shown in the Fortunes of a Family of Pilgrims and Genealogies and Biographical Sketches of the Ancestry and Descendents of Richard Sears* (Boston: Crosby, Nichols, and Company, 1857); ———, *Revolution or Reform: A Discourse Occasioned by the Present Crisis* (Boston: Crosby, Nichols, and Company, 1856); Simon, Henry W., ed., *A Treasury of Christmas Songs and Carols* (Boston: Houghton Mifflin, 1955). ***Selected Secondary Sources:*** Cooke, George Willis, *Unitarianism in America: A History of its Origin and Development* (Boston: American Unitarian Association, 1902); Eliot, Samuel A., ed., *Heralds of a Liberal Faith*, vol. 3 (Boston: American Unitarian Association, 1910); Wright, Conrad, *The Liberal Christians: Essays on American Unitarian History* (Boston: Beacon Press, 1970).

Thomas L. Herakovich

SECCOMBE, JOSEPH (1706–1760)

Joseph Seccombe, one-time missionary to Native Americans, third minister of the Congregational church in Kingston, New Hampshire, poet, and literary theorist (of sorts), is best known for a sermon, "*Business and Diversion inoffensive to God . . . A Discourse utter'd in Part at Ammauskeeg-Falls, in the Fishing-Season.*" However, he also holds an important place in early American poetry, both as a possible influence on the poetry of **Phillis Wheatley** and as a poet in his own right.

Joseph Seccombe was born on June 14, 1706. His parents, who were not prosperous, were John, an obscure innkeeper, and Mehitable (Simmons) Seccombe from Boston. Although Joseph was baptized at the North Church of Boston, which his father attended, he joined his mother's church, the Old South, where Joseph Sewall was the principal minister and Thomas Prince was his assistant, on October 6, 1723, at age seventeen.

Because of his keen intelligence and gentlemanly bearing, Seccombe soon caught the attention of the generous communicants of the Old South who decided to fund his education. Perhaps already drawing on the wealth of books, maps, and manuscripts that Thomas Prince had long been collecting, Seccombe was dispatched to Reverend Samuel Wigglesworth, a descendant of the famous Wigglesworth family and a 1707 Harvard graduate, for the purposes of preparing him to enter Harvard. Seccombe began at Harvard in 1728 and was soon advanced a full year so that he eventually graduated with the class of 1731.

After a brief stint as a schoolmaster and holder of a graduate fellowship at Harvard, in 1732 he was selected by the Edinburgh Society for Propagating Christian Knowledge among Native Americans (SPCK) to serve as a missionary to Native Americans. Seccombe's services were judged by his peers to be distinguished. It was during his tenure as a missionary that Seccombe came to the attention of Benjamin Colman (Harvard BA, 1692), an accomplished minister, the father of Jane Turell, and an agent in the Colonies for the SPCK. Considering that all Colman's reports regarding Seccombe are superlative, that Colman, upon his death, became the subject of a **pastoral elegy** by Seccombe should come as no surprise.

Following Seccombe's service as missionary, he accepted a call to minister to the congregation at Kingston, New Hampshire, where he wrote the first tract to appear in America on sport, "Business and Diversion Inoffensive to God . . . in the Fishing Season" (1739), and where he remained until his death in 1760, just a year before the arrival of Phillis Wheatley in Boston. Through Sewall, the principal minister at Old South church who had delivered the ordination sermon for the young Seccombe in 1733, we can draw a straight line between these two poet-thinkers, Seccombe and Wheatley. Because Sewall served Wheatley as her spiritual "monitor" as she phrased it, and because Wheatley composed in 1769 an elegy on the death of Sewall, it is reasonable to posit the African American poet would have been familiar with Seccombe's pastoral elegy and with his many published homilies.

Seccombe's pastoral elegy, "On the Death of the Reverend Benjamin Colman, D.D. . . . An Eclogue," is important, not just because it does not imitate Milton's *Lycidas*, but also because it is later imitated by two other colonial American poets, thereby ascertaining a pattern of referentiality that proves so crucial to an understanding of a distinctly early American classicism, one decidedly not derived from Britain or the Continent. Another reason to pay attention to this piece is its representation of a confluence of literary and intellectual exemplars of thought.

For example, references in the poem to specific literary figures—Edmund Spenser's Pastorella, a shepherdess from Book VI of the *Faerie Queene*; Maecenas (whose name later serves Phillis Wheatley as a sort of collective patron—anyone who purchases her 1773 *Poems*), a poet and wealthy Roman patron of such figures as Vergil,

Horace, and Ovid; and Eusebrius (ca. 264–340 A.D.), author of *The Ecclesiastical History*, which exercised a considerable influence throughout the Middle Ages and the Renaissance—suggest the range of Seccombe's learning. This pastoral elegy, which Seccombe chooses to call an eclogue, thereby calling up Vergil's ten *Eclogues* (his first major work), contains virtually all the components of Vergil's eclogue (or selection) on Daphnis (the fifth), which established the central paradigm for the praxis of the genre from the time of Vergil to the present day (though the twentieth century's American praxis of the genre manifests some fascinating variations).

Seccombe's elegy includes a pathetic fallacy ("All Nature smiles" as the poem opens, but later a storm presages the announcement of Colman's death after which "rustic Cotts [cottages] and lonely Rocks lament"); mourning that sounds in the voices of shepherds such as Clericanor and Tyro, and here including the voice of the shepherdess Pastorella; a procession of mourners in which Seccombe numbers Joseph Sewall, Thomas Prince, **Mather Byles**, and Charles Chauncy, all famous American clergy of the day; and a final consolation.

Seccombe accomplishes this consolation with arresting economy; rather than having a protracted, reassuring exhortation to the living to seek the heavenly state of the newly ascended subject, as was characteristic of Puritan funeral laments, Seccombe writes the following:

> Thus varying passes Life, with each Event;
> Hence warmly urge we, Hope and calm Content,
> 'Till Grace in Glory give a Friendship permanent.

This triplet, only the second in a poem largely composed of couplets, resembles a syncretization of Horation aspirations toward sweet contentment with the Christian promise to the faithful of glorification by means of God's grace. But Seccombe's emphasis on "Life's" variety and the practice of friendship resonates provocatively with classical virtues and mores. So one is moved to query, just how Christian is this thoroughly classical pastoral elegy?

Seccombe's pastoral elegy on Colman has the additional distinction of establishing a paradigm for composition in this genre for two other early American poets, **Jeremy Belknap** and **Joseph Green**. Rather than imitate Milton in *Lycidas*, as nearly all critics have held until very recently, these three—Seccombe, Belknap, and Green—clearly reference one another. Since Belknap and Green (1766) follow Seccombe in chronology, it is logical to conclude that the pattern Seccombe uses was adopted by Belknap and Green. This pattern entails using the word "eclogue," conjuring Vergil somewhere in their title, and preceding the text with an argument or description of the poem's action (here Seccombe is almost certainly following Spenser once again, since he opens each of his twelve pastorals comprising *The Shepherdes' Calendar*, including a pastoral elegy, with an argument), which few, if any, other early American pastoral elegies do. All three poets employ lightning or its results to announce each of the three subjects' deaths, and the pattern also includes the evocation of famous authors, either by allusion (Seccombe's Pastorella alludes to Spenser) or by quotation (Belknap and Green quote a few phrases from Milton—his *Paradise Lost*, not *Lycidas*—and from Pope's *Essay on Man*, respectively).

As a literary theorist, Seccombe once again serves as a nexus for the dispensation of knowledge. In his homilies or sermons, for example, which often read more like treatises, Seccombe mentions or cites such figures as the skeptic Pierre Charron, such classical historians as the Greek Herodotus and the Roman Livy, and the British philosopher and political theorist John Locke. That Seccombe quotes from Charron's *de la Sagesse* (Concerning Wisdom) signals Seccombe's career-long search, outside the Holy Circle (Peter Gay's term), for the idea and practice of wisdom. Indeed, one of his sermons was entitled *A Specimen of the Harmony of Wisdom and Felicity*.

The quotation from Charron comes out of his discussion of imagination, whose use Pope had labeled "a dangerous art." Whereas Charron called imagination a "blustering and restless Faculty [which] never lies still" (9), Seccombe, in his *Some Occasional Thoughts* (1742), finds that imagination "is a very useful and powerful Faculty," for even "the Divine Spirit makes Use of the imagination" (9). Samuel Cooper, who baptized Phillis Wheatley, found imagination in *Pietas et Gratulatio* (1761) to be a "heav'n born maid," so we can draw a straight line regarding the imagination from Seccombe to Joseph Sewall, to Samuel Cooper, and finally to Phillis Wheatley.

Because Wheatley's "On Imagination" represents the most emphatic declaration in early America about the imagination as the poet's reason, we may easily conclude that Seccombe's role in Wheatley's arriving at her declaration in literary aesthetics was pivotal. Additionally, his importance to the evolution of an American classicism prompted an episode in American self-referentiality (a refusal to seek out British or Continental examples to imitate) that makes a strong case for American literary independence long before the American Revolution's accomplishment of political independence. It is time that Seccombe be recognized for much more than his contribution to sport history.

Further Reading. ***Selected Primary Sources:*** Seccombe, Joseph, *Business and Diversion Inoffensive to God . . . in the Fishing Season* (Boston: 1743); ———, "On the Death of the Reverend Benjamin Colman, D.D. . . . An Eclogue" (Boston: 1747); ———, *Some Occasional Thoughts on the Influence of the Spirit* (Boston: 1742); ———, *A Specimen of the Harmony of Wisdom and Felicity, in Relation to Our Civil,*

Moral, and Spiritual Behavior (Boston: 1743). ***Selected Secondary Sources:*** Shields, John C., *The American Aeneas: Classical Origins of the American Self* (Knoxville: University of Tennessee Press, 2001); ———, "Seccombe, Joseph," in *ANB* 19 (Oxford University Press, 1999, 574–575); Shipton, Clifford K., "Joseph Seccombe," in *Biographical Sketches of Those Who Attended Harvard College*, Vol. IX (Boston: Massachusetts Historical Society, 1956, 87–96).

John C. Shields

SEEGER, ALAN (1888–1916)

Given the general run of so much of his work—vague, derivative, burdened by an obsolete poetic diction, and its rampant idealism untempered by any measure of irony—Seeger might have been forgotten long ago. But two facts, taken together, ensure that he will be remembered: He died young as an enlistee in the French Foreign Legion (three years before the United States entered the war in 1917), and he wrote "I Have a Rendezvous with Death." He also garners respect for the purity of his intentions and for his willingness to die for his idealism. At the very least, Seeger deserves to be remembered with the other doomed poets of War World I, to mention only the British writers Rupert Brook and Wilfred Owen. From another perspective, Seeger is an intriguing contrast to Ernest Hemingway, who, also drawn to the war early, shared with him an attraction to the grim romanticism of war. Hemingway lived and enjoyed the opportunity to write prose that would shape our vision of that horrific event. Seeger did not, so we are left with the sometimes-callow words that he could never revise.

Born in 1888, Seeger lived with his family on Staten Island and then in New York City, where he attended the Horace Mann School. In 1900 the family moved to Mexico for two years before returning to the United States. Seeger spent 1906 through 1910 at Harvard, graduating in Italian studies. After spending two unfocused years in New York City—but writing poetry—he moved to Paris, where he enthusiastically embraced its glamorous life. Writing there, he produced the bulk of "Juvenilia," but could not find a publisher. In 1914, shortly after the outbreak of World War I, he enlisted in the French Foreign Legion, along with many other young Americans. He managed to continue writing poetry, now drawing inspiration from the war in which he fought. In 1916, battling for the village of Belloy-en-Santere, he died under German machine-gun fire. His collected poems were published posthumously in 1917.

His enduring poem, "I Have a Rendezvous with Death," is included in the section labeled "Last Poems." It is a short work of three eight-line stanzas in modified ballad form, with an additional rhyming couplet at the end of the third. The speaker of the poem accepts an inevitable confrontation at "some disputed barricade" with personified Death, who will lead him into "his dark land." He sees the event as occurring in the spring, when "apple-blossoms fill the air." He acknowledges that remaining with a lover is preferable, but maintains that he has a deeper obligation—"I to my pledged word am true"—that he cannot fail.

The themes—the inevitability of death, the soldier's obligation, the proud acceptance of fate—are strung throughout much of his other work, but they show up here uncharacteristically concrete, vivid, and dramatic. The poem is evidence that he was in the process of shedding some of the derivative qualities that mark his work. Still, his poetry largely remains of one piece in his insistence on expressing the idealism of a previous age, the great abstract virtues—beauty, duty, courage, destiny, fate, and so on.

Many of his early poems—labeled "Juvenilia" (or works the artist produces in youth) by Seeger himself—yield these predictable sentiments. In "The Sultan's Palace," the speaker declares, "My spirit only lived to look on Beauty's face." And in this quest for beauty, he sees "no dread in death, no horror to abhor."

"The Torture of Cuauhtemoc," reflecting his time in Mexico, is different enough from the derivative poems to attract interest. As the Spanish conquerors torture the Aztec nobility in order to learn the location of their treasure, one young prince is ready to give in to avoid the pain (they are being burned alive). When rebuked by a fellow sufferer (who asks, pointedly, "And am—I—then / Upon a bed of roses?"), the prince, "Stung with shame," then "turned his face against the wall—and died." The sense of duty in the poem, the choice of death over shame, is a thematic commonplace in Seeger's work. Weighed down with ponderous diction and static imagery, the poem is still a welcomed relief from the bulk of "Juvenilia."

Though many of the "Last Poems" are based on his experience in the war, Seeger's writing is thematically consistent with his earlier poetry. While the later poems are marked by fatalism, it is a romantic fatalism, not much out of temper with the rest of his work. One improvement in the later poetry is in the diction, which does become somewhat more concrete in describing actual events. What before had been lofty expression and vague abstraction is brought closer to experience with which the reader can identify. For example, in "The Aisne" he announces in the first line, "We first saw fire on the tragic slopes." The directness and clarity are an important development in his work. "Maktoob" makes even further advances; the opening stanza presents a clear scene and uses (at least for that stanza) straightforward language: "A shell surprised our post one day / And killed a comrade at my side. / My heart was sick to see the way / he suffered as he died." This opening is evocative of Thomas Hardy, though the tone is not sustained.

In the "Last Poems," though the voice of the speaker is direct and clear, the ideas remain the familiar ones. In "Sonnet IV," he restates his basic position: "My creed is simple: that the world is fair, / And beauty the best thing to worship there."

The last poem in the collection, "Ode in Memory of the American Volunteers Fallen for France," was requested by a group of American residents. Seeger had hoped to read it on Decoration Day, May 30, 1916, in Paris at the statue of Lafayette and Washington, but did not receive permission in time. The poem gives thanks to France for "That chance to live the life most free from stain / And that rare privilege of dying well."

Further Reading. ***Selected Primary Sources:*** Seeger, Alan, *Letters and Diary of Alan Seeger* (New York: Scribner's, 1917); ———, *Poems*, ed. William Archer (New York: Scribner's, 1917). ***Selected Secondary Sources:*** Penney, Clara L., "A Letter of Alan Seeger (1888–1916)" (*Bulletin of the New York Public Library* 78 [1975]: 393–396); Southam, B.C., "Whispers of Immortality (*Times Literary Supplement* [22 June 1973]: 720–721); Werstein, Irving, *Sound No Trumpet: The Life and Death of Alan Seeger* (New York: Crowell, 1967).

Steve Anderson

SEIDEL, FREDERICK (1936–)

Few recent poets are as ruthlessly contemporary as Frederick Seidel. In his often terse, sometimes elegiac poetry, Seidel confronts an epoch that is saturated with varying and competing forms of media, rampant consumerism, and a collective ethos bordering on the pornographic. He captures the allure of the surface and juxtaposes the fashionable with inescapable realities; indeed, this is "what a poem does," writes Seidel in the title poem of his 1998 collection, *Going Fast*: "It explosively reanimates / By oxygenating the tribe." As the poet **Lawrence Joseph** wrote in *The Nation*, Seidel brings a mix of subjects not found before in American poetry: "the politics of the American empire, moneyed and unmoneyed class, Judaism in the Diaspora, racial oppression and violence. Seidel combine[s] a classical historian's eye for the details of human behavior with a sophisticate's poetics" (314).

Son of a business executive, Frederick Lewis Seidel was born on February 19, 1936, in St. Louis, Missouri. He received his BA from Harvard in 1957; after nine years of marriage, he and his wife Phyllis Munro Ferguson divorced in 1969. The New York resident's collections of poetry include *Final Solutions* (1963); *Sunrise* (1979); *Poems, 1959–79* (1989); *These Days* (1989); *My Tokyo* (1993); *Going Fast* (1998); and *The Cosmos Trilogy* (2003), which incorporates three collections, *The Cosmos Poems* (2000), *Life on Earth* (2001), and *Area Code 212* (2002). Seidel received the 1979 Lamont Prize for *Sunrise*, the 1980 National Book Critics Circle Award in poetry, and a Guggenheim Fellowship in 1993; *Going Fast* was nominated for the Pulitzer Prize in poetry; and in 2002, he received the PEN/Voelker Award for Poetry. In addition to writing poetry, Seidel has written screenplays with Mark Peploe for the 1985 film *Samson and Delilah*, based on D.H. Lawrence's work, the acclaimed 1992 film *Afraid of the Dark*, and the 2002 film *Victory*, based on Joseph Conrad's novel.

Edward Mendelson, in his introduction to the Vintage edition of **W.H. Auden**'s poems, states that "Auden was the first poet writing in English who felt at home in the twentieth century. He welcomed into his poetry all the disordered conditions of his time, all its variety of language and event" (ix). Mendelson's statement could apply equally to Seidel and the late twentieth and early twenty-first centuries. Indeed, Auden could be seen as Seidel's essential predecessor: Auden's ironic tone coupled with his understanding of the obligations of citizenship and the ethical demands of history inform Seidel's work.

Seidel's first collection has been criticized for being too deeply influenced by **Robert Lowell**'s style and references; however, Lowell's position as a public poet owes much to Auden and the belief in one's responsibility for addressing the conditions the poet finds present. Seidel challenges us with historical choices and representations through the very title of his first book, *Final Solutions*, with its reference to the extermination of Jews, gypsies, communists, and homosexuals by the Nazis. By changing the term to a plural, Seidel risks the heresy that the Nazi's project was not historically specific, but repeated and repeatable. Taking on racial politics, as in "The Negro Judge"; Europe's cold war politics, as in "A Year Abroad" or "'The Beast is in Chains'"; or sexual discontent, as in "The Widower," against the awareness of his mother's long, terminal illness during his youth, Seidel's first collection can be harrowing. *Final Solutions*, however, also risks shocking for the sake of shock.

Seidel's next collection, *Sunrise*, contains poems addressed to Robert Lowell, Mandelstam, Robert Kennedy, Mayakovsky, and **Hart Crane**, as well as poems invoking a privileged life, motorcycles, and the late 1960s with its assassinations, riots, and escalating Vietnam war. Reviewers point to the prophetic and angered voice of *Sunrise*, as in the opening poem "1968," wherein the "the beginning of a new day" becomes the date of the assassination of Robert Kennedy. As Lawrence Joseph has noted, the poem, like many of Seidel's, is constructed through the selection of scenes and images; thus, although Seidel eschews the authoritative "I" of Lowell, Seidel is the one who sees, the one who then is the prophet. The title poem, composed of forty nine-line stanzas, reflecting Seidel's "forty Easters of life," appraises the United States, "Bicentennial April, the two hundredth / Lash of the revolving lighthouse wink," in an avalanche of referents and motifs. Sacrifice, sexuality, autobiographical fragments, countdowns, destitution, and the galactic all fuse into a hymn of sunrise, echoing Hart Crane's *The Bridge* in its tendency to move toward texturing of sound: "Organizations of gravity and light, / . . . / In an incomprehensible -1 of might."

New York City is the locus of much of Seidel's poetry. "Wanting to Live in Harlem," "The Future," "The New Frontier," and "Pressed Duck" share in the sense that "The City was our faith— / Ah we knew now the world need not end," as Seidel writes in "The New Frontier." The depravities and excesses of humans and of the elite and political classes of the United States that Seidel depicts in his first collections of poems continue in *These Days*, yet there is also an element of exhaustion; this is apparent in the repetition of "I don't believe in anything"—as in "Stanzas" and "The Last Poem in the Book"—and in the awareness of our insignificance in geologic and cosmic time, as he writes in the opening poem "Scotland": "The sun will expand a billion years from now / and burn away the mist Caithness." Seidel is far more taut and critical in this collection, as illustrated in the concluding lines of "Empire," in which he compares the rank smell in urine "Of asparagus from the night before, / This is empire waking drunk, and remembering in the dark." Seidel's world is that of experience and betrayal; "Gethsemane" fuses personal anguish and frustration with the century's horrors. The rapaciousness, and the repression, of sexuality become synonymous with the betrayal of all that is human. Not since **T.S. Eliot**'s "The Love Song of J. Alfred Prufrock" has the banal come to be incorporated into a visionary skepticism about human possibility.

Seidel's next book, *My Tokyo*, continues his skepticism and ironic tone: "The universe begins, / And look what happens" (from "The Complete Works of Anton Webern"). Throughout *My Tokyo* there exists a tension between disconnection and the reportage of events. The anonymity of "Untitled" is juxtaposed with the scathing confession that during the civil rights movement, "I had no time. They lynched and burned. / I played squash drunk." The poem suggests cohesion through its use of six-line stanzas and villanelle-like repeated lines, yet those very repetitions, such as "Nothing has been the same since the Zapruder film," create a sense of political and moral discordance. If "Untitled" is typical of many of the poems of the collection, there are also the enigmatic, erotic poems such as "Autumn," "The Lover," "The Second Coming," and "The Lighting of the Candles."

Divided into eight sections that seem to move across the surface of the globe with sections titled "New York," "London," "Paris & Tahiti," or "Milan," for example, Seidel's collection *Going Fast* veers between the gentle and the grim witness. In "Prayer" Seidel links childhood with the Crayola yellow taxi cabs and his act of generosity (as poet and witness): "Dear friend, get in. / I will take you where you are going for free." In "Heart Art," Seidel opens the poem stating, "A man is masturbating his heart out," and continues a grim reportage of mediation and depletion of the senses through the Internet, cyberspace, and "Information, zeros-and-ones, whitecaps of." The title poem, divided into six sections, closes the collection; its final section titled "Killing Hitler" combines Seidel's ironic elevation of machismo, as emblemized by the Ducati motorcycle, sexual desire, his Jewish identity, and history: "How to be a work of art and win. / How to be Supermono and marry Lois Lane in the synagogue, and love."

The Cosmos Trilogy combines *The Cosmos Poems* (written in honor of the 2000 opening of the American Museum of Natural History's Hayden Planetarium in New York City), *Life on Earth*, and *Area Code 212*, in a Dantean journey in reverse, from contemplations of the celestial to the inferno of the twenty-first century. Divided into one-hundred titled sections, each section consisting of eight quatrains, except for the final one-hundredth poem, which is twenty-five stanzas long, *The Cosmos Trilogy* is written mainly in the present tense as a way of placing the narrator, Seidel himself, among the objects of our world, and thereby constructing his identity. The trilogy ends just after the attacks on the World Trade Center in 2001; Seidel does not write *about* this event, but rather it becomes part of his shaping of his identity, the precarious balancing of love for the world and contempt for himself and that same world: Watching people decide to leap from the upper floors of the twin towers rather than perish within them, "The man stands at his childhood window saving them," and this line is countered by the final line of the poem's ninety-eighth section, "God is great. Love is hate." Indeed, as Calvin Bedient wrote in *The Boston Review*, Seidel may be not only the poet the twentieth century deserved but also the poet the millennium deserved.

Further Reading. ***Selected Primary Sources:*** Seidel, Frederick, *The Cosmos Trilogy* (New York: Farrar, Straus, and Giroux, 2003); ———, *Final Solutions* (New York: Random House, 1963); ———, *Going Fast* (New York: Farrar, Straus, Giroux, 1998); ———, *My Tokyo* (New York: Farrar, Straus, Giroux, 1993); ———, *Poems: 1959–1979* (New York: Knopf, 1989); ———, *These Days* (New York: Knopf, 1989); ———, *Sunrise* (New York: Knopf, 1979). ***Selected Secondary Sources:*** Bedient, Calvin, "Review of *The Cosmos Poems* and *Life on Earth*" (*The Boston Review* [October/November 2001]); Creswell, Robyn, "On Frederick Seidel" (*Raritan* 21.2 [Fall 2001]: 68–84); Joseph, Lawrence, "War of the

Worlds" [review of *Poems: 1959–1979* and *These Days*] (*The Nation* [24 September 1990]: 314–318); Mendelson, Edward, "Preface" to *W.H. Auden: Selected Poems* (New York: Vintage, 1979); Phillips, Adam, "A New Kind of Visionary" (*Raritan* 18.2 [Fall 1998]: 120–127).

James McCorkle

SELVA, SALOMÓN DE LA (1893–1959)

Although Salomón de la Selva is one of the most important poets in Nicaraguan literary history, he began his career writing poems in English in the United States. His first book, *Tropical Town and Other Poems*, published in New York in 1918, neatly expresses the bifurcation of his career and cultural interests. The volume's first two sections are called "My Nicaragua" and "In New England and Other Lyrics." The Nicaraguan poems reveal a nostalgia for the poet's homeland, complemented by a fascination with its images and complexities and a dissatisfaction with its subordination to the interests of the United States. The poems of New England suggest a sense of displacement and exile in the snowy terrain of inland Massachusetts. Taken together, the poems reveal a unique instance of pan-American awareness by a poet gifted in plangent imagery, social awareness, and emotional yearning.

Born in León, Nicaragua, to a physician's family, Selva came alone to the United States at the age of eleven or perhaps thirteen to live with the family of a wealthy patron. He studied for several years at Williams College in Western Massachusetts and eventually took a job teaching Spanish and French there. He also began writing poetry. As a fledgling poet, he befriended **Stephen Vincent Benét**, Alice Meynell, **Edna St. Vincent Millay** (who memorialized their relationship in her poem "Recuerdo"), and the great Nicaraguan poet Rubén Darío (whose poetry Selva praised in the pages of *Poetry* magazine). Selva's work appeared in anthologies such as Edwin Markham's *The Book of American Poetry* (1926), in which he seemed one of the leading voices of a new generation. He also had close ties to the American union movement, working for a time as the secretary of Samuel Gompers.

Many of the poems in the "My Nicaragua" section of *Tropical Town and Other Poems* reflect Selva's longing for the Nicaraguan landscape and culture. In the sonnet "Tropical Town," for example, the speaker begins the initial octet by recalling

> Blue, pink, and yellow houses, and, afar,
> The cemetery, where the green trees are.

In the concluding sestet, he tells us that "I come from there" and that his thoughts often return to where "the lonely green trees and the white graves are." The poem reflects a loss of both nation and childhood through visual and auditory images of rural Nicaragua. In another such poem, "Tropical Childhood," the speaker recalls his imaginative play as a "thin" and "restless" young child. In such poems, Selva attempts to create a distinctly modern poetry that is at once formally intricate, autobiographically resonant, and pan-American in flavor.

Other poems in the "My Nicaragua" section of Selva's book take up political and social issues. "A Song for Wall Street" laments Nicaragua's enduring poverty, despite the richness of its agriculture and culture:

> In Nicaragua, my Nicaragua,
> What can you buy for a penny there?—
> A basketful of apricots,
> A water jug of earthen ware.

The poem concludes by lambasting the exploitation of his native land by the United States, with its "dirty dollar" and cultural "leprosy." In the last poem of this section, "The Dreamer's Heart Knows Its Own Bitterness," the poet assesses his medial position between North and Central America, declaring that he has "shattered the walls of creed and race" so that both "North and South would hear me sing." He attempts to resolve the tensions within his identity by positing that "my flags are two," but despite this conscious effort at self-unity, a cry from his plundered homeland continues to haunt him: "Lest ye forget!" The poem expresses a confused sense that the United States is righteous in relation to the Allied cause in World War I, but oppressive in relation to the nations south of its border.

The poems of "In New England and Other Lyrics," the second section of Selva's book, focus on the immigrant's wish to fit in while still feeling an outsider. "Deliverance," for example, asks, "What am I doing here in New England?" Looking over the alien landscape he waits to see "the universal moon." A stranger in a strange land, he thus searches out a symbol of commonality that would unite the two halves of his personal history. Although "The Secret" pays tribute to the beauty of a New England birch tree, it ends by acknowledging the speaker's cultural distance from the human beings around him:

> But the good folk grew sulky
> Because I would not pay
> A compliment to the Springtime
> In that New England day;
> And they murmured because I wanted
> To pack my things and run away.

In the concluding two sections of *Tropical Town and Other Poems*, Selva focuses first on the United States at war (in a section called "In War Time") and then on ostensibly timeless themes (in a section called "The Tale from Faerieland"). Yet the poems of these sections continually return to the central issue of cultural displacement. In "I Would Be Telling You," the speaker states that he would be telling of the exotic tamarind tree, but "what is that to me?" On the other hand, writing under an "alien sky," he finds it impossible to articulate a convincing vision of home. Such poems evoke the feeling of not belonging and the sense of imaginative abjection that so frequently underlies the **modernist** ethos.

Unhappy about the continued occupation of Nicaragua by the United States Marines, Selva moved to England soon after publication of his book. He fought briefly with the British army in World War I, which became the central focus of his second collection, *El soldado desconocido* (The Unknown Soldier), written in Spanish and published in Mexico in 1922. From this point onward, Selva wrote his poems and essays primarily in Spanish. He spent the 1920s living in England, with occasional return visits to New York. By 1930 he was again residing in Nicaragua, where he supported the leftist guerrilla leader Augusto Sandino. After Sandino's execution in 1934, Selva lived primarily in Mexico, though he also spent time in Costa Rica and Panama. A vocal opponent of both U.S. imperialism and Nicaraguan authoritarianism, he nonetheless accepted an ambassadorial position at the end of his life from the Nicaraguan dictator Anastasio Somoza. He died in Paris of a heart attack at the age of sixty-five.

Selva's poetry attests to the difficulties and opportunities of a multinational identity. It also suggests that traditional **poetic forms** may subsist with modernist alienation, intensity, and boundary-crossing. In the U.S. context, Selva's accomplishment was sidelined to some extent by the experimentalism of **Eliot**, **Pound**, **Stein**, and **Williams**. But it waits to be rediscovered. Along with the poetry of **Martí** and **Williams**, it attests to the interconnectedness of the literature of the Americas.

Further Reading. ***Selected Primary Sources:*** Selva, Salomón de la, *Antología mayor*, ed. Julio Valle-Castillo (Managua: Editorial Nueva Nicaragua, 1993); ———, "Edna St. Vincent Millay" (*América: Revista Antológica* 62 [January 1950]: 7–32); ———, "Rubén Darío" (*Poetry: A Magazine of Verse* 8 [1916]: 200–204); ———, *Tropical Town and Other Poems*, ed. Silvio Sirias (Houston, TX: Arte Público Press, 1999). ***Selected Secondary Sources:*** Arellano, Jorge Eduardo, *Los tres grandes: Azarías H. Pallais, Alfonso Cortés y Salomón de la Selva* (Managua, Nicaragua: Ediciones Distribuidora Cultural, 1993); Gutiérrez, Ernesto, ed., *Homenaje a Salomón de la Selva: 1959–1969* (León, Nicaragua: Cuadernos Universitarios, 1969); Sirias, Silvio, "Introduction" to *Tropical Town and Other Poems*, by Salomón de la Selva (Houston, TX: Arte Público Press, 1999, 1–56).

Steven Gould Axelrod

SELYNS, HENRICUS (1636–1701)

Henricus Selyns, a Dutch minister, is one of the earliest voices in American literature. Selyns was regarded as a man of genius and learning, and his poetry served as an extension of his sermons and intellectual discourses on matters of the foundation of the Dutch Church in the New World. Although his poetry consists solely of one slim collection, his poems provide historical insights into the pressing social, political, and religious issues of his day.

Selyns was born in Amsterdam, Holland, in 1636. He attended the University of Leyden and in 1660 was ordained a minister in the Reformed Dutch Church. He then set sail for New Amsterdam—now New York—and established a congregation in Brooklyn. In 1664 Selyns was summoned back to Holland, where he remained until 1682, when he returned to head the First Reformed Dutch Church of New York City. His influential connections and dedication to the growth of the Dutch Church as the preeminent religious organization resulted in the Dutch Reformed Church's receiving the first church charter issued in the colony in 1696. Under his inspirational leadership, Selyns's congregation strove to realize the true mission of their church and to establish a network of moral and social services, which appealed to the colonists and enabled the church to grow in stature and members.

Selyns was one of the most accomplished philosophers, orators, and scholars of his time. He was not a prolific poet; only nineteen poems are credited to his name, written in Dutch. During his lifetime he published one Latin poem in a selected edition of his close friend **Cotton Mather**'s famous work, *Magnalia Christi Americana* (1702). It was not until 1865 that Selyns's collected poetry was translated and published by Henry C. Murphy in the *Anthology of the New Netherlands.* However, Selyns did achieve acclaim for his popular hymn "O Kersnacht" ("O Christmas Night" [1663]), originally named "Nuptial Song," composed for the wedding of Rev. Ægidius Luyck and Judith Van Isendoorn. In six stanzas with a combination of rhyming couplets and quatrains, "O Christmas Night" is an analogy of Christ's birth and his creation of the church.

His poetry marked significant occasions—weddings, deaths, and musings of the moral dilemmas of the day—and also served as public commentary on leading political and religious figures. **Puritan** writers such as **Edward Taylor** and **Michael Wigglesworth** shared Selyns's literary concerns, which constituted a doctrine of righteousness. Social and political events of the day, such as the ongoing battles between Native Americans and European settlers, served as the inspiration for Selyns's **epic** portrayal of the futility of war, "Bridal Torch" (1865). Wrestling with themes of revenge and forgiveness, he writes, "Although the harmless rogue nor service does, nor good, / 'Tis best to leave the savage children sleeping." In addition to calming the colonists' fears of the uncertainty of the land, he also editorialized his views on the developing church.

Key figures in his own life served as inspiration for his work. In honor of the twentieth birthday of his first wife, Matilda Specht, he composed, "Birth-Day Garland" (1865), employing classical Greek form with designated verses labeled "Strophe," "Anti-Strophe," and "Epode." Selyns praises his wife, stating that since her birth, she "is the aim of ev'ry mortal."

Selyns uses his poetry not only to praise but also to imbue morals and humor. The poem "To My Friend" (1865) was written as a warning to parishioners who are neglecting the church. He states, "The world goes up; / God's church and worship / going under."

Ruminations on social practices are the central themes of the majority of his work. His poem "Reasons For And Against Marrying Widows" (1865) presents both sides of the argument by titling the first stanza "Pro" and the second stanza "Con," and wherein he asserts that to wed a widow is "not to marry trouble." The poem "Of Scolding Wives and the Third Day Ague" (1865) states that scolding wives "the greatest evils are" and advises the reader to suffer with great patience their wrath. "On Mercenary and Unjust Bailiffs" (1865) warns of the trappings of being "wrong with power." In addition to social issues, economic woes are also addressed. In "Upon the Bankruptcy of a Physician" (1865), he blames financial mismanagement and reckless spending as the causes that brought the "doctor under."

He wrote a short series of epitaphs, which included one for Peter Stuyvesant, the Governor General of New Netherland, which wistfully laments the land around New York that "unto the foe, the land did he give over." To honor Selyns's relative and successor, Willem Niewenhuysen, he wrote "On the Ministry" (1865), which concludes with the lines, "Now is New Netherland, by Nieuwenhuysen's / mission / And Nieuwenhuysen, by New Netherland's contrition, / Led to the New Jerusalem for new delights. / What church more safety finds than in renewed rites?"

The work of Henricus Selyns sheds necessary light upon a significant period in early America's cultural and political history and upon the development of the Dutch Reformed Church.

Further Reading. ***Selected Primary Sources:*** Murphy, Henry, *Anthology of New Netherland; or Translations from the early Dutch poets of New York, with memoirs of their lives* (New York: 1865); Mather, Cotton, *Magnalia Christi Americana* (New York: 1687). ***Selected Secondary Sources:*** The Holland Society of New York, www.hollandsociety.org.

Jayanti Tamm

SENTIMENTALITY

Although an object of suspicion throughout the nineteenth century, sentimentality enjoyed enormous prestige from its inception as a keyword in poetics in the late eighteenth century until the rise of **modernism** in the early twentieth century. Closely associated throughout its long history with a poetry of strong feelings freely expressed, its identifiable characteristics have varied considerably over time, as have the particular cultural projects with which it is associated. Only after World War I did sentimentality's shifting definitions stabilize into a single, wholly negative form. Linked by modernist poets and critics with Victorian culture and the figure of the "poetess," sentimental poetry was effectively written out of literary history and became (as Jerome McGann persuasively argues) unreadable in its own terms. Although we still speak approvingly of the "sentimental value" of personal possessions, sentimentality in a literary context is now understood as a synonym for *false* feeling and *clichéd* expression. Yet despite this repudiation, sentimentality survives as a living tradition both within and beyond modernism, sometimes in easily recognized form (as in the work of **e.e. cummings** or **Edna St. Vincent Millay**) and often in surprising disguise (as in the emotional extravagance of **confessional poetry**). At issue in this survival, from a philosophical point of view, are the proper relationship between thought and feeling and the value placed on feeling within that relationship. At the same time, because the charge of sentimentality is so often leveled against writing by women—or against writing concerned with topics associated with women, topics such as family and the home—the adjudication of this relationship is not only a philosophical problem but a cultural one as well.

An important starting point for all discussions of sentimental poetry is the German poet, dramatist, and philosopher Friedrich von Schiller's 1795 distinction between the "naïve" and "sentimental." Of crucial concern in this distinction is the poet's relation to nature, which for Schiller included human nature as well as the natural world. What was requisite was that the object "stand in contrast to art and put it to shame." Those poets whose writings fit this description, Schiller labeled "naïve." Their writings, artless as nature, will make the reader feel shame for his or her fallen condition of civilization. This shame Schiller labeled "sentimentality." It did not matter for him that the notion of an artless work of art was ultimately insupportable. The naïve belonged for him to an age now past. The sentimental poet—the poet of consciousness—was the only kind of poet that a modern age such as Schiller's own was capable of producing. Though traces of the naïve survive in "children," "the customs of country folk," "the primitive world," and "the monuments of ancient times," as well as in "the open air," "the country," "flowers and animals," and "simple gardens," poems that take up these traces invariably present them through the mediations of consciousness. Thus, in a sentimental poem, "we are never given the object, only what the reflective understanding has made of it, and even when the poet is himself the object, if he would describe his feeling to us, we never learn of his condition directly and at first hand, but rather how he has reflected it in his own mind, what he has thought about it as an observer of himself."

Sentimentality in Schiller's sense was ubiquitous in nineteenth-century America, evident in such canonical works as **William Cullen Bryant**'s "Thanatopsis" (1817), which welcomed death as a reabsorption of consciousness into nature, and **Emily Dickinson**'s "The Tint I cannot take—is best" (1863), which accepted consciousness as a precondition and limit. Reflections on the naïve were also common, whether presented in idealized form (as in **Henry Wadsworth Longfellow**'s *The Song of Hiawatha* [1855]) or mourned as a lost possibility (as in **Herman Melville**'s *Clarel, A Poem and Pilgrimage in the Holy Land* [1876]). The influence of the sentimental mode is especially evident in "The Jewish Synagogue at Newport" (1867), **Emma Lazarus**'s earliest treatment of a Jewish theme. Although the Touro Synagogue, erected in 1759, was still active—Lazarus and her family worshipped there—the poet presents this site as the relic of a vanished people, a place where "the very prayers / Inscribed around are in a language dead." Less well-known examples include **Lydia Huntley Sigourney**'s "Indian Names" (1834), which uses place names to summon the memory of lost American Indian tribes, and **Bayard Taylor**'s "Hylas" (1851), which frees itself from the shame of civilization by casting its portrait of ideal male beauty in mythic terms and setting it in the ancient world. This fascination with the naïve also survives into modernism with e.e. cummings's "Chansons Innocents" (1923) and the publication of actual **children's poetry** such as Hilda Conklin's **free-verse** *Poems of a Child* (1917), introduced by **Amy Lowell**, as well as with **H.D.**'s evocations of ancient Greece in *Sea Garden* (1916) and the Orientalism of **Ezra Pound**. Closer to Schiller's sense of the sentimental are such twentieth-century poems of reflective consciousness as **Randall Jarrell**'s "The Lost World" (1965) and **Lyn Hejinian**'s *My Life* (1980; 1987).

Schiller's definitions notwithstanding, sentimentality is most commonly understood as a mode of writing in which deeply felt emotions and their florid expression are given free rein. In this conception, the reflective consciousness so important for Schiller is deemphasized and even repudiated in favor of a strict obedience to feeling. This view, like Schiller's, is a product of eighteenth-century aesthetics and more especially a product of the "Age of Sensibility," Northrop Frye's term for the period immediately preceding Romanticism, in which (as Janet Todd notes) literary conventions functioned as "a kind of pedagogy . . . clarifying when uncontrolled sobs or a single tear should be the rule, or when the inexpressible nature of the feeling should be stressed." **Phillis Wheatley**'s *Poems on Various Subjects, Religious and Moral* (1773) belongs to this age. Her "To a Lady on the Death of Her Husband" enjoins the reader to "see the softly-stealing tears apace / Pursue each other down the mourner's face," and her "Niobe in Distress" observes of its heroine, "How strangely chang'd!—yet beautiful in woe, / She weeps, nor weeps unpity'd by the foe." This presentation of the object of pity as an aesthetic object persists in such later poems as Lydia Sigourney's "The Suttee" (1827) and **Adah Issacs Menken**'s "Resurgam" (1868). For other poets, extravagant emotion held an aesthetic charm in its own right. Mark Twain's Emmeline Grangerford in *The Adventures of Huckleberry Finn* (1885) offers a parody of this kind of writing.

As Janet Todd's use of the word "pedagogy" suggests, however, the pleasures that a reader might take in this kind of writing were not simply an aesthetic indulgence. The manipulation of emotion could also be placed in the service of social reform. Obedience to feeling, in these cases, was shaped by an ethical impulse: In a society dominated by self-interest, in which cruel policies and corrupt behavior were justified through the use of abstract reasoning, sympathy could offer an answer to the lure of the marketplace and induce readers to act on their consciences. Thus, in **Frances Ellen Watkin Harper**'s "The Slave Mother" (1854), the poet delineates the mother's grief even before she explains its cause, knowing that scenes of suffering educate the reader more forcefully than facts do. Paula Bernat Bennett describes this kind of writing as "high sentimentality" (as opposed to "literary sentimentality") and suggests that its ablest nineteenth-century practitioners—she singles out **Sarah Louisa Forten**, Sarah Mapps Douglass, and Lydia Sigourney—were aware of its limitations. The most significant of these limitations, as Bennett remarks, was "the substitution of feeling for a recognition of rights." Having offered feeling as a corrective to thought, the sentimental poets faced the problem of thinking through their own prejudices.

Sentimental poetry in the nineteenth century was shaped by a moral impetus, quite apart from its engagement with specific moral issues. As Mary Louise Kete has shown through her study of consolation verse, sentimentality was a collaborative practice. Poetry provided a medium for sharing feelings, and shared feelings provided a basis for forming or sustaining community. Community in this context followed the model of family, and this emphasis on family and shared feelings led Ann Douglas to equate the cultural project of sentimentality with "the feminization of American culture." So significant was domesticity to this culture that its most honored practitioners were called the "**Fireside Poets**," and, true to their name, their work was often shared aloud at the family hearth. **Walt Whitman** fittingly eulogized Longfellow as the "poet of all sympathetic gentleness—and universal poet of women and young people," and Longfellow's diminished reputation after modernism was preceded by that of all other poets of "sympathetic gentleness," most notably the popular women writers associated more directly with sentimentality: Lydia Sigourney, **Helen Hunt Jackson**, **Lizette Woodworth Reese**, and **Ella Wheeler Wilcox**.

The modernist repudiation of sentimentality was thus, in part, a repudiation of the literary culture in which women played a dominant role. This is especially clear in the work of I.A. Richards, whose *Practical Criticism* (1929) registered and then codified the twentieth century's transformation of "sentimentality" from description of a mode of writing to "expression of contempt." According to Richards, susceptibility to sentimentality was a sign of "disorder of the automatic nervous system," a gender-coded criticism first raised against women writers in the eighteenth century. His earlier *Principles of Literary Criticism* (1925) was even more explicit. There Richards cited Ella Wheeler Wilcox as his principal example of "Badness in Poetry," allowing that "even a good critic at a sufficiently low ebb of neural potency might mistake" her work for something better. In *Modern Poetry and the Tradition* (1939), Cleanth Brooks was likewise dismissive of **Genevieve Taggard**, a practitioner of what Bennett calls "high sentimentality." Clearly, the figure of the "poetess" did not conform to the scientific posture of the modernist poets and their allied academic movement, the **New Criticism**. **Allen Tate**'s judgment of Edna St. Vincent Millay is in this sense representative: "Miss Millay's success . . . is precariously won; I have said that she is not an intellect but a sensibility: if she were capable of a profound analysis . . . she might not use it." Other sentimental poets excluded from this self-conscious process of **canon formation** include **Sara Teasdale**, **Léonie Adams**, and **Elinor Wylie**—the last of these an important influence on **James Merrill**.

The reduction of sentimentality's complex meanings to a single dismissal has made it difficult to identify continuities between the nineteenth and twentieth centuries, and has blinded readers to sentimentality's ongoing evolutions within and beyond the twentieth century. In addition to those survivals already mentioned, these evolutions have taken two principal forms, both of which begin in confessional poetry. First, sentimentality's emphasis on the family and community survives in the poetry of middle-class culture, commonly associated with the "workshop poem" of contemporary MFA programs. Second, sentimentality's emphasis on deeply felt emotions and their florid expression survives in the poetry of exaggerated affect, practiced by poets as different in their procedure as **Sharon Olds** and **Leslie Scalapino**. In some respects, of course, the confessional poets were as anti-sentimental as their modernist predecessors, but unlike these predecessors—against whose impersonality and difficulty **W.D. Snodgrass**, **Robert Lowell**, **Anne Sexton**, and **Sylvia Plath** were reacting—the confessionals situated their critique within a recognizably sentimental frame. Thus, whereas nineteenth-century sentimental poets lauded the family as a basis for social order more generally, Snodgrass in *Heart's Needle* (1959) and Lowell in *Life Studies* (1959) exposed the family as a place of *dis*order—while affirming the correlation between family and society. Likewise, whereas the sentimental "poetess" drew moral and poetic authority from her deployment of conventions, Sexton in *To Bedlam and Part Way Back* (1960) and Plath in *Ariel* (1965) flouted convention and outraged morality—while affirming the power of a pedagogy of exaggerated emotion.

Sentimentality's recuperation as an object of serious study originates in the feminist literary criticism of the 1980s, much of which focused on the rediscovery, republication, and reevaluation of neglected writings by women. As a consequence of this scholarship, we are now able to appreciate the power and variety of this work and to view its blanket condemnation as "rancid writing" as the narrow consequence of a modernist sensibility. Although the word "sentimentality" is not likely to shed its negative connotations, sentimental poetry itself—its history, philosophical underpinnings, and generic conventions—remains a rich field for scholarly study.

Further Reading. ***Selected Primary and Secondary Sources:*** Bennett, Paula Bernat, *Poets in the Public Sphere: The Emancipatory Project of American Women's Poetry, 1800–1900* (Princeton, NJ: Princeton University Press, 2003); Clarke, Suzanne, *Sentimental Modernism: Women Writers and the Revolution of the Word* (Bloomington: Indiana University Press, 1991); Dillon, Elizabeth Maddock, "Sentimental Aesthetics" (*American Literature* 76 [2004]: 495–523); Douglas, Ann, *The Feminization of American Culture* (Avon Books, 1977); Haralson, Eric L., "Mars in Petticoats: Longfellow and Sentimental Masculinity" (*Nineteenth-Century Literature* 51 [1996]: 327–355); Howard, June, "What Is Sentimentality?" (*American Literary History* 11 [1999]: 63–81); Kete, Mary Louise, *Sentimental Collaborations: Mourning and Middle-Class Identity in Nineteenth-Century America* (Durham, NC: Duke University Press, 1999); McGann, Jerome, *The Poetics of Sensibility: A Revolution in Poetic Style* (Oxford: Oxford University Press, 1996); Schiller, Friedrich von, *Naïve and Sentimental Poetry and On the Sublime*, tr. Julius A. Elias (Frederick Ungar, 1966); Todd, Janet, *Sensibility: An Introduction* (London:

Methuen, 1986); Walker, Cheryl, *The Nightingale's Burden: Women Poets and American Culture before 1900* (Bloomington: Indiana University Press, 1982).

Benjamin Friedlander

SERVICE, ROBERT W. (1874–1958)

A folkloric balladeer and a wanderer, Robert Service was an **anti-intellectual**, a rough and ready traveler of the early Pacific Northwest frontier, and the most popular poet in North America during the first half of the twentieth century. His travels were the source for his writing, whose goal was to create something "the man in the street would take notice of and the sweet old lady would paste in her album; something the schoolboy would spout and the fellow in the pub would quote" (Klinck, 73). His ballads are dramatic monologues that celebrate the Northwestern frontier's vernacular aspects: saloons, the winter cold, and the dirt and loneliness of the frontier. His first two collections of poetry (*The Spell of the Yukon* [1907] and *Ballads of a Cheechako* [1909]) and a novel (*The Trail of Ninety-eight: A Northland Romance* [1910]) draw heavily on his northern years' experience. The poetry volumes hit sales figures up in the two millions by 1940, before their most popular poems were published independently. One poem, *The Shooting of Dan McGrew,* was also the basis of a Hollywood film. His *Rhymes of a Red Cross Man* (1916) was based on his wartime experience and offers a forceful view of what happens to soldiers on the front lines when politicians choose war.

Born in Lancashire, England, Service moved with his family to Glasgow, Scotland, in 1882. At age twenty-one, he immigrated to British Columbia, Canada, and traveled down the Pacific coast to Los Angeles. He worked a series of itinerant jobs on the West Coast including logger, dishwasher, farm hand, and bank clerk, and in 1901 took a bank teller position in Victoria. This latter position led to transfers to British Columbia and the Yukon.

Just before World War I, Service traveled to the Balkans as a foreign correspondent, and from there, he moved to France in 1913. He married Germaine Bourgoin and the couple lived first in Paris and then on the coast of Brittany and in Monte Carlo. One of the early North American expatriates of the generation before Hemingway and **Fitzgerald**, he was not a part of any bohemian or high art group, perhaps because he so appreciated his independence. During World War I, he served as a volunteer ambulance driver for the American Red Cross and later as an officer of a Canadian Army intelligence unit. During World War II, Service moved his family to Hollywood.

Published in New York in 1907 as *The Spell of the Yukon* (and in Toronto as *Songs of Sourdough*), Service's first book of poetry sold nearly a million copies and was an overnight success. It included the two most popular poems of his career, "The Shooting of Dan McGrew" and "The Cremation of Sam McGee." The first four lines of "The Shooting of Dan McGrew" were familiar to most people in the United States and Canada soon after publication:

> A bunch of the boys were whooping it up in the Malamute saloon;
> The kid that handles the music box was hitting a jag-time tune;
> Back of the bar, in a solo game, sat Dangerous Dan McGrew,
> And watching his luck was his light-o'-love, the lady that's known as Lou.

Service thought of himself as a versifier rather than a poet, a slinger of ink who used cadence and rhyme scheme to stitch his ballads together. Usually in rhymed couplets, Service's poetry is a masculine, unsophisticated, adventurous verse, never far from nature "red in tooth and claw," and always very far from social pretension and refinement. The influences of Robert Browning, Alfred Tennyson, Robert Burns and Rudyard Kipling in Robert Service's work are strong, especially with regard to form. In content, though, Service's poetry moves beyond the chauvinistic qualities of Kipling's poetry and toward an appreciation of character formed by experience in nature that is found in **Henry David Thoreau**. Especially when Service describes the isolation of the pioneer in a breathtaking and potentially deadly natural world, there is a simple, clear vigor and emotional depth:

> There where the mighty mountains bare their fangs unto the moon,
> There where the sullen sun-dogs glare in the snow-bright, bitter noon,
> And the glacier-glutted streams sweep down at the clarion call of June.
>
> ("The Heart of the Sourdough" [1906])

One senses that Service was the kind of person Thoreau would have liked to have been. Service was in fact strongly influenced by Thoreau, seeing in *Walden* a simplicity and clarity toward which he could aim and a life directed by principle in which he could find a model.

The works in *Rhymes of a Red Cross Man* focus on the experience of war and serve as a basis for the claim that Robert Service is a poet of significance whose works have contributed to our understanding of war and its social impact. Biographer Carl Klinck observes that *Rhymes of a Red Cross Man* is

> less jingoistic than one might expect from a poet still strongly influenced by Kipling; the verses here tell of

> lost limbs, blindness, dirt, and separation from loved ones—sometimes sentimentally, sometimes with a rough, grim humor, but always in the familiar rhymed forms that Service admires. (1976)

In the volume's introduction, Service asks the reader to forgive his curses, asserting that the "red resentment of the guns" might bring the reader to similar behavior.

Perhaps because Service's poetry is intentionally anti-intellectual, it has, for the most part, been overlooked by literary critics and the academy. Yet in terms of popular culture and artistry, the work of Robert W. Service deserves our attention because it is masterfully crafted and set squarely within popular culture and the oral tradition. Judged by its own standards, its continued inclusion in anthologies, and its market popularity, Robert W. Service's poetry deserves our acquaintance.

Further Reading. ***Selected Primary Sources:*** Service, Robert W., *The Collected Poems of Robert Service* (New York: G.P. Putnam's Sons, 1940); ———, *The Trail of Ninety-eight: a Northland Romance* (New York: Dodd Mead, 1910). ***Selected Secondary Sources:*** Hellman, Geoffrey T., "Profiles: Robert Service, two part series" (*The New Yorker* [30 March 1946, 6 April 1946]); Klinck, Carl F., *Robert Service: A Biography* (New York: Dodd, Mead & Company, 1976); MacKay, James, *Vagabond of Verse* (Edinburgh, Scotland: Mainstream Pub. Co., 1995).

Jeanne McNett

SETH, VIKRAM (1952–)

Vikram Seth (pronounced "sate") has transcended the boundaries of several literary genres and cultures. He has published notable poetry, fiction, and travel literature in India, Britain, and America. The themes of Seth's poetry and fiction make him a typical postcolonial writer. Largely due to the impact of *The Golden Gate* (1986), his celebrated novel in narrative rhymed verse that focuses upon the lives of California yuppies, he also ranks as a major American poet associated with the **New Formalism** movement. Utilizing rhyme, meter, and classical wit, Seth's poems steadily challenge the course of post-1960s mainstream American poetry.

Seth was born in Calcutta, India, to a prominent family. His mother served as the first woman chief justice of India; his father became a successful businessman. Seth was educated at prestigious institutions in India, Great Britain, the United States, and China. After receiving a BA from Oxford, he undertook graduate study in economics, demography, and poetry at Stanford (obtaining an MA in economics). Later he also studied at Nanjing University in China. Although he never completed his Ph.D. dissertation on Chinese economy, his interest in Chinese culture and poetry deepened. Seth eventually settled in New Delhi, India.

Seth's first poetry collection, *Mappings*, was privately published by the author in Saratoga, California, in 1980 and was then reissued by a press in Calcutta a year later. This apprentice work brings poems that are influenced by the formalist poets associated with Stanford (such as **Yvor Winters**, **J.V. Cunningham**, and **Timothy Steele**). Although the style is derivative, Seth's command of a broad range of forms and themes is interesting—family life in India is highlighted in "Panipat" and "Rakhi," and poems such as "Home Thoughts from the Bay" and "Sea and Desert" portray the customs of California. There are melancholic poems on the loss of love and friendship ("To a Fellow Traveller" and "Sonnet") as well as an autobiographical poem, "Departure Lounge," that deals with cross-cultural problems in a father-son relationship. In "Quaking Bridge," the themes of memory, loss, and adopted landscape find moving expression in the form of a sonnet. *Mappings* features both **lyric** and **narrative poems**, a translation of a Chinese poem, and poems on Asian history and myth—modes and themes that Seth later developed in his poetry and fiction.

The next book, *From Heaven Lake: Travels Through Sinkiang and Tibet* (1983), is an award-winning travel essay about an adventurous trip. In 1981, instead of flying back home, he hitchhiked from eastern China through Tibet and Nepal to Delhi, India. As a student of Chinese economy and a speaker of the language, Seth was able to paint an intimate portrait of China, describing everyday details and cultural curiosities that few foreign tourists experience. The riveting prose account is spiced with lyric poems in the tradition of Chinese poet wanderers.

The Humble Administrator's Garden (1985) is Seth's second collection of poetry, which was published by Carcanet, a major British poetry publisher. As with *Mappings*, this volume contains poems inspired by the author's experiences in China, India, California, and England. The poems present universally applicable feelings instead of relying on the exoticity of the portrayed locations. The book is divided into three sections named after trees that are emblematic of the respective countries—"Wutong" for China, "Neem" for India, and "Live Oak" for California. The language of the poems is penetrative, the forms are traditional and well-mastered, and the tone is one of unassuming sincerity. Seth introduces a changeable voice (which reappears in his later works)—he gets, in turn, deceptively easy, intelligent, and sophisticated to the point of flippancy. Although the book received favorable reviews and won Seth the Commonwealth Poetry Prize, it hardly gave an idea of what was to follow.

Seth's next book, *The Golden Gate* (1986), is a novel in verse set in California. This unlikely popular and critical success is a thirteen-chapter sequence of 590 sonnet-like poems of fourteen line stanzas set in iambic tetrameter and *ababccddeffegg* rhyme scheme. The jumpy meter allows Seth to be both comic and serious, both colloquial and literary. This style was perfected by Pushkin in *Eugene Onegin*—a book whose excellent and faithful 1977 English translation by Charles Johnston provided Seth with a formal and thematic model. Widely hailed as a tour de force, *The Golden Gate* focuses on the story of several young San Francisco yuppies whose lives are brought together against the backdrop of the Whitmanian symbol of the bridge. The emptiness of suburban life, the limits of sexual prudishness, and workaholism are exposed to complement the traditional quest for love in which the main character, John Brown, and his friends participate. Included are trendy social topics such as anti-nuclear activism, a critique of Silicon Valley and its corporate culture, and the **avant-garde** art scene. Some of the formal pleasures of the book are its strikingly original rhymes, its pacing, and the rewarding experience of reading some of the sections aloud. Mixing the public and private, the attributes of high and pop culture, Seth tells a moving and memorable story that resonates beyond its immediate milieu. By reviving narrative verse with humanism, wit, and complexity, Seth's book cuts against the grain of mainstream American poetry, which has since the 1960s privileged **free-verse confessional poetry**.

All You Who Sleep Tonight (1990) is a volume of shorter lyric poems. This American volume was badly received for it failed to match the achievement of *The Golden Gate*. The approach that Seth brought to perfection in the previous book rendered his lyric poems emotionally narrow and formally stilted, as in "A Doctor's Journal Entry for August 6, 1945," a narrative spoken in the voice of a Japanese doctor who tries to understand the effects of the nuclear bomb attack on Hiroshima: "My right side bled, my cheek torn, and I / Dislodged, detachedly, a piece of glass, / All the time wondering what had come to pass."

After eight years of work, Seth published his first prose novel, *A Suitable Boy* (1993). The 1,349-page novel is a family saga set in 1950s India. It became an international bestseller despite its length, its complexity, and the author's conservative reliance on traditional storytelling techniques. *An Equal Music* (1999) was his next novel. It explored the world of classical music and got lukewarm reviews.

Seth is a talented mixed-genre author whose eclectic work defies easy categorization. He swings the realms of poetry, fiction, and nonfiction with formal elegance and classicist poise that is often lacking in most current American literature. As a New Formalist poet with a rich postcolonial heritage, his voice is unique among the other crusaders who wage the battle against free verse confessionalism in contemporary American and postcolonial poetry.

Further Reading. ***Selected Primary Sources:*** Seth, Vikram, *All You Who Sleep Tonight* (New York: Knopf, 1990); ———, *Beastly Tales from Here and There* (New Delhi and New York: Viking, 1992); ———, *An Equal Music* (New York: Broadway Books, 1999); ———, *From Heaven Lake: Travels Through Sinkiang and Tibet* (London: Chatto & Windus/Hogarth, 1983); ———, *The Golden Gate* (New York: Random House, 1986); ———, *The Humble Administrator's Garden* (Manchester, England: Carcanet, 1985); ———, *Mappings* (Calcutta: Writers Workshop, 1981); ———, *A Suitable Boy* (New York: HarperCollins, 1993). ***Selected Secondary Sources:*** Disch, Thomas, "Onegin's Children: Poems in the Form of a Novel" (*Parnassus: Poetry in Review* 17/18 [1993]: 166–186); Hill, Rowena, "Vikram Seth's The Golden Gate: A Quick Look" (*Literary Criterion* 21.4 [1986]: 87–90); Hollander, John, "Yuppie Time in Rhyme" (*New Republic* 194 [21 April 1986]: 39–47); Ianonne, Carol, "Yuppies in Rhyme" (*Commentary* 82.3 [1986]: 54–56); King, Bruce, "Postmodernism and Neo-Formalist Poetry: Seth, Steele, and Strong Measures" (*Southern Review* 23 [1987]: 224–231); Mungo, Raymond, "Modern Love in Rhythm and Rhyme" (*New York Times Book Review* [11 May 1986]: 11); Perloff, Marjorie, "'Homeward Ho!': Silicon Valley Pushkin" (*American Poetry Review* 15.6 [1986]: 37–46).

Jiri Flajsar

SEUSS, DR. *SEE* GEISEL, THEODORE.

SEWALL, SAMUEL (1652–1730)

Known primarily as a diarist and as one of the judges at the Salem witch trials, Samuel Sewall also wrote a good deal of verse, both in English and in Latin, which he recorded in his diary, circulated among friends, and published in broadsides and newspapers.

The son of a successful merchant in England, Sewall came to New England at the age of nine when his family moved to Boston. Sewall attended Harvard College, graduated in 1671, and served as a tutor starting in 1673. He married for the first time in 1675 (old calendar) and became a "freeman" in 1679. Having long debated whether to pursue a career as a minister or as a merchant, Sewall launched a long and famous political career in the 1680s, when he managed the colonial printing press and later began serving in the General Court. Sewall traveled to England but spent most of his time in public office. In 1692 Sewall was appointed one of the judges for the infamous Salem witch trials; he was the only judge ever to publicly acknowledge error in regard to the proceedings. Sewall's varied writings include the millenialist defense of New England *Phaenomena Quaedam Apocalyptica* (1697) and the anti-slavery tract *The Selling of Joseph* (1700). As a writer, he is best known for his voluminous diaries, first published more than a century after his death (1878–182). Much of his poetry appears in his diary; some was published, and some was circulated in manuscript. He had fourteen children by his first wife, and toward the end of his life, the widowed Sewall famously courted and married twice more; he had no children by the latter two unions. He died in 1730.

Sewall wrote verse for a variety of public and private reasons. His published poetry, which appeared both in newspapers and in broadsides, generally offers moral observation, be it on births and deaths in prominent Boston families or on auspicious occurrences (for example, reflections on New Year's day 1701; the return of a leading preacher to the pulpit after an illness; a celebration of the celibacy occasioned by the death of an unmarried minister). Sewall's regard for the natural beauty of New England, evident in the often-cited passage on Plum Island from his otherwise exceedingly scholarly *Apocalyptica*, is also apparent in his public poetry, such as his short verse on Plymouth beach or his poem on the Merrimack River. Unlike complete books of poetry, broadsides and newspapers provided a wide and immediate local audience, and Sewall's preference for these venues of publication indicate something of how he saw his status as a public figure. Also indicative of his stature in the community, however, was his participation in the tradition of manuscript circulation of poetry among friends. He often sent lines of verse in letters, as commemorative mementos, or inscribed in gift books to other prominent men of his time. Verse writing was a regular habit for Sewall; his diary contains many other examples of reflective verse, often short two-line distichs that epitomize a thought or observation that particularly struck him during the course of a day.

Much of Sewall's poetry remains relatively unknown, not only because so much is scattered throughout various manuscripts but also because much is written in Latin—as are the majority of the distichs that appear in his *Diary* as well as much of his privately circulated verse. Latin composition was part of the standard training in both England and New England; ministers and university-educated men alike composed poetry in Latin, especially in "the expansive and hospitable genres of epigram and occasional verse" (Rosenwald, "Voces," 304). **Cotton Mather**, for example, not only composed his own Latin verse but also collected and transcribed the verses of many other leading figures in his *Magnalia Christi Americana* (1702). Lawrence Rosenwald notes, "Sewall himself left more Latin poems than any other Puritan, and on a greater variety of subjects" ("Voces," 305). There is critical disagreement over the relative merit of Sewall's Latin verse. In general, New England **Puritan poetry** is considered, though usually technically proficient, inferior in quality to the work of John Milton. Without disagreeing with this basic assessment of a "curious intertness" of New England Latin verse ("Voces," 313), Rosenwald makes a useful distinction between the goals of the humanist and the Puritan traditions, suggesting that whereas the former valued metrical virtuosity and the creative use of classical influences, the latter restricted itself almost exclusively to the even sobriety of elegiac couplet and dactylic hexameter, choosing standard vocabulary and phrasing as stock generic resources ("Voces," 310–313). Rosenwald further suggests that whereas New England Puritans used Latin verse primarily for private circulation among a relatively restricted society, Sewall appeared to be an "exception" by virtue of the "great diversity and abundance" of his public verse, demonstrating aspects of both the humanist and Puritan tradition, as was "consonant with other traits of what one might call Sewall's cultural profile" ("Voces," 316–328).

A habitual poet in both his public and his private life, Sewall reveals some of the wide range of reasons Puritans of the late seventeenth century and early eighteenth century turned to poetry. Both his English and his Latin verse invite further consideration of the role of poetry in New England Puritan society during a period of dramatic cultural change.

Further Reading. ***Selected Primary Sources:*** Meserole, Harrison T., ed., *American Poetry of the Seventeenth Century* (University Park: The Pennsylvania State University Press, 1985); Sewall, Samuel, *The Diary of Samuel Sewall*, ed. M. Halsey Thomas (New York: Farrar, Straus and Giroux, 1973). ***Selected Secondary Sources:*** Rosenwald, Lawrence, "Sewall's *Diary* and the Margins of Puritan Literature" (*American Literature* 58.3 [1986]: 325–341); ———, "*Voces Clamantium in Deserto*: Latin Verse of the Puritans," in *Puritan Poets and Poetics: Seventeenth-Century American Poetry in Theory and Practice*, ed. Peter White (University Park: The Pennsylvania State University Press, 1985, 303–317).

Meredith Neuman

SEXTON, ANNE (1928–1974)

Anne Sexton's poetry presents a vivid record of a life lived in the context of mental illness and at the beginning of women's liberation. Sexton, along with **Robert Lowell**, **Sylvia Plath**, and **W.D. Snodgrass**, is considered part of the **confessional** movement in postwar poetry. Confessional poetry offered the reader an intimate and often shocking perspective on personal experience. Inspired largely by Freudian analysis, it emphasized the creation of a first-person voice driven to the extremes of ecstasy and despair in the presence of an intimate listener. Sexton's poetry embraced the virtues of candor and directness to articulate personal pain and suffering. Though nearly all of the poets associated with confessional poetry endured mental illness, Sexton's work was singular in its direct linkage of poetry and therapy: She started writing in earnest when she was twenty-nine, on the advice of her psychiatrist, after having a nervous breakdown and entering treatment (though she had also dabbled in poetry and the arts in high school). Many of her poems record apparent psychosis, breakdown, and hospitalization, and many directly address her various doctors. Sexton is often paired with **Sylvia Plath**, who also broke historical silences about women's experience, and who also suffered from mental illness and committed suicide. Like Plath, Sexton turned honesty into a form of charisma, combining autobiographical detail with religious emblems, surreal imagery, and the incantatory cadences of spell-like verse. Sexton spoke with unprecedented frankness about the physical experience of womanhood, writing poems on the themes of pregnancy, motherhood, masturbation, and adultery. Her consistently engaging voice and storyteller persona allow her work to combine the clarity of an autobiographical record with the mannered intensity of the dramatic monologue. She may, therefore, be the poet who most clearly dramatizes the risks and dares of truth-telling that the confessional mode inspired writers to take.

Anne Gray Harvey was born in Newton, Massachusetts, in 1928 to wool merchant Ralph Harvey and his wife Mary Gray Staples. Her childhood had all the trappings of middle-class comfort, but her family had an unavoidable history of alcoholism and mental illness. Though Sexton would later become a voracious reader, she did not enjoy school, and after attending a finishing school, at age nineteen she married Alfred Muller Sexton II, called "Kayo." She worked briefly as a model and gave birth to a daughter in 1953. Shortly afterward, she suffered her first breakdown and hospitalization. This was followed by the birth of a second daughter in 1955, a second breakdown, and Sexton's first suicide attempt, on her birthday of that year. In those years, Sexton's therapist encouraged her to express herself in poetry. For the rest of her life, Sexton remained in treatment for depression and instability, and for the rest of her life, Sexton wrote. Her participation in a number of Boston area writers' workshops introduced her to several prominent poets, notably **Maxine Kumin**, who would become her lifelong friend. Sexton also participated in Robert Lowell's writing seminar during this time. Sexton's poems became critically and commercially successful, and in 1966 she won the Pulitzer Prize. In the later years of her life, success and illness took their toll on her personal life. After divorcing her husband in 1970, Sexton's instability grew, but she continued to produce poems. By the year of her suicide, 1974, at age forty-six, she had written ten books of poems and a play, as well as four books for children with her friend Maxine Kumin.

The poems of *To Bedlam and Part Way Back* (1960) were enthusiastically received by critics. In many of the lyrics, Sexton's deeply personal voice reports her condition directly from the asylum, with her therapist as interlocutor. "Said the Poet to the Analyst," deals with poetic self-expression in the context of therapy. "My business is words," the speaker begins the first stanza, and she goes on to address her therapist in the first line of the second stanza: "your business is watching my words." Many of the poems are surreal self-portraits. A poem that would become one of Sexton's signature works is "Her Kind," in which she establishes her persona as powerful, sexual, uncontrollable, and dangerous. "I have gone out, a possessed witch, / haunting the black air, braver at night," she begins, infusing the lyric with dark and almost melodramatic imagery. Sexton speaks here on the brink of madness but within self-imposed bonds of rhyme and stanzaic order. In Sexton's frank treatment of familial relationships, she explains the sources of her pain. The final section of *To Bedlam and Part Way Back* includes the **long poem** "The Double Image," in which Sexton speaks with narcissistic candor about her relationship with her daughter Joy. Examining her in reference to Sexton's own pain, Sexton concludes, "this was my worst guilt; you could not cure / nor soothe it. I made you to find me." Throughout the book, Sexton's voice grows in confidence and effortlessness and buoys its vulnerability with an emerging wise, wry wit.

In *All My Pretty Ones* (1962) Sexton remained focused on issues of womanhood and family but expanded her subject matter to the religious as well. Sexton's voice is more controlled and traditional in the elegies that begin the book. The title poem is a very personal **elegy** for Sexton's father. The poem honors his memory and tries at the same time to speak frankly about his alcoholism and abusive temperament. At the end, Sexton uneasily resolves to remember him and forget him: "Now I fold you down, my drunkard, my navigator, / my first lost keeper, to love or look at later." The book's most shocking poem, "The Abortion," describes in lucid detail that medical procedure (illegal at the time of its composition) but also incorporates fantastic elements. Comparing the illegal abortion doctor to Rumpelstiltskin, Sexton repeats a haunting, spell-like refrain: "*Someone who should have been born / is gone.*" Sexton's letter to a Catholic friend in "With Mercy for the Greedy" ends with a characteristic blend of pride and shame as she describes herself born "doing reference work in sin, and born / confessing it." Sexton's developing interest in religious imagery turns her voice towards satire. In "For God While Sleeping" Sexton refashions a Christian crucifixion into a raw and anonymous scene: "Skinny man, you are somebody's fault." In this poem and in others Sexton emphasizes a direct and physical encounter with an imagined Christ and places Christ firmly in the present moment.

Live or Die (1966) sounds the most triumphant note in Sexton's career. Winner of a Pulitzer, the volume begins with a quote from Saul Bellow that admonishes and encourages Sexton's suffering persona: "Live or die, but don't poison everything!" The final poem, "Live," ends with a renunciation of the poet's former self. Resolving to leave the asylum and cast off her language of pain and sorrow, Sexton concludes the book, "I say *Live, Live,* because of the sun, / the dream, the excitable gift." *Live or Die* includes some of Sexton's best-known work, including "Little Girl, My String Bean, My Lovely Woman," in which the poet addresses her daughter with magisterial tenderness, imagining her body blossoming into adult womanhood. The dynamic address of the poem indicates how Sexton increasingly relies on an intimate and specific listener, edging her poems nearer to dramatic monologues. "Menstruation at Forty" continues Sexton's record of women's experience and insists again on an erotic tie between mother and child. Speaking of the son she never had Sexton cries, "I would have possessed you before all women, / calling your name." Sexton's poems grow increasingly dependent on voice by the end of the book; her old formalism is nearly gone.

The simple title of *Love Poems* (1969) declares her fourth book to be about the genre that Sexton had been revolutionizing all along. Throughout her career, addresses to beloveds, children, and therapists had all been explorations of desire. In *Love Poems* Sexton reconnects with the simplicity of that form. The book scandalized critics because it traced the narrative of an extramarital affair and breakup. "Eighteen Days Without You," the longest poem, charts the speaker's loneliness and abandonment against the backdrop of current events; in the poem, Sexton sees her private life of desire clearly in the context of history for the first time. Remembering a clandestine meeting with her lover, she recalls Kennedy's assassination: "And we cried and drank our whiskey straight / and the world remembers the date, the date." However, the most accomplished poems in *Love Poems* concern women without men, women relieved of the burden of relationship. "In Celebration of My Uterus" is less a sexual poem than a symbolic one: In its middle section, Sexton lists women and their occupations all over the world. Some of Sexton's best lines can be found in "The Ballad of the Lonely Masturbator," a poem in which she returns to ballad form. Her ironic tone carries the clear authority of independence. Addressing her beloved, who has abandoned her, she asserts, "You borrowed me on the flowered spread. / At night, alone, I marry the bed."

Sexton made a lasting contribution to the folk tradition with her revisions of Grimm's fairy tales in the best-selling *Transformations* (1971). Macabre and sexual, Sexton's versions of the tales combine Gothic elements and Freudian psychology. These "fiendish cartoons" (as critic Helen Vendler called them) also place the tales in contemporary context, using demotic diction and references to popular culture. "The Twelve Dancing Princesses" compares those lost adolescents to a contemporary drifter. "If you danced from midnight / to six A.M. who would understand," Sexton asks, and she answers that the strung-out boy on speed and saltines in Boston Common is the only one who would. The most successful poems in *Transformations*, "Snow White," "Cinderella," and "Briar Rose," rewrite their tales with a wry, cynical perspective on the idea of marriage and happy domesticity. Sexton concludes "Cinderella" with deep irony: "their darling smiles pasted on for eternity. / Regular Bobbsey Twins." In *Transformations* Sexton takes the volatile witch's voice of "Her Kind" and transforms it into a less personal, more narrative instrument for fictional subject matter. With a new authority and wisdom, Sexton's poems grow in length and effortlessness. Though they still use rhyme, they eschew traditional forms for a more diffuse and prose-like presentation.

Sexton's later work took a visionary turn incipient in the fantastic subject matter of *Transformations. The Book of Folly* (1972) does repeat much of the subject matter of Sexton's first volumes: Poems like "The Doctor of the Heart" and "Anna Who Was Mad" again frame the speaker as someone attempting to stay mentally healthy. Sexton continues to trace her relationship with her daughter in "Mother and Daughter," and her insights are as keen, brave, and honest as in her first poems about the subject. Her nest empty, Sexton accuses her daughter of depleting her poetic resources: "you've racked up all my / poker chips and left me empty." For the most part, however, the poems of *The Book of Folly* employ a more mystical voice and inhabit less realistic terrain. In "The Silence," Sexton uses surreal imagery to describe an outside force destroying her body piece by piece. The book includes "Angels of the Love Affair" and "The Jesus Papers," two groups of short lyrics saturated in Christian imagery. Sexton continues to push the limits of decorum in both sets of poems. In "Jesus Asleep," she describes Jesus sleeping and having an erotic dream about Mary. But she is also aware of a new set of conventions in her own work. The title of the book indicates the growth of a new self-consciousness and of Sexton's impatience with her own traveled ground and with the seemingly endless succession of unstable mental episodes in her own life. Calling herself Ms. Dog, she situates her self-deprecation in bitter irony.

Ms. Dog is, of course, "God" in reverse, and Sexton's poems, at the end of her career, become almost single-mindedly focused on God and on the possibility of transcendent experience. Sexton's penultimate published volume, *The Death Notebooks* (1974), includes a long section divided into "psalms" called "O Ye Tongues." Based on Christopher Smart's eighteenth-century praise poem *Jubilante Agno*, the poem is written in prose sentences and uses anaphora, the imperative, and ritual diction to speak about America, religion, and sexuality. The end of the long poem "Hurry Up Please It's Time" reflects Sexton's change in topic and persona. "Bring a flashlight, Ms. Dog, / and look in every corner of the brain," she insists at the end of a search for spiritual understanding. Sexton still peppers her visionary voice with domestic detail and casual diction, always attempting to encounter God with striking directness. "Rats Live on No Evil Star" revises the creation myth not merely in description but in narrative—in Sexton's version, Adam breaks his own rib in half, and Eve gives birth to a rat. Many of the poems of *The Death Notebooks* are ominous and macabre. Strained resistances to the unknown, they imagine forces of death that threaten the speaker. In the final section of "The Death Baby," Sexton addresses lifelong friend Maxine Kumin, saying that someday death will come in the form of an infant. As a poem from one mother to another, its choice of a baby for a figure of death is haunting and revolutionary. However, the poem reads less as a confessional poem than as a direct, performative, and dramatic ritual text. It dares and threatens to go forward in action as much as it confesses. In *The Death Notebooks* many of Sexton's poems act as present-tense litanies of suffering, doubt, and pain. Pain has nowhere to go, and cannot be extinguished—the purpose of the poem is to give the pain shape, not to heal it.

The Awful Rowing Toward God (1975) was the last book Sexton herself organized before her death from carbon monoxide poisoning in 1974. She returns to a storyteller persona, framing the book as a narrative that begins with "Rowing" and ends with "The Rowing Endeth." Invoking Christian discipleship and a mythic New England seascape, Sexton posits herself as a spiritual mariner, sailing on a rough ocean of faith. She takes a more distanced perspective on sexual love in "When Man Enters Woman." Referring to the "double hunger" of man and woman, Sexton claims that intercourse brings the sexes together until God "in His perversity / unties the knot." While the terrain of the poem is still sex, Sexton is less interested in shock than she is in wisdom. Though the visionary orientation of the book proves that Sexton's range is greater than that of personal trauma, by and large the poems are not memorable. Her confidence in ideas often verges on cliché, as in "Words." Comparing words to eggs, Sexton warns, "Once broken they are impossible / things to repair." Still, the crystalline wit and comic timing in her dialogue with God in "The Rowing Endeth" show Sexton to be a poet of great dexterity, and at times, to be still working at the height of her powers. In the poem the speaker and God are playing poker, and God wins because of a wild card unknown to the speaker. "I win because I hold a royal straight flush. / He wins because He holds five aces." The poker metaphor, a familiar one across Sexton's career, indicates how luck-driven and out of control the poet often feels life to be. However, here, she elevates that game of chance to the level of a religious ritual. This allegorical vision has much in common with the seventeenth-century Calvinist poems of **Edward Taylor** and other dramatic devotional poems. Though Sexton's fame may have come from her innovations in subject matter and voice, her poetics retains its New England roots. Sexton links the purpose of the lyric to an engaged understanding of the difficult and sometimes incomprehensible nature of fate. Reckoning with one's own fate brings the necessity of spiritual reckoning and transcendent vision.

Sexton left two unpublished books composed in her last years, *Words for Dr. Y* and *45 Mercy Street.* A notable section of *45 Mercy Street* treats her divorce, and much of the rest of the volume focuses on her relationship with her parents. *Mercy Street* is also the title of the successful off-Broadway play Sexton wrote that was produced in 1970, which also treated family themes from a visionary perspective, saturated in religious imagery. Though Sexton began her career as a confessional, by the end of her life, her penchant for iconic and religious imagery gave her poems a new dramatic density. Of all confessional poets, Sexton may have been the most influenced by a Freudian concept of the "unconscious," and the uncanny images that pepper her later work reflect her interest in that idea as much as they chart her growing interest in ideas of belief and disbelief.

In spite of, or because of, her mental illness, Sexton was extraordinarily prolific. Since she wrote to relieve and express suffering, she wrote through it and during it, and nearly all of the important experiences of her life are recorded by her poems. Her lasting contribution to American poetry may not be best expressed by an evaluation of a select number of poems, though she created many individual lyrics of great genius. Instead, her body of work considered as a whole shows great range as it fluctuates between an instinct for self-preservation and an urge towards self-destruction. Though Sexton is known for her confessional stance and her treatment of women's issues, her poems broke new ground in their treatment of religion and their treatment of family relationships. However, Sexton's poetry has proved inseparable from her life, and critics have struggled with how to describe a relationship between the two. Diane Middlebrook's controversial biography of Sexton even used tapes from the poet's therapy sessions (with the permission of her therapist) in order to understand the poet and her work. Sexton's own insistence on accessible clarity made her poems popular in her lifetime, even if their value has fallen in past decades.

Further Reading. ***Selected Primary Sources:*** Sexton, Anne, *The Complete Poems* (Boston: Houghton Mifflin, 1981); Sexton, Linda Gray, and Lois Ames, eds., *Anne Sexton: a Self-Portrait in Letters* (Boston: Houghton Mifflin, 1977). ***Selected Secondary Sources:*** Forbes, Deborah, *Sincerity's Shadow: Self-consciousness in British Romantic and Mid-Twentieth Century American Poetry* (Cambridge, MA: Harvard University Press, 2004); George, Diana Hume, *Oedipus Anne: The Poetry of Anne Sexton* (Urbana: University of Illinois, 1987); McClatchy, J.D., ed., *Anne Sexton: The Artist and Her Critics* (Bloomington: Indiana University Press, 1978).

Katie Peterson

SHAPIRO, ALAN (1952–)

The poetry of Alan Shapiro reflects an urgent desire to give artistic shape to chaotic experience, to contemplate suffering in a way that will perhaps allow the reader, as well as the author, to rise above the destitution of loss. Shapiro's poems display a serious intellect in their learned allusions to classical myth and literature as well as a commitment to direct delivery that makes the work accessible to virtually all readers. Shapiro's most persistent and powerful themes are loss and grief, feelings with which the poet has had extensive personal experience. Numerous poems in his most recent books deal with the serious illnesses and premature deaths of his sister and brother. Although these poems take as their subject personal experience, their central concern is trying to make sense of loss and finding ways to transcend grief from a more universal and less self-interested perspective. Shapiro's stoic yet emotionally resonant poetry illustrates the resilience of the human spirit in the face of suffering.

Shapiro was born in 1952 in Boston. He was educated at Brandeis University, where—in addition to playing freshman basketball—he studied poetry writing throughout his undergraduate years under **J.V. Cunningham**. He was a Stegner Fellow at Stanford in 1975 and then a Jones lecturer in creative writing from 1976 to 1979. While at Stanford in 1978, he did extensive research in the library's microfilm room, assembling material that would lead to the poems of his first collection, *After the Digging* (1981). That volume was followed by *The Courtesy* (1983), *Happy Hour* (1989), and *Covenant* (1991). *Mixed Company*, the poet's fifth collection, won the 1996 *Los Angeles Times* Book Prize for poetry, and his next book, *The Dead Alive and Busy*, received the Kingsley Tufts Award in 2001. The collection *Song and Dance* appeared one year later. In addition, Shapiro has also published two memoirs, *The Last Happy Occasion* and *Vigil*; a collection of essays on poetry, *In Praise of the Impure: Poetry and the Ethical Imagination*; and a translation of the *Oresteia* of Aeschylus. He has received the Academy Award in Literature from the American Academy of Arts and Letters, as well as fellowships from the National Endowment for the Arts and the Guggenheim Foundation. He has taught poetry workshops at the Bread Loaf Writers' Conference, the Sewanee Writers' Conference, and the Provincetown Fine Arts Work Center, and he became the William R. Kenan, Jr. Distinguished Professor in the Department of English at the University of North Carolina in 2002.

After the Digging consists of two groups of poems, the first dealing with the Irish Famine of the mid-1800s and the second with the subject of demonic possession in early Puritan New England. These historically placed poems reflect the themes of loss, suffering, grief, and human misunderstanding that the poet would continue to explore in each of his subsequent books. The poems also indicate Shapiro's early interest in using poetry to illustrate the universal and grand nature of individual human pain and endurance.

Happy Hour contains many poems that delve into the nature of human relationships and the disappointment to which so many of them lead. The ironic title poem displays the profound but quiet unhappiness of a married couple at a bar. The wife, having gotten drunk, taunts and tries to provoke her too-sober and perhaps too-self-conscious husband, who maintains his cool and treats her with a reserved kindness in return. Readers may assume that the long-suffering husband is the one deserving their sympathy, but the speaker reveals that the man is carefully calculating his behavior in order to build emotional capital, to insure that his wife feels so guilty that the next day "will be *his* happy hour. There won't be / anything she wouldn't do for him." Shapiro often turns such a penetrating eye on human motive and self-interest. His poems frequently show that, despite good intentions, people are most often the cause of, or at least complicit in, the suffering of those to whom they are closest. The volume's remarkable centerpiece, "Neighbors," traces the desperate suffering of a mentally unstable shut-in from the perspective of a married couple who have moved into the apartment above her. Throughout the poem's ten sections, it becomes clear that the husband and wife themselves are drifting apart into the distance and loneliness that is painfully apparent in the woman who lives below.

Mixed Company further develops the theme of distance—the distance felt between couples, between parents and their children, and between the races of people. The book's first poem, "The Letter," examines the failure of human communication as the speaker contemplates the seemingly changing message of a letter from his mother over the length of twenty-five slant-rhymed couplets. Many of the volume's poems continue this theme of the difficulty of communication between lovers, spouses, family members, and friends. But the final five poems take such concerns to a more universal level, as they explore the at-times disheartening complexities of American race relations. In the last of these poems, "Between Assassinations," a white speaker recounts the harmony found in a pick-up game of basketball with a group of young black men in the late 1960s. In the graceful movements and necessary teamwork of the game, the people find a wordless communication for which actual language cannot account. At the end of the poem, the speaker regrets that the time on the court was only an "[o]ld dwindling cease fire, with no hope for peace, / that we silently turn away from when the game is over."

With a number of accomplished books already to his credit, Shapiro attained his full artistic maturity in 2000 with *The Dead Alive and Busy.* In this Kingsley Tufts Award–winning collection, the poet again visits the themes of suffering, loss, and grief, but never has his treatment been so personal; nor has it ever achieved quite such a degree of universality. In many of the poems of this book, Shapiro deals with the physical and mental decline of his aging father and the early death of his sister while incorporating a motif of mythical allusion that helps to reveal the broader human implications of his own narrow, individual experience of loss. In the book's striking and emotionally devastating first poem, "Old Joke," he invokes the god Apollo as a muse of suffering and death, asking, "what do you know about us?" After telling of his aging parents' physical sufferings, and particularly of his father's indignity of trying to convince his old penis to urinate and then, having missed the toilet bowl when it did, having to get onto his hands and knees to wipe up the floor, he can only say to Apollo, in the poem's concluding line, "You don't know anything about us." In fact, he sees classical descriptions of suffering as nothing next to his own experience of the real thing, and he sees his parents' endurance of—and even brief ability to rise above—their pain as "godlike, better than gods, if only for a moment." Near the end of the book, in a poem titled "Air," Shapiro poignantly recounts how the dying patients in a hospital, including his sister Beth, turn away from the faces of visitors and only look out the window "not for grace, or mercy, of for any otherworldly / health, but only this, the air outside." The purely implied personal grief of this poem is palpable.

Song and Dance, Shapiro's seventh book of poems, continues the theme of personal loss out of a sad necessity. As a collection, the book can be read as an extended **elegy** for the poet's brother David, who died of brain cancer. What is remarkable is that in dealing with personal tragedy in these two most recent books, Shapiro has at the same time grown artistically in significant steps. The poems of *Song and Dance* deliver the same deft treatment of emotional material as those of *The Dead Alive and Busy*, but they also display a free and confident formal experimentation. This is a book that shows the poet fully stretching his artistic wings. From the familiar two-line stanzas of "Transistor Radio" and "Scan" to the staggered indentions of "The Match" and "The Last Scene" to the Q&A format of "Sleet" and "Song and Dance" to the extraordinary mixture of joy and sorrow in the concluding **prose poem** "Last Impressions," Shapiro demonstrates his broad skills in a truly eclectic collection. As a whole, the book is almost certainly his finest achievement to date.

Alan Shapiro's abilities to convey deep emotion without incurring the first charge of sentimentality, to create profound meaning through direct and simple language, and to find an expression for the kind of grief so frequently endured in silence have made him one of the most important of late twentieth-century American poets.

Further Reading. ***Selected Primary Sources:*** Shapiro, Alan, *After the Digging* (Chicago: University of Chicago Press, 1998; rpt. from 1981 orig. ed.); ———, *The Courtesy* (Chicago: University of Chicago Press, 1983); ———, *The Dead Alive and Busy* (Chicago: University of Chicago Press, 2000); ———, *Happy Hour* (Chicago: University of Chicago Press); ———, *Covenant* (Chicago: University of Chicago Press, 1991); ———, *Mixed Company* (Chicago: University of Chicago Press, 1996); ———, *Song and Dance* (New York: Mariner Books/Houghton Mifflin, 2002). ***Selected Secondary Sources:*** Hallberg, Robert von, "Poetry, Politics, and Intellectuals," in *The Cambridge History of American Literature, Vol. 8: Poetry and Criticism, 1940–1995*, ed. Sacvan Bercovitch (New York: Cambridge University Press, 1996, 9–259); Pfefferle, W.T., "Poets on Place" (*Poets & Writers* 33.1 [January/February 2005]: 38–41); Shetley, Vernon, [On Shapiro's "The Sweepers"], in *After the Death of Poetry: Poet and Audience in Contemporary America* (Durham, NC: Duke University Press, 1993, 188–190).

Dan Albergotti

SHAPIRO, DAVID (1947–)

David Shapiro's imaginatively agile and erudite poems make him one of the most eloquent poets of the **New York School**'s second generation. Shapiro wrote the first dissertation on **John Ashbery**'s poetry and was the editor, with the poet **Ron Padgett**, of *An Anthology of New York School Poets* (1970), and he therefore brings an inspired and scholarly knowledge of their work to his own. He develops the New York School's penchant for vivid, surreal surprise and its fluid play with and between metaphoric depths and quotidian surfaces. Notice, in this section from *A Man Holding an Acoustic Panel* (1971), the ease with which Shapiro layers the ordinary and the imaginative to refresh the lyric's capacity to express sentiment; the speaker remembers taking a "mental walk" on New Year's:

We had a long white talk
And your voice was a bouquet.

Words, ideas, and images become wonderfully supple within the frame of Shapiro's poetry; subjects and their definitions slide quickly into unexpected realms. As Joanna Fuhrman writes, "To read a David Shapiro poem is to enter a space in which 'emotion' is as abstract as theory and an 'idea' is as visceral and tender as the best pop song." Shapiro's poems are highly imaginative landscapes that not only expand the range of discourses a poem can include but also experiment with and meditate upon poetry's reach into the spiritual and the metaphysical. Each Shapiro poem testifies to poetry's vital and necessary work, highlighting the imaginative dimensions that link the spirit and the mind.

Shapiro was born in Newark, New Jersey; his childhood was immersed in the arts. In an interview, Shapiro recalls the creative milieu of his childhood and states, "One of the great influences of my life was my father constantly memorizing Virgil, Shakespeare, Milton, and he had me do the same, as soon as I could speak" (Fuhrman). As this statement makes clear, The New York School poets are by no means Shapiro's only influence. Shapiro critically and creatively restages the works and figures of Western art so that they can be developed and explored in the imaginative present of poetry. Before he became a published poet, Shapiro was an accomplished violinist, and music informs and inspires his poetry in both formal and thematic ways. Thomas Fink writes that his poems "abound" in "subtle, complex, often unpredictable tonal shifts" (13 [1993]). Music often serves as a sensual and tactile stage, a place from which imaginative transformation begins. In *The Page-Turner* (1972) Shapiro writes, "On the music-stand the music stands like softened skin. / And outside the peony burning with silent thirst." At age eighteen, Shapiro published his book *January* (1965). *January* is full of dream-like allegories for faith and unrequited love; it is as though the poet sees "all of a world so simply made of usual and unusual detail," and the poems rush to render the world's usual and unusual making. A prolific and lauded poet, Shapiro's collection *A Man Holding an Acoustic Panel* was nominated for a National Book Award in 1971. Among many other honors, Shapiro received the American Academy of Arts and Letters Morton Dauwen Zabel Award in 1977.

Painting is another of Shapiro's resources for rendering supple images and transforming the shapes of imagination, perception, and memory. His work as a critic and theorist of the visual arts continually and productively dovetails with his poetry: Looking is a transformative act, and lines of poetry play freely with the imagination's spatial possibilities. Many of the Shapiro poems that engage with painting call attention to both art forms' distance from, rather than their proximity to, the objects, ideas, or emotions they represent. In an essay entitled "Poets and Painters: Lines of Color" (1980), Shapiro writes that "[b]oth poetry and painting may be said to be a reticence, an opacity, and a separation." In "Sestina," from the collection *To an Idea* (1983), Shapiro plays with opacity and its possibilities. After the speaker asks his mother "for a new form / from Paradise," he states that he "saw a sestina in lines of / color, like a magic marker on a lake." Under this vivid image are the sestina's six "lines," but they are actual lines without words. In "A Book of Glass," which appears in *House (Blown Apart)* (1988), Shapiro bestows a visuality and materiality on the writing to evoke language's inspiring but fragmented evanescence:

And I see a book in glass—the words go off
In wild loops without words. I should

As the title of his collection *After a Lost Original* (1992) suggests, Shapiro's poems investigate, but do not lament, art's range when a stable source of reality cannot be found. In "After" (1994), **postmodern** ironies split representation into possibility: "The twentieth century falls off below and fragility / and the kitsch of flowers above, finesse of heaven / No one can enter here, and there is nothing but hope." Shapiro's work alludes to many artists "who have mischievously concocted ironies about the perils of referentiality" (Fink, 29 [1998]), and he often reconfigures expected images of artists to defamiliarize concepts of reality. In "A Realistic Bar and Grill" (1983), Shapiro explores the habits through which literature is written, read, and experienced: "So we descended to meet / In the old opinions / Having given up nothing." The conclusion of the poem opens into strange delight: "Shelley was a fire balloon / Or Shelley was a fireballon lover." Even if his lines take disjunctive turns or plunge deliberately into the outlandish, impossible, or the absurd, Shapiro's voice maintains a level or sincerity that betrays the seriousness he brings to literature's imaginative acts.

One of many poems that reflect upon literature's imaginative terrain, "To an Idea" (1983), from the book of the same name, explores a poet's mind in the act of composition. He begins by articulating and then revising a desire to write out of the experience of possibility that an abstract nothingness represents: "I wanted to start *Ex Nihilo* / I mean a review of sorts." The poem transforms itself into an ode for poetry, which has "carried me like mail / From one house to another." Shapiro's work attests to art's potential for taking readers into meaningful uncertainties.

Further Reading. ***Selected Primary Sources:*** Shapiro, David, *After a Lost Original* (New York: Solo Press, 1992);

———, *House* (*Blown Apart*) (Woodstock, NY: Overlook Press, 1988); ———, *January* (New York: Holt, Rinehart and Winston, 1965); ———, *Man Holding an Acoustic Panel* (New York: E.P. Dutton & Co, 1971); ———, *The Page-Turner* (New York: Liverwright, 1972); ———, *To an Idea* (Woodstock, NY: Overlook Press, 1983). ***Selected Secondary Sources:*** Fink, Thomas, *The Poetry of David Shapiro* (Madison, NJ: Farleigh Dickinson University Press, 1993); ———, "The Poetry of David Shapiro and Ann Lauterbach: After Ashbery" (*American Poetry Review* 17 [January/February 1988]: 27–30); Fuhrman, Joanna, "Plurist Music: An Interview with David Shapiro" (*Rain Taxi Review of Books* [Fall 2002], www.raintaxi.com/online/Fall2002/Shapiro.shtml); Shapiro, David, *John Ashbery: An Introduction to the Poetry* (New York: Columbia University Press, 1979); ———, "Poets and Painters: Lines of Color," *Poets & Painters* (Washington, D.C.: Smithsonian Institution Press, 1984); Shapiro, David, and Ron Padgett, eds., *An Anthology of New York School Poets* (New York: Random House, 1970).

Kimberly Lamm

SHAPIRO, KARL (1913–2000)

Karl Shapiro shaped American poetry and poetics in a number of ways. He brought a Jewish consciousness into the mainstream of American poetry that had previously been largely Protestant. In the "Introduction" to *Poems of A Jew* (1958), Shapiro says that the poems in this collection "are documents of an obsession. This obsession, I believe is universal and timeless; the Jew is at its center, but everyone else partakes of it." Beyond this so-called obsession is an impressive range and diversity of subject matter derived from experience. With the publication of *Person Place And Thing* (1942), Louis Bogan predicted that Shapiro's work would "become a touchstone for his generation." He was praised for his "acute sense of form," for his satirical powers, and for his wit, and he made that which was ordinary (in this case, a glutton) poetic: "The jowls of his belly crawl and sell like the sea / When his mandibles oily with lust champ and go wide." Shapiro wrote of war and of soldiering in "V-Letter," and he brought his knowledge of **prosody** into play in *Essay On Rime* (1945), in which the lines of the poem are a disputation on the art of poetry. *White-Haired Lover* is a collection of sonnets, and *The Bourgeois Poet* (1964), in contrast, eschews rhyme and regular versification and includes **prose poems** that begin at the left margin and follow with lines of hanging-indents. Shapiro showed that American poetry was open to invention while yet adhering to masterful craftsmanship.

Karl Shapiro was born to Joseph and Sarah Omansky Shapiro on November 13, 1913, in Baltimore, Maryland, where he grew up a middle-class Southern Jew. In his memoir, *The Younger Son*, Shapiro says that he "could not remember much of what is called mothering." There were maids who "did the bathing and changing and scolding." A brother, a year and five days older, was the beautiful child whose photograph appeared in the Baltimore paper, but Carl (the name was originally spelled with a C) was jokingly called "a defect in manufacture." "The poet," as he refers to himself in his memoirs, married three times: to Evalyn Katz, by whom he had three children, to Teri Kovach, and lastly to Sophie Wilkins, whose essay "Seriously Meeting Karl Shapiro" in the festschrift so named is one of the most delightful accounts of Karl Jay Shapiro's life.

Poet, editor, and critic, Shapiro's numerous awards include *Poetry* magazine's Levison Prize, the Contemporary Prize (1943), the Pulitzer Prize for *V-Letter*, the Shelley Memorial Prize for *Essay on Rime*, and a Guggenheim fellowship (1945). Shapiro also served as Poetry Consultant at the Library of Congress (1946–1947), a position that is now classified as U.S. Poet Laureate. In spite of his notable awards, however, Shapiro's reputation suffered because of incidents of his sometimes antagonistic outspokenness, not the least of which was his opposition to **Ezra Pound**'s 1948 Bollingen Prize. Shapiro claimed that Pound's anti-Semitism tainted his poetry.

Since his early days at the University of Virginia (1932–1933), Shapiro expressed strong feelings about exclusion. He complained that the curriculum "hurt the Negro" and avoided the Jew. The "free modern Jew," he wrote, "is neither hero nor victim. He is a man left over, after everything that can happen has happened (*Poems of a Jew* [1958]). A number of quotes from Shapiro's work highlight his forthright objections to policy and politics in military, social, academic, and poetic circles. In "The Death of Randall Jarrell," Shapiro claims that his, Shapiro's, anti-cultural-committee activities spanned many years, and he writes that he Shapiro "tried to sabotage organized culture whenever possible." He objected to the ponderousness of modern criticism that weighed down the academy. In "The Decolonization of American Literature" in *To Abolish Children and Other Essays* (1968), Shapiro indicates that he tried many years "to loosen the hold of the academic or colonial mind over poetry." He felt it served to encourage "a poetry as well as an entire literature of reference, the kind that refers back in every case to prior commitments, historical, religious, or philosophical." Shapiro explains in "The Decolonization" that "a literature is the expression of a nation's soul, and a great literature leaves nothing out—that is its greatness. But to leave nothing out means to go against the grain, it means to dissent."

Criticism of Shapiro's work has been a little less than kind considering that the author's poetic and critical legacy defined poetics in America for many years. In addition to numerous and prestigious awards, Shapiro honorably served as the editor of two of America's most notable publications: *Poetry* and *The Prairie Schooner*. He published eighteen books of poetry, a novel, and two memoirs, *The Younger Son: The Youth And War Years Of A Distinguished American Poet* (1988) and *Reports Of My Death: A Distinguished American Poet Looks At The Literary Life Of Our Times.* The latter title refers to two false and mistaken articles about the poet's suicide. A craftsman and expert on prosody, Shapiro is also known for his literary criticism. Such works include *English Prosody and Modern Poetry* (1947), *A Bibliography of Modern Prosody* (1942), *Beyond Criticism* (1953), and *A Primer for Poets (1965). In Defense of Ignorance* (1960) argued for poetic vitality, for realness, and for experiencing the world via the senses. Shapiro additionally wrote two collections of essays: *To Abolish Children and Other Essays* (1968) and *The Poetry Wreck: Selected Essays 1950–1970* (1985).

Shapiro's teaching drew acclaim. **Ted Kooser**, in *Seriously Meeting Karl Shapiro,* says that as a young student, he applied to the University of Nebraska because Shapiro was teaching there. Shapiro was then fifty years old, and Kooser describes him as "wiry and energetic, witty and charming." Hans Ostram, in "'This Isn't A Poem Yet': Karl Shapiro The Teacher" says that he transferred to the University of California–Davis "to study with Karl Shapiro." He refers to Shapiro as an academic poet who wasn't really academic; an Easterner with a curious *empathy* for the West; a critic who took potshots left (the Beats) and right (Pound and Eliot); a writer who refused to join any "school" (particularly one that would want him); a person who always thrived on the anomalies of being a "white-haired lover," a "bourgeois poet," and a well-read poet unconcerned about showing off what he had read. "I remember him as a teacher who didn't seem to be teaching, but who, by saying things like 'This isn't a poem yet,' gave . . . hundreds of . . . young writers precisely the sort of clear advice we most needed to hear" (*Seriously Meeting Karl Shapiro*).

It might be said that Karl Shapiro was the "real thing." Never an imposter, he championed whatever he believed in. He thought that "war is an affection of the human spirit, without any particular reference to 'values'" ("Introduction," *V-Letters*). In "The Geographers" (*V-Letters*), he wrote that "[w]ars cannot change the shapes of continents," and in the poem, "V-Letter," he said, "Give me the free and poor inheritance / Of our own kind, not furniture / Of Education, nor the prophet's pose, / The general cause of words, the hero's stance, / The ambitions incommensurable with flesh."

An American, Southern, Jewish poet, Shapiro describes his sense of being a Jew in the "Introduction" to *Poems Of A Jew*: "The religious question is not my concern. I am one . . . who views with disgust and disappointment the evangelism of the twentieth century and the back-sliding of artists and intellectuals toward religion." The poems are not religious poems, but rather they are the poems of a Jew, a word, he says "[n]o one has been able to define . . . [f]or to be a Jew is to be in a certain state of consciousness."

Karl Shapiro's canvas, displaying a panorama of human experience, is one that features the commonplace—such American things as the drug store with its "packages with wiles" that say, "Buy me, buy me"; an auto wreck with "[s]tretchers . . . laid out, the mangled lifted / And stowed into the little hospital"; and the fly, that "hideous little bat, the size of snot," that man swats with hate. Anything in Shapiro's vernacular can be a subject for poetry.

Wit and playful delight are also aspects of Shapiro's poetry. In lighthearted verse, he claims he never got the hang of love-making," and he complains about being yanked from a favorite anthology, crying, "Fame gave me a wrench and I cried *Ouch! / That hurt!* who used to use a silky touch, / Called me illustrious, caressed my name, / Made me an indispensable." He said in a poetic "interview" (*The Old Horsefly*), that "validation [should] bury itself / Deep in the loam of the poem." The loam of Shapiro's poetry is exceedingly rich and attests to his expansive talent. His reputation will live long beyond his death, and the work he left behind will continue to be the rich mine of creativity that made Karl Shapiro, as Robert Phillips says, a national monument.

Further Reading. ***Selected Primary Sources:*** Shapiro, Karl, *Collected Poems 1940–1978* (New York: Random House, 1978); ———, *Love and War, Art and God: The Poems of Karl Shapiro*; ———, *New and Selected Poems 1940–1986* (Chicago: University of Chicago Press, 1987); ———, *Reports of My Death* (Chapel Hill, NC: Algonquin, 1990); ———, *The Younger Son* (Chapel Hill, NC: Algonquin, 1988). ***Selected Secondary Sources:*** Pinsker, Sanford, "Recalling Karl Shapiro, Jewish poet against the grain" (*N.J. Jewish News*, www.jewishsf.com/bk00061/usshapiro/shtml); Reino, Joseph, *Karl Shapiro* (Boston: Twayne Publishers, 1981); Walker, Sue, ed., *Seriously Meeting Carl Shapiro* (Mobile, AL: Negative Capability Press, 1993).

Sue Brannan Walker

SHOMER, ENID (1944–)

Enid Shomer's poems give a clear, emotionally convincing picture of women's experience, especially in the 1960s and 1970s, but also in other historical eras from the ninth century to the present. Her poems about Pope Joan and her book-length collection *Stars at Noon*, which describes the life of an early pilot, provide close readings of women's lives, and their strong **narrative** line provides the satisfactions of fiction as well as poetry. Thus, Shomer's work prods the border between poetry and fiction and, much like Robert Browning's work, provides complex character sketches that also reflect societal values.

Born in Washington, D.C., Shomer (pronounced sho-MER) found an aptitude for writing in childhood. She graduated from Wellesley College in 1965 and then received an MA from the University of Miami (1967). Her subsequent career has consisted of writing and teaching in writing programs, including the Antioch Writer's Workshop and programs at Florida State University and Ohio State University. Her many awards include two National Endowment for the Arts Fellowships, the Word Works Washington Book Prize, and the Jubilee Press Prize. In 2002 she was appointed Series Editor for the University of Arkansas Press Poetry Series. In addition to her major poetry books, she has published fiction, essays, and interviews.

Stars at Noon is based in part on the autobiography of Jacqueline Cochran, whose exploits as one of the first women pilots were eclipsed by those of her friend Amelia Earhart and were blurred by a host of other circumstances. This complicated woman's character and the intense opposition she faced as pilot, reporter, entrepreneur, and politician are brought to life in a chronological sequence of poems tracing her abandonment as a baby through her late, unsuccessful foray into politics and through her death and detailing the link between Cochran and her poetic biographer. The poems display a variety of forms, from sonnet to **free verse**, and the sequence reads like a novel, with brief informative sections introducing each new era of her life. David Wojahn commented, "As a work of visionary hagiography, it is comparable to Robert Penn Warren's great Audubon poem." And **Maxine Kumin** wrote, "[*Stars at Noon*] may break the sound barrier between historical facts and passionate feelings."

What Shomer's work does most clearly is clothe complex concepts and paradoxes in language, so that the reader can feel them. "What logic can't grasp, metaphor can," Shomer says. "Poems enable us to redeem the language in which we were lied to." This is a distinctive way of reclaiming the language for the woman poet and, indeed, for poetry in general. Shomer often uses familiar forms, the lyrical repetitions of the villanelle and the formal closure of the sonnet; the forms are always clearly recognizable and appropriate to the content, so that they become part of the poetic metaphor.

Shomer's earlier work also engages women in their time. Pope Joan takes a legend—the ninth-century woman pope—and uses it to explore realities of women in history, what was expected of them and how the exceptional woman might be dealt with by a society that did not allow exceptions. Her other poems are rich with history made immediate, whether it is an era she experienced or one she read about; her perspective is always a woman's view. Some of her poems are shot through with humor; her style is relaxed and flexible, as she slips easily back and forth between formalism and a controlled, lyrical free verse.

At the heart of Shomer's woman-centered work is the issue of the mind-body split: To what extent is biology destiny and to what extent is possibility socially determined and limited? Shomer's books provide a definition of **feminism** that is essentialist without being aggressive; there is a luminous sadness in her work as she comments on women's fragility and the strength of her needs and desires. The women in her poems are varied; her metaphors often bring delight because they are clear but subtle, and they often inhabit an entire poem. One such metaphor is the dummies all named Annie that the children are practicing on in "Learning CPR"; the Annies become others and selves. Another is the cows in "Among the Cows," in which the woman speaker is told to get herself regrounded in the power and verve of earth by breathing "with the Holsteins." Shomer's are felt metaphors, not hidden but powerful; it is for this reason that her work is read and appreciated more than it is analyzed. The accessibility of her poetry does not detract from its often-startling originality.

Other women poets have chosen the extended dramatic monologue form to give voice to marginalized women. Shomer's monologues are different in that the narrative is so grounded in history that we see her characters in their time and of their time as much as we see them as individuals. Her moving among very different historical situations and eras reminds the reader of the commonalities of all women's experiences. Enid Shomer's poems tell clear and moving, sometimes shocking stories of women living their varied and shared lives.

Further Reading. ***Selected Primary Sources:*** Shomer, Enid, *Black Drum* (Fayetteville: University of Arkansas Press, 1997); ———, *Florida Postcards* (Tampa, FL: Jubilee Press, 1983); ———, *Stalking the Florida Panther* (Washington, D.C.: Word Works, 1988); ———, *Stars at Noon: Poems from the Life of Jacqueline Cochran* (Fayetteville: University of Arkansas Press, 2001); ———, *This Close to the Earth* (Fayetteville: University of Arkansas Press, 1992). ***Selected Secondary Sources:*** Mason, David, "Subdividing Parnassus" (*The Hudson Review* 51.1 [Spring 1998]: 265–275); Yezzi, David, "Black Drum" (*Poetry* 171.5: 291–293).

Janet McCann

SHORE, JANE (1947–)

In more than thirty years of serious writing, beginning in the late 1960s and the 1970s, Jane Shore has maintained a consistent focus on the things of this world: family, location, weather, and *stuff*—games, clothes, food—a world that she called in the title of a poem in *Eye Level* "This World Without Miracles." But there are miracles in her vision of these materials, "a kind of radiance" that the dark takes on in that poem, giving everything "an elegant human shape." Recovery is not a bad word for this process. It is, in fact, a word that Shore herself uses for the poet's genius in her tribute to **Elizabeth Bishop**'s love for the hapless, scaled-down aspects of Nova Scotia, a world of scarecrow children and a "tight-lipped but cheerful" curator in a local crafts museum. So many things are lost to shipwrecks, "lost, all lost, and then recovered."

Born in 1947, Shore grew up in New Jersey and graduated from Goddard College and the University of Iowa Writer's Workshop. The author of five books of poetry, Jane Shore achieved tenure as a professor at George Washington University and also became a faculty member in 1999 at the famed Bread Loaf Writers' Conference at Middlebury College in Vermont. In addition to her many and various teaching activities and poetry readings, she has served as a literary judge for several prestigious awards, has held a Guggenheim Fellowship (1991–1992), and has received two National Endowment for the Arts grants (1978 and 1987) and an Alfred Hodder Fellowship at Princeton University (1989–1990). Most recently, Shore helped organize Washington, D.C., area poets to speak out against the war in Iraq, contributing to the *Poets Against the War* anthology, which she and others attempted to deliver to First Lady Laura Bush in a public demonstration at the White House on February 12, 2003.

Shore published *Lying Down in the Olive Press*, a chapbook, in 1969 at the age of twenty-two, but her first major publication was *Eye Level*, which won the Juniper Prize and went into a third printing after being first published by the University of Massachusetts Press in 1977. *The Minute Hand* (1986) was a Lamont Poetry Selection and was reprinted in 2000 in the Carnegie Mellon Classics Contemporary Series. *Music Minus One* (1996) was cited by the Detroit Free Press as one of the Best Books of the Year and was a finalist for the National Book Critics Circle Award. In 1999 Picador USA (a division of St. Martin's Press) published *Happy Family*.

Elizabeth Bishop, whom Shore knew and wrote about in a perceptive 1979 essay entitled "Elizabeth Bishop: The Art of Changing Your Mind," has been a central influence for Shore's work, not only, as **Rachel Hadas** has pointed out, in the strange distortions of perspective (large to small, small to large) but also in the deadpan rendering of incident that has increasingly come to the fore as a feature of Shore's sure-footed comic style. In "God," for example, from *Happy Family*, Jewish Jane recalls her Catholic childhood babysitter, Mary, showing her a white plastic statue "of a bearded man wearing a bathrobe," and telling her "This is God." The unsettling effect of this statement is that Jane blows into Mary's ashtray, causing a stinging and burning whirlwind of ashes to assail her eyes. "I had to cry the ashes out, every last one," she says, a response that unsurprisingly leaves her with some confusion about the relationship between revelation and pain. In its deadpan contrast between different points of view, this poem reminds one of the ending of Bishop's "Santarém," in which a fellow passenger on a boat trip down the Amazon responds to Bishop's treasured memento (a wasp's nest) by asking, "What's that ugly thing?"

In addition to Elizabeth Bishop, the influence of **Randall Jarrell** on Jane Shore's work is noticeable. In calling attention to this connection, Robert Boyers mentions the similar "equable" accent in the two poets:

> It is an accent I associate with Jarrell, more than with any other American poet, and of course Jane celebrates that link in *Happy Family*, giving one of her poems, 'Next Day,' the title of one of Jarrell's most famous dramatic monologues, and allowing herself now and again discreet echoes of images and tropes wittily lifted from Jarrell and made into startlingly original passages and poems.

However, Boyers also sees that Shore achieves a wholly different attitude toward experience in her poem, an attitude that is much mellower than Jarrell's. Similarly, in her poem "The Reader" from *Eye Level*, which responds to **Wallace Stevens**'s "The House Was Quiet and the World Was Calm," Shore's reader—a young woman beginning to recognize herself in the achievement of a style—is a more particularized and intimate portrait than Stevens's philosophical abstraction.

Increasingly, Jane Shore identifies herself with a particular history and location having to do with her background as the daughter of Jewish parents who owned a clothing store in North Bergen, New Jersey. Both *Music Minus One* and *Happy Family* recount this history. Yet, as several critics have noted, Shore treats this background with both humor and candor. Rachel Hadas writes, "there is never the feeling of an agenda, that the poems' *real* significance is historical rather than personal. With an art that conceals art, Shore appears to be concerned only with getting the details right" (166). In one humorous poem, "Shit Soup," for example, Shore plays off the Yiddish expression *shit-arein* (to pour in) to suggest (discreetly) the need to acknowledge and transform the full range of human experience, not leaving anything out, but rendering it, like the meat and vegetables in the soup, wholly palatable by simmering it for two hours "on the lowest possible flame." Like many of the subtleties of these poems, this recipe enacts Shore's effective strategy of combining understatement and illuminating description.

Further Reading. ***Selected Primary Sources:*** Shore, Jane, "Elizabeth Bishop: The Art of Changing Your Mind" (*Ploughshares* 5:1 [1979]: 178–191); ———, *Eye Level*

(Amherst: University of Massachusetts Press, 1977); ———, *Happy Family* (New York: Picador USA, 1999); ———, *The Minute Hand* (Amherst: University of Massachusetts Press, 1987; reprinted Carnegie-Mellon Classics Contemporary Series, Spring 2000); ———, *Music Minus One* (New York: Picador USA, 1996). ***Selected Secondary Sources:*** Boyers, Robert, *A Book of Common Praise* (Keene, NY: Ausable Press, 2002); Hadas, Rachel, "Four Voices Thinking Out Loud" (*Kenyon Review* 20:3/4 [1998]: 157–173); Kaufman, Janet, "Life, Freedom, and Memory: The Poetry of Jewish American Women," in *Jewish American Poetry*, ed. Jonathan N. Barron and Eric Murphy Selinger (Hanover, NH: University Press of New England, 2000).

Cheryl Walker

SIGOURNEY, LYDIA HUNTLEY (1791–1865)

According to the website of Sigourney, Iowa (population 2, 209), the town, founded in 1843 and "named after the distinguished poetess, Lydia Huntley Sigourney," went into a severe decline at the start of the twentieth century. Beginning in 1990, however, it underwent a physical and mental "metamorphosis," a rehabilitation so successful that not only was the town the first to win Iowa's coveted "Spirit of Main Street" award in 1995, but two years later, it was also a finalist for the National Main Street Center's Great American Main Street Award (1). In a way hard to view as simply fortuitous, the fortunes of "the distinguished poetess" after whom Sigourney, Iowa, was named have, in this same period, undergone a similar rehabilitation. A poet whose popularity and name-recognition once rivaled that of **Henry Wadsworth Longfellow**, Lydia Sigourney quickly sank into oblivion after her death in 1865. With the groundbreaking publication of Nina Baym's "Reinventing Lydia Sigourney" in 1990, however, years of neglect came to an end. Today, at least among scholars of nineteenth-century American literature, Sigourney is a figure to be reckoned with—ranked among the most influential women writers that nineteenth-century America produced.

Born on September 1, 1791 to Ezekiel Huntley, caretaker of the Lathrop estate in Norwich, Connecticut, and his second wife, Zerviah, Lydia Huntley Sigourney was an exceedingly quick child, whose precocity caught the attention of her father's employer, Mrs. Daniel Lathrop. The widowed and childless Mrs. Lathrop took the little girl under her wing, nurturing her intellectual ambitions, giving her access to the Lathrops' private library, guiding her reading, and encouraging her attendance at the local public school. From her earliest days, Sigourney wanted to be a teacher. Although her own formal education ended when she was thirteen, in 1811, with a close friend, Nancy Maria Hyde, she opened a small private school in the Norwich area. When the school folded in the course of a difficult winter the next year, Sigourney and Hyde continued to teach, imparting free religious instruction two days a week to indigent white children and those, as Sigourney puts it in her posthumously published memoir, *Letters of Life* (1866), "of sable hue" (200). Two of the three great passions that would rule Sigourney's life and work—religion, aiding the oppressed, and poetry—had fallen into place. In 1815, four years after the Norwich venture, she published her first book of verse, *Moral Pieces, in Prose and Verse*, completing the picture.

Sigourney's career as a teacher, the vocation for which she prepared from childhood on, ended abruptly in 1819 with her marriage to Charles Sigourney, a hardware merchant and widower with three children. Much older than his bride, and far more conservative, Charles Sigourney disapproved of wives displaying their talents in public. When Charles's business began to fail in the 1820s, Sigourney, by then a mother herself, defied him, as she had not over her teaching, and turned to writing as her best means of support. Although she already had two books of poetry to her credit (*Moral Pieces* [1815] and *Traits of the Aborigines of America* [1822]), it was her 1827 *Poems* that launched her new career as one of the early nineteenth century's most beloved and best-paid writers.

By 1840 Sigourney, now tagged "the American Hemans," after the hugely popular British woman poet of that name (Haight, 78), had twenty-nine publications with titles ranging from *How to be Happy* and *Letters to Mothers* to *History of Marcus Aurelius, Emperor of Rome* and *Sketch of Connecticut Forty Years Since*. If poetry volumes per se constituted less than half this output, her poems nonetheless were seeded through the culture, appearing regularly in all the leading periodicals (including the *Dial*) and in newspapers from the East Coast to Kentucky, Michigan, and beyond. If one counts newspaper reprints—although copyright legislation was on the books, its implementation had yet to smother poetry's free circulation—the yearly number of her poetry publications was at its height well in the hundreds. Indeed, by 1840 her work was so popular that Louis Godey paid $500 a year simply to have her name on the title page of his magazine, the *Lady's Book*. Ever the shrewd businesswoman, Sigourney nurtured her popularity by being extremely generous with her writing, frequently contributing poems for charitable causes that touched on her own deep-rooted religious and political commitments—temperance, peace societies, missions among the Cherokee and Choctaw Indians, and so on—in this way satisfying her three great passions at once.

Sigourney had no illusions about the price she paid for this popularity. In a now famous passage in her memoir, *Letters of Life*, she gives a hilarious account of the requests she received from ardent admirers, including one for an **elegy** on "a canary-bird, which had accidentally been starved to death," and another for an elegy on a child who had "drowned in a barrel of swine's food" (373). She was the first American woman poet who made a living from her writing; but with a sense of irony for which she is rarely credited, she summed her career up by saying, "If there is any kitchen in Parnassus, my Muse has surely officiated there as a woman of all work, and an aproned waiter" (376). How can one argue with a judgment like that?

Yet all the evidence suggests that if Sigourney wrote for money, she also wrote because she loved to, because as a daughter of the Republic she believed in hard work and self-reliance, and because she had causes she wished to support and viewed poetry, correctly, as an effective means of supporting them. After Charles died in 1854, Sigourney, who had moved to Hartford, Connecticut, in 1814, lived comfortably on her own income until her death in 1865; and when she died, Hartford's church bells tolled for an hour to mourn her passing. For a caretaker's—or, as her biographer Gordon Haight cattily insists, a gardener's—daughter, she went a long way, perhaps too long a way for those, like Haight, who were convinced that the desire to rise above her class was the chief fuel sustaining her (otherwise unwarranted) ambition. But even if, as Sigourney herself acknowledged, much of what she wrote, she wrote for money, the magnitude of her poetry's literary contribution and its influence on other writers, especially women writers, are simply too great and too important to pass off.

So what kind of a poet was Lydia Sigourney? Excepting Baym, most scholars, at least until quite recently, have followed Haight, if not in despising Sigourney herself, then in homogenizing her writing, typically, under the rubric of the **sentimental**, treating her elegies as the key to her oeuvre. As Baym argues, Sigourney's poetry is, however, best understood as plural. That is, it is an eclectic mix of eighteenth-century wit, post-Revolution republicanism, Miltonic epic, German Romanticism, American jeremiad, evangelical sermonizing, and pious domestic sentimentalism. Not only does Sigourney write many different kinds of verse, but because she does, she also lacks that prized achievement of twentieth-century poets, a "voice" of her own—unless, that is, one calls such a mélange, so very Victorian in its way, a voice in itself. When composing, she adopted one or another of these discourses, alone or in combination, depending on her subject and what kind of effect(s) she wished to achieve, subordinating the idiosyncrasies of her own tongue, as it were, to the idiosyncrasies of her subject. She would, as Grace Lathrop Collin observes when speaking of Sigourney's prose, even use dialect when employing rural New England speakers, leading Collin, writing in 1902, to call her a "realist" before her time (29).

Given this variety and given Sigourney's productivity, there is no way to encompass all that Sigourney wrote in a brief discussion. However, two of the texts deserving of attention are "Traits of the Aborigines of America" (1817, 1822), written very early in her career, and *Illustrated Poems* (1849), a representative collection brought together at the height of her career. Taken together, these two works—one a single poem of, literally, **epic** dimensions, the other, a highly heterogeneous collection of Sigourney's "best," that is, most popular, verse—give some sense of her range and of the significance of the specific contribution to American literature her poetry made.

One can hardly imagine a twenty-five-year-old setting out today to write a five-canto **blank-verse** epic of, by Nina Baym's count, four thousand lines. Nonetheless, two years before Sigourney's marriage to Charles Sigourney in 1819, this is precisely what the poet—who had all of one slender volume to her credit at the time—did. According to Sigourney's *Letters of Life*, her effort was not met with applause, "there existing in the community no reciprocity with the subject." Dry though Sigourney's account of the poem's failure is, however, her commitment to the subject—the genocide practiced by European settlers against the continent's aboriginal peoples—never weakened over a lifetime. On the contrary, she concludes her brief description of the debacle with yet one more condemnation of her country's unjust and "hard-hearted policy" toward those whom she (defiantly?) identifies as "the original owners of the soil." "[O]ne of our greatest national sins," she calls it, slavery, no doubt, being the unnamed other (327).

Although "Traits of the Aborigines" came early in Sigourney's career, it represents one of the most persistent and deepest strains in her writing: her very-late-eighteenth-century commitment to republican communality and a functionalist aesthetic. Adapting her voice to her subject, and not, as most poets do today, the reverse, in this poem, as in those like it—"Imitation of Parts of The Prophet Amos," for example, and "The Man of Uz," a retelling of the Book of Job—she adopts the impassioned voice of the (male) prophet to speak authoritatively to those who, she believes, had gone astray. As Wendy Dasler Johnson shrewdly observes in one of the few recent essays to take Sigourney's range seriously, for a "poetess," she did a surprising amount of "cross-gendering" where her speakers are concerned (para 29).

As in "Traits," what Sigourney achieves thereby can also be stunningly effective. What one hears in this poem is not Haight's sentimental elegiast or any other stereotype of the nineteenth-century poetess, but a woman poet writing squarely and unapologetically in the tradition of what Sacvan Bercovitch called the American jeremiad, that secular reshaping of Hebraic or Edwardsian discourse and vision to serve republican ends. In this passage, Sigourney, still in her early twenties and living (by then) in Hartford, dons the mantle of the prophet as surely as ever the great Calvinist preacher did, to limn out her own apocalyptic vision:

O'er calcin'd ruins, steep'd in gore,
Stalks Desolation; while no sound disturbs
His drear dominion, save the heavy tramp
Of haughty victors, save the shrill response
Of pipe, and drum, and clarion, clamouring loud,
Triumphant joy I see the thronging band
Emerging from the vale; their banners float
Amid the forest, and a captive train
Helpless, and weeping, follow.
Who are these,
Red from the bloody wine-press, with its stains
Dark'ning their raiment? Yet I dare not ask
Their clime and lineage, lest the accusing blasts,
Waking the angry echoes, should reply
"Thy Countrymen!" (Canto Third, lines 945–960)

Embedding the fate of North America's aboriginal tribes in the larger narrative of Western imperial aggression from Alexander the Great's conquest of Persia to Cortez's conquest of Mexico, Sigourney is unsparing in her critique of the New World project, both its cost in blood and the price paid in the moral corruption of conquerors and victims alike. As **Helen Hunt Jackson** would do sixty-four years later in *Century of Dishonor*, Sigourney uses her epic, with its voluminous burden of informational notes, to spell out, chapter and verse, the multiple ways in which Europeans betrayed the American Indians again and again in the course of taking this continent from them.

Although toward the end of the epic Sigourney claims to find hope in Christianity as a means of healing the wounds conquest had incurred, this hope, embedded as it is in a narrative of slaughter and betrayal, takes on an irony that inevitably destabilizes the speaker's putatively Christian point of view. Did Sigourney intend the irony? Was she even aware of it? A note appended to the fifth canto suggests that, sincere though her piety was, the irony is deliberate. Sounding very much like **Phillis Wheatley** in her famous letter to the Mohegan minister, Samson Occom—also a friend of Sigourney's—the poet dryly asks, "While we urge that the just claims which our aborigines have on us for religious instruction should no longer be slighted, can it be thought of inferior importance, that those christians who have intercourse with them, should strive to exemplify the moral virtues which their faith enjoins?" (Canto Fifth, note 3) That is, what would finally convert the American Indians was not preaching virtues to them, but living by the virtues we preached.

Like so many American authors writing in the jeremiadic tradition, Sigourney, as Pogo succinctly but wisely put it, had met the enemy and discovered it was we. Sigourney, Baym writes, "faced the insoluble *political* and *moral*, problem that the triumphs of Christianity and republicanism in America were achieved at the cost of their own basic tenets" (394). More than that, she wrote this insolubility into her texts, exposing what Wheatley in the Occom letter so eloquently called that "strange Absurdity of . . . Conduct whose Words and Actions are so diametrically opposite" (177), which continues to baffle observers of the American mind to this day. No wonder, then, that Sigourney's compatriots did not snap her epic up. Far from ducking the consequences of the American proneness to cognitive dissonance, she savaged this capacity for self-contradiction for the self-blind hypocrisy it was.

"Traits of the Aborigines of America," both as epic and jeremiad, forces readers to rethink, as Baym says, how we see antebellum American women's "literary aims" and their achievements (397). In particular, it puts into question the assertions of nineteenth-century litterateurs like Rufus W. Griswold—no friend of Sigourney's poetry—that women, being creatures of emotion, were incapable of producing serious or, as he viewed it, masculine verse. Given its ostensible reason for being, one would think that Sigourney's later volume, *Illustrated Poems* (1849), would have measured itself by the Griswoldian standard. That is, in contrast to the unpopular "Traits," it should have been conventional not provocative, feminine not masculine, full of feeling, not thought. According to *Letters of Life,* the Philadelphia publishing firm, Carey & Hart, solicited the edition as part of a luxury series that already boasted **William Cullen Bryant**, **Henry Wadsworth Longfellow**, and **Nathaniel Willis** among its authors. Sigourney was told to include her most popular poems in the book, together with new poems as she saw fit. The book was priced at a remarkable five dollars a copy, seven dollars for the turkey morocco bound version. It was an offer Sigourney could hardly refuse; and, canny lady that she was, she used the volume unabashedly to showcase her prolific and various wares.

In its 1849 version, *Illustrated Poems* includes 105 poems, taking up more than four hundred pages, and including fourteen engravings by Felix O.C. Darley. The poems selected run the gamut of Sigourney's styles from the domestic sentimental in "The Ancient Family Clock" and "Farewell to a Rural Residence" to nature poems in the European romantic tradition such as "Niagara," and "The Coral Insect"; the volume includes biblical re-writes such as "Aaron on Mount Hor" and "Abraham at Machpelah"; political poems such as "The Return of Napoleon" and "On the Admission of Michigan into the Union"; hymns to the Republic such as "Connecticut River," "The Thriving Family," and "Our Country"; poems on Native American subjects, such as

"Oriska," "Pocahontas," and "The Lost Lily"; poems purveying moral lessons from history, such as "Bernadine du Born" and "Harold and Tosti"; and sermonic poems such as "Scotland's Famine" and "The Bell of the Wreck."

The poems themselves come in a wide variety of meters, from iambic pentameter to common meter, and in rhyme schemes of all sorts, along with blank verse. The majority of the poems are incontestably sentimental by one standard or another, although some are far too complex tonally for an easy fit—including "The Lost Lily," "the Western Immigrant," "A Scene at Sea," and a number of the non-domestic poems cited above. Sigourney also wrote social satire, and she includes a few examples, though not her best, here—"To a Goose" and "Gossip with a Bouquet." Interestingly, however, and possibly indicative, this gallimaufry of **lyric** verse does not include a single example of the one lyric genre—the elegy—that one would, if anything, expect to see the most of, given not only what Haight said about the poet but also what Ann Douglas (Wood) wrote both in her 1972 article on Sigourney and "Inner Space" and in *The Feminization of American Culture.* None of the poems in *Illustrated Poems,* not even the oft-commented upon "Death of an Infant," actually mourns the passing of a specific person or thing, although a significant number—"Death of an Infant," "Indian Names," and "Farewell to a Rural Residence," for example—are inarguably elegiac in tone.

Is it possible, then, that even though Sigourney wrote numerous elegies, she (and maybe even her readers) did not prize this particular lyric as much as we have been led to believe? Given the witty, not to say mordantly cynical, way in which Sigourney treats her readers' requests for elegies in *Letters of Life*—as she herself might say, a child "drowned in a barrel of swine's food," forsooth!—it seems quite possible that she did not prioritize the form, especially if, as the evidence suggests, she produced many of her elegies on demand. They were indeed written for money, in rather the same way that professional mourners made money from their tearful wails when Roman nobles hired them for funerals. But was moneymaking how she also viewed the rest of the poetry that she included in this moneymaking volume—her "most popular" verse? Was all she wrote, at least from 1827 on, if not before, a way to make money and, as both Haight and Douglas (Wood) argue, a way to get above her class and nothing more?

There is no way to answer such questions definitively. However, it is worth noting that although *Illustrated Poems* was no high-minded epic and was not written out of passionate zeal, its differences from "Traits of the Aborigines" are in the end far less interesting than its similarities to the earlier volume—not the least of such similarities being the presence of a number of so many poems sympathetic to American Indians, including "Pocahontas" in its 500-line entirety. True, none of the poems in the later work carry the full weight of historical, religious, and political learning that "Traits of the Aborigines" does, with its pages on pages of learned notes. None is so literarily ambitious either. Nor are subsequent poems as scathing in their anger. But, sentimental or not, lyric in form or not, these are not lightweight poems; nor is *Illustrated Poems* a lightweight (read: mindlessly sentimental) volume. Rather, it is a volume constructed in such a way as to make its readers think, not just about the state of their own souls but about the state of the world, about values, about pleasures, about God and his all-too inscrutable ways, and about the history of the country in which they lived. It teaches and preaches at once.

Drawing on eighteenth-century republican precedents, Sigourney followed writers like Wheatley and **Sarah Apthorp Morton** in filling volumes like *Illustrated Poems, Zinzendorf and Other Poems,* and *The Man of Uz, and Other Poems* with poems on "issues" of weight, thus assigning to the long tradition of American women poets' public verse, a tradition Griswold nowhere acknowledges, but whose presence and importance recent scholars have finally begun to explore, the same aesthetic value men assigned to their own political, historical, and socially-engaged poetry. For other nineteenth-century American women poets, this was a political move of immense proportion, which, given Sigourney's position as the United States's premier woman poet, legitimated the right of all women writers to write with the head, not just the heart, as male litterateurs like Griswold had insisted they do. If the male literati of her period had little good to say of Sigourney, the reason in all likelihood lies here, not in the "sentimental" quality of her verse, or even in her social-climbing per se, but in the fact that she successfully challenged men on grounds they believed securely theirs. No only that but she won—at least within her own lifetime, raising the interesting possibility that, had Sigourney's considerable contribution to American women's verse not been so thoroughly erased after her death, the history of American women's poetry in the twentieth century might have taken a very different, possibly less tortured, path than it did.

Further Reading. ***Selected Primary Sources:*** Sigourney, Lydia Huntley, *Traits of the Aborigines of America: A Poem* (Cambridge, MA: from the University Press, 1822); ———, *Illustrated Poems* (Philadelphia: Carey and Hart, 1849); *Letters of Life* (New York: D. Appleton and Company, 1866). ***Selected Secondary Sources:*** Baym, Nina, "Reinventing Lydia Sigourney" (*American Literature* 62.3 [September 1990]: 385–404); Bennett, Paula Bernat, "Laughing All the Way to the Bank:

Female Sentimentalists in the Marketplace, 1825–50" (*Studies in American Humor* 3.9 [2002]: 11–25); Bercovitch, Sacvan, *The American Jeremiad* (Madison: University of Wisconsin Press, 1980); Collin, Grace Lathrop, "Lydia Huntley Sigourney" (*New England Magazine*, N.S. 27 [May 1902]: 15–30); Douglas, Ann, *The Feminization of American Culture* (New York: Anchor Press, Doubleday, 1988); (Wood) Douglas, Ann, "Mrs. Sigourney and the Sensibility of the Inner Space" (*New England Quarterly* 45.2 [June 1972]: 163–187); Griswold, Rufus W., "Preface," in *Female Poets of America*, ed. Rufus W. Griswold (Philadelphia: Parry & McMillan, 1854, 7–10); Haight, Gordon, *Mrs. Sigourney: The Sweet Singer of Hartford* (New Haven, CT: Yale University Press, 1930); Johnson, Wendy Dasler, "Reviving Lydia Huntley Sigourney" (*Romanticism on the Net* 29–30 [February–May 2003], www.erudit.org/revue/ron/2003/v/n29/007722ar.html); "Welcome to Main Street Sigourney," www.mainstreetiowa.org/towns/sigourney.html; Wheatley, Phillis, "To the Reverend and Honoured Sir [Samson Occom]," in *The Collected Works of Phillis Wheatley*, ed. John Shields (New York, Oxford: Oxford University Press, 1988, 176–177).

Paula Bennett

SILKO, LESLIE MARMON (1948–)

Leslie Marmon Silko is among a group of highly influential Native American writers whose works have changed the American literary landscape. Silko was one of the first Native American women authors to gain public attention with her poetry and novels, making American Indian realities, histories, and visions part of a general American consciousness of itself. With a finely grained sense of the history of conquest and colonization, of specific tribal consciousness and cultures, and of marked links to the earth, American Indian writers have helped shape aesthetic and critical thinking in postcolonial, ecocritical, feminist, and cultural studies fields of scholarship and literature. Attention to indigenous ways of knowing, which include spiritual and material intimacy with the earth, is primary in these writers, who include **Joy Harjo, Simon Ortiz, N. Scott Momaday,** Paula Gunn Allen, and **Wendy Rose** from the American Southwest and **Louise Erdrich,** James Welsh, **Linda Hogan, Carter Revard**, and Diane Burns from other regions.

Silko was born in Albuquerque, New Mexico, daughter of photographer Lee Marmon (Silko, Harjo, and Ortiz collaborated on a collection of Marmon's photographs and their writings, *The Pueblo Imagination* [2003]) and Mary Virginia Leslie. Her mixed heritage of Laguna Pueblo, Mexican, and white, and her upbringing on the Laguna Pueblo Reservation inform her poems and novels. She attended day school on the reservation and in Albuquerque. She began her secondary education at the University of New Mexico in English. She graduated with honors in 1969 and published her first short story, "The Man to Send Rain Clouds." She went to law school briefly but then returned to literary study and took some graduate courses. Her consciousness of the struggles of Native Americans led her to leave the university and teach on a Navajo reservation in Arizona. Seven of Silko's short stories appeared in an anthology *The Man to Send Rain Clouds* (1974), including the hugely popular "Yellow Woman." Her celebrated novel *Ceremony* (1977) brought her to the attention of the American reading public. She moved to Ketchikan, Alaska, the setting of her mesmerizing revenge narrative "Storyteller," which appeared in *Storyteller*, her collection of poems, life-writings, traditional stories and photographs in 1981. Her interdisciplinary ways and variety of artistic interests are demonstrated in her achievements. These include novels (*Almanac of the Dead* [1991] and *Gardens in the Dunes* [1999]); essays (*Yellow Woman and a Beauty of the Spirit: Essays on Native American Life Today* [1996]); the letters she exchanged with **James Wright**, published in the prize-winning *Delicacy and Strength of Lace Letters* (1986); and her ventures into film, the short film *Running on the Edge of the Rainbow: Laguna Stories and Poems* (1978), in which she played herself as a Laguna storyteller, and "Arrowboy and the Witches," an hour-long video of her short story "Estoy-eh-moot and the Kunideeyahsa," which appeared in *Storyteller*. She is impatient with questions of genre, asserting that for her purposes, "it's just useless . . . it doesn't interest me at all" and declaring, "What I'm interested in is getting a feeling or an idea that's part of a story" (Barnes Interview, 59). Despite this disclaimer, Silko's attention to language, sound, and rhythm won her a National Endowment for the Arts Discovery Award in 1971, a NEA award for her first collection of poetry, *Laguna Women Poems* (1974), and the Pushcart Prize for Poetry (1977). A MacArthur Foundation Prize Fellowship (1981) supported her writing of *Almanac of the Dead*. She was declared a "Living Cultural Treasure" by the New Mexico Humanities Council (1988) and in 1994 was awarded the Wordcraft Circle of Native Writers and Storytellers Lifetime Achievement Award.

The position of the mixed-blood person informs much of her writing as she examines the nature of purity and hybridity, authenticity, identity, and community. Silko emphasizes the power of stories and storytelling as the connective tissue in culture and memory and brings all her writing into the terrain of story, integrating poems into her novels and writing stories that read like **narrative poems**. Although Silko brings the old stories of the Laguna people into her writing, she resists the view that she is reinterpreting the legends. Explaining the oral tradition and the view of indigenous people that time is round rather than linear, she says, "If time is round, if time is an ocean, then something that happened 500 years ago may be quite immediate and real" (Interview, Irmer). The old stories that appear in her writings are thus happening now, as in the "Yellow Woman" story, often told by Yellow Woman's Aunt Mary and her beloved Grandmother, Grandma A'mooh. Yellow Woman is the name given a young woman who finds herself enthralled by a mysterious new lover while walking along the riverbank. She goes off with him and returns home to husband and family only when she is ready to. In Silko's tale, the narrator's unsanctioned sexual desire and hunger for freedom are enmeshed with contemporary western scenes, such as the encounter with the fat, sweaty rancher who accuses her lover of rustling cattle and the jet trails marking the pale blue sky. Her adventure with this spirit-being ends with her belief that he will return to the riverside where they met and with her own return home. The narrator says, "I decided to tell them that some Navajo had kidnapped me, but I was sorry that old Grandpa wasn't alive to hear my story because it was the Yellow Woman stories he like to tell best" ("Yellow Woman," 43). This gentle, comic tale brings the elements of women's autonomy, the land, and storytelling together in the voice of a narrator who is at once a modern woman and Yellow Woman of time immemorial. Many of Silko's poems carry this evocation of doubleness as well. In "Indian Song: Survival," for example, the speaker says, "I have slept with the river and / he is warmer than any man," but she is told by some indeterminate voice, "It is only a matter of time, Indian / you can't sleep with the river forever. / Smell winter and know" (*Storyteller*, 35–37). Nature here, as in all Silko's writing, is knowable as the self is knowable, through attention to stories, and is imaginative, intellectual, and sensory.

Poems are integral to *Ceremony*, providing an intelligible context to young Tayo's unintelligible and intractable trauma. Tayo, a young man of mixed blood has returned, after serving as an American soldier and being held captive by Japanese in World War II, to the reservation where he was raised. The novel opens with a poem about "Ts'its'tsinako," the "Thought-Woman," whose thoughts appear: "She is sitting in her room / thinking of a story now // I'm telling you the story she is thinking" (1). These poems from ancient legends, rituals, and ceremonies provide a counterpoint to the struggles of Tayo against the racism in the white world and on his reservation, against the poisoning of the people's land with uranium mining, and against the grip of evil that was called into being by the witch whose conjuring brings "*white skin people / like the belly of a fish / coved with hair*" who are ruled by fear and death (135). For Silko evil is not an abstraction but an active force of hatred, destruction of the earth, and pleasure in cruelty. Only active resistance can combat it effectively, and for that the old truths must be reenacted in the old stories made new. Once the ceremony is complete, individual and community are healed and Tayo can at last come home.

Almanac of the Dead (1991) is Silko's most complex work on several fronts, including her own account of the process of writing the novel. She explains that although she had intended to write a simple, commercial crime story, she "began to lose control of the novel and to feel that all of the old stories came in" (Interview, Irmer). These she experienced as spirits, requiring of her the fulfillment of a task. The novel is the articulation of the revolutionary energy rising from the spirit forces of indigenous peoples of North, Central, and South America. The contemporary world in which these forces are gathering is characterized by the degradation of the earth and its people. Characters are pathetic junkies and vicious drug dealers; cruelty addicts and pornographers specializing in infants and snuff films; sellers of body organs harvested from poor people; and land developers draining the water from Arizona to build a Venice in the desert. Also present are the crazies, the ex-Vietnam vets, the homeless, the Indians—some recognizing a modified Marxism—and, of course, the old stories, some caught on fragments of an almanac saved from destruction by the conquistadores. Silko tracks the politics of Mexico, Central America, and the United States along with her inevitable echo of ancient stories. Although the narrative is grim, even grisly at times, it is also comic in its sharp satire of contemporary America. Her revolutionary Indians, for example, gather at Tucson's "International Holistic Healers' Convention," where every commodity known to the New Age is available for ready money. Silko has produced one of the few contemporary novels that take on the corruption of greed that underpins a global economy. She names an indigenous socialism as a necessary corrective to both capitalism and Marxism, a socialism that is inclusive and rigorous.

Silko says that her 1999 novel, *Gardens in the Dunes*, was intended to be a story about "two women and their gardens and flowers. Absolutely no politics." But when she began to study the history of plants in her region, she discovered that "right behind the conquistadores came the plant collectors . . . it turns out gardens are very political" (Interview, Irmer). Silko's sense of politics, however, is very broad. She hopes for a "new consciousness in the hearts of all human beings, the idea that the earth is shared and finite, and that we are naturally connected to the earth and with each other" (Interview, Irmer). Silko is not, however, unrealistic. She sees change as an "organic transformation . . . slow and interior" (Interview, Irmer), and that belief alone has allowed her to confront the present world and face the future.

Further Reading. ***Selected Primary Sources:*** Silko, Leslie Marmon, *Almanac of the Dead: A Novel* (New York: Simon

& Schuster, 1991); ———, *Ceremony* (New York: Viking Press, 1977); ———, *The Delicacy and Strength of Lace: Letters Between Leslie Marmon Silko & James Wright*, ed. Anne Wright (Saint Paul, MN: Graywolf Press, 1986); ———, *Laguna Woman: Poems* (Greenfield Center, NY: Greenfield Review Press, 1974); ———, *Laguna Woman: Poems*, 2nd ed. (Tucson, AZ: Flood Plain Press, 1994); ———, *Gardens in the Dunes, A Novel* (New York: Simon and Schuster, 1999); ———, *Running on the Edge of the Rainbow: Laguna Stories & Poems* [video recording], prod. Larry Evers (Tucson: University of Arizona Radio-TV-Film Bureau, 1978); ———, *Sacred Water: Narratives and Pictures* (Tucson, AZ: Flood Plain Press, 1993); ———, *Storyteller* (New York: Seaver Books, 1981); ———, *Yellow Woman*, ed. Melody Graulich (New Brunswick, NJ: Rutgers University Press, 1993); ———, *Yellow Woman and a Beauty of the Spirit: Essays on Native American Life Today* (New York: Simon & Schuster, 1996). ***Selected Secondary Sources:*** Barnett, Louise, and James Thorson, eds., *A Laguna Woman: Leslie Marmon Silko: A Collection of Critical Essays* (Albuquerque: University of New Mexico Press, forthcoming); Brewster, Fitzgerald, *Silko: Writing Storyteller and Medicine Woman* (Norman: University of Oklahoma Press, 2004); Silko, Leslie, *Conversations with Leslie Marmon Silko*, ed. Ellen L. Arnold (Jackson: University Press of Mississippi, 2000); Silko, Leslie Marmon, "Interview" by Kim Barnes, in *"Yellow Woman" Leslie Marmon Silko*, ed. Melody Graulich (New Brunswick, NJ: Rutgers University Press, 1993, 47–65); ———, "Interview" by Thomas Irmer (1993, www.altx.com/interviews /silko.hmtl).

Jeanne Perreault

SILL, EDWARD ROWLAND (1841–1887)

Teacher, poet, and idealist, Edward Rowland Sill was born in Windsor, Connecticut, the son of Theodore Sill, a physician, and Elizabeth Rowland. He lost his only sibling in 1847, and then his mother died in 1852, and his father in 1853. The tragedy in Sill's young life perhaps contributed to his lack of clear purpose. As an orphan, supported by his uncle, Elisha Sill, Sill attended Phillips Exeter Academy in New Hampshire. Afterwards, he attended the preparatory school at Western Reserve College in Cleveland, Ohio; he temporarily lived with relatives in Pennsylvania and Cuyahoga Falls, Ohio. At seventeen, he was accepted to Yale College, where he made several close acquaintances, adopted unorthodox opinions of church dogma, and distinguished himself as poet, writer, and editor for the *Yale Literary Magazine*. His primary influence was Tennyson, although he was also influenced by **Ralph Waldo Emerson**. One of his classmates wrote in his diary that Sill was "somewhat a genius." He graduated in 1861.

Following his graduation, Sill sailed for California with his friend, Sextus Shearer, who shared Sill's rebellion against conservatism and materialism. Sill's voyage experiences were recorded in *Around the Horn; A Journal: December 10, 1861 to March 25, 1862*. For the next several years, Sill sought employment as a teacher. He also considered medicine, law, and reporting. With the assistance of family and friends, he found positions in a post office and a bank. Meanwhile, he continued to develop his interest in poetry.

Later, Sill and Shearer decided to return to New England. Prior to their voyage towards the East Coast, Sill began collecting poems and translating them from German. As a result of his work, he produced *The Hermitage and Other Poems* (1867) and *Mozart: An Historical Romance* (1868), translated from the German of H. Rau.

Arriving back in the East, Sill published his poems and entered divinity school at Harvard. In 1867 he married his cousin, Elizabeth, in Cuyahoga Falls; they had no children. Sill attended Harvard for its liberal religious atmosphere. After only a few months, however, he became disenchanted with Harvard's liberals who, as Sill explained, "had forgotten that truth is always safe" and had "made religion mockery." He worked briefly as an editor for the Evening Mail in Brooklyn, New York, but still dissatisfied, he took other unfulfilling positions and discovered that he strongly disliked city life. The Sills soon returned to Ohio, where Edward Sill taught at a small country school. Later, he became a principal of the high school and then the superintendent of schools in Cuyahoga Falls. During this time, his poetry was published on a regular basis.

Not finding contentment in Ohio, finding the Midwest intellectually impoverished, finding Harvard too liberal, and finding the East in general too conservative, Sill and his family moved to California. In 1871 Sill became assistant principal of a high school in Oakland. There he taught Latin, Greek, history, art, music, natural sciences, physical geography, and rhetoric. His teaching requirements kept him extremely occupied. From 1874 to 1882, he was professor of English literature at the University of California at Berkeley. Along with his teaching obligations, Sill worked to improve the school's library, recruited new students, mentored talented writers, revised the English curriculum, and hired philosopher, teacher, and leading American exponent of idealism Josiah Royce as his assistant. Although his academic schedule kept him busy, he did find a little time to work on his personal interests. Sill published more than forty poems, including his most popular works, "Opportunity," "Tree of My Life," and "The Fool's Prayer." He engaged cultural and social concerns in essays such as "The Doctrines of Ralph Waldo Emerson," "The Best Uses of Wealth," "Shall We Have Free Schools?" and "What is a University?" In 1882, at only forty-one, Sill was persuaded by his father-in-law to resign from his position and return to Ohio. He privately published *Venus of Milo and Other Poems* as a farewell to California.

Back in the Midwest, Sill devoted his resources and hard work to establish the first circulating library in Cuyahoga Falls. Because his family strongly disapproved of his literary endeavors, Sill was forced to write and publish anonymous and pseudonymous works. He published poems such as "Anthony Morehead" in the *Century Magazine* and the *Overland Monthly* and "Andrew Hedbrook" in the *Atlantic Monthly*. He was an activist for female education and various topics including nature, science, memories, dreams, language, and music.

Most of Sill's poems and sonnets reflect his love of God and man and of faith and practice. However, he was not devoted to a narrow view of Christianity, but to many realms of life. In "The Hermitage," Sill teaches the truth of the "inching and outshining" of God. His poem "Sunday" explores the worth of the Sabbath and worship. He continued to influence his audiences with his writings on the spirit and truth of Christianity.

Sill's health began to fail him in 1886 and 1887. Several days after a surgery in Cleveland, Ohio, he suffered a stroke and died just when he was prepared and ripe for his work. **John Greenleaf Whittier** observed, "Beyond the poet's sweet dream lives the eternal epic of a man." Sill accomplished only a hint of what he had hoped to achieve.

Sill's contemporaries considered him one of the most modest and charming men of his era. His publications brought him fame and identified him as a graceful writer among minor American poets. Even though his contribution to American poetry was limited, it was of fine quality. **Elizabeth Stuart Phelps Ward** recalled Sill as "personally beloved as I believe few men of our day have been." Sill continued to receive praise from critiques into the mid-twentieth century. Newton Arvin considered Sill one of the "worthwhile" poets of the post-Civil War era, and Alfred Kreyborg defined Sill as the "purest artist in Nineteenth Century Poetry." However, his work has not received critical notice in recent decades.

Further Reading. ***Selected Primary Sources:*** Parker, William Belmont, ed., *The Poetical Works of Edward Rowland Sill* (Boston, New York: Houghton, Mifflin and Co., 1906); Phelps, Elizabeth Stuart, "Edward Rowland Sill" (*Century Magazine* 36 [September 1888]: 704–708); Sills, Edward Rowland, Edward Rowland Sills papers (Bancroft Library, University of California; John Hopkins University Library; Yale University Library; and Houghton Library of Harvard University). ***Selected Secondary Sources:*** Arvin, Newton, "The Failure of E. R. Sill" (*Bookman* 62 [February 1931]: 581–589); Damon, Barbara Simison, "Letters to Yale friends from Edward Rowland Sill" (*Yale University Gazette* 41 [April 1967] and 42 [July 1967]: 21–33); Dix, William F., "The Poems of Edward Rowland Sill" (*Outlook* 72 [November 1902]: 554–556); Ferguson, Alfred Riggs, *Edward Rowland Sill: The Twilight Poet* (1955); Kreyborg, Alfred, *A History of American Poetry* (1934); Parker, William Belmont, *Edward Rowland Sill: His Life and Work* (1915).

Melvin G. Hill

SILLIMAN, RON (1946–)

Ron Silliman has since the mid-1980s been recognized as one of the most important **Language poets** now writing. His many books, from *Ketjak* and *Tjanting* to the longer series of books comprising a project called the *Alphabet*, as well as his essay *The New Sentence* (1987) and other polemical writings, have constituted a sustained attack on the shibboleths of self, voice, narrative, and coherence in mainstream American writing. His most distinctive formal contribution, besides his emphasis on prose sentences (and the space between them), is his selection of nearly-chance forms based on numerical patterns such as the Fibonacci series to determine the lengths of his paragraphs. Such formal decisions serve the larger purpose of foregrounding the constructedness of illusory wholes, such as a self or a meaning; and such attention to construction serves to prod the reader into an awareness of the tacit nature of all natural-seeming ideologies. Ultimately, a program of this kind puts the responsibility for the way things are squarely on the reader, the last bastion of the unexamined "self."

Perhaps a childhood lived in straitened circumstances planted the seeds of social critique in Silliman. He was born August 5, 1946, in Pasco, Washington, and grew up in Albany, California, just outside of Berkeley. He has remarked that his family was poor; he later pursued a college education in various California schools but never finished his degree. Silliman has taken direct action in political and social causes throughout his career, from teaching in prisons to editing the *Socialist Review*. He married Krishna Evans, with whom he has twin sons, Colin and Jesse, and the family settled in San Francisco. Though Silliman began publishing work as early as 1965, *Ketjak* (1978) is regarded as his breakthrough poem. His alliance with the Language poets in the 1980s, the publication of *Tjanting* in 1981, and his editing of *In The American Tree*, an anthology of the new poetries on the East and West coasts that included a collection of statements of intent or theory by the poets themselves, clinched his position in the new American pantheon.

Silliman's work, despite its theoretical underpinnings, is surprisingly accessible, perhaps because the poet is ultimately interested in fostering democracy. His lines, his selection of prose, and even his jokey tones are derived from the homespun and quotidian vernaculars of **William Carlos Williams** and the capacious cataloguing of

Whitman; his predilection for structures full of exposed seams (and requiring a high degree of reader participation and self-awareness) is profoundly indebted to the not-so-accessible syntactical investigations, juxtapositions, and experiments of **Gertrude Stein**'s *Tender Buttons.* Perhaps his greatest contribution to literary history will be the fact that he made such use of Stein's discoveries and renovated her work.

Ketjak and *Tjanting* instantiate the theory Silliman articulated later in *The New Sentence,* a theory that states that, in effect, once sentences are combined into paragraphs, the illusion of syllogistic progression and logical coherence overrides the individual power of the sentence to form new contexts, associations, and meanings. Silliman writes, therefore, a "new" sentence that does not link up easily with its neighbors to produce narrative. Instead, sequence activates reader awareness of the habits we employ to make sense. The happy results in Silliman's prose are often both theoretically astute and "silly, man." As *Ketjak* has it, "A deliberate refusal to perform the normal chores of verse. Silverfish, potato bugs" (8). The poet produces jokes, puns, and strange encounters with skewed truths because our reading habits force us to put disparate elements together as we drive toward closure—a drive Silliman delights in thwarting. What's so bad about closure or narrative coherence? If the reader is allowed to roll over, gratified by the text, nothing in the world is likely to change, including the reader.

"Not this. What, then?" (11) So begins *Tjanting.* Silliman has described this two-paragraph opening as a dialogue, but it is also the restless beginning of a very long bus ride; the answer to the question, "what is a poem"; and the first two integers, one and then one again, of the Fibonacci series, which adds the last number to all the preceding numbers in a series to generate the next number. But the Fibonacci series is the mathematical foundation for one of the most lyrical forms in nature, the spiral. And the poem itself, it turns out, is full of voice, self, miniature narrative, and that sly dog, realism.

Or perhaps each member of that list should be pluralized, qualified—selves, narratives, realisms—because the prose effortlessly slips between registers: "Would it be different with a different pen? Of about to within which what. Poppies grew out of the pile of old broken-up cement. I began again & again. These clouds are not apt to burn off. The yellow room has a sober hue. Each sentence accounts for its place. Not this" (11). Although the poppies certainly look "real" from here, "each sentence" focuses our attention at the level of the material text in hand; we cannot look through it, as through a window, to a transparently visible reference beyond the sentence. And yet we can't stay at the text-level either because the question arises: Is the "place" of "each sentence" perhaps in the "yellow room"? Or does each sentence account for "a sober hue"?

Like the brilliant *Ketjak* before it, books after *Tjanting,* such as *What* (1988) and *Demo to Ink* (1992) (parts of the *Alphabet*), ply similar waters, though the repetition of sentences and phrases is not a salient feature of their meaning-making. The books seem increasingly comfortable with autobiographical elements, private joking, and the sense of a person behind the words—which comfort is not to be confused with a Romantic self, suddenly revealed. Silliman's genius has been to make the theoretical concerns of Language poetry—ruptures of subject and syntax, narrative and coherence—accessible, even pleasurable. What is good and true is perhaps also, finally, beautiful.

Further Reading. ***Selected Primary Sources:*** Silliman, Ron, ———, *ABC* (Berkeley, CA: Tuumba Press, 1983); ———, *The Age of Huts* (New York: Roof Books, 1986); ———, *Bart* (Hartford, CT: Potes & Poets press, 1982); *Crow* (Ithaca, NY: Ithaca House, 1971); ———, *Demo to Ink* (Tucson, AZ: Chax Press, 1992); ———, *Jones* (Mentor, OH: Generator Press, 1993); ———, *Ketjak* (San Francisco: This Press, 1978); ———, *LIT* (Hartford, CT: Potes & Poets Press, 1987); ———, *Manifest* (Tenerife, Canary Islands: Zasterle Press, 1990); ———, *Mohawk* (Bowling Green, OH: Doones Press, 1973); ———, *The New Sentence* (New York: Roof Books, 1987); ———, *N/O* (New York: Roof Books, 1994); ———, *Nox* (Providence, RI: Burning Deck, 1974); ———, *Paradise* (Providence, RI: Burning Deck, 1985); ———, ® (New York, NY: Drogue Press, 1999); ———, *Sitting Up, Standing Up, Taking Steps* (Berkeley, CA: Tuumba Press, 1978); ———, *Toner* (Elmwood, CT: Potes & Poets Press, 1992); ———, *Tjanting* (Berkeley, CA: The Figures, 1981); ———, *What* (Great Barrington, MA: The Figures, 1988); ———, *Xing* (Buffalo, NY: Meow Press, 1996); ———, Bruce Andrews, Charles Bernstein, Ray DiPalma, and Steve McCaffery, *Legend* (New York: L=A=N=G=U=A=G=E/Segue, 1980); ———, Michael Davidson, Lyn Hejinian, and Barrett Watten, *Leningrad* (San Francisco: Mercury House, 1991); ———, and Karen MacCormack, *Multiplex* (Bray County, Wicklow, Ireland: Wild Honey Press, 1998). ***Selected Secondary Sources:*** Beckett, Tom, ed., *The Difficulties: Ron Silliman Issue* 2.2 (1985); Hartley, George, *Textual Politics and the Language Poets* (Bloomington: Indiana University Press, 1989); McGann, Jerome, *Social Values and Poetic Acts: The Historical Judgment of Literary Work* (Cambridge, MA: Harvard University Press, 1988); Parsons, Marnie, *Touch Monkeys: Nonsense Strategies for Reading Twentieth Century Poetry* (Toronto: University of Toronto Press, 1994); Perelman, Bob, *The Marginalization of Poetry: Language Writing and Literary History* (Princeton, NJ: Princeton University Press, 1996); Perloff, Marjorie, *Radical Artifice: Writing Poetry in the Age of Media* (Chicago: University of Chicago Press, 1991); Ross, Andrew, "The New Sentence and the Commodity Form: Recent

American Writing," in *Marxism and the Interpretation of Culture*, ed. Cary Nelson and Lawrence Grossberg (Urbana and Chicago: University of Illinois Press, 1988); Silliman, Ron, ed., *In the American Tree* (Orono: National Poetry Foundation/ University of Maine Press, 1986); Vogler, Thomas, ed., *Quarry West 34: Ron Silliman and the Alphabet* (Santa Cruz: University of California at Santa Cruz, 1998).

Melanie Hubbard

SIMIC, CHARLES (1938–)

Charles Simic developed the reputation, along with **Russell Edson**, of being one of the foremost surrealist poets of his era. Surrealism in any medium always has to struggle to overcome a certain staginess, a sense that the artist has assembled apparently dissonant objects or images just to show that he can do it. But Simic created an organic surrealism in which the real melded almost seamlessly with the strange, just as he evolved a persona in which the America of **blues**, **jazz**, highways, and cities blended with the Eastern Europe of dark folk tales. Perhaps the only other writers who combine these strains are Vladimir Nabokov and **Andrei Codrescu**. But Nabokov, who first came to America at the age of forty, writes about America from the point of view of a European cosmopolite. Codrescu was only a few years older than Simic (twenty to Simic's sixteen) when he emigrated from Eastern Europe, but that seems to have been enough to make a difference. Codrescu, who has become a radio personality, retains his Romanian accent and views America as a bemused and deeply fascinated outsider. Only Simic brings such a complete blend of American and old world sensibility to his work. Even his speaking voice seems to naturally combine flat American vowels with a Balkan lilt.

Charles Simic was born May 9, 1938, in Belgrade, Yugoslavia. His earliest memories are of World War II, and the destruction that rained around him. He remembers being hurled from his bed by an exploding German bomb at age three. He has said, "my travel agents were Hitler and Stalin": His father, an engineer, immigrated to Italy in search of work right after the war and later to America. The rest of the family was unable to leave Yugoslavia then, but America, specifically American music, became a part of Simic's life early. He describes first hearing jazz, and falling in love with it, over Armed Forces radio in 1944–1945 and then having jazz outlawed under Communist rule. Simic, along with his mother and brother, finally left Yugoslavia for Paris in 1953. They remained in Paris, where he studied English, for a year, and then the family was finally reunited in Chicago.

Simic was drafted into the U.S. Army in 1961, and then upon his discharge, he attended New York University, where he received his BA in 1966. He began teaching at the University of New Hampshire in Hanover, New Hampshire, in 1973. He received the PEN International Award for Translation (1970, 1980), and he has been a fellow of the Guggenheim Foundation (1971–1972), the National Endowment for the Arts (1974–1975), the Fulbright Foundation (1982), the Ingram Merrill Foundation (1983–1984), and McArthur Foundation (1984–1989). He received the Edgar Allan Poe Award from the Academy of American Poets (1975) and awards from the National Institute of Arts and Letters and the American Academy of Arts and Letters (1976). He was elected a Chancellor of The Academy of American Poets in 2000.

Simic has published extensively—by 2004 he was credited with more than sixty books, including *Charon's Cosmology* (nominated for the National Book Award in 1977). His award-winning publications include *Classic Ballroom Dances* (Harriet Monroe Award from the University of Chicago and di Castagnola Award from the Poetry Society of America in 1980), *The World Doesn't End: Prose Poems* (Pulitzer Prize for Poetry in 1990), *Walking the Black Cat* (National Book Award finalist in 1996), and *Jackstraws* (*New York Times* Notable Book of the Year in 1999). Other books include his first poetry collection, *What the Grass Says* (1967), *Dismantling the Silence* (1971), *Return to a Place Lit by a Glass of Milk* (1974), *Austerities* (1982), *Unending Blues* (1986), *The Book of Gods and Devils* (1990), *Hotel Insomnia* (1992), *A Wedding in Hell* (1994), *Night Picnic* (2001), and *The Voice at 3 A.M.: Selected Late and New Poems* (2003). He has also published translations of French, Serbian, Croatian, Macedonian, and Slovenian poetry and several books of essays and autobiography, including *Wonderful Words, Silent Truth* (1990), *Dime-Store Alchemy: The Art of Joseph Cornell* (1992), *A Fly in the Soup* (2000), *Unemployed Fortune Teller* (1994), and *Orphan Factory* (1998). He was guest editor of *The Best American Poetry 1992.*

Simic began writing poetry in high school, for a not unusual reason. There was another kid in his school who wrote sappy poems as a way to impress girls, and Simic decided he would try it, too. Interesting about this is that Simic, even as a recent immigrant, was drawn to American-style sappy poetry rather than exotic European sophistication as a mechanism to attract girls. Additionally, many poets or musicians with similar stories follow it up with a variant of "soon, I became more interested in the poetry (or the guitar) than the girl," but Simic, looking back, still remembers the girls with as much pleasure as the poems ("I still tremble at the memory of a certain Linda listening breathlessly to my doggerel on her front steps"), and characteristically, he also remembers his early indoctrination in poetry with as much passion as his sexual awakening: "The way Don Juan adored different kind of women I adored different kind of poets. I went to bed, so to speak, with ancient Chinese, old Romans, French Symbolists, and American Modernists individually and in groups. I was so promiscuous. I'd be lying if I pretended that I had just one great love."

Unlike Polish-born English novelist Joseph Conrad, who stated that he could never have become a writer had he not learned English, Simic has stated that he really does not know the effect of the English language on his creative output, or whether his work would have been substantially different if he had written in Serbian. This is not meant as a dismissal of the pull and power of languages, but as an acknowledgement of how deeply rooted both cultures are within him.

He is much more emphatic about the influence of American music, which has been part of his experience since his first night in the United States, when his father, also a music lover, took him out on a tour of late-night jazz clubs. Simic found in jazz an expression of artistic daring built on a foundation of craft:

> It wasn't just that they were being reckless. Instead it was only a kind of seeming recklessness. Underneath there was a structure. But still, I think what appealed to me before I even learned about the structure was the sheer recklessness of it, the freedom, the wildness . . . I have been listening to [jazz] for more than forty years. And when you pay attention to something for a long period of time . . . you begin to . . . realize what mastery means in an art form.

From blues Simic says that he came to understand "how much you can say with a minimum of moves. It doesn't take much . . . and an incredible context is established. That economy is something I always try to emulate." At the same time, he acknowledges his deep debt to Eastern European folk tales, and he finds a connection between his two cultural godmothers: the minor key. He recalls his father as dividing the world into those who could hear the minor key and those who could not, and he puts the Nazis, and other totalitarian consciousnesses, into the latter camp.

Unlike other poets deeply influenced by jazz, such as **Billy Collins**, **William Matthews**, or **Yusef Komunyakaa**, Simic rarely uses music as subject matter. His poems are more often about things or about people set in relation to things and places. In his early work, he frequently fastened on objects, seen close-up and in a focus so sharp as to be distorted or surreal. There is an Eastern European ancestor here—the Rainer Maria Rilke of the "seeing poems," inspired by Rodin's advice that Rilke go to the zoo and look at an animal until he truly saw it. Simic looks at a fork, for example, until he sees it as a "strange thing [which] must have crept / Right out of hell. / It resembles a bird's foot / Worn around the cannibal's neck" (*Somewhere Among Us a Stone Is Taking Notes*). Or he may focus even closer, on part of an object, like the fingers of his hand, from the "Thumb, loose tooth of a horse," through the middle finger, "An old man at birth. It's about something / That he had and lost," and through the smallest finger, "perpetually at the point / Of birth" (*Somewhere Among Us*).

Simic's near-microscopic precision of language and his minor-key blending of two cultures can be seen in a poem like "Mother Tongue" (from *Return to a Place Lit by a Glass of Milk*), in which he conflates the tongue as physical object "Sold by a butcher" with the symbol for language, traveling in the bag of a stooped widow to a new place, a new environment, "a dark house / Where a cat will / Leap off the stove / Purring / At its entrance." The stooped widow, the dark house, and the cat on the stove are all Eastern European in reference, but they move, especially in the cases of the dark house and the cat, toward specifics that can as easily be jazz-centered America. He generally avoids specific details of place—he will put a poem on a street, or in a kitchen, but not in Chicago or Kukujevci—and this adds to the ever-present duality of his experience. Consider the details in "Brooms," from the same collection. The poem begins, "Only brooms / Know the devil / Still exists," an almost perfect blend of the superstition-shrouded Eastern European cottage and the imagery of Robert Johnson. When Simic turns political, which he often does, his politics are humanist and not locked into the current events of a specific country or series of incidents. A poem like "We All Have Our Hunches" (from *Night Picnic*) gives us the image of a president's picture, on a rolled-up newspaper, "Already speckled by the blood / Of warm-weather flies and mosquitoes." The "President" could be from any country; the blood is home-grown, collected by flies and mosquitoes from the newspaper reader in her own kitchen.

Although Simic has acknowledged the European roots of his surrealist vision, he makes a point of also rooting his vision in his American experience, "a country like ours where supposedly millions of Americans took joyrides in UFOs. Our cities are full of homeless and mad people going around talking to themselves. Not many people seem to notice them. I watch them and eavesdrop on them." In "Early Evening Algebra" (from *The Voice at 3 A.M.*), his eavesdropping gaze fixes on a madwoman who "went marking X's / With a piece of school chalk / On the backs of unsuspecting / Handholding, homebound couples." The madwoman may be an angel of death, but she could just as easily be real, part of the world that Simic notices and incorporates.

The "certain Linda" of Simic's adolescence is not forgotten in his mature poetry, where the erotic is celebrated in a variety of ways. "Body and Soul" (from *Weather Forecast for Utopia and Vicinity: Poems 1967–82*) plays with the double entendre of the blues: "He fiddled with her radiator, / Diddled with her radio. / He even creamed her wheat / And threaded a needle." The women are often glimpsed in vivid but uncertain memory, wearing a red bikini and waving from a train window. Like all else, eros has its dark side in Simic's work. A beautiful woman in a white dress is surrounded by masked men wearing black capes and carrying knives; a couple is seen in wild sexual embrace on a television screen which has recently been showing war and the denial of accountability.

Simic, who has written that the "scandal" of American poetic culture is its neglect of the poetry of other countries, has translated a number of poets from different languages, including the Yugoslav poets Ivan V. Lalic, Vasko Popa, Slavko Janevski, and Novica Tadic. He has also edited collections of poetry in translation, including *Another Republic, an anthology of European and South American Poetry* (1976, with Mark Strand) and *The Horse Has Six Legs, An anthology of Serbian Poetry* (1992).

Further Reading. ***Selected Primary Sources:*** Simic, Charles, *Austerities* (New York: George Braziller, 1982); ———, *The Book of Gods and Devils* (New York: Harcourt Brace Jovanovich, 1990); ———, *Charon's Cosmology* (New York: George Braziller, 1977); ———, *Classic Ballroom Dances* (New York: George Braziller, 1980); ———, *Dime-Store Alchemy: The Art of Joseph Cornell* (Hopewell, NJ: The Ecco Press, 1992); ———, *Dismantling the Silence* (New York: George Braziller, 1971); ———, *A Fly in the Soup* (Ann Arbor: University of Michigan Press, 2000); ———, *Hotel Insomnia* (New York: Harcourt Brace Jovanovich, 1992); ———, *Jackstraws* (New York: Harcourt Brace, 1999); ———, *Night Picnic* (New York: Harcourt, Inc., 2001); ———, *Return to a Place Lit by a Glass of Milk* (New York: George Braziller, 1977); ———, *Unending Blues* (New York: Harcourt Brace Jovanovich, 1986); ———, *The Voice at 3 A.M.: Selected Late and New Poems* (New York: Harcourt, Inc., 2001); ———, *Walking the Black Cat* (New York: Harcourt Brace, 1996); ———, *A Wedding in Hell* (New York: Harcourt Brace, 1994); *What the Grass Says* (San Francisco: Kayak, 1967); ———, *The World Doesn't End* (New York: Harcourt Brace Jovanovich, 1989). ***Selected Secondary Sources:*** Craig, J. Patrick, Eric D. Williams, et al., "Artful Dodge," www.wooster.edu/artfuldodge/interviews/simic.htm; Spalding, J.M., Interview (*Cortland Review* 4 [August 1998], www.cortlandreview.com/issuefour/interview4.htm).

Tad Richards

SIMMS, WILLIAM GILMORE (1806–1870)

William Gilmore Simms is best remembered as the author of two dozen novels, among them *The Yemassee* (1835), *Woodcraft* (1854), and *Martin Faber* (1833). In his own time, although he was known also for his short fiction, his literary criticism, his biographies, and his editing of numerous periodicals, his reputation as a novelist was paramount. In fact, he was so well regarded for his novels that **Edgar Allan Poe** wrote in 1846 that no American writer exceeded Simms "in the aggregate of the higher excellences of fiction" (qtd. in Guilds, 47). Nevertheless, Simms always considered poetry his forté and believed that he would eventually "assert a better rank in verse than" he currently did "in prose" (*Letters*, 3:190). Contemporary opinion lends some support to this assumption, for reviews highly praised his poetry, including those by **William Cullen Bryant** and Poe (Guilds, 185–186). As prolific in poetry as in prose, Simms published more than 2,000 poems and brought out no fewer than sixteen volumes, some of the poems, like *Atalantis: A Story of the Sea* (1832, rev. 1848), being book-length works. Significantly, he incorporated elements of British Romanticism into poetry before **Emerson**, **Thoreau**, and **Longfellow**; in addition, he was among the earliest American poets not only to use native materials and American settings but also to treat them in a realistic manner.

Simms was born in Charleston, South Carolina, on April 17, 1806. In 1808, however, his mother died giving birth to another baby who also died. Subsequently, his grief-stricken father set out for Mississippi, leaving his son to the care of the maternal grandmother. Though his father later attempted to retrieve the boy several times, Simms chose to stay put. His belief in rootedness would shape his work significantly. His grandmother sent him to a school run by the College of Charleston, which nurtured his literary interests. He published his first poem at age sixteen. After trying out both medicine and law, Simms devoted himself to a career in literature, as both writer and editor. By 1832 he had published six books of poetry, and before turning thirty-one, he had authored his first five novels, which brought him to national prominence. His first marriage to Anna Malcolm Giles resulted in a daughter, but Simms's spouse died in 1832. Flush with the success of his early works, he remarried at age thirty and moved to Woodlands, a family plantation of his well-heeled new wife, Chevillette Eliza Roach. This union engendered fourteen children, though only five survived their parents. Simms remained productive as a poet and novelist throughout the 1840s and 1850s. Hardship, however, marked his last decade. After losing their young boys Beverley and Sydney in 1859, Simms and his wife lost two more toddlers in 1861, and then Chevillette died soon after; moreover, their home burned twice, by accident in 1862 and by stragglers of Sherman's army in 1865, during their march downstate. The Civil War also complicated Simms's publishing efforts and thus limited his earning power. In 1859 he published his last book of fiction, *The Cassique of Kiawah*, and in the following year, he released his final collection of verse, *Areytos or Songs and Ballads of the South.* Broke and suffering from cancer and heart disease, Simms died in Charleston in 1870.

From the beginning Simms's poetry participated in the movement of American Romanticism. When the nineteen-year-old poet anonymously published his first book, *Monody, on the Death of General Charles Cotesworth Pinckney* (1825), he followed the moribund fashion of neoclassical couplets. Nevertheless, Simms's initial poems as well as his next books—*Lyrical and Other Poems* (1827) and *Early Lays* (1827)—manifest his affinity to the British Romantics, especially Byron and Keats. For instance, his first proved published poem, "Sonnet—To My Books" (1823), betrays Keats's influence. As James Kibler observes, the poem's subject, form, and use of simile in the sestet all parallel Keats's "On First Looking into Chapman's Homer" (*Selected Poems,* 314). Keats continued to be a presiding spirit to Simms. Sonnets from the 1827 volumes, such as "'If From the Morning of Thy Days'" and "Invocation," stylistically recall the luxurious, sensuous diction of Keats's immature work. Later poems incorporate Keats's mature themes: Like "Ode to a Nightingale," "To a Mock-Bird" from *Poems Descriptive, Dramatic, Legendary and Contemplative* (1853) juxtaposes grief and transcendent joy, and "The Beauty of Departing Objects" from *Grouped Thoughts and Scattered Fancies* (1845) rehearses the frequent Keatsian theme of how transience underlies and enhances the beautiful.

Simms's Romanticism inheres as well in his lifelong employment of the sonnet and in his longer philosophical poems, especially those works expressing personal experience, spirituality, and connection to nature. *Grouped Thoughts,* a collection of sixty-one sonnets, includes many examples that achieve a Wordsworthian brand of Romanticism by emphasizing nature's endurance, sublimity, and power to free one from the world of practicality and work: "Flowers and Trees," "The Same Subject," "Solace of the Woods," and "Religious Musings," to list a few. "The Wreath" (1838), first collected in *Selected Poems,* is similarly framed. In this sonnet Simms characteristically approaches the Shakespearean rhyme scheme but diverges from it: He alters the middle quatrain with envelope rhymes of *cddc* rather than *cdcd*; he allows the final quatrain to overflow syntactically into the couplet; and he extends the final line from pentameter to hexameter. Through conversational syntax and diction, Simms makes the point that what is most authentic is often not the conventionally elevated, but rather the common, not the rose but "the poorest of the flowers."

Simms's **blank-verse** contemplative poems such as "The Inutile Pursuit" from *Poems* (1853) develop the romantic theme that nature compensates and provides salve for the soul-diminishing effects of commerce, teaching that "things of highest profit to the heart / Are never things of trade." Following Coleridge and Wordsworth in these poems, Simms often evokes the unity of all things, natural and human, and characterizes nature as teacher, nurse, foster parent, agent of childhood memory, and ground of ultimate being. For instance, "Harmonies of Nature" (1866), never collected until *Selected Poems,* epitomizes this Romantic faith in sublime experience: "with the choral songs of wind and forest, / The very soul grows lifted into stature, / Feeling the effusion of a sovereign God." Similarly influenced by Coleridge, Wordsworth, and Shelley, Simms's critical defense of poetry, *Poetry and the Practical* (1851–1854), both cements his lifelong connection to the Romantic tradition and lays out his theory of poetry and its cultural importance.

Another element of Simms's Romanticism reveals his pioneering realism, namely his use of native subjects and local landscapes. His concrete settings include not only local places, such as Sullivan's Island, the Charleston harbor, the plantation at Woodlands, and the Saluda Mountains on the Carolina border, but also areas that in Simms's youth constituted the American West. Simms visited his father in Mississippi in 1824–1825 and produced several poems based on this western experience. "The Streamlet" was first published in 1829, but Simms expanded it from twelve to twenty-two stanzas in *Poems* (1853). Centering on the father's romantic faith in memory and nature, Simms symbolizes the capacity of nature to bring renewal and healing. He does this by dramatizing the mysterious voice of the stream: Though like a "hundred streams . . . / From Santee to Savannah," for the speaker this one in Mississippi uniquely manifests his dead father's presence. In addition, *Lyrical and Other Poems* (1827) contains "The Wilderness," whose speaker rests in the Choctaw Nation. He notes that the white man "has scarcely ever come" here to experience such native wildlife as the mockingbird and the red deer. In writing of the American West, Simms also provided some of the earliest sympathetic portrayals of Native Americans. And unlike Cooper's, Simms's depictions of American Indians were often based on firsthand experience, not books. One prime example is "The Broken Arrow" (1827), a historical account of the assassination by the Upper Creeks of a Lower Creek chief, William McIntosh; another poem in this vein is "The Indian Village" from *Southern Passages and Pictures* (1839), which through realism satirizes the sentimental myth of "the noble savage." Above all, the ambitious **narrative** "The Cassique of Accabee," the title poem to an 1849 volume, shows Simms's use of local landscape and legend to underscore the power of place and the past and their joint endurance, even as the white man's plantation house has replaced the ghostly chief's wigwam. Here Simms blends a romantic theme with Southern materials that combine existing place names and oral history of the displaced American Indians. Notable too in this poem is Simms's formal dexterity as he introduces a seven-line stanza with varying iambic meters and a rhyme scheme of *ababccb*.

Indeed, Simms's handling of form and revision in the writing process further indicates his romantic sensibility. In his numerous sonnets Simms rarely follows strict traditional patterns, but instead, like Keats in his last experiments, Simms invents his poems' nonce rhyme schemes during spontaneous lyrical expression. Simms believed that lyrics should be "unpremeditated" improvisations. However, he also stated that the initial outpouring should be "refined subsequently by exquisite art" (*Letters*, 4: 432). In fact, like **Whitman**, he revised poems throughout his life and often created new and better versions, such as his turning "The Indian Village" (1839) into the more complex "Chilhowee," published in a magazine thirty years later. As David Newton has remarked, Simms considered his poems not as fixed products but rather as drafts in an ongoing organic process (34).

As a poet, Simms was not only prolific but also versatile. Though proficient in the forms and themes inherent to Romanticism, he also wrote effective songs, love poems, **light verse**, **verse drama**, religious poems, war poetry, epigrams, and even adaptations of Horace. *Selected Poems* (1990), the first edition of Simms's poetry since 1860, provides a cross-section of these varied types of poems, as well as his works of Romanticism. Moreover, as Kibler asserts in his preface, by including significant poems never before collected and in some cases never published under Simms's name, this volume makes true evaluation of Simms's broad-ranging and bulky poetic canon finally possible (xii). Accordingly, John C. Guilds concludes that among nineteenth-century American poets, Simms falls between Bryant and **Whittier** (346), whereas Kibler places Simms with Bryant, Emerson, and Longfellow (xvi).

Further Reading. ***Selected Primary Sources:*** Simms, William Gilmore, *The Letters of William Gilmore Simms*, ed. Mary C. Simms Oliphant, et al. (Columbia: University of South Carolina Press, 1952–1982); ———, *Poems Descriptive, Dramatic, Legendary and Contemplative* (1853; New York: Arno, 1972); ———, *Poetry and the Practical*, ed. James Everett Kibler, Jr. (Fayetteville: University of Arkansas Press, 1996); ———, *Selected Poems*, ed. James Everett Kibler, Jr. (Athens: University of Georgia Press, 1990). ***Selected Secondary Sources:*** Guilds, John C., *Simms: A Literary Life* (Fayetteville: University of Arkansas Press, 1992); Kibler, James Everett, Jr., "Perceiver and Perceived: External Landscape as Mirror and Metaphor in Simms's Poetry," in *"Long Years of Neglect": The Work and Reputation of William Gilmore Simms*, ed. John C. Guilds (Fayetteville: University of Arkansas Press, 1988, 106–125); ———, *The Poetry of William Gilmore Simms: An Introduction and Bibliography* (Columbia, SC: Southern Studies Program, 1979); Newton, David W., "Voices from the Enchanted Circle: Simms and the Poetics of the American Renaissance" (*Southern Quarterly* 41.2 [Winter 2003]: 23–36).

Matthew C. Brennan

SIMON, MAURYA (1950–)

In the poems of Maurya Simon, the theories of making poetry and of interpretation overlap; the work concerns the language and art of truth. Her sources are history, religion, memory, geopolitics, myth, and language itself; the voicing is lyrical and sometimes ecstatic for hers is a vision of potentiality; and the stance is inclusive, as **Whitman** is inclusive.

Simon teaches and writes in California, where she was also educated: She earned her MFA in English and creative writing at the University of California, Irvine, in 1984; she received her BA in English literature from Pitzer College in 1980; and she was an honor student at the University of California, Berkeley, from 1968 to 1971. She began teaching in the 1980s at the University of California, Riverside, where she since 1997 she has been a professor of creative writing. Simon has been a visiting poet at the California Institute of California (1990–1997), at University of Redlands (1988), and at Pitzer College (1982–1983).

Maurya Simon's first book of poems, *The Enchanted Room* (Copper Canyon Press [1986]), introduces her deft use of natural imagery, as in "small furnishings of wind" and "fat as new potatoes," imagery in which the natural world and the rich inner world of memory and spirit collide to form the latent enchantment that Simon seeks and simultaneously offers to her readers. In "Dream of a Red Chamber" the doorway into the enchanted room is "in the wind opened up," and we have already "sailed through effortlessly." But after entering, one must "forfeit old diversions" to fully know and to feel the "enchantment." The play between the initial ease of access and the necessity to behave differently, to forfeit something, in order to "open different doors" offers the conundrum at the book's center. Each threshold offers another, and passage is unending.

The book explores both "everything" and "nothing" and in perhaps the most affecting section, "Madra Bhavan," the particulars of an experience with Indian culture. One sees in the ordinary details of a place and people like and unlike us something of the magic of experience that is the enchantment of which Simon speaks. The beauty of it is that no hocus-pocus is necessary. The imagination's power is to be able to really see a wedding and carefully listen to a conversation ("Conversations in Madra)"; and in other sections of the book, the power is in the ability to remember one's first tooth or to dwell where "The deer is not only a deer but a woman."

In *Days of Awe* (1989), Simon's generous vision continues though the poems are darker, the delight of the early poems having deepened into reverence and fear. Awe in "Breakwater" is elemental, concerning the daylight and moonlit journeys of two small girls to the edge of the ocean to fish for crabs:

> We lived to see them foam wildly at the mouth,
> Their curved claws clacking like pinking shears.

She goes on to note, "We hated and loved them zealously, as we did / The sand sharks who wore firm faces on their backs." Simon's phrase "hated and loved" expresses the mixed emotions associated with awe; the crabs depicted with their eyes on black stems and the image of jellyfish bodies trailing purple barbs are a wonderment to the children, who comfort themselves with a likeness from the sewing room ("their curved claws clacking like pinking sheers") and are drawn back to the dangerous ocean and its "something / vast and ageless, like an old grief, ever singing / its salt in our veins, the ocean calling us home." The imagery in the poem is both materially exact and exacting, as when the ocean tugs at the girls in their nightgowns, and the girls feel the "thrumming swells undulating their bellies / over the closed womb of the blackened sea." The correlation suggests a mother ocean ("womb") and also death ("blacked sea"). We know that the girls won't drown, can't enter the "closed womb," but the effect of the metaphor is chilling.

Awe's origin is different from poem to poem, always attended by a mixture of imagery and diction, so that what is lovely leans against what is: "A pi-dog snores, half her golden fur gone / From asofoetida or mange . . . / . . . clouds rearrange themselves / In a flotilla of sails whitening the horizon" ("Madra Lament"); "Our dark hope in its golden case" ("The Atomic Psalm"); "Gone the singing flesh, fever / Of light, the sands of eternal grief ("The Pharaohs").

In essence, Simon enacts in the crafting of the poem what awe is—a mixed feeling. In another poem in the collection, "Boy Crazy," the euphoria of virginal love is accompanied by "hot ice" and "a melting and stiffening, a strange tug in my thighs, blood rushing everywhere" during the sexual encounter. In "The White Cockroach" Simon's grandfather, who dreams "of a pure wealth, a kind of white power" to save him from loneliness, strokes the insect's thorax for luck while it sings. And in "Days of Awe," a psalm to a mother, the poet must either come to the acknowledgment that the lovely dream of looking into the eyes of a hummingbird is only a dream or realize that either she or the hummingbird is a mirage. Beautiful as the possibility is, reality counters.

Speaking in Tongues (1990) discusses the origins of language in the high diction appropriate to religious meditation. "God or god" is in language, Simon says, in "that breath that speaks in us," and language is holy, "respoken from mouth to mouth / like a blessing."

In the first section of the book, "Origins," Simon imagines the invention of language as belonging to a female scribe, the first scribe, whose first pictograph is of "a stick-figure man, his penis shafted downward, / a thick finger pointing to earth" as a symbol for her people. Her second is of a woman whose shape and body are carved out of stone by the scribe; creation of the torso, arms, and legs is followed by creation of the woman's "second mouth that calls to the earth like a lover." The scribe next "makes the breasts vast, pendulous, like great teardrops / . . . / Balanced over the rim of the world, over belly-mound. / And it is finished."

What is finished is not only the pictograph in stone and a word that she can roll on her tongue to taste as "an eloquence / there, a sweetness as powerful as god's name." The potential for the rest of language has also been created now that there are woman and man, "vulva" and "penis." Language, Simon tells us, is bodied, alive, and fertile and offers the lasting (the woman is made from the "rock-page") possibility of understanding in the dualities of mind and body, silence and song, self and other, zero and zenith.

The second section, "Spellbound: An Alphabet," explores the permutations of Simon's explorations of what words mean. If God is the Word but cannot be spoken, then "what is God" is one of the poet's fascinations. And what is the Word? What of the ineffable—death's "hugeness," for instance? The poet isn't interested in riddles or in *a priori* answers. The poet's answers are *a posteriori*, built on the idea of language as a tool of discovery, "when all the circuitry's in flames, // when all the cells clasp hands / electrifyingly and sing."

The Golden Labyrinth (1995) returns Simon to her earlier interests in realism. Her "examination of the 'breakdown' of nature and culture," Dorothy Barresi tells us in a review of Simon's book in the Winter 1996 issue of *The Gettysburg Review*, "is located in South India, where she sets her poems' speakers amidst poverty and disease" (60). The spiritual epiphanies of *Speaking in Tongues* have been undermined by stark contemporary realities though transcendence is ever a possibility in Simon's sensibility and approach, as in "Meditation at Twilight," in which the speaker watches as, after a cobra is run over by a truck, a baby cobra emerges from the grass on the side of the road to run "its delicate body up and down" the body of its dead mother, "As if trying to coax it back to life." The speaker reports that all the world and all the nature seemed to stand still in that moment: "Every death records the silence / of a single, amazed mourner."

Several of Simon's signature notions of poetry and the world collide in this short **lyric poem**—first, the lyric voice. That death leads to something new and, like almost everything in Simon's fertile cosmology, is ground for the imagination is another concern carried over from earlier books. The writer asks us to appreciate the cobra in terms that approach animism insofar as the actions of the cobra and the cicadas seem "willed" and reverent in the response to death, as if more than a body had been extinguished.

A catalogue of phrases in the poems shows the stark realities of human existence in South India: "an armless child," decaying loincloth," "naked toddler squatting," "blackened cathedrals and crumbling minuets," "a crippled man," "a boy wags his tongue stump at me," "toothless beggars," "an aged man, draft-wary, his right eye gone out," and "urchins leaving their magotty sacks, / side-stepping disease, hunger, disembowled cats." Still, Simon finds amid the squalor examples in the religious men of transcendence: "Each small world," she says in "The Bishop of Mysore," "transforms itself."

A danger in Simon's approach is a too-easy lift, to be "blessed and afflicted, / delivered, condemned in one breath," instead of two. But as in all her work, Simon finds a balance between mystery and accuracy, hopefulness and a clear-eyed presentation of our realities, in the books before *The Golden Labyrinth*, and especially in *Ghost Orchid* (2004), where the poems are filled with reverence, wonder, and "razzamatazz." The poems also wrestle with God, who she says loses "meaning, losing me," and politics. Simon's voice is unique in a marriage of opposites that is believable. In her vision the world consists of body and soul, religion and politics, man and woman, and above all of it, imagination, largely secular, which feeds her very fertile personal language and results in a sense of magic, awe, epiphany, and the ineffable.

Further Reading. ***Selected Primary Sources:*** Simon, Maurya, *Days of Awe* (Port Townsend, WA: Copper Canyon Press, 1989); ———, *The Enchanted Room* (Port Townsend, WA: Copper Canyon Press, 1986); ———, *Ghost Orchid* (Granada Hills, CA: Red Hen Press, 2004); ———, *The Golden Labyrinth* (Columbia: University of Missouri Press, 1995); ———, *Speaking in Tongues* (Salt Lake City, UT: Gibbs Smith Publishers, 1990). ***Selected Secondary Sources:*** Barresi, Dorothy, "The World as We Know it (*New England Review* [Winter 1996]: 60–63); Graham, Neile, "Speaking in Tongues" (*Calyx* 14.1 [Summer 1992]: 107); Wakoski, Diane, "Words of Power" (*The Woman's Book Review* 8.9 [June 1991]).

Carol Frost

SIMPSON, LOUIS (ASTON MARANTZ) (1923–)

The literary career of Louis Simpson spans poetry, fiction, journalism, and criticism. The major themes of his poems include war, civil society, and nationhood. His early poetry is modeled after Elizabethan and Metaphysical poets. In late 1950s he made the transition from regular **poetic forms** toward **free verse**. In the later poems he challenges the optimistic vision of **Walt Whitman**'s America. Simpson is a democratic poet who also has the landscape imagination of William Wordsworth and other English Romantics. He has been grouped with American **Deep Image** poets **Robert Bly**, **James Wright**, and **Donald Hall**. In his later work, Simpson shows a strong bend for **narrative poems** and for a multiplicity of lyric voices.

Louis Simpson was born in Kingston, Jamaica, in 1923. He spent his youth in the British West Indies. His father was of Scottish origin and his mother came from a Jewish family. At the age of seventeen, Simpson came to theUnited States to attend Columbia University in New York. Although his studies were interrupted by service in the U.S. army during World War II, he returned to Columbia to finish his bachelor's and master's degrees and finally, in 1959, his doctoral degree. He worked first as an editor and then taught at Columbia University, the University of California at Berkeley, and the State University of New York.

Simpson's first volume of poetry, *The Arrivistes: Poems 1940–1949* (1949), was privately published in Paris. He utilizes here his experience from the war battlefield and gives realist description of soldier psychology. His celebrated ballad "Carentan O Carentan" shows the emotions, fear, depression, and despair of young Americans who are left to die needlessly by their officers. Other poems in the collection, such as "Song: Rough Winds Do Shake the Darling Buds of May," have an erotic undertone. Simpson's second collection, *Good News of Death and Other Poems* (1955), broadens the scope of subject matter. The poet scrutinizes contemporary American society by contrasting it with its idyllic, harmonious past. Simpson's ideological debt to Walt Whitman, especially his *Democratic Vistas*, is apparent. The early formalist phase of Simpson's poetry is complete with the collection *A Dream of Governors* (1959).

The Pulitzer Prize–winning collection *At the End of the Open Road* (1963) marks the second period of Simpson's poetry. Following this publication, he turned toward free verse and a wider range of speakers. In the frequently anthologized "Walt Whitman at Bear Mountain," the poet contrasts the idealism of Whitman's time to the disillusionment of 1960s America: "Where are you, Walt? / The Open Road goes to the used car lot. / 'Where is the nation you promised?'" "In California" is another poem exploring the theme of cultural decline: "Lie back, Walt Whitman / . . . / We cannot bear / The stars any more, those infinite spaces. / Let the realtors divide the mountains, / For they have already subdivided the valley." Simpson uses an ironic tone to emphasize the moral emptiness of middle-class American life. Other notable collections from the middle period are *Selected Poems* (1966) and *Adventures of the Letter I* (1971).

In 1976 Simpson published *Searching for the Ox*. Here he draws remarkable character sketches and observes mundane details that acquire unique meaning. In his next collection, *Caviare at the Funeral* (1980), Simpson again heavily alludes to Walt Whitman. In addition, he shares an interest in common objects and simple language with **William Carlos Williams**. In *People Live Here: Selected Poems 1949–1983* (1983), the poems are not organized chronologically but are divided by topics: "Songs and Lyrics," "The Fighting in Europe," "A Discovery of America," "Modern Lives," "Tales of Volhynia," "Armidale," and "Recapitulation." Each of these sections represents one dominant field of Simpson's thematic interest. Five years later, Simpson's *Collected Poems* (1988) was published.

In the Room We Share (1990) is Simpson's exploration of his mother's memories and of his own Jamaican boyhood. Simpson draws on Chekhov in his mastery of characterization. Russian motives are balanced out by the recollections of Simpson's early years in the British West Indies. Although the poet refused to physically visit Jamaica for fifty-one years, he returns to his native island in *Jamaica Poems* (1993). In the following collection, *There You Are: Poems* (1995), Simpson merges narrative and prose elements with poetry. In *The Owner of the House: New Collected Poems 1940–2001* (2003), Simpson focuses on the vices of contemporary Americans such as fake intellectualism, materialism, and cultural emptiness. He has thus documented ways in which the American Dream has failed. His poems have always benefited from frequent epiphanic moments whose intensity highlights the joys and weaknesses of American democracy. Moreover, Simpson has written fine lyric poems of Romantic sensitivity that further testify to his humanist belief in poetry as a vital intellectual activity. As he states in "The Unwritten Poem," once we put concern with "popularity out of the way, / we can get on with art. It's long."

Simpson is also the author of autobiographies—*North of Jamaica* (1972) and *The King My Father's Wreck* (1995), for example. In addition, he has published a novel, *River Drive* (1962), and a volume of *Selected Prose* (1988). His early plays include *The Father Out of the Machine: A Masque* (1950) and *Andromeda* (1956). Regarding Simpson's literary criticism, he strongly supports the historical-biographical approach. Such is the method of his book-length studies *James Hogg: A Critical Study* (1962), *Three on the Tower: The Lives and Works of Ezra Pound, T.S. Eliot, and William Carlos Williams* (1975), and *A Revolution in Taste: Studies in Dylan Thomas, Allen Ginsberg, Sylvia Plath, and Robert Lowell* (1978). In *Ships Going into the Blue: Essays and Notes on Poetry* (1994), he argues against the death of poetry. Simpson has also worked as an editor and translator. He continues to translate from the French—*Modern Poets of France: A Bilingual Anthology* (1997).

Further Reading. ***Selected Primary Sources:*** Simpson, Louis, *The Arrivistes: Poems 1940–1949* (Paris: privately printed, 1949); ———, *At the End of the Open Road* (Middletown, CT: Wesleyan University Press, 1963); ———, *Caviare at the Funeral* (New York: Franklin Watts, 1980); ———, *Collected Poems* (New York: Paragon House, 1988); ———, *In the Room We Share* (New York: Paragon House, 1990); ———, *Out of Season* (Old Deerfield, MA: Deerfield Press, 1979); ———, *The Owner of the House: New Collected Poems* (Rochester, NY: BOA Editions, 2003); ———, *People Live Here: Selected Poems 1949–1983* (Rochester, NY: BOA Editions, 1983); ———, *Searching for the Ox* (New York: Morrow, 1976); ———, *Selected Poems* (New York: Harcourt, Brace & World, 1966). ***Selected Secondary Sources:*** Lazer, Hank, ed., *On Louis Simpson: Depths beyond Happiness* (Ann Arbor: University of Michigan Press, 1988); Lensing, George S., and Ronald Moran, *Four Poets and the Emotive Imagination: Robert Bly, James Wright, Louis Simpson, and William Stafford* (Baton Rouge: Louisiana State University Press, 1976); Moran, Ronald, *Louis Simpson* (New York: Twayne, 1972); Makuck, Peter, "The Simpson House: Sixty-One Years in Construction" (*The Hudson Review* 57.2: 335–345).

Pavlína Hácová

SLAM POETRY

Slam poetry, also known as "spoken word" or "performance poetry," is largely an American poetry phenomenon with scenes growing out of several urban metropolises in the early to mid-1980s. Slam poetry is meant to be spoken or performed—never simply read. Poetry Slams often blend multimedia performance techniques such as film, video, music, and art. Slam poets attempt to break down the boundary between academic poetry (the realm that has taken poetry away from the masses) and what they see as **commonplace** or everyday poetry. As such, their attempt to bring poetry back to the streets or masses is largely seen as a continuation and reinvention of **oral tradition**. Slam readings are usually organized as poetry matches or Slams—pitting two poets against each other. The poets try to out-duel each other while playing to audience members and judges. Through grassroots efforts, Slam poetry has become a staple of local poetry scenes in coffee houses, bars, and lounges.

Poetry Slams are attributed to poet Marc "So What" Smith, who coined the term in the mid-1980s in Chicago. Other key figures in the movement include **Sherman Alexie**, **Marvin Bell**, Reggie Gibson, **Edward Hirsch**, Jerry Quickly, Patricia Smith, Quincy Troupe, Jr., and Saul Williams, among others. Although it is difficult to narrow down such a diversity of poets and poetic interests, most Slam poets are united by a rejection of academic poetry and a celebration of poetry performance. They seek to add performance as a formal and aesthetic criterion to the making of poetry. They want to make poetry not only erudite and academic but also entertaining, liberating poetry from what they see as stuffy, static classrooms. According to founder Smith, "[Slam poetry] is about expanding the possibilities of poetry instead of limiting them, about injecting performance into the art of poetry, and most importantly about creating community amongst poets and audiences of diverse natures" (Eleveld, 116).

Slam is best thought of as an amalgamation of various strains and schools in American poetry and cultural history. Many people attribute the birth of Slam to the legacy of the **Beat poets**—specifically to **Allen Ginsberg** and also to other Beat poets, such as **Gregory Corso**, **Bob Kaufman**, and **Jack Kerouac**, who valorized spontaneous readings of their work in front of audiences. We can also see Slam's origins much earlier than this: in Walt Whitman's urging for a "democratic" art, in the everyday aesthetic of **William Carlos Williams**, in the poetry readings of **Robert Frost**, and in African American vernacular and **oral traditions**. Mostly, however, Slam poetry is an inheritor of the counter-culture of the 1960s and 1970s. Artistic and cultural movements, such as the protest movement; racial and minority movements, such as the **Black Arts Movement**; and happenings and other performance art techniques can be seen as foundational to Slam poetry. As a largely urban phenomenon, Slam poetry can also be seen to grow out of the 1970s punk and hip-hop scenes in New York, sharing the DIY ("do-it-yourself") philosophies of these underground movements. With these various precursors, Slam shares a philosophy of experimentation, revolution, and political activism. Slam seeks to challenge conventional **poetic forms**, putting pressure on the limits and boundaries of what poetry is. With its celebration of community and breakdown of the traditional boundary between audience and poet, Slam poetry shares the aesthetic agenda of the classical **avant-garde**, which, according to Peter Brger, seeks to reintegrate art with everyday life (*Theory of the Avant-Garde*).

The primary thing that Slam poets share with the historical avant-garde is the willingness to challenge the academic biases that have controlled poetry since the periods of high **modernism** and since the **New Critics** have fully canonized the modernists. Probably the main thematic preoccupation of Slam is a radical attack on traditional poetic conventions. For instance, in "Hip Hop Hollas," poet Jerry Quickley questions the scholarly bias that separates elite poetry from hip-hop music: "A scholar recently asked me about / the relevance of hip hop." To the contrary, Quickley asserts that musical practice came before institutionalized forms of poetry: "All I could say was that I remember field hollers / before the preachers got a hold a them." Quickley valorizes popular or folk practices (hip-hop and field hollers) at the expense of institutionalized or conventional practices (scholars and preachers). Slam poets believe, above all else, in the power of poetry as folk or popular artform to affect change in the world. Moreover, they hope to reawaken America's middle-class and working-class citizens to the revolutionary potential inherent in the poetic art form. Thus we have **Bob Holman**'s "Praise Poem for Slam: Why Slam Causes Pain and Is a Good Thing." Holman answers the poem's question by saying, "Because poetry is an endangered species Slam / finds and revivifies."

This "revivification," in Holman's words, had been taking place throughout the 1980s and had grown by the end of the decade to epic proportions. Marc Smith's founding of Slam during "Monday Night Poetry Readings" at Chicago's Get Me High Lounge in 1984, and afterward at The Uptown Poetry Slam at the Green Mill Bar, has established Chicago as the center of the Slam world. Developing from this seminal Chicago scene, other scenes have grown all across of the nation. Although different scenes emphasize different subject matter, they share an emphasis on a unique urban experience, a strong political stance, multiculturalism, and an ethics of activism. Important Slam scenes have developed in Boston with the help of the ardently political poetry of Lisa Buscani and Patricia Smith; in New York, where poets have come together around the Nuyorican Poets Café; and in Taos, New Mexico, where the World Heavyweight Poetry Championship was first held in 1982. This first poetry bout featured legendary Beat poet Corso against up-and-coming Tery Jacobus. That Jacobus defeated Corso in this historical first "match" served as a kind of triumph for the new scene and gave notice that Slam was here to stay. These poetic boxing matches, largely originating from Taos, have been a staple in all of the various Slam scenes. As Slam has grown in popularity to have nationwide appeal, Chicago has still remained at the center of it all, giving birth to important new scenes, such as the Asian American poetry ensemble Two Tongues, and also housing the Chicago Poetry Ensemble and important events like the National Poetry Slam.

Edward Hirsch's "Song," along with Taylor Mali's "How to Write a Political Poem," encapsulates the basic thematic and formal techniques of poetry Slams. Hirsch's poem demonstrates some of the thematic concerns of Slam poets, including a strong empathizing voice for the plights of marginalized peoples. Thus, Slam poets hope to draw attention to and through poetry and performance, making visible the lives of the culturally underrepresented and invisible: for example, minorities, sexually nonnormative groups, and other castaways from society's mainstream. Hirsch writes, "This is a song for the speechless, / the dumb, the mute and the motley." Furthermore, Mali's poem also demonstrates the key formal elements of Slam poets. Incorporating Slam poetry's emphasis on political activism and social justice, Mali's poem has a manifesto-like feel. According to Mali, a "political poem" must be "loud," have "rhyme," and be filled with "platitudes of / empowerment." We can imagine Mali performing this poem to a raucous audience: "Because this is how you write a political poem / and how you deliver it with power." This poem, along with many of the poems in the Slam tradition, is a call to action of sorts, urging audience members to become poets of their own and write political poetry. Thus the poet, the poem, and the audience all become equals, collaborators, and are urged to stand up for political action.

Perhaps Saul Williams is the best choice to begin talking about the legacy and cultural impact of Slam poetry. Widely considered the most famous and popular of Slam poets, Williams wrote and starred in a feature-length movie called *Slam* (1998). The film features Williams as Joshua, a young man trapped in the ghetto, who spends time in prison due to a drug deal. In prison he finds a way out of the ghetto through a new, truthful, gritty, and urban style of poetry called "Slam." In the film Williams performs his own hip-hop poetry. Williams's best-known poem is titled "Amethyst Rocks," which according to Marc Smith, is the "model and standard" for aspiring Slam poets. To write about the poem is really to do it a disservice because the poem's appeal lies primarily in its performance. The tight rhymes, the hip-hop stylizations, the humorous punning, and double entendre are difficult to convey on the written page. Above all, it is enjoyable to listen to "Amethyst Rocks." One can easily hear the effort and thought that Williams puts into it before a live performance. Williams's poetics differ from traditional Slam poetry, while sharing some of its characteristics. He increasingly uses parody and other forms of irony in order to subvert traditional cultural narratives. For instance, in a line like "I spoon powdered drum beats into plastic bags / sellin' kilos of kente scag," Williams gives you imagery commonly associated with drug culture, but subverts these common associations by giving a ridiculous reference ("kente scag"). Williams continually ironizes everyday experiences or common perceptions: "the Feds are also plottin' me / they're tryin' to imprison my astrology." Incredibly literate of popular culture, Williams continuously draws upon pop culture, but always with a twist or a sense of irony meant to undermine traditional conceptions. For example, he says, "i need a fix of that purple rain," mixing references to drug culture and popular music.

A unanimous winner of the 1998 Grand Jury Prize at the Sundance Film Festival, *Slam* helped to bring Slam poetry into the mainstream. It increased the popularity of Slam, causing an outburst of Slam readings in coffee shops and bars throughout the country. The increased popularity of Slam poetry has also added to growing concerns about its commercialization and commodification. Starting with Williams's 1998 film, followed by Paul Devlin's documentary *SlamNation* (1999), and, perhaps most significantly, in music producer Russell Simmons's bringing Slam poetry to television in the HBO series, "Def Poetry Jam" and "Hip Hop Poetry Jam," the increasing commercialization of Slam is apparent.

At best, we can see Slam's emphasis on performance and its reintegration of poetry into everyday life as positive in themselves, causing a growing number of established poets to rethink their attitudes toward poetry readings and performance. **Jim Carroll**, for example, has recorded a "spoken word" album, thanks in large part to the phenomenal success of Slam poetry. Carroll and other famous poets have also started to perform regularly on cable television stations MTV and VH-1. At worst, we can see the increasingly commodification of Slam as damaging to its reputation, especially when its potentials were constructed in many ways against mainstream consumer culture. In the furor, charges of selling out have become commonplace.

Insofar as its lasting influence is concerned, the jury may still be out. Although growing exponentially from audiences in the hundreds at Chicago's Green Mill to audiences in the millions on HBO's Def Poetry Series, it seems that the fever-pitch of popularity that Slam garnered in the mid- to late 1990s has since waned. Moreover, it has not yet permeated academic discourse, which (though it would certainly cause most Slam poets to scoff) might ultimately control whether it will have a significant enduring legacy.

Further Reading. ***Selected Primary and Secondary Sources:*** Algarín, Miguel, Bob Holman, and Nicole Blackman, *ALOUD: Voices from the Nuyorican Poets' Café* (New York: Owl Books, 1994); Eleveld, Mark, ed., *The Spoken Word Revolution: (slam, hip hop & the poetry of a new generation)* (Naperville, IL: Sourcebooks, 2003); Glazner, Gary Max, *Poetry Slam: The Competitive Art of Performance Poetry* (San Francisco, CA: Manic D Press, 2000); Medina, Tony, and Louis Reyes Rivera, eds., *Bum Rush the Page: A Def Poetry Jam* (New York: Three Rivers Press, 2001); Smith, Mark Kelly, and Joe Kraynak, *The Complete Idiot's Guide to Slam Poetry* (New York: Alpha Books, 2004).

Jeremy Kaye

SMALL PRESS BOOK PUBLISHING

"Small press" is a general term that alludes to a range of approaches to editing, printing, and publishing poetry. Independent, Micro, Limited Edition, Fine, Private, and the Literary Fine Press are all forms of small press publishing. There are several distinctions between small press and commercial publishers. Small presses are independently owned and operated, they print their books in limited editions out of financial necessity (typically fewer than 1,000 copies), and they often use fine materials and creative publishing formats. These books appeal to a community of loyal readers and are distributed through an organic network composed of independent bookstores and collective homepages (such as Jerrold Shiroma's Duration) and at poetry readings. Small Press Distribution (SPD) in Berkeley, California, remains at the center of small press culture in the United States. Perhaps the most important distinction between the small press and commercial press is the fact that the former are committed to bringing emerging, esoteric, or **avant-garde** poets into print, thereby altering the face of contemporary literature and perpetually redefining the aesthetic precepts and reading practices that make poetry a dynamic, evolving medium.

The first small press operation coincided with Johannes Gutenberg's invention of the printing press in Germany approximately 450 years ago. As Gutenberg reached the closing stages of the first printing of the Bible, his associate John Fust foreclosed on their venture, forcing Gutenberg out of the business. Hoping to turn a quick profit, Fust took the Bibles to Paris, where he sold several (misrepresenting them as hand-copied manuscripts) to Louis XI. The King's officials observed that individual letters were identical in appearance and claimed that the ornamental caps, in their sensuous redness, were written in blood. Fust was accused of witchcraft, imprisoned, and later freed by Louis after he disclosed the secrets of letterpress printing. From the outset, print was relatively inexpensive, and posed a threat to the longstanding monastic practice of copying by hand. Skeptics maintained that Fust was in cahoots with Satan, and to this day, "black art" remains synonymous with the practice of printing.

The printing press has been a transformative social force since its inception, and this is particularly true of its function in shaping modernist writing. In the late 1800s, the English printer, poet, artist, and social reformer William Morris complicated the distinctions between art and craft in his desire to publish luxurious books in response to the decline of print quality that had become acceptable to industrial society. At the Kelmscott Press, he designed the type, page borders, and bindings of fine books. Morris had a profound influence on the printing industry with his brilliant graphic contrast of ink with page and his elegantly designed type. In the era of **modernism**, writers who served as both editors and publishers (William Butler Yeats, **Ezra Pound**, and Virginia Woolf, among the most influential) had more control over their textual production than did their literary predecessors. Following Pound's infamous formulation of 1913, the *printed* poem is an image that is "an intellectual and emotional complex in an instant of time." Responding to the popularity of the genteel and typically innocuous poetry of the twentieth century's second decade, Pound and Wyndham Lewis published the first issue of *Blast* on June 14, 1914. The unadorned cover announces its assault on Victorian order and ornamentation. "BLAST" appears in a bold sans serif against a violent pink page—its angle reminiscent of a cannon or missile (missive) launcher.

In 1927 the wealthy expatriates Harry and Caresse Crosby were living in Paris when they established the Black Sun Press, known for its beautifully bound, handset books. Early on, the Crosbys commissioned the fine printer Roger Lescaret to produce Harry Crosby's *Red Skeletons*, with illustrations by Hans Henning von Voight. The Black Sun Press continued to publish Crosby's poems, lavish reprints of obscure editions of the editors' choosing, and most importantly, magnificent first editions by D.H. Lawrence, **Charles Olson**, **Hart Crane**, James Joyce, and **Archibald MacLeish.** In 1929 the Crosbys published fourteen books before Harry Crosby's tragic suicide in December, and Caresse Crosby went on running the Press in his wake.

James Laughlin, founder of New Directions, issued his first anthology in 1936. Laughlin recollects Pound's advice: "He had been seeing my poems for months and had ruled them hopeless. He urged me to finish Harvard and then do 'something' useful." Following the first anthologies, New Directions began publishing experimentalist novels, plays, poetry, and short story collections, including works by Pound, **William Carlos Williams**, and Tennessee Williams as well as a wide variety of translations of Apollinaire, Rilke, and Lorca.

Using a hand press, Harry Duncan began publishing books of contemporary poetry under The Cummington Press imprint at the Cummington School of the Arts in Cummington, Massachusetts, in 1939. Duncan's refined typographic practices set a precedent for generations of small press operations in the Midwest, including The Stone Wall, Perishable Press Limited, and Toothpaste Press. Duncan has published William Carlos Williams, **Wallace Stevens**, and **Armand Schwerner**, among other innovators. In both its historical and conceptual engagement with postmodern aesthetics, the Cummington Press transcends the hiatus between the eras of American modernism and **postmodernism**, endowing writers such as Stevens and Williams with a visual form that would cast their words in a timely, yet timeless mode.

Five centuries after Gutenberg gave rise to the printing press, his country was leveled, and the first photocomposition devices (the French Photon and Intertype's Fotosetter) made their debut. The principles of printing with moveable type have undergone relatively little change since the practice's inception in 1454, but by the time the atomic dust began to settle, the handpress was nestled comfortably under a veil of obsolescence. In the aftermath of the unimaginable, poets and printers were simultaneously reconfiguring the possibilities and limits of expression within the space of the printed page—and beyond. In the 1950s, typeface masters for photocomposition were produced on film.

Beatrice Warde's controversial essay "The Crystal Goblet, or Printing Should be Invisible" made its appearance in London less than a decade after World War II. Warde metaphorically presents the reader with two goblets of wine, the first goblet made "of solid gold, wrought in the most exquisite patterns." The second is a transparent construction "of crystal-clear glass, thin as a bubble." Warde's advocacy for a return to the precious transparency of Victorian print is thinly veiled. She succinctly explains the moral of her allegory: "if you are a member of that vanishing tribe, the amateurs of fine vintages, you will choose the crystal, because everything about it is calculated to reveal rather than hide the beautiful thing which it was meant to contain." Over fifty years have passed, and transparency remains the ruling convention of typographic practice.

Few major American publishers of the pre-war years were eager to embrace radical poetries or politics with a necessary urgency. Jack London's command in 1906, "Let us not destroy those wonderful machines that produce efficiency and cheaply. Let us control them. Let us profit by their efficiency and cheapness. Let us run them for ourselves," captures the spirit and motivations behind most small press initiatives. Frances Butler has evocatively written of Poltroon Press, "Instead of collectibles we have produced our own lives, lives which are their own satisfaction, not defined by exchange for money, power, or the trappings of a glorious career." In many respects, the impetus for independent publishing in the postwar years was not unlike that of preceding decades, nor even of the eras leading to the industrial revolution—a minority of writers working outside of the mainstream literary milieu took publishing into their own hands.

The Untide Press was conceived in the midst of a broken world. **William Everson** was stationed in a conscientious objectors' camp at Waldport, Oregon, where he published poetry in an unofficial newsletter, *The Untide,* launched in 1943. In a time of unrest, Everson and company produced this alternative periodical in a response against the camp's official newsletter, *The Tide.* The purpose of *The Untide* was decisive: "This is the time of destruction, against which we offer the creative act." Everson and company ran the mimeograph machine to produce Everson's own *X War Elegies,* among other small volumes. **Kenneth Patchen**'s *An Astonished Eye Looks out of the Air* (1945) was the last book Everson printed in the company of the conscientious objectors at the camp. When World War II came to an official halt, Everson moved to Berkeley and acquired a Washington hand press. Patchen's book has gained credence as a benchmark in the small press revolution.

In 1955, **Lawrence Ferlinghetti** launched City Lights Publishers, paving the way for the infamous Pocket Poets Series associated with writers of the **Beat** generation. City Lights continues to publish a wide range of writers and genres, exhibiting an ongoing "commitment to innovative and progressive ideas, and its resistance to forces of conservatism and censorship" that began with the publication of **Allen Ginsberg**'s controversial poem *Howl.*

In 1946 poet, playwright, and printer Claude Fredericks met Anaïs Nin, who offered him work at her press. He left the Obelisk Press half a year later, and in December established The Banyan Press in New York with the writer Milton Saul. Banyan published sumptuous books by **Gertrude Stein** and **Wallace Stevens**, and afterFredericks began to accept longer commissions in 1958, Banyan printed **Robert Duncan**'s poems, *Letters,* for **Jonathan Williams**'s Jargon Society. Williams was a former student of **Charles Olson** at **Black Mountain** College in North Carolina. After receiving a small inheritance while stationed in Germany, Williams had Olson's *Maximus Poems I-X* printed in Stuttgart, a landmark among the many innovative publications issued by Jargon. The Black Mountain Review was edited by **Robert Creeley** and was printed by the same jobbers that produced Creeley's Divers' Press books in Mallorca, Spain. Divers' published Canadian poet Irving Layton, Japanese poet Katué Kitasono, **Paul Blackburn**, **Larry Eigner**, and Robert Duncan as well as Creeley's own poems.

Robert Hawley met Charles Olson when he enrolled as a student at Black Mountain College in 1956—an instant before it closed. Olson (not unlike Pound's advice to the young Laughlin) was discouraging of Hawley's desire to become a poet and suggested that publishing would be a more productive vocation. This initial series of Oyez publications by Hawley consists of ten broadsides by Everson, **Gary Snyder**, Olson, **Michael McClure**, and others. The first Oyez book was a collection of poetry by David Meltzer. Not being a printer himself, Hawley sought out the skills of Graham Mackintosh, who worked for other acclaimed California presses such as John Martin's Black Sparrow. Black Sparrow has published almost all of **Charles Bukowski**'s writings, as well as the works of writers as disparate as **David Antin**, **Michael Palmer**, **Ed Dorn**, **Jack Spicer**, Paul Blackburn, and Richard Grossinger.

Keith and **Rosmarie Waldrop**, poets, translators, and founders of Burning Deck Press, have written:

> Since being eclectic is not always taken for a virtue, we would note that our eclecticism—besides simply reflecting personal ranges of appreciation—is based on an inability to believe that the history of, for instance, poetry can possibly be clear before the poems are written. It is not denying the importance of 'movements,' to insist that there is another importance in moving beside or apart from them. After all, there are many judgments, none of them the last. ("Forty years of Burning Deck Press, 1961–2001")

Together, the Waldrops have published sturdy and affordable first-edition poetry by established and emerging writers of three generations, including books by **Jackson Mac Low**, Lisa Jarnot, **Lyn Hejinian**, and **Peter Gizzi**.

The establishment of various centers for the book—venues for poetry readings and publishing alike, such as the Poetry Project at St. Mark's Church in the Bowery or Clifford Burke's open studio at the Cranium Press in San Francisco—contributed to the economic and technical viability of bringing the private voice into the public sphere with efficiency, flair, and immediacy. Fascinating changes in "typographic typology" (as Alastair Johnston puts it in his *Musing on the Vernacular*) were taking place along the West Coast. Joe Dunn and Graham Mackintosh began making books and broadsides under the White Rabbit impression in 1957, a year before Dave Hazelwood published **John Wieners**'s *The Hotel Wentley Poems,* the first book to appear under the sign of the Auerhahn Press. Cranium has published hundreds of books and broadsides, including works by Asa Benveniste, Robert Duncan, **Theodor Enslin**, Michael McClure, David Meltzer, Lewis Welch, and Ferlinghetti. It was at Burke's studio that Michael Myers and Holbrook Teter met and later conceived of the renegade Zephyrus Image Press, which flourished under the growth of the NEA under the Nixon Administration. They published Tom Raworth, **Tom Clark**, Jeremy Prynne, Michael McClure, Louis Garcia, Bob Callahan, and Lewis MacAdams in *Bean News,* as well as in chapbooks, broadsides, and ephemera.

The year 1963 brought the Vancouver Poetry Conference and the emergence of conceptual artist Ed Ruscha's *Twenty-Six Gas Stations,* a milestone in the history of the artists' book. The Broadside Press (1965–1975) was established by **Dudley Randall** in Detroit. He described the place of poetry in the **Black Arts Movement** in broadside number 28: "In the present circumstances, it helps in the search for black identity, reinforces black pride and black unity, and in helping to create the soul, the consciousness, and the conscience of black folk." The broadside has a public quality, and the words of **Gwendolyn Brooks**, James A. Emanuel, **Etheridge Knight**, Raymond Patterson, and Kuweka Amiri Mwandishe were coupled with striking calligraphy and complimentary illustrations produced by prominent black artists. After Andrew Hoyem's partnership with Hazelwood came to a head, he began working with the legendary Bay Area printer Robert Grabhorn. Together, they printed an excess of fifty editions by Olson, **Ted Berrigan**, Pound, Creeley, H.D., Ginsberg, and **Ronald Johnson** among others before Grabhorn's death in 1973. Shortly thereafter, Hoyem established the Arion Press, specializing in deluxe limited editions that often contain original works by prominent artists.

The Five Trees Press was established when five women (Cheryl Miller, Kathy Walkup, Ellen Callahan, Cameron Bunker and Jamie Robles) set up shop in a San Francisco storefront. The proprietors were particularly interested in publishing writing by women, and they produced glorious first editions of **Djuna Barnes**'s *After the Fall of Satan* (1974), H.D.'s *The Poet and the Dancer* (1975), Susan McDonald's *Dangerous as Daughters* (1976), and **Denise Levertov**'s *Modulations for Solo Voice* (1977), in addition to titles by Paul Metcalf, Olson, and Gino Clay. Also, in 1973 Tree Swenson and Sam Hamill moved the Copper Canyon Press from Denver to the grounds of old Fort Worden in Port Townsend. Copper Canyon remains one of the largest small press operations in America.

By the late 1970s, works by subversive Bay Area presses such as Zephyrus Image and Poltroon had been displayed at the "Printer's Choice Exhibition" hosted by the Grolier Club (America's oldest and largest society for bibliophiles), and "The Page as Alternative Space" exhibition had gone up at the Franklin Furnace Archive. Frances Butler and Alastair Johnston established Poltroon on April Fool's Day, 1975, on the ground floor of their home in Berkeley. The origin of their press's name is "lost in the labyrinthine layers of lore beyond their motto, from Horace, '*Dulce est desipere in loco*' ('Tis sweet to play the fool on meet occasions)." Their Modern Poets Series introduced vibrant books by Larry Fagin, Tom Raworth, Tom Clark, **Phillip Whalen**, Jim Nesbit, Darrell Gray, Jess, Dawn Kolokithas, and Lucia Berlin.

Douglas Messerli's alternative publishing venture, Sun & Moon Press, is dedicated to **experimental poetry**, fiction, and drama; it began in 1976 in College Park, Maryland, and is now associated with **Language poetry**, a movement historicized after **Charles Bernstein** and **Bruce Andrews** established the influential *L=A=N=G=U=A=G=E* mimeograph magazine. James Sherry's Roof Books, based in New York City, has published trade editions by other poets associated with this movement, including Fiona Templeton, Abigail Child, and Nick Piombino. In 1984 the poet and book artist Charles Alexander founded Chax Press after his move from Madison, Wisconsin, where he studied with Walter Hamady. Alexander writes:

> The work of Chax Press is directly related to (my) work as a poet and participation in specific currents of contemporary American poetry, primarily movements that have included Black Mountain Poetry, Language Poetry, and the works of many independent writers invigorated by these two movements, if not a part of them. Yet the work of Chax Press is fiercely independent and can not be classified according to any limited poetic identity. (n.p.)

Granary Books, established by Steve Clay, is one of the most productive publishers of books of enduring quality and experimentation today. Charles Bernstein has written:

> At Granary, books are not neutral containers but are invested with a life of their own, conceived as objects first and foremost, entering the world not as the discardable shell of some other story but piping their own tunes on their own instruments. Nothing is taken for granted—the binder is as much a star as the printer or writer. The design is an extension of (not secondary to) the content, just as the content is an extension of the design. (n.p.)

Granary has published a wide range of artists and writers, including **Joe Brainard**, **John Cage**, **Johanna Drucker,** Alison Knowles, **Jerome Rothenberg**, and John Zorn**.**

When considering the spectrum of forces acting on the transitional face of contemporary poetry, the revolutionary value of the small press merits full acknowledgement. Ironically, texts that now appear in glossy anthologies at university bookstores and corporate retailers would not have transcended their subaltern status were it not for the desires of small press publishers such as those mentioned previously. One need only glance at the credits of anthologies such as **Ron Silliman**'s *In the American Tree*, Donald Alan's *New American Poetry*, or Paul Hoover's *Postmodern American Poetry* to confirm that the first editions were indeed largely the products of small literary presses. The socialization of these texts is the fundamental attribute of the collective capital, labor, and distribution methods initiated by poets and publishers.

Further Reading. ***Selected Primary and Secondary Sources:*** Alexander, Charles, "Beginnings, Education, and Support" (Chax Press, 2005, www.chax.org/history.htm [accessed 1 March 2005]); Badaracco, Claire Hoertz, *Trading Words: Poetry, Typography, and Illustrated Books in the Modern Literary Economy* (Baltimore, MD, and London: The Johns Hopkins University Press, 1995); Bernstein, Charles, "Claymation: A Reader's Guide" (Granary Books, 2005, www.granarybooks.com/books/when_will_the_book/bernstein.html [accessed 1 March 2005]); Bornstein, George, ed., *Representing Modernist Texts: Editing as Interpretation* (Ann Arbor: The University of Michigan Press, 1988); Clay, Steven, and Rodney Phillips, *A Secret Location on the Lower East Side: Adventures in Writing, 1960–1980* (New York: The New York Public Library and Granary Books, 1998); Dana, Robert, ed., *Against the Grain, Interviews with Maverick American Publishers* (Iowa City: University of Iowa Press, 1986); Johnston, Alastair, and Frances Butler, *Trance and Recalcitrance: 20 Years of Poltroon Press: The Private Voice in the Public Realm* (Berkley, CA: Poltroon Press, 1995); Laughlin, James, "A Brief History of New Directions" (New Directions Publishing Corp., 2005, www. wwnorton.com/nd/BriefHistory.htm [accessed 1 March 2005]); McGann, Jerome, *Black Riders: The Visible Language of Modernism* (Princeton, NJ: Princeton University Press, 1993); Perloff, Marjorie, *Radical Artifice: Writing Poetry in the Age of Media* (Chicago and London: University of Chicago Press, 1991); Sullivan, James D., *On the Walls and in the Streets: Poetry Broadsides of the 1960s* (Urbana: University of Illinois Press, 1997); Waldrop, Keith, and Rosmarie Waldrop, *A Century in Two Decades* (Providence, RI: Burning Deck Press, 1981 http://www.brown.edu/facilities/university_library/exhibits/burningdeck/); Warde, Beatrice, "The Crystal Goblet, or Printing Should Be Invisible" (Typo-L, 2005, gmunch.home.pipeline.com/typo-L/misc/ward.htm [accessed 1 March 2005]).

Kyle Schlesinger

SMITH, ANNA YOUNG (1756–1780)

Anna Young Smith, niece of **Elizabeth Graeme Fergusson**, published only one poem in her lifetime. "An Elegy to the Memory of the American Volunteers" appeared in the *Pennsylvania Magazine* (1775) shortly after the Massachusetts Bay Militia and British troops exchanged fire in Lexington, Massachusetts, on April 19, 1775. Smith's poetry addresses a broad range of topics, both personal and political. She wrote about family, gratitude, grief, and sensibility. She also composed political pieces, such as "Elegy" and "On Reading Swift's Works" (1774).

Smith was born on November 5, 1756. Her mother, Jane Graeme Young, died when Smith was an infant. Smith and her brother, John, were raised by their mother's sister, Elizabeth Graeme Fergusson, at the Graeme family estate, Graeme Park, near Philadelphia. From Smith's writing, both poetry and prose, one can infer a close relationship between aunt and niece. "Ode to Gratitude" (1770) expresses Smith's thanks to Fergusson for care of the "orphan" Smith: "Teach me to thank the gracious maid, / Who rear'd my infant years." Fergusson, a leading intellectual of the day, most likely influenced Smith's writing and politics. Fergusson's writing provides much of the biographical information about Smith that exists today. For example, Fergusson once observed that her niece was a Whig. This progressive political stance is supported by themes in Smith's poetry.

In "Elegy," Smith demonstrates strong political opinions. In the poem she addresses the political conflict between Britain and the North American colonies. She reprimands Britain for the killing of American militiamen in April of 1775: "This deed in bloody characters enroll'd / Shall stain the luster of their [Britain's] former name." The language of the poem confirms that Smith is a revolutionary, as she addresses the fallen soldiers: "Your memories, dear to every free-born mind, / Shall need no monument your fame to raise." Her discussion in the poem of her "much-lov'd country," of its "native skies," and of "liberty and peace" reveals strong patriotic feelings.

In "Swift's Works," Smith displays an early feminist attitude. The poem takes to task Irish writer Jonathan Swift for his mistreatment of women in his work: "Say when thou dipp'st thy keenest pen in gall, / Why must it still on helpless woman fall?" A fine piece of rhetorical writing, "Swift's Works" expresses admiration of Swift's wit while criticizing the sexist content of his compositions: "And what we now admire, we then had loved . . . / Awakes too oft our anger or disgust." As the piece was obviously not meant to influence Swift himself (he died in 1745), Smith must have had a different motive in mind. The poem advises its reader to allow "the milder virtues [to fill] thy breast" and to "on vice thy lash bestow." The poem could be read as a primer for the virtuous behavior of men during the revolutionary period. Similarly, "Ode to Sensibility" (1774) provides more gentle guidance to its readers. The poem argues the necessity of sensibility as a personal virtue: "Without thee Beauty's lifeless form / But coldly we approve."

Smith's poetry was published under a pseudonym, "Sylvia." Most of the other magazine poets of the late 1700s similarly used pseudonyms when publishing their work. On November 30, 1775, Smith married Dr. William Smith of Philadelphia; her father did not consent to the match. The majority of Smith's extant poems were composed prior to her marriage, before she was twenty years old. Most scholars believe that Smith died on April 3, 1780, at the age of twenty-four, shortly after the birth of her third child. However, there is some scholarly disagreement about the date and cause of her death. After Smith's death, eight more of her poems appeared in print, in the *Universal Asylum and Columbian Magazine.* Many of Smith's poems were recorded by Fergusson in Fergusson's **commonplace** book, there preserved for future generations. Despite her death at such a young age, Smith composed poetry that demonstrates a broad range in both style and content.

Further Reading. ***Selected Secondary Sources:*** Cowell, Pattie, *Women Poets in Pre-Revolutionary America, 1650–1775: An Anthology* (Troy, NY: Whitston, 1981); Davis, Cynthia J., and Kathryn West, *Women Writers in the United States: A Timeline of Literary, Cultural, and Social History* (New York: Oxford University Press, 1996); Harris, Sharon M., *American Women Writers to 1800* (New York: Oxford University Press, 1996); Mainiero, Lina, *American Women Writers: A Critical Reference Guide from Colonial Times to the Present,* vol. 4 (New York: Frederick Ungar, 1979–1994); Watts, Emily Stipes, *The Poetry of American Women from 1632 to 1945* (Austin: Texas University Press, 1977).

Katie Rose Guest

SMITH, CAPTAIN JOHN (1580–1631)

Captain John Smith was a soldier, a geographer, a cartographer, an ethnographer, a governor, a historian, an autobiographer, and a poet. Though Smith never actually held the rank of captain in the service of his king, James I, he was prone to exaggerate, and he continued to refer to himself as "Captain" throughout his life. Smith's writings cover a wide range of topics and move between various genres, demonstrating his great versatility. Poems often interrupt prose, blurring the lines between poetry and other genres. Although he wrote only a handful of poems, he would become a key figure for later American poets, particularly **Charles Olson**, who emphasized writing out of an experience of America's geography and history.

Smith was born in Willoughby, Lincolnshire, England, in 1580. His father, George Smith, was a farmer and a member of the gentry. Because of a close friendship with their landlord, Lord Willoughby de Eresby, the Smith family enjoyed special privileges, including educational opportunities for John. His success in school helped to secure an apprenticeship with an established merchant, but Smith soon found merchant life tedious, and around 1596 he left his apprenticeship to become a solider. Over the next decade Smith fought in the Netherlands, Belgium, France, and Eastern Europe. During this period he also participated in piracy on the Mediterranean, traveled extensively from Russia to Morocco, and was enslaved in Constantinople. Smith describes this early period of his life in *The True Travels, Adventures, and Observations of Captaine John Smith* (1630). When he returned to England, Smith was awarded membership in the governing council in Virginia, and in 1606 he sailed with the Virginia Company. After reaching North America and founding Jamestown in 1607, the colonists encountered numerous problems, including food shortages, Native American raids, and disagreements between members of the governing council. Later that same year Smith was captured by Native Americans and sent to the Algonquian Indian chief,

Powhatan, Pocahontas's father. Though in *The Generall Historie of . . . Virginia* (1608) Smith claims that Pocahontas "got his head in her armes, and laid her owne upon his to save him from death," this is one of Smith's many embellishments. As president of Jamestown's governing council, Smith instituted programs that strengthened defense, enforced laws, and increased agriculture. While these measures did improve life in Jamestown, Smith's rivals forced him to give up his office, and he returned to England. His experiences in Virginia are described in *A True Relation of . . . Virginia* and *A Map of Virginia* (1612). *The Generall Historie of Virginia, New England, and the Summer Isles* (1624) includes an account of these experiences as well, but it also describes Smith's last visit to North America. During this final trip, Smith surveyed (and named) New England. He spent the final sixteen years of his life in England, writing. Despite the wide range of his work, Smith did not profit from his writings. He died in poverty on June 21, 1631.

Poems are scattered throughout Smith's work, but most of them are not his own. Rather, he includes excerpts from poems he admires, and he prefaces much of his writing with poems written in his honor. This was not uncommon in his day, and Smith himself wrote at least two commendatory verses—one for engineer and gunner Robert Norton, and another for poet John Taylor. In his poem "The Sea Marke," which is found in *Advertisements for the Unexperienced Planters of New England, or Any Where* (1631), Smith commemorates his own life, portraying himself as a "marke," or warning, for sailors who might be passing through dangerous waters. While this poem reflects the thirst for adventure that characterized Smith's life, it also hints at his sense of failure: "If in or outward you be bound, / doe not forget to sound; / Neglect of that was cause of this / to steare amisse." Olson includes this poem in *The Maximus Poems*, and in "Captain John Smith" Olson writes, "Why I sing John Smith is this, that the *geographic*, the sudden *land* of the place, is in there" (319). In addition to praising "The Sea Marke," Olson celebrated Smith's attention to language and his naming capabilities. Smith named numerous North American locales, and his work often has a lexicographical element. *A Sea Grammar* (1627), a work on seamanship, pays particular attention to the terminology used in sailing, and *A Map of Virginia* includes a list of key Native American words. Smith is also celebrated in **Henry David Thoreau**'s *Cape Cod* and **Hart Crane**'s *The Bridge*.

Further Reading. ***Selected Primary Source:*** Smith, John, *The Complete Works of Captain John Smith (1580–1631)*, 3 vols., ed. Philip L. Barbour (Chapel Hill: University of North Carolina Press, 1986). ***Selected Secondary Sources:*** Barbour, Philip L., *The Three Worlds of Captain John Smith* (Boston: Houghton Mifflin, 1964); Lemay, J.A. Leo, *The American Dream of Captain John Smith* (Charlottesville: University Press of Virginia, 1991); Olson, Charles, "Captain John Smith" and "Five Foot Four, but Smith Was a Giant," in *Collected Prose*, eds. Donald Allen and Benjamin Friedlander (Berkeley: University of California Press, 1997, 318–323).

Sasha Steensen

SMITH, DAVE (1942–)

Labeled by many critics as a "giant" of Southern poetry in the second half of the twentieth century, Dave Smith has cemented his reputation as a writer with tremendous appeal nationwide. His work has fruitfully been compared to the writers he often mentions with great fondness—**Richard Hugo**, **James Wright**, **James Dickey**, **Robert Penn Warren**, and **Charles Wright**, among others. Recognized early on as a prolific writer in the vein of **Walt Whitman**, Smith has produced a dozen books of poetry marked with a distinctive voice that fuses the visionary with a Southern back-woods sensibility. They are written in a plain-spoken style yet also feature hyphenated tangling à la Gerard Manley Hopkins, **Robert Lowell**, or Warren (e.g., "Swamp-sheen, a dew-gilt mast" and "Plank-seep blood-freckles them"). These are poems unabashed by male desire or the vulgar manifestations of it, poems that champion storytelling and "living figures" above all. Smith regards poems as the playing out of a Yeatsian internal struggle that results in what he calls "a gesture of acceptance."

David Jeddie Smith (who also goes by the pseudonym Smith Cornwell) was born in Portsmouth, Virginia, on December 19, 1942. He attended the University of Virginia, where he earned his BA in 1965; he then received an MA from Southern Illinois University in 1969. After being drafted into service in the U.S. Air Force during the Vietnam War, and serving a full tour of duty from 1969 to 1972, he returned to graduate school, completing his doctorate at Ohio University in 1976. Before his long-term position at Louisiana State University, Smith taught in several locations: the University of Utah, SUNY–Binghamton, the University of Florida, and Virginia Commonwealth University. He currently occupies the Elliott Coleman Chair of Poetry at Johns Hopkins University, and has been involved in the revival of the *Johns Hopkins Review*, last published in the 1950s. Smith was twice runner-up for the Pulitzer Prize in poetry, and was short-listed for the National Book Critics Circle Award in 1979. He has held fellowships from the National Endowment for the Arts twice, the Guggenheim Foundation, the Bread Loaf Writers' Conference, and the Lyndhurst Foundation.

Although Smith has forever thought of himself as a poet, he has also written fiction, and he has published one novel. *Onliness* is a richly textured and comic allegorical tale, whose protagonist, the unassuming giant

Billy Luke Tomson, navigates a broad cast of characters, from his employer, a loud-mouthed, conspiracy buff auto-shop owner, to a tellingly named love interest, Promise Land. Smith has continued to write fiction in spurts, including a recent stint at the Yaddo colony.

Smith spent twelve years as co-editor of the *Southern Review.* In thinking about being a poet and an editor simultaneously, he commented in an interview with Ethan Gilsdorf that other such poet-editors—including his forebear at the *Southern Review,* Warren, as well as **Allen Tate** at the *Sewanee Review,* **Howard Moss** at the *New Yorker,* Daniel Halpern at *Antaeus,* and David Bottoms at *Five Points*—have benefited from the convergence of roles in that "it is natural on one hand to stick to your aesthetic convictions in what you accept and on the other hand one wants to stay up to date, even ahead of date" (Gilsdorf). As editor of the *Southern Messenger Poets* at the Louisiana State University Press, Smith published a range of poets hailing from Southern states: **Fred Chappell**, **Jay Wright**, Lisel Mueller, **Marilyn Nelson**, Daniel Hoffman, and Judy Jordan.

Smith's early poetry in *The Fisherman's Whore* (1974) and *Cumberland Station* (1977) is thoroughly regional in its outlook, rhythms, and subject matter, capturing the essence of a particular place. It is a place where "Calm as a snake, the Bay / moves, phosphor on dark coils," where one can find a boy "among the broken hulls" of boats, men grunting, "hammerheaded." Smith's fourth collection, *Goshawk, Antelope* (1979), bears the imprint of his change of scenery as a consequence of short-term academic contracts outside of Virginia and the South. This poetry takes on the task of mimetically rendering the landscape, although always in reference to the Virginia of his childhood; even the inverted Apollo and Daphne story of "Hawktree" invokes Southern flora.

In 1981 Smith published two full-length collections, *Dream Flights* and *Homage to Edgar Allan Poe.* The latter reflects Smith's growing conviction that while Tate was correct in declaring that the South must generate its own literature, the true progenitor of Southern poetry was the Richmond-raised **Edgar Allan Poe**. Indeed, Smith's relation to the South is summed up in the title poem, which tells how as a bookish fourteen-year-old he was excluded from "nekkid" swimming, partly by social dictum, partly by choice. This is the age-old story of the isolation of the poet. He explains in the poem how he climbed some rocks nearby "because I wanted to *see*" and, racing for his life after seeing a couple copulating in the bushes, he wishes that he "was not weird," that he was "not a son of a bitch / flung like spit into the universe."

In a similar, somewhat contrarian stance in the collection *Gray Soldiers* (1984), Smith covers a subject previously untouched in his poetry, the legacy of the Civil War. For example, the quandaries of a father regarding his children's education are rendered with sharp clarity in "Night Traffic, Near Winchester, Virginia," where the speaker recalls his own father stopping at Winchester for food, and to pay respects to the Confederate memorials. Now, his own children in tow, the speaker passes by the memorial, telling them—as much as himself—"we'll stop another time."

Smith's poems of the late 1980s and early 1990s appear in *Cuba Night* and *Fate's Kite.* The former book reveals a poet honest in his self-estimation, setting himself against the political commitments of Neruda and his peers in the Vietnam Era, much in the way that **Seamus Heaney**, whose work Smith admires, has done with Irish politics. He again settles into what he calls the "antipastoral" mode from *The Roundhouse Voices,* with the anger of losing a half-born pinto set in juxtaposition to Cold War Era fighter jets roaring overhead.

Fate's Kite (1996) is made up of poems similar to those **John Hollander** termed "thirteeners" in his 1983 collection *Powers of Thirteen*—thirteen-line poems—the exception being that Smith's poems hover around iambic pentameter, whereas Hollander was committed to thirteen-syllable lines. Smith's poems have strong resonances—with Lowell's extended trilogy of unrhymed sonnets (*History, The Dolphin, For Lizzie and Harriet*); with their predecessors, the volumes titled *Notebook*; with Heaney's liberties of sound in the Glanmore sonnet sequences; and with the work of his long-standing friend Charles Wright.

Smith's two "new and selected" collections, *The Roundhouse Voices* (1985) and *The Wick of Memory* (2000), show him at work in the Whitman tradition ceaselessly revising previously published work. For example, the aforementioned section, "Nekkid" from the "Homage to Edgar Allan Poe" sequence, shows signs of an ear seeking greater confluence of sound and image ("the nearly white streaks / of foam" becomes "the thick pollution of foam"), and the drama of the concluding scene is magnified with a glance (for example, "while underneath her face went from flat to a grin. She grinned as he hurried" becomes "while I watched her face roll toward me and wink. / She grinned, whispered, while he plunged"). But these collections also contain major new works, such as "The Roundhouse Voices," an elegiac piece for Smith's uncle, set in the train yard: "Words we all we ever were and they did us / no damn good. Do you hear that?" The uselessness of the lyric against death is a common enough element of the elegy, but the imperiousness of the demand stands out. In *Little Boats, Unsalvaged,* Smith's latest collection of verse, his poetry exhibits a new brevity and clarity, as when he describes how "his keys poke my pocket like a need. / Still, I don't want to leave" ("In the Library").

Smith continues to write criticism in addition to his poetry. Helen Vendler has characterized his critical work as moving between a "lay sermon" and the "academic," and as being marked by a "refusal to take a single position or to accept a single form of critical writing"; in her assessment of *Local Assays*, Vendler observes that Smith's writing challenges genre: "Is an essay on poetry an anecdotal conversation between friends, or a critical description, or an exhortation to a higher self-scrutiny? Does it descend from the familiar letter, from the gloss on the sacred text, or from the sermon?" ("Looking for Poetry in America," 54–55).

Smith's newest book of essays, due out in 2006 from Louisianna State University Press, to be titled *Hunting Men: A Life in the Life of Poetry*, covers familiar territory—Poe, Dickey, Warren, Whitman—but also considers contemporary poets such as **Stephen Dunn**, **William Matthews**, and **Stephen Dobyns**. According to Smith, "The joy is in the writing, in the present moment, not in what is on the horizon. And it is, it must be, entirely personal, writing to the self's sense of what matters" (Gilsdorf, n.p.). His writing—whether poetry or prose—reflects this attitude both in its subject matter and its stylistic elegance.

Further Reading: ***Selected Primary Sources:*** Smith, Dave, *Cumberland Station* (Urbana: University of Illinois Press, 1976); ———, *Dream Flights* (Urbana: University of Illinois Press, 1981); ———, *Fate's Kite: Poems, 1991–1995* (Baton Rouge: Louisiana State University Press, 1995); ———, *The Fisherman's Whore* (Athens: Ohio University Press, 1974); ———, *Goshawk, Antelope* (Urbana: University of Illinois Press, 1979); ———, *Homage to Edgar Allan Poe* (Baton Rouge: Louisiana State University Press, 1981); ———, *Little Boats, Unsalvaged: Poems, 1992-2004* (Baton Rouge: Louisiana State University Press, 2005); ———, *Local Assays: On Contemporary American Poetry* (Urbana: University of Illinois Press, 1985); ———, *Onliness* (Baton Rouge: Louisiana State University Press, 1981); ———, *The Roundhouse Voices: Selected and New Poems* (New York: Harper & Row, 1985); ———, *The Wick of Memory: New and Selected Poems, 1974–2000* (Baton Rouge: Louisiana State University Press, 2000). ***Selected Secondary Sources:*** Gilsdorf, Ethan, "Dave Smith on Twelve Years of Editing the *Southern Review*" (*Poets & Writers*, http://www.pw.org/mag/dq_smith.htm); Vendler, Helen, "Looking for Poetry in America" (*New York Review of Books* 32.17 [7 November 1985]: 53–60); ———, "Oh I Admire and Sorrow" in *Part of Nature, Part of Us* (Cambridge: Harvard University Press, 1980), 289–302.

Douglas Basford

SMITH, ELIZABETH OAKES PRINCE (1806–1893)

Elizabeth Oakes Smith was a poet, essayist, novelist, lecturer, and women's rights advocate who achieved considerable reknown in the 1840s and 1850s for her romantic **narrative long poem** "The Sinless Child" (1842), which **Edgar Allan Poe**, among others, admired for its beauty, scope, and "novelty" (if not necessarily for its rigor). She was also known for a series of feminist lectures and essays collected under the title *Woman and Her Needs* (1851). The latter book has been identified, along with the work of her contemporary, **Margaret Fuller**, as an influential source for later feminist and suffragist writings in America. Oakes Smith's reputation as a political writer, in fact, has often overshadowed her accomplishments as a poet, novelist, and author of children's stories, as well as her contributions to nineteenth-century writing about Native Americans.

Elizabeth Oakes Prince was born on August 12, 1806, in North Yarmouth, Maine. Her father, a sea captain, died at sea when she was two, after which her mother remarried and settled in Portland. A traditionalist and religious conservative, her mother urged Elizabeth's early marriage to the thirty-one-year-old Seba Smith, a writer and newspaper editor, when she was only sixteen. She had six sons, four of whom survived to adulthood. Oakes Smith later wrote about her resentment of this forced marriage in a number of essays advocating more "equitable" unions based on love, mutual respect, and financial independence (Rose, 208). In addition to raising her children, Oakes Smith managed a household of servants and apprentices, assisted her husband with editorial duties, and contributed poetry and essays to his publications. In 1837, as a result of bad investments and a stock market panic, Seba Smith lost his fortune. Two years later the family moved to New York, where both husband and wife hoped to find success as writers.

Although Seba Smith earned some recognition for his humorous *Jack Downing Letters*, it was Oakes Smith who established herself, both as a literary figure and as the principal breadwinner in the family. After the success of "The Sinless Child," which she published under the name "Mrs. Seba Smith," Oakes Smith adopted a number of pseudonyms, including "Ernest Helfenstein" (a character in one of her novels), "Oakes Smith," and eventually, "Elizabeth Oakes Smith." She even managed to have her sons' names legally changed to "Oakesmith." Through the 1840s Oakes Smith produced three volumes of **verse**, a number of children's stories, and two serialized novels. In the 1850s she discovered the financial and political benefit of public lectures, and began her career as an influential voice for such causes as abolition, women's rights, educational reform, universal suffrage, and other progressive movements. She was one of the first American women to speak on the prestigious Lyceum circuit, which typically featured such notables as **Ralph Waldo Emerson** and Henry Ward Beecher. Oakes Smith was also a delegate to several women's rights conventions in the 1850s. In the late 1850s and 1960s, she continued to write essays and fiction, particularly adventure stories and romantic tales of

Indian captivity, which, while popular, also challenged the racial and gender assumptions of her time. Later in life she began work on an unpublished autobiography, and contributed a number of largely nostalgic letters and articles to popular magazines. After the death of her husband and two of her sons in the 1860s, Oakes Smith turned to religion, particularly spiritualism, and served briefly as minister to an independent congregation in Canastota, New York. She died in 1893, at the age of eighty-seven.

Oakes Smith's most famous poem, "The Sinless Child" (1842), has sometimes been cited as a classic archetype of what has become known as "the cult of True Womanhood"—a set of cultural values and assumptions that defined the domestic roles of nineteenth-century women as keepers of the moral and spiritual hearth—and the inspiration for Harriet Beecher Stowe's sentimental heroine, "little Eva" in *Uncle Tom's Cabin.* Indeed, Oakes Smith's protagonist, also named "Eva," does rely heavily on the conventions and values of nineteenth-century sentimentality: She is young and innocent, sexually naive, spiritually "pure," nurtured by an idealized natural world, and presented primarily through melodramatic and nostalgic evocations of emotion:

> Thou art my spirit's cherished dream, its pure ideal birth;
> And thou hast nestled in my heart, with love that's not of earth. (*The Poetical Works*)

Recent critics, however, in an effort to reconcile this early work to her later, decidedly "un-traditional" feminist writings, have argued that, while Oakes Smith does share a certain aesthetic and moral vision of womanhood with other sentimental writers of the period, her treatment of women even in this early poem displays a far more complex ideology, which Jane Rose calls "noble womanhood" (209). While Oakes Smith emphasizes the domestic duties of women as wives,. mothers, and teachers, as well as the moral and spiritual superiority of women, her attitude is, according to these critics, more in keeping with Fuller's vision of women as potentially "self-reliant" visionaries and metaphysical guides. Her Eva, although innocent, somehow transcends the corrupt materialism and spiritual "blindness" of those around her, including her would-be lover with whom she achieves spiritual union while remaining physically and morally independent. Through her death, Eva offers a Christ-like redemption to her lover and serves as an exemplary figure to others, but, unlike the typical sentimental heroine, she is not confined by masculine expectations or domestic roles. Similar re-visions of Oakes Smith's later poetry suggest a number of correspondences between her progressive politics and her poetic vision.

Among Oakes Smith's later poems, two others stand out. "The Drowned Mariner" (1845), a haunting ballad about a sailor lost in the mystical depths of the sea, is quoted by **Herman Melville** in the extracts preceding *Moby-Dick.* It may serve as an homage, not only to her own seaman father, but also to those German gothic tales and frontier adventure stories that inspired much of her fiction. In a similar vein, "The Summons Answered" (1845) was apparently among Poe's favorites. It deals with a supernatural encounter between a group of intoxicated tavern-hoppers and the figure of Death—a reflection, perhaps, of Oakes Smith's own supernatural beliefs and spiritualist philosophy.

Further Reading. ***Selected Primary Sources:*** Smith, Elizabeth Oakes Prince, *The Autobiography of Elizabeth Oakes Smith*, ed. Mary Alice Wyman (Lewiston, ME: Lewiston Journal Company, 1924); ———, *The Poetical Writings of Elizabeth Oakes Smith* (New York: J.S. Redfield, 1845; 2nd ed. 1846); ———, *Woman and Her Needs* (New York: Fowlers and Wells, 1851; Reprint, New York: Arno Press, 1970). ***Selected Secondary Sources:*** Kirkland, Leigh, "Elizabeth Oakes Smith," in *19th-Century American Women Writers: A Bio-Bibliographical Critical Sourcebook*, ed. Denise D. Knight (Westport, CT: Greenwood Press, 1997); Rose, Jane E., "Expanding Woman's Sphere, Dismantling Class, and Building Community: The Feminism of Elizabeth Oakes Smith" (*CLA Journal* 45.2 [December 2001]: 207–230); Wiltenberg, Joy, "Excerpts from the Diary of Elizabeth Oakes Smith" (*Signs* 9 [1984]: 534–548); Woidat, Caroline M., "Puritan Daughters and 'Wild' Indians: Elizabeth Oakes Smith's Narratives of Domestic Captivity" (*Legacy: A Journal of American Women Writers* 18.1 [2001]: 21–34).

John Edward Martin

SMITH, JOAN JOBE (1940–)

Californian poet and small press publisher Joan Jobe Smith has since the 1970s made a significant contribution to the writing scene in Los Angeles and Long Beach—first as founding editor of *Pearl* magazine in 1974, later the Pearl Editions imprint, and most recently as editor of the *Bukowski Review.* She is widely published, especially in Britain, and has created an authentic working-class female poetic voice. Her poems about family life can be usefully compared to those of Wilma Elizabeth McDaniel, the Okie "biscuits and gravy poet" whom she greatly admires, but Smith's describe a far more fraught and unbuttoned existence. Moreover, Smith has a witty manner, frequently relating her experiences ironically to popular song lyrics and movie stars. Her best-known book, *Jehovah Jukebox* (1993), a sequence about being a go-go dancer in tough West Coast clubs and bars, is not only a well-observed account of the

1960s but also the first poetic account of the sex industry from a woman's perspective. *Bukowski Boulevard* (1999) memorializes Smith's important friendship and literary correspondence with **Charles Bukowski**.

Smith was born in Paris, Texas, in 1940. Her parents were Depression era Dust Bowl survivors who migrated to California in that decade. Since then, in her own phrase, she has led a strange and hectic life as a mother, multiple divorcee, dancer, law student, graduate of the Writing Program of the University of California–Irvine (MFA 1977), teacher, and secretary, as well as caring for her mother during a terminal illness. The latter was memorialized in *The Pow Wow Café* (1998). Smith was encouraged in her writing early on by acceptances from *Wormwood Review*, as well as by writing friends Ann Menebroker and Linda King, who was then Bukowski's partner. Three issues of *Pearl* appeared between 1974 and 1975, initially as a magazine for women writers. The magazine was re-launched in 1987 (co-edited with Marilyn Johnson and Barbara Hauk) as a more eclectic publication featuring poets such as **Gerald Locklin** and **Billy Collins**. Smith won the $500 Mary Scheirman award in 1996 with her poem "How You Taste the Apples." She has made successful reading tours of Britain with her husband, machinist and poet **Fred Voss**, collaborating with him on several chapbooks.

Smith's collections form what is essentially a discontinuous autobiographical sequence, distilling her life experiences and showing a clear-eyed compassion for others. Poignant and humorous about herself, the poems also examine American society, often highlighting the sexual and economic exploitation of women. Smith's appreciation of Bukowski's direct language and raucous personality was immediate and has proved long lasting. As she relates in *Bukowski Boulevard*, he invited her to "feed your brain on me," and certainly inspired her tightly packed **free verse narrative** style, one flavored by occasional profanities. She has since moved away from his bohemian stamp into broader themes. Her first (shared) publication, *The Habit of Wishing* (1977), was characteristic in presenting vignettes of her parents, grandparents, childhood, and her own daughter, noting sardonically the gap between real life and Hollywood fantasies. "Sadie Thompson Lives on Elm Street," for instance, imagines her movie fan aunt's "vicarious lovelife of a harlot" with the stars, telling us that she later married a private, lived in a tract home and had "a son named after Little Joe / in the 'Bonanza' tv show." In "Life is But a Dre-am" the naïve hopes of a girlfriend who drops out of high school in 1955 are conveyed by her misspelled note to "Dear MISS Jobe," which ends: "it sure is / fun being marryed. SH-BOOM!" *The Coolest Car in School* (1994) continues Smith's story into the 1950s, when at fifteen, "anxious for my first diamond ring," she is still confused by a boy's sexual advances ("The Gonad Story"). In the title poem she rides serenely to the junior prom in the aquamarine leather tuck and roll back seat of "Tinker Christensen's '56 Olds," observing that never again "would the moon, pearls, or gardenias / glow as white." "The Girls of the Chickie Runs," however, debunks youthful romance by recounting what happened to the girls in later life. Some have been forced into early retirement from the phone company, and "four wear Eva Gabor wigs to hide / what chemo did."

Jehovah Jukebox dramatizes the seven years (roughly 1965 to 1972) that Smith worked as a go-go dancer at nightclubs and beer-bars in the Los Angeles area. It conveys not only the mixed sexual attitudes of the 1960s but also the discrepancy between the dancers' daily reality and the male customers' fantasies: "We were Delilah, Salome, Jane Avril, / and Gypsy Rose Lee" ("Intimacy"). Readers are brought up close and personal to observe drunken men's verbal and physical abuse, as in "Tits for Tat" and "The Crotchwatchers." The narrator is, however, generally sympathetic toward the men, despite a rogues' gallery including the boss Dirty Dave, covert homosexual Crazy Ted, "Smitty the scared shitless marine" on his way to Vietnam, and "the famous astronaut" who propositions her. The dancers are depicted in the title poem as workers with an insecure and exhausting job, with no vacation pay, no sick leave, no overtime pay, and no pension. Yet they too have their fantasies, such as dancing to "Purple Haze" while secretly being "The Ladies of the Fred Astaire Fan Club." Brandi Blue's own fantasy, while she endures silicon breast injections, is that "the topless craze / would cure us all—even The Establishment." In the end, the dancers are laid off: One club becomes a dental clinic, "the Playgirl Club" becomes a video rental store, and "Daisy Mae's" is bulldozed ("You Should've Seen This Place a Year Ago").

The title poem in *The Pow Wow Café* describes another worker, Smith's mother, wearing a low-cut blouse as a waitress at a truck-stop. But during the 1940s, it observes, a woman's attempt at independence could be cut short by an outraged husband. The collection relates events from Smith's childhood, along with a bittersweet account of her parents' marriage. Starting as "the stuff of romantic comedies," the relationship eventually disintegrates into a series of conflicts and separations. Smith's father joined the army and her mother went to stay with relatives in California, living in a tent city and working as a date picker. She tells her little girl, after watching *The Grapes of Wrath* on screen a few years later, "we're Jobe, like / Job in the Bible" ("Handsomer than Henry Fonda"). The bond between mother and daughter is symbolized by their shared love of dancing during the Rock n' Roll era, as they teach each other the Jitterbug and the Bop to the latest records. The book concludes movingly with poems about caring for her mother during the 1980s, and coming to terms with her parents' legacy in "Trying On Their Souls for Size." Smith's achievement has been not only her resilience in the face of adversity but her ability to narrate it in verse that is both haunting and humorous. In "At Terror Street & Reincarnation Way," the last poem in *Bukowski Boulevard*, she remarks that it has taken all her life to find enough clothes to keep "My skin and soul warm and / I still don't know what to wear."

Further Reading. ***Selected Primary Sources:*** Smith, Joan Jobe, *Bukowski Boulevard* (Long Beach, CA: Pearl Editions, 1999); ———, *The Coolest Car in School* (Long Beach, CA: Pearl Editions, 1994); ———, *The Habit of Wishing* [with Rosemary Capello and Ann Menebroker] (Pasco, WA: Goldermood Press, 1977); ———, *Jehovah Jukebox* (Desert Hot Springs, CA: Event Horizon Press, 1993); ———, *The Pow Wow Café* (Huddersfield, UK: Smith/Doorstop Books, 1998). ***Selected Secondary Sources:*** Stein, Julia, "Those Love Bird Poets: Are They the Future?" in Rolfe, Lionel, *Literary LA* (Los Angeles: California Classics, 2002); Smith, Jules, *"Art, Survival and So Forth: The Poetry of Charles Bukowski"* (North Cave, UK: Wrecking Ball Press, 2000).

Jules Smith

SMITH, SAMUEL JOSEPH (1771–1835)

A writer of both poetry and prose, Samuel Joseph Smith enlivens American poetry's relatively fallow years between the most popular work of **Philip Freneau** and the early work of **William Cullen Bryant**. Smith wrote in a variety of **verse** genres, such as occasional poetry, hymns, lines for children, and **graveyard poetry**. While he generally adhered to the rather strict conventions governing language and form in the poetry of eighteenth-century America, his verses more often than not tend to transcend these limitations and strike the reader as more graceful and natural than those of many of his contemporaries.

Smith was born in 1771 to a Quaker family residing near Burlington, New Jersey. According to the few biographical details available, he was a strong-willed child who would not be kept in school. So, with the benefits of a good library at Hickory Grove, his father's estate just outside Burlington, young Smith was largely self-educated. He never married and remained at Hickory Grove almost his entire life, first as heir and then as master. There he lived and wrote with as low a profile as he could manage, maintaining and improving his estate, doing what public good his patrimony allowed, and writing poetry and prose for the local literary market. For all intents and purposes, he seems to have lived the quiet and reclusive life about which the speaker of **William Livingston**'s "Philosophic Solitude" only dreams. Smith died in 1835 at the age of sixty-four. The following year a member of Smith's extended family collected for publication in Philadelphia and Boston *Miscellaneous Writings of the Late Samuel J. Smith, of Burlington, N.J. . . .* (1836). Including a biographical sketch about the poet's life, the collection offers almost two hundred pages of Smith's poetry and prose.

Smith participated in the eighteenth century's understanding that instruction ought to be poetry's primary concern. In a representative topical poem from *Miscellaneous Writings*, 1791's "On Dress—To the Ladies," Smith suggests the connection between the female fashion of novel-reading and that of weighing herself down with "transatlantic frippery . . . and nick-nacks." Smith's "advice in rhyme" suggested that American women should instead dress in "lasting fabrics from Columbian [American] looms" and win their lovers' hearts with "substantial merit" and with an "economic, . . . industrious spirit."

Smith directed his advice to larger social and political topics as well. His blank verse poem "Scraps; Or a Page from My Port Folio," for example, appears to praise America for its high opinion of itself, its pioneer spirit, its virtue, and its Christian morality. At the same time, Smith's speaker suggests that an ironic dissonance exists between the "tuneful wolves" displaced by America's push west and the pioneers who dance to squeaky fiddles. The displacement of the tribal peoples—"tawny, two legg'd, and inferior vermin"—consciously undermines the speaker's praise of America's "virtuous and enlightened population." As for "proof" of America's wisdom and morality, unidentified lands boasting "floods of milk and honey" provide an idyllic contrast to the "whiskey-streaming land" that is the United States. In the final sections of "Scraps," America's Christian character—its promotion of equality under God and its valorization of law—is troubled by the institution of slavery and many instances of dueling.

Smith's most popular poem was "Eulogium on Rum." This curious work is one of only six American poems to appear in all three of the first major poetry anthologies that were printed in America and included works by American poets—Mathew Carey's *The Beauties of Poetry, British and American* (1791), Elihu Hubbard Smith's *American Poems, Selected and Original* (1793), and James Carey's *The Columbian Muse: A Selection of American Poetry, from Various Authors of Established Reputation* (1794). "Eulogium on Rum" is a delightful yet haunting piece that complicates its eighteenth-century moral lesson with the ambiguity of its conclusion.

From the poem's beginning, its mock-heroic language rises playfully above its subject: "Arise, ye pimpled, tippling race, arise! / . . . / Show your red noses, and o'erflowing eyes." As the poem progresses toward its central stanzas, the drink receives tongue-in-cheek praise for its supposed virtues: that it inspires the bard, that it warms in winter and cools in summer, and so on.

In the center of the poem, rum's dark side receives attention as well in lines laced with dramatic irony:

Hail, mighty Rum! to thee the wretched fly,
And find a sweet oblivion of their woes;
Locked in thy arms, as in the grave they lie,
Forget their kindred, and forgive their foes.

Careful readers could not help but catch the poet's condemnation in this stanza and those that follow. Smith allows his speaker to continue by praising the Euro-American's destruction of the native tribes through the devastating effects of alcohol. The poet's derision, sarcasm, and horror at this devastation ooze between the haughty speaker's lines throughout this portion of "Eulogium."

Ultimately, the drink is "spurned from table . . . and the public eye" and forced to be hidden away in a closet. But it will not necessarily be there in the darkness alone. In an act perhaps more characteristic of later literary artists, Smith turns the decision to do good or not over to the individual. Once he has presented the lesson, he allows his audience to witness the drunken speaker as he emerges from the dark closet of his ruler, rum, and—beautiful in his own mind but terrible in the reader's—stumbles off to bed.

Smith engaged his cultural milieu as a gentleman farmer and author in late eighteenth- and early nineteenth-century America. From his detached vantage point at Hickory Grove, he commented on the sources of beauty and corruption in the early life of the United States. He created his verse not for fame and fortune, as he writes in his poem "The Bachelor," but rather to celebrate his "happy fire-side."

Further Reading. ***Selected Primary Source:*** Smith, Samuel Joseph, *Miscellaneous Writings of the Late Samuel Joseph Smith, of Burlington, N.J.* (Philadelphia, PA: Henry Perkins, 1836). ***Selected Secondary Source:*** Smith, John Jay, "A Brief Memoir of One of New Jersey's Neglected Sons, Samuel J. Smith, 'A Lost Poet,' with Some Reminiscences of Burlington, by a Sexagenarian" (n. p., 1860).

Michael Cody

SNODGRASS, W(ILLIAM) D(EWITT) [PSEUDONYM S.S. GARDONS] (1926–)

William DeWitt Snodgrass is said to have inaugurated **confessional poetry** with the publication of *Heart's Needle* (1959), although he "dislikes the term." He notes that at the time he was writing what **Anne Sexton** called a "searingly personal" kind of poetry ("Note on W.D. Snodgrass"). *The Penguin Dictionary of Literary Terms And Literary Theory,* however, names Snodgrass's *Heart's Needle*, along with **Robert Lowell**'s *Life Studies* ((1959), four volumes of Sexton's work, and a number of **Sylvia Plath**'s poems as illustrative of this genre. Overall, Snodgrass's body of work is impressively diverse. For example, in 1977 he published *The Führer Bunker*, which is constructed as a series of dramatic monologues featuring Adolf Hitler, Albert Speers, Joseph Goebbels, Martin Bormann, and Eva Braun, and takes place during the regime' final days. In addition to more than twenty books of poetry, Snodgrass has written literary criticism. He has also published six volumes of translations, including *Selected Translations* (1998), which won the Harold Morton Landon Translation Award.

William DeWitt Snodgrass, known as W.D., was born in Wilkinsburg, Pennsylvania, on January 5, 1926. He attended Geneva College from 1943 to 1944 and again from 1946 to 1947 prior to graduating from the University of Iowa with a BA in 1949. He received an MA in 1951 and an MFA in 1953. Snodgrass additionally holds an Honorary Doctorate of Letters from Allegheny College. He taught at a number of colleges and universities in the course of his career, including Cornell University, the University of Rochester, Wayne State University, Syracuse University, Old Dominion University, and the University of Delaware, where he was professor of writing and contemporary poetry from 1979 to 1994, when he retired from teaching. He lives with his fourth wife, the writer Kathleen Browne Snodgrass. Snodgrass's *After-Images: Autobiographical Sketches* was published in 1999.

The poems of *Heart's Needle*, Snodgrass's best-known work, are a rendering of the poet's personal state of mind and feelings, many recounting the difficulties associated with his divorce. The volume contains some of Snodgrass's most notable poems and gives a glimpse into the poet's life. Some pieces address his return from service in the U.S. Navy during World War II. Others, like "April Inventory," are reflections on teaching and the nature of being. Snodgrass writes: "In one whole year I haven't learned / A blessed thing they pay you for." He then concludes that "'Gentleness' and 'loveliness' provide reason enough for all we do in education, and this, in essence, preserves us."

The concluding section of *Heart's Needle* features poems dealing with the loss of and separation from his wife and daughter, Cynthia, and contains some of Snodgrass's most poignant verse. His work in this confessional mode ranks with that of Sexton (whom Snodgrass taught at the University of Iowa), Plath, and Lowell. The volume won the Pulitzer Prize for poetry in 1960 and the British Guinness Award in 1961. In "Time and the Tragic in the Poetry of W.D. Snodgrass and Wallace Stevens" Ronald Pies likens Snodgrass's work to that of Matthew Arnold and "rejects the common misclassification of Snodgrass among the 'confessional' school of verse." He claims that Snodgrass's poetry is universal and that it portrays a self in conflict with a "thieving world" (*Poetrybay*).

Snodgrass's second volume of poetry, *After Experience: Poems and Translations* (1968), was published eleven years after *Heart's Needle.* It again blends the personal and the traditional, although the poet was already starting to move away from the confessional mode at this point. In "A Flat One," for example he writes with both poignancy and humor about "Old Fritz," a veteran who dies over the course of seven long months. Told from the perspective of a hospital attendant who provides some of the care for the dying man, and who is critical of the expense and time spent on someone who will not survive, the poem is a striking commentary on death and dying. The narrator observes of Old Fritz, "You whispered you would not die," but at night he hears the man crying "Like a whipped child." In "September," from the same volume, Snodgrass returns to the effects of divorce: "I don't know where. I can't remember/Your face or anything you said."

Snodgrass next published *The Remains* (1970) under the pseudonym/anagram **S.S. Gardons**. The poems in this volume again deal with difficult subjects: the suicide of Snodgrass's sister as well as the tensions that existed between Snodgrass and his parents. In a poem called "The Mother" Snodgrass writes, "If evil did not exist, she would create it / to die in righteousness, her martyrdom." The use of the pseudonym was apparently in deference to his parents, although Snodgrass released the book again under his own name once they had passed away.

The Führer Bunker, Snodgrass's infamous poetry cycle, was a complete departure from the poet's earlier confessional/personal work. The dramatic monologues were first published as a work in progress in 1977, and subsequent poems were added in 1983 and 1985. The complete cycle of poems was published in 1995. The terrain of these poems, that of historical memory, suggests the way poetry can interpret the past and render it in a present ever threatened with war. The poems were adapted into a play that was performed off Broadway at American Place Theatre in May 1981. The volume was also nominated for the National Book Critics Circle Award for Poetry. Drawing both condemnation and praise, the book created a certain furor in the United States, and in "The Enigma of W.D. Snodgrass" Gilbert Wesley Purdy quotes Snodgrass as saying the book "in effect ruined my career. . . . Magazines refused all my work. I've had no awards for twenty years. In this country. Out of the country I have, yes. I must say that my reputation continues to pick up in England."

Snodgrass is a versatile writer, whose work manifests his interest in music and art. *6 Minnesinger Songs* (1983) is an adaptation of original medieval songs, while *W.D.'s Midnight Carnival* (1988) is a collaboration with artist Deloss McGraw in which Snodgrass wrote poems in response to McGraw's paintings. The work focuses on the theme of the carnival, and in the book's introduction Robert L. Pincus writes that the character W.D. is "something akin to a ringleader of his own carnival."

In addition to being a poet, Snodgrass is an astute and capable critic. *De/Compositions: 101 Good Poems Gone Wrong* (2001) was nominated for the New York Critics Circle Award in Criticism, while *To Sound Like Yourself: Essays on Poetry* (2002) includes six essays on the craft of poetry. Thomas F. Dillingham writes that in this text, "Snodgrass seeks to demonstrate the deep connections between the sound and meaning, energy and form, the artistry and the bodily sensations of the poet, found in the best poetry" (n.p.). In his earlier volume, *In Radical Pursuit* (1975), Snodgrass wrote one of the more brilliant commentaries on D.H. Lawrence's "The Rocking Horse Winner," in which he says, in the vein of Lawrence himself, that "the sexual area is more basic to the story—is, indeed, the basic area in the pattern of living which the rocking-horse symbolizes" (134–135).

Robert Phillips, Moores Professor of English at the University of Texas and author of *The Confessional Poets* writes that *W.D. Snodgrass in Conversation with Philip Hoy* (1998) is a seminal text for understanding Snodgrass's work and that this "conversation" will help establish Snodgrass as a major **postmodern** American poet (http://interview-with-poets.com/william-snodgrass).

Among other awards Snodgrass has received are a Hudson Review fellowship (1958), a special citation from the Poetry Society of America (1960), an Ingram Merrill Foundation award (1968), as well as awards from the Ford Foundation, the Guggenheim Foundation, the National Institute of Arts and Letters, and the National Endowment for the Arts.

Further Reading. ***Selected Primary Sources:*** Snodgrass, William DeWitt, *De/Compositions* (Saint Paul, MN: Graywolf Press, 2001); ———, *Each in His Season* (Brockport, NY: BOA Editions,1993); ———, *Führer Bunker* (Brockport, NY: BOA Editions, 1990); ———, *In Radical Pursuit* (New York: Harper & Row, 1975); ———, *Selected Poems 1957–1987* (New York: Soho Press, 1987). ***Selected Secondary Sources:*** Dillingham, Thomas F., Review of *To Sound Like Yourself* (http://www.cmsu.edu/eng/phil/snodgrass.html); Haven, Stephen H., *The Poetry of W.D. Snodgrass: Everything Human* (Ann Arbor: University of Michigan Press, 1993); Hoy, Phillip, "A Note on W.D. Snodgrass" (London: Between the Lines, http://www.interviews-with-poets.com/william-snodgrass/snodgrass-note.html); ———, *W.D. Snodgrass in Conversation with Philip Hoy* (London: Between the Lines, 1998); Pies, Ronald, "Time and the Tragic in the Poetry of W.D. Snodgrass and Wallace Stevens" (*Poetrybay*, Summer 2001, http://www.poetrybay.com/summer2001/summ2001_21.html); Purdy, Gilbert Wesley, "The Enigma of W.D. Snodgrass" (*Limestone Magazine*, http://www.limestonemag.net/theenigmaofwdsnodgrass.html); Raisor, Philip, *Tuned and Under Tension: The Recent Poetry of W.D. Snodgrass* (Newark: University of Delaware Press, 1998).

Sue Brannan Walker

SNYDER, GARY (1930–)

Gary Snyder, one of the most acclaimed literary figures of the postmodern era, is known as a poet of the wilderness and of alternative culture. He is often identified as a member of the **Beat** generation and was one of the poets whose work helped make it famous, though he more accurately belongs to the **San Francisco Renaissance**—a West Coast equivalent of the predominantly East Coast Beat movement. His eighteen volumes of poetry and eight volumes of essays, influenced by deep interests in environmental issues, Native American myths and culture, and the poetry and philosophy of the Orient, celebrate the natural world and recommend a meditative relation to that world. Recognitions of his work include a Pulitzer Prize for Poetry (1975) and a Bollingen Prize for Poetry (1997).

Gary Snyder was born in San Francisco, California, on May 8, 1930, but his family soon moved north to Washington and subsequently (when Snyder was twelve) to Portland, Oregon. Growing up in the general hardship of the Depression era, which in the Snyder family meant long-term unemployment for his father, Snyder knew poverty from the beginning and learned early the necessity of working for a living. But the young Snyder also found opportunities for camping, mountain climbing, and other activities that satisfied his love of the outdoors. He was also intrigued by the tribal cultures of Native Americans. With the aid of scholarship funding, he attended Reed College in Portland and graduated with an interdisciplinary degree in anthropology and literature. His undergraduate thesis was a study of Native American myth that he published many years later as *He Who Hunted Birds in His Father's Village* (1979). While at Reed, he married and divorced for the first time and held jobs in a logging camp, on an ocean-going ship, and as part of an archeological dig. He also established friendships with **Philip Whalen** and Lew Welch, both of whom would later develop reputations of their own as poets.

After leaving Reed College, Snyder spent one semester in a graduate program in anthropology at Indiana University, and then returned to the West Coast with the intention of devoting his attention to poetry. At the same time he began to study Chinese and Japanese languages and culture (at the University of California–Berkeley)—an interest that began as a fascination with Chinese landscape painting that predated his teenage years. Particularly notable was his discovery of the seventh- and eighth-century Chinese poet Han-shan, whose "Cold Mountain" poems he began translating during this period. Meanwhile, Snyder continued to put in stints working in logging operations and also as a fire lookout for the Forest Service. In 1956 he left California to continue his study of the Japanese language and Zen Buddhism in Japan. He remained in Japan, for the most part, until 1968. His residence there was interrupted by several extended trips: eight months working on an oil tanker (1957–1958), during which time he wrote *Sappa Creek* (1957–1958); six months in India (1961–1962) with his second wife, Joanne Kyger (to whom he was married from 1960 to 1964); and several extended visits to the San Francisco Bay area, during which he taught English at the University of California–Berkeley (1964), participated in poetry conferences, and gave poetry readings at various colleges. For much of his stay in Japan, Snyder studied under a Zen master and even at times lived in a monastery. In 1967 he married Masa Uehara, a Japanese graduate student who was studying English literature, and they, with their first child, Kai, moved back to the United States the following year. A second son, Gen, was born in 1969, and in 1971 Snyder built a home in the Sierra Nevadas. He continues to live in California and, having been divorced from Masa in 1987, married a fourth time, to Carole Koda. Besides continuing to write poetry and essays, he teaches at the University of California–Davis, where he has been a member of the faculty since 1986.

Snyder's career as a poet received its first great boost when he was suddenly catapulted into celebrity in 1955 as a result of participating in a poetry reading in San Francisco billed as *6 Poets at 6 Gallery.* With poet **Kenneth Rexroth** as master of ceremonies, Snyder joined his friend Philip Whalen, **Allen Ginsberg** (a then-unknown poet who read his poem *Howl* publicly for the first time), and three others in this communal reading. Snyder read last, immediately following Ginsberg (whose reading was an overwhelming sensation), presenting his poem "A Berry Feast," a mythologizing treatment of Native American culture featuring the stock trickster figure Coyote, which he later published in the 1968 volume *The Back Country.* Besides forming a friendship with Ginsberg, the quintessential Beat poet (who jokingly labeled Snyder a "forest beatnik"), Snyder made the acquaintance of **Jack Kerouac**, the great Beat novelist, who used Snyder as model for the character Japhy Ryder in his 1958 novel *The Dharma Bums.* This circle of friends—Snyder, Ginsberg, Whalen, Kerouac, and Welch—emerged in the late 1950s as a major **avant-garde** force in poetry, and in Kerouac's case, fiction. The poetry featured counter-cultural themes and bold experimentation in style and subject matter, of which Snyder's contribution of Eastern and Native American elements was an important part.

In this period Snyder produced the material for his first two volumes of poetry, *Riprap* (1959) and *Myths and Texts* (1960). The former volume's title poem, "Riprap," is probably Snyder's most anthologized. He employs the substance "riprap," a rough paving material used for logging roads, as an emblem for his poetic intention—emphasizing a palpable interchange between thoughts and things in which common objects generate meditation and words become "like rocks. / placed solid, by hands." This relation between solid objects on one hand and the products of the mind on the other is evident in haiku-like poems such as "Mid-August at Sourdough Mountain Lookout," where precise renderings of the weather, the view, and the swarms of flies mix with and crowd out the hazy recollections of absent people and things. Another poem, "Milton by Firelight," juxtaposes the reading of *Paradise Lost* with the hard realities and necessary skills of mining and living close to nature and with a vision of the earth's evolution toward some barren future in which the fruits of human endeavor have been erased by time's ravages. All three poems celebrate a simple existence in their focus on natural objects, physical exertion, and the beauties of transient things. Snyder says of *Riprap* that he wanted to write poems composed of "tough, simple, short words, with the complexity far beneath the surface texture."

In 1965 Snyder published a second edition of *Riprap*, this time titled *Riprap and Cold Mountain Poems*, incorporating the translations of Han-shan's poems that he had begun in the mid-1950s and continued to revise while living in Japan. The resulting poems are part Han-shan and part Gary Snyder and demonstrate the remarkable melding of the two that Snyder, in his immersion in Oriental culture, had been able to achieve. Like *Riprap*, the complexly structured poem sequence *Myths and Texts* shows the influence of his fascination with Native American culture as a source of mythic substructure, as well as with Oriental poetry and philosophy for their models of thought and articulation. As with *Riprap*, it is also solidly grounded in Snyder's experiences in logging work and as a fire lookout, and more generally in his tenacious attachment to the severe but richly stimulating life he had lived as an outdoorsman.

Besides *Riprap and Cold Mountain Poems*, in 1965 Snyder published *Six Sections from Mountains and Rivers Without End*, beginning a poem sequence that would be expanded and finally published in its totality in 1996. What followed was a period of productivity that resulted in thirteen volumes of poetry and one prose volume. Snyder's work was partly supported during this period by a Bollingen grant (1965–1966) and a Guggenheim fellowship (1968), and in 1968 he was awarded the Levinson Prize for "Eight Songs of Clouds and Water." The books of poetry published in these years continue to feature not only Sierra Nevada settings and various aspects of Native American mythology and culture but also add Japan as a locale. The underlying influence of Oriental thought is complemented by the hardness, and sometimes the squalor, of reality. In volumes such as *The Back Country* (1968), the Zen Buddhist in the Sierra Nevadas is counter-pointed by the exile whose everyday, often urban, Japanese reality is colored by the memory of American locales, demonstrating a structure of meditation in which pairings such as presence/absence, solitude/society, and thought/activity take on a greater reality than the actual setting itself. *A Range of Poems* (1966) includes translations of poems by the Japanese poet Miyazawa Kenji, and *Regarding Wave* (1970) conjures images of the great eighteenth- and nineteenth-century Japanese artist Hokusai's most famous work, *Great Wave Off the Coast of Kanagawa*. The image of the ocean wave—an image of powerful movement captured in the glance of an eye, a woodcut by Hokusai, or a poetic meditation, yields a picture of the changing world frozen in a moment of meditative comprehension. *Regarding Wave*'s poems range from the pure meditation of the title poem (concluding with "om ah hum") to "Kai, Today's" poetic description of Snyder's wife Masa's giving birth to their first son. *Regarding Wave* marks the apogee of Japanese-ness in Snyder's poetry.

Snyder's first prose volume, a collection of essays titled *Earth House Hold: Technical Notes and Queries to Fellow Dharma Revolutionaries* (1969), marks a move from the implied environmental activism of his early poetry to a more explicit, more politically active phase. Coupled with this, he was conspicuous in the celebration of the first Earth Day in 1970, serving as guest speaker at Colorado State College. In his speech he proclaimed the "ecological battle"—the battle to save the environment—as "the only battle that counts now, the only thing that matters to me anymore." In 1972 he traveled to Stockholm, Sweden, representing the publishers of the *Whole Earth Catalog*, to attend the "United Nations Conference on the Human Environment"; subsequently, he wrote an article on the proceedings, which was published in the *New York Times*. This turn toward the ecological reflects backward on his already published poetry as well as forward to the unpublished, ensuring his characterization as an "eco-poet" whose works has a political intent in combination with the aesthetic.

Snyder in the early 1970s was still to some degree a regional poet, with his reputation largely confined to the West Coast. However, his volume *Turtle Island* (1974) earned him national recognition when he was awarded the Pulitzer Prize for Poetry in 1975. *Turtle Island* pursues Snyder's ecological interest, combining it with his long-standing fascination with Native American culture. He identifies "Turtle Island" as "the old / new name for the continent," meaning North America, which he refers to as "this continent of watersheds and life-communities." This identification abandons the political divisions of the continent in favor of its character as a single landmass whose "natural boundaries" are the only ones that matter. This notion reflects Snyder's belief in the value of tribal relationships as opposed to the European idea of nationhood with fixed political boundaries and of private property with similarly fixed dividing lines. The name also alludes to the myth of the earth, or as Snyder says, "even cosmos," supported on the back of a great turtle, suggesting the oneness of the cosmos and of human origin and destiny. The language and the movement of thought in the poems in *Turtle Island* are, for the most part, more celebratory and less hard-bitten than in his previous volumes, perhaps reflecting his newly acquired role as parent to two sons. The predominant myth is that of the earth as the mother-goddess—"the Great Mother," as he says in "No Matter, Never Mind"—who nurtures us and gives meaning to simple existence. The mother-goddess myth is a myth of shared effort and shared destiny, as opposed to the Greco-Roman patriarchal myths of heroic individualism and competitive struggle that form an ideological basis for European and American civilization. The return to a culture that reverences the earth is, as "I Went into the Maverick Bar" suggests, "the real work"; it is "[w]hat is to be done." Poems such as "The Bath," which describes the experience of Gary and Masa together bathing their son Kai, also express a reverence for the human body. "The Bath," with its refrain "this is our body," echoing the phrases of the Christian communion, expresses appreciation for the way the body's natural processes are a part of the great cycles of nature and its sexual nature incites a bond between man and woman that goes beyond the physical.

It could be said that *Turtle Island*, with its strong emphasis on the particular context of North America, was also a signal of Snyder's resolve to be repatriated after his sojourn in Japan. The poems identify with America as a place, if not with its current social and political systems, an identification that continues in *Axe Handles* (1983). Here the focus is less grandly ecological and more on community and family, once again returning to the poet's advocacy of tribal, more communal living. At the same time, the motif of work as a source of meaningfulness, established in his first volumes many years earlier, continues to be an important part of his view of human existence. As in his earlier works, practical skills are often showcased, but the rough companions and rugged settings of the earlier volumes are largely replaced by domestic ones. In the title poem Snyder describes showing Kai how to use one hatchet to shape the handle of another and, recalling quotations from **Ezra Pound** and the third-century Chinese painter and poet Lu Ji about axe handles and the patterns that shape them, he thinks of himself as the axe and Kai as the handle: "model / and tool, craft of culture"—the momentary occupants of certain current positions in a continuing pattern in the chain of human interdependence. In other poems such domestic skills as plastering ceilings and driving nails into wood lead to meditative moments, and these are supplemented in poems such as "Changing Diapers" by domestic skills of a less traditionally masculine sort, emphasized by the poem's ironic citations of "Geronimo" and "Sharp's repeating rifle." The poems repeatedly show how seemingly trivial experiences can bring moments of vision of the universal and the profoundly unchanging shape of things.

Since 1983 Snyder's full-length volumes of poetry have included *Left Out in the Rain* (1988), *No Nature: New and Selected Poems* (1992), and *Mountains and Rivers Without End* (1996). The poem sequence that comprises *Mountains and Rivers Without End* moves among various locales, including not only his most usual ones, the Sierras and Japan, but also Manhattan. In his own comments on the poem, Snyder has termed its motif of travel a "metaphor for impermanence," representing the changes in the earth over time and the cultural changes of the human beings inhabiting it. The task in the face of that impermanence is to find some grounding—to be, as he says, "deeply placed." *Mountains and Rivers Without End* also again exhibits Snyder's deep ongoing concern for the environment. He offers the poem sequence as a continuation of his effort to redefine, in the public mind, the word "wild"—from the usual connotation, he says, of "out of control, undisciplined," to the more profound understanding of the natural as "'in control'—self-organized, self-maintaining." According to Snyder, "That's the nature of our planet: it regulates itself."

Snyder can be compared to **Henry David Thoreau** for his meditative relation to nature and to solitude, his love of physical labor, and his faith in the oneness of the earth and its creatures. However, though Thoreau found meaning in primitive existence, he had little admiration for primitive peoples. Snyder, with his interests in myth and in tribal culture, adds to the love of non-human nature a dimension of emphasis on social organization and interpersonal relationships. He says of the human role in the movement of time and the evolution of nature, "We are all composite beings, not only physically but intellectually, whose sole individual identifying feature is a particular form or structure changing in time." When Snyder, subsequent to the publication of *Mountains and Rivers Without End*, was awarded the Bollingen Prize for Poetry in 1997, the selection committee said of his poetry, "He has brought together the physical life and the inward life of the spirit to write poetry as solid and yet as constantly changing as the mountains and rivers of his American, and universal, landscapes."

Snyder's poetic influences—other than the Chinese Han-shan, the Japanese haiku tradition, and his fellow poets of the San Francisco Renaissance—are most pertinently Ezra Pound, with his poetry's intercultural mixings and often elliptical conciseness, and **William Carlos Williams**, with his poetic renderings of "things" as the locus of ideas. Pound and Williams were, of course, mainstays of the **modernist** movement in poetry. Snyder, as their poetic heir, has been one of those responsible for shaping **postmodernist** poetry. His poetry not only questions American and Western European social and political values but also—in its embrace of the mythological and the existential, that is, of free-form as opposed to patterned experience—it calls into question the Western tradition of linear, logical thinking. In place of the practicality of purposive action, his poetry celebrates the practicality of attention to the moment and receptivity to whatever is to come. In *Myths and Texts* he speaks of his values as "the most archaic values on earth," identifying them with fertility rites, animal magic, prophetic vision, Dionysian ecstasy, and "the communal work of the tribe." In his later work, however, he complicates this by adding a more argumentative element, recognizing that within the cultural context of American life, political action is necessary in order to effect meaningful change. The Gary Snyder that results is part solitary visionary, part political activist, part artist, and part ordinary man living a quiet domestic life and finding meaning in the common tasks and situations that confront him from day to day.

Further Reading. ***Selected Primary Sources:*** Snyder, Gary, *Axe Handles* (San Francisco: North Point, 1983); ———, *The Back Country* (New York: New Directions, 1968); ———, *Earth House Hold: Technical Notes and Queries for Fellow Dharma Revolutionaries* (New York: New Directions, 1969); ———, *The Gary Snyder Reader: Prose, Poetry, and Translations, 1952–1998* (Washington, DC: Counterpoint, 1999); ———, *He Who Hunted Birds in His Father's Village: The Dimensions of a Haida Myth* (San Francisco: Grey Fox, 1979); ———, *Left Out in the Rain: New Poems 1947–1985* (San Francisco: North Point, 1986); ———, *Mountains and Rivers Without End* (Washington, DC: Counterpoint, 1996); ———, *Myths & Texts* (New York: New Directions, 1978); ———, *No Nature: New and Selected Poems* (New York: Pantheon, 1992); ———, *The Old Ways: Six Essays* (San Francisco: City Lights, 1977); ———, *A Place in Space: Ethics, Aesthetics, and Watersheds: New and Selected Prose* (Washington, DC: Counterpoint, 1995); ———, *A Range of Poems* (London: Fulcrum, 1966); ———, *The Real Work: Interviews & Talks, 1964–1979* ed. Scott McLean (New York: New Directions, 1980); ———, *Regarding Wave* (New York: New Directions, 1970); ———, *Riprap and Cold Mountain Poems* (San Francisco: Four Seasons, 1965); ———, *Turtle Island* (New York: New Directions, 1974). ***Selected Secondary Sources:*** Molesworth, Charles, *Gary Snyder's Vision: Poetry and the Real Work* (Columbia: University of Missouri Press, 1983); Murphy, Patrick, ed., *Critical Essays on Gary Snyder* (Boston: G.-K. Hall, 1990); ———, *Understanding Gary Snyder* (Columbia: University of South Carolina Press, 1992); Schuler, Robert, *Journeys Toward the Original Mind: The Long Poems of Gary Snyder* (New York: Peter Lang, 1994); Steuding, Bob, *Gary Snyder* (Boston: Twayne, 1976).

James S. Leonard

SOBIN, GUSTAF (1935–)

Gustaf Sobin writes an **experimental poetry** that uniquely incorporates the poetic strategies of a number of slightly earlier experimental poets. As he himself notes in an interview with **Edward Foster**, he combines the Orphic sense of **Robert Duncan** (for an understanding of language as "the generator, the mother, the source of all being") with the "focused intensity" of **George Oppen** (for "investing the particular with its all-too-lost significance") (127). Since literary historians group the former with the **Black Mountain** poets and the latter with the **Objectivist poets**, and since Sobin's poetry so seamlessly absorbs just what he admires in each, Sobin is a poet who is difficult to place in terms of traditional American literary history. Obviously experimental, Sobin's poetry is both expansive *and* condensed; it makes space for both the tangibly present *and* the ephemeral, the present *and* the potential. Sobin accomplishes this by consistently indicating the very real presence and effect of the "conditional" in the midst of what we have learned to call the "actual."

Born in Boston, Massachusetts, in 1935, Sobin attended Choate School in Connecticut, a secondary school for boys, and later attended Brown University. Growing up in New England in the 1950s, he responded to the sense of stricture in that time and place by reading the expatriate writers of the 1920s. As a young man, he studied French and regularly visited the **Gertrude Stein** Collection at Yale. Such experience surely planted the seed for his own expatriation because, in 1962, he moved permanently to France. Having read the work of the French poet Rene Char, Sobin was drawn to Provence and, once there, actually met Char himself. Char became a crucial influence on his writing and, through him, Sobin met other European writers and intellectuals, including the philosopher Martin Heidegger. Sobin found that he very much identified with the expansive landscape of Provence and settled there, writing all his books in a small, eight-by-eleven–foot *cabonon.* He continued to read widely—not only literature but also nonfiction, such as philosophy and anthropology—and in December of 1972 wrote what he called his "first poem," finding direction for a distinctive voice. This development sparked work on his first collection of poetry, *Wind Chrysalid's Rattle,* which actually did not appear until 1980, published by the Montemora Foundation. Sobin, even while living in France, never ceased to find useful models in American poets and specifically mentions both **Michael McClure** and **Robert Creeley** as important influences. While poetry has certainly been the longest commitment of his writing career, Sobin has also more recently published well-received fiction, such as *The Fly-Truffler* (1999) and *In Pursuit of a Vanishing Star* (2001), as well as the nonfiction *Luminous Debris* (2000), a reflection on the French landscape he admires so much.

Sobin's poems are, for the most part, made up of compact lines with a heightened attention to enjambment. This should not be surprising, considering the influence of Oppen and Creeley, and Sobin speaks of this approach—again, in the Foster interview—as seeing the poem as a "vertical gesture," comparing it to a "waterfall falling over its own ledges" (129, 130). Even though he speaks of the effect of this condensing as quickening the reader's pace and relieving sustained attention, the line breaks themselves call attention to the materiality of language, underscoring its vital parts: each syllable, each prefix or root, each article or preposition. The reader then experiences at once a rush of language *and* cause to slow and note what constitutes that rush. Sobin will also occasionally, especially in his longer poems, punctuate this more common short line with lines that span the entire page, once again choreographing the reader's attention by bringing him or her back to a more prosaic form of reading. The poems are often full of dashes and hyphens, and section breaks are often indicated with tildes or long, black lines of varying lengths. As a result, the poems visually present themselves as series of crucial and short units within a much larger, dynamic whole.

This method is crucial to Sobin's most recurrent theme concerning the function of language. He prefers the verb to the noun, seeing the world in constant movement rather than as static substance. The structure and pacing of his poems, then, barely allow attention to linger on a single image or phrase before shuttling off to the next, giving a sense of motion in the process of reading. This preference for the fleeting would explain, also, why the majority of his images are abstract or ephemeral: breath, light, wind, and water. In "Tracing a Thirst," from *Breath's Burials* (1995), Sobin expands upon this theme by adding his understanding of the potential. He addresses the work of a poem directly, writing that it "edges / towards its / own / . . . / ob- / fuscated source." For him, the world—with all its moving parts—is animated by constant dialogue with the ideas that precondition it, by the intangible, but very real, concepts that embody its potential. The work of the poem, then, according to "Tracing a Thirst," is to tap into the abstract and transient realm of this potential so as to engage with this originating force. Logically, this poetic work is represented by a return to vital origins, as the poem ends with breath's returning to its "pleated lip."

Sobin's writing process consciously reflects this goal. In the Foster interview he says, "In my own work . . . I find myself moving, in nearly every poem I write, and usually somewhat towards its conclusion, from a place, a locus, a set of material circumstances, to a proposition. A postulate. And, in so doing, going—in terms of verbal time—from the present to the conditional. From an 'is' to a 'would,' a 'could,' to the ever-present possibility of a 'might'" (124). His goal becomes clear in a long poem such as "Reading Sarcophagi: An Essay in *Towards the Blanched Alphabets* (1998), where he expresses nostalgia for "an age in which all things, once, in counterpoint, thrived echoic, reflex- / ive: in which image substantiated substance." He longs for a time where language—by its images and narratives—"substantiated substance." The role of the poet is to use language to do such again. Such a project requires the poet to throw his or her weight in with either the less substantial or the absent—the unspoken, the invisible. As Sobin writes in the last poem of this same collection, "Called It Space," "we'd only happen, here, in our own / self- / induced elaborations.

The poetry of Sobin is both elusive and exacting. He uses a very calculated poetic experimentation to lend our potential—our imagination—the same weight as stone and flesh. Such a project—drawing a map of where we have not been, articulating what we have yet to say—requires a careful moving away from the physical coordinates we already trust and away from any language set in habit. Interested as he is in anthropology and geography, Sobin consistently sets his poems in landscapes full of artifacts, only to dissolve such satisfying markers and reveal the very real and strange potential that lies underneath. If this project is specific, it is also very rich, and earns Sobin his unique place among contemporary American experimental poets.

Further Reading. ***Selected Primary Sources:*** Sobin, Gustaf, *Breath's Burials* (New York: New Directions, 1995); ———, *By the Bias of Sound: Selected Poems: 1974–1994* (Jersey City, NJ: Talisman House, 1995); ———, *Towards the Blanched Alphabets* (Jersey City, NJ: Talisman House 1998). ***Selected Secondary Source:*** Foster, Edward, "Gustaf Sobin," in *Postmodern Poetry: The Talisman Interviews* (Jersey City, NJ: Talisman House, 1994).

Samuel Jason Ezell

SONG, CATHY (1955–)

Cathy Song writes poems that explore her family history and the complexity of family relationships, while also evoking her Korean American background. Critical evaluations of her poetry are as varied as her wide range of poems. Song's continuous rejection of restrictive ethnic identity has been a hallmark of her cultural, personal, and familial poems. Paradoxically, even though she refuses to define and limit her poetic muse to ethnic frames, she often uses metaphors and symbols that reflect her complex ethnicity.

Born in Honolulu, Hawai'i, to a mother of Chinese descent and a father of Korean descent, Song inherited a rich cultural heritage. She graduated with a BA from Wellesley College in 1977 and an MA from Boston University in 1981. She won the Yale Series of Younger Poets Award for her first book, *Picture Bride*, and has received numerous other awards, including the Shelley Memorial Award and the Hawai'i Award for Literature. Her poems have been anthologized in *The Norton Anthology of Modern Poetry* and *The Heath Anthology of American Literature*. Her works have also appeared in such publications as *Hawaii Review*, *Poetry*, *Shenandoah*, and *Bamboo Ridge*. She lives in Honolulu with her husband and three children, where she writes and teaches.

Picture Bride, broadly records the history of the first Hawaiian immigration from Korea. In these poems, Song depicts plantation culture, picture bride customs (an arranged marriage through the exchange of photographs), unique Asian filial pieties, and strong family relationships. In the first three lines of the title poem, "Picture Bride," Song recounts the meeting and subsequent marriage of her grandmother, a picture bride, to her grandfather, who was much older, and how the couple came to America from Korea. While Song rejects the strictures of her ethnic and regional background, she also recognizes the value of attendant family structures that have allowed immigrants to survive and even thrive. Apart from the subject of the family, whether past or present, another hallmark of Song's poetry is a sensuality of language, which is present in many of the poems included in *Picture Bride*.

Song's evocative language, used with a careful painterly eye, is evident in "Primary Colors," with its vivid images of flowers. The section "Orchids" uses lush and exotic language to depict a Japanese wood-block print by Kitagawa Utamaro ("Girl Powdering Her Neck"), while "The White Trumpet Flower," the last poem in this volume, shows Song's appreciation of the work of artist Georgia O'Keeffe. The poem "Seamstress" tells the stories of four unmarried daughters and a father, and returns Song to her traditional theme of family relationships. Thus, the book opens with with a poem about Song's paternal grandparents and ends with a poem about her father ("Someone Very Quiet Once Lived Here").

Frameless Windows, Squares of Light (1988) and *School Figures* (1994) continue Song's exploration of the themes of childhood and family; the poems in these volumes are filled with a variety of relatives—aunts, uncles, parents, grandparents—who together create a fabric of interrelationships against which Song can explore themes such as intimacy, love, and community. With *The Land of Bliss* (2001), Song returns again to the themes of love, flowers, and religion, this time including elements of Zen Buddhism and Taoism. She invokes a Chinese ancestor in the poem "Ghost," which resonates with Maxine Hong Kingston's *The Woman Warrior*. The poem "A City of Sleeves" evokes the Chinese *yinyuan*, of which East Asian countries—China, Japan, and Korea—have similar versions. The single act of the brushing of sleeves reveals an ancient, deep connection to the past, one that is also evoked in other poems in the collection.

Song has won numerous awards, including the Frederick Bock Prize from *Poetry*, the Shelly Memorial Award from the Poetry Society of America, the Hawai'i Award for Literature, a fellowship from the National Endowment for the Arts, and a Pushcart Prize.

Further Reading. ***Selected Primary Sources:*** Song, Cathy, "Beginnings (For Bok Pil)" (*Hawaii Review* 6 [Spring 1976]: 55–65); ———, *Frameless Windows, Squares of Light* (New York: Norton, 1988); ———, *The Land of Bliss* (Pittsburgh, PA: University of Pittsburgh Press, 2001); ———, *Picture Bride* (New Haven, CT: Yale University Press, 1983); ———, *School Figures* (Pittsburgh, PA: University of Pittsburgh Press, 1994). ***Selected Secondary Sources:*** Cobb, Nora Okja, "Artistic and Cultural Mothering in the Poetics of Cathy Song" in *New Visions in Asians American Studies*, ed. Franklin Ng et al. (Pullman: Washington State University Press, 1994, 223–234); Kim, Elaine H., "Korean American Literature," in *An Interethnic Companion to Asian American Literature*, ed. King-Kok Cheung (New York: Cambridge University Press, 1997, 156–191); Lim, Shirley, "A Review of *Picture Bride*" (*MELUS* 10.3 [Fall 1983]: 95–99).

Geun Young Jang

SORRENTINO, GILBERT (1929–)

Gilbert Sorrentino is a prolific **avant-garde poet**, novelist, and essayist who argues that "despite the recrudescence of such aesthetic nonsense as Moral Responsibility, Great Themes, and Vast Issues, . . . form determines content" ("Le Style de Queneau," *Something Said*, 200). Accordingly, Sorrentino emphasizes the very process of writing. In "The Act of Creation" he claims that "the process is sublime" and the writer's task "is the recapture . . . of this sublime state" (*Something Said*, 7). Like the OuLiPo, the French experimental group with whom he is frequently associated, Sorrentino often incorporates "constraints" into his writing that are meant to generate what he calls "imaginative writing," such as reading a tarot deck to determine chapter order and content (*Crystal Vision*, 1981). The use of such aleatory devices, he argues, allows him entry into the "magic state [in which] things that are unknown to the writer in his everyday life are *found*" (*Something Said*, 9). He calls himself a "troubador," referring to the French Provençal poets, meaning literally a "finder."

Sorrentino was born in Brooklyn, New York, in 1929. He attended New York public schools and entered Brooklyn College in 1950, although his education was interrupted by two years of service in the U.S. Army

Medical Corps (1951–1953). Much of his early work is set in New York and indebted to its literary scene, of which he was an integral part. He founded the literary magazine *Neon* in 1956, edited and contributed to *Kulchur* magazine in the early 1960s, and served as an editor for Grove Press in the late 1960s and early 1970s. He came into contact with and was influenced by such poets as **William Carlos Williams**, **Robert Creeley**, and **Amiri Baraka**, and later Edward Dahlberg, **Allen Ginsberg**, **Frank O'Hara**, **Charles Olson**, **Kenneth Rexroth**, **Paul Blackburn**, and **Harry Mathews**. In 1960 Sorrentino published his first volume of poetry, *The Darkness that Surrounds Us*, which was reviewed by **Denise Levertov** for the *Nation*. Through Baraka, he published *Black and White* in 1964. Since then, he has published seven more volumes of poetry as well as a multitude of fiction and criticism and is perhaps most famous for his playful **prose** work in *Mulligan Stew* (1979), whose title is borrowed from an early page of James Joyce's *Ulysses*.

Like Williams, a poet to whom he frequently alludes, Sorrentino is interested in a distinctly American "language," stating in his collection of essays, *Something Said* (1984), "I conceive of American poetry as that poetry which has most daringly junked the paraphernalia of 'the beautiful,' as conceived by aesthetes and professors" (13). In order to capture this American language, Sorrentino is, like the **Objectivists**, an observer—his poems are descriptive but concrete and not symbolic; he rejects conventional lyricism and always prefers metonymy to metaphor. This emphasis often leads to bracing conclusions: In 1970, he wrote in *The Nation*, "We Americans . . . are such saps for the grand statement, the allegory, the symbolic gesture, the 'truth that lies beneath the surface' . . . [yet] there is nothing but surface, over which the imagination plays: and the master of the imagination is the artist" (quoted in "William Carlos Williams," *Something Said*, 22). Always privileging surfaces, his poetry tends to be highly self-conscious, often self-reflexive, and his prose writing is frequently qualified as metafiction.

For Sorrentino, then, the work of art aims at what he calls "the imaginative qualities of actual things," a Williams phrase from *Kora in Hell*, which serves as the title of Williams's 1971 novel. This concern with where art or the imagination meets reality lends much of his writing a kind of artificial, sometimes impersonal, aesthetic. In his poem "Rose Room," from *Corrosive Sublimate* (1971), he encapsulates this idea: "Strange memorable objects: / caught in the most elegant turn of / the mind." In an interview with Barry Alpert, Sorrentino states, "Life is right in front of you. Mysterious because it is not hidden. I'm interested in surfaces and flashes, episodes" (10). Sorrentino's poetry indeed captures a mysterious or nebulous quality that he believes only poetry can convey about the surfaces of the concrete world, a quality that cannot be revealed when it is assumed that these surfaces harbor some hidden depth. It is this, the mystery of the everyday, the destruction of our assumptions, that Sorrentino embraces in poetry.

In what is probably his best-known volume, *The Orangery* (1978), Sorrentino brings together all of his interests in writing and imagination with personal history. This is a collection of unrhymed, metrically varied sonnets organized around "orange"—the color, the object, and, most importantly for Sorrentino, the English word that cannot be rhymed—a kind of "prime" word. The volume explores the essentially arbitrary relationship of language to experience as the proper subject of writing, and Sorrentino plumbs his own life experiences for the material to fill out this poetic investigation. So the poems in *The Orangery*, some of which come from earlier collections such as *A Dozen Oranges* (1976) and *White Sail* (1977), are heavily autobiographical, concerning themselves with the past, such as the relationship with his mother, his childhood, his upbringing, and, inevitably, with loss (e.g., "Everybody would soon change / or die" and "At twenty love disintegrates with perfect ease"). However, this is no memoir, which would be to construct a depth where there is none; so while the poems are colorful ("Green fruit in the trees and / in the green trees oranges") and lively, even self-reflexive ("Nothing rhymes with orange"), they are each as contained as the sonnet form itself, suggesting no overarching narrative, no "grand statement." As David Andrews says of the volume, "orange" becomes a colorful "counterweight to loss and despair" (23).

Sorrentino has taught at New York's New School for Social Research and is Professor Emeritus of English and creative writing at Stanford University. He has been the recipient of two Guggenheim fellowships, a National Endowment for the Arts grant in 1974, a Samuel S. Fels Award for the short story "Catechism" also in 1974, a Creative Artists Public Service grant in 1975, a Lannan Literary Award in 1992, and the John Dos Passos Prize for Literature in 1981.

Further Reading. ***Selected Primary Sources:*** Sorrentino, Gilbert, *Black and White* (New York: Totem Press, 1964); ———, *Corrosive Sublimate* (Los Angeles: Black Sparrow Press, 1971); ———, *The Darkness Surrounds Us* (Highlands, NC: Jonathan Williams, 1960); ———, *A Dozen Oranges* (Los Angeles: Black Sparrow Press, 1976); ———, *Mulligan Stew* (New York: Grove, 1979; reprint 1987; Norman, IL: Dalkey Archive Press, 1993); ———, *The Orangery* (Austin: University of Texas Press, 1978; Los Angeles: Sun & Moon Press, 1995); ———, *Selected Poems: 1958–1980* (Santa Barbara, CA: Black Sparrow Press, 1981); ———, *Splendide-Hôtel* (New York: New Directions, 1973; Elmwood Park, IL: Dalkey Archive Press, 1984); ———, *Sulpicæ Elegidia: Elegiacs of Silpicia*

(Mt. Horeb, WI: Perishable Press, 1977); ———, *White Sail* (Santa Barbara, CA: Black Sparrow Press, 1977). ***Selected Secondary Sources:*** Alpert, Barry, "Gilbert Sorrentino—An Interview" (*Vort*, 6 [Fall 1974]: 3–30); Andrews, David, "The Art Is the Act of Smashing the Mirror: A Conversation with Gilbert Sorrentino" (*RCF* XXI.3 [Fall 2001]: 60–68); ———, "Gilbert Sorrentino" (*RCF* XXI.3 [Fall 2001]: 7–59); Sorrentino, Gilbert, *Something Said: Essays by Gilbert Sorrentino* (San Francisco: North Point Press, 1984; rev. ed. Norman, IL: Dalkey Archive Press, 2001).

Stefanie E. Sobelle

SOTO, GARY (1954–)

Gary Soto is the award-winning author of ten books of poetry, including *New and Selected Poems*, which was a finalist for the 1995 National Book Award as well as a finalist for the Los Angeles Times Book Award. Soto's well-received first book, *The Elements of San Joaquin*, received the U.S. Award from the International Poetry Forum and was published by the University of Pittsburgh Press in 1977. Yet even before publication of his first collection, Soto's prodigious talent was recognized with the 1974 Discovery/*The Nation* Prize and a 1975 Academy of American Poets Prize. Among many awards, Soto has received the Bess Hokin Prize and the Levinson Prize from *Poetry*, two NEA grants (1981 and 1991), a Guggenheim fellowship (1979), and a California Arts Council fellowship (1989). In 1990 Soto published *A Fire in My Hands*, a selection of poems with **prose** commentary and an interview designed for young beginning poets. In addition to his poetry, Soto is a prolific author of books of creative nonfiction, novels, and short stories for young adults and children, and biographies of César Chávez and Jesie de la Cruz. In recognition of his accomplishment in his writing and his commitment to community-based organizations, and of his efforts to support literacy among Chicano communities through his many readings and appearances at primary, secondary, and high schools, Soto received, in his opinion, his most prestigious awards: the 1999 Literature Award from Hispanic Heritage Foundation, the 1999 Human and Civil Rights Award from the National Education Association, and the 2001 appointment as Young People's Ambassador for California Rural Legal Assistance and the United Farm Workers of America.

Gary Soto was born April 12, 1952, in Fresno, California, and lived across the street from a broom factory and the Sun Maid Raisins plant. His father died in a work-related accident when Soto was five and a half. In his early teens, he and his brother Rick often worked in the fields so they would have money for school clothes. Soto attended the local schools, and it was at Fresno City College, concentrating on Geography, that he one day picked up a book of poetry by **Edward Field**, and that book changed his life. The poems he read there were direct, sad, and humorous, and were not cast in the **prosody** of the poetry he was made to study in high school. Soto began to fill a notebook with his own poems and would soon move on to study at Fresno State College and become a student of **Philip Levine**. By the time he graduated and entered the MFA Program at University of California–Irvine, he was already publishing in many of the most notable literary journals, such as *Poetry*, the *Iowa Review*, and the *Nation*.

As a young poet, Soto emerged from obscurity with his subject well in hand—poverty: the day-to-day poverty of food on the table, clothing, and shelter, as well as the poverty of the spirit as a result of lost family members and social and racial injustice.

Writing in *Poetry*, Alan Williamson offered: "Zest for concrete experience, and for the figures of speech that often have the trick of reanimating it. . . . At his frequent best, Soto may be the most exciting poet of poverty in America to emerge since James Wright and Philip Levine." And Peter Cooley commented in *Parnassus: Poetry in Review* that "His voice possesses the kind of unaffected honesty we experience only in conversation with friends." And so it was that the hallmarks of Soto's poetry were established in his first book, *The Elements of San Joaquin*, a book steeped in control of language. Soto's poems have a keen eye for the particular and he holds them up shining like totems. His choice of verbs as well was startling and inventive, and his fresh phrasing and imagery balanced the narrative grit and gravity of his subjects. Soto's early poetry speaks with an objective authority that is almost visionary, the imager arising naturally and subtly from the concrete details of his environments. Just beneath the skin we have the pain of personal and spiritual loss, as well as the suffering of the field worker, factory worker—the physical deprivation of the poet. The section from which the book receives its title gives us the poet as farm worker, as part of the landscape of the central valley of California. His stance and voice are elemental as he shows us the pain that the land wears into him after a long day working the grape fields near Rolinda: "Already I am becoming the valley, / A soil that sprouts nothing / For any of us."

In his second book, *The Tale of Sunlight*, Soto continues to explore the conditions of the poor, which expand to illuminate the larger strengths and failings of us all. Using the persona of his childhood friend Molina, Soto allows us to enter the child's mind as he attempts to conjure and interpret the world. The book is also remarkable for a section of poems titled "The Manuel Zaragoza Poems." This work extends Soto's methods to further develop the persona poem in light of magical realism.

Where Sparrows Work Hard, Soto's third book of poetry from the University of Pittsburgh Press, is noteworthy for its realism as well as its humor. Drawing from his own experience as a teenager, homeless and working in Los Angeles, Soto is witness to the lives of the street and factory, doing what they can to survive. In one of his most poignant poems, "Mission Tire Factory, 1969," Gary is there when a fellow worker falls from his machine and is critically wounded. Manny, bleeding through his clothes, actually thinks his fellow workers have saved his life as they lay him down, but he is too hurt to make sense of his situation. Soto finds the perfect and spare dramatic detail and dialogue to make the poem work, and the irony and pathos of the last line, as Manny takes three dollars from his wallet and offers them to his friends, is inescapable: "Buy some sandwiches. You guys saved my life."

It is Soto's ability to pay close attention to the lives of others, as well as to his own, that carries a reader through the progression of the rest of his books to date. *Black Hair* continues to examine the work through the eyes of Gary the child in poems like "Behind Grandma's House" and other poems from his youth growing up in Fresno. But here also we find the subject of fatherhood emerging and many poems for his young daughter.

In 1990 Soto moved from the University of Pittsburgh Press to Chronicle Books, and his first two books with Chronicle demonstrate Soto expanding his style and interests. In *Who Will Know Us?* a more meditative tone surfaces and there is an inkling of metaphysical concern. The title poem, dedicated to and influenced by the great Czech Nobel Laureate poet Jaroslave Seifert, shows the heights Soto can reach with a poem that is cast in the **lyric** vein as opposed to the **narrative**. *Home Course in Religion* (1991) shows us Soto pushing his craft in new directions. These poems work in longer lines than anything before (or after) and are generally longer poems. Again, Soto is able to enter and sustain the view from the mind of the child or adolescent, and he investigates the tenets of religion with humor and sincerity.

Soto's three most recent books from Chronicle are various and wonderful, and each gives us work best described by **Joyce Carol Oates** in her blurb on the back of *Junior College*: "Soto's poems are fast, funny, heartrending, and achingly believable, like Polaroid love letters or snatches of music heard out of a passing car; patches of beauty like patches of sunlight; the very pulse of a life." The poetry of Gary Soto is never without a sense of humor and wonder, and those qualities are anchored firmly in a mind and voice that value the spirit and dignity of the individual.

Further Readings. ***Selected Primary Sources:*** Soto, Gary, *Black Hair* (Pittsburgh, PA: University of Pittsburgh Press, 1985); ———, *The Elements of San Joaquin* (Pittsburgh, PA: University of Pittsburgh Press, 1977); ———, *Home Course in Religion* (San Francisco: Chronicle Books, 1991); ———, *Junior College* (San Francisco: Chronicle Books, 1997); ———, *A Natural Man* (San Francisco: Chronicle Books, 1999); ———, *New and Selected Poems* (San Francisco: Chronicle Books, 1995); ———, *One Kind of Faith* (San Francisco: Chronicle Books, 2003); ———, *The Tale of Sunlight* (Pittsburgh, PA: University of Pittsburgh Press, 1978); ———, *Where Sparrows Work Hard* (Pittsburgh, PA: University of Pittsburgh Press, 1981); ———, *Who Will Know Us?* (San Francisco: Chronicle Books, 1990). ***Selected Secondary Sources:*** Buckley, Christopher, "Keeping in Touch—*The Elements of San Joaquin* by Gary Soto" (*Abraxas* 16/17 [1979]); ———, "Resonance and Magic: Gary Soto's *The Tale of Sunlight*" (*Slow Loris Reader* [Fall 1979]); Day, Frances Ann, "Gary Soto," in *Latina and Latino Voices in Literature*, (Westport, CT: Greenwood Press, 2003).

Christopher Buckley

SOUND POETRY

Sound, like music, has always played a role in traditional poetry. Poetic devices of sound, such as rhyme, alliteration in its various forms, and onomatopoeia, have long been used by poets to add to and re-enforce the semantic content of their language. Sound poetry takes this one step further, creating work that relies on sound/sound structures rather than semantic structures to produce its primary aesthetic/syntactic sense. Sound poetry is closely associated with **visual poetry**, the two often co-existing within the same text/visual score. One of the first such experiments in English was Lewis Carroll's "A Fragment of Anglo Saxon Verse" (1855), which later in an extended form became his famous onomatopoetic, nonsense piece, "Jabberwocky" (1871), characterized by whimsical neologisms and fantastical imaginative inventions. Soon after the turn of the twentieth century, several groups associated with **modernism** began experimenting with sound as a primary meaning maker. The futurists both in Italy and in Russia, F.T. Marinetti, in particular, with his experiments in typography and sound, which, in his polemic literature and **poetry manifesto** "Technical Manifesto of Futurist Literature" (1912), he called "words-in-freedom," produced visual and onomatopoetic portraits of World War I. **Dada** groups in Zurich around the Cabaret Voltaire and in Germany (both in Cologne and Berlin) were also experimenting with sound. Hugo Ball's eclectic performances at the Cabaret Voltaire often consisted almost entirely of neologisms and non-normatively semantic sounds arranged in the rhythmic patterns of poetic verse. Similarly, Raoul Hausmann in Berlin was writing and performing Dadaist sound poems that experimented with both visual aspects of the page (font variations in face and size) as well as neologisms and nonsensical constructions. More important, during the period between the wars, Kurt Schwitters in Cologne was working on his masterpiece of sound poetry, *Ursonate* (1932). The contemporary Canadian **Christian Bök**'s work plays with these kinds of sonic/phonic treatments.

After World War II, with the more widespread use of sound recording and playback devices, most notably the reel tape recorder, poets such as Henri Chopin and Bernard Heidsieck in France and Arne Mellnas and Sten Hanson in Sweden began producing sound texts made by the manipulation of the recorded human voice. These sound poems were often produced by running the same tape through several recorders, all recording a single voice. The tape then might be cut and spliced in physical parallel to William S. Burroughs and Brion Gysin's Cut-Up techniques, then played at different speeds and re-recorded. The resultant sound poems were eerie, often almost mechanical-sounding pieces which, although frequently very pleasing to the ear, essentially engaged in a practice of alienating poetry from both the poet and the voice itself. A current American practitioner operating in this vein is Charles Amirkhanian, whose sound poetry radio programs in the 1970s on KPFA in Berkeley, California, were quite remarkable.

During the same time period that saw an explosion of technologically mediated sound poetry, the more traditional approach to reading a text as a sound performance made great advances in terms of how texts might be read and what exactly constituted a text for reading. Poets such as **Jackson Mac Low** and Bob Cobbing began experimenting with ideas of visual and aleatoric scores, often written with more than one voice in mind for performance. This led, in the late 1960s and early 1970s, to the formation of several important sound poetry performance groups: the English groups Koncrete Kanticle (Cobbing, Paula Claire, and Michael Chant or Bill Griffiths at various times) and JGJGJGJGJGJGJGJGJGJGJG (As Long As You Can Say It That's Our Name) (cris cheek, Lawrence Upton, and P.C. Fencott) on the one hand; and from Toronto the Four Horsemen (**Steve McCaffery**, **bp Nichol**, Rafael Barreto-Rivera, and Paul Dutton) and from Baltimore the far more radically performative CoAccident (Chris Mason, Marshall Reese, Kirby Malone, and Alec Bernstein) on the other. These groups explored a different kind of musicality, one often characterized by improvisatory elements mixed with rhythmically arranged language and phonemes. The idea of a score became something altogether different for these groups, with Koncrete Kanticles' famous reading of a stone at the Eleventh International Sound Poetry Festival in Toronto. All of these groups consistently tried to render visual form into acoustic expression through voice and language; however, they all tended toward **performance art**, **Fluxus**, and theater, with less and less to do with normative poetry. The Rochester-based F'loom continues in this vein, although their work has a marked rehearsed quality to it in that their performances are repeatable and much more like a rehearsed musical piece than the marginally controlled anarchy of their predecessors.

Coincident with the rise of the sound poetry performance groups, there was a growing international interest in sound poetry that produced a series of international sound poetry festivals (centered around the Fylkingen radio station in Stockholm, Sweden). The First International Festival of Sound Text Composition was held in 1967 and events occurred regularly for the next ten or so years, culminating in the Eleventh International Sound Poetry Festival in Toronto, organized by McCaffery and Nichol in 1978. The pair also produced one of the major sound poetry anthologies of critical and aesthetic statements, *Sound Poetry: A Catalogue* (1978). At that festival, along with many of the practitioners noted above, were **Jerome Rothenberg**, Bill Bissett, and **Dick Higgins**. Although not as widely known as it was in its heyday, the festival is alive and well in contemporary practice. mARK oWEns in Portland, Oregon, has revived to an extent the festival format for sound poetry, having organized two annual festivals and produced one anthology CD of performances, *phoneticathon* (2004), to date.

In its most interesting current form, sound poetry has moved into what Higgins would have called intermedia. North American practitioners, such as Michael Basinski, John M. Bennett, Wendy Kramer, Mikel And, William R. Howe, Ric Royer, and Chris Fritton, all use sound poetry as one element of a combined strategy investigating, among other things, the materiality of language and our relationship to it. They often use visual scores, collage, performance, multiple voices, live writing practices, performance residue-as-text, non-repeatable reading practices, technological intervention, theatrical props, and musical instruments (as **John Cage** would see it) in order to realize a text. As a consequence, contemporary sound poetry is not so much a movement, as it was in the 1960s and 1970s, but rather an integral element of an ongoing and developing poetic practice, just like other, more traditional forms such as **free verse** or the **prose poem**.

Sound poetry has been consistently overlooked by the contemporary criticism of **avant-garde** poetic practices for arguably some of the same reasons that it has moved so smoothly into intermedial forms and that some of its older practitioners, such as Cobbing and Mac Low, readily adopted/appropriated **Language poetry** and other forms of left-wing avant-garde-ism. Sound poetry covers a broad spectrum of work and engages multiple genres of artistic production. To innovative practitioners this can be quite interesting, but one of the draw-backs to critically exploring this work in a literary context is that a critical framework and vocabulary does not exist with which to discuss all of the elements that are at play (sonic/phonic, technological, visual, performative, as well as semantic and linguistic); and, unlike the context of musicology, where critical practitioners are used to dealing with textualities that are fundamentally intermedial, literary criticism is uncomfortable dealing with one or more of these elements. As a consequence, much of the critical work done on sound poetry either has investigated it as a form of music or has been relegated to alternative avenues of publication. For instance, in addition to Amirkhanian's radio programs mentioned above, Martin Spinelli's *Radio Radio* series of experimental radio programs (which all can be found on *UBUWEB*) examining current poetic practice spends nearly half of the sixteen programs talking with practitioners heavily invested in the exploration of sound (*Bufflux*us, cheek, Cobbing, Upton, Basinski, and others). Websites like *UBUWEB* and *Factory School* have large collections of recordings of sound poetry performances and sound events, along with critical essays and aesthetic statements by practitioners.

Further Reading. ***Selected Primary Sources:*** Amirkhanian, Charles, "History of Sound Poetry: An Introduction" (radio program broadcast originally on KPFA in the early 1970s, now archived at *Other Minds Archive,* http://www.archive.org/audio/collection.php?collection=other_minds,2005); Hedling, Erik, and Ulla-Britta Lagerroth, eds., *Cultural Functions of Intermedial Exploration* (Amsterdam: Rodopi, 2002); MacCaffery, Steve, and bp Nichol, eds., *Sound Poetry: A Catalogue* (Toronto, CA: Underwhich Editions, 1978); oWEns, mARK, ed., *phoneticathon* (Portland, OR: Sad Penguin Records, 2004); Schwitters, Kurt, *Ursonate* (published as entire issue of *Merz* 24 [1932]). ***Selected Secondary Sources:*** Bernstein, Charles, *Close Listening: Poetry and the Performed Word* (Tuscaloosa: University of Alabama Press, 1998); *Factory School* (http://www.factoryschool .org, 2005); Morris, Adalaide, ed., *Sound States: Innovative Poetics and Acoustical Technologies* (Chapel Hill: University of North Carolina Press, 1997); *Ubu Web* (http://www.ubuweb.com).

William R. Howe

SPENCER, ANNE (1882–1975)

Anne Spencer was one of the most important female poets of the **Harlem Renaissance**. Her poems appeared in Alain Locke's *The New Negro*, **Countee Cullen**'s *Caroling Dusk*, and **James Weldon Johnson**'s *The Book of American Negro Poetry*, as well as in two of the most important journals of the renaissance, *The Crisis* and *Opportunity*. She was close friends with Johnson and **Langston Hughes**, and figures such as **W.E.B. DuBois**, George Washington Carver, and Paul Robeson were among the many guests at her home. Spencer lived a dynamic and unconventional existence, working actively for civil rights in her small hometown of Lynchburg, Virginia, and refusing to conform to proscribed roles of blackness or womanhood. She was not given the same critical attention as her male colleagues during the Harlem Renaissance, and she published relatively few poems during her lifetime. Nevertheless, she has left us with a small but impressive selection of poetry, and the recovery work of scholars such as J. Lee Greene, Maureen Honey, and Erlene Stetson has helped to raise awareness of her contribution to American poetry.

Anne Bethel Bannister was born in Virginia in 1882 and attended the Virginia Theological Seminary and College, where she met her future husband Edward Spencer, with whom she had three children. In addition to her roles as poet, activist, wife, and mother, she worked as a librarian and was an accomplished gardener, a fact evident in poems such as "Lines to a Nasturtium" and "For Jim, Easter Eve," which are filled with images from her garden. Like many of the writers involved in the Harlem Renaissance, Spencer chose to employ rather than overturn existing literary structures, and she clearly saw herself as writing within a white male tradition; as she writes of herself in a short poem, "Chatterton, Shelley, Keats and I— / Ah, how poets sing and die!" (Greene, 197). However, her work constantly brings into play her own voice and concerns as a black woman, and many of her poems make sharp political statements in spite of their quiet **lyricism**.

In "Before the Feast at Shushan," for example, Spencer employs the formal conventions of a dramatic monologue and a loose iambic line to retell the biblical story of Vashti. The queen and wife of King Ahasuerus, Vashti refuses to be put on display for the pleasure of her husband and his drunken men, preserving her self-respect even though the king has her banished for her disobedience. Spencer's poem tells the story from the point of view of the husband-king, who struggles between his passion for Vashti and his fear of appearing weakened by a woman: "Am I, the King, to bend and kiss with sharp / Breath the olive-pink of sandaled toes between." Vashti has tried to guide him toward a more spiritual understanding of love, telling him "love is sacrament . . . love is both bread and wine"; it must be shared equally and cannot be forced by power. He finally resists her enlightened view of love and insists upon his traditional role as male and king, telling her "Love is but desire and thy purpose fulfillment." But Vashti's strength and courage in the face of conventional gender roles, as well as her intelligence and insight into the nature of love, come through clearly in contrast to the king's narrow-minded attempts to assert his power.

In other poems Spencer's feminist political concerns come through more overtly. In "Letter to My Sister" she claims "It is dangerous for a woman to defy the gods." The male gods in the poem own all instruments of power, from the physical violence of "searing lightning" to the guilt and "anger of red sins." And while they enjoy their tormenting as a game, for the women involved the suffering is real. The only option, the speaker tells her fellow woman, is silence and concealment. "Lock your heart" and "Raise no shade for sun," she encourages her, suggesting a sort of artistic and emotional death in order to preserve a sense of self.

One of Spencer's best-known poems, "Lady, Lady," explores issues of race as well as gender through a portrait of a washerwoman who has "borne so long the yoke of men." In spite of the physical and ideological oppression she has endured, the woman has maintained a powerful and even god-like presence. In this poem Spencer reverses the ideological notions that associate whiteness with the superior and sought-after; it is in the "darksome place" of the woman's heart, not the "bleached poor white" of her hard-working hands, that the speaker finds "the tongues of flames the ancients knew, / Where the good God sits to spangle through." Similarly, in "White Things" Spencer inverts ideological notions that associate whiteness with purity, innocence, and desirability. She celebrates color in a series of striking natural images. But the white men have blanched everything they have come into contact with, draining the world of its color and life and burning black men down to white ash. The poem relates whiteness with cowardice, violence, greed, and finally with death: "For the skull of a black is white, not dull, / But a glistening, awful thing."

While it is less obviously political than some of her other works, Spencer's "At the Carnival" continues to forge a black female aesthetic. The poem presents a portrait of a young woman artist, a diver whom the speaker encounters at a carnival diving tank. Most scholars have found in "At the Carnival" the possibility of beauty and redemption in the ugliest places, as the "Gay Little Girl-of-the-Diving-Tank" seems to burst forth from the "unholy incense" of the sausage booth and the "sordid life" of the carnival. Like the Lady, whose heart is connected to the seat of god, the diving girl possesses a form of holiness—she is "Leaven for the heavy ones of earth"—in spite of the negative forces that surround her. The girl is an original wonder, elevated to the role of goddess, but the poem suggests that she will not remain so. The speaker recognizes that the girl's destiny, like her own, is one of silence and a loss of innocence.

Even though the girl's future may hold the same frustrated isolation as the women in "Letter to My Sister," the poem announces the girl's success, telling her, "The wonder is that you are here." Likewise, the fact that Spencer and other women poets of the Harlem Renaissance managed to survive as artists and to produce such works of beauty as the poems they left behind provides for many contemporary readers the type of wonder that the diver offers for the speaker of the poem. In poems such as "At the Carnival," Spencer's skillful use of traditional poetic devices, along with her experience and perspective as a black woman, combine to create a powerful voice that surprises and complicates the landscape of twentieth-century American poetry.

Further Reading. ***Selected Secondary Sources:*** Drake, William, *The First Wave: Women Poets in America, 1915–1945* (New York: Macmillan, 1987); Ford, Charita M., "Flowering a Feminist Garden: The Writings and Poetry of Anne Spencer" (*SAGE* 5 [1988]: 7–14); Greene, J. Lee, *Time's Unfading Garden: Anne Spencer's Life and Poetry* (Baton Rouge: Louisiana State University Press, 1977); Honey, Maureen, ed., *Shadowed Dreams: Women's Poetry of the Harlem Renaissance* (New Brunswick, NJ: Rutgers University Press, 1989); Hull, Gloria T., "Afro-American Women Poets: A Bio-Critical Survey," in *Shakespeare's Sisters: Feminist Essays on Women Poets*, ed. Sandra M. Gilbert and Susan Gubar (Bloomington: Indiana University Press, 1979); ———, *Color, Sex, and Poetry: Three Women Writers of the Harlem Renaissance* (Bloomington: Indiana University Press, 1987). Stetson, Erlene, "Anne Spencer" (*College Language Association Journal* 21 [1978]: 400–409); ———, ed., *Black Sister: Poetry by Black American Women, 1746–1980* (Bloomington: Indiana University Press, 1981); Wall, Cheryl A., *Women of the Harlem Renaissance* (Bloomington: Indiana University Press, 1995).

Holly Karapetkova

SPICER, JACK (1925–1965)

Jack Spicer is a major figure in post–World War II American poetics and was a distinguished member of the group of innovative poets often referred to as the Berkeley or **San Francisco Renaissance**. The group was diverse and made up of a variety of different writers and factions, but Spicer's immediate group mostly involved **Robin Blaser** and **Robert Duncan**. The three poets met in 1946 at the University of California, and their strong bond and distinct poetic sensibilities helped establish a flourishing community of writers in and around San Francisco from the mid-1950s to early 1960s. Spicer's poetry, and his legacy as a teacher, innovator, and cult figure, has had a significant influence on **modern** and contemporary American poetry that includes writers such as the **Language poets** and prominent writers in the **gay and lesbian** community.

Born in Los Angeles, California, on January 30, 1925, Spicer has remained a largely marginalized figure in the Western literary **canon**, but his impact and popularity continue to grow as his poetry becomes more widely read and discussed. In his first collection, *After Lorca* (1957), Spicer used intertextual and collage techniques that were unique at the time and deviated radically from conventional and even progressive ideas about poetry. To begin, the poet writes a kind of "false" introduction, whereby he attributes the introduction that he himself wrote to the already dead Spanish poet Frederico Garcia Lorca. Much of the book includes a fabricated dialogue with Lorca, as well as translations, or perhaps, more correctly, versions of some of Lorca's poems. "Versions" might serve as better descriptions of these individual pieces throughout the book, because some of the poems depart drastically from the original work and are often intentional mistranslations more indicative of Spicer's poetry than straight translations of Lorca's work. The book also challenges the distinction between poetry and literary criticism and, as a result, serves as a powerful indication of Spicer's philosophy and poetics. In one section, he calls a poem "a collage of the real" (34) and suggests that "poetry discloses" (15) rather than invents.

Subsequent publications by Spicer are difficult to track since they include privately printed series poems, posthumously published books, scattered journal publications, and small chapbooks. Several of these chapbooks and series poems were published by White Rabbit Press, which is a press Spicer was closely and personally involved with, even if somewhat in the background. Spicer's complex publication history was partly complicated by Spicer himself, who often derided the national publishing houses, and focused on a very local community of writers and readers. Spicer also defined a "book" more as a mode and method of composition rather than a collection of poetry. However, his publication record was somewhat clarified by the publication of *The Collected Books of Jack Spicer* by Black Sparrow Press (1975), edited by Blaser, which republished many of these collections and, therefore, provides a clearer indication of Spicer's work and evolution as a poet.

Spicer began work on *After Lorca* in 1957 while conducting his "Poetry as Magic Workshop" in San Francisco, which was instrumental in shaping the poetry community in the North Beach area of San Francisco. As Blaser notes, "magic, it became clear, was a matter of disturbance, entrance and passion, rather than abracadabra" (*Collected*, 353). Spicer's assignments would often involve difficult tasks to stimulate both the intellect and the imagination. For example, he would ask the participants, which included Duncan, George Stanley, Joe Dunn, Helen Adam, and others, to "Create a Universe" or "Become a flesh eating beast" and then write a poem. From this workshop there arose a kind of aesthetic that revealed Spicer's poetic sensibility; that is, a very impersonal impulse that somehow reveals more of the personal through a kind of engagement with language itself and that which exists outside of the self.

Following *After Lorca* Spicer wrote *Admonitions* (1958), where he furthered his poetic experiments and showed a strong contention that the author and the work are inextricably linked to a specific social community. Most of the poems in this collection are dedicated to various friends and members of Spicer's poetry group, including several love poems. However, they are not love poems in a traditional or conventional sense, because they tend to amplify the inadequacies and inabilities of relationships, while also conflating these problems with the same difficulties experienced in the attempt to produce coherent meaning through language. *A Book of Music*, *Billy the Kid*, and *Fifteen False Propositions Against God* were also published in 1958. In each of these serial poems, Spicer continues a kind of radical regionalism whereby the poem is itself the site of a kind of shared understanding through language. In *Billy the Kid* Spicer once again uses collage techniques, mixes prose and poetry, and conflates pop cult figures with personal friends. The character Billy the Kid, for instance, seems to suggest the infamous outlaw, as well as Spicer's friend and onetime lover, Russell Fitzgerald. Although Spicer's text invokes these figures, his language is certainly more complex than only actual or symbolic references. The characters in his poetry point to a difficulty in perception, memory and meaning that somehow becomes intertwined with notions of alienation, loneliness, and love: "So the heart breaks / Into small shadows / Almost so random / they are meaningless" (83).

Spicer's next several "books" or serial poems, all published between 1959 and 1961, include *Apollo Sends Seven Nursery Rhymes to James Alexander* (1959), *A Red Wheelbarrow* (1959), *Lament for the Makers* (1961), and *The Heads of the Town Up to the Aether* (1961). Also at this time, Spicer's "Imaginary Elegies I–V" were included in Donald Allen's famous anthology, *The New American Poetry: 1945–1960*, which also published such poets as **Allen Ginsberg**, **Frank O'Hara**, **John Ashbery**, and **Jack Kerouac**. Spicer's inclusion revealed that the poet had moved beyond the regionalism of San Francisco and had begun to receive national recognition. In these poems and most of his poetry from this period, especially *The Heads of the Town*, Spicer's notion of the poem as something that is dictated or received from a source outside of the self became most evident. This concept of the poem as dictation is considered one of his most radical and influential ideas. In a series of lectures given in San Francisco and Vancouver in 1965, Spicer explains that the poet is similar to a radio receiving various waves from outside. He uses this metaphor to assert that the poet is merely a conduit or a kind of vessel for ideas that originate from somewhere else: "essentially you are something which is being transmitted into, and the more that you clear your mind away from yourself, and the more also that you do some censoring—because there will be all sorts of things coming from your mind, from the depths of your mind, from things that you want, which will foul up the poem" (*House*, 7). Spicer also relates several, mostly metaphorical, possibilities as to who or what actually dictates the poem, ranging from ghosts and spooks to "Green Martians" to dead baseball players to various poets throughout history.

Although some critics have found these ideas quite unbelievable, Spicer did effectively challenge the established paradigms regarding identity within a poem. In other words, he questioned the relationship between the poet and others, and how this relation is mediated through language. His ideas subverted the dominant assumption put forward in academic and poetry circles that the ego or "I" is at the center of the poem. His challenge ultimately meant a radical reordering of the way in which identity and the self is perceived and constructed through the poem. Moreover, some of the supposed sources of poetry (e.g., spooks and Martians) are largely figurative for Spicer and represent a kind of hyperbolic expression to challenge the poet as the source of the poem. In addition, Spicer's sources are radically different than the idea of a divine or spiritual muse that is often connected to a kind of vigorous interiorization put forward by various poets in different epochs, but especially the British Romanticists of the nineteenth century (e.g., William Wordsworth, Samuel Taylor Coleridge, William Blake). For Spicer, the ghosts, Martians, or radio transmissions are not so much inspirational as they are disruptive. That is, the dictation subverts meaning and conventional structures of language. The dictation becomes an added destabilizing gesture that challenges the relationship of literature to reality and the relationship between language and human experience. Spicer argues that both the content and the form of the poem are dictated, and, therefore, language, meaning, structure, and shape are all subject to the voices from outside. This problematizes the idea of the poet as a visionary and, instead, places him or her within a shared community. Thus, the poem becomes less a private artifact than a public, historical, and cultural text. The subject is no longer at the center of the poem and, therefore, other forces become a factor in shaping the direction and content of the poem.

Spicer also emphasizes a kind of mistrust in language. In the poem "Sheep Trails Are Fateful to Strangers" he writes, "What I mean is words / Turn mysteriously against those who use them" (125). This demonstrates Spicer's suspicion of language, as well as his interest in subverting existing paradigms and structures about literature and poetry. As critic Peter Gizzi argues, Spicer's vision consistently involves dissent. The poet's next three books, *The Holy Grail* (1962), *Language* (1965), and *Book of Magazine Verse* (1966), exemplify this notion of subversion and dissent, as well as Spicer's idea of the serial poem. The serial poem, his next most influential idea after the notion of the poem as dictation, involves a group of connected poems that are dictated in chronological order. The "seriality" of the poem is essentially synonymous with the direction of the book or a kind of intuitive map of the text itself. However, for Spicer, intuition involves knowing and acknowledging the work as dictated from outside and not the ideas of the poet. Spicer further suggests that the poet must enter the process of creation in a serial poem first by not knowing what to expect and without looking back. He asserts that the best thing the poet can do in composing a poem is "to try to keep as much of yourself as possible out of the poem" (8). What follows in a serial poem, then, is a kind of unit that is not a totalizing structure but that is somehow related poetically. In other words, the serial poem is the form that the poet writes within, but that he or she is ignorant of. These texts also reveal Spicer's impulse to use everyday language and events to represent and explore complex ideas. In *The Holy Grail* Spicer reworks the Arthurian Grail legend into a contemporary pastiche that simultaneously critiques and celebrates the classic quest narrative. The tension in this text involves a struggle with understanding and with ideas about love, as well as an attempt to reconcile the visible and the invisible. In *Language* Spicer despairs that "[n]o one listens to poetry" (217), yet he is compelled to continue writing. In this text the poet explores the purpose of poetry and the impact of language on the imagination and perception. The poet writes, "Let us tie the strings on this bit of reality" (*Collected*, 240), and then later concludes that "time leaves us / Words, loves" (*Collected*, 243). In his final book Spicer invents a kind of dialogue between magazines from the *Nation* to *Poetry Chicago* to the *St. Louis Sporting News*. Spicer explores one of his ongoing obsessions—baseball—and he revisits a kind of regionalism. He concludes the poem with what some critics have argued is an address to Allen Ginsberg, one of the prominent figures in the **Beat movement**: "At least we both know how shitty the world is. You wearing a beard as a mask to disguise it. I wearing my tired smile" (267).

Spicer's influence on contemporary American poetry continues to expand. Many critics argue that Spicer directed a new kind of focus toward the materiality of language and the textual aspects of the poem. This seems to be echoed in his last words to Robin Blaser: "My vocabulary did this to me." His untimely death as a result of alcoholism has created a kind of mythic aura about the poet, and one he would most likely explicitly reject, but secretly relish.

Further Reading. ***Selected Primary Sources:*** Spicer, Jack, *The Collected Books of Jack Spicer* (Santa Rosa, CA: Black Sparrow Press, 1975); ———; *The House That Jack Built: The Collected Lectures of Jack Spicer* (Hanover, NH: University Press of New England, 1998). ***Selected Secondary Sources:*** Davidson, Michael, *The San Francisco Renaissance: Poetics and Community at Mid-Century* (Cambridge: Cambridge University Press, 1989); Ellingham, Lewis, and Kevin Killian, *Poet Be Like God:*

Jack Spicer and the San Francisco Renaissance (Hanover, NH: University Press of New England, 1998); Foster, Edward Halsey (Boise, ID: Boise State University, 1991); Spanos, William V., ed., Jack Spicer issue, (*boundary 2* 6.1 [Fall 1977]).

Mark Tursi

SPIRES, ELIZABETH (1952–)

Elizabeth Spires belongs to the younger generation of post-World War II American poets. An acclaimed author of five volumes of poetry and children's books, in her verse she draws on the American canon, both nineteenth- and twentieth-century, for her inspiration: **Edgar Allan Poe**, **Walt Whitman**, **Emily Dickinson**, **Robert Frost**, **W.D. Snodgrass**, **Josephine Jacobsen**, **John Berryman**, **Robert Lowell**, **A.R. Ammons**, and especially **Elizabeth Bishop**. In 1977 Spires conducted an interview with Bishop for the *Paris Review*, the last Bishop ever gave. Spires is also influenced by the English metaphysical poet John Donne. Her poetry employs both rhyme and **free verse** to depict her prevailing themes of memory, imagination and the flow of time. Spire's work ranges from riddles for the young, to meditative poetry, to the rewriting of myths.

Elizabeth Spires was born on May 28, 1952, in Lancaster, Ohio. She received her education at Vassar College in New York, where she was awarded a BA in English in 1974, and at Johns Hopkins University in Baltimore, Maryland, where she earned her MA in 1979. Between 1977 and 1981 she worked as an assistant editor in the Charles E. Merrill Publishing Company, and then as a freelance writer. Later Spires accepted several teaching jobs as a professor of English. In 1981 and 1982 she was a poet-in-residence at Loyola College in Baltimore. In 1985 she married the novelist Madison Smartt Bell. During her academic career, she has taught a number of courses in creative writing at Johns Hopkins University and Goucher College. She currently lives in Baltimore.

When she was twelve years old, Spires read the short story "Everything that Rises Must Converge" by Flannery O'Connor. That experience led to Spires's decision to become a fiction writer. However, during her university study she switched from short stories to poetry writing and published *Globe*, her first collection of poetry, in 1981. The book is influenced by both metaphysical and transcendental poetics, as the opening poem "Tequila" shows: "taking the only road / out of the valley, / the one that leads everywhere." Four years later Spires published her next collection, *Swan's Island* (1985), which contains poems based on photographs of New Orleans by E.J. Bellocq. In 1989 Spires's third collection, *Annonciade*, followed. The poems are meditations on the possible relationship between life and death and concentrate on objects, topoi, and landscapes. Her best-known collection, *Worldling* (1995), introduces the theme of motherhood. For Spires, becoming a mother has been a transforming experience. Since then she has acquired more philosophical depth, while her poetry has remained as lucid as ever. The opening poem, "The First Day," includes a striking line: "I have had a child. Now I must live with death." Spires explains in an interview: "I know that that's a line that makes some readers cringe, but . . . that line connects to what I'm still thinking about: my own mortality and the mortality of those close to me." The final poem, "Life Everlasting," prefers death to immortality: "Our only paradise is here, / and we are rich as misers, rich in change! Spires is increasingly preoccupied with death and loss: "I see where the next book is heading; it is preoccupied with these losses [parents, mentors, close friends]."

The prevailing theme of death has also brought Spires to the exploration of myths and archetypes. She tries to give them a contemporary context and people them with modern personae, as did Frost. Such adaptations of Greek and Roman myths are included in her book *I Am Arachne* (2001).

Spires's next collection, with the Whitmanian title *Now the Green Blade Rises* (2002), continues to address the mortality theme. It is cast in an elegiac tone as the speaker witnesses the process of dying and ultimate death of her mother. Grief and despair are balanced with the reconciliation provided by Zen.

Spires is frequently included in anthologies, such as *Best American Poetry* (five volumes), and periodicals, such as the *New Yorker*, *American Poetry Review*, *Yale Review*, *Partisan Review*, *New Criterion*, and *Paris Review*. Spires prefers tight formal structures but does not obey them strictly. Occasionally, she uses rhyme, sometimes off-rhyme, and there is a strong tendency to use repetition of words at irregular intervals, which produces an echoing effect. She claims that her writing technique has not changed over the years: "I am still just writing poems about what is directly in front of me that's all-engrossing, trying to write really directly. I've never been prolific; for me poems are like major events. Even if they're about something small—that something may seem small to other people, but it doesn't feel small to me."

Besides poetry, Spires is the author of popular children's books, including *With One White Wing* (1995) and *Riddle Road: Puzzles in Poems and Pictures* (1999). Brainteasers in verse are accompanied by illustrations by Erik Blegvad. Critics praised her next book, *The Mouse of Amherst* (1999), a story about a mouse named Emmeline who lives in the house of Emily Dickinson. The mouse becomes acquainted with Dickinson's poetry, and, inspired by the poet, Emmeline responds with poetry of her own; she even develops a friendship with Dickinson. The story is not mere entertainment; it also supplies valuable historical background to Dickinson's writing and thus pays tribute to her. Spire's most recent children's book is *The Big Meow* (2002).

No survey of Spires's writing is complete without acknowledgment of her editorial work. In *The Instant of Knowing* (2002) she collected lectures, criticism, and prose, as well as three previously uncollected poems, by the poet Josephine Jacobsen, a writer Spires believes is still very under-appreciated.

Spires has received numerous awards, including a Whiting Award, a Guggenheim fellowship, the Amy Lowell Traveling Poetry scholarship, and two fellowships from the National Endowment for the Arts. She received the Witter Bynner Prize for Poetry from the American Academy of Arts and Letters in 1998, and the Maryland Author Award from the Maryland Library Association.

Further Reading. ***Selected Primary Sources:*** Spires, Elizabeth, *Annonciade* (New York: Viking, 1989); ———, *The Big Meow* (Cambridge, MA: Candlewick, 2002); ———, *Globe* (Middletown, CT: Wesleyan University Press, 1981); ———, *The Mouse of Amherst* (New York: Farrar, Straus and Giroux, 1999); ———, *Now the Green Blade Rises* (New York: W.W. Norton, 2002); ———, *Riddle Road: Puzzles in Poems and Pictures* (New York: M.K. McElderly Books, 1999); ———, *Swan's Island* (New York: Holt, 1985); ———, *With One White Wing* (New York: Schuster, 1995); ———, Worldling (New York: W.W. Norton, 1995); ———, *The Instant of Knowing* (Ann Arbor: University of Michigan Press, 1997). ***Selected Secondary Sources:*** Christie, A.V., "About Elizabeth Spires" (*Ploughshares* 25.4 [Winter 1999–2000]: 10–15); ———, "The Power of the Visible Is the Invisible" (*Southwest Review* 80.1 [Winter 1995]: 35–57); Taylor, Henry, "In the Everlasting Present: The Poetry of Elizabeth Spires" (*Hollins Critic* [April 2002]: 1–19).

Pavlína Hácová

SPIVACK, KATHLEEN (1938–)

Kathleen Spivack was part of the generation of American poets who came of age and whose creative work first blossomed during the counter-culture and feminist movements of the 1960s. Although she began publishing her work in magazines and newspapers while still an undergraduate, it was during her senior year of study with the poet **Robert Lowell** that she began to write in the **Imagistic** and personal style that she has continued to hone throughout her career. Encouraged by Lowell to develop her own voice and following an inner urgency to render her experience as a woman in **lyrical** and accessible language, Spivack has for thirty years continued to write and publish poetry, fiction and nonfiction, and to support and mentor a younger generation of poets in the United States and Europe.

Born in New York City in 1938—on a fire truck in the midst of a hurricane—Kathleen Spivack grew up in North Bennington, Vermont, one of four children in a family of writers, artists, and intellectuals. Her parents were Austrian-German refugees who had recently arrived in America, and from an early age Spivack was exposed to literature and music, as well as to the events of World War II being discussed by the adults in her childhood home. Her father, the renowned economist and political scientist Peter Drucker, read to her from Greek mythology and encouraged her early desire to become a writer. She also studied cello from the age of eight, learned to play a variety of other musical instruments, and sang and performed as a young woman. All of these influences are evident in her poetry, which is musical, dramatic, and direct; it is also personal and deeply engaged with the world, attempting to situate the individual in the historical and political context of her time.

After high school, Spivack attended Oberlin College in Ohio, where she majored in English and history and minored in music. Although the curriculum at that time did not include a formal creative writing program, she flourished in the progressive environment there, leading creative writing classes for fellow undergraduates, editing the campus literary magazine, and writing for the Cleveland *Plain Dealer.* In 1959, during her senior year, she was awarded a Gage Foundation fellowship for her journalistic work with the *Plain Dealer.* The fellowship allowed her to go to Boston to study with Lowell at Boston University; later, she would participate in Lowell's "office hours" at Harvard University, which were attended by poets from all over the northeastern United States. Spivack studied in a private tutorial with Lowell and attended his classes, which also included **Sylvia Plath**, **Anne Sexton**, and others. Lowell was instrumental in supporting a variety of young writers and exposing them to the work of **modern** and postmodern poets. While **Ezra Pound** and **T.S. Eliot** had paved the way for poets to write about historical and political events, Lowell encouraged his students to do so in a more direct and immediate way, to address the impact of those events on the individual, and to discover their own most compelling material. For Spivack that material would come to include the concerns of women and children, particularly in times of upheaval and war, and specifically in the era of U.S. involvement in the war in Vietnam.

Spivack's first book, *Flying Inland*, was published by Doubleday in 1971 and praised by critics for the freshness of its imagery and the directness of its speech. In poems such as "But You, My Darling, Should Have Married the Prince," the language is conversational, relaxed, and fluid; yet the work retains an echo of formality, with occasional rhyme or slant rhyme and carefully crafted lyricism. Yet the stirrings of dissatisfaction with convention are evident here, as well. At the end of "But You, My Darling," "the apples rot with wishes" and "there is no magic." In "Mythmaking" "Beauty is never satisfied / with beauty." Spivack's second volume, *The Jane Poems*, published by Doubleday in 1973, was a more dramatic departure from tradition in terms of both subject matter and style. Although occasional rhyme still appears, it does so in a darker context here, and more for the sake of irony than beauty: "Jane lies with her man in a downtown shack / she hears the gunmen going ack ack" ("Jane the Victim the Lovely One"). In other poems from the volume, the lines are jaggedly broken, the syntax fractured. Spivack's creation of the "crazy Jane" persona allowed her to write about the violence that was occurring domestically and internationally in a way that was both immediate and at one remove from the purely personal; the effect was controversial. Spivack also presented the text in **performance** with **blues** and **jazz** musicians in clubs and theaters around the United States in the 1970s. Also in the 1970s, her work was included in the groundbreaking anthology *No More Masks* (edited by Florence Howe and Ellen Bass), placing Spivack among those American women poets for whom a trail had been blazed by Plath and Sexton, and who addressed and validated women's experience from a distinctly female perspective. During those years, Spivack was living in Boston, teaching and raising two children. A Bunting fellowship in the early 1970s afforded her time to write. Her third and fourth collections, *Swimmer in the Spreading Dawn* (1981) and *The Breakup Variations* (1985), continued to explore the themes of sexual struggle, as well as the struggle between women and men, female and male; the poems reincorporated the imagery from the natural world of her earlier work, as well as musical structuring. In 1986 Scarecrow Press published *The Beds We Lie In: Selected and New Poems*, which was nominated that year for the Pulitzer Prize. Her collection of short stories, *The Honeymoon*, was also published in 1986 by Graywolf Press. In the early 1990s Spivack began living part time in Paris, where she is a visiting professor of American literature and creative writing in the French university system. She continues to give lectures and readings and lead conferences in Europe and the United States. Her most recent work, published in magazines and literary journals, includes **ekphrastic** poetry, formal poetry, and **free verse** poems in prose. She has also completed the manuscript of a memoir about her years spent studying with Robert Lowell.

Further Reading. ***Selected Primary Sources:*** Spivack, Kathleen, *The Beds We Lie In* (Lanham, MD: Scarecrow Press, 1986); ———, *Swimmer in the Spreading Dawn* (Boston: Applewood Press, 1981); ———, *The Jane Poems* (New York: Doubleday, 1973); ———, *Flying Inland* (New York: Doubleday, 1971); ———, *The Honeymoon* (short stories; also translated into French [1992]) (St. Paul, MN: Graywolf Press, 1986). ***Selected Secondary Sources:*** Kennedy, Terry, "An Interview with Kathleen Spivack" (*Massachusetts Review: A Quarterly of Literature, the Arts and Public Affairs* 21.3 [Fall 1980]: 540–547).

Cecilia Woloch

SPOFFORD, HARRIET PRESCOTT (1835–1921)

Harriet Prescott Spofford's writing career spanned sixty years, during which time she published extensively in periodicals, including the *Atlantic Monthly*, *Harper's Bazaar*, *Scribner's Magazine*, and *Lippincott's Magazine*. She first gained a wide audience with the 1859 publication of her short story "In a Cellar" in the *Atlantic Monthly*, and would continue to publish prolifically until her death in 1921. Her vast body of work has yet to be compiled in contemporarily accessible volumes, but she produced more than thirty novels, volumes of poetry and plays, as well as over 275 short stories throughout her career.

While Spofford's first love was poetry, she found that prose afforded more publishing opportunities. Nonetheless, Spofford's lush and vivid descriptive language in her stories and novels retained a poetic quality she believed intrinsic to the artistic merit of her work. As a woman who initially wrote to support her family, Spofford was always painfully aware of the changing tastes of American readers and strove to accommodate them. While her early writing reflected the ideals of romanticism, Spofford found herself required to shift toward the aesthetic tenets of realism championed by Henry James in the late nineteenth century in order to continue to find publication outlets for her writing. Spofford eventually did create realist fiction, however, she never lived up to the high expectations that marked her literary debut. With the publication of "In a Cellar," she was heralded as a newcomer with tremendous potential. By the time of her death in 1921, the prolific nature of her writing had led to the publication of work that was of an uneven quality, and she was quietly forgotten.

Harriet Elizabeth Prescott was born in Calais, Maine, on April 3, 1835, the first child of Joseph Newmarch Prescott and Sarah Jane Bridges Prescott. She displayed an early love of literature and began composing poetry at age thirteen. With the once prosperous family in financial straits, Joseph Prescott moved west to Oregon in 1849 to seek his fortune, leaving his wife and four children on the East Coast. Spofford was sent to live with her Aunt Elizabeth Betton in Newburyport, Massachusetts, in the same year, where she was afforded the opportunity to attend the prestigious Putnam Free School and Pinkerton Academy. Her education in Newburyport furthered her literary aspirations and put her in contact with the man who would be her lifelong friend and mentor, **Thomas Wentworth Higginson**. At sixteen Spofford won a prize sponsored by Higginson with an essay on *Hamlet*, which Higginson described as "very daring and original" (quoted in *Halbeisen*, 40). By the late 1850s Spofford had graduated and found herself the sole breadwinner for her family due to her parents' illness. Her father had returned from Oregon nearly an invalid and her mother was gravely ill as well. Faced with dire financial hardship, Spofford supported her family by writing over one hundred anonymous stories for Boston story-papers at a frantic rate and for little money. Spofford's biographer, Elizabeth K. Halbeisen, tells of a time Spofford wrote all night to finish a story for which she hoped to win a prize. Failing in her efforts, all she was left with was a swollen arm the next day. In 1858 Spofford's literary career began to garner critical acclaim with the publication of "In a Cellar" in the *Atlantic Monthly*. Spofford's story was in good company as the *Atlantic* was publishing work by Harriet Beecher Stowe, **Henry Wadsworth Longfellow**, **John Greenleaf Whittier**, **Julia Ward Howe**, **Ralph Waldo Emerson**, **James Russell Lowell**, and Elizabeth Stuart Phelps during the same time period. Lowell, then editor of the *Atlantic*, initially suspected "In a Cellar" to be a translation from the French rather than Spofford's own work, and Higginson had to be called in to verify that "a demure little Yankee girl could have written it" (quoted in *Halbeisen*, 53).

Two novels and a number of short stories quickly followed her initial success: *Sir Rohan's Ghost* (1860), "Circumstance" (1860), "The Amber Gods" (1863), and *Azarian* (1864). While "The Amber Gods" and "Circumstance" are masterpieces in many ways, her novels received mixed reviews. These included a harsh critique of *Azarian* by James, who had praised "The Amber Gods" just a year earlier. James objected to Spofford's reluctance to embrace a realist aesthetic, and his devastating review in the January 1865 *North American Review* was both fair and scathing and foreshadowed the downturn Spofford's literary reputation was to take. Spofford had prominent admirers as well, however, including **Emily Dickinson**. After reading "Circumstance," Dickinson told her sister-in-law, "it is the only thing I ever read in my life that I didn't think I could have imagined myself" and later instructed her to pass on everything Spofford wrote (quoted in Halbeisen, 80).

In 1865 Spofford married her longtime beau Richard S. Spofford, and the couple shared an idyllic marriage until Richard's death in 1888. While the years from 1868 to 1890 were marked by prolific publication, the extensive and often hastily written nature of Spofford's work gave it an uneven quality. At its best, Spofford's poetry earned favorable reviews for its lushness and comparisons to Ben Jonson and Robert Herrick for its wit and emotion, while her prose demonstrated a remarkable gift for Romanticism and the supernatural. At its worst, her tendency to cater to shifting audience expectations led her to rely often on banal **sentimentality** or clumsy realism. After her husband's death, Spofford became increasingly religious and the work she produced for the rest of her life frequently contained elements of this faith. Her later writing included *A Scarlet Poppy and Other Stories* (1894), *In Titian's Garden and Other Poems* (1897), *Old Madame and Other Tragedies* (1920), and *The Elder's People* (1920), the latter a collection of previously published short stories about New England life. Spofford died on August 14, 1921, at her home on Deer Island located on the Merrimack River in Massachusetts.

Compared with her prose output, Spofford's poetry appears minor, but it was well received by her contemporaries. It is fair to say that while she wrote prose out of necessity, she wrote poetry out of passion. A brief mention of Spofford's poems in *Harper's Bazaar* noted: "she writes from real love of them, and values them far above her prose" (quoted in *Halbeisen*, 159). While many of Spofford's magazine poems remain uncollected, she published four volumes of poetry in her lifetime: *Poems* (1882), *Ballads about Authors* (1887), *In Titian's Garden and Other Poems* (1897), and *The Great Procession and Other Verses for and about Children* (1902). The subject matter of her work ranges from poems describing the people and places of her beloved New England, to love, death, and religion. Marked by Spofford's penchant for sumptuous description and detailed imagery, many of her **lyrical poems** feature the vivid use of color, alliteration, and onomatopoeia. In "A Sigh," which was reprinted in *Poems*, Spofford romantically describes a rose, symbolic of a lover's intentions and desire, as "Withered, faded, pressed between the pages, / Crumpled fold on fold," and in "Ballad," a poem found interspersed in the prose of *Sir Rohan's Ghost*, she effuses about "plucking purple pansies" one summer evening "Till [her] love should come to shore." In contrast to such vibrant verse, Spofford's poetry also frequently reflected her personal joys and tragedies in simple, unadorned language. "Lament," which appeared in *In Titian's Garden*, relates the loss of a child in infancy that the Spoffords endured in 1867: "The child is gone, and I grow gray and old. / And still I murmur to my angry grief, / How meager is the life so briefly doled!" In both poetry and prose, Spofford's imagery often contained an erotic, sensual component. In "Pomegranate-Flowers," which appeared in the May 1861 issue of the *Atlantic*, Spofford articulates female sexual desire through descriptions of a woman admiring a pomegranate tree given to her by a lover: "That damasked half of the rounding cheek / Of each bud great to bursting grown." Such sexualized descriptions set Spofford's writing apart from the typically sedate poetic renderings of many of her female contemporaries. Although Spofford published over three hundred poems in her lifetime, critical work on her poetry is limited.

She remains an obscure writer whose work is not widely read. Recent work by feminist critics such as Judith Fetterley, however, have sought to reclaim Spofford as a nineteenth-century author who dealt unconventionally with issues of domesticity, violence, sexuality, and autonomy through evocative language and characters who challenged or subverted prevalent, limiting stereotypes of sentimental femininity.

Further Reading. ***Selected Primary Sources:*** Spofford, Harriet Prescott, *The Amber Gods and Other Stories* (Boston: Ticknor & Fields, 1863); ———, *Azarian: An Episode* (Boston: Ticknor & Fields, 1864); ———, *Ballads about Authors* (Boston: D. Lothrop Co., 1887); ———, "Circumstance" (*Atlantic Monthly* [May 1860]); ———, *The Elder's People* (Boston: Houghton Mifflin, 1920); ———, *The Great Procession and Other Verses for and about Children* (Boston: Badger, 1902); ———, "In a Cellar" (*Atlantic Monthly* [February 1859]); ———, *In Titian's Garden and Other Poems* (Boston: Copeland and Day, 1897); ———, *Old Madame and Other Tragedies* (Boston: Badger, 1900); ———, *Old Washington* (Boston: Little, Brown, 1906); ———, "Pomegranate-Flowers" (*Atlantic Monthly* [May 1861]); ———, *Poems* (Boston: Houghton Mifflin, 1882); ———, *A Scarlet Poppy and Other Stories* (New York: Harper, 1894); ———, *Sir Rohan's Ghost: A Romance* (Boston: J.E. Tilton, 1860). ***Selected Secondary Sources:*** Bendixen, Alfred, "Introduction," in *"The Amber Gods" and Other Stories*, by Harriet Prescott Spofford, ed. Alfred Bendixen (New Brunswick, NJ: Rutgers University Press, 1989), ix–xxxiv; Fetterley, Judith, ed., "Introduction," in *Provisions: A Reader from 19th-Century American Women* (Bloomington: Indiana University Press, 1985); Halbeisen, Elizabeth K., *Harriet Prescott Spofford: A Romantic Survival* (Philadelphia: University of Pennsylvania Press, 1935); Rodier, Katharine, "Astra Castra: Emily Dickinson, Thomas Wentworth Higginson, and Harriet Prescott Spofford" in *Separate Spheres No More: Gender Convergence in American Literature, 1830–1930*, ed. Monika M. Elbert (Tuscaloosa: University of Alabama Press, 2000).

Jessica Metzler

ST. JOHN, DAVID (1949–)

David St. John is unusual among American poets of his generation for his adherence to a Continental tradition originally espoused by **T.S. Eliot** and **Ezra Pound**. Unaffected by the tenets of the **New Formalism**, his basic unit of composition remains the musical phrase as opposed to the decasyllabic line. Indeed, he delights in the pure sensuality of words as they accrue meaning within a larger **narrative** frame.

W.S. Merwin describes St. John's poetry as "distinguished from the start by its intimacy and subtlety, and by a disturbing force, the work of an urgent sensibility and a true ear."

The son of professional educators, David St. John was born on July 24, 1949, in California. He earned his baccalaureate degree at California State University–Fresno. In 1974 he received an MFA from the University of Iowa Writers' Workshop. His numerous grants and awards include the Discover/*The Nation* Prize, the Prix de Rome fellowship in literature, and the Award in Literature from the American Academy and Institute of Arts and Letters. He has taught at Oberlin College in Ohio and the Johns Hopkins University in Baltimore, Maryland. St. John is presently professor of English and director of creative writing at the University of Southern California.

Steeped in the European literary tradition and influenced by such diverse writers as John Keats, William Butler Yeats, Georg Trakl, and Stephane Mallarme, St. John is a leading proponent of what has been called "the international voice." His pursuit of the exotic and strange within the context of the mundane resonates throughout his first volume, *Hush* (1976).

Few poets manage the transition from talented neophyte to accomplished master as quickly as St. John did. Most significantly, selections from his second book, *The Shore* (1980), highlight his growing distrust of rich wordplay as an end itself. This does not mean that he relinquishes Imagistic verve or declines to explore the full register of sounds available to the human ear. On the contrary, his facility with language increases as he confronts the challenge of narrative sequence. A questing imagination informs each line of "Until the Sea Is Dead," a dramatic monologue whose speaker searches for the poetic marvelous at the heart of the living world. He begins by describing the landscape of a former whaling community, "its jagged sockets of rock / And sudden gullies." Desolate among drifts named the Dunes of Abraham by local legend, the speaker tells of a Russian trader who goes mad when his Spanish bride abandons both him and their two-year-old son. The man lashes the boy to the ribbed and rotting hull of an overturned skiff with the intention of cutting his throat. Phospor-lit, the child resembles the fresco of a cherub "painted high / Across the dome of a cathedral ceiling." The awestruck Russian turns the blade on himself, severing the reed of his "Own windpipe." According to the speaker, the Russian's ghost still paces the dunes, and his wife waits in one of the whaler's shacks: "drawing a black / Comb out of her hair." St. John anchors every poem from *The Shore* in the phenomenal world, and demonstrates a Yeatsian gift for combining a terrible beauty with a mythopoetic sensibility.

In *No Heaven* (1985) St. John relies on the exotic and strange elements of an otherwise quotidian existence to divulge the innumerable mysteries of life. "A Hard and

Noble Patience" offers a tantalizing anecdote about a girl who chooses to drown herself in a Swiss lake "[f]ed by a glacier said in local myth / To be a pool of the gods." Fettered by the ringing cold of the glacial current, she sustains an unspoiled comeliness even in death. When her body is recovered, the speaker notices that "even her eyelashes seemed to quiver / Beneath my breath." The speaker endures an exquisite torment as the drowned girl thaws lash by lash in the cadence of his breathing. However, the awakening belongs solely to him: "A man made lonely / By such beauty."

Terraces of Rain (1991), set in Italy, heralds St. John's arrival at full poetic maturity. Like **Edgar Allan Poe** and the French **Symbolists** before him, St. John deliberately rejects the corporeal in a desire for the spiritual. "Last Night with Rafaella," for example, focuses on the speaker's tryst with a woman who flares "rouge along the white cheekbones / Of the most beautiful women in the world." Rafaella imparts certain lofty secrets, such as how "artists' models" wear tattoos "like badges against the daily nakedness." Only after describing these emblems of a fleshly aesthetics does the speaker venture to explore with his fingertips the angel delicately emblazoned on the curve of Rafaella's hip. But we lose interest in the diminutive seraph that danced its brief hour on the point of an electric needle, as the speaker moves past the wispy allurements of the lady's hair to the ultimate inspiration—a sharp intake of breath—an animating principle more singular than any cosmetic or fetish.

In his fifth volume, *The Red Leaves of Night* (1999), St. John achieves a vision that affirms the primacy of aesthetic experience. "Fleurs Mystiques," a series of lyric vignettes, explores his identification with Charles Baudelaire, tracing the Symbolist poet's passage through the trials of erotic love in language that is uncompromisingly sensual and inevitably haunting. In the poem St. John relives vicariously the liaison between Baudelaire and Jeanne DuVal, a mulatto actress immortalized by the French poet as "Black Venus." All her life, DuVal remained for Baudelaire the incarnation of beauty, sensuality, melancholy, and exotic sexuality. By proxy of his protagonist, St. John strives for transcendence through fleshly indulgence and spiritual suffering. Absinthe, opium, intellectual and moral sloth, even carnal delight become various aspects of "Les Fleurs du Mal": "He could smell the blossoming of Jeanne's body / The familiar fragrance of sex that would arise / . . . / & fill the entire landscape" of his soul. But in the poem's sixth section, St. John couples Baudelaire's ultimate vision of redemption through art with his own. He describes a priceless Renaissance lute "[c]arved of rosewood & maple / Its mouth a necklace of precisely tooled roses." The lute is a marvel of artisanal workmanship, an instrument patiently carved and cunningly embellished. Despite intimations of blight and lapsed arboreal splendor—the archetypal fall from grace—the lute becomes an emblem of the poet's self-recognition, an apotheosis.

Further Reading. ***Selected Primary Sources:*** St. John, David, *Hush* (Baltimore, MD: Johns Hopkins University Press, 1976); ———, *No Heaven* (Boston: Houghton Mifflin, 1985); ———, *Prism* (Sausalito, CA: Arctos Press, 2002); ———, *The Red Leaves of Night* (New York: HarperPerennial, 1999); ———, *The Shore* (Boston: Houghton Mifflin, 1980); ———, *Study for the World's Body: New and Selected Poems* (New York: HarperCollins, 1994); ———, *Terraces of Rain* (Santa Fe, NM: Recursos, 1991); ———, *Where the Angels Come Toward Us: Selected Essays, Reviews and Interviews* (Fredonia, NY: White Pine Press, 1995). ***Selected Secondary Source:*** St. John, David, Interview, December 1999 (*Cortland Review* 11 [May 2000], http://www .cortlandreview.com/issue/11/stjohn11htm).

Floyd Collins

STAFFORD, WILLIAM (1914–1993)

From the same generation that produced **John Berryman**, **Randall Jarrell**, and **Robert Lowell**, William Stafford stands apart from poets of the so-called **confessional** school even as his work largely is concerned with the place of men in relation to society, modernity, and the environment. Stafford's usually short lyrics are carefully crafted, frequently meditative pieces reflecting a close attention to human thought, memory, and meaningful act, and throughout his body of work we see a strong undercurrent of spirituality and moral wrangling with the human condition. Unlike Lowell, Berryman, and others, however, Stafford maintains a steady, even tone and mannerly style, rarely venturing into vernacular or the artfully fragmented styles of many of his contemporaries. Rather than deal with political issues of his time in language indicative of desperation, mania, or distress, Stafford handles issues such as war, nuclear armament, Native American displacement, and human encroachment on the wilderness in a quieter, calmer tone, avoiding judgments or easy answers in favor of open spaces where ambiguity, contradiction, and a sense of mystery are allowed to reside. Although Stafford was originally from Kansas and although his work deals with diverse landscapes he experienced, in later years he came to be known as the quintessential poet of the American West. This designation is partially the result of his overriding concern with the natural world and his specific naming of western places, but also because of his clear privileging of the wilderness-as-such over human experience, as well as his evident belief in a higher, natural order of things, all of which can be said to reflect a spiritualist frontier mentality.

William Stafford was born in Hutchinson, Kansas, in 1914 and earned his BA and MA at the University of

Kansas in Lawrence. Like Lowell, Stafford was a conscientious objector during World War II, and he spent time working in the civilian public service camps. In 1954, at the age of forty, he completed his Ph.D. at the Writers' Workshop at the University of Iowa, although by then he had already been teaching poetry at Lewis and Clark College in Portland, Oregon, a position he held from 1948 until he retired in 1980. Stafford's first book of poetry, *West of Your City*, was published in 1960 when the poet was forty-six years old; he would go on to publish more than sixty-five volumes of poetry and prose, including two memoirs on the craft of writing. He won many awards and designations throughout his career, among them a National Book Award for *Traveling Through the Dark* (1962), a Shelley Memorial Award, a Guggenheim fellowship, and a Western States Lifetime Achievement Award in Poetry. In 1970 he was the Consultant in Poetry to the U.S. Library of Congress, a position now called the Poet Laureate. Throughout his life, Stafford rose every morning before dawn and wrote in the dark, a practice his admirers cite as the primary reason behind his sheer volume of work. He also traveled extensively and read his work widely, and he was particularly active in writing programs geared toward younger writers. He married Dorothy Hope Frantz in 1944, and the couple had four children. In 1988 his eldest son, Brett, committed suicide. Stafford's second son, Kim Stafford, is also a poet. Following Stafford's death in 1993, his literary executors—including Kim Stafford—published *The Way It Is: New and Selected Poems* (1998), as well as a collection of his pacifist writings titled *Every War Has Two Losers: William Stafford on Peace and War* (2003).

One of Stafford's most anthologized poems, "Traveling Through the Dark" (1960), showcases the poet's customary style and tone as well as his ongoing concern with human violence in relation to the wilderness. Composed of four quatrains and an ending couplet all in **free verse**, this brief **lyric poem** charts the male narrator's encounter with a dead, pregnant deer on a winding country road. The narrator muses on the doe, "a recent killing," as he drags her toward the edge of the road to pitch her over the side. On discovering that "her fawn lay there waiting, / alive, still, never to be born," the narrator hesitates in the glare of his car's headlights before declaring, "I thought hard for us all—my only swerving—, / then pushed her over the edge into the river." A seemingly straightforward narrative of one man alone making a decision amid his own internal conflict, "Traveling Through the Dark" has been read as indicative of Stafford's environmentalism and mistrust of the man-made world as discreetly emblematic of the poet's deep pacifism, and as a simple meditation on modern man's relationship to nature. In form and style the poem is quintessentially Stafford: tightly controlled, formal, yet accessible in tone and language, and resonant with several weighty silences that invite the reader to meditate on the small but significant experience recounted.

Perhaps because of its very popularity and pervasiveness in anthologies of modern American poetry, "Traveling Through the Dark" also is situated at the crux of an ongoing debate between increasingly divisive poetic camps, the lyric and language schools of poetry. In 1980 as formally disjunctive and linguistically opaque **Language poetry** gained ascendancy in New York and Bay Area circles, poetry critic and *language* writer **Bob Perelman** cited Stafford's "Traveling Through the Dark" as the epitome of the inherently disingenuous and necessarily moribund "voice poem." Citing the way in which Stafford's narrator—ostensibly in spite of his visible efforts at sorting out the situation he is in—exhibits complete control over the content and trajectory of the narrative, thereby forcing the reader into the passive role of mere witness to one individual's linguistic and physical mastery over his environment, Perelman set Stafford's poem up as the model Language poets everywhere should eschew. Ironically, Stafford is on record as saying he understood and agreed with Perelman's criticism, or at least the part about humans' mastery over their natural surroundings (Barnes, 35). Responding to his own independent concerns with excessive human ego, Stafford wrote *Things That Happen Where There Aren't Any People* (1980), a collection in which people and their opinions are noticeably absent as the physical landscape and "you" (the implied reader) occupy the foreground. For example, he writes in "Notice What This Poem Is Not Doing" that "the light / along the hills has come, has found you. / Notice what this poem has not done", concluding a vignette in which "the people are gone" with direct reference to the absence of denotative, descriptive language. Although Stafford never abandoned his chosen lyric form and use of everyday, accessible language, his work in *Things That Happen* and beyond is increasingly marked with irresolution, indeterminacy, and open silences indicative of meditative contemplation shared by writer and reader. In his own way, Stafford too believed in the toxic implications of too much "voice" in literature.

Stafford's progression away from his early opinions about humanity and nature can be traced—with intriguing political implications—through comparison of two poems he wrote about Native Americans, "Report to Crazy Horse" (1973) and "Tourist Country" (1983). In the earlier poem Stafford's narrator is a modern Sioux Indian addressing his fallen chief/ancestor, Crazy Horse. The narrator "reports" to Crazy Horse about the condition of the tribe at the time of his speaking, recounting how the children are taking on the white man's ways; the narrator himself married "a Christian," outside the tribe. The narrator claims to be revealing "a new vision" to his chief, one in which Christian values are saving the people; he further declares how he proudly salutes "the white man's flag" in affirmation of "our generous sayings to each other." Perhaps the most problematic assertion of this misguidedly utopian poem is the narrator's description of his found spirituality in the context of "a religious / colony at prayer in the gray dawn / in the deep aisles of a church." Coupled with the concluding lines of the poem—last-minute references to nature that the narrator and his tribe presumably hold dear—these declarations of Christian spirituality coming from the body of a forgiving, "saved" Sioux are particularly jarring to today's audiences. Indeed, the imposition of white Christian faith onto a member of a historically marginalized and persecuted people, and the presumption of being able to speak for such an individual at all, are practices few if any politically aware poets would embark upon now. They are also practices Stafford himself eventually abandoned as he transitioned away from heavy reliance on literary persona and his earlier, more assertive/declarative style.

Stafford's "Tourist Country" would seem to make amends for the earlier "Report to Crazy Horse," reflecting as the later poem does an acute awareness of the inherently imperialistic nature of the gaze and white man's desire to fix and locate Native America in an objectified state. Invoking language of the shaping properties of sight in the first line, Stafford's abstracted narrator declares, "Shadows, like Navahoes, wear velvet," thereby juxtaposing the Native Americans of the poem with the concealing properties of the viewer's own gaze. Proceeding in this more self-conscious vein, the narrator reflects on light, the glance, and the turning of objects toward or away from the sun; the Navajo do not come under the lens at all, but rather, the act of looking and trying to see is the object of study here. In a concluding meditation on rocks, the only reified objects of the poem, the narrator declares "Each one / cools fast in the dark and re-learns at night / —Oh so sincerely—its local part." These final lines underscore the informing role of the tourist/viewer's perspective and unspoken desire for authenticity, at the same time that they speak to the performativity surrounding "authentic" representations of Native Americans. Concisely and with sensitivity, Stafford has re-positioned himself and his audience away from the privileged, all-knowing position offered in "Report to Crazy Horse" in favor of this self-consciously compromised, always uncertain position of tourist in relation to Native American peoples and culture.

Numerous critics have pointed out that Stafford was primarily a craftsman of and a listener to language, a poet of process as opposed to a poet of final product. Indeed, Stafford's extensive body of work would seem to suggest that he valued and enjoyed the *act* of writing, not letting excessive concern with perfection interrupt or shut down his creativity. In several interviews—which he gave freely—that have been collected in *Writing the Australian Crawl*, Stafford describes the process of writing variously as the act of trying to start a car on ice, gaining "traction on ice between writer and reader" (65); as swimming, "sweep[ing] that yielding medium [i.e., water / language]" (25–26) as he propels himself along; and often as a form of listening—to himself, to the world around him. In "After Arguing Against the Contention That Art Must Come from Discontent" (1982), a supremely triumphant poem implicitly comparing the act of writing to that of rock climbing, Stafford writes, "Oh how I love this climb! / —the whispering to stones, the drag, the weight," the narrator straining against his own weight and the abyss below as he struggles to achieve his goal. His final cry of victory on attaining the summit resonates deeply throughout Stafford's prolific career as a keen and sensitive listener attuned to the world around him: "'Made it again! Made it again!'"

Further Reading. ***Selected Primary Sources:*** Stafford, William, *Even in Quiet Places* (Lewiston, ID: Confluence Press, 1996); ———, *Every War Has Two Losers: William Stafford on Peace and War* (Minneapolis, MN: Milkweed Editions, 2003); ———, *The Rescued Year* (New York: Harper & Row, 1966); ———, *Stories That Could Be True: New and Collected Poems* (New York: Harper & Row, 1977); ———, *Things That Happen Where There Aren't Any People* (Rochester, NY: BOA Editions, 1980); ———, *Traveling Through the Dark* (New York: Harper & Row, 1962); ———, *The Way It Is: New and Selected Poems* (St. Paul, MN: Graywolf, 1998); ———, *West of Your City* (Los Gatos, CA: Talisman, 1960); ———, *Writing the Australian Crawl: Views on the Writer's Vocation* (Ann Arbor: University of Michigan Press, 1978). ***Selected Secondary Sources:*** Averill, Thomas Fox, "The Earth Says Have a Place: William Stafford and a Place of Language" (*Great Plains Quarterly* 21.4 [Fall 2001]: 275–286); Axelrod, David, "Poetry of the American West: Review of *Even in Quiet Places*" (*Western American Literature* 31.3 [November 1996]: 255–263); Barnes, Dick, "The Absence of the Artist" (*Field* 28 [Spring 1983]: 27–37); Shigley, Sally Bishop, "Pax Femina: Women in William Stafford's West" (*Rocky Mountain Review* 54.2 [Fall 2000]: 77–84).

Amy Moorman Robbins

STAND-UP POETRY

Although originally associated with a small group of Los Angeles poets, stand-up poetry is best understood not as a poetic school but as an increasingly widespread aesthetic tendency in contemporary American verse. The term "stand-up" suggests **performance** and humor, as in the phrase "stand-up comedy," and trustworthiness and integrity, as in the phrase "he's a stand-up kind of guy." Although stand-up poems are often humorous, they are chiefly characterized by a conversational voice and manner that locates them in a populist tradition that has rejected the primacy of linguistic complexity, obtuse referentiality, and narrative fragmentation as fundamental aesthetic values. Gritty, feisty, sexy, and irreverent, the poems showcased by **Suzanne Lummis** and **Charles Harper Webb** in their original 1990 *Stand Up Poetry* anthology are clearly literate, though relatively unornamented, intent on straightforward narrative presentation, and written in idiomatic American English. Such poetry tends to be anecdotal and casual, voiced in or around the conversational register, and though it occasionally aspires to the illusion of artlessness, it is the product of intellectually resourceful poets who have firmly rejected central values of **modern** and **postmodern** poetics: Here there is no hankering after difficulty, little inclination toward the foregrounding of language, and an adamant rejection of the aesthetics of difficulty and indeterminacy. Nor are such poets interested in what Lummis has characterized as the "grave, sonorous tone of pious solemnity" associated with the main streams of twentieth-century poetry (Tarling, 20). They are thus very much "antipoets" in Nicanor Parra's sense of that term and can trace back their roots far earlier than Swift and Villon to the scabrous and piquant Latin of Catullus. Lummis, who has a background in theater, and Webb, a former rock musician (now a practicing psychotherapist and university professor), were concerned as well with a poem's performability, although for them that quality is more effectively achieved through intelligibility and narrative virtuosity than through rhetorical or declamatory histrionics. At their most lapidary and concise, stand-up poems aspire to something akin to the incandescent anecdote—a kind of Zen or Sufi tale—delivered with impeccable timing by an incisive stand-up comedian.

It would not be unfair to say that the most salient characteristic of such verse is the adherence to the illusion of "the real language of men," as William Wordsworth characterizes his own experiments at the beginning of his preface to the *Lyrical Ballads*. **Walt Whitman**, in his famous preface to the 1855 edition of *Leaves of Grass*, makes the case for the unequivocal level of accessibility that stand-up poetry represents when he insists that he would "not have in my writing any elegance or effect or originality to hang in the way between me and the rest like curtains. I will have nothing hang in the way, not the richest curtains" (vii). In his introduction to *The Maverick Poets*, a 1985 California anthology that attempted to showcase the various strands of accessible poetry in the United States, **Steve Kowit** quotes the **small press** publisher Alex Scandalios, who characterizes such writers as "easy poets," with the caveat that such poetry is easy to read, not easy to write (1).

According to Webb, the term "stand-up poetry" was first used in an essay written in 1967 by **Gerald Locklin** and Charles Stetler about **Edward Field**'s 1962 Lamont Poetry Prize collection *Stand Up, Friend, with Me*, an essay in which the authors refer to Field as a "stand-up poet." Field's collection seemed to many of its readers to be unusually free of the complex rhetorical environment that marked the dominant poetic modes of the era, both the university-based mainstream verse that had derived from **T.S. Eliot**, **W.H. Auden**, and **New Criticism**, and, even more pronouncedly, the **Ezra Pound**- and **William Carlos Williams**-oriented **avant-garde** that was gaining great influence in the 1960s, a poetry that was associated with **Robert Creeley**, **Robert Duncan**, **Charles Olson**, **Louis Zukofsky**, and the **projectivist** aesthetic. In contrast, Field's poems were reader-friendly, straightforward, chatty, anecdotal, irreverent, and devoid of the acutely intellectualized diction, narrative pastiche, sophisticated allusiveness, and endemic complexity that marked the dominant modes. Locklin and Stetler have themselves been closely associated for many years with the insistently intelligible and conversational verse that has since become known as stand-up poetry.

Another seminal influence on the emerging stand-up phenomenon was the relentlessly hard-edged and hard-boiled verse of **Charles Bukowski**, who had fashioned a tough-guy, plain-spoken poetic line and an anti-lyrical diction that seemed influenced more by Louis Ferdinand Celine and Henry Miller than by William Carlos Williams and Ezra Pound. Two paradigmatic Los Angeles stand-up poets, **Ron Koertge** and Gerald Locklin, both of whom had been publishing since the 1960s, were also considerably influential and, along with Bukowski, made it logical that the stand-up phenomenon would find a congenial home in the Los Angeles region.

Certainly the **Beat poets** were important precursors. Given to the comic and the outrageous, a street-smart poetry peppered with pop culture and tuned to the vernacular, poets such as **Allen Ginsberg**, **Lawrence Ferlinghetti**, and **Gregory Corso** similarly relished breaking down the rhetorical postures and high seriousness of modernist verse. Corso's "Marriage" is nothing if not a stand-up poem. And no doubt the burgeoning public poetry readings that came in the wake of the Beat revolution of the 1960s and 1970s helped open poetry to more public modes of expression. Both first- and second-generation **New York School** poets such as **Kenneth Koch** and **Ted Berrigan** often employed an urban, anecdotal vernacular as a central aesthetic strategy, though the New York School poets, self-consciously avant-garde, were not always committed to a poetry hospitable to the general reader. The more multi-ethnic poetry that was starting to be written during that same era, and which evolved under the influence of rap and hip-hop into the spoken word/**slam poetry** movement, was also influential though it might be more accurate to say there was, among all these aesthetic persuasions, a great deal of cross-fertilization.

Koertge's "I Went to the Movies Hoping Just Once the Monster Got the Girl" (*Diary Cows*, 1981) is a representative stand-up poem, the lengthy, colloquial and somewhat humorous title itself indicative of the poet's aesthetic orientation. In the opening stanza the speaker, mulling over his disastrous high school years, tells us that while the movie monster longed for the archeologist's "terrific assistant" he himself hid in his bedroom "acne lighting up the gloom like / a spotlight." Needless to say, in the movies, the irresistible ingenue ends up in the arms of the handsome hero. The poem concludes "with this stereotypical image: the weeping 'Sweater Girl' \ running to the 'rolled-up sleeves \ of the hero; but the narrator's response is to cry as well, 'afraid for myself, lonely as \ a leftover thumb.' \ A group of cheerleaders \ ask some "high scorers \ what's wrong with him, to which the latter reply, 'He's weird.'"

Though one could mention the metonymous use of "rolled up sleeves," the striking and complex metaphor of the leftover thumb, and the witty ambiguity of "high scorers," it is the ear for colloquial phrasing and both the charm and transparency of the narrative that are most striking. However crisp and inventive, the language is ever at the service of the narrative content, which itself is often, as in this poem, a brilliantly incisive metaphoric conceit. That Hollywood monster movies have replaced Greek legend as the poem's mythological ground is also indicative of the pop-culture ambience of stand-up poetry.

If the 1990 edition of *Stand Up Poetry* was focused almost exclusively on the Los Angeles region, with only a few poets representing other parts of the country (most significantly, Ed Field and **Billy Collins**), the enlarged 1994 edition, edited solely by Webb, had a decidedly more national flavor. The number of poets tripled and the volume included work by **Stephen Dobyns**, **Denise Duhamel**, Terry Hertzler, **Tony Hoagland**, **David Kirby**, **Dorianne Laux**, **Thomas Lux**, Paul Zimmer, and Al Zolynas—among other poets committed to a poetry at once unpretentious and accessible. In a further expanded edition, published by the University of Iowa Press in 2002, Webb added still more poets working in that mode. A review of that edition in the *Crab Orchard Review* (Summer 2002) commented: "Maybe the answer to **Dana Gioia**'s 'Can Poetry Matter?' has finally come to this: a glass of wine flung in the face of high snobbery, a pair of bunny ears over the head of theory, a cacophony of class clowns with something to say" (Dusseau, 258–259).

It is of some interest that the poets included in Webb's anthology are not all associated with a vernacular, conversationally voiced, straight-on verse. The 1994 edition, for example, contains a poem by **Galway Kinnell** ("Oatmeal"), and the University of Iowa Press version includes poems by **Russell Edson**, **B.H. Fairchild**, **Albert Goldbarth**, **Edward Hirsch**, Paul Hoover, and Pattianne Rogershardly writers one thinks of as stand-up poets. But such selections suggest that the tendency described as stand-up is both fluid and permeable and that American poets of remarkably different persuasions are occasionally given to writing poems that have about them no scent of the high-toned, fragmentary, erudite, classically allusive, and impenetrable. It is likely that stand-up poetry, a disposition that was once the province of a small body of rebellious anti-modernists in the last decades of the twentieth century, has now become the common property of American poetry in general, so that poets of diverse predilections, both traditional and experimental, occasionally find themselves writing poems in that conversational, unambiguous, and reader-friendly mode sometimes referred to as stand-up poetry.

Further Reading. ***Selected Primary Sources:*** Dusseau, Melanie, Book Review (*Crab Orchard Review* 7.2 [Spring/Summer 2002]: 258–259); Field, Edward, *Stand Up, Friend, with Me* (New York: Grove Press, 1963); Kowit, Steve, ed., *The Maverick Poets* (San Diego, CA: Gorilla Press, 1988); Lummis, Suzanne, and Charles Harper Webb, eds., *Stand Up Poetry: The Poetry of Los Angeles and Beyond* (Los Angeles: Red Wind Books, 1990); Webb, Charles Harper, ed., *Stand Up Poetry: The Anthology* (Long Beach: California State University Press, 1994); ———, ed., *Stand Up Poetry: An Expanded Anthology* (Iowa City: University of Iowa Press, 2002); Whitman, Walt, *Leaves of Grass* (New York: Library of American Poet, 1992). ***Selected Secondary Source:*** Tarling, Sandra, "Imperative: Stand Up Poetry in Los Angeles and Beyond" (*Poets & Writers* 32.2 [March/April 2004]: 19–21).

Steve Kowit

STANSBURY, JOSEPH (1740–1809)

Like most Loyalist writers, Joseph Stansbury has been largely ignored in American literary history. Born in London in 1740, he emigrated from England in 1767, shortly before the build-up of hostilities. A poet and merchant in Philadelphia, Stansbury spoke out openly against the Revolution. He served as a liaison between Benedict Arnold and John André, and was arrested for espionage in 1780. He spent the remainder of the war in New York, as did many other Loyalists, and moved to Nova Scotia, Canada, after the war, returning to New York later in life.

Stansbury was the author of both political songs and satires, and his work has been usefully compared to that of Francis Hopkinson. He was equally capable of producing an ode, a comic ballad, or a song. A typical work is his "Town Meeting," a satirical ballad of over 150 lines. However, Stansbury also writes poignantly about the loss and disruption occasioned by the Revolution. His most often anthologized poem, "To Cordelia," paints a picture of exile in frontier Nova Scotia, suggesting that it's no place for women and children, but ends by inviting the addressee to join him in his exile: "Here, Cordelia, bend your pensive way, / And close the evening of Life's wretched day." This poem, along with other poems of protest and exile, were printed in *The Loyal Verses of Joseph Stansbury and Doctor Jonathan Odell; Relating to the American Revolution* (1860); taken with the work of a poet such as **Ann Eliza Bleecker**, who grieves her family losses after the invasion of the British, this volume offers the not surprising but always important insight that war can wreak personal havoc as much for those on both the "right" and "wrong" sides.

Further Reading. ***Selected Primary Sources:*** Sargent, Winthrop, ed., *The Loyal Verses of Joseph Stansbury and Doctor Jonathan Odell; Relating to the American Revolution* (Albany, NY: J. Munsell, 1860); Stansbury, Joseph, "To Cordelia" in *Early American Writings*, ed. Carla Mulford (New York: Oxford University Press, 2002, 972).

Angela Vietto

STARBUCK, GEORGE (1931–1996)

George Starbuck's poems are calculated to surprise, delight, and shock, playing word games through extravagant conceits, making rhymes sometimes for the sake of rhyme, and always experimenting with the possibility of form. At present he is a critically undervalued poet, although he was acclaimed in the 1960s and 1970s. He won the Yale Series of Younger Poets prize, four years after **John Ashbery**, for his first book, *Bone Thoughts* (1960). Starbuck was a much-admired friend of **Maxine Kumin**, **Sylvia Plath**, and **Anne Sexton**, attending **Robert Lowell**'s and also John Holmes's poetry workshops in Boston, Massachusetts. Two posthumous collections of his poems have recently been published: *The Works: Poems Selected from Five Decades* (2003) and *Visible Ink* (2002), containing late, previously uncollected material.

Starbuck was born in Columbus, Ohio, in 1931, but moved when he was four; as he says in "Magnificat in Transit from the Toledo Airport," he always like[d] to tell it that way, acting / as if I'd sized the place up and skedaddled" (*The Argot Merchant Disaster*). Starbuck grew up in Illinois and California and entered Caltech as a precocious mathematician at the age of sixteen. He dropped out after two years, deciding instead to devote himself to poetry. He studied for two years at the University of California–Berkeley, for three years at the University of Chicago, and for one more year at Harvard University, attending Lowell's seminars, before discontinuing his formal education without gaining a degree. In 1960 Starbuck published his first award-winning book of poems, *Bone Thoughts*, which was followed by a half-dozen later collections, including *White Paper* (1966), *Elegy in a Country Church Yard* (1975), and *The Argot Merchant Disaster: Poems, New and Selected* (1982). After he left Harvard, Starbuck remained in Boston, working as a junior editor at Houghton Mifflin, occasionally taking time off to meet Plath and Sexton after Lowell's class. Sexton would drive them all to the Ritz, illegally parking her old Ford in a "Loading Only Zone," telling the nonplussed porters, "It's okay, because we are only going to get loaded!" Starbuck had an affair with Sexton and was editor of her first book, *To Bedlam and Part Way Back* (1960). He also worked as a librarian at the State University of New York in Buffalo before becoming a professor of English at the University of Iowa and director of the university's Writers' Workshop. From 1971 to 1988 Starbuck directed the graduate writing program at Boston University. In 1990 he was made the Coal Royalty Chairholder in Poetry for a semester at the University of Alabama in Tuscaloosa, where he remained until his death from Parkinson's disease in 1996. The poet's widow, Kathryn Starbuck, with the help of Elizabeth Meese, has edited the two important posthumous collections of his poetry.

In "What Works" Starbuck poses a Zen Ko-an: "There is a live goose in a bottle. How does one remove the goose without hurting it or damaging the bottle?"(*The Argot Merchant Disaster*). One "admired" answer to this problem is, "Behold, I have done it!" In "Poetry Defined" John Holmes suggests another solution: "I put it in with my words. / I took it out the same way." Starbuck's early poem "What Works" offers both problem and his friend's response so that neither will do. After the speaker has "*Thunk*" the "*Thunk*" of his goose, trying to escape his "lovely bottle" (each time "they came out, goose and bottle, neck and neck"), he takes matters into his own hands, "Seizing the pot-lid, *Thwack!*" Thus the "Kind Reader" is presented with "our bruised goose." This exercise works for Starbuck when after the Ko-an–defying "*Thwack!*" he is edified by a splintered vision of what poetry could be, in which his eyes "buzzed as the blue-green bits like sizzling flies / diamond-drilled them." If Starbuck is a formalist and expert stylist, it is because he smashes bottles; he makes his own forms because his poems explore the creative relation between freedom and restraint, as they, by turns, strain and are constrained by traditional models.

In "Tuolomne," written in the 1970s, Starbuck stops to camp on the way home from a trip west to see his married daughter; he builds a poem out of his shifting, regretful ruminations on parables from the Gospels: "I let my seed fall on the rocky ground. / I never laid my talents out to found / The many-mansioned condominium" (*The Argot Merchant Disaster*). His greatest fear as a poet is that he has built, as he has here, his "space-age pup tent on the sand." While Starbuck scratches out "one verbal razzmtazz / And heavy up my notebook with another," he also grieves: "There's nothing I would gladlier achieve / than poetry. I mean the serious thing." In fact, he means Wordsworthian poetry of "pure Organic Form, / . . . / Where not one word malingers from the norm." Critics should be wary of the poet's half-confessions in "Tuolomne." Starbuck builds on sand, but that sand is "a standard / Of competition and comparison / In counting up the offspring of the dutiful." He is not often a poet "[a]s bad as any of those silly gooses / Who put the right thing to the wrong thing's uses." As sand can also be fused with soda and potash to make glass, so poetry that shifts words brilliantly, undermining and reconfiguring form, makes the poet go "glass-eyed onto my knees."

This "spectacle of devastations" in "Tuolomne" becomes the setting for Starbuck's conversation with Wordsworth in the 1980s, as in "Magnificat in Transit from the Toledo Airport": "Merciful Muchness, Principle of Redundance, /. . . / the world *is* too much for us, wait and see!" (*The Argot Merchant Disaster*). Knowing that "The world has a glass center," Starbuck sees Wordsworth through the lens of poems that can "[p]olish [him] off. Take measurements. Melt in." For Starbuck the Romantic way of looking at the world, along with every poetic form that we inherit (including songs and sonnets, ballades and sestinas), must go "into what they call a 'solid solution.' / 'Doping the mix,' they call it" in glassmaking. Starbuck's poems half-disgustedly and half-delightedly explore what Wordsworth abhors in his sonnet: "The World Is Too Much with Us." Starbuck's work is fascinated, as dutiful speculum of late twentieth-century cultural and social devastation, with "late and soon, getting and spending" or what he calls "Power. Dough" in "Washington International" (*Visible Ink*). Developing the innovations of Edward Lear's fluid nonsense verse, in "Sunday Brunch in the Boston Restoration" Starbuck is consumed with the nonsense of shopping and eating in 1980s America, although this poem is also on the road to truth. He surveys a late capitalist world in which chocolate shrimps are chocolate shrimps but wrapped in aluminum foil and for sale: "Everybody a billboard! Certo! Chiapan or is it Belizian /. . . / comparison shopping the toveracks, the quarkbins, the wampeteropenerbarrels."

Such a tendency to verbal jiggery pokery is exploited by Starbuck in the humorous quatrains of double dactyls and double double dactyls from the 1970s and in his many cryptograms and double acrostics. His technical wizardry also turns an ode into a "bad joke" in the first quatrain of his sonnet "The Commencement Address" (*The Argot Merchant Disaster*), and he compresses fourteen lines of Shakespeare's pentameters into fourteen syllables of rhymed paraphrase in the "Space-Saver Sonnets." Starbuck is also quite capable of writing "Sonnet with a Different Letter at the End of Each Line,"—dedicated to the formalist critic Helen Vendler, with each line beginning with the letter "O" and rhyming with the same sound—and of weaving "A Tapestry for Bayeux" in dactylic monometer, with a 156-letter rhymed acrostic threaded through it. But Starbuck is not just a "Belial-the-Kid" as he puts in "The Universe Is Closed and Has REMs" (*The Argot Merchant Disaster*). "[T]hough his tongue / Dropt manna, and could make the worse appear / The better reason," Starbuck is unlike John Milton's Belial in Book II of *Paradise Lost* or Billy the Kid, because he does not "perplex and dash / Maturest counsels." During the 1960s Starbuck could focus the lens of his art on the futility of "demonstrations" in "Dear Fellow Teacher" (*The Argot Merchant Disaster*) and he produced in "Of Late" what Anthony Hecht has described, in his Introduction to *The Works*, as "not merely the best 'protest poem' about the Vietnam War . . . but the only one of any merit whatever." For all of his technical pyrotechnics, Starbuck is intent on truth. His words, well disposed, burnish with an American gloss, sprouting thoughts or second thoughts that swell in and out of forms, beyond the self, but composed, as Dudley Fitts understood in his foreword to *Bone Thoughts*, "passionately and learnedly from the ground up" (viii).

Further Reading. ***Selected Primary Sources:*** Starbuck, George, *The Argot Merchant Disaster: Poems: New and Selected* (Boston: Little, Brown, 1982); ———, *Bone Thoughts* (New Haven, CT: Yale University Press, 1960); ———, *Desperate Measures* (Boston: D.R. Godine, 1978); ———, *Elegy in a Country Church Yard: Another in a Line of Complete Authentic Decorator Kits* (Cambridge, MA: Pym-Randall Press, 1975); ———, *Space-Saver Sonnets: Purged of Accretions and Newly Published in the Corrected Hemimeter Version* (Cleveland, OH: Bits Press, 1986); ———, *Visible Ink* (Tuscaloosa: University of Alabama Press, 2002); ———, *White Paper: Poems* (Boston: Little, Brown, 1966); ———, *The Works: Poems Selected from Five Decades* (Tuscaloosa: University of Alabama Press, 2003). ***Selected Secondary Source:*** Davidson, Peter, *Fading Smile: Poets in Boston from Robert Lowell to Sylvia Plath: 1955–1960* (New York: Knopf, 1994).

Edward Clarke

STEDMAN, EDMUND CLARENCE (1833–1908)

Edmund Clarence Stedman's influence on American poetry was greater as a critic and editor than as a poet. Nonetheless, his unusual vantage point as a broker for thirty-one years on the New York Stock Exchange enabled him to comment in **verse** on some of the most salient characteristics of urban life in the industrialized North. Despite his close association with the **New York School** of genteel poets (**Bayard Taylor**, Richard Henry Stoddard, and **Thomas Bailey Aldrich**), Stedman was less encumbered by the diffuse classicism and aesthetic idealism that now makes many productions of that school appear sentimental and forced. Much of his poetic output can be classified as "magazine verse," short lyrics on occasional topics that were more notable for their evocations of mood than their philosophical critique. In his later years Stedman became one of the foremost architects of America's literary heritage by editing influential anthologies, publishing essays and volumes of perceptive criticism on his more successful poetic contemporaries, and nurturing emergent poets by championing their works with other editors and publishers.

Edmund Clarence Stedman was born in Hartford, Connecticut, to Major Edmund Burke Stedman and Elizabeth Dodge Stedman. Major Stedman died two years later, and his widow and children were subsequently separated due to financial exigencies and Elizabeth's remarriage. Robert J. Scholnick, Stedman's only twentieth-century biographer apart from his wife, argues that these early trials caused Stedman to prioritize his Wall Street practice over his literary pursuits when later in life he had a family of his own to support. Stedman's interest in poetry was nurtured by his mother, who for a time supported her family with her earnings as a writer.

After a brief tenure at Yale University, Stedman first entered the New York literary scene as a journalist. Some of his most successful comic and political pieces stem from this period. "How Old Brown Took Harper's Ferry" (1859) and "The Diamond Wedding" (1859) illustrate Stedman's gift for turning reportage into social commentary. Stedman's lampooning of a wealthy Cuban suitor's pursuit of a beautiful New York socialite in "The Diamond Wedding" earned him both a challenge from the aggrieved suitor and literary notoriety when the poem sold in great numbers as a newspaper pamphlet. Despite maintaining a light tone for most of the poem, Stedman closes his satire with the diamond-bedecked bride and groom standing in "naked equality" when after death they cross the Styx in company with plebeian New Yorkers "most used to a rag and bone." This harsh egalitarian vision also energizes Stedman's account of the 1869 Stock Market Crash in "Israel Freyer's Bid for Gold." The fanciful "Pan in Wall Street" (1867) depicts the fate of the transliterated Greek deity on the streets of New York. Stedman keenly observes the cultural conflict between the classical pretension of Wall Street's architecture and its hardheaded commitment to getting and spending. In the short span between two quarter-chimes from "Trinity's undaunted steeple," Pan draws a crowd of truant "bulls and bears," only to be driven off as a "vagrant demigod" by the "legal baton" of a policeman.

Although Stedman observed the Civil War at close quarters as a front line reporter for New York's *Evening World*, his war poems lack a sense of immediacy and insight into the exigencies and motivations of the war. While the meter of poems such as "Sumter" and "Gettysburg" convey a martial sense of urgency, Stedman adopts a diction that associates the war with the chivalric conflicts of the Crusades. In "Gettysburg" Stedman refers frequently to Confederate forces as "grey-clad hosts" and "Southern hosts" in contrast to a reporter-like accounting of the heroic acts of individual Union soldiers and units. The war did inspire Stedman to write one of his longest **narrative poems**, "Alice of Monmouth" (1863). The eponymous heroine of the piece is a poor field worker chosen as a wife by the son of a landowning and class-conscious lawyer. The family breach that results is healed when Hugh, the son and husband, is mortally wounded in battle, and his repentant father embraces Alice as a true daughter. Despite the chivalric depiction of combat in the poem and other archaic Romanticisms, the poem's theme is not as sentimental as it appears. Stedman displays keen historical and financial insight by compressing the significance of the War into that of a therapeutic balm for healing the class divisions of the North.

The most notable section in Stedman's collected works is titled "The Carib Sea," and it contains poems written under the influence of trips to the Caribbean in 1875 and 1892. These fourteen poems depict the mingled violence and beauty of a region scarred by European and American imperialism, and Stedman uses the region's ambiguous heritage to express his dark reflections on the emotional and physical costs that he has paid as an urban author and worker in the American economic system. The Darwinian tones of "Sargasso Weed" conclude by characterizing humankind as "parasites soon to be gone." In "Castle Island Light" the sterile solitude of a lighthouse in the Bahamas leads two of the keeper's three daughters to abandon him. The poem ends with the "gray old man / Digging a grave in the sand" for the third, an image that conveys the impermanence and desolation of European influence in the Caribbean. "Astra Caeli," the final poem in the sequence, extends this melancholy tone even to the poet's journey "Toward the one small part ourselves inherit / Of this lone darkling world—and call our home."

Stedman's literary criticism established him as the foremost proponent of an objective style of criticism that considered an author in the context of his society and the literary tradition in which he worked. Stedman's essays on **Whitman** and **Poe** did much to refute the calumnies that had been laid on both men for their purported morbidity and grossness. *Poets of America* (1885) collected Stedman's magazine essays on **Longfellow**, **Emerson**, **Lowell**, **Whittier**, and others into one influential volume that enumerates the strengths and weaknesses of these American poets in terms that are still relevant to criticism today.

Further Reading. ***Selected Primary Sources:*** Stedman, Edmund C., *The Poems of Edmund Clarence Stedman* (Boston: Houghton Mifflin, 1908); ———, *Poets of America* (Boston: Houghton Mifflin, 1885). ***Selected Secondary Sources:*** Scholnick, Robert J., *Edmund Clarence Stedman* (New York: Twayne, 1977); Stedman, Laura, and George M. Gould, *The Life and Letters of Edmund Clarence Stedman* (New York: Moffat, Yard & Co., 1910).

Liam Corley

STEELE, TIMOTHY REID (1948–)

Timothy Steele is a metrical poet whose use of traditional forms and precise, accessible language has repositioned formal prosody into the rich palette of contemporary poetry. Steele has published several collections of poetry, principally *Uncertainties and Rest* (1979), *Sapphics Against Anger and Other Poems* (1986), and *The Color Wheel* (1994). Known for addressing a rich variety of topics, Steele writes about his native Vermont and his adopted California home with elegance and wit. He is also a well-regarded literary critic who has written cogently about the development of modern poetry, among other topics.

Born on January 22, 1948, in Burlington, Vermont, Timothy Reid Steele was the eldest son of three children to Edward William Steele, a college professor, and Ruth Reid Steele, a nurse. He credits his mother's readings of Mother Goose, Robert Louis Stevenson's *Child's Garden of Verses*, and Alfred Lord Tennyson's "Locksley Hall" for engendering his earliest appreciation for poetry. This interest deepened in grade school when Steele was introduced to the works of local poet **Robert Frost**: "He wrote with spellbinding accuracy about a world my friends and I saw around us every day," writes Steele in his 1992 essay "The Forms of Poetry" (29). Readings from his grandmother's home-based library with Keats, Shelley, and **Longfellow** as well as works from his father's political science library by George Orwell, John Steinbeck, Dos Passos, and James Baldwin further enriched his upbringing.

Steele attended Stanford University, whose English program was strongly influenced by **Yvor Winters**, and received his BA in 1970. At Brandeis University, he studied with **J.V. Cunningham**, a rigorous scholar and formalist poet, and received his MA in 1972. Steele was then awarded a Wallace Stegner Fellowship in Poetry at Stanford (1972–1973) and was later appointed a Jones Lecturer in Poetry at Stanford (1975–1977). During this productive time writing poetry and teaching, Steele also completed his dissertation on the history and conventions of detective fiction under Cunningham's direction. He received his Ph.D. in English from Brandeis in 1977. On January 14, 1979, Steele married Victoria Lee Erpelding, a rare books librarian, currently head of special collections at UCLA. Steele held visiting appointments at the University of California–Los Angeles from 1977 to 1983 and at the University of California–Santa Barbara in 1986. Since 1987 he has been a professor of English at California State University–Los Angeles.

In addition to Frost and Cunningham, Steele draws inspiration from a wide range of poets, for example, Shakespeare, Ben Jonson, Sir Philip Sidney, Keats, **Emily Dickinson**, Thomas Hardy, **E.A. Robinson**, **W.H. Auden**, **Richard Wilbur**, Philip Larkin, **X.J. Kennedy**, **Louise Bogan**, **Anthony Hecht**, **Thom Gunn**, Janet Lewis, and Edgar Bowers. Steele's honors include a Guggenheim fellowship (1984–1985), Academy of American Poets Award (1986), Commonwealth Club of California Medal for Poetry (1986), and a Los Angeles PEN Center, Literary Award for Poetry (1987). Though **pastoral** by subject, poems such as "Family Reunion" (*Uncertainties*) speak to frailties that go beyond landscape: to vistas of blue hills, / Or the silence of a still and dripping field." In "Summer" (*Sapphics*) he recounts the season's rich beauty: "Lakes windless with profound sun-shafted water; / Dense orchards in which high-grassed heat grows thick." In "December in Los Angeles" (*The Color Wheel*) Steele keeps his gaze toward Vermont, which brings a certain bemusement, if not poignancy to his verse: "The tulip bulbs rest darkly in the fridge / To get the winter they can't get outside." In "Near Olympic" he describes a diverse Los Angeles culture: "The neighborhood, part Japanese and part / Chicano, wears poverty like art / Exotic in its motley oddities." Steele's love poems are particularly striking. In "Eros," for example, he blends nature and intimacy: "Yet the soul loves the braided rope of hair, / The sense of heat and light, the cheek's faint flush." Donald E. Stanford's review of *The Color Wheel* echoes similar critiques when he praises the collection for its "fresh, perceptive look at ordinary (frequently domestic) events with a tone sometimes ironic, sometimes whimsical, sometimes merely sympathetic. The excellence of the poems is in their language" (385). Indeed, Steele's precision in image and word lends his verse a quiet, definitive strength.

Steele is also an important literary critic, whose seminal study *Missing Measures: Modern Poetry and the Revolt Against Meter* (1990) lucidly traces the developments that led **modernist** poets **T.S. Eliot**, **Ezra Pound**, and **William Carlos Williams** to abandon traditional forms in pursuit of new styles. X.-J. Kennedy elaborates, "With lightly wielded knowledge, Steele revises accepted histories of modern poetry, seeking to explain how meter, formerly the dominant force of English and classical poetry, can have become so widely neglected by most poets today" (299). Steele's analysis, while sympathetic to the modernist's reaction to ornate Victorian diction, is mindful that meter and rhyme not only distinguish poetry from prose but allow it to sing, what Samuel Johnson calls the poet's unique power to join "music with reason." Thus, counter to the notion that writing in form is restrictive, Steele writes in "The Forms of Poetry" that he finds "no greater joy than hearing a fine poet harmonize the infinitely variable rhythms of human speech with the fixed patterns of **poetic form**" (28). To write, then, in meter is quite natural and, for Steele, inspiring, as he states in *Missing Measures*: "I believe that our ability to organize thought and speech into measure is one of the most precious endowments of the human race" (24). Steele's second critical study, *All the Fun's in How You Say a Thing: An Explanation of Meter and Versification* (1999) has been widely adopted by poets and teachers as an authoritative text on **prosody**.

Steele draws upon the rhythms of language and brings form to bear naturally and gracefully upon his subjects. He is a central figure in contemporary poetry, one whose poems bring the world into focus through a beautiful, reverent lens concentrated on our connection to nature and to the everyday with a powerful eloquence wherein, as he writes, "peace rests in form" ("Love Poem," 19).

Further Reading. ***Selected Primary Sources:*** Steele, Timothy, *All the Fun's in How You Say a Thing: An Explanation of Meter and Versification* (Athens: Ohio University Press, 1999); ———, *The Color Wheel* (Baltimore, MD: Johns Hopkins University Press, 1994); ———, "The Forms of Poetry" (*Brandeis Review* 12 [Summer 1992]: 28–33); ———, *Missing Measures: Modern Poetry and the Revolt Against Meter* (Fayetteville: University of Arkansas Press, 1990); ———, *Sapphics Against Anger and Other Poems* (New York: Random House, 1986); ———, *Sapphics and Uncertainties: Poems 1970–1986* (Fayetteville: University of Arkansas Press, 1995); ———, *Uncertainties and Rest* (Baton Rouge: Louisiana State University Press, 1979). ***Selected Secondary Sources:*** Baer, William, "An Interview with Timothy Steele" (*Formalist* 14.1 [Summer 2003]: 20–40); Kennedy, X.J., *Dictionary of Literary Biography, Volume 120: American Poets Since World War II* (Detroit, MI: Gale, 1992); Stanford, Donald E., "American Formalism" (*The Southern Review* 31 [Spring 1995] 381–387); Walzer, Kevin, "The Poetry of Timothy Steele" (*Tennessee Quarterly* [Winter 1996]: 15–30).

Susan Clair Imbarrato

STEERE, RICHARD (1643–1721)

Richard Steere was a merchant and ardent Whig whose poetry was typically written in response to political events of the day. While varied in terms of its quality, his **verse** indicates a willingness to experiment both with form and theme.

Born in Chertsey, Surrey, England, in 1643, Steere probably attended the local grammar school before being apprenticed in 1658 as a cordwainer in London. In 1666, at the end of his apprenticeship to Master Henry Brown, Steere was admitted to the Cordwainer Corporation and became a Citizen of London, a title he proudly bore the rest of his life. As a religious dissenter, he was in time attracted to the political arena and became an ardent supporter of the Whigs and their political agenda. Steere's religious and political views prompted his first literary productions. His first effort was *The Babylonish Cabal; or the Intrigues, Progression Opposition, Defeat, and Destruction of the Daniel-Catchers: In a Poem* (1682), an anti-Catholic poem written in answer to John Dryden's *Absalom and Achitophel*. Steere followed with two broadsides: *A Message from Tory-Land to the Whig-Makers in Albian* (1682) and *Romes Thunder-Bolt, Or, Anti-Christ Displaid* (1682). Steere's political activities and his dissenting religious views certainly drew unwanted and dangerous governmental attention and likely led to his first voyage to New England sometime in late 1682 or early 1683. However, Steere returned to England in December 1683. During the voyage his ship was nearly sunk off the English coast by violent storms. These experiences formed the basis for his *A Monumental Memorial of Marine Mercy* (1684). Steere then returned to New England in December 1684, settling for a time in New London, Connecticut, and engaged in mercantile activities.

However, Steere left neither his strongly held religious beliefs nor his political tendencies behind in England. By 1695 he was involved in another furor, the Rogerene Controversy, writing in defense of Baptist minister John Rogers and protesting mandatory taxes for Connecticut's state-supported Presbyterian Church. Steere's efforts earned him a fine of £5 from the Connecticut Court. In 1710 Steere moved for the last time to Southold, Long Island. Three years later his final known work, *The Daniel catcher. The life of the prophet Daniel: in a poem* (1713), was published in Boston. Steere's longest poetical production makes minor revisions to the earlier anti-Catholic *The Babylonish Cabal* and *Romes Thunder-Bolt*, but more importantly adds poems that show a mature and capable craft.

Steere's earlier politically inspired poems are uneven. For example, *The Babylonish Cabal* has moments of biting satirical wit, but overall the work labors under the constraints of the political allegory and never rises to the level of Dryden's work. However, *A Monumental Memorial of Marine Mercy* is a much more capable production. The poem is lively and dramatic with striking details: "The Chests between Decks swim as in a flood, / Where men up to their knees in water stood." *A Monumental*

Memorial is not only a traditional **Puritan** meditation on God's providence, it is also an important early addition to the tradition of American sea literature. "On a Sea-Storm nigh the Coast" (1713), a much shorter poem included in *The Daniel catcher*, continues the maritime theme, but is a taut and naturalistic rendering of the storm experience, as evidenced by the opening lines: "All round the Horizon black Clouds appear; / A Storm is near." The poem lays aside traditional religious themes to focus on the acts of a powerful nature: "Night, Thunder, Lightning, Rain, and raging Wind, / To make a Storm had all their forces joyn'd." "Upon the Caelestial Embassy Perform'd by Angels, to the Shephards" (1713) is a rare example of Puritan writing of a Nativity poem (they generally did not observe the Christmas holiday). However, "Earth's felicities, heaven's allowance" is even more unique as one of the period's few poems written in blank verse and for its aesthetic meditations, which call into question stereotypic views of the Puritans as a dour and otherworldly group. The narrator advises his readers to enjoy all the pleasures the world has to offer, "our Eyes, our Ears, and all our Sense," and to do so without guilt. Since we have toleration from Above; / Still keeping pace with Time and Moderation." As with the maritime poems, "Earth's felicities" shows not only Steere's willingness to experiment with form, but also his keen appreciation of the physical universe.

Steere died on June 20, 1721, in Southhold, Long Island. His resting place is marked by a simple black slate headstone: "Here lyes buried the body of Mr Richard Steere Citizen of London."

Further Reading. ***Selected Primary Sources:*** Steere, Richard, *The Babylonish Cabal; or the Intrigues, Progression Opposition, Defeat, and Destruction of the Daniel-Catchers: In a Poem* (London: R. Baldwin, 1682); ———, *The Daniel catcher. The life of the prophet Daniel: in a poem. To which is added, Earth's felicities, heaven's allowances, a blank poem. With several short poems* (Boston: John Allen, 1713). Online version: *Archive of Americana: Early American Imprints, 1st Series: Evans, 1639–1800.* No. 1650 [filmed]; ———, *A monumental memorial of marine mercy being an acknowledgement of an high hand of Divine deliverance on the deep in the time of distress, in a late voyage from Boston in New-England to London, anno 1683. In a poem. By Richard Steere. To which is added another occasioned by several remarkable passages happening at the birth of a male child on board the same ship in her voyage returning 1684. By the same author then a passenger* (Boston: Richard Pierce (printer) for James Cowse (stationer), 1684). Online version: *Archive of Americana: Early American Imprints, Series I: Evans, 1639–1800.* No. 377 [filmed]. ***Selected Secondary Sources:*** Miller, Perry, and Thomas H. Johnson, eds., *The Puritans* (New York: American Book, 1938), 667–669; Wharton, Donald P., "The Poet as Protester: Richard Steere's 1695 Defense of Liberty of Conscience" (*Seventeenth-Century News* 34.2/3 [Summer/Fall 1976]: 46–50); ———, *Richard Steere: Colonial Merchant and Poet* (University Park: Pennsylvania State University Press, 1979).

Walt Nott

STEIN, GERTRUDE (1874–1946)

Dubbed "the Mother of **Modernism**," Gertrude Stein was one of the most influential writers of the twentieth century, inspiring the stylistic innovations of such writers as Sherwood Anderson, Thornton Wilder, and Ernest Hemingway. Perhaps more remarkable has been her importance to contemporary authors as well. Writers associated with **Language poetry**, for example, point to Stein as the revolutionary who spawned current **experimental** work. Stein's principal project was to revitalize the English language, which she believed was in a state of atrophy:

> You had to recognize words had lost their value in the Nineteenth Century, particularly towards the end, they had lost much of their variety, and I felt that I could not go on, that I had to recapture the value of the individual word, find out what it meant and act within it. (*Primer,* 17–18)

The compositional strategies Stein deployed generated writing that radically changed the experience of reading; at every turn, one's expectations are challenged by a word that is surprising either in its novelty or in its recurrence. Such unfamiliarity has prompted many, champions and detractors alike, to call her work non-representational. Yet her writing is often fiercely engaged with representation, as her interest in portraits would suggest. Her poetics seek not only to make language fresh again, but to make the world fresh againl. Commenting on what became her signature phrase, "rose is a rose is a rose is a rose," she claimed that "in that line the rose is red for the first time in English poetry for a hundred years" (*Four,* vi).

Born in Allegheny, Pennsylvania, on February 3, 1874, Stein moved with her family later that year to Vienna, where they lived for four years. Stein's radical disposition toward language was likely nurtured by the polylingual envirinment of her early childhood years. The precocious toddler learned German and, in 1878, French, when the family moved to Paris. It was a creative gift to her that in these early years German and French were always on hand to render English fresh, strange, and in a state of defamiliarization she continued to provoke throughout her career. Interestingly, she spent the greater part of her writing life in France, where she was keenly aware, on a daily basis, of the differences between languages, and thus more aware not only of the concreteness of words (their sounds and shapes) but of the unstable connection between word and thing in the world.

On their return from Europe, the Steins settled in Oakland, California, where her father worked as a stockbroker, making some wise investments (including in San Francisco's Omnibus Cable Car Company) that would provide financial security for the family. Stein had plenty of time to read and benefited from the employment of tutors. Neither she nor her brother Leo, who spent their days reading, eating, and wandering in the California countryside, could ever contribute much when asked to report good deeds in their school's Lend a Hand Society. Of the five siblings, it was with Leo—the closest to her in age and intellect—that Stein formed the surest bond; this relationship became even more central when they lost their parents; both Amelia and Daniel Stein died while Stein was still a teenager.

After visiting Leo at Harvard University in 1892, Stein herself enrolled the following year in Harvard Annex (later Radcliffe). There she studied under psychologist William James, whose influence she touted until her death. He inspired her interest in consciousness and human typology, and in the paradoxical notion of simplicity through complexity that propelled her life and work. She credited him with fostering her enthusiasm for all manner of people, experiences, and ideas, quoting him as saying, "Never reject anything. Nothing has been proved. If you reject anything, that is the beginning of the end as an intellectual" (*Primer,* 34). In her third-person memoir, *The Autobiography of Alice B. Toklas* (1933), she delights in reciting anecdotes that betray his favoritism toward her as a pupil. Students who read the *Autobiography* take special pleasure in her recollection of an examination in James's course: "Dear Professor James," she wrote at the top of the paper. "I am so sorry but really I do not feel a bit like an examination paper in philosophy today," and left. The next day she had a postal card from James saying, "Dear Miss Stein, I understand perfectly how you feel. I often feel like that myself." And underneath it he gave her work the highest mark in his course (88).

It was James who suggested Stein move on to medical school, with an eye to becoming a psychologist. Stein attended Johns Hopkins medical school, but lost interest in her courses. She was far more engaged with her summer travels; she and Leo toured Italy, France, Morocco, Spain, and England. In 1903 she started two writing projects, the novel *The Making of Americans* (1925) and *Q.E.D.* (1971), a novella based on an unhappy love affair she had while at Johns Hopkins. That year also marked her fateful move to 27 rue de Fleurus in Paris, where she and Leo lived together for several years, cultivating a mutual interest in modern art and collecting paintings by now-renowned artists, including Cezanne, Renoir, Matisse, and Picasso. They held weekly salons, which quickly became famous, attended by cultural luminaries residing in or visiting Paris.

During these years Stein met people who would prove formative in her life and career. Shortly after developing an interest in his work, she met Cubist pioneer Pablo Picasso, with whom she shared an enduring and passionate friendship based on mutual professional respect. His famous portrait of her, now hanging in the Metropolitan Museum of Art, was executed in the early months of their relationship. She and Alice Babette Toklas were introduced in 1907 and soon became devoted to one another. Alice was her lifelong love, secretary, and homemaker. As these relationships developed, Stein's bond with Leo began to unravel. Leo respected neither her work nor that of the Cubists, and in 1913 the siblings divided up their art collection and he moved to Italy, never to speak to his sister again.

Stein did attract some critical notice at this time, thanks to the publication of *Three Lives* (1909), which she paid New York's Grafton Press $600 to publish, and *Tender Buttons* (1914), which appeared in part through the efforts of another lifelong friend and supporter, Carl Van Vechten. But although she had a number of enthusiastic champions, particularly among young writers, it would be many years before she received popular attention, and it was a struggle to get her work into print. She was very prolific, but much of her work was published after her death, notably in the eight-volume Yale Edition of *The Unpublished Writings of Gertrude Stein* (1951–1958). In 1930 she sold one of her Picassos to finance Plain Edition, a press that would be dedicated to printing her own work. As was the case with many women artists of her time, the public was more interested in her as a character than in her work.

It is not surprising, then, that public curiosity about Stein was both satisfied and further provoked by *The Autobiography of Alice B. Toklas,* a quirky yet accessible memoir written from the point of view of her lover. *Autobiography,* written in the fall of 1932, was Stein's breakthrough book, bringing her fame that unfortunately induced a dark season of writer's block. While she struggled with the crises of identity and audience reception attending her sudden high visibility, she did enjoy the new monetary rewards and contracts to publish manuscripts both past and future. The buzz created by *Autobiography* also primed American audiences for the 1934 productions of the opera *Four Saints in Three Acts* (1932), the work she had written for composer Virgil Thomson in 1927. The attention garnered by this opera is evidenced by its profile as popular reference; in the Spring of 1934, for example, a window display in Gimbel's on Fifth Avenue bore the title "4 SUITS IN 2 ACTS." Thomson and Stein would collaborate on another memorable opera as well, *The Mother of Us All* (1947), although Stein would not live to see its premiere. She died of stomach cancer on July 27, 1946.

Public fascination with Stein in the mid-1930s led to her American lecture tour in 1934 and 1935, and the publication of those talks, *Lectures in America* (1935). These engaging statements of poetics are classic Stein: full of complex simplicity, bravado, paradox, and humor. In "Poetry and Grammar" she begins with the question, "What is poetry and if you know what poetry is what is **prose**?" (209). Such an opening promises answers and, indeed, she offers distinctions between the genres, but then promptly undermines them, finding examples from her own work to test her theories. The result is an exploration that turns on the subtleties of grammar—the role of nouns, for example, or the "gentle tender insinuation" of an apostrophe (216)—and the unstable boundaries among genres. As she continues to tease out the question of prose versus poetry, she reveals the generative interaction of these modes in her work. In her lecture she discusses the poetic aims of *Lucy Church Amiably* (1930), which she introduces on the original cover as "A novel of Romantic beauty." Conversely, of her short prose portraits in *Tender Buttons* (1914), she writes, "I did not mean it to make poetry but it did" (235). Her numerous plays often lack the usual generic markers of drama, such as speech prefixes and stage directions. If one insisted on categorizing Stein's work, most of it might be considered prose poetry, for its dynamic interplay of the verse **line** and the sentence. **Ron Silliman**, in fact, points to Stein as an important early practitioner and theorist in his book on the contemporary unit of composition, *The New Sentence.* Isolating Stein's "poetry" would be difficult and inappropriate; this entry, therefore, addresses some works manifesting the features of traditional prose, especially where these works occasion a discussion of the signature compositional modes that propel all of Stein's oeuvre.

"Continuous present" and "insistence" are the two terms most often associated with Steinian style. Stein locates their development in her important early works, *The Making of Americans* and *Three Lives.* In both, the use of gerunds, the slightly vertiginous orchestration of syntax, and the recurrence of phrases succeed in keeping the reader's attention in the now. In her lecture "How Writing Is Written" (1974), Stein offers another way of characterizing the continuous present; in a discussion of *The Making,* she declares, "from that time I have been trying in every possible way to get the sense of immediacy, and practically all the work I have done has been in that direction" (*How Writing,* 155–156). Such immediacy was vital to the project of portraiture undertaken in these books. *The Making* tracks the history of a family (based on her own family's chronicle), offering dynamic renderings of all the players, then proceeds ambitiously to "describe every kind of human being that ever was or is or would be living" (*Lectures,* 142). *Three Lives* comprises three novellas, each featuring the extended portrait of a woman. Moving beyond staid description, Stein sought to bring her subjects into being, to enact them through language.

"Insistence" is the term Stein favored over "repetition," which she claimed did not exist, explaining, "It is very like a frog hopping he cannot ever hop exactly the same distance or the same way of hopping at every hop" (*Lectures,* 167). In the insistence she heard patterning people's speech, in their way of repeating with change their stories, Stein found the motivation for her style of portraiture. Likening her method to that of the new film technology, she observes, "The cinema goes on the same principle: each picture is just infinitesimally different from the one before" (*How Writing,* 158). "Melanctha" is the most celebrated of the *Three Lives.* This portrait of a young African American woman is made complex and mobile through sustained insistence in both **narrative** and dialogue. Several of Stein's African American contemporaries admired the work; Nella Larsen, author of *Passing,* wrote to her about the story: "I never cease to wonder how you came to write it and just why you and not some one of us should so accurately have caught the spirit of this race of mine" (quoted in Brinnin, 121). One of the poignantly repeated lines in the story deals with repetitive behaviors: "Melanctha Herbert was always seeking rest and quiet, and always she could only find new ways to be in trouble." This behavior recalls Freud's theory of our compulsion to repeat moments of trauma. Recollecting the influences on her work of this time, Stein writes, "I doubt whether at the time I had ever seen a cinema but, and I cannot repeat this too often any one is of one's period" (*Lectures,* 177). Freudian psychology was also of her period, and among the forces shaping her poetic.

The contemporary influence Stein was most conscious of, indeed declared, was Cubism. It is productive to consider the difficult poetics of the prose poems in *Tender Buttons* through the lens of Cubist painting. *Tender Buttons* is a collection of portraits in the tradition of the "still life"; Stein offers three categories of subject: objects, food, and rooms. Like the compositions by Picasso of the time, Stein's poems are anything but still. Where in Picasso we see a new geometric inflection and a shift in the vocabulary of forms, in Stein we see shifts in syntactical order. An adjective or preposition can take the place of a noun, as in "A little" and "a beside." Specific nods to the Cubist aesthetic can be read in phrases such as "A piece of coffee" and "a little corner of ham." Where in Picasso we see the disappearance of a conventional focal point and the democratization of components, in Stein we see the disappearance of the verb, so that we become more aware of the less gregarious parts of speech. "Butter" concludes with "Make a little white, no and not with pit, pit on in within." In Picasso the background and foreground register as equally important; in Stein we do not find the independent/subordinate clause structure, but rather a paratactic model, as in "Orange In":

> Cocoa and clear soup and oranges and oat-meal.
> Whist bottom whist close, whist clothes, woodling.

Another useful approach to *Tender Buttons* has been proposed by Margueritte Murphy, who suggests that a passage such as this marks Stein's engagement with contemporary guides to domestic life. Cookbooks and books on etiquette, keeping house, and fashion, for example, act as intertexts, with Stein both celebrating the domestic and poking fun at the authoritative voice of such manuals. The fruitful results of both this reading and a Cubist analysis evidence the richness of *Tender Buttons.* Stein recalls the genesis of this project as a moment when she "became more and more excited about how words which were the words that made whatever [she] looked at look like itself were not the words that had in them any quality of description (*Lectures,* 191). The portrait of "A Dog," for instance, does not include the appropriately descriptive word "dog." Instead we read: "A little monkey goes like a donkey that means to day that means to say that more sighs last goes. Leave with it. A little monkey goes like a donkey." Creating a portrait that results in something "doggier" than "dog" demanded an acute, new sense of language, one that transcended semantic value. While the book inspired ridicule upon its publication, it also inspired admiration. Anderson applauded her method, saying "She is laying word against word, relating sound to sound, feeling for the taste, the smell, the rhythm of the individual word" (*Notebook,* 49).

The combination of disdain and appreciation was typical of the public reception of Stein's works. While *Tender Buttons* was met with polarized reviews soon after it was written, however, many works lay in wait, sparking controversy years after Stein's death. Many posthumously published works were erotic in nature, and incited discomfort even decades after their composition. In *Gertrude Stein in Pieces* (1970) Richard Bridgman suggests that the lesbian relationship in the poem "Lifting Belly" (composed 1915, published 1953) is "luridly" portrayed. Paradoxically, he also notes the obliqueness of the work, and participates in the popular critical game of "decoding" Stein (many readers argue that "cow" = orgasm, etc.). Such erotic decoding is inadequate to Stein's language play, the semantic indeterminacy itself contributing to a kind of Barthesian textual eroticism. Articulating textual pleasure, Barthes explains, "the word can be erotic on two opposing conditions, both excessive: if it is extravagantly repeated, or on the contrary, if it is unexpected, succulent in its newness" (42). This combination of insistence and surprise aptly characterizes the engine of "Lifting Belly." In the poem the words "Lifting Belly" are hinged to over four hundred different phrases, definitions, and qualifiers. Sometimes these words appear to identify a person, as in "Lifting belly knows this" or "Lifting belly is kind and good and beautiful." In other instances they clearly denote an act, generally a sexual one, as in "Lifting belly is a special pleasure," "Lifting belly was very fatiguing," or the pornographic "A magazine of lifting belly. Excitement sisters." Repeatedly tagged to a copula, "Lifting Belly" simultaneously resists and insists on definition: "Lifting belly is a way of sitting," "Lifting belly is a miracle," "Lifting belly is sugar." Also operant in the poem are instances of mutation engaging the concrete, or visual and aural, resources of language. "Rest" becomes "Arrest," "A door" turns into "adore," "Caesar" reappears as "seize her."

What drives this persistent variability is a radically paradoxical representational stance. While Stein has an interest in representing lesbian eroticism, she repeatedly overturns moments of clear referentiality, thus complicating the very notion of representation. Such a stance anticipates current **feminist** and queer theories, as it actively negotiates the vexed notion of visibility. One of the reasons for Stein's growing popularity in the latter decades of the twentieth century was feminist scholarship, in particular the rearticulation of a literary canon that traditionally admitted few women. Marianne De Koven's *A Different Language* (1983) offered the important claim that an "anti-patriarchal" energy lies in the very experimentalism of Stein's form. Less recognized are texts in which the content is overtly feminist. Stein's final opera, *The Mother of Us All,* for example, honors suffrage activist Susan B. Anthony, critiques gender stereotypes, and challenges androcentric cultural traditions. When Indiana Elliot marries her husband Jo, she declares, "I think all the same he will have to change his name, he must be Jo Elliot, yes he must, it is what he has to do, he has to be Jo Elliot." *Mother* was the final work in a series of operas and plays; the dramatic form was attractive to Stein because "in the poetry of plays words are more lively than words in any other kind of poetry" (*Lectures,* 111). The liveliness of words is particularly striking in Stein's plays, where language, rather than action, attracts the spotlight. She decided to confront what she saw as the troubling "syncopated" (*Lectures,* 93) relationship between audience and stage. The viewer of drama has no control over pace, might still be thinking about the last scene while the action proceeds, might anticipate a climax and miss a line. Stein made a concerted effort in her early plays to avoid linear narrative, "to tell what happened without telling stories" (*Lectures,* 121–122). Her motive was akin to that driving her portraits, which aimed to show whom someone was without description. Catharsis is evaded in her plays. *They Must. Be Wedded. To Their Wife* (*Last Operas,* 1949) includes no wedding scene; in fact, the title reflects the torqued chronology of the play, as the phrase "*To Their Wife*" pre-empts a wedding. Even *Mother,* perhaps her most narrative play, fails to dramatize its defining moment, the victory of women's suffrage. Stein chose "landscape" as guiding figure for drama, making clear her desire to spatialize a temporal medium. Declaring that "story is not the thing," she preferred "landscape not moving but being always in relation, the trees to the hills the hills to the fields the trees to each other" (*Lectures,* 125).

She considered *Four Saints in Three Acts* her most successful landscape play. To constitute a landscape, her subjects would have to act as elements in relation through space rather than characters in development through time. Saints were the perfect choice, she decided, because "A saint a real saint never does anything" (*Everybody's Autobiography,* 112). At the level of content, Stein thematizes her motive throughout the opera. During the prelude we are told, "It is very easy to be land. / Imagine four benches separately." Those for whom "being land" is "very easy" are likely the titular four saints, a reading confirmed by the subsequent "four benches," which suggest the saints can be arranged concretely like furniture. Soon after, indeed, we come upon "Four saints born in separate places. / Saint saint saint saint," in which the four saints are mapped physically on the page. As much as Spain is setting for the play, the page is a kind of landscape upon which the elements of the script are arranged and rearranged. Aural concretization is effected as well, in phrases such as "As loud as that as allowed as that," "Scene once seen once," and "Enact end of an act." Here language comprises a dynamic landscape in which shapes and sounds function in relation to each other rather than in transparent service to story. Stein's emergence from traditional "syncopated" drama was inspired in her youth, when she discovered the thrill of watching theatre in a language she only partly understood. Imperfect understanding of words' denotative values highlighted their material resources, released her from a play's linear narrative, so that "it all being so French [she] could rest in it untroubled" (*Lectures,* 115).

While such experiences contributed to her choice to live as an expatriate, and her love for France and Spain were evident, Stein held a lifelong fascination and passion for all things American. Many of her works, both long and short, evidence a fierce interest in American character. A sampling: *Four in America* (1947) (meditations on Ulysses S. Grant, Wilbur Wright, Henry James, and George Washington), "Thoughts on an American Contemporary Feeling" (*Reflection,* 1973), "American Food and American Houses" (*How Writing,* 1974), *Brewsie and Willie* (1946) (about American GIs). American-ness was something she could perceive uniquely and with acuity from her vantage point in Europe. In 1935 she made the provocative statement that while British writers "just went back to the nineteenth century and made it a little weaker," American writers "are the twentieth century literature" (*Lectures,* 49). If this is so, it is due in large part to her exceptionally innovative body of work, which continues to surprise and stimulate in the twenty-first century.

Further Reading. ***Selected Primary Sources:*** Stein, Gertrude, *The Autobiography of Alice B. Toklas* (1933) (London: Penguin, 1966); ———, *Brewsie and Willie* (New York: Random House, 1946); ———, *Everybody's Autobiography* (1937) (Cambridge, MA: Exact Change, 1993); ———, *Four in America* (introduction by Thornton Wilder) (New Haven, CT: Yale University Press, 1947); ———, *Four Saints in Three Acts: Operas and Plays* (Paris: Plain Edition, 1932); ———, *How Writing Is Written*, ed. Robert Bartlett Hass (Los Angeles: Black Sparrow Press, 1974); ———, *Last Operas and Plays* (New York: Rinehart & Co., 1949); ———, *Lectures in America* (1935) (Boston: Beacon Press, 1957); ———, "Lifting Belly" in *The Yale Gertrude Stein*, ed. Richard Kostelanetz (New Haven, CT: Yale University Press, 1980); ———, *The Making of Americans* (Dijon: Maurice Darantière, 1925); ———, *The Mother of Us All* (New York: Music Press, 1947); ———, *A Primer for the Gradual Understanding of Gertrude Stein*, ed. Robert Bartlett Haas (Los Angeles: Black Sparrow Press, 1973); ———, *Q.E.D. Fernhurst, Q.E.D., and Other Early Writings* (New York: Liveright, 1971); ———, *Reflection on the Atomic Bomb*, ed. Robert Bartlett Haas (Los Angeles: Black Sparrow Press, 1973); ———, *Tender Buttons* (1914) (New York: Dover, 1997); ———, *Three Lives* (New York: Grafton Press, 1909). ***Selected Secondary Sources:*** Anderson, Sherwood, *Notebook* (Mamaroneck, NY: Paul P. Appel, 1970); Barthes, Roland, *The Pleasure of the Text*, trans. Richard Miller (New York: Hill and Wang, 1975); Bridgman, Richard, *Gertrude Stein in Pieces* (New York: Oxford University Press, 1970); Brinnin, John Malcolm, *The Third Rose: Gertrude Stein and Her World* (Boston: Little, Brown, 1959); DeKoven, Marianne, *A Different Language: Gertrude Stein's Experimental Writing* (Madison: University of Wisconsin Press, 1983); Murphy, Margueritte S., "'Familiar Strangers': The Household Words of Gertrude Stein's Tender Buttons" (*Contemporary Literature* 32.3 [Fall 1991]: 383–402); Silliman, Ron, *The New Sentence* (New York: Roof, 1977).

Susan Holbrook

STEPANCHEV, STEPHEN (1915–)

A New York poet and professor, Stephen Stepanchev writes lucid, urbane poems rooted in place and exact situation, and characterized by vivid **imagery** that depicts dreams or cityscapes, remembers parents and childhood, recounts lovers, and observes fellow humans with sympathy. Although his poems strongly reflect his longtime residency in New York City, Stepanchev's work does not conform to the generations of the so-called **New York School**. Rather his **verse** is notable for the craft and search for meaning typical of **New Criticism**, although his strong first person narrators, while mostly serious, often exhibit the wit and playfulness that distinguishes the New York School. He has produced eleven collections of poems and contributes regularly to the *New Yorker*, *Poetry*, and *American Poetry Review*. A longtime faculty member at Queens College of the City University of New York (1949–1985), Stepanchev became the poet-in-residence at a time when that position became established in many American colleges and universities. He served as the first poet laureate of the Borough of Queens in New York City from 1997 to 2000.

Stepanchev was born in Mokrin, Yugoslavia, on January 30, 1915. His mother brought him to Chicago when he was seven, where he quickly picked up English in his immigrant neighborhood. Stepanchev would later turn his experiences as an immigrant and naturalized American citizen into a significant subject of his verse. On a scholarship, he went to the University of Chicago, received his AB (1937), was elected to Phi Beta Kappa, and then completed his MA (1938). He taught at Purdue University and while there was drafted into the U.S. Army during World War II, working in the Adjutant General's Office in London, Paris, and Frankfurt. He received a Bronze Star Medal for his war service. War appears as a subject in many of his significant poems. After the war, he resumed graduate studies at New York University receiving a Ph.D. in American literature (1949). In 1949 he began his long tenure at Queens College of the City University of New York, where he conducted the creative writing workshops before retiring in 1985. He was Fulbright Professor of American Literature at the University of Copenhagen in 1957. His awards include the Society of Midland Authors Prize (*Poetry*, Chicago) in 1937, a National Endowment for the Arts grant in 1968, and the Oscar Blumenthal Prize (*Poetry*, Chicago) in 1995.

In his first book, *Three Priests in April* (1956), Stepanchev presented himself as a consummate poetic craftsman, writing tight, short lyrics that use first-person narrators who are usually wry, detached observers: "Me, poking among dead men's words" ("A Visit"). Before his next poetry collection, *Spring in the Harbor* (1967), Stepanchev published one of the first major critiques of the emerging trends and schools of post–World War II American poetry, *American Poetry Since 1945: A Critical Survey* (1965). This study, including essays on **Robert Lowell**, **Elizabeth Bishop**, **Charles Olson**, **Robert Duncan**, **Robert Creeley**, **Denise Levertov**, **James Wright**, **John Ashbery**, LeRoi Jones (**Amiri Baraka**), and **William Stafford**, has been viewed as a milestone analysis of **modern** American poetry.

A Man Running in the Rain (1969) is the first of four texts published by the influential (now defunct) Black Sparrow Press, which established Stepanchev's reputation as a master of the concise lyric. These collections contain the subjects that pervade most of his work. The lovers in his poems often are women who are both physically and emotionally distant. The narrator of "In the Gallery" from *The Mad Bomber* (1972) observes a female guest at an art gallery whom he can only encounter as, "I mix her in my martini and drink her down at the window." *The Mad Bomber* also strongly reinforced Stepanchev's use of imagery. Poems such as "Monday" employ a rapid montage of images rendered in a succession of simple declarative sentences: "The windows open / On solid geometry." *Mining the Darkness* (1975), arguably Stepanchev's finest work, is particularly notable for his reliance on clever similes to create images that, nevertheless, almost always yield emotional responses: "Nerves arrange themselves like piano keys" ("The House") and "Light slips through his fingers / like water." ("Older"). *Mining the Darkness*, as the title suggests, introduced a darker strain in Stepanchev's work. The narrators in this collection are painfully aware of their aging. Even normally happy events become inverted, as exemplified by the narrator's despondency in "Losing a Friend." Despite having come from the wedding of his best friend, he nevertheless has "an appetite for grief." He describes three old men sitting on a bench who "look like tombstones in the cemetery of the poor: /. . . / They are my future, hurrying on like hunger."

Stepanchev's work is also notable for its pervasive use of images of the moon, the sun, night, day, and the seasons to describe the emotions of his narrator. For example, "Old" from *Medusa and Others* (1975) begins with an image of "melting" stars, then "The whitening trickle of morning / Washes the night out." Water is a constant image throughout Stepanchev's canon. Few poets have been as effective in describing the oceans, rivers, bays, and harbors that surround New York City, where Stepanchev resided. As the narrator says in "Cousin" (*The Mad Bomber*), "Living on an island, I can always hear the water." Stepanchev also places many of his poems in clearly identifiable places throughout the five boroughs of New York, especially Queens County: the Botanical Gardens, LaGuardia Airport, and the East River.

After publishing three chapbooks, *The Dove in the Acacia* (bilingual edition, translation by Rasa Popov, 1977), *What I Own* (1978), and *Descent* (1988), Stepanchev published a full-length collection, *Seven Horizons* (1997), with poems that are cosmopolitan, ironic, tender, and philosophical. The location of the title poem is Stepanchev's longtime Queens neighborhood: "Here in Flushing I let the rain / Wash away my rotting selves." Stepanchev's new collection, *Beyond the Gate: New and Selected Poems*, appeared in 2005.

Further Reading: ***Selected Primary Sources:*** Stepanchev, Stephen, *American Poetry Since 1945: A Critical Survey* (New York: Harper, 1965); ———, *Beyond the Gate: New* *and Selected Poems* (Washington, DC: Orchises Press, 2005); ———, *The Mad Bomber* (Los Angeles: Black Sparrow Press, 1972); ———, *A Man Running in the Rain* (Los Angeles: Black Sparrow Press, 1969); ———, *Medusa and Others* (Los Angeles: Black Sparrow Press, 1975); ———, *Mining the Darkness* (Los Angeles: Black Sparrow Press, 1975); ———, *Spring in the Harbor* (Flushing, NY: Amity Press, 1967); ———, *Seven Horizons* (Washington, DC: Orchises Press, 1997); ———, *Three Priests in April* (Baltimore, MD: Contemporary Poetry, 1956). ***Selected Secondary Sources:*** *Poetry* (165.3, [December 1994]); ________, "Stephen Stepanchev," in *Contemporary Poets*, 7th ed. (London: St. James Press, 2001); ________, "Stephen Stepanchev" in *Writer's Directory*, 20th ed. (London: St. James Press, 2004).

Stephen Marino

STERLING, GEORGE (1869–1926)

George Sterling is remembered primarily as the central figure of San Francisco's turn-of-the-century bohemian culture rather than for his poetic achievement. Yet in the years prior to World War I, he attained a national reputation as a poet. His unconventional themes offered a welcome contrast to the **sentimentality** of his **genteel** contemporaries. His style, however, remained entrenched in nineteenth-century **poetics**, and just as his popularity peaked, he was deemed old-fashioned by the standards of the nascent **modernist** movement to which he refused to conform.

George Sterling was born into a prominent family in Sag Harbor, New York, on December 1, 1869. An early affinity for both literature and mischief seemed to foreshadow his future as a bohemian poet. In 1886 he entered a Catholic seminary where he met the poet Father **John Banister Tabb**, whose primary influence, however, was in encouraging Sterling to quit the seminary. In 1890 Sterling's parents sent him to California to work for his wealthy uncle. But his uncle's influence was overshadowed after Sterling met the frontier poet Joaquin Miller, whose passion, spontaneity, and individualism he found irresistible. Sterling did not write poetry, however, until he was twenty-six and had become the protégé of **Ambrose Bierce.** While Bierce helped Sterling focus his poetic sensibility, another friend, Jack London, introduced him to the barrooms and brothels. In 1907 Bierce catapulted Sterling to national attention by publishing "A Wine of Wizardry" in *Cosmopolitan* and proclaiming him the greatest living American poet. By this time Sterling had moved to Carmel, California, and, with **Mary Austin**, established a bohemian colony, that was more famous for its hedonistic revelry than for its artistic output. In 1912 *Poetry*, the avant-garde **literary magazine**, featured Sterling's work, but in 1916 an assault from its editor, accusing him of clinging to archaic Victorian rhetoric, signaled his impending critical decline. Sterling refused to write in **free verse** but remained popular among conservative critics, in particular H.L. Mencken, who frequently published Sterling's poems in his *American Mercury.* Sterling and Mencken also shared a love of liquor, and while awaiting a visit from Mencken, Sterling became unbearably ill from excessive drinking and ingested cyanide, which he always carried with him in case life became too painful. He was found dead in his room at the San Francisco Bohemian Club on November 17, 1926.

Like most of Sterling's work, the title poem of his first book, *The Testimony of the Suns* (1903), straddles the gap between the late nineteenth century and the modernist movement. While sustaining Alfred Tennyson's *In Memoriam* rhyme scheme for 161 stanzas, the poem is filled with the alienation and moral uncertainty that would define **T.S. Eliot**'s *The Waste Land.* In "Testimony" the poet apostrophizes the night sky, craving "from the silence of the stars / solution" to the mystery of existence, which he suspects has plagued "thy sons on worlds destroyed" and will trouble "thy seed on worlds to be." He portrays the cosmos as an infinite battleground with no "dream of end and plan" to be deciphered from its "syllables of fire." Skeptical of any transcendent meaning in this vast deep, he ponders whether anything permanent abides "Beyond the veil the senses draw," concluding that the eons of generations who have asked such questions have joined the nebular dust at which he gazes. The short lyrics in this collection, however, offset the pessimism of "Testimony" with their exaltation of beauty, however illusive or transient. Sterling believed that the pleasure that beauty offered was man's antidote to an otherwise tragic existence. His poetry, therefore, coupled with his hedonistic lifestyle, helped him "forget all that we dread we are," as he would write in "Illusion" (1916). This idea of escape is at the heart of the title poem of *A Wine of Wizardry* (1909). After sipping a potent wine, the narrator follows his starving imagination, personified as "Fancy," on a journey through enchanted, often grotesque, realms but is never fully satisfied. In "A Mood" the poet, "grown weary of permitted things," would "for a moment's rapture welcome death." In *The House of Orchids* (1911) Sterling's notion of man's insignificance begins to resemble misanthropy. "The Midges" compares humans and their "progress" to gnats, "tiny folk, / Who dart, and hum, and make so much ado." Sterling's most anthologized poem, "The Black Vulture," a sonnet about man's mastery of air travel, is less hostile toward "the human swarm," yet still foreboding.

More optimistic, the title poem of *Beyond the Breakers* (1914) finds Sterling facing the "blind sea" in search of the consolation he had sought in the "silence of the stars," but instead of alienation he discovers "the thrill and union of earth." A tinge of optimism also appears in his **verse drama**, *Lilith* (1919), generally considered his finest achievement. The hero, Tancred, is hideously demoralized by the seductress Lilith, who teaches him that human ideals are an illusion and only pleasure and pain matter. Facing execution for refusing to compromise his last shred of honor, Tancred finds value in the fact that "The dust in man hath lived and loved," and he understands that death allows man to "know the worth of life." Ironically, he is rewarded by being flayed alive while two lovers in a nearby garden block out his moans, implying that man's cruelty is far more demeaning than the indifference of the cosmos. While poems such as "The First Food" and "Sails," from his final collection, *Sails and Mirage* (1921), are nostalgic for more innocent times, others continue to espouse the importance of finding refuge in sensual and aesthetic pleasure. "Dance," he writes in "To a Girl Dancing," "for the time comes when the dance is done." Sterling penned hundreds of sonnets during an endless succession of love affairs. One hundred of these, written to the future wife of Upton Sinclair, were published posthumously as *Sonnets to Craig* (1928).

Sterling regretted having spent more energy on living than on writing and saw the best of himself in the young, austere poet **Robinson Jeffers**. The last book Sterling wrote was a critical appraisal of Jeffers, whom he helped to bring to national recognition—an act some critics consider his greatest legacy.

Further Reading. ***Selected Primary Sources:*** Sterling, George, *Beyond the Breakers and Other Poems* (San Francisco: Robertson, 1914); ———, *The Caged Eagle and Other Poems* (San Francisco: Robertson, 1916); ———, *The House of Orchids and Other Poems* (San Francisco: Robertson, 1911); ———, *Lilith* (San Francisco: Robertson, 1919); ———, *Sails and Mirage and Other Poems* (San Francisco: Robertson, 1921); ———, *Selected Poems* (New York: Holt, 1923); ———, *Sonnets to Craig* (New York: A. and C. Boni, 1928); ———, *The Testimony of the Suns and Other Poems* (San Francisco: W.E. Wood, 1903); ———, *The Thirst of Satan: Poems of Fantasy and Terror*, ed. S.T. Joshi (New York: Hippocampus Press, 2003); ———, *A Wine of Wizardry and Other Poems* (San Francisco: Robertson, 1909). ***Selected Secondary Sources:*** Benediktsson, Thomas E., *George Sterling* (Boston: Twayne, 1980); Joshi, S.T., ed., *From Baltimore to Bohemia: The Letters of H.L. Mencken and George Sterling* (Rutherford, NJ: Farleigh Dickenson University Press, 2001); Noel, Joseph, *Footloose in Arcadia: A Personal Record of Jack London, George Sterling, Ambrose Bierce* (New York: Carrick and Evans, 1940).

John Cusatis

STERLING, JAMES (1701–1763)

James Sterling was one of the few colonial British American poets who immigrated to the colonies with a reputation as a poet already established. He wrote occasional poems celebrating the marriage of dignitaries, but he more frequently focused his poetry on celebrating and encouraging Britain's expanding empire. Poetry was only one of Sterling's literary efforts. Before he came to America, indeed, by the time he was twenty years old, Sterling was a rising literary star in his native Ireland. He wrote *The Rival Generals*, one of the very first tragedies by an Irish native, and saw it have a successful run in Dublin. Sterling wrote a second play and translated another, each of which was in sufficient demand to be printed multiple times. When he gained a reputation for the quality of his poetry in the New World, Sterling became one of the few American writers before the Revolution to achieve a substantial literary reputation for work that he did on both sides of the Atlantic.

James Sterling was born in 1701 at Downrass, King's County, Ireland, to a well-known family with a distinguished line. He entered Trinity College in 1716 and graduated in 1720. Sometime before 1723, he married Nancy Lyddel, an actress. In addition to appearing in plays written by Sterling, she performed to great acclaim in London and Dublin productions, including *Richard the Third* and *The Tragedy of Lady Jane Grey*. Failing health made the *Beggar's Opera* in 1732 Lyddel's last performance, and she died soon after. In the aftermath of his young wife's death, Sterling began studying for a master of arts degree and turned his attention to becoming a minister. Rather than remain in Ireland, though, Sterling sought work in America. In 1736 he applied to become minister to a church in Boston. This was not to be. Sterling's literary background and sympathies troubled Boston's church leadership. A minister who thought it acceptable to write plays and marry actresses cast doubt, in their eyes at least, on his fitness to minister to a congregation. Instead, Sterling received an appointment as a missionary in Maryland. He was inducted as rector of All Hallows Parish, in Anne Arundel County, on November 16, 1737. His travels through Maryland's churches had only just begun, however, and after two years at All Hallows he left to become rector of St. Anne's in Annapolis. In 1740 Sterling was named chaplain to the Maryland General Assembly. In August of 1740 he moved again, accepting the rectorship of a wealthier parish, St. Paul's in Kent County. Sterling ultimately settled in Chestertown on Maryland's Eastern Shore, where he remained for the final twenty years of his life. In 1743 he married a second time, to Rebecca Holt. Not long thereafter, on November 22, 1744, the couple's first child, Rebecca, was born. Rebecca Holt Sterling died soon after giving birth. In September 1749 Sterling married Mary Smith. Throughout his life in Maryland, Sterling's work, location, and reputation brought him into contact with some of the most renowned or soon-to-be renowned individuals of the period, including the great revivalist minister George Whitefield. In his role as minister, Sterling also baptized Charles Wilson Peale.

Colonial Maryland has a distinguished tradition of poetry, including **verse** produced by **George Alsop**, **Ebenezer Cooke**, and **Richard Lewis**, but Sterling is perhaps the most prolific of all the colonial Maryland poets. He published his first book of poetry, *The Poetical Works of the Rev. James Sterling*, in Dublin in 1734. In the colonies he published works in the leading magazine of the day, William Smith's *American Magazine or Monthly Chronicle.* Of Sterling's poetic output, two pieces are particularly interesting. *An Epistle to the Hon. Arthur Dobbs, Esq. in Europe, from a Clergyman in America* engages with one of the most important concerns for Britain's eighteenth-century empire, the existence of the Northwest Passage. Sterling wrote the poem in approximately 1750, circulated it in England in manuscript form, but did not publish it until 1752. The approximately 1600-line poem is divided into three cantos: Commentators have praised the work for its portrait of whales, one of the earliest in American literature, and of other scenes of nature. In addition, the poem provides a striking example of how American writers saw themselves in relation to China, India, and the East, for Sterling spends a good deal of time presenting a vision of England and America transformed by Asian goods once Arthur Dobbs succeeds in discovering the passage. The poem's enthusiastic celebration of the Northwest Passage seemed to serve another function for Sterling as well. When in London to try to secure a publisher for the poem, he joined with a group of merchants in seeking a monopoly on trade along the Labrador coast, a key trading post for all goods that would be sent through the passage. The application was denied, but his efforts drew the ire of Benjamin Franklin, who also hoped to profit from the discovery of such trade routes.

A Poem. On the Inventions of Letters and The Art of Printing was first published in 1728 in Dublin, then reprinted in Boston and Philadelphia that same year before Sterling published a revised version in the *American Magazine* in 1757. The poem begins with a history of the art of letters and moves on to a discussion of the rise of printing. This is a particularly interesting poem not only for the quality of the verse itself but also for the often surprising conceptual implications it gives print and letters in the figures of speech Sterling uses to bring these subjects to life for his readers. In addition, the poem provides an important historical perspective on the role of print in a culture's development, a subject that would play a key role in Revolutionary writing but was, as Sterling's poem demonstrates, a great concern for earlier colonists as well.

Further Reading. ***Selected Primary Sources:*** Sterling, James, *An Epistle to the Hon. Arthur Dobbs, Esq.* (Dublin, 1752);———, *A Poem on the Art of Printing* (Dublin, 1728); ———, "A Poem on the Inventions of Letters and the Art of Printing . . . " (*American Magazine or Monthly Chronicle* 1 [March 1758]: 281–290); ———, *The Poetical Works of the Rev. James Sterling* (Dublin, 1734); *The Rival Generals* (Dublin, 1722). ***Selected Secondary Sources:*** Davis, Richard Beale, *Intellectual Life in the Colonial South 1585–1763*, 3 vols. (Knoxville: University of Tennessee Press, 1978); Lemay, J.A. Leo, *Men of Letters in Colonial Maryland* (Knoxville, University of Tennessee Press, 1972); Wroth, Lawrence, "James Sterling: Poet, Priest, and Prophet of Empire" (*American Antiquarian Society Proceedings* 41 [1931]: 25–76).

James Egan

STERN, GERALD (1925–)

A poetry of ecstasy, joy, and unbridled passion has been Gerald Stern's single most important gift to American literature. Through long lines, punchy imagery, and rolling cadences Stern's poetry celebrates what he has termed "a place that no one else wanted, because it was not noticed, because it was abandoned or overlooked" (1978). His work is filled not only with "weeds, and waste places and lovely pockets" but also with wonderful maniacs dancing on the edge of precarious existence. Skirting the edge of realism, Stern uses often surreal and symbolic language to probe the deeper mysteries of his and the American psyche. His impact on poetry since the mid-1970s, when he first began publishing, is wide ranging. For many years a teacher in the famed Iowa Writers' Workshop, Stern taught a visionary core of younger American poets. Among early twenty-first–century poets he has influenced are **Kim Addonizio** and **Li-Young Lee.**

Gerald Stern was born in Pittsburgh, Pennsylvania, on February 22, 1925. Along with an older sister, he grew up in an immigrant Jewish household. His mother, Ida Barach Stern, was born in Biaylstock, Poland, where her father had been a kosher butcher and something of a scholar. His father, Harry Stern, was born in the Ukraine near Kiev. In Pittsburgh he was manager and buyer for a department store that mostly served a minority and immigrant population. Stern's was a traditional Jewish childhood, but following his bar mitzvah at the age of thirteen, he rejected institutionalized religion. Of all the events of his childhood, perhaps the most traumatic was the death of his older sister, about which he has written movingly in the essay "Some Secrets" and the **long poem** "Sylvia."

Stern went to college at the University of Pittsburgh expecting to be a labor lawyer. He described that period as follows: "I didn't hang out with poets. I was straight. I wore wing-tip shoes, white shirts, double breasted suits, neckties. I played pool, I was on the football team" (1993). In 1946, following college, Stern entered the U.S. Army Air Corps. There, after a fight with an officer, he ended up with both a court-martial and jail time, another experience about which he has written movingly in his autobiography, *What I Can't Bear Losing* (2003). After leaving the Army in 1947, he married his first wife, a young artist, Patricia Miller. With money from the GI Bill, Stern went to Europe where, he says, he got his real literary education.

On his return, he entered graduate school at Columbia University, earning his master's degree in 1949. He then made another trip to Europe with two friends, **Jack Gilbert**, who would become a well-known poet himself, and Richard Hazley. When Stern returned to the United States this time, he entered the Ph.D. program at Columbia, only to leave after one year to begin an erratic career as a teacher. Initially, he became headmaster of a private school in New York. This was followed by a period as a high school teacher in Glasgow, Scotland. After the Scottish excursion, he taught at Temple University in Philadelphia (1956–1963); Indiana University of Pennsylvania (1963–1967); Somerset County College in Somerset, New Jersey (1968–1982); and the University of Iowa (1982–1995). He has two children, David and Rachel.

Like **Robert Frost**, Stern made a dramatic late entrance into the world of American poetry; his first success came in the late 1970s when he was already in his sixth decade. Although he had been writing poems since college, he had by his late thirties reached an artistic crisis that would produce his first published collection, *Rejoicings* (1973). That book received almost no critical notice and no acclaim. In 1977, however, his second book, *Lucky Life*, was widely reviewed and praised for its love of life, striking imagery, relentless honesty, and compelling rhythms. It came as a welcome antidote to the cynicism and despair of post-Watergate, post-Vietnam poetry. Ultimately, the book won the Academy of American Poets' Lamont Prize. At the same time, however, a few critics complained about the excess of emotionalism in Stern's poetry; a complaint that would dog him throughout his career.

That emotionalism owed as much to Stern's understanding of his own Jewish heritage as it did to his understanding of the Romantic poetic tradition. In his next book, *The Red Coal* (1981), he included poems that drew their inspiration from both sources. In the title poem, whose central image comes from Percy Bysshe Shelley's definition of poetry, Stern found a symbol for the sort of poetry he had come to write: intense, imaginative, fully lived, **lyric** outbursts. The visionary aspects of Judaism are fully invoked in such poems as "The Shirt Poem," "Joseph Pockets," "The Angel Poem," and "The Poem of Liberation." *The Red Coal* won the prestigious Poetry Society of America's Melville Cane Award. One reviewer, Peter Stitt, declared Stern to be "a spiritual reincarnation of Whitman" (1981).

Following *The Red Coal*, Stern returned his attention to the **long poem** and the **epic** tradition. In 1982 he published in the *Paris Review* the long poem "Father Guzman," which won the Bernard F. Conners Poetry Prize (1982). Rather than continue in that vein, however, he published more lyric collections, such as *Paradise Poems* (1984), which included three Holocaust poems—"The Dancing," "Soap," and "Adler"—and *Lovesick* (1987). In the latter collection, Stern reflects on his divorce as well as a new lover. Of his books, this provoked the most divided appraisals: Poets such as Robert McDowell and **Louis Simpson** complained about the overly emotional language, while others, such as Jane Miller, defended it, arguing that it "must spontaneously combust in the imagination of the reader rather than illustrate the known" (1988).

In 1990 Stern brought together his first five books and published *Leaving Another Kingdom: Selected Poems* (Harper & Row). This collection, in conjunction with *Two Long Poems* (Carnegie-Mellon), which reprinted both "The Pineys" (1969) and "Father Guzman" (1982), offered reviewers the first chance to assess Stern's career. One result was the first scholarly book on Stern's poetry, *Making the Light Come: The Poetry of Gerlad Stern*, by Jane Somerville. The 1990s were also notable for the resurgence of the long poem as a focus of Stern's poetic imagination. With the long poem, Stern combined the lyric imagination and a discursive, meandering **narrative** style. In the books from this decade, *Bread without Sugar* (1992), *Odd Mercy* (1995), and *This Time* (1998), critics singled out such long poems as "Sylvia," an **elegy** to his sister, "The Bull-Roarer," an elegy to his father (both from *Bread*), and "Hot Dog," a tour de force at forty-five pages and more than one thousand lines (from *Odd Mercy*). That poem, Stern declared in 1995, "is about salvation. It's about God. It's about redemption. It's a comic poem too." It opens in lower Manhattan around Tomkins Square Park, where Stern meets an African American woman—a street person named Hot Dog. Its characters also include Saint Augustine and **Walt Whitman**. Of the poem, Stern said in a 1998 interview, "it is the longest poem I've ever written, and it's as if I have been preparing to write that poem all my life." *Odd Mercy* won the prestigious and lucrative $75,000 Ruth Lilly Poetry Prize.

In 1998 Stern published his second collection of selected poems, *This Time.* The reviews sealed his reputation as one of America's leading poets. He was praised precisely for the ecstatic vision his poetry had brought to contemporary verse. The book also won the 1998 National Book Award.

In the new century, Stern has returned to the short lyric with *Last Blue* (2000), a series of fifty-two poems divided into six sections, and *American Sonnets* (2003), a free ranging collection of his own unique sonnet form, a short lyric often of fifteen to seventeen unrhymed lines.

Stern has also published his first extended **prose** collection, *What I Can't Bear Losing: Notes from a Life* (2003).

Further Reading. ***Selected Primary Sources:*** Stern, Gerald, *American Sonnets: Poems* (New York: Norton, 2003); ———, *Bread Without Sugar* (New York: Norton, 1992); ———, *Last Blue* (New York: Norton, 2000); ———, *Leaving Another Kingdom: Selected Poems* (New York: Harper & Row, 1990); ———, *Lovesick* (New York: Harper & Row, 1987); ———, *Lucky Life* (Boston: Houghton Mifflin, 1977); ———, *Odd Mercy* (New York: Norton, 1995); ———, *The Red Coal* (Boston: Houghton Mifflin, 1981); ———, *Rejoicings: Selected Poems 1966–1972* (Fredericton, New Brunswick: Fiddlehead Poetry Books, 1973); ———, *This Time: New and Selected Poems* (New York: Norton, 1998); ———, *Two Long Poems* (Pittsburgh, PA: Carnegie-Mellon, 1990); ———, *What I Can't Bear Losing: Notes from a Life* (New York: Norton, 2003); ———, "What I Have to Defend, What I Can't Bear Losing" (*New England Review* 15.2 [1993]: 94–103). ***Selected Secondary Sources:*** Abbate, Francesca, Karin Schalm, and Robert Firth, "Five Questions: An Interview with Gerald Stern" (*Cutbank* 43 [1995]: 88–102); Barron, Jonathan N., "New Jerusalems: Contemporary Jewish American Poets and the Puritan Tradition" in *The Calvinist Roots of the Modern Era*, eds. Aliki Barnstone, Michael Tomasek Manson, and Carol J. Singley (Hanover, NH: University Press of New England, 1997, 231–249); "Gerald Stern," in *Contemporary Authors*, vols. 81–84 (Detroit, MI: Gale Research, 1978, 535–536); "Interview with Gary Pacernick" (*American Poetry Review* 27.4 [1998]: 41–48); Miller, Jane, "Working Time" (*American Poetry Review* 17.3, [1988]: 9–16); *Poetry East* (issue containing fifteen essays and poems about Stern) (26 [1988]: 32–162); Somerville, Jane, *Making the Light Come: The Poetry of Gerald Stern* (Detroit, MI: Wayne State University Press, 1990); Stitt, Peter, "Engagements with Reality" (*Georgia Review* 35.4 [1981]: 874–881).

Jonathan N. Barron

STEVENS, WALLACE (1879–1955)

Wallace Stevens is a major poet of the American **modernist** period whose poetic career, roughly from 1915 to 1955, almost exactly matches the span of that era. He is known as a poet of academia and of the erudite. Though he maintained that he never intended his writing to be unclear, casual readers often find his work difficult. Their difficulty springs from Steven's subtle turns of thought and diction and from the sophistication of his poetry's philosophical grounding, the same qualities that make it fascinating to the more sophisticated reader. Stevens is sometimes referred to as a "poet's poet," not only because his poetry appeals to other poets but also because he often takes poetry as his subject. However, this is not merely the practicing poet's interest in the details of his own craft; Stevens uses poetry as a symbol, a synecdoche (in which the part stands for the whole) for humankind's symbolizing capacity: the way we imbue objects and events with meanings and live in a world enriched by our own comprehensions. Stevens's most anthologized and therefore best-known poems are the short, often exuberant, richly imaged poems that characterize his first volume, *Harmonium* (1923). His later poetry, which tends to attract the greater amount of critical attention, is known for its much longer, intricately structured poetic meditations. Stevens was awarded the Bollingen Prize for Poetry (1950), the Pulitzer Prize for Poetry (1955), and two National Book Awards for *The Auroras of Autumn* (1950) and *The Collected Poems of Wallace Stevens* (1954). These awards are an indication both of the poetic vigor Stevens maintained during his final years and of the stature he had attained as a poet by the end of his life.

Wallace Stevens was born in Reading, Pennsylvania, son of Garrett Stevens, a lawyer, businessman, and aspiring poet; and Margaretha Zeller, with whom, as his letters indicate, he had a warm and playful relationship. The second of five children, he led an active life, full of swimming, hiking, and other outdoor activities, but he was also an outstanding student. He entered Harvard University in 1897 as a special three-year student, presumably in preparation for law school. While at Harvard he contributed poetry and short stories to student publications and in his final year was president of the *Harvard Advocate.* After leaving Harvard in 1900, Stevens worked briefly as a journalist in New York City, then attended New York Law School and was admitted to the bar in New York in 1904. He briefly attempted to establish his own law practice, and when that failed, he worked in other law offices in New York City until 1908, when he took a job with the American Bonding Company and began to develop a specialty in surety bonds.

In 1909 he married Elsie Kachel Moll, a twenty-three-year-old piano teacher from Reading, who would later, while they were living in New York, be the model for a bust by sculptor Adolph Weinman that is reproduced on the Liberty dime. Stevens's parents, especially his father, disapproved of Elsie and did not attend the wedding, even though it took place in Reading, where they still lived. Stevens and his father were still not reconciled when Garrett died in 1911. His mother, to whom Wallace had been closer emotionally, died in 1912. Stevens and Elsie continued to live in New York City until 1916, when they moved to Hartford, Connecticut, so that he could take a job with The Hartford Insurance Company, where he was employed for the remainder of his life. With The Hartford, Stevens quickly achieved a position of responsibility. He also found it necessary to spend much of his time traveling. Meanwhile, Elsie remained homesick for Reading and often returned there for visits. The Stevens's only child, Holly, was born in 1924. In the late 1920s Stevens continued to devote a great deal of time to his work with The Hartford and also took the job of fatherhood seriously. During the 1920s and 1930s he often vacationed, usually without Elsie and Holly, in Key West, Florida, where he associated with, among others, **Robert Frost** and Ernest Hemingway. He had a now-famous fistfight with Hemingway in Key West in 1936 and came away with a broken hand. In 1933 he purchased an expensive home in Hartford, and in 1934 he was promoted to executive vice president for The Hartford Insurance Company. He died in 1955 of stomach cancer.

Stevens was a late bloomer as a poet. Although he was very much a part of the poetry scene as a student at Harvard, including an exchange of sonnets with philosopher, poet, and faculty member **George Santayana**, and although he wrote two small books of poetry as presents for his future wife during their courtship, his poetry remained imitative and somewhat sentimental until its sudden flowering in 1914 and 1915, when he published "Sunday Morning" and "Peter Quince at the Clavier," two of his best medium-length poems, and several excellent shorter ones in various little magazines. "Sunday Morning," a blank verse meditation consisting of eight fifteen-line sections, portrays a female protagonist enjoying the sensuous pleasures of a quietly nonreligious Sunday morning and spins from that scene a consideration of the competing claims of transient earthly delights versus the eternal concerns of religion. "Peter Quince at the Clavier," taking its name from the leader of the "rude mechanicals" in *A Midsummer Night's Dream*, proposes that music, and by extension art in general, is "feeling . . . not sound" and that, therefore, what the speaker feels for the woman he addresses "is music." The poem then examines this proposition by considering—using musical terminology—the case of Susanna, from the Book of Daniel in the Apocrypha. Besides the matching of written text to musical **imagery**, the poem also appears to be related to sixteenth-century painter Jacopo Tintoretto's *Susanna Bathing*, thus effecting analogies among music, visual art, and literary art, supporting the poem's conclusion that while abstract beauty is momentary, beauty "in the flesh" (that is, in accurate artistic representation) is "immortal."

How this sudden development into full poetic maturity at the age of thirty-seven occurred remains a mystery. A part of the explanation is that the death of Stevens's parents, the responsibilities of marriage, and the demands of his professional life all combined to purge any elements of adolescent silliness from his personality so that he emerged as an adult sufficiently grave and confident to handle the weighty aesthetic and philosophical issues that his poetry raised. Probably more important still was his discovery of modern art. He attended the 1913 Armory Show in New York City, which brought the latest trends in European visual art to the United States. He also formed acquaintances with Cubist painter Marcel Duchamp (whose *Nude Descending a Staircase* may have inspired various Stevens poems in which "nudes" appear, as well as some poems whose effects might be defined as "Cubist"), poet **William Carlos Williams**, and others in the **avant-garde** artistic community in New York. Whatever the cause, he was able to leave behind the Victorian and Romantic influences that had dogged his earlier efforts and began to produce poetry that was truly modern. He continued to write poetry fairly intensively during the next few years and also wrote three **verse** plays.

The poetry from this period is collected in Stevens's first volume, *Harmonium*, published by Alfred A. Knopf in 1923. *Harmonium* contains one **long poem**, "The Comedian as the Letter C," which Stevens had written for a poetry contest sponsored by the Poetry Society of South Carolina and judged by **Amy Lowell**. The poem, a burlesque poetic autobiography, eventually became one of the standards of the Stevens canon; it finished second in the contest. Other outstanding poems in the volume include "Thirteen Ways of Looking at a Blackbird," a grouping of thirteen haiku-like lyrics centering on the blackbird as an object of perception; "The Snow Man," which uses its winter setting as an emblem for the desire to strip away past mythologies and see things as they are; "The Emperor of Ice-Cream," a brief meditation on life's transience; "Anecdote of the Jar," a parable of the relation between the human and the natural; and "Domination of Black," which uses perceptions of the sameness of things to evoke a sense of inevitable fatality and "the cry of the peacock" to suggest the human struggle, especially through the use of the creative faculty, against that fatality. Another short poem, "A High-Toned Old Christian Woman," playing musical imagery against religious imagery, introduces what would become the most distinctive and enduring concept in Stevens's poetry: the "supreme fiction." Playing off "supreme being," the notion of "supreme fiction" converts the object of belief from something purely external to something humanly created. In this first incarnation, the "supreme fiction" is specifically identified as poetry itself, vis-à-vis religious (the comparison that the poem expressly examines), political, and other "fictions" on which human beings base their lives.

Following the publication of *Harmonium*, Stevens wrote little poetry for the next decade. In 1931 Knopf published a new edition of *Harmonium* that contained only a few new entries; however, one of those was the notable "Sea Surface Full of Clouds," which offers five descriptions of a November morning "off Tehuantepec," meditating on the relation between inner and outer reality. The next new volume was *Ideas of Order* (1935), whose most important contribution to the Stevens canon is "The Idea of Order at Key West," a medium-length poem exploring relations among human perception, human creativity, and brute reality. The poem centers on a woman singing as she walks beside the sea and questions whether it can be said that her song reproduces the sounds of the sea (representing reality as a whole), or that the song, on the contrary, may be simply a reflection of the singer. The meditation then continues into the aftermath of the song and notices the way in which the world seems to have taken on a new shape, perhaps as a result of the song, suggesting the way we create the world in which we live. The poem proposes a "blessed rage for order" as a sacred human characteristic, thus establishing the "poetic" faculty—the ability to "sing" the world—as fundamental to humanity's best possibilities.

Ideas of Order was published in the midst of the Great Depression, a time when fundamental social assumptions in the United States and other countries were being questioned and poets were being exhorted to produce work with greater social relevance. Some American intellectuals were flirting with communism, which in an essay titled "Imagination as Value" Stevens later referred to as a "grubby faith" that tried to take "the measure of humanity." It was, in his view, a phenomenon of the imagination "on its most momentous scale"—an attempt at a "supreme fiction," a rival to religion, poetry, and other ideological frameworks. Out of this context of social concern Stevens constructed two long poems, "Owl's Clover" (1937) and "The Man with the Blue Guitar" (1938), that examined the place of art in the real (that is, the social and political) world and the question of the artist's social responsibility. "Owl's Clover," which was first published by Alcestis Press as a separate volume and then reprinted in 1938 in a Knopf volume titled *The Man with the Blue Guitar*, has the curious distinction of being the only major poem that Stevens chose to exclude from his *Collected Poems* (1954), probably because he regarded it as too argumentative instead of being, in **Archibald MacLeish**'s modernist phrase, "palpable and mute as a globed fruit." "The Man with the Blue Guitar," whose title is probably related to Picasso's Blue Period paintings, makes a more successful foray into the subject of social responsibility, portraying the opposition between "things as they are" and the imaginative products of the artistic process, represented by "the blue guitar." The poem sets up a dramatic tension in which the poet/musician tries to reproduce the common reality but finds that effort incompatible with aesthetic transcendence. Yet the poem affirms that in the end the imagined reality is the one in which we most vitally live. In this poem Stevens experiments stylistically with two-line stanzas and uses more rhyme than usual. In addition to its poetic interest, it is one of Stevens's poems most often cited as a treatment of aesthetic issues.

The 1930s were for Stevens primarily a decade of transition, as he returned to poetry after a period of inactivity and tried to readjust to the demands of the time. The 1910s, when he wrote his first great poetry, had been a time when aesthetics dominated, and the Stevens of that period had been an aesthete, often characterized as a dandy. The Stevens of the 1930s was a much more sober member of society, perhaps reflecting changes in his own life, but surely also reflecting the character of the age and current views of the artist in that age. The Stevens of the 1940s, on the other hand, was an artist who, despite writing a number of poems that he considered "war poems," largely transcended the social, political, and even artistic currents of the time and more successfully followed the momentum of his own poetic genius. This change was evident in two volumes published in 1942, *Parts of a World*, published by Knopf, and *Notes toward a Supreme Fiction*, published by Cummington Press. *Parts of a World* is a miscellany that contains no major poem to anchor the volume. Many of the poems, such as "On the Road Home," "The Latest Freed Man," and "A Rabbit as King of the Ghosts," pursue, often with remarkable poignancy, the "death of God" theme so eloquently established decades earlier in "Sunday Morning." For example, "On the Road Home" proposes that it is only when notions of the inhuman "truth" have been discarded that "the grapes [seem] fatter" and only when the truth of finite vision has been accepted that the "fragrance of the autumn" is most richly perceived. Other poems in the volume assert the importance of the subjective aspect and the potential profundity of imaginative seeing. For instance, "Study of Two Pears" abstracts from the pears their shapes and colors, making them not discreet objects but a focus of the visual field; "The Glass of Water" turns light into "a lion that comes down to drink"; and "Woman Looking at a Vase of Flowers" renders the seeing as comparable to the aesthetic moment "when thunder took form upon / The piano."

But it is in "*Notes toward a Supreme Fiction*," initially published in a limited edition as a separate volume and later incorporated into *Transport to Summer* (1947), that Stevens makes the great leap of this extraordinary poetic period. Here he takes up the notion of the "supreme fiction" and refines it from poetry in general to a specific object of belief which is believed in with full knowledge of its fictionality. As such, the supreme fiction becomes not an external truth (a "supreme being") but the truth of human knowing, tempered by human desire, that provides what the poem "Of Modern Poetry" (in *Parts of a World*) refers to as "what will suffice." Thus, it is a truth of a higher order (and a definitively aesthetic one) because it understands and acknowledges its own nature. The poem opens with a brief prologue in which an unspecified "you" is identified as the sole object of the speaker's love. This "you" could be the muse of poetry, or the Greek "Sophia" (wisdom), or the earth. In fact, it seems to be all three at once, since what Stevens pursues in the poem is not the project of actually creating a particular "supreme fiction," but an outline of the principles by which such fictions, in his view, have always been produced. He offers three dicta, which function as the headings for the poem's three major sections: "It Must Be Abstract," "It Must Change," and "It Must Give Pleasure." The poem does not attempt a sustained argument but instead offers a series of poetic meditations on the topics of abstraction (a focus on universal structural principles as opposed to specific incarnations), change (the replacement of outmoded ideas and images with those that match current conditions), and pleasure (the satisfaction that comes from a fully conceived, fully accepted fiction). "Notes" is peopled by male and female figures who represent, respectively, the masculine myth of power, heroic action, and rational thinking, and the feminine myth of sensuous presence, love, and nonlinear comprehension. The interactions between these two mythic tendencies lead to an image of resolution in which "the irrational is rational" and the speaker's "fluent mundo" (his fully expressive world) revolves "in crystal"—that is, the transient moment is understood and appreciated within the framework of eternal principle.

In 1945 the Cummington Press published another small, limited-edition volume of poems by Stevens, this one titled *Esthétique du Mal*. The title poem is a medium-length meditation whose title (playing off Charles Baudelaire's *Les Fleurs du Mal*) means "aesthetic of pain/evil/misfortune." The poem brings all three of these meanings of "mal" into play. Just as Stevens tried in the 1930s to deal with the economic hardship of that era in his poetry, he here takes on the suffering associated with World War II, considering the humanness of pain and misfortune and introducing Satan himself as the representative of evil (the "genius of misfortune"). The "death of God" motif is inverted here, becoming the "death of Satan," which the poem terms "a tragedy for the imagination." This suggests both Satan's role as a tragic character (as in *Paradise Lost*) and that his death, which comes through "negation" (that is, non-belief), is a great loss for the imagination itself since the character of Satan is a way of comprehending evil and human misfortune. However, the poem proposes, in Nietzschean fashion, that after the negation there must come an affirmation, a new "yes" which is the creation of a new "supreme fiction" (though that term is not used in the poem). This must include the negative term, equivalent to Satan, as well as the positive, equivalent to God. Thus, in spite of pain, evil, and misfortune, the poem affirms the richness of the "physical world" and the "metaphysical changes" that give it its human character.

Transport to Summer, published by Knopf in 1947, includes "Notes toward a Supreme Fiction" and "Esthétique du Mal" and adds, in addition to many excellent shorter poems, two major ones: "Description without Place" and "Credences of Summer." "Description without Place," originally composed for reading at Harvard's 1945 Phi Beta Kappa gathering, returns to the two-line stanza used in "The Man with the Blue Guitar" (as opposed to the three-line stanza used in "Notes" and the variable-length stanzas of "Esthétique") and like "Blue Guitar" makes a (more or less) sustained argument. In this case the thesis is announced in the first line: "It may be that to seem—it is to be." The poem argues, in fairly familiar Stevensian fashion, that we live within our conceptions of things—that the way things seem creates a reality of its own, a "description without place." Stevens introduces images of "Nietzsche in Basel" and "Lenin by a lake," as well as more cursory references to John Calvin, Queen Anne, and Pablo Neruda as examples of individuals who by their imaginings have created realities and/or have become characters within imagined worlds. Thus, ours is a "world of words" since we live within the articulations of ourselves and others. The assertion in "Description without Place" that the "seeming of a summer's day" creates a reality provides a theoretical framework for "Credences of Summer," a poem that richly evokes the image of a summer day as an emblem of perfection. The poem's opening words, "Now in midsummer come," plays off Shakespeare's *Richard III*'s "Now is the winter of our discontent / Made glorious summer," and also brings into play the mythology of midsummer's eve as a magical time. Here it is high noon, and although the time is midsummer, the day is identified as the "last day of a certain year." In other words, this is a finality; in its midst is the "final mountain," and the poem is as ripe with biblical imagery as the scene is with life. And yet in the reality of the fully satisfying summer day, the poem insists that its perfection is as much imagined as real, and the closing lines, like the first, present the scene as a dramatization—a fictionalization, suggesting once again that we live within our conceptions of things.

Stevens's next volume, *The Auroras of Autumn*, published by Knopf in 1950, includes two highly regarded longer poems: "The Auroras of Autumn" and "An Ordinary Evening in New Haven." "The Auroras of Autumn" takes the aurora borealis as its imagistic center and finds in the aurora's shifting shapes an emblem of the passing and reappearance (or, more precisely, replacement by a successor) of ideologies (represented in the poem by "the father") and the images that give them sensuous presence (represented by "the mother"). The poem envisages the aurora as "a theatre floating through the clouds," and as in "Esthétique du Mal," the tragedy is enacted, passes, and begins again. "An Ordinary Evening in New Haven" can be seen as the second half of a pair, in which the first, "Notes toward a Supreme Fiction," sketches out a program for grasping the nature of human transcendence. "An Ordinary Evening in New Haven" complements this with a program for the comprehension of common reality—as the poem says, "not grim / Reality but reality grimly seen." Again the poem explores the relation of objective to subjective, of the transcendent to the down-to-earth, and of changes of era as changes in reality. Like "Notes," "An Ordinary Evening" is composed in blank verse, the form that Stevens's most stately poems tend to be written in, grouped into three-line stanzas, and like most of Stevens's poetry, it relies heavily on alliteration, anaphora (repetition), and subtle internal rhymes for aesthetic effect. Its argument probes the world of objects for the human significance that creates a "world of words"—that is, a reality inseparable from our articulations of it. The lover of reality is seen as "a serious man without the serious," a person with the transcendent impulse but determined to find his transcendence in the near-at-hand rather than evade it with outworn myths from the past.

Stevens's next book was his only volume of **prose**, a collection of essays mostly composed to be delivered as speeches on various occasions and given the collective title *The Necessary Angel: Essays on Reality and the Imagination* (1951). As the volume's subtitle and such essay titles as "Imagination as Value," "Effects of Analogy," and "The Relations Between Poetry and Painting" make clear, the essays are mainly on aesthetic issues. The views he articulates exhibit mainstream modernist attitudes toward art, but they also include a substantial component of the philosophical, demonstrating, as his poems themselves do, a surprisingly subtle understanding of important philosophical issues.

The Collected Poems of Wallace Stevens, published by Knopf in 1954, the year before Stevens's death, reprints nearly all the poems from the previous Knopf volumes, which had, in turn, absorbed the volumes printed first by smaller publishers. In addition, *Collected Poems* includes some new poems written after *The Auroras of Autumn*, grouped under the title *The Rock*. The title poem is divided into three sections, of which the first, "Seventy Years Later," muses on the seeming unreality of the past, then shifts to a meditation on its meaningfulness nonetheless. The second section, titled "The Poem as Icon," uses the image of the rock as bare reality and the image of leaves covering the rock as the imagination's conversion of that bare reality into meaningfulness, such that our articulations of reality become indistinguishable from ourselves. The third section gathers the religious associations of "the rock" (as in the "Rock of Ages") and "icon," offering "Forms of the Rock as a Night-Hymn." The rock, the foundation of our existence, is here defined as "the habitation of the whole." That is, the rock, which may at first seem to consist only in an external reality, in fact is equally composed of our "hymns" of (or to) it. Other important poems in this group include "To an Old Philosopher in Rome," a tribute to Stevens's old acquaintance from his Harvard days, George Santayana, written as Santayana lingered near death at a convent in Rome, and also a meditation on mortality and transcendence; and "Final Soliloquy of the Interior Paramour," a love poem to the human ability to create an ultimate meaningfulness that can stand as a sufficient comfort against mortality.

In 1957, two years after Stevens's death, *Opus Posthumous*, edited by Samuel French Morse and published by Knopf, collected Stevens's previously uncollected poems, including some written too late to appear in *The Collected Poems of Wallace Stevens*, his three verse plays, and some uncollected prose pieces. Among the very late poems, "Of Mere Being" (sometimes identified as "Stevens's last poem," though it is not clear that that label is factually accurate) has attracted attention for the way it uses the brilliant image of a "gold-feathered bird" singing in a palm tree to stake out the farthest reach, whether temporal or conceptual, of human consciousness ("the end of the mind") as it bleeds into an image of heaven, giving a sort of closure, so it seems, to Stevens's many meditations on the earthly and the heavenly.

Because Stevens composed his poetry in his spare time, at home in the evening, as he walked to and from work, or in odd moments as he sat at his desk at The Hartford, he produced a relatively modest quantity of poetry. However, the quality of the poems he published is so uniformly high that the number of them that seem destined to endure is great. The poems reveal him to be among the purest of modernists in his belief in art's ability to symbolically represent profundities far beyond the reach of discursive articulation. But he also pushes this insight toward the postmodern by his insistence on human metaphorizing, as opposed to external reality, as the origin of belief and by his search not for a new belief but for the structural principles according to which belief is created. He sees the world we live in as a structure of the human mind, and though his poetry speaks longingly about arriving at a new locus of faith, its author seems finally more interested in understanding that longing, perhaps more poignantly than it has been understood before, than in actually satisfying it.

Further Reading. ***Selected Primary Sources:*** Stevens, Wallace, *The Collected Poems of Wallace Stevens* (New York: Alfred A. Knopf, 1954); ———, *Letters of Wallace Stevens*, ed. Holly Stevens (Berkeley: University of California Press, 1996); ———, *The Necessary Angel: Essays on Reality and the Imagination* (New York: Vintage, 1965); ———, *Opus Posthumous*, ed. Milton J. Bates (New York: Vintage,

1990); ———, *Wallace Stevens: Collected Poetry and Prose*, ed. Frank Kermode and Joan Richardson (New York: Library of America, 1997). ***Selected Secondary Sources:*** Bloom, Harold, *Wallace Stevens: The Poems of Our Climate* (Ithaca, NY: Cornell University Press, 1977); Brazeau, Peter, *Parts of a World: Wallace Stevens Remembered* (New York: Random House, 1983); Leggett, B.J., *Early Stevens: The Nietzschean Intertext* (Durham, NC: Duke University Press, 1992); Lensing, George, *Wallace Stevens: A Poet's Growth* (Baton Rouge: Louisiana State University Press, 1991); Leonard, James S., and Christine E. Wharton, *The Fluent Mundo: Wallace Stevens and the Structure of Reality* (Athens: University of Georgia Press, 1988); MacLeod, Glen, *Wallace Stevens and Modern Art: From the Armory Show to Abstract Expressionism* (New Haven, CT: Yale University Press, 1993); Stevens, Holly, *Souvenirs and Prophecies: The Young Wallace Stevens* (New York: Random House, 1977).

James S. Leonard

STEWART, SUSAN (1952–)

Susan Stewart's work provides a dramatic alterative to the self-centered poetry that has dominated the contemporary landscape for the last quarter of a century. Her poetry refuses the details of autobiography and concentrates instead on universal, mythic stories. Her work therefore emerges from a deep belief in the comprehensible and shareable nature of those stories for her readers. Stewart's poetic voice conducts itself with intelligence, gravity, and considered philosophical steadiness. She also excels at inventing and perfecting new and musical **poetic forms**.

Poet and critic Susan Stewart was born in 1952. She was educated at Dickinson College in Carlisle, Pennsylvania, and received a master's degree from Johns Hopkins University, where she studied poetry. She went on to receive a doctorate in Folklore and Folk Life Studies at the University of Pennsylvania. She has published four books of poetry: *Yellow Stars and Ice* (1981), *The Hive* (1985), *The Forest* (1995), and *Columbarium* (2003). Stewart's body of work also includes four dense and painstakingly researched books of **prose**, and one translation of a Greek tragedy, *Andromache*. Strongly regarded as one of academia's most eloquent defenders of poetry, she currently teaches English and aesthetics at Princeton University.

Stewart's poetry is preoccupied with memory and history, and her poems frequently attempt to access a collective intellectual past. Stewart's frequent classical allusions rarely seem restrictive and never present themselves as unrecoverable elegiac fragments of culture. Instead, Stewart writes into the frame of myth in order to speculate on vital philosophical and universal questions. Her lack of interest in autobiography is a striking aspect of her body of work. Unlike many of the poets of her generation, she rarely rehearses the specifics of her own personal history, or asserts her cultural location or identity. Instead of using personal experience to make myth personal, Stewart invokes mythic **narratives** and **epic** fragments to make personal experience general. She imagines characters, cities, and predicaments with a deliberate generality that often borders on anonymity. Consistently, Stewart avoids using the first person singular until she reaches the end of a poem. Her poems ultimately seek to reconnect the isolated individual self with a communal imagination. They also argue that the human subject is best seen as an integrated part of the larger world of nature, emphasizing the universality and organic nature of the passing of time and the seasons.

Though Stewart composes, for the most part, short **lyric poems**, her impulse to create book-length themed works connects her work closely to classical traditions of epic and narrative. For example, her first book, *Yellow Stars and Ice*, begins with a poem set at dawn and ends with a lyric about the speaker's descent into sleep. The book effectively frames itself as a single day in the life of the poetic subject. One striking **long poem**, "Four Questions Regarding the Dreams of Animals," speculates on the imaginative lives of non-human creatures, as if to attempt to bring the reader closer to animal life, but ends with a terse answer to the question, how can we learn more: "This is all we will ever know." Stewart often chooses to explore both sides of a question or idea, inscribing the limits of her knowledge while at the same time asserting what she knows. "Yellow Stars and Ice" is a kind of love poem between the speaker and the reader. The refrain establishes distance and connection at the same time, "you are as far as invention, and I am as far as memory." The repetition and cadences of the poem are reminiscent of a sestina, or a song, and remind the reader of Stewart's training as reader of folksong. The "you" and "I" of the poem begin in abstraction, free from context or name, but achieve a striking intimacy and tenderness reminiscent of the bare love poems of **Emily Dickinson**.

Throughout her work Stewart rings changes on the theme of memory. The title poem of *The Forest* urges the reader to remember the forest and worries about its possible permanent disappearance. Memory for Stewart is a tool of potential communal understanding and a force that fights against loss. Though the poem's eleven stanzas are full of lush description, the speaker is forced to conclude, "Once we were lost in the forest . . . / but the truth is, it is, lost to us now." Stewart again uses repetition and regular stanza form to bring her voice nearer to a kind of choral song. The various repeated lines insist that we see its speaker not as a single individual but as someone channeling the feelings of the community at large.

Still, Stewart has no illusions about the easy creation of communal narratives, and her poems often play on the inconsistency of different versions of a situation. One central series of poems in *The Forest* concerns a rape and its difficult consequences for memory and representation: Though the poems are dated from the middle of the century, their scenes and characters stay anonymous to us, and we never find out their relation to the poet. Stewart returns to song in "Medusa Anthology," a series of eight-line spell-like poems that incorporate various classical, Shakespearean, and nineteenth-century allusions, a strangely contemporary voice, and a direct address to an absent god. "Medusa Anthology" and many of Stewart's other long poems insist on repeating and revisiting tropes as a way of questioning and understanding them. Though they deal with abstractions such as history and memory, they ground them with deliberate sonic effects and pointed allusive moments.

One of Stewart's greatest contributions to contemporary verse is the inventive nature of her poetic forms. *Columbarium*, her most recent book, experiments with form even as it follows classical sources. Many of the poems in the book are called "shadow georgics" and try to explore a philosophical question or concept from Virgil's georgics from one side and then from another. They use shape as well as stanza length, and sometimes move from one side of the page to another. These fantasias on Virgil's famous poems about farming treat the nature of loss, the passing of the seasons, loneliness, and love. *Columbarium*, like Stewart's second book, *The Hive*, takes as its central image a place in which a group of animals thrive and breed. A hive is a natural construction, however, and a columbarium, or dovecote, breeds birds to kill them. In poem after poem in *The Hive,* Stewart finds herself considering fertility and death together. Consistently, she refuses to make old forms and voices new by infusing them with contemporary personality. Instead, she seeks to create a vatic voice whose roots are in the poetry and images of the ancient world.

Stewart's most recent book of prose criticism, *Poetry and the Fate of the Senses*, argues for the spiritual and social value of poetry as the metaphorical fight of light against darkness. She creates a theory of poetry that celebrates sensory perception, memory, and expression as positive and life-affirming values inscribed by the lyric. The book's wide-ranging treatment of poetry across the centuries and its comprehensive look at how the senses are enacted and engaged by lyric predicaments has helped advance Stewart as one of the foremost critics of her generation. Like her contemporaries **Susan Howe** and **Jorie Graham**, Stewart is committed to creating an ambitious body of work in a magisterial, prophetic, and philosophical voice.

Further Reading: ***Selected Primary Sources:*** Stewart, Susan, *Columbarium* (Chicago: University of Chicago Press, 2003); ———, *The Forest* (Chicago: University of Chicago Press, 1995); ———, *The Hive* (Athens: University of Georgia Press, 1985); ———, *On Longing* (Durham, NC: Duke University Press, 1993); ———, *Poetry and the Fate of the Senses* (Chicago: University of Chicago Press, 2002); ———, *Yellow Stars and Ice* (Princeton, NJ: Princeton University Press, 1981). ***Selected Secondary Sources:*** McLane, Maureen N., "A Sustained Meditation on Creation" (*Chicago Tribune* [22 August, 2004]); Thompson, Jon, "Interview with Susan Stewart" (*Free Verse* [Spring 2003], http://english.chass.ncsu.edu/freeverse); Review of *Columbarium* (*Free Verse* [Spring 2004], http://english.chass.ncsu.edu/freeverse).

Katie Peterson

STICKNEY, TRUMBULL (1874-1904)

Trumbull Stickney died of a brain tumor on October 11, 1904, at the age of thirty, shortly after publishing *Dramatic Verses* (1902), his only volume of poetry. One year later the first of many efforts to establish Stickney's literary reputation began when his friends **William Vaughn Moody** and **George Cabot Lodge** published *The Poems of Trumbull Stickney*, a volume containing all the poems in *Dramatic Verses* as well as many unpublished poems and fragments. In many respects Stickney was a classic *poete maudit*—sensitive, melancholy, handsome, cosmopolitan, and sickly. And yet Stickney's poetry, like that of the later **T.S. Eliot**, drew inspiration from Greek literature, Jacobean drama, Indian philosophy, and French aestheticism. In Eliot these elements eventually flowered into a **modernist** aesthetic, and despite the unmistakable fin de siècle quality of Stickney's poetry, critics attempting to resuscitate his reputation—including **Conrad Aiken**, Edmund Wilson, **W.H. Auden**, and most recently **John Hollander**—can rarely resist the temptation to speculate about what Stickney's role in American poetry might have been had he lived another forty years.

Trumball Stickney was born in Geneva, Switzerland, on June 20, 1874. His father, Austin Stickney, was a classical scholar, and his mother, Harriet Champion Trumbull, was descended from a wealthy and prominent New England family. Stickney was educated by his father during a childhood spent traveling throughout Europe, where the family lived in Rome, Paris, Nice, London, Dresden, Venice, Florence, and Geneva. In 1891 Stickney entered Harvard University and immediately distinguished himself academically. He was the first freshman ever elected to the editorial board of the *Harvard Monthly*, the journal that published most of his poems. In those early years at Harvard, Stickney also became fascinated by Greek tragedy, writing to his sister Lucy that he planned to be lost in it "for the next 2000 years." Despite his academic successes, however, Stickney's European upbringing and aestheticism proved a poor fit for Harvard, where many students and faculty dismissed his manners and poetry as effete. **George Santayana**, for example, recounts that Stickney was rejected from a student poetry circle after referring to a sunset as "gorgeous"—an observation that Santayana describes as "too literary and ladylike for Harvard." After graduating, Stickney continued his study of Greek poetry in France, becoming the first American awarded *doctorate es letters* by the Sorbonne. While in Paris, Stickney befriended fellow expatriates Santayana, **Henry Adams**, and Bernard Berenson.

Stickney wrote two dissertations while at the Sorbonne, one on Ermolao Barbara and a longer work on gnomic elements in Greek poetry. While completing these dissertations, Stickney composed his own tragedy, the blank **verse drama** *Prometheus Pyrphoros* (1900). In Stickney's version of the myth, Prometheus never doubts that his gift of fire will result in eternal punishment and never hopes that light will bring happiness to the play's characters. Instead, he acts only to assert his will in a dark world saying that whatever we achieve "[s]tands in defiance, and we at Nature's heart / Register signs of our nobility." Also notable in the *Prometheus Pyrphoros* are the songs of Pandora. Always heard from offstage, these songs give voice to a chthonic female power older than the gods. In addition to the *Prometheus*, Stickney wrote several other verse plays, including fragments on Julian the Apostate (1901) and on Benvenuto Cellini (1904), the sixteenth-century Italian sculptor and goldsmith. As these works suggest, Robert Browning was a significant influence on Stickney's poetry, especially in dramatic monologues such as "Lodovico Martelli" (1898) and "Requiescam" (1900).

Stickney had intended to call his second collection *Dramatic Scenes*, suggesting he concurred with Moody's assessment that "his career as a dramatic poet [had] only begun." It is, however, largely through his **lyric poems** that Stickney survives today. These lyrics owe much, especially their melancholy tone and autumnal settings, to French **Symbolist** poets such as Paul Verlaine. Even when set in the bright light of the Mediterranean, Stickney's poems are somber, their speakers cut off, as Edmund Wilson suggested, from a classical tradition that represented for Stickney a source of joy and vitality. In the opening lines of "In Ampezzo," for example, Stickney transforms Milton's confident deployment of classical tropes—"Yet once more, oh ye laurels"—into an invocation that portends the final gasp of poetic utterance: "Only once more and not again." Stickney's "Sonnets from Greece" display a similar inadequacy or belatedness before the classical world's natural power. The wind that blows in the poem "Mt. Lykaion" should transform the poet into an Aeolian harp; instead it threatens to annihilate him. He fears that antiquity's "great wind [will] kill my little shell with sound." A more domestic image of the poet severed from inspiration occurs at the conclusion of "Near Helicon" where "a migrant bird in passing sung / And the girl closed her window not to hear."

Of all Stickney's lyric poems, certainly the best known is "Mnemosyne," a meditation on time and memory in which tercets recalling a vernal landscape are interrupted by a refrain re-inscribing the autumnal present. The poem's rhymed tercets and refrains recall the echoes of a villanelle, and yet "Mnemosyne" deploys its refrain unlike any villanelle, signaling significant temporal and tonal shifts between strophe and repetend. The poem's diction also ranges across a variety of registers; lines such as "I had a sister lovely in my sight" clearly recall the Song of Songs, while other lines in their plainspokenness seem to prefigure **Robert Frost**, as when the speaker asks of the landscape, "how came such wretchedness to cumber / The earth and I to people it alone." The poem ends in a deluge that extinguishes the "perished ember" of remembrance that the poet was able to "stare . . . into flames" a few stanzas earlier. Though many commentators have likened this line to Verlaine's "*Il pleure dans mon coeur*," Stickney's line is less about the poet's subjective despair and more a recognition of time's power to eradicate even the memory of past happiness.

In the fall of 1903 Stickney returned to America to teach at Harvard. His melancholy at the provincialism of Cambridge life was aggravated by his growing physical pain. Stickney soon developed severe headaches and by 1904 had become blind. Despite his blindness, he continued to write, composing fragments that, as Hollander notes, might have been claimed for **Imagism** a decade later:

> The green and climbing eyesight of a cat
> Crawled near my mind's poor birds.

Stickney was widely mourned. In addition to publishing Stickney's collected works, George Cabot Lodge wrote a twenty-six–sonnet cycle lamenting his death, and William Vaughn Moody said that he dreaded returning to Paris without Stickney. As always, **Edwin Arlington Robinson** was more direct. Writing about Stickney's death to a friend, he set the elegiac tone that would mark Stickney scholarship for years to follow, writing simply "We could not afford to lose him."

Further Readings. ***Selected Primary Source:*** Stickney, Trumbull, *The Poems of Trumbull Stickney*, ed. Amberys R. Whittle (New York: Farrar, Straus and Giroux, 1972). ***Selected Secondary Sources:*** Hollander, John, "Far Space and Long Antiquity: Trumbull Stickney's Autumns" in *The Work of Poetry* (New York: Columbia University Press, 1997); Whittle, Amberys R., *Trumbull Stickney* (Lewisburg, PA: Bucknell University Press, 1973); Wilson, Edmund,

"The Country I Remember" (*New Republic* 103 [October 14, 1940]: 529–530).

Thomas Hawks

STOCKTON, ANNIS BOUDINOT (1736–1801)

Annis Stockton's significance as an eighteenth-century American poet was seldom appreciated until the late twentieth century. She finds new readers as a result of feminist recovery projects that began in the 1970s and also from new understanding of the importance of manuscript culture to literary history that date from the 1990s. Regionally known in her own day as a skilled practitioner of an American neoclassicism much influenced by British contemporaries, Stockton's works were scattered among a variety of manuscript networks and pseudonymous or anonymous periodical publications. Buried in a variety of archives through most of the nineteenth and twentieth centuries, her poetry was lost to readers. Pattie Cowell's gathering of *Women Poets in Pre-Revolutionary America, 1650–1775* (1981) and Carla Mulford's scholarly edition *"Only for the Eye of a Friend": The Poems of Annis Boudinot Stockton* (1995) have retrieved Stockton's work for contemporary audiences.

Stockton's recovered writing and its significance come into focus as readers learn that manuscript culture was at least as important to the development of eighteenth-century American poetry as the growing print culture. Throughout a long writing life, Stockton relied less on periodical and book publication than on manuscript networks to circulate her work. More than 130 of her poems have now been pulled from colonial archives, and she emerges as among the most prolific of eighteenth-century American poets, a notable practitioner of the neoclassical aesthetic as it evolved in the American colonies and the new republic.

Born in Darby, Pennsylvania, on July 1, 1736 to Elias Boudinot, a merchant and silversmith of French Huguenot descent, and Catherine Williams, Annis Boudinot Stockton left few records of her youth. Her family lived in Philadelphia during much of her childhood, moving to New Brunswick in the early 1750s to pursue a copper mining business and then in the mid-1750s to the Princeton area, where Elias Boudinot served as postmaster and ran a tavern. Stockton's extant manuscripts and correspondence suggest that her education, especially in the popular English literature of the day, was not neglected, but of her training or formal schooling (if she had any) nothing is known. Her first datable poem is marked "New Brunswick May the 22nd 1753" (Stockton, 71), indicating that she was writing poetry even as a young woman of sixteen. She married Richard Stockton, prominent New Jersey lawyer, landowner, and signer of the Declaration of Independence. Though the date of their marriage is unknown, it was most likely late in 1757 or early in 1758; some of her earliest surviving poems celebrate their courtship. "The Dream," a 1756 courtship ode, hints that the marriage may have met with familial disapproval: "I found thee all my own in spite of those / Whose cold unfeeling minds would bid us part" (Butterfield, "Morven," 11). After she moved with her new husband to the Stockton estate near Princeton, Annis Stockton began to call her home "Morven," drawing the name from the imaginary land of Ossian's (James Macpherson's) Fingal. The elaborately stylish gardens she cultivated at Morven share their aesthetic with her verse: **pastoral**, formal, patterned on popular British modes.

Stockton's quiet world of family, friends, and poetry was shattered by the turmoil of the American Revolution. When Richard Stockton's Quaker politics of moderation and pacifism gave way to a public declaration of support for the patriots, the Stocktons found themselves on the military as well as the political battlefront. Morven was occupied by the British under Cornwallis during the Battle of Princeton in December 1776. Annis Stockton had carefully secreted the records of the American Whig Society at Princeton before the British arrived, a service for which she was later named an honorary member of the society. No such foresight could have preserved Morven: The estate was ransacked. Papers, including some of Stockton's early poems, were stolen. Son-in-law Benjamin Rush estimated the losses at £5000. Although the family had evacuated, Richard Stockton was taken prisoner soon after their escape and held until January 1777. Washington's quick recapture of Princeton enabled the Stocktons and their unmarried children to return to their ruined home in early 1777. Richard Stockton had signed a British oath that he would no longer participate actively in pro-Revolutionary work. He kept that oath until his death from cancer in 1781. Annis Stockton stayed at Morven until sometime around 1795, when she moved to a smaller place in Princeton. By 1796 she was living with her youngest daughter, Abigail Field of White Hill. She died there on February 6, 1801.

Despite the burdens of raising six children and managing a sizeable household, Annis Stockton continued writing throughout her lifetime, often using the pseudonym Emelia (sometimes spelled "Amelia"). She published at least twenty-one poems, mostly in colonial periodicals. Her first known publication, "To the Honorable Col. Peter Schuyler," appeared in the *New York Mercury* for January 9, 1758, and was immediately reprinted by the *New American Magazine* for January 1758. Schuyler was commander of a troop known as the Jersey Blues that was sent to Canada during the French and Indian War. Stockton's poems continued to be published from time to time until 1793, mostly in mid-Atlantic periodicals such as the *Pennsylvania Magazine*, the *American Museum*, and the *Columbian Magazine*.

After the early poem to Schuyler, Stockton wrote many occasional pieces to leading military and political figures, among them Benjamin Franklin, Alexander Hamilton, Joseph Warren, Richard Montgomery, and Henry Laurens. Sometimes she wrote a few lines in celebration of writers such as historian Catherine Macaulay Graham or poet-philosopher James Beattie. She wrote at least ten poems celebrating George Washington, four of them published—two each in the *New Jersey Gazette* and the *Gazette of the United States.* Published or not, Stockton sent fair copies of these poems directly to Washington. He warmly acknowledged many of them and kept them among his papers. Uncertain about the propriety of publication for women, Stockton hedged her apparent desire to publish her work with careful rationalization. In a letter to her brother, Elias Boudinot, dated May 1, 1789, about one of her several odes to Washington, she explained that "if you think it will only add one sprig to the wreath, the country twines—to bind the brows of my heroe, I will run the risk of being sneered at by *those* who criticise female productions, of all kinds" (Stockton, 10). Two particularly moving poems elegizing Richard Stockton's death were appended to the Reverend Samuel Stanhope Smith's *Funeral Sermon on the Death of the Hon. Richard Stockton* . . . (Trenton, NJ: Isaac Collins, 1781).

Despite this evidence of Stockton's readiness to find readers through print media, the vast majority of her poems were circulated in manuscript. She sent fair copies through a series of friendship and kinship networks, fully expecting that those with whom she shared her poems would read them aloud to their family and friends and perhaps even send them to others. Her correspondence with poet **Elizabeth Graeme Fergusson**, for example, resulted in frequent exchanges of verse; one of Fergusson's poetic commonplace books, apparently written in 1787, was addressed to Annis Stockton. A friend and fellow resident of Princeton, Esther Edwards Burr copied two of Stockton's poems into her regular letter-journals to Sarah Prince, one of them written "To my Burrissa" in 1757. Another lengthy exchange between Stockton and Princeton tutor Benjamin Young Prime developed a version of the centuries-old *querelle des femmes*, a series of attacks on and defenses of woman. Prime praises Stockton by making her unlike other women, exceptional among "the lovelier Sex" who "[t]he wild Commands of Vanity obey / And in dull Trifles waste their Time away." Stockton responds that she "will not purchase at your Cost my Fame," going on to suggest that "while Men against us rise / And Female Learning in the Kitchen lies," his criticisms may be unjust (Stockton, 275, 278–279).

Stockton's work is consistently part of a neoclassical tradition much in vogue in the eighteenth century. American neoclassicists such as Stockton knew the work of Dryden, Pope, Young, Thomson, and Gray. The aesthetic at the core of this tradition celebrated poetry as the most important of the literary genres because its capacity for elevated language could convey, in the words of Alexander Pope, "[w]hat oft was Thought, but ne'er so well Exprest." Neoclassical poetry was a public poetry, valuing didactic and communal purposes. Idealizing the literature of ancient Greece and Rome and the Christian epics of Spenser and Milton, neoclassicists promoted the imitation of classical forms rather than originality. They sought an order in poetry that could inspire an order in society. Perhaps the regularity of line in their odes, elegies, eclogues, epithalamia, sonnets, and hymns was designed as a counterweight to the social chaos that led to war and revolution. But whatever their rationale, neoclassicists preferred a poetry of emotional restraint and decorum, a poetry that moved away from particularized detail to generalized observations of human character and condition.

Stockton embraced neoclassical conventions, developing in her work broad themes of friendship, courtship, marriage, nature, patriotism, old age, and grief. She wrote to celebrate friends' birthdays, mourn the deaths of those she loved or admired, create pastoral scenes of idealized rural nature, commemorate special events for community or nation, and use her considerable wit to tease and play. Early works sometimes chafed against the gendered restraints she faced. She responded to a piece in the *Pennsylvania Chronicle* (1768) critical of women, for example, by mounting a strong defense of more education for girls and women. She reminded her readers that the frequent sarcasms directed at educated women—"the odium of a *bookish fair*, / Or *female pedant*, or *'they quit their sphere'*"—inhibited women's learning, forcing them to "sigh for sweet instruction's page in vain" (Stockton, 90). However, a later "Poetical Epistle . . . to her Niece, upon her Marriage" (1786) revealed a growing social conservatism (Stockton, 134–137).

Stockton's manuscripts indicate few revisions except for those poems that were subsequently published. A comparison of the manuscript "To Mr. Stockton in England, An Epistle, 1769" to "By a Lady in America to her Husband in England" (1775) from the *Pennsylvania Magazine,* for example, reveals the addition of four lines and the reworking or omission of several others. Comparisons between other manuscript poems and published versions indicate similar reworking, perhaps a signal that her attention to poetry was more than the necessity to "jingle" when "the fit is on [her]," as she had indicated to Elias Boudinot in 1781 (Stockton, 195).

Because Stockton circulated her verse freely among her friends, her extant manuscripts are widely scattered. The largest collections of her verse are housed at the New Jersey Historical Society and Princeton University. Other manuscripts are distributed among the Historical Society of Pennsylvania, the Rosenbach Museum and

Library, the Washington Papers at the Library of Congress, the Fergusson commonplace book at the Dickinson College Library, and the Esther Burr journal in Yale University's Beinecke Library.

Further Reading. ***Selected Primary Sources:*** Cowell, Pattie, ed., *Women Poets in Pre-Revolutionary America, 1650–1775: An Anthology* (Troy, NY: Whitston Publishing Company, 1981, 87–100); Stockton, Annis Boudinot, "*Only for the Eye of a Friend": The Poems of Annis Boudinot Stockton,* ed. Carla Mulford (Charlottesville: University Press of Virginia, 1995); Mulford, Carla, "Annis Boudinot Stockton and Benjamin Young Prime: A Poetical Correspondence, and More" (*Princeton University Library Chronicle* 52.2 [Winter 1991]: 231–266). ***Selected Secondary Sources:*** Bill, Alfred, *A House Called Morven: Its Role in American History*, rev. Constance M. Greiff (1954; reprint Princeton, NJ: Princeton University Press, 1978); Butterfield, Lyman H., "Annis and the General: Mrs. Stockton's Poetic Eulogies of George Washington" (*Princeton University Library Chronicle* 7 [November 1945]: 19–39); ———, "Morven: A Colonial Outpost of Sensibility. With Some Hitherto Unpublished Poems by Annis Boudinot Stockton" (*Princeton University Library Chronicle* 6 [November 1944]: 1–16); Mulford, Carla, "Political Poetics: Annis Boudinot Stockton and Middle Atlantic Women's Culture" (*New Jersey History* 111 [1993]: 66–110); Shields, David S., *Civil Tongues and Polite Letters in British America* (Chapel Hill: University of North Carolina Press for the Institute of Early American History and Culture, 1997).

Pattie Cowell

STODDARD, ELIZABETH (1823–1902)

Elizabeth Stoddard's poetry is difficult to categorize even one century after her death. In many respects, Stoddard found herself caught between two major groups of writers: those who were traditional and more aesthetically oriented, and the emerging women artists who broke with convention by addressing social concerns. She resisted both of these movements: the traditional for its censorship of the female voice, and the emerging women writers for their conventional morality. Instead, Stoddard, through her collected *Poems* (1895), brings forth a pioneering voice of female individuality that addresses the passion, independence, and sexuality of the speaker. Through exploring these aspects of the speaker, Stoddard exposes the effects of subjectivity on nineteenth-century American women artists.

Elizabeth Drew Barstow was born in Mattapoisett, Massachusetts, to a wealthy shipbuilder, Wilson Barstow, Sr. Though the family was wealthy, Elizabeth's father would go bankrupt three times. Nonetheless, Elizabeth and other family members were encouraged to enjoy their affluence. The family, however, was excluded from the "genteel" society of the New England elite. Stoddard would later poke fun at such families in her writing. Young Elizabeth would have a limited formal education, but, unlike many girls her age, she was free to read in minister Thomas Robbins's library. Elizabeth chose to read many eighteenth-century novels as well as drama. Though fiercely independent, she had a strong attachment to her immediate family. When her sister Jane died in 1848 and her mother died a year later, Elizabeth turned to her brother, Wilson. Through her travels, she became interested in literature. In 1851 she went to a literary ball in New York, where she became acquainted with many literary figures, including her future husband, Richard Henry Stoddard. In 1852 Elizabeth and Richard were secretly married. Her husband encouraged her creative interests, and she began writing poetry in 1853. Discouraged by the poetic constraints her husband put on her, however, she turned to prose writing. She became a correspondent for the *Daily Alta California* in 1854. Through the connection with her husband and the newspaper, she became acquainted with other writers. She would begin writing short stories and longer prose after 1858. During1860 Stoddard published three novels: *The Morgesons* (1862), *Two Men* (1865), and *Temple House* (1867). All would have disappointing sales, but Stoddard continued to write, although never another novel. In the coming decades, she would go on to publish poems, essays, and short stories. In 1895 Stoddard's selective *Poems* was published by Houghton Mifflin.

Stoddard's passion and independence can be felt through the speaker in her poem "The Wolf-Tamer." The poem is about a musician who tames wolves through his pied pipers, but some critics suggest that the poem mimics Stoddard's resistance to the restrictions placed on her own poetic creativity. In fact, the speaker of the poem is a wolf that tries to break out of itsspell several times, which is evident by the breaks in the rhyme scheme. The wolf's struggle echoed in the rhyme scheme, may reference Stoddard's own frustration while attempting to write poetry. She felt forced to make her ideas fit into a metric pattern. The resistance to being tamed is evident in the poem as the wolf says, "When your lips shall cease to blow / . . . / We shall fall upon your race" (quoted in Smith, 46). Whether it is a poem that simply references the musical influence that the skilled piper has over the wolves or if the poem is a reference to a woman poet's subservience to traditional male poetics, the poem illustrates the speaker's frustration over the powerless position she finds herself in.

In another poem, "Before the Mirror," Stoddard rewrites Lord Tennyson's "Lady of Shalott." In the original, Tennyson creates a female persona to represent imagination. The poetic imagination is limited because if it is not protected from the human condition, it will become preoccupied with human life and be unable to create true art. Imagination will die. This is precisely what happens in the poem. In Stoddard's version, Lady Shalott, is more than an allegory, however; Stoddard's Shalott chooses to remain in her room and will not be tempted to come out. Unlike Tennyson's allegory, she is successful in her isolation. But this success is rather morbid because it does not provide freedom for the woman. She has maintained her creative seclusion and will forever "weave," but she cannot escape from the confines that society has placed on her. In other words, being an imaginative woman can be dangerous and oppressive.

Like her "Lady Shalott," Stoddard did resist the pressure to focus on social conditions. Many women poets wrote about such issues as temperance, slavery, and women's suffrage, but Stoddard's poems avoided the sentimental language that was so common in other works of the era. Even when she did use sentiment, she always stopped short of optimism. In a poem she wrote shortly after the death of her first child, the speaker describes the episode. The speaker says that she left him one morning and later heard that he had died. Then the speaker describes how "We made him ready for his rest" (quoted in Smith, 52). In another poem about her son, titled "Unreturning," the flower imagery and sentiment return. What is absent in both poems, however, is any reassurance that the child will go to heaven, where the family will be joined together. Such confirmation during a time of loss was common if not expected. But Stoddard resisted this device because she was critical of such an evangelical Christian reading.

Stoddard's poetry was unexpected and outside the conventions of the time. "In-between" two poetic traditions, she encompasses the subjectivity of women in general. In "Nameless Pain" the speaker asks herself why she is not content. She notes that her needs are taken care of. She also states that she has "no power" or "healing art." In fact, the poem's speaker claims she has nothing but an uneventful and discontented life, a life that she has little control over. In "I Love You, but a Sense of Pain," the speaker struggles with her desire, her love, and her dream. She loves her husband, yet wishes for one unlike him. Should she remember only her past, her wedding, in order to be fulfilled? But to do so, to be content, would mean that she would have to give up her dream. Whether the dream was a traditional life or the life of a writer was one with which Stoddard struggled, in her poetry.

Further Reading. ***Selected Primary Sources:*** Smith, Robert McClure, and Ellen Weinauer, eds., *American Culture, Canons, and the Case of Elizabeth Stoddard* (Tuscaloosa: University of Alabama Press, 2003); Stoddard, Elizabeth, *The Morgesons* (New York: Penguin, 1997). ***Selected Secondary Sources:*** Baym, Nina, *American Women Writers and the Work of History, 1790–1860* (New Brunswick, NJ: Rutgers University Press, 1995); Kete, Mary Louise, *Sentimental Collaborations, Mourning and Middle-Class Identity in Nineteenth-Century America* (Durham, NC: Duke University Press, 1999).

Earl Yarington

STONE, RUTH (1915–)

In 2002, at the age of eighty-seven, Ruth Stone's eighth collection of poetry, *In the Next Galaxy*, won the National Book Award. A few weeks later, the Academy of American Poets presented her with its **Wallace Stevens** Prize, an annual recognition of mastery in the art of poetry. Many in the literary world thought the acknowledgments were long overdue. It wasn't that Stone hadn't won several prestigious awards. The collection *Ordinary Words* (1999) received the National Book Critics Circle Award, and over the decades she had also received the Bess Hokin Award, a Bunting fellowship, the Delmore Schwartz Award, two Guggenheim fellowships, the Shelley Memorial Award, and the Vermont Cerf Award for lifetime achievement in the arts. But Stone's long life had been bereft of either economic or creative security. Widowed at forty-one, Stone had spent decades cobbling an existence for herself and her three daughters from her poetry and her work as an itinerant writing instructor, teaching at a dozen or more colleges and universities over her long career. Despite her own hardships, her generosity to other writers was legendary. In 1956 she bought a run-down farmhouse in Vermont with $4000 from a poetry prize. Over the years, she made her home available to an ever-changing assembly of writers from Tillie Olson to **Sharon Olds**. At age eighty, laser surgery designed to improve her failing eyesight had instead exacerbated the problem. But she never stopped writing, instead developing techniques to create poems in giant script that her daughters helped render back onto the page. Despite near blindness and hearing loss, Stone published a ninth volume, *In the Dark*, in 2004.

Perseverance was not only the hallmark of Stone's life; it also contributed to highly personalized poems whose emotional content translated into universal themes easily accessible to the reader. As Pulitzer Prize–winning poet **Galway Kinnell**, one of the judges for the Academy of American Poets Award, said of Stone's poems, "They are experiences, not the record of experiences. They are events, interactions between the poet and the world. They happen—there on the page before us and within us—surprising and inevitable" (Daley, 258). Those experiences are not tainted by self-pity or maudlin metaphor but rather are expressed with a brutal honesty, with wit, and with a deep belief in the power of poetry to heal.

A feminist and amateur scientist, Stone's poems unflinchingly examine the pathos of the human condition, especially the female struggle in a patriarchal society. But nature and the wider world are never far away, and it is from these, along with family, music, and art, that she took and gave solace. Stone's work is rich with scientific detail—keen observations about wild plants growing where she lived, records of native birds and animals inhabiting her environment, and personal observations about astronomy, biology, and genetics. These details imbue her poems with multiple levels of reference, especially when juxtaposed against her outrage over the stupidity of many human acts—from war to petty cruelties. Yet Stone's work is rarely preachy. As she aged, she took on the voice of the wise mother who had seen and suffered much, but she balanced finger-pointing and lamenting with forgiveness and humor.

Beyond that, Stone's use of ordinary, everyday items and explicit language to describe amorphous emotional responses to the world around and within her give her poems an uncanny openness. In "This Is How It Is" (*In the Dark*), she compares the imagination's night wanderings to "walk[ing] through the corridors of my thoughts." Her computer is something to love because "it's full of my words" ("Tools of the Psyche," *In the Dark*). In her poem "Loss" (*Cheap*, 1975) she writes of the persistence of heartache, a "pain that would wake me / Or like a needle it would stitch its way into my dreams." And when she writes, "In the night each foot has nothing to love / but the other foot" ("Sorrow," *Sextet One*, 1996), the reader shares her candid loneliness.

Stone was born in 1915 in Roanoke, Virginia. As a child, her family moved often to pursue her father's prospects as a musician, first from Roanoke to Norfolk, Virginia, and later to Akron, Ohio, and finally to Indianapolis. There she was doted on by an extended family of poets, painters, teachers, and musicians. She claimed to remember her mother reading Alfred Lord Tennyson's "In Memoriam" to her while she nursed. She told the National Book Foundation at her acceptance speech that by the time she was two her mother, "had taught me a thick book of poems by heart and she used to give me a penny to say them. I'm not very commercial about my work so I guess it didn't sink in." She read by age three, climbing into the stacks of her grandparents' library to fetch "the big books." Her father, a drummer who made ends meet by setting type for the *Indianapolis Star* and other newspapers, practiced at home; Stone believed the rhythm of poetry and music were interlaced into the oldest recesses of her brain. She published her first poem at age five, and then published regularly in the *Indianapolis Star*, the *New York Times*, and *Golden Book Magazine*.

After meeting novelist and poet Walter Stone at the University of Illinois, where she had studied, the two became devoted writing partners. He typed the poems that eventually appeared in her first book, *In an Iridescent Time* (1959). In 1953 Stone won Poetry Magazine's Bess Hokin Prize and a Kenyon Review Fellowship in Poetry. She had seen an ad for a Vermont farmhouse in the *New York Times* and, quite impulsively, drove north to view it. As she drove along the bumpy dirt road through the woods leading to the place, she told the real estate agent she would buy the farm, sight unseen, using her prize money to do so. At the time, she and Walter Stone were part of an elite group of writers that included **Sylvia Plath**, Ted Hughes, and Dylan Thomas. Life was exhilarating—and exhausting. She wanted the Vermont house to be their haven—a place to write and raise the children.

By the fall of 1959, however, Walter Stone was dead. He was found hanging from a cord thrown over the doorway of a London rooming house he had rented while conducting research for a novel he had a contract to write. The Vermont house became her sanctuary. When not traveling to teach or read, she holed up there, heating by wood, hauling water in winter after the water pipes had frozen, and raising her daughters to appreciate the power of art to heal. The house had more than five thousand books and no television. Early on, she invented the Poetry Game, in which all participants (which often included developing and already acclaimed writers) contributed a word and wrote a poem using all the offerings. Stone's daughters Abigail Stone and Phoebe Stone are successful writers, as are several of her grandchildren.

From childhood on, Stone's poems often came to her whole, "riding in like a freight train, the words appearing at full speed in my mind, sometimes from the bottom up" (Daley, 256). But, like a traveler rushing to catch a departing train, she had to write the lines down fast before they passed on by. The poems were far from finished products when they arrived. Stone painstakingly revised, honed, read the words aloud, dreamt about her poems, put them aside, then worked on them again and again before she considered them finished. "There are so many words," she said, explaining her creative process. "What I'm after is the right words. I like to live with a poem for a while, get to know it, get to know its language" (Daley, 256). She worked on one poem for a decade, then gave up on finding the right ending line. One day, while doing some menial task, the perfect ending came. Inspiration is a necessary partner, she believed, but you have to write it down.

In an Iridescent Time was published shortly after her husband's suicide. It captured the innocent happiness of the years before her husband's death and began to explore the unfathomable reality of his act, an oft-repeated theme throughout her work. In 1963 Stone was awarded a two-year Radcliffe Institute fellowship and worked on poems for her second collection, *Topography and Other Poems* (1971). She developed lifelong ties to other Radcliffe fellows, including **Maxine Kumin** and Olson. Over the next thirty years, she repeated the wanderings of her own family, teaching at Old Dominion, Cooper Union, New York University, the University of California–Davis, the University of Virginia–Charlottesville, Brandeis University, Indiana University, the University of Wisconsin, Wellesley College, and Harvard University before finally settling down at SUNY–Binghamton, where she taught from 1998 to 2004. *The Oxford Companion to Women's Writing in the United States* calls Stone the "mother poet" for many contemporary writers, especially women, because of her lifelong devotion to teaching and mentoring. Poet and scholar **Willis Barnstone**, co-author of *A Book of Women Poets from Antiquity to Now*, describes Stone as "a legendary teacher of poetry like no one on this side of the century, which has led to many ardent converts to poetry. . . . Her poverties have, like all adversity, kept her lean and real and made her wealthy" in her dual professions of writing and teaching (Daley, 257).

In an Iridescent Time reflects a mastery of formal conventions that include rhythmic sonnets and balanced pentameters, along with a reliance on classical themes. By *Topography*, Stone's poems had become more flexible and she had abandoned traditional themes for stories about people like herself, people pushed to the margins of society, whether by economic adversity or gender bias. One reason she moved from one university to another was her inability to play the academic game or stifle her criticism about the treatment of lecturers hired for only a semester or two. In "Madison in the Mid-Sixties" (*Ordinary Words*, 1999), she writes of arriving at the University of Wisconsin after "a long drive from the East . . . penniless" only to have the chairman of the department who had hired her for the semester urge her "to get a motel" for the night. As the two talked on the phone, she could hear "the background dinner party" she had not been invited to. She spent the night in her old Oldsmobile, with "my mother in the backseat / and the hamster and Abigail."

It's the inconspicuous elegance of lines like "the birch trees are wrapped in their white bandages" ("What We Have," *In the Next Galaxy*) or her ability to describe silence as "the large comfortable casket of snow" ("Blizzard," *In the Dark)* that readers find so engaging. Because Stone employs elements of daily life, describing, for example, the job of a poet as inventing the universe with a handful of alphabet written on a few blocks ("What Is a Poem?" *In the Dark*), the average person does not feel intimidated. Even when the subject is death and the loneliness of the person left behind, Stone's poetry remains rich in tangible meaning while also being fresh and inventive. In "Mantra" (*In the Next Galaxy*), she expresses the lasting incredulity of her husband's death: "Love lies asleep / and dreams that everything/ is in its golden net."

Such stark candor is balanced with delightful good humor. In the title poem of *Second Hand Coat* (1987), she writes of the peculiar connection between the new owner of a secondhand coat and its previous owner. The narrator of the poem instinctively knows that its previous owner "kept a handkerchief box, washed her undies, / ate at the Holiday Inn, had a basement freezer." When she awakens, the poem's narrator thinks she has turned into the other woman. As she slips the coat over her arms, she thinks about the previous owner "and her coat says, / Get your purse, have you got your keys."

Further Reading. ***Selected Primary Sources:*** Stone, Ruth, *Cheap* (New York: Harcourt, 1975); ———, *In an Iridescent Time* (New York: Harcourt Brace, 1959); *In the Dark* (Port Townsend, WA: Copper Canyon Press, 2004); ———, *In the Next Galaxy* (Port Townsend, WA: Copper Canyon Press, 2002); ———, *Ordinary Words* (Ashfield, MA: Paris Press, 1999); ———, *Second Hand Coat* (New York: David R. Godine, 1987); ———, *Simplicity* (Ashfield, MA: Paris Press, 1995); ———, *Topography* (New York: Harcourt, 1971); ———, *Who Is the Widow's Muse* (Sommerville, MA: Yellow Moon Press, 1991). ***Selected Secondary Sources:*** Barker, Wendy, and Sandra M. Gilbert, eds., *The House Is Made of Poetry: The Art of Ruth Stone* (Carbondale: Southern Illinois University Press, 1996); Barnstone, Aliki, and Willis Barnstone, eds., *A Book of Women Poets from Antiquity to Now* (New York: Shocken Books, 1987); Daley, Yvonne, *A State of Mind: Writing in Vermont* (Hanover, NH: University Press of New England, 2005); Davidson, Cathy N., et al., eds., *The Oxford Companion to Women's Writing in the United States* (Oxford: Oxford University Press, 1995).

Yvonne Daley

STRAND, MARK (1934–)

If the work of Mark Strand lies squarely in the main line of contemporary American poetry during the last quarter of the twentieth century, it is because he has in fact been central in establishing that era's most recognized model of what constitutes a contemporary poem. When he began publishing in the early 1960s, poetry was in the crest of the confessional mode, in which poets submitted the most painful details of their private experiences to the merciless judgment of public speech. The **confessional** poets thus offered personal exposure as an antidote to the vast, impersonal mythic structures in which the **modernist** poets of the years between the wars famously escaped from the burden of personality.

Strand is among the first poets who found a way to resist the temptations both toward grand mythic vision and intensely personal self-revelation. He marked what has since become a heavily trafficked path by his early development of a poetic diction that disavowed effusion and adornment, mimicking the sort of plain, interior meditation one might hold with oneself. His poetry avoids any direct description of subjective states, scrupulously crafting images of the exterior world to serve as metaphors for experiences at once intensely private and essentially impersonal: time, loss, distance, desire, and the momentary compensations of poetry chief among them.

A late heir to **Imagism** and to **Wallace Stevens**, Strand has defined the less hubristic boundaries that so much recent poetry respects; his poems are more apt to delineate the opacities behind which the self and the gods may lurk than to try to shove them into the uncertain light of words. One gauge of Strand's centrality is the almost unseemly number of awards he has garnered, from Guggenheim, Rockefeller, and NEA fellowships to a Pulitzer (for *Blizzard of One*), a MacArthur fellowship, and the Poet Laureateship of the United States (1990). Poetry, indeed, has been Strand's nearly sole intersection with public life. Born to American parents on Prince Edward Island in 1934, educated at Antioch, Yale, and Iowa, a husband, father, and teacher who has lived in many cities around the Americas, Strand has never made news by the manner of his life. Neither has he inscribed its turning points in his poetry. His poems return often to his boyhood as a source of imagery but not of incident; similarly, "For Jessica, My Daughter" and even his long "Elegy for My Father" struggle to articulate the difficulty of absence in the face of love rather than recounting any narrative particularities of either life. Strand's lyrics are not anecdotal. Trained as a painter before he studied poetry with **Donald Justice**, he has also published books on Edward Hopper (to whose work his own poetry has frequently been compared) and William Bailey. Indeed, Strand might serve as a model for the poet as man of letters, having spent most of his adult life in the university system, occupying a wide variety of appointments at such institutions as Harvard, Yale, Princeton, Johns Hopkins, the University of Chicago, and the University of Utah, while not only pursuing his poetic career but also working occasionally as an editor, translator, and essayist. A close friend of Octavio Paz, Strand has been especially active in the translation and dissemination of Latin American poetry.

Strand's life as a poet divides aptly into three periods. The volumes *Sleeping with One Eye Open* (1964), *Reasons for Moving* (1968), and *Darker* (1970) largely consist of short, very involuted lyrics, poems in which the speaker, often addressing an unnamed "you" or "he" who may as well be his other self, records rather than escapes his incapacity to express himself in any other way than by passing hints and shadows. Indeed, the imagery of shadows haunts these direct, unadorned poems, which suggestively evoke emotional states without trying to name, evaluate, or moralize them. Strand's line lengths vary in his early work as they would throughout his career, but many of his earlier compositions use short, tense, declarative lines to create a sense of the compression of what can be said amid the gulf of what can only be implied. The poem "Keeping Things Whole" (1964), from his first book, begins with nine words cut into three lines that still probably constitute Strand's best-known formulation of the opacity of human experience: "In a field / I am the absence / of field." To be human, the poem goes on to hint, is to be the missing element in the phenomenal world we observe, an eye outside its own field of vision.

In *The Story of Our Lives* (1973), *The Late Hour* (1978), and the "New Poems" section of *Selected Poems* (1980), Strand grows more expansive; not only do his poems literally lengthen, they address definable others for virtually the first time, attempting, for instance, to word the inner life of Strand's dying father (though objectively, as always, through observed detail) in "Elegy for My Father" (1973). From this point on, it is at least as likely for Strand to use the word "you" to refer to an identifiable person outside himself as to use it in self-address to betoken the incurable alienation of self-consciousness. Whether under the pressure of this attempt to make contact or for more mundane reasons, Strand experienced a long, self-described "dry period" in the early 1980s during which he wrote no poetry, publishing the collection of short stories *Mr. and Mrs. Baby* in 1985 as well as a number of translations, children's books, and essays on art.

Ten years after the appearance of *Selected Poems*, Strand published *The Continuous Life*; his original work in the 1990s, which also includes the forty-five-section poem sequence *Dark Harbor* (1993) and the volume *Blizzard of One* (1998), engages the meaning of his own enterprise as a poet more openly than ever before. The poetic resources Strand has employed in this latest phase of his career have suitably been more various. For the first time, he has published work in such traditional forms as the villanelle ("Two de Chriricos," 1998); for the first time, he has welcomed into his poetry the figures of myth, formerly exiled, one imagines, for implying submission to modernist canons of taste. In both method and matter, though, the continuity of Strand's work is more striking than its departures. This sense of unity arises in part from the narrow view Strand has always taken of what constitute fit subjects for poetry. He rules the world of public events out of bounds, for instance, never using poetry to examine the changing social circumstances of our times; one could hardly deduce from the volumes he published in the 1960s that it had been a decade of any particular ferment. Questions of social identity never arise in Strand's work either; ethnicity, sexuality, and class are simply disregarded as formative elements of experience. Opening any of Strand's books assures one of entering a world of purely individual (though not personal) concerns. Such assumptions regarding the appropriate province of poetry, indeed, have been widespread enough in the last quarter of the twentieth century to underlie the judgments of a substantial portion of the established poetic community.

But apart from its exclusions, Strand's work also cleaves to a consistent thematic line in its own right. The surreal landscapes his poems so lovingly create generally turn out to be time-scapes as well, the initially static picture concealing unexpected depths of before and after. Here, Strand finds absence in presence and presence in absence; he reveals, that is, the evanescence of what seems solid and known while affirming the substantiality things may have in our recognition of the moment of their passing. In "Where Are the Waters of Childhood?" (1978), for instance, Strand begins with the injunction to "Enter the kingdom of rot," passing through a series of fleeting images of the past before he at last simultaneously loses and discovers what he seeks, an affirmation of some continuity beneath the flux of self that is simultaneously a recognition of the utter disappearance of the original place from which that self has proceeded. Indeed, place seems best known in memory for Strand, which means best known in absence. Frequently, too, what seem at first natural, observed landscapes slide into the kingdom of dreams, as in "Here" (1998), which opens with a description of the light that is utterly plain and natural, shifts into a vision of a surreal city of deserted spaces, and ends with the image of an imaginary presence having survived a dragon "Curled up before its cave in saurian repose."

One of Strand's most anthologized poems, "Pot Roast" (1978), shows with special clarity the nexus of time and desire—which is by necessity for what is absent—at the heart of his work. The pot roast Strand eats in the present moment of the poem is valuable primarily for its evocation of the past, so that he may declare the moment of his anticipation of what he is about to eat identical with the memory of the same meal in vanished childhood: The two absent moments—anticipation and memory—create the powerfully present experience of both meal and poem. Strand carefully pairs this instant of connection with a quiet acknowledgment that the normal condition of life in time is precisely the opposite, a perpetual regret for that which one desires but cannot hold on to. Furthermore, the poem's celebration of this moment of the roast's overwhelming presence also conceals an admission of limitation by the very dailiness of its subject; indeed, Strand wryly admits, both in "Pot Roast" and elsewhere, that with the great poetic themes of eternity and heroism grown stale or suspect, such moments may be all that are left for the poet to celebrate. The "meat of memory" in "Pot Roast" might serve as Strand's image for poetry itself.

Another of his most anthologized pieces, in fact, is titled "Eating Poetry" (1968). The compensation of poetry for a life in time is nowhere more happily portrayed than in this short lyric. The poem imagines the act of reading, as its title indicates, not as a process of interpretation with the aim of deriving meaningful guidance through life (a conventional idea of poetry that the horrified librarian of the poem would presumably endorse), but as a self-consuming process. After the speaker of the poem has devoured his reading, he notes, "The poems are gone," by which one might understand that their value is also time bound; rather than being the eternal artifacts poems have traditionally been imagined to be, in this reading (or eating), a poem disappears into the life of its reader. What a poem does is crucial, not what it "says." The feast, in any case, is transformative; the poem ends with its narrator on all fours, his inner canine released at last. Poetry in this conception does not enlighten, but offers a secret, inner release, an atavistic alternative to being human in the usual sense and so subject to the pain of lost desire. To eat a poem is to escape the snare of intellectual understanding, the pretense of stable meaning in our world and in our language, and to revel in the momentary connection that the evocative, poetic use of words can provide.

By the care of his finely crafted images, Mark Strand has been instrumental in spreading the idea of poetry as a private compensation for the afflictions of life. He has been among the leading poets to establish the most influential vision of what poetry itself is for readers and writers of the late twentieth century—not a revelation of truth or a repository of value, but an art of suggestion, in which the silent gaps between speech tell as much as the words themselves. One sees most clearly, after all, when looking slightly from the corner of the eye.

Further Reading. ***Selected Primary Sources:*** Strand, Mark, *Blizzard of One* (New York: Knopf, 1998); ———, *The Continuous Life* (New York: Knopf, 1990); ———, *Dark Harbor* (New York: Knopf, 1993); ———, *Darker* (New York: Atheneum, 1970); ———, *The Late Hour* (New York: Knopf, 1978); ———, *Reasons for Moving* (New York: Atheneum, 1968); ———, *Selected Poems* (New York: Atheneum, 1980; exp. ed. 1990); ———, *Sleeping with One Eye Open* (Iowa City: Stone Wall Press, 1964); ———, *The Story of Our Lives* (New York: Atheneum, 1973); ———, *Mr. and Mrs. Baby* (New York: Knopf, 1985). ***Selected Secondary Sources:*** Berger, Charles, "Reading as Poets

Read: Following Mark Strand" (*Philosophy and Literature* 20.1 [April 1996]: 189–192); Bloom, Harold, ed., *Mark Strand* (New York: Chelsea House, 2003); Jackson, Richard, "Charles Simic and Mark Strand: The Presence of Absence" (*Contemporary Literature* 21 [1980]: 136–145); Kirby, David, *Mark Strand and the Poet's Place in Contemporary Society* (Columbia: University of Missouri Press, 1990); Olsen, Lance, "Entry to the Unaccounted for: Mark Strand's Fantastic Autism," in *The Poetic Fantastic*, ed. Patrick D. Murphy and Vernon Ross Hyles (Westport, CT: Greenwood Press, 1989).

Robert Squillace

STRYK, LUCIEN (1924–)

Lucien Stryk, a poet of the American Midwest, is also one of the principal Zen poets of the United States. His poetry displays the transcendental quality of lyric observation of objects. Stryk is also a translator of Chinese and Japanese poetry, which has profoundly influenced his own verse. Other influences include **Walt Whitman**, with whom Stryk feels great affinity, and twentieth-century French poets such as Paul Eluard.

Lucien Stryk was born in 1924. After receiving a BA from Indiana University, he pursued his graduate studies at the Sorbonne. His stay in Paris meant an artistic awakening for him. He studied old and new French poets, surrealism, and the philosophy of existentialism. He continued his studies at the University of Maryland, the University of London, and, finally, the University of Iowa. He began his career as a freelance writer, later becoming a professor of English. Two stays in Asia proved stimulating for his poetry. He was a visiting lecturer at Niigata University between 1956 and 1958, and spent a year teaching at Yamaguchi University in 1962. Stryk taught poetry and Asian literature at Northern Illinois University until his retirement in 1991. He still frequently gives poetry readings on the radio and lectures throughout the United States. He also contributes to journals such as *American Poetry Review*, *Encounter*, *New Statesman*, and *Partisan Review*.

Stryk published his first book on Zen in 1965. Zen poetry does not offer ready-made solutions to human observation or questions. Rather, it leads the reader into recognition. As Stryk says, "Do not look *at* things, look *as* things." His creed is to portray ordinary things as realistically and naturally as possible. On the other hand, he claims that every poem should include a metaphor that will engage the imagination of the reader. After his first book on Zen, the publisher Doubleday suggested that he write a book on Zen and Buddhism. This idea materialized in *World of the Buddha: A Reader* (1968), later published as *World of the Buddha: An Introduction to Buddhist Literature* (1982).

In 1976 Stryk's *Selected Poems* appeared. The book encompassed all his previous collections—*Taproot* (1953), *The Trespasser* (1956), *Notes for a Guidebook* (1965), *The Pit and Other Poems* (1969), and *Awakening* (1973)—as well as new poems. There is a considerable variety of topics, from everyday experience of Midwest America, to poems inspired by travels in Europe and Asia, to translations of the Japanese Zen poet Takahashi.

The philosophy of Zen continued to inspire Stryk's work. In 1980 he published *Zen Poems* (1980) and a year later *Encounter with Zen: Writings on Poetry and Zen* (1981), later published as *The Awakened Self: Encounters with Zen* (1995). The book presents essays, poems, and interviews with Asian writers about the nature of their poetry and the practitioners' Zen Buddhism. For Stryk, Zen is a religious philosophy combining meditation with epiphany that lead to enlightenment. Zen Buddhism in particular aims at meditations that sustain the complex discipline of an individual.

Stryk has long admired Asian literature for its discipline and concise presentation of ideas. He adopted one of the most prolific forms—haiku. Stryk embraces the form, which is limited to seventeen syllables and expresses a single idea or image that is not disturbed by unnecessary detail. His comments on his own work and that of both contemporary and past Zen poets of Japan and China emphasize the distillation of experience, heightened awareness and acceptance, and communion with nature that is not governed by time—in essence, a world returned to stillness. Stryk introduced the seventeenth-century master Matsuo Bashō in his book *Birds of Time: Haiku of Bashō* (1983). There Stryk brings his translations and sets the poet in the historical context of Japanese poetry.

In his later career Stryk published various selections from his work. In 1984 *Collected Poems: 1953–1983* appeared, which contains 205 poems and shows the variety of Stryk's work. The unifying theme is the flow of life that is universal: "A mower sputters— / cat leaps from the shade, / into the moment, where we are." The quote from this poem became the title of the next collection, *Where We Are: Selected Poems and Zen Translations* (1997). Included are his finest Zen poems, Chinese and Japanese masters in his translation, and Japanese haiku. The volume contains a useful introduction to Stryk by Susan Portfield as well as Stryk's essay on the Japanese poet Takahashi, who is commemorated in "June 5, 1987": "The phone rings, bringing / word Shinkichi Takahashi / died last night. / And so / the world goes on." Stryk's own poetry is grouped not chronologically but thematically, divided into three sections: "The Duckpond," "Willows," and "Voyage." Stryk is at his best when he applies his talent for detail to minimalist phrasing. His last volume was *And Still Birds Sing: New and Collected Poems* (1998). Stryk incorporates images from small-town life in the Midwest in his so-called neighborhood poems. He observes the activities of the country and transforms these into lyrics of universal meaning. His poetry is accessible to international readership and it has been translated into many languages, including Chinese, German, French, Japanese, Russian, and Swedish.

Lucien Stryk simultaneously writes his own poetry and translates Asian masters. There is a continuous interaction between these activities. Altogether, he has translated fifteen books of Chinese and Japanese literature. He started translating from Asian languages during his academic lectureships in Asia. He worked on the poems by old masters, but he was also searching for new poets. He contacted the poet Takashi Ikemoto, who helped him with translations and introduced him to current writers. They cooperated on such books as *Twelve Death Poems of the Chinese Zen Masters* (1973), *Zen Poems of China and Japan: The Crane's Bill* (1973), *Three Zen Poems, after Shinkichi Takahashi* (1976), and *The Penguin Book of Zen Poetry* (1977). In 1995 they published *Zen Poetry: Let the Spring Breeze Enter* (1995), for which Stryk wrote an introduction, translated the poems, and supplied an afterword. In addition, Stryk has translated many haiku poems, which are collected in *Haiku of the Japanese Masters* (1977), *The Duckweed Way Haiku of Issa* (1977), *Traveler, My Name: Haiku of Bashō* (1984), *On Love and Barley: Haiku of Bashō* (1985), *The Dumpling Field: Haiku of Issa* (1991), and *Cage of Fireflies: Modern Japanese Haiku* (1993).

Stryk's work is not limited to poetry and translation. He has served as an editor and author of introductions. He collected the most prominent poems by authors of the Midwest in two volumes, *Heartland I* (1967) and *Heartland II* (1975). He has been the recipient of many awards, such as the Society of Midland Authors Poetry Award, and fellowships from the National Endowment for the Arts and the Ford and Rockefeller foundations. He has also served as a Fulbright scholar.

Further Reading. ***Selected Primary Sources:*** Stryk, Lucien, *And Still Birds Sing: New and Collected Poems* (Athens, OH: Swallow Press, 1998); ———, *Awakening* (Athens, OH: Swallow Press, 1973); ———, *Birds of Time: Haiku of Bashō* (Vermillion, SD: Flatlands Press, 1983); ———, *Collected Poems: 1953–1983* (Athens, OH: Swallow Press, 1984); ———, *The Duckpond* (London: Omphalos Press, 1978); ———, *Encounter with Zen: Writings on Poetry and Zen* (Athens, OH: Swallow Press, 1981; later published as *The Awakened Self: Encounters with Zen,* 1995); ———, ed., *Heartland: Poets of the Midwest,* 2 vols. (DeKalb: Northern Illinois University Press, 1967, 1975); ———, ed., *The Penguin Book of Zen Poetry* (Harmondsworth: Penguin, 1977); ———, *The Pit and Other Poems* (Athens, OH: Swallow Press, 1969); ———, *Selected Poems* (Athens, OH: Swallow Press, 1976); ———, *Taproot* (Oxford: Fantasy Press, 1953); ———, *Where We Are: Selected Poems and Zen Translations* (London: Skoob Books, 1997); ———, *Willows* (Cambridge: Embers Handpress, 1983); ———, ed., *World of the Buddha: A Reader* (New York: Doubleday, 1968; later published as *World of the Buddha: An Introduction to Buddhist Literature,* 1982); ———, *Zen Poems* (Cambridge: Embers Handpress, 1980); ———, ed., *Zen Poetry: Let the Spring Breeze Enter* (New York: Grove Press, 1995). ***Selected Secondary Sources:*** Abbott, Craig S., "Lucien Stryk: A Bibliography" (*Analytical & Enumerative Bibliography* 5.3–4 [1991]); Deming, Richard A., "Finding the Way: An Interview with Lucien Stryk, Part I" (*ELF: Eclectic Literary Forum* 7.2 [Summer 1997]: 6–10); ———, "Finding the Way: An Interview with Lucien Stryk, Part II" (*ELF: Eclectic Literary Forum* 7.3 [Fall 1997]: 6–10); Guillory, Daniel L., "The Oriental Connection: Zen and Representations of the Midwest in the Collected Poems of Lucien Stryk" (*Midamerica: The Yearbook of the Society for the Study of Midwestern Literature* 8 [1986]: 107–115); Porterfield, Susan, ed., *Zen, Poetry, the Art of Lucien Stryk* (Athens, OH: Swallow Press, 1993); ———, "The War Poetry of Lucien Stryk" (*Journal of the Midwest Modern Language Association* 33–34.3–1 [Fall/Winter 2000–2001]: 152–169).

Pavlína Hácová

STUART, RUTH MCENERY (1849–1917)

Well known at the end of the nineteenth century for her Southern local color fiction, Ruth McEnery Stuart contributed about fifty poems—many of them narrated in black dialect—to national magazines between 1893 and 1916. She collected most of this poetry, along with new material, in *Daddy Do-Funny's Wisdom Jingles* (1913) and *Plantation Songs and Other Verse* (1916). In contrast, her first book of verse was *Gobolinks or Shadow Pictures for Young and Old* (1896), an unusual pairing of inkblots with short rhymes in standard English that Stuart created in collaboration with Mark Twain's biographer, Albert Bigelow Paine. The three volumes reflect a turn-of-the-century fashion for **light verse** and other comic poetry, and Stuart's humor—like that of **Mary Mapes Dodge**, Rudyard Kipling, **Carolyn Wells**, Gelett Burgess, and Oliver Herford—was often directed to a combined audience of children and adults.

Mary Routh McEnery was born in Marksville, Louisiana, in 1849, the oldest of eight children. Her father, James McEnery, emigrated from Ireland as a boy; her mother, Mary Routh Stirling McEnery, was the daughter of a Scottish immigrant. Perhaps this ancestry heightened Stuart's appreciation for the ethnic mixture of New Orleans, where the family relocated from their rural plantation when she was a girl. Stuart's daily walks through many distinctive neighborhoods anticipated her stories and poems about the city's Irish, African American, German, Italian, and French Creole residents. After the Civil War, she became a schoolteacher to help offset her father's financial losses. At thirty, she married Alfred Oden Stuart and moved to Washington, Arkansas, which appears as Simpkinsville, Arkansas, in her fiction.

Returning to New Orleans with her young son after her husband's death, Stuart associated with many Louisiana writers, including George Washington Cable, Katherine Nobles, and Dorothy Dix. In 1888, encouraged by Charles Dudley Warner of *Harper's Monthly*, she began to publish black dialect tales in the tradition of Sherwood Bonner, **Joel Chandler Harris**, and other Southerners. Stuart moved North in the early 1890s to develop her career; in New York, she soon became known as a "pet of the Harper set" and a popular hostess to artists and writers. Like Cable and Mark Twain, she began to travel on the platform reading network, presenting her works to audiences in Boston, Chicago, Denver, and other cities.

When Stuart lived in Arkansas in the early 1880s, she wrote a parody of **Edgar Allan Poe**'s "The Raven" for a local women's club, but her first published poetry was dialect verse. Like her fiction, such poems often combined pathos and humor, appealing to Victorian tastes for both **sentimentality** and **minstrelsy**. The eleven stories in Stuart's *A Golden Wedding and Other Tales* (1893) are accompanied by two black dialect poems. "'Oh, Shoutin's Mighty Sweet': Plantation Parting Hymn" was previously unpublished; "Lucindy" (1892), illustrated with a cakewalk scene, had first appeared in *Harper's Monthly*. *Harper's Weekly* printed another early dialect piece, "Winnie: A Verse Romance" (1893), narrated—like "Lucindy"—by a beau who is teased by the flirtatious young woman he loves. "De way she'd pervoke me was *killin'*," says Winnie's sweetheart, whose lament is included in Stuart's second story collection, *Carlotta's Intended and Other Tales* (1894), along with two other poems, "Rose: Plantation Love-Song" and "Voices." The aging narrator of this last selection admits he "ain't got educatiom" or a "white pusson's knowledge"; but he does hear heavenly voices and his "mammy's ole hymns" in the sounds of the katydids and the pine trees.

Stuart's plantation songs, representing her larger fascination with folklore, responded to a national interest in the music of white songwriters such as Stephen Foster and African American touring groups like Fisk University's Jubilee Singers. Retitled "Plantation Love Song: My Rose," her early poem was set to Deems Taylor's melody and published as sheet music in 1917. Although much of Stuart's black dialect poetry reinforced such stereotypes as the cheerful washerwoman, the comforting mammy, the mischievous boy, and the singing field hand, these images were quite different from the portrayals of bestial African Americans in the contemporaneous work of writers such as Thomas Dixon. In fact, early discussions of Stuart often cite Joel Chandler Harris's remark that she "got nearer the heart of the negro than any of us."

Stuart's most famous dialect poems are the verses of Daddy Do-Funny, many of which appeared in *Century* and *St. Nicholas* magazines beginning in 1910; they were collected in *Daddy Do-Funny's Wisdom Jingles*, with drawings by G.H. Clements. Reminiscent of both Aesop and Harris's Uncle Remus, Daddy imparts moral lessons from the natural world in pithy lines on "Judge Owl," "The Giraffe," "The Ambitious Cow," and a few-score other animals and plants. Daddy Do-Funny consistently rejects hypocrisy and pompous behavior. In "The Mosquito," he laments that this insect, despite all the "Christian blood in 'is veins," takes no pains to love his neighbor; instead, he is always "p'izenin' an' backbitin'." In a refrain that recurs throughout the book, the old man concludes that the mosquito "ain't by 'isself in dat, in dat— / No, he ain't by 'isself in dat."

Daddy Do-Funny's Wisdom Jingles and Stuart's earlier comic volume, *Gobolinks or Shadow Pictures*, are both profusely illustrated, eye-catching to a young audience. The short verses for the inkblot book, however, are more descriptive than didactic, in the manner of **children's poetry** by Lewis Carroll and Edward Lear. Gobolink swimmers in "The Divers," for example, are gathering "water-roses" from the ocean on a "sweet summer day," when two lobsters come along and bite them "on their toeses." Stuart's affection for silly images is evident, too, in the "Just for Fun" section of her third poetry collection and final published book, *Plantation Songs and Other Verse*. The volume is further divided into the black dialect verses of "Plantation Songs" and the standard English of "Songs of Life and Love." This latter group includes such conventional verses as "The Sea of Peace" (1910), first published in *Century*, and "Sitting Blind by the Sea" (1914), from *Poetry* magazine. The book's longest section is the plantation poetry, illustrated by E.W. Kemble—hymns, love songs, lullabies, and other dialect pieces that emphasize Stuart's role as an "interpreter of the South," as one obituary called her after her death in 1917. When scholars such as Helen Taylor and Kathryn B. McKee examined Stuart's work at the end of the twentieth century, they criticized the dialect poems and fiction as nostalgic in tone and racist in their portrayals of slaves and former slaves. In her own time, however, Stuart was complimented not only by white associates like Harris and Kate Chopin but also by the African American authors Anna Julia Cooper, Charles Chesnutt, and **Paul Laurence Dunbar**. Dunbar's praise is especially significant because the black dialect verse of his *Lyrics of Lowly Life* (1896), *Poems of Cabin and Field* (1899), and other works established his reputation as the nineteenth century's most successful writer of **African American poetry**.

Further Reading. ***Selected Primary Sources:*** Stuart, Ruth McEnery, *Daddy Do-Funny's Wisdom Jingles* (New York:

Century, 1913); ———, *Plantation Songs and Other Verse* (New York: D. Appleton, 1916); Stuart, Ruth McEnery, and Albert Bigelow Paine, *Gobolinks or Shadow Pictures for Young and Old* (New York: Century, 1896). ***Selected Secondary Sources:*** Hall, Joan Wylie, "Ruth McEnery Stuart (1849–1917)" (*Legacy: A Journal of American Women Writers* 10.1 [1993]: 47–56); McKee, Kathryn B., "Ruth McEnery Stuart," in *Dictionary of Literary Biography, Volume 202: Nineteenth-Century American Fiction Writers*, ed. Kent P. Ljungquist (Detroit: Gale, 1998, 242–250); Taylor, Helen, *Gender, Race, and Region in the Writings of Grace King, Ruth McEnery Stuart, and Kate Chopin* (Baton Rouge: Louisiana State University Press, 1989).

Joan Wylie Hall

SUBLIME

Background and Context

In conversational usage the term "sublime" often functions as a simple superlative, a meaning that derives in part from its origins in an anonymous Greek treatise (attributed to Longinus) "On the Sublime," where it meant "high" or "lofty" as regards a work of literature. The abiding influence of this seminal work, however, was to define the lofty in literature as a function of more than form or style. For the author of "On the Sublime," sublimity is a pleasurable experience of greatness internal to both writer and reader, and the style or form of the work is only the medium that carries it: "sublimity is the echo of a great soul."

Aesthetics largely ignored questions of the sublime until the eighteenth century, when Edmund Burke gave the term its modern meaning: an awe-inspiring greatness that is paradoxically both fearsome and pleasurable to behold. At this point, sublimity became associated with natural objects, and with literature in which the subject of the writing is itself sublime. Immanuel Kant, the most important theorist of the sublime, follows "On the Sublime" by squarely locating the sublime "not . . . in anything of nature, but only in our own mind," even if nature often provides the loci for our encounter with sublimity. He also provides a compelling explanation of the contradictory response the sublime engenders. Although Mont Blanc (a touchstone of the sublime for English Romantics) may suggest the puniness of humankind by comparison, and may defy the mind's capacity to imagine it, for Kant we leave such an encounter augmented by our ability to withstand, and, if not imagine, then apprehend and represent its limitlessness in the mind. For it is not Mont Blanc alone that we have encountered, but the baffling and incomprehensible totality of the universe itself. "Nature," writes Kant, "is sublime in those of its phenomena whose intuition brings with it the idea of infinity." For poets such as Wordsworth and Shelley, who were indirectly influenced by Kant, sublime nature leaves the poet with a renewed sense of poetic promise and power and also, at the same time, a deeper awareness of their mortality and insignificance.

The American Sublime in the Nineteenth Century

Critic Harold Bloom, who has made substantial contributions to our understanding of the genre, argues in his *The Anxiety of Influence* that the "American sublime (which is always a counter-sublime)" is a reaction not only to European notions of the sublime but also to the sublimity of canonical works by such towering writers as Milton, Wordsworth, and Shelley (103). On the one hand, **Ralph Waldo Emerson**, who can be said to inaugurate the tradition of the American sublime, extends the Romantic project by further interiorizing what Kant had already made a largely internal phenomenon, referring to the "aboriginal self" as a "science-baffling star, without parallax, without calculable elements." On the other hand, however, Emerson seems to react to earlier writers' stance toward sublimity in nature. In opposition to earlier Romantic writers, Emerson claims that "vast spaces of nature, the Atlantic Ocean, the South Sea; long intervals of time, years, centuries, are of no account. This which I think and feel underlay every former state of life and circumstance." He admonishes the person who would behold the sublime in nature but "not stand in awe of man" or "put himself in communication with the internal ocean." As critic Rob Wilson has pointed out, the American sublime in its original formulation is an internal sublime.

Although Emerson wrote poems, none of them did as much to figure the American sublime in poetic language as did **Walt Whitman**, whose poems are, to a large degree, poetic applications of Emersonian principles. But the Whitmanic sublime, confounding the binary of inner and outer life, motivates a much more extensive encounter with the material universe. In opposition to some of the tenets set down in "Self-Reliance," Whitman experiences transcendence both through an encounter with the self and with the object world, two means to the same end. Whitman's poems also demonstrate a deeper struggle with the terror that the sublime engenders. In the climactic middle of "Song of Myself," the speaker, encountering the entirety of creation and whirled "wider than Uranus flies," describes himself as "[s]teeped amid honeyed morphine . . . [his] windpipe / Squeezed in fakes of death." But for the most part, Whitman vanquishes such terrors of the external, and is "[l]et up again to feel the puzzle of puzzles, / And that we call being." Like Emerson, Whitman "contain[s] multitudes" and because the sublime is within him as well as without, he need not fear it: "Dazzling and tremendous how quick the sun-rise would kill me, / If I could not now and always send sun-rise out of me." Whereas for

Kant the imagination in confronting the sublime "sinks back into itself," the Whitmanic sublime elicits a correspondent discharge of counter-power.

In defining the American poetic sublime, it is useful to look at American paintings of sublime nature. Frederic Church's "Niagara" is perhaps the quintessential visual representation of the American sublime. Vertiginously horizontal, with the viewer flung out over the rapids above the falls, the painting characterizes the inward-plunging sublime of Whitman and Emerson. Whereas in the European paintings of J.W. Turner or Caspar David Friedrich the viewer must often contend with an imposing, mountainous verticality, here a panoramic sweep wider than eye (akin perhaps to Whitman's long lines) subsumes the viewer in the vast and open American spaces.

As different as **Emily Dickinson**'s gnomic poetry is from Whitman's, it might be tempting to think her opposed to the notions of the sublime previously described, or perhaps not even concerned with the subject at all. Certainly, Dickinson's poetry does not enact formally the horizontal expansiveness, but to expect all the poetry of the American sublime to do so would be to fall victim to the **imitative fallacy**. Dickinson does, along with Emerson and Whitman, confront a bottomless and endless interiority, and sometimes also an exterior just as infinite. Dickinson "dwells in Possibility / A fairer House than Prose." Her task as a poet is "—This— / Spreading wide my narrow Hands / To gather Paradise." Dickinson's series of sunset poems, in particular, dwell lingeringly upon the sublime possibilities of the American landscape. Even if some of these poems characterize nature as innocently playful, others present the "Western Mystery" of the sunset in starkly Kantian terms, with pleasure and terror inextricably commingled: "It's Amber Revelation / Exhilarate—Debase." Here, too, as in Kant, the initial emotional shock modulates to a triumphal repose. "When the solemn features / Confirm—in Victory—" the speaker of the poems "start[s]—as if detected / In Immortality—." It is worth noting that, in this poem, Dickinson's encounter with the sublime does not motivate the extremes of self-reliance and self-transformation that we see in Whitman and Emerson. Although many of her poems do suggest an inner sublime and its accompanying triumphs, they are much more familiar with despondency in the face of the infinite than are Whitman's.

The American Sublime in the Twentieth Century

As with any mode in which great talents participate, the American sublime rightly appears almost as various as those talents themselves. Rather than speaking sophomorically of a single "American sublime," we must instead discuss tendencies, some taken up and others not. Looking at it this way, the American sublime seems distinguished by one or more of the following characteristics: (1) a deep and sometimes absolute interiority, (2) a fearlessness in the face of the externally sublime object, and (3) a raising of the self to the level of the sublime object. In the twentieth century no poet explored such poetic possibilities more than **Wallace Stevens**, who, in fact, named the tradition of the American sublime in his eponymous poem. For Stevens, the internal sublime is no longer a choice, as it was with Emerson (for whom nature still presented a seductive sublimity), but rather a necessity, since "one grows used to the weather, / The landscape and that." Nature has been emptied of its sublimity—the poles reached, most of the great mountains climbed—and what was once its province is located firmly within humanity. Stevens does "stand in awe of man" but not always in the way that Emerson imagined, as seen here by the figure of the genocidal and nature-trampling Andrew Jackson. After the early part of the twentieth century, the internal sublime is no longer a plenum, but rather the action of "The spirit and space, / The empty spirit / In vacant space." It is a sublime nothingness, sublime because of its infinite and fearful potential for the poetic creator. Stevens no longer wonders where to find the sublime, but rather asks, "How does one stand / To behold the sublime?" He wonders, in fact, how we might withstand and respond to such internal meaninglessness with its immense potential for human violence. One might almost hear Stevens asking, "How *can* one stand / To behold the sublime?"

After World War II, and the twin traumas of the Holocaust and the atomic bomb, the sublime became increasingly both irredeemably negative and technological in conception. As **Adrienne Rich** writes in "Waking in the Dark," "The thing that arrests me is / how we are composed of molecules." In this sublime, the astonishment of the subject is figured as an oppressive (arresting) social force, "arranged without our knowledge and consent" and the infinite interiors (molecules) no longer allow the kind of transcendence that they once did. Rich's poem suggests an intimate relationship between poetic conceptions of the sublime and the contemporaneous scientific conception of the universe: the advent of particle physics, genetics, and the Byzantine complexities of neurochemistry has fueled postwar poetic conceptions of the interior sublime. For **A.R. Ammons**, who trained as a chemist, scientific observations motivate an encounter with the sublime that, unlike the case for Rich, allows for redemptive and Emersonian possibilities. In his widely anthologized poem "The City Limits," the subject and object of sublime experience reverse, the sublime "radiance" is both considered and considering, both an object of scientific and poetic inquiry and the spirit of inquiry and truth-seeking itself. The sublime in this poem is both external and internal; in fact the radiance with its "storms of generosity" and penetrating "abundance" dissolves such distinctions, considering the "weaving heart" and the "coil of shit" equally. By the end of the poem, though, these antinomies resolve to an almost Kantian formulation: "fear lit by the breadth of such calmly turns to praise."

Some poets, however, have reacted to upheavals of the twentieth century by turning away from direct, Emersonian confrontation with both nature and the world-historical. **John Ashbery**, for instance, whose wry, ironic, post-Stevensian poems have earned him both accolades and contempt, inhabits better than any poet of his generation the grandeur of Romantic and Whitmanic attitudes toward the sublime, writing of "the whole incredible / Mass of everything happening simultaneously and pairing off." Ashbery's fearless occupation of these modes, however, derives from the fact that his aim is parodic, an emptying out or "decreation" of the sublime, which becomes "something one can / Tip one's hat to and still get some use out of." Ultimately, however, Ashbery's goal is to revitalize the vitiated sublime, what Rob Wilson calls the "unspeakable totalities of commodity-infinitude and sign-glut" (219) that fill Ashbery's poems to bursting. His project is "a vast unraveling . . . / To these bare fields, built at today's expense." The difficulty, it seems, for Ashbery and for the generation of **Language** and avant-garde poets who follow in his wake, is not to erect monuments to the sublime such as "Song of Myself" or "Notes toward a Supreme Fictions," but to create through destruction a ground for poetic possibility and play, at the expense of "everything happening." Many of these poets fail, however, to create that sublime emptiness, stalling out in the process of fragmentation and willful destruction of established orders and orthodoxies.

If the sublime is a part of the repertoire of today's poets, it is also an intellectual and emotional muscle that has suffered a certain degree of atrophy. As Wilson and others have pointed out, images of the earth from space have long since become a commonplace; the violent power of nuclear weaponry is a constant to which many have become inured; and, in North America, the media inundate us with images of a violent sublime that become, through repetition, mere titillation, incapable of eliciting the mixture of awe and pleasure particular to the true sublime. As such, American poets, should they choose the assignment, must reinvent the sublime object in language not yet fatigued by such malaise, while at the same time contending with the sublimity of a tradition that contains many of the English language's greatest poems. For some poets, the sublime might seem part and parcel of a notion of subjectivity and linguistic coherence against which they have chosen to rebel, either by engaging in a pornography of the sublime or by avoiding the mode altogether. Other poets might choose to protect this venerable mode by redirecting our attention to new sublimities, inside and out. It is still too early to tell if, in the post-9/11 age (when the spectacle of the Twin Towers became infused with that dread vital to the sublime), poets will turn toward or away from such a modality. Either way, the sublime seems likely to persist, by this or other names, as long as poets retain the capacity for wonderment, and as long as humans remain less than fully at home in the world.

Further Reading. ***Selected Primary Sources:*** Ammons, A.R., "The City Limits," in *Collected Poems 1951–1971* (New York: W.W. Norton, 2001); Bloom, Harold, *The Anxiety of Influence* (Oxford: Oxford University Press, 1997); Burke, Edmund, *A Philosophical Enquiry into the Origin of Our Ideas of the Sublime and the Beautiful* (New York: Penguin, 1999); Dickinson, Emily, *The Poems of Emily Dickinson,* ed. Thomas Johnson (Cambridge: Belknap Press, 1951); Emerson, Ralph Waldo, "Self-Reliance," in *The Essays of Ralph Waldo Emerson* (Cambridge: Belknap Press, 1987); ———, "Nature," in *The Essays of Ralph Waldo Emerson* (Cambridge: Belknap Press, 1987); Kant, Immanuel, *Critique of Judgment,* trans. Werner Pluhar (Indianapolis: Hackett Publishing, 1987); Longinus, *On Great Writing (on Sublime)* (Indianapolis: Hackett Publishing, 1991); Stevens, Wallace, *The Collected Poems of Wallace Stevens,* ed. Holly Stevens (New York: Vintage Books, 1990); Whitman, Walt, *Leaves of Grass,* ed. John Hollander (New York: Vintage/Library of America, 1992); Wilson, Rob, *American Sublime: The Genealogy of a Poetic Genre* (Madison: University of Wisconsin Press, 1991). ***Selected Secondary Source:*** Arensberg, Mary, *The American Sublime* (Albany: SUNY Press, 1986); Wilton, Andrew, and Tim Barringer, *American Sublime: Landscape Painting in the United States, 1820–1880* (London: Tate Publishing, 2002).

Jasper Bernes

SWENSEN, COLE (1955–)

The poetry of Cole Swensen has clear affinities with the contemporary French poets she translates, as well as to contemporary American experimentalism. There is a commitment to formal exploration, intellectualism, and surface that in no way compromises her equally clear emotional connection to her subjects. Seeing the book itself as a primary aesthetic unit, her collections range substantially in terms of form—from, say, the shorter, compact poems of *New Math* (1988) to the visually constellated and syntactically disjunctive poems of *Such Rich Hour* (2001). Where her readers may encounter—for example—prose combined with verse, English melded with foreign languages, vocabulary with various disciplinary origins, a spectrum of art and historical references, or associative meetings of apparently disparate thoughts, those readers will also surely find a consistent return to key images, phrases, and tactics that serve as guideposts toward the ideas that the author is so obviously passionate about. And Swensen's books return again and again to the very crucial and complex business of perception.

Swensen was born in San Francisco in 1955, her mother a painter and her father an engineer. The visual, especially in terms of art, then, has long been familiar territory to her, as has a mathematical or scientific understanding of her subjects. She started writing seriously fairly early—around age eleven—and later, while dropping out of several undergraduate programs, she deepened her commitment to the arts by running a number of café reading series, working in the Marin County Poets-in-the-Schools program, and living in a variety of Bay Area communal living situations. She then completed her undergraduate work at San Francisco State and spent her last year studying bookbinding and calligraphy at a small arts college in London, an experience that strengthened her understanding of the connection between the textual and visual arts. Returning to San Francisco, she entered the MA program in creative writing and studied with—among others—Nanos Valaoritis, **C.D. Wright**, and **Ron Silliman**. She continued studying bookbinding, working with the Poets-in-the-Schools program, and waitressing and bartending while she pursued certification in English as a Foreign Language. In 1987, she went to Paris, for about six months, for the first time. She entered the Ph.D. program at the University of California–Santa Cruz in 1989, where she eventually focused her dissertation on a comparative study of contemporary French and American poetry, looking particularly at the work of Claude Royet-Journoud, Anne-Marie Albiach, **Susan Howe**, **Michael Palmer**, and **Rosmarie Waldrop**. In the early 1990s she began attending collaborative translation sessions at the Foundation Royaumont, just outside Paris, the first step in a continued work of **translating** contemporary French poets and a continued pattern of returning to Paris for extended periods of time almost yearly since then. She has been the director of the creative writing program at the University of Denver and is now full-time faculty at the University of Iowa.

Swensen's books have consistently garnered awards and have shown a deep attention to the act of perception, especially seeing. *New Math* was chosen as a National Poetry Series winner by Michael Palmer and begins with the line "Let me get this picture straight—." Swensen sets herself a complex project with this opening and ends that poem—"The Immigrant Carries Her Painting"—by observing of the immigrant's new country that "Later, evening may be the only / way we have of proving it's there." The poems here are short, tight, and incisive—if visually unpresuming—but hold within them surprising shifts in perspective and thought. This form is appropriate, seeing as Swensen portrays both the seeming simplicity of vision while emphasizing how it is also full of blurred and sometimes conflicting "readings" of what is before the eye. Observer, subject, and memory overlap, blend, and distinguish themselves in surprising turns of vision. The very materiality of sight—light, color, and line–is foregrounded, as in "Background," which says both that "God is a color" and that "Later I'll dissolve within the picture." Such a thorough atomization of the act of sight might be assumed to disorient the viewer or the reader, but Swenson's answer is ultimately calming in the final poem of the collection, "Fade to Light": "A search for clues / encounters bliss." There is something exciting about this release—this "new math" of vision—from the too-easy habits of ordinary seeing.

Noon (1997), which was selected for the New American Poetry Series by Rae Armantrout, deepens this complex understanding of perception while adopting a more experimental form. The book is composed of nine sections, each of which is divided into smaller parts. Each of the nine larger sections alternates between prose and verse, most being dedicated to a person represented by his or her initials. This form reflects an understanding of the world Swensen puts forth here: a world that is infinitely divisible and definable in the act of seeing, counting, and naming. The dedications add another dimension, pointing outside the book in the direction of others who assumedly perceive and name just as the poems' speaker does. Observation of landscape and animals is expanded upon by the inclusion of historical personages—Einstein and Wittgenstein—joining the scientific study of "objects" to the philosophical study of language. This last move makes *Noon* more intensely personal in an odd way, picturing the world as a field of beings all negotiating their own definitions, boundaries, and relations in the ever-shifting now of perceiving each other (the "noon" of the title). Again, as daunting as such perceptual tasks must seem, Swensen finds the silver—or gray—lining when at the end of the book she writes, "Some rivers burn—they say this isn't good, but I'm no one to judge, and I think it's got its points."

Later collections go further into an examination of the human within this complicated world by taking a unique approach to **ekphrasis**. *Try* (1999)—winner of the Iowa Prize—deals with visual arts from the medieval and Renaissance periods; *Oh* (2000) is a poetic encounter with opera; and *Such Rich Hour* (2001) is a dialogue with the illuminations from a famous book of hours, *Tres Riches Heures du Duc de Berry*. Ekphrasis for Swensen—as might be expected by her understanding of observation—is a highly dynamic experience. Speaking of the ekphrastic project in an interview with Jon Thompson, she observed that "looking at paintings—you get assumed by the painting. You live in the painting for a little while, become a part of the composition." If for Swenson, looking at a landscape, say, is very complex, then observing—or entering into—a work of *art* has the potential to be even more so. With a work of art, there is not only the material itself (paint, light, frame, and so forth) to engage with, but there is also the subject of the art and even the artist and his or her historical context to encounter as well. And all this occurs not as traditionally imagined, with a viewer's objective distance, but with the active viewer's own immersive perception being altered in the very process of looking. The experience is dynamic and multivalent. As a result, Swensen's poetry becomes even more complicated and experimental, especially in *Such Rich Hour.* The lines are often lengthened, the page is used like a canvas, there are disjunctive internal line breaks, languages are mixed, and time periods overlap. It is exactly this sort of richness of technique that is required to perform the kind of multivalent looking that Swensen engages in when she enters into the act of ekphrasis.

Her latest book, *Goest* (2004), focuses less on ekphrasis in order to delve more directly into history, especially the history of early invention and discovery that have fundamentally defined the way we perceive the world. Current projects, though, see her working on a collection that encounters Pierre Bonnard's paintings of windows, and another that treats Andre Le Notre's French garden designs. Swenson's poetry continues to elaborate on the kind of faithfulness of attention that might be seen in **Gertrude Stein**'s *Tender Buttons* or in the work of the **Objectivist poets** by making room for and engaging with the very history of such a careful attention.

Further Reading. ***Selected Primary Sources:*** Swenson, Cole, *Goest* (Farmington, ME: Alice James Books, 2004); ———, *Noon* (Los Angeles: Sun & Moon Press, 1997); ———, *Such Rich Hour* (Iowa City: University of Iowa Press, 2001). ***Selected Secondary Sources:*** Thompson, Jon, "Interview with Cole Swenson" (*Free Verse* 5 [Winter 2003], http://english.chass.ncsu.edu/freeverse/Archives/Winter_2003 /Interviews/interviews.htm).

Samuel Jason Ezell

SWENSON, MAY (1919–1989)

May Swenson is an important figure in American poetry because of the depth and conspicuousness of her perception. The poet's wide range of subject matter reflects her interest in different phenomena and creatures, which are expressed in vivid and intricate images, with colorful and detailed descriptions reminiscent of the poetry of **Marianne Moore** and **Elizabeth Bishop**, to whom she is frequently compared. The poet also tackles epistemological and metaphysical questions in spite of the deceptively simple appearance of her poetry, a characteristic also shared by the works of William Blake. Swenson's experimental approach to poetry and her verbal and visual inventiveness, moreover, situate her in the category of such leading poets as **Emily Dickinson**, **e.e. cummings**, and George Herbert. Most notably, Swenson is known for the way she de-familiarizes everyday objects and concepts. She achieves this mainly through breaking random angles of perceptions and suggesting less common ways of looking at the world. Swenson has been the recipient of many awards, including a Guggenheim fellowship in 1959 and an Academy of American Poets fellowship in 1979, among others.

May Swenson was born in Logan, Utah, to parents of Mormon background. She was the oldest of her ten siblings. After earning a Bachelor of Science degree from Utah University in 1939 Swenson started a job as a reporter in Salt Lake City. Her career began when she accepted a job as an editor at New Directions Press in 1959. She worked in this position until 1966. After quitting her job as editor, she took on writing and served as writer-in-residence and taught poetry in a number of colleges and universities, including the University of North Carolina Greensboro and the University of California–Riverside. She died in 1988 after a prolific life as a poet.

Many of the poems in Swenson's first collection of poetry, *Another Animal* (1954), explore the theme of perception and reflect the poet's sheer interest in objectively examining human and animal behavior. Many of these poems juxtapose the physical and mental characteristics of animals and human beings, demonstrating an impartial persona unable to make up her mind about the superiority of one species to the other. Swenson can see beauty in everything and everywhere. In her philosophy nothing is meaningless and no creature is insignificant; therefore, all objects, creatures, and phenomena have to be carefully looked at in an atmosphere not influenced by previous opinions and prejudices. As indicated by Susan Mitchell in the foreword to *Nature: Poems Old and New* (1994), "Any object can become an entry into a larger world, any one small piece or part of the whole evoke a universe. So experience is always complex, layered, laminated, with image superimposed on image, as if several slides had been simultaneously jammed into the projector" (xxi).

Closely related to the theme of perception is the technique of blending together the objects of description in these poems. In Swenson's poetry, animals and natural objects are frequently described in terms of other creatures, and quite often they merge into the background, a technique highly suggestive of the unreliability of human perception. The relativity of the act of human observation is a subject Swenson also considers in her later poems. In all these poems, the poet seems to be suggesting new ways and different angles of looking at everyday phenomena, animals, and objects for a heightened degree of awareness and a more profound appreciation of life and its components. In "His Secret," published in *Poems to Solve* (1966), the subject matter is the speaker's cat that attracts his owner's attention as she is eager "to see what made him purr." The speaker then "[takes her] cat apart" and examines him "[l]ike an electric clock" and "a warming kettle" to find out the source of "the snore" that "fizzed and sizzled in him." The metaphor of comparing the cat to "a soft car" that is "the engine bubbling sounds" at the end of the second stanza and a series of other comparisons following it finally help deconstruct the image of the cat and portray the animal in a new light.

Following the theme of perception are epistemological questions that focus mostly on the subjects of death and love in Swenson's early work. In many of the poems that reflect on death, the speaker is hesitant about its nature and keeps oscillating between the two opposing poles of desiring it and disliking it. On the one hand, there is comfort, calm, and peace enjoyed after death in becoming one with nature, and on the other, there is the pleasure of living and the senses. As with other conceptual poems, the persona in these poems presents a series of questions without providing any answer to them.

In a similar way, love is often treated from an objective viewpoint in Swenson's poetry. In her love poems the poet barely addresses the topic in an explicit manner and almost always refers to it in an impersonal tone, and even then only as a physical attraction that exists between creatures of different species. In "A Couple," published in *The Love Poems of May Swenson* (1991) after the poet's death, for instance, the choice of words and the image at the heart of the poem erotically embody the sexual act.

Probably the most conspicuous characteristic of the poems both questioning and revealing the possibilities of love is their obliqueness. Love in all of these poems is almost always described in vividly visual images. *A Cage of Spines* (1958) returns to the question of human perception and its limitations. Following this theme, many of the poems in this collection consider mankind's futile attempt to properly name and define phenomena, creatures, and objects. This failure is subtly contrasted with the speaker's reluctance to name creatures, a characteristic also seen in nature. The riddle poems in Swenson's next collections have their roots in these poems. Together with the poems that probe the theme of definition, the riddle poems aim at removing the dust of custom and definition from mankind's eyes in order to heighten his level of awareness. Swenson also juxtaposes nature and art in this group of poems, suggesting the superiority of art due to its artificial nature. The reader is reminded of John Keats and a similar preference for art expressed in his "Ode on a Grecian Urn." One of the other dominant themes in this early collection of poems is the juxtaposition of modernity and the desirable serenity of nature. In accordance with the persona's preference for nature and simplicity, the language of these poems, although still highly figurative, continues to be unaffected and straightforward. Yet the most prominent characteristic of Swenson's first two collections of poems is their vivid imagery and the intricate way in which objects are described in terms of color and shape.

To Mix with Time (1963) is a compilation of poems, old and new. As also highlighted by their titles, the first few poems in the collection, "The Universe," "God," "Out of My Head," and "Downward," all undertake questions of metaphysics and epistemology. Many other poems, such as "Notes Made in the Piazza San Marco" and "The Pantheon, Rome," take the reader to European settings with vivid descriptions and colorful details, as seen in these lines from "Italian Sampler": "A mast. A horn. A bramble. A bride. / Lombardy, Tuscany, Umbria, Calabria."

A host of other poems in this collection emphasize the significance of perspective in understanding the world around us. Probably the most memorable poem capturing this theme is "Cat & the Weather," in which snow, through vivid descriptions, is experienced for the first time from the viewpoint of a cat. The cat of the poem sees "[i]nsects are flying, fainting down," and further notices that "[t]hey have no body and no buzz, / and now his feet are wet." Through these actual descriptions, snow is seen from a different perspective and hence freshly reintroduced.

A related topic is the importance of imagination to man's psychological well-being, a subject treated allegorically in a poem about man's first space flight. This theme will recur in Swenson's later poems that highlight the deteriorating effect of modernity and scientific advancement on mankind's psyche, leaving him without a proper refuge in his confrontations with the harsh reality outside.

The poems in *Half Sun Half Sleep* (1967) once again reflect Swenson's profound attention to detail and the significance of close observation in coming to grips with reality. Again often grounded in metaphysics and epistemology, the poems in this collection follow themes explored in previous poems. The collection also includes riddle poems and poems about man's flight into space. Most of the ideas reflected in these poems are augmented by the typographical arrangement of words and a noticeable rebellion against punctuation and grammatical rules.

Iconographs (1970) reflects the visual inventiveness of the artist to the fullest. The shapes of almost all the poems included in this collection impart their subject matters. In "The Blue Bottle," a conspicuous shape poem, for instance, the arrangement of the words on the page effectively represents the shape of a bottle. Moreover, the playfulness of the poet is seen in the use of words with similar or identical pronunciations in consecutive lines.

Alliteration, onomatopoeia, careful use of internal rhyme, and other verbal and visual tricks heighten the figurativeness of language and form in these poems. Probably the most conspicuously unconventional use of punctuation in this group of poems is seen in "Wednesday at the Waldorf." The punctuation marks and arithmetic signs typed over the words and between the lines in this poem do not seem to have any particular significance attached to them, yet they function as a means of de-automatizing the reader's understanding of them and enhancing his or her perception of the subject matter. It is, however, in *Iconographs* that the poet for the first time addresses the subject of human relationships in a more personal tone and with less obliqueness. The slight autobiographical note seen for the first time in this collection of poems expands vastly in Swenson's next collections, including *New and Selected Things Taking Place* (1978). In accordance with this growing voice emphasizing more personal themes, Swenson's work becomes less visually compelling and benefits less from the technical devices so extensively used in the poet's earlier works. Yet, despite her more mature perspective and the decreasing attention she pays to visual inventiveness and typography, the poet continues to present colorful descriptions of the world she sees around her.

Since the time of her death in 1989, four collections of Swenson's poems have been published; these include poems that have appeared before and those being published for the first time. The collections include *Nature: Poems Old and New* (1994), and *May Out West* (1996).

Further Reading. ***Selected Primary Sources:*** Swenson, May, *Another Animal* (New York: Scribner's, 1954); ———, *A Cage of Spines* (New York: Rinehart, 1958); ———, *Half Sun Half Sleep: New Poems* (New York: Scribner's, 1967); ———, *Iconographs: Poems* (New York: Scribner's, 1970); ———, *The Love Poems of May Swenson* (Boston: Houghton Mifflin, 1991); ———, *May West Out* (Logan: Utah State University Press, 1996); ———, *Nature: Poems Old and New* (Boston: Houghton Mifflin, 1994); ———, *New and Selected Things Taking Place* (Boston: Little, Brown, 1978); ———, *Poems to Solve* (New York: Scribner's, 1966); ———, *To Mix with Time: New and Selected Poems* (New York: Scribner's, 1963). ***Selected Secondary Sources:*** Arditi, Neil, "'In the Bodies of Words': The Swenson-Bishop Conversation" (*Parnassus: Poetry in Review* 26.2 [2002]: 77–93); Howard, Richard, "Banausics" (*Parnassus: Poetry in Review* 25.1–2 [2001]: 411–424); Schulman, Grace, "Life's Miracles: The Poetry of May Swenson" (*American Poetry Review* 23.5 [1994]: 9–13); Zona, Kristin Hotelling, "A 'Dangerous Game of Change': Images of Desire in the Love Poems of May Swenson" (*Twentieth Century Literature: A Scholarly and Critical Journal* 44.2 [Summer 1998]: 219–241); ———, *Marianne Moore, Elizabeth Bishop, and May Swenson: The Feminist Poetics of Self Restraint* (Ann Arbor: University of Michigan Press, 2002).

Manijeh Mannani

SYMBOLISM

During the late nineteenth century and early twentieth century, Paris was the hub of the avant-garde and modernist movements. Symbolism, a leading fine art and literary movement, started as a reaction to the naturalism and realism movements of the period. The Symbolists emancipated their writing style and subject matter from a scientific description that eliminated all fantasy, emotions, and inconsistencies. Symbolism shook the foundations of naturalism by rejecting, though not entirely, the use of the law of cause and effect in literature. Pythagorean and Kantian concepts were introduced to explain the movement's disdain with a constricting approach to fiction, and to advance the writing on the mystical realm of human existence. Even though many Symbolists showed an affinity to Catholicism and Christian mysticism, Liberalism thrived in the new movement. Socially, being a Symbolist implied a bohemian lifestyle, laden with loud philosophical and ideological debates in the small cafés of Paris's Latin Square.

The French Symbolist school began with the writings of Charles Baudelaire (1821–1867) and Stéphane Mallarmé (1842–1898). Baudelaire's poems concentrate on themes of death, sex, and decay. His prose poem "Les Fleurs du Mal" ("Flowers of Evil," 1857) brought him lasting fame, but when first published it met with scandals, persecution, and censorship due to accusations of obscenity and blasphemy. Interestingly, Baudelaire was inspired by the work of the American writer **Edgar Allan Poe** (1809–1849), whom he called his "twin soul." In 1854 and 1855 he published several translations of Poe's writings: *Histoires extraordinaires* (1852), *Nouvelles histoires extraordinaires* (1857), *Aventures d'Arthur Gordon Pym, Eureka,* and *Histoires grotesques et sérieuses* (1865). He did not live to witness the rising controversy on the artistic merit of the Symbolist movement and its subsequent immense influence on world literature.

On September 18, 1886, infuriated by critics who associated the decadent writers with the Symbolists, Jean Moréas (1856–1910) published the manifesto of *Symbolisme* in *Le Figaro.* Moréas claimed that naturalism had disintegrated and cleared the way to a new form of creative expression: "opposed to 'teaching, declamation, flase sensibility, objective description,' symbolic poetry seeks to clothe the Idea in a perceptible form" (quoted in Chipp, 48). Though Moréas published the manifesto of the emerging movement, Mallarmé, who lectured extensively on the philosophy of the movement, is considered its leading theoretician. As Herschel Chipp writes, Symbolist theories "centered in a rejection of the world of the commonplace middle-class people meticulously described in Zola's 'scientifically' probing novels. They believed that the greatest reality lay in the realm of the imagination and fantasy" (48–49). Symbolist poetics was further elucidated in the writings of Paul Verlaine (1844–1896), Arthur Rimbaud (1854–1891), and Gustave Kahn (1859–1936).

At the end of the nineteenth century Symbolism lost its dominance in France. Yet the movement's popularity increased and spread to continental Europe, England, Russia, the United States, and South America. The Symbolists' experimental methods appealed to many English, Irish, and American poets, such as W.B. Yeats (1865–1939), **Ezra Pound** (1885–1972), **T.S. Eliot** (1888–1965), and **Wallace Stevens** (1879–1955). Additionally, some critics argue that at this point the English language was a fertile ground for the basic principles of Symbolism: free verse, dense syntax, figurative language, and rhythm.

Translations of the French Symbolist poets emerged in England during the 1890s. The Irish writer George Moore (1852–1933) was the first to write in English about the Symbolists. Moore, who studied art in Paris, renders his accounts of Verlaine, Rimbaud, Mallarmé, and Jules Laforgue in *Impressions and Opinions* (1891). In 1893 Edmund Gosse (1849–1928) published three essays on Mallarmé, whom he afterward dismissed as "hardly a poet" (Wellek, 340). Evidently, the onset of Symbolism in English literature was clouded with skepticism and to some degree unfavorable criticism. Even so, thanks to Oscar Wilde (1854–1900), W.B. Yeats, John Millington Synge (1871–1909), and James Joyce (1882–1941), French Symbolism had an immeasurable impact on modernist English and American literature.

Responding to Arthur Symons's *The Symbolist Movement in Literature* (1899), William Butler Yeats, who won the Nobel Prize for Literature in 1923, published an essay titled "The Symbolism of Poetry" (1900). Yeats admits that in his previous article, "Symbolism in Painting," he failed to describe "the continuous indefinable Symbolism which is the substance of all style." Yeats defines the Symbolist poem, in his "The Symbolism of Poetry," as a short lyric, perpetuating an emotion that is then transformed into "some great epic," empowered by symbols, and compared to a "ring within ring in the stem of an old tree." According to Yeats, poetry is a powerful emotional energy, and poets receive their "creative impulse from the lowest of the Nine Hierarchies [referring to the Nine Choirs of Angels, also found in Dante's *Paradiso*]," making and unmaking the human experience," and even "the world itself" (ibid.). Besides, claims Yeats, emotional symbols cannot create a distinct meaning; when combined with intellectual symbols, however, they denote an enduring poetical impression. In "Aedh Tells of the Rose in His Heart," from his *The Wind Among the Reeds* (1899), Yeats wrote: "The wrong of unshapely things is a wrong too great to be told; / I hunger to build them anew and sit on a green knoll apart."

Yeats and Ezra Pound, who was twenty years Yeats's junior, met in London in 1909. Pound became Yeats's secretary, and their relationship could be viewed as the meeting point of English and American Symbolism. Reports on French Symbolism surfaced in the United States in the early 1890s, mostly in the writings of American journalists, who were impressed by the avant-garde culture in Paris. Critics regard Poe's essay "The Philosophy of Composition" (1846) as the starting point of the French Symbolist movement, but Poe's influence on American poetry is at best controversial. The French literary historian René Taupin, whose book *The Influence of French Symbolism on Modern American Poetry* (1985) is a classic in the field, observes that the American **Imagist** movement, by surpassing the model of French Symbolism, is to a large extent the extension of the latter. However, it was not until Wallace Stevens, Ezra Pound, **T.S. Eliot,** and **Hart Crane** (1899–1932) had embraced Symbolism that it actually gained admittance into American literature.

Like the decadent French Symbolists, Wallace Stevens composed philosophical poetry as well as essays. In his essay "The Irrational Element in Poetry," Stevens writes that "Pure poetry is both mystical and irrational. If we descend a little from this height and apply the looser and broader definition of pure poetry, it is possible to say that, while it can lie in the temperament of very few of us to write poetry in order to find God, it is probably the purpose of each of us to write poetry to find the good which, in the Platonic sense, is synonymous with God. One writes poetry, then, in order to approach the good in what is harmonious and orderly" (*Opus Posthumous*, 222). While Stevens often appears to be writing a "pure poetry," in his work he often eschews the Symbolist techniques of correspondence and rather constructs a poem operating on its sonic possibilities, such as "The Emperor of Ice Cream," and that is hence resistant to thematic incursions and prose equivalents. The pure poem, for Stevens, detaches us from reason, though not experience, and moves us to another plane. As Stevens asks rhetorically in "The Irrational Element in Poetry," "If the poem had a meaning and if its explanation destroyed the illusion, should we have gained or lost?" (223).

Ezra Loomis Pound, an American **expatriate** since 1908, used his formal education in Romantic literature to found the Imagists, a group that included emerging poets such as **H.D.** (**Hilda Doolittle**, 1886–1961), **William Carlos Williams** (1883–1963), and **Amy Lowell** (1874–1925). The Imagists, following in the footsteps of the Symbolists, embarked on the task of remaking poetry. As outlined by Amy Lowell and more loosely related to Pound's definition of the image, the poems collected in Amy Lowell's anthologies value the use of common speech, creating new rhythms and modes, free choice of subject matter, the use of exact and clear images, producing lucid and definable poetry, and a brevity and economy of language. Pound's early poems were influenced by several of his contemporaries: Robert Browning (1812–1889), W.B. Yeats, Ford Madox Ford (1873–1939), T. E. Hulme (1883–1917), and his protégé, T.S. Eliot. Pound's short lyric "In a Station of the Metro" (1916), which was originally published with no spaces between words so as to emphasize the pullness of the apprehended moment, mirrors the language of Imagism and attests to the prevalence of Chinese and Japanese elements in his early poetry: "The apparition of these faces in the crowd; / Petals on a wet, black bough."

Perhaps the most remarkable of the American Symbolists is another expatriate, T.S. (Thomas Stearns) Eliot, 1948 Nobel Laureate in Literature. While reading Arthur Symons's book, he was introduced to Jules Laforgue's work. Henceforth, Eliot changed his poetic style, but still retained Elizabethan and Jacobean dramatic elements. During his long career, Eliot appropriated materials from several past and contemporary writers: Henry James (1843–1916), **Ralph Waldo Emerson** (1803–1882), F.H. (Francis Herbert) Bradley 1846–1924), Jules Laforgue, Charles Baudelaire, Rémy de Gourmont, T.E. Hulme, James Joyce, and Ezra Pound, his friend and mentor. Eliot's famous comment, "Immature poets imitate, mature poets steal," belies Eliot's own conscious and close examination of tradition and the necessity of integrating one into that tradition in order to renew it, as he expresses in his essay "The Social Function of Poetry": "The greatest poets have aspects which do not come to light at once; and by exercising a direct influence on other poets centuries later, they continue to affect the living language. Indeed, if an English poet is to learn how to use words in our time, he must devote close study to those who have used them best in *their* time; to those who, in their own day, have made the language new" (*On Poetry and Poets*, 11). Indeed, his early poems "Preludes" and the "Rhapsody" resemble the poetry of Laforgue and Baudelaire, as exemplified in the closing lines to "Preludes":

> Wipe your hand across your mouth, and laugh;
> The worlds revolve like ancient women
> Gathering fuel in vacant lots. [T.S. Eliot, *Prufrock and Other Observations* (London: The Egoist, 1917): 24–26.]

Eliot's main contribution to American poetry is his well-known poem "The Waste Land" (1922, edited by Ezra Pound and dedicated to him) which depicts the redeeming journey of the human soul. At this juncture, Eliot departs from many conventions of traditional poetic style and subject matter, creating a new poetic form replete with literary and historical allusions. The barrenness of the land in the poem symbolizes the meaninglessness and lack of spirituality in European culture. Human existence, according to the poem and the philosophy of French Symbolism, is sterile, decadent, isolated, and devoid of faith. However, deliverance is imminent in the form of rain that will feed the waste land and its inhabitants. In "The Waste Land" religion is clearly absent; yet five years after its publication, Eliot joined the Church of England, an event that profoundly altered his perspective on life and writing.

The role Pound and Eliot played in spreading the Symbolist message is illuminated by the words of Frank Kermode, the editor of Eliot's *Selected Poems* (1975): "[W]e think of the Pound group as a historical necessity, and of Pound and Eliot in particular as the founders of modernist poetry in English" (*Voices & Visions*, 284).

The popularity of free verse and the prose poem in American poetry is largely due to the influence of French Symbolism. In *Sacred Wood* (1920), Eliot intuitively observes, "Free verse is no longer an experiment, no longer even a new movement. Nearly every modern poet uses it either exclusively or in addition to its counterpart, regular verse" (*Voices and Vision*, 14–15). On many levels, the French Symbolists showed modern American poets how to break away from tradition, express intense and discontented emotions, and use irony in verse. Their influence went far beyond the poetic realm, pervading prose, drama, music, and visual art as well. The appeal of French Symbolism and its poetic innovations transcended national boundaries and contributed to what modern critics call the universal language of poetry.

Further Reading. ***Selected Primary Sources:*** Baechler, Lea A., Walton Litz, and James Longenbach, eds., *Ezra Pound's Poetry and Prose: Contributions to Periodicals* (New York and London: Garland, 1991); Eliot, T.S., *The Complete Poems and Plays of T.S. Eliot* (London: Faber, 1969); ———, *On Poetry and Poets* (New York: Farrar, Straus and Giroux, 1961); Stevens, Wallace, *Selected Poems* (London: Faber and Faber, 1953); ———, *Collected Poems* (New York: A.A. Knopf, 1954): ———, *The Necessary Angel: Essays on Reality and the Imagination* (A.A. Knopf, 1951); ———, *Opus Posthumous: Poems, Plays, Prose* (New York: Knopf, 1980); Yeats, W.B., *Essays and Introductions* (New York: Collier Books, 1961). ***Selected Secondary Sources:*** Balakian, Anna, ed., *The Symbolist Movement in the Literature of European Languages* (Budapest: Akadémiai Kiadó, 1984); Chipp, Herschel, *Theories of Modern Art: A Source Book by Artists and Critics* (Berkeley: University of California Press, 1968); Feidelson, Charles, Jr., *Symbolism and American Literature* (Chicago: University of Chicago Press, 1953; Phoenix Books, 1966); Taupin, René, *The Influence of French Symbolism on Modern American Poetry*, trans. William Pratt and Anne Rich Pratt, rev. ed. (New York: AMS Press, 1985); Vendler, Helen, ed., *Voices & Visions: The Poet in America* (New York: Random House, 1987); Wellek, René, "Symbol and Symbolism in Literature," in *The Dictionary of the History of Ideas: Studies of Selected Pivotal Ideas*, ed. Philip P. Wiener (New York: Charles Scribner's Sons, 1973–1974).

Dina Ripsman Eylon

SZE, ARTHUR (1950–)

Arthur Sze is the author of seven collections of poetry, including one book of **translations** from Chinese. In a career spanning over thirty years, Sze has garnered awards from the Guggenheim Foundation, the Lannan Foundation, and the Witter Bynner Foundation for his work as a poet and esteemed translator of classical and contemporary Chinese poetry. With the publication of *The Willow Wind* (1972), Sze broke into the world of poetry as one of the first **Asian American poets** to publish in this country. *Two Ravens* (1976), *Dazzled* (1982), and *River River* (1987) followed, continuing Sze's exploration of the imagistic **lyric** poem. Sze's fifth book of poems, *Archipelago* (1995), is widely regarded as the poet's breakthrough collection, marking a shift in Sze's poetic practice toward a longer line and more complex poetic structure. *The Redshifting Web: Poems 1970–1998* (1998) gathered together several new poem sequences alongside work from Sze's previous collections. Sze's most recent work, *The Silk Dragon: Translations from the Chinese* (2001), brings together poems ranging from translations of the classic T'ang Dynasty Masters to contemporary poets.

The son of Chinese immigrants, Sze was born in New York City in 1950. He attended public elementary school in Garden City, Long Island, and was educated at a private high school in Lawrenceville, New Jersey. In 1968 Sze enrolled at the Massachusetts Institute of Technology (MIT) where from 1969 to 1970, he attended a poetry workshop led by **Denise Levertov**. After two years at MIT, Sze transferred to the University of California at Berkeley where he majored in poetry. At Berkeley, Sze self-designed a program of study under **Josephine Miles**, which included intensive study of Chinese language and literature. Sze graduated from UC Berkeley in 1972, simultaneous with the publication of his first book, *The Willow Wind*. Sze's poems began to appear in publications including *Hanging Loose*, *Mother Jones*, and *Puerto del Sol*. He began teaching during this period as a Poet-in-the-Schools through the New Mexico Arts Division; from 1974 to 1984 he taught in twenty different schools and pueblos throughout the state.

Under John Brandi's Tooth of Time imprint, Sze published his second collection of poems, *Two Ravens* (which was later republished in 1984 in an expanded version) and a revised version of *The Willow Wind: Translations and Poems* (1981). Sze eventually became a board member for Tooth of Time, and helped to publish books by such poets as Carolyn Lau and Rosemary Catacalos until the press ceased publication in 1988. From 1985 to 1990, Sze served as contributing editor to *Tyuonyi*, a publication founded at the Institute of American Indian Arts by **Phillip Foss.** Sze's third collection, *Dazzled*, was published in 1982, the same year that the National Endowment of the Arts awarded Sze a creative writing fellowship. Attracting the interest of Lost Roads Publishers, **C.D. Wright** and **Forrest Gander**'s independent publishing project, *River River* followed. In 1995 Copper Canyon Press published *Archipelago*, which is widely regarded as Sze's landmark collection and which garnered Sze an American Book Award the following year. *The Redshifting Web: Poems 1970–1998* gathered together new poems, excerpts from *The Willow Wind* and *Two Ravens*, and collected together the complete poems of *Dazzled, River River*, and *Archipelago. The Redshifting Web* tracks the progress of the poet's evolution and growth from restrained, short, lyric works to more complex **ecopoetic** structures. The publication of *The Silk Dragon: Translations from the Chinese* marked Sze's arrival as a translator of exceptional quality. Sze is former director of the **creative writing program** at the Institute of American Indian Arts, where he has taught since 1984. Sze currently serves as contributing editor to *Manoa*. He lives in Pojoaque, New Mexico, with his wife, the poet Carol Moldaw.

The poems in Sze's first two collections, *The Willow Wind* and *Raven Raven,* are painterly tableaux composed in short, lyric form. "The Wood Whittler," "The Taoist Painter," and "Brueghel" meditate on the artistic process and reflect an interest in **ekphrasis**, whereas poems such as "Li Po" and "Wang Wei" point directly to a Chinese influence. Commenting on Sze's early work in *Raintaxi*, Tony Barnstone writes that Sze "blends Chinese techniques with the archetypal imagery of **Deep Image** poetry."

The poems of Sze's middle period begin to move away from the shorter, imagistic poems that characterized his earlier work, while retaining his signature style—language rich with the imagery and vocabulary of the sciences and the natural world. Scenes from contemporary China are juxtaposed alongside images of the cultural past in "Viewing Photographs of China" (*Dazzled*), which provides a glimpse into Sze's approach. In *River River*, Sze begins experimenting with the extended serial poem. Written in six sections, "The Leaves of a Dream Are the Leaves of an Onion" continue the poet's exploration of collage juxtaposition to create a sense of the simultaneity of experience: "No single method can describe the world / therein is the pleasure."

Sze's breakthrough collection is widely regarded as *Archipelago*. The centerpiece of *Archipelago* is a long poem built around the concept of the Zen garden at Ryoanji Temple in Kyoto. Composed of fifteen stones and a sea of raked gravel, the Ryoanji garden is structured in such a way that from a fixed perspective, a viewer is never able to see all of the stones in the garden at once. Similarly, the poems in *Archipelago* are mini-epics and complexly linked poetic sequences arranged to continually reveal connections and resonances between individual poems. Sze's poems from this period weave together various disparate elements to create a parallax view, allowing for a continual discovery and rediscovery of the poem.

Spanning Sze's interests in **Chinese poetr**y from the T'ang Dynasty Masters to contemporary poets, *The Silk Dragon* gathers together Sze's translations from three major periods: 1971–1972, 1982–1983, and 1995–1996. Sze includes Wen I-to's **long poem** "Miracle," a poem that helped Sze to "discern a new stage" for his own writing in finding a way to extend the lyric poem. In his introduction to *The Silk Dragon*, Sze credits the Chinese poets as being a "source of inspiration" for his own evolution as poet, feeling that by struggling with and translating the great poems of the Chinese literary tradition, he could best develop his voice as a poet.

Although some critics have compared Sze's tendency for juxtaposition to surrealist or **Dadaist** techniques, Sze draws from the very juxtaposition of the Chinese language itself and the essence of how complex ideographic characters are rendered and constructed.

Further Reading. ***Selected Primary Sources:*** Sze, Arthur, *The Redshifting Web: Poems 1970–1998* (Port Townsend, WA: Copper Canyon Press, 1998); ———, *The Silk Dragon* (Port Townsend, WA: Copper Canyon Press, 1998). ***Selected Secondary Sources:*** Barnstone, Tony, "A Revelation Waiting to Happen: A Conversation with Arthur Sze on Translating Chinese Poetry" (*Translation Review* 59 [2000]: 4–19); ———, Review of *The Redshifting Web: Poems 1970–1998* (*Rain Taxi* 3.3 [Fall 1998]: 30); Zhou, Xiaojing, "The Redshifting Web: Arthur Sze's Ecopoetics," in *Ecopoetry: A Critical Introduction*, ed. Scott Bryson (Salt Lake City: University of Utah Press, 2002).

Shin Yu Pai

T

TABB, JOHN BANISTER (1845–1909)

John Banister Tabb achieved popularity and critical success with the publication of his short poems in the late nineteenth and early twentieth centuries. The prolific Roman Catholic priest-poet employed short verse forms to a variety of ends, often writing humorous and **children's verse**. His greatest successes came when he covered a range of topics and moods, however, as he did in his bestselling *Poems* (1894). The renown that Tabb achieved with his intense, epigrammatic verse signified a trend in popular taste and publishing practices at the turn of the century.

Tabb was born March 22, 1845, to a wealthy and well-connected Episcopalian Virginia family. He identified himself as a Southerner throughout his life, serving as a blockade runner during the Civil War, lamenting the destruction of his family's estate during the war, and calling himself an "unredeemed rebel." While a Civil War prisoner at Point Lookout, Maryland, in 1864, Tabb met the poet **Sidney Lanier**, also a prisoner. Tabb later dedicated *Poems* (1894) to Lanier. After Tabb was released from prison, he pursued an education in musical performance in Baltimore, Maryland, until, for financial reasons, he was compelled to leave school and support himself with a number of temporary teaching posts. During this period, Tabb converted to Roman Catholicism, formally joining the church in 1872. His ordination in 1884 was as a member of the secular clergy; however, "he chose rather to live the retired life of the priests of the Society of St. Sulpice, whose sole purpose it is to conduct seminaries and prepare young men for the priesthood" (Litz, *Father Tabb*, 37). After attending St. Mary's Seminary, Tabb returned to St. Charles's College in Maryland, where he had worked earlier, and taught there for the remainder of his life. Accounts that recall Tabb fondly as a teacher relate how he intermixed his poetry with his teaching, most notably verses that he composed for grammar lessons. Tabb suffered from poor vision throughout his life; he died November 19, 1909, at St. Charles's College after suffering a debilitating illness and going blind.

Tabb claimed that, despite a longstanding interest in poetry, he did not seriously attempt writing it until 1872. Five years later, his first published poem, "The Cloud," appeared in the July 1877 *Harper's New Monthly Magazine.* Additional poems followed in *Harper's Monthly* and in *New England Magazine*, the *Atlantic Monthly*, and the *Century.* Tabb's breakout volume, *Poems* (1894), followed two privately published ventures, *Poems* (1882) and *An Octave to Mary* (1893). The 1894 *Poems* was highly successful, with sales figures reportedly second only to **Emily Dickinson**'s *Poems* (1890). In fact, Tabb in part owed his 1890s success to the same machinery that promoted Dickinson. His appeal to **Thomas Wentworth Higginson** for help led Tabb to Higginson's friend, prominent Unitarian John White Chadwick. Both Higginson and Chadwick compared the two poets in their reviews. In an 1895 *Nation* article, Higginson found Dickinson's verse less sentimental, more "terse and vigorous," and capable of greater depth, but he found in Tabb "a far greater variety of interests" and more "finish" and "form." Tabb's later volumes included *Lyrics* (1897), *Child Verse* (1899), *Two Lyrics* (1900), *Later Lyrics* (1902), *The Rosary in Rhyme* (1904), and *Quips and Quiddits; Ques for the Qurious* (1907).

Although Tabb wrote a number of poems dealing directly with **religious** themes, and two of his books (*An Octave to Mary* and *The Rosary in Rhyme*) feature overtly religious titles, his poetry avoids pressing particular doctrines and instead forges links between natural subjects and religious language. "The Cloud" (1877), for instance, reveals the divine-like properties of a cloud that opens the day with "prophetic" "visage" and later becomes like a "sheltering" and "soothing" angel. But the cloud's almost human expiration at the close of day provides the poem's central analogy: Like the cloud, the speaker's soul is nothing, "a vapor foul," without "the light of Heaven."

Tabb's later poems continued to derive controlling images from religion. In Tabb's 1897 *Lyrics*, an "Echo" is a "famished Prodigal," and the "waves" and "hills" in their activity and stillness are "Martha" and "Mary" ("The Sisters"). Tabb, who suffered from insomnia, emphasized a divine presence and plan in his life, writing of his sleepless state that "e'en this, Lord, didst thou bless—" ("Insomnia"). But Tabb largely eliminated moral conclusions to his poems as he increased his use of compressed forms such as quatrains and octaves. In "Victims," for instance, published in Tabb's 1910 *Later Poems*, he infuses an autumn landscape with images of martyrdom and sacrifice: "[M]aple-martyrs" are "ablaze in autumn fire" on "many a smoking pyre"; the final fall of leaves signals that "[t]he sacrifice is done." The short, eight-line poem never moves beyond that comparison to suggest a moral lesson, however, and instead seems to prefigure **Imagism** in its focused and concentrated metaphor.

Tabb's greatest publishing success corresponded with his switch to forms such as the quatrain, sestet, octave, and sonnets. Francis Litz variously credits **Poe**'s theoretical tenets and Dickinson's 1890s success with Tabb's interest in short forms. In fact, the 1890s success of both Dickinson and Tabb attests to the popular interest in short poetry catered to and fostered by the day's literary periodicals (*see* **Literary Magazines**). The *Atlantic Monthly*, for example, published Tabb with others in two quatrain samplings ("Quatrains by Different hands" in December 1885 and "Four Quatrains" in November 1892). When not offered in groups, such poems were no doubt attractive because they adapted easily to a magazine's space requirements. Critic M.A. De Wolfe Howe even casts Tabb's poems as better served by that context than by the context of a book: "The little poems are things best read, where many of them first appeared, at the end of a page of prose in a magazine," he wrote in a review of Tabb's *Poems* (1894). "There they are welcome bits of fancy; here their effect is to leave one feeling as if one had arisen from a dinner of crumbs" (quoted in Litz, *Father Tabb*, 101).

Tabb's 1894 *Poems* reveals the range and flexibility of his poetry in short forms. By turns serious, morose, playful, and **sentimental**, Tabb's short poems offer pithy observations on the natural world and the human condition. His quatrains configure "Stars" as "seeds of golden light" that "bear the heaven-full harvest, Dawn"; define "Whisper" as the sister of "Silence"; and compare "The Shadow" to a "friend of fortune"—there in "flattering light," gone in "darkness." Some early twentieth-century scholars predicted for Tabb a staying power that he failed to have. Still, his extensive experimentations with short forms both guaranteed some lasting recognition for him and revealed the depths and variations of his era's "welcome bits of fancy."

Further Reading. ***Selected Primary Sources:*** Tabb, John Banister, *Later Poems* (New York: Mitchell Kennerley, 1910); ———, *Lyrics* (Boston: Copeland and Day, 1897); ———, *Poems* (Boston: Copeland and Day, 1894). ***Selected Secondary Sources:*** Litz, Francis E., ed., *Letters—Grave and Gay: And Other Prose of John Banister Tabb* (Washington, D.C.: Catholic University of America Press, 1950); ———, *Father Tabb: A Study of His Life and Works* (Baltimore: The Johns Hopkins Press, 1923).

Ingrid Satelmajer

TAGGARD, GENEVIEVE (1894–1948)

Genevieve Taggard's poetry reflected the two major poetic currents existing between the world wars: one that emphasized an **avant-garde poetics** of experimentation and aestheticism, and one that emphasized the political and social challenges to the status quo such art often presented. As a **feminist** and outspoken socialist, Taggard was concerned with social struggle, and her poems often consider this subject from a woman's perspective. At the same time, she believed that the "artist's concern is not to persuade or educate, but to overpoweringly express" (*May Days*, 14), and she was widely recognized for her formal control and superior craftsmanship by prominent critics including Louis Untermeyer, Edmund Wilson, and Mark Van Doren. Taggard's poetry addresses both formal and social issues; this has perhaps contributed to her relative obscurity today, as the major critical schools of the twentieth century have tended to view these poetic concerns as antithetical.

Genevieve Taggard was born in Waitsbug, a rural town in southeastern Washington state, in 1894. Her parents were both teachers and missionaries. The family moved to Hawai'i in1896, but, because of financial difficulties, they returned intermittently to Waitsburg. She was educated at Oahu College, Hawai'i, and the University of California–Berkeley. At Berkeley, Taggard studied with **Witter Bynner** and became a socialist. After receiving her degree in 1919, she moved to bohemian New York City and lived in Greenwich Village. Taggard helped found and co-edited the poetry journal *The Measure: A Journal of Poetry.* In 1921 she married novelist and poet Robert Wolf, with whom she had her only child, Marcia. Wolf and Taggard were contributing editors of the *New Masses. For Eager Lovers* (1922) was the first of eighteen books Taggard published in her brief career. She taught at Mount Holyoke from 1929–1931, where she published the very well-received *The Life and Mind of Emily Dickinson* (1930). She was awarded a Guggenheim fellowship for poetry in 1931, and spent one year writing abroad before returning to teach at Bennington College, where she taught from1932–1934. Taggard and Wolf divorced in 1934; in 1935 she married the socialist journalist Kenneth Durant. Taggard concluded her teaching career at Sarah Lawrence, where she worked from 1934–1947.

The most prominent theme of Taggard's poetry is women's emotional, physical, social, and political relationship to the larger world. "With Child," an early lyric that appeared in her first volume of poetry, is one of her better-known poems, and was translated into French by Eugène Jolas. Her speaker begins by musing, "Now I am slow and placid, fond of sun, / Like a sleek beast, or a worn one," an image that contrasts with the concluding lines, which focus on the quickening child she carries: "Defiant even now, it tugs and moans / To be untangled from these mother's bones." The speaker's attempt to occupy her child's perspective prompts the poem's meditative vacillation between two individual voices. This technique emphasizes the speaker's awareness of the natural yet strange state in which two beings occupy the same body. In Taggard's poetry, the double-voiced speaker recurs consistently, especially in poems that imagine a woman's subjectivity. "Evening Love-of-Self," a **long**, surreal, **narrative poem** from *Not Mine to Finish* (1934), acknowledges the second voice embedded in her speaker's head as a social one: Her speaker futilely wishes someone would "take, take away," "the mirrors of friends' faces like their fine eyes; / Showing: *to me you are this.* Mirrors of limitation."

Friends, lovers, children, and the world at large make demands upon women's quest for self-realization throughout Taggard's work, including in "The Little Girl with Bands on her Teeth," from her last volume of poetry, *Slow Music* (1946). In this poem, her speaker refuses to "return the triple mile" to rescue a crying child, and discovers that she must "finish the journey" on her own rather than perform acts of self-sacrifice out of pity. This revelation underscores the dilemmas of individual conscience and consciousness that mark much of Taggard's work. "At Last the Women Are Moving," and "A Middle-Aged, Middle-Class Woman at Midnight," poems from *Calling Western Union* (1936), interrogate the particular tension between these two stances from a woman's point of view, and register Taggard's own socialist worldview and concern for humankind more generally.

Taggard published much of her work in the *Nation* and the *New Masses,* belonged to various left-oriented groups, and served as a member of the executive council of the League of American Writers. Her socialist perspective is implicitly indicated in many of her best poems in their images of revolution and rebirth. The most evocative of these appear in *Not Mine to Finish,* including "Lark," and "Image." "Lark," a poem set to music by Henry Leland Clarke, begins with the invocation, "O, Lark, from great dark, arise!" and celebrates the lark's song. The lark, "sprung like an arrow from the bow of dark," will "shock ears and stun our eyes" by its welcome to a new day. This poem and "Image," two of her best known, exude energy and vitality at the formal level through her playful experimentation with repetition, rhyme patterns, and tone changes. The rhythmic propulsion of "Image" is striking: "Joy, red on tongue with wind on frozen forehead; / Mouth open, Joy just-spoken, grief just-broken."

Taggard became increasingly innovative with the lyric form. The playful experiments with **sound** prominent in *Slow Music* suggest the influence of her friend **Wallace Stevens**. In one such poem, "Problem of Evil into Cocoon," a worm connives, "malignant as eel, / As stinging, as male" This sound-derived humor is featured throughout the volume, as in "The Geraniums" and "A Sombrero Is a Kind of Hat—This Poem Is a Kind of Nonsense." Taggard's emphasis on "teaching the joy of the song, not the letter" in "Definition of Song" (*Calling Western Union*), indicates how such experiments in sound may actually make singing the "best" medium for public expression. Taggard's interest in sound led her to write for music, and her poems appeared in compositions by William Shuman, Aaron Copeland, Roy Harris, and Henry Leland Clarke.

Further Reading. ***Selected Primary Sources:*** Taggard, Genevieve, *Calling Western Union* (New York: Harper, 1936); ———, *Collected Poems 1918–1938* (New York: Harper, 1938); ———, *For Eager Lovers* (New York: Selzer, 1922); ———, *The Life and Mind of Emily Dickinson* (New York: Knopf, 1930); ———, ed., *May Days: An Anthology of Verse from Masses-Liberator* (New

York: Boni & Liveright, 1926); ———, *Not Mine to Finish: Poems 1928–1934* (New York & London: Harper, 1934); ———, *Slow Music* (New York: Harper, 1946). ***Selected Secondary Sources:*** Allego, Donna M., "Genevieve Taggard's Sentimental Marxism in *Calling Western Union*" (*College Literature,* 31.1 [Winter 2004]: 27–51); Berke, Nancy, *Women Poets on the Left: Lola Ridge, Genevieve Taggard, Margaret Walker* (Gainesville, FL: University Press of Florida, 2001); Miller, Nina, "The Bonds of Free Love: Constructing the Female Bohemian Self" (*Genders* 11 [Fall 1991]: 37–57).

Geneva M. Gano

TAGGART, JOHN (1942–)

John Taggart is a contemporary **experimental** poet who stands apart from the usual groupings of experimentalists. Taggart did his doctoral dissertation on **Objectivist poetics**, and thus his work shares certain concerns with the writing of **Louis Zukovsky** and **George Oppen**. Other influences—most notably, a life-long engagement with music and the visual arts and an unabashed use of spiritual language—have blended with the Objectivist aspects to make for a recognizably unique voice in contemporary American experimental poetry. Long overlooked by mainstream anthologists and publishers, Taggart garnered heightened visibility when Sun & Moon Press published *Loop* in 1991 and, in 1998, when **Jerome Rothenberg** and **Pierre Joris** included two of his poems in their crucial **anthology** of **modern** and **postmodern** poetries, *Poems for the Millennium.* Both books put Taggart in the company of the **Language poets**, a pairing that makes a certain sense in terms of very general poetics but that also only serves to highlight more fundamental differences between them.

The son of a Methodist minister, Taggart was born in Guthrie Center, Iowa, in 1942. In high school, he showed an interest in writing fiction, but at Earlham College, where he double-majored in literature and philosophy, his interest shifted to poetry. There he began reading widely—especially **Wallace Stevens**, **Charles Olson** (and other **Black Mountain poets**), and **William Bronk**. During the summer following his junior year, he attended the Aspen Writers' Workshop in Colorado, where he met his lifelong friend, Toby Wilson, as well as **Paul Blackburn** and **Robert Creeley**. His first poems appeared in *Crucible* in 1965, and sometime in 1966 he was editor and publisher of the **literary magazine** *MAPS*, which appeared intermittently from then until the mid-1970s. His experience as an editor not only underscored the potential for dialogue between writers' work, but also brought him closer to the physical act of publishing, in terms of his work with the printing process. At the suggestion of **Donald Justice**, he went to Syracuse University, where, in 1974, he received a Ph.D. in the Humanities Interdisciplinary Studies Program; the primary focus of his dissertation was the work of Zukovsky. In 1969 he began teaching English at Shippensberg University in Pennsylvania, where he taught literature and creative writing and directed the interdisciplinary arts program. Aside from his collections of poetry, he has also written critical works: *Songs of Degrees*, a collection of essays on poetry and **poetics**, and *Remaining in Light*, an extended look at a painting by Edward Hopper.

A central characteristic of Taggart's aesthetic is an active dialogue with artists and their work. Because of his interdisciplinary background, he is familiar with a range of art forms, and the methods and concerns of those works are central to many of his poems. What particularly interests Taggart, though, no matter what the art form, is the method of composition. Admittedly sympathetic with the experimental spirit of the 1960s, much of his poetry gravitates toward the innovations of the mid-twentieth century: **jazz**, abstract expressionism, rhythm and **blues**, and pop/rock. The ways in which such forms are composed—in terms of rhythm, repetition, variation, or improvisation—provide occasions for Taggart to explore what language is capable of, thereby stretching its own similar compositional potential.

While this experimentation justifies comparison with the Language poets, the latter often emphasize the unfortunately alienating effect of language—as a needed corrective to common usage—while Taggart consistently emphasizes how such experimentation with language is not alien to human expression at all. Taggart traces these compositional methods to some of our most well-known and admired artists—John Coltrane and Marvin Gaye, John Rothko and Edward Hopper—and stresses how repetition and improvisation are fundamental to how memory, desire, and change are experienced and expressed. He connects compositional experimentation with what it means to be human; this marriage is what lies behind the unabashedly spiritual language of his poetry.

Taggart's spirituality is by no means conventional. For example, the poem "Monk," from *Loop*, written in response to the death of jazz musician Thelonious Monk, uses the familiar hymn "Abide With Me" as a kind of template, and performs a variation not unlike the kind typical of jazz. The poem begins just as the hymn does but introduces a brokenness, a stutter: "A-bidea-a- / bide." As the poem continues, internal line breaks alter the rhythm of the hymn, and certain words are omitted while others are repeated. This variation is at once an homage to Monk and a reflection of the way the pain of loss may effect utterance. Interestingly, the poem is not addressed to the "Lord" of the original song but to Monk himself. What "abides" is Monk's aesthetic example of how to make that utterance one's own. The living artist is lost, however, leaving the speaker alone to speak to himself or herself in the final repetition of the poem: "Abide with / me me." In an interview with Brian Haas, Taggart spoke of the effect of musical variation, saying that the effect is one he would call "transformation" even though others would call it "transcendence." In Taggart's spirituality, there is no mystical escape from the givens of daily existence; there is only the transformation that creation and communication can—and do—afford.

The benefits of such spirituality are considerable for Taggart, and throughout his career he has demonstrated the power of transformation in the way he has approached the composition of his own poems. Whether it is the shorter, Objectivist-inspired approach of his first collection, *To Construct a Clock* (1971); the nearly mathematical "weaving" of images in works such as *Dodeka* (1979); or the creation of longer-lined poems with internal repetition as seen in his Vietnam War poem *Peace On Earth* (1981) and in *Dehiscence* (1983), Taggart has pursued variety as he explores how we might actively engage language so as to transform ourselves. How highly he esteems this ability to change ourselves and others through creativity can be seen in his later collection, *When the Saints* (1999), a book in memory of his sculptor friend Bradford Graves. In it, Taggart returns several times to Saint Colombe, who added a string to the viol, which "added a vibration and changed the vibration / . . . [and] changed the destination of the music." Later, he writes, "There can be change by way of subtraction // it is no secret what I am doing." Here again, Taggart stresses the options available for causing change, shows how the smallest of changes has a proliferative effect, and demonstrates how such work can be honest and clear.

These changes, these transformations, relate to human needs: how we deal with loss, how we act upon desire, and how we build relationships and community. Fundamental to all these is how we construct meaning. In the Haas interview, he says, "The creation of meaning is . . . a fabulation. . . . Otherwise . . . you are subject to a construction that will always come into conflict with the reality of the external universe, if not spiritual reality." John Taggart's poetry continues to provide an example of how to construct such meaning, and does so with an active and earnest experimentation. Whether by indicating the recognizable historical occurrences of this experimentation, by using familiar spiritual imagery and language, or by addressing everyday concerns, Taggart's is a poetry that demonstrates how language can be stretched to fit our needs.

Further Reading. ***Selected Primary Sources:*** Taggart, John, *Dodeka* (Milwaukee, WI: Membrane Press, 1979); ———, *Loop* (Los Angeles: Sun & Moon Press, 1991); ———, *Songs of Degrees: Essays on Contemporary Poetry and Poetics* (Tuscaloosa: University of Alabama Press, 1994). ***Selected Secondary Sources:*** Daly, Lew, *Swallowing the Scroll: Late in a Prophetic Tradition with the Poetry of Susan Howe and John Taggart* (Buffalo, NY: M Press, 1994); Haas Brad, "John Taggart *FlashPoint* Interview" (*FlashPoint* [Spring 2002], Web Issue 5: www.flashpointmag.com/taggart.htm); Ratner, Rochelle, "The Poet as Composer: An Inquiry into the Work of John Taggart" (*Paper Air* 1.2 [1979]: 59–63).

Samuel Jason Ezell

TALLMOUNTAIN, MARY (1918–1994)

Mary Demoski, a Koyukon Athabaskan, fashioned her pen name in honor of a mountain near her childhood home of Nulato, Alaska, on the banks of the Yukon River, one hundred twenty miles west of Fairbanks and one hundred miles south of the Arctic Circle. Childhood memories greatly influenced TallMountain's writing as an adult. Her childhood was the beginning of a life of struggle that she was able to manage through writing. TallMountain's work demonstrated the juxtaposition that many Native American poets experienced between celebrations of traditional indigenous cultures and life in urban twentieth-century America. Hers was the voice of a child uprooted from one culture who is forced to live in another, and who survived. She continues to speak for many Native Americans who are trying to find their places in contemporary America.

At the age of six, TallMountain was removed from her family and community because of a tuberculosis epidemic that eventually killed her mother and brother. She was adopted by a white doctor and his wife, who moved her to Oregon and later to California, and who refused to allow her to speak her Athabaskan language. The resulting isolation became a thread that continued throughout her life. Her birth mother had died when she was eight; her adoptive father died when she was sixteen, soon followed by the suicide of her adoptive mother. TallMountain married and divorced twice, and moved several times trying to find her place. When she finally returned to Nulato in her mid-fifties, she found that she no longer fit in with the members of her home village. It was after this visit that she began to write seriously.

"The Figure in Clay," the first poem in her collection *There is No Word for Goodbye* (1990), which is based on her return to Nulato, has, according to an interview TallMountain conducted with **Joseph Bruchac**, "nothing to do" with what she learned about her tribe, but "more what I found out about myself" (*SAIL* 1.1 [Summer1989]: 13). Nevertheless, nostalgic for her family and community, she began to deal with the dichotomies of her life through poetry and short stories. The poem "Schizophrenia" (*The Light on the Tent Wall*, 1990) is an example of the anguish suffered by someone caught between two cultures. The poem also reflects her decision to choose life over death and her refusal to give in to the effects of isolation and displacement. Instead of despairing, TallMountain celebrates her ancestors, particularly her mother. In "Matmiya" (*The Light on the Tent Wall*), she celebrates her grandmother and, in other poems and short stories, the people she lived with in the Tenderloin district in San Francisco.

In addition to dealing with the feeling of isolation and the need to develop a sense of place, TallMountain also experienced dichotomies of native spirituality and Roman Catholicism. A strong spirituality helped her survive her sense of isolation, and saw her through alcoholism, battles with cancer, and quadruple heart bypass surgery. Her teacher and mentor, Paula Gunn Allen, writes in *The Sacred Hoop* (1986, 1992) that TallMountain's "tribal consciousness is tempered with a mystical Roman Catholic perspective" that Allen found to be "a difficult and uneasy alliance" (172). However, Allen's opinion changed by the time she wrote the Foreword to TallMountain's collection of poems, *The Light On the Tent Wall*, in which she described TallMountain as being skilled at balancing and incorporating both types of spirituality in her life and in her work (2).

TallMountain's Catholicism is evident in the fact that her first book, a chapbook of nine poems, was published in the 1970s by the Friars Press. In the early 1970s, she began writing a regular column titled "Meditations for Wayfarers" for the Franciscan magazine the *Way of St. Francis* (the *Way*). She won second place in the 1970 Catholic Press Association writing awards for her poem "Ashes Unto Eden" (originally published in the *Way* and later included in *Continuum*, 1988).

TallMountain saw similarities between Native American spirituality and Roman Catholic mysticism, finding in both lessons on how to live. Her poem "The Last Wolf," which has been often anthologized and is included in *The Light on the Tent Wall*, acknowledges the influence of animal spirits on indigenous peoples, even those who have left their tribal homeland for the cities. TallMountain told Bruchac that the poem was both about the destruction of civilization and a possible rebuilding, and about the loss of her people because of the loss of their language (19).

After becoming a student of Paula Gunn Allen in the mid 1970s, when she was in her late fifties, TallMountain committed herself to writing. Through her writing she wrestled with her demons. She wrote about grief, anger, and abandonment; yet, she also wrote about joy, love, and hope. She learned to accept what life offered and deal with it the best she could. In "There is No Word for Goodbye," the title poem of a collection that won the Pushcart Prize (originally published in 1988 and reissued in 1990), she comes to accept her separation from the village of her birth while at the same time recognizing that her village land will always remain a fundamental part of who she is as a woman. In *Continuum*, she begins to see herself as a bridge between the many divergencies in her life.

Near the end of her life, TallMountain reveled in the positive things in life, what she called "good grease" because celebrations always included food, particularly greasy caribou meat (*The Light on the Tent Wall*). At the time of her death, she was working on a novel, tentatively titled *Doyon,* about a child uprooted from one culture and placed into another. In her will, TallMountain left the proceeds of her published works to benefit low-income writers. The TallMountain Circle, a project of the Tenderloin Reflection and Education Center, a community-based, nonprofit, spiritual and cultural center in San Francisco where TallMountain served as poet in residence, publishes and promotes her literary works and sponsors the annual TallMountain Awards for Creative Writing and Community Service. The Rasmussen Library at the University of Alaska in Fairbanks houses her archives, including her journals and unpublished works. (*See also* **Native American poetry**.)

Further Reading. ***Selected Primary Sources:*** TallMountain, Mary, *Continuum* (Marvin, SD: Blue Cloud Quarterly, 1988); ———, *The Light On the Tent Wall: A Bridging* (Los Angeles: UCLA Press, 1990); ———, *Listen to the Night*, ed. Ben Clarke (San Francisco: Freedom Voices, 1995); ———, *Nine Poems* (San Francisco: Friars Press, 1977); ———, *A Quick Brush of Wings* (San Francisco: Freedom Voices, 1991); ———, *There is No Word for Goodbye* (Oakland: Red Star Black Rose, 1990). ***Selected Secondary Sources:*** Allen, Paula Gunn, Foreword, in *The Light on the Tent Wall: A Bridging* (Los Angeles: UCLA Press, 1990, 1–4); ———, *The Sacred Hoop: Recovering the Feminine in American Indian Traditions* (1986; Boston: Beacon Press, 1992); Bruchac, Joseph W., "We Are the Inbetweens: An Interview with Mary TallMountain" (*Studies in American Indian Literature* 1.1 [Summer 1989]: 13–21).

Susan L. Rockwell

TAPAHONSO, LUCI (1953–)

Luci Tapahonso was born to the Salt Water Clan for the Bitter Water Clan on the Diné (Navajo) reservation at Shiprock, New Mexico, on November 8, 1953, the sixth of eleven children born to Lucille Deschenne Tapahonso and Eugene Tapahonso, Sr. Her first language was Diné; she did not become fluent in English until she attended the Navajo Methodist Boarding School in Farmington, New Mexico, when she was eight. She began to write poetry in high school (**Bruchac**, 86). Her poetry celebrates Diné culture and its location in the natural and spiritual worlds, and offers an integrative view of that culture within the American context.

The author of five books of poetry and short stories, Tapahonso purposely mixes English and Diné prose and storytelling styles in her work. She often creates her poems in Diné, later translating them into English. When an appropriate English translation is not possible, she retains the Diné phrasing. Poetry as **performance** is a fundamental concept for Tapahonso, showing the cultural influence of oral Diné songs and rhythms. "Don't marry a man who can't sing," she warns in the poem "Listen." "There's something wrong if a man can't sing in Indian" (*Seasonal Woman*).

As a student at the University of New Mexico, where she earned a BA in English in 1980 and an MA in English and creative writing in 1983, Tapahonso came under the tutelage of renowned **Native American** writer **Leslie Marmon Silko**, who both influenced and encouraged Tapahonso in her writing. She claims that as a writer she would not have done much if she had not met Silko: "I didn't take what I was doing to be something important to the general community" (Bruchac, 86). Tapahonso published her first two books of poetry while a student at the University of New Mexico (*One More Shiprock Night* in 1981 and *Seasonal Woman* in 1982). The poems in these volumes address what it is like to be a modern Diné woman, a daughter, a wife, and a mother. Family is very important in her work. The poems also express a love for the beautiful land of Dinétah, and many poems are written about specific places.

Tapahonso remained at the University of New Mexico as an associate professor of English, American studies, and American Indian studies from 1983 to 1989. In 1987 she published her third volume of poetry, *A Breeze Swept Through*. In this volume, she continues the recurring themes of her earlier volumes: the role of Diné women and the importance of Diné place and tradition. Her works, apparently simple, are rich with social and political comments regarding modern Native American life, both on and off reservation.

In 1989 Tapahonso moved to University of Kansas, where she keenly felt the estrangement from her family and her home, a suffering made evident in many of the poems of her fourth volume, *Sáanii Dahatall: The Women Are Singing* (1993). The poems in this collection provide a deeper look at the connection of history and place to family and individual well-being. In "Shaa Ako Dahjiniteh Remember the Things They Told Us," Tapahonso remembers the lessons passed down on a myriad of topics from how to pray, to how to cook, to when to cut one's hair. "It Has Always Been This Way" also provides lessons in time-honored child-rearing practices.

In addition to the longing for home and family expressed in "A Whispered Chant of Loneliness," in the *Sáanii Dahatall* collection, Tapahonso consciously experiments with style and language, blending poetry and prose, song and prayer. She emphasizes Diné spiritual traditions in addition to cultural traditions. In particular, her **narrative prose poem** "In 1864" connects the present with the past, reflecting on the painful experiences and the lessons learned by the Diné. The powerful images of the people's forced removal to Bosque Redondo heighten readers' awareness that the Diné exist today because of survivors in the past.

This emphasis on Diné tradition continues in *Blue Horses Rush In* (1999), her fifth volume of poetry. In "Notes for the Children," she continues to pass on important cultural lessons, from a story about the Holy Ones building the first "hooghan" to the reason why Diné women have always worn skirts ("In the old way . . . Asdzani—'woman' means the same thing as a skirt") to the best flour for making frybread (Bluebird or Red Rose brands of flour). Historical events are recounted in present-tense poems, emphasizing the Diné belief that past, present, and future are all part of the same circle.

Currently, Tapahonso is a professor of English at the University of Arizona, and her papers are housed at the University of New Mexico Center for Southwest Research. She is an advocate for community involvement and has served on the editorial boards of *wizcazo sa review*, *Frontiers*, and *Blue Mesa Review*. She also assists her community by serving on both the New Mexico and Kansas arts commissions, the board for Habitat for Humanity, the United Way Allocations Panel, and the board of trustees for the National Museum of the American Indian (Smithsonian Institution); she was a Newberry Library fellow in 1995.

Tapahonso has been recognized widely for her poetry. In 1999 she received the Wordcraft Circle of Native Writers Storyteller of the Year award for her readings and performances. She was named a Woman of Distinction by the American Girl Scout Council in 1996 and an Outstanding Native American Woman by the City of Sacramento, California, in 1993. She received the 1998 Regional Book Award from the Mountains and Plains Booksellers Association, a 1981 Southwestern Association for Indian Affairs literature fellowship, and a Hall Center Creative Fellowship Award in 1995, among other awards and recognitions.

Further Reading. ***Selected Primary Sources:*** Tapahonso, Luci, *Blue Horses Rush In* (Tucson: University of Arizona Press, 1997); ———, *A Breeze Swept Through* (Albuquerque, NM: West End Press, 1989); ———, *Navajo ABC: A Diné Alphabet Book* (New York: Macmillan Books for Young Readers, 1995); ———, *One More Shiprock Night* (San Antonio, TX: Tejas Art Press, 1981); ———, *Sáanii Dahatall: The Women Are Singing* (Tucson: University of Arizona Press, 1993); ———, *Seasonal Woman* (Santa Fe, NM: Tooth of Time Books, 1982); ———, *Songs of Shiprock Fair* (Walnut, CA: Kiva Publishing, Inc., 1999). ***Selected Secondary Sources:*** Allen, Paula Gunn, *The*

Sacred Hoop: Recovering the Feminine in American Indian Traditions (1986; Boston: Beacon Press, 1992); Balassi, William, John F. Crawford, and Annie O. Eysturoy, eds., *This is About Vision: Interviews with Southwestern Writers* (Albuquerque: University of New Mexico Press, 1990); Bruchac, Joseph W., "A *MELUS* Interview: Luci Tapahonso" (*MELUS* 11 [Spring 1984]: 88–91); Radar, Dean, "Luci Tapahonso and Simon Ortiz: Allegory, Symbol, Language, Poetry" (*Southwestern American Literature* 22.2 [1997]: 75).

Susan L. Rockwell

TARN, NATHANIEL (1928–)

Despite a prodigious and highly acclaimed poetic output, Nathaniel Tarn remains best known for his **translations** of Pablo Neruda and his involvement with the founding of the Cape Edition series. Although he has garnered little critical attention in recent years, Nathaniel Tarn has consistently proven himself to be among the most eclectic and erudite poets in contemporary American letters. Throughout his poetry, Tarn is dedicated to navigating, in all their complexities and contradictions, the myths, feelings, and rituals that grant humanity its myriad forms and identities. Greatly influenced and informed by his training as an anthropologist, Tarn incorporates a seemingly endless variety of sources into his work, producing a body of poetry that is difficult to categorize or define. Tarn never steps into the same room twice. He boldly experiments with structures and voices, rendering each of his collections—and each of his poems—as particular entities, with visions and forms that are uniquely their own.

Perhaps the only theme that carries through all of his work is that of change, be it the constant change of geographical or cultural place, or the constant switching of theme and style. Although he is a poet of the world, Tarn is also very much an American poet, strongly influenced by America's **modern** poetic tradition—especially the work of **Ezra Pound**, **Charles Olson**, and **William Carlos Williams**—and fascinated by its promises and its multitude of myths and histories.

Born in Paris, France, in 1928, Nathan Tarn's childhood in Belgium was disrupted by the World War II, which forced his family to flee to England in 1939. After graduating in English and history from Cambridge University, Tarn studied anthropology under Claude Levi-Strauss at the Sorbonne and with Robert Redfield at the University of Chicago. As an anthropologist, Tarn traveled throughout Asia and the American continents, studying and writing on such diverse subjects as initiation rituals, secret societies, Gnostic phenomena, and Burmese Buddhism, subjects and locales to which he has frequently returned in creating his poetry. Although he had been writing poetry intermittently since childhood, Tarn did not fully dedicate himself to the task (and begin to relegate his work as an anthropologist to the side) until the late 1950s, when he became involved in the surrealist movement in Paris. He later co-founded and served as the editor in chief (from 1967 to 1969) of the Cape Edition Series in London, and first translated and introduced Pablo Neruda into English. Following the literary and cultural tradition that he had long admired, Tarn immigrated to the United States in the late 1960s for the express purpose of becoming an American citizen and defining himself as an American poet. Along with Dennis Tedlock and **Jerome Rothenberg**, Tarn is one of the key figures in the **ethnopoetic** movement of the late 1960s, to which his status as an anthropologist provided some further validity. He has produced numerous collections of poetry, authored dozens of essays, and taught at several colleges throughout the United States and Europe.

Highly praised in New York and London upon its release in 1964, *Old Savage/Young City*, Tarn's first collection of poetry, demonstrates a remarkable degree of seriousness and range of themes for a first book. In poems such as the decidedly modernistic "Ranger Spacecraft," in which the poet observes a space capsule at Cape Canaveral and "cannot help thinking of it / as a creature outbound in heart-breaking loneliness," and "The Last of the Chiefs," in which an ancient, disembodied voice from America's precolonial history speaks of the "far-away races / who wrecked us," Tarn attempts to mediate between America's oldest myths and cultures and its newest. Although Tarn's second collection, *Where Babylon Ends*, is his most thematically traditional piece, employing themes typical of the English **lyrical** tradition, it is perhaps his most novel in terms of its technical experiments, complex allegories, and compounded metaphors.

The Beautiful Contradictions is the most widely read and representative of Tarn's works. One of the beautiful contradictions that the title alludes to is undoubtedly the fact that although the collection is, to a significant measure, Tarn's most American work in terms of is influences and attitudes, it is also, at least thematically, his most worldly collection. Tarn claims, at the outset, that he plans to take the whole world as his mother in this collection, and that he must confront the cosmos in their entirety. Yet the influence of the **Beat** school and the **Black Mountain** poets is apparent throughout the entire book, as Tarn warmly embraces unfettered realizations and **open poetic forms**. Tarn's central concern in this work is with locating the poet as an agent of cultural preservation, rendering and conserving a record of humanity's achievements and movements throughout the world. Tarn imagines us all as exiles, no matter our time or place, with a mission to continue to search and discover ourselves through the intersections of our histories and myths, with the poet functioning as our navigator and interpreter, who "it is up to . . . to call into being everything that is."

Although such books as *Lyrics for the Bride of God* and *The House of Leaves* are remarkable for their emotional honesty and forthrightness, Tarn is certainly not a poet operating in the **confessional** vein. In poems such as "Stalemate in the City" and "Thinking Her Name," personal trials and tribulations are framed and expressed as universal experiences common to all of humanity. *Seeing America First* takes the bold step of reversing the general direction of *Old Savage/Young City* as it recounts Tarn's spiritual journey to discover a vision of America as the new world, an open, unknown space, and not simply to locate but to invent for himself a personal vision and myth of America.

Further Reading. ***Selected Primary Sources:*** Tarn, Nathaniel, *The Beautiful Contradictions* (London: Cape Goliard Press, 1969); ———, *The House of Leaves: Poems* (Santa Barbara, CA: Black Sparrow Press, 1976); ———, *Lyrics for the Bride of God* (New York: New Directions, 1975); ———, *Old Savage, Young City* (New York: Random House, 1965); ———, *Seeing America First: Poems* (Minneapolis: Coffee House Press, 1984); ———, *Selected Poems: 1950–2000* (Middletown, CT: Wesleyan University Press, 2002); ———, *Where Babylon Ends* (London: Cape Goliard Press, 1968). ***Selected Secondary Sources:*** Bartlett, Lee, *Nathaniel Tarn: A Descriptive Bibliography* (Jefferson, NC: McFarland, 1987); Corngold, Stanley, "Where Babylon Ends, Nathaniel Tarn's Poet Development" (*boundary 2* 4.1 [Autumn 1975]: 57–75); Lensfet, David, "Notes Towards a Study of Nathaniel Tarn's *The Beautiful Contradictions*, the Poetry of Material Transmigration" (*boundary 2* 4.1 [Autumn 1975]: 76–95).

James Fleming

TATE, ALLEN (1899–1979)

Allen Tate, a major figure in twentieth-century American letters, achieved fame in the 1920s as one of the **Fugitives**, a group of poets and critics associated with Vanderbilt University. His poetry seeks to embody the aristocratic and **agrarian** principles Tate and his friends believed were essential to a Southern culture threatened by Northern commercialism and irreverence for the past. Tate's poems are consciously traditional, and they assert the value of the philosophical perspective of the educated Southerner, a perspective which lays claim to the authority of experience. Often meditative and dignified, the voice of Tate's poems is that of the traveled, small-town academic, wise and sometimes world-weary, but yet cosmopolitan, sometimes stuffy, and always with at least a modest air of dog-eared nobility.

John Orley Allen Tate was born on November 19, 1899, in Winchester, Kentucky, and he matriculated at Vanderbilt University in 1918. He soon associated himself with a group of intellectuals, including his English professor **John Crowe Ransom**, that was engaged in literary pursuits. By the time of his official graduation in 1923, he was involved in producing this group's magazine, the *Fugitive.* Primarily a poet in this early period, Tate was influenced by two powerful forces: Southern tradition on the one hand, and, on the other, literary **modernism**. His own artistic and philosophical development can be described as the working out of a personal identity related both to his regional origins and to his recognition of a spiritual kinship to such American expatriate modernists as **T.S. Eliot** and **Ezra Pound**. Having graduated from Vanderbilt in 1923, Tate found an editorial job in New York the next year, where he came into contact with various writers, including **Hart Crane**, and married the aspiring novelist Caroline Gordon.

In 1928 Tate was awarded a Guggenheim fellowship, and he and his family went to England and then to Paris, where for some time they shared Ford Madox Ford's apartment with the poet **Léonie Adams**. Having met **Gertrude Stein**, F. Scott and Zelda Fitzgerald, and Ernest Hemingway, the Tates concluded 1929 by returning to New York, which, after France, seemed uncomfortable and distracting; they soon returned to Tennessee.

Tate had published a biography of the Confederate general Thomas J. "Stonewall" Jackson in 1928, and he followed it in 1929 with another biography, this time of Jefferson Davis, president of the Confederate States of America. Tate was also publishing poetry (*Mr. Pope and Other Poems*, 1928) and reflecting upon the perspective he had gained on his native South by living in New York and Paris. His reflections were energized by his return and by the dialogue he continued with his friends; this dialogue soon took the form of a collaborative book, *I'll Take My Stand*, in which this group of Southern loyalists, including Ransom, Cleanth Brooks, **Robert Penn Warren**, and Donald Davidson, expressed their commitment to agrarian values in opposition to the commercialism they attributed to Northern interests. The publication of this book was a significant event for Tate and the other contributors, as they were identified with the agrarian position at least to some extent for the rest of their lives.

In 1932 *Poems 1928–1931* appeared, and four years later Tate published *The Mediterranean and Other Poems.* While poetry remained a preoccupation, he became engaged in teaching as he continued his work in literary criticism, and much of his energy was devoted to tasks other than poetic composition. He taught at the Woman's College of the University of North Carolina before accepting a fellowship at Princeton University in 1939. Leaving Princeton in 1942, Tate accepted the chair of poetry at the Library of Congress, a post he held from 1943 to 1944.

Tate's growing reputation soon brought him a succession of editorial positions and faculty appointments. His connections with such luminaries as T.S. Eliot offset to some extent the limitations that might otherwise have been attributed to his regionalism, and he was careful in both prose and verse to maintain a detached sophistication of tone that would separate him from the naive or sentimental enthusiasm associated with the more vulgar adherents of the Old South. A prolific writer, he occupied himself with criticism and reviewing; although his composition of poetry was typically painstaking and deliberate, he continued to write poems, issuing a new volume, *Poems: 1922–1947*, in 1948.

Tate finally reached a measure of professional security with his appointment at the University of Minnesota in 1951. At Minnesota, Tate settled into the academic position he was to hold until his retirement. Continuing his role as a major voice of American criticism, he taught, published, and, over the years, received a number of prestigious awards for his poetry and for his critical contributions. These included the Bollingen Prize (1956), the Brandeis University Medal for Poetry (1961), and the Academy of American Poets Award (1963). He retired from the University of Minnesota in 1968 and returned to Sewanee, Tennessee, where he continued to teach. In 1979, he died in Nashville, Tennessee.

As a poet, Tate produced a body of work that many have found difficult, perhaps because of its obscurity or because of Tate's evident devotion to a region under increasing pressure for its resistance to civil rights. The importance of Tate's involvement in the poetry of his time cannot be dissociated entirely from his personal history, in which three biographical periods may usefully be considered: when Tate and Caroline Gordon shared a New Jersey farmhouse with Hart Crane; when Tate and Gordon shared a Paris apartment with Léonie Adams; and when the Tates occupied their Tennessee house, Benfolly, with young **Robert Lowell** living in a tent on their lawn.

Tate's body of poetic work centers on two key themes. One of these is the urgency of the past, which for Tate sometimes took shape in Virgilian reflections that enabled him to assume the role of Trojan hero, thus connecting his own perspective as heir of the defeated Confederacy with that of the survivors of defeated Troy who went on, in Virgil's myth, to found the civilization of Rome. This metaphorical maneuver enabled the poet to connect to the heroic world of Homer, the arch-poet of the West, and to place himself in the mainstream of literary tradition (as opposed to the commercial attitudes of the Northern victors of 1865). Another theme is the human need for spiritual satisfaction, particularly as that need is celebrated in the great literature of the past. Although for Tate mere nostalgia is reprehensible, he believed that literature at its best directs its readers toward a spiritual satisfaction essential to all human experience.

Both these themes are present in "Ode to the Confederate Dead." In viewing the cemetery that holds the dead heroes of the Confederate lost cause, the narrator, like Virgil's Aeneas, is a survivor who bears the burden of great loss. His contemplation is an engagement of memory, which also poses for the poet the urgent question of creative potency. The ordered stone memorials, with their deteriorating ornaments and inscriptions, suggest the gradual erasure of memory (the goddess Mnemosyne having been for the Greeks the mother of the Muses). As the monuments "yield their names to the elements," to a wind that is "without recollection," the narrator confronts this seeming annihilation with a symphony of echoes from his literary tradition. The poem moves forward awash in echoes and allusions. Percy Bysshe Shelley's "Ode to the West Wind," a prayer for poetic inspiration, is one allusive link, suggested by the autumn setting, the flying leaves, and the deep fear of the loss of poetic power. William Wordsworth's "Tintern Abbey" seems to be evoked by the focus upon memory, and Tate's "think of the autumns that have come and gone!" may well echo Wordsworth's "five years have past; five summers, with the length / Of five long winters!" Tate's description of the underground bodies nurturing the grass of the cemetery recalls the passage in Lord Byron's *Childe Harold's Pilgrimage*, in which a similar point is made of the blood shed at Waterloo, and the phrase "like an old man in a storm" suggests Shakespeare's *King Lear.* Most significant, however, is the similarity of Tate's poem to T.S. Eliot's "The Love Song of J. Alfred Prufrock," for Eliot's poem also describes a quest for poetic identity while incorporating through allusion some fundamental fragments of the Western intellectual tradition. Tate's "blind crab" echoes Eliot's "pair of ragged claws," and Tate's "ribboned coats of grim felicity" surely resemble Prufrock's attire. (*See also* **Graveyard Poetry**.)

The two poems also conclude in a similar fashion, the apparent subsidence of hope at the end of Eliot's poem resembling the absurdity of Tate's narrator's final question: "Shall we, more hopeful, set up the grave / In the house? The ravenous grave?" Tate himself declared that "[t]he two first lines of 'The Love Song of J. Alfred Prufrock' were the first gun of the twentieth-century revolution" (Preface, *Essays of Four Decades*). Both poems incorporate allusion and fragmentation into their structure, and both express doubt that the poet's work in a diminished world is possible, although each implicitly makes a case for the poet's prospects. Tate's narrator describes an owl whose cry "seeds the mind" with the nobility of the dead soldiers' purpose, a romantic metaphor much less pessimistic than Prufrock's comment on the mermaids in his imagination: "I do not think that they will sing to me."

The "Ode" remains Tate's most famous poem, a work that he revised over a period of some twelve years (1925–1937). Within the frame of a conventional **elegy** for courageous young compatriots, Tate was able to create a poem that addresses his desire to create an artistic identity along with his desire to preserve and honor the literary tradition in which he hoped to establish that identity.

After leaving Nashville, Tate worked to establish himself as a poetic voice with a message for the larger world. His first collection of poems, *Mr. Pope and Other Poems* (1928), communicates his desire to speak personally from his own regional experience, as well as claim the putatively larger perspective of a citizen of the republic of letters . The poem "Mr. Pope" embodies this latter claim.

While the revulsion of the Romantic poets against the conscious artificiality of Alexander Pope's public poetry may be understandable, Tate's Southern circle shared some of Pope's prejudices, including a preference for formality in poetic expression and a repudiation of **sentimentality**. Tate and Pope shared an appetite for satirical wit, and neither was averse to acknowledging the claims of aristocracy. Although Pope was generally out of favor early in the twentieth century, Tate appreciated the gifts of the earlier poet and recognized the forces that had shaped Pope's creative perspective. Just as Pope's celebration of the status quo reflected a horror of the disorder of the English Civil War, so the attitude of the Nashville agrarians, discomfited by the ravages of war and Reconstruction, led to a defensive posture. In his poem "Mr. Pope," Tate exerts his poetic detachment in sententious commemoration of his predecessor's inadequate fame.

The four quatrains of "Mr. Pope" function by means of understatement; only the first stanza is a positive assertion, and it is qualified by its paradoxical announcement that Pope, the poet of order and supposed reason, was actually a goat-like object of fear for the ladies of his day. The following two stanzas sardonically lament the emptiness of Pope's funeral urn. The striking phrase "dribbled couplets like the snake / Coiled to a lithe precision in the sun" seems to point out that Pope's venomous wit was actually natural, and not a product of the artificiality he treasured.

In the final stanza, the impersonal narrator disavows knowledge of Pope's motivation, although the phrase "wit and rage" suggests grim approbation, and the backhanded compliment of the closing line and a half again employs natural metaphors to describe both Pope and his "moral." It is difficult not to think that Tate is alluding to a poem Pope wrote for inscription upon the royal dog collar. "Mr. Pope" uses understatement, allusion, suggestive metaphor, detachment, and wit to review the reputation of Alexander Pope and, in so doing, manifests Allen Tate's claim to kinship with the great poet of the eighteenth century.

Selected Poems (1937) includes the final version of "Ode to the Confederate Dead" as well as "To the Lacedemonians." This latter poem is a dramatic monologue, the embittered fulmination of an aged Confederate veteran who believes the postbellum world has lost the saving vision that animated the conflict. Maimed in combat, the old soldier finds himself dazed by the alien aspect of those around him ("my own people but strange") and the sound of engines, a "dull commotion" that reflects the growth of technology in the years since the South's defeat. He speaks of a secret, then proclaims "gentlemen, my secret is / Damnation . . . ," explaining that now, as he says, "all are born Yankees of the race of men"; in other words, everyone is now a citizen of the United States.

Here, Tate is playing on the theme of the incorrigible oldster whose opinionated tirades reflect intolerance of a deteriorating world, a stock character who dates back to Homer's Nestor. There is a comic dimension to this effusion against modern youth. Grouchy and crippled, the veteran is mentally preparing his discourse for those of his old comrades who yet survive and can be expected to sympathize with his point of view. Although his memory may be failing, he retains the passion of his youth as well as contempt for those who have yielded to such new preoccupations as budgets. This generation, having forsaken the outdoor work of agriculture, wears "the white face / Eyeless with eyesight only," since for them vision is merely a physical rather than a spiritual phenomenon.

Offsetting the mild comicality of this ornery but sympathetic character is the poem's governing allusion, the reference to the Spartan (Lacedemonian) heroes who unhesitatingly sacrificed their lives in obedience to their city's laws. Although the poem's narrator fumbles momentarily when he alludes to the Spartans' epitaph, the juxtaposition of this classical instance of pathetic heroism with the character of the old soldier produces a powerful and unsentimental reminder of the catastrophic dimension of the Civil War.

In "Last Days of Alice," Lewis Carroll's Alice finds herself in old age and unhappily unable to find fulfillment, for in passing through the looking glass she has destroyed her own identity. The final pair of this poem's nine rhymed quatrains points out the moral of this fairy tale without magic. The narrator explains that "we," like Alice, are trapped in a physical, mathematical universe in which there is no escape "back to the world." In the last three lines, the unbelieving narrator waxes desperate enough to pray: "O God of our flesh, return us to Your wrath!" The grimly witty conclusion, which echoes poems by John Donne ("Oh, to vex me, contraries meet in one") and Gerard Manley Hopkins ("Carrion Comfort"), suggests wryly that even divine grace is better than the continued meaninglessness of Wonderland.

Narrated by the hero of Virgil's *Aeneid*, "Aeneas at Washington" personifies the heroic Roman tradition that derived its origins from the destruction of Troy and the construction of the classical civilization whose wisdom made possible the development of a nation of laws in North America. Aeneas, however, is not only "a true gentleman, valorous in arms, / Disinterested and honorable," but he is also an aristocrat who deplores the work of the destructive "many" (Greek *hoi polloi*), and, like a Southern aristocrat betrayed by the Northern interests, he regards the Capitol and sadly declares, "The city my blood had built I knew no more."

Like other poems by Tate that deliberately invoke Virgil, "The Mediterranean" also suggests the affinities between civilized Southerners and the classical tradition. The modified Latin epigraph from the first book of the *Aeneid* is Venus's complaint to Jupiter about the enforced wandering of her son Aeneas, who has yet to focus on his divinely appointed mission of founding Rome. The poem is based on a picnic expedition by Tate, Caroline Gordon, Ford Madox Ford, and friends to a Mediterranean beach, and the Homeric feast gives the American celebrants a visionary sense of identity with their legendary, heroic ancestors. Yet, in the last quatrain, the poem describes a movement westward to the New World, and the final words, "in that land were we born," complete the sense of identification with the destined mission of the migrating Trojans.

"The Swimmers" (*Poems*, 1960), is one of a group of poems Tate wrote after a long period of inactivity. The description here is of the aftermath of a lynching as observed by a young boy. Although Tate's personal conservatism had restrained him from dealing with Southern bigotry to the extent that William Faulkner or Flannery O'Connor did, his position at Minnesota in the years following the various political attempts by Southern politicians from 1948 onward to sideline civil rights reforms must have afforded him occasion for reflection on the behavior of many of his countrymen. Tate had also become a Roman Catholic in 1950, which may have had an effect on his perspective.

"The Swimmers" is a **narrative** from the point of view of a twelve-year-old boy, whose trip to a creek on a hot day is interrupted by the appearance of a posse on its way somewhere. The boy investigates and finds the sheriff by the body of a lynched black man. One of the men helps the sheriff tie the body to a horse, and the body is dragged off to the courthouse square, at which point the boy's perception becomes visionary: "There were three figures in the dying sun / Whose light were company where three was crowd." The boy is frozen by the sight, and at the close of the poem he recognizes the town's responsibility for what has happened.

As in other poems, Tate employs classical allusion here, with details such as "mullein . . . Soft as Nausicaä's palm," and the *terza rima* stanza form echoing that of Dante, but the essential effect of the poem depends upon the fact that the only character who is at all sympathetic is the lynched man, about whom no information is given other than that he has been killed and that his body is treated with contempt. The boy's recognition is morally neutralized by the confused language in which he describes what he sees, but, beyond the boy's narration, is the theme of memory and of the long-developing recognition that has set the poet to work to record the event. This poem forms a group with the poems "The Maimed Man" and "The Buried Lake," all of which were written in *terza rima* in the early 1950s.

Further Readings. ***Primary Sources:*** Tate, Allen, *Collected Poems, 1919–1976* (New York: Farrar, Straus & Giroux, 1977); ———, *Mr. Pope and Other Poems* (New York: Minton, Balch, 1928); ———, *Poems, 1922–1947* (New York: Scribners, 1948); ———, *Poems: 1928–1931* (New York: Scribners, 1932); ———, *Selected Poems* (New York: Scribners, 1937). ***Secondary Sources:*** Bishop, Ferman, *Allen Tate* (New York: Twayne, 1967); Coley, Lem, "Memories and Opinions of Allen Tate" (*Southern Review* [Autumn 1992]: 944–964); Cowan, Louise, *The Fugitive Group: A Literary History* (Baton Rouge: Louisiana State University Press, 1959); Dupree, Robert S., *Allen Tate and the Augustinian Imagination: A Study of the Poetry* (Baton Rouge: Louisiana State University Press, 1983); Malvasi, Mark G., *The Unregenerate South: The Agrarian Thought of John Crowe Ransom, Allen Tate, and Donald Davidson* (Baton Rouge: Louisiana State University Press, 1997); Squires, Radcliffe, ed., *Allen Tate and His Work: Critical Evaluations* (Minneapolis: University of Minnesota Press, 1972); Tate, Allen, *Essays of Four Decades* (Chicago: Swallow, 1968).

Robert W. Haynes

TATE, JAMES (1943–)

James Tate is considered one of the preeminent contemporary American surrealist writers and is the author of over twenty-five books of poetry and fiction. He is the recipient of some of the most prestigious awards in American literature, including the Pulitzer Prize (1991) and the National Book Award (1994). Tate is perhaps best known for his wit, humor, and irony, as well as his unique use of surrealist strategies. Diverging from the surrealism of early French **modernists** and later Latin American surrealists, Tate combines the phantasmagoric with the quotidian and writes a subversive and irreverent poetry that has been called "conversational surrealism." His poetry combines the events and language of everyday life with dream logic, free association, and the juxtaposition of seemingly incongruous images. His often bizarre narratives and oneiric imagery reveal a world where the unconscious mind seems to collide with day-to-day life.

Born in Kansas City, Missouri, in 1943, Tate first gained literary notoriety when, at the age of twenty-three, his first collection, *The Lost Pilot* (1967), was selected by Dudley Fitts for the Yale Series of Younger Poets competition. At the time, he was still a student in the University of Iowa's graduate writing program. The title poem from this book, "The Lost Pilot," offers a brief glimpse into Tate's early biography, since it was dedicated to his father, who was killed while flying a combat mission over Germany when Tate was a baby. However, most of Tate's work resists autobiography and subverts the **confessional** style that was popular in American poetics at the time his writing career began. Therefore, little about his biography has been made public except for his many awards and literary accomplishments. Tate attended the University of Missouri (1963–1964) and received a BA from Kansas State College (1965). He then attended the University of Iowa and, after receiving his MFA in poetry (1967), taught at the University of California–Berkeley (1967–1968) and at Columbia University (1969–1971). Since 1971, he has been a professor at the University of Massachusetts–Amherst.

Following the success and acclaim of his first collection came the publication of *The Oblivion Ha-Ha* (1970) and *Hints to Pilgrims* (1971). In these texts, the poet moves further away from autobiographical impulse and toward comic surrealism, creating a **narrative** spectacle full of both humor and horror, an often zany but unsettling jaunt through what seems to be someone's private and bewildering dreamscape. In the poem, "Dear Reader," from *The Oblivion Ha-Ha*, he writes: "I am trying to pry open your casket / with this burning snowflake" (87). Such psychically revealing imagery is similar to that of the early surrealists, but Tate's work is more preoccupied than theirs with humor and kitsch. The poems submerge the reader in a universe strewn with day-to-day events comingling with grotesque or wickedly funny and impossible occurrences.

Tate's next book, *Hottentot Ossuary* (1974), which is sometimes considered **prose poetry** or short fiction, involves a similar exploration of dream logic. In the poem "Leaping Woman," he writes: "The leaping woman arrives in an ambulance of starlight" with "her foaming team of white Cadillacs" (13). These lines demonstrate Tate's oneiric impulse his macabre sense of metaphor, and his interest in the capacity of language to challenge our perceptions of reality.

Tate frequently submerges ideas about the self and personal identity into a dizzying array of wordplay or bizarre comedic narratives. However, the work retains a sense of urgency that is both sympathetic and horrifying, disturbing and hopeful. In *Viper Jazz* (1976), the poet writes that "dreamy cars graze on the dewy boulevard. / Darkness is more of a feeling inside the drivers." He then observes that "the city is welded together / out of hope and despair" (62). As this example demonstrates, Tate can fluctuate from comic absurdity to profound statements to straightforward candor. Drawing as it does on images of pop culture and contemporary life, the language seems natural and unpretentious.

Tate does not attempt to use symbolism elicit the same reaction in every reader, as did the French surrealists, but he does attempt to excite the irrational element of human experience, thereby disrupting dominant assumptions about reality. This is especially true of his recent collections such as *The Shroud of the Gnome* (1997) and *Memoir of the Hawk* (2001), in which plain, conversational language describes peculiar and freakish events. In the prose poem "Somehow Not Aware That She Was Heaven-Born," he writes about the second coming of a one-eyed beast: "I was just sitting in my chair growing a beard, my brain lit up like a pinball machine and I prayed for order" (69).

Tate's other books of poetry include *Return to the City of White Donkeys* (2004); *Worshipful Company of Fletchers* (1994), which won the National Book Award; *Selected Poems* (1991), which won the Pulitzer Prize and the William Carlos Williams Award; *Distance from Loved Ones* (1990); *Reckoner* (1986); *Constant Defender* (1983); *Riven Doggeries* (1979); and *Absences* (1972). He has also published a novel, *Lucky Darryl* (1977), and a collection of short stories, *Dreams of a Robot Dancing Bee* (2001). His *Selected Poems* includes work from *The Lost Pilot* (1967) to *The Reckoner* (1986) and is considered to include his most significant work through that period.

Further Reading. ***Selected Primary Sources:*** Tate, James, *Hottentot Ossuary* (Cambridge, MA: Temple Bar Press, 1974); ———, *The Oblivion Ha-Ha* (Boston: Atlantic Monthly Press, 1967); ———, *Selected Poems* (Hanover, MA: Wesleyan University Press, 1991); ———, *Viper Jazz* (Hanover, MA: Wesleyan University Press, 1979); ———, *Worshipful Company of Fletchers* (Hopewell, NJ: Ecco Press, 1994). ***Selected Secondary Sources:*** Gioia, Dana, "James Tate and American Surrealism" (*Denver Quarterly* 33.3 [Fall 1998]: 70–80); Harms, James, "Clarity Instead of Order: The Practice of Postmodernism in the Poetry of James Tate" (*Denver Quarterly* 33.3 [Fall 1998]: 81–88); "James Tate" (*Poetry Exhibits,* Academy of American Poets [13 June 2001], www.poets.org).

Mark Tursi

TAYLOR, BAYARD (1825–1878)

Primarily known as a journalist and world traveler by his contemporaries, Bayard Taylor professed poetry to be his highest occupation as a writer. His rise from farmer's son to cosmopolitan litterateur, his knowledge of numerous cultures and peoples from both firsthand experience and scholarly study, and his varied social and professional relationships provided him with a range of subject matter for his poetry matched in the nineteenth century only by **Whitman** and **Melville**.

Taylor's poems range from brief **lyrical** descriptions of the sights encountered during his many journeys abroad to metaphysical speculations cast in dramatic verse plays. **Poe** judged Taylor to be the finest prosodic craftsman in American literature in his time. His verse is notable for the diversity and fluidity of its metrical patterns and rhyme schemes. Although Taylor was honored as the nation's poet laureate at the 1876 Centennial Exposition in Philadelphia, his book-length verse **narratives** and plays published in the 1870s were not popular. Taylor's reputation went through a sharp decline soon after his death, but interest in his writing has revived as readers have recognized Taylor's engagement with male-male sexuality and with global influences on American political and religious cultures.

Ambition and financial need motivated Bayard Taylor to be a prolific writer. His oeuvre includes seventeen volumes of occasional and narrative verse, four novels, eight critical works and translations of German classics, nineteen travel books, and innumerable magazine essays, short stories, and reviews. His success on the public lecture circuit and the popularity of his travel writing made him one of the best-known men of his day. Taylor's diplomatic career enhanced his reputation and influence as a literary interlocutor of foreign places and peoples to an American audience, and included service as a writer for the Perry Expedition to Japan, chargé d'affaires to Russia during the Civil War, and ambassador to Germany in 1878.

Taylor established himself as a writer of note without any of the traditional benefits of college education, inherited family wealth, or government sinecure. Born on January 11, 1825, to Joseph and Rebecca Way Taylor, Taylor entered a world that was remarkable for its stability in the midst of widespread social change. He grew up in Kennett Square, a small village thirty-five miles northwest of Philadelphia, surrounded by neighbors belonging to the Society of Friends. Although marrying a German non-Quaker had caused his paternal grandfather to be read out of the local Quaker meeting house, and none of the family ever rejoined the sect, the habits of the Taylor family were strongly influenced by the surrounding Quaker community. Living in the midst of a conformist community with which he and his family were not entirely in sympathy affected Taylor's sense of himself as one set apart from the common lot of a farmer's sons. Taylor's wanderlust mirrored the social mobility that characterized American life in the Jacksonian era. If Taylor's sense of separation drove him out of Kennett Square into the world, it just as inexorably drew him back. When he finally earned enough money to build Cedarcroft, his long-dreamed-of family estate, he chose to build it in Kennett Square. Several of Taylor's most powerful poems, such as "The Quaker Widow" and "The Old Pennsylvania Farmer," drew on his familiarity with Quaker community life and used it as a microcosm to express the poet's alternating sense of bewilderment, resignation, and serenity in the face of rapid social change.

Taylor escaped farm life at age seventeen when he apprenticed himself to the printer of the *West Chester Register*. Although his restless spirit led him to buy out his contract after only two years, Taylor gained important knowledge of the publishing trade and popular tastes during this time. The money to buy out his apprenticeship came from the proceeds of his first book of poetry, *Ximena: or The Battle of the Sierra Morena* (1844). "Ximena," the title poem of the collection, is set in southern Spain during the Crusades, and its dependence on chivalric ideals and foreign settings made it an ideal vehicle for Taylor's introduction into the mid-nineteenth–century literary world. Taylor parlayed the modest success of this volume (sold by subscription) and the literary connections he had developed with Rufus Griswold, editor of *Graham's Magazine*, into a long-cherished dream of traveling to Europe. With one hundred dollars in advances from two different periodicals and a vague promise from Horace Greeley to purchase additional letters, Taylor embarked in 1844 on a two-year tour that made his career as a writer. Often penniless and reduced to scraps and the kindness of strangers, Taylor paid his way primarily by the labor of his pen, submitting regular travel letters to the *New York Tribune*, the *Saturday Evening Post*, and the *United States Gazette*. The book that resulted from this journey, *Views Afoot, or Europe Seen With Knapsack and Staff* (1846), catapulted Taylor into minor literary fame at the age of twenty-one. The book went through nine editions in the first year of its publication, and it established Taylor as the center of a New York literary circle that included poets such as R.H. Stoddard, **George Boker**, and **E.C. Stedman**.

Poems of the Orient (1854), the most celebrated and bestselling of Taylor's seventeen volumes of poetry, was published close on the heels of his well-received triptych of foreign travel narratives set in the Middle East, Africa, and Asia. Poems such as "The Temptation of Hassan Ben Khaled" treat readers to exotic depictions of Islamic society while simultaneously identifying the poet with the physical and spiritual yearnings experienced by his Muslim characters. In "L'Envoi," Taylor claims that his Eastern experiences enabled him to find "the cipher of my nature—the release / Of baffled powers, which else had never won / That free fulfillment, whose reward is peace." This "release" was both the physical restoration that resulted from the journey and the aesthetic license it afforded him for a passionate expression of sensuality in his verse.

The best-known poems in this collection include "Bedouin Song," "Hassan to His Mare," and "To a Persian Boy." These poems contain elements of sublimated passion and male-male sexuality, extending themes Taylor first explored in his magazine verse. One such poem, "Hylas" (1850), has been identified by Robert K. Martin as an important contribution to the tradition of **gay poetry** in the United States. In 154 lines of iambic pentameter, Taylor relates the death by drowning of Heracles's squire and lover, Hylas. Taylor dedicates fully half of the poem to a detailed and nearly lascivious description of Hylas's body: "Naked, save one light robe that from his shoulder / Hung to his knee, the youthful flush revealing / Of warm, white limbs, half-nerved with coming manhood, / Yet fair and smooth with tenderness of beauty." The presence of intense sensuality and intimations of homoerotic love, albeit in a poem with obvious Tennysonian influences and a traditional form, remind one of those elements in Whitman's verse that elicited charges of crudity from some readers. Taylor's relative freedom to explore human sexuality within accepted poetic forms distinguishes him among mid-nineteenth–century American poets publishing in mainstream magazines like *Grahams* and the *Atlantic Monthly*.

In 1855 Taylor collected his published works into *Poems of Home and Travel*. The earlier poems included in the collection were mostly landscape descriptions written while "afoot" in Europe. Other poems, such as his extremely successful California ballads, were fictional creations that he had published before an 1849 journey to California, despite Taylor's claim in print that the poems were authentic descriptions of California life. "The Fight of Paso Del Mar" is typical of these poems in its use of Spanish names and words as the principal means of establishing its California setting. In the poem, "Stout Pablo of San Diego" encounters "Bernal, the herdsman of Chino," who is going the opposite direction on a narrow cliff-side path. Both men prove to be so hotheaded and violent that, grappling desperately on the slippery path, they fall off the cliff together.

> A cry of the wildest death-anguish
> Rang faint through the mist afar,
> And the riderless mule went homeward
> From the fight of the Paso del Mar.

In addition to its romantic depiction of passionate conflict, the poem contributes to a convenient fantasy of the "Vanishing Californian," in the same vein as much American writing about Native Americans at that time.

By 1865, having published nearly twenty books of poetry, travel, and fiction, Taylor felt ready to attempt projects of greater seriousness and sustained thought, including book-length narrative poems, verse dramas, and masques. His first longer work, *The Poet's Journal* (1865), is a pastiche of lyric snapshots woven by means of lengthy verse passages into an autobiographical narrative of the poet's journey from grieving widower to husband in a second marriage. *The Picture of St. John* (1866), a poem of 2,840 lines written in *ottava rima*, concerns the wisdom gained by an artist through the difficult circumstances of his life. Taylor used the poem to explore the ways that tragedy and beauty could contribute to an artist's aesthetic development. In *Lars: A Pastoral of Norway* (1873), Taylor drew on his familiarity with Quaker beliefs and customs to craft a quaint love story that hinges on the doctrine of pacifism.

Taylor's greatest scholarly achievement was the **translation** of Goethe's *Faust* in its original meters (*Part 1* in 1870; *Part 2* in 1871). Translating *Faust* was an ideal task for a poet with Taylor's formidable technical skills, and it served as the standard American translation for nearly eighty years. The three major poetic works that Taylor produced after his immersion in Goethe—*The Masque of the Gods* (1872), *The Prophet* (1874), and *Prince Deukalion* (1878)—represent his attempt to extend the force of Goethe's Romantic genius to an American context. All three books are **verse dramas**, none of which were intended for the stage.

David Starr, the protagonist of *The Prophet*, is loosely modeled on Joseph Smith, the founder of Mormonism, but the force of Taylor's theological and sociological critique of Starr's sect was directed at the conservative Christian groups that opposed the metaphysical vision espoused in the other two dramas. In *The Masque of the Gods*, a pantheon of ancient gods from diverse cultures bewail their abandonment and question the validity of their individual claims to divine supremacy. The poem integrates Taylor's experiences as a traveler and observer of non-Western cultures and religions with a critique of the spiritual aridity he observed in the urbanized and industrialized cities of the United States. It ends with a chorus of spirits that celebrates the triumph of men over their anthropomorphic gods: "They have conquered the phantoms themselves created; / They have torn the masks from the gods aforetime, / To find the mock of the face of Man." (*See also* **Religon and Poetry**.)

Prince Deukalion presents a more affirmative vision of humanity's relationship with the Divine. The four acts of the play follow Deukalion and Pandora on a Faustian quest through four stages of human history: the ancient world, medieval Europe, industrialized Europe, and an unknown future. Deukalion and Pandora serve as the personifications of humanity's romantic and spiritual longings. Their quest for divinity is consummated in an agnostic vision of immortality that is "proven by its need":

By fates so large no fortune can fulfil;
By wrong no earthly justice can atone;
By promises of love that keep love pure;
And all rich instincts, powerless of aim,
Save chance, and time, and aspiration wed
To freer forces, follow!

In few other passages of Taylor's work can the relationship between genteel idealism and industrial abjection be seen this clearly. The powerlessness and alienation experienced by those who lack "fortune" and "justice" demands, in Taylor's mind, a religious consolation.

By the time of his death in 1878, Taylor had amassed a formidable literary heritage, buttressed in part by his network of professional and personal connections in the worlds of literary publishing and reviewing. His friends remembered him as a witty and urbane world traveler, and he was eulogized by the likes of **John Greenleaf Whittier** and **Henry Wadsworth Longfellow**. Taylor had been warmly embraced by the older generation of New England poets as a literary heir apparent, but their long tenure overshadowed Taylor during his lifetime. His untimely death gave greater emphasis to the proof of immortality offered in *Prince Deukalion*: "The trust / Of the chilled Good that at life's very end / Puts forth a root, and feels its blossom sure!"

Further Reading. ***Selected Primary Sources:*** Taylor, Bayard, *The Dramatic Works of Bayard Taylor* (Boston: Houghton Mifflin, 1880); ———, *The Poetical Works of Bayard Taylor* (Boston: Houghton Mifflin, 1880). ***Selected Secondary Sources:*** Martin, Robert, *The Homosexual Tradition in American Poetry* (Iowa City: University of Iowa Press, 1998); Smyth, Alfred, *Bayard Taylor* (Boston: Houghton Mifflin, 1896); Wermuth, Paul, *Bayard Taylor* (New York: Twayne, 1973).

Liam Corley

TAYLOR, EDWARD (CA. 1642–1729)

Edward Taylor is the most accomplished poet of the American colonial period. Unpublished until the 1930s, his poetry interests readers less for its expression of expected Calvinist beliefs than for its unexpected Renaissance sensibility combined with a Reformed religious point of view.

Probably born in the farming community of Sketchley, Leicestershire, England, Taylor was educated as a religious nonconformist. His earliest verse, including a dialogue on maypoles and a defense of Protestants accused of setting the London fire of 1666, indicate his fervid rejection of both Anglican and Roman Catholic beliefs. It is likely, however, that during the early years of the Restoration of King Charles II, Taylor attended Cambridge University, where he encountered rich cultural material that would later contribute to his poetic meditations. In response to a loss of employment as a result of measures designed by the King to persecute nonconformist believers, Taylor became an émigré who settled in Massachusetts Bay in 1668.

He graduated with a BA from Harvard College in 1671, the same year he accepted an invitation to serve as the Congregational minister and physician in Westfield, Massachusetts. While serving this frontier settlement in the western part of the state, he raised a family with Elizabeth Fitch of Norwich, whom he had courted in verse and then married in 1674. Three years after the death of his wife in 1689, he married Ruth Wyllys of Hartford.

Early in his Westfield ministry Taylor felt discontented because of the distance from the cultural milieu of Boston, especially Harvard. But he came to accept his frontier calling as divine will and also managed to participate in the intellectual issues of his day by maintaining correspondence with such East Coast figures as Increase Mather and **Samuel Sewall**. He read books given or loaned to him by such friends, copied extensive passages from borrowed books, and by the end of his life possessed a library consisting of at least two hundred works. In what might be described as "sermon wars," he participated in heated religious controversies, particularly concerning the liberal interpretation of the church sacraments advanced by Solomon Stoddard (1643–1729). During the last four years of his life, Taylor was very ill and benefited from the ministerial assistance of Nehemiah Bull. He died and was buried in Westfield in 1729.

Ranging from the four **elegies** written as a Harvard student to "Verses on Pope Joan" written late in life, Taylor's writings remained in manuscript during his lifetime. Although his sermons appear to have been prepared for the press and his poetic meditations were carefully revised and hand-bound, only stanzas five and seven of his "Upon Wedlock and Death of Children," which **Cotton Mather** included in *Right Thoughts in Sad Hours* (1689), ever appeared in print during his lifetime. Had Taylor stayed in Boston, his many writings, possibly even his potentially controversial meditations, doubtless would have been published. His corpus includes eight sermons written about 1694 in reply to Solomon Stoddard (published in 1965 as *Edward Taylor's Treatise Concerning the Lord's Supper*), thirty-six sermons written between 1693 and 1706 on typology (published in 1989 as *Edward Taylor's Upon the Types of the Old Testament*), fourteen sermons written between 1701 and 1703 on the nature of Christ (published in 1962 as *Edward Taylor's Christographia*), and various other writings spanning his lifetime (collected in 1981 as *The Unpublished Writings of Edward Taylor* and in 1982 in *Edward Taylor's Harmony of the Gospels*). These sermons, conforming to the Ramist formula of discourse Taylor learned at Harvard, frequently identify the specific occasions for select poetic mediations, and comprise a valuable resource for identifying the ideas and **biblical** imagery found in his poetry.

Not much of Taylor's early poetry would likely have seen print. His English nonconformist verse, his Harvard elegies on Richard Mather and others, and his Westfield love letters in verse offer little of artistic interest. Many of his later poems, such as "The Great Bones Dug Up at Clavarack" and "The Metrical History of Christianity," remain unfinished. His thirty-eight paraphrases of the Psalms, which follow the metrical patterns of the earlier Sternhold-Hopkins Psalter, suggest Taylor's particular interest in this Old Testament book. The characteristic psalm sequence—from lament, to supplication, to thanksgiving—possibly served as a general structural model for Taylor's later poetic meditations. Taylor's verse paraphrases of the book of Job are even more extensive, perhaps an indication of his enduring interest in the theatrical properties of drama.

A theatrical poem that Taylor almost certainly intended for a public audience is *God's Determinations Touching His Elect*, a lengthy doctrinal work composed around 1682. Critics have reasonably speculated that this poem was written to encourage baptized members of the Westfield parish to consider full communion in their church. The poem personifies severe Justice and compassionate Mercy, and it also dramatizes the contest between sophistic Satan and wise Christ for the souls of sinners, who are represented in various states of emotional turmoil over their elect or damned spiritual status. Paradoxes pertaining to the intertwining of doubt and faith contribute to the drama of the poem, especially whenever Satan's wiles advance rather than impede the divine scheme for creation. Besides morality and English Renaissance plays, other influences upon *Gods Determinations* might include debate paradigms, Theocritan song contests, Ignatian meditative practices, and homiletic tradition.

Although neither the structure nor the varied style of *Gods Determinations* is well understood, its long sequence of parts does exhibit unifying motifs. One notable instance occurs in the poet's reference to a pair of jawbones, an image that schematizes the overall pattern of the poem. The upper jaw represents Christ (mercy and the Gospel), while the lower part of the jaw represents Satan (justice and the law). The elect and the damned alike find themselves inside these jaws, and, in effect, they are divinely chewed as they incline emotionally both upward in hope and downward in despair during the course of their lives. Only the elect survive this divine mastication, but Taylor's point is that the elect never know of their redeemed status until the end of their lives. So, the poet urges, those in the church who exhibit any of the positive signs of salvation dramatized in *Gods Determinations* should present themselves for full church membership.

Several miscellaneous poems, probably written between 1674 and 1689, interpret natural events as a school in which the divine teacher instructs humanity. "Upon a Spider Catching a Fly" allegorizes how easily the fly-like, obtuse Christian falls victim to the spider-like devil, while "Upon a Wasp Child with Cold" draws spiritual support from observing the sun-influenced recovery of a nearly frozen insect. "Upon a Sweeping Flood" (1683) discerns an expression of divine displeasure in the consequences of a storm. Tidal movements provide an apt image for the soul's emotional fluctuation between despair and hope in "The Ebb & Flow." "Huswifry" extends the metaphor of the spinning wheel to depict how the redemptive destiny of the elect is divinely woven.

During this time, as throughout his adult life, Taylor wrote elegies. "Upon Wedlock, & Death of Children" (1683), including an extended metaphor based on garden flowers, responds to the death of two of his children from his first marriage. The poet admits that the six-weeks-long "[v]omit, Screechings, groans" of one of the dying children aroused feelings in him that almost made him berate the Creator. Instead, he accepts divine will: "Take, Lord, they're thine. / I piecemeale pass to Glory bright in them." The painful loss of his thirty-nine-year-old first wife six years later (July 7, 1689) is memorialized in "A Funerall Poem," in which the poet apologizes to God for shedding "a Tear, or two" at her grave. In this poignant elegy, recalling as well the deaths of five of his eight children, the poet cherishes detailed memories of his spouse.

Taylor's reputation as the most outstanding colonial American poet derives from *Preparatory Meditations before My Approach to the Lord's Supper*, a manuscript introduced by Thomas H. Johnson in 1937 and fully transcribed by Donald E. Standford in 1960. Begun in 1682, this series of over two hundred poems was written mostly in conjunction with the poet's scheduled sermons on the nature of Christ, the sacrament of the Lord's Supper, and the prophetic fulfillment of biblical typology, among other religious subjects. Influenced by the meditative traditions of the sixteenth and seventeenth centuries, these **devotional poems** aided the poet in preparing himself for the Lord's Supper, the more sacred of the two Puritan sacraments. Evidence also suggests, however, that Taylor revised and recast several of these poems on later occasions.

From the 1930s to the present, these poems have puzzled readers. They are difficult to read. Their language often includes words and meanings long forgotten, their sequencing of thought and image is highly elliptical, and their collage of biblical and cultural allusions denies easy access. To some extent, especially whenever they echo George Herbert's poetry, Taylor's verse meditations recall the tradition of obscurity, rough verse, and extravagant imagery associated with seventeenth-century English metaphysical poetry (*see* **British Poetry**). But whereas this late-Renaissance verse tradition featured a protean sense of identity, Taylor's poetry evinces a carefully controlled and Puritan-defined aesthetics of imperfection.

Taylor apparently reveled in a self-portrait of poetic incompetence, a point established in his "Prologue." There he asks whether a crumb-of-dust poet can be relevant to the resplendent divine scheme of things when, at his best, all the author can do is "hand a Pen whose moysture doth guild ore / Eternall Glory with a glorious glore." The disagreeable word "glore" conveys exactly the poet's situation. Taylor represents himself as disabled by sin-engendered ineptitude, which results in the utterance of an unattractive word while he futilely tries to celebrate divine glory. The best he can do is get it half right, achieving the "glore" part of "glory" without attaining an aesthetically pleasing ending.

Taylor's use of "glore" may playfully represent the pitiful best of a poet besotted by his fallen condition, but it also remains as potentially redeemable as does the sinful author. Only divine intervention is needed, since the hand of the Master Artist can change the position of a poet's word or a poet's soul, and hence make manifest its latent capacities. "Glore," in other words, could be redemptively repositioned by the Deity so that its silent final "e" would suddenly resound. This potentiality inheres in the fallen state represented by the ill-sounding word because, in pre-standardized English, "glory" may alternately be spelled "glorie," "glori" and even "glore." So, the use of "glore" is designed to underscore the need for a divine positioning of the poet into a better place in the redemptive rhyme scheme. Then the poet's words would meet the obligation to celebrate "Eternall Glory." Taylor consciously practiced a Puritan decorum of imperfection—an observance of various biblical injunctions pertaining to artistic representation and, as well, an awareness of the fallen self's incompetence when undertaking any creative act, particularly in relation to the Deity. This carefully managed form of imperfection amounts to a paradox similar to that of Taylor's technique in *Gods Determinations.* In this case, the poet's voice paradoxically achieves an assertive identity through its self-humiliation.

Such an understanding of Taylor's practice revises early critical observations about the stylistic features of his verse. Much of the linguistic awkwardness in his meditations is the product of artistic intention rather than ineptitude. In "Meditation 1.8" (1684), for example, the poet writes: "Which Bread of Life from Heaven down came and stands / Disht on thy Table up by Angells Hands." The syntax here, highlighted by oddly positioned prepositions, is indeed inelegant. The predominating metrical iambs (an unstressed syllable followed by a stressed syllable) are marred by the need to elide the two syllables of "Heaven," by the reverse trochaic stress of "Disht on," and by the uncommon conjunction of the two prepositions "up by" (neither of which would be stressed in normal oral syntax). These prosodic effects are not accidents. They are, instead, designed like character-revealing lines delivered by a player in a stage production. The lines from "Meditation 1.8" dramatize the speaker's precedent point: being unable to reason or to sing well because of the wracking pangs of his spiritually famished soul.

The exuberant metaphors featured in the *Meditations* have also led to critical suspicions that Taylor was not properly Puritan, that he was either consciously or unwittingly sympathetic to Anglican sources and Roman Catholic culture. The poet does value Renaissance ideas considerably more than is customary in his Puritan milieu at the end of the seventeenth century. On the other hand, his Puritan world was more pluralistic than is commonly appreciated today. Especially concerning the Lord's Supper, the usual occasion for Taylor's meditations, Puritans enjoyed a deep sacramental awareness of the connection between the material and the spiritual world. Such liturgical objects as the communion cup suggested symbolic implications that enabled the Puritan believer to visualize Christ's spiritual presence without crossing into idolatry. In the light of such Reformed practice, the sacramental intensity of Taylor's imagery seems less radical.

There is no question that the Calvinistic theology and meditative disposition expressed in these poems are orthodox. A strong Augustinian current runs throughout Taylor's meditations. These poems emphasize predestination and election—the insistence that God alone determines the fate of each soul. Taylor may playfully represent himself as a wheedling or finagling character who tries to manipulate his Maker's decision concerning the speaker, but his poems end with only a hope of election, a proper disposition concerning his own salvation rather than a presumptuous assurance of it. His poems acknowledge a supply-side divine economy, in which the Deity controls all the spiritual resources, predetermines who will be the fortunate beneficiaries, and then dispenses saving grace only to those elect individuals.

Taylor is also orthodox in his use of typology, the study of the prophetic relationships between Old Testament and New Testament people and events. In the late *Meditations*, which are focused on the Song of Songs, the poet inclines toward an allegorical disposition that more readily applies biblical types to the present world. In these instances, the image of the pleading saint appears to be more personally included in the typological scheme. For the most part, however, Taylor seems to have preferred a conservative understanding of typology, according to which Christ is the sole fulfillment of the Old Testament types. In the earlier *Meditations*, then, humanity (represented by the poet's voice) is outside this closed scheme, at least in terms of traditional biblical commentary.

Taylor can be clever, however, when depicting a biblical scene. Often he will apply another feature of Renaissance biblical exegesis, which customarily included brief observations on specific small objects mentioned in Scripture (such as Mary Magdalene's alabaster box). The emphasis on small details that can take on surprisingly significant roles is also an element of Renaissance painting, another factor in Taylor's English cultural inheritance. When Taylor depicts a typological scene, he visualizes a rich array of surrounding detail that plays a minor, almost insignificant, role in the central action of the story—debris floating around Noah's ark ("Meditation 2.29" [1698]) or a coal burning in an altar ("Meditation 2.83" [1708]). However, for the self-deprecating poet, these seemingly small objects provide possible points of identification, a way for him to be peripherally included (imaginatively, not presumptively) in the redemptive typological picture.

"Meditation 2.23" (1697), for example, features Aaron, the first Israelite high priest, participating in a ritual sacrifice. He is well prepared and richly attired, in contrast to Taylor's self-described sorry state as he anticipates administering the Lord's Supper. Since the Aaron-type is fully completed by Christ, the last high priest, the poet (unlike George Herbert in "Aaron') cannot identify with this Old Testament figure. Instead, he focuses on details in the biblical scene, including the vessels used by Aaron to collect the sacrificial blood. The poet cherishes such peripheral yet necessary accessories because they are minor types not exhausted by Christ. It is possible, then, that such minor typical instruments of divine service might apply to him. He does not claim the vessel Aaron uses to catch the sacrificial blood, but he hopes that it might prophetically type his own role in life: "Lord let my Soule the Vessell be of thine."

As this poem implies, the biblical commentaries of Taylor's day are crucial to understanding his *Meditations*. These same exegetical traditions enable the reader to find a greater coherence in his verse, which seems on its surface to cascade haphazardly from image to image. This exegetical context, for instance, makes clear the otherwise unperceived connection between the poet's own writings and the biblical type of burnt offerings in "Meditation 2.25" (1698). The contexts for Taylor's verse, however, are extraordinarily extensive, including Christianity, Renaissance art, science, history, medicine, folklore, economics, agriculture, and domestic life. Beneath the seeming hodgepodge of images in "Meditation 2.61" (1704), for example, biblical types and Paracelsian medical theory combine to suggest the compatibility of religion and science. A similar compatibility between typology and astronomy emerges in "Meditation 2.10" (1694) and "Meditation 2.21" (1697). Scientific and folkloristic herbalism coalesce in "Meditation 2.62" (1704), which exhibits a thrice-reiterated progression from purgation, through improving health, and finally to regeneration.

The sense of "Meditation 2.3" (1693) is characteristically difficult to discern beneath its seemingly out-of-control proliferation of unrelated images, but this is a particularly interesting poem. This meditation, in particular, demonstrates a very original application of emblem tradition—the use of images to visualize moral truths. In this case, the poet reads the dire topography of his own aging face—hardly an exercise in narcissism. This self-portrait of the poet in his early fifties reveals hair once blond and now "hoared" with gray, cheeks once apple-red and now ashen-pale beneath a weedy beard, and skin once healthy and now afflicted by splotches of depigmentation, a "Leprosie of Sin." In this poem, the author's entire face becomes an emblematic *memento mori*, a sobering reminder of death.

The seemingly free-associative manner of Taylor's *Meditations* is always deceptive. It is a feature of the poet's decorum of imperfection—a self-humiliating demonstration of post-fall incompetence in comparison to divine majesty. The poet's self-characterization as someone vying desperately against the odds to control his art is actually a well-intentioned act designed to draw God's attention. The poet hopes that the Deity will see through such humorous awkwardness and detect certain worthwhile and redeemable potentialities deep within his soul (imprinted by the image of God). Read closely and contextually, the *Meditations* reveal underlying patterns that impart organizational sense to the abrupt transitions and the proliferation of images. These underlying patterns, such as the poet's reliance on the emblematic circle, are divinely ordained principles of order, and, as such, they give the poet hope concerning the Creator's disposition toward him.

The typological poems of *Preparatory Meditations* are found in the Second Series, which Taylor began in 1693 and continued until 1725. Why the poet abruptly started a new series is unclear, but there are significant differences between the two units. The turn to typology in the second series corresponds to a greater restraint in the poet's creativity than is found in the First Series (1682–1692). Although Taylor's creativity is manifest throughout the Second Series, its imaginative reach is somewhat inhibited by the demands of typology and its biblical commentary. The poet's need to include the many doctrinal details of whatever type is being used decreases the overall aesthetic range and resonance of the Second Series meditations.

In contrast, the First Series, which remains much closer to Taylor's Renaissance heritage even as it conforms to

Reformed dogma, contains his best poetry. In their use of strategic details, these early poems are as indebted as the later ones to Renaissance illustration, but they surpass the typological meditations in their management of narrative voice. Because of Puritan hostility toward the theater, it is easy to overlook the relationship between Taylor's theatrical self-representations and Renaissance drama. As his theater-inspired meditations and *Gods Determinations* suggest, the poet reveals knowledge of and deep engagement with late-Renaissance stage performance. Taylor doubtless had some contact with the theater when he was a student in Restoration England. Besides viewing popular secular stage works, he might also have encountered Renaissance-influenced English Calvinistic plays that situated their audience in various narrative positions. The English metaphysical verse that influenced his use of imagery and nuance would likewise have provided a late-Renaissance model for the dramatic voicing of subjective points of view. Puritan culture, moreover, encouraged dramatic presentations of personal testaments of faith, both private and public.

The First Series is particularly noteworthy for its various narrators, each of whom enacts Reformed versions of otherwise proscribed theatrical models. Each of these poems represents the poet in the guise of some character (persona), whose performance recalls the soliloquies of Elizabethan drama. These narrators are maladroit, if well-intentioned, sinners, who have failed at the trade or profession that defines them. Their rambling apologies expressed in seemingly indiscriminate imagery exhibit habits of mind (such as a mercenary disposition) beyond their own awareness. As with the speech of stage comedy characters, the First Series soliloquies are often humorously undercutting in ways not perceived by their speakers. Taylor, of course, controls such humorous effects, which finally are self-deprecatingly aimed at the **Puritan poet** behind the invented voice.

"Meditation 1.8" (1684) opens with a stargazer meditating on the night sky. The celestial bodies are a beautiful yet also depressing sight to him; they suggest a Creator who can be known only secondhand through the reflected light of nature and the Bible. These positive and negative feelings run through the poem in a dizzying array of imagery, suggesting the narrator's confused state of mind and the paradoxical inversions associated with Christ's redemption. Unknown to the narrator, an implicit emblematic circle (symbol for divine wholeness) organizes his seemingly unrelated series of semi-circle images as he speaks of the horizon as a bird-cage, an empty barrel, God's bowel, leavened dough, and an overturned crystal bowl.

A frightened prostitute is suddenly awakened by a knock on her door in "Meditation 1.12" (1685). She furtively peeks from behind the curtains of her shuttered windows—her eyes—and wonders whether the law or a client is looking for her. She knows she has a "pimping" heart, but she says she cannot change. While observing the unidentified figure's signs of wealth, she fantasizes that he could be a lover who might rescue her from her fallen state. She would like to love him, but something inside her would have to be changed first (justification by God). Her soliloquy ends in uncertainty: will the visitor greet her with a legal blow (divine justice) or a spousal kiss (divine mercy)?

The narrator in "Meditation 1.15" (1685) is drawn from seventeenth-century crime literature. Although this speaker once was heir to an ancestral estate (Eden), he was born poor (unjustified) and has already been legally sentenced for an ancestral capital offence (Adam's fall). He confesses that he is a hardened criminal, a repeat offender who has been imprisoned for failure to pay his many debts (sins). He has been sentenced to a penal colony (life on earth). Consistent with his disposition and situation, his inadvertently humorous language reveals that even as he asks for forgiveness, he fixates primarily on the signs of this Lord's wealth. The poem ends ambiguously: Does the debtor's final bold entreaty for one of his Lord's gems suggest a progression to higher spiritual affections or a regression to a lower preference for material things?

"Meditation 1.19" (1686) opens at dusk with the narrator staring into a freshly dug grave. He is a pale-faced gravedigger (as is every sinner), who refers to the deceased as a "glorious Sun, what whilom shone so bright." It is easy for the narrator to read the grave as a *memento mori*, but in the lost light (the fallen state) he also imagines, at the bottom of this hole, "Devills, Crowding men to Hell" through the mouth of the Revelations dragon. The emblematic image of the pit recurs in the gravedigger's seemingly disordered soliloquy, which also indicates (perhaps more than the speaker knows) that just as the sun that sets rises again, so, too, buried elected suns/sons are resurrected from the grave. (*See also* **Graveyard Poetry**.)

The unwittingly hilarious narrator in "Meditation 1.28" (1688) is a drunken sea captain who confesses his failure to discharge his duty. Instead of sending his homeland Lord a proper bounty (praise) from the narrator's colonial outpost, he has only "[b]its of Glory packt in Shreds of Praise" (meaning this awkwardly written letter-poem). He complains of bad weather as the reason, but when he suggests that his Lord send an intoxicant so he can "drinke thy Health," he inadvertently reveals another, more personal reason for his derelict performance. As he imagines the arrival of this gifted drink (grace), the narrator's confusing sequence of images intensifies, as if he gets increasingly drunk on the very idea of his cup overflowing with such an intoxicating largesse.

A medieval crusader speaks in "Meditation 1.30" (1688), a poem that refers to such Roman Catholic matter as the knights of Christ, the martyr's crown, and the sign of the cross. Describing his body as a ruined ship, the crusader laments his inability to join his Lord in holy war (the Reformation). Asking to be re-outfitted—to bear the Lord's sign (election)—he promises to manage his equipment better than he has done so far. The poem ends with a fantasy of waging a final war at his Lord's side.

The discordant appeal of "Meditation 1.39" (1690) dramatizes a disoriented narrator stricken by illness (the fallen state). He vomits at the opening of the poem, and then explains why he has not been able to discharge his duty of looking after his lord's flock (his affections). He needs Christ the physician to cure him, Christ the advocate to plead his case for the damage done by uncared-for animals, and Christ the carpenter to fix once and for all the barn of his body. And, with a theatrical naiveté typical of Series One narrators, he hopes to secure all of this divine service on a mere promise to do better, sealed by a gentleman's handshake. The creative brio of this poem and the other First Series meditations has no match in colonial American poetry.

Further Reading. ***Selected Primary Sources:*** Taylor, Edward, *Edward Taylor's Gods Determinations and Preparatory Meditations,* ed. Daniel Patterson (Kent, OH: Kent State University Press, 2003); ———, *Edward Taylor's Minor Poetry,* ed. Thomas M. and Virginia L. Davis (Boston: Twayne, 1981); ———, *The Poems of Edward Taylor,* ed. Donald E. Stanford (New Haven: Yale University Press, 1960). ***Selected Secondary Sources:*** Davis, Thomas M., *A Reading of Edward Taylor* (Newark, University of Delaware Press, 1992); Gatta, John, Jr., *The Meditative Wit of Edward Taylor* (Columbia: University of Missouri Press, 1989); Grabo, Norman S., *Edward Taylor* (Boston: Twayne, 1988); Hammond, Jeffrey A., *Edward Taylor: Fifty Years of Scholarship and Criticism* (Columbia, SC: Camden House, 1993); Keller, Karl, *The Example of Edward Taylor* (Amherst: University of Massachusetts Press, 1975); Rowe, Karen E., *Saint and Singer: Edward Taylor's Typology and the Poetics of Meditation* (Cambridge: Cambridge University Press, 1986); Scheick, William J., *The Will and the Word: The Poetry of Edward Taylor* (Athens: University of Georgia Press, 1974).

William J. Scheick

TEASDALE, SARA (1884–1933)

Sara Teasdale was fortunately "cursed" to be born to middle-aged parents; as their last child, she had three older siblings aged twenty, seventeen, and fifteen to nurture and shelter her as she grew up. As an adult, Teasdale was frequently frustrated by an inability to re-create the youth she missed under their watchful eyes. Teasdale's poetic gift was recognized early at Hosmer Hall, a "young ladies' academy," when one of her poems was published in a local religious paper, much to her parents' surprise. From this first publication, Teasdale went on to publish seven collections of original poems and to edit two **anthologies**. Teasdale achieved vast critical and popular success in her own time, a success that made it possible for other women poets to succeed; unfortunately, Teasdale is often overlooked today for inclusion in major anthologies.

Sara Teasdale was born August 4,1884, in St. Louis to the well-off John Warren Teasdale and Mary Elizabeth Willard, who were both in their forties. After graduation from Hosmer Hall in 1902, Teasdale joined a group known as the Potters. The eight women in this group had both artistic and scientific interests. As a member of the Potters, Teasdale explored innovative ideas, read about new views and people, and gained leadership skills that would serve her later in her career. The Potters produced a monthly magazine, called the *Potters Wheel,* completely by hand, including poetry, drawings, and articles, challenging the imposed norms of society and the stereotypical roles women were expected to play. Teasdale's contributions to the *Potters Wheel* led to her being noticed by William Marion Reedy, a leader in American journalism, who published Teasdale's "Guenevere" in the May 30, 1907, issue of his *Reedy's Mirror.* Supported by the attention of a wider audience and more approval, Teasdale compiled her first volume of poems, *Sonnets to Duse and Other Poems* (Poet Lore, 1907), a tribute to the actress Eleanora Duse. Even though this collection was available in limited distribution, Teasdale was daring enough to send a copy to the renowned English critic Arthur Symons, who responded with a favorable notice in the *Saturday Review.* This positive review cemented Teasdale's belief in her choice of vocation; with her poor health in mind, she created a regime to complement her work, with time for rest, writing, and visits with friends.

Teasdale's popularity grew between 1908 and 1910, as did the market for poetry prior to World War I. Teasdale was published in *Putnam's, Harper's,* and *Scribner's,* helping her become nationally known. New York called her to join its literary circle, and she was nominated for the Poetry Society of America. Her next collection, *Helen of Troy and Other Poems* (Putnam's, 1911), earned her additional acclaim. The collection begins with monologues concerning love as "spoken" by Helen, Beatrice, and Sappho. Different phases of woman's love are dramatized in the monologues with an intensity that gained Teasdale recognition as a new Romanticist. While spending time with her widening circle of New York friends, she met John Hall Wheelock for the first time, although she had earlier begun a friendship with him through letters, a practice she often followed. Throughout her life, Wheelock remained her friend and unofficial advisor. Later, she commented that the man she married was similar to Wheelock in appearance, spirit, and understanding.

Another important poet, **Vachel Lindsay,** came into Teasdale's life in 1914. Teasdale had admired Lindsay's poetry and had written him to say so. After a failed attempt by **Harriet Monroe** to arrange a meeting during a brief visit by Teasdale to Chicago, Lindsay called on her at her parents' home in St. Louis. Lindsay beagn to fall in love with Teasdale, whom he saw as an Elizabeth Barrett Browning look-alike with himself in the role of Robert Browning. Teasdale knew from the start that the love and passion Lindsay was offering her had a depth she had not encountered before. Vachel Lindsay had forsaken all the safety and security of family in order to find inspiration for his poetry, traveling and doing odd jobs so that he could be free to explore and seek insight about life. Teasdale's sheltered upbringing did not allow her to encourage Lindsay as a suitor; however, she found his need for her affection and the adoration he showed her appealing. Furthermore, their relationship mattered to her as a poet, for they were able to read and criticize each other's work candidly and honestly.

Teasdale's indecision about initiating a relationship with Lindsay was complicated by her having met Ernst Filsinger, a successful St. Louis businessman she met in April of the same year. Having loved Teasdale from afar since reading *Sonnets to the Duse*, Filsinger revealed a romantic side that Teasdale valued along with high ideals. Like John Hall Wheelock, and like Vachel Lindsay, Filsinger was also capable of great passion. Teasdale struggled with the choice between Filsinger and Lindsay: Who would make a better husband, and for whom would she make a better wife? In the end Teasdale's common sense helped her choose Filsinger over Lindsay, knowing that Lindsay needed to maintain his poet's freedom and that she would not be able to live a nearly impoverished life.

Teasdale and Ernst Filsinger were married on December 18, 1914, with her family present, surrounded by all the fanfare appropriate for a woman of her social class. Unfortunately, the happiness of her wedding day did not last. Teasdale was torn between her need to give and receive love and her need for solitude in which to think and work. Filsinger tried to smooth the way for her, making excuses about her health whenever she failed to appear at social functions, but refuge and solitude became increasingly more important for Teasdale. Moreover, the demands of business in the chaos of a postwar world required that Filsinger travel out of the country for extended periods of time. Unable to accompany him on trips, Teasdale shrank into herself more and more, and the couple drifted apart. This sense of alienation is reflected in her poetry: "Earth is hostile and the sea hostile / Why do I look for a place to rest? / I must fight always and die fighting / With fear and unhealing wound in my breast." Teasdale discussed getting a divorce with Filsinger, but he refused because he loved her and feared losing her. However, by late summer 1929, Teasdale felt she could no longer sustain the marriage. She believed Filsiner must be free, since their marriage could no longer bring him happiness. While Filsinger was on a trip abroad, she wrote him a letter explaining her decision. She then went to Reno and obtained a divorce decree, which was granted on September 5, 1929.

Despite the turmoil Teasdale felt during her marriage, she wrote some of her best poetry during the period and gained increasing acclaim. Her successes led the way for other women poets such as **Edna St. Vincent Millay**, Margaret Widdemar, and **Elinor Wylie**. Teasdale supported her female peers and used her popularity to publish an anthology of their verse, *The Answering Voice: One Hundred Love Lyrics by Women* (1917). Her next collection, *Rivers to the Sea* (1915), was an intensely personal collection of poems where, instead of using surrogates, she spoke in her own voice for the first time. Critics commented that she echoed poets Christina Rosetti (the poet she loved as a child), William Blake, and A.E. Houseman and praised Teasdale's ability to convey both joy and wistfulness with delicate simplicity. "The Look" and "I Shall Not Care" are two often-anthologized poems from this collection. *Rivers to the Sea* (1915) received such a positive reception in both America and Britain that a German translation was necessary at the end of World War I.

Teasdale, now the leading Romantic poet of the time, continued her lyrical praise of beauty in the collection *Love Songs* (1917). In "Barter" she writes, "Spend all you have for loveliness, / Buy it and never count the cost." This volume of poetry was selected by Columbia University as the best book of poetry for that year, the nation's highest honor at the time and the forerunner to the Pulitzer Prize for poetry (which was not awarded until 1922). As a result of this new recognition and her identification with new Romanticism, she became a judge for the 1918 prize, a competition that resulted in a tie between **Carl Sandburg** and Margaret Widdemar.

A maturing Teasdale was affected by the country's entry into World War I, and, although she continued her love themes in *Flame and Shadow* (1920), she tempered her Romanticism with hints of fear and references to the conflict between the mind's purity and life's mundane realities. This collection includes poems about death, grief, loss, and inescapable time; critics noted her new focus and praised her mature wisdom, which reflected the postwar audience's change in mood. During this period, Teasdale's health continued to decline, which darkened her work further. There was a six-year gap before *Dark of the Moon* (1926) was published, and critics observed the lack of light in the title, noting that, as with her previous book, the poems were somber. Again critics praised the depth of feeling within Teasdale's sonorous **lyricism**. Seven more years passed before her last book, *Strange Victory* (1933), was published posthumously. Another critical and popular success, it served as a tribute to her memory.

The maturity in these last two volumes of Teasdale's poetry resulted from her suffering and from the wisdom she developed throughout her life. Her poems were enhanced by her soberness, graciousness, and acquiescence, as well as her lack of self-pity or resentment. Written just before Teasdale took her own life on January 29, 1933, *Strange Victory* was published exactly as she wished it to be. It included her **elegy** for Vachel Lindsay, who, on December 5, 1931, had also taken his own life. In addition to her own poetry collections, Sara Teasdale edited two anthologies: *The Answering Voice: One Hundred Love Lyrics by Women* (1917) and *Rainbow Gold: Verses Old and New for Boys and Girls* (1930).

Critics agreed that Teasdale's last three collections of poetry were her best. She continued to grow and develop as a poet without losing the delicate lyricism that made her a critical and popular success. Teasdale used her success as a poet to help launch the careers of other women poets; it is impossible to overlook her contributions to the genre of poetry.

Further Reading. ***Selected Primary Source:*** Teasdale, Sara, *The Collected Poems of Sara Teasdale* (1937; New York: Macmillan, 1969). ***Selected Secondary Sources:*** Carpenter, Margaret Haley, *Sara Teasdale: A Biography* (Norfolk, VA: Pentelic Press, 1960); Drake, William, *Sara Teasdale: Woman & Poet* (San Francisco: Harper & Row, 1979); Izzo, David Garrett, "Sara Teasdale (1884–1933)," in *American Women Writers, 1940–1945: A Bio-Bibliographical Critical Sourcebook*, ed. Laurie Champion (Westport, CT: Greenwood Press, 2000, 343–347); Schoen, Carol B., *Sara Teasdale* (Boston: Twayne Publishers, 1986); Sprague, Rosemary, *Imaginary Gardens: A Study of Five American Poets* (Philadelphia: Chilton Book Company, 1969).

Alisa M. Smith-Riel

TERRY, LUCY (1730–1821)

Abducted from Africa as a child, Lucy Terry was brought to Rhode Island as a slave, and by the age of five was sold to Ebenezer Wells of Deerfield, Massachusetts. She was baptized and admitted to her master's church in 1744; in 1756 she married a freeman named Obijah Prince who purchased her freedom, and the couple relocated to Guilford in the then-disputed territory that became Vermont. Later in life, Terry argued with the trustees of Williams College in an attempt to get them to change their racial segregation practices and admit one of her six children. When a neighbor tried to claim some of the Princes' land, Terry spoke in her own defense, and won her case. After her husband's death, she relocated to Sunderland, Vermont, where she died in 1821.

According to current knowledge, Terry is the first **African American** from whom we have a poetic text. She is known for the poem "Bars Fight," apparently written in or around 1746, when she was about sixteen years old. The tetrameter scheme of the poem suggests it was written to be sung. "Bars" here means meadow or field, and the title refers to a 1746 raid on Deerfield, Massachusetts, by Native Americans. The poem names and pays tribute to the settlers who died there, describing how each met his or, in at least one stance, her fate:

> Eunice Allen see the Indians coming
> And hoped to save herself by running
> And had not her petticoats stopped her
> The awful creatures had not catched her
> And tommyhawked her on the head
> And left her on the ground for dead.
> (Josiah Holland, *History of Western Massachusetts*)

The poem has been dismissed by some critics as imitative doggerel that shows a musical sensibility but little literary skill. Some have suggested that the poem shows a lack of critical and political distance from slave-owning society. Still others have stressed that the poem demonstrates Terry's confidence in her ability and right to express herself, while also speaking on behalf of the Deerfield community. Certainly, Terry's later life shows that, like many African Americans of the colonial and post-Revolutionary periods, she did not hesitate to pursue her rights through petitions and legal suits. Terry's husband, and perhaps her son as well, fought the British in the American Revolution, and the family's location in Vermont may be significant as well: In the 1777 constitution declaring Vermont a free and independent state, Article I banned slavery. When situated historically and biographically, then, "Bars Fight" evokes a life of engaged vernacular expression.

Further Reading. ***Selected Primary Source:*** Holland, Josiah, *History of Western Massachusetts* (Springfield: n.p., 1855). ***Selected Secondary Sources:*** Bruce, Dickson D., Jr., *The Origins of African American Literature* (Charlottesville, University Press of Virginia, 2001); Foster, Frances Smith, *Written by Herself: Literary Production by African American Women, 1746–1892* (Bloomington: Indiana University Press, 1993); Proper, David R., *Lucy Terry Prince* (Pocumtuck Valley Member Association, 1997).

Ed White

THAXTER, CELIA LAIGHTON (1835–1894)

Although perhaps the most widely published American woman writing poetry in the second half of the nineteenth century, Celia Laighton Thaxter has until recently been dismissed as unworthy of serious attention. The challenge for critics, as Jane Vallier has argued, lies in transcending conventional readings of Thaxter's poetry. Indeed, re-reading Thaxter reveals her contributions to key nineteenth-century discussions of humankind's relationship to nature, love, and religion.

Celia Laighton was born on June 29, 1834, in Portsmouth, New Hampshire. Her father, Thomas, dabbled in everything from politics to lighthouse-keeping before building the famous Appledore Hotel on one of the Isles of Shoals. Growing up in an often-isolated location, with sometimes only her parents and brothers as companions, had a profound effect on Celia, who became a close observer of nature and grew to know every inch of the islands. At sixteen, she married Levi Thaxter, her father's business partner and her former tutor. This marriage to a man eleven years her senior was an unhappy one; it produced three sons, one of whom suffered brain damage after birth and required Celia's constant care. Despite these circumstances, Celia managed an active literary career, publishing poetry, nonfiction, children's literature, and local history. Her first poem, "Land-Locked," appeared in the prestigious *Atlantic Monthly* in 1861, and afterwards her poetry appeared regularly in major periodicals. Her best-known book, *Among the Isles of Shoals*, a prose work combining autobiography, local history, and naturalist writing, was published in 1873. After her husband moved his family to mainland Massachusetts, Celia could only return home to the Isles of Shoals during the summers. While there, she hosted her famous salons at the Appledore, with guests including **Ralph Waldo Emerson**, **Sarah Orne Jewett**, Nathaniel Hawthorne, **Thomas Wentworth Higginson**, **John Greenleaf Whittier**, James and Annie Fields, and Mark Twain. Known as the "Sweet Singer of the Shoals" and "our Island Miranda" (a title Hawthorne gave her), Thaxter moved in the most important literary circles of her time.

Thaxter wrote largely to make money, and, as a result, much of her poetry shows the characteristics popular audiences appreciated. Marked by didacticism, as well as conventional language and meters, the majority of these works strike modern readers as unexceptional. Nevertheless, there are many poems deserving close attention even today. Nature plays a key role in almost all of Thaxter's noteworthy poetry. Poems such as "Wherefore" (1874) and "At the Breaker's Edge" (1874) demonstrate the ambivalent relationship between humans and nature. For example, in "Wherefore," a ship full of sleeping passengers moves ever closer to an iceberg, "a trap of Death's contriving / Waiting remorseless for its easy prey." In such poems, Thaxter's realism emerges, as nature is portrayed as both beautiful and terrifying, awe-inspiring and peaceful, and ultimately unconcerned with the fates of humans. At the heart of this conflict lies Thaxter's skepticism about traditional religion and the apparent irrationality of life and death, a skepticism she would maintain until her conversion to a more traditional theology later in life.

Thaxter also wrote about nature in more positive terms, often using it as an objective correlative for her feelings. The sea figures prominently in many of these works, including "Remembrance" (1896), in which the speaker is constantly drawn to the ocean, even when surrounded by the beauty of land. In pieces like "Impatience" (1896) and even "Land-Locked," Thaxter, who always keenly felt the time away from her mother, explored the love between women, especially mothers and daughters. "Alone" (1896), a tightly constructed, sixteen-line poem, begins with a vivid description of a beautiful woman surrounded by flowers and ends with a dramatic shift: "I would have given my soul to be / That rose she touched so tenderly! / I stood alone, outside the gate, / And knew that life was desolate." These intense poems, in which the speaker is separated from her beloved, rely on concrete detail and emotional restraint that seem more modern than sentimental.

Moving comfortably from one poetic form to another, Thaxter's verses show her wide technical range. Her "Two Sonnets" (1896) is both a passionate and controlled exploration of the classic form. "In Kittery Churchyard" and "The Spaniards' Graves," two of her dramatic monologues modeled after Robert Browning, were among her most commercially successful poems and show her abilities as a **narrative poet**. The former poem, in which the speaker visits the grave of a wife who died over one hundred years before and imagines the grief her husband might have felt, moves effortlessly between the two perspectives, yet resists and even gently rebukes **sentimentalism**: "And in my eyes I feel the foolish tears / For buried sorrow, dead a hundred years!"

Although "Among the Isles of Shoals" remains Thaxter's most widely studied work, her poetry offers equally fruitful ground for critical inquiry. Continued critical interest in nineteenth-century women's writing, Transcendentalism, regionalism, and eco-feminism assures a healthy future for Thaxter scholarship.

Further Reading. ***Selected Primary Sources:*** Thaxter, Celia, *The Cruise of the Mystery, and Other Poems* (Boston: Houghton Mifflin, 1886); ———, *Drift-Weed* (Boston: Houghton, 1878); ———, *Poems* (New York: Hurd and Houghton, 1872); ———, *The Poems of Celia Thaxter* (Boston: Houghton Mifflin, 1896). ***Selected Secondary Sources:*** Vallier, Jane, *Poet on Demand: The Life, Letters, and Works of Celia Thaxter* (Camden, ME: Downeast Books, 1982); White, Barbara A., "*Legacy* Profile: Celia Thaxter (1835–1894)" (*Legacy* 1 [1990]: 59–64);

Woodward, Pauline, "Celia Thaxter's Love Poems" (*Colby Library Quarterly* 23.3 [1987]: 144–155).

Heidi M. Hanrahan

THAYER, ERNEST LAWRENCE (1863–1940)

Ernest Lawrence Thayer is the author of "Casey at the Bat," the favorite poem of many Americans. There are a number of parodies of this poem, and a parody cannot be successful unless its audience knows what is being parodied. "Casey at the Bat" has been recorded, and has been made into silent movies and animated cartoon films. William Schuman used the poem for an opera, *The Mighty Casey*, which premiered in 1953. In the 1970s, Frank Proto wrote a popular musical score for it. The poem is now available on videotape and CDs. It has been read and recited countless times in American settings: theaters, churches, classrooms, and homes.

Thayer, the author of "Casey," was a reporter for the *San Francisco Examiner* in 1887 and 1888. An additional assignment on the paper was to write one humor column for each Sunday edition. "Casey at the Bat," was written for that Sunday column and was the last piece Thayer submitted to the *Examiner*. Earlier, as a Harvard student, he had published humorous work in the *Harvard Lampoon*. That work at Harvard, his news reporting, and the Sunday columns for the Hearst publications represent the extent of his published writings.

Thayer was born in Lawrence, Massachusetts, and was raised in Worcester, Massachusetts. He graduated magna cum laude from Harvard. After graduation and travel in Europe, he was hired by a *Harvard Lampoon* friend, William Randolph Hearst, as a reporter for the *San Francisco Examiner*. In early 1888, Hearst brought part of his *Examiner* crew, including Thayer, to Washington, D.C., to lobby for San Francisco to be the site of the upcoming Democratic National Convention. Thayer, rather than returning to California, traveled home to Massachusetts. He composed "Casey" at home in Worcester in May of 1888 and mailed the copy to the *Examiner*. He went to work in his family's mill business near Worcester and, in 1912, at age forty-nine, moved to Santa Barbara, California, and married. He died at age seventy-seven on August 21, 1940.

When first published on June 3, 1888, the poem was titled "Casey at the Bat," with the subtitle "A Ballad of the Republic, Sung in the Year 1888," and was signed simply "Phin." According to **Donald Hall** in his afterword to the David R. Godine centennial edition of *Casey at the Bat*, Thayer had arrived at the name "Phin" by "abbreviating his college nickname of Phinny." The piece caught the attention of editors around the country and was republished, not always using the "Phin" signature. Jim Moore and Natalie Vermilyea, in their discussion of Thayer and "Casey," titled *Ernest Thayer's "Casey at the Bat,"* a McFarland publication, report that Jim Kennedy, editor of the *New York Sporting Times*, substituted "Kelly" for Casey and "Boston" for Mudville, cut the first five stanzas, and published the poem in his paper as "Kelly at the Bat." Mike "King" Kelly, perhaps the best known baseball player of the day, was in the news since he had been recently hired away from the West Coast league for $10,000 by the Boston Red Stockings.

It was over ten weeks after the *Examiner* publication of "Casey," on August 15 of 1888, that the New York Giants and the Chicago White Stockings, according to Moore and Vermilyea, as guests of the management of Wallack's Theater in New York City, heard De Wolf Hopper, a young comic star, recite the piece between the acts of a comic opera. It was an ad lib performance of "Casey." Before the show, writes Donald Hall, Hopper had announced backstage that he wished he had a baseball piece "he might perform in the ballplayers' honor." A friend handed him a clipping from the *San Francisco Examiner*. It was "Casey at the Bat," and it was a hit with the audience. He was asked to repeat it between the acts of future performances, and it became a signature piece for him. As word of Hopper's Broadway success with the poem became news, another wave of newspaper reprintings began. This type of "borrowing" of material by editors was common at the time. Thayer, a Harvard graduate in philosophy, was not eager to promote himself as the author of "Casey" until others began to claim that they had written the increasingly popular piece.

"Casey" displays a wonderful sense of literary suspense. In the opening line, Thayer announces, "The outlook wasn't brilliant for the Mudville nine that day." The third stanza reveals that most of the spectators believed there was "little chance of Casey's getting to the bat," for the hopeless Flynn and Blake "preceded Casey." Then, Flynn and Blake surprised everyone by getting hits, with "Johnnie" [Blake] even hitting a double. Casey comes up to bat in stanza six. With "haughty grandeur," he lets the first two pitches go by. But in stanza eleven, he grows "stern and cold," "his muscles strain[ed]." Stanza twelve presents the crisis: with the tying two runs on, there are two outs, and the batter has two strikes. Casey takes his mighty swing and the stanza ends. Was it a hit or a strike out? Three lines delay the verdict. How often has one heard "there is no joy in Mudville"? Why? "For Casey, mighty Casey," who "wouldn't let that [third pitch] go by again," has failed. The "mighty Casey has struck out."

In fifty-two lines, Thayer brings the Mudville spectators from the "sickly silence" of despair to the edge of triumph. Flynn and Blake, a hopeless pair, have kept the game alive. And then the mighty Casey—obviously a major power in the league—arrogantly abuses his power by taking two pitches as strikes. His arrogance is rewarded with defeat. Yet, there is always next year. Today's loss is only one loss, and there will be another game tomorrow or the day after that will bring a chance for redemption. It is Thayer's dramatic development and presentation of "Casey" that enables us to accept the defeat of Casey and "the Mudville nine," yet allows us to continually enjoy the drama of "Casey at the Bat."

Further Reading: ***Selected Primary Source:*** Thayer, Ernest Lawrence, *Casey at the Bat, A Centennial Edition*, afterword by Donald Hall (Boston: David R. Godine, 1988). ***Selected Secondary Sources:*** Moore, Jim, and Natalie Vermilyea, *Ernest Thayer's "Casey at the Bat"* (Jefferson, NC: McFarland & Co., 1994); Gardner, Martin, *The Annotated "Casey at the Bat": A Collection of Ballads About the Mighty Casey*, 2nd. ed. (1967; Chicago: University of Chicago Press, 1984).

Carle Johnson

THOMAS, EDITH M. (1854–1925)

In 1881 Edith M. Thomas first visited New York City as an aspiring poet. It was not long after this exciting initial visit that she left behind her Midwestern upbringing in order to pursue a literary career on the East Coast. Her talent was quickly discovered and introduced to the poetic community by the successful poet **Helen Hunt Jackson**. By the 1890s, Thomas was regularly contributing poems, critical essays, and reviews to several New York periodicals. Thomas's volumes of poetry were published contemporaneously with posthumous editions of the poems of **Emily Dickinson**, and, along with Dickinson, she took her place among a group of turn-of-the-century American women poets, almost all of whom pushed against the boundaries of such a category. The sensitive tributes to nature and the treatment of romance in Thomas's poetry reveal her literary connections to **British** Romanticism, and most distinctly to the Romantic poet John Keats. Her intimate knowledge of classical mythology along with her meticulous attention to craft allowed Thomas to enliven myth through her poetry.

Edith Mathilda Thomas was born on a farm in Chatham, Ohio. Her father was a successful teacher until his early death in 1861. Her mother, a native of Connecticut, then moved her two children to the Ohio town of Geneva, near Lake Erie. There, Thomas studied at the Normal Institute and was able to pursue her interest in Greek through special courses that were arranged for her. Thomas attended Oberlin College for a term, but then she withdrew and sought other forms of employment such as teaching and type-setting. At the same time, Thomas was trying her hand at poetic composition. She was successful in publishing some early poems in Ohio newspapers such as the Cleveland *Leader* and *Herald*. In 1881, her uncle, James Thomas, returned from building his fortune in California and took notice of Thomas's poetic gift. While in California, James Thomas had become acquainted with the work of Joaquin Miller (*see* **Miller, Cincinnatus Heine**) and others of this California group. He recognized that his niece Edith would benefit from the experience of visiting the New York literary scene.

Literary salon culture was at its height in New York at the time, and Edith Thomas was introduced to Mrs. Vicenzo Botta, host of one of the salons in which **Edgar Allan Poe** had given readings of "The Raven." Upon reading samples of Thomas's verse, Botta arranged a meeting with Helen Hunt Jackson. It was Jackson, then, who brought Thomas's verse to the attention of the editors of *Scribner's Monthly*. These editors, J.G. Holland and Richard Watson Gilder, were about to launch a new magazine, *Century*, and in June of 1881, Edith M. Thomas and her verse were introduced to New York in this new magazine. After her initial appearance in *Century*, Thomas was sought out by editors for contributions of poems, essays, and reviews. In 1887, after the death of her mother, Thomas made permanent her home in New York City. She befriended Dr. Samuel Elliot and his wife, and lived in their patronage for ten years. Elliot was a scientist and a musician, and also contributed essays to periodicals such as the *Atlantic* and *Harper's Weekly*. While with the Elliots, Thomas secured a position at *Harper's*, and, after Dr. Elliot's death, she was able to support herself through publishing and writing. In 1925 Thomas died of a cerebral hemorrhage at the age of seventy-one.

Four years after Thomas's initial publication in *Century* magazine, her first book, *A New Year's Mask and Other Poems* (1885), was published by Houghton, Mifflin & Company. Thomas was developing a reputation as a skilled poet, and this first volume was generally well received, although the reviews reflect her categorization as an American "poetess" by referring to her dainty volume as a collection of feminine verse in which the language was almost too pretty. Criticism of the lightness of her verse continued to haunt Thomas as she went on to publish several more volumes, some only a year apart from each other.

Thomas's obvious mastery of poetic form was not ignored in these initial reviews, although the implication was that this mastery was mere artifice without the substantial content needed to provide a deeper poetic meaning. Certainly, one can find plenty of light verse among the many collections of poetry by Thomas, and it is likely that Thomas's readers appreciated such verse. Her famous sonnet "Frost To-Night," included in the opening section of the *Selected Poems of Edith M. Thomas,* is one example of the simple, beautiful, and sorrowful language with which Thomas brought natural landscapes to life. As the speaker is given the bittersweet permission to cut any flowers from the garden, she concludes:

In my garden of Life with its all-late flowers,
I heed a Voice in the shrinking hours:
"Frost to-night—so clear and dead still..."
Half sad, half proud, my arms I fill.

Thomas had deeper aesthetic ties than some of her critics were willing to acknowledge. Poems like "The Life Mask of Keats" and "On Severn's Last Sketch of Keats" suggest that by modeling her poetic practice on Keatsian notions of beauty, Thomas was seeking to incorporate this aesthetic into American verse.

It is Thomas's dependence on beauty as truth that can make her verse somewhat inaccessible to the modern reader. Her strict adherence to the formal qualities of verse along with her affinity for mythological settings make Thomas's work seem old-fashioned next to that of the **modernists** of the twentieth century, yet Thomas's emphasis on poetry as art and her insistence on classical settings helped to set the stage for the myth-making projects of modernists like **H.D.** (Hilda Doolittle) and **T.S. Eliot**. At the time, she was certainly an inspiration, even a "foremother" figure for aspiring female poets. Unfortunately, Thomas is not widely read today either as a poet or as a critic. Her contributions to American poetry through her work with poetry journals and magazine verse are certainly underestimated.

Further Reading. ***Selected Primary Sources:*** Thomas, Edith M., *The Dancers* (Boston: Richard G. Badger, 1903); ———, *Fair Shadow Land* (Boston: Houghton, Mifflin, 1893); ———, *The Guest at the Gate* (Boston: Richard G. Badger, 1909); ———, *In Sunshine Land* (Boston: Houghton, Mifflin, 1895); ———, *The Inverted Torch* (Boston: Houghton, Mifflin, 1890); ———, *Lyrics and Sonnets* (Boston: Houghton, Mifflin, 1887); ———, *A New Year's Mask and Other Poems* (Boston: Houghton, Mifflin, 1885); ———, *The Round Year* (Boston: Houghton, Mifflin, 1886); ———, *Selected Poems of Edith M. Thomas*, ed. Jessie B. Rittenhouse (New York: Harper and Brothers, 1926); ———, *The White Messenger and Other War Poems* (Boston: Richard G. Badger, 1915); ———, *A Winter Swallow and Other Verse* (New York: Charles Scriber's Sons, 1986). ***Selected Secondary Sources:*** Bennett, Paula Bernat, *Nineteenth-Century American Women Poets* (Malden, MA: Blackwell Publishers, 1998); Gray, Janet, ed., *She Wields a Pen: American Women Poets of the Nineteenth Century* (Iowa City: University of Iowa Press, 1997); Rittenhouse, Jessie B., ed., "Memoir" in *Selected Poems of Edith M. Thomas* (New York: Harper and Brothers, 1926).

Anne Keefe

THOMAS, LORENZO (1944–2005)

Lorenzo Thomas began his writing career as a member of the Umbra workshop, which included Tom Dent, Calvin Hernton, David Henderson, **Ishmael Reed**, Joe Johnson, Askia Muhammad Toure, Steve Cannon, and other young writers, who met in New York's Lower East Side between 1962 and 1965. The workshop was instrumental in beginning the **Black Arts Movement** of the 1960s as well as the movement known as cultural black nationalism. Thomas's poetry comments on popular culture and simultaneously displays an atavistic interest in the folklore and religious beliefs of ancient African culture. He believes that the arts of the African diaspora are indelibly influenced by memories of the African past. He is also an **experimental poet** using new forms of poetry, new forms of syntax, and vernacular diction to convey the contemporary **African American** experience. His experimentation makes use of a wide knowledge of the musical heritage of African Americans and the language of the folk. In fact, his poems are unique in their original interplay of music, film, and visual art.

In his article in the *Dictionary of Literary Biography*, Tom Dent notes how the poetic style of Lorenzo Thomas "gives the reader the feel of a camera gliding through a maze of sensual impressions and memories" (Dent, 318). It is a surrealistic approach that shows the influence of Aimé Césaire. Thomas says that his poems are also influenced by **Frank O'Hara** and **John Ashbery**, **Amiri Baraka** and Calvin Hernton. "I think what I learned from Ashbery reinforced what I learned from **Wallace Stevens** and both Ashbery and Baraka reinforced what I found interesting about the colloquial language that I found in **Langston Hughes** and **Carl Sandburg**" (*New Journal*).

Lorenzo Thomas was born on August 31, 1944, in the Republic of Panama and moved with his parents to New York in 1948. He graduated from Queens College (City University of New York) and worked with the Umbra workshop. He left New York in 1968, joining the U.S. Navy and going to Vietnam in 1972. After completing his tour of duty, he settled in Houston, Texas, where he became a writer-in-residence at Texas Southern University and was involved in writing workshops in the community. He later became professor of English at the University of Houston–Downtown and has been instrumental in bringing art to the schools—as an active member of the Texas Commission of Arts and Humanities, as one of the first black writers to work as an artist in the schools, as a member of the board of directors of the Coordinating Council of Literary Magazines, and as an organizer of the Juneteenth Blues Festivals in Houston and other Texas cities.

A widely published poet and scholar of poetry, Thomas's books include *Fit Music: California Songs* (1972), *Dracula* (1973), *Framing the Sunrise* (1975), *The Bathers: Selected Poems* (1978), *Chances Are Few* (1979, repr. 2003, [1992]), *Es Gibt Zeugen/There Are Witnesses* (OBEMA Series, 1996), and the critical study, *Extraordinary Measures: Afrocentric*

Modernism and 20th Century American Poetry (2000). He is also editor of *Sing the Sun Up: Creative Writing Ideas from African American Poetry* (1998). His poetry and critical essays have appeared in many journals, including *Callaloo*, the *African American Review*, *Arrowsmith*, *Blues Unlimited* (England), *Living Blues*, *Partisan Review*, *Ploughshares*, *Xavier Review*, and *Popular Music and Society*. He is a regular book reviewer for the *Houston Chronicle*, and has contributed scholarly articles to the *African American Encyclopedia*, *American Literary Scholarship*, *Gulliver* (Germany), and the *Dictionary of Literary Biography*.

The Bathers, 1981, is a chronological selection of Thomas's poems from his experiences in New York, Vietnam, and Houston. The title poem juxtaposes images of the fire hoses that police turned on civil rights demonstrators in Alabama with Egyptian religious symbols and hieroglyphics, the Egyptian symbols giving new meaning to the events in Birmingham. The demonstrators are suffering and angry, but some are feeling the cooling waters of baptism and the bath of Horus, Egyptian god of the dead.

The theme of "Dracula," another poem in *The Bathers*, which was published separately in 1973, is an indictment of ordinary American life and its need to sublimate itself in the more ghastly, although often shallow, movie representations of Dracula, a creature "whose heritage and biography was death" (1981). The pent-up anger of the American white man, the poet suggests, could just as easily cause him to join a lynch mob after the "necessary black negro" as find release indulging in the gore of a Dracula movie, very popular in the 1930s, 1950s, and 1960s (1981). "Dracula is a real person," says the "real man" who "[w]alks in the luncheonette / Grinning over the sandwich" (1981).

Thomas's innovative, edited volume, *Sing the Sun Up*, is a collection of essays by teachers and writers detailing how they use African American literature as a resource to teach reading, the skills of writing, and the understanding of real-life experiences, as well as to broaden the range of the readers' imagination. Contributors discuss ways of conveying to readers and writers of all ages and ethnic groups the craft of language and the use of the oral tradition, the vernacular, music, and folklore through the reading of African American literature.

Thomas's *Extraordinary Measures: Afrocentric Modernism and Twentieth-Century American Poetry* presents a scholarly overview of African American poetry, from the innovative work of **Fenton Johnson** at the beginning of the last century to the work of new writers like **Harryette Mullen** in the early twenty-first century. He points out continuities in African American writers' contributions to literary **modernism** in their Afrocentric sense of identity and diasporic consciousness—a consciousness that is "both spiritual and nascently political" (Thomas, *Extraordinary*, 175).

Thomas also authored the poetry collection *Dancing on Main Street*, published by Coffee House Press in 2004. He died of emphysema in Huston, Texas, in 2005.

Further Reading. ***Selected Primary Sources:*** Thomas, Lorenzo, *The Bathers* (New York: Reed Books, 1981); ———, *Chances Are Few*, 2nd. ed. (Berkeley: Blue Wind Press, 2003); ———, *Extraordinary Measures: Afrocentric Modernism and Twentieth-Century American Poetry* (Tuscaloosa: University of Alabama Press, 2000); ———, *Sing the Sun Up: Creative Writing Ideas from African American Literature* (New York: Teachers and Writers Collaborative, 1998). ***Selected Secondary Sources:*** Dent, Tom, "Lorenzo Thomas," in *Dictionary of Literary Biography*, 41 (n.p.: 315–326); Thomas, Lorenzo, "Alea's Children: The Avant-Garde on the Lower East Side, 1960–1970" (*African American Review* 27.4 [1993]: 573-78); ———, "'Classical Jazz' and the Black Arts Movement" (*African American Review* 29.2 [Summer 1995]: 237–240); "Talking to Lorenzo Thomas (Virtually)" (*New Journal* [2001; 16 July 2003], http://www.thenewjournal.com/html/interviews/Thomas_interview.htm).

Violet Harrington Bryan

THOMPSON, DUNSTAN (1918–1975)

There have been many holy sinners in history—more accurately, repentant sinners—but they became a rarer breed in the tolerant, post-Freudian atmosphere of the mid- to late twentieth century. Dunstan Thompson was a man who went on a wild spree during World War II, after which he reversed gears and spent the rest of his life atoning for it. About 1950, Thompson rejected his life of excess and promiscuity, and, unlike other poets of the time who returned to religion—**T.S. Eliot** and **Robert Lowell**, for instance—renounced the worldly aspects of his poetry career and effectively disappeared from the literary world, although he continued to write prolifically until his death.

Virtually forgotten today, in the 1940s Dunstan Thompson was, according to Gregory Wolfe "often mentioned in the same breath as Dylan Thomas as one of the most promising poets of his time" (*Image* #14, 3–4). Of Thompson's two books published in the United States in the 1940s, poet and gay scholar David Bergman called Thompson the gayest poet of World War II. But when introduced to Thompson's later poems of repentance, the poet **Dana Gioia**, a Roman Catholic himself, said he thought Thompson was the best Roman Catholic poet of his time. (*See also* **Graveyard Poetry**.)

Dunstan Thompson was born in 1918 in New London, Connecticut, the son of a naval officer. According to Gioia, "[H]e was the rarest sort of American Catholic author— a patrician. That was a huge anomaly for his generation, especially with his lineage [of] Catholic aristocrats" (personal correspondence with the author).

Thompson was descended from the brother of Archbishop Carroll of Baltimore, the first Roman Catholic bishop of the United States. But his life went into its secular phase in 1936 when he went to Harvard, where he studied under the prosodist Robert Hillyer and, during a summer abroad, with the poet **Conrad Aiken**. At Harvard he edited the *Harvard Monthly* and founded, with classmate Harry Brown, a lively, if short-lived, **poetry magazine** *Vice Versa*. After he entered the army in 1942, he worked for the Office of War Information in London where he joined the Gargoyle Club, a literary hangout, and met British poets Stephen Spender and George Barker, as well as old friends from Harvard who were also stationed abroad. In 1943 his first book was published in the United States. Although it contained only twenty-four poems, *New York Times*'s reviewer, Abbot Martin proclaimed it "a brilliant display of verbal fireworks" (12 October 1947: 30–31).

It was during the war in London that Thompson met Philip Trower, who was in the British armed forces and who was to become his life companion. At the end of the war in Europe, Trower was posted to Egypt, and Thompson was sent back to the United States, where he was discharged from the army. But Thompson got a contract to write a book about the Middle East and, in 1947, traveled to Cairo, where Trower was stationed, as well as throughout the Holy Land. Although the American publisher rejected the book, *The Phoenix in the Desert* was later published in London in 1951. It is notable for its description of an early transatlantic flight, as well as for its scenes of the luxurious life of the British colonial class in Cairo.

Trower was demobilized in March 1947, and the two men, reunited, soon moved to a seaside village in Norfolk, Cley-Next-The-Sea. It was there that they attended a pilgrimage, held in thanksgiving for the end of the war, to nearby Walsingham, the principal shrine of St. Mary in England, an experience that led Thompson to begin reading widely in Roman Catholic history and theology. Crucially, in 1952, he visited an old priest in London whom he had heard preaching during the war; he decided then that if he ever wanted to return to his childhood faith that was the priest to whom he would go to for confession.

Although he and Trower lived a quiet life in Norfolk, Thompson continued to see his friends throughout his remaining years. Dunstan Thompson hoped to be remembered for the poems from the last twenty-five years of his life, his devout years, that rather than by the poems published in the 1940s, which, as he informed Trower, he did not want to be reprinted (personal correspondence between Philip Trower and the author). It was a decade after Thompson's death in 1975 that his surviving partner privately printed *Poems 1950–1974*, following Thompson's wishes in the matter of the early poems.

It is true that the subject matter of Thompson's earlier works was limited largely to his love affairs with soldiers, sailors, and airmen, often tragically cut short by death. A few of the earlier poems dealt with friendship, such as "Largo" (1943) addressed to William Abrahams and "Glittering Phaeton" (1943) to George Barker. Much in evidence in the early work is the influence of **Hart Crane**, as in "In All the Argosy of Your Bright Hair" (1943), the title a quote from Crane, and of Gerard Manley Hopkins, whose tongue-twisting rhetorical devices Thompson takes to the limit: "[b]raided like bravo, gold as day gay gallant" (*Poems*). The stanzaic and metaphysical complexities of John Donne are also evident. The exacting versification Thompson uses so skillfully, almost obsessively, demands enormous work, and its effect is staggering.

Although Thompson may have used the word "gay" more than any poet of his time—in fact, the word in its homoerotic sense was not yet in general use—guilt was also a recurring theme during these supposedly carefree years. In "Tarquin" (1943), while the homosexuality is open, sexual activity is seen as a despoilment of the body, even as murder; the religious sensibility shines through. The poem begins with "[t]he Red-haired robber in the ravished bed," but soon "[t]his bellboy beauty, this flamingo groom" is "afraid he / Has lost his lifetime in a moment's murder," and "[t]his dark night makes him wish that he were dead." The extravagant language, with its metrical intricacies, whips a mere sexual episode into a Dante-esque Inferno.

It is startling to see the change in Thompson's poetry after his return to Roman Catholicism. With his religious reawakening, as evidenced in the posthumous book, his style became much less baroque; nonetheless, there is a greater variety of form and subject matter, including the use of **free verse**, in which Thompson is able to write more autobiographically, even **confessionally**. Most notable are his intense **religious** poems, some inspired by the nearby shrine that he continued to visit. If this poetry is less rigorous, less formal, the **open forms** seem to allow **narrative**, nostalgia, and even breast-beating over past sins and the predicament his homosexuality appeared to cause in his life (as in "To My Mother," *Poems 1950-1974*). Curiously for a poet who gave up the worldly side of the literary life, he also writes in "Images and Reflections" (ca. 1948) of **T.S. Eliot**'s winning the Nobel Prize, parodying Eliot's own style to mock him for his pretensions.

Thompson published eight books in the twenty-five years before his death in 1975. Despite the availability of his work, only when the proscription against publishing all his work in one volume is lifted can a fair assessment of this conflicted poet be made.

Further Reading. ***Selected Primary Sources:*** Thompson, Dunstan, *The Dove with the Bough of Olive* (New York:

Simon & Schuster, 1943, 1947); ———, *Lament for the Sleepwalker* (Boston: Dodd, Mead & Co., 1947); ———, *The Phoenix in the Desert* (London: John Lehmann, 1951); ———, *Poems* (New York: Simon & Schuster, 1943); ———, *Poems* (London: Secker & Warburg, 1946); ———, *Poems, 1950–1974* (Bungay, Suffolk: Paradigm Press, 1984). ***Selected Secondary Sources:*** Borland, Hal, "Verse in Varied Keys" (*New York Times Book Review* [23 January 1944]: 14); Field, Edward, "Poet of the Month" (*Poetry Pilot, Newsletter of the Academy of American Poets* [October 1980]: 1, 9); Martin, Abbott, "The Poets in Review" (*New York Times Book Review* [12 October 1947]: 30–31).

Edward Field

THOREAU, HENRY DAVID (1817–1862)

Although renowned in American letters as a nature writer, philosopher, and social critic, and celebrated internationally as the inspirational author of *Walden; or, Life in the Woods* (1854) and "Resistance to Civil Government" (also titled "Civil Disobedience" 1849), Henry David Thoreau is seldom studied as a poet. In fact he published relatively few poems separately during his lifetime, although he composed enough verse to warrant a volume titled *Poems of Nature*, collected and published posthumously in 1895. Thoreau wrote most of his poems as a young man between 1837, when he undertook the vocation of writing and began composing his journal, and 1850. For a short time, friend and mentor **Ralph Waldo Emerson** encouraged Thoreau to cultivate his talent and submit poems to the *Dial*, a short-lived Transcendentalist literary journal (*see* **Literary Magazines**). While editors **Margaret Fuller** and Emerson published a few of his poems, they in turn critiqued and rejected many others.

Frustrated by Emerson's waning enthusiasm, Thoreau destroyed nearly half of his early poems and turned his attention to prose. As it turns out, however, he had not altogether abandoned the poet's craft, for he interlaced sixty poems or poetic fragments throughout his first book, *A Week on the Concord and Merrimac Rivers* (1849). Throughout the journal, his commentary on the strengths and weaknesses of the many poets he read comprised a theory of poetry as well. What is more, many readers would agree that *Walden,* although it contains little verse, has many of the characteristics of great poetry; for a work of prose, it is remarkably compact, highly evocative, and profoundly symbolic. Today, all of his surviving poems and fragments appear in the *Collected Poems of Henry Thoreau*, a volume that affords a perspective on the poet's progress that he himself may not have seen. Many of the works are untitled, and thus are referenced by the first lines. Despite being a rather small collection, Thoreau's poems shed light on the strivings and principles of an extraordinary thinker.

Born on July 12, 1817, in Concord, Massachusetts, David Henry Thoreau reversed the order of his first and middle names sometime during the 1830s. Although his parents were poor, Henry was able to attend Harvard College from 1833–1837. While at college he read Emerson's *Nature*, the manifesto of Transcendentalism that urges the young thinker to seek essential spiritual truths in nature rather than in religious doctrine. The two men became friends, despite their fourteen-year age difference. As Thoreau began what would turn out to be a fleeting career as a Concord schoolteacher, he and Emerson discussed writing, philosophy, and history. For a while, Thoreau also participated in meetings of the local Transcendentalist Club along with Emerson, **Amos Bronson Alcott**, **Theodore Parker**, Margaret Fuller, George Ripley, and **Jones Very**. Eventually, however, Thoreau went his own way; he quit the teaching profession, worked briefly in his father's pencil-manufacturing business, and then settled on a life of subsistence as a surveyor, day laborer, and handyman so that he could devote more of his time to writing.

From 1845 to 1847, Thoreau lived at Walden Pond, putting Transcendentalism into practice by closely studying the natural environment and living independently. In the midst of this "experiment," he went to jail for not paying his poll tax, an act of protest on his part against the government's use of federal tax dollars to support the Mexican War. These experiences provided the inspiration for his most famous works. After completing *Walden* and "Resistance to Civil Government," Thoreau published a number of powerful reform essays (many of which began as lectures), among them "Slavery in Massachusetts" (published in **William Lloyd Garrison**'s *Liberator* in 1854), "A Plea for Captain John Brown" (1860), and "Life Without Principle" (posthumously published in 1863). Having struggled with poor health for most of his adult life, Thoreau died of tuberculosis on May 6, 1862.

Inspired by the poetry of William Wordsworth and Emerson (whose ideas were influenced in turn by the philosophy of Immanuel Kant, Samuel Taylor Coleridge, and Thomas Carlyle), Thoreau's verse explores themes and values associated with Romanticism and its American counterpart, Transcendentalism. Following Emerson's teachings, Thoreau embraced nature as the origin of moral laws and guiding principles for a just life. Like Emerson, he maintained that human beings had erred in distancing themselves from the primal source and could no longer decipher the universal and ethical truths manifest in the natural world. Believing that poets and philosophers were visionary individuals who lived their day-to-day lives in perfect correspondence with nature, Emerson urged the spiritually bereft masses to look to these individuals for instruction. In an effort to become just such a philosopher/poet, Thoreau devoted himself to the daily practice of transcendence, that is, to overcoming the socialized mind's limitations—prescribed values and orthodox beliefs—by communing directly with nature. In most of his writings, therefore, he lavishes praise on the natural world while he painstakingly engages in the scientific observation of her particulars, taking notice of every detail as he searches for correspondence.

The principle of correspondence, the belief in the individual mind's capacity for the intuitive apprehension of truth, is the subject of many of Thoreau's poems. A winter sunrise provides an apt analogy for the soul's illumination in "The Inward Morning," for example. The speaker's "inmost mind," somewhat awkwardly likened to a satchel "packed" with "all the clothes / Which outward nature wears," corresponds to nature's diurnal process. Like the woodland birds that respond to the "new light" each day, the mind is also awakened, but the source of inspiration for bird or man is one in the same: nature within and without.

Sunlight is also the metaphoric vehicle in "I Am the Autumnal Sun," a poem in which the speaker's emotional state corresponds to seasonal transformation, particularly the approaching darkness of winter. Like the foliage and fruits of late fall, he declares, "I am all sere and yellow, / And to my core mellow," suggesting a state of mind that is both ripe and sympathetic. Although he was a young man when he wrote this poem in 1842, Thoreau portrays his speaker as one who has reached a level of emotional and spiritual maturity. Ironically, the imagery of autumn and death is linked to the idea of unity rather than severance. The speaker simply *is* the sun; he is one with the natural order in which death and darkness are cyclic rather than terminal. Similarly, in a short poem titled "On Fields O'er Which the Reaper's Hand Has Pass[e]d," the speaker likens his thoughts to the "stubble floating in the wind" after the fields have been harvested. Subtler than the "finest summer haze," these ethereal autumnal thoughts are disassociated from both leisure and labor. They arise neither as a result of one's temporary freedom from obligations nor in response to the necessities of production; rather, they are the post-harvest gleanings of life in the absence of toil. The sight of empty fields in October allows the speaker to embrace almost existentially the very essence of nature once human efforts to control and cultivate have ceased. Using one of his favorite techniques, that of redefinition, Thoreau transforms the significance of "harvest" to imagine the possibilities of genuine spiritual freedom amidst a society rooted in materialistic pursuits.

In addition to rejecting the ideology of business, which he sometimes refers to as his preference for life over work, Thoreau also repudiates society's efforts to control and domesticate human nature. In his journal, he writes, "What is peculiar in the life of a man consists not in his obedience, but his opposition, to his instincts." Preparing the way for **Walt Whitman**'s celebration of selfhood, Thoreau argues that instinct should not be repressed but embraced. In the poem that begins with the line "conscience is Instinct Bred in the House," the speaker celebrates the thoughts of the instinctual individual while poking fun at the pious conformist. "Feeling and Thinking" must be turned out of doors to avoid committing a kind of mental incest. The truly conscientious mind must, in a sense, breed with nature to give birth to genuine independence and free itself from petty social concerns with civility and conformity. Such a mind will be "true to the backbone / Unto itself alone, / and false to none." Mired in unnatural and hypocritical thinking, a rigidly Calvinist society tries to suppress instinct and squelch spontaneity. Baptism "drowns" genuine emotions of the present moment with promises of a rebirth "to-morrow," while predestination does away with truly free will and promotes a narrow concept of good versus evil. The disingenuous doctrine of good works encourages people to interfere with the natural world, and thereby results in the destruction rather than completion of God's design. In true Wordsworthian fashion, therefore, Thoreau rejects the dutiful, domesticated bourgeoisie in favor of "simple laboring folk, / Who love their work, / Whose virtue is a song / To cheer God along."

Along similar lines, the speaker of Thoreau's ode "To a Stray Fowl" observes the behavior of a lost bird as a means of reflecting on instinct as the very essence of life. Fearing "imprisonment has dulled thy wit, / Or ingrained servitude extinguished it," he is heartened to discover that the transplanted creature retains a "dim memory" of its indigenous origins in the Brahmapootra River region of India. Inadvertently barred from its coop for the night, the bird does not panic but returns to its instincts and takes shelter in "friendly trees." If a non-native chicken can revert to its primeval state in the woods, Thoreau suggests, so humans may transcend their repressive social conditioning and rekindle their aboriginal senses by communing with nature. Given Thoreau's abolitionist views, one can also perceive in this poem a veiled attack on the institution of slavery. Stolen from their homelands in the East and forced into a system of bondage and domestic servitude that violates the very laws of nature, slaves are utterly dehumanized as chattel, yet they, too, might recuperate their lost, unrepressed selves by seeking refuge in the more hospitable North.

As a Romantic thinker, Thoreau valorized nature as the basis of true liberty and rejected social mores, conventions, and religious practices as stultifying and unnatural. He saw an increasingly urbanized and governed nineteenth-century America as inimical to the cultivation of the free individual championed by the democratic ideologies and revolutions of the eighteenth century. The institutions of American society, government, and law were artificial and oppressive, he realized; not only did they demand allegiance to an economic system founded on materialism and greed, but they also blunted the individual's innate capacity for moral action in the face of such blatant injustices as slaveholding and territorial expansionism.

Even though they were inspired by Emerson's call for "self-reliance," many of Thoreau's poems were early attempts to develop his own bolder concept of the individual as an autonomous being, compelled to revolt against the immoral State. In "Independence," for example, the speaker declares his freedom from the "civil polity" that offers him nothing he truly wants. "Penurious states lend no relief / Out of their pelf," he reminds the reader. What little support they dole out to their subjects comes from loot obtained at the expense of others. A truly free person must shun alliances with "realms" and "circumscribed power," including any "band" or party, despite its claims to righteousness. The nation's "nobles," the speaker playfully implies, may don the shimmering trappings of chivalric virtue, but they are little more than plunderers. Allusions in this poem to medieval knights and the courtly tradition might at first seem anachronistic, but Thoreau's independent speaker sees a link between the feudal past and the present. Southern plantation society often described itself in terms of Arthurian legends and Anglo-Saxonism, employing chivalry as an ideology to rationalize the expanding slaveholding system. In the final lines of the poem, the speaker declares his aspiration to live independently—free from the "emblazonry" of "trade upon the street." He refuses to participate in the political economy of a state that shields its true motives behind heroic images of a progressive, democratic Republic, yet fills its coffers with profits from the trade in human flesh.

Similarly, in the poem "Wait Not Till Slaves Pronounce the Word," Thoreau advises abolitionists and ordinary citizens to free themselves. Building on the idea that only an individual can achieve genuine freedom, this poem promotes the argument of "Resistance to Civil Government." Here, the speaker rejects government and the state in favor of self-rule based on conscience rather than politics. "Think not the tyrant sits afar," he warns. On the contrary, tyranny lies "in your own breasts," but the power to enslave and the power to emancipate are one in the same. The "captive" within each of us—that which puts faith in the idea of a "republic" or submits to the state's authority—must be emancipated. We are all slaves so long as we allow ourselves to be ruled by political systems and thus deny "the things / Which only conscience knows." As Thoreau argues in "Resistance to Civil Government," truly conscientious abolitionists must immediately "withdraw their support, both in person and property," from the State.

Although Thoreau believed firmly that he had to separate himself entirely from the corrupt institutions of society in order to ascertain nature's higher truths, some of his poems evoke a sense of doubt about transcendence. One of his best works, "Light Winged Smoke, Icarian Bird," conveys the failure of vision through a succession of aerial metaphors. Beginning as a meditation on smoke, the speaker alludes to the mythic Icarus, whose wax wings failed to transcend human limits for very long. This smoke that seems to melt away as it rises is also likened to a "lark without song," suggesting an inarticulate poet. The voiceless bird nonetheless strives to be the source of enlightenment, a "messenger of dawn," but it emanates from the chimneys of the domestic hamlet below rather than from some natural or divine source, rendering the "message" ambiguous. "Or else," he says, this smoke is but a "departing dream" or "midnight vision, gathering up thy skirts," a fading fantasy that obscures the stars at night and darkens the sunlight by day. The speaker's smoke seems to obstruct or inhibit vision. Revelation fails. Perhaps, too, the speaker feels his muse may collect herself and abandon him. And so, as the poem closes, the meditation becomes a prayer, and the smoke turns out to be an offering to "ask the gods to pardon this clear flame." The word "pardon" is somewhat ambiguous here, but, given the preceding imagery, it seems to connote release rather than forgiveness. The liberty-seeking "flame," although clear about his destination, remains bound to earth. A more direct expression of Thoreau's fear of failure can be found in the poem that begins with the lines, "Great God, I ask thee for no meaner pelf / Than that I may not disappoint myself, / That in my action I may soar as high, / As I can now discern with this clear eye." Although he measured himself by his own standards, Thoreau often despaired of meeting them.

In choosing to pursue a life of relative solitude, attempting to act on principles guided by the laws of nature, and refusing to compromise, rationalize, or conform for the sake of expediency, Thoreau became an iconoclast. The decision to live life simply and "deliberately," his expressed motive for retreating to Walden Pond, was no meager undertaking, for it meant rejecting all of the materialistic values of the business world, along with its puritanical work ethic, its blind acceptance of stratified social classes, its false religious values, and its blatant immorality. Yet, what seemed to worry Thoreau the most was not that he might falter in his challenge to the status quo, but rather that he would fall short in his attempt to become a true poet of nature, one who, by his own definition, "nailed words to their primitive senses" and "transplanted them to the page with earth adhering to their roots," as he writes in "Walking." Whether he saw his poetic self as an Icarus incapable of ascending to the heights of his vision or an uninspired groundling at a loss for meaningful language, Thoreau ultimately chose to abandon what was for him the restrictive genre of poetry in favor of the unfettered, uncompromising, and courageous prose for which he is known. The world would have to wait a few more years for Whitman to invent a poetic form both inspired by and expressive of Thoreau's Transcendentalist vision.

Further Reading. ***Selected Primary Source:*** Thoreau, Henry David, *Collected Poems of Henry Thoreau*, ed. Carl Bode (Baltimore: Johns Hopkins Press, 1964). ***Selected Secondary Sources:*** Harding, Walter, *The Days of Henry Thoreau* (1962; Princeton, NJ: Princeton University Press, 1992); McGregor, Robert Kuhn, *A Wider View of the Universe: Henry Thoreau's Study of Nature* (Urbana: University of Illinois Press, 1997); Richardson, Robert D., *Henry Thoreau: A Life of the Mind* (Berkeley: University of California Press, 1986); Robinson, David M., *Natural Life: Thoreau's Worldly Transcendentalism* (Ithaca, NY: Cornell University Press, 2004); Tauber, Alfred I., *Henry David Thoreau and the Moral Agency of Knowing* (Berkeley: University of California Press, 2003).

Krista Walter

TILLINGHAST, RICHARD (1940–)

A Southern poet by virtue of birth and early education, Richard Tillinghast has become a nationally recognized poet of great versatility. His works use a number of traditional and experimental techniques to explore the place of the individual within the landscapes of America and Europe. He is also interested in the exploration of personal relationships, and in the nostalgic presentation of memories.

Richard Tillinghast was born and raised in a prominent family in Memphis, Tennessee. His father was an inventor and businessman; his mother taught French and Latin. In high school, Tillinghast proved a talented student with an interest in history, literature, drumming, and painting. He received his BA from the University of the South in 1962. He then pursued graduate studies in English at Harvard, where **Robert Lowell** was one of his teachers. Tillinghast earned his MA from Harvard in 1963 and Ph.D. (his dissertation dealt with the poetry of Lowell) in 1970. He has taught creative writing and literature at several universities, including Berkeley (1968–1973), Sewanee (1979–1980), and Harvard (1980–1983). In the 1970s, Tillinghast held a number of menial jobs and then returned to teaching through his affiliation with the College of Marin and the college program at San Quentin State Prison. Since 1983, he has taught at the University of Michigan in Ann Arbor, where he was named professor of English in 1992. He has remarried and has four children with his second wife, Mary Graves.

Tillinghast placed poems in prestigious magazines early in his career. In 1969 his first collection of poems, *Sleep Watch*, was published by Wesleyan. The volume contains remarkably mature poems reflecting the poetic influence of **James Wright**, **W.S. Merwin**, **James Dickey**, and Robert Lowell. The personal element is prominent in poems about the breakup of Tillinghast's first marriage. Another major theme is the quest for spiritual fulfillment, which brought him to travel to the holy places of Asia in the early 1970s. Finally, the poems represent Tillinghast as a socially engaged poet who has been involved with social activism since the early 1960s.

Tillinghast's next book did not appear until 1980 when *The Knife and Other Poems* was published. The volume is full of haunting images of cherished objects, family memories, and the poet's former selves, all of which are irretrievably gone. They present a typical Southern vision of a lost, idealized America to which one cannot return but which one tries to recreate through poetry. In the title poem, Tillinghast commemorates the dropping and retrieval of an old family knife that fell into a river and was recovered through a flash of insight: "David burst into the upper air / gasping as he brings to the surface our grandfather's knife," a knife "shaped now, for as long as these words last, / like all things saved from time." The preoccupation with time and the poet's wish to stop it in a moment of suspended epiphany is reminiscent of the poetry of **Robert Penn Warren**. Tillinghast proves himself to be an **elegiac** poet with a deep allegiance to family and cultural history. His poems often use rain as a potent backdrop for a variety of emotions.

In 1981 Tillinghast published *Sewanee in Ruins*, a long, historical poem that focuses on the American South in the 1870s as the Confederacy tried to recover from the aftermath of the Civil War, in which everything had burned "but the brick chimneys / and a way of talking." The memorable and moving portrait of the plight of a small Tennessee community was reprinted in Tillinghast's next volume, *Our Flag Was Still There* (1984). Besides the patriotic note of the title poem, which was inspired by the text of the national anthem, the book also features poems on Americans and their involvement in war, technology, and popular culture.

Tillinghast's next book, *The Stonecutter's Hand* (1994), was mostly written during his stay in Ireland (1990–1991), where he spent a fruitful year on a travel grant. The local landscapes, people, and culture provided a perfect environment for the poet who had spent his life meditating, traveling, and searching for answers to his experiences and memories. The historical topics include the effects of war and slavery in America, the collapse of the Ottoman Empire in Turkey, and the decline of the Irish aristocracy. The poet takes his readers to these countries as he pursues his constant search for "home." In "Southbound Pullman, 1945," Tillinghast portrays the ambivalent feelings of American soldiers on the triumphant train journey back home after World War II has ended: "Tomorrow, bands and a convertible. / Then fresh mistakes begin." The future of postwar America lures with erotic possibility, yet the prediction of mistakes that will most likely be repeated by future generations lends the poem a bittersweet quality. The book was praised as a showcase of Tillinghast's mature voice that mixes meter, rhyme, and **free verse** with an authority that is unparalleled among most poets of his generation. The poet expresses his love of travel and boundary-crossing in an effort to understand and celebrate the temporal and metaphysical dimensions of American history.

In 2000 Tillinghast published *Six Mile Mountain*, a volume of deceptively simple poems about places that add up to a compassionate picture of the spiritual rootlessness of contemporary America. In "Departure," the speaker leaves his anguished past to drive through "the defeated landscape / that buys and sells, that smiles and photosynthesizes," finally choosing to pursue "the methodical achievement of distance / into the ink-wash of a thundery sky." The quest for self-acceptance is not a failed one, however. In "A Visit," the poet honors the tomb of his forebears and notes with surprise that he is finally reconciled with his uneasy heritage.

Tillinghast has become a major American poet who reveals an emotional involvement with both the personal and public aspects of love, politics, and history. In addition to his volumes of poetry, he has written numerous reviews and articles on American and Irish literature, as well as travel and art pieces. In 1995 he published *Robert Lowell's Life and Work: Damaged Grandeur,* a book-length study of his 1960s teacher, mentor, and friend. In 2004 a volume of his essays, *Poetry and What Is Real*, was published as part of the Poets on Poetry series.

Further Reading. ***Selected Primary Sources:*** Tillinghast, Richard, *The Knife and Other Poems* (Middletown, CT: Wesleyan University Press, 1980); ———, *Our Flag Was Still There* (Middletown, CT: Wesleyan University Press, 1984); ———, *Poetry and What Is Real* (Ann Arbor: University of Michigan Press, 2004); ———, *Robert Lowell's Life and Work: Damaged Grandeur* (Ann Arbor: University of Michigan Press, 1995); ———, *Sewanee in Ruins* (Sewanee, TN: University of the South, 1981); ———, *Six Mile Mountain* (Ashland, OR: Story Line Press, 2000); ———, *Sleep Watch* (Middletown, CT: Wesleyan University Press, 1969); ———, *The Stonecutter's Hand* (Boston: David R. Godine, 1995); ———, *Today in the Cafe Trieste* (Chester Springs, PA: Dufour Editions, 1997). ***Selected Secondary Sources:*** Bawer, Bruce, "Borne Ceaselessly into the Past" (*Hudson Review* 54 [2001]: 513–520); Grosholz, Emily, "Arms and the Muse: Four Poets" (*New England Review* 5 [1983]: 634–646); Ward, Scott, "No Vers Is Libre" (*Shenandoah: The Washington and Lee University Review* 45.3 [1995]: 107–119).

Jiri Flajsar

TOLSON, MELVIN (1898–1966)

Well regarded during his lifetime, Melvin Beaunorus Tolson received the highest award in a national poetry contest sponsored by the American Negro Exposition for his poem "Dark Symphony" (1939), which was subsequently published in the *Atlantic Monthly*. Named poet laureate of Liberia in 1947, Tolson went on to win *Poetry*'s Bess Hokin Prize in 1951 and a prize in literature from the National Institute of Arts and Letters in 1965. Tolson's work was reviewed in major critical journals and received largely positive reviews in 1954 from the *Nation* and the *Times Book Review*, in 1955 from *Poetry*, and in 1965 from the *Saturday Review* and *Times (London) Literary Supplement*. Nonetheless, critics have had a difficult time categorizing Tolson, and two of his major works, *Libretto for the Republic of Liberia* (1953) and *Harlem Gallery: Book I, The Curator* (1965), went out of print in 1980 and 1987 respectively. After his death, Tolson's work fell into obscurity until the University of Virginia Press issued *"Harlem Gallery" and Other Poems of Melvin B. Tolson* in 1999, with an introduction by **Rita Dove**. In addition to "Harlem Gallery" and "Libretto," the Virginia edition contains *Rendezvous with America*, a book originally published in 1944, of which "Dark Symphony" is a part, as well as previously uncollected poems including "E. & O.E."

Historically, and perhaps aesthetically, Tolson falls between the **Harlem Renaissance** and the **Black Arts Movement**, although he is now being recognized as a major figure in African American **modernism**. Writing from the 1930s through the 1960s, Tolson lived far from major urban centers and arrived on the poetic scene somewhat late for the Harlem Renaissance. However, he was highly aware of writers associated with this movement, taking them as the subject for his MA thesis. Tolson, although not a black nationalist, shares several political concerns with Black Arts Movement writers; nevertheless, some proponents of the black aesthetic objected to what they saw as Tolson's wholesale adoption of European poetic forms. "Harlem Gallery," Tolson's final work, demonstrates the commitment he had made by about 1948 to modernism, a modernism that in his hands continually investigates and complicates readings of African American identity. Alongside a striking display of reading and cultural knowledge from Africa, Europe, Asia, and the Americas, "Harlem Gallery" also foregrounds Tolson's concern with the artist's role in the community and his interest in African American vernacular forms. The recognition of Tolson's contributions to a distinctively American modernism will only continue to grow as more and more poets and scholars become familiar with his work, placing him rightfully as a major poet in the lineage of **African American poetry**.

Born to parents Alonzo and Lera (Hurt) Tolson in 1898 in Moberly, Missouri, Tolson showed early interest in poetry and other arts. He published his first poem, "The Wreck of the Titanic," in 1912 in the Oskaloosa, Iowa, local newspaper. Tolson's father was an itinerant Methodist minister, and Tolson grew up in small towns throughout Missouri and Iowa. His mother, an accomplished seamstress, encouraged Tolson's goals to attend college and to become a poet. Tolson reported that on her deathbed she said to him, "Son, I always wanted to write. I had many things to tell people. But now that I am going to die, you'll have to do it for me" ("Odyssey," 6). As senior class poet at Lincoln High School in Kansas City, Missouri, Tolson published two short stories and two poems in his high school yearbook, the *Lincolnian*. He attended Fisk University from 1918 to 1919, and then transferred to Lincoln University in Pennsylvania, the first historically black college/university. The transfer may have been prompted by Lincoln University's interest in giving Tolson necessary scholarship support. During this time, he met Ruth Southall, whom he married in 1922. According to his wife, Tolson purchased her wedding ring with the ten-dollar prize that he won as the best individual debater during the academic year 1921–1922. The couple went on to have three sons and a daughter. Tolson graduated cum laude from Lincoln with a BA in journalism and theology in 1923.

After graduation, Tolson was hired as an instructor of speech and English, and he taught for more than forty years at historically black colleges: from 1924 until 1947 at Methodist-affiliated Wiley College in Marshall, Texas, and then at Langston University in Langston, Oklahoma, beginning in 1947. In 1965, the year before his death from stomach cancer, Tolson had accepted an appointment to the first Avalon Chair in the Humanities at Tuskegee Institute. Tolson was a dedicated and rigorous teacher. Among his activities at Wiley College, which included coaching the junior varsity football team and directing the theater club, Tolson co-founded the black intercollegiate Southern Association of Dramatic and Speech Arts, and organized the Wiley Forensic Society, a debate team that earned a national reputation, losing only one debate over the course of ten years competing against both black Southern schools and integrated schools in the West. The members of the intercollegiate drama association that Tolson organized competed both in the North and in the South. Wiley College's debate squad further distinguished itself by defeating the national champions from the University of Southern California in 1935.

Tolson's efforts to break the color-barrier extended to his dedication as a social activist. During the 1930s he organized both black and white sharecroppers in southeastern Texas within the Southern Tenants Farmers Union. For his family's protection, Tolson kept the details of this work from them as much as possible. Three published poems are concerned with sharecropping: "The Battle of the Rattlesnake," in *Rendezvous with America*, and "Zip Lightner" and "Uncle Gropper," in *A Gallery of Harlem Portraits* (1979). Tolson also served as mayor of the all-black town of Langston, Oklahoma, from 1954 to 1960.

Supported by a Rockefeller fellowship, Tolson enrolled in Columbia University's master's degree program in comparative literature in 1930–1931. Tolson's year in New York had a long-lasting effect on his career as a poet, and he subsequently visited the city many times, with Harlem assuming mythic proportions both in his life and in his imagination. Encouraged by a fellow student at Columbia to write a "Negro **epic**," Tolson began composing *A Gallery of Harlem Portraits* during his stay in New York. This collection of poems was modeled after *The Spoon River Anthology* of **Edgar Lee Masters**. Tolson also cited **Walt Whitman** as an influence during this time. *A Gallery of Harlem Portraits* was probably completed in 1935, although, since Tolson could not find a publisher, it was not published until 1979, thirteen years after Tolson's death. The series of poetic character sketches written to represent the rich variety of life in Harlem begins with a poem titled "Harlem," probably written after the portraits and intended to anchor the collection.

Tolson received the MA in 1940, after submitting final revisions of his thesis, "The Harlem Group of Negro Writers." Though Tolson was one of the first African Americans to conduct a study of the Harlem Renaissance, mention of his work is absent from subsequent major studies because "The Harlem Group of Negro Writers" went unpublished for more than sixty years. In 2001 Greenwood Press published the thesis, which includes individual chapters on **Countee Cullen**, **Langston Hughes**, **Claude McKay**, **W.E.B. DuBois**, **James Weldon Johnson**, and others. Tolson stated that his goals for the thesis were three-fold: "First, to give the social background of the Harlem Renaissance and the various forces that scholars say operated in the black metropolis to bring about the artistic and literary development of 'The New Negro'; second, to emphasize the lives and works of the leading contemporary Negro writers, novelists, and poets in the light of modern criticism; and third, to interpret the attitude and stylistic methods discovered in the Harlem Renaissance" ("Harlem Group," 35). The final goal in particular had an influence on Tolson's poetic development. For example, Tolson asserts that Hughes "is the most glamorous figure in Negro literature" (57) and goes on to praise Hughes's use of the **blues** as a poetic form.

Tolson, too, became interested in what he called authentic forms of folk expression, and his use of the blues is evident in the poem "Harlem": "When a man has lost his taste fer you, / Jest leave dat man alone."

In his thesis, Tolson also praises Hughes as a "defender of the proletariat." Tolson himself often stressed the commonalties that workers in a capitalist system share with one another across racial lines ("Harlem Group," 57). Tolson never joined the Communist Party, although there are indications that he identified himself as a Marxist. Tolson's political views are explored in his column, "Caviar and Cabbage," that ran in the African American newspaper the *Washington Tribune* from October 8, 1937, to June 24, 1944. In a column dated October 19, 1940, Tolson emphasizes the importance of both economic and racial equality: "There can be no democracy without economic equality. Thomas Jefferson said that when he wrote the Declaration of Independence. There can be no brotherhood of man without a brotherhood of dollars. I have another theory. It is based on economic and racial brotherhood" ("Caviar," 91).

The immersion in contemporary poetry that Tolson began in the 1930s continued into the 1940s, developing into his affiliation with modernism. This self-conscious change is evident in a 1948 address Tolson gave at Kentucky State College: "Now the time has come for a New Negro Poetry for the New Negro. . . . The standard of poetry has changed completely. Negroes must become aware of this. This is the age of **T.S. Eliot** who has just won the Nobel Prize in Literature. If you know Shakespeare from A to Z, it does not mean you can read one line of T.S. Eliot! But Negro poets and professors must master T. S. Eliot!" (Berubé, 63–64). Tolson's "New Negro Poetry" includes "E. & O.E.," published in *Poetry* magazine in 1951, "Libretto," and his masterwork "Harlem Gallery." During the 1950s and 1960s, a critical controversy developed around Tolson's modernist works. **Allen Tate**'s preface to the *Libretto for the Republic of Liberia* (1953) states that Tolson "assimilated completely the full poetic language of his time, and by implication, the language of the Anglo-American tradition." **Karl Shapiro** countered with the assertion in the introduction to *Harlem Gallery* (1965) that "Tolson writes and thinks in Negro" (13). An ongoing argument as to whether Tolson's work is authentically African American continued at least into the 1980s, despite the facts of Tolson's life and the content of his works.

Tolson conceived of "Harlem Gallery," a poem that differs markedly in style from the earlier *Gallery of Harlem Portraits*, as an epic in five books representing the black diaspora. Sadly, Tolson only lived to complete *Book I: The Curator*. The other planned books were *Book II: Egypt Land, Book III: The Red Sea, Book IV: The Wilderness*, and *Book V, The Promised Land*. In "Harlem Gallery: Book I," the main character in the poem is the Curator, a character mentioned but not developed in *A Gallery of Harlem Portraits*. In a radio interview conducted in 1965, Tolson described the Curator: "The Curator is of Afroirishjewish ancestry. He is an octoroon, who is a Negro in New York and a white man in Mississippi. Like Walter White, the late executive of the NAACP, and the author of *A Man Called White*, the Curator is 'voluntary' Negro. Hundreds of thousands of Octoroons like him have vanished in the Caucasian race—never to return. This is a great joke among Negroes. So Negroes ask the rhetorical question, 'What man is white?'" ("Gallery," 260). In constructing a central speaker who is physiologically racially indeterminate, Tolson removes the so-called biological determinates of race and forces the reader to confront the ways in which race is socially and culturally constructed. The Curator occupies a liminal space in which he could be "Negro" in New York, but at the same time "white" in Mississippi. Yet it is this very liminality that gives the Curator the perspective and insight to evaluate art.

The Curator discovers the secret, modernist poem written by one of Tolson's other characters, Hideo Heights, "the vagabond bard of Lenox Avenue" ("Gallery," 258). The discovery of the poem leads the Curator to observe that the "color line" "splits an artist's identity" (337). Significantly, Heights's secret work is titled "E. & O.E." the same title as Tolson's poem. The fact that the poet's modernist work must be kept secret indicates the split identity black modernist artists confronted. The Curator describes Heights's dilemma as follows: "The racial ballad in the public domain / And the private poem in the modern vein" (335). Tolson's Afro-modernist work consciously interrogates the splits policed by both the "color line" and the "party line." His complex, nuanced approach to representations of racial identity prefigures modernist work by black writers late into the twentieth century, such as **Will Alexander**, and will continue to influence writers well into the next century.

Further Reading. ***Selected Primary Sources:*** Tolson, Melvin B., *Caviar and Cabbage: Selected Columns by Melvin B. Tolson from the* Washington Tribune, *1937–1944,* ed. Robert M. Farnsworth (Columbia: University of Missouri Press, 1982); ———, *Gallery of Harlem Portraits* (Columbia: University of Missouri Press, 1979); ———, *"Harlem Gallery" and Other Poems of Melvin B. Tolson,* ed. Raymond Nelson (Charlottesville: University of Virginia Press, 1999); ———, *The Harlem Group of Negro Writers,* ed. Edward J. Mullen (Westport, CT: Greenwood Press, 2001); ———, Interview with M.W. King, "A Poet's Odyssey, " in *Anger and Beyond: The Negro Writer in the United States,* ed. Herbert Hill (New York: Harper & Row, 1966, 181–195); ———, *Libretto for the Republic of Liberia* (New York: Collier, 1970); ———, "The Odyssey of a Manuscript" (*New Letters* 48 [Fall 1981]: 5–17); ———, *Rendezvous with America* (New York: Dodd, Mead, and Co., 1944). ***Selected Secondary Sources:*** Berube, Michael, *Marginal Forces/Cultural Centers: Tolson, Pynchon, and the Politics of the Canon* (Ithaca: Cornell University Press, 1992); Farnsworth, Robert M., *Melvin B. Tolson 1898–1966 Plain Talk and Poetic Prophecy* (Columbia: University of Missouri Press, 1984); Flasch, Joy, *Melvin B. Tolson* (New York: Twayne Publishers, 1972); Nielsen, Aldon L., "Melvin B. Tolson and the Deterritorialization of Modernism" (*African American Review* 26.2 [1992]: 241–255); Russell, Mariann, *Melvin B. Tolson's "Harlem Gallery": A Literary Analysis* (Columbia: University of Missouri Press, 1980).

Kathy Lou Schultz

TOMLINSON, CHARLES (1927–)

The work of English poet, critic, translator and artist Charles Tomlinson looks before and after, in transit, as he passes between the Old World and America. He sets out his poems to descry his own and foreign landscapes from their boundaries. Tomlinson's poems are acclaimed in North America and continental Europe, but they have so far received less academic recognition in his own country. Jonathon Minton and other recent commentators have suggested that Tomlinson remains one of the major examples of the "transitory poetics" at the center of the American **modernism** from which his work emerges. This means that, within the distinctive movement of his poetry, every border becomes suddenly the center at which point a new and larger view is discovered.

Tomlinson was born in 1927 in Stoke-on-Trent, an industrial town forming part of "the Potteries" in North Staffordshire, England. After receiving a grammar school education, he studied English at Cambridge (1945–1948), where he was tutored by the poet and critic Donald Davie. Upon leaving the university, he taught in an elementary school in London. In 1951, he published a pamphlet of poems, *Relations and Contraries*, which, except for its title and "Poem" ("Wakening with the window over fields"), he has since dismissed. In the same year, he accepted a secretarial post in northern Italy, where he composed poems later published in *The Necklace* (1955). On returning to London, Tomlinson embarked on his MA thesis at the University of London, which he completed in 1955. In 1956 he joined the department of English at the University of Bristol as a lecturer (later as a reader and eventually as a professor, holding a chair).

Tomlinson's academic career in England was punctuated by many visits abroad as reflected in his numerous volumes of verse. He traveled widely in Europe, the United States, and Mexico, spending a year as visiting professor at the University of New Mexico. His 1958 collection of poems, *Seeing Is Believing*, was published first in the United States. *A Peopled Landscape* followed in 1963 and *American Scenes and Other Poems* in 1966; since then, he has averaged one collection every three years. His first *Collected Poems* was published in 1985. Tomlinson retired from academic life at Bristol University in 1992, devoting himself to reading, writing and translating, traveling and lecturing occasionally. His *Selected Poems: 1955–1997* appeared in 1997. In 1998 he became a member of the American Academy of Arts and Sciences, and a Companion of the British Empire in 2002. *Skywriting* appeared in 2003 and *Cracks in the Universe* is forthcoming in 2006. Tomlinson and his wife, Brenda, have two daughters and live mainly at their home above the banks of the river Severn in Gloucestershire, England.

In 1981, at the American critic Hugh Kenner's behest, Tomlinson published *Some Americans* (now incorporated as part of *American Essays: Making It New* [2001]), his chronicle of "the way certain American poets . . . helped an English poet to find himself" (117). For the young Tomlinson, these poets were **Ezra Pound**, **Marianne Moore**, **Wallace Stevens**, and **William Carlos Williams**, whom he encountered and absorbed in that order. Along the way, he labored through **Walt Whitman** and he admired **Hart Crane**, albeit grudgingly, since Crane's "suicidal" (121) vision of paradise reminded Tomlinson of his growing dissatisfaction with Whitman, **Ralph Waldo Emerson**, and **Edgar Allan Poe**.

According to this memoir of poetic influence and encounters, Tomlinson's often frustrated awakening into American modernist poetry began with his first puzzled reading in a copy of the Sesame Book selection of Ezra Pound, found by chance in a Staffordshire bookshop in the 1940s. He later encountered Marianne Moore in Michael Roberts's *Faber Book of Modern Verse*, eventually coming across her poem "The Fish" in Anne Ridler's *Little Book of Modern Verse.* When he was introduced to Stevens's "Thirteen Ways of Looking at a Blackbird" by his tutor Davie in a pub near Cambridge, he simultaneously "muffed" (119) the chance to read Williams for the first time, and he did not seriously read the latter poet until the autumn of 1956. Thus this narrative of a poet finding himself by slowly finding American poets only culminates for Tomlinson after he has written "Sea Poem" (*A Peopled Landscape*), which emulates the "three-ply cadences" of late Williams. Eventually Tomlinson corresponded with Stevens and visited Moore and Williams among others during his first visit to America, funded by a travel grant for European writers in 1959. In later years, he forged connections with American **Objectivist** poets such as **Louis Zukofsky** and **George Oppen**, **Robert Duncan** and **Robert Creeley**.

As Tomlinson wrote in 1981, "The 1950s were an unpropitious time to write the kind of verse that interested me, and England an unpropitious place in which to publish it" (124). He recalls and wryly reverses Stevens's half-jocular sense of displacement, which Stevens felt in the America of the mid 1930s, noting in "Sailing After Lunch" that he was "a most inappropriate man / In a most unpropitious place" (*Ideas of Order*). However, Tomlinson as an inappropriate young Englishman in an unpropitious postwar Britain, found the American Stevens to be an appropriate master. Tomlinson discovered early that Stevens, along with Pound, Moore, and Williams, had already made out of America the propitious place of American modernist poetry. His precocious and passionate need to cross over to embrace these appropriate American poets has developed during his long career into a profound understanding of transatlantic poetic relations. For the older Tomlinson, neither American nor **British poetry** exist in isolation, but they come into being, as he remembers Williams saying of marriage, in an "anthology of transit."

In "Some Americans," which Tomlinson considers his very first poem, he not only approaches a place "where space represented possibility" (*Collected Poems*, vii), but also approaches a place where he can embrace Pound. Thus, "wakening with the window over fields" continues with lines in which Tomlinson's "unstopped ear" is "caught" by Poundian syncopation in "Ode Pour l'Election de Son Sepulchre": "Each succeeding hoof fall, now remote, / Breaks clean and frost-sharp on the unstopped ear." In this English version, involving a quaint horse float delivering milk in the late 1940s, Tomlinson implies his "own variation that the ear was unstopped not to the sirens' song, but to the sharpness of sense experience" (122). Later, Tomlinson's unstopped ear will imitate Stevens's "Thirteen Ways of Looking at a Blackbird" (*Harmonium*) in such poems as "Nine Variations in a Chinese Winter Setting" in *The Necklace*, where Stevens's "it was evening all afternoon" becomes "it is afternoon—interminably." He will also become accustomed to Moore's scrupulousness in his conversations with her about her repeated revisions of "The Steeple-Jack."

Tomlinson's haphazard but increasingly perceptive and creative conversations with American modernist poetry in the late 1940s and 1950s were played out against the backdrop of his more conventional English studies under the aegis of Donald Davie at Cambridge. Thus, although the "tonality" of his early poems "sounded American, the tradition of the work went back to Coleridge's conversation poems" (*Collected Poems*, 125). However, it is on this border between Old World and the New World that Tomlinson found his distinctive voice as a poet. This border became, for the developing poet, transfigured as the sea. Tomlinson read Stevens's "The Comedian as the Letter C" (his poem of the ocean, which allows the letter C to merge with the sea), Crane's "Voyages," Pound's second *Canto*, Moore's "The Fish" and "The Steeple-Jack," and, retrospectively, Whitman's "Sea Drift." It seemed to the poet that these poems "propose a moral terrain where you must confront nature, and they implied for me a moral atmosphere that itself partook of the sharpness of brine and sea breeze" (123). This liquid, moral terrain, which is also a moral atmosphere, is the border upon which critics are now tempted to read Tomlinson on both sides of the Atlantic. For Tomlinson, the place of national literature is transatlantic.

"The Atlantic," the opening poem in *Seeing Is Believing*, makes its title the subject of the first sentence of the poem, in the manner of Moore's "The Fish." Like Moore, Tomlinson is also enthralled by the liminal site of the shore, the beach, and the waves: "A whitening line, collapsing / Powdering-off down its broken length." As Michael Kirkham says in *Passionate Intellect*, the first exclusive critical study of Tomlinson's poetry, "The Atlantic" "provides a very clear demonstration, on the one hand, of the separate existence of natural processes and human actions and, on the other, of the unity that overrides those differences" (73). In "Sea Poem," from his next collection, *A Peopled Landscape*, Tomlinson transmutes Williams's distinctive three-tiered "measure" "in a multiple monody / crowding towards that end." This movement makes the poem both less and more generous toward the American idiom than Williams imagined.

By the time of "On Water," published in *Written on Water* in 1972, Tomlinson suggests his sense of transitory identity and nationality in the figure from Keats's epitaph of having one's name "writ on water." In Tomlinson's poem his identity is written "with illegible depths / and lucid passages," a writing which "confers / as much as it denies" what he knows of Stevens's "noble accents / And lucid inescapable rhythms" (lines from Stevens's "Thirteen Ways of Looking at a Blackbird"). Later in life, Tomlinson gazes at the Atlantic, near his dead mother's house on the English border with Wales but across the river Severn from his own home in Gloucestershire and describes the Severn "[f]lashing its sign inland, its pulse / Of light that shimmers off the Atlantic" (*The Flood*, 1981). The Atlantic has become for this transatlantic poet at once a liquid, illimitable border and an inward-flooding pulse of light. For Tomlinson, American and European poetics exist in a state of mutual modulation, each attending to and measuring the other.

Tomlinson's poems engage with place, but this Objectivism is also a realization that space represents what he calls, in the Preface to his *Collected Poems*, "possibility" (vii). As Tomlinson's work approaches the force of this possibility, the human self puts aside, as he says, "the more possessive and violent claims of personality" (vii). His poems embrace not objects so much as relations. Tomlinson works to interrupt but also to centralize these spatial and phenomenological, or temporal and national, borders; at once, he is dividing and conjoining man and world or Old and New Worlds, as the self expands, "somewhat self-forgetfully" (vii), to embrace such possibility.

Further Reading. ***Selected Primary Sources:*** Tomlinson, Charles, *American Essays: Making it New* (Manchester: Carcanet, 2001); ———, *American Scenes and Other Poems* (Oxford: Oxford University Press, 1966); ———, *Collected Poems* (Oxford: Oxford University Press, 1985; expanded paperback edition, 1987); ———, *The Flood* (Oxford: Oxford University Press, 1981); ———, *The Necklace* (Swinford, England: Fanatasy Press, 1955); ———, *A Peopled Landscape* (Oxford: Oxford University Press, 1963); ———, *Seeing Is Believing* (New York: McDowell, Oblensky, 1958; 1960); ———, *Selected Poems* (Oxford: Oxford University Press, 1978); ———, *Selected Poems: 1955–1997* (Oxford: Oxford University Press, 1997); ———, *Skywriting* (Manchester: Carcanet, 2003); ———, *The Way of a World* (Oxford: Oxford University Press, 1969); ———, *Written on Water* (Oxford: Oxford University Press, 1972). ***Selected Secondary Sources:*** Clark, Timothy, *Charles Tomlinson* (Plymouth: Northcote House, in association with the British Academy, 1999); Kirkham, Michael, *Passionate Intellect: The Poetry of Charles Tomlinson* (Liverpool: Liverpool University Press, 1999); Minton, Jonathon, "Review of *American Essays*" (*Free Verse* [n.d.]); Saunders, Judith P., *The Poetry of Charles Tomlinson: Border Lines* (London: Associated University Presses, 2003).

Edward Clarke

TOMPSON, BENJAMIN (1642–1714)

Benjamin Tompson was the first British American colonial poet of distinction who was American born. Although Tompson wrote many works commemorating the deaths of distinguished New Englanders, he is perhaps best known for his work defining, defending, and celebrating British America's colonial and commercial efforts. Much of his poetry appears as introductory matter for histories and maps of the region or as tributes to distinguished businessmen and leaders of British American military campaigns. His most famous work provides a New Englander's perspective on the most devastating war of the period, King Philip's War. The work gained considerable attention on both sides of the Atlantic, so much so that an English printer came out with a pirated edition of the poem before Tompson's own work appeared. His work was well regarded enough during his own lifetime that he was dubbed "the renowned poet of New England" on his tombstone.

Little is known about the details of Tompson's life. He was born in Braintree, now Quincy, Massachusetts, on July 14, 1642, to Abigail and the Reverend William Tompson, a minister of great influence in the colony. His mother died in 1654 while his father was in Virginia, and Tompson was adopted by the Blanchard family of Charlestown. His father, subject to fits of melancholy and depression throughout his life, never reclaimed his son. Tompson's adoptive family had the financial resources to send him to Harvard, where he received his degree in 1662. Although the expectation was almost certainly that Tompson would go into the ministry upon graduation, he embarked instead on a career that included a number of different occupations. Tompson practiced medicine, sought to earn his living as a poet, and worked as a teacher in various New England communities, sometimes suing those communities in disputes over compensation. In his battles with local authorities, Tompson did not shy away from even the most powerful of New Englanders—for instance, he sent letters soliciting land grants from members of the most famous family in Massachusetts Bay, the Mathers. He was married twice, first in 1667 to Susanna Kirkland and then in 1698 to Prudence Payson.

His most famous poem, *New England's Crisis*, uses the mock **epic** form to provide a brief history of King Philip's War. In its American version, the poem begins with a jeremiad on the moral backsliding of late-seventeenth-century New Englanders. The war, the poem contends, should be seen as God's attempt to chasten the community for failing to maintain the high standards of religiosity that defined the colonies' original inhabitants. In spite of these flaws, the poem contends that if New Englanders reformed their ways, the war might produce a new, even more zealous brand of colonist and a return to the ways of the founders. To communicate these ideas, Tompson uses an innovative structure for the poem. Rather than tell the chronological story of the war, Tompson concludes his poem with a series of **elegies** to the towns that were destroyed, or nearly so, during the conflict. In so doing, Tompson provides a fundamentally different way of understanding community in New England. Whereas other writers had cast New England solely in terms of exemplary individuals or purely in relation to English ways, Tompson's focus on towns as bodies for which elegies are appropriate gives the colonial community a collective identity that is entirely derived from local conditions.

The English version of this poem, in both its pirated and authorized editions, retains the closing elegies but omits the opening stanzas that bluntly criticize the supposed materialist leanings of New Englanders. The removal of this section shifts the poem's focus and theme from a demonstration of God's attempt to purify and reclaim what New Englanders hope is a chosen land, to an attempt to demonstrate to a skeptical English audience the Indians' treacheries against a largely innocent colonial population.

Tompson never wrote anything quite as ambitious again. Of the various elegies and dedicatory poems Tompson composed following that *New Englands Crisis*, perhaps the most interesting is "To Lord Bellamont when entering Governour of the Massachussets." Written in 1712 to commemorate the arrival of Lord Bellamont, the new governor of the colony, Tompson's poem shows that colonial British American writers were beginning to think about the writing of previous colonists as part of a distinct tradition. Tompson's poem contains many references to other works by New England writers. In addition, when Thompson delivered the poem to the new governor, he dressed as one of the characters from an earlier work, Nathaniel Ward's *The Simple Cobbler of Aggawam.* In dressing as a self-declared American who feels compelled to sound off to the king, Tompson began the work of drawing other New England writers into a literary tradition.

Further Reading. ***Selected Primary Sources:*** Tompson, Benjamin, *Benjamin Tompson: Colonial Bard, A Critical Edition,* ed. Peter White (University Park: Penn State University Press, 1980); ———, *New Englands Crisis. Or a Brief Narrative of New Englands Lamentable Estate at present, compar'd with the former (but few) years of Prosperity* (Boston: n.p., 1676). ***Selected Secondary Sources:*** Franklin, Wayne, "*The Harangue of King Philip* in *New Englands Crisis* (1676)" (*American Literature* 51 [1980]: 536–540); White, Peter, "Cannibals and Turks: Benjamin Tompson's Image of the Native American," in *Puritan Poets and Poetics: Seventeenth-Century American Poetry in Theory and Practice,* ed. Peter White (University Park: Pennsylvania State University Press, 1985, 198–209).

James Egan

TOOMER, JEAN (1894–1967)

Jean Toomer is one of the twentieth-century's more enigmatic literary figures. His first major work, *Cane* (1923), garnered immediate attention with its sensual descriptions of black life and its experimental mixture of poetry and prose. American proponents of **modernism** saw in this previously unknown talent something new and unique in both subject matter and style. Then, almost immediately after *Cane*'s publication, Toomer disappeared from the literary scene to focus on his philosophical and religious interests. He continued writing throughout his life, but most publishers found his work too esoteric to risk printing it. The emergence of African American studies in the early 1970s brought Toomer renewed attention, with many critics viewing *Cane* as an inaugural text of the **Harlem Renaissance**. Ironically, Toomer rarely associated himself with this movement's leading figures and, for most of his life, did not identify himself as black—casting himself instead as a "New American," a mixture of several races and nationalities. Despite ambivalence about his own racial heritage, Toomer portrayed **African American** experience, particularly as occurring in the South, with a lyrical beauty and spiritual passion that few writers of his time would match.

Biographers have characterized Toomer's early years as a period of literal and figurative wandering. He was born Nathan Eugene Toomer on December 26, 1894, to Nathan and Nina Pinchback Toomer. After Nathan abandoned his family, Nina returned to her father's Washington, D.C., home. She remarried a few years later, moving young Eugene to New Rochelle, New York. She died in 1909, leaving the boy in the care of his grandparents. Toomer's grandfather, Pinckney B.S. Pinchback, had earned fame as the son of a planter and slave, who achieved financial success through shrewd business acumen and then rose to political power with a brief stint as governor during Louisiana's turbulent Reconstruction days. By the time Jean Toomer was born, Pinchback's fortunes had begun to decline, and in 1910 he moved his family from an affluent Washington neighborhood to much more modest accommodations. The move brought Toomer to the famous M Street High School, where activist Anna Julia Cooper was principal and writer **Angelina Weld Grimké** taught English. Despite a solid education and a relatively privileged life, Toomer never finished college. After graduating from high school in 1914, he attended four universities in four years, with frequent changes in major. Finally dropping out of New York's City College in 1917, Toomer spent the next few years moving from job to job and wound up collapsing from physical exhaustion in 1919. His recuperation from the 1919 incident brought a renewal of his attention to literature, initially developed when he missed a year of school and spent his time reading. He soon resolved to be a writer.

Toomer took his literary apprenticeship seriously. His reading list included Russian novelists Fyodor Dostoyevsky and Leo Tolstoy, French writers Charles Baudelaire and Gustave Flaubert, and American contemporaries Sherwood Anderson, Theodore Dreiser, **Robert Frost**, and Sinclair Lewis. He read the top magazines of his day, such as the *Dial*, the *Nation*, and the *New Republic*, and he read widely in religion, philosophy, and psychology. Toomer also made contacts with important literary figures who lived near him in Greenwich Village, including Van Wyck Brooks, **Hart Crane**, **Edwin Arlington Robinson**, Lola Ridge, and Waldo Frank. The latter two became instrumental in shaping the work that led to *Cane.*

During this time, Toomer produced what he called a "trunk full of manuscripts" representing all genres, yet he still had trouble finding a focus. That opportunity came in 1921, while he was living in Washington, D.C., and caring for his aging grandparents. The principal of a small, black, agricultural and industrial school in Sparta, Georgia, passed through town seeking a temporary replacement, and Toomer took the job. The time he spent in the South defined his work thereafter. Struck by the rich folk spirit that persisted among the people, despite lives made difficult by poverty and racial violence, Toomer began to write about what he saw and, more important, what he heard. The music of spirituals, work songs, and **blues** became the basis of *Cane*, both thematically and structurally. The day before he left Sparta, he sent a poem, "Georgia Dusk" (1922), to the *Liberator*; on the train home he started work on the prose sections of the book, and, within a year, *Cane* was complete. Waldo Frank helped Toomer secure publication by Boni and Liveright. Excerpts from the book came out in the *Crisis*, *Double Dealer*, *Modern Review*, and *Broom* (where Lola Ridge worked as an editor), convincing many readers that a new literary star had been born. Pleased with his critical success, Toomer was dismayed by the book's slow sales and also by the publishing world's insistence upon describing him as a promising "Negro" talent rather than as an "American." Toomer had already begun turning his attentions elsewhere, to the philosophies of a man named George Ivanovitch Gurdjieff.

Gurdjieff provided what Toomer believed he had been missing: a rigorous system of spiritual and physical practices that would bring harmony to his fragmented soul. Gurdjieff's teachings had attracted many followers to his Institute for the Harmonious Development of Man, located near Paris in Fontainebleau, where students would learn to reach their full potential as human beings by balancing mind, body, and spirit. Toomer was an eager recruit and soon became a teacher, working for the Gurdjieff organization for the next decade. While leading a group in Portage, Wisconsin, in 1932, he met and married novelist Margery Latimer, who died in 1933 while giving birth to their daughter. In 1934 he married Marjorie Content, who remained with him until his death. This turbulent period of the early 1930s contributed to Toomer's break with Gurdjieff, whom he wrote shortly after his marriage to Content to say that his responsibilities as husband and father prevented him from participating more actively. Although Gurdjieffian philosophies continued to influence Toomer after his formal break with the group, he began to explore other spiritual paths—making a pilgrimage to India, becoming a Quaker in 1939, beginning Jungian analysis in 1949, and, in 1950, taking up Scientology.

Toomer's writing during the post-*Cane* years paralleled his spiritual quest, focusing on the search for wholeness, human potential tragically unrealized, and the possibility of transcendence. These writings also mirror Toomer's pre-*Cane* years as he produced another "trunk full" of manuscripts. Some works—such as the **Whitmanesque long poem** "Blue Meridian" (1936), the play *Balo* (1927), and the short stories "Easter" (1925), "Mr. Costyve Duditch" (1928), and "York Beach" (1929)—found their way into magazines and anthologies. Others—the novels *Caromb* and *The Gallonwerps*, and several draft versions of an autobiography—remained unpublished until Darwin Turner's 1980 edition, *The Wayward and the Seeking: A Collection of Writings by Jean Toomer*. Unfortunately, Toomer never recaptured the genius he exhibited in *Cane*, nor did he seem to find the harmony he sought in life. From the 1940s on, he was beset with physical problems and, consequently, emotional ones. He spent his final years in and out of nursing homes, succumbing to arteriosclerosis on March 30, 1967.

The tension between harmony and fragmentation that makes Toomer's life appear tragic ironically makes *Cane* an intriguing book. A collection of poems, sketches, and stories, some with elements of drama, *Cane*'s unifying structure is circular. Its first two sections are preceded by drawings of arcs, and the final section pulls the two arcs together into a circular form whose lines do not fully meet. These drawings visually represent the book's movement through different locations, imagery patterns, and themes. The first part, set in the South and comprising ten poems and six narratives, focuses on stories of women who cross traditional sexual boundaries. Karintha is a "growing thing ripened too soon"; Becky is a white woman whose two sons are black; Carma and Louisa drive men to kill. This section's tone is correspondingly sensual: Karintha and the others inhabit a world of sugarcane and cotton, smelling of pine needles and smoke, colored by dusk, and accompanied by folk songs hummed in the background. *Cane*'s second section moves north, to Washington, D.C., and Chicago, a world of asphalt and interiors, where men never fully connect to their own emotions or to the women they love. Avey falls asleep as the narrator speaks of his feelings. Characters in "Theater" and "Box Seat" maintain an emotional as well as literal distance across the aisles, while Bona and Paul are driven apart by race. The middle section's seven sketches and five poems are followed by "Kabnis," *Cane*'s entire third section. Here, the book returns to the South, with its northern-educated schoolteacher Ralph Kabnis, whose experience mirrors in many ways Toomer's in Sparta. Both are struck by the land and its people, which exude a poetic beauty that is offset by the ugliness of poverty and racism. Both struggle to give voice to this tension but find that words cannot capture the complicated essence of such a place.

"Kabnis" ends with a man trying to overcome an emotional breakdown, and, in a similar way, *Cane* is a book whose various threads always seem to be on the verge of pulling apart. Holding the book together are not just the visual elements of the circle and the geographical movement from the South to the North and back, but also the poems that act as Toomer's primary transitional device—the chorus to the song that *Cane* ultimately becomes.

In the first section, two poems separate each narrative, reinforcing the action, themes, and imagery. Karintha gives birth in the woods, and the child's fate remains mysterious, but the following poem, "Reapers," describes a field mouse cut down by a scythe while men continue mowing without noticing the bloodstained blade. The next poem, "November Cotton Flower," echoes descriptions of Karintha's beauty, as both bloom suddenly, and sets up Becky's death in the next sketch by referring to the flower as an omen of a deathly winter. "Carma," beginning with the image of a woman wearing overalls who is "strong as any man," follows the work rhythms of "Cotton Song," in which men chant "[c]ome, brother, roll, roll" as they heave the bales. "Blood-Burning Moon," in which a black man is lynched after fighting with a white man over a woman, is preceded by "Portrait in Georgia," which describes a woman whose braided hair coils "like a lyncher's rope," and whose body is the color of "black flesh after flame." Poetry can be found within sketches as well. "Karintha" is punctuated by a four-line verse at the beginning, middle, and end, comparing her skin to "dusk on the eastern horizon." "Blood-Burning Moon" has a similar structure, with each of its three sections ending in a cry for the "sinner" to "come out that fact'ry door," just as the lynch mob might have chanted for their victim, Tom Burwell.

Both the second and the third, "Kabnis," sections of *Cane* also use poetry within their narratives. Six lines reminiscent of a spiritual recur in "Kabnis," promising "rest, and sweet glory / In Camp Ground"—an ironic commentary on a story whose main character seeks but does not find rest or redemption. Similarly, the natural imagery of poems such as "Beehive" and "Storm Ending" provide counterpoint to the second section's urban tones. The second section's poetry, on the other hand, often echoes its stories just as the poems do in the first. The lines that form the beginning and end of "Seventh Street," a main thoroughfare in Washington, D.C., describe "bootleggers in silken shirts" and "ballooned, zooming Cadillacs, / Whizzing, whizzing down the street-car tracks." A poem such as "Her Lips are Copper Wire" speaks of an erotic electricity quite different from the blooming flowers and rising moons that accompany the dusky rural beauties of the book's first section, emphasizing the second's more streetwise and sophisticated women. In keeping with *Cane*'s primary tension between fusion and fragmentation, as well as its use of poetry as chorus, it could be said that the poems in this second section sometimes work in harmony and sometimes create dissonance. This section's overall rhythms differ as well. Rather than the regular beat of the narrative/two poems/narrative pattern found in the first section, the second section forms an irregular cadence of poetry occurring sporadically, with the whole structure working very much like the arcs that divide *Cane*'s three parts: the circle comes close but never fully fits together.

Cane is ultimately a book about mourning and morning, an outcry that comes from a fragmented soul as well as the music that holds the promise of a new day. Each of the book's three sections reflects this theme through images of sunset and sunrise, hunger and sustenance, and, especially, the poet and his song. Two poems lying at the literal and metaphorical center of *Cane*'s first section speak to music's healing power. The people Toomer writes of in this section of the book are not far removed from slavery: They toil in sawmills and cotton fields, they combat poverty and lynch mobs. In "Georgia Dusk," they leave that world behind as they gather at night amid the pine trees and the swamps in a parade evoking "race memories of king and caravan, / High priests . . . and a juju-man." Their song reaches back through the ages, upward to the heavens, and back down again to nourish them, in the poem's final lines, bringing "dreams of Christ to dusky cane-lipped throngs." In "Song of the Son," Toomer speaks of the poet's responsibility to record that song before it is too late. The lines "the sun is setting on / A song-lit race of slaves" echo a statement Toomer made after *Cane* was published, explaining that he wanted to write about a way of life before it died out. "Song of the Son" figures that sentiment as a "plum" saved for the poet, from which he takes a seed that becomes "[a]n everlasting song."

Cane's second section demonstrates the emotional price characters pay when they lose touch with their roots and with themselves. In the spiritual wasteland of the ironically titled "Harvest Song," placed near the end of this section, the refrain is one of hunger. The speaker puts grain into his mouth and tastes nothing. His throat is dry to the point that he cannot sing, and his ears are so caked with dust that he cannot hear others' songs. The need to mourn the loss of song also appears in "Kabnis," as the title character, like *Cane*'s poet, seeks the right words to convey his Southern experience, but finds that words elude him. Yet "Kabnis" does not end on an entirely tragic note. Despite the inadequacies of language, and the book's movement from harmony into a fragmented dissonance, Toomer holds out promise for the future. "The sun arises," *Cane*'s final lines read, and "sends a birth-song slanting down gray dust streets."

The book concludes with a hope that Toomer struggled to believe in until the end. His search for creative expression was often thwarted but found its most poignant realization in *Cane*. In that sense, he fulfills the poetic role described in "Song of the Son": recording and transmitting for future generations an everlasting song with the respect and beauty that it deserves.

Further Reading. ***Selected Primary Sources:*** Toomer, Jean, *Cane* (New York: Boni and Liveright, 1923); ———, *The Collected Poems of Jean Toomer*, ed. Robert B. Jones and Margery Toomer Latimer (Chapel Hill: University of North Carolina Press, 1988); ———, *A Jean Toomer Reader: Selected Unpublished Writings*, ed. Frederik L. Rusch (New York: Oxford University Press, 1993); ———, *Jean Toomer: Selected Essays and Literary Criticism*, ed. Robert B. Jones (Knoxville: University of Tennessee Press, 1996); ———, *The Wayward and the Seeking: A Collection of Writings by Jean Toomer*, ed. Darwin Turner (Washington, D.C.: Howard University Press, 1980). ***Selected Secondary Sources:*** Fabre, Geneviève, and Michel Feith, eds., *Jean Toomer and the Harlem Renaissance* (New Brunswick: Rutgers University Press, 2001); Kernan, Cynthia Earl, and Richard Eldridge, *The Lives of Jean Toomer: A Hunger for Wholeness* (Baton Rouge: Louisiana State University Press, 1987); McKay, Nellie Y., *Jean Toomer, Artist: A Study of His Literary Life and Work, 1894–1936* (Chapel Hill: University of North Carolina Press, 1984); O'Daniel, Therman B., ed., *Jean Toomer: A Critical Evaluation* (Washington, D.C.: Howard University Press, 1988); Woodson, Jon, *To Make a New Race: Gurdjieff, Toomer, and the Harlem Renaissance* (Jackson: University Press of Mississippi, 1999).

Julie Buckner Armstrong

TRANSLATION

"There is no one way to translate" is an adage especially true in the domain of poetry. For Walter Benjamin, the translator's task is the accurate transmission of an inessential content, thus placing the poet-translator in a complex double-bind. Questions of general strategies and specific semantic and sound choices must be raised: Who is the translation for? Will it serve as a crib for the reader who partially speaks the source language? Is it to be a stand-alone poem? Is a prose summary required, or a poetic translation? How should the repetition of the French *schwa* sound be rendered? Is the color known as gray the same in English and Welsh? And so on. One primary concern, except when the translator's purpose is purely academic, is to avoid spoon-feeding the reader a mere paraphrase. The target text should remain as open as the original. Translating poetry is anything but a mechanical task; it involves the poet-translator with the very materials of his/her trade. For these reasons, generations of American poets have been attracted to this onerous activity, sometimes seen as an apprenticeship to writing new poetry.

The poet-translator's double-bind is stickier than that of the prose translator. Beyond maintaining the balance between faithfulness and target text readability, the poet-translator must deal with questions of rhyme and rhythm, rarely central in prose translation. It is all too easy to supply quick answers and lead the reader into a false sense of security, for example by rhyming the translation of a poem merely because the source text was in rhyme. The assumption that rhyme in different languages works in similar ways is erroneous. French rhyme (bound to metrical and morphological considerations) is not English rhyme. The native French structure of the alexandrine (twelve syllables) is as inherently tied to the French language as the iambic pentameter is to English. Beyond and behind such formal differences lies the fundamental otherness of a foreign language. How greatly a language is inflected, the number of nasal vowels, and a host of other linguistic realities inform the structural possibilities of formal poetry. Rhythm, too, is language-specific. Transposing foreign rhyme or rhythm either directly or using unjustified displacement compensation generally results in a skeleton translation. Conversely, the importing of foreign poetic forms, as exemplified by **Elizabeth Bishop**'s use of the sestina and the sonnet, stands as another form of indirect translation.

Free-verse translation is now often the poet's choice for how best to render rhyme and rhythm. Although the promotion of free-verse translation by figures such as Yves Bonnefoy and **Robert Lowell** may seem like a very recent phenomenon, the refusal of word-for-word translations, and the preference for something more akin to imitation, can be traced back to classical sources, notably Cicero's *De optimo genere oratorum* and Quintilian's *Institutio oratoria*, where the appropriateness of stylistic devices within the target language are of primary importance. St. Jerome later formulated his approach in similar terms, noting that he translated "not word for word, but sense for sense." Dryden, too, long before the advent of what is now recognized as free verse, insisted on the importance of focusing on the text as a whole, not merely on minute questions of faithfulness. The choice of a free-verse translation is not (except when it is poorly executed) to be confused with translation into prose; this approach is closer to crib notes, often invaluable for the academic or researcher, but generally losing much of the source text's true being.

The history of translation undertaken by American poets offers only a few moments of interest before the twentieth century. Many early American poets (especially from New England) were part of the church and thus were versed in the languages of classical antiquity. **Edward Taylor**, whose poetry was only discovered in the 1930s, read Greek, Latin, and Hebrew, and authored a *Metrical History of Christianity* (ca. 1720), wherein the influence of his knowledge of translation is clear. **Cotton Mather**'s *Magnalia Christi Americana* (1702) demonstrates its proximity to European models, and alongside **Roger**

Williams, among his many books, authored one of the first phrase books of Native American languages, *A Key Into the Languages of America* (1643). In the nineteenth century, translation moved away from the clergy, and a new interest developed in poetry from around the world. **Emerson**, for example, was fascinated by the legends of Arabia, India, and Persia. His short poem "Brahma," published in the November 1857 *Atlantic Monthly*, stands as an epitome of Hindu philosophy. It has its roots in Emerson's own translations of the *Vishnu Purana* and the *Katha Upanishad*, with direct links, too, to the *Bhagavadgita*. Not only did Emerson's reading and translation provide him with much of the philosophical content for his own poetic production, but his renderings and adaptations have continued to influence later translations of Eastern texts in both tone and content. **Longfellow** was another nineteenth-century poet equally involved in the process of translation. As a professor of modern languages at Harvard (1835–1954), Longfellow studied and taught Dante. He later produced a poetic translation of Dante's *Divine Comedy* (1867).

It is the twentieth century that clearly stands as the century of translation for American poets. Building on Emerson and Longfellow as well as the history of poetry translation in England (including translators such as King Alfred, Chaucer, Sidney, Donne, Milton, and especially Dryden), it was most specifically **Ezra Pound** who revolutionized poetry translation. Without him, the translation of poetry as now understood would be unimaginable. Although Pound wrote widely on the translation of poetry, he was by no means a theorist. Nor was he a systematic translator. Yet, Pound's impact on all translators who followed him cannot be overestimated.

Early in his career, Pound rendered classical **Chinese** poems into free verse (*Cathay*, 1915), using as a basis the literal word-for-word translations of Ernest Fenollosa. As a translation, *Cathay* underscores that to translate a poem successfully, the translator needs more than merely a knowledge of the source language, as the collection's full title suggests: *Cathay: . . from the Chinese of Rihaku, from the notes of the late Ernest Fenollosa, and the Decipherings of the Professors Mori and Ariga*. The resultant construction is thus neither transposition, nor imitation, but a fresh creation from the "ruins" of a demolished poem, a space where the poet-translator, between languages, deals with what Benjamin calls "pure language." The importance of *Cathay* for Pound's own creative output was immense: The concrete nature of Chinese ideograms represented for Pound a model of juxtaposition that had already become apparent to him through his interaction with artists of **vorticisim**, and which also paved the way for the extensive use of quotations in foreign languages throughout *The Cantos*.

In 1919 Pound published his *Homage to Sextus Propertius*. The first-century Roman poet is invoked as a fellow satirist, but the relationship between the original text's author and modern translator is unclear. This is what creates such a heady feeling of unease: Was Pound translating? Was he merely using Propertius as a model? There is no definitive answer, unless Pound was doing both things simultaneously, a possibility that the poem itself touches upon in its concluding verses. This link between new poetry and a literary continuum informs much of Pound's poetry, and the uncertainty of the poet-translator's identity is one more element in the eternal debate over a poet's sources and the relationship between history, reality, and poetry.

About the same time, Pound translated the Anglo-Saxon poem "The Seafarer." Lee Apter (85–88) analyses two English versions of the same poem: one translation (by Charles W. Kennedy) strictly follows the metrical rules of the original; Pound's, on the other hand, does not, and yet Pound's poem sounds much more like the original than does Kennedy's—an irony that might be seen as proof of Pound's genius. Compare, for example, Kennedy's "a song I sing of my sea-adventure" to Pound's "may I for my own self song's truth reckon / Journey's jargon." Kennedy's version seems to resemble a chain of iambs rather than the Anglo-Saxon model, where each half-line is composed of two stressed and a variable number of unstressed syllables, creating a very heavy and tail-dragging rhythm. Pound breaks with the specific model and reduces the number of unstressed syllables, thus adding weight to the line—one consequence of which is to bring out the heavy sound of the caesura in the original.

Pound's legacy as a translator is large and protean, eclipsing other twentieth-century poets also actively involved in the translation of poetry, such as **Marianne Moore** (who translated La Fontaine's *Fables*) and a host of others. Beyond Pound's translations and his other poetic works, which directly and indirectly grew from and around them, perhaps his most significant contribution was the concretization of the notion that a poem-translation should have the status of independent text. Pound gave to the poet-translator the right to create a text that shared in the original text's sounds and meanings without replicating them unit for unit.

Pound's influence has led to the situation in which today's commercial translations generally emphasize the fact that the poems in translation are also valid as independent texts. In the introduction to his **anthology** of foreign poetry translated into English, George Steiner defines a translated poem as "[one for] which a poem in another language . . . is the vitalizing, shaping presence." The new poem can thus "be read and responded to independently" although it is "not ontologically complete," given that its genesis is situated in a previous text (Steiner, 34) In a similar vein, **W.S. Merwin** notes in the introduction to his recent translation of Dante's *Purgatorio* that, although he wanted a translation "as close to the meaning of the Italian words [as possible]," he also wanted very keenly to produce a "poem in English."

The notion of translations as readable poetry (because the translation is a poem) sometimes meshes with the notion that readability must also guarantee accessibility—not, however, one of Pound's concerns. **Robert Pinsky** produced a version of Dante's *Inferno* (1996) that received the Harold Morton Landon Translation Award from the Academy of American Poets and introduced Dante's masterpiece to a new generation of readers, making it accessible by providing a poem both readable and clear. Pinsky's role as translator here overlaps with his wider concern to make poetry more accessible, illustrated for example by his editing of *Slate*, an online, weekly poetry magazine published by Microsoft. Moreover, Pound's approach to translation is at the origin of a continuing trend of poets collaborating (as did Ezra Pound for *Cathay*) with others better versed in the knowledge of the source language. The translations of Polish poet **Czeslaw Milosz**, for example, were collaboratively realized by Renata Gorczynski, **Robert Hass**, and Robert Pinsky (*The Separate Notebooks*, 1984). It is indeed increasingly common to read at the bottom of an English translation "translated by," followed by an American poet's name, concluded by "and the author."

Pound's contribution to translation lies as part of the history of twentieth-century American poetry. Robert Lowell's progression from rigorously formal poetry (under the influence of **Allen Tate** and the **New Critics**) to a new style in the mid-1950s (under the influence of **W.D. Snodgrass** and **Ginsberg**, as well as personal trauma) picks up on the possibilities made available to translators by Pound, leading to his *Imitations* (1961), a collection of "loose" translations of Rilke, Rimbaud, and others. *Imitations* won the Bollingen Poetry Translation Prize in 1962.

One of the many poet-translators on whom Pound's influence was most radical is **Louis Zukofsky**. Although often overlooked, Zukofsky is essential for understanding the relationship of, and history between, translation and American poetry. Zukofsky saw in Ezra Pound the finest writer in English, and had regular exchanges with him from the 1920s on. In his rendering of *Catullus*, Zukofsky privileged the sounds of the original text over the semantic content: "Pedicabo ego vos et irrumabo" thus slides into "piping, beaus, I'll go *whoosh* and I'll rumble you" (*Catullus*, 16); "minister vetuli" morphs into "minister wet to lee" (27); and "Amabo" becomes "I'm a bow" (32). This approach made Zukofsky's *Catullus* as provocative to classicists as had been Pound's *Homage to Sextus Propertius*. Zukofsky's guiding principle was that for the modern reader to experience the poem in as *Catullus's* readers might have, the reader's vocal organs (mouth, tongue, throat) should be in similar positions to those required to speak the Latin text. It is all too easy to assume that Zukofsky's approach was not grounded in a sure knowledge of Latin, or that the original text's narrative content was completely abandoned, but this is much too simple a conclusion. Catullus's poem 58, for example, sings of the poet's love for Lesbia: "Lesbia nostra, Lesbia illa, / illa Lesbia" (rendered as "Lesbia new star, Lesbia a light / all light, Lesbia"). Calling Lesbia a "new star" is, obviously, motivated more by the sound of the Latin text than by the meaning of "nostra," and yet the poet's intention in both cases is the same: to claim and praise Lesbia. Catullus's statement that Lesbia is "unam / plus quam se atque suos amavit omnes" is rendered as Lesbia being one "whom his eyes caught so as avid of none." The idea of loving Lesbia more than himself and all his own is no longer present, and yet, while following primarily the sound of "suos amavit omnes," in "so as avid of none," Zukofsky still conveys the poet's infatuation and desire, the exclusive nature of his love. This technique, crystallized in this long and important translation project, is present elsewhere throughout Zukofsky's oeuvre through transliterations of words in various modern and ancient languages, from Hebrew to Welsh. Zukofsky's translation stands as an exemplary monument to Pound's influence.

The individuality of each translation makes theorizing or even summarizing the achievements of American poet-translators almost impossible. Although trends can be highlighted, only a focus on individual poets and translations can be of real relevance. The variety and continued interest in translating poetry confirms that it is still a vibrant source of the public's reading pleasure, and of the poet's own exercise and creative output. The variety in approaches to translation is also currently accompanied by an increase in the sources of translated poetry. Although there are still more poems translated from languages such as French, Spanish, and German, a growing number of poets in America are exploring literary traditions less explored by previous generations: poet Charles Cantalupo collaborating with Eritrean poet Reesom Haile on the English version of his poems (*We invented the wheel* 2002), and **Charles Simic** translating the work of Serbian poet Novica Tadic (*Night Mail* 1992) are but two of the many examples of this ongoing work.

Further reading. ***Selected Primary Sources:*** Lowell, Robert, *Imitations* (New York: Noonday Press, 1965); McClatchy, J. D., *The Vintage Book of Contemporary World Poetry* (New York: Vintage Books, 1996); Pound, Ezra, *The Translations of Ezra Pound*, ed. Hugh Kenner (New York: n.p., 1953); Steiner, George, ed., *Poem into Poem: World Poetry in Modern Verse Translation* (Harmondsworth: Penguin, 1970); Zukofsky, Celia and Louis, *Catullus* (London: Cape Goliard, 1969). ***Selected Secondary Sources:*** Apter, Lee, *Digging for the Treasure: Translation* *after Pound* (New York: Peter Lang, 1984); Benjamin, Walter, *Illuminations* (New York: Schocken Books, 1969); Gasparov, Mikhail, *A History of European Versification*, ed. G.S. Smith and Leofranc Holford-Stevens, trans. G.S. Smith and Marina Tarlinskaja (Oxford: Clarendon Press, 1996); Hooley, Daniel, *The Classics in Paraphrase* (London: Associated University Presses, 1988); Steiner, George, *After Babel: Aspects of Language and Translation* (London: Oxford University Press, 1975).

Phillip John Usher

TRASK, KATRINA (1853–1922)

Best known for her role in founding Yaddo, the artists' colony in Saratoga Springs, New York, Katrina Trask was also a writer of poems, essays, short stories, and novels. Although her poetry often suffers from an excess of **sentimentality** and a lack of psychological depth, it is also notable for its considerable formal sophistication and rich variety of subject matter.

The daughter of George Little Nichols, a merchant, and Christina Mary Cole, Trask was born Kate Nichols in Brooklyn, New York, and educated in private schools and by tutors. In 1874 she married Spencer Trask, a Wall Street banker and philanthropist whose financial generosity made possible the resurrection of the *New York Times* in 1896. After the death of their first son in 1881, the Trasks moved to Saratoga Springs. Inspired by their young daughter's mispronunciation of "Shadow," the inn on the grounds of the three-hundred–acre estate where they had stayed during previous summers, they decided to name the estate Yaddo. But tragedy soon followed: In 1888 two of the Trasks' children died from diphtheria, and their last child, twelve days old, died in 1889.

Shortly thereafter, in Yaddo's peaceful precincts, Trask began writing. Several plays about her children were performed privately, and she started publishing poetry in 1892, at first anonymously, and then as Katrina Trask, the name she adopted after being crowned "Katrina, Queen of Yaddo" at a Halloween party. Her first collection, *Under King Constantine*, consisting of three, blank verse, Arthurian-era love poems, was published in 1892 and met with popular success.

In 1891 the mansion at Yaddo burned down, but two years later the Trasks contracted the architect William Halsey Wood to build a fifty-five–room palace of various architectural styles. In this new, stately home, Trask continued to write prolifically: Among her numerous works are *Sonnets and Lyrics* (1894), another volume of poems; *Lessons in Love* (1900), a collection of stories; *Free, Not Bound* (1903), a novel; *Night and Morning* (1906), poems; the blank **verse drama** *King Alfred's Jewel* (1909); and the 1913 anti-war play, *In the Vanguard*, in which she condemned killing in the name of patriotism (eight editions of the play were published, and it was frequently performed by church groups). Trask's anti-war stance was reflected not only in her writing but in her actions: When the United States entered World War I, she cultivated a large plot of land on Yaddo's grounds to provide support to the Allied Forces.

The heirless Trasks, concerned about Yaddo's future, decided that after their deaths, the estate would be transformed into a refuge for artists. "Here," Trask wrote, "will be a perpetual series of house parties—of literary men, literary women, and other artists. Those who are city-weary, who are thirsting for the country and for beauty" would be seen "walking in the woods, wandering in the garden, sitting under the pine trees—men and women—creating, creating, creating!" (quoted in Furman, "The Benign Ghosts of Yaddo"). The Trasks began inviting eminent artists, scientists, and politicians to their estate, and erected marble fountains, planned pine groves, and installed artificial lakes to enhance its picturesque charm.

When Spencer died in a train crash in 1909, Trask devoted herself fully to converting Yaddo into a creative retreat. Increasingly infirm as a result of heart disease and the lingering effects of a childhood spinal injury, she lived from 1916 on in the estate caretaker's cottage in order to preserve Yaddo's endowment. She also opened the mansion to residents of Saratoga Springs, and arranged lectures and conferences on the estate for both children and adults; additionally, she was the benefactor of a parish house for the Bethesda Protestant Episcopal Church, and of the Christina School and Christina Hospital for handicapped children. In 1921 she married Spencer's friend and business partner, George Foster Peabody, and she died a year later in Saratoga Springs.

Although Trask had not chosen someone to carry out her plans for Yaddo before her death, Elizabeth Ames visited the mansion in 1926 and remained as its executive director until 1970, selecting the writers, artists, and musicians who would most profit from the time and space it offered. Poets who have attended Yaddo include **Langston Hughes**, **Robert Lowell**, **Sylvia Plath**, and **William Carlos Williams**, and to this day it remains a serene haven where, in Trask's own words, "calm, majestic, midst the Yaddo pines, / Unconquered, waits unconquerable peace" ("April 1918").

The strengths and weaknesses of Trask's own poetry are perhaps most clearly seen in her collection *Sonnets and Lyrics*. Her love poems can be cloying, as in these lines from untitled sonnets: "Thy love is like an armor for my soul, / A burnished armor glitteringly white"; "I know that sweeter than aught else to me, / Is the tense silence of Love's breathless hush." Her devotional lyrics are marked by neither original language nor convincing crises of faith, as in this untitled poem: "Our darkened hearts grow white, / Bathed in his holy light." But alongside these mediocre poems, there are delights and surprises. As she demonstrates in the sonnets "Iseult to Tristram" and "Paolo to Francesca," Trask is an adept impersonator of other voices. She is capable of a bracing, epigrammatic terseness, whether scolding foes of those who "rejoice"—"Ah, why should your voice, / To mock him, be raised?" ("To a Pessimist")—or, in this untitled poem, bluntly urging people who cannot find "a just and righteous man" to "vindicate your creed and be one." She exhibits a flair for sonnets of many kinds, and often puts refrains to effective use. Her descriptions of nature can be quite powerful: "The rain-drops shed / Their sullen damp defiance on my head" ("Autumn"); "The fleece-specked sky is a vivid blue" ("Morning"). And "Contrasts," the volume's most original and interesting section, contains a memorable suite of poems that imagines certain scenes from two different perspectives: the sea as seen by a speaker whose lover leaves and then returns ("The Sea"), and the trees, whose rustling is alternately heard as a "doleful song" and a "wondrous symphony" ("The Pines"). Although Trask's artistic legacy is undeniably dimmer than that of many writers who visited her utopian home, she was nevertheless a gifted and resourceful poet.

Further Reading: ***Selected Primary Sources:*** Trask, Katrina, *Sonnets and Lyrics* (New York: Randolph and Company, 1894); ———, *Under King Constantine* (New York: Knickerbocker Press, 1892); ———, *Yaddo* (privately printed, 1923). ***Selected Secondary Sources:*** Furman, Laura, "The Benign Ghosts of Yaddo" (*House and Garden* [June 1986]); "In Memory, Katrina Trask" (record of her memorial services, possession of Skidmore College, 1922); *Six Decades at Yaddo* (n.p: publication in honor of Yaddo's sixtieth anniversary, 1986).

Rachel Wetzsteon

TRUMBULL, JOHN (1750–1831)

One of the great satirists of the early republic, Trumbull, together with fellow Connecticut Wits **Timothy Dwight**, **Joel Barlow**, **David Humphreys**, and **Lemuel Hopkins**, helped articulate the patriotic fervor and political anxiety of the early days of the American republic. His two great satires, *The Progress of Dulness* and *M'Fingal*, targeted reactionary forces that threatened the new nation's stability and future prosperity.

Trumbull was born in Westbury, Connecticut, where his father was a Congregationalist minister. A precocious youth, he spent his boyhood learning Latin and Greek, reading in his father's library, and writing verse. He entered Yale College at thirteen and spent the next nine years there, staying on as a master's student and tutor after completing his undergraduate studies. In 1773 he moved to Boston to study law but soon returned to Connecticut. There, he embarked on a successful legal and political career that included stints as state representative and judge. Six years after retiring from public office in 1819, he left Connecticut to live out his remaining years with his daughter's family in Detroit.

As a student, Trumbull composed competent but imitative **elegies** and other poems in the neoclassical mode. He also wrote occasional comic pieces, many of which hinted at the satiric flair that would later win him literary fame. His "Epithalamium" (1769, 1805), exemplifies the learning and wit that would later characterize his greatest poetic successes. It was his experience as a tutor, however, that inspired his first lasting literary triumph. In *The Progress of Dulness* (1772–1773), he mocks lazy Tom Brainless, sheltered by his parents and promoted by a conservative educational system more interested in social convention than intellectual and moral instruction. Although Trumbull ridicules the student, his most biting criticism is directed toward the scholars and clerics responsible for his training. The dullard, although he "scarcely knows to spell or write," is nevertheless ordained because "he's orthodox, and that's enough." In the second and third parts of the poem, Trumbull aims his satire toward the fops and coquettes of colonial America, though his portrait of Dick Hairbrain in Part II lacks the social dimension of the satire in Part I. In Part III, however, Trumbull again uses an individual type to expose social conventions for satirical correction. The coquetry of Harriet Simper, he argues, is produced by a society that declares "by antient rule / The Fair are nurst in Folly's school."

In addition to lesser poems, both comic and serious, Trumbull wrote a series of prose essays during his years as a tutor. After his sojourn in Boston, however, he returned to satiric verse, this time taking aim at the passionate politics of the times. His comic **epic**, *M'Fingal* (1776; revised 1782), lampoons the British and their loyalist supporters, although not without revealing some anxiety about the violence unleashed by patriotic fervor. The poem's first two cantos are staged as a debate between a predictably level-headed Whig and the irascible Tory, M'Fingal. Many of the positions M'Fingal espouses are obvious distortions of Loyalist principles. Despite this ridiculousness, his attacks against the Whigs often contain a sharp warning against democracy's tendency toward anarchy. "For Liberty in your own bysense," he tells his Whig opponents, "is but for crimes a patent licence." Even as the poem triumphs in the hoisting up of a tarred and feathered M'Fingal onto a liberty pole, its depiction of a mob animated by passion and violence tempers the patriotic pride evoked in canto four's glorious vision of American independence and imperial expansion: "Th' Amer'can empire proud and vaunting, / From anarchy shall change her crasis, / And fix her pow'r on firmer basis." Perhaps sensing that such unstable times demanded his political rather than poetic skill, Trumbull published little poetry after 1782. Of this, the most significant is his collaboration with other Connecticut Wits in *The Anarchiad* (1786–1787).

As one of the great satiric poets of the Revolutionary period, Trumbull helped sway opinion against the British and their supporters. At the same time, his unflinching criticism of social attitudes and institutions that threatened stability and progress made him one of the most visible literary proponents of political moderation. The lasting success of Trumbull's best satire lies in his ability to delve beneath the superficial follies of particular people, places, and times to expose the frailties that characterize humanity in general.

Further Reading. ***Selected Primary Sources:*** Humphreys, David, Joel Barlow, John Trumbull, and Lemuel Hopkins, *The Anarchiad: A New England Poem*, ed. Luther G. Riggs (1861; repr. Gainesville, FL: Scholars' Facsimiles & Reprints, 1967); Trumbull, John, *The Poetical Works* (1820; repr. Grosse Pointe, MI: Scholarly Press, 1968); ———, *The Satiric Poems of John Trumbull:* The Progress of Dulness *and* M'Fingal, ed. Edwin T. Bowden (Austin, TX: University of Texas Press, 1962). ***Selected Secondary Sources:*** Briggs, Peter B., "English Satire and Connecticut Wit" (*American Quarterly* 37.1 [Spring 1985]: 13–29); Cowie, Alexander, *John Trumbull, Connecticut Wit* (Chapel Hill: University of North Carolina Press, 1936); Gimmestad, Victor E., *John Trumbull* (New York: Twayne, 1974); Grasso, Christopher, "Print, Poetry, and Politics: John Trumbull and the Transformation of Public Discourse in Revolutionary America" (*Early American Literature* 30.1 [March 1995]: 5–31).

Michael Householder

TUCKER, ST. GEORGE (1752–1827)

Best known as the "American Blackstone," St. George Tucker was an eminent Virginia jurist whose edition of *Blackstone's Commentaries* had an important influence on the direction of early nineteenth-century American jurisprudence. Like many lawyers of his day, he also wrote a considerable amount of poetry. His patriotic poems celebrating George Washington or castigating Benedict Arnold reflected a strong commitment to the Whig cause during the Revolution, and his occasional verses, touching **elegies**, witty epigrams, bawdy doggerels, and satirical tales were in great demand among an elite circle of friends and fellow belletrists in Williamsburg during the 1790s and the early nineteenth century. But his most significant works were political satires, particularly *The Probationary Odes of Jonathan Pindar, Esq.* (1793), a series of poems criticizing Alexander Hamilton, John Adams, and the Federalists.

Tucker is often confused with a number of descendents influential in law and letters who shared his name, including his son, Henry St. George Tucker (1780–1848), also a judge and professor of law, and his nephew, George Tucker (1775–1861), a lawyer, novelist, and professor of moral philosophy. Although his poetry had no lasting influence, St. George Tucker was, in fact, among the first of a group of lawyer-authors—including **Jonathan Trumbull**, Thomas Jefferson, **Royall Tyler**, **Hugh Henry Brackenridge**, Charles Brockden Brown, Washington Irving, and **William Cullen Bryant**—whose polite but politically-resonant works had a profound impact on the shape of early American national literature.

Born in 1752 to a wealthy English family that had founded a plantation in Port Royal, Bermuda, during the mid-1600s, Tucker came to Virginia in 1771 to attend the College of William and Mary. Upon graduation, he studied law under George Wyeth, the teacher of Jefferson, and was admitted to the Virginia Bar in 1774. When the Revolution interrupted his law practice, he aided both the patriots' cause and his father's business by running indigo and arms between the West Indies and Bermuda. Once back in Virginia, he served as a colonel in the local militia and participated in several battles, including the siege of Yorktown. In 1778, he shrewdly married Frances "Fanny" Bland Randolph, the wealthy widow of John Randolph, thereby gaining both stepsons and large estates. But his passionate poems to her—calling her "Stella," in the manner of William Shenstone—suggest that it was more than a marriage of convenience.

After the Revolutionary War, Tucker's law practice prospered, and, in 1788, the year Fanny died giving birth to his sixth child, he became judge of the General Court of Virginia. Two years later, he succeeded Wyeth as professor of law at William and Mary, and married Lelia Carter, another socially prominent widow. In 1804 he left teaching and returned to the bench when Jefferson appointed him a justice of the Virginia Court of Appeals. In the mean time, Tucker wrote numerous occasional poems for his friends and himself, essays for William Wirt's *Old Bachelor* series (1812), musical dramas and verse adaptations of popular songs, and an impressive body of political and legal works, including a proposal for the gradual abolition of slavery in 1796, the first systematic commentary on the U.S. Constitution in 1803, and, in 1811, his edition of *Blackstone*. His legal career was both distinguished and rewarding; however, as he admitted in an 1810 poem, "The Sorry Judge," it was also tiring and even tedious, for "he drudged and judged from morn to night, no ass drudged more than he." In 1813, President James Madison appointed him to the U.S. District Court, an office he held until shortly before his death in 1827.

As an educated gentleman in late-eighteenth-century America, Tucker believed in the political efficacy of poetry, and, like much republican poetry, his work aimed largely at facilitating elite sociability, advocating virtue, and criticizing the excesses of government institutions. The tone of his poetry is consistently urgent and spontaneous, lacking metrical precision but rife with classical and colloquial allusions. His most widely read poems were political satires, such as "The Alarm" (1777), a lampooning of Tory reactions to a rumored attack on Bermuda by Admiral Esek Hopkins. Although the attack never came, Tucker playfully depicts the chaotic scene of an interrupted feast: "A general panic now prevails / And every Tory breast assails / With hideous fears—each doughty Whig." In "Liberty" (1780), dedicated to Washington, the eponymous goddess moves across Europe, chased by "Tyranny" and "Oppression," finally arriving where "Columbia's rising states appear." When threatened by Britain, she calls Americans to arms and predicts victory, but with the caution that they must avoid letting "internal broils thy strength destroy" if the new nation is to "live to deathless fame / Unrivalled or by Rome or Britain's vaunted name."

Tucker's most influential work, *The Probationary Odes of Jonathan Pindar, Esq.*, appeared in **Philip Freneau**'s *National Gazette* in 1793. Consisting of fourteen poems written in opposition to what he saw as overreaching by the new federal government, the *Odes* were understood by their readers to be inspired by such British Whig writers as George Ellis and John Wolcott (using the pseudonym of Peter Pindar), whose *Probationary Odes for the Laureateship* (1785) and *Ode Upon Ode* (1787) criticized William Pitt's administration and the foibles of King George III, respectively. Such a tradition, for Tucker, aptly contextualized his views on the self-interested and "monarchical" tendencies of the Federalists. In one ode, Pindar offers to use his laureate's gifts to shill for Federalist schemes, such as the establishment of a national bank and federal assumption of state debt: "I'll swear—that nation's debt's a blessing vast / Which far and wide its genial influence sheds." In another, Adams is called a "would-be great man" and "Daddy Vice," and his *Discourses on Davila* is ridiculed for its defense of monarchy and aristocracy: "On Davila's page / Your discourses so sage, / Democratical numbskulls bepuzzle."

After the Democrats defeated the Federalists in the election of 1800, Tucker's poetry often took a **sentimental** turn. His 1807 lyric, "Resignation," for example, put his earlier political battles in perspective: "Days of my youth! Ye have glided away; Locks of my youth! Ye are frosted and gray." Although Adams was a frequent target of Tucker's *Odes*, he unwittingly praised the poem as comparable to the works of Home, Shakespeare, and Pope.

Further Reading. ***Selected Primary Sources:*** Tucker, St. George, *The Poems of St. George Tucker of Williamsburg, Virginia, 1752–1827*, ed. William S. Prince (New York: Vantage Press, 1977); ———, *The Probationary Odes of Jonathan Pindar, Esq.* (Philadelphia: Benjamin Franklin Bache, 1796). ***Selected Secondary Sources:*** Coleman, Mary Haldane, *St. George Tucker: Citizen of No Mean City* (Richmond, VA: Dietz, 1938); Dolmetsch, Carl, "The Revolutionary War Poems of St. George Tucker" (*Tennessee Studies in Literature* 26 [1982]: 48–65); Prince, William S., "St. George Tucker: Bard on the Bench" (*Virginia Magazine of History and Biography* 84.3 [1976]: 267–282).

Edward Cahill

TUCKERMAN, FREDERICK GODDARD (1821–1873)

Frederick Goddard Tuckerman was the son of a prominent merchant in the Boston community of the early 1800s. A native of Massachusetts his entire life, Tuckerman's early years were mixed with education and leisure. Like most males belonging to wealthy Boston-area families during the first half of the nineteenth century, Tuckerman attended the Boston Latin School, receiving training in the classics along with other traditional subjects. Completing his education at the Latin School permitted him to study at Harvard starting in 1837. However promising the start of Tuckerman's education, he left college a year later, only to return to study law within the same educational institution; finally, in 1842, Tuckerman obtained a law degree (Golden, 21–26, and Momaday, xvii–xx).

Although Tuckerman's early educational efforts are often baffling, especially the exact reasons for his continual bouncing in and out of school, the developing poet never fully committed to the law profession either, quickly quitting a job after having served in the legal field for only one year. This same life of leisure, particularly after the poet and his wife moved out of the Boston community to the more rural Greenfield, Massachusetts, in 1847, allowed his critics to characterize him as a social outcast. Despite two trips abroad and to Cambridge, Tuckerman, as Samuel A. Golden states, "never returned permanently to the opulent surroundings of his boyhood" (31). It was during this isolated state, which lasted for the majority of his life, that he produced poems while simultaneously pursuing his other interests in the sciences, especially botany and astronomy (England, 911).

Although Tuckerman's poetic achievements were unknown to the general reading public until the first part of the twentieth century, he published various editions of his *Poems* in 1860, 1864, and 1869 (Cady, 141). A review of the poet's output reveals his preoccupation with the sonnet, a genre that required "regularity in form and restraint in expression," both still relevant elements of eighteenth-century neoclassical era aesthetics (126). The sonnets also contain a distinct autobiographical flavor; as one critic suggests, personal elements appear "not because they are rare or recondite but because they are so voluminous and apparent" (Golden, 49).

A sonnet from the *Second Series, 1854–1860* illustrates this autobiographical preoccupation. "How oft in schoolboy-days, from the school's sway / Have I run forth to Nature as to a friend . . . to spend / My school-time in green meadows far away," reminisces the speaker at the beginning of Sonnet XXIX. Both Tuckerman's preoccupation with nature and the idea of isolation appear within the first four lines of this poem. Much like **Walt Whitman**'s "When I Heard the Learn'd Astronomer," the speaker then reveals a preference for direct experience with nature over textbook learning. The speaker proclaims that the same eye that "shrank from hated hours" of "decimal and dividend" also "[k]new each bleached alder root that splashed across / The bubbling brook, and every mass of moss." As is typical of many of Tuckerman's sonnets, the autobiographical elements project the importance of nature.

But to identify Tuckerman as only an overly disciplined sonneteer would be too great a generalization. In fact, a number of other poems illustrate the poet's interests in other genres and topics. For example, in "Ode: For the Greenfield Soldiers Monument," Tuckerman uses the personalized, lyrical aspect of the ode to memorialize the fallen soldiers of the Civil War. At first the speaker asks, "[i]n half-light of the autumn day, / Meet we to mourn for what has been, / A tale, a triumph passed away?" After posing this question, he responds: "Yes, more: our gift is generous /As theirs who gave their lifeblood free; / Not to the dead alone, to us / Ourselves, and ours that yet shall be." While operating within conventional patriotic rhetoric, the speaker reminds the reader that the outcomes of the war, although at times painful, are for the sake of present and future generations.

"Anybody's Critic," a relatively early poem, lampoons a literary critic. At first, the critic is extolled in the exclamation "Behold the Scholar now, the Judge profound!" However, these lines of praise are followed by an important qualification: "Yet, feeling with his foot precarious ground, / He stands to fly, or with a borrowed jest / To blink the question when too closely pressed." Here, the speaker creates an ironic picture of the knowledgeable critic, who seemingly waivers and even wishes to escape when pressed with difficult questions. Later, the speaker, thinly veiled as Tuckerman himself, seems to create another moment of self-parody. When a boy hands the critic a poem for commentary, the critic points out that "no man can stand aside without rebuke / To prate of bubbling brooks and uplands grassy," thereby criticizing the conventional natural settings so often employed within Tuckerman's own work.

After initiating brief correspondences in 1861 with two prominent figures of American literature, **Nathaniel Hawthorne** and **Ralph Waldo Emerson**, Tuckerman once again returned to the seclusion with which he was so familiar; eleven years later, the poet passed away, relatively unknown to his contemporary American readers. It was not until 1909 that Walter Prichard Eaton, developing an interest in a forgotten **anthology** of poems, rejuvenated interest in Tuckerman (**Momaday**, xvii). This recognition of Tuckerman's poetry continued into the 1950s and 1960s. Tuckerman's status has continued to increase as his poems have been included in other anthologies (England, 912).

Further Reading. ***Selected Primary Source:*** Tuckerman, Frederick Goddard, *The Complete Poems of Frederick Goddard Tuckerman*, ed. and intro., N. Scott Momaday (New York: Oxford University Press, 1965). ***Selected Secondary Sources:*** Cady, Edwin H., "Frederick Goddard Tuckerman," in *Essays on American Literature in Honor of Jay B. Hubbell*, ed. Clarence Gohdes (Durham, NC: Duke University Press [1967]: 141–151); England, Eugene, "Frederick Goddard Tuckerman," in *American National Biography* (New York: Oxford University Press, 1999, 911–912); ———, *Beyond Romanticism: Tuckerman's Life and Poetry* (New York: State University of New York Press, 1991); Golden, Samuel A., *Frederick Goddard Tuckerman* (New Haven, CT: College and University Press, 1966).

Eric D. Lamore

TURNER, FREDERICK (1943–)

Frederick Turner, perhaps best known as the founder of, and spokesman for, the **New Formalist** and **New Narrative** movements, is a prolific and wide-ranging author who has published books of poetry, Shakespearean criticism, Renaissance philosophy, cultural criticism, biopoetics, science fiction, and **translation**. His mature poetry is known for its use of strict meter, often **epic** scope, and, in at least two books, subject matter drawn from the world of science fiction. Turner's work is heavily interdisciplinary, often drawing from contemporary studies in evolutionary biology, folklore, space exploration, futurism, and information theory. Turner also views his work as restorative: He aims to return to "a 'natural classicism' in human arts that is based on culturally universal art forms and genres (Williams, 294)." No less an eminence than Edward O. Wilson, widely considered to be the founder of the fields of evolutionary psychology and sociobiology, has praised Turner's work for " [taking] us past the wreckage of **postmodernism** to revive the dream of the unification of science and the humanities—and hence of culture" (back cover blurb for *The Culture of Hope*).

Frederick Turner was born in Northamptonshire, England, on November 19, 1943, to the anthropologists

Victor Witter Turner and Edith Davis Turner. In his youth, Turner lived in central Africa, where his parents conducted field research. He earned three degrees (BA, MA, and B.Litt.) in English language and literature at Christ Church College, University of Oxford, between 1962 and 1967. Oxford University Press published his dissertation, *Shakespeare and the Nature of Time*, in 1971.

After marrying Mei Lin Chang in 1966, Turner immigrated to the United States, where he taught at the University of California–Santa Barbara until 1972. He published his first full-length volume of poetry, *Between Two Lives*, in 1972. Turner taught at Kenyon College from 1972 to 1985 and was naturalized as a United States citizen in 1977. He published *Shakespeare's Romeo and Juliet*, a student edition of the play with notes and introduction, in 1974.

From 1978 to 1982, Turner served as editor of the *Kenyon Review*. During his tenure as editor, Turner gained fame (and in some quarters, infamy) as an advocate for the New Formalist and New Narrative movements. He published both the science fiction novel *The Double Shadow* and *Counter-Terra*, a book of poems, in 1978. The **long narrative poem** *The Return* followed in 1979. His essay, "The Neural Lyre," written with the psychophysicist Ernst Pöppel, which explores poetic meter in the light of brain science and information theory, won *Poetry* magazine's Levinson Prize in 1983. In 1985 Princeton University Press published his **epic** science fiction poem, *The New World*.

In 1984–1985, Turner was a visiting professor at the University of Exeter, and, since 1985, he has been the Founders Professor of Arts and Humanities at the University of Texas–Dallas. In 1988, Turner published *Genesis*, a second epic, which imagined the future terraforming of Mars and further developed Turner's philosophy of natural classicism. Since 1985, he has also written four volumes of shorter poems, mostly using strict metrical forms: *The Garden* (1985), *April Wind* (1992), *The Ballad of the Good Cowboy* (1997), and *Hadean Eclogues* (1999).

While at the University of Texas–Dallas, Turner has written five volumes of cultural criticism: *Natural Classicism: Essays on Literature and Science* (1985, repr. 1992); *Rebirth of Value: Meditations on Beauty, Ecology, Religion and Education* (1991); *Tempest, Flute, and Oz: Essays on the Future* (1992); *Beauty: The Value of Values* (1992), and *The Culture of Hope: A New Birth of the Classical Spirit* (1995). In 1999, he edited a volume of essays, *Biopoetics: Evolutionary Explorations in the Arts*, with Brett Cooke.

He has also published two volumes of translations, both co-authored with Zsuzsanna Ozsvath: *Foamy Sky: The Major Poems of Miklos Radnoti* (1992) and *The Iron-blue Vault: Selected Poems by Attila Jozsef* (2000). *Foamy Sky* won the Milan Fust Prize, Hungary's most prestigious literary honor. Turner has also revisited Shakespearean criticism, publishing *Shakespeare's Twenty-first Century Economics: The Morality of Love and Money*, an examination of "evolutionary economics" based on Shakespeare's plays, in 1999.

Turner's work has been published in French, German, Japanese, Spanish, Hungarian, Italian, Rumanian, Macedonian, Russian, Turkish, and other languages. In addition to the prizes already listed, he has also won the Golden Pen Award from PEN, Dallas chapter, and the *Missouri Review* essay prize. He has lectured or given poetry readings at over a hundred institutions in the United States, Canada, and Western and Eastern Europe. Turner currently lives in Richardson, Texas, with his wife and his two sons, Daniel and Victor.

Critical reception to Turner's work has been mixed. Reviewers of the early epics, for example, seem unable to agree on even basic assessments of its worth. **Alfred Corn,** writing in the *New Republic*, says that Turner, in *The New World*, "has written an entertainment in verse and not a great epic (40)." Yet, Judith De Luce, writing in the *Humanist*, calls *Genesis* "a remarkable poem" and a "skilled manipulation of tradition (19–20)." This sort of disagreement routinely occurs in Turner criticism, and the argument is by no means settled. Quite recently, Scott Cutler Shershow, writing in *Medieval and Renaissance Drama in England*, judges *Shakespeare's Twenty-First Century Economics* "not a serious study of Shakespeare, or even a work of literary scholarship (333)." Yet, Paul Canter, writing several years earlier in *Reason,* hailed *Twenty-First Century Economics* as "a fundamental reconception of Shakespeare (62)." What seems certain is that Turner will continue his ambitious project, one that he expects, as he wrote in *The Culture of Hope*, will "rejoin artist with public, beauty with morality, high art with low, art with craft, passion with intelligence, art with science, and past with future (quoted in Williams, 294)."

Further Reading. ***Selected Primary Sources:*** Turner, Frederick, *The Culture of Hope: A New Birth of the Classical Spirit* (New York: Free Press, 1995); ———, *Genesis* (New York: W.W. Norton, 1988); ———, *Hadean Eclogues* (Ashland, OR: Story Line Press, 1999); ———, *The New World* (Princeton, NJ: Princeton University Press, 1985); ———, *Shakespeare's Twenty-first Century Economics: The Morality of Love and Money* (New York: Oxford University Press, 1999); Turner, Frederick and Zsuzsanna Ozsvath, *Foamy Sky: The Major Poems of Miklos Radnoti* (Princeton, NJ: Princeton University Press, Lockert Series, 1992; augmented ed., Budapest: Corvina, 2000). ***Selected Secondary Sources:*** Canter, Paul A., "Capitalism's Poet Laureate" (*Reason* 31 [March 2000]: 62); Corn, Alfred, "The New World, an Epic Poem" (*New Republic* 193 [25 November 1985]: 38); De Luce, Judith, "Genesis: An Epic Poem" (*Humanist* 53.6 [November–December 1993]: 190); Shershow, Scott

Cutler, *Medieval and Renaissance Drama in England, vol. 15* (n.p.: Associated University Press, 2003); Williams, Sonny, "Frederick Turner," in *Dictionary of Literary Biography*, vol. 282 (Detroit: Gale Research, 2003).

Joe Ahearn

TYLER, ROYALL (1757–1826)

Lawyer and public servant by profession, Royall Tyler is best known as America's first successful dramatist. His play, *The Contrast*, was performed by the American Company at the John Street Theatre in New York City on April 16, 1787. Tyler wrote other plays, among them *May Day in Town* (1787) and *The Georgia Spec* (1797). He was also a novelist (*The Algerine Captive*, 1797) and a prolific, if mostly undistinguished, poet.

Royall Tyler was born in 1757 in Boston. He graduated from Harvard College in 1776 and received a degree from Yale the same year. After studying law with John Adams (whose daughter, Nabby, he courted unsuccessfully) he was admitted to the Massachusetts Bar in 1780 and opened an office in Braintree. Tyler served in the militia in 1778, and in 1787 he became an aide to General Benjamin Lincoln during Shays's Rebellion. His success as a negotiator during the rebellion caused the Boston city council to send him to New York on related business. Although the circumstances surrounding its composition are hazy, *The Contrast* appears to have been written during that trip in 1787, and the play was produced in New York five weeks later.

Tyler established a law practice in Guilford, Vermont, in 1791 and served as state's attorney for Windham County, Vermont, from 1794–1801. He served as justice of the Vermont Supreme Court from 1801 to 1807, and chief justice of the state's highest court from 1807 to 1813. He taught law at the University of Vermont from 1811 to 1814. In 1794 he married Mary Palmer, and together they had eleven children. Tyler died in Brattleboro, Vermont, in 1826 after a protracted struggle with facial cancer.

The Contrast is a comedy of manners that contrasts two representative characters—the sophisticated but dishonest Billy Dimple, who admires all things European, and the honest open-hearted Manly, who stands for the red-blooded American. While critical attention and acclaim for this play has been consistent since it was first produced in 1787, an assessment of Tyler's body of poetry—the best of which is satiric or light verse—is much more difficult. First of all, most of Tyler's contributions to newspapers and magazines over the years appeared anonymously. Secondly, his publication record—many poems remained in manuscript at his death, and he appeared not to have been overly driven to see many of them in print—indicate that Tyler saw his poetry primarily as entertainment, and as a way to maintain contact with the energetic literary community of which he was a part. Even so, Tyler contributed to a number of **periodicals**, and much of his poetry was both witty and popular. G. Thomas Tanselle lists the principle periodicals to which he contributed as follows: *Eagle or Darmouth Centinel* (1794); Boston *Federal Orrery* (1794–1795); Boston *Tablet* (1795); Walpole, New Hampshire, *Newhampshire and Vermont Journal, or The Farmer's Weekly Museum* (1796–1799); *Port Folio* (1801–1804); and *Polyanthos* (1806–1807). Tanselle attributes over 2900 lines of verse—roughly fifty poems—to Tyler, the majority of which are in iambic tetrameter quatrains or couplets. He wrote primarily in three categories: satire, occasional poems, and reflective or moralizing poems.

After moving to Vermont, Tyler began a literary partnership with Joseph Dennie, as "Colon & Spondee," in 1794. Dennie, one of the best known essayists and editors of the early republic, was, like Tyler, a lawyer. Among the poetic forms the two promised their readers in the first "advertisement" for their column in the *Eagle, or Dartmouth Centinel,* were these:

> Anagrams, Acrostics, Anacreontics; Chronograms, Epigrams, Hudibrastics, & Panegyrics; Rebuses, Charades, Puns and Conundrums, by the *gros,* or *single dozen.* Sonnets, Elegies, Epithalamiums; Bucolics, Georgics, Pasterals; Epic Poems, Dedications, and Adulatory Prefaces, in *verse* and *prose.*

Dennie and Tyler's collaboration was successful, with Dennie responsible primarily for prose output and Tyler the verse.

During Dennie's editorship of the *Farmer's Museum* (1796–1799), Tyler contributed approximately twenty-five poems, ranging from satire to patriotic odes. Between April 1806 and July 1807, Tyler published thirteen poems in the *Polyanthos,* founded in 1805 by Joseph T. Buckingham. Tanselle ranks these poems, written in a variety of forms and meters, as Tyler's best. Among them are a tetrameter fable, "The Wolf and Wooden Beauty," **lyrics**, epigrams, and three **long poems** in pentameter.

Although a collection of Tyler's poems and essays was reprinted in his lifetime in *The Spirit of the Farmer's Museum* (1801), no comprehensive collection was available until Marius B. Peladeau's *The Verse of Royall Tyler* was published in 1968.

Further Reading. ***Selected Primary Sources:*** Tyler, Royall, *The Algerine Captive* (Gainesville, FL: Scholars' Facsimiles & Reprints, 1967); ———, *Four Plays,* ed. Arthur Wallace Peace and George Floyd Newbrough, in *America's Lost Plays,* vol. 15 (1940; Bloomington: Indiana University Press, 1965); ———, *The Prose of Royall Tyler,* collected and ed. Marius B. Peladeau (n.p.: Charles E. Tuttle Co., Inc., 1972); ———, *The Verse of Royall Tyler,* collected and ed. Marius B. Peladeau (Charlottesville: University Press of Virginia, 1968). ***Selected Secondary***

Sources: Carson, Ada Lou, and Herbert L. Carson, *Royall Tyler* (Boston: Twayne, 1979); Silverman, Kenneth, *A Cultural History of the American Revolution* (New York: Columbia University Press, 1976); Tanselle, G. Thomas, *Royall Tyler* (Cambridge: Harvard University Press, 1967).

Ann M. Brunjes

U

UPDIKE, JOHN (1932–)

John Updike is one of America's most celebrated and prolific novelists, with a wide audience and equally wide acclaim over almost half a century. However, he has also written in many other genres, including poetry, short fiction, essays, drama, memoir, and literary criticism; in fact, Updike's first published book was a book of poetry, *The Carpentered Hen and Other Tame Creatures* (1958). Although his fiction is highly regarded both by many academic critics and by literary reviewers, his poetry has often been dismissed as light and facile. It is true that Updike employs word play and novelty in some of his poems and that much of his poetic output consists of **light verse**. However, he has written substantial poetry, especially in his later years. Updike's poetry frequently appears, as does his fiction and criticism, in major publications such as the *New Yorker* and the *Atlantic Monthly*, and he has also published several volumes of his poems. As Updike entered his seventies, he continued to publish several poems a year.

John Updike was born on March 18, 1932, in Reading, Pennsylvania, and was brought up in nearby Shillington, a largely agricultural area. Updike's father taught mathematics, and his mother was a well-read person who encouraged her son's reading, writing, and drawing. Updike attended Harvard as a scholarship student. He majored in English and graduated summa cum laude in 1954. While still an undergraduate, he married Mary Pennington. They had four children, two daughters and two sons, by 1960. From 1955 to 1957, Updike worked as a full-time staff member for the *New Yorker* magazine, but he quit that position to become a self-employed writer, even though his first book would not be published for another year. Fortunately for the welfare of his growing family, Updike not only published *The Carpentered Hen and Other Tame Creatures* in 1958, but also followed that poetry collection with two successful novels, *The Poorhouse Fair* (1959) and *Rabbit, Run* (1960). These publications began Updike's critical and popular success. He won the National Book Award in 1964 for his novel *The Centaur*, which was the first of many major awards and honors for Updike. Although he divorced Mary Pennington in 1974 and married Martha Bernhard in 1977, his personal upheavals did not diminish his literary output. He has continued to write prolifically over the decades and published the novel *Villages* (2004) when he was seventy-two.

Updike's series of novels about the working-class Rabbit Angstrom, which began with Rabbit's young adulthood in *Rabbit, Run* and culminated thirty years later with Rabbit's aging and death in *Rabbit at Rest*, have received perhaps the most critical and popular esteem of any of his novels. In fact, two of the Rabbit novels, *Rabbit Is Rich* (1981) and *Rabbit at Rest* (1990), earned Pulitzer Prizes for Updike. John Updike has also written novels updating or recasting famous literary works, such as *The Centaur* (1963), which recasts the Prometheus and Chiron myth; *A Month of Sundays* (1975), *Roger's Version* (1986), and *S.* (1988), which retell Nathaniel Hawthorne's *The Scarlet Letter* from the perspective of Hawthorne's characters Dimmesdale, Chillingsworth, and Hester Prynne, respectively; and *Gertrude and Claudius* (2000), which is a prequel to William Shakespeare's *Hamlet*. This technique of re-visioning literary works from a different perspective is a strategy that appears in Updike's poetry, as well.

Some of the key elements in John Updike's poetry include clever exploitation of the comic possibilities of verse, immense facility with language, and broad knowledge of the works of other writers, which he variously satirizes, pays homage to, and recasts.

The Carpentered Hen and Other Tame Creatures (1958), primarily comprises the light verse that Updike became known for in the first decades of his literary career. Perhaps the most significant poem in this collection is "Ex-Basketball Player," about a gas-station attendant, Flick Webb, who has long since outlived his glory days as a high school basketball star. Updike treats Flick Webb sympathetically, observing that when he handled the basketball, "his hands were like wild birds," but now, "His hands are fine and nervous on the lug wrench. / It makes no difference to the lug wrench, though." Adulation has long since passed Flick by, and instead of listening to cheering crowds, he spends his leisure hours at a diner where he sees "bright applauding tiers" of candy, a tenuous reminder of his former glory. This poem eschews the light verse and novelty forms of many of the early poems, instead focusing on a serious and poignant subject. Beyond its poetic significance, "Ex-Basketball Player" has additional significance within Updike's oeuvre, since Flick Webb undergoes a name change to Rabbit Angstrom and becomes the central character of Updike's four Rabbit novels, *Rabbit, Run* (1960), *Rabbit Redux* (1972), *Rabbit Is Rich* (1981), and *Rabbit at Rest* (1990), as well as a novella about his survivors, "Rabbit Remembered," that became part of Updike's collection of short fiction, *Licks of Love* (2001).

Other poems in this collection rely more extensively on Updike's characteristic use of wordplay and of altering the appearance of the poem on the page to achieve particular effects. For instance, in Updike's series of short poems, one for each letter of the alphabet, collectively titled "A Cheerful Alphabet of Pleasant Objects," the poem "Mirror" includes a literal mirror image of the text of the poem, beginning:

When you look kool uoy nehW
into a mirror rorrim a otni

Similarly, "Pendulum" features lines angled down the page like the swing of a pendulum, and "Apple" jests, "My child, take heart: the fruit that undid Man / Brought out as well the best in Paul Cézanne." This verbal fluency and wit have brought praise from many critics, but others feel that Updike's skills have been used for trivial subjects.

Updike has also incorporated more elaborate nontraditional techniques into his poems. "Midpoint," the central piece in *Midpoint and Other Poems* (1969), uses drawings, photographs, and text to create an autobiography of Updike's life from babyhood to early middle age. Although this poem could be dismissed as a mere novelty, it also has elements of self-reflection reminiscent of **Walt Whitman** or **Ralph Waldo Emerson**.

When Updike does turn his hand to more serious subjects, critics often deem this work less successful than his lighter verse. For example, in his collection *Americana: and Other Poems* (2001), a poem entitled "Death in Venice" (its title itself an homage to Thomas Mann's novella) has as its subject two women attempting, and failing, to resuscitate a dying man. The narrator remarks of the two women, "My wife thought they were doing it wrong, / this pair slaving like whores at their client." This jarring simile comparing public death with commercial sex is characteristic of much of Updike's later poetry, in which melancholy concern with aging and death is combined with sometimes-coarse sexuality.

Other major volumes of poetry include *Collected Poems 1953–1993* (1993), a collection of poems from Updike's youth to his maturity. Included in this collection are many of the poems from earlier collections, as well as otherwise uncollected poems. Many of these poems are written in traditional forms such as odes and sonnets, yet they often concern themselves with nontraditional and light subjects such as eyeglasses and bugs. However, not all the poems are lightweight. "Seven Stanzas at Easter" muses on the mechanism of Christ's death and resurrection, arguing that to accept the resurrection is to accept the physical reality of Christ's dead "cells," "molecules," and "amino acids" coming to life again, overseen by an "opaque" angel "robed in real linen / spun on a definite loom."

In his poetry, Updike encourages his readers to reflect upon their inner selves and upon the minutiae of everyday life. He explores these minutiae not only as trivia, but also as microcosms for the larger philosophical issues we must all explore: the purpose of life, the nature of death, and, the importance of finding humor in it all.

Further Reading. ***Selected Primary Sources:*** Updike, John, *Americana: and Other Poems* (New York: Knopf,

2001); ———, *The Carpentered Hen and Other Tame Creatures* (New York: Knopf, 1958); ———, *Collected Poems 1953–1993* (New York: Knopf, 1993); ———, *Midpoint and Other Poems* (New York: Knopf, 1963); ———, *Telephone Poles and Other Poems* (New York: Knopf, 1963). ***Selected Secondary Sources:*** De Bellis, Jack, *The John Updike Encyclopedia* (Westport, CT: Greenwood, 2000); Greiner, Donald J., *The Other Updike: Poems/ Short Stories/ Prose/ Play* (Athens: Ohio University Press, 1981).

J. Robin Coffelt

V

VALENTINE, JEAN (1934–)

A distinguished poet supported by a small but fiercely loyal following, Jean Valentine is the author of ten collections of poetry, including *Door in the Mountain* (2004), a volume of new and collected poems, which was nominated for a National Book Award. A member of no school, she has been called a "poet's poet" more than once. It is difficult to class her with other poets currently writing, although **Adrienne Rich** and **Jane Cooper** are among her closest contemporaries and friends, and, for her unadorned style, **Emily Dickinson** and **W.C. Williams** are clear predecessors. Seen by some as obscurantist, Valentine's work moves by a kind of fluid dream logic, leaping from image to image and always remaining within the archetypal sphere of mothers, lovers, and the life cycle from birth to death.

Born on April 27, 1934, in Chicago to John and Jean Valentine, Valentine was raised in affluent but emotionally distant surroundings. The family moved to New York when the poet was three and then to the suburb of Bedford, in Westchester County. For her final years of high school, Valentine attended Milton Academy, a private boarding school, a departure that she has described as a relief. Valentine then attended Radcliffe College, graduating in 1956. Married twice to the historian and foreign policy analyst James Chace, she has two children, Sarah and Rebecca. After her second divorce from Chance, she married and divorced the Irish painter Barrie Cooke. Valentine has struggled with alcoholism and depression, and her writing, which has grown increasingly autobiographical, reflects her emotional journey.

Valentine's career is an object lesson for the rewards of persistence. Roundly rejected by magazines for ten years, she had nearly decided to give up writing altogether when, at the age of thirty, she received the Yale Younger Poet's prize for *Dream Barker* (1965). Three more books quickly followed, but then Valentine experienced a long silence during the 1980s (during which she underwent recovery for alcoholism). At the end of that decade, her volume of selected poems, *Home Deep Blue* (1988), was brought out by Alice James Books. Book publication led to teaching posts: Valentine has taught at numerous colleges on the East Coast, including Swarthmore College, Hunter College, Sarah Lawrence, and New York University. She has also received a number of honors, in addition to the Yale Younger Poet's Prize: a Guggenheim fellowship, a Shelley Memorial Award from the Poetry Society of America, and grants from the National Endowment for the Arts, the Rockefeller Foundation, and the Bunting Institute.

Although the early work—*Dream Barkers*, in particular—is somewhat more accessible than the later, all of her poems are marked by a quality of mysterious ineffability, what **James Merrill** once described as "the world beneath the world." It is this quality that has most likely limited Valentine's readership—her poems, which are heavily influenced by the Russian poets Osip Mandelstam and Anna Akhmatova, are rarely straightforward or linear. In *Pilgrims* she writes, "all come giant-stepping / out into some wide, light merciful mind." Valentine's poems, which also seem inflected by Jungian depth psychology, are perpetually in search of the divine and often document the strangeness of dreams or visions. "How deep we met, how dark," she writes in a love poem in *Dream Barker*, "How wet! before the world began." However, this pursuit of the divine often takes place in the realm of the domestic; even a poem about Cain is situated in the family scene: "The first life's blood. Now day / lies at the door, the clocks tick, / the smoky kitten nurses at my salty fingers."

The year 1992 saw the publication of *The River at Wolf*, which is considered by some to be one of Valentine's finest works. Characteristically spare in diction and structure, the poems operate through a tension between the pain of human life and the constant pursuit of redemption and inner peace. "Maybe not today the amazing loveliness but it won't be long for us to wait," she writes in a poem titled "The Free Abandonment Blues." Her poems are nearly always short and written in quotidian plain speech. The spareness of the poems is invigorated and made more musical by her habit of employing repetition: "I ask you Emily Dickinson, / water spider rowing danger and death: four white lines / four white lines: nothing over nothing." Another poem, on the subject of the speaker's mother's death, concludes with the line "Who died?" repeated three times.

The most persistent theme of Valentine's work—it might be called the underlying impulse of her work—is the desire to articulate a true female subjectivity. This is seen clearly in one of her most important poems, "Trust Me" (*Home Deep Blue*). The poem commences with the question, "Who did I write last night?" and proceeds to interrogate the female self as writer, concluding with a metaphysical assertion: "my shining, your shining life draws close, draws closer, / God fills us as a woman fills a pitcher." In *The Cradle of the Real Life* (2000), her most autobiographical work to date, she writes "I ask for a dream / about my marriage/ 'Ink'. Ink. Ink. Ink." The same book contains a series of short poems describing her experience as a young wife and mother in the 1960s. These are quick snapshots of the tension between the societal expectation to fulfill a traditional woman's role and the responsibility to the self as a writer. Although the later work documents a feminist perspective in more realistic verse, her poetry in general is engaged in an exploration of the mythologically or archetypally feminine nature of the world: "Every rock was a green womb," she writes, "lit from inside" (*The River at Wolf*). Valentine's legacy to American poetry is surely this representation of female subjectivity, as well as her expression of interior experience metaphorically rendered through a mixture of dream dialogue and concrete images of the natural world. (*See* **Feminist Poetics**.)

Further Reading. ***Selected Primary Sources:*** Valentine, Jean, *The Cradle of the Real Life* (Hanover, NH: Wesleyan University Press, 2000); ———, *The Door in the Mountain* (Middletown, CT: Wesleyan University Press, 2004); ———, *Home Deep Blue* (Cambridge, MA: Alice James Books, 1988); ———, *The River at Wolf* (Cambridge, MA: Alice James Books, 1992). ***Selected Secondary Sources:*** "Jean Valentine: An Interview by Michael Klein" (*American Poetry Review* 20.4 [1991]: 39–44); Turner, Alberta, "Standing in the Whole Stare" (*Field* 40 [Spring 1989]: 78–85); Upton, Lee, "'Dream Barker': Preoedipal Fusion and Radiant Boundaries in Jean Valentine," in *The Muse of Abandonment* (London: Associated University Presses, 1998).

Amy Newlove Schroeder

VAN DUYN, MONA (1921–2004)

Mona Van Duyn's poetry is filled with the things of our everyday, bourgeois lives: animals in a zoo, carwashes, backyard gardens, and trips to the hospital. A lifelong resident of the Midwest, Van Duyn wrote poetry that—like the region she called home—refuses affectation, grounding her extensive knowledge and insight in both memory and personal experience as well as in the objects and images that surround her. In almost five decades, she produced hundreds of poems, most of which illuminate the self through close inspection of humans' relationships to one another and the world. Compared at times to Wordsworth, **Walt Whitman**, **Elizabeth Bishop**, and **Marianne Moore**, Van Duyn made use of the domestic and quotidian to explore poetry's timeless subjects.

Despite the limited scope of her world—she lived and taught in St. Louis for most of her adult life—her vision remained large. Like her friend and colleague **Howard Nemerov**, van Duyn remained, in the words of one critic, "optimistic in the face of the terror and beauty of the world." That attitude was developed and refined from the start in the poems she produced.

Born in Waterloo, Iowa, in 1921, Van Duyn was raised the only child of middle-class parents. As her poems indicate, she grew up under the eye of a protective mother who was always fearful for her child's health. The result seems to have been a turning inward, a discovery of the imagination and of poetry, which she secretly wrote all through her childhood and teen years. She earned a BA from Northern Iowa University in 1942 and an MA from the University of Iowa in 1943. That same year, she wed fellow poet Jarvis Thurston. Their sixty-one year union was the inspiration for many of Van Duyn's poems, since marriage, as her readers have noted, is her fundamental metaphore for the self's relation to the world. In 1947 Van Duyn and Thurston founded *Perspective: A Quarterly of Literature and the Arts*, which they edited until 1970.

Over the course of her career, Van Duyn published ten collections of poetry, including *Near Changes*, which won her the Pulitzer Prize in 1991. The award opened up a bitter and public debate about contemporary poetry, prompting **Allen Ginsberg** to deride the contemporary privileging of smaller, more domestic subjects. His condemnation did not, however, have a lasting effect on the Pulitzer committee or on Van Duyn's career: In 1992 she became the first woman to be appointed Poet Laureate of the United States.

Her poems, rooted as they are in the human body, tend to be formal, as if to declare that part of life's project is to set boundaries around ourselves, so that our lives—and our verse—take on shapes we can recognize and ponder. Rhymes and half-rhymes abound, as do witticisms and stanzaic patterns that structure individual poems. But her language remains casual, conversational.

Her first collection, *Valentines to the Wide World,* established both the style and some of the themes and tropes that would appear thereafter in her poems, using the opportunities opened up by seemingly normal moments in an ordinary person's life, often her own, to get at larger questions of human frailty, mortality, and love. In the title poem, she trains her eye first on an eight-year-old girl, busy pulling scabs off her knee as she grows awkwardly into herself, who asks, seemingly out of nowhere, "'Mother, is love God's hobby?'" which prompts the observation, "[at] eight you don't even / look up from your scab when you ask it." Metaphysics in mid-sentence, a lesson learned—"Such absurd / charity of the imagination has shamed us, Emily"—from an unexpected source, leads, in the second section, to a consideration of poetry itself. "It starts with the creature / and stays there, assuming creation is worth the time / it takes, from the first day down to the last line on the last page." The world in this poem reveals itself as beautiful and merciless, composed of pain and aging and death, but it offers the possibility of an embodied wisdom, learned through innocence and art, and for that it deserves our love.

Van Duyn and Thurston remained childless, a situation that, although not belabored in her poems, remains close to the surface, erupting every so often, as when in "Late Loving," from *Near Changes*, she declares, "[our] dogs are dead, our child never came true." In place of the mother-child relationship, she wrote about friendship and most often, her own evolving marriage, as in "Notes from a Suburban Heart," from her second book, *A Time of Bees*, in which she considers, in the wry humor that is typical of her verse, the relative superiority of "Philadelphia sewage" over her native St. Louis sewage to fertilize her garden, which leads her to ponder the mystery of growing anything, a plant or a relationship with another person. In the progress of the year, from planting season to planting season, she ends up back where she started, claiming to have learned that "I love you, in my dim-witted way."

Like other women poets writing in the late twentieth century, Van Duyn engaged in a project of discourse with history, both mythic and literary, oftentimes revising tales in which women have been treated cruelly or, worse, have been merely vehicles for men's aims. Lot's wife, Midas and his wife, and Miranda all take their turns, but Van Duyn's most famous offering, "Leda," from *To See, To Take*, begins where Yeats's famous poem left off. She answers his closing questions—"Did she put on his knowledge with his power / Before the indifferent beak could let her drop?"—forcefully: "Not even for a minute." Van Duyn gives Leda her humanity and puts her into a domestic sphere of children and home, as a real woman with the ability to survive after her one great trauma, melting "into the storm of everyday life."

Her final collection before her death, *Firefall* (1993), represented something of a departure for Van Duyn—although she had diverged stylistically in the past, too, most notably in *Bedtime Stories.* Here, she writes many of what she termed "minimalist sonnets" and "extended minimalist sonnets." These fourteen- or eighteen-line poems are more epigrammatic than most of her work, with shorter lines that reveal the more perfect rhymes. The resulting poems seem less substantial, even though she covers familiar material: cooking with a spouse, kids at a mall, and a mantelpiece ornament. Still, the collection is haunted by the deaths of friends and colleagues, and by the poet's own inexorable, if accepted, aging. Even here, though, Van Duyn remains true to her central attitude: love for the world and its wonders and its cycles of renewal that bring new babies into being, new families to an old block, and new things to learn. As ever, her poems testify to what she has long advocated: "The heart makes its presence known, disheveled but whole."

Though Van Duyn's *Selected Poems* was published in 2003, the poet, according to her husband, stopped writing around 1996, and following a battle with bone cancer, Van Duyn died at her St. Louis, Missouri, home on December 1, 2004.

Further Reading. ***Selected Primary Sources:*** Van Duyn, Mona, *Bedtime Stories* (Champaign, IL: Ceres Press, 1972); ———, *Firefall* (New York: Knopf, 1993); ———, *If It Be Not I: Collected Poems, 1959–1982* (New York: Knopf, 1993); ———, *Letters from a Father, and Other Poems* (New York: Atheneum, 1982); ———, *Merciful Disguises* (New York: Atheneum, 1973); ———, *Near Changes* (New York: Knopf, distributed by Random House, 1990); ———, *Selected Poems* (New York: Alfred A. Knopf, 2002); ———, *A Time of Bees* (Chapel Hill: University of North Carolina Press, 1964); ———, *To See, To Take* (New York: Atheneum, 1970); ———, *Valentines to the Wide World* (Cummington, MA: Cummington Press, 1958). ***Selected Secondary Sources:*** Burns, Michael, ed., *Discovery and Reminiscence: Essays on the Poetry of Mona Van Duyn* (Fayetteville: University of Arkansas Press, 1998); Goldensohn, Lorrie, "Mona Van Duyn and the Politics of Love" (*Ploughshares* 4.3 [1978]).

Michal M. Lemberger

VANGELISTI, PAUL (1945–)

An outsider even to the **avant-garde** that he promoted as editor of the seminal West Coast journal *Invisible City*, Paul Vangelisti was first characterized as a "parasurrealist" for his combination of whimsical imagery and political realism. This characterization suggests Vangelisti's disregard for American pragmatism, for personal psychology, and for the literary nationalism prevalent in his youth. Vangelisti's internationalism as well as his use of collage have allowed him to both evoke and criticize the transcendent spirituality of popular American **prose poem** writers such as **Robert Bly** and **James Tate**. Looking to Europe, Vangelisti absorbed French influences as did **John Ashbery** and his decendents, but his interest in Italy and particularly its avant-garde set him apart. He learned early to augment and side-step surrealism. He also drew from **concrete poetry**, futurism, and his own work as a **translator** of Adriano Spatola, Amelia Rosselli, and Antonio Porta, among others for whom parataxis and broken syntax could never be divorced from historical conditions.

Vangelisti's early work combines his interest in Italian heritage with his interest in the serial poems of **Jack Spicer** and **George Oppen** and in Marxist theory. A poem called "Air" was quite unique in 1973, as it extended tactics used in Spicer's "Book of Magazine Verse" to Marxist theory, distancing Vangelisti from those who were also inquiring into the play of signifiers but who did not share his emphasis on place, concrete situations, and comedy. Even his prose collages in such work as "Events" drew their logic more from Adriano Spatola and Antonio Porta than from the more popular Robert Desnos or Caesar Vallejo. Vangelisti's collages have been compared to Proust's notion of "fragments without anything lacking" because they refer back to one another in a comic fashion, both defying psychological interpretation and questioning the relation of consciousness to commodified language. "Air"'s collaged elements are modified to create a sense of continuity, especially in regard to syntax, even if the sections themselves remain "parts," and this distinguishes Vangelisti's work from **modernist** disjunctive fragments that remained tied to a search or voyage that could not lead anywhere beyond father, mother, and liberal notions of freedom. The search theme in Vangelisti leads only to further dialects and idioms, more ephemera, and quotidian detail, events that can only be captured in real material relationships, not their explication. Even the poems that embrace detective language and themes of investigation lead not so much to issues of crime as to community. In "Gof in Singapore," for example, Vangelisti's detective hero forgets that he has prior knowledge of the crime and thus becomes an accomplice. Work in this fashion, which would include the early *The Extravagant Room* and the more recent *Nemo*, are novels-in-verse, a form Vangelisti became interested in by translating and collaborating with French Algerian novelist Mohammed Dib. Like Dib's works, Vangelisti's poems are concerned simultaneously with humanity's natural innocence and with notions of personal responsibility, and by extension, with "art as oppositional dream." These concerns become clearer in later work like "Gold Mountain," which is a poem about Japanese prostitutes in Southern California during the Gold Rush, but which is collaged in part from Van Gogh's letters, thereby linking historical accomplishments and cultural heritages to recent events such as Japanese internment camps and westward expansion.

Other late work involves even more complex collages and includes strict formal structures that surpass much of the most involved work of the Oulipo group. The middle period's *Rime* also reflects his interest in constraint but less overtly. It relies on the rare use of "subject rhyme" and other often-hidden constraints to produce work that performs lyrically and accents quotidian concerns, another aspect of his anti-pragmatism. *Rime* anticipates the later *Villa*, an epistolary series of poems between an educator and student, ostensibly set in Rome even as it invokes contemporary Los Angeles as a city of displacement and alienation: "the only game in town, exile." This is a theme that returns both in his later "Book of Life" and in *Alphabets*, a book composed of four abcdarian variants, again full of anachronistic language and technique or "medieval synchronizations," used to critique contemporary American society and its poetic trajectory. But exile is also the position of Vangelisti's contemporaries in Los Angeles. The characterization of the West in general and Southern California in particular as an incoherent and anti-intellectual segment of America undoubtedly explains Vangelisti's interest in the book-length poem, in cohesive work that both evokes and defies notions of "the blank slate," "the melting pot," and the infertile desert. In opposing beatnik dandyism and East Coast elitism, he acknowledges Los Angeles's complicity and writes that its inauthenticity is a product of Hollywood: "Who can deny a city that gives nothing back / where the rain always leaves at night / and only leprechauns and gaffers whistle at the end of a rainbow." To this, he adds that Los Angeles is also the product of excessive sincerity: "who can deny the sincerity of / hot dog stands envisioned as hot dogs / checks emblazoned with skiers and / snow-capped Sierras who can deny." Finally, there is also a profound, if comic, concern for community: "who can deny / a communion of lovers a eighty / miles per hour shot once through the head . . . ten million / sincere words still missing still arriving / to die among strangers once and for all." That these seemingly mutually exclusive concerns—inauthenticity, sincerity, and community—are spread throughout a career of relentless experimentation suggests the difficulty not only in categorizing an avant-garde, but also in realizing human potential itself.

Further Reading. ***Selected Primary Sources:*** Vangelisti, Paul, *Alphabets* (Los Angeles: Littoral Books, 1999); *Embarrassment of Survival: Selected Poems 1970–2000* (New York: Marsilio/Agincourt, 2001); *Rime* (Los Angeles: Red Hill, 1984); *Villa* (Los Angeles: Littoral Books, 1991). ***Selected Secondary Sources:*** Davidson, Michael, *The San Francisco Renaissance* (Cambridge: Cambridge University Press, 1991); Mohr, Bill, "Likelihood of Survival: Paul Vangelisti's Poetry" (*Chicago Review* [22 March 2005]).

Standard Schaefer

VARIABLE FOOT

Because twentieth-century poet **William Carlos Williams** sought to create poetry that better reflected both the manner of American speech and the nature of modern life, he experimented with new **prosodies** in attempts to break free from the constraints of traditional European forms that used the metrical line. His "variable foot," an approach that appears in a number of his later poems, relied on time-based line lengths containing one strong beat and a shifting number of unstressed syllables—a varying rather than a standardized metrical foot.

Many modern poets, among them **T.S. Eliot**, **Marianne Moore**, and **Allen Ginsberg**, have noted the conflicts created by imposing upon a strongly Germanic language like English a metrical system based upon the rhythmic features of Romance languages. In his *Rethinking Meter: A New Approach to the Verse Line*, Alan Holder argues that the metrical rules of Latin and later Romance-based poetry were systematically applied to English poetry beginning in the fourteenth century as writers sought to give their English language the heft and tradition of classical forms. Although a discussion of the variable foot will not settle such a debate, it is worth noting that Williams sensed American English as having different rhythms, shapes, and impulses than Romance languages or even than British English. With this in mind, he set out to create prosodies that mirrored contemporary American practices.

The variable foot, one of the poet's later developments, devises lines of poetry that take a certain predetermined amount of time and that contain only one strong beat—usually placed on a concrete image or word in the line. Williams's isochronous line, as it is often called (see **Charles O. Hartman**'s *Free Verse: An Essay on Prosody*), used time as a means of imitating the rhythms of common American speech. Jessica Levine quotes lines from Williams's poem, "Sunday in the Park," in Book II, Part I of *Paterson* (1948), as an example of his use of this new American prosody:

> The descent beckons
> as the ascent beckoned
> Memory is a kind
> of accomplishment
> a sort of renewal
> even

Employing a triadic stanza as the poem's structural foundation, Williams uses his lines to propel his readers downward with the "descent" of the poem. His ideas on the variable foot ask us to think of each line in the triad as expending the same amount of time. Thus, the final, one-word line must slow to meet the time used by the longer earlier lines. This slowness reflects an uncertainty in the speaker—a questioning of his own words—that would not be embodied in a more traditional metrical line-unit. Also, each line draws our attention to one significant focus because each line contains but one strong beat. Note how in the first two quoted lines the stress falls upon the words "descent" and "ascent." The lines themselves reveal, within their structure, the central issues the poem is exploring. Williams's famous argument for "no ideas but in things" underlies his variable foot, asking of readers that they see the ways in which American speech, as well as American understanding, draws from the things of the world and not from abstract concepts about which we might disagree.

Fellow American poet **Robert Creeley** noted in an interview with Smartishplace.com that Williams's short lines, like his own in the 1950s, contain the edginess, the unsettled nature of modern existence. Rejecting the formal structures of traditional metrical poetry, these lines unsettle the readers' expectations of an underlying and familiar order given the poem by the standardization of the meter; this underlying order would suggest that experience, too, could be made orderly. Indeed, Hartman wondered in *Free Verse* whether readers could even find Williams's variable feet without the poet himself explaining his prosody first.

This question anticipates much of the reason for later poorly written **free verse** by young and established authors alike—who thought mistakenly that free-verse lines have no form. Even so, the variable foot is among a small number of twentieth-century prosodies for American poetry that offered a new *system* at once rebellious and disciplined.

Further Reading. ***Selected Primary Sources:*** Williams, William Carlos, *The William Carlos Williams Reader* (New York: New Directions, 1969). ***Selected Secondary Sources:*** Hartman, Charles, *Free Verse: An Essay on Prosody* (Evanston, IL: Northwestern University Press, 1996); Levine, Jessica, "Spatial Rhythm and Poetic Invention in William Carlos Williams's 'Sunday in the Park'" (*William Carlos Williams Review* 21.1 [Spring 1995]: 23–31).

Steve Wilson

VAZIRANI, REETIKA (1962–2003)

Reetika Vazirani was a poet caught between two different worlds, two different cultures. Her poetry explores her South Asian, North American, and Caribbean heritages, geographies, and languages. She uses several different voices to accomplish this, questioning issues of citizenship, the effects of migration, and Eastern versus Western culture. Her love of mythology and the art of her storytelling are the two distinguishing features of her poetry. She was on her way to becoming a major cross-generational voice among the young immigrants from the Indian subcontinent when her life was cut short at at the age of forty.

Reetika Vazirani was born in India in 1962. Her parents immigrated to the United States when she was six years old, moving to Maryland. Reetika was the second of four children. Her family was multicultural even in India; her father was Sindhi from Punjab and her mother was a Bengali, representing different cultures and regions in India. Reetika graduated from Wellesley College in 1984 and later received a Thomas J. Watson fellowship for travel and study in India, Thailand, Japan, and China. She then received her MFA from the University of Virginia, where she was a Hoyns Fellow. She received several prestigious literary awards including the Pushcart Prize, the Discovery/*The Nation* Award, the Poets & Writers Exchange Program Award, and fellowships from the Bread Loaf and Sewanee Writers' conferences. Vazirani's first book, *White Elephants* (1996), received a Barnard New Women Poet Prize in 1996, and her second book, *World Hotel* (2002), won the 2003 Anisfield-Wolf-Book Award. She had a troubled relationship with Pulitzer Prize–winning poet and Princeton University professor **Yusef Komunyakaa**, and the couple had a child together. Behind all this apparent success lurked a deep sadness and despair, roots of which can be traced back to her father and his suicide. On July 16, 2003, Reetika took her own life along with the life of her two-year-old son Jehan. In February 2004, the *Washington Post* published an important and sympathetic article titled *Failing Light*, which sheds light on Vazirani's troubled life.

Many of Vazirani's early poems are about elders remembering their past in the home country, the burden of that past that the young children feel, and the childrens' natural curiosity about their history. In "Chanel Lipstick" she uses the voice of her grandmother for the character of Mrs. Biswas, who is also a transplanted Indian woman in the Western world. She observes, "When I bought my first / Chanel lipstick, it was as if / I might have bought a cow in India." The overall effect is tragicomic: "last week I sent my sari / to new dry cleaner, and I was in shock / to be billed for two tablecloths." Her later works explore the rootless nature of contemporary American life. Vazirani was devoted to the language and craft of poetry, revising consistently, and had a keen eye for details about character and landscape. She also used a variety of voices with different inflections.

About her first book of poetry, *White Elephants*, Vazirani said in a note to PoetryNet, "*White Elephants* also began and ended as a funeral for my father." The book was an act of closure for her. Vazirani experiments extensively with the sonnet form in this collection. Her next book of poems, *World Hotel*, is divided into two parts. The poem sequence, "Inventing Maya" forms the first half of the book. The poems take Maya through her north Indian childhood to Washington, D.C., through an eventful adult life. The fictional character Maya is based on Vazirani's mother. The sequence portrays the experience of every immigrant, which comes with a sense of alienation and adventure at the same time. Many of the memories are typical of the people of the Indian diaspora. In "Memory I" she talks of a father who "just as the British withdrew . . . was finally British, (he was forty-two / and had finished changing)" and who then has to change in America all over again. "He grew strange, my father, / caught between two accents and two worlds." In the second part, "It's Me I'm Not Home," she experiments with many different poetic forms: villanelles, pantoums, a sestina, ghazals, and others. The poems of this collection are layered with stories within stories.

Vazirani used many Hindi words in her poetry for their musical effect, without any loss of accessibility to the readers. Witness these lines from "Days in Punjab, 1960–67": "Mali watered the lawn morning and night and reported on / the rose / bushes: blooming memsahib." Vazirani's poems show how much the old world finds its way into the new world. No matter how hard one tries to "replace a former accent," there is "always the scent of spices on our breath, / and bronze elephants waiting on the front steps."

Further Reading. ***Selected Primary Sources:*** Vazirani, Reetika, *White Elephants* (Boston: Beacon Press, 1996); ———, *World Hotel* (Port Townsend, WA: Copper Canyon Press, 2002).

Pratibha Kelapure

VERSE DRAMA

Although American verse drama has never enjoyed the popularity it deserves, its history is well worth examining, not only because of the intrinsic interest of the genre, but also because many of the greatest American poets have tried their hands at it. But first a clarification of terms is in order. Poetic monologues from Robert Browning to **Frank Bidart** are certainly dramatic, but they are not written to be performed, nor do they include the cast of characters that nearly all plays possess. Many playwrights—from the gently lyrical Thornton Wilder to the magnificently profane David Mamet—might be labeled "poetic," but they do not make systematic use of poetic techniques like rhyme and meter. Numerous poets have written "closet dramas"—plays written for the page rather than the stage—which must for this reason be disqualified from the category of verse drama as well. Librettos are often in poetic form but are not performed without musical accompaniment. A verse drama, then, can be defined as a nonmusical play with more than one character, written to be staged, and featuring some use, however experimental, of poetic techniques.

Plays were written in poetic form throughout Europe for centuries, reaching their high point in the Elizabethan Age. Shakespeare's habit, however, of using prose for comic scenes (the Porter's speech in *Macbeth* and the gathering of "rude mechanicals" in *A Midsummer Night's Dream*) indicated that prose was increasingly employed for comedies, even though poetry remained the standard form for tragedies: Dryden's dramatic oeuvre, for example, contains both prose comedies and verse tragedies. During the nineteenth century, verse drama experienced a Renaissance with the plays of Goethe and Schiller, and the genre enjoyed some popularity in England, as attested by Byron's *Werner* (1830), Shelley's *The Cenci* (1886), and Tennyson's *Becket* (1893). But eventually—due mostly to the increasing commercialization of the theater—most plays were written in prose. And the naturalistic dramas of Ibsen, Chekhov, and their British counterparts dealt a further blow to verse drama.

Nevertheless, around the turn of the century, the genre enjoyed a revival on both sides of the Atlantic thanks to such varied influences as the Noh drama of Japan, French **Symbolism**, and the Irish literary revival. William Butler Yeats, by far the most influential British poetic dramatist of this period, wrote numerous plays in verse, including *On Baile's Strand* (1903), *Dierdre* (1907), and *The Death of Cuchulain* (1939), and with his friend Lady Augusta Gregory, he founded the Abbey Theatre in Dublin to stage plays by himself and others. Although he also wrote plays in prose, Yeats's renovation of verse drama paved the way for later British playwrights as diverse as Christopher Fry, **Glyn Maxwell**, John Masefield, Dorothy Sayers, and Stephen Spender.

In America the first significant verse dramatist was **William Vaughn Moody**, who had his greatest success with the prose play *The Great Divide* (1906), but who also wrote a trilogy of poetic dramas: *The Masque of Judgment* (1900), *The Fire-Bringer* (1904), and the *Death of Eve* (incomplete on his death in 1910). All three plays deal with religious themes in a highly stylized manner that does not age well, though they also contain splendid lines: The angel Raphael, in *Masque*, remarks as he watches a sunrise, "Another light like this would change my blood / To human" (*Poems and Plays*, 247).

No American poet did more to reinvigorate verse drama than **T.S. Eliot**, who wrote—in addition to the fragments "Sweeny Agonistes" and "The Rock"—five full-length poetic plays: *Murder in the Cathedral* (1935), *The Family Reunion* (1939), *The Cocktail Party* (1950), *The Confidential Clerk* (1954), and *The Elder Statesman* (1959), all set and first performed in his adopted England. In Eliot's own 1951 essay "Poetry and Drama," the most useful introduction to his dramatic works, he charts the evolution of the plays he had written so far. "When I wrote *Murder in the Cathedral*," he admits, "I had the advantage . . . of an occasion which called for a subject generally admitted to be suitable for verse" (Eliot, *Selected Prose*, 138–139): the murder of Archbishop Thomas Becket. "Verse plays, it is generally held," Eliot continues, "should either take their subject matter from some mythology, or else should be about some remote historical period, far enough from the present for the characters not to need to be recognizable as human beings, and therefore for them to be licensed to talk in verse" (139). Talk in verse they do: a Chorus who speaks in various meters; a haunting series of Priests, Knights, and Tempters; and the staunch, impassioned Thomas ("Now my good Angel, whom God appoints / To be my guardian, hover over the swords' points"). But Eliot remarks that "the play was a dead end" and that he was "determined in [his] next play to take a theme of contemporary life." The result was *The Family Reunion*, which features a family, members of which speak sometimes as individuals, sometimes as a chorus inspired by Aeschylus's *Eumenides*, and sometimes in "lyrical duets" of shorter lines—a device Eliot came to find "too much like operatic arias" and that is therefore absent from his last three plays. *The Cocktail Party*, perhaps the most completely successful of Eliot's plays, is an extremely moving story of marital estrangement and reconciliation containing "no chorus, and no ghosts," though, like his earlier work, it is based on a classical play, Euripides' *Alcestis.* Here the blank verse is both deeply elegant and bracingly contemporary: "There's no memory you can wrap in camphor / But the moths will get in. So you want to see Celia." Eliot's last two plays, written in similarly natural blank verse, continue his devastating exploration of the clash between outer and inner lives, the struggles of the present and the ghosts of the past, and the agony of guilt and the gift of forgiveness.

Around the time that Eliot started to write plays, the poet **W.H. Auden**—who moved to the United States in 1939—and the novelist Christopher Isherwood began collaborating on a series of equally inventive poetic dramas, including *The Dog Beneath the Skin* (1935), *The Ascent of F6* (1936), and *On the Frontier* (1939). These plays, inspired as much by Brecht's "epic theater" as by the recent innovations of Yeats, move between poetry and prose and between music-hall hijinks and lacerating social satire with majesterial ease. Auden's solo works also reflect an interest in verse drama, as can be seen in his "charade" *Paid on Both Sides* (1928); his "Christmas Oratorio," *For the Time Being* (1941–1942); his **long poem** *The Sea and the Mirror* (1942–1944), in which Shakespeare's Prospero and his "supporting cast" reflect on their lives after *The Tempest*; and his baroque eclogue "The Age of Anxiety" (1944–1946), in which four characters speak in a bravura rendering of Anglo-Saxon accentual-syllabic meter.

Edna St. Vincent Millay, another great twentieth-century poet who wrote verse dramas, indelibly stamped the genre with her vast range of forms and subjects. Since she lacked a strong native tradition on which to draw, Millay often looked to medieval and Renaissance playwrights for inspiration, but her contemporary themes, coupled with her imaginative approach to verse forms, make her plays unmistakably modern. After writing and acting in several plays at Vassar, Millay moved to New York and became involved with the Provincetown Playhouse, which produced her folktale-inspired verse dramas *Two Slatterns and a King* and *The Prince Marries the Page* (which she had written in college). When these plays received critical acclaim, Millay went on to write—and direct—perhaps her best and most influential verse drama, *Aria Da Capo* (1919), whose *dramatis personae* include two commedia dell'arte characters, Pierrot and Columbine; an allegorical figure, Cothurnus, who represents tragedy; and two shepherds, Corydon and Thyrsis, who, for the majority of the play, battle over two different treasures—water and jewels—on opposite sides of a wall they have built. Corydon strangles Thyrsis with the jewels, Thyrsis poisons the water, and both die. *Aria Da Capo* has been labeled an anti-war play, but it can be read in more broadly metaphorical terms—conflict between the sexes, races, and classes—as well. Millay wrote several other plays, including the experimental *Conversation at Midnight* (1937), a dialogue in verse based on real conversations among Millay, her husband, Eugen Boissevain, and their friends at Steepletop, a farm in Austerlitz, New York. Over the course of the play, nine men discuss their habits, families, religions, and worldviews in a dazzling variety of rhyming and metrical schemes. This fascinating and inventive play was not produced until after Millay's death, running for only four nights on Broadway.

Many other modern American poets have written verse dramas. **Wallace Stevens**'s "Three Travelers Watch a Sunrise" (1916) contains little plot but many passages of powerfully dramatized imagism (sunrise "filled my doorway / Like whispering women" [*Opus Posthumous*]). **Robert Frost**'s *A Masque of Reason* (1945) and *A Masque of Mercy* (1947), though not written for performance either (the stage directions are part of the blank verse), reveal the great lyric poet—who, after all, created such memorable embedded dialogues as "The Witch of Coos" and "West-Running Brook"—to be a gifted dramatist as well. Poet **e.e. cummings**'s *Santa Claus* (1946), also written in blank verse, draws, as Millay's work had, on medieval morality plays like *Everyman* to present a confrontation between Death and Santa Claus. **Delmore Schwartz**, heavily influenced by Eliot, wrote several intriguing and idiosyncratic plays in which verse and prose mingle, including *Choosing Company* (1936), an "oratorio" featuring the voice of a radio as a character; *Shenandoah* (1941), an account of how Schwartz's alter ego Shenandoah Fish got his name; and *Paris and Helen* (1941). Alfred Kreymborg wrote too many brief and fanciful poetic plays—animal fables, political allegories, and metaphysical meditations—to count; **Robinson Jeffers** and **Gertrude Stein** wrote vibrant poetic plays; and **Ezra Pound**'s verse translation of Sophocles's *Women of Trachis* appeared in 1954. **Archibald MacLeish** wrote stirring and original verse dramas throughout his long career, including most memorably *JB* (1956), a modernized version of the story of Job in which the title character broods on the mysterious ways of God. The strength of MacLeish's play lies in his marriage of biblical fidelity (a "Distant Voice" asks Job, "Where wast thou / When I laid the foundations of the earth") and demotic vigor: The faithful servant Job remarks, "God is God or we are nothing— / Mayflies that leave their husks behind—." MacLeish wrote many other verse plays on religious and political themes, including *Nobodaddy* (1926), *Air Raid* (1938), and *The Trojan Horse* (1952), a radio play about the dangers of McCarthyism. Maxwell Anderson composed numerous verse dramas—some, like *Elizabeth the Queen* (1930), based on history and others, like *Winterset* (1935), a searching exploration of the Sacco and Vanzetti case, inspired by more recent events. And **Richard Eberhart**'s charmingly eccentric verse plays—reflections on the competing claims of art and life in which an energetic and opinionated author-figure often makes a metadramatic appearance—serve as further proof of the enduring power of the medium.

Sadly, verse drama fell into decline in the second half of the twentieth century; the demise of the Federal Theatre Project in America in 1939 and the rise of movies and television—with their tendency toward realism—made it less and less likely that a play's characters would speak in poetry. Even so, institutions devoted to verse drama such as the Poet's Theater in Cambridge and university theaters have insured the continued—albeit dimmed—existence of the genre. And several recent verse dramas have shown both the genre's lasting ability to rivet and delight and the great variety of subjects and forms it can accommodate. Barbara Garson's *MacBird!* (1966), a political satire of Lyndon Johnson's rise to power modeled on Shakespeare's *Macbeth*, employs blank verse that occasionally modulates into bitingly effective couplets (Mac Bird: "I git to be a-weary o' this show / And wish my country didn't need me so"). Ntozake Shange's *For Colored Girls Who Have Considered Suicide When the Rainbow Is Enuf* (1974), a hugely popular "choreopoem" about the struggles and stories of black women, featuring seven women who each play multiple roles, is written in edgy, fast-moving **free verse**. Finally, David Hirson's 1991 *La Bete*, which enjoyed great critical success despite its brief Broadway run, demonstrates how, in Hirson's own words, "an undeniably American, undeniably contemporary piece of writing" can "be set in a neoclassical frame" (v). *La Bete*, composed in rhyming pentameter couplets and concerning a seventeenth-century acting troupe whose members clash regarding the nature and purpose of art, is an engaging blend of breakneck dialogue and breathless philosophical monologues: One character mourns the loss of "real morals or real wisdom or real art: / We can't tell truth and travesty apart!" That verse drama indeed contains "real art" is on powerful display in these three very different plays, and it can only be hoped that writers acknowledge and nourish this truth in generations to come.

Further Reading. ***Selected Primary Sources:*** Auden, W.H., *Complete Works: Plays and Other Dramatic Writings, 1928–1938*, ed. Edward Mendelson (Princeton, NJ: Princeton University Press, 1988); Eliot, T.S., *The Complete Plays* (New York: Harcourt, Brace and World, 1967); Yeats, W.B., *Eleven Plays* (New York: Collier Books, 1964). ***Selected Secondary Sources:*** Donoghue, Denis, *The Third Voice: Modern British and American Verse Drama* (Princeton, NJ: Princeton University Press, 1959); Hassall, Christopher, *Notes on the Verse Drama* (London: Curtain Press, 1948); Peacock, Ronald, *The Poet in the Theatre* (London: Routledge, 1946).

Rachel Wetzsteon

VERY, JONES (1813–1880)

Among the works of writers constellated as members of the Transcendentalist Club in the late 1830s and 1840s, the poetry of Jones Very appears distinctly, if briefly, as the product of a mystical experience (1838–1840) that, though expressed in sonnets whose language is derived almost entirely from New Testament writings, defies categorization within any orthodoxy. Yet his body of work extends over a much longer career. Represented in the twentieth century in successive editions of *The Oxford Book of American Verse* by a selection of more than a dozen poems, Very remains a poet worth the attention of readers desiring a more than passing acquaintance with Transcendentalism and the ferment of ideas and poetic expression in the American Renaissance. While it was not until 1993 that a complete modern scholarly edition of his poetry was published (Deese, *Jones Very: The Complete Poems*), his place among writers of this milieu was established by **Yvor Winters** in an influential essay first published in 1936 and reprinted in several editions thereafter (e.g., *Maule's Curse*). Winters identified Very as a Calvinist whose authentic religious experience put to shame the merely putative experiences of Emerson and others. (For a condensed critical genealogy, see Deese, xxxviii ff.) One might also suggest, however, that **Thoreau**'s comment in *Walden* that "we may be beside ourselves in a sane sense" gains resonance from the example of Very's ecstatic lyrics (their careers at Harvard overlapped, and both were members of the informal "Transcendentalist Club"); and many years later, Elizabeth Palmer Peabody, who had befriended Very in the ecstatic period, used the similar phrase "beside himself" to describe his disposition during this time. Unfortunately, having defined this mystical period as the distinct epoch of Jones's poetic career, and bearing an awareness that Winters used Very's ecstatic utterances as an example to deprecate the more ordered discourse of Emerson and other Transcendentalists, the critical tradition has tended also to deprecate Very's poetry in its earlier Romantic and later pietistic Unitarian modes. Critical and biographical treatments have therefore tended toward endorsements, disparagements, and attempts to reconcile supposedly dichotomous positions (Transcendentalism versus Calvinism versus Unitarianism) without establishing deeply convincing estimates of the whole career of the poet.

Very was born in Salem, Massachusetts, on August 28, 1813, the first son of Captain Jones Very (1790–1824) and his first cousin Lydia Very (1794–1867), nearly two centuries after the nonconformist Very family had immigrated to a somewhat interior section of southeastern

Essex County and a scant six months after Jones Very's parents' supposed marriage. (Documentation of their marriage became a matter of intrafamilial dispute in probate after the death of Captain Very at an early age, when Isaac Very—Captain Very's father and Louisa's uncle—made claims upon the estate and disputed the existence of a legal marriage between Louisa and the elder Jones.) The history of the family poses several chief points of interest for readers of Very's poetry besides establishing the family as long-standing inhabitants of New England. First, his father's occupation as a sea captain, the presence of his two sisters and one brother who survived into adulthood (two other children died in infancy or before the age of five), and his father's early death meant that Very grew up in an environment largely defined by women, among whom his mother was obviously central as she managed the affairs of the household during the father's intermittent and then permanent absence. Biographical treatments differ in speaking of Lydia on one hand as an "atheist" (Gittleman, basing his view solely on passages in the letters of Elizabeth Palmer Peabody) and on the other as a woman of religious sensibility (Bartlett; Reeves), and it is difficult to discern and evaluate the evidence for such assertions. (Early biographers could have had access to people in the Salem community who remembered the family—Lydia Louisa Ann, the youngest daughter, died in 1901—and oral traditions regarding contentions about individuals and families could persist in the community without ever being publicly adjudicated; and Salem was a community in which decided opinions and judgments about others were themselves something of a tradition. Moreover, the charge of "atheism" in this environment could signify nothing more than an exaggerated reaction to Lydia's declining to affirm an established creed or to confess to a conversion experience.) Since the sources of Very's religious disposition are of obvious interest, his mother's disposition is also of interest; but definition is lacking. Second, at about the age of ten, young Jones accompanied his father on a voyage to northern Europe, Russia, and—returning to the United States—New Orleans, where he met Captain James Cook. This voyage was a common initiation experience of the time; yet, though common for young men of a certain class, the experience was unique for each individual, and Very remembers his own in an unfinished poem (Bartlett, 10). Third, but perhaps not finally, the death of Captain Jones Very at an early age meant a disruption of continuity in the development of young Jones. He was cut off from following his father's occupation or, for want of resources, from immediately proceeding toward higher education, and he was called upon to help support his mother and three younger siblings. This he did by working for an auction house (where he was able to procure books) and by eventually working in a private college preparatory school as an assistant—where he collaterally prepared for college. Already his literary bent was evident and noted; he published poems in local papers.

Very entered Harvard at the age of twenty with advanced standing, but still discontinuously, since his classmates were typically much younger than he was. He showed extraordinary promise, being one of the few students to win the Bowdoin Prize twice for essays that are still remarkable examples of the mastery of the elements of nineteenth-century rhetoric and composition. Following his graduation in August 1836 (**Thoreau** graduated in 1837), Very gained preferment as a Greek tutor and then experienced what was perhaps the most disruptive event of his life. A dedicated scholar, he diverted from the course of instruction and began to preach to his students in oracular ways: "Flee to the mountains, for the end of all things is at hand!" (Reeves, "Making of a Mystic," 14). Very was dismissed (replaced by Charles Stearns Wheeler, his and Thoreau's mutual friend), and he returned to Salem and convalesced in a mental hospital and at home. He eventually regained his mental composition to the degree that, having been licensed as a Unitarian preacher in 1833, but not ordained, he earned much if not all of his living as a Unitarian "supply preacher," replacing absent ministers for short terms and variable remuneration over the next forty years. He continued to publish poems and other writings locally.

Very's early poems reflect, as might be expected, the diction, form, and ethos of late-eighteenth- and early-nineteenth-century precursors such as Wordsworth and Keats and sometimes of their common precursor Milton. Both "North River" (1835)—beginning "How sleep the silent waves!"—and "Memory" (1836), in its lines "Soon the river, brightly gleaming, / Rolls its dark forgetful wave," recall the ambiance and diction of Wordsworth's "Lines, Written in a Boat when Sailing at Evening" and "Lines, Composed upon the Thames near Richmond." "The Snow-Bird" (1835) echoes Keats's "To a Nightingale" in its interrogative mood and diction and its circumstance in concluding, "Thou'rt fled. . . . / I bless thee—for thou'st left behind / Thine image ere thou'st past." If simpler in theme and prosody, and more homely, than the poems to which they partly (and perhaps not entirely consciously) allude, Very's poems are not embarrassingly so. Indeed, it would not be out of place to consider them in a tradition that extends from these precursors through Hardy and **Frost**.

The poems of what may be called the religiously ecstatic period, roughly from 1838 to 1840, break with the typically Romantic themes of the earlier poems, and allusiveness becomes another thing altogether. Many of these poems are titled with key phrases from the gospels or other New Testament writings, which could set up the expectation that, like sermons, the poems are meant as explications or exemplifications of the biblical (or liturgical) trope invoked by the title. For critical tradition, then, another lineage would be engaged, such as that of Herbert or Milton or American **Puritan poets**. But these poems, most of them in sonnet form, raise peculiar issues of voice (see Deese, citing Buell, xli), even when compared to the tradition of meditative verse. The typical religious verse that takes the form of prayer ("Avenge O Lord thy slaughter'd Saints," Milton, Sonnet 18) or of the soul's questioning redounding to itself, as in Herbert, is not typical here. In poems of 1838–1839 such as "The Kingdom of God Is within You" and "The Church" ("This is the rock where I my Church will build"), the lyric "I" of the sonnet speaks in the persona of God or, what is equivalent, of Christ, and the poems weave biblical tropes into a new utterance that is neither a supplication nor an explicit commentary on scripture or distanced engagement with scripture, but that sounds like a scriptural representation of the voice of God. What one makes of such poems depends, of course, upon a tradition of reception—and it was probably more startling around 1840 in New England than it could possibly be now—and upon one's knowledge of the author. At least partly, one suspects, the reaction to Very's verse was informed by a knowledge that the author during this period spoke, apart from the bracketing conventions of poetry, in a similar way in daily discourse. Whatever one makes of the doctrinal controversy surrounding Very, following Winters, the issue presented by these poems seems in retrospect to be less their doctrinal tendency than their audacity.

Almost half of Very's more than eight hundred poems were written after the period of enthusiasm or inspiration—or of insanity, as some would have it—in the late 1830s and early 1840s. What is remarkable about the later poems is an accomplishment of poetic form and diction in relation to the topic of the poem. Moreover, there is a consistency of vision with what is expressed in his undergraduate essay "Epic Poetry": "we do reverence and honor those motives which even in the infancy of the human mind served to raise it above the dominion of sense, and taught it to grasp at a life beyond the narrow limits of its earthly vision" (*Essays and Poems*, 10). One can find this vision exemplified in nearly any of the later poems, if only in a homely way, but explicitly in "True Knowledge Necessary for the Voyage of Life" (1866), "The Teachings of the Spirit" (1867), and "The Revelation of the Spirit Through the Material World" (1873). If the thought and sentiment of these poems can be considered somewhat ordinary, and therefore overshadowed by what one might think of as the extraordinary expression of the poems of the ecstatic period, then one might pause to consider how these oddly abstract titles and even the subjects of the poems compare, even if by the way of subsequent parody, to the oddly abstract titles (and the subjects) of a later poet like **Wallace Stevens**.

Very's poetry both benefits and suffers from a literary-critical form of American exceptionalism. In ordinary critical acceptance, to the degree that he is remembered and acknowledged, it is as an example of the perturbations of religious and philosophical enthusiasms of his time. The major bio-critical treatments of his work have become dated and his poetry calls out for reconsideration.

Further Reading. ***Selected Primary Sources:*** Very, Jones, *The Complete Poems*, ed. Helen R. Deese (Athens: University of Georgia Press, 1993); ———, *Essays and Poems*, ed. R.W. Emerson (Boston: Charles C. Little and James Brown, 1839); ———, *Poems and Essays*, ed. James Freeman Clarke (Boston: Houghton, Mifflin, and Co., 1886); ———, *Selected Poems*, ed. Nathan Lane (New Brunswick: Rutgers University Press, 1966). ***Selected Secondary Sources:*** Bartlett, William Irving, *Jones Very: Emerson's "Brave Saint"* (Durham, NC: Duke University Press, 1942); Gittleman, Edward, *Jones Very: The Effective Years, 1833–1840* (New York: Columbia University Press, 1967); Levernier, James A., "Calvinism and Transcendentalism in the Poetry of Jones Very" (*ESQ* 24.1 [1978]: 30–41); Reeves, Paschal, "The Making of a Mystic: A Reconsideration of the Life of Jones Very" (*Essex Institute Historical Collections* 103 [January 1967]: 3–30); ———, "Jones Very as Preacher: The Extant Sermons" (*ESQ* 57 [1969]: 16–22); Robinson, David, "The Exemplary Self and the Transcendent Self in the Poetry of Jones Very" (*ESQ* 24.4 [1978]: 206–214); Winters, Yvor, *Maule's Curse* (Norfolk, CT: New Directions, 1938).

Stephen Hahn

VILLA, JOSÉ GARCÍA (1908–1997)

José García Villa was known in the United States as an important **modernist** poet, particularly in the New York literary scene of the 1940s and 1950s, and was hailed in his home country of the Philippines as one of the major patrons of Filipino letters in the twentieth century. His controversial and complicated poetical experiments led him to be appreciated among modernist poets such as Edith Sitwell, Mark van Doren, and **Marianne Moore**. Nonetheless, by the late 1950s his prominence began to fade and he fell into obscurity in the United States, although his influence in the Philippines continued to grow. Critics regard him as the founder of modern Philippine literature in English. Villa's position as a crucial player in Philippine letters was made official when he was named Philippine National Artist in Literature in 1973.

Villa was born on August 5, 1908, in Malate, Manila. He published his first story in the *Manila Times* at the age of fifteen. In his second year of law school, his "Man-Songs" appeared in the *Philippines Herald*, causing him to be suspended from the university because of the poems' "immorality." He immigrated to the United States in 1929, with the money from a prize he won for a short story, "Mir-i-nisa." He lived in the United States for the rest of his life, except for brief visits to the Philippines. In New York he worked as associate editor of *New Directions* (1949–1951), as Poetry Workshop Director of the City College of New York, and as a lecturer at the New School for Social Research (1964–1973). The awards he received include the Poetry Award of the American Academy of Arts and Letters (1942), a Guggenheim fellowship in poetry (1943), a Poetry Society of America fellowship (1959), and a Rockefeller fellowship for poetry. He died in New York City on February 7, 1997.

In the United States, Villa published his only collection of short stories, *Footnote to Youth: Tales of the Philippines and Others* (1933), which recalls Sherwood Anderson's *Winesburg, Ohio.* After his experiment with fiction, and influenced by poets such as Robert Blake, **e.e. cummings**, **Marianne Moore**, Dylan Thomas, **Elinor Wylie**, and Edith Sitwell, he devoted his career to rethinking forms of poetry and, in particular, experimenting with the sounds and the appearance of words on paper. His first collection of poetry published in the United States, *Have Come, Am Here* (1942), outlines the themes that would be taken up repeatedly in his later writing.

Villa's poems are characterized by revolt in content and in form. God is the prime object of the poet's rebellion, as Villa negotiates the connections among God, love, death, and identity. In Villa's personal theology, Man is the creator of God through the human—and especially the poetic—power of thought and poetry. As he writes in "Poem 95," "In the chamber of my philosophy God is instructed." Love is another recurrent theme. In "Poem 21" he argues that the heart that cannot love cannot be cured by death, nor sleep, "nor splendor of wound." He views romantic love as a release of the soul and repeatedly posits it as superior to even God, who "shall not be able to put out Love at all" ("Poem 15").

Villa repeatedly engages the structures of traditional poetic diction in order to discover what he considers the language of pure poetry. In his multiple definitions of poetry, he consistently privileges the power of the word: "Poetry is a struggle between a word and silence; between an eternal word and an eternal silence" ("Definitions of Poetry," 224). In his most famous poetic description of a poem ("Poem 15"), Villa requires that a poem be magical, musical, elusive, and even secretive, like the bride who hides what she seeks, stressing the universality of the poetic craft. Preoccupied with developing an essentially poetic language that would achieve effects akin to music and painting, Villa negotiated three experimental strategies. First, he developed "reversed consonance," a rhyme method which required that the last consonants of the last syllable, or the last principal consonants of a word, be reversed for the corresponding rhyme, making the rhyme for *near* words like *run, rain, green, reign.* His second major innovation was his creation of "comma poems," published in his second book of poetry, *Volume Two* (1949). He inserted commas and eliminated the spaces between all the words in the poem, contending that the commas would regulate the poem's verbal density and movement, heighten appreciation for each word, and achieve fuller tonal effects. Thus, in "Poem 20" he sees Life "Clean,like,iodoform," between the letters of "death." The comma poems also appear to allow him a deeper introspection: "At,the,in,of,me" begins "Poem 11." His third poetic experiment in this volume involved adaptations, experiments in converting prose to poems with specific line movements and shape. Villa's adaptations developed from sources that included letters, newspaper reports, book reviews, short stories, and novels.

Villa stopped writing poetry in the early 1950s; his last poem was "The Anchored Angel," written in 1953, which may be considered his poetic valedictory. After this, he devoted himself to critical and philosophical writing.

Although Villa lived in the United States for most of his adult life, his influence on Philippine literature in English far outweighs his influence on American letters. Yet, paradoxically, he appears to have been better appreciated as a poet in his country of adoption than in his homeland, where Filipino critics accused him of solipsism. Though American poets responded enthusiastically to the originality of Villa's early poetry, they judged concepts such as reversed consonance as esoteric and exhibitionist, impossible to discern by the average reader. The "comma poems" were also received with skepticism and disapproval because of their clumsiness and the tediousness of the technique's invariability. Nonetheless, recent Asian American criticism is revising the role and position of Villa in the context of transnational writing, as a poet and cultural figure, and is reconsidering the context of his production and reception in the United States.

Further Reading. ***Selected Primary Sources:*** Villa, José García, *The Essential Villa* (Manila: A.S. Florentino, 1965); ———, *Footnote to Youth: Tales of the Philippines and Others* (New York: Charles Scribner's Sons, 1933); ———, *Have Come, Am Here* (New York: Viking, 1942); ———, *Volume Two* (New York: New Directions, 1949); ———, "Definitions of Poetry," in *Filipino Essays in English 1910–1954, Vol. 1: 1910–1937,* ed. Leopoldo Y. Yabes (Quezon City: University of the Philippines Press, 1962). ***Selected Secondary Sources:*** Tabios, Eileen, ed., *The Anchored Angel: Selected Writings by José García Villa* (New York: Kaya Press, 1999); Tinio, Rolando S., "Villa's Values: Or,

The Poet You Cannot Always Make Out, Or Succeed in Liking Once You Are Able To," in *Brown Heritage: Essays on Philippine Cultural Tradition and Literature*, ed. Antonio G. Manuud (Quezon City: Ateneo de Manila University Press, 1967, 722–738); Yu, Timothy, "Asian/American Modernisms: José García Villa's Transnational Poetics," in *Pinoy Poetics*, ed. Nick Carbó (New York: Meritage Press, 2004).

Rocío G. Davis

VIOLI, PAUL (1944–)

Paul Violi, an American Metaphysical, often yokes totally dissimilar concepts to reveal the otherworldly in the everyday. He is "one of the few genuinely funny poets around, not merely witty, *funny*" (North, 96). His poems combine "the relaxed unpredictability of **Frank O'Hara**, the shadowy wisdom of Rimbaud, and the urban angst of Jerry Seinfeld" (Muratori), mixing humor, history, and traces of poems by Samuel Daniel or Michelangelo Buonarroti with fascinating pop-culture trivia.

Born in New York City in 1944, Violi grew up in Greenlawn, Long Island; studied English literature and art history at Boston University (BA 1966); served in the Peace Corps (Nigeria); traveled through Africa, Europe, and Asia (1966–1967); married Ann Boylston (New York, 1969); worked for WCBS-TV News (1968–1970) and as managing editor for the *Herald* (1970–1972) and *Architectural Forum* (1972–1974); and served as interim director for the St. Mark's Poetry Project and as Chairman of Junior Council Poetry Committee (Museum of Modern Art). His daughter, Helen, was born in 1972 and his son, Alex, in 1977. He has taught at New York University and Columbia University. His five art book collaborations with British printmaker Dale Devereux Baker are in major collections. His awards include grants from the New York Foundation for the Arts, the Foundation for Contemporary Arts, the Fund for Poetry, and the Ingram Merrill Foundation; the Creative Artists for Public Service Award (New York State Council on the Arts); two National Endowment for the Arts fellowships in poetry; the John Ciardi Award for Lifetime Achievement in Poetry (Italiana Americana / National Italian American Foundation); and the Morton Dauwen Zabel Award (American Academy of Arts and Letters).

Violi's poems fearlessly document miracles, dark passions, fierce tenderness, and all-too-human follies. Besides O'Hara, his poetic influences include other **New York School** poets—James Schuyler, **Kenneth Koch, John Ashbery**, **Ron Padgett**, Tony Towle, and **Charles North**. Violi's rare editions—*She'll Be Riding Six White Horses* (1970), *Automatic Transmissions* (1970), *Waterworks* (1972), *In Baltic Circles* (1973), and *Some Poems* (1976)—underscore his vibrant **lyricism**, provocative imagination, satiric humor, and radical experimentation with a range of appropriated and invented forms and personae. He turns a "Coda" into a sexy love poem: "roll off you / off a wave," to "dream awhile scheme awhile," lying still beside the wave that brought the lover there. "To Cisco in the Swamps" is a faux translation of Wolfram de Zorro. "Exacta" reports on a day at the races—"And they're off! / Babe Wittgenstein takes the lead"—and the much-noted "Index" unveils Sutej Hudney's life: "Disavows all his work 120" or "Complains of 'a dense and baleful wind / blowing the words I write off the page' 165." "Triptych" is a day in a *TV Guide*: "'Bugs Bunny' (9 a.m.), 'VIGIL. 8 people on train platform reading little books' (2 p.m.), 'TIME AND TOLERANCE. An invisible nude enters the elevator. She's chewing gum' (10:30 p.m.)." Violi stretches forms in "Industrial Sonnet" and "Tanka" and appropriates forms in "Alba," "Saga," "The Chronicles of a Space Cadet," "*from* Campaign Journals," "On the Surface" (a poem of definitions), and "Calendar"—with verses of Edgard Debris translated for each month, as in April's popular topic, "On Lust."

Harmatan (1977)—with Paula North's drawings of dancing nails, a Coca-Cola bottle, and a thermometer—is a canticle of Nigerian joys and sorrows. Early poems reappear in *Splurge* (1982), Schuyler's "favorite book of poems" that year (Hillringhouse). "Haiku" (*Likewise* [1988]) depicts a mugging: "No change, just large bills. / One wrong move will be your last." "Self-Portrait" claims, "I feel like someone who has swum the ocean / only to drown in the muck offshore." Violi's **translation** of Leopardi's "L'Infinito" declares, of a gust of wind in the trees, "I see how far into that infinite silence / this voice can go, and then in an instant / I know what eternity is." Koch thought Violi's translation of Cecco Angiolieri's "Sonnet" ("If I were fire, I'd burn the world away") was the best he'd seen and called from his hospital bed in Houston, Texas, to ask Violi to send it. "Little Testament" quotes "**Ezra Pound**'s translation of Arnaut Daniel" and "parodies François Villon's lament for the 'snows of yesteryear' in *Le grande testament*" (Diggory): "Dead-Eye Dick, / the jubilant realist, where did he go?"

The Curious Builder (1993), with William Wegman's fire-creature cover, also blends seriousness and humor: The **sublime** verse of the Renaissance poet Samuel Daniel—"Like to the curious builder who this year / Pulls down, and alters what he did the last"—and poetic-biography ("I, Paul Violi, being of sound mind") follow the skidmarks back to Manhattan "through Suburbia and the footfalls of Tyrannosaurus Bronx" (another Violi poem). "Tanka" is a ransom note. "From Provender Books," a rare-book listing, comments on Violi's contemporaries: "536 Welish, Marjorie. The Modern Poem, N.Y. 'Fierce / devotion to the ideals of a classic calm.' $260." In "Police Blotter," Officer "444 reports youths have turned darkly / sarcastic, requests back-up. All units." In "Haitian Quatrains," lines of proper names are classical musical motifs. In "Errata," editing is erotic: Page 11, line 6 reads, "After 'her body,' add 'Pythagorean, flotilla, nocturne, scramble.'" In *Fracas* (1998), Violi returns to Canal Street in New York City, like some famous Parisian boulevard, announcing in "Inscribed on the Gates to Canal Street," "*This* is where New York / buries its jittery poets," and "The Hazards of Imagery" tours artworks in arcane places: "In the Gift Shop at the Lunatic Asylum" or "At the Cottage of Messer Violi," where "In the kitchenette is a statuette / of Ceres, Goddess of Wheaties."

Long poems reprinted in *Breakers* (2000) "demand a double reading of this 'curious builder' as not only 'strange, singular, odd' but also, in the Renaissance sense, 'careful, studious, attentive'" (Diggory). Often lighthearted, Violi turns "whatever provides the impulse into poems which give evidence of his curiosity and learning, feelings, wit, and struggle to come to terms with private demons" (North, 101). Best known for innovation in form, Violi is a **postmodern** Raymond Roussel, charting the waters of cultural highs and lows in America and often, to our astonishment, in a restless republic of dreams.

Further Reading. ***Selected Primary Sources:*** Violi, Paul, *Breakers: Selected Long Poems* (Minneapolis, MN: Coffee House Press, 2000); ———, *The Curious Builder* (Brooklyn, NY: Hanging Loose, 1993); ———, *Fracas* (Brooklyn, NY: Hanging Loose, 1998); ———, *Hamartan* (New York: Sun Press, 1977); ———, *In Baltic Circles* (New York: The Kulchur Foundation, 1973); ———, *Likewise* (Brooklyn, NY: Hanging Loose, 1988); ———, *Selected Accidents, Pointless Anecdotes* (Brooklyn, NY: Hanging Loose, 2002); ———, *Some Poems* (Putnam Valley, NY: Swollen Magpie Press, 1976); ———, *Splurge* (New York: Sun Press, 1982); ———, *Waterworks* (Iowa City, IA: Toothpaste Press, 1972). ***Selected Secondary Sources:*** Diggory, Terrence, "A Maze of Openings" review of *Breakers: Selected Poems*, by Paul Violi) (*American Book Review* 22.4 [May/June 2001], www.litline.org/ABR/issues/Volume22/Issue4/abr224.html); Hillringhouse, Mark, Review of *Selected Accidents, Pointless Anecdotes*, by Paul Violi (*Literary Review* [Fall 2002], www.findarticles.com/p/articles/mi_m2078/is_1_46/ai_94983807); Muratori, Fred, Review of *Breakers: Selected Poems*, by Paul Violi (*Rain Taxi*, online edition [Winter 2000/2001], www.raintaxi.com/online/2000win ter/violi.shtml); North, Charles, *No Other Way: Selected Prose* (Brooklyn, NY: Hanging Loose, 1998).

Eugene Richie

VISUAL POETRY

Visual poetry may be defined as poetry that is meant to be seen, poetry that presupposes a viewer as well as a reader. Combining visual and verbal elements, it not only appeals to the reader's intellect but also arrests his or her gaze as well. To be sure, every poem consists of visual elements, since the eye must process the words before the mind can interpret them. Where visual poetry differs from ordinary poetry is in the extent of its iconic dimension, which is much more pronounced, and in its degree of self-awareness. Visual poems are immediately recognizable by their refusal to adhere to a rectilinear grid and by their tendency to flout their plasticity. In contrast to traditional poetry, visual poems are conceived not only as literary works but also as works of art. Although, like traditional poems, they provide cues that aid in deciphering the text, they function simultaneously as visual compositions. Whether the visual elements form a rudimentary pattern or whether they constitute a highly sophisticated design, they transform the poem into a picture.

Although visual poetry has a lengthy and varied history, going back to the *technopaegnia* of the ancient Greeks (and perhaps even earlier), it has flourished during the modern period as never before. Refined, redesigned, and redefined, it has been the object of countless schools and movements from 1914 to the present and has spread to every corner of the globe. As much as anything, the rise of modern visual poetry reflects a new awareness of the printed page. Words are no longer perceived as transparent signs but assume the destiny and shape of objects. This distinctly modern perspective was adopted by two important precursors toward the end of the nineteenth century: William Morris in England and Stéphane Mallarmé in France. Like other members of the Arts and Crafts movement, Morris sought to counter the dehumanizing effects of mechanical reproduction by creating a long line of handcrafted items, including books of poetry that were meticulously designed and executed. Similarly, Mallarmé revealed a whole new realm of possibilities in 1896, when he published *Un Coup de dés jamais n'abolira le hasard* (*A Throw of the Dice Will Never Abolish Chance*). Employing each word, indeed each letter, as a visual counter, he brilliantly demonstrated just how radical visual poetry could be.

These developments were not lost on F.T. Marinetti in Italy and Guillaume Apollinaire in France, who grasped their profound implications and who invented modern visual poetry more or less independently in 1914. Inspired by such inventions as the phonograph, the telephone, radiotelegraphy, and the cinema, they were among the first to explore the poetic possibilities of modern means of transmission and reproduction. Under the guidance of Marinetti, who encouraged them to express their "wireless imagination," the Italian Futurists experimented with *parole in libertà* ("liberated words"). In addition to a large variety of typographical effects, they utilized *analogie disegnate* ("visual analogies") in their poetry. In "Fumatori II" ("Smoking 2nd Class"), for example, Francesco Cangiullo lengthened the word *fumare* to "FUUUUUMARE" and made each letter progressively larger to evoke a puff of cigarette smoke. By contrast, Apollinaire's visual compositions, which he first called *idéogrammes lyriques* and then *calligrammes*, were largely figurative. Utilizing filled forms as well as outlined forms, they reproduced the physical appearance of objects. In contrast to traditional visual poetry, which tended to portray a single object, most of Apollinaire's calligrammes contained multiple figures arranged in unified compositions.

Visual poetry was cultivated initially in the United States by members of the New York **avant-garde** during World War I. Created by Marius de Zayas and several of his associates, the first examples appeared in *291* in 1915 and were condemned by **Amy Lowell**. The best-known visual poet in America is doubtless **e.e. cummings**, who was inspired by Zayas's and his contemporaries' example (and Apollinaire's) to try his hand at the genre. His poems derive surprisingly sophisticated effects from a few elementary typographical devices.

Invented in Europe and Brazil, **concrete poetry** is a special variety of visual poetry that invaded the United States during the early 1950s. Emmett Williams, Mary Ellen Solt, **Aram Saroyan**, and the Canadian **bp Nichol** were among the first to experiment with this new form, which attracted a great many poets. **Dick Higgins** was another pioneer who, like **John Cage**, helped to shape the **Fluxus** movement. More recently, **Charles Bernstein** has explored the concrete legacy within the framework provided by the **Language poets**. Visual poetry continues to elicit widespread interest. The general availability of computers has inspired poets to experiment with new technological forms such as visual hypertexts, kinetic poetry, and holography.

Further Reading. Bohn, Willard, *The Aesthetics of Visual Poetry, 1914–1928* (Cambridge, Cambridge University Press, 1986; reprint Chicago: University of Chicago Press, 1993); ———, *Modern Visual Poetry* (Newark: University of Delaware Press, 2001); Drucker, Johanna, *The Visible Word: Experimental Typography and Modern Art, 1909–1923* (Chicago: University of Chicago Press, 1994); Jackson, K. David, Eric Vos, and Johanna Drucker, eds., *Experimental-Visual-Concrete: Avant-Garde Poetry Since the 1960s* (Amsterdam: Rodopi, 1996).

Willard Bohn

VOIGT, ELLEN BRYANT (1943–)

Ellen Bryant Voigt trained as a pianist before becoming a poet, and her highly trained musical ear is evident in her poetry, with its subtle orchestrations of sonic patterns and its intricate interweaving of lyric and narrative elements. The author of six collections of poetry as well as a collection of essays on craft, *The Flexible Lyric*, she also founded the nation's first low-residency master of fine arts program in creative writing at Goddard College in 1976, a design for graduate study that has been emulated by colleges and universities across the country.

Born in Danville, Virginia, in 1943, Voigt grew up on a farm, in a large, extended and close-knit Southern Baptist family. She studied music and performed as a pianist from an early age—at church, in school, and for her father's barbershop quartet. After graduating from high school, she attended Converse College in South Carolina, an all-women's college that included a music conservatory. Late in her undergraduate career, she stumbled upon poetry and began taking more literature and fewer music classes. Her professors there were proponents of **New Criticism**, so they championed a poetry that transcended the "merely personal"—an attitude that initially suited Voigt's urge toward language for its own sake and the purity of the musical phrase. In her own poetry, however, she would soon combine that musical purity with subject matter firmly rooted in the physical—and most often the natural—world. In the 1960s, Voigt was one of the few women participants in the Iowa Writers' Workshop. She earned an MFA in music and literature from the University of Iowa, taught briefly at Iowa Wesleyan College, and arrived on the Goddard College campus at the height of the late 1960s counter-culture movement. She founded the low-residency MFA program there from a desire to provide access to graduate study for talented writers, particularly women, who had little opportunity to attend conventional graduate programs or were not well served by them. The program—six-month tutorial semesters conducted via correspondence with practicing poets and writers and initiated by a two-week residency on campus—became the model for other "low-residency" writing programs and was eventually reincarnated at Warren Wilson College in North Carolina. Voigt has continued to direct the Warren Wilson program, to teach and to mentor younger writers. She settled with her husband in rural Vermont—in a small town much like the one in which she grew up—where she has raised a family and produced a steadily growing body of work that continues to garner increasing critical acclaim. She has recently served as poet laureate of the state of Vermont.

Voigt's first collection of poems, *Claiming Kin*, was published in 1976. The poems are filled with the dense and fertile imagery of rural life—"the vast, disordered world" ("At the Piano")—honed to precision in language both carefully measured and richly musical. The poet's vision, here as in her later poems, is clear-eyed, stripped of all sentimentality, almost brutal, at times, in its rendering of the cycles of birth and death, of the violence and beauty of the natural world. And her ear is ever attuned to the rhythms and trills of that world, sonic patterns that run through our experiences, ordering our lives and driving the poems forward—just as the girl at the piano drives "triplets against the duple meter" while, outside, the calves taken from their mothers "bawl and hoot all night." Voigt's subsequent volumes, *The Forces of Plenty* (1983) and *The Lotus Flowers* (1987), similarly draw on scenes from her Virginia childhood and rural life in Vermont, while her imagery grows increasingly concise and her lyricism simultaneously more subtle and more intense. In *Two Trees* (1992), the two chords that sound throughout her work—dark and bright, physical and spiritual, transforming pain and transcendent pleasure—intertwine in poems that invest scenes of daily life with a haunted and haunting resonance. In "Fish," a woman engaged in the simple task of changing the water in a fish tank is "thrown back ten years" when she lifts one of the fish in her net from the water. She pictures her baby daughter with "hands tied at her side, / writhing and tossing in her transparent cage" as a nurse approaches to momentarily "cut off the air" in order to suction the mucus from the infant's throat. Unable to make a sound, the baby's "mouth closed and opened without a sound / on the M, the dark ah—." The beginning of utterance, the child's silent mouthing of "the M, the dark ah—" when she can't speak or call out for "mama," harks back to the bawling calves in the earlier poem; we're reminded that all utterance is rooted in the body, as is music, as is longing. In "Blue Ridge," the speaker finds herself standing "among the paired / bodies, the raw pulsing music driving / loneliness into the air like scent." And then she is standing beside a man she wishes would touch her, a friend with whom she watches fireworks, "so little ease between us, / I see that I have armed myself; / Fire charges everything it touches."

In her later poems, Voigt's fierce attention is sharpened further, as if the poet is refusing to look away from even the most devastating scenes of suffering. And yet the poems are quietly restrained, never melodramatic; they give to human pain, if not "meaning," at least a measure of dignity. With *Kyrie*, published in 1995 and nominated that year for the National Book Critics Circle Award, Voigt reaches beyond her own experience into a collective past, a shared tragedy. A book-length sequence of loosely structured sonnets—"little songs"—*Kyrie* paints a portrait in mosaic of the influenza epidemic of 1918–1919, which killed twenty-five million worldwide, set against the background of World War I. The poems' various speakers—most not precisely identified—present a variety of perspectives to show the impact of world events on individual lives and the life of a small town. Here again, the tension between form and subject and between lyricism and narrative invests the poems with an almost brutal tautness and energy.

Voigt's 2002 collection, *Shadow of Heaven*, may also be her most grave and starkly accessible. These tightly crafted poems examine, in straightforward language, the subjects of illness, dying, and grief; they explore the themes of mourning and memory; and they employ details of the natural world balanced with pared down emotional insights. Those insights are conveyed with such authority that they sometimes sound almost like commands, as in "High Winds Flare Up and the Old House Shudders," which begins, "The dead should just shut up." But then the poem sweeps across a landscape in which the dead continue to make their presence known: A "new-plowed field" "looks like a grave," and within the "dark room" created by walls of "pine-woods," "a birch, too young to have a waist, / practices sway and bend, slope and give." In the end, the poet seems to feel some camaraderie with the dead, after all, and with their unwillingness to let go of the physical world—"they lodge / in your throat like a stone, or they descend / as spring snow . . . frantic for more, more of this earth." Voigt's deft use of sonic devices—internal rhyme, slant rhyme, alliteration, subtle metrical patterns—and the universality of her subject matter have helped to place her among those contemporary poets responsible for the current renaissance of popular interest in poetry in America.

Further Reading. ***Selected Primary Sources:*** Voigt, Ellen Bryant, *Claiming Kin* (Middletown, CT: Wesleyan University Press, 1976); ———, *The Flexible Lyric* (Athens: University of Georgia Press, 1999); ———, *The Forces of Plenty* (New York: Norton, 1983); ———, *Kyrie* (New York: W.W. Norton, 1995); ———, *The Lotus Flowers* (New York: W.W. Norton, 1987); ———, *The Shadow of Heaven* (New York: W.W. Norton, 2002); ———, *Two Trees* (New York: W.W. Norton, 1992). ***Selected Secondary Source:*** Orr, Gregory, and Ellen Bryant Voigt, eds., *Poets Teaching Poets* (Ann Arbor: University of Michigan Press, 1996).

Cecilia Woloch

VORTICISM

One of the major though short-lived literary and artistic movements of the early twentieth century, Vorticism was on its American side an outgrowth of **Ezra Pound**'s dissatisfaction with developments of **Imagism** and on its British side a response, primarily by the writer and painter Wyndham Lewis, to Italian futurism, Franco-Spanish Cubism, and German Expressionism, making it the first truly pan-Atlantic **avant-garde** modernist movement. Though its theoretical and aesthetic principles remain disputed, its foremost vehicle, the two issues of the London-based journal *Blast* (June 1914 and July 1915, cut short by World War I), makes at least some overarching characteristics clear: It vehemently attacked late Victorian complacency and **sentimentalism**, embraced artistic abstraction, was attracted by motion and modern machinery, and employed an excessively aggressive tone in expounding its ideas as well as in the content of its literary manifestations. Above all, it stressed an acute awareness of form in art: the arrangement of planes in sculpture, the line and color in painting, and the juxtaposition of images in poetry, all of which would become important creeds for many derivative movements later in the twentieth century and into the twenty-first.

Following in the wake of artistic excitement in Europe after the publication of the first "Futurist Manifesto" in 1909, the Italian futurist, master publicist, and later fascist F.T. Marinetti gave a series of lectures in London at the Dore Galleries in the summer of 1914. In April of the same year, Lewis had founded the soon-to-be-defunct Rebel Arts Center, and during his stay in England, Marinetti published an article entitled "Vital English Art" in the *Observer* (7 June 1914), in which he appropriated the names and works of Lewis and his circle into the futurist movement without their permission, infuriating Lewis. During roughly the same period, the **expatriate** American Ezra Pound, who once held the banner for Imagist poetry, with its famous primary tenet "An 'Image' is that which presents an intellectual and emotional complex in an instant of time," was appalled by the way the movement was developing under the guidance of **Amy Lowell** and sought to replace it with a more dynamic aesthetic. He explained, "The image is not an idea. It is a radiant node or cluster; it is what I can, and must perforce, call a VORTEX, from which, and through which, and into which, ideas are constantly rushing. In decency one can only call it a VORTEX" (*Gaudier-Brzeska*, 92).

Lewis and Pound joined forces and—with the input of the French sculptor Henri Gaudier-Brzeska, Richard Aldington, and others—together published a collection of prose, poetry, and paintings in the first issue of *Blast: Review of the Great English Vortex* (dated June 1914, but published in July). In the issue, Lewis set out his own program in plain and aggressive terms:

> We stand for the Reality of the Present—not for the sentimental Future or the sacrosanct Past.
> We believe in no perfectibility except our own. . . .
> We do not want to change the appearance of the world, because we are not Naturalists, Impressionists or Futurists (the latest form of Impressionism), and do not depend on the appearance of the world for our art.
> WE ONLY WANT THE WORLD TO LIVE, and to feel its crude energy flowing through us. (*Blast I*, 7–8)

Pound, for his part, coined the word "Vorticist" and published in *Blast* **T.S. Eliot**'s four "Preludes" and the "Rhapsody of a Windy Night" for the first time, as well as a few scathing pieces against his literary contemporaries and his and **H.D.**'s quasi-Imagist poetry.

The issue, in which the markedly futurist use of dramatically large typographical settings should be noted, included poems by Pound, Lewis's drama *Enemy of the Stars*, Rebecca West's story *Indissoluble Matrimony*, the opening of Ford Madox Hueffer's *The Saddest Story* (later published as *The Good Soldier*), a review by Edward Wadsworth of Kandinsky's *Über das Geistige in der Kunst insbesondere in der Malerei*, and numerous reprints of Vorticist paintings and designs. Among the things and people to be "blasted," according to the Vorticists, were English weather, Galsworthy, Dean Inge, Croce, Bergson, the British Academy, and William Archer; among the things and people to be "blessed" were French vitality, skepticism, pornography and females, the Pope, Barker (John and Granville), the Salvation Army, Charlotte Corday, castor oil, James Joyce, Lloyd George, and the Commercial Process Company. These tongue-in-cheek lists have led some readers to question the seriousness of the proto-Vorticists.

In the second issue of *Blast* (July 1915), the beginning of World War I seems to have toned down the vigor if not the humor with which the Vorticists set out to change the literary and artistic face of early **modernism**. Gaudier-Brzeska contributed his last writings from the trenches, in perhaps the most humane and compassionate manifestos of the movement:

> With all the destruction that works around us, nothing is changed, even superficially. *Life is the same strength*, the same moving agent that permits the small individual to assert himself. . . .
> This war is a great remedy. (*Blast II*, 33–34)

Just a few short months later, Gaudier-Brzeska died in the trenches. Among the other casualties of World War I was the publication of *Blast* and, with it, Vorticism itself.

Further Reading. *Blast I* (June 1914; rpt. Santa Barbara, CA: Black Sparrow Press, 1981); *Blast II* (July 1915; reprint Santa Barbara, CA: Black Sparrow Press, 1981); Fletcher, John Gould, *Life Is My Song* (New York: Toronto, Farrar & Rinehart, 1937, 136–137); Goldring, Douglas, *South Lodge* (London: Constable & Co., 1943, 65–70); Norman, Charles, *Ezra Pound* (New York: Macmillan, 1960, 146–162); Pound, Ezra, *Gaudier-Brzeska: A Memoir* (New York: New Directions, 1974); Ross, Robert H., *The Georgian Revolt, 1910–1922: Rise and Fall of a Poetic Ideal* (Carbondale: Southern Illinois University Press, 1965, 39–46).

Antony Adolf

VOSS, FRED (1952–)

Fred Voss has been called a poet of alienated labor and can be regarded as the foremost verse chronicler of blue-collar working life in America, preeminently in his first full-length collection, *Goodstone* (1991). This is a multifaceted dramatization of his experiences as a machinist in the factories of the Los Angeles area, where he has worked, and at times been laid off, for more than two decades. He continued a powerful poetry of social witness in *Carnegie Hall with Tin Walls* (1998), expanding his scope to look outside the workplace, sympathizing with the economically vulnerable in society. The masculine environment and implicitly political undertones of Voss's writing place it in a line of descent from the proletarian poets of the 1930s as well as Californian novelists such as John Steinbeck and Louis Adamic. It is also characterized by a **Whitman**-like embracing of the human spirit. His prolific output, humor, and hammered-down vernacular language recall **Charles Bukowski**, the contemporary poet whom Voss most admires.

Voss was born in Long Beach, California, in 1952, and has remained in the city for his adult life. He dropped out of the Ph.D. program in English at the University of California–Los Angeles to take jobs in a gasket factory and steel mill before becoming a machinist in an aircraft factory. During the 1980s he became active on the Long Beach poetry scene, socializing with and learning from writers such as **Gerald Locklin** and **Joan Jobe Smith**, whom he married in 1990. By his own account, Voss began writing poems six months after the death of his father, having previously written seven unpublished short novels. In the last of these, called *Goodstone Aircraft Company and the Acid*, he discovered his true subject matter. Little magazines such as *Wormwood Review* and *Poetry LA* encouraged him with acceptances, but the major breakthrough came in Britain during 1989–1990, when more than a hundred of his poems were published in successive issues of the literary magazine *Bete Noire*, whose editor hailed Voss's factory poems as without parallel in contemporary Anglo-American verse. *Goodstone* was enthusiastically reviewed in the *London Review of Books* and in British national newspapers. Voss has made several successful reading tours, and his richly resonant voice has been broadcast on BBC Radio. In America, however, his writing has thus far had a lower profile.

In each of his collections, Voss creates what is essentially a **long poem**, made up of compelling vignettes that focus on his fellow workers' masculinity, quirks, life stories, ethnicity, and psychological vulnerability. Much as he appreciates Bukowski's **narrative** style and exploration of the social margins, he largely breaks with the latter's machismo and obtrusive ego. Voss writes about unvarnished humanity, but formally his poems have something of a machine-like quality, relentlessly propelled down the page by Whitmanic lists, reiterations, and lines that vary greatly in length, often ending in a satirical punch line. His perennial subject is the daily grind of machine shop and factory work and the ways in which industrial confines make individuals react, frequently in boredom or frustration, as in "8 Hours at Goodstone Aircraft Company." The poems depict an abrasive atmosphere full of profanities and sexual taunts, as well as danger, farce, confrontations, and racial tensions between groups. They amount to a stark picture not only of blue-collar working conditions, but also, in their class conflicts, of financial insecurity, racism, and homophobia, an implied microcosm of American society itself.

Goodstone is itself a product of the Reagan era, when large Air Force contracts for the manufacture of aircraft were awarded, and connections are made explicit by blackly ironic titles such as "Making America Strong," in which workers play K-20 bomber parts like musical instruments, and "What You Got for Your Tax Dollars." Voss has a satirical way of depicting both bureaucracy and managerial incompetence: Old hammers explode in "Less than Zero," respirators are impossible to obtain ("Safety"), and falling tool cabinets nearly crush a man in "Too Good to Be True." He adds up the cost to individual lives: A steel mill worker under threat of dismissal carries a heavier burden each day, driving his neck and his head down into his shoulders, "as if he were a shaft being driven through concrete / by a jackhammer" ("Termination"). Politically, the workers are "Asleep": "we believe that we are powerless / as we sit in bars" while watching the president on television. The book ends as the contracts run out, with inevitable layoffs despite the supervisor's assurances, and in the office "they were smiling at us" ("Keep the Faith").

In "Outside," from the chapbook *Maybe It's All True* (1995), he remarks that after a year of unemployment, the alley "begins to reach right up into your apartment." Voss's own experience of layoffs widened his emotional scope, leading him to consider the plight of abused women in "How Long Can They Last?" and that of the poor in "Community," stating that "none of us can ever really be defeated." He often juxtaposes shop-floor reality with art and artists who lift the spirit, observing in "Priceless" that a poem is worth less than a thrown-out chair or than a cigarette butt ground into a factory floor, yet this "is what makes a poem in America / so valuable." "Alchemy" achingly lists what "Art can be made out of," including a beautiful girl who left him, with empty dresser drawers and blank walls, and concludes, "I don't think / I would be alive today / if it couldn't."

Carnegie Hall with Tin Walls is set during the 1990s and presents more men under competing pressures, returning to the obnoxious Curly and to Big Ed. Others rivet "World Class Asshole" plaques onto their toolbox lids in "One of the Joys of the Job," and they cut corners or use air-guns to fire pellets into each other's backs ("Improvising"). But some of the best poems are set outside the factory, recollecting Voss's Sunday softball games among social misfits in "Down but Not Out." Perhaps with a nod toward his wife's book *Jehovah Jukebox*, he observes machinists in nude dance bars "with all that $22-an-hour 50-hour-a-week money / in their wallets" ("Aircraft Factory Love"). Surely, one of his most moving and memorable poems is "When All the Electric Lightbulbs in the World Won't Help," whose repeated phrase, "the sun goes down," serves to link together all those suffering in America, from suicidal welfare mothers to men who used to own homes and "disowned 17-year-olds in strange cities." In "I Know This Man," he peers into an alley to look at a down-and-out man picking through garbage, and he recognizes himself: "for he is me / if I had not somehow stumbled across that job." Voss has universalized the harsh lessons learned in the factory; he continues to portray Americans with sympathy and humanity.

Further Reading. ***Selected Primary Sources:*** Voss, Fred, *Carnegie Hall with Tin Walls* (Newcastle, UK: Bloodaxe Books, 1998); ———, *Goodstone* (Long Beach, CA: Event Horizon Press, 1991); ———, *Maybe It's All True* (Long Beach, CA: Pearl Editions, 1995). ***Selected Secondary Sources:*** Stein, Julia, "Those Love Bird Poets: Are They the Future?" in *Literary LA*, by Lionel Rolfe (Los Angeles: California Classics, 2002); Voss, Fred, "Title" (*Bete Noire* 10/11 [Autumn 1990]: 1–32); ———, "Title" (*Bete Noire* 8/9 [Autumn 1989]: 103–122).

Jules Smith

WAGONER, DAVID (1926–)

Although David Wagoner has authored ten novels and several plays (along with pursuing occasional acting and magic performances), his eighteen books of poems form the core of his legacy. These poems best display his love of language, his respect for formal structure, his social concerns, and most important, his connection to the natural world, often with a lover as a fellow participant. If a core theme could be attributed to Wagoner, it would be the psychic freedom that can occur when the constrained and overly civilized self begins to be cleansed by a quiet immersion in the forest or the seashore. Wagoner's vistas may not be those of **Emerson**, but his keen observations of and serene participation in the natural world continue to offer a sustaining vision.

Born in 1926, David Wagoner spent his first seven years in Massilon, Ohio, and his most formative years in Whiting, Indiana, in the bleak industrial area between Gary and Chicago. He graduated from Penn State in 1947, and while there studied poetry with **Theodore Roethke**. He has observed that "it was Roethke's workshop that really changed the direction, quality, and meaning of my life" (*Contemporary Authors*, 402). After finishing his MA in creative writing at Indiana University in 1949, Wagoner, at Roethke's invitation, took a position at the University of Washington in 1954, where he taught for almost fifty years before retiring in 2003.

Wagoner's first book, *Dry Sun, Dry Wind* (1953), reflects the barrenness of his early midwestern experience. Perhaps because of this background, the move to Washington proved cathartic: "I had never seen or imagined such greenness, such a promise of healing growth. Everything I saw appeared to be living ancestral forms of the dead earth where I'd tried to grow up" (*Contemporary Authors*, 406).

Although his next volume, *A Place to Stand* (1958), shows little influence of the Pacific Northwest, his 1963 *The Nesting Ground* clearly does so. In 1966 Wagoner published his most noteworthy early book, *Staying Alive*, and took over as editor of *Poetry Northwest*, where he remained until its last issue in 2002. The title poem of *Staying Alive* is quintessential Wagoner. Starting with the advice to someone lost in the forest that "staying alive in the woods is a matter of calming down," the poem offers a practical but profound commentary on physical survival that leads to psychic stability Three years later, Wagoner published his well-received *New and Selected Poems*, and in 1972 he edited *Straw for the Fire*, a selection from Roethke's notebooks. *Sleeping in the Woods* appeared in 1974 and was nominated for the National

Book Award. Two years later his *Collected Poems 1956–1976* saw print and was also nominated for the National Book Award. A number of other volumes followed, including *Who Shall Be the Sun?* (1978), which incorporated a number of Native American myths, and then *Landfall* (1981) and *First Light* (1983). In 1987 Wagoner published *Through the Forest: New and Selected Poems* and a decade later *Walt Whitman Bathing: Poems.* He published *Traveling Light: Collected and New Poems* in 1999 and *The House of Song* in 2002.

Throughout his career Wagoner has garnered numerous awards and fellowships, including an American Academy of Arts and Letters award, the Sherwood Anderson Award, the Fels Prize, the Ruth Lilly Poetry Prize, the Eunice Tietjens Memorial and English-Speaking Union prizes from *Poetry*, and fellowships from the Ford Foundation, the Guggenheim Foundation, and the National Endowment for the Arts.

Wagoner is often categorized as a nature poet, but he is also eloquent on many other themes. For instance, although he has written a number of poems directly invoking the natural world ("A Guide to Dungeness Spit" and "The Nesting Ground") and others firmly critical of industries that destroy nature ("Working Against Time" and "Valedictory to Standard Oil of Indiana"), he also writes regularly about his boyhood and his father, a man he remembers as detached and difficult, and often about his troubled relationships with his second wife, Patt, to whom he remained married for twenty years, and his third wife, Robin. Other common topics include the deceptive beauty of magic (his most successful novel is called *The Escape Artist*) and historical events ("The March of Coxey's Army" and "The Shooting of John Dillinger Outside the Biograph Theater, July 22, 1934").

Perhaps Wagoner's most effective organizing technique is the sequence, and most of his volumes include one. "Traveling Light" from *Collected Poems* is a nine-poem series that directly addresses surviving in the woods but that also serves as a commentary on relationships and the act of writing poetry. "Sea Change" in *Landfall*, "Sleeping in the Woods" from the volume of the same name, and "Landscapes" from *Walt Whitman Bathing*, are three other notable sequences.

Wagoner also has a fine comedic touch, often displayed through his sprightly punning, a talent he exhibits in poems such as "Neighbors," "Note to a Literary Club," and "The Man Who Spilled Light." The poet **James Dickey** praised Wagoner's "curious, sardonic and often authentically wild comic imagination" (4). A fine example can be found in "Elegy for a Woman Who Remembered Everything," wherein Wagoner writes that the woman's ears were as "perfectly pitched" as those of a piano tuner; gifted with "total recall," the woman "absorbed the absorbing facts and the absorbent / Fictions of everyone's life but her own."

David Wagoner remains a poet of careful observation and compelling language. His first play was produced as he approached age eighty, and a new volume of poetry titled *Good Morning and Good Night* was released in 2005. Ron McFarland has wondered why Wagoner, over the course of his long and distinguished career, has not "attracted greater critical and scholarly interest" (10). This lack of attention may be corrected in the coming years as more readers come to appreciate the quiet beauty and sharp observation at the heart of his poetry.

Further Reading. ***Selected Primary Sources:*** "Wagoner, David," in *Contemporary Authors Autobiography Series*, vol. 3 (Detroit: Gale Research, 1986, 397–412); Wagoner, David, *Collected Poems 1956–1976* (Bloomington: Indiana University Press, 1976); ———, *Dry Sun, Dry Wind* (Bloomington: Indiana University Press, 1953); ———, *New and Selected Poems* (Bloomington: Indiana University Press, 1969); ———, *Staying Alive* (Bloomington: Indiana University Press, 1966); ———, *Through the Forest: New and Selected Poems, 1977–1987* (New York: Atlantic Monthly, 1987); ———, *Walt Whitman Bathing: Poems* (Urbana: University of Illinois Press, 1996). ***Selected Secondary Sources:*** Dickey, James, Review of *The Nesting Ground* (*New York Times Book Review* [22 December 1963]: 4); Dobyns, Stephen, Review of *New and Selected Poems* (*Poetry* 117 [March 1971]: 397–398); Lieberman, Laurence, *Unassigned Frequencies* (Urbana: University of Illinois Press, 1977); McFarland, Ron, *The World of David Wagoner* (Moscow: University of Idaho Press, 1997); Waggoner, Hyatt, *American Visionary Poetry* (Baton Rouge: Louisiana State University Press, 1982).

Justin Askins

WAH, FRED (1939–)

Fred Wah's writings combine and complicate the categories of reception of at least three poetics tendencies and moments: new American poetry, **Language poetry**, and Asian–North American poetry. Wah's writings exist largely in the relations between, and in the margins of, Canada's and the United States' national poetic cultures. Wah's writings affirm the relevance of **Charles Olson**'s poetics for imagining racialized and gendered subjectivities. Olson's anti-humanist idea of a "human universe," in the broadest historical and geographical senses, marks an important departure point for Wah's poetic explorations of race and racialization, citizenship, diaspora, and ideologies of multiculturalism. Wah's earlier writings enact an exemplary range of new American poetic techniques, and his later writings are notable for their formulations of racial hybridity, especially for tropes of fakery and mimicry, which insist on complicating identity.

Wah's diasporic, biracial family, particularly on his father's side, significantly informs his writing trajectory.

Wah's parents successively owned and operated several Chinese Canadian cafes in Swift Current, Saskatchewan, where the poet was born, and in the Nelson area of British Columbia, where the poet grew up. Wah's paternal grandfather emigrated from China when the U.S. government was seeking cheap labor to build the Canadian Pacific Railroad, which was vital to national unity. Once the railroad was completed in 1885, the government denied citizenship and imposed a prohibitive head tax (equal to two years of a laborer's salary by 1903) on new immigrants from China, followed by an outright exclusion act (1923). Wah's father is of mixed Chinese and Scottish-Irish ancestry. Wah's mother's family emigrated from Sweden when she was a child, at a time when the government sought European settlers and offered prairie land. So Fred Wah is half Swedish—like Charles Olson. Wah's Swedish-born grandfather was a carpenter who built grain elevators. Olson's Swedish-born father was, for a time, an ironworker who built New England factory stacks.

Wah attended courses by Olson and by **Robert Creeley** as an undergraduate at the University of British Columbia (BA 1962), co-founding *TISH: A Poetry Newsletter, Vancouver* (1961–1963) while there. *TISH* was sympathetic to contemporary United States poetic models rather than to traditional British poetic models. Wah founded *Sum* magazine, publishing New American and Canadian contemporaries, while undertaking graduate studies with Creeley at the University of New Mexico. The young Wah's two-page open letter to **Louis Zukofsky** in *Sum* 3 (1964) characterizes his dialogic poetic address. Wah became a contributing editor to *Niagara Frontier Review*, the *Magazine of Further Studies*, and *Open Letter: A Canadian Journal of Writing and Theory* while studying with Olson at SUNY–Buffalo (MA 1967). After graduate studies, Wah returned to teach in the Nelson area. He then became instrumental in the 1980s in founding the Kootenay School of Writing; he won the Governor General's Award for Poetry in 1985.

Wah's first five books engage elementary spatio-temporal coordinates for the body via Charles Olson's idea of writing as an integrally proprioceptive function—a notion fundamental to all Wah's work. Wah enacts a notion of the body at one with nature by attuning writing to his own body's proprioceptive balance, affect, and movement. Achieving such "natural" poise requires "getting rid of the lyrical interference of the individual as ego" (Olson, 247) and distrusting the "solid lyric subject ground" (Wah, *Faking*, 109) of a socialized, humanist "I." Wah aligns the body *against* society.

George Bowering remarks how the "integration of consciousness and surroundings" in Wah's early writings is unparalleled in any other writer (Wah, *Loki*, 11). Wah stylistically invokes a tendency of new American poetry to prioritize a complex primitivist, as much as **modernist**, idea about culture. In the poem *Mountain* (1967), the "I" becomes interchangeable with birds encountered on a cliff-face—"Birds of the Mountain lift me"—until experiencing vertiginous shock—"where the birds on the way out / hang."

Among (1972) displays, in its informal address to friends, a **New York School** aesthetic transposed to the British Columbian backwoods. The ecological and rural concerns of *Tree* (1972) emphasize—as does all Wah's work—"you, the intermingler," a communal agent of poetic and political practice. There is an insistent formal inventiveness throughout Wah's writings—in the numbered **prose poem** paragraphs of *Earth* (1974), for example: "The idea of it. Pictures form and the topography gets carried around in a head. Sometimes the feet find out what a trick the mind is." *Earth* was published approximately a year after **Ron Silliman**'s recorded first instance of the "new sentence" form in Language poetry (Silliman, "Tight Corners"). Wah continued to engage with the paratactically democratic vistas of Silliman's "new sentence" in two ongoing prose poem series, "Music at the Heart of Thinking" (1987) and its continuation, *Alley Alley Home Free* (1992).

An **ethnopoetics** sensibility (as in **Jerome Rothenberg**'s world tribal poetry translations and formulation of an ethnopoetics) is evident in *Pictograms from the Interior of B.C.* (1975), which features improvisations on drawings of aboriginal cave paintings. In *Lardeau* (1965) storytelling comes to the fore. The poem "Gold Hill," in which the speaker and companions are standing in the forest of Gold Hill and looking around at the rocks, one of which they pick up and see is gold, is **Edward Dorn**–esque, but with a twist.

In the 1980s and 1990s Wah's writing indicated evidence of a diasporic, racialized memory and the linguistic and cultural differentials and critiques of Asian Canadian identity politics and poetics. *Breathin' My Name with a Sigh* (1981) marks a thematic and formal departure from Wah's earlier books. Wah begins to give equal attention to words as signifiers, beginning with his surname, which may signal the influence of **bp Nichol**'s nominal letter-play as much as it does Wah's need to differentiate himself from his former teacher, Robert Creeley, on the subject of "names . . . [that] never hurt me" (as the nursery rhyme has it). Theme and form are linked via racialization, as this autobiographical statement suggests: "I can pass for white until I have to explain my name" (*Faking*, 76). Wah's last name provides the formal permission, in **Robert Duncan**'s exploratory mindful sense, to begin a multiform (and multi-book) thematic investigation of mixed-race family roots in relation to ideologies of Canadian uniculturalism, biculturalism, and multiculturalism. Self as signifier is still a hesitant prospect in *Breathin'*; in the following excerpt from an untitled poem, the pronoun "it" remains productively ambiguous: "It's not enough. I think it should be. / . . . How does it go? Did it?"

In Wah's most widely celebrated book, *Waiting for Saskatchewan* (1985), which won the Governor General's Award, the hesitancy is gone, but melancholia is present instead. The narrating self cannot become transparent to itself, due to insurmountable historical fractures: The story of Chinese migration to Canada is not Wah's first-hand account but, rather, is a reconstruction of the account of his father, who had passed away well before Wah wrote these poems. *Waiting*'s persona searches for family history by expressing "colonial mimicry" (Kamboureli, quoted in Sugars) without irony, expressing the internalized racism (as in the statement "Chinese always sounds so serious, emotional, angry" [*Waiting*, 61]) and exotic othering (as in *Waiting*'s formal experiments with the haiku-like *haibun* and the *utaniki*, or poetic diary) of the dominant white culture. An underlying motive for this melancholic and conflicted turn becomes apparent in a later book, *Diamond Grill* (1996), a prose memoir Wah prefers to describe as a "biotext" (the term is a "hedge" against "being hijacked by ready-made generic expectations, the cachet exuded, at least for [Wah], by those other two terms, life writing and autobiography" [*Faking*, 97]). In vividly depicted scenes and anecdotes combined with historico-theoretical aperçus, the book finds a language for the racism and anger Wah has experienced growing up and living in Canada.

Wah's later writings affirm the importance of Olson's cultural and scientific prognosis that there is "bios ahead: ex. *blood*" (Olson, 309). By addressing and problematicizing racial hybridity, Wah extends Olson's critique of America and of the "Western box" beyond Olson's own best insights. Whereas Wah's early writings align the proprioceptive body with nature against society and against the humanist, white self, his later writings construct an alternative, hybridized, faking-it self, in order to directly confront Canadian society's "fake imagination" on its own terms. In the early poem, "Gold Hill" (excerpted previously), there is no direct mention of the West as Gold Mountain. To read the poem allegorically that way would be mistaken, yet the bitter, dashed hopes of Chinese immigrants to the West nevertheless seem to comprise the poem's political unconscious and unstated historical referent. By contrast, Wah's later writings shift toward enacting political and historical consciousness—yet do not shift toward representational transparency of subjectivity (commodified identity). In, for example, *High ~~(bridi)~~ Tea* (2000), a collaboration with artist Haruko Okano, "Chinook jargon and Japanese-Canadian Pidgin," puns, malapropisms, racialized mispronunciation, pluralism's conflation of racial-cultural differences with food and consumption, and the alphabet as an indexed litany of past wrongs meet on the page in a layout resembling a restaurant menu. "F" is for "Fake / die / fusion / fuss / w/ / foreign- / icity." "J" is for "Jargon / tongues / wch half / to jangle." On the page that notes, "Y" is for "Yellow / down the / middle— / that's the road," "Special Chinese Dishes" include "Shanghaied World View" for "4.60," "Chow Mein Kampf" for "4.35," "Sweet 'N Sour But Still No Vote" for "8.25," and "Chop Sewer" for "6.50."

Wah said in an interview that "Good poetry should bring language to the fore" (Tostevin, 170), a comment resonating with Language poetry's emphasis on the material sound and look of language ideologically coded in everyday use, but the statement might be easily taken as Wah's writing slogan for over forty years.

Further Reading. ***Selected Primary Sources:*** Wah, Fred, *Alley Alley Home Free* (Red Deer, AB: Red Deer College Press, 1992); ———, *Breathin' My Name with a Sigh* (Vancouver, BC: Talonbooks, 1981); ———, *Diamond Grill* (Edmonton, AB: NeWest, 1996); ———, *Faking It: Poetics & Hybridity, Critical Writing 1984–1999* (Edmonton, AB: NeWest, 2000); ———, *Lardeau: Selected First Poems by Fred Wah* (Toronto, ON: Island Press, 1965); ———, *Loki Is Buried at Smoky Creek: Selected Poems*, ed. and intro. George Bowering (Vancouver, BC: Talonbooks, 1980); ———, *Mountain* (Buffalo, NY: Audit / East-West, 1967); ———, *Music at the Heart of Thinking* (Red Deer, AB: Red Deer College Press, 1987); ———, *Pictograms from the Interior of B.C.* (Vancouver, BC: Talonbooks, 1975); ———, *Waiting for Saskatchewan* (Winnipeg, MB: Turnstone Press, 1985); Wah, Fred, and Haruko Okano, *High ~~(bridi)~~ Tea* (Vancouver, BC: self-published, 2000). ***Selected Secondary Sources:*** Creeley, Robert, "The Names," in *The Collected Poems of Robert Creeley, 1945–1975* (Berkeley: University of California Press, 1982, 179); Derksen, Jeff, "Making Race Opaque: Fred Wah's Poetics of Opposition and Differentiation" (*West Coast Line* 29.3 [Winter 1995–1996]: 63–76); McCaffery, Steve, "Fred Wah's *Pictograms from the Interior of B.C.*," in *North of Intention: Critical Writings 1973–1986* (Toronto and New York: Nightwood/Roof, 1986, 30–38); Olson, Charles, *Collected Prose*, ed. Donald Allen and Benjamin Friedlander, intro. Robert Creeley (Berkeley: University of California Press, 1997); Silliman, Ron, "Tight Corners" (*The Difficulties: David Bromige Issue* 3.1 [1987]: 47–53); ———, "The New Sentence," in *The New Sentence* (New York: Roof Books, 1987, 63–93); Sugars, Cynthia, "'The Negative Capability of Camouflage': Fleeing Diaspora in Fred Wah's Diamond Grill" (*Studies in Canadian Literature* 26.1 [2001]: 27–45); Tostevin, Lola Lemire, "Lost Presence: Fred Wah Interviewed by Lola Lemire Tostevin," in *Dream Elevators: Interviews with Canadian Poets*, ed. Beverley Daurio (Georgetown, ON: Mercury Press, 2000, 167–186).

Louis Cabri

WAKOSKI, DIANE (1937–)

Diane Wakoski's poetry is noted for its feminist and its modernist stances, though Wakoski's is a **modernism** without the detached irony. Her work has also been noted for its early adherence to the **deep image** movement associated with **Jerome Rothenberg.** Deep imagery conjoins the physical and the spiritual and evokes the work of Frederica Garcia Lorca and the Spanish *canto jondo*, or "deep song." **Robert Bly** says that in a deep image poem, "Something surprising happens often during the writing . . . . It is as if the object itself, a stump or an orange, has links with the human psyche, and the unconscious provides material it would not give if asked directly. The unconscious passes into the object and returns" (*Georgia Review* [Spring 1980]).

Wakoski's poetry seeks to find its own identity and to map its own deep roots in the particularities of the poet's time and place. She said in a Poetry Society of America interview that she writes out of the "tradition" of **Walt Whitman**, **William Carlos Williams**, and **Allen Ginsberg**, claiming a space for the personal and autobiographical, as well as for the American landscape and its cultural myths, popular culture, and expressions of ethnicity. In "What is American About American Poetry?" she writes,

> American poetry is always about *defining oneself individually*, claiming one's right to be different and often to break taboos. Distinctly American poetry is usually written in the context of one's geographic landscape, sometimes out of one's cultural myths, and often with reference to gender and race or ethnic origins. American poets celebrate their bodies, very specifically as Whitman did. America may be a melting pot, but most American poets think of themselves as separate, different, and while very specially identified with some place in American or some set of cultural traditions, it is usually about the ways in which they discovered their differences from others and proudly celebrate them. (http://www.poetrysociety.org/wakoski.html)

Diane Wakoski was born in Whittier, California, on August 3, 1937, to Marier Elvira Cora Mengel and John Joseph Wakoski. Her father, following a three-year stint in the Navy, and seeing no other opportunity, reenlisted in the Navy after his daughter's birth and became a career military man. Her mother was a bookkeeper for an automobile agency.

Wakoski attended grade school in California and in Bremerton, Washington, where, for a brief time, her father's ship was in dry dock. She was recognized as a "brain," and she graduated from Fullerton Union High School with a scholarship to Berkeley, which she turned down to be near a boyfriend, by whom she became pregnant. She turned down the boyfriend's offer of marriage and gave up her son, born in 1956, for adoption. She then entered the University of California–Berkeley and worked a number of jobs to support herself. During her senior year at Berkeley, history repeated itself; Wakoski found herself pregnant and again gave up her child, this time a daughter, for adoption. In subsequent decades, she found her children and has been in contact with both of them, with her son by letter and personally with her daughter, whom she has met on several occasions. Wakoski's third husband is Robert Turney. She became writer-in-residence at Michigan State University in 1976.

Wakoski's work probes the human psyche and popular culture. "High and low culture," she says "come together in all Post Modern art, and American poetry is not excluded from this." **Hayden Carruth** claims that Wakoski is "one of the two or three most important poets of her generation in America." She has published more than forty books of poetry, among them "The Archaeology of Movies and Books" series, which was published by Black Sparrow Press and consists of *Argonaut Rose* (1998), *The Emerald City of Las Vegas* (1955), *Jason the Sailor* (1993), and *Medea the Sorceress* (1991). *Emerald Ice: Selected Poems 1962–1987* won the Poetry Society of America's William Carlos Williams Award in 1988. In addition to her books of poetry, Wakoski has published collections of essays: *Toward a New Poetry* (1979), *Variations a Theme* (1976), *Creating a Personal Mythology* (1975), and *Form Is an Extension of Content* (1972). Her awards and honors include a Fulbright fellowship, a Guggenheim Foundation grant, and an award from the National Endowment for the Arts.

Wakoski's created mythology is especially evident in *Medea*, a **postmodern** pastiche that constructs a world playing itself out amid Niels Bohr's doctrine of established physics. Wakoski shows that the imagination forms an alternate reality as she transforms an orange into the state of Michigan. She expresses her infatuation with sex, and in "Nuns" she witnesses the everyday reality of black lace and black pumps and belts, but a letter to her correspondent, Craig, laments that "you have to lose everything as your grow older."

Growing older is a motif that appears in such Wakoski poems as "Having Replaced Love with Food and Drink, a poem for those who've reached 40." She writes that she has given up love in exchange for things made with love, such as a poem, "an orchid," and "this pasta, green and garlicky / made with my own hands." In "Moneylight," she muses over knowing in middle age that youth will not come again and finding that knowledge satisfying: "You / can dance with the shadow partner / and not feel you have failed."

Mythmaking as well as Wakoski's experience as a pianist and her continued interrogation of loss and desire are central to the poems in *The Man Who Shook Hands* (1978). The poems in *Cap of Darkness* (1980) advocate both reading and listening because, Wakoski says, "some rehearsal of the past is always with me." Her poetry is the music that makes this past sing, but in new, conservative ways.

Wakoski critics, like those of Flannery O'Connor, will find that letters are a part of her **canon**. They provide insight into her creative world and are a culinary delight. In a December 1996 letter she writes,

> A Saturday several months ago was one of those days I value so much in my life. I had the whole day to cook and prepare a meal for friends who were coming to dinner. . . . I love my cooking days, for they are the days when I order the world and totally interact with it as a physical person. . . . Would I make soup or create some other kind of appetizer plate? Would I find a way to use the fresh Calamyra figs that I had found at the market the day before, and would [they] be for an appetizer or for dessert? What dessert would I bake[?] . . . a pear version of Tarte Tatin . . . or would I go for the Pear Chocolate Tart I had only made once before? How would I cook the pork loin I had purchased?

Readers with a taste for Wakoski's virtuosity will relish *The Butcher's Apron: New and Selected Poems* (2000), a five-course-meal cookbook that asks where our roots start: "In what we eat / or what we read?" The first section of the book, titled "Preparation," begins with the poem "Breakfast." The book ends with a chapter titled "Greed," in which Wakoski serves dessert and ties together the previous sections.

Asked what she would like to be remembered for, Wakoski, in a May 3, 1999, conversation with Alan Fox, named "half a dozen poems: 'Blue Monday,' 'Father of My Country,' 'I Have Had To Learn To Live With My Face,' maybe a few poems from the *Archeology of Movies and Books*, like 'Medea and the Sorceress.'" Wakoski plans to retire from MSU in 2007. In 2005, she was working on a project entitled *Noir*, a work that she likens to Katherine Anne Porter's *Ship of Fools*.

Further Reading. ***Selected Primary Sources:*** Wakoski, Diane, *Argonaut Rose* (Santa Rosa, CA: Black Sparrow Press, 1998); ———, *The Butcher's Apron: New And Selected Poems* (Santa Rosa, CA: Black Sparrow Press, 2000); ———, *The Collected Greed, Parts 1–12* (Santa Rosa, CA: Black Sparrow Press, 1984); ———, *Emerald City of Las Vegas* (Santa Rosa, CA: Black Sparrow Press, 1995); ———, *Emerald Ice: Selected Poems* (Santa Rosa, CA: Black Sparrow Press, 1989); ———, *Jason The Sailor* (Santa Rosa, CA: Black Sparrow Press, 1993); ———, *Medea The Sorceress* (Santa Rosa, CA: Black Sparrow Press, 1991); ———, *Toward A New Poetry* (Ann Arbor: University of Michigan Press, 1980). ***Selected Secondary Sources:*** Fox, Alan, "Conversation with Diane Wakoski and Alan Fox" (*Rattle: Poetry for the 21st Century* 6.1 [3 May 1999], http://www.rattle.com/rattle13/poetry/dwakoski interview.html); "Wakoski, Diane," in *Contemporary Authors: Autobiography Series* 1 (Detroit, MI: Gale Research, 1984); Wakoski, Diane, "What Is American About American Poetry?" (*Poetry Society of America*, www.poetrysociety.org /wakoski.html); Walker, Sue, "Interview with Diane Wakoski" (*Negative Capability* 10.1 [1990]).

Sue Brannan Walker

WALCOTT, DEREK (1930–)

Derek Walcott is the most celebrated poet of the Caribbean and one of the most important postcolonial writers of the world. Acclaimed principally for his more than twenty books of poetry, he is known additionally for his many plays—from *Henri Christophe* in 1950 to his stage version of the *Odyssey* in 1993. He is an accomplished painter, whose watercolors adorn the covers of several of his books and who in his poetry often explores the problems of representation through the metaphor of painting, most notably in *Tiepolo's Hound* (2000). Walcott won the Nobel Prize for Literature in 1992, on the five-hundredth anniversary of Columbus's landing in the New World; he was the second Caribbean Nobel Laureate in Literature (the first being St.-John Perse in 1960). In addition to his poetry and drama, Walcott has published a book of essays, *What the Twilight Says*, which collects numerous articles written for the *New York Review of Books* as well as his Nobel lecture, "The Antilles: Fragments of Epic Memory."

While many critics see Walcott's poetry, with its allusiveness and command of form, as conservative and "literary," it is markedly contemporary in its exploration of identity and displacement in the New World. The principal critical question about Walcott's work has concerned the poet's subject position with regard to his Caribbean birthplace and the cosmopolitan world of European capitals and Ivy League universities he also inhabits. This is a question more interestingly taken up in the poems themselves and reflected in their titles, the titles both of volumes—*The Castaway* (1965), *The Gulf* (1969), *Another Life* (1973), *The Fortunate Traveler* (1981)—and of individual poems or sequences, such as "A Far Cry from Africa," "Tales of the Islands," "Homecoming: Anse La Raye," "The Schooner *Flight*," "The Spoiler's Return," and many others. The subject is also developed through book-length poems such as *Midsummer* (1984), *Tiepolo's Hound* (2000), and *The Prodigal* (2004). Indeed, the book-length poem, as opposed to the lyric, has become the genre for which he is best known, particularly since the publication of *Omeros* (1990), his Caribbean recasting of the *Iliad.*

Walcott's poetry is famous for its lush verbal texture, in contrast to the flat and unadorned style that was the dominant mode in poetry in English of the twentieth century. Indeed, in spite of the inevitable critical emphasis on themes in Walcott's work, the most striking dimension of his poetry may be its style, which is characterized by abundant allusion and metaphor, adaptation of widely varied forms and meters, and linguistic play in general. Walcott has attributed his replete style to the influences of calypso and carnival. For his thick linguistic texture and for sheer length, he also has Caribbean antecedents in St.-John Perse and Aimé Césaire, both of whom he discussed at length in *What the Twilight Says.*

Derek Alton Walcott was born on January 23, 1930, in the town of Castries on the former British colony of Saint Lucia, one of the windward islands of the Lesser Antilles. He is of English, Dutch, and African ancestry; both of his grandmothers were descended from slaves. His father, Warwick, a civil servant and amateur painter, died when Derek, his sister, and his twin brother Roderick were children. His mother ran the town's Methodist school. Walcott studied at St. Mary's College, on Saint Lucia, and at the University of the West Indies in Jamaica, after which he moved to Trinidad, where he worked as a theater and art critic and where he founded the Trinidad Theatre Workshop in 1959. In 1981 he began teaching poetry and playwriting at Boston University, with one year at Harvard as visiting professor.

Critics have sometimes sought to determine whether Derek Walcott is subverting European poetic conventions with new, Caribbean content, or rather is re-colonizing the Caribbean with the "master's" language. Walcott rightly rejects such binary terms and observes that the problem of conflicted identity is not one with a solution; it is rather "an ambiguity without a crisis," as he says in an early essay ("The Caribbean: Culture or Mimicry," 3). As regards his own poetics, Walcott feels no apparent **anxiety of influence**. In "What the Twilight Says," he comments,

> The writers of my generation were natural assimilators. We knew the literature of Empires, Greek, Roman, British, through their essential classics; and both the patois of the street and the language of the classroom hid the elation of discovery. If there was nothing, there was everything to be made. With this prodigious ambition one began. (4)

Although Walcott may appear "traditional" in his homage to canonical Western literature, he is candidly **postmodern** in his repudiation of originality. "I may have not wanted to be a poet but an anthology," he has remarked (Montenegro, 211). One hears in his work the echoes of numerous poets he admires, from Dylan Thomas, W.B. Yeats, and **Robert Lowell** to Pablo Neruda and **Walt Whitman**.

Derek Walcott made his literary debut at age eighteen with the publication of *25 Poems*, but it was his first commercial publication, *In a Green Night* (1962), that announced him as a major voice of the Caribbean. The book's first poem, "A Far Cry from Africa," raises the question of an allegiance split between colonized and colonizer. Writing in the wake of the Mau Mau reprisals against the British colonists in the 1950s, Walcott asks, "I who am poisoned with the blood of both, / Where shall I turn, divided to the vein?" The ambivalence continues to occupy Walcott in subsequent books.

Another Walcottian topic introduced in *In a Green Night* is that of island life as static and enervated, a depiction often associated with Walcott's fellow Caribbean Nobel laureate, the novelist V.S. Naipaul. In "Tales of the Islands" Walcott speaks of "malarial light," "urine-stunted trees," and poor inhabitants who "must breed, drink, rot with motion." The scene is rewritten in later books and has often elicited disapproval, as it has in Naipaul's case, from postcolonial critics. The conclusion of "Tales of the Islands" establishes a scene—that of the poet looking out the airplane window at the receding landscape—that is repeated in such later volumes as *Another Life, The Gulf, Midsummer*, and *The Fortunate Traveler*, in the title poem of which the jet plane becomes a metaphor for privileged mobility. Finally, *In a Green Night* introduces another postmodern feature of Walcott's work: an obsession with viewing the world as text. In the title poem, islands are "like words . . . Erased with the surf's pages." Walcott later describes "shelves forested with titles, trunks that wait for names" ("A Map of the Continent," *The Gulf*), "the monotonous scrawl of the beaches" (*Another Life*), and hundreds of similar phrases. This mutual enfiguring of nature and language transcends wordplay, constituting an inquiry into the relation between reality and representation, and asserting Walcott's sense of the world as mythic, existing outside of linear history. (See especially the essay "The Muse of History," in *What the Twilight Says.*)

Walcott's next three books exhibit the kind of overlap that characterized the publications of Robert Lowell during the same period. *The Castaway and Other Poems* is included, partly revised, in its entirety in *The Gulf* (1970), as is a shorter book, published a year earlier, titled *The Gulf and Other Poems* (1969). The "gulf" in the title poem is, first, the Gulf of Mexico, over which the poet is flying, but it is also the gulf between Walcott's craft and his commitment to representation, and, crucially, the widening gulf between the poet and his native island. The poem "Homecoming: Anse La Raye" illustrates the latter, introducing the figure of the poet as a tourist in his own land, a poignant scene that recurs often in later volumes. In this poem the children "swarm like flies / round your heart's sore." The tourist-speaker gives them "nothing"; they curse and walk away. The "nothing" here is not only the absence of money; it is also the nothing of the rotted sea grapes and beach-wrack and of the tropic island as absence, and finally, it is "nothing" in the sense that his poetry has not touched them—this latter anxiety, again, reappears in numerous later poems.

Another Life (1973) is a book-length autobiographical poem, at times addressing family and childhood friends and at times populating a world, in the style of William Faulkner or Gabriel García Márquez, with town characters sketched with affectionate detail. In *Another Life* one finds that sense that Walcott locates in the New World "Adamic" poets he admires (Neruda, Whitman, Perse, and Césaire): There is the sense of a landscape not yet named, a world in which entire generations "died, unchristened," a world of "forests / of history thickening with amnesia." This absence is, as always, a positive incitement for Walcott, not a negative lack, as it is for V.S. Naipaul. Walcott has unquestionably Naipaulian moments, as in his many descriptions of the islands as torpid and impoverished, but he argues that, in the Caribbean, history "has never mattered, what has mattered is the loss of history, the amnesia of the races, what has become necessary is imagination, imagination as necessity, as invention" ("Caribbean," 6).

The often-overwrought rhetoric of *Another Life* (which arguably exists also in *Midsummer* and later books such as *Tiepolo's Hound* and *The Prodigal*), a symptom of Walcott's poetics of excess, may reduce the poems' significance in Walcott's oeuvre. Paul Breslin has complained that reading *Another Life* is "rather like listening to an organist who leaves the diapason stop on for the whole recital" ("I Met History," 178).

Walcott has often used narrators who speak in dialect; He does so in several sections of "Tales of the Islands" and, notably, in two of his best-known **long poems**, "The Schooner *Flight*" (*The Star-Apple Kingdom* [1979]) and "The Spoiler's Return" (*The Fortunate Traveler*). "The Schooner *Flight*" is a sea yarn, a meditation on travel and responsibility, and a poignant poem of departure, spoken by Shabine, a Caribbean seaman and poet, who describes himself in terms that suggest Walcott's own autobiography, particularly in the famous lines, "I have Dutch, nigger, and English in me / and either I'm nobody or I'm a nation." The latter choice is more serious than the choice between the collective and the individual; it is a choice between the collective and nothingness. It suggests that no identity will suffice that does not reflect all the history that Shabine embodies. But Shabine has rejected his "nation," as it has rejected him. (The whites "chain my hands and apologize, 'History'"; the blacks "said I wasn't black enough for their pride.") This untenable situation is Shabine's spur to travel, suggesting that Freud was correct in theorizing that travel's impetus is dissatisfaction. In the sense that "The Schooner *Flight*" presents the individual as collective or communal—a "nation" rather than "nobody"—the poem is, as Rei Terada calls it, "a Caribbean universal history" (112).

"The Schooner *Flight*," in one passage of metaphorical excess, conceives islands as peas on a plate, as stars in the sky, as meteors, and as fruit—"star-apples"—falling around the ship. The long title poem "The Star-Apple Kingdom"—reintroducing this latter figure—closes the book. The poem depicts a Caribbean cut into parts by politicians, who have turned the lovely star-apples into "a tree of grenades." The poet is accused at one point of lacking revolutionary commitment, of wanting to escape history—a fair charge, given Walcott's many repudiations of linear history. Grenades and star-apples, in such a context, become virtual insignia flown over the two terrains of the engaged and the aesthetic. Since Walcott generally favors the latter, the conclusion, in which "Star-apples rained to the ground in that silence," is foregone and perhaps difficult to accept in a poem that set out to grapple with moral and historical problems.

The traveler in "The Fortunate Traveler," the title poem of Walcott's next book (1981), contrasts with Shabine socially and professionally. "The Fortunate Traveler," unlike most of Walcott's poems of travel and displacement, places the anxiety of travel on a more obviously global field. Early in the poem, the comfort of the airborne narrator is contrasted with the misery of millions in the developing nations. A former academic, now a government broker of Third World economic interests, the narrator ironically remarks, "One flies first class, one is so fortunate," deploring his own detachment from the sorrows he sees below and comparing himself and his colleagues to cockroaches "riddling the state cabinets." Armed with graphs and World Bank forms, the narrator conducts his tractor sales, absconds with the money, and hides in the Third World, where he waits for his enemies to find him.

"The Fortunate Traveler" draws on Conrad's *Heart of Darkness* as well as on imagery of the Holocaust, but what confers its unity is in large part a biblical motif: The phrase "*and have not charity*" (Walcott's italics), from I Corinthians 13, which is repeated throughout the poem, occurs three times in the last section, where the poem adopts its powerful prophetic tone. In this poem anxiety about travel as a sign of the failure to love becomes global prophecy, even while Walcott plays on words to the last moment—"thin stalks" referring to the wasteland of famine becoming "stalks / grasshopper: third horseman" as a verb, signaling the approach of the Apocalypse. The insects, which appear only as a metaphor earlier in the poem, now make their literal entrance as harbingers of the end of humanity on earth.

The Fortunate Traveler, one of Walcott's strongest volumes, also contains the long poem "The Spoiler's

Return," a poem in dialect spoken by a calypso singer come back from Hell to lampoon Caribbean social and political corruption. The poem with its darkly funny turns ("I decompose, but I composing still") reveals the function of calypso as satire while it epitomizes the worldly role Walcott sees for the poet. Like Shabine in "The Schooner *Flight*," and like the poet Walcott in innumerable poems, the Spoiler pays homage to his forebears—Juvenal, Quevedo, Pope, Dryden, Swift, and others—who "salted my songs, and gave me their high sign."

Walcott's next book, *Midsummer* (1984), is a book of sketches in which the poet lets his "imagination range wherever / its correspondences take it." The subjects are often "scenic"—seascapes, plazas, and old forts—but one section of the book stands out for its depiction of the Anglophone Caribbean poet traveling in the Hispanic Caribbean. Walcott has written other poems about the Spanish Caribbean, but this eight-page section of *Midsummer* titled "Tropic Zone," written in and about Puerto Rico, is the most extended and most complex treatment.

The first two sections of the sequence explore the poetic possibilities of a new island and a new language, but in the third section an apparently aesthetic, even painterly, subject becomes political. The narrator sits in a hotel bar, facing a mural that, he says, gestures toward "a remorseful past," a mural painted by artists who must stay revolutionary "even when commissioned." As he views the mural, he hears a jingle for a new beer and conflates the beer's gold color with New World gold mines and with "the gold of their bodies," invoking uses of the Caribbean by those who see "our two tropics as erogenous zones." The artist's supposedly revolutionary stance, the traveler reflects, is what makes him commissionable: The Edenic mural must depict a revolutionary history in order to sell beer, whose gold evokes the other golds of a pre-Columbian golden age and of touristic fantasy. Walcott's frequent argument against history-as-victimization may seem to rear its head here in the poem's critique of the fall into co-optation—with Eden nationalized and the beer blotting out the "revolution"—but in the end it is the visitor himself who has fallen, who "doubts the murals and trusts the beer."

Although Walcott's versions of Latin America are frequently predigested, he does not pass them off as anything else. He is as interested in scenery that folds up as he is in that which is "natural." Yet the poet's musings in these Puerto Rican poems can seem careless. Do tropical settings as backdrops for yanqui psychodramas, for example, reveal the tourist's ignorance of tropical realities, or is the narrator himself condescending to the "snoring peon," the tacky pseudo-revolutionary mural, and so on? There are easy barbs such as the one aimed at the "gringo with his Wasp's rage at tedium," but throughout "Tropic Zone," cliché Latin-Americanisms are presented without a tone, to suggest an unreliable narrator.

In an early essay, Walcott writes that "In the New World, servitude to the muse of history has produced a literature of recrimination and despair. . . . The great poets of the New World," on the other hand, "from Whitman to Neruda, reject this sense of history. Their vision of man in the New World is Adamic" (*Twilight*, 37). It is not hyperbole to say that this idea runs through every volume of Walcott's poetry. *Arkansas Testament* (1987), for example, is divided into two parts, "Here" and "Elsewhere," the "Here" section consisting of poems about Saint Lucia, and the "Elsewhere" of poems about Cambodia, the Holocaust, Central America, and global crisis. One of the themes of the book is the unfathomability of suffering and the error of making "a career of conscience." If this position seems reproachable, as in lines such as "There is sometimes more pain in a pop song than all of Cambodia," one must consider this sense of history in Walcott—quite unpopular in postcolonial or historicist studies—as myth rather than as struggle. He wrote, in *Midsummer*, of wishing to write "lines as mindless as the ocean's of linear time, / since time is the first province of Caesar's jurisdiction." Although this may sound revolutionary as a strike against Caesar, it is, from a historicist point of view, quite the opposite.

The most remarkable poem of the "Here" section of *Arkansas Testament* is "The Light of the World," another poem about estrangement, with a more complicated version of the travel-as-betrayal theme than the early "Homecoming: Anse La Raye." In the first line of the former poem, the poet boards the bus or "transport"—a word that will take on several senses—to hear the reggae singer Bob Marley's voice on the stereo. He sees a beautiful woman, whom he names "the light of the world," humming to the music. As the bus begins to pull away, an old woman shouts to the driver to wait for her: "Pas quittez moi à terre!" she shouts in French Creole. The narrator offers several quick glosses on this phrase, but the immediate sense of "Wait for me!" is quickly dropped in favor of one that makes the old woman the voice of "her people." She and they want to be included in the "transport," an experience the poet has not been able to offer. The poet feels he has failed, as he did in "Anse La Raye," to be his people's poet, particularly in the way that Marley is—popular, danceable, "transporting." He has, again, abandoned them. This theme of abandonment, however, is inextricable from the earlier theme of erotic desire, since the first of the poem's "transports" occurs while the poet-traveler gazes longingly at the young woman's body. What he offers as a response to the old woman's cry not to be left behind is, then, a poem involved not so much in transporting as in mulling over sexual and poetic frustrations.

The last verse paragraph contains a poignant reversal. The transport stops, and a man shouts the poet's name and holds out a pack of cigarettes he had dropped. The poet turns away in tears, regretting that there is "nothing I could give them / but this thing I have called 'The Light of the World.'" In these lines the poet refits the metaphor he had used for the beautiful woman at the poem's beginning, applying it now to the poem itself, the art that mediates that woman's presence for us. The anxiety about the value of the gift (the poem), however, is not diminished. It is perhaps for this reason that Walcott's poems, no matter how rhetorically impressive, are most predictable when their narrators seem to be Derek Walcott and most fascinating when they are invented or drawn from history.

Omeros (1990) is Walcott's most celebrated book in part because of the nature of its project, a New World re-imagining of Homer's *Iliad*. The superimposition of the Caribbean on the Aegean seems, handily, to illustrate Walcott's own career and his own poetics, as well as his deep and candid affinity with his precursors—in this case Homer, Dante, and Joyce, among others.

Omeros is a poem of about 8,800 terza rima lines, in seven untitled books. While its narrative design is circular, the book nevertheless describes, again, a homecoming. The Greek word for Homer, "Omeros," is introduced early in the book by a Greek girl in exile in America, who announces her desire to go back to Greece and thus introduces the story of a return journey, through a web of places and histories, for the poem's chief characters. Achille, an island fisherman and the protagonist of the poem, who is setting out on a fishing expedition from the island of Saint Lucia, is carried across the centuries to his ancestral home on the West African coast. On the journey, he is forced to leave behind his friend Philoctete, who suffers from an incurable leg wound. Philoctete's wound, the central trope of *Omeros*, is the wound of his race—the inherited swelling of his grandfather's ankle, punctured by a slave manacle—and is, for this reason, incurable. Philoctete is, like Caliban (and arguably like Walcott creations such as Shabine or the nameless old woman in "The Light of the World"), a figure for a more general loss.

In its convoluted course, the poem takes up global historical events and migrations—the losses of the American Indian and the passage of African slaves to the New World—as well as the trials of deracinated individuals. Among the many characters who populate *Omeros* are Helen, the silent and remote black waitress whom Achille tries to please, and the ex-Raj Colonel Plunkett who, with his wife, has adopted the island as home but who feels, as do the others, lost and left out of history. Homer himself appears as a character, as does James Joyce.

The two texts, collective and individual, are interwoven through two sets of archipelagoes, Greek and Antillean. For both of these oceans, as one of Walcott's poem titles has it, "The Sea Is History." Indeed, when all else has transpired, *Omeros* ends, "When he left the beach the sea was still going on."

The title of Walcott's subsequent book, *The Bounty* (1997), evokes its subjects: Captain Bligh, breadfruit, and mutiny, and, less obviously, Freud, the Bible, the Tourist Board, and the mad John Clare. Like its formal and thematic predecessor *Midsummer*, it is a book of verbal and aesthetic abundance as much as a book of abundance of themes. "Homecoming"—as a final example of that genre—offers a particularly clear example of the Walcottian genre in which the traveler is called to account for his estrangement from home. The poem consists of an argument between the uprooted prodigal and the rooted trees of his homeland. Recalling the opening pages of *Omeros*, where the trees were "the old gods" of the island, cut down to provide fishing canoes, these trees have religious authority. As they complain of the poet's "turned leaves," all the metaphors for turning are invoked: the tropism of leaves, literary tropes as turns, the acts of turning pages or phrases, and, perhaps most of all, the turning of a turncoat. The trees hear the poet's reply, "I have tried to serve both" (home and abroad), as a betrayal.

Beyond these hurtful accusations, the trees charge that, because of the poet's squandering of his talent abroad, they "remain unuttered, undefined." Although the material world may be unutterable by definition, the charge is scarcely credible in the context of Walcott's work, which rivals that of both Pablo Neruda and St.-John Perse in its loving catalogues of island minutiae. We begin to see that it is nature's appetite for signs that is in question. No matter how extensive the naming, the trees will remain unuttered because they are untranslatable presence. Thus, linguistic nature takes on a meaning beyond that of the poet's accustomed tropes. From the poet's standpoint, Nature's demand for transformation into language is its principal feature. He faces a world of objects that demand to be something other than themselves.

Tiepolo's Hound is Walcott's most extended poetic treatment of painting. It tells at least two stories: that of the nineteenth-century painter Camille Pisarro, born in 1830, who left his native St. Thomas to pursue his career in Paris; and that of the painter and poet Derek Walcott, born 100 years later, who left St. Lucia for New York and who, in this poem, travels to Venice in pursuit of a detail, a brushstroke glimpsed in New York's Metropolitan Museum of Art—"a slash of pink on the inner thigh / of a white hound entering the cave of a table." The epiphany so disorients him that he afterward cannot remember whether the painter was Veronese or Tiepolo; he travels in pursuit of understanding this detail.

Pisarro's story is inevitably Walcott's. The choice facing them is "the same crisis every island artist . . . / must face in these barren paradises." The defense against charges of betrayal ("There was no treachery if he turned his back / on the sun") once again rises up, as does the old dialogue between home and abroad. Like *Omeros*, *Tiepolo's Hound* is both a global poem—tracing the empires of Rome, Paris, and Venice as well as African and Jewish diasporas—and a personal one, with long passages indulging the subject of the poet's own failure as a painter, even though the book is illustrated by twenty-six of Walcott's luminous watercolors, including one of Gauguin in Martinique. The poem is nothing if not painterly, with long passages descriptive of Parisian streets, country markets, and, of course, paintings—by Cézanne, Gauguin, Turner, and others.

Just as *Omeros* changed the way Homer is read, and perhaps the way "epic" in general is read, so *Tiepolo's Hound* is likely to change our views of the relation between visual and verbal, poetry and painting. It may be the most extended and theoretically sophisticated example of **ekphrastic poetry** of the twentieth century.

In Walcott's "last" (as he says) book-length poem, *The Prodigal* (2005), the poet again uses a self-descriptive title—as he did in *The Castaway*, *The Fortunate Traveler*, and, arguably, *Omeros*—this time raising explicit questions about the meaning of his travels. "Prodigal, what were your wanderings about?" he asks in the twelfth book, or section, of the poem. The question is rhetorical; the long meditation on it meanders through 100-odd pages, but as in other book-length meditations, such as *Midsummer* and *The Bounty*, the theme is an occasion for the play of language and association rather than for summations or analysis.

The Prodigal is a globe-trotting discursion—through Boston, Milan, Paris, and New Jersey—but the poem is bathed principally in the light of Italy. Toward the end of the book, Walcott again answers the demons of duty that he has interiorized, writing defensively that he is not "made subtly Italian, there is no betrayal, / there is no contradiction in this surrender."

Formally, *The Prodigal* returns to the big blocks of poetic lines, occasionally rhymed or slant-rhymed, that Walcott deployed in *Midsummer* and *The Bounty*, leaving behind the more rigorous demands of *Omeros'* terza rima or the *abab* couplets of *Tiepolo's Hound.* It is his most capacious if also his slackest vehicle of expression. As in *Midsummer*, the imagination ranges where it lists, and no observation, however slight, fails to find a place. This is the other meaning of prodigality, as it was of "bounty" in the book of that title. Walcott's has always been a poetics of process, whether in the writing of free verse, sonnets, or rhymed quatrains. His talent has always been such that he has never had to struggle toward perfection. When he has wanted, he has been able to fashion the well-wrought urn of the **New Critics'** dream. He has never had to worry language, and he often has seemed to let content take care of itself. He has always cast his net wide, increasingly so in later volumes, and has never troubled unduly over the extraneity of what he has pulled in.

If *The Prodigal* really is Walcott's "last" book, as he declares in that poem, he has left behind a poetic oeuvre of enormous significance. Although other Anglophone Caribbean poets have received wide critical acclaim—**Edward Kamau Brathwaite**, **Louise Bennett-Coverly**, and **Lorna Goodison** among them (*see also* **Caribbean Poetry**)—Walcott is unquestionably the Caribbean poet whose work has attracted the most sustained critical attention and the largest readership. His astonishing technical prowess, his wide and unusual frame of reference, his erudition and sensibility, the uses to which he has put Caribbean lore and culture, his understanding of the conditions of displacement, and his nuanced explorations of identity formation make him one of the most important poets in English of the twentieth and early twenty-first centuries.

Further Reading. ***Selected Primary Sources:*** Walcott, Derek, *Another Life* (New York: Farrar, Straus and Giroux, 1973); ———, *The Arkansas Testament* (New York: Farrar, Straus and Giroux, 1987); ———, *The Bounty* (New York: Farrar, Straus and Giroux, 1997); ———, "The Caribbean: Culture or Mimicry?" (*Journal of Interamerican Studies and World Affairs* 16.1 [February 1974]: 3–13); ———, *The Castaway and Other Poems* (London: Cape, 1965); ———, *Collected Poems* (New York: Farrar, Straus and Giroux, 1986); ———, *Dream on Monkey Mountain and Other Plays* (New York: Farrar, Straus and Giroux, 1971); ———, *The Fortunate Traveler* (New York: Farrar, Straus and Giroux, 1981); ———, *The Gulf* (London: Cape, 1969); ———, *In a Green Night* (London: Jonathan Cape, 1962); ———, *Midsummer* (New York: Farrar, Straus and Giroux, 1984); ———, *Omeros* (New York: Farrar, Straus and Giroux, 1990); ———, *The Prodigal* (New York: Farrar, Straus and Giroux, 2005); ———, *Sea Grapes* (New York: Farrar, Straus and Giroux, 1976); ———, *The Star-Apple Kingdom* (New York: Farrar, Straus and Giroux, 1979); ———, *Tiepolo's Hound* (New York: Farrar, Straus and Giroux, 2000); ———, *What the Twilight Says: Collected Essays* (New York: Farrar, Straus and Giroux, 1998). ***Selected Secondary Sources:*** Breslin, Paul, *Nobody's Nation: Reading Derek Walcott* (Chicago: University of Chicago Press, 2001); ———, "'I Met History Once, But He Ain't Recognize Me': The Poetry of Derek Walcott" (*TriQuarterly* 68 [Winter 1987]: 168–183); Brown, Stewart, ed., *The Art of Derek Walcott* (Bridgend, Wales: Seren Books, 1991); Burnett, Paula, *Derek Walcott: Politics and Poetics* (Gainesville: University Press of Florida,

2001); Gray, Jeffrey, "The Problem of Witness: The Travels of Derek Walcott," in *Mastery's End: Travel and Postwar American Poetry* (Athens: University of Georgia Press, 2005); King, Bruce, *Derek Walcott: A Caribbean Life* (Oxford: Oxford University Press, 2000); Montenegro, David, "An Interview with Derek Walcott" (*Partisan Review* 57.2 [1990]: 202–214); Terada, Rei, *Derek Walcott's Poetry: American Mimicry* (Boston: Northeastern University Press, 1992).

Jeffrey Gray

WALDMAN, ANNE (1945–)

Long celebrated as one of the few women writers associated with the so-called **Beat** movement and aligned with the Beat poetics of **Allen Ginsberg** and **Diane di Prima**, Anne Waldman is increasingly recognized as a highly prolific and influential poet, editor, and founder of numerous poetry projects that mapped significant directions within post-Beat and **postmodernist** American poetry. Most significant has been her impact on a confluence, in contemporary poetry, of Western and non-Western literary, cultural, and philosophical traditions and on a revival of oral and performative modes of poetic expression. Though cherishing spontaneous writing and free forms, Waldman has tended to mediate between different schools in her writing, realigning, for instance, the openness of a sound-centered **ethnopoetics** with the politics of 1970s and 1980s **feminist** poetry and the aesthetics of the **New York School**. A central concern of Waldman's poetics is to dissolve established boundaries between cultures, thought systems, and forms of representation and to evolve new modes of perception and artistic production that accommodate multiple differences. In the course of her career as a writer, performer, teacher, and initiator of various projects, this concern has been played out in a variety of media and has taken multiple poetic shapes, ranging from breath-lines and cut-ups across classical forms such as sestina and canzone to texts of **epic** scales. In this way Waldman has managed to redefine poetry as both "voyage" and "dream," as an "experience" that takes the reader in a multitude of directions, empowering him or her to draw on ancient as well as current voices deflected in different tongues.

Born in Millville, New Jersey, in 1945, and raised in New York City's Greenwich Village, Waldman traveled in Europe and met **Frank O'Hara** before attending the 1965 Berkeley Poetry Conference, where hearing **Charles Olson**, **Robert Duncan**, and Ginsberg read from their work had an impact on her own sense of her future profession as a writer. After graduating with a BA from Bennington College in 1966, she became the co-founder of *Angel Hair* magazine and books and served from 1968 to 1978 as the director of St. Mark's Church-in-the-Bowery Project, where she organized readings of Ginsberg, William Burroughs, and **Gregory Corso,** as well as Patti Smith and Lou Reed. Waldman then co-founded, with Ginsberg and Chögyam Trungpa Rinpoche, the **Jack Kerouac** School of Disembodied Poetics at the Naropa Institute in Boulder, Colorado, which was modeled after Buddhist learning centers that flourished in India between the fifth and eleventh centuries. These centers were described by Waldman and Andrew Schelling as "part monastery, part college, part convention hall or alchemist's lab." Waldman also served as the editor of *World* magazine during the late 1960s and early 1970s.

She has published numerous collections of poetry, including *On the Wing* (1968), *Fast Speaking Woman and Other Chants* (1975), the two-part epic *Iovis* (1993, 1997), and *In the Room of Never Grieve: New and Selected Poems, 1985–2003* (2003). In addition, she has edited a number of anthologies, among them *Out of This World: The Poetry Project at the St. Mark's Poetry Project, an Anthology 1966–1991* (1991), *Nice to See You: Homage to Ted Berrigan* (1991), and, most notably, *The Beat Book: Poetry and Fiction from the Beat Generation* (1996). Among her sound recordings are collaborations with Ginsberg (*Beauty and the Beast* [1976]) and John Giorno (*Anne Waldman and John Giorno* [1977]) and work attributed to various projects she supported, like that of *The Dial-a-Poem Poets*. Waldman has also starred in videos and films, including **Bob Dylan**'s experimental *Renaldo and Clara* (1978) and *Live at Naropa* (1990). She featured with Ginsberg, Burroughs, and Meredith Monk in the documentary *Fried Shoes, Cooked Diamonds* (1978) and has collaborated with visual artists, including Elizabeth Murray and Yvonne Jacquette. Waldman has received numerous honors and awards for her poetry, including the Dylan Thomas Memorial Award, the Poets Foundation Award, the National Literary Anthology Award, and the Shelley Memorial Award for poetry, as well as grants from the National Endowment of the Arts and the Foundation for Contemporary Performance Arts. Her poetry has been translated into Spanish, French, German, Norwegian, and Turkish, among other languages. As Waldman's career progressed, she became the director of the MFA Writing and Poetics program at the Naropa Institute and established homes in Boulder, Colorado, and New York City.

Like most poets of her generation, Waldman rejected high **modernist** models provided by **T.S. Eliot**'s classicism and **New Critical** hermeneutics while also radicalizing certain moments of American modernist poetics and revising its interest in myth, primitivism, and Asian as well as Native American cultures. Compared with her writing of the mid-1970s, her first volumes capitalized on local and national rather than intercultural and transhistorical issues. Whereas her second collection, *Giant Night* (1970), for instance, celebrated the Lower East Side poetry circle with which Waldman had become involved, the collection *Baby Crackdown* (1970) evolved from a

1960s American counter-culture and its resistance to the Vietnam War. Playing personal and political concerns off of each other and projecting an "Altogether Another World," the latter volume eventually turns away from drugs and revolution alike and falls back on poetry itself as ultimate energizer and medium of change. Although *Life Notes: Selected Poems* (1973), recalling **Robert Lowell**, strikes a **confessional** note, Waldman's poetry from the mid-1970s onward reflects her sense of the poet as a "tribal shaman" ("My Life a List" [1979]) as well as an indebtedness to Buddhist principles and to Olson's conception of **projective verse**. Her interest in non-Western archaic rituals and Asian philosophies, especially Buddhist notions of a sacred and unified body, speech, and mind—an interest shared with Ginsberg and growing, in part, out of 1960s alternative cultures—directly relates to Olson's sense of poetry as a field of energy. Redesigning the poem as a kind of mantra, a continuity of sound, Waldman meant to evolve a poetics that both acknowledges the impermanence of existence and extends experience beyond that which is immediately perceived. In this way Waldman's writing has situated itself between seemingly incompatible cultural traditions, and the elements of repetition, for instance, that dominate her poetry may be traced back to the writing practices of **Walt Whitman** and **Gertrude Stein** as well as to the orality of non-Western shamanic rituals.

Following Ginsberg's recommendation that she write **long poems**, Waldman produced her best-known work, *Fast-Speaking Woman and Other Chants* (1975), which appeared in enlarged editions in 1978 and 1996. In its first edition *Fast Speaking Woman* (1974) consisted of a book-length catalogue poem that emerges Waldman's particular Beat sensibility while at the same time transforming that Beat poetics by way of a growing feminist consciousness. The explicitly oral quality of the poem that comes to life in Waldman's public readings is due to both its catalogue aesthetics and its adaptation of Mazatec shamaness cultural practices, which reflect the poet's anthropological interests. In the composition of this text, Waldman was inspired by and transformed into writing a mushroom-induced curing ritual, a vigil or *velada* involving prolonged chanting, performed in 1956 by the non-literate Mazatex poet-priestess Maria Sabina from Oaxata, Mexico. While this shamanic practice was meant to provide guidance for young Mazatec women, the guidance that Waldman's poem offers is multi-voiced and highly ironic. Claiming a variety of speaking positions and professions, as well as stereotypical and pejorative labels assigned to women ("I'm the aimless woman / I'm the average woman / I'm the woman adoring"), the poem offers a feminist critique while asserting the power of the female voice, of the woman who "know[s] how to shout," "how to sing," and "how to lie down" (1978).

Drawing on oral traditions and diverse ethic cultures, as **Jerome Rothenberg** has done in his own way, Waldman became a significant force within the revival of **performance poetry** in the United States, Europe, and Asia. In fact, her particular sense of poetry as an oral and public art catalyzed an **avant-garde** that revitalized acts of performance, public ritual, and theatricality as essential moments of poetic practice. Even the recent prominence of **slam poetry** may in part be traced to Waldman's work. Her own poetry performances and appearances, taking place all over Europe as well as in Canada, Bali, India, and Nicaragua, have gained a reputation for being highly spirited, energized, and reminiscent of shamanic ceremonial practices. Frequently, Waldman engaged with other writers during these readings, among them Ginsberg, Gregory Corso, **Gary Snyder**, di Prima, Burroughs, **Kenneth Koch**, and **Clark Coolidge**, and performed and collaborated with musicians, composers, and dancers as well. In this way Waldman kept mediating between art forms that, as the author emphasizes, "originally . . . were inextricably combined" (*Talking Poetry*, 268).

Throughout, Waldman's work presents the speaking subject as well as the artist's project itself as an ever-changing process in time that dissolves the boundaries between forms of representation as well as between life and art. The poems collected in *Journals and Dreams* (1976), for instance, all of which experiment with typography and the visual effects of the printed page, are presented as "a collage of work coming directly out of journal writing, reading, & dreams." Likewise, Waldman's "Number Song," which is part of the *First Baby Poems* (1982), celebrates motherhood as much as acts of multiplication and moments of repetition: "I'm 2, he's my art, / . . . / He art one. I'm still one. I sing of my son. I've multiplied."

Waldman's work *Iovis: All Is Full of Jove* (Book I [1993], Book II [1997]), a long poem drawing on Virgil's verse "*Iovis omnia plena*" and published in two parts, has been considered both a turn away from beatitude and a transformation of Beat feminism. Revising modernist mythopoetics and its inscriptions of gender, Waldman recalls the work of modernist writers such as Hilda Doolittle, known also as **H.D.** Unlike Doolittle, however, whose poetics attempts to mediate what the poet conceives of as a fundamental difference between the sexes, Waldman in her texts exposes these differences as gendered constructions that, in the course of her epic poem, get displaced by conceptions of male and female energies. Whereas the second book of *Iovis* (1997) focuses its attention on the powers of the feminine, opening with an invocation to Sappho ("So Help Me Sappho"), the first book presents a multilingual and multi-generic exploration of masculinity and its various cultural manifestations, of manifold personal and public voices and authorities, and of destructive as well as creative energies. As much a feminist manifesto as a journey into the traditions of poetry and poetic imagination and the position of the female writer within male-dominated pretexts, including those of prominent modernist poets such as **William Carlos Williams** and **Ezra Pound**, *Iovis* redefines the poet as a female shamanist hero. Working on the principle of inclusion and plenitude, this poet acknowledges male energies as a significant part of female creativity, thus deconstructing gender polarities and evolving the spectre of a multi-gendered imagination and an "androgynist poetics" in the process ("Feminafesto," *Kill or Cure*). Highlighting the materiality of language, Waldman's text at the same time evolves a visual and verbal texture that builds on and develops the typographical and polysemantic qualities of modernist and **Language poetries**. Waldman's work thus circumscribes, in its very own way, a process that leads from a rejection to a reengagement of modernist poetics, a process that has been characteristic for many postmodernist poets.

Further Reading. ***Selected Primary Sources:*** Waldman, Anne, *Baby Breakdown* (New York: Bobbs-Merrill, 1970); ———, *Fast Speaking Woman and Other Chants* (San Francisco: City Lights, 1975; 2nd enl. ed. 1978 and 1996); ———, *First Baby Poems* (Cherry Valley, NY: Rocky Ledge, 1982); ———, *Giant Night* (New York: Corinth, 1970); ———, *Helping the Dreamer: New and Selected Poems, 1966–1968* (Minneapolis, MN: Coffee House Press, 1989); ———, *Iovis: All Is Full of Jove. Book I, Book II* (Minneapolis, MN: Coffee House Press, 1993, 1997); ———, *Journals and Dreams* (New York: Stonehill, 1976); ———, *Kill or Cure* (New York: Penguin, 1994); ———, *Life Notes: Selected Poems* (Indianapolis: Bobbs-Merrill, 1973); ———, *Marriage: A Sentence* (London: Penguin, 2000); ———, *Skin Meat Bones* (Minneapolis, MN: Coffee House Press, 1985); ———, *Vow to Poetry* (Minneapolis, MN: Coffee House Press, 2001). ***Selected Secondary Sources:*** Knight, Brenda, *Women of the Beat Generation: The Writers, Artists, and Muses at the Heart of the Revolution* (Berkeley, CA: Conari Press, 1996); Puchek, Peter, "From Revolution to Creation: Beat Desire and Body Poetics in Anne Waldman's Poetry," in *Girls Who Wore Black: Women Writing the Beat* Generation, ed. Ronna C. Johnson and Nancy M. Grace (New Brunswick, NJ: Rutgers University Press, 2002, 229–250); Roarck, Randy, "Vow to Poetry: Anne Waldman Interview," in *Disembodied Poetics: Annals of the Jack Kerouac School*, ed. Anne Waldman and Andrew Schelling (Albuquerque: University of New Mexico Press, 1994, 22–67); Tonkinson, Carole, ed., *Big Sky Mind: Buddhism and the Beat Generation* (New York: Riverhead, 1996).

Sabine Sielke

WALDROP, KEITH (1932–)

Although he is celebrated most as a poet, translator, and editor, Keith Waldrop's fascination with theater leaves its mark in his public readings. His long involvement with **avant-garde** theater first began in Ann Arbor, Michigan, where he, **X.J. Kennedy**, James Camp, and Dallas Wiebe founded the Wolgamot Society for production of off-beat and anti-establishment plays by the French absurdist Alfred Jarry, the anarchist Paul Goodman, the alcohol-besotted German Christian Dietrich Grabbe, and others. Later, after he and his wife **Rosmarie Waldrop** had moved to Providence in 1968 to teach at Brown University, he played an integral part in the Wastepaper Theatre for twenty years. While reading from his collection of poetry and prose, *The Real Subject: Queries and Conjectures of Jacob Delafon*, he interrupts himself just as Jacob comes across the word "orthoepy" ("the correct pronunciation of words"), produces a card-stock sign with the word printed on it, and continues without saying the word. This and the occasional song recital (often bordering on mock-cabaret) only confirm that theater was Waldrop's first love, developing side-by-side with a lyric of introspection.

Keith Waldrop was born in Emporia, Kansas, in 1932. His father, Arthur Waldrop, was a worker on the Santa Fe railroad and, as the poet notes in his autobiography *Ceci n'est-pas Keith*, an inventor who claimed to have beaten Lord Kelvin to the design of the refrigerator. Opal Waldrop née Mohler, his mother, later in life turned to piano teaching and nursing. Waldrop attended a fundamentalist parochial high school in South Carolina, and in 1953 his studies in the pre-med program at Kansas State Teachers College were interrupted by the draft; he served as an Army engineer specializing in water purification in Germany. After he completed his four-year tour of duty, he enrolled in the comparative literature program at the University of Michigan, where he earned his doctorate in 1964. For four years Waldrop co-edited the magazine *Burning Deck* with James Camp and D.C. Hope; this subsequently led to the founding of the Burning Deck Press, which he has continued to run with his wife after over four decades. Foundational texts of experimental poetry and fiction, particularly of the **Language poetry** movement, were published here, including work by **Jackson Mac Low**, **Lyn Hejinian**, **Bruce Andrews**, **Ron Silliman**, **Marjorie Welish**, **Robert Creeley**, **Robert Kelly**, **Barbara Guest**, **Harry Mathews**, **Larry Eigner**, and **John Yau.**

Waldrop's prolific production—thirty collections of poetry, twenty-two books of translations, and three edited books—reached a peak in 2002, but his steady record of publishing makes it possible to do as he did in his introduction to Gertrude Stein's *Useful Knowledge*: identify style as the dominant feature of his writing. As with Stein, a focus on style is a more fruitful form of investigating Waldrop's writings than the parsing of minute meanings. His sense is that Stein's style results from interest in the "being" of individuals or in the "essence" of events; similar emphases are to be found in Waldrop's work. He speaks in his "Notes Towards a Preface" in *The Opposite of Letting the Mind Wander* of states or facets of being "inattentive" (where the mind "lets in strays"), of being unconsciously aware of "background." He finds roots in André Breton, quoting him in an essay on the image in **modernism**: "*light from the image*, to which we find ourselves infinitely sensitive." The absolute lightness, to use Italo Calvino's term, of his books is reflected in the subtitles—"no-boundary proposals," "self-portrait as mask," "transcendental studies," "serious variations"—always indicating some form of the provisional utterance, subject to verification. His first book, *A Windmill Near Calvary*, indicates his love of Raymond Queneau's procedural work (the book is alphabetized by title), while the narrative stance and layering of such lines as "I have come a long way, and the long way / round" point toward his future work. There is a touch of the absurdist in Waldrop, as well as what he terms the Hegelian Spirit. Using puns and quips, he revels in the "objective humor" of the surrealists. *A Windmill Near Calvary*, composed of the "queries and conjectures" of Waldrop's bookworm alter-ego Jacob Delafon (whose name is that of a French manufacturer of sanitary fixtures), continues the pattern of the hapless yet determined whimsy found in *House Seen from Nowhere* ("Vampires, he has heard, are visible to twins wearing their clothes inside out"). While he declares, "I say no wise sayings, no dark sentences," Waldrop's work takes comfort in the idea that "the end of poetry is knowing and the end of knowing is joy."

Waldrop was named Chevalier of Arts and Letters by the French government in 2000. His translations, almost exclusively from French and Chinese, have tended to foreground the avant-garde, the real movers of the French literary scene: Edmond Jabès, Claude Royet-Journoud, Anne-Marie Albiach, André Breton, Paul Eluard, René Char, Pierre Reverdy, and others. Waldrop's **translations** of Xue Di (most in collaboration with Wang Ping, some with other translators, and a handful with Xue Di himself) have made available to an English-speaking audience the work of this writer.

Occasionally, in keeping with his use of collage in his poetry, Waldrop has worked in the graphic mode. In particular, *Bomb* by Clark Coolidge (2001) is peppered with Waldrop's off-center collages of cut-up and scuffed photographs of the Manhattan Project.

Further Reading. ***Selected Primary Sources:*** Waldrop, Keith, *The House Seen from Nowhere* (New York: Litmus Press, 2002); ———, *The Opposite of Letting the Mind Wander: Selected Poems and a Few Songs* (Providence, RI: Lost Roads, 1990); ———, *The Real Subject, Queries and Conjectures of Jacob Delafon with sample poems (Richmond, CA: Omnidawn, 2004);* ———, *A Windmill Near Calvary* (Ann Arbor: University Press of Michigan, 1968); Waldrop, Keith, and Rosmarie Waldrop, *Ceci n'est pas Keith—Ceci n'est pas Rosmarie* (Providence, RI: Burning Deck, 2002). ***Selected Secondary Sources:*** Drucker, Johanna, "Books as a Way of Life: Rosmarie & Keith Waldrop" (*The Journal of Artists' Books* 9 [Spring 1998]: 15–20); Gizzi, Peter, "Interview with Keith Waldrop" (*The Germ* 4 [Spring 2000]: 275–305, 5 [Summer 2001]: 270–319); Kelly, Robert, Review of *Haunt*, by Keith Waldrop (*Rain Taxi* 6.2 [Summer 2001]); Lasher, Susan, Review of *The Opposite of Letting the Mind Wander: Selected Poems*, by Keith Waldrop (*Parnassus* [1993]).

Douglas Basford

WALDROP, ROSMARIE (1935–)

The German-born experimental poet, novelist, translator, and essayist Rosmarie Waldrop devotes her texts to the indissoluble connections between language, the body, and knowledge. In her poetry, which ranges from short **free verse** to extensive **prose poems**, she blurs the generic borders between poetry and prose as well as between poetry and philosophy. The language and structure of the two historiographic novels she has written, *The Hanky of Pippin's Daughter* (1986) and *A Form / of Taking / It All* (1990), also are highly poetic and philosophical. The text of the latter novel even turns into a **long poem** in its last section.

Waldrop writes in the tradition of U.S., French, and German **modernism** and **postmodernism**. **Gertrude Stein**, **Charles Olson**, **Robert Creeley**, Walter Abish, **Susan Howe**, and **Lyn Hejinian** are among the U.S. writers who have influenced the style, the structure, and the poetics of her work. Ludwig Wittgenstein's philosophy of language is the main philosophical context of her poetry, which might be fruitfully, although not at all exhaustively, regarded as a challenging rereading of the Austrian philosopher. Yet Waldrop's poetic experiments are not reducible to the one or the other existing literary method or philosophical theory. Playfully, ironically, and self-reflexively, she intertwines European and American poetic and philosophical traditions.

Waldrop was born in Kitzingen, Germany, in 1935. In 1954 she began to study comparative literature in Würzburg, where she met her future husband, the American **Keith Waldrop**, who served in the Allied Forces stationed in Germany. After spending a year at the Université Aix-Marseille and another year at Freiburg University, Waldrop moved to the United States, where she married and earned an MA (1959) and a Ph.D. (1966) at the University of Michigan. Both she and her husband, who is also a poet, have since taught at various American universities. In the 1980s she began teaching primarily as visiting lecturer and visiting associate professor at Brown University, and she established her home in Providence, Rhode Island. Together with her husband she operates the small press Burning Deck, which promotes international innovative writing. Since its foundation in the early 1960s, Burning Deck has published more than 160 titles of **experimental poetry** and fiction in English. The **translations** from German and about half of the translations from French are hers. She has received numerous awards and fellowships for her poetry and translations, including the NEA and the Lila Wallace–Reader's Digest Writers' Award. The French government has made her a "Chevalier des Arts et Lettres."

Waldrop began translating literary texts from German and French into English after her move to America. Among her very first translations was Edmond Jabès's *Le livre des questions* (*The Book of Questions* [1976]). Her work on the enigmatic and prophetic text was the beginning of a lifelong translation project that led to her fourteen Jabès translations. In her 2002 memoir *Lavish Absence: Recalling and Rereading Edmond Jabès*, she connects her personal reminiscences of Jabès, whom she first met in Paris in 1970, with her introduction to his writing. She has also translated, from the French, Jacques Roubaud and Emmanuel Hocquard and, from the German, Friederike Mayröcker, Elke Erb, Ernst Jandl, and Oskar Pastior. Translations of her works have been published in France, Germany, Denmark, Norway, Sweden, Italy, Spain, Serbia, and Mexico.

Waldrop started to write poetry in English in the middle of the 1960s. After her first poems appeared in various American poetry journals, she published *A Dark Octave* (1967) at Burning Deck, and after publishing several other poetry collections with small presses, *The Aggressive Ways of the Casual Stranger* was published by Random House in 1972. In her poetry, Waldrop claims a transcultural space and a transnational poetic tradition. The speakers of the short-lined free-verse poems of the first two sections of *The Aggressive Ways of the Casual Stranger* are clearly personae for the young poet. She fashions a poetic self that might be understood as the title's "stranger," one who tries to position herself within, or rather vis-à-vis, family, national, or literary traditions that are either strange or estranging. For example, the volume's title is a quote from Gertrude Stein's *The Autobiography of Alice B. Toklas*, one of the poems is titled "Like Hölderlin," and others have Wittgensteinian overtones. The poem "Between" features a speaker who is "not quite at home / on either side of the Atlantic." This alludes to Waldrop's own search for a position as a German woman in America and is typical of the volume. Yet "Between" exceeds many of the other poems in its final embrace of the state of being-in-between when the speaker determines to live as "a creature with gills and lungs" between "shallow water" and "the land." This acceptance of indeterminacy is carried over into the poem's formal structure, with rapid changes in point of view and unexpected line breaks in its middle section. "Between" cautiously anticipates Waldrop's movement into radical linguistic experimentation that is characteristic of her subsequent work.

Her 1971 study *Against Language?: 'dissatisfaction with language' as theme and as impulse towards experiments in twentieth century poetry* was devoted to radical formal changes in twentieth-century poetry, to "the devices that break rules of language" (12). In this analysis of primarily German and French poetry, published one year prior to *The Aggressive Ways of the Casual Stranger*, Waldrop had come to the conclusion that "a more general aesthetic change" in contemporary poetry was at hand, "and the direction seem[ed] to be away from the pole of expressiveness towards greater emphasis on composition, towards a kind of formalism" (123). In *Against Language* she investigates this redirection by foregrounding metaphoricity and symbolism ("expressiveness") and stressing the ways in which poetic meaning is produced by the arrangement and contextualization of formal poetic devices—language, syntax, line breaks, and the arrangement of words in a line and lines on the page ("formalism").

The poetic sequence "As If We Didn't Have to Talk" in the third part of *The Aggressive Ways of the Casual Stranger* was Waldrop's first consistent formalist experiment with one of these devices, the **line**. As the first three lines of the sequence demonstrate, the main compositional principle of the sequence is the grammatical double, wherein individual lines serve both as the object of the preceding line and as the subject of the following one:

I want to stay and look at
the mess I've made
spills over

With this use of the line, which Waldrop dubbed "pivotal," the flow of reading is both interrupted (the reader has to pause to perform the functional transformation of the phrase from object to subject) and enhanced (the reader does not have to take in a new subject phrase). This, in turn, leads to both the enhancement and interruption of metaphoric reference, which, far from being abandoned, is structurally multiplied and denaturalized. "As If We Didn't Have to Talk" illustrates that we must "talk" to interact with and understand the world, yet that there is no way to arrest "talk's" meaning.

In her next book, *The Road Is Everywhere or Stop This Body* (1978), Waldrop used her experiments with the "pivotal line" to explore the linguistic limits and possibilities of understanding and expressing the dialectic of technology and the human body. With the metaphor of "the road," she explored an archetypal American image, immortalized in countless books, songs, and movies; but her adaptation of the image balances the *On the Road* symbolism of limitless freedom and openness with more sober concepts of the road as monitored system of traffic circulation. The other half of the title, which focuses on the body, turns to a prominent topic of feminist writing of the period, although Waldrop's strategy of foregrounding the linguistic to fabricate poetic embodiment (whether male or female) goes against the grain of **feminist poetry** in the 1970s.

The anti-essentialist feminism underlying Waldrop's poetry also informs her 1978 volume *When They Have Senses.* With these poems, she abandoned the technique of the "pivotal line," using instead predetermined structures or vocabularies as frames for poetic arrangements. Thematically, the text plays upon the dual meaning of "sense" as "being sensible" and "being sensuous" and the related gender connotation of this opposition in Western culture. The stereotypical roles ascribed to women (and men) according to a binary gender code are highlighted in poetic "snapshots" or "scenarios" showing the interaction of men and women. Although her sources, Shakespeare's texts most obvious among them, supply her with common representations of women as passive, subservient, marginalized, and gazed upon, Waldrop's radical rearrangement, fragmenting, and splicing of the source texts deconstructs the cultural ascription of minor roles to women and at the same time appropriates "what perhaps / isn't meant / for [her]." In her 1987 long prose poem *The Reproduction of Profiles,* Waldrop applied her cultural-critical collage technique to literary modernism and the philosophy of language, the two fields that have been her major inspiration. Wittgenstein's *Philosophical Investigations* and Franz Kafka's short prose writings served as source texts. The two authors both focused on the centrality of language for knowing and being in the world, yet they held diametrically different views of the function of language within this context; Wittgenstein thought to dissolve all misunderstanding by a methodical investigation of language and its grammar, whereas Kafka came to the unsettling belief that Being could not—but should—be expressed in words. Waldrop's poems splice phrases from Wittgenstein's terse and methodical linguistic investigations with scenes from Kafka's colorful and surreal texts, thereby supplementing the abstract logic of grammatical analysis with the referential concreteness of modernist fiction.

Yet Waldrop did not just assemble bits and pieces from her sources; she used two further methods to bind the material together and multiply its meaning. On the one hand, she arranged the material so as to suggest two speakers who inhabit the linguistic universe of Wittgenstein and Kafka and who communicate it to the reader. These two speakers are literally "made" out of the language of the philosopher and the writer. They result from the phrase "I/you said" and the reader inadvertently fills the position of each speaker with "someone" according to the linguistic-fictional scenario at hand. Literary criticism has tended to read the speakers as a man and a woman, but the genders are not necessarily clear. The figures could also be Wittgenstein and Kafka, or the earelier and later Wittgenstein. On the other hand, Waldrop used the method of "semantic sliding" (as stated on the book's dust jacket) between incompatible discursive areas such as philosophical speculation, mundane activities, and politics. She thereby transformed what philosophers call "category mistakes" into a poetic method.

Put into a theoretical framework, Waldrop's *The Reproduction of Profiles* is an "interactive deployment of [Wittgenstein's] language games" (Perloff, 208) and a demonstration of the validity of Althusser's, Barthes's, Benveniste's, Derrida's, Foucault's, and Lacan's theories on the ways in which subjects are constructed and controlled in language. As poetry, this demonstration becomes a highly entertaining and funny, if ambiguously serious, poetic tour de force—the playful enactment of Wittgenstein's and Kafka's language via unstable speaking positions and constant stylistic and referential slides.

The linguistically produced yet feeling, thinking, and physically embodied "Self" evolves as the central theme of a number of Waldrop's further books of poetry. The 1990 collection *Peculiar Motions,* which is written in verse and stanzas again, traces the ways in which "the Self" is constructed and made culturally intelligible. The title is borrowed from William James's idiosyncratic definition of the self as "*peculiar motions in the head or between the head and throat*" in *Principles of Psychology.*

The making of "a Self" is inspected with specific emphasis on the production of gender in the 1993 prose poem *Lawn of Excluded Middle* The title plays upon a law of logic, the "law of excluded middle," and the text plays Wittgenstein's language games to investigate the cultural fashioning of femaleness on the basis of linguistically produced speaking positions. It is Waldrop's most overtly feminist text. On the last page she explains in ten neatly numbered (but illogical) propositions how *Lawn of Excluded Middle* subverts the neat binary order of "true or false" by "playing with the idea of woman as the excluded middle" and thereby coding as female that which, by the laws of logic, is excluded from existence.

The construction of Waldrop's own "Self" is briefly highlighted in the third and central section of the 1998 *Split Infinites,* which collects five technically diverse poetic sequences that all criticize in one way or another the mind-body split characterizing contemporary Western thought. The prose poem "Memory Tree" is a reminiscence, or rather a reconstruction, of her youth in

Germany in the 1930s, when she "was six or seven dwarfs, the snow was white, the prince at war . . . Hitler on the radio, followed by Léhar" (58). On two pages Waldrop arranges her personal recollections out of fragments from German fairy tales, wartime memories, and Freudian analytical terms. The historically specific yet openly autobiographical poem not only ingeniously exemplifies the famous feminist slogan that "the personal is the political" and therefore is never innocent but also illustrates that both the personal and the political are always already discursive, and thereby collective and historic.

This dialectics of history had already been explored by Waldrop in her 1994 *A Key into the Language of America*, which was devoted to a text of the same title from America's colonial period. By turning to Roger Williams's 1643 cultural guide to the Narragansett Indians and their language, Waldrop took her poetic investigation of the links between language, knowledge, and power to the historic "clash of Indian and European cultures," which she highlights in the text "by a violent collage of phrases from Williams with elements from anywhere in [her] Western heritage" (*Key*, xxii).

Waldrop experiments with poetic form and its function to explore the possibilities and limits of language as a means of cognition and power. She searches for, invents, and investigates—in the words of the title of her 1997 volume of selected poetry—*Another Language.*

Further Reading. ***Selected Primary Sources:*** Waldrop, Rosmarie, "Alarms and Excursions," in *The Politics of Poetic Form: Poetry and Public Policy*, ed. Charles Bernstein (New York: Roof, 1990, 45–72); ———, *Blindsight* (New York: New Directions, 2003); ———, *Reluctant Gravities* (New York: New Directions, 1999); ———, *Shorter American Memory* (Providence, RI: Paradigm, 1988); ———, *Love, Like Pronouns* (Richmond, CA: Omnidawn, 2003); Waldrop, Rosmarie, and Keith Waldrop, *Ceci n'est pas Keith—Ceci n'est pas Rosmarie* (Providence, RI: Burning Deck, 2002); ———, *Well Well Reality: Collaboration* (Sausalito, CA: Post- Apollo, 1998). ***Selected Secondary Sources:*** Bergvall, Caroline, "Writing at the Crossroads of Languages," in *Telling It Slant: Avant-Garde Poetics of the 1990s*, ed. Mark Wallace and Steven Marks (Tuscaloosa: University of Alabama Press, 2002, 207–223); Freitag, Kornelia, ed. "'Truth While Climbing the Stairs'—A Rosmarie Waldrop Feature" (*how2* 1.8 [2002], www.scc.rutgers.edu/however/ v1_8_2002/current/readings/index-waldrop.shtm); Keller, Lynn, "'Nothing, for a Woman, Is Worth Trying': A Key into the Rules of Rosmarie Waldrop's Experimentalism," in *We Who Love to Be Astonished: Experimental Women's Writing and Performance Poetics*, ed. Laura Hinton and Cynthia Hogue (Tuscaloosa: University of Alabama Press, 2002, 103–115); Retallack, Joan, "A Conversation with Rosmarie Waldrop" (*Contemporary Literature* 40.3 [1999]: 329–377); Perloff, Marjorie, "Running Against the Walls of Our Cage: Toward a Wittgensteinian Poetics," in *Wittgenstein's Ladder: Poetic Language and the Strangeness of the Ordinary* (Chicago: University of Chicago Press, 1996, 181–218).

Kornelia Freitag

WALKER, MARGARET (1915–1998)

The work of Margaret Walker is a bridge between eras in African American writing, spanning the distance from the Chicago Renaissance of the 1930s to the **Black Arts Movement** of the 1960s and beyond. Walker's career is marked by peaks of great success—*For My People* (1942), which won the Yale Younger Poets Prize, and the novel *Jubilee* (1966), which became a best seller—and marred by periods of public inactivity, when the frustrations of illness and the demands of motherhood and making a living kept her from writing. Her tenaciousness, however, and the consistency of her black humanist vision have made her both a model and a sparring partner for a later generation of African American women writers.

Walker was born in 1915 in Birmingham, Alabama, where her father was a Methodist minister and her mother a musician; both were also teachers. The couple instilled in Walker a sense of Christian responsibility, deep self-worth, and the importance of education. Her parents' occupations are significant, for Walker's verse is didactic as well as musical and is rich with the rhetoric of Southern preaching. At the age of ten, Walker moved with her family to New Orleans, and Walker was given a daybook for her birthday. She was soon writing poems. In 1930 Walker enrolled in New Orleans University, where she met and received encouragement from **Langston Hughes**. She moved to Chicago to finish college at Northwestern, where she met **W.E.B. DuBois**, who invited her to submit to *Crisis*, the NAACP magazine. "Daydream," Walker's first published poem, appeared there in 1934. She also met **Harriet Monroe**, the editor of *Poetry*, where her most important poem, "For My People," was published in 1937. After graduating from Northwestern, Walker joined the Federal Writers Project, an arm of the WPA. There she began a brief but intense friendship with Richard Wright, recounted in her critical biography, *Richard Wright: Daemonic Genius* (1989). By 1940 Walker had completed an MA from the University of Iowa, using as her thesis the manuscript of *For My People.* The book, judged by **Stephen Vincent Benét**, went on to win the Yale Younger Poets Prize in 1942, the first by an African American woman to do so. Her next publication, *Jubilee*, a novel of the Civil War seen through African American eyes, was, like her first book, used to fulfill degree requirements at Iowa, this time for the Ph.D. The twenty-four years between books saw the birth of three children, stints as a teacher (most notably at Jackson State in Mississippi, where she taught until 1979), and the undertaking of the research necessary for completing her historical novel. The 1970s and 1980s were fruitful for Walker, who attended speaking engagements and published poems and essays with increased frequency. *This Is My Century: New and Collected Poems* (1989), which republished all of Walker's books of verse, was a valedictory culmination of five decades of poetry. She went on to oversee the publication of two collections of essays while receiving a steady stream of late-life honors. Walker died of cancer in 1998 and was buried in Jackson, Mississippi.

Already in her first book Walker displayed the full range of her poetic repertoire. *For My People* is divided into three sections distinctly different in form: **free verse** dominated by long, strophic lines; folk-influenced ballads; and sonnets, evidence of Walker's facility for traditional verse. The inaugural title poem is as powerfully anaphoric as the Old Testament and **Walt Whitman** and has the latter's way with a list: "For my people everywhere singing their slave songs repeatedly: their dirges and their ditties and their blues and jubilees." Walker alternates between general racial pronouncements and specific personal moments, from an unnamed people "never gaining never reaping" to remembered "playmates in the clay and dust and sand of Alabama backyards." Having spent significant time in Chicago, Iowa City, and New York, Walker struggles with a desire to return to a loved but treacherous South. It is the land and its fruits that she desires, apparent in the poem "Delta" or in the aptly-named "Sorrow Home": "I want the cotton fields, tobacco and the cane." What Walker despises is the prevalent racist act, to which she alludes in "Southern Song": "I want no mobs to wrench me from my southern rest; no forms to take me in the night and burn my shack and make for me a nightmare full of oil and flame."

The wrenching ambivalence of Walker's strophic poems is absent from her folk ballads. With dialect and a subtle sense of humor, Walker portrays characters such as the witch "Molly Means," the "Bad-Man Stagolee," the pimp "Poppa Chicken," and "Kissie Lee" ("Toughest gal I ever did see"). This early use of folk materials shows a strength that Walker would exploit in *Jubilee*, where each chapter begins with snatches of blues and ballads. Less demotic are the sonnets at the end of *For My People*. These poems move from Walker's "Childhood" to her time in Chicago ("Whores" begins, "When I grew up I went away to work / where painted whores were fascinating sights") to her encounter with an "Iowa Farmer." The volume closes with "Our Need" and "The Struggle Staggers Us," sonnets that return to the intentions of the title poem, with Walker speaking again to her "people" as their poet.

Walker's next collection, *Prophets for a New Day* (1970), continues in the political mode of those poems of three decades before. In the intervening years, the "struggle" had moved to the fore of the country's mind. Walker's poems represent the Civil Rights Movement in various ways. "Street Demonstration," "Sit-Ins," and "Girl Held Without Bail" are direct reports from the front. Alongside these pictures of the participation of regular people are portraits of public figures and events, such as "At the Lincoln Monument in Washington, August 28, 1963," and "For Andy Goodman, Michael Schwerner, James Chaney," an **elegy** for slain Civil Rights workers. Returning to the sonnet in "For Malcolm X," Walker also elegizes, and humanizes, the powerful Muslim leader: "Gather round this coffin and mourn your dying swan." Of formal interest is the series of what R. Baxter Miller calls Walker's "typological" poems (*Fields*, 93). Here the title of her collection bears fruit, as Adam Clayton Powell, Jr., becomes "Jeremiah," Martin Luther King, Jr., becomes "Amos," and other movement leaders are represented as "Joel," "Isaiah," and "Micah."

Despite the topicality of *Prophets* and the inherently radical nature of taking a prophetic stand, there is a way in which Walker's deep-seated Christian humanism forced her to argue against the bitter anger typifying the more radical branches of the movement. This conflict is best seen in the heated but mutually respectful 1972 interviews Walker did with **Nikki Giovanni**, published as *A Poetic Equation: Conversations between Nikki Giovanni and Margaret Walker* (1974). Matching the argumentative fire of the younger poet, Walker demands reconciliation beyond violence. In "For My People" Walker had called for "martial songs" and "a second generation full of courage," and she had spoken in the rhetoric of revolution: "Let another world be born. Let a bloody peace be written in the sky." But by *October Journey* (1973), a more autumnal mood had taken hold. Walker is still political, as the ballad "Harriet Tubman," with its stabbing of the overseer with "his rusty knife," harshly proves. But the politics are less those of the prophet than of the artist and daughter. Poems for **Gwendolyn Brooks**, **Paul Laurence Dunbar**, and **Phillis Wheatley** draw an African American literary lineage, and her lovely and muted "Epitaph for My Father" shows how his hard work and love of learning helped lead to her success. Starting from his native Jamaica, "an Island full of Bays / Like jeweled tourmaline set in the sea," Walker drifts in and out of a flexible blank verse, recounting one black man's difficult attempt to retain his integrity in the American South. "October Journey," the title poem, shows that region once again in all of its natural beauty and hateful history.

The new poems collected in 1989 in *This Is My Century* continue Walker's strategy of social protest mixed with autobiographical lyric. More pronounced, however, is a critique of capitalist exploitation ("Money, Honey, Money," "Inflation Blues") and media manipulation ("The Telly Boob-Tube on the Idiot Box"), although the former was always implicit in Walker's sometimes Marxist-inflected work. The final poems in the volume return to the long and expansive lines with which Walker began her career.

Further Reading. ***Selected Primary Sources:*** Walker, Margaret, *"How I Wrote Jubilee" and Other Essays on Life and Literature*, ed. Maryemma Graham (New York: Feminist Press, 1990); ———, *Jubilee* (Boston: Houghton Mifflin, 1966); ———, *On Being Female, Black, and Free: Essays by Margaret Walker, 1932–1992*, ed. Maryemma Graham (Knoxville: University of Tennessee Press, 1997); ———, *This Is My Century: New and Collected Poems* (Athens: University of Georgia Press, 1989). ***Selected Secondary Sources:*** Graham, Maryemma, ed., *Conversations with Margaret Walker* (Jackson: University Press of Mississippi, 2002); ———, *Fields Watered with Blood: Critical Essays on Margaret Walker* (Athens: University of Georgia Press, 2001).

Andrew DuBois

WARD, DIANE (1956–)

Diane Ward notes that she realized she wanted to become a poet when she one day heard a local Radio Pacifica broadcast in which Peter Inman described what he felt a poet was. By the age of eighteen, Ward had won a National Endowment for the Arts grant for poetry. Although influenced, in part, by writers associated with **New York School** poetry, such as **Bernadette Mayer** and **Clark Coolidge**, Ward notes that she was most influenced by **Gertrude Stein** and conceptual artists of the period: "I realized that poetry could be like drawing, it could be thinking itself, a conceptual activity, and not just an end product."

Born in Washington, D.C., in 1956, Diane Ward grew up in the Virginia suburbs of that city. She was one of six children, one of whom died in infancy, and in order to support his family, her father worked as an accountant for the General Accounting Office of the U.S. government during the day and worked in numerous other jobs in the evenings. He died when Ward was twelve years old. Finances became difficult for the family, and Ward's two brothers dropped out of school. Her mother worked as a seamstress and for a savings and loan institution.

Ward was determined, however, to become an artist, and she enrolled in the Corcoran School of Art, which was then an unaccredited institution. There she took art courses and met Doug Lang and Terence Winch, both of whom taught creative writing. Ward began writing poetry, and with Doug Lang moved into a large house whose other tenants included local poet Bernard Welt. At this time, Lang began a reading series at a local bookstore, Folio, whose guests included **John Ashbery**, **Charles Bernstein**, and many others. The series influenced several local poets, including **Douglas Messerli**, **Joan Retallack**, Lynne Dreyer, and Phyllis Rosenzweig, a curator at the Hirschhorn Museum of Art and Sculpture.

Meanwhile, Lang's Folio readings had expanded to weekly "workshops" in which several Washington, D.C., and Baltimore writers read their work to one another. Poets in those workshops included Ward, Lang, Welt, Rosenzweig, Dreyer, Retallack, Messerli, Tina Darragh, Julie Brown (later a curator at the Museum of Contemporary Art in Los Angeles), **Anselm Hollo**, Kirby Malone, Chris Mason, Marshall Reese, and others.

The loss of the communal house and the closing of the Folio bookshop brought an end to this important D.C. group; and, ultimately, Ward moved with a young artist friend to New York City in 1979. There she worked as a freelance typesetter and helped with distribution and production for Roof Books, which was one of the major sources of **Language poetry** and whose publisher and editor was James Sherry. While working on the night shift at a typesetting house near Union Square, Ward met Chris Hauty, the man she would later marry. Hauty also wanted to be a poet, but after writing plays and reviewing scripts, he began to focus more heavily on film and began scripting his own films.

Meanwhile, Ward took a job as a production associate at Pantheon Books in 1982. In 1987 she moved with Hauty to Los Angeles, where they had two children, George and Jackson. Hauty began working for various film studios, and Ward worked for a while at the University of California–Los Angeles, before turning her attention full-time to motherhood.

Ward's poetry is highly abstract and yet contains a quiet emotional intensity which, like her own reading voice, transforms the abstract language into seeming encounters with the poet's state of mind. Among her books are *On Duke Ellington's Birthday* (1977); *Trop-i-dom* (1977); *The Light American* (1979); *Theory of Emotion* (1979); *Never Without One* (1984); *Relation* (1989); *Imaginary Movie* (1992); *Human Ceiling* (1995); *Portraits and Maps* (2000); and *Portrait As If Through My Own Voice* (2001). Her work has appeared in numerous periodicals and in anthologies such as *The Norton Anthology of Postmodern American Poetry* and *From the Other Side of the Century: A New American Poetry 1960–1990.*

Further Reading. ***Selected Primary Sources:*** Ward, Diane, *Human Ceiling* (New York: Roof, 1995); ———, *Imaginary Movie* (Elmwood, CT: Potes & Poets Press, 1992); ———, *The Light American* (Seattle, WA: Jawbone, 1979); ———, *Never Without One* (New York: Roof, 1984); ———, *Portrait as If Through My Own Voice* (Margin to Margin, 2001); ———, *Portraits and Maps* (Los Angeles: Sun and

Moon Press, 2000); ———, *On Duke Ellington's Birthday* (1977); ———, *Relation* (New York: Roof, 1989); ———, *Theory of Emotion* (Segue/O Press, 1979); ———, *Trop-i-dom* (Seattle, WA: Jawbone, 1977).

Douglas Messerli

WARD, ELIZABETH STUART PHELPS (1844–1911)

Elizabeth Stuart Phelps Ward was a prolific author of poetry, novels, short fiction, and nonfiction that focused on themes of spirituality, social reform, and feminism. To modern readers she is best known for her realist novel *The Story of Avis* (1877), a female kunstlerroman, but her poetry has received little critical attention and is rarely anthologized. Although much of her poetry may be considered too didactic or religious for current tastes, Ward also wrote poems with the psychological realism and nuanced portrayals of women that she exhibits in her best prose.

Ward's father was a professor at Andover Theological Seminary in Massachusetts, and her mother, Elizabeth Stuart Phelps, was a popular novelist. Ward was christened Mary Gray Phelps, but at the age of eight, after her mother died, she took her mother's name as an act of devotion. At the age of thirteen, Ward published her first story, and she later became part of the literary circle connected with **James Fields**, editor of the *Atlantic Monthly*, and his wife, **Annie Adams Fields**. Ward, who wrote twenty-five novels, became internationally famous with the publication of *The Gates Ajar* (1868), which offered a utopian vision of the afterlife as a consolation to women's life in postbellum America. In the mid-1880s, after both Ward's brother and her close friend Dr. Mary Briggs Harris died, Ward's health began to deteriorate. In 1888, she married Herbert Dickinson Ward, who was seventeen years her junior. As a well-known and self-supporting writer, she apparently hoped to further the literary aspirations of her husband, but his career was not a successful one, and the couple lived apart much of the time. Ward published two volumes of poetry, *Poetic Studies* (1875) and *Songs of the Silent World and Other Poems* (1885).

Ward's poetry can best be understood as exemplifying her literary aesthetic of "art for truth's sake," which she delineates in her autobiography, *Chapters from a Life* (1896). In "George Eliot: Her Jury" (1881), Ward passionately defends the British novelist against charges of immorality by portraying the goodness and spirituality of Eliot's best-known characters. The poem closes with a rhetorical question, asking how is it possible that Eliot's "immortal" characters could "Possess the life eternal, and not *She*?" In "New Neighbors" (1885), the speaker, a single woman, watches with wondering pity as a married woman "sits and sews, and sews and sits" at home, waiting for her husband to return from work each day. The poem is remarkable for its reversal of nineteenth-century conventions of sympathy; instead of a young bride expressing pity for an "old maid," the single woman wonders at the daily emptiness of her married neighbor's life. Rather than relying solely upon satiric reversal, however, the poem shows respect for both women. Although the speaker enjoys "the untamed thoughts / Of free and solitary days," she recognizes, albeit with perplexity, that her domestic neighbor is "gloriously transfixed" upon her husband's return and "throws my unasked pity back." Ward further explores the popular theme of the waiting woman in the "Stone Woman of Eastern Point" (1892), but in this poem the tone is bleak. The "stone woman," a granite outcropping along the shore, becomes a symbol of coastal women. The poem plays upon the trope of the beautiful woman as artistic statue but instead depicts the stone woman as "stunted of stature and thin" because "coast women alive look so." The speaker asks the stone woman, "Waiting and watching and gray; / Growing old, poor and alone; / Was it worth living for?" No answer is possible, however, because the woman is "Dumb in her life and her death."

In the poems "A Woman's Mood" and "A Man's Reply" (1875), Ward presents gendered views of male-female love and friendship. The woman, who speaks first, chastises the man for missing much of the beauty of life because of his need for ownership: "Because you cannot pluck the flower, / You pass the sweet scent by." Though she is willing to offer him "the hand / Of a woman's faithful friendliness," she knows that he will reject it because he wants romantic love. She argues that if she were a man, she would not reject such friendship but would "wait, and keep / steel-loyal and steel-true." At the poem's closure, the female speaker senses that she has angered her male friend and adopts a playful, ironic tone, stating that if she has upset his "fancy," he should remember that "we're talking about flowers / And thinking about stars!" In the poem "A Man's Reply," the male speaker argues that a woman's heart is "something cold" if she can rely upon "the light of stars" for "daily fire." He explains that "Man loveth in another way! / He is too strong or weak." His reply takes on the form of seduction as he argues that if he "could taste, just taste before I die" her "sacred, sheltered mystery" and call her "for one hour mine," then he could live "in the woman's nobler way." In the end, no resolution seems possible because both the woman and the man fail to meet one another's gender ideals. Ward's complex, psychological portrayals of women's lives are as compelling in verse as they are in prose, and should encourage readers to examine her work as a poet.

Further Reading. ***Selected Primary Sources:*** Ward, Elizabeth Stuart Phelps, *Chapters from a Life* (Boston: Houghton Mifflin, 1896); *Poetic Studies* (Boston: Osgood,

1875); ———, *Songs of the Silent World and Other Poems* (Boston: Houghton Mifflin, 1885). ***Selected Secondary Sources:*** Bennett, Paula Bernat, *Nineteenth-Century American Women Poets* (London: Blackwell, 1998); Kessler, Carol Farley, *Elizabeth Stuart Phelps* (Boston: Twayne, 1982).

Denise Kohn

WARD, NATHANIEL (1578?–1652)

Rev. Nathaniel Ward, a Congregationalist minister in colonial Ipswich, Massachusetts, a frontier transatlantic community, was a writer with a wicked wit, a Latinate vocabulary, and a proto-Swiftian sense of social criticism. Ward was also a minor poet, probably best known to modern readers for his commendatory verse in **Anne Bradstreet**'s first volume of poetry, *The Tenth Muse Lately Sprung Up in America* (1650), which was published three years after his own quirky polemic, *The Simple Cobler of Aggawam in America* (1647). Both *The Simple Cobler* and *The Tenth Muse* were printed by Stephen Bowtell in London during the Interregnum. Indeed, Ward's connections to Bradstreet, besides sharing a publisher and contributing to her book, was probably in editing or collating some of the works in *The Tenth Muse.* Ward may also have been involved in choosing the title and in advocating or arranging for its printing in London. Publication of Bradstreet's text was evidence of the solidarity of the Massachusetts Puritans with the Cromwellian Roundheads, a cause that Ward championed strenuously. Ward was also Bradstreet's pastor in Aggawam, now known as Ipswitch.

Nathaniel Ward was born in Haverhill, England, between the years 1578 and 1580. He studied at Cambridge University and entered the ministry in 1618. He served as pastor for a London Anglican parish until he was dismissed for his Puritan beliefs. He emigrated to Massachusetts Bay Colony in 1634, where he wrote The Body of Liberties (1641) and *The Simple Cobler of Aggawam in America* (1647). In these pamphlets he expressed his hostility toward other religious sects. Ward eventually returned to England; he died in Shenfield in 1652.

In *The Cobler,* Ward's persona and eponymous nom de plume ("Theodore de la Guard") wants "to help Mend his Native Country, lamentably tattered, both in the upper-Leather and sole, with all the honest stitches he can take." Ward's shoe-repair conceit, however, becomes less important as *The Cobler* unfolds and he reveals the true nature of his message, one of extreme partisanship for what he sees as the single, pure, English theocratic cause. Ward vociferously opposed religious experimentation in New England and was so committed to political Puritanism that he returned to England during England's Civil War. Among his many righteous quips, Ward asserts, "Poly-piety is the greatest impiety in the world."

Ward was also critical of women's dress. He wrote, "I honour the woman that can honour her selfe with her attire: a good Text alwayes deserves a fair Margent" (454). He argued that women should not "disfigure themselves with such exotick garbes . . . [as] the French flurts of the pastery, which a proper English woman should scorne with her heels, . . . [unless she hath] a few Squirrels brains to help them frisk from one ill-favour'd fashion to another" (455). Ever the prickly pundit, Ward continued his critique of women in his commendatory verse to Mrs. Bradstreet, a grudging acknowledgment of the exceptional talent and high quality of the mostly quaternion-style poems in *The Tenth Muse.* His praise was not without a caveat: "To see a woman once do ought that's good; / And shod by Chaucer's boot's, and Homer's furs, / Let men look to't, lest women wear the spurs" (Hensley, 4).

The poem is an intriguing window into seventeenth-century gender conventions, in addition to being an artistic assessment of Bradstreet and a barometer of Ward's aesthetic, religious, and political priorities. Ward lets Mercury and Minerva proffer to Apollo, the mythical judge of poesy, Guillaume Du Bartas's *Divine Weeks* (1567; trans. Joshua Sylvester, 1605), and Bradstreet's *Tenth Muse,* respectively. Du Bartas's book was a staple for Renaissance Protestant and Puritan readers, and to compare Bradstreet's book to it was a compliment indeed. However, the admonition to men that such a woman-poet might usurp a typically male domain shows that Ward was ambivalent about Bradstreet's achievement.

What we know of Ward as writer, poet, editor, and social commentator comes from his own texts. As "the Cobler of Aggawam" and as an editor of Bradstreet's poems, Ward presents himself as a partisan Puritan theocrat invested in the promotion of an Anglophone aesthetic.

Further Reading. ***Selected Primary Source:*** Ward, Nathaniel, *The Simple Cobler of Aggawam in America.* (London: Stephen Bowtell, 1647; "Le Project Albion," http://puritanism.online.fr/puritanism/ward/ward.html). ***Selected Secondary Sources:*** Dean, John Ward, *A Memoir of the Rev. Nathaniel Ward* (Albany, NY: J. Munsell, 1868); Hensley, Jeannine, ed., *The Works of Anne Bradstreet* (Cambridge, MA: Belknap Press of Harvard University, 1967); Jehlen, Myra, and Michael Warner, eds. *The English Literatures of America 1500–1800* (New York: Routledge, 1997).

Elizabeth Ferszt

WARREN, MERCY OTIS (1728–1814)

Mercy Otis Warren, known as the first historian of the American Revolution, was also an important playwright and poet who drew on political events, as well as her experiences as a wife, mother, and writer in Massachusetts colonial society. Her poetry displayed both wit and political acumen, exemplifying the early American preoccupation with forming a national identity through a unique poetic voice, distinct from European precedents, through the use of classical form and allusion. In this latter regard, Warren's work is characteristic of the genre of **literary independence poems**. Her most substantial prose work was her three-volume *History of the Rise, Progress, and Termination of the American Revolution* (1805).

Mercy Otis Warren was born in Barnstable, Massachusetts, on September 25, 1728, to Colonel James Otis and Mary Allyne Otis. She was the third of thirteen children and the eldest daughter of the illustrious Otis family. Although she began writing poetry as early as 1759, she did not announce herself as the author of her poems ("Mrs. M. Warren") until 1790, when she published her *Poems, Dramatic and Miscellaneous*, dedicated to George Washington. In addition to her poetry, the book contained two previously unpublished and never-performed political dramas, "The Sack of Rome" and "The Ladies of Castile." Striking a balance between political epyllia (short epics) and **elegies**, Warren's poetry was admired by such contemporaries as **John Adams**, Benjamin Franklin, Catherine Macaulay, and **Sarah Wentworth Morton**. The book established Warren as a poet well before she was acclaimed as the historian of the American Revolution. However, writing, whether poetry or prose, was considered outside an eighteenth-century woman's sphere, and despite the earlier accomplishments of such poets as **Anne Bradstreet** and **Phillis Wheatley**, Warren's poems and her ability to publish them challenged eighteenth-century society's conception of women. Indeed, Warren could not own the copyright to her books, since, as a married woman in early Boston, she could not hold property of any kind. Consequently, Warren could neither make a profit from her works nor, while her husband lived, escape the domestic sphere.

Warren criticized British abuses in her epyllia and elegies. Her epyllia, however, were distinct from the mock epics of English Augustan poets, exemplified by Pope's *The Rape of the Lock*, in which the poet burlesques traditional **epic** by addressing trivial subject matter in a grandiose style. Warren's "The Squabble of the Sea Nymphs" (*Boston Gazette* [April 1774]), for example, requested by John Adams to celebrate the events of the Boston Tea Party, burlesques the niceties of society by relating a squabble between classical deities, but unlike Pope's *Rape*, Warren deploys traditional epic conventions when depicting the "heroes" of this nation-shaping event. After all, the Boston Tea Party could hardly be compared to a stolen lock of hair; it was, rather, a national event to be celebrated. In "Squabble of the Sea Nymphs," the sea deities who plan to "rob and plunder every neighb'ring vine" represent the British, who, like the deities, care only for their luxury, to the detriment of the American colonies. In her representations of the Tea Party, Warren is careful not to dismiss the influence of women, since "females have their influence o'er kings," and wives and mistresses were never "useless things." In fact, according to Warren's account, women are both the aggressors and the champions behind the event. By giving the events of the Tea Party a classical form and setting, Warren relates the event as an important historical episode worthy of inclusion in the American classical tradition (*see also* **Poetics, Seventeenth- and Eighteenth-Century**).

Also important in the development of an American classical tradition are the poems Warren wrote after the style of Ovid and Catullus. In these poems, she achieves a delicate balance between a "proper" colonial woman's viewpoint and a subversive voice that decries British abuses as well as contemporary perceptions of a woman's place. For example, pioneer physicist, patriot, and Harvard Professor John Winthrop, impressed with the poetic skill of Warren's "Squabble of the Sea Nymphs," requested from her "a poetical List of the Articles the Ladies might consider as 'Necessaries' in the suspension of trade with Britain in all nonessential goods." Warren took up the challenge by composing "To the Hon. J. Winthrup, Esq." (*American Magazine* [June 1774]), which was subtitled "Who, on the American Determination, in 1774, to suspend all Commerce with Britain, (except for the real Necessaries of life) requested a poetical List of the Articles the Ladies might comprise under that Head." Winthrop's request for a mock epic on trivial goods that "Ladies might consider as 'Necessaries'" is transformed by Warren into a discussion of virtue, with allusions both to Ovid's Book IV of the *Metamorphoses* and to Pope's *Rape*. Warren refers to a British woman named Clarissa and "her wanton pride," who "reigns no more a favorite toast" with so many "costly trappings." Like Ovid's Silenus, who is hampered by drink and the encumbrance of a swaybacked ass, and who eventually loses his way out of sheer drunkenness, Clarissa is weighed down with "female ornaments" and pride, losing favor because of her vanity. Warren characterizes Clarissa as adorned by "foreign looms," or more precisely, American "looms" that "refuse" her "costly trappings." The "looms" are significant because Ovid's Maenads weave as they tell their stories, creating an analogy between the acts of weaving and writing poetry. However, this analogy is subversive in Warren's hands; here the weavers "refuse" to weave for Clarissa (or Britain) but weave instead for "Columbia."

The release of *Poems, Dramatic and Miscellaneous* became the topic of discussion for half of the twelve issues of *Massachusetts Magazine* and created a forum for discussion of the idea of "female genius" (Richards, 81). Soon after the collection was published, George Washington responded to the book's dedication, explaining, "I am persuaded of [the book's] gracious and distinguished reception by the friends of virtue and science." Warren also received applause from Thomas Jefferson and Samuel Adams, among many others.

During the mid-1780s, Warren turned away from poetry and began writing prose, most notably her three-volume *History of the Rise, Progress, and Termination of the American Revolution* (1805) and her *Observations on the New Constitution, and on the Federal and State Conventions. By a Columbian Patriot* (1788). Her political prose, critical of the non-egalitarian government, was not as readily accepted, but her poetry continued to be recognized by her contemporaries. Warren continued to write with the help of her son, even after losing her sight, until her death on October 19, 1814. By using her writing in the fight against British oppression, among other causes, Warren also helped to undermine the social conventions that confined women to the domestic sphere and contributed to the formation of a uniquely American culture.

Further Reading. ***Selected Primary Sources:*** Butterfield, L.H., ed., *The Adams Family Correspondence*, 6 vols. (Cambridge, MA: Belknap Press of Harvard University Press, 1963); Taylor, Robert J., ed., *The Papers of John Adams*, 10 vols. (Cambridge, MA: Belknap Press of Harvard University Press, 1977); Warren, Mercy Otis, *History of the Rise, Progress, and Termination of the American Revolution*, 3 vols. (Boston: Larkin, 1805); ———, *Mercy Otis Warren Papers* (Massachusetts Historical Society, 1968); ———, *Poems, Dramatic and Miscellaneous* (Boston: Thomas and Andrews, 1790). ***Selected Secondary Sources:*** Anthony, Katharine, *First Lady of the Revolution* (New York: Kennikat Press, 1972); Brown, Alice, *Women of Colonial and Revolutionary Times: Mercy Warren* (New York: Scribner's Sons, 1896); Hutcheson, Maud Macdonald, "Mercy Warren, 1728–1814" (*William and Mary Quarterly* 10.3 [July 1953]: 378–402); Richards, Jeffrey H., *Mercy Otis Warren* (New York: Twayne, 1995).

Maureen Anderson

WARREN, ROBERT PENN (1905–1989)

Robert Penn Warren left his mark in many areas of American letters, so much so that he has often been called a Renaissance man. As an editor he founded, along with Cleanth Brooks and Charles Pipkin, the *Southern Review*. Also with Cleanth Brooks, he wrote the revolutionary poetry textbook *Understanding Poetry* (1938), a book that pioneered **New Criticism** as a method for reading poems and brought this manner of thinking and reading into countless American classrooms. *Understanding Poetry* pushed students to approach texts as "close readers," mindful, most of all, of the importance of the text. As teacher and friend, Warren's influence on American letters was extensive. The members of the **Fugitives** group, Warren, **John Crowe Ransom**, **Allen Tate**, and Donald Davidson, influenced some of the major writers of fiction and poetry of the twentieth century, including poets **Robert Lowell**, **John Berryman**, and **Randall Jarrell** and fiction writers Katherine Anne Porter (who was the godmother to Warren's daughter Rosanna), Caroline Gordon, Eudora Welty, Flannery O'Connor, Peter Taylor, and Warren's second wife, Eleanor Clark.

As a novelist Warren was responsible for *All the King's Men* (1946), a look into Louisiana politics and a thinly veiled portrayal of the governorship of Huey Long. This novel met with tremendous success, bringing Warren the first of his Pulitzer prizes in 1947, and eventually was made into a film, a stage play, and an opera. But Warren's primary love was for poetry, and *All the King's Men* was first conceived by Warren as a **verse drama**.

As a poet, Warren won many awards, including two Pulitzer prizes for poetry: one for *Promises: Poems, 1954–1956* and the other for *Now and Then: Poems, 1976–1978.* From 1972 until 1988 he was the Chancellor of the Academy of American Poets. He served as the first United States Poet Laureate from 1985 until his death in 1989. In the years since his death, the appreciation for Warren as a poet has only grown.

Robert Penn Warren was born in Guthrie, Kentucky, on April 24, 1905, the first child of Robert Franklin Warren and Anna Ruth Penn Warren. His father was a merchant, banker, and sometime poet. His mother was a schoolteacher. Together, they provided Warren with the best education available. Because Warren graduated from the local Guthrie School at the age of fifteen, he was sent away to relatives in Tennessee for one more year of high school. Warren said that he felt Guthrie, Kentucky, was an ideal place to begin and from which to move out into the world, an ideal place to be a boy. Tennessee was also a beloved place for Warren, although it never occupies quite the position in his work that Kentucky does. His every intention was to leave Tennessee for an appointment to the United States Naval Academy. Instead, his left eye became injured in an accident when his younger brother pitched a cinder into the air, not knowing that Warren was behind some shrubbery. The damage to his eye was severe enough to cost him the Academy appointment, and Warren entered Vanderbilt University instead, at the age of sixteen.

At Vanderbilt Warren quickly distinguished himself among the undergraduates, and he began the friendships that were to define his career and his life. It was there that he met John Crowe Ransom, Andrew Lytle, and Allen Tate. He and Tate shared a room that Warren painted with scenes from **T.S. Eliot**'s *The Waste Land.* These friends together became associated with the **Agrarian** movement, and they later came to be called, collectively, the Fugitives, after the magazine they published together, where Warren's verse first appeared. After graduation from Vanderbilt with high honors, Warren left his friends behind while he pursued graduate study at the University of California. He earned an MA there and met a student of Italian, Emma "Cinina" Brescia, who would eventually become his wife. Warren matriculated at Yale for graduate work toward a Ph.D., but left for Oxford as a Rhodes Scholar the following year. He received his BLitt from New College at Oxford in 1930. He never returned to Yale as a student, but he had a distinguished career as a teacher, culminating at Yale University. Warren was married to Emma Brescia for twenty-two years, from 1929 until their divorce on June 28, 1951. There were no children from this marriage. His later marriage to novelist Eleanor Clark produced his two children, Rosanna Phelps Warren and Gabriel Penn Warren. **Rosanna Warren** is a distinguished poet in her own right. Warren's son Gabriel, a sculptor, succumbed to cancer on September 15, 1989.

Robert Penn Warren produced sixteen books of verse, ranging in form from the book-length **narrative poem** to compilations of traditional lyrics. Warren's poems revel in his history as a Southerner and a Kentuckian and tend to employ a rough "manliness" of language, sometimes bordering on the coarse. Beloved of critics since his undergraduate years, Warren seemed to reverse the trajectory of so many poets' careers, becoming a better poet as he grew older. His devotion to poetry is reflected in his decision to concentrate exclusively on poetry after his retirement from Yale in 1973. Harold Bloom compared Warren to "Thomas Hardy, William Butler Yeats, and Wallace Stevens" in the great strides he made in his poetry late in his life, calling the *Collected Poems* in his introduction "Warren's center, and his lasting glory" (xxiii).

Warren's first two published volumes, *Thirty-Six Poems* (1935) and *Eleven Poems on the Same Theme* (1942), both employ traditional forms in the service of the folklore of Warren's native Kentucky. These early works introduce one theme that was to characterize all of Warren's poetry: the fall of innocence into experience. Victor Strandberg believes that *Eleven Poems* in particular occupies "a crucial place in the Warren canon, for its metaphor of a repressed shadow self that was slain and buried in the dank cellar of the house of the psyche"(148).

Selected Poems 1923–1943 (1944) represents twenty years of poetry writing and shows Warren grappling with ideas of guilt, crime, and original sin. "The Ballad of Billie Potts" is concerned with all of these. It is based on a Kentucky folktale of a murderous innkeeper who mistakenly kills his own son, and it is one of Warren's most quoted poems. Young Billie has a birthmark in the shape of the lucky four-leaf clover, but he meets his death at home at the hands of parents who do not recognize him until it is too late. His parents kill their child as they have killed many other travelers, breaking the bonds of hospitality, morality, and—this time—blood. The poem asks readers to contemplate which they might be, the murdered or the murderer, and to finally wonder if they might not be both. Young Billie's four-leaf clover thus becomes synonymous with the black spot we all carry in our hearts.

Brother to Dragons (1953) is based upon another Kentucky story, and again treats the theme of the sins of the fathers visiting themselves upon the sons. A slave is murdered in anger by Lilburn Lewis, the nephew of Thomas Jefferson. One of the founding fathers, Jefferson must also bear the shame of the act, as all Americans must bear the shame of slavery and the evils it engendered. *Brother to Dragons* is also something of an autobiography in verse. The narrator, identified as R.P.W., revisits the events from the perspective of the twentieth century. When Robert Lowell reviewed it, he remarked that it was fit for the company of such major works as Eliot's *Four Quartets*, **Pound**'s *Pisan Cantos*, and **Williams**'s *Paterson*.

Promises: Poems, 1954–1956 (1957) is the volume for which Warren won his first Pulitzer Prize in Poetry. It also won the National Book Award. This book seems to respond directly to Warren's new roles as husband to Eleanor Clark and as father to Rosanna and Gabriel. *Promises: Poems 1954–1956* also represents Warren's return to the **lyric**. The relation of the child to his parents and the parent to the child are central concerns of these poems. As he writes in "Founding Fathers, Nineteenth Century Style, Southeast U.S.A.," we must forgive those who came before us, "For we are their children in the light of humanness, and under the shadow of God's closing hand." Many of the poems in *Promises* are addressed to his children, such as "To a Little Girl, One Year Old, in a Ruined Fortress," "Infant Boy at Midcentury," "Lullaby: Smile in Sleep," and "Lullaby: A Motion Like Sleep." *You, Emperors, and Others: Poems, 1957–1960* (1960) did not receive the same praise accorded to *Promises.* What has been chiefly singled out from it is "Mortmain," a poem written on the death of Warren's father.

Tale of Time: Poems 1960–1966 is perhaps best represented by Warren's lovely "Homage to Emerson, On Night Flight to New York." In this poem Warren moves between the elevated and the low, between dream and memory. In the first section of this poem of seven sections, the poet considers the smile of Emerson. The last line of this segment seems to come from the blue: "When I was a boy I had a wart on the right forefinger." The speaker, aboard a plan headed to New York, considers the possibility of death and what that might entail. He tries instead to think of what is below: "to my right, far over Kentucky, the stars are shining," as are his friends. "I love them, I think."

Morality is a central concern of Robert Penn Warren's poetry, as is the question of how to be a moral man in a fallen world. As Harold Bloom wrote in his introduction to Warren's *Collected Poems* (Bloom was a close friend of Warren during Warren's later years), although Warren was "*not* a Christian believer, [he] nevertheless had Augustinian convictions as to sin, error, guilt, and history"(xxiv). The poem "Masts at Dawn" from *Incarnations: Poems 1966–1968* (1968) speaks to one aspect of Warren's moral searching and his desire, ultimately, to believe. The speaker of the poem says, "We must try / To love so well the world that we may believe, in the end, in God." As Strandberg observes, "Implying a love of the world, joy is the surest mark of grace for the Warren persona; it is his sign of a religious redemption—redemption not in the sense of immortality, but in the sense that the world has come to seem permanently meaningful" (226).

Audubon: A Vision (1969) is a poetic sequence that reflects on the life and career of John James Audubon and the nature of time. It is also a meditation on the desire to fix the world into permanence. Audubon, in his desire to preserve his birds, had to shoot them in order to paint them. In this figure of a man bringing death to life in order to convert the living thing into art, Warren recognizes something of the poet. He concludes that "the human filth, the human hope" is the true province of the poet. Section VII of the poem deals with Warren's boyhood in Kentucky and contains the refrain, "Tell me a story." He notes that "the story will be Time" and connects it to the sound of geese moving northward. Warren, like Audubon, arrests the birds of his boyhood, though they are certainly long dead.

Or Else: Poem/Poems 1968–1974 (1974) is considered by Bloom to be Warren's "finest single volume" (xxiv). It explores the life of its narrator, identified as R.P.W.

Can I See Arcturus from Where I Stand? (1974) takes its title from the last line of "Old Nigger on One-Mule Cart Encountered Late at Night When Driving Home from Party in the Back Country." The black man the speaker meets in the dark Louisiana night, moving slowly with his mule cart on the wrong side of the road, says nothing. At least he says nothing the poem's speaker can hear, although the speaker sees the man's mouth move, "Wide open, the shape of an O, for the scream / That does not come." The speaker finds in this image the beginning of his poem, but the words to the poem do not come easily. He asks, finally, if he will have the words he needs at the end, if he will find himself with the final and most important word, his name, held in his hand, something with which to understand Time (so often capitalized in Warren) and truth.

In 1975 Warren published his *Democracy and Poetry*, essays that explore the relationship between poetry and a democratic society, and also his *Selected Poems, 1923–1975* (1975). *Selected Poems, 1923–1975* was singled out for special praise by Hilton Kramer in the *New York Times Book Review*, who said that it validated Warren's position among the most lauded of twentieth-century American poets and that Warren is a poet "who speaks to us with a moral intensity few others have even attempted"(9 January 1977: 26).

Now and Then: Poems, 1976–1978 (1978) opens with a poem that revisits Warren's boyhood. "American Portrait: Old Style," like "Audubon: A Vision," is in seven sections. In the third the poet asserts that "What imagination is—it is only / The lie we must learn to live by." *Now and Then* also contains Warren's "Red Tail Hawk and Pyre of Youth," described by **Dave Smith** as "one of the great poems of our language" (78). It is a poem that owes a debt to Samuel Coleridge's "The Rime of the Ancient Mariner." A young boy shoots a red-tail hawk and preserves the bird through the act of taxidermy (again, we sense shades of Audubon). The hawk is a symbol that runs throughout Warren's work, and part of his admiration is directed at the hawk's keen vision. Over time the stuffed hawk is put away with other childish things, forgotten until the poet finds him eventually, in a much poorer state and with one eye gone. The poet reflects, "I reckoned / I knew how it felt with one gone," and he makes a funeral pyre for the bird and the other remnants of his youthful self. Still, the poet feels he will be connected to the bird even in death, knowing that in youth he was "ignorant," as all youths are. Warren received his second Pulitzer Prize for this volume.

After Warren's retirement from Yale, he concentrated exclusively on poetry, and his production until the end of his life reflects this dedication. In 1980 he published *Being Here: Poetry, 1977–1980*, followed in 1981 by *Rumor Verified: Poems, 1979–1980* and in 1983 by the book-length poem, *Chief Joseph of the Nez Perce*, which was dedicated to **James Dickey**. Dickey is often mentioned as Warren's heir to the mantle of Southern poet, and Dave Smith is often considered the successor to both.

Altitudes and Extensions (1985) was the last book of poems published in Warren's lifetime. In this collection Warren continues to explore ideas and memories that have followed him throughout his life. The motif of flight and return, the hawk, the passage of time, and the innocence of youth are all recurring elements. In "Old Time Kentucky Childhood" Warren returns to memories of boyhood explorations of the Kentucky landscape, this time in the company of his uncle and his beloved grandfather. This poem also invokes the history of the land in the form of fossils, myths, rumors, and family. In it the boy asks how he should live now that he no longer sees the world as simply what it is, but instead feels "the past and future" crowding and moving all about him. Nothing is without echo and nothing is without meaning, although the meaning may not be clear.

Warren's *New and Selected Poems, 1923–1985* (1985) appeared just after his death. The order of the poems from the most recent to the more remote past underscores the feeling that Warren's strongest work came late in his career. *The Collected Poems of Robert Penn Warren* appeared in 1998.

In Floyd C. Watkins and John T. Hiers's volume of Warren's interviews, *Robert Penn Warren Talking: Interviews 1950–1978* (1980), Warren is asked many times to discuss what he is trying to do in his poems and what he looks for in the work of others. One answer he gives is the following:

> If I had to say what I would try to hunt for in a poem—would hunt for in a poem, or would expect from a poem that I would call a poem—it would be some kind of vital image, a vital and evaluating image, of vitality. That's a different thing from the vitality you observe or experience. It's an image of it, but it has the vital quality—it's a reflection of that vital quality, rather than a passing reflection, but it has its own kind of assurance, own kind of life, by the way it's built. (Watkins, 14)

In his introduction to *Critical Essays on Robert Penn Warren*, William Bedford Clark describes the situation presented in much of Warren's work: "imperfect man, finding himself in a predicament that is at once painful and absurd, longs for transcendence, knowing all the while that he will eventually be called to account for being who and what he is" (1). Warren, in showing us that vitality, the blood and trouble of living in the world, also reveals how the imperfect man might transcend, how the hawk, though dead, might still soar.

Further Reading. ***Selected Primary Sources:*** Warren, Robert Penn, *All the King's Men* (New York: Harcourt, 1946); ———, *Audubon: A Vision* (New York: Random House, 1969); ———, *Brother to Dragons* (New York: Random House, 1953); ———, *The Collected Poems of Robert Penn Warren*, ed. John Burt (Baton Rouge: Louisiana State University Press, 1988); ———, *New and Selected Essays* (New York: Random House, 1989); ———, *New and Selected Poems: 1923–1985* (New York: Random House, 1985); ———, *Promises: Poems 1954–1956* (New York: Random House, 1957); ———, *A Robert Penn Warren Reader* (New York: Random House, 1987); Warren, Robert Penn, and Cleanth Brooks, *Understanding Poetry* (New York: Holt, 1976). ***Selected Secondary Sources:*** Beck, Charlotte H., *The Fugitive Legacy* (Baton Rouge: Louisiana State University Press, 2001); Blotner, Joseph, *Robert Penn Warren* (New York: Random House, 1997); Clark, William Bedford, ed., *Critical Essays on Robert Penn Warren* (Boston: G. K. Hall & Co., 1981); Cowan, Louise, *The Fugitive Group: A Literary History* (Baton Rouge: Louisiana State University Press, 1959); Lowell, Robert, "Prose Genius in Verse" (*Kenyon Review* 15 [1953]: 619–625); Madden, David, ed., *The Legacy of Robert Penn Warren* (Baton Rouge: Louisiana State University Press, 2000); Smith, Dave, *Local Assays: On Contemporary American Poetry* (Chicago: University of Illinois Press, 1985); Strandberg, Victor H., *The Poetic Vision of Robert Penn Warren* (Lexington: University Press of Kentucky, 1977); Watkins, Floyd C., and John T. Hiers, eds., *Robert Penn Warren Talking: Interviews 1950–1978* (New York: Random House, 1980); Watkins, Floyd C., John T. Hiers, and Mary Louise Weeks, eds., *Talking with Robert Penn Warren* (Athens: University of Georgia Press, 1990).

Anna Priddy

WARREN, ROSANNA (1953–)

An accomplished translator, Rosanna Warren fashions her poetry from sources in world literature, from the art of the past and present, and from personal experience. Her poems reflect a depth wherein the interaction between author and subject is always personal, yet objectified, allowing the reader a space in which to enter. When *Stained Glass* was published in 1993, Harold Bloom claimed Warren for his canon of the top dozen living American poets. The strength of her poetry has been confirmed by *Departure* (2003), and the American Academy of Arts and Letters honored her work with the Award of Merit in 2004.

The first child of her father's second marriage, and daughter to two prize-winning literary figures, Eleanor Clark (National Book Award for *The Oysters of Locmariaquer*) and **Robert Penn Warren** (recipient of three Pulitzer prizes and the first U.S. Poet Laureate, 1985–1988), Rosanna Warren was born July 27, 1953, in Fairfield, Connecticut. At the time, her father was teaching at Yale in the company of his lifelong friend Cleanth Brooks. As she said in a recent interview, "I grew up in a house with a poet who murmured lines from Blake and Hardy to me before I even knew what the words meant. We all read and recited poetry aloud as part of family life: it was like breathing" (Wong). At age seven she was given a typewriter. Three years later, her story about receiving a puppy was published by Random House at Bennet Cerf's insistence. Classifying her childhood as "a little bit itinerant," Warren explains that she lived with her family in Magagnosc in southern France in 1965 and attended a lycée in Grasse, where she learned to memorize and recite poetry in French (McHenry). During her training as a visual artist, from 1971 to 1975, she studied at the Accademia delle Belle Arti in Rome, the Skowhegan School of Painting and Sculpture in Maine, and the New York Studio School's Paris program, and she obtained her BA in comparative literature and painting from Yale University in 1976. Her MA in creative writing was completed at Johns Hopkins University in 1980.

Keenly aware of the privileges of her childhood, Rosanna Warren has committed herself to sharing with others by practicing a particular type of generosity in her teaching. Assistant professor at Vanderbilt University until she began organizing translation seminars for the University Professors Program at Boston University in 1982, from 1995 to 2000 she was an associate professor in the University Professors Program and Department of English. In 2000 she was named Emma Ann MacLachlan Metcalf Professor of the Humanities. Involved in a prison writing program that she added to Boston University's education program curriculum in 1995, she edited *In Time: Women's Poetry from Prison* (1995) and *Springshine: Poetry from Prison* (1998), and with Meg Tyler she co-edited *From This Distance* (1996). A member of PEN International, she was named Chancellor for the Academy of American Poets in 1999. Warren's vivacity at poetry readings (Library of Congress with **Mark Strand** in 1998, the University of Caen in 2000, the Village Voice in Paris in 2000, Western Kentucky University in 2000, Boston University Radio with Geoffrey Hill in 2002, and Roanoke College in 2003) makes her a popular speaker. During a year's leave, as the New York Times Resident in Literature at the American Academy in Rome in 2000, she composed some of the poems included in *Departure* (2003). She is also involved in editorial work for the periodicals *Daedalus* and *Literary Imagination* and is in the process of completing a long-term project on the literary biography of Max Jacob. Warren's activity in **translation** ranges from teaching to theorizing to editing (*The Art of Translation: Voices from the Field* [1989]) to translating (Carducci, Catullus, Jacob, Nerval, Reverdy, and a joint effort with her husband for *The Suppliants*, a verse rendition of Euripides' play). She established her home in Roslindale, Massachusetts, with Stephen Scully, a classicist who also professes at Boston University, and their two children.

Warren's first book of poems, the chapbook *Snow Day*, was published in a limited edition in 1981 and was dedicated to her parents. Those poems were included in *Each Leaf Shines Separate* (1984); the second poem, "World Trade Center," now reads as prophetic: "We have not been consulted on these laws." The poems are in three parts, punctuated by three charcoal drawings on aquatic subjects by Heddi Vaughan Siebel. Warren writes poems about the visual, as in "Funerary Portraits," a poem mentioned in the notes as "Hellenistic Period, bas-relief" and bearing the epigraph "In a world of stone, they grieve in stone." Poems about painting include two poems about Turner, "The Field (from Chagall)," "Through the East Door," "Renoir," and "Painting a Madonna." Preoccupations with history and memory are evident in "Illustrated History" and "History as Decoration," which speaks of the "gorgeous crimes we cannot feel." "Antietam Creek" specifies "(22,000 dead: September 17, 1862)" and seems to dialogue with Geoffrey Hill's "Shiloh Church, 1862: Twenty-three thousand" as well as his "Funeral Music" from *King Log* (1968). Warren's discovery of Max Jacob when she was twenty resulted in "To Max Jacob" and "Max Jacob at Saint Benoît." The third section focuses largely on domestic life with "Jigsaw Puzzle in the Suburbs," "Child's Room in Autumn," and "The Back Yards," yet this is not typical mainstream America: The reader also visits Tuscany, Rocamadour, and Maine.

Stained Glass (1993) was the Lamont Poetry Selection of the Academy of American Poets. In four distinct parts it strikes a delicate balance between personal and universal experience. The first section is concerned with responsibilities—of adults toward children in poems such as "Child Model," "Eskimo Mother," "Pornography," and "The Cost." The poem "Hagar" probes what it means to be on the apparent wrong side of providence. Hagar pointedly asks, "Bonded to Abraham, did I guess / his wilderness?" The bitterness of the situation ends with a virtuoso curve when the praying Hagar, who is addressing a god of stone, utters the same words as Moses in front of the burning bush: "Here I am." The poems of the second part vary between what might be poems about her parents ("Girl by Minoan Wall" and "Ice") and other poems that explore aesthetic morality. In "Jacob Burckhardt, August 8, 1897," Burckhardt is quoted as saying, "history is poetry on the grandest scale," which can be juxtaposed to the following poem, "In Creve Coeur, Missouri," where the photo of an infant that a fireman could not save wins a Pulitzer Prize "though it couldn't revive *her.*" In the third section, devoted primarily to poetry and painting, Max Jacob returns in the company of Pierre Reverdy in poems translated by Warren. In Jacob's "Christ at the Movies" the point seems to be that "outside of church, God's everywhere, and speaks with us." The final section, as in her previous book, contains a series of poems alluding to family. There are the **elegies** wrought from the care that Warren provided for her father before his death in 1989 ("His Long Home," "From New Hampshire") and the very tender poems "for ECW," her mother. In "The Broken Pot" Rome is "the internal city," a place shared by mother and daughter. The following poem, "Umbilical," expresses the anxiety and bonding felt when her own daughter was injured in an accident.

Departure (2003) takes its title from the triptych painted by Max Beckmann, and the title poem of the volume "splices quotations" from Beckmann and the thirteenth-century Italian poet Guido Guinizelli. Beyond subject matter, a brushstroke can be felt in the use of words that suggest visual perceptions, as in the imagist "until dawn flushed away clots of night" (in "Cyprian"). "Bonnard" reads like a critical evaluation of a painting where passion is lacking. Warren told Eric McHenry, "Poetry for me is very linked to drawing, very linked to the activity of the hand moving on the page in response to some sort of unease in the soul." In "Sicily" the place is bound up with artistic representations of the great scenes of Judaism, Christianity, and Islam: the woman at the well, Jacob wrestling with the angel, Abraham ready to sacrifice Isaac where "Dawn polishes the silver blade of the sea's horizon." The prefatory poem "Cassandra" speaks as much to what art can become as it does to the world situation. "Mud" begins "It's not as simple as rhyming 'mud' and 'blood'" and mentioning Wilfred Owen. The artistic representation of war interests Warren, and in "Dark Knowledge, Melville's Poems of the Civil War" (1999), she writes, "Melville's Battle-Pieces labor for their knowledge, and engage the reader in that struggle. Poem after poem pursues its quarry of truth, casting off illusory knowledge along with conventional poetic solutions." This is also what Warren's poetry does.

The third section is composed of two long, romantically passionate sequences. "Intimate Letters" is based on a true story about a Czechoslovakian composer and his muse, a married woman forty years younger than he. "From the Notebooks of Anne Verveine" presents Warren's "etheric double" (to borrow an expression from *Stained Glass*, 16). The imaginary fate of this unknown French poetess may represent what can happen to the talented who do not have the advantage of social status. The pull of Warren's poetry is both epic and elegiac, in which "a man must labor through much practice / to adjust his words," as Socrates puts it in "Eclogue," so that "Bonfires," a translation of *Aeneid* XI, reads like a description of present horrors: "the stunned / still bleeding human victims."

Further Reading. ***Selected Primary Sources:*** Warren, Rosanna, ed., *The Art of Translation: Voices from the Field* (Boston: Northeastern University Press, 1989); ———, "Dark Knowledge: Melville's Poems of the Civil War" (*Raritan* 19:1 [Summer 1999]: 100–121; reprinted in *Battle Pieces and Aspects of the War: Civil War Poems* [Amherst, NY: Prometheus, 2001, 269–293]); ———, *Departure, Poems* (New York: W.W. Norton, 2003); ———, *Each Leaf Shines Separate* (New York: W.W. Norton, 1984); ———, *Snow Day* (Winston-Salem, NC: Palaemon Press, 1981); ———, *Stained Glass* (New York: W.W. Norton, 1993); Warren, Rosanna, and Stephen Scully, *The Suppliants, verse translation of Euripides* (Oxford: Oxford University Press, 1995). ***Selected Secondary Sources:*** McHenry, Eric, "Departure and Arrivals" (*Bostonian* [Spring 2004], www.bu.edu/alumni/bostonia/2004/spring/ departure); Simic, Charles, "Difference in Similarity" (*New York Review of Books* [11 March 2004]: 21–23); Sisson, C.H., "How Would It Look in English" (*New Criterion* 8.2 [October 1989]); Wong, Allegra, "An Interview with Rosanna Warren" (*Full Circle, A Journal of Poetry and Prose* [2003], http://fullcirclejrnl.com/warrenintvu .html?1055442088010).

Jennifer Kilgore

WATERS, MICHAEL (1949–)

Poet, editor, and translator, Michael Waters has been consistently praised for devotion to craft, precision of language, and intimacy of subject matter. With the publication of his critically lauded fifth volume of poetry, *Bountiful* (1992), his reputation as a poet was solidified, and his reputation as a talented teacher and notable person of letters had begun to develop. In 1999, he succeeded A. Poulin, Jr., as editor of a classroom staple, the influential anthology *Contemporary American Poetry.* Along with his wife, Mihaela Moscaliuc, Waters has translated the work of Romanian poets; he has also co-edited *Perfect in Their Art: Poems on Boxing from Homer to Ali* (2003). His other books of poetry include *Green Ash, Red Maple, Black Gum* (1997), *Parthenopi: New and Selected Poems* (2001), and *Darling Vulgarity* (2006). "I cannot call to mind anyone of Waters' generation who is currently writing better poetry," wrote Floyd Collins in 1992 (*Gettysburg Review*).

Born in Brooklyn in 1949, Michael Waters moved with his family to Queens in 1963; the gritty New York boroughs provide many of Waters's poems with landscape and tension. After attending the State University of New York at Brockport and the University of Nottingham, England, he received an MA degree from SUNY–Brockport, as well as an MFA from the University of Iowa, where his classmates included such contemporaries as **Larry Levis**, Michael Ryan, **David St. John**, **Tess Gallagher**, and John Skoyles. In 1975 Waters published his first book of poetry, *Fish Light.* He later earned a Ph.D. in American literature with a creative dissertation from Ohio University, where he taught in the creative writing program. He began teaching at Salisbury University on the Eastern Shore of Maryland in 1978; his daughter, Kiernan, was born in 1988; and his first marriage, to Robin Irwin, ended in divorce in 1992. Waters has also taught at the University of Maryland; the University of Athens, Greece; the Writers' Center at Chautauqua; the Catskill Poetry Workshop; and the Prague Summer Program. Waters has served as Banister Writer-in-Residence at Sweet Briar College and Stadler Poet-in-Residence at Bucknell University. Additional honors include a fellowship in creative writing from the National Endowment for the Arts, Individual Artist awards from the Maryland State Arts Council, and three Pushcart prizes.

The poems of his first book, *Fish Light*, reflect a period style and are tinged with surrealistic gestures that rely more on associative imagery than on narrative structure. "What I believed then . . . was that it was the power of the poet that made the poems, and it was the poet's idea that informed the poem," explains Waters in a 1995 interview in *Kestrel.* "But now I disagree entirely with that method," Waters continues, "and . . . I came to believe more in the power of the language rather than in the power of the poet" (22).

Waters's second book of poetry, *Not Just Any Death*, appeared in 1979, and that collection begins to point toward his mature style. Image, though still important, is no longer central, and with the introduction of narrative focus comes the revelation of Waters's skill at telling stories and at producing sites where plot and lyrical intensity might fruitfully coexist. Apparent, too, are traits that continue to inform Waters's poetry: the idea that, with some appropriate risk or sacrifice, something like transcendence is possible, as well as intense explorations of the strata of human desire, communion, and loss. Waters sees the interplay of these intimate themes as having its roots in nineteenth-century American Transcendentalism and as coming "close, for me, to a religious sensibility" (*Kestrel*, 25). Because these themes fully reveal themselves in *Anniversary of the Air* (1985), Waters has said that it feels like a first book to him. In *Anniversary of the Air*, there is also a conscious movement toward "trying to move outside myself a bit instead of being I, I, I" (*Kestrel*, 24.) One of Waters's most anthologized poems, "Singles," aptly demonstrates this impulse. Although it uses first-person narration, the poem is clearly much more about the story of the lonely, almost pitiful, woman that is its subject than it is about the omniscient speaker. Although the woman spends her hours "memorizing baseball scores" and "sets two places at the table / though no one ever comes," she seems hesitant to take any sort of risk, and on her drive to work fails to see possibility in front of her, the equally lonely toll-booth attendant, who is thankful just to be "touching fingers," however fleetingly, "with such a beautiful stranger" (17). In poems such as "Negative Space," "Mythology," and "The Stories in the Light," *Anniversary of the Air* reveals another frequent concern of Waters's poetry, the creation of art. Other such poems include "Horse," which begins Waters's next collection, *The Burden Lifters* (1989); all the poems in the first section of *Bountiful*; and several poems in *Green Ash, Red Maple, Black Gum*, including "God at Forty," where several lines might function as an ars poetica for Waters. God, though he "prefers free verse," is checking the syllables of his poems in the "traditional forms" that "lend emotional restraint" and that keep him from slipping "over / the border of sentimentality where minor / post-modernists stray" (18).

Indeed, the poems of *Green Ash, Red Maple, Black Gum*, as well as later poems in *Parthenopi* and *Darling Vulgarity*, demonstrate Waters's growing interest in syllabic structure, either utilizing decasyllabic lines or alternating lines of thirteen and seven syllables. Such formality provides Waters with an additional check on **sentimentality** and easy gesture. This restraint is particularly crucial in *Green Ash, Red Maple, Black Gum*, since many of the poems found there consciously deal with explicit sexuality, "not shying away from sex, not having some sort of cinematic fade-out but staying with it and finding the language with which to express it, a language that means to be both sensual and respectful and not sentimental or pornographic" (*Kestrel*, 40).

Further Reading. ***Selected Primary Sources:*** Waters, Michael, *Anniversary of the Air* (Pittsburgh, PA: Carnegie Mellon University Press, 1985); ———, *Bountiful* (Pittsburgh, PA: Carnegie Mellon University Press, 1992); ———, *The Burden Lifters* (Pittsburgh, PA: Carnegie Mellon University Press, 1989); ———, *Darling Vulgarity* (Rochester, NY: BOA Editions, 2005); ———, ed., *Dissolve to Island: On the Poetry of John Logan.* (Houston, TX: Ford-Brown & Company, 1984); ———, *Fish Light* (Ithaca, NY: Ithaca House, 1975); ———, *Green Ash, Red Maple, Black Gum* (Rochester, NY: BOA Editions, 1997); ———, *Not Just Any Death* (Brockport, NY: BOA Editions, 1979); ———, *Parthenopi: New and Selected Poems* (Rochester, NY: BOA Editions, 2001). ***Selected Secondary Sources:*** Collins, Floyd, "The Power of Language" (*Gettysburg Review* 13.4 [Winter 2000]: 653–670); Hoppenthaler, John, "'From Nothing to a Thrumming Architecture': An Interview with Michael Waters" (*Kestrel* 11 [1998]: 22–42); Mann, John, Review of *Parthenopi: New and Selected Poems*, by Michael Waters (*World Literature Today* 76.2 [Spring 2002]: 158–159).

John Hoppenthaler

WATTEN, BARRETT (1948–)

Through his poetry, editing, and critical theory, Barrett Watten has been an articulate and prolific practitioner of and advocate for an **experimental poetry** that acts as both aesthetic innovation and political resistance. A key figure in the **Language poetry** network that developed in the Bay Area during the early 1970s, Watten has forged a dizzingly abstract nonnarrative poetic style influenced by mid-century poets such as **Robert Creeley**, **John Ashbery**, and **Allen Ginsberg**; avant-garde **modernism** (**Gertrude Stein**, **Louis Zukofsky**, Russian formalism, and French surrealism); and philosophy (from Ludwig Wittgenstein to Slavoj Zizek). Credited by **Ron Silliman** as the progenitor of the "New Sentence," Watten has been included in such anthologies as *In the American Tree* (1986), *"Language" Poetries: An Anthology* (1987), *From the Other Side of the Century: A New American Poetry, 1960–1990* (1994), and *A Norton Anthology of Postmodern American Poetry* (1995). Watten's later work still employs the radically dissociative, defamiliarizing procedures of his early poetry, but it also more fully engages various intersecting planes of history—personal, local, national, and global. Notably, *Bad History* (1998) is at once a telling of the American 1990s (the Gulf War, the LA riots, and so on)and a meditation on the death of his mother.

Born in Long Beach, California, in 1948, into a military family (his father was a research physician in the

U.S. Navy), Barrett Watten moved numerous times throughout his childhood, living in California, Japan, and Taiwan. Graduating from high school in Oakland, California, Watten attended both MIT and University of California–Berkeley, where he graduated with a BA in biochemistry in 1969. Most importantly, it was at Berkeley where Watten began his longtime poetic affiliations with fellow experimental poets **Robert Grenier** and Ron Silliman, two key figures in what is now known as Language poetry By 1972, when Watten graduated from the Iowa Writers' Workshop with an MFA, he had already begun editing *This*, one of the key poetry journals that laid the groundwork for Language poetry as a theoretical and aesthetic counterforce to the **lyric** tradition. Throughout the 1970s and 1980s, Watten's poetry and poetics became one of the crucial practical and theoretical nodes in the network of experimental writing that reached mainstream attention by the 1990s.

"The turn to language," to borrow the title of Watten's essay on the origins of Language poetry, began in the cultural ferment of the late 1960s Berkeley anti-war movement. Watten's participation in the war resistance and his concomitant frustration with the discourse of oppositionality embodied in the content-driven political writing of poets like **Denise Levertov** led him to find other ways of intervening in the crisis of language that was the Vietnam War. The poets who became Language poets practiced a heterogeneous poetry that, according to **Bob Perelman** in his *The Marginalization of Poetry: Language Writing and Literary History*, "was (sometimes) nonreferential, (occasionally) polysyntactic, (at times) programmatic in construction, (often) politically committed, (in places) theoretically inclined, and that enacted a critique of the literary I (in some cases)" (21).

From his first published book, *Opera—Works* (1975), Watten's poetry has deconstructed the notion of poetry as a discourse of transparency: the transparency of subjectivity (the lyric self), the transparency of language (common language made pure), the transparency of narrative (plot), and the transparency of image (the image as window into the real). In the short poem "Story," Watten's deconstruction of subjectivity, plot, and image operates through his typical collision of hyper-self-consciousness, nonnarrative distanciation, and occluded signification. The speaker observes that he always tries to "walk forcefully into a room." In response, "[t]he ten men at the table tipped their hats. / This was not a gesture, but a sign." Echoing René Magritte, this poem suggests the way in which Watten's project is centrally an interrogation of a certain mode of language, the masculine and circular non-communication of a Robert McNamara or a Lyndon Johnson.

Throughout the 1970s and 1980s, Watten and the other West Coast poets affiliated with experimental writing (among them Steve Benson, **Carla Harryman**, **Lyn Hejinian**, **Michael Palmer**, Bob Perelman, Kit Robinson, **Leslie Scalapino**, and Ron Silliman) supported each other's work through **small-press** publication. During this period, Watten published *Opera-Works* (1975), *Decay* (1977), *Plasma/Paralleles/"X"* (1979), *1–10* (1980), *Complete Thought* (1982), the book-length poem *Progress* (1985), *Conduit* (1988), and the collectively authored *Leningrad* (1989). The latter book suggests the importance that Watten and the other Language poets placed on collaboration, as both antidote to what Silliman has called "the pathology of the individual" and as means of collective literary production. Watten's remark in *Leningrad* cuts to the heart of the problem of lyric subjectivity—that it is the poetic version of empire: "Isn't there a complicity with power, however at odds one may be with it, behind the sense that one is at the center of things?"

Watten's poetry obsessively evades the tendencies toward narrative closure and singular meanings, at times by miming and subverting the very syntax of "complete thoughts," as in the opening couplet of "Complete Thoughts": "The world is complete. / Books demand limits." From *Decay* (1977), the poem "Chamber Music" manifests what Silliman named the first use of "New Sentence"—that formal technique associated with Language poetry that involves the rigorously disjunctive employment of the sentence as its central measure. A few lines demonstrate the disjoint, but also the subtle associations that inevitably emerge in that disjunctiveness: "I found my new life to be hard, constant attention but great joy. / Two hundred black boxes, delivered to his new address, haunted his life."

Watten's *Total Syntax* (1985), the first-book length critical study of Language poetry, articulates the theoretical basis for the kind of poetry in which Watten and other experimental poets have engaged in order to expand the limits of the genre. Displacing the notion of the poetic text as a discrete universal object (as per the **New Criticism**), a total syntax—that is, a more fully realized interpenetration of all the layers of syntax (grammatical and socio-cultural)—proposes a radically new frame from which to conceive of and understand the polyvalency of the work of art.

In "Aesthetic Tendency and the Politics of Poetry: A Manifesto" (1988), Watten, Carla Harryman, Lyn Hejinian, Bob Perelman, and Ron Silliman offer two aims of their collective project: (1) to dissociate the "marginal isolated individualism" of the mainstream lyric, and (2) to write a "contaminated" rather than a "pure" language. True to his poetics, Watten's poetry pursues a rigorously disjunctive, depersonalizing strategy that may indeed perform the absolute negation of the lyric. Watten's unremitting linguistic project of working through negativity by means of a deconstructive poetry that is anti-lyric, anti-mimetic, and nonnarrative—is at once the most innovative, and the most critiqued, aspect of his poetics. David Hess has described Watten's early work as full of "dryness and uniformity . . . death-simulating"—in short, mechanical and lacking affect. Fredric Jameson's important, though flawed, reading of Language poetry in *Postmodernism* suggests the way in which this kind of writing may actually participate in, rather than provide resistance to, the culture of late capitalism.

Watten's poetry has consistently demonstrated a full awareness of the vexing relationship between language and the culture of late capitalism. The paradox of his writing is that its confounding abstraction and its resistance to "affect" work to foreground the materiality of language and thereby deconstruct—as poststructuralist and Marxist theories have suggested—the illusions of a transcendental language. In *Bad History* (1998), Watten's poetic project may have found its ideal mediating subject—the 1991 Persian Gulf War. His use of poetry as a mode of theoretical inquiry, his obsession with the problem of the frame, his working through negativity, and his employment of a kind of traumatized "I" all combine to address the problem of being witness to an event whose framing almost entirely blocked representation. *Bad History* (1998)—itself constructed like a newspaper column—cuts diagonally through the discourses of art criticism, print journalism, romantic lyric, dream language, and financial prospectus. Watten's disjunctive sentences stretch, harry, and subvert the discourses they invoke. Poetry becomes a complicating procedure, using the subjective knife of language toward and within those discourses. The poet is, among other things, a dissenting journalist: "each new war being the culmination of our old belief in the supersession of a new technology. . . . Only later did we find out that the success rate for Patriot missiles was only 6 percent. How can we be so thoroughly trained to disbelieve the evidence of our senses?"

In his work as an editor alone, Watten figures centrally in the story of Language poetry. From 1971 to 1974, Watten co-edited *This* with Robert Grenier, whose opening salvo, "I HATE SPEECH," heralded a poetry at odds with the mainstream lyric tradition's emphasis on voice and in tune with a re-emphasis on poetry as writing, as language. Bob Perelman has called the first issue of *This* "an originary moment" for language writing. Watten continued editing *This* magazine and produced books as part of This Press until 1982. He also co-edited the influential *Poetics Journal* with Lyn Hejinian from 1982 to 1998 and was an associate editor for the New Historicist *Representations* between 1984 and 1994 and a corresponding editor for *Artweek* from 1989 to 1995.

Receiving his Ph.D. in literature from the University of California–Berkeley in 1995, and having gained increasing recognition for his work (he received a Guggenheim fellowship and a MacArthur Foundation fellowship in 2001), Watten continues to extend the practical and theoretical implications of avant-garde modernism into the twenty-first century.

Further Reading. ***Selected Primary Sources:*** Watten, Barrett, *Bad History* (Berkeley, CA: Atelos, 1998); ———, *The Constructivist Moment: From Material Text to Cultural Poetics* (Middletown, CT: Wesleyan University Press, 2003). ———, *Frame: Poems 1971–1990* (Los Angeles, CA: Sun & Moon Press, 1997); ———, *Total Syntax* (Carbondale: Southern Illinois University Press, 1985); Watten, Barrett, Michael Davidson, Lyn Hejinian, and Ron Silliman, *Leningrad: American Writers in the Soviet Union* (San Francisco: Mercury House, 1991); Watten, Barrett, Carla Harryman, Lyn Hejinian, Bob Perelman, and Ron Silliman, "Aesthetic Tendency and the Politics of Poetry: A Manifesto" (*Social Text* 19/20 [Fall 1998]: 261–275). ***Selected Secondary Sources:*** Debrot, Jacques, "Barrett Watten," in *Dictionary of Literary Biography* (Farmington Hills, MI: Gale Research, 1998); Hess, David, "No Surprises: On Barrett Watten" (*Jacket* 12 [July 2000], http://jacketmagazine.com/12/hess-david.html); Jameson, Fredric, *Postmodernism, or, the Cultural Logic of Late Capitalism* (Durham, NC: Duke University Press, 1991); Metres, Philip, "Barrett Watten's *Bad History*: A Counter-Epic of the Gulf War" (*Postmodern Culture* 13.3 [Winter 2003]); Perelman, Bob, *The Marginalization of Poetry: Language Writing and Literary History* (Princeton, NJ: Princeton University Press, 1996); Smith, Rod, ed., *Aerial 8: Barrett Watten* (Washington, DC: Edge Books, 1995).

Philip Metres

WEBB, CHARLES HARPER (1952–)

Charles Harper Webb was a rock musician as well as a poet from the late 1960s through the 1970s. He abandoned both pursuits around 1980, but returned to poetry eight years later. He went on to become a prominent figure in Los Angeles poetry and one of the more exciting poets on the national scene—widely published, editor of four anthologies (three entitled *Stand Up Poetry*), and professor of English at California State University, Long Beach, where he helped to start the MFA program. Like the rock music he composed and played, Charles Webb's poetry is accessible and informal, yet complex, challenging, and full of energy. It is also frequently humorous and introspective. Among Webb's publications are six books of poetry and over 1,000 individual poems. His many awards include the Kate Tufts Discovery Award, a Whiting Writer's Award, and a Guggenheim fellowship.

Webb was born in Philadelphia in 1952, but grew up in Houston, where he learned to love fishing, hunting, and the outdoors—interests reflected in early poems. He also learned to sing and play guitar. At the time he graduated magna cum laude from Rice University, he was publishing poems and playing music professionally. After graduate study at the University of Washington (MA in English), Webb lived in Seattle for ten years, supporting his poetry habit by playing in rock bands. He also edited the literary magazine *Madrona.* During this time, his work appeared frequently in "underground" and "outsider" magazines such as *Wormwood Review* and *Poetry Now.* His first collection of poetry, *Zinjanthropus Disease,* won the Wormwood Review Award for 1978. In 1980, disillusioned with both the poetry establishment and the music scene, Webb left Seattle for Los Angeles. During the next eight years, he received an MFA in professional writing and a Ph.D. in counseling psychology from the University of Southern California. He wrote no poetry, but published a novel, *The Wilderness Effect* (1982), and wrote screenplays—several optioned, none produced.

In 1984, Webb began teaching at Cal State Long Beach. He also opened a practice as a psychotherapist and returned to writing poetry. In 1989 he published a new collection, *Everyday Outrages.* In 1990, inspired to collect poems that students were sure to enjoy, he edited (with **Suzanne Lummis**) the first edition of *Stand Up Poetry.* Two more solo-edited editions arrived in 1994 and 2002. A key to Webb's approach to poetry is found in his introduction to the 2002 edition: "Entertainment isn't always art, but the best art always entertains, while the worst struggles self-consciously to edify."

Between 1992 and 2001, Webb published four books of poetry. The first, *A Weeb for All Seasons* (1992), celebrates Weeb, described by Webb as "the dweeb in all of us. (I hope it's not just me.)" Many of these poems display the sexual energy characteristic of Webb's poems. Of the 1997 Morse Poetry Prize–winning *Reading the Water* (Northeastern University Press), contest judge **Edward Hirsch** states, "Charles Harper Webb has a wild inventive energy, a quirky, at times even manic, wit and a deep sense of wonder at the world." Webb's next collection, *Liver,* won the 1999 Felix Pollak Prize in Poetry from the University of Wisconsin Press Poetry Series. **Robert Bly**, the judge that year, wrote, "Charles Harper Webb has a strong voice; he doesn't back away in order to say safe things. He is a poet of complicated and brave feelings."

Much of Webb's early poetry took the form of either surreal **prose poems** or **narratives**, as in the Bukowski-inspired "Meat Poetry." Webb's background in fiction writing is evident in his use of intriguing characters, premises, and conflicts, along with strong narrative drive and psychological exploration. *Everyday Outrages* mixes all of these ingredients with the cadence and feel of the rock music that he performed in Seattle.

During this period, Webb also published a number of Weeb poems. These operate as comedy, fantasy, and serious psychological investigation of maleness. In some poems, Weeb the underdog miraculously triumphs. In others, reality hits hard. Titles set up the narratives: "A Bean Burrito Momentarily Knocks Young Weeb Out of the Park," "Of Necessity, Weeb Jokes About His Height," "Hoping for an Orgy, Web Attends a Witchcraft Class," and "Weeb's Amours Interrupted by Nature's Call."

Reading the Water and *Liver* mark a widening of Webb's poetic reach. His clear imagery, wit, imaginative leaps, and active language persist and even intensify in these poems. At the same time, their more formal qualities—including a frequent "ghost pentameter"—emphasize the unconventionality of Webb's mind and voice. Poems such as "Prozac" and "Prayer for the Man Who Mugged My Father, 72" reflect his experience as a psychotherapist. Of Webb's new work, Hirsch observes, "His poems are filled with curiosities and odd facts and details, with unlikely anecdotes—all of which he takes personally."

Webb's 2001 book, *Tulip Farms and Leper Colonies,* continues the evolution of his work. Each line is lean and tightly crafted, with strong, purposeful rhythms. Poems such as "Waking at 3 A.M." ("Now is the time humans feel closest to the grave"), "Socks" (about making love with them on), and even "Cocksucker" display a new poignancy, and tenderness. The first poem in the book, "To Make My Countrymen Love Poetry," ends with the hope that poetry will open the hearts of his countrymen to the possibilities of compassion and kindness.

Hot Popsicles, a forthcoming book of prose poems from University of Wisconsin Press, promises a return to the surreal Webb. A woman falls in love—literally—with a house; Werner Heisenberg confronts his own uncertainty; a rat (the rodent kind) runs for president; Hamlet has trouble with his prostate. These prose poems, coupled with the verse he continues to publish in **literary magazines**, tend to confirm Maura Stanton's assessment of Webb as "a major poet of the twenty-first century."

Further Reading. ***Selected Primary Sources:*** Webb, Charles Harper, *Everyday Outrages* (Los Angeles: Red Wind Press, 1989); Webb, Charles Harper, *Liver* (Madison: University of Wisconsin Press, 1999); ———, *Reading the Water* (Boston: Northeastern University Press, 1997); ———, ed., *Stand Up Poetry: The Anthology* (Long Beach: California State University Press, 1994); ———, *Tulip Farms and Leper Colonies* (Rochester, NY: BOA Editions, 2001); ———, *A Weeb for All Seasons* (Long Beach, CA: Applezaba Press, 1992). ***Selected Secondary Sources:*** Kaufman, Alan, ed., *The Outlaw Bible of American Poetry* (New York: Thunder's Mountain Press, 1999).

David Widup

WEINER, HANNAH (1928–1997)

Although primarily associated with **Language poetry**, Hannah Weiner's work spans the aesthetic and historical range of the **New York School** through to her posthumous influence on the New Narrative movement of the late twentieth and early twenty-first centuries. Weiner came late to writing poetry and was better known as a **performance** and conceptual artist in the late 1960s. Beginning in the early 1970s, Weiner began composing journals, eventually scored for live performance and organized formally around her peculiar aesthetic response—which she figured as "clairvoyance"—to mental and physical illnesses from which she suffered for more than twenty-five years before her death from cancer in 1997.

Weiner was born in 1928 in Providence, Rhode Island, where she graduated from Classical High School. After graduating from Radcliff College in 1950, she worked as a lingerie designer in New York City. In the early 1960s she began giving performances, one of which was entitled "Hannah Weiner at Her Job"; it consisted of a sort of open house hosted by her employer, A.H. Schreiber Co. Other performance pieces in the late 1960s and early 1970s included "Street Works" and "World Works." Most significantly, after studying poetry with **Bill Berkson** and **Kenneth Koch** at the New School for Social Research in 1963, and through working friendships with second-generation New York School poets such as **Ted Berrigan** and **Bernadette Mayer**, Weiner composed and performed a series of Code Poems, collected as such for her second published book of poetry in 1982. Using a nineteenth-century system of visual signals for communication at sea, these works, along with similar early works by **Jackson Mac Low**, brought **avant-garde** forms of translation to bear upon contemporary sociopolitical issues, particularly 1970s American feminism and the American Indian Movement (AIM). Weiner's first book of poetry, however, was basically a New York School attempt to write verse in response to the paintings of René Magritte; *The Magritte Poems* was published in 1970. By the end of the 1960s, all the hallmarks of Weiner's later work were in place—the mundane, everyday experiences in her personal life; playful and personal responses to high and official cultural artifacts; and theoretical and practical forms of ideological critique—and she had found a way to syncretize them.

Weiner spent the first three years of the 1970s finding the poetic form for her work in three voices, the underground masterpiece *Clairvoyant Journal*. The larger *Clairvoyant Journal* project is preceded by four early journals, *The Fast* (1992), *Country Girl* (2004), "Pictures and Early Words," and "BIG WORDS." A small edition of the first several months of the *Clairvoyant Journal* itself was published by Angel Hair in 1978. The majority of the material, although essential to understanding the book's achievement, was never put into print. Audio recordings from the book, featuring Weiner and fellow poets, were released the same year and now reside at her home page: http://epc.buffalo.edu/authors/weiner.

Much has been made of Weiner's claims to possess special powers to predict, heal, and teach through the medium of "clairvoyance," to the detriment of the work's power. Clairvoyance signifies two interlacing aspects of Weiner's work. Poet-critic Judith Goldman describes it as a claim that demonstrates the aspect of belief prejudicing any reader or "seer" of words, and hence it is a critical engagement with the fundamentals of experiencing language so mundane as to become extraordinary under sustained scrutiny by the poet and her reader (121). But it also became a poetic form, and as such it has been highly influential, particularly among Language poets. Any of Weiner's works from the mid-1970s onward, which she describes as clairvoyantly written, are organized as "large-sheet poetry," in which the sentence, frequently interrupted by "seen" words and inner voices supposedly outside the control of the narrator (except insofar as they are strictly scored as such on the page), becomes the poetic measure.

Most lyric poetry uses the verse line as its basic measure, within which other factors, such as accents and syllables, provide nuance. Weiner's clairvoyant writings rarely use such conventions. Instead, she visually organizes the language experienced by the narrator, ostensibly her "self," across the entire page, leaving a prose-like, but significantly skewed, layout that can be used as a vocal score for performing the works. Although this form is influenced by **concrete poetry,** it is also akin to the revolution in poetic form initiated by **Gertrude Stein** in the **modernist** period. One can see the influence of both of these approaches to clairvoyance in the works of younger authors such as **Charles Bernstein** and **Ron Silliman**.

Little Books/Indians, published in 1980, lived quite literally by its name. The "large-sheet" poems were organized into "little books," and the sentences were more often cut short so as to resemble verse. Weiner's interest in the AIM became the focus of the ideological theme of the collection, moreover providing a more easily recognized narrative thrust. *Spoke* (1984), *Silent Teachers / Remembered Sequel* (1993), and *We Speak Silent* (1997) are closer to the *Clairvoyant Journal* in form and theme, but they further develop the aspect of clairvoyance pertaining to interpersonal relations mediated by language the author called "silent teaching." This theme is essentially a means of inquiry into global, holistic politics inspired by avant-garde art in the West and Eastern religious practices often alluded to in the *Clairvoyant Journal*. Weiner's last major work, *page* (2002), is a complex series of poems closer to normative lyric verse yet highly disjunctive in terms of grammatical forms. It is also a deeply personal work in which the deaths of her aunt and mother become an allegory for an intrapersonal examination of silent teaching.

Further Reading. ***Selected Primary Sources:*** Weiner, Hannah, "Capitalist Useless Phrases after Endless," in *The L=A=N=G=U=A=G=E Book*, ed. Bruce Andrews and Charles Bernstein (Carbondale: Southern Illinois University Press, 1984); ———, *Clairvoyant Journal* (Lenox, MA: Angel Hair, 1978); ———, *The Code Poems* (Barrytown, NY: Open Studio, 1982); ———, *The Fast* (New York: United Artists, 1992); ———, *Little Books/ Indians* (New York: Roof Books, 1980); ———, *Magritte Poems* (Sacramento, CA: Poetry Newsletter, 1970); ——— , "Mostly about the Sentence" (*Jimmy and Lucy's House of "K"* 7 [1986]: 54–70); ———, *Nijole's House* (Needham, MA: Potes & Poets Press, 1981); ———, *page* (New York: Roof Books, 2002); ———, *Silent Teachers / Remembered Sequel* (Providence, RI: Tender Buttons, 1993); ———, *Sixteen* (Windsor, VT: Awede Press, 1983); ———, *Spoke* (College Park, MD: Sun & Moon Press, 1984); ———, *Weeks* (Ann Arbor, MI: Xexoxial, 1990); ———, *We Speak Silent* (New York: Roof Books, 1997); ———, *Written In/The Zero One* (Victoria, Australia: Post Neo, 1985). ***Selected Secondary Sources:*** Bernstein, Charles, "Excerpts from an Interview with Hannah Weiner," in *The Line in Postmodern Poetry*, ed. Robert Frank and Henry Sayre (Urbana: University of Illinois Press, 1988, 187–188); Damon, Maria, "Hannah Weiner Beside Herself: Clairvoyance After Shock or The Nice Jewish Girl Who Knew Too Much" (*East Village Web*, www.fauxpress.com/t8/damon/p3.html); Durgin, Patrick F., "Journalism" (*Kiosk* 2 [2002]: 243–255); Goldman, Judith, "Hannah=hannaH: Politics, Ethics, and Clairvoyance in the Work of Hannah Weiner" (*differences: A Journal of Feminist Cultural Studies* 12.2 [Summer 2001]: 121).

Patrick F. Durgin

WEISS, THEODORE (1916–2003)

After America's golden era of "little magazines" in the first half of the century, when names like **Harriet Monroe** and Philip Rahv resonated with almost the same mystique as those of **Wallace Stevens** and **William Carlos Williams**, and anthologists like Oscar Williams and Louis Untermeyer helped shape the public cultural consciousness, American letters entered a time in which **literary magazines** came to proceed from the consciousness of semi-anonymous boards or to represent schools or styles rather than the powerful individual voice of a great and literate editor. Theodore Weiss's *Quarterly Review of Literature* stands out as an exception. Weiss made a significant place for himself in American poetry as a master of long-form **narrative poetry** and as a blender of classical consciousness and vernacular American voice. But the *Quarterly Review*, which he and his wife, Renée Karol Weiss, founded and edited for nearly sixty years, may be the achievement for which he is most remembered.

Weiss was born on December 16, 1916, in Reading, Pennsylvania, in, he notes for an autobiographical essay, "that supposedly most lucky of things, a caul" (*Contemporary Authors 189*, 421), a protective cushion created by amniotic membrane. This detail came to excite Weiss when he read that Byron had been born in the same way. Weiss's father was a businessman and man of action who named his son after Theodore Roosevelt. Weiss traces his own literary bent to his maternal grandfather, a Polish immigrant peddler, socialist, and rabbinical scholar.

Weiss graduated from Muhlenberg College in 1938, and received his MA from Columbia University in 1940. He married Renée Karol in 1941. His early teaching career included positions at the universities of Maryland and North Carolina and at Yale University. In 1946 Weiss joined Bard College in Annandale-on-Hudson, New York, where he was professor of English for twenty years. In 1966 he moved to Princeton University, where he would spend the rest of his academic life. He was first brought in as a poet-in-residence and was then appointed professor of English and creative writing in 1968. In 1977 he was named the William and Anne S. Paton Foundation Professor of Ancient and Modern Literature, a position that he held until his retirement in 1987. His awards include the Wallace Stevens Award (1956), the Brandeis Creative Arts Award in Poetry (1977), the Poetry Society of America's Shelley Memorial Award (1988–1989), and, appropriately, the Oscar Williams and Gene Derwood Award (1997). He has been a fellow of the Guggenheim, Ford, and Ingram Merrill foundations and of the National Foundation of the Arts and Humanities. He read at the White House in 1980 and was the subject of two documentary films, *Living Poetry: A Year in the Life of a Poem* and *Living Poetry 2: Yes, With Lemon*, by Harvey Edwards. The first film tracks Weiss from initial inspiration through the completion of a poem over the course of a year, following the creation and evolution of his poem "Fractions." The second film includes revisions to and a discussion of the poem.

Weiss's first collection, *The Catch*, was published in 1951; his first book-length poem, *Outlanders*, came out in 1960. Another **long poem**, *Gunsight* (1962), became his best-known work. Begun in the early 1940s as a short poem about a wounded soldier, it grew over the years to become a meditation on war and suffering that centers on the interior monologue of the soldier undergoing surgery, but reaches out to include a multitude of viewpoints, denoted by typographic changes, incorporating both created characters and the meditative persona of the poet. The sensual immediacy of youth and the unsentimental realism of guns intertwine, as do the voices: "the gun-struck thing I am. / Admire sores, black gaping gums, these sockets / filled with nothing."

Subsequent books, including *The Medium* (1965) and the collections *The World Before Us: Poems, 1950–1970* (1970), *Views and Spectacles: Selected Poems* (1978), and *Fireweeds* (1976), found Weiss working in the shorter forms more typical of his era. These poems often echo the fascination of *Outlanders* with icons of American individuality like **Henry David Thoreau** and Albert Pinkham Ryder. "Simples of the Moon" lauds an unsuppressible will like that of "Ryder (the thin caul / of a wide-eyed moon between you / and the city, and a field." **Hayden Carruth**, in reviewing *The World Before Us*, found himself cast back into the time of his youth, when language mattered and poets used words to capture precise nuances of emotion.

Weiss returned to the long form again in *Recoveries* (1982), in which an art restorer engages in a colloquy with the subjects of the fresco he is restoring. He would publish three more books of shorter poems and a *Selected Poems* (1995) before his death. He also published several collections of essays.

The Weisses founded *Quarterly Review of Literature* in 1943. The magazine quickly became, and remained, one of the most influential in its field and, with the six-decade stewardship of the Weisses, a voice of consistent and sophisticated taste. In addition to being an important outlet for the later work of Stevens and Williams (including segments of *Paterson* in progress), the *Quarterly Review of Literature* published early poems by **James Merrill**, **Denise Levertov**, **Robert Duncan, James Dickey**, **W.S. Merwin**, and others.

Further Reading. ***Selected Primary Sources:*** Weiss, Theodore, Autobiographical essay, in *Contemporary Authors 189*, ed. Scott Peacock (Farmington Hills, MI: Gale Group, 2001, 420–449); ———, *The Catch* (New York: Twayne, 1951); ———, *Fireweeds* (New York: Macmillan, 1970); ———, *Gunsight* (New York: New York University Press, 1962); ———, *The Man from Porlock, Selected Essays 1941–1981* (Princeton, NJ: Princeton University Press, 1982); ———, *The Medium* (New York: Macmillan, 1965); ———, *Outlanders* (New York: Macmillan, 1960); ———, *Recoveries: A Poem* (New York: Macmillan, 1982); ———, *Views and Spectacles: Selected Poems* (London: Chatto and Windus, 1978; New York: Macmillan, 1979); ———, *The World Before Us: Poems, 1950–1970* (New York: Macmillan, 1970). ***Selected Secondary Source:*** Gibbons, Reginald, "Interview with Theodore Weiss" (*American Poetry Review* 30.3 [May/June 2001]: 33–40).

Tad Richards

WELCH, JAMES (1940–2003)

James Welch was a leading figure in the Native American Renaissance, which began in the late 1960s, but he sought to avoid being characterized as a "spokesman" for Native Americans and did not view social criticism or political activism as a focus of his writing. When asked in an interview about the intersections of his culture and subject matter, Welch replied, "I used to object to being called an Indian writer, and would always say I was a writer who happened to be an Indian, and who happened to write about Indians" (Lee, 193). Although Welch resisted ethnic labeling, the subject matter for nearly all of his work emerged from a specifically Native American experience, and the setting of both his poetry and his prose is frequently reservation land on the Montana plains. Welch began to write about his experiences growing up on both the Blackfeet and Fork Belknap reservations as a graduate student when he thought no one would be interested in reading about such things. Welch quickly discovered, however, that his poetry and fiction found a ready readership, both in the United States and in Europe. His career spanned thirty years and saw the publication of a volume of poetry, five novels, and a book of nonfiction. A contemporary of **N. Scott Momaday**, **Leslie Marmon Silko**, **Simon J. Ortiz**, and **Louise Erdrich**, Welch taught at the University of Washington, the University of Montana, and Cornell University during his career and received numerous awards, including an American Book Award (1986), the John Dos Passos Prize for Literature (1994), and a Lifetime Achievement Award from the Native Writers Circle of the Americas (1997).

James Welch was born in 1940 in Browning, Montana, headquarters of the Blackfeet reservation. Welch was of Blackfeet descent on his father's side and Gros Ventre on his mother's. After spending his youth on the Blackfeet and Fort Belknap reservations, Welch graduated from high school in Minneapolis in 1958. He received a BA in liberal arts from the University of Montana at Missoula in 1965. Welch then pursued an MFA at the university and studied with poet **Richard Hugo**. Hugo strongly influenced and encouraged Welch, who cites his time in Hugo's writing workshop as the point at which he became serious about his writing. In 1969 Welch received a National Foundation for the Arts grant to work on his first and only poetry collection, *Riding the Earthboy 40* (1971). *Riding the Earthboy 40* won a Pacific Northwest Booksellers Award in 1975, and a revised edition of this volume including new material was published in 1976. Although he did not complete the MFA, Welch was awarded honorary doctorates from both Rocky Mountain College in Billings in 1993 and the University of Montana in 1997. In 1981 Welch began teaching in the English and Indian Studies departments at the University of Washington.

Welch's work is often described as surreal, and he prominently uses dreamscapes, visions, juxtapositions of the absurd and the everyday, and the presentation of fractured time in his poetry. *Riding the Earthboy 40*, his only volume of poetry, derives its name from a Fort Belknap reservation family and their forty acres of land. Several poems from this collection have been heavily anthologized, and the most frequently discussed of these include "The Man from Washington," "Magic Fox," "Surviving," "Grandma's Man," and "Harlem, Montana: Just off the Reservation." Most of Welch's poems are lyrically sparse and composed in **minimalist free verse** with a deliberate "sense of economy of language," as Welch described his style (Coltelli, 188). Welch's stylistic influences include Ernest Hemingway, John Steinbeck, Elio Vittorini, Cesar Vallejo, and **John Berryman**.

"The Man from Washington," which depicts a history of broken land treaties, serves as a compelling example of Welch's surreal imagery. The government representative is described as "a slouching dwarf with rainwater eyes," and the onlookers are "packed away in our crude beginnings / in some far corner of a flat world." Similarly, "Magic Fox" exemplifies Welch's fondness for dreamscapes and stark imagery: "He turned their horses into fish, / or was it horses strung / like fish . . . ?"

Critics have noted a theme of hopelessness that runs throughout Welch's work, one often mirrored in his depictions of windy, wintry landscapes. Such characteristics emerge in "Surviving," a poem that begins with a description of "the day-long cold hard rain" and ends with the lament that the moon disappeared that night, "just long enough / for wet black things to sneak away our cache / of meat." Such dismal, ambiguous endings became precursors to Welch's fiction, especially *Winter in the Blood* and *The Death of Jim Loney*.

In contrast with such despondency, "Grandma's Man," a linear narrative, displays Welch's wry humor as the poem's grandmother hurls a goose that bit her hand over a cowshed roof and uses it to stuff a favorite pillow. Meanwhile, her foolish husband ineptly attempts to capture the incident in amateurish paintings as his farm goes untended. The life and death of this artist who "never ever got things quite right" are portrayed in an equally humorous fashion as Welch puns on the word "well" in the final lines of the poem: "Well, and yes, he died well, / but you should have seen how well his friends took it." "Harlem, Montana: Just off the Reservation," displays a sharper ironic edge as it addresses futile hopes and the illusory nature of a touted American meritocracy: No one needs to run for office because "booze is law. / and all the Indians drink in the best tavern." Although Welch's reputation today largely rests on the strengths of his novels, the often poetic quality of his fiction finds its source in his early poetry, and his work remains frequently taught in American and Native American literature courses.

Further Reading. ***Selected Primary Sources:*** Welch, James, *The Death of Jim Loney* (New York: Harper & Row, 1979; London: Gollancz, 1980); ———, *Fools Crow* (New York: Viking, 1986); ———, *The Heartsong of Charging Elk* (New York: Doubleday, 2000); ———, *The Indian Lawyer* (New York: Norton, 1990); ———, *Riding the Earthboy 40* (New York: World, 1971; rev. ed. New York: Harper & Row, 1976); ———, *Winter in the Blood* (New York: Harper & Row, 1974; Toronto: Bantam, 1975); Welch, James, and Paul Stekler, *Killing Custer: The Battle of the Little Bighorn and the Fate of the Plains Indians* (New York: Norton, 1994). ***Selected Secondary Sources:*** Coltelli, Laura, *Winged Words: American Indian Writers Speak* (Lincoln: University of Nebraska Press); Lee, Don, "About James Welch: A Profile" (*Ploughshares* 20.1 [Spring 1994]: 193–200); McFarland, Ron, ed., *James Welch* (Lewiston, ID: Confluence Press, 1986); ———, *Understanding James Welch* (Columbia: University of South Carolina Press, 2000).

Jessica Metzler

WELISH, MARJORIE (1944–)

Marjorie Welish's poetry frequently develops from her understanding of the theoretical questions of modern art. Welish works with a shrewd repertoire of **postmodern** strategies, but her work's clearest predecessors are the **modernist** poets compelled by representing visual perception in language. When Welish unfastens the words and images through which perception is conventionally shaped, one hears echoes of **Wallace Stevens**. Lines in "Setting, or Farewell" (1981) suggest Stevens's austere, contemplative formality: "There is night in the mirror surrounding the lake. / This is a mirror you say." When she plays with the decorative surface of diction and extends the logic of cultural expression, Welish's poems exhibit an intellectual agility that could outwit **Marianne Moore**. In "Macbeth in Battle" (2000) she observes that wondering where her wallet is "is not a question / but an implicit temptation trafficking / in interrogatives."

Though Welish's work analyzes rather than responds to the concepts at stake in modern art, the **New York School** poets' engagement with painting is another antecedent. Of these poets, Welish's poetry aligns best with the work of **Barbara Guest**. Both write associative, meticulous, self-consciously *written* poems that critically and lyrically enact the process of making a poem. As Welish explains in her essay on Guest, poetry about writing poetry involves twisting words away from their referents, "taking things apart to assemble them afresh," and making the poem a compositional field in which "language responds to and revises itself."

Welish was born, raised, and educated in New York City. She received a degree in art history from Columbia University and an MFA in studio art from Vermont College of Norwich University. A cosmopolitan upbringing exposed her to a wide array of aesthetic forms and practices, which accounts not only for her expansive concept of poetry but also for Welish's being an accomplished painter and art critic as well as a poet. In a correspondence with **Carla Harryman**, Welish writes, "Early on, modern music, dance, and theories of these, together with New Wave film, had a decided impact on my expectations for the nature of the verbal artifact we call a poem." Many of Welish's poems are speculative answers to questions that intersect aesthetic forms and ideas, and the "image" of painting becomes an imaginative surface upon which one can visualize the material outcomes of ideas. Welish highlights the visual, material, spatial aspects of lines, stanzas, and sentences, composing poems analogous to paintings that defamiliarize perception.

Welish's work resists falling into the emotional booby traps of personal narrative by following the logic of associative patterns to their conclusions. Yet *Handwritten* (1979), her first collection, explores the possibilities for linking individual perceptions to recognizable codes. In "Among Them All" (1979) Welish renders a car turning into a driveway through layers of spatial, aural, and tactile inscriptions and then allows this detailed scene to move into a metaphor for painting: "the wet, the partially wet sounds of paint rollers / pushed from the gutter of tray are the tires also." "Greenhouses and Gardens" meditates on the pastoral melancholy in the letters of painter Arshille Gorky. After writing that Gorky "always exaggerated his states of feeling" and comparing his phrases to "an imitation oriental carpet," Welish records the moment of seeing how his written expressions have corollaries in painting: "I realized his colors suspend in the same way, / in a solvent, permissive yet starved." Gorky's letters recollect family gardens, but Welish compares them to greenhouses, which suggest that the exaggerated representation of feelings emerge from expressions condensed and kept in almost transparent but artificial forms.

The poems in *The Windows Flew Open* (1991) engage with the fact that concepts are not outside of representation, but that the latter eclipses artistic originality. And yet, as the title of the collection suggests, the idea of a transcendent outside can unexpectedly open perception. "Veil" (1991) begins with an "enchanted frame" that "assures the image of a loved one" and then follows the relationship between an image and the frame that made it possible into metaphysical speculations: "Then there is this question / Of existence." The poem enacts a process of extending beyond and then circling back to frames of recognition, though it ends with an image of a "starstruck blue" sky layered with expansive "beyonds" and "you / not even among them in question form." A sky that does not reveal and only veils is linked to representation's endless unfolding. In "Crossing Disappearing Behind Them" (1991) Welish represents the perceptual events that take place after writing a poem that is "original if late": "I saw myself / stepping onto a movie set of rain imitating rain / a central fiction."

Casting Sequences (1993) underscores painting as a "central fiction" in Welish's work. The poem "Scapel in Hand" (1993) begins with a series of compelling propositions for beginning a painting through negation—"Let us effect a moratorium on things"—and borrows from the suggestions that emerge from painting's unique mesh of color, texture, proximity, and form: "the flutter of nearby bleeding does not render charcoal lemon tragic." In "Suppressed Misfortunes" (1993), part of a series entitled "Of a Display," which "completes" Michaelangelo's poetry of fragments, Welish opens each line with the word components of a phrase and then places the phrase's recognizable form in italics, creating a pattern of doubled lines that enact the shift into syntactical convention: "Breath tired my or *or my tired breath* / Hour evil the or *or the evil hour.*" After establishing this pattern, Welish plays with the expectation it sets up, intertwining it with a sequence of phrases that are not "mirrors" of others; the stanzas become composed of sentences in enjambed lines, arriving at the question of where meaning is and what purpose it serves: "Or is it conception *carried within* / Incessant meriting, *Consoling Heaven?*"

With a depersonalized austerity, "*The Annotated "Here"*" (2000) takes up the question of an artwork's existence in time and space. The subject of this book is radically contingent and slippery; each line is a fragment that both refers to and defers the guiding concept, which is often the abstraction of composing a poem. For example, the poem "This Near That" (2000) ends with and arrives at the phrase "Our professed subject." Responding to this collection, Forrest Gander writes, "Welish relishes rerouting our bias. In her lines, disclosure seductively defers itself." Even less tangibly present than in previous collections, Welish transforms the idea of the author into a deft compositional hand that sifts and arranges from afar. *Word Group* (2004) continues to experiment with ideas about repetition as representation; the poems thread through the layers of language tangled between self, gesture, idea, and word, allowing these elements to surface and submerge in time: "'That's me, in hardware' / . . . / a person is gesticulating at a thing through a thing thing." Named the 2004–2005 Judith E. Wilson Visiting Poetry Fellow at Cambridge University, Welish shows no sign of compromising her scrupulous exploration of poetry's continual engagement with the pressures the most challenging theoretical ideas place on representation.

Further Reading. ***Selected Primary Sources:*** Welish, Marjorie, *The Annotated "Here" and Selected Poems* (Minneapolis, MN: Coffee House Press, 2000); ———, *Casting Sequences: Poems* (Athens: University of Georgia Press, 1993); ———, *The Windows Flew Open* (Providence, RI: Burning Deck Press, 1991); ———, *Word Group: Poems by Marjorie Welish* (Minneapolis, MN: Coffee House Press, 2004). ***Selected Secondary Sources:*** Gander, Forrest, Review of *The Annotated "Here"* (*Poetry Project Newsletter* 186 [October/November 2001]: 21–22); Harryman, Carla, and Marjorie Welish, "Of, and/or Through: Correspondence," in *Of the Diagram: The Work of Marjorie Welish*, ed. Jean-Michel Rabaté and Aaron Levy (Philadelphia: Slought Foundation, 2003, 201–217); Welish, Marjorie, "On Barbara Guest," in *Moving Borders: Three Decades of Innovative Writing by Women*, ed. Mary Margaret Sloan (Jersey City, NJ: Talisman House, 1997, 561–565).

Kimberly Lamm

WELLS, CAROLYN (1862–1942)

An early collector and bibliographer of **Walt Whitman**, Carolyn Wells published almost 200 books in several genres, from detective fiction and Mother Goose adaptations to autobiography and rhymed charades. In the memoir *The Rest of My Life* (1937), Wells claimed that she wrote so many jingles for the *World's Fair Puck* at the 1893 Columbian Exposition in Chicago that a large number were printed under pseudonyms. Throughout the 1890s, her comic poetry appeared in mass-market periodicals and in **literary magazines**, including the *Yellow Book*, the *Cornhill Booklet*, and the *Chap Book*. She soon began publishing volumes of her own poems and editing collections of works by other poets. In the 1920s, Thomas L. Masson, an editor at *Life* magazine, described Wells as "our chief woman humorist, and a quite ubiquitous argument against that foolish declaration that women have no sense of humor."

Born in Rahway, New Jersey, in 1862, to William E. Wells and Anna Woodruff Wells, Carolyn Wells grew up in a prosperous household similar to those portrayed in the series books she wrote for girls. Wells could read before she went to school, and she and her three siblings were fascinated by word games. Scarlet fever damaged her hearing, a condition that worsened in adulthood. Although Wells was class valedictorian, she rejected college as "waste motion" and instead sought out private instruction in French, astronomy, natural history, religion, and other subjects. As Rahway's town librarian, she ordered a steady supply of books and periodicals with funding from a large endowment. Wells published her first volume, *At the Sign of the Sphinx* (1896), at the suggestion of Shakespeare scholar William J. Rolfe, who shared her love of riddles. Rolfe arranged for Wells to meet **Emily Dickinson**'s sister Lavinia, an encounter that she records humorously in *The Rest of My Life*, along with her parody of Dickinson's "To make a prairie." The sphinx-verses of Wells's first book were followed by *The Jingle Book* (1899), a volume of **children's poetry** in the tradition of *Rhymes and Jingles* (1874) by **Mary Mapes Dodge**, her editor at *St. Nicholas* magazine.

Oliver Herford's frontispiece drawing for *The Jingle Book* accompanies Wells's best-known limerick, "The Tutor" (1898). Originally published in *Life*, this alliterative piece describes a flute player who "tried to teach two young tooters to toot." Herford and his colleague Gelett Burgess, of "Purple Cow" fame, became important mentors and friends of Wells; she included their work in *A Nonsense Anthology* (1902), the first of the several poetry collections she edited. In the early decades of the twentieth century, when universities were just beginning to consider American literature as an academic discipline, such anthologies were significant texts of **canon formation**. Wells was a serious student of comic writing, and her collections gathered authors from both sides of the Atlantic, from classical Greeks to a diverse range of her contemporaries. She was personally acquainted with many American poets, including **Edgar Lee Masters**, whose *Spoon River Anthology* (1915) she parodied for *The Bookman* in the "The Styx River Anthology" (1916); and Peter Newell, whose wry pairs of lyrics and illustrations she admired.

Much as Wells's *The Technique of the Mystery Story* (1913; 1929) provides a practical guide to writing and reading many types of mysteries, her introductions to her anthologies analyze the sometimes-overlapping varieties of humorous poetry, such as **light verse**, satire, vers de société, parody, limericks, and nonsense verse. Some of these volumes reprint works by John Milton, Alfred Lord Tennyson, and other authors who are rarely considered humorous. At times, Wells makes careful distinctions, explaining, for instance, why **James Whitcomb Riley**'s "Spirk Troll-Derisive" is nonsense poetry, but his "Little Orphant Annie" is a different sort of comic writing. The compendium that especially reveals the breadth of Wells's reading is *An Outline of Humor: Being a True Chronicle from Prehistoric Ages to the Twentieth Century* (1923). In contrast to her other anthologies, the *Outline of Humor* includes several examples of prose humor along with comic poems, and Wells incorporates her selections into a running commentary on humor up to the year 1900.

Wells moved from New Jersey to New York City in 1918, when she married Hadwin Houghton, a businessman related to the well-known publishing family. He died a year later, and Wells describes their time together as her "most blessed memory." She continued to write and edit prolifically until her death on March 26, 1942; some publishers incorporated her name into titles, such as *Carolyn Wells' Book of American Limericks* (1925), an indication of her great appeal as a comic poet.

Throughout her career, Wells reacted to fads and fashions in a witty, often graceful style. Elegantly illustrated, her *Rubáiyát of a Motor Car* (1906) and *Rubáiyát of Bridge* (1909) parodied the popular verses of *The Rubáiyát of Omar Khayyam* while satirizing a national fascination with cars and card games. In *Laughing Their Way: Women's Humor in America* (1934), Martha Bensley Bruère and Mary Ritter Beard call Wells the outstanding female parodist at the start of the twentieth century. "The Poster Girl," from her *Idle Idyls* (1900), is both a parody of Dante Gabriel Rossetti and a comment on the popularity of poster art, one of Wells's own collecting manias. Other aspects of modern culture that evoke Wells's humorous verses include Cubistic art, **Imagistic** poetry, and the shirt-waisted "summer girls" memorialized in her friend Charles Dana Gibson's magazine illustrations.

Carolyn Wells's comic spirit is also evident in such prose works as *Folly in Fairyland* (1901); *Abeniki Caldwell: A Burlesque Historical Novel* (1902); and *Ptomaine Street: A Tale of Warble Petticoat* (1921), her parody of Sinclair Lewis's *Main Street* (1920). Although her scores of detective books won her the title "Dean of American Mystery Stories," Wells's humorous work was a more lasting contribution, and comic poetry was her area of expertise. Her skillful parodies of such predecessors as **Edgar Allan Poe**, **Henry Wadsworth Longfellow**, and Walt Whitman helped to strengthen these poets' status as American icons. During an era when many literary collections overlooked women's work, Wells anthologized **Phoebe Cary**, **Ruth McEnery Stuart**, Josephine Dodge Daskam Bacon, Caroline Duer, and several other female poets. Arthur Bartlett Maurice, the *Bookman* editor, counted Wells among the modern humorists whose sharp perceptions countered the **sentimentality** of much nineteenth-century literature.

Further Reading. ***Selected Primary Sources:*** Wells, Carolyn, *A Nonsense Anthology* (New York: Scribner's, 1902); ———, *An Outline of Humor: Being a True Chronicle from Prehistoric Ages to the Twentieth Century* (New York: Putnam's, 1923); ———, *The Rest of My Life* (Philadelphia: Lippincott, 1937). ***Selected Secondary Sources:*** Dresner, Zita Zatkin, "Carolyn Wells," in *Dictionary of Literary Biography, Volume 11: American Humorists, 1800–1950, Part 2: M–Z*, ed. Stanley Trachtenberg (Detroit, MI: Gale, 1982, 556–560); Hall, Joan Wylie, "Carolyn Wells (c. 1862–1942)" (*Legacy: A Journal of American Women Writers* 13.2 [1996]: 142–151); Masson, Thomas L., *Our American Humorists* (New York: Moffat, Yard, 1922).

Joan Wylie Hall

WHALEN, PHILIP (1923–2002)

Philip Whalen, best known as one of the original **Beat** writers, was also associated with the **San Francisco Renaissance**. He was included in Donald Allen's seminal anthology of avant-garde poets, *The New American Poetry* (1960), where his notable statement on poetics, "Since You Ask Me" (1959), appeared, defining poetry as a "picture or graph of a mind moving . . . from the particular to the general." Perhaps the most formally **experimental** of the Beat poets, Whalen tended to emphasize the process of writing in his poems. He was interested in the nature of perception, the relation of daily life to art, and the function of the poet in society. In addition, he is known for his playful wit and humor, his range of tone and voice, and the visual elegance of his calligraphic poems and drawings.

Whalen was born into a working-class family in Portland, Oregon, in 1923, and shortly after, he moved with his parents to The Dalles, a small town on the Columbia River, where he lived until graduation from high school. His father was a salesman; his mother died when Whalen was sixteen. After high school he lived with his father in Portland, taking on odd jobs until enlisting in the Army. Released from service, he used the GI Bill to attend Reed College, where he formed friendships with **Gary Snyder** and Lew Welch and first met **William Carlos Williams**, who had come to Reed on a 1950 reading tour.

After graduation in 1951, Whalen wandered the West Coast picking up odd jobs, staying with friends, and working as a fire look-out in the summers. It was during one of these stints that he wrote "Sourdough Mountain Lookout" (1955–1956), one of his best-known poems. Invited by Snyder, Whalen took part in 1955 in the Six Gallery poetry reading in San Francisco, where he met **Allen Ginsberg**, **Jack Kerouac**, and **Michael McClure**, among others. He was published in numerous small-press magazines during this time, appearing most notably in the *Chicago Review* Zen issue and *Evergreen Review*'s issue featuring West Coast poets. The following decade was also a prolific period for Whalen. In 1960 his first two volumes of poetry were published: *Like I Say* and *Memoirs of an Interglacial Age*. He also wrote three novels, subsequently published by **small presses**: *You Didn't Even Try* (1967), *Imaginary Speeches for a Brazen Head* (1973), and *Diamond Noodle* (1980). More significantly, Harcourt Brace brought out a major collection of Whalen's poems, *On Bear's Head* (1969), affording him a wider audience. Despite this recognition, Whalen's financial situation was unstable.

In 1967 Whalen traveled to Japan to teach English in Kyoto, returning to the United States in November of that year. He made a second trip to Japan, living in Kyoto from 1969 to 1971. It was during this time that he wrote his **long poem**, *Scenes of Life at the Capital* (1971), and began to practice Zen Buddhism seriously. After his return to the United States, he was invited to move to the San Francisco Zen Center, shortly thereafter becoming a monk. Three new poetry collections were published in the 1970s, along with a volume of selected poems. However, both because of his increasing commitment to meditation and teaching and his deteriorating health, his poetic output declined in the last decades of his life. In a talk given to Buddhist followers, he noted that the habits of meditating and writing poetry were "mutually destructive" because in meditation one watched words go by and in poetry one caught them. After the 1980 volume, *Enough Said*, his later collections were primarily selections of previously published work: *Heavy Breathing* (1983), collecting the books published in the 1970s, *Canoeing Up Cabarga Creek* (1996), a volume of selected Buddhist poems, and *Overtime* (1999), a final selected volume. In 1987 Whalen was given dharma transmission, subsequently becoming abbot of the Hartford Street Zen Center. He retired in 1996, staying on there as resident teacher until his death in 2002.

Whalen acknowledged the influences of **e.e. cummings**, **Kenneth Patchen**, **Gertrude Stein**, William Carlos Williams, **Charles Olson**, and Allen Ginsberg. Williams became a mentor for Whalen, especially in his emphasis on a poetry based on American speech. In the memorial poem "Plums, Metaphysics, an Investigation, a Visit, and a Short Funeral Ode" (1963), Whalen moves between memories of Williams and a description of a plum tree outside the window, the plums recalling one of the elder poet's most famous poems. Whalen also acknowledged the wider community of writers of which he was a part in dedicatory and epistolary poems demonstrating his conversational tone at its most effective. "Letter to Charles Olson" (1958) carries on a philosophical conversation by poem, and "Homage to William Seward Burroughs" (1965) is a **prose poem** employing Burroughs' cut-up methods. "Life in the City In Memoriam Edward Gibbon" (1968) demonstrates Whalen's wide reading and familiarity with the British literary tradition as well as the American.

Another important influence on Whalen was the Zen Buddhist spiritual and aesthetic tradition, with its idea that when someone deeply experiences everyday objects, spiritual insight occurs. For example, "Sourdough Mountain Lookout" records meditations on the view from the fire lookout as the speaker realizes his part in the flux of the universe. The poem incorporates quotes from Western and Eastern philosophies and ends with a mantra or chant from the Prajnaparamitra Sutra, a key Zen text. Other early poems, such as "Metaphysical Insomnia Jazz, Mumonkan XXIX" (1958), refer to Zen koans, the paradoxical statements or questions traditionally given by Zen teachers to practitioners on which to meditate. Zen also has its own tradition of priests who practiced poetry and calligraphy. "Hymnus ad Patrem Sinensis" (1958) pays homage to these Chinese forefathers, who, "conked out" among cherry blossoms and wine jars, "saved us all." Whalen was also interested in haiku, evident in his shorter poems that juxtapose images of the natural world with self-reflection, such as "Early Spring" (1964) or "Dharmakaya" (1981).

Later poems incorporate fewer specific allusions to Buddhism, while demonstrating the interconnectedness of all beings, a major theme of Whalen. He begins "What's New" (1978) with the observation, "We keep forgetting the world is alive," a world that includes inanimate objects such as kimonos or rugs. Another poem—with the playful title, "Hot Springs Infernal in the Human Beast" (1979)—opens with the poet looking out a window, observing that he is "saved by the real world." The poem ends simply with the names and colors of flowers. The last line, "Four nasturtiums (ORANGE)," with its mix of upper- and lowercase type lets us hear an emphatic and exclamatory tone of voice, contributing to the oral and performative nature of this poem, a hallmark of Whalen's work in general.

Experimentation is evident here in the mixing of typefaces, an example of Whalen's attention to poetry's visual aspect. In other poems, he used lines, dots, asterisks, brackets, and columns to space text on the page. For example, "One of my Favorite Songs Is Stormy Weather" (1961) presents a list of natural objects and foods down the left margin and bottom half of the page, juxtaposed with three meditative stanzas on the speaker's mental attitude while composing the list on the right. Both sides of the brain are thus represented. Such careful layouts show a literal composition by field as suggested by Olson's theory of **projective verse**.

An emphasis on process is further evident in Whalen's methods of composition. Most of his poems were originally journal entries, from which he later selected lines or pages that, typed up and arranged, became poems. In addition, Whalen's skill in calligraphy allowed him to combine words and playful images in short, pithy poems, reproduced in published texts as they first appeared in his notebooks. Process is likewise emphasized in poems composed while walking. "America Inside and Outside Bill Brown's House in Bolinas" (1968) combines the speaker's observations of the world on a morning walk with reflections about life in America where "we can afford this emptiness and the color of dawn."

Another experimental form included in his collections was the prose take, which presented the speaker's perceptions of the moment in stream-of-consciousness fashion. For example, "Prose Take-Out, Portland 13:IX:58" (1958), a record of the aftermath of a drinking bout with Kerouac, mixes mind chatter; quotes from Shakespeare, Paul Bowles, and Henry James; and ambient sounds of rain "drip" or fireplace "pop." His most experimental novel, *Diamond Noodle*, developed out of such prose takes.

Although Whalen's poetry has been considered esoteric and self-centered by some critics, much of his work exhibits a political stance and a keen interest in changing society. He protested the Vietnam War in his poetry, most notably in "The War Poem for Diane di Prima" (1966). Living in Kyoto, Whalen wrote about the war from the perspective of an American in Asia who stood for nonviolence. Whereas the poem's first section specifically protests the war, the second addresses the war within humans, fueled by desire and anger. In the last section he returns to the idea that the war is driven by capitalism, concluding that "only the money fights on, alone."

Whalen's wry, ironic comments are often directed both at himself and at American society's conformism and materialistic values. An early poem, "If You're So Smart, Why Ain't You Rich" (1955), addresses these issues along with thoughts of the speaker's own inadequacy. Of this poem, Whalen said it was a breakthrough enabling him to move away from imagism and the influence of **Wallace Stevens** represented by such early poems as "The Road-Runner" (1950), to a longer, more inclusive poetry influenced by Ginsberg's *Howl.* Whalen took a common American saying for the title, applicable to the college-educated poet who, if smart, in America should also be rich. Instead the speaker has nothing, except a sensibility that notes the color of marigolds in front of a garage door. In so spending his time registering beauty, he may be considered by some to have, as the poem concludes, "squandered every crying dime."

This poem also presents a theme Whalen returned to often in his poetry, the poet's survival in America, a society that does not particularly value poetry, at least not the experimental variety. The early poem, "Further Notice" (1956), attempts to validate an anti-conformist stance. Here the speaker compares himself to the buffalo and the American Indian and vows to continue to be both a "genius and an embarrassment." A later poem that celebrates the outsider status of Beat writers in general is "Chanson d'Outre Tombe" (1979). The poem begins with what society has claimed about the Beats, "that we was nowhere," and ends with the promise to chant from beyond the grave dug for them by reviewers, "wrecking your white expensive world."

Another important and related theme for Whalen was the relation of art to life, as evident in the early poem "All About Art and Life" (1959). Here the poet moves from the idea of art as a "compulsion," which separates him from his friends, to the idea that the artist can turn others "ON." "Homage to Rodin" (1960–1961) also addresses this issue, contrasting the speaker's comments on Rodin's sculpture with both the world he passes through and memories of a lover. Resolution and renewal are ultimately found through the contemplation of the art object.

With the passing of time, Whalen's poetry has become of interest not only in the context of the Beat revival but also for its **postmodern** qualities and affinity with **Language poetry**. He seemed less interested in a poetry constructed around a central, unified, and lyric voice. Instead, the many voices and unique tonal qualities of American speech that Whalen included in his poetry—his own voice, remembered voices, and found and heard sounds—play with and deconstruct a unified, central consciousness. He also shared the postmodern interest in disrupting narrative flow, foregrounding the language of the poem. However, Whalen differed from most other postmodernists in having Zen Buddhism as a philosophical basis for his deconstructions with its teaching that there is no unified self or ego in the state of enlightenment. From the Pacific Rim, Whalen participated in two great poetic traditions, Western and Eastern, perhaps his unique contribution to American letters.

Further Reading. ***Selected Primary Sources:*** Whalen, Philip, *Off the Wall, Interviews with Philip Whalen* (Bolinas, CA: Grey Fox Press, 1978); ———, *On Bear's Head* (New York: Harcourt Brace, 1969); ———, *Overtime* (New York: Penguin, 1999). ***Selected Secondary Sources:*** Christensen, Paul, "Philip Whalen," in *The Beats: Literary Bohemians in Postwar America,* ed. Ann Charters (Detroit, MI: Gale Research, 1983, 554–572); Davidson, Michael, *The San Francisco Renaissance* (Cambridge, UK: Cambridge University Press, 1989); Robertson, David, "The Circumambulation of Mt. Tamalpais" (*Western American Literature* [Spring 1995]: 3–27); Suiter, John, *Poets on the Peaks* (Washington, DC: Counterpoint, 2002); Thurley, Geoffrey, "The Development of the New Language: Michael McClure, Philip Whalen, and Gregory Corso," in *The Beats: Essays in Criticism,* ed. Lee Bartlett (Jefferson, NC: McFarland, 1981, 165–180).

Jane E. Falk

WHARTON, EDITH (1862–1937)

Edith Wharton, Pulitzer Prize winner and author of two volumes of poetry, *Artemis to Actaeon* (1909) and *Twelve Poems* (1926), published poems in such places as *Atlantic Monthly* and *Scribner's* long before she earned fame and considerable recognition for her fiction, with novels such as *The Age of Innocence* (1920) and *Ethan Frome* (1912). Whereas her fiction often depicts wealthy upper-class families and explores the romance and sexual awakenings of women of the nineteenth century, Wharton's poetry addresses loss, independence, and the sexual awareness of the feminine, as well as the representation of women of myth and history, often using historical or mythical figures in order to reshape and redefine the role of women.

Born to Lucretia Stevens Rhinelander and George Frederic Jones, Edith Newbold Jones entered the world on January 24, 1862, during the height of the American Civil War. She was the third and youngest child of an old and socially prominent New York family, whose wealth was acquired predominantly through Manhattan landholdings. However, due to a reduction in real estate values, the family moved to Europe in 1866, living well in such places as England, France, Italy, and Germany. In 1872 the family returned to the United States and established residence in both New York and Newport, Rhode Island.

As a child, Wharton was educated at home with private tutors and with open access to her father's extensive library. By the time she was sixteen, she was already composing a significant amount of poetry, and in 1878 her mother financed the publication of a private volume of her daughter's poetry, *Verses* (1878). One poem from the collection was published by **William Dean Howells** in the *Atlantic Monthly*, initiating Wharton's long publishing career. Between 1879 and 1880, Wharton published five poems in the *Atlantic Monthly* after **Henry Wadsworth Longfellow** expressed admiration for some of her early work.

The engagement between Edith Jones and Henry Stevens, the son of a prominent Newport family, was announced on August 19, 1882, in Newport's *Town Topics*. However, Stevens's mother withheld her approval and the engagement fell through. On October 28, *Town Topics* published a correction to the previous announcement, stating, "The marriage of Mr. Henry Stevens, Mrs. Paran Stevens's son, to Miss Edith Jones, which was announced for the latter part of the month, has been postponed, it is said, indefinitely." Gossip and rumors quickly followed the young woman's broken engagement until the Newport's *Daily Times* published a statement on the matter, claiming that the reason for the break between Stevens and Edith Jones was "an alleged preponderance of intellectuality on the part of the intended bride." "Miss Jones," the statement continues, "is an ambitious authoress, and it is said that, in the eyes of Mr. Stevens, ambition is a grievous fault."

Though scarred by the experience, Edith Jones soon met Edward Robbins Wharton, "Teddy," a Harvard graduate from Boston; a close friend of Edith's older brother, Harry Jones; and an adamant outdoorsman. Edward, however, had no money of his own and lived off of an annual two-thousand-dollar allowance from his parents. Still, in March 1885, *Town Topics* again announced an engagement for Edith. Soon after, Edward and Edith were married.

The Whartons traveled often to Europe, where they spent most of their time in Italy. In 1889 Wharton published poems in *Scribner's*, *Harper's* and *Century Magazine* and soon began publishing short stories. The couple then bought a New York townhouse and an estate in Newport. During this time, Wharton studied art and interior design. Wharton's interest in interior design and architecture prompted her to apply her writing talents to her newfound interest, and she collaborated with architect Ogden Codman to write *The Decoration of Houses* (1897). By 1898, however, Wharton had suffered both mental and physical breakdowns and was prescribed the "rest cure" under the supervision of the infamous Dr. S. Weir Mitchell. Wharton survived her breakdown as well as her "rest cure" treatment, and in 1899 she settled for four months in Washington, D.C., where she developed a close friendship with Walter Berry. During the same year, she published her short story collection *The Greater Inclination* with great success. In 1901 the Whartons bought property and had constructed a large house, "The Mount," in Lenox, Massachusetts. Wharton also published her second short story collection that year, *Crucial Instances* (1901); and in 1902 she published her first historical novel, *The Valley of Decision*. Within the same year, Wharton met Theodore Roosevelt, initiating a long friendship while she and her husband moved into "The Mount." Soon after, however, her husband suffered the first of a series of nervous collapses. Wharton often spent her time in both Lenox and England. As well, Wharton toured Sussex with Henry James. While at "The Mount," she enjoyed houseguests that included Brooks Adams, **George Cabot Lodge**, and a host of other distinguished guests.

Although her writing career was well under way, Wharton's marriage began to suffer. In 1908 Wharton reportedly began an affair with journalist William Morton Fullerton. In 1909 her husband admitted to embezzling money from Wharton's trust funds. During this time, Wharton published a collection of her poetry, *Artemis to Actaeon* (1909). Much later, in 1913, she was granted a divorce on the grounds of adultery.

Regardless of her personal strife, Wharton continued to publish fiction, including *The House of Mirth* (1905), *Ethan Frome* (1911), *The Reef* (1912), and *The Custom of the Country* (1913). She also published her third collection of poems, *Twelve Poems*, in 1926.

Wharton's interests hardly confined her to her prosperous writing career, however. In 1914 she traveled to North Africa and Spain. With great compassion for American soldiers during World War I, she established American Hostels for Refugees. During that same year, she was made Chevalier of the Legion of Honor, deciding to settle in Europe by buying a house in St. Brice-sous-Forêt, a village outside of Paris. Moreover, in 1923, Wharton became the first woman to receive an honorary doctorate from Yale University.

She published her autobiography, *A Backward Glance*, in 1934. In 1937 the author suffered a stroke. Unfortunately, Wharton's health failed to improve and two months later, on August 11, the world lost a literary giant when Wharton died at her home in St. Brice, France.

During her lifetime, Wharton was blessed by a rich array of friends, including Paul Bourget, Teddy Roosevelt, Howard Sturgis, Percy Lubbock, **Henry Adams**, and Bernard Berenson. Wharton received her primary recognition and applause as a fiction writer, and few scholars have examined her poetry at length. Her poems explore not only broader feminist themes and figures but also her own life.

Wharton's poetry is provocative in that it often interweaves story and allusion in order to explore the feminine persona, particularly stories of women and lovers who are frequently portrayed as bad or grotesque. Perhaps one of the most interesting of Wharton's poems is her Petrarchan sonnet, "Phaedra" (1898), wherein the infamous seducer and betrayer, Phaedra, speaks from her perspective beyond the grave to the gods. Phaedra, well known from the story of Hippolytus in both Seneca's *Phaedra* and Euripides's *Hippolytus* and later treated by French dramatist Jean Racine in *Phèdre* (1677), is the wife of Theseus and sister of Ariadne, who, during Theseus's absence, falls in love with her stepson, Hippolytus. However, as a devotee of the goddess Artemis, Hippolytus rejects her advances. Phaedra consequently hangs herself for shame, but only after writing a letter to Theseus condemning Hippolytus as her seducer.

Though Euripedes constructs Phaedra as a tragic and sympathetic character, subjected to her own passions and the fates, Wharton reaches beyond constructing the figure as one to be scorned or pitied by asserting her perspective as a passionate woman, unwilling to admit shame for her natural desire. Indeed, Phaedra announces herself as the "Last martyr of [her] love-ensanguined race," emphasizing that instead of characterizing herself as victim or villain, she instead identifies herself as a "martyr," dying by choice for the sake of passion. Furthermore, Phaedra describes the gods as "baffled" as to what exactly makes their triumph and her pain. Phaedra lists common outside perceptions of her state, answering the gods' queries with an assertive repetition of the word "not." Her repetition not only suggests that the common perceptions of Phaedra are wrong but also asserts her right to be passionate. She continues by stating that not even the death of Hippolytus causes her grief: "Not that I slew him!—yet, because your goal / Is always reached." The sonnet unfolds as a rhythmic declaration in which Phaedra disowns the perceptions of others in firm and definitive statements.

In the poem "Chartes," Wharton again champions a feminine figure, the Black Virgin. Written as a meditatio, Wharton visits the realms of memory, understanding, and will. However, unlike the traditional trinity presented by Saint Augustine, which proposes that the trinity of the meditatio is representative of God the Father, the Son, and the Holy Spirit, Wharton utilizes the form to venerate the Black Virgin of Chartes Cathedral.

Wharton's poetry often treats feminine figures in nontraditional ways, exploring the concepts of love, sensuality, and spirituality and providing a voice to both classical and contemporary female figures. Her exploration of the feminine in her writing frequently leads her to investigate stories wherein women are customarily portrayed as victims, complicating traditional perspectives. For example, in "Artemis to Acteon," she challenges the version presented by Ovid in his *Metamorphoses* by giving Artemis a voice through which to convey her plight. As a goddess, she has "man's wealth, man's servitude, but not himself"; hence, for "lack of warmth" she "wane[s]."

Although she may be best remembered as an innovative and provocative writer of fiction and nonfiction, Wharton's poetry is also indicative of her feelings about the female perspective. Wharton is one of the few authors in her day to address the complexities of womanhood and to challenge traditional perspectives of femaleness; she did so by revisiting traditional forms and figures.

Further Reading. ***Selected Primary Sources:*** Wharton, Edith, *Artemis to Acteon and Other Verse* (New York: Charles Scribner's Sons, 1910); ———, *A Backward Glance* (New York: D. Appleton–Century Company, 1934; New York: Scribner's, 1998); ———, *Twelve Poems* (London: Medici Society, 1926); ———, *Verses* (1878). ***Selected Secondary Sources:*** Bauer, Dale M., *Edith Wharton's Brave New Politics* (Madison: University of Wisconsin Press, 1994); Benstock, Shari, *No Gifts From Chance: A Biography of Edith Wharton* (New York: Scribner's, 1994); Lewis, R.W.B., *Edith Wharton: A Biography* (New York: Harper & Row, 1975); Lewis, R.W.B., and Nancy Lewis, eds., *The Letters of Edith Wharton* (New York: Scribner's, 1989); Wolff, Cynthia Griffin, *A Feast of Words: The Triumph of Edith Wharton* (New York: Addison-Wesley, 1977, 1995).

Maureen Anderson

WHEATLEY, PHILLIS (CA. 1753–1784)

Born probably in 1753, Phillis Wheatley was enslaved in Boston but became an internationally published poet while still in her teens. Her *Poems on Various Subjects, Religious and Moral*, published in London in 1773, was the first book-length collection of English-language poetry by an African American writer. That is not her only historical distinction. Much celebrated during her lifetime and often controversial since, she was also—following Anne Bradstreet—the second poet from Great Britain's North American colonies to publish poems that remain in print, continuing to attract significant critical and popular readership.

Abducted in West Africa and sold in 1761 at the Boston slave market, Phillis Wheatley was, as she herself later wrote, though fragile of health, a child "whose lot it was to fall into the hands of a *generous* master and *great* benefactor" (*Collected Works*, 191). She was purchased by John Wheatley, a wealthy merchant, as a present for his wife, Susanna; they thought the African girl would be a useful servant. Her intellectual ability was recognized immediately by the family. John Wheatley claimed that the girl learned English within sixteen months of her arrival and was soon able to read the Bible. Her studies would also include literature as well as texts in Latin. Wheatley was probably tutored in English by Mary Wheatley, one of the twins, who were six years older than Phillis. For Latin she would have required the instruction of J. Sewall, Mather Byles, or Samuel Cooper, all three of whom she knew intimately.

Writing poetry became Phillis's most important duty, superseding household chores. By all accounts Susanna Wheatley encouraged Phillis to write poems and helped get them published in newspapers throughout New England. Mrs. Wheatley also passed the young poet's work along to her correspondents in England. One of these was Selina Shirley Hastings, Countess of Huntingdon (1707–1791). The countess supported Rev. George Whitefield's work, employing him as her personal chaplain, and provided funds to support his evangelical ministry in the North American colonies and such projects as the Bethesda orphanage in Savannah, Georgia.

The evangelist died suddenly in 1770, a week after an appearance in Boston. It is likely that Whitefield was a guest in the Wheatley mansion and therefore that Phillis enjoyed verbal exchanges with this voice of the Great Awakening. Mrs. Wheatley forwarded Phillis's elegy for Rev. Whitefield to the Countess, who was pleased enough by the young poet's work to agree, eventually, to support the publication of a book of her verses. The elegy itself was extensively circulated in Britain and in America as a broadside, causing Wheatley to be recognized internationally as a poet. Wheatley prepared a manuscript of thirty-eight poems and eventually traveled to London in June 1773 for the publication of her book. Though she did not see the Countess of Huntingdon in person (Hastings was ill at the time), she did meet other luminaries, including the Earl of Dartmouth, abolitionist Granville Sharp, and American ambassador Benjamin Franklin. She received honors and generous gifts (e.g., five guineas from Dartmouth), enabling her to obtain bound copies of *Don Quixote* and the collected works of Alexander Pope. Brook Watson, MP, who, as a merchant, had visited New England and was apparently known by the Wheatley family, and who would become Lord Mayor in 1774, bequeathed Phillis a folio copy of John Milton's *Paradise Lost.* She was forced to cut the visit short, however, upon learning that Mrs. Wheatley was suffering a serious illness.

After the publication of her book and her return to Boston, by October 18, 1773, Phillis was granted her freedom but continued to serve Mrs. Wheatley until the elder woman's death in March of 1774, and she remained close to the family afterward. She also continued to write and publish poems. On April 1, 1778, she married a free African man named John Peters. Even after the American Revolution, however, free Africans had few opportunities for success in eighteenth-century Boston. The couple experienced extreme poverty and may have been forced to sell the handsome book collection Wheatley had brought back from her sojourn in London. According to a number of accounts, she herself took employment as a maid in a rooming house. The Peters had three children who all died in infancy. Soon after the birth of her last child, Phillis died on December 5, 1784; she was found holding her third child, also dead.

Wheatley's earliest works exhibit tremendous talent, and her later manuscripts demonstrate that she learned how to revise her poems effectively. Wheatley's first published poem, "On Messers. Hussey and Coffin," appeared in the *Newport Mercury* on December 12, 1767, and was written after Phillis, tending to her duties at table, overheard the dinner guests' tale of sailing out from Nantucket and being shipwrecked in a storm. While the exciting incident would impress any twelve-year-old boy or girl, what interested this poet was the state of the survivors' souls, whether they would find their home in the bosom of God or, rather, make "their Beds down in the shades below / Where neither Pleasure nor Content can flow" (*Collected Works*, 133). The orthodox Christian position is notable, but the reference to "the shades below" bespeaks Wheatley's career preoccupation with ancient classicism and her tendency to syncretize classicism with Christianity.

The attestation page included in Wheatley's *Poems on Various Subjects, Religious and Moral* (1773) was unique for its time. In the autumn of 1772, John Wheatley assembled a panel of dignitaries to conduct an oral examination to ascertain that Phillis was indeed the author of the poems published under her name. The status of the men on this jury attests both to John Wheatley's social eminence and to the seriousness with which he and his wife viewed the young woman's poetic activity. As Henry Louis Gates, Jr., has pointed out, the jury included the most prominent figures in Boston, including political leaders such as Thomas Hutchinson, the governor of Massachusetts; lieutenant governor Andrew Oliver; and James Bowdoin, who would also serve as governor of Massachusetts and founder of Bowdoin College. Prominent businessmen included John Hancock, signer of the Declaration of Independence and a wealthy merchant and city official who was also involved in litigation for protesting British colonial tax policies. Additionally, there were three poets—Rev. Mather Byles (a nephew of the famed Cotton Mather), Joseph Green, and Rev. Samuel Cooper (who had baptized Phillis in 1771). Rev. Andrew Elliot and businessman Harrison Gray were staunch opponents of slavery. Although some, like John Wheatley himself, would become loyalists, others would soon align themselves with the revolutionary cause. The group was, therefore, something of a cross-section of the colony's intellectual elite.

The neoclassical style that characterizes Wheatley's poetry valorized artifice, wit, decorous formality, and erudite allusion. The poetry of the late eighteenth century abounded in intellectual divertimentos, formal elegies, devotional expression, hymns, and philosophical arguments cast in rhymed couplets and traditional forms such as sonnets and odes. Wheatley mastered these forms and techniques not only by reading English poets such as Alexander Pope and popular Boston poets, but more particularly from her immersion in the work of such American colonial poets as Joseph Green, Joseph Seccombe, Samuel Cooper, and especially Rev. Mather Byles, whose 1744 *Poems on Several Occasions* served as the model for Wheatley's 1773 *Poems on Various Subjects, Religious and Moral.* Wheatley was also an excellent student of Latin and achieved a firsthand understanding of the modes that Byles and other poets had used. For example, Byles's 78-line biblical paraphrase of 1 Samuel 17 (the pericope of David and Goliath) becomes in Wheatley's hands a 222-line epyllion (short epic) that includes Christian machines (God and cherubim), interpolations of long speeches, and an 8-line invocation to the muse, none of which appears in the Bible or in Byles. Mentors such as Byles and Green clearly influenced Wheatley's choice of poetic style, though not her politics of revolution. Others in Wheatley's circle of acquaintance were sympathetic to the democratic and libertarian principles that informed the American Revolution—such persons as Samuel Cooper, John Hancock, and James Bowdoin, named previously. Wheatley developed a personal relationship with Rev. Samuel Occom, a Native American of the Mohegan nation who had become an evangelist and a graduate of Dartmouth College, which was founded as a college for Native Americans. According to John Wheatley's own testimony in the prefatory matter to the 1773 *Poems*, Wheatley's first correspondence was addressed to Occom in 1765 (*Collected Works*, 6). Later, Wheatley's letter to Occom of February 11, 1774, in which she delivers an emphatic and elegant declaration for freedom—"in every human breast, God has implanted a Principle, which we call Love of Freedom; it is impatient of Oppression and pants for Deliverance" (*Collected Works*, 177)—was widely circulated among colonial American newspapers (printed at least twelve times).

Although Wheatley was an excellent practitioner and skilled master of the neoclassical style, some readers have found her work overly imitative or impersonal. Thomas Jefferson, in *Notes on the State of Virginia* (1785), commented that her work lacked quality. It would have been surprising, though, if Jefferson—an Enlightenment intellectual and Deist philosopher as well as an astute politician—had praised a writer widely known in the early 1770s as "Phillis, the Christian Poetess" (*Collected Works*, 190). Indeed, several of Wheatley's early poems, which appear to have served as catechistical exercises designed to convince white readers that she was "good" enough to be baptized, were challenges to Deists and atheists. "To the University of Cambridge in New England," written in 1767, would certainly not have endeared her to Mr. Jefferson. In this poem, Wheatley chastises Harvard students for placing scientific studies ahead of religion and, revealing an ironic edge, warns the students to avoid sin:

> An *Ethiop* tells you 'tis your greatest foe;
> It transient sweetness turns to endless pain,
> And in immense perdition sinks the soul.

Average readers of the day would not have missed the implications of an African girl correcting Harvard scholars, just as Wheatley's admirers would have delighted in this situation.

One important aspect of Wheatley's popular appeal was the novelty of her precociousness, which was intensified by her race and gender. Wheatley was clearly aware of the implications of her work and the fact that she was, as Gates aptly says, "auditioning for the humanity of the entire African people" (27). More concerned with sales than with the Great Chain of Being, Wheatley's publisher also invested in the stereotypes of the day, advertising that her poem might be more expected from someone who "had the happiness of a liberal education than from one born in the wilds of Africa" (*Complete Works*, xviii). The fact of the matter is that, whether as an extraordinary expression of Christian charity or as a social experiment, a liberal education is exactly what Phillis Wheatley had.

The elegiac poem on George Whitefield that brought Wheatley international notice best exhibits her personal concerns and poetic skills. "The very act of choosing to write a poem on Whitefield is a political statement," argues Dwight A. McBride, "since he was known in colonial America and in England as a friend to the African" (McBride, 114). The poem is in four sections: a ten-line apostrophe to the deceased in rhyming couplets; a seventeen-line section that personifies the preacher and his sermon in metaphors of ascent ("He leaves the earth for heav'n's unmeasur'd height"); a ten-line stanza presented as if a verbatim quote from Rev. Whitefield's sermon; and two five-line stanzas of condolence addressed to the Countess of Huntingdon, ending the poem on a note of Christian faith in resurrection. The poem's proportions are both logical and elegant.

Wheatley's felicity of phrase and metaphor and careful management of meter and alliteration are superior to much that was being published in the period. Further, in the matter of content, this impressive performance reveals Wheatley's familiarity with Rev. Whitefield's sermons and demonstrates also why she, as an enslaved African, might have found his message particularly attractive. Christ is literally central in this poem. In the third section, Rev. Whitefield calls out to "the num'rous throng" gathered to hear him:

"Take him, ye *Africans*, he longs for you / *Impartial Saviour* is his title due." As elegies were a standard genre of the period, Wheatley wrote several more to mourn other church leaders, as well as relatives and children of acquaintances. As an achievement of perfectly balanced form and content, however, "On the Death of the Rev. George Whitefield" stands unquestionably higher than the rest. In Africa, elegiac dirges were the province of women; so we should not be surprised to discover that Wheatley composed eighteen extant elegies, her most frequently recurring genre.

Unlike the Whitefield elegy, few of Wheatley's poems refer explicitly to Africans. But these poems and letters were not casual productions and must be given close reading. Many contemporary critics follow Dwight A. McBride's interpretation of Wheatley's poetry and assume that, even though Phillis Wheatley *seems* at times to accept slavery, her writing represents a poetics of resistance to slavery, at the center of which is her Christian faith. McBride, like Sondra O'Neal, suggests that Wheatley found it necessary to write in a manner that would reach a white Christian readership, hence giving her an opportunity to express her viewpoint. As is evident in many of her poems, religion was her deepest concern.

Within days of October 18, 1773, John Wheatley manumitted Phillis, and she was soon offered an opportunity to travel to Africa as a missionary. In a letter to John Thorton (1720–1790), a Wheatley family friend in London, she speaks of gratitude to Mr. Wheatley for granting her freedom, but also writes, "If this had not been the Case, yet I hope I should willingly submit to Servitude to be free in Christ.—But since it is thus—Let me be a *Servant of Christ* and that is the most perfect freedom" (*Collected Works*, 184). Though this play on words offers conflicting possibilities of interpretation, nothing in the statement can be said to be an endorsement of slavery. If anything, the statement might best be described as a demand for *freedom* that recognizes different concepts of that word.

This letter also employs humorous exaggeration in declining an invitation to return to Ghana in West Africa with two other young male missionaries. "Upon my arrival," she jests, "how like a Barbarian Should I look to the Natives; I can promise that my tongue shall be quiet for a strong reason indeed being an utter stranger to the Language of Anamaboe" (*Collected Works*, 184). The three letters Wheatley wrote to Thorton as a group read like cleverly crafted refusals that carry a subtext of protest. In the first of the three, she asserts that both African Americans and Native Americans have found themselves to be "despised on earth on account of our colour" (*Collected Works*, 174). Given that Wheatley's personal idea of God was not strictly Christian but was a syncretized version of her beloved classicism, her mother's Islam combined with her hierophantic solar worship, and New England Christianity (see the analysis in *African-American Writers* II, 774–783), her efforts to appear strictly Christian to a powerful, white, British, evangelical philanthropist may be construed as a gesture of survival.

Wheatley's work was known to other literate Africans, including Jupiter Hammon, the enslaved poet in New York, who wrote "An Address to Miss Phillis Wheatley." Published as a broadside in Hartford, Connecticut, on August 4, 1778, the poem consists of twenty-one stanzas, each glossed with a Bible verse. Such a compositional plan seems logical since Hammon was a preacher as well as a poet. In stanza VI, meditating upon the statement in 2 Corinthians 5:10 that "we must all appear before the judgment seat of Christ," Hammon implores Christ to set Wheatley free from sin so that she might serve as a model of devotion and piety "to youth of Boston town" (O'Neale, 76). Hammon, born in the American colonies, lectures Wheatley, as a displaced African, to cast off heathenism (perhaps here addressing Wheatley's use of classicism in her poetry), cautioning his subject that it is through Christ that she has left "the heathen shore" and hopes that she will "Among the heathen live no more" (O'Neale, 77).

In Wheatley's poem "To the Right Honorable William, Earl of Dartmouth," an address to William Legge (1731–1801), she exploits the political measure of the word "freedom" as it circulated in some circles in pre-Revolutionary Boston. The poet, speaking for that community, hails Dartmouth as newly appointed secretary of state for the colonies. Because the new official was a patron of education who participated in philanthropic projects supported by the Countess of Huntingdon and the Wheatleys, Bostonians who had harbored grievances against the crown looked forward to more sympathetic treatment: "While in thine hand with pleasure we behold / The silken reins, and *Freedom's* charms unfold." These lines might express the political sympathies of Mary Wheatley, John Hancock, and others; but the poet now personalizes her dramatic message, describing her own trauma of living in Africa under "wanton Tyranny with lawless hand," before being "snatch'd from Afric's fancy'd happy seat." This poem presaged Wheatley's open and enthusiastic support of the coming Revolution. As might be expected from her familiarity with journals and newspapers, she understood the rhetoric of the revolution and the ideals that would be presented in the Declaration of Independence.

Wheatley's October 26, 1775, poem in praise of General George Washington was accompanied by a letter wishing "success in the great cause you are so generously engaged in" (*Collected Works*, 185). The poem is a careful neoclassical address, beseeching that heavenly beings—including the nation metaphorically personified, as if an ancient Greek or Roman goddess, under the name Columbia—attend the general and bring him victory. Wind, ocean, and indeed all of nature are in a state of excitement, and the poet merely joins in. On the day of expected triumph, the poet hopes to see the general awarded more than mere glory: "A crown, a mansion, and a throne that shine, / With gold unfading WASHINGTON! be thine!"

Replying with modesty, Washington wrote, "however undeserving I may be of such encomium and panegyric, the style and manner exhibit a striking proof of your poetical talents" (*Collected Works*, 304). Intended to rally support for the Revolutionary cause, the poem was published in April 1776 in Thomas Paine's *Pennsylvania Magazine* and brought Wheatley an invitation to visit General Washington at his headquarters in Cambridge, Massachusetts. She did so sometime in mid-March of 1776 and was received cordially as a free woman and patriot. Years later, in "Liberty and Peace" (1784), a broadside published under her married name, Phillis Peters, she cited her poem to Washington, celebrating victory. Pleased that "kind Heaven, indulgent to our Prayer / In smiling Peace resolves the Din of War," she also takes the opportunity to denounce tyranny and to mourn soldiers who have paid "with guiltless Blood for Madness not their own."

As a poet, Phillis Wheatley is notable for her technical precision and mastery of her age's dominant literary forms. Her elegy for Rev. George Whitefield has been seen by Dwight McBride and others as a political statement since the poem praised a religious figure who was close to those who supported progressive educational efforts for orphans, Native Americans, and African slaves. The poem found an encouraging audience in its own day; indeed, the wide newspaper publication of Wheatley's poem in the colonies and in England "made her the Toni Morrison of her times" (22), wrote literary critic Henry Louis Gates, Jr. Her elegy "On the Death of General Wooster" contains these inflammatory lines placed in the mouth of the dying general:

> But how, presumptuous shall we hope to find
> Divine acceptance with th' Almight mind—
> While yet (O deed ungenerous!) they disgrace
> And hold in bondage Afric's blameless race?

Wheatley's ultimately was a poetics of liberation. Despite Thomas Jefferson's negative assessment of her book, Wheatley was praised throughout the nineteenth century as an example of African American aptitude and the benefits of education. Her career and example suggested to her supporters that slavery, as practiced in North America and the Caribbean, tragically wasted the talents of men and women who might make great contributions to society if given the education and opportunity to do so.

Beginning in the Harlem Renaissance of the 1920s, some critics began to complain about the lack of explicit protest against slavery in Wheatley's verse. By the 1960s, this evaluation often resulted in the charge that Wheatley had been "brainwashed" or so deceived by religious fervor that she did not understand the cruelties of slavery. What was missing from this assessment, during the period from the 1920s through the 1960s, was any awareness of the 1774 letter to Occom and the elegy to David Wooster, just cited. The appearance of these two texts, in 1974 and 1975, brought about a dramatic reevaluation of Wheatley. Now her serious readers have discovered a dynamic subversive subtext in her work, a focus firmly on liberation. In the 1990s the critical approach was again modified when Wheatley began to be seen through a feminist lens and as an important figure in the context of a black transatlantic intellectual diaspora. Wheatley is, of course, a poet of her era. The neoclassical style allows her to employ irony, and her poetry's condemnation of hypocrisy and arrogance is appropriately modest. However, as Wheatley wrote in a letter to Rev. Samuel Occom on February 11, 1774, she was well aware of those activities "whose Words and Actions are so diametrically opposite" (*Collected Works*, 166–167), referring to the lip service paid by white people to the ideals of equality. Regardless of the critical perspective taken toward her work, there is no dispute that Phillis Wheatley represents the beginning of African Americans' participation in the nation's formal literary activity.

Further Reading. *Selected* ***Primary Sources:*** Carretta, Vincent, ed., *Complete Writings: Phillis Wheatley* (New York: Penguin, 2001); Mason, Julian D., Jr., ed., *The Poems of Phillis Wheatley*, 2nd ed. (Chapel Hill: University of North Carolina Press, 1989); O'Neale, Sondra, ed., *Jupiter Hammon and the Biblical Beginnings of African-American Literature* (Metuchen, NJ: Scarecrow Press, 1993); Robinson, William H., *Phillis Wheatley and Her Writings* (New York: Garland Press, 1984); Shields, John C., ed., *The Collected Works of Phillis Wheatley* (New York: Oxford University Press, 1988). ***Selected***

Secondary Sources: Bennett, Paula, "Phillis Wheatley's Vocation and the Paradox of the 'Afric Muse'" (*PMLA* 113.1 [January 1998]: 64–76); Gates, Henry Louis, Jr., *The Trials of Phillis Wheatley* (New York: Basic Books, 2003); Isani, Mukhtar Ali, "The British Reception of Wheatley's *Poems on Various Subjects*" (*Journal of Negro History* 66.2 [Summer 1981]: 144–149); Levernier, James A., "Style as Protest in the Poetry of Phillis Wheatley" (*Style* 27.2 [Summer 1993]: 172–193); McBride, Dwight A., *Impossible Witnesses: Truth, Abolitionism, and Slave Testimony* (New York: New York University Press, 2001); O'Neale, Sondra, "A Slave's Subtle War: Phillis Wheatley's Use of Biblical Myth and Symbol" (*Early American Literature* 21.2 [Fall 1986]: 144–165); Robinson, William H., ed., *Critical Essays on Phillis Wheatley* (Boston: G.K. Hall, 1982); ———, *Phillis Wheatley: A Bio-Bibliography* (Boston: G.K. Hall, 1981); Shields, John C., "Phillis Wheatley and Mather Byles: A Study in Literary Relationship" (*CLA Journal* 23 [June 1980]: 377–390); ———, "Phillis Wheatley's Subversive Pastoral" (*Eighteenth-Century Studies* 27.4 [Summer 1994]: 631–647); ———, "Phillis Wheatley," in *African American Writers* II, 2nd ed., ed. Valerie Smith (New York: Scribner's Sons, 2001, 773–792).

Lorenzo Thomas
John C. Shields

WHEELER, SUSAN (1955–)

Susan Wheeler's poetry attempts to mediate between the disjunctive, experimental mode of **postmodern** poetry since **Gertrude Stein** and the **confessional** domestic realism of the broadest band of American self-expression. Her poems, which began appearing in a variety of experimental and mainstream journals in the early 1990s, braid several strands of American postwar poetry, including the confessionals (through **Berryman**), the **New York School** (**Ashbery**, Schuyler, **O'Hara**, and inheritors such as **David Lehman** and **Joe Brainard**), and the **Language poets** of both the East and West coasts (especially **Bernstein**, **Hejinian**, and **Andrews**). These American ancestries, combined with flavors of Renaissance English and modern European poetry in translation, bespeak Wheeler's catholicity of derivation and effect. Wheeler's poetry has consequently found a large and eager audience (as evidenced by her poems' appearance in numerous volumes of *The Best American Poetry* series) sophisticated enough to enjoy and even expect jump-cuts, nonce words, arcane expressions, torqued verbals, slang, tonal monstrosity, and other shocking effects; but jaded enough by the dry excesses of pure linguistic experiment to crave a poetry that can express and contain emotion, however indirectly.

Wheeler was born in Pittsburgh, Pennsylvania, in 1955, and she grew up in small-town Minnesota and the suburbs of Boston and New York in the 1960s and 1970s. She received a BA in literature from Bennington College in Vermont (1977) and attended the University of Chicago from 1979–1981 to pursue postgraduate work in art history. The transition from the homogeneity of middle-class America to the vibrancy of voices in Chicago can be heard in Wheeler's pastiches of dialogue, tone, and vernacular expression. Chicago also exposed her to **jazz**—a music whose competing tempos energize her own verse—and to contemporary painting's concern with surfaces and representation. She married Philip Furmanski in 1991 and they established their home in New York City, where Wheeler joined the creative writing faculty at the New School for Social Research and at Princeton University. *Bag 'o' Diamonds* (1993), Wheeler's first book, was selected by **James Tate** to receive the Norma Farber First Book Award through the Poetry Society of America; her second book, *Smokes*, was selected by **Robert Hass** for Four Way Books in 1998. *Source Codes*, her third book, appeared in 2001 with Salt Publishing. Wheeler had two more books published in 2005, *Ledger* and *Record Palace*, a novel.

Probably the most important contribution of Wheeler's poetry is its resolute attachment to emotion, voice, and statement in the face of Language poetry's broad critique of these elements of the linguistic status quo. What Wheeler derives from Language poetry is the awareness of linguistic artifact, the voice print juxtaposed to the computer printout, the ability of the language itself to generate startling effects, surreal statements perfectly "normal" in context, and an almost limitless palette of competing tones and perceptions. In *Bag 'o' Diamonds*, Wheeler's poems slyly celebrate the persons we have become, persons who say such things as "*Damn it, Graw, you've got the sponge / on the wrong side of the ketchup bottle. / Have not shithead*" ("Debates"). Further, Wheeler's poems do not, by adding forward emotional thrust, undermine the ability of such a pastiche aesthetic to subvert the self's normalization of experience. If this is "normal," it comes at a price: "The senses they forego, / stapling each thumb in place, for a long campaign."

Wheeler is perhaps the first of a generation now being called the Elliptical poets, poets whose roots are as deep in the dandyism of **Wallace Stevens** as in Gertrude Stein's program to liberate words from stultifying syntactical convention; poets who derive their force from the cryptic compression of **Emily Dickinson**, the cankered desperation of John Berryman, the aesthetic clarity of perception in **Elizabeth Bishop**, and the refusal to resolve the chord in David Lehman's early poetry. Ellipticals also owe a great deal to the New York School's integration of European surrealism, pop art, and everyday life in kaleidoscopic perception, pronoun shifting, and other performances of a self at home somehow in displacement. As

Wheeler remarks in "Clock Radio," a poem in *Smokes*, "Its drive is for the offbeat, the cack-handed, the apocopated. It sings with regret for its thrum."

Stylistically all over the map, sourced from Burton's *Anatomy of Melancholy* to Francis Ponge's French **Objectivism**, Wheeler's poetry restlessly turns over period furniture in the key of **John Cage**. She mines the voice as much as the dictionary, aleatory forms as well as traditional forms just corrupted enough to be serviceable. Upon its publication, *Source Codes* became Wheeler's most ambitious and perhaps riskiest book; its poems forgo titles and are listed by number and source instead. For instance, "Ten" is derived from Burton and turns out to be a randomized sampling of his prose: "Every lover admires his mistress / eyes / look like a squis'd cat." Three appendices include drafts for the poems in the book, drafts for poems in *Bag 'o' Diamonds*, and a run of HTML. It is unclear whether the HTML is to be read as computer language (reportedly, it is missing vital syntax), fractured English (in which case it may represent a demented Robert Burns's wistful instructions to his mouse: "startmoving . . . keepmoving . . . stopmoving"), or as an abstract entity in itself, a comment on the sources of linguistic action. Perhaps Wheeler's singular insight is that words do, in fact, animate as well as represent a reality and that in this most vibrant period in the history of English, comparable to the efflorescence of the Renaissance, these invented and demented ways of speaking and seeing come closest to succor and truth.

Further Reading. ***Selected Primary Sources:*** Wheeler, Susan, *Bag 'o' Diamonds* (Athens: University of Georgia Press, 1993); ———, *Ledger* (Iowa City: University of Iowa Press, 2005); ———, *Record Palace* (St. Paul, MN: Greywolf Press, 2005); ———, *Smokes* (Marshfield, MA: Four Way Books, 1998); ———, *Source Codes* (Cambridge, UK: SALT Publishing, 2001). ***Selected Secondary Sources:*** Burt, Stephen, "Smokes" (*Boston Review* [Summer 1998]); Keller, Lynn, "Susan Wheeler's Open Source Poetics," in *American Poets in the 21st Century: The New Poetics*, ed. Lisa Sewell and Claudia Rankine (Middletown, CT: Wesleyan University Press, forthcoming); Ramke, Bin, "Enhanced and Instrumentalized Looking: Poetry as/and Visual Art" (*American Letters and Commentary* [2003]).

Melanie Hubbard

WHEELWRIGHT, JOHN (1897–1940)

John Wheelwright, scion of a Boston Brahmin family and founding member of the Socialist Workers Party, produced complex, contradictory poems in a voice so genuine as to sweep readers past confusion and doubt into, if not clarity, a heartbreaking sense of trust in the writer's passionate beliefs. He died early but was accorded significant status in the last quarter of the twentieth century, most notably by **John Ashbery**, who addressed Wheelwright's life and work in a Harvard Norton Lecture, saying, "He is a poet from whom one takes a great deal on faith, but one does it voluntarily. His conviction is contagious" (72).

Wheelwright was born in 1897 in Milton, Massachusetts; his mother was from a wealthy merchant family, and his father was a noted architect whose works include many public buildings in Boston. Wheelwright grew up in Europe and on the maternal estate at Medford, sold during his lifetime to developers. When he was in his mid-teens, writing poetry at St. George's prep school in Newport, Rhode Island, his father had a breakdown and committed suicide. This tragedy led the young Wheelwright into religious conversion, turning him from Unitarianism to Anglicanism, but his years at Harvard (1916–1920) found him at the center of the Harvard Aesthetes, with S. Foster Damon (later his brother-in-law), Robert Hillyer, **e.e. cummings**, John Dos Passos, and Malcolm Cowley. Although he was expelled from Harvard for cutting classes, his work was included in the anthology *Eight More Harvard Poets* (1923). He then spent two years in Europe, publishing and working as an editor for the magazine *Secession*. Financial disasters at the onset of the Great Depression sent him home to his mother on Beacon Street. He maintained appearances, dressing in sleek suits, bowler hat, and Malacca cane, and carried along fourteen pairs of shoes through Europe. In later life, he attended socialist meetings in a full-length raccoon coat. Matthew Josephson recalls the blonde, blue-eyed poet's thin, long-legged figure, with a prominent nose inherited from his mother. Europe had provided some adventures, as did Boston, with romance and sexuality, but Wheelwright's temperament seems to have been unsuited to success in love. What most inspired his imagination were his sense of outrage at injustices and his hope for a Promethean leader among the workers. In his ancestral city, he pursued a double course of religious heresy and political radicalism that led him finally out of orthodox Christianity and into the Socialist Party, Trotskyism, and the Rebel Arts Society.

A pamphlet, *North Atlantic Passage* (1925), was privately printed in Florence and was then reprinted in *Rock and Shell* (1933), his first collection, which, with *Mirrors of Venus: A Novel in Sonnets* (1938), was published for him by Bruce Humphries, Boston. The well-received *Rock and Shell* includes "Why Must You Know," an exquisite lyric that demonstrates, according to Ashbery, Wheelwright's perfect balance of clear mystery, cold passion, and warm intelligence: "'One who turns to earth again / finds solace in its weight; and deep / hears the blood forever keep / the silence between drops of rain.'" *Mirrors of Venus*, a sequence of thirty-five sonnets, eulogizes human friendship and abandons hope of

Christian immortality, linking Ned Couch, a Harvard friend killed in World War I, with Wheelwright's father, also named Ned: "Ned. Ned. / Snow on a dome, blown by night wind." In *Political Self-Portrait* (1940), "Bread-Word Giver" celebrates the radical Puritan Rev. John Wheelwright (ca. 1592–1679), the poet's ancestor: "make our renunciation of dominion / mark not the escape, but the permanent of rebellion." But in 1940 Wheelwright died at age forty-three in an automobile accident, on the threshold of major recognition for the power and originality of his work. The posthumous *Selected Poems* (1941) offered some unpublished pieces and promised that more poems would appear later, but despite Wheelwright's important literary connections, *Collected Poems* (1972) did not appear for over thirty years. It includes his last collection, *Dusk to Dusk*, finished just before the poet's death, with poems dedicated to such notable writers as **Archibald MacLeish**, **Allen Tate**, **Howard Nemerov**, Horace Gregory, and **James Laughlin.** A "novel" of poems, including "Twilight" in *Rock and Shell* and "Morning" in *Dusk to Dusk,* retells the story of Doubting Thomas, Wheelwright's favorite saint.

Wheelwright's wrestling with language to illustrate his exquisite perceptions, to illuminate the convictions of a mind under tremendous pressures of meaning, produced poems of nearly mathematical elegance and eccentricity. **R.P. Blackmur** praises the poems' disparities in their quick associative progressions, but the chaotic surface irritated and confused some. One early critic wrote that "he leaves the mind in a state bordering on collapse": Wheelwright endorsed this assessment enough to include it in a self-published brochure advertising his work (Ashbery, 71). Though Wheelwright would have labeled such critics Philistines, in fact he eschewed what he called the nihilism of apolitical poetry and the disengagement of surrealism, as in "To Wise Men on the Death of a Fool," a **eulogy** warning against the choices of the aesthete Harry Crosby. One may live for art, but should not try to live art. While Wheelwright's breadth of intellect and his religious and revolutionary agendas add to the magnificent difficulties of his poetry, the work offers not only gorgeously complex soundscapes but also greatness of spirit: As he recorded in an unpublished notebook, "The only art worth bothering with" is not one "that adorns and softens life but art which is at once a benediction and a judgment." He believed poets, like priests, should serve society as ethical guides; many find his poems dazzling with visions, authority, and urgency worthy of Revelations.

Not only does Wheelwright's poetry seem less daunting for readers today than when it first appeared, but its agonized themes also are more relevant than ever. His late philosophic poem "Train Ride," with its haunting refrain "Always the enemy is the foe at home," speaks with most eloquent clarity to contemporary America.

Further Reading. ***Selected Primary Source:*** Wheelwright, John, *Collected Poems of John Wheelwright*, ed. Alvin H. Rosenfeld (New York: New Directions, 1983). ***Selected Secondary Sources:*** Ashbery, John, *Other Traditions* (Cambridge, MA: Harvard University Press, 2000); Wald, Alan M., *The Revolutionary Imagination: The Poetry and Politics of John Wheelwright and Sherry Mangan* (Chapel Hill: University of North Carolina Press, 1983); Warren, Austin, *New England Saints* (Ann Arbor: University of Michigan Press, 1956).

Rosanne Wasserman

WHITMAN, SARAH HELEN POWER (1803–1878)

Sarah Helen Whitman was one of the most versatile and intellectually wide-ranging literary women of the nineteenth century. Recognized by her contemporaries as a skillful poet and translator, a significant critical voice, a spiritual and philosophical explorer, and a vehement champion of women's rights, universal suffrage, educational reform, and animal rights, among other causes, Whitman is perhaps most famous to literary historians as "Poe's Helen." The distinction arises from her friendship with, and brief engagement to, **Edgar Allan Poe** in 1848 and from the series of poetic flirtations that each published in the popular **literary magazines** of the day. Though Whitman herself encouraged and cultivated the association with Poe (and with Poe's memory), it has often had the effect of obscuring her own literary accomplishments and contributions, particularly to **feminist poetics** and gender-writing in America. Whitman published two volumes of verse, *Hours of Life and Other Poems* (1853) and *Poems* (1879) and numerous critical essays on contemporary poetics, social issues, and philosophical movements, as well as an important personal and literary defense of Poe in *Edgar Poe and His Critics* (1860).

Sarah Helen Power was born on January 19, 1803, in Providence, Rhode Island, to Nicholas and Anna Marsh Power. Her father, though a successful merchant, lost his fortune during the War of 1812 and was captured at sea by British forces. Upon release, Nicholas Power chose to remain at sea, abandoning his family as well as his legal and financial obligations. Though her family struggled to survive without a husband and father, Sarah Power managed to receive a standard education for young ladies of the time, including study of the classics, geography, history, astronomy, and languages. Unlike many young ladies, however, Sarah developed a particular interest in the works of Byron and the Romantics, and began writing similar verses of her own. In 1828 she married John Winslow Whitman, a lawyer, poet, and editor of the *Boston Spectator*, in which she published some of her early poetry under the name "Helen." After a short and apparently unhappy marriage, John Whitman died in 1833, leaving Sarah Whitman, once again, without the support of a male provider. As before, Whitman flourished—this time as a poet and essayist, as well as a frequent contributor to popular anthologies. She became an advocate of Transcendentalism and later explored a number of radical philosophical and social movements, including Fourierism, Unitarianism, and Spiritualism. Whitman's affinity for radical philosophies and her literary defenses of such controversial figures as Shelley, Byron, Goethe, and, of course, Poe, mark her, along with **Margaret Fuller**, as one of the most independent and liberal female intellectuals of the day. That liberal spirit continued to the end of her life, when she publicly defended such notions as "free love" and divorce. Though her poetry was, by the latter half of the century, known only to a relatively small circle of literati, Whitman retained her status as an important mentor, critic, and biographer of Poe. Sarah Helen Whitman died on June 27, 1878, in Providence, Rhode Island, at the age of seventy-five.

Whitman's early poetry follows many of the conventions of nineteenth-century **sentimentality** and Romantic nature poetry, with an emphasis on the spiritual affinity between the natural world and the individual imagination. Such poems typically feature solitary figures—often women or children—seeking spiritual and emotional comfort in an imagined communion with nature or, more rarely, with other sensitive spirits. Such were the "Sonnets" that Whitman famously dedicated to Poe, celebrating the "mystic converse" that she felt would transcend even their earthly deaths (*Hours of Life* [1853]). Most of this writing is distinctly melancholic in tone, though it is a melancholy tinged with idealism, spiritual aspiration, and earthly sensuality, much like the Romantic poets that she so admired. Whitman does have more playful moments, particularly in those poems dedicated to friends and family, such as "Apple Blossoms" (1861) and "A Pat of Butter" (1877). Whitman's later poetry moves away from her Romantic origins and tends toward more philosophical and social concerns. She retains, though, an abiding interest in the power of imagination and memory to transcend the limitations of mortal life, and, perhaps, to reconcile us to earthly losses, as in these lines from "Night Wanes" (1861):

> Be patient, O my heart; look through the gloom
> Of the sad present, look through all the past,
> And learn how, out of sin and death and doom,
> And mournful tragedies, august and vast,
> The world's great victories are achieved at last.

Although Whitman, like most sentimental poets, has often been dismissed by critics as derivative, Eliza Richards (1999) argues that the strategy of "lyric mimicry" is in fact central to Whitman's uniquely social poetics (one strongly influenced by her spiritualist beliefs), in which "emulation operates as a mode of spiritual communion" (270). Far from detracting from her own genius, Whitman sees such echoing as the most powerful testimony to a shared vision of aesthetic and moral transformation.

Whitman's most influential contribution to literary history remains her vehement defense of Poe's reputation against the slanders of his executor, Rufus Griswold. In *Edgar Poe and His Critics* (1860), Whitman contends that Poe, like other geniuses of his age, had a "peculiar mission" in the world—one that "represents, or rather anticipates, with more or less of consciousness and direct volition, those latent ideas which are about to unfold themselves in humanity" (60). Though Whitman was motivated by her love and admiration for the man and a genuine belief in his prophetic status, recent critics have suggested that Whitman's own reputation and literary legacy are as much at stake in her defense of Poe as his own (Baker [1999]). As a woman of great ambition, imagination, and social vision in her own right, it is not unlikely that Whitman sees her own "peculiar mission" as comparable, though not identical, to that of the great male poets she frequently championed.

Further Reading. ***Selected Primary Sources:*** Miller, John Carl, ed., *Poe's Helen Remembers* (Charlottesville: University of Virginia Press, 1979); Whitman, Sarah Helen, *Hours of Life and Other Poems* (Providence, RI: George H. Whitney, 1853); ———, *Edgar Poe and His Critics* (New York: Rudd & Carlton, 1860); ———, *Poems* (Boston: Houghton, Osgood and Company, 1879). ***Selected Secondary Sources:*** Baker, Noelle A., "'This slender Foundation . . . Made me Immortal': Sarah Helen Whitman vs. Poe's Helen" (*Poe Studies/Dark Romanticism* 32.1–2 [1999]: 8–26); Richards, Eliza, "Lyric Telegraphy: Women Poets, Spiritualist Poetics, and the 'Phantom Voice' of Poe" (*Yale Journal of Criticism* 12.2 [1999]: 269–294); Ticknor, Caroline, *Poe's Helen* (New York: Scribner's, 1916); Varner, John Grier, "Sarah Helen Whitman: Seeress of Providence" (Ph.D. diss., University of Virginia, 1940).

John Edward Martin

WHITMAN, WALT (1819–1892)

Walt Whitman, author of *Leaves of Grass*, was one of America's most innovative and influential poets. He devoted his career to defining and enacting a new poetics that would be distinctive to the American nation and its democratic aspirations. His impact was such that virtually all American poets after him have in some way been forced to engage him—to build upon his ideas of what an American poet should be or to argue against those ideas and push off from him in a different direction. "I make a pact with you, Walt Whitman," wrote **Ezra Pound** in "A Pact" (1913), noting, "It was you that broke the new wood, / Now is a time for carving." Twentieth-century poets have carved the wood Whitman broke into a dizzying variety of shapes, but, as Pound grudgingly admitted, it usually has been Whitman's original material with which American poets after him have worked. His influence has extended far and wide, across race and social class and ethnicity and poetic style. Poets as diverse as **Hart Crane**, **Carl Sandburg**, **T.S. Eliot**, Michael Gold, **Wallace Stevens**, **Langston Hughes**, **Muriel Rukeyser**, **William Carlos Williams**, **Allen Ginsberg**, **Robert Creeley**, **June Jordan**, **Gary Snyder**, **Adrienne Rich**, and Rudolfo Anaya have all talked back to Whitman eloquently and directly, as they extend, refine, rewrite, battle, endorse, and sometimes reject the work of the writer who strove so insistently to define national identity, to speak with an open democratic voice, and to imagine an inclusive society.

Whitman's influence has extended well beyond poetry. He has been examined seriously by political scientists and cultural theorists as a philosopher of democracy; his work has been set to music by over five hundred composers, more often than that of any other American poet; he has been the subject of, and inspiration for, paintings and sculptures by American artists from Thomas Eakins to Ben Shahn; and he has inspired the architects Louis Sullivan and Frank Lloyd Wright, photographers like Alfred Stieglitz and Edward Weston, and filmmakers from D.W. Griffith to Jim Jarmusch.

Walt Whitman was born into a working-class family in West Hills, New York, a village near Hempstead, Long Island, on May 31, 1819. His father, Walter Sr., was of English stock, his mother, Louisa Van Velsor, was of Dutch and Welsh heritage; this mix led to what Walt always considered a fertile tension in himself and his siblings between a brooding Puritanical temperament and easier-going Dutch disposition. When Walt was a young boy, his father moved the family to the growing city of Brooklyn, across from New York City, or "Mannahatta" as Whitman would come to call it in his celebratory writings about the nation's emerging major urban center. Whitman attended the newly founded Brooklyn public schools for six years, but most of his meaningful education came outside of school, when, often crossing over to Manhattan on the Brooklyn ferry, he visited museums, went to libraries, and attended lectures by speakers like the radical Quaker leader Elias Hicks.

Through with school at age eleven, he began his life as a laborer, working first as an office boy for some prominent Brooklyn lawyers, who gave him a subscription to a circulating library, where his self-education began. In 1831 Whitman began a series of apprenticeships at newspaper offices, where he learned the printing trade and was first exposed to the excitement of putting his words into print for thousands of readers; his first signed piece appeared in the fashionable New York *Mirror* when he was fifteen. Those early years in Brooklyn and New York on his own—the rest of his family had moved back to Long Island—remained a formative influence on his writing, for it was during this time that he developed the habit of close observation of the ever-shifting panorama of the city, and a great deal of his journalism, poetry, and prose consisted of catalogs of urban life and the history of New York City, Brooklyn, and Long Island.

By the time he was sixteen, Whitman's future career seemed set in the newspaper and printing trades, but then two of New York's worst fires wiped out the major printing and business centers of the city, and, in the midst of a dismal financial climate, Whitman briefly rejoined his family in rural Long Island. Rebelling at his father's attempts to get him to work on the new family farm, he took a series of itinerant teaching jobs in at least ten different Long Island towns. These were some of the unhappiest years of his life: He missed the excitement of Brooklyn and New York, and the isolated towns and unenlightened people depressed him. But his teaching style was progressive; he rejected corporeal punishment, engaged his students with games like "twenty questions," and read them his own poetry, which at the time was quite conventional romantic verse. His interactions with these young people had a lasting impact on his work: His greatest poem, "Song of Myself," is generated by a child's wondering question, "What is the grass?" and "A Child Went Forth" is a testament to Whitman's fascination with the infinite capacity of children to absorb and learn.

After a failed attempt to start his own newspaper on Long Island, and after taking some time to work for Martin Van Buren's presidential campaign, Whitman in 1841 returned to New York City to resume his career in printing and journalism, as well as to try his hand writing fiction. In the early 1840s, Whitman's fiction appeared in over ten different newspapers and magazines, including several stories in the prestigious *Democratic Review*, and in 1842 he published a temperance novel, *Franklin Evans*, as an extra to *The New World*. Although some of the concerns of *Leaves of Grass* are traceable in Whitman's fiction, most of the volume, like his early poetry, lacks the innovation and radical experimentation of his later work. In 1845 he moved to Brooklyn, where he edited the Brooklyn *Daily Eagle* and earned widespread respect as a journalist who wrote about a wide range of civic and cultural issues, including slavery. Whitman subscribed to "free-soil" ideas, opposing the spread of slavery to the new western territories (in large part because he believed slavery denigrated and devalued white labor) but stopping short of endorsing the abolition of slavery in Southern states. Whitman's views on this subject got him in trouble with the pro-slavery owner of the *Daily Eagle*, and Whitman lost his job in 1848.

Acting impulsively on an unexpected offer to edit the New Orleans *Daily Crescent*, Whitman abruptly left with his young brother Jeff for Louisiana, where for three months he experienced Southern culture, witnessed slave auctions, and absorbed the multilingual mix of the Creole city. His sojourn there would have lasting effects, from his love of mixing occasional French terms into his poetry to his powerful evocation of the slave market in "I Sing the Body Electric" to his portrayals of the South in poems like "I Saw in Louisiana a Live-Oak Growing." His round-trip included a steamboat ride up and down the Mississippi River, giving Whitman his first glimpse of the vast expanse of the growing nation that he would catalogue so frequently in *Leaves of Grass.* Once back in Brooklyn, Whitman founded and edited a free-soil newspaper, but he quit in 1849 and tried out several different occupations, including house building, job printing, and running a bookstore. He continued writing freelance newspaper pieces, but during these years leading up to the appearance of the first edition of *Leaves of Grass* in 1855, he mostly gave himself time to read, to write incessantly in the small notebooks he always carried with him, and to allow his roiling ideas to evolve. In a burst of creative energy, still discernible in the notebooks he left behind, he discovered his revolutionary new vehicle, a long-lined **free verse** organized by a vast and absorptive "I" who would speak for all of America in a brash and nondiscriminating voice.

Whitman's notebooks and surviving manuscripts reveal the intensity and fluidity of the development of his poetic style. Images, phrases, and whole lines of what would become *Leaves of Grass* can be found in his prose jottings, and only a year or two before *Leaves* appeared, Whitman was unclear what shape—even what genre—his new expression would take: In one notebook from the early 1850s, where prose lines appear that would later take their place in the poetry of *Leaves*, Whitman writes "Novel? Work of some sort / Play? . . . Plot for a Poem or other work . . . A spiritual novel?" Still thinking of himself as a fiction writer, Whitman initially thought his new work might take that form. Some of his other notes indicate he thought his ideas would best emerge as speeches, and he imagined going on the lecture circuit. Only gradually do the notebooks edge toward his discovery of his poetic line, but once that discovery comes, he moves quickly toward his finished book. The **line** becomes his basic unit; as a professional typesetter, he was used to thinking of lines of type as movable units, and as a poet, he tended to revise by rearranging entire lines. Some early manuscripts are composed of lines that would later appear in *Leaves*, but that are arranged in an entirely different order. Throughout his career, he would continue to revise by literally cutting and pasting lines in new arrangements.

In July of 1855, Whitman took his still-in-flux manuscript to his friends the Rome brothers, who ran a small print shop in Brooklyn and specialized in printing legal documents. Setting some of the type himself, Whitman chose a large legal-sized page, so that the first edition of *Leaves*, with its bold typeface and rough finish, looks like what it in fact is: a declaration of **literary independence**, a proclamation of a new kind of literature fit for a new democracy. He omitted his name from the title page, intensifying the sense of the book as a public document. He included as a frontispiece an engraving of himself in laborer's garb, with his hat on, staring at the reader with a challenging look. The portrait is unlike any previous frontispiece representation of an author: The full-body pose, with the torso as the center of focus, suggests that *this* poetry emerges not just from the intellect but furthermore from the experience of a body at work in the world, hat on, shirt open, ready to be inspired and ready also to perspire.

At the last minute, Whitman added a prose preface to the book, defining the new American poet. He composed the preface by culling from his notebooks passages where he had theorized about the nature of a new poetry, and he connected these statements with his idiosyncratic ellipses, avoiding standard punctuation for a more loose and fluid syntax controlled by a variable number of dots, the same eccentric punctuation he would use in the poetry itself. Following the preface were twelve poems, the first six all called "Leaves of Grass," the last six untitled. Since he was paying for the publication, he squeezed the last six poems tightly onto the page so that he would not have to pay for an extra signature. He printed 795 copies, stopping the press a couple of times to correct errors and once to change an entire line, and then had the pages bound on three different occasions in progressively cheaper bindings.

The opening poem took up forty-three pages, beginning with "I celebrate myself, / And what I assume you shall assume," and ending with "Missing me one place search another, / I stop some where waiting for you." This **long poem**, which Whitman would title "Poem of Walt Whitman, an American" in 1856, "Walt Whitman" in 1860, and finally "Song of Myself" in 1881, became his best-known work, an epic of American individualism, setting out to expand the boundaries of the self to include all of one's fellow Americans, then the entire world, and ultimately the cosmos. Whitman keeps probing the question of how large the self can become before it dissipates into contradiction and fragmentation, and each time he seems to reach the limit, he dilates even more: "My ties and ballasts leave me . . . I travel . . . I sail . . . my elbows rest in the sea-gaps, / I skirt sierras . . . my palms cover continents, / I am afoot with my vision." Cataloguing a huge array of urban and country scenes, portraying people at work in myriad occupations, incorporating vast geographical stretches, redefining life and death as one continuous and evolving dynamic process, Whitman's "I" takes the reader on a dizzying journey through religions, American history, and geological and biological evolution, absorbing everything and rejecting nothing. His plea is for his readers to learn to accept and live in plurality, difference, and contradiction, which he defines as the necessary democratic condition: "Do I contradict myself? / Very well then . . . I contradict myself; / I am large . . . I contain multitudes."

Whitman's two great characters in this poem are "I" and "you." The "I" becomes a model voice of American democracy, indiscriminate in its acceptance of people, ideas, and experience, discriminating against nothing but discrimination itself. The "you" becomes an open-identity space the reader is invited to occupy. Translators of *Leaves* often note that the "you" is impossible to capture in other languages, because Whitman plays on the peculiar nature of the English second-person pronoun—an all-purpose word that can indicate singular or plural, formal or informal. It is possible to hear the "you" in *Leaves* as addressed to the entire nation or the entire world, and it is also possible to hear it as intimately addressed only to the individual reader in this particular moment of encounter. "Song of Myself" opens with "I" and ends with "you," and the poem enacts a transfer of absorptive energy from poet to reader, the latter of whom by the final lines is sent off alone to continue the journey the poem began. The journey is one of liberation, and Whitman's concern with slavery is everywhere evident in this first edition, from the way the "I" identifies with a captured slave ("I am the hounded slave, I wince at the bite of the dogs") to the highly charged moment in the poem he would later call "The Sleepers" when the "I" turns the narration of the poem over to an incensed slave whose wife and children have just been sold down the river ("I hate him that oppresses me, / I will either destroy him, or he shall release me / Damn him! how he does defile me"). The whole book plays on chattel slavery as a cultural metaphor for the various kinds of enslavement—religious, economic, moral—from which all readers must craft an escape.

Once the first edition of *Leaves* was printed, Whitman immediately began a thirty-five-year process of rethinking and revising his book: "As long as I live the Leaves must go on," he once said. The result is a textual nightmare for anyone studying the evolution of *Leaves* from 1855 to Whitman's final deathbed edition. He would add and delete poems; combine, revise, and retitle them; and cluster them in different arrangements. *Leaves of Grass* is not so much a single, changing book as it is a series of at least six different books, each with the same title, but each responding to a particular set of biographical and historical circumstances, and each structured in radically different ways. To add to the complexity, each edition had multiple issues, with each issue containing significant differences—different covers, different illustrations, even different contents. Whitman, late in his life, began to think of the different editions almost as individual children: "They all count," he said. "I don't know that I like one better than any other." Three of the editions (1855, 1856, and 1860) are antebellum and three (1867, 1871–1872, and 1881) postbellum. The three editions after the Civil War struggle with absorbing Whitman's haunted war writings while retaining the celebratory sense of the first three editions, which set out to absorb and embrace the nation's differences.

Whitman had become friendly in the 1850s with the publisher, social reformer, and phrenologist Lorenzo Fowler, who gave Whitman's skull bumps a generous reading, finding him to be a man of large appetites. Fowler's firm, Fowler and Wells, had distributed the first edition, and in 1856 they took on the publication of Whitman's second edition of *Leaves*, though they withheld their name from the title page. For this edition, Whitman added twenty new poems to the original twelve. But as the book grew in the number of poems, it shrank in page size; the paper for this edition is less than half the size of that of the first edition. The new size indicates Whitman's changing attitudes toward his book and toward the goals he had for his work. He gave up the spacious pages that would easily accommodate his long and flowing lines in order to get a pocket-size edition, something more akin to a devotional book than a proclamation. His dream now was to have working people carry his poetry with them to work and read it during breaks. About a thousand copies of this edition were printed.

It is in this edition that we most clearly see **Ralph Waldo Emerson**'s influence on Whitman. Whitman owed a great deal to Emerson, whose essay "The Poet" seemed in many ways to prophesy the poet Whitman became (some critics have argued that Whitman simply modeled himself on Emerson's essay). Whitman reportedly said that by the mid-1850s he was "simmering, simmering, simmering; Emerson brought me to a boil," and this edition is the most furious roiling of the waters. Whitman here prints the supportive letter that Emerson had sent him after reading the 1855 *Leaves*, prints his own twelve-page response to Emerson (addressing him as "Master"), and brazenly features Emerson's name and endorsement—"I greet you at the beginning of a great career"—on the spine of the book. In his letter to Whitman, Emerson had praised *Leaves* for its "wit and wisdom" but neglected to refer to the work as poetry, and, as if to set the record straight, Whitman now underscored the genre that he had decided to claim for himself: He titled every one of his thirty-two pieces in the new edition "Poem" ("Poem of Women," "Sun-Down Poem," "Poem of the Road," and so on), and he began his open letter to Emerson by referring to his,

Whitman's, work as "poems" seven times in the first paragraph.

Two of Whitman's greatest poems first appeared in this edition: "Poem of Wonder at the Resurrection of the Wheat" (later titled "This Compost") and "Sun-Down Poem" (later called "Crossing Brooklyn Ferry"). The first poem explores the poet's deep faith in the process of composting, the idea that all of life is a resurrection out of death, an unending cycle of things breaking down to their elements, out of which new creations are made. The speaker worries about how the earth can absorb so much death and not become poisonous, but the poem comes to celebrate the "chemistry" that turns that death back into life, that "grows such sweet things out of such corruptions." Here is the ecological mystery that lies behind *Leaves of Grass* and explains the book's title: The leaves of grass are the first sign of new life emerging from the graves of the dead, the proof that there is no such thing as death. Whitman would often address his poems to readers who would be living decades or centuries after he was dead, and his faith was that his own *Leaves of Grass* would, like the organic leaves, be the sign of ongoing identity after his physical demise. "Sun-Down Poem" would be his great testament to the power of his poetry to transcend time and space, to allow the poet, living in his present when the poem was written, to communicate with a reader who was not yet born when the poem was written: "We understand, then, do we not? / What I promised without mentioning it, have you not accepted? / What the study could not teach—what the preaching could not accomplish is accomplished, is it not?" All the preaching about the afterlife could not be as effective as this poem's actual *demonstration* of an afterlife, as the living poet talks intimately to the unborn reader, as the living reader responds to the dead poet.

In the years following the 1856 edition, Whitman continued his sporadic work with Brooklyn newspapers and began frequenting Pfaff's beerhall, a bohemian hangout on Broadway, where he socialized with Henry Clapp, editor of the *Saturday Press*, who became a great supporter of the poet, and other radical writers and artists. He worked hard on revising and expanding *Leaves*, and in 1860, with the country heading inexorably toward war, Whitman's poetic fortunes took a sudden positive turn. He received a letter from the Boston publishers William Thayer and Charles Eldridge, whose aggressive new publishing house specialized in abolitionist literature; they wanted to become the publishers of the new edition of *Leaves of Grass*. Whitman, feeling confirmed as an authentic poet now that he had been offered actual royalties, readily agreed, and Thayer and Eldridge invested heavily in the stereotype plates for Whitman's idiosyncratic book—over 450 pages of varied typeface and odd decorative motifs, a visually chaotic volume all carefully tended to by Whitman, who traveled to Boston to spend his days with the typesetters and oversee the printing. Emerson came in from Concord to see Whitman and tried to talk him out of including his new "Enfans d'Adam" cluster of poems (later "Children of Adam"), which celebrated sex in remarkably direct terms ("O hymen! O hymenee! Why do you tantalize me thus?"; "It is I, you women, I make my way, / . . . I pour the stuff to start sons and daughters fit for these States, I press with slow rude muscle"). Emerson worried that the poems would sensationalize the book and blind readers to the wisdom there, but Whitman argued that sex was central to his vision and that to cut the sex out of *Leaves* would be to destroy it.

There was another new cluster in the book, one that Emerson did not comment on: "Calamus," a group of poems that quietly explored male-male affection. Deriving from a sequence of poems that Whitman uncharacteristically left only in manuscript, called "Live Oak, with Moss," these poems seem to trace a love affair between the poet and a young man, sometimes identified as Fred Vaughan, a friend of Whitman in the 1850s. But there is little biographical evidence beyond the poems themselves. In order to create his "Calamus" cluster, Whitman rearranged the "Live Oak" poems and supplemented them with other new poems; the sequence caused little reaction at the time, though toward the end of Whitman's life and throughout the twentieth century, these poems would come to be read as Whitman's admission of or endorsement of homosexuality. In recent decades, they have been read as a courageous early articulation of gay identity. Whitman described the poems as his most political; in an age of advancing U.S. capitalism, Whitman realized that something would have to offset the fierce competition that males were increasingly taught was crucial to their success. Whitman's solution was what he called "camaraderie," an intense affection between men that would temper competition and bind the nation through love. Democracy could not thrive, he believed, in a brutal competitive economic environment: men needed to learn to love each other for the republic to endure.

The 1860 *Leaves*, carrying this innovative message of men loving men, appeared in May 1860, less than a year before the outbreak of the Civil War. Whitman had put the date "1860–61" on the title page of this edition of *Leaves*, and the broken date proved prophetic, since it marked the transition between a troubled but still unified nation and a nation fractured. Suddenly, Whitman's "Calamus" poems took on a greater urgency as American men began killing other American men, fathers sons, sons fathers, brothers brothers. Whitman stayed in New York until the end of 1862, continuing to go to Pfaff's, but also visiting hospitals where wounded soldiers were already being brought from the battlefields. When he learned that his brother, George, had been wounded in the battle of Fredericksburg, he went to Virginia to check on him, and in another characteristically impulsive move, he simply abandoned New York and settled in Washington, D.C., so that he could be at the political heart of the war.

During the next two years, Whitman lived in a series of rooming houses, worked as a clerk in the Army Paymaster's office, served as a correspondent for New York newspapers, and almost daily visited the ubiquitous war hospitals that filled the nation's capital. He once estimated that he visited up to 100,000 wounded soldiers, for whom he would write letters, run errands, provide treats, and offer comfort. Still keeping notebooks, he jotted down the battlefield stories the young soldiers told him. Out of those notes emerged a series of poems about the Civil War, unlike any poems he had written before—quieter, more somber, with a more subdued "I" who now witnessed and observed and nursed and listened: poems like "A Sight in Camp in the Daybreak Gray and Dim," capturing the thoughts of a soldier-persona as he lifts the blankets off the faces of three dead comrades, finding "the face of the Christ himself," with the suggestion that each anonymous death in this war was the crucifixion of a soul as valuable as any in history. Whitman had written some early Civil War poems when he was still in New York, but these had been boisterous recruitment poems—like "Beat! Beat! Drums!"—almost giddy in their excitement over the impending war. After he had seen the battlefield at Fredericksburg and the pile of amputated limbs outside the battlefield hospital there, his tone changed, and poems like "The Wound-Dresser" (originally called simply "The Dresser") turned the war inside out, shifting our attention from the battlefield to the hospital, from heroic deeds in battle to the horrific after-effects of those battles: "The crush'd head I dress, (poor crazed hand tear not the bandage away,) / . . . (Come sweet death! Be persuaded O beautiful death! / In mercy come quickly)." Death, cast in the earlier *Leaves* as a vital part of the composting process, churning up new life, was now putting Whitman's compost-faith to its sternest test, as nearly a million young Americans decomposed in the soil, rivers, and seas of the North and South. Out of this vast compost, Whitman realized, America would have to grow its future.

His extraordinary hospital service took a toll on Whitman's own health. He took sick leave for the last half of 1864 and returned to his mother's house in Brooklyn, where he continued to write short war poems, some of them based on newspaper accounts of battles. He returned to Washington in early 1865 in time for **Lincoln**'s second inauguration and took a new job as a clerk in the Indian Bureau of the Department of the Interior. He now turned his attention to *Drum-Taps*, his book of poems about the war. This book, another self-published one, was almost entirely set in type when Lincoln was assassinated. He quickly added a brief poem, "Hush'd Be the Camps To-Day," acknowledging the assassination, and bound a few copies before deciding to put the publication on hold so that he could absorb the ending of the war and the momentous events surrounding it.

That summer he wrote two of his best-known poems, "O Captain! My Captain!" and "When Lilacs Last in the Dooryard Bloom'd," both **elegies** to Lincoln. The first was written in conventional meters and rhymes, perhaps capturing the voice of a sailor imagining the loss of Lincoln in terms of a ship losing its captain. The second poem is one of the greatest elegies in the language, beginning with a complex evocation of the moment the poet first heard of the assassination: Whitman was with his mother in Brooklyn and went outside to her dooryard where the early lilacs were in bloom; inhaling deeply out of his grief, his senses registered the smell of lilacs and forever bound that aroma with Lincoln's death and the deaths of all the soldiers of the war. The poem—with its talismanic images of the drooping evening star and the hidden thrush that sings, from deep in the swamp, a death carol the poet must translate into lasting language—becomes Whitman's great statement of faith in the composting process. Following Lincoln's death train across the blooming spring landscape of America, the poem is finally drawn deep into the swamp, the very site of composting, and the poet finds there "retrievements out of the night," fragments on which he will build a future, based on the natural fact that the lilacs will continue to bloom in the annual cycle of renewal, carrying in their aroma the memory of death bound always to the hope of a fresh beginning. He would even go back to his 1856 compost poem, which he named "This Compost" in 1867, and poignantly add a half-line to his long catalogue of nature growing out of death: "the lilacs bloom in the door-yards."

Whitman printed a "Sequel to Drum-Taps" containing these two elegies along with other late Civil War poems, including his powerful call for a national healing, "Reconciliation," in which he kisses the corpse of his enemy, trusting again in the powerful process of compost: "Beautiful that war, and all its deeds of carnage, must in time be utterly lost; / That the hands of the sisters Death and Night, incessantly softly wash again, and ever again, this soil'd world." On the title page, he dated the sequel "1865–6," marking another transitional moment in American history, the break between the last year of the Civil War and the first year of reconciliation.

The "Sequel" marks the end of Whitman's great poetic output. He would continue to write for the next twenty-five years, and he would produce a few memorable poems like "Passage to India" (1871), with its increasingly global concerns, along with innovative and important prose works like *Democratic Vistas* (1871), his meditation on the failures of and hopes for American democracy, and *Specimen Days* (1882), his self-described "wayward, spontaneous, fragmentary book" that contained his previously published *Memoranda During the War* (1875–1876), a prose account of his encounters with soldiers during the last years of the conflict. But his major poetry was now behind him.

In 1865 Interior Secretary James Harlan dismissed Whitman from his job, and, although Whitman was quickly hired in the Attorney General's office, the firing became a national scandal thanks to Whitman's passionate friend and supporter, William Douglas O'Connor. O'Connor, a government worker and writer, was outraged at Harlan's actions and was sure that Whitman was the victim of Harlan's conventional and cramped morality. Harlan had found Whitman's working copy of the 1860 *Leaves* in his desk and was shocked at some of the language. O'Connor wrote a diatribe against Harlan and called it *The Good Gray Poet: A Vindication* (1866), portraying Whitman as a kind of saint because of his service in the Civil War hospitals and extolling the "intellectual and moral grandeur of this work." Whitman soon *became* the Good Gray Poet, less and less the radical and outrageous artist and more and more the sage old prophet.

After the war, Whitman became very close to a young former Confederate soldier named Peter Doyle, who became Whitman's regular companion for years. He now devoted more and more of his time to rearranging and revising what he had already written. He was particularly concerned with absorbing the Civil War into *Leaves of Grass*, and he began doing that with the 1867 edition, a cheaply printed version, into many copies of which he sewed *Drum-Taps* as a kind of appendix. In 1870 he published another edition (dated 1871) with major rearrangements and with the *Drum-Taps* poems now fully absorbed into *Leaves*. Whitman had thought of starting a new book, called *Passage to India*, that would be a book of the soul to balance the emphasis on the body in *Leaves*, but once again he decided that *Leaves* was large enough to contain it all, and so in the 1870 edition, he bound in *Passage to India* as an annex.

The year 1873 was Whitman's worst year. He suffered a stroke, followed quickly by the death of his mother, and he went to Camden, New Jersey, where his brother, George, lived. As abruptly as he left New York for D.C., he now left Washington behind and took up residence in Camden, first with his brother and then in a small house of his own. It was in Camden that he worked on *Specimen Days* and his 1881 edition of *Leaves*, where he achieved the final ordering of his poems and created the version that most readers after his death would come to know. After 1881 he would add poems to *Leaves*, but only as annexes; he would never rearrange the poems of the main book or have them reset in type again. The 1881 edition was published in Boston by the prestigious firm of James R. Osgood, but the book was immediately attacked by moral reformers in the city and was ruled obscene and banned from the mails. Osgood tried to get Whitman to expurgate the book; when the poet refused, Osgood transferred the plates to Whitman, who had the book printed in Philadelphia, which became his publishing home for the rest of his life. Fueled by the banned-in-Boston scandal, sales of *Leaves* were more robust than ever before.

Living in very modest surroundings in a dirty industrial city, visited by a growing number of disciples from the United States and abroad, and steadily declining in health, Whitman continued appending poems to *Leaves* up to his death in 1892, including some moving brief poems focusing on his aging body. The final version of his book, in paper covers, was brought to him for his inspection on his deathbed. He was buried in Camden's Harleigh Cemetery, in a tomb he himself designed. Over the door are two words, "Walt Whitman."

Further Reading. ***Selected Primary Sources:*** Whitman, Walt, *The Collected Writings of Walt Whitman*, 25 vols., ed. Gay Wilson Allen et al. (includes *The Correspondence of Walt Whitman*, vols. 1–6, ed. Edwin Haviland Miller [New York: New York University Press, 1961–1977], vol. 7, ed. Ted Genoways [Iowa City: University of Iowa Press, 2004]); ———, *Daybooks and Notebooks*, 3 vols., ed. William White (New York: New York University Press, 1977); ———, *The Early Poems and Fiction*, ed. Thomas L. Brasher (New York: New York University Press, 1963); ———, *The Journalism*, 2 vols., ed. Herbert Bergman, Douglas A. Noverr, and Edward J. Recchia (New York: Peter Lang, 1998–2003); ———, *Leaves of Grass: Comprehensive Reader's Edition*, ed. Harold W. Blodgett and Sculley Bradley (New York: New York University Press, 1965); ———, *Leaves of Grass: A Textual Variorum of the Printed Poems*, 3 vols., ed. Sculley Bradley, Harold W. Blodgett, Arthur Golden, and William White (New York: New York University Press, 1980); ———, *Notebooks and Unpublished Prose Manuscripts*, 6 vols., ed. Edward F. Grier (New York: New York University Press, 1984); ———, *Prose Works 1892*, 2 vols., ed. Floyd Stovall (New York: New York University Press, 1963–1964). ***Selected Secondary Sources:*** Allen, Gay Wilson, and Ed Folsom, eds., *Walt Whitman and the World* (Iowa City: University of Iowa Press, 1995); Erkkila, Betsy, *Whitman the Political Poet* (New York: Oxford University Press, 1980); Folsom, Ed, *Walt Whitman's Native Representations* (New York: Cambridge University Press, 1994); Folsom, Ed, and Kenneth M. Price, eds., *The Walt Whitman Archive* (www.whitmanarchive.org); Kummings, Donald D., and J.R. LeMaster, eds., *Walt Whitman: An Encyclopedia* (New York: Garland Press, 1998); Loving, Jerome, *Walt Whitman: The Song of Himself* (Berkeley: University of California Press, 1999); Reynolds, David, *Walt Whitman's America* (New York: Knopf, 1995).

Ed Folsom

WHITTIER, JOHN GREENLEAF (1807–1892)

For more than half of his long life, John Greenleaf Whittier was known—and often vilified—as a controversial editor and Quaker spirit roused by the abolitionist movement to anger and ceaseless poetic activity to restore dignity to all people. Like Samuel Johnson, Whittier regarded as an offense to God and humankind the notion that one person could own another. After the Civil War brought an end to slavery, Whittier gave voice in such works as *Snowbound* and *The Tent on the Beach* to his lifelong love of nature and his fascination with events that had shaped his native New England. If his early work helped bring manumission to American slaves, then his later work enabled him to reach the apogee of fame as a poet. Whittier's eightieth birthday occasioned a national celebration, including a testimonial book signed by the majority of U.S. senators and representatives and by the entire bench of the Supreme Court, as well as by other dignitaries such as Frederick Douglass and James G. Blaine. Whittier is remembered today mainly for such **sentimental** lyrics as "The Barefoot Boy," "Maud Muller," and "Barbara Freitchie," and sometimes he is even considered the poet of a bygone way of life. In his time, though, Whittier's was a uniquely American poetic voice—the voice of freedom and equality, of the natural beauty of his native New England, and of the richness of the American heritage—and for the last thirty years of his life, Whittier was a poet whose works were known and loved almost everywhere.

Whittier was born in 1807 near Haverhill, Massachusetts. His family's Quaker faith taught him that all human beings are created equal; as well, it informed the fervor of his abolitionist poetry and the gentleness of tone that would characterize many of his lyric utterances. In 1826 Whittier's sister, Elizabeth, sent one of his poems, "The Exile's Departure," to the *Newburyport Free Press*, then edited by **William Lloyd Garrison**, and by 1828 Whittier had published nearly 150 poems. A year later, Garrison secured for Whittier the editorship of the *American Manufacturer*. In the 1830s Whittier began to devote his exclusive editorial and poetic attention to the abolitionist movement, fully aware that in so doing he might well be cutting himself off from both editing a major newspaper and becoming a poetic voice of the American people. Along with **James Russell Lowell**, **Henry Wadsworth Longfellow**, **Ralph Waldo Emerson**, and **Oliver Wendell Holmes**, Whittier in 1857 founded the *Atlantic Monthly*, in part to publish the abolitionist views of its founders and of many other northern intellectuals who by this time had begun openly to favor the cause of abolitionism. The passage of the Thirteenth Amendment in 1865 ended both slavery and the cause to which Whittier had devoted so much psychic and poetic energy. Whittier turned his poetic attention to reminiscence of his New England boyhood in *Snowbound* (1866), the first poem to bring him lasting fame and financial security. This poem was followed by the similarly successful *The Tent on the Beach* (1867). At the time of his death in 1892, Whittier was remembered not only as a pillar of the victorious abolitionist movement but also as a poet of national stature who spoke for the dignity of the common person.

Whittier's revulsion at human slavery and his commitment to its abolition are apparent in hundreds of his poems that appeared in newspapers and magazines all over the eastern states. That he was victimized several times by mob violence and his Philadelphia newspaper office burned down intensified Whittier's visceral sense of injustice and strengthened his resolution to oppose slavery with all the forces at his disposal. In "To William Lloyd Garrison" (1832) Whittier tells Garrison, "Thy very wrath from pity grew, / From love of man thy hate of wrong." Like Garrison, Whittier believed that America had become the subject of "the Christian's scorn, the heathen's mirth" because she seemed unable to respond to the national disgrace of "Slaves, crouching on the very plains / Where rolled the storms of Freedom's war!" ("Expostulation").

Whittier's "Pastoral Letter" (1837) denounces clergy who refuse to discuss controversial topics for fear of dividing their congregations or exposing women to unpleasant truths. His "Massachusetts to Virginia" (1843) takes up the case of George Latimer, insisting that Massachusetts remain free of slavery and, with considerable prescience, anticipating the Fugitive Slave Act (1850), the Dred Scott case (1857), and the secession that began the Civil War. The final lines sum up Whittier's position: "No slave-hunt in our borders,—no pirate on our strand! / No fetters in the Bay State,—no slave upon our land!"

"Texas" (1844) and "To a Southern Statesman" (1846) attack John C. Calhoun for advocating the admission of new slave states. "Ichabod" (1850) laments Daniel Webster's support for the Compromise of 1850 and, more generally, the error of placating exponents of a morally indefensible cause in the hope of preserving civil concord. As late as 1880, Whittier was still returning to this important theme:

> Thou should have lived to feel below
> Thy feet Disunion's fierce upthrow;
> The late-sprung mines that underlaid
> Thy sad concessions vainly made. ("The Lost Occasion")

In *The Pennsylvania Pilgrim* (1872), Whittier presents his most developed argument for an inclusive philosophy and, in his description of **Daniel Pastorius**, offers his most attractive and compelling picture of someone who translated that philosophy into practical action.

Deeply imbued with the spiritual traditions of the medieval Friends of God, Pastorius in the 1690s had sought to establish an ideal community in a woodland Pennsylvania setting. Whittier's poem recalls Thomas Gray's "Elegy Written in a Country Churchyard" because Whittier's Pastorius values a godly life and an unblemished conscience more than what Gray calls "the boast of heraldry, the pomp of power, / And all that beauty, all that wealth e'er gave." Whittier's aim is to offer to the memory of Pastorius "the garland which his meekness never sought."

Whittier's tribute to Pastorius reflects clearly his own passionate commitment to the anti-slavery movement and, more generally, to a vision of social justice in which all human beings possess a native dignity that must be recognized and lifted up. As described in Whittier's poem, Pastorius's home in Germantown, though removed from the urban setting, is no hermit's cell but rather the meeting place at which all types of people gather. Included among such guests are "Indian chiefs with battle-bows unstrung" and even "the black boy . . . by the hearth." Pastorius's learning and personal faith lead him to see unity where others see only difference, and, respecting his inclusive vision, guests put aside their quarrels when they visit Pastorius's home, where his spiritual vision unites them as members of the human family. For Whittier this spiritual vision possesses powerful appeal because it seemed to transcend the Puritan faith familiar to him from his earliest memories. A xenophobic narrowness, Whittier believed, lay behind Puritan persecution of those who believed and lived differently. The result of this persecution, he said elsewhere, was to dissolve in acid the Christian pearl of charity.

By contrast, Pastorius's faith allowed him to live among "many-creeded men" without becoming either a zealot or a trimmer. To men "frozen in their creeds like fish in winter's pool," Pastorius conducted himself with respect and dignity. Whittier's conviction that narrow creeds emphasize individual purity only by endorsing hurt to others, a major theme in *The Pennsylvania Pilgrim,* informs earlier poems as well. "St. John" (1841) describes events from 1647 in which Protestants and Catholics use creedal differences to justify killing one another for temporal possessions. "Mary Garvin" (1856) minimizes the deeds of a woman who went to dwell among the Indians: "Creed and rite perchance may differ, yet our faith and hope are one." On a more positive note, "The Exiles" (1841) tells the story of the Quaker Thomas Macy's clash with a sheriff and a Puritan preacher because he will not give up to their bigotry a man to whom he has extended hospitality. "Marguerite" (1870) describes events of 1760 that led to the relocation of Acadian peasants to Massachusetts, where they were bound to do forced labor. In this poem, Marguerite's "hard-faced mistress" denounces her as "the Papist, the beggar, the charge of the town." Her son, by contrast, sees Marguerite as an angel. As she dies, he kisses her and "words the living long for he spake in the ear of the dead."

Pastorius's commitment to human dignity, Whittier contends, led him at once to respect the values of the community in which he lived and, if need be, to quietly ignore that community. In one episode of Whittier's tribute, Pastorius laments that his friends refuse to oppose slavery, supposedly because they respect authority and wish to live for God alone, but really, Pastorius recognizes, because they are selfish and afraid. Anna Pastorius, counseling patience, conjures up the day when "slave and slave-owner shall no longer meet, / But all sit equal at the Master's feet." Pastorius respects Anna's quiet faith but continues to offer assistance to fugitive slaves—and Anna, despite her earlier counsel, joins him. When "the human hunter" comes in search of a runaway slave, Anna mounts a delaying action while Pastorius "speed[s] the black guest safely on his way." Whittier's decision to embrace the abolitionist cause may have owed much to Pastorius's conviction that time, itself morally neutral, would never put an end to slavery. At the same time, Whittier's account of Pastorius clearly reflects his own belief that God used human efforts and human hands to work for social justice.

The cause for which Whittier worked so hard was won with the ending of the Civil War, and Whittier turned to the poetry of memory and nature, producing his best-known poem, "Snowbound." Immediately arresting is the initial "mute and ominous prophecy" of snow, the need to bed down the farm animals before the snow makes outdoor work impossible, the "whirl-dance of the blinding storm," the lightless next day, the roar of the nearby sea as it is roiled by the east wind, and the transformative power of the storm—in all, a masterful piece of scene painting. The isolation created by the storm is palpable: No church bells ring, no one works outside for long, and even the running brook cannot be heard. In contrast to this silent, frozen world is the sudden blaze that causes "the old, rude-furnished room / Burst, flower-like, into rosy bloom." Whittier's power here to contrast the white cold of the outdoors and the rosy warmth of the room rivals the juxtaposition of "black purgatorial rails" and passionate "argent chivalry" in Keats's "Eve of St. Agnes."

From this contrast of setting, the speaker's mind wanders to the alterations wrought by time—only Whittier and his brother, Matthew, are still living, a perception that opens out into a long Tennysonian affirmation:

> Yet Love will dream, and faith will trust,
> (Since He who knows our need is just,)
> That somehow, somewhere, meet we must.
> . . .

Who hath not learned, in hours of faith,
The truth to flesh and sense unknown,
That Life is ever lord of Death,
And Love can never lose its own!

Then follow what Whittier calls "Flemish pictures of old days." Whittier's father tells such stories of old New England as one might find in "Sewel's ancient tome" or "Chalkley's Journal, old and quaint." After referring briefly to his Uncle Moses ("innocent of books") and to his unmarried aunt is (a serious contrast to Oliver Wendell Holmes's jocular treatment in "My Aunt"), Whittier mentions his elder sister and then launches into a powerful tribute to his beloved younger sister, Elizabeth Hussey Whittier, once his close companion and a poet of note in her own right who is "now bathed in the unfading green / And holy peace of Paradise." Acknowledgment of Elizabeth's recent death prompts a graceful meditation on the passage of time and an affirmation that one day he will again experience Elizabeth's nurturing presence:

And when the sunset gates unbar,
Shall I not see thee waiting stand,
And, white against the evening star,
The welcome of thy beckoning hand?

Whittier's apparent reverie turns finally to such an assertion of urgency as one sees in his anti-slavery poems, yet Whittier has sounded a note heard more insistently in his later poetry, in which value lies in looking back upon yesterday "with the few who yet remain." There is an almost Wordsworthian sense that past "spots of time" offer perspective and sanity to the person beset by urgent present causes. These expressions affirm what Whittier's social conscience and religious convictions affirm: the value of perspective and tradition as standards against which to measure actions in the present to identify those that are most just and most right.

The last forty years of the century saw an increased interest in cultures outside the New World. Henry Wadsworth Longfellow had been hard at work on a translation of Dante's *Divine Comedy,* and he and James Russell Lowell had been teaching Dante to a small but determined group of Harvard University students. The legends of Northern Europe had also received increased attention, one mark of which was Francis James Child's work on what eventually would be *The English and Scottish Popular Ballads.* Most illustrative of this varied narrative interest is Whittier's *The Tent on the Beach* (1867). Whittier originally planned to imitate the *Decameron* by having each poet read her or his own poem, but he abandoned this idea in favor of a modified version in which a "lettered magnate" (**James T. Fields**), a "free cosmopolite" (**Bayard Taylor**), and Whittier camp on the beach, watching sisters, brothers, lovers, carters, fishers, hunters, schooners at sea, and the distant fort and lighthouse, the latter providing with its light the first signal that day is waning. Gradually their observation of passing local characters slips into an exchange of stories about far-off time and places.

Two poems from this collection, "The Wreck of Rivermouth" and "The Changeling," both look back to Eunice Cole, who was arraigned as a witch in 1680. In "The Wreck of Rivermouth," Goody Cole mutters ominously to a group about to set off on a nautical jaunt that going out to sea is easier than coming back. The inevitable storm arises, and Goody weeps and exclaims, "Lord forgive me! my words were true!" But no one sees how conscience-stricken she has become. At the funeral, she exclaims, "Lord forgive us! we're sinners all!" But what she says falls on deaf ears, partly, we are led to believe, because the inbred faith of the community demonizes Goody because she is different—a mumbling, eccentric, lonely old lady, not a church-going family woman. "The Changeling" addresses more directly the belief that infected early New England. In this poem, Anna Favor becomes convinced that witches have stolen her baby and left in its place an ugly changeling that, when it nurses, sucks her blood. Believing that the witches will restore her baby if she endangers theirs, Anna prepares to set the changeling in the fire. In response to her husband's prayers for her healing, Anna suddenly looks down at the baby, sees it smile, and knows that it is her own child and not a changeling at all. Only after this happens do we learn that Anna, in her madness, had procured Goody Cole's imprisonment on a charge of witchcraft. Now she seeks Goody's release. But the case is exceptional, not normative. The poem does not suggest that this superstitious, witch-hunting culture has been permanently altered for the better.

Two other poems from this collection embody Whittier's continued interest in Native American legend. "The Maids of Attitash" describes two young women by Attitash Lake who think about their future husbands. One seeks riches, the other love. The maid who sought riches finds that love and riches are one and that the other maid, who sought love first, is now also rich. "The Grave by the Lake" is more substantial and, like **Philip Freneau**'s "Indian Burial Ground," muses on the equality of all people in death and the implied irony that this equality is too seldom recognized in life. The poem opens out into an extended meditation on the legions of numberless dead whose identities are lost to us, but it then concludes with an affirmation that the dead are not lost to God, who loves everyone equally, regardless of creed.

"The Brother of Mercy" transports the listeners from "the land of hackmatack and pine" to the fields of Tuscany. The porter Piero Luca is dying after a lifetime of good works. To the monk who consoles him with the prospect of living a life of endless ease in Heaven, Piero objects that this sounds like the lazy excuse of someone who is using his reward as an excuse to avoid helping the needy. The monk departs, totally scandalized, but an angel blesses Piero: "For heaven is love, as God himself is love; / Thy work below shall be thy work above."

"Kallundborg Church" is set on an island in the Baltic Sea. The Lord of Nesvek promises his daughter to Esbern Snare only if he will build a church at Kallundborg. Snare consults a troll, who tells him that he will do the job, but that if Snare cannot name him after the church is built, Snare will have to forfeit his heart and eyes. As the church nears completion, Snare, feeling doomed, laments, "I have sinned, O Helva, for love of thee!" However, "more than spell of Elf or Troll / Is a maiden's prayer for her lover's soul," and the troll knows that something is countering his evil intention. At this point, Snare hears the troll's wife singing underground to her baby, "Tomorrow comes Fine, father thine," who will bring Snare's eyes and heart for the baby to play with. Armed with this information, Snare names and defeats the troll. Later at night, harvesters hear the troll blaming his sobbing wife for having divulged his name in an unguarded moment. The Kallundborg Church still stands, and Zealand fishers still hear the troll scolding his wife.

Looking back on Whittier's poetic career, one sees that his commitment to the anti-slavery movement led him to publish poems wherever he could, preferably newspapers or magazines that would permit him to reach the largest number of readers. One result of this practice was that Whittier's books were to some extent afterthoughts. As early as 1843, the publishing firm of Ticknor and Fields issued *Lays of My Home, and Other Poems,* a collection of Whittier's previously published verse. In 1849 B.B. Mussey and Company issued the first comprehensive edition of Whittier's poems, following up this commercial success in 1850 with Whittier's *Songs of Labor.* But the day-to-day urgency of his cause left Whittier with only negligible royalties. Not until 1858 did Sanborn, Carter, Bazin, and Company publish the "blue and gold" edition of Whittier's works in proud imitation of Whittier's friend Longfellow.

After 1865 Whittier no longer needed to devote his life to ceaseless activism because slavery had at last been abolished. Very quickly he assumed the role for which he remains best known: the poetic voice of a newly united America and the champion of nature, New England history, and the legends of other cultures. Coincident with this redirected poetic vocation was an altered approach to publication. Whittier's earlier volumes had been collections, often *publishers'* miscellanies, of poems printed in various places, often in the distant past. By contrast, *The Pennsylvania Pilgrim, Snowbound,* and *The Tent on the Beach* and the volumes that follow mark Whittier's resolve to publish volumes *intended* as books by Whittier himself.

Readers of Whittier's anti-slavery poems still respond positively to their range of moods, their denunciation of social evils, and the incandescent passion for justice with which Whittier infused them. By contrast, Whittier's later pronouncements on human nature and human institutions have at times been assessed as naive or merely sentimental. This perception possesses some validity. Whittier's promise in *Snowbound* that education will replace internecine strife with universal freedom and unity has yet to be realized. His assurance that the transatlantic cable will put an end to war because "round the world the thought of all / Is as the thought of one" certainly rings hollow after over a century of world war and bloodshed. Nevertheless, Whittier's conviction that the quality of life depends upon the quality of one's ideals and the amount of work one is willing to devote to them (recalling Crevecoeur's industrious American) suggested to millions of his readers—and can suggest now—that his was a poetic voice not lightly to be put aside in the rush of modern times.

Further Reading. ***Selected Primary Sources:*** Whittier, John Greenleaf, *The Complete Writings of John Greenleaf Whittier,* 7 vols. (vols. 1–4, poetry; vols. 5–7, prose), ed. Horace E. Scudder (Boston: Houghton Mifflin, 1888–1889); Pickard, Samuel T., *Life and Letters of John Greenleaf Whittier,* 2 vols. (Boston: Houghton Mifflin, 1895); Pickard, John B., ed., *The Letters of John Greenleaf Whittier,* 3 vols. (Cambridge, MA: Harvard University Press, 1975). ***Selected Secondary Sources:*** Mordell, Albert, *Quaker Militant: John Greenleaf Whittier* (Boston: Houghton Mifflin, 1933); Currier, Thomas Franklin, *A Bibliography of John Greenleaf Whittier* (Cambridge, MA: Harvard University Press, 1937); Frank, Albert J. von, *Whittier: A Comprehensive Annotated Bibliography* (New York: Garland, 1976); Kribbs, Jayne E., ed., *Critical Essays on John Greenleaf Whittier* (Boston: G.K. Hall, 1980); Whittier Club website, www.johngreenleafwhittier.com.

Russell Rutter

WIENERS, JOHN (1934–2002)

The poetry of John Wieners is quietly defiant. Although his poetic voice is, at its best, diffident and unassuming, it also sets out to powerfully challenge poetic complacency and the degrading effects of modern urban life. Against all the odds, Wieners's poetry is celebratory; it tells of a hard-won life given up to the poetic. Despite his descriptions of personal trauma, lost lovers, and desperate love affairs and of loneliness, mental illness, and various addictions, Wieners never quite loses sight of the basic generosity of his poetic impulse. The lyrical power of his best writing rests on its ability to temper devastating and seemingly overwhelming personal experience with a delicate sense of poetic care and precision of detail. Wieners's influences are wide and various: He has been claimed by various poets and critics as a **Beat** writer, as a **Black Mountain** poet, as part of the **San Francisco Renaissance**, as a Boston poet or even part of the **New York School**, as a prototypical **Language poet**, and as a gay activist poet. His work is important, however, precisely because it resists the categorizations and divisions that have characterized postwar American poetry.

John Wieners was born into a working-class Catholic family in Milton, Massachusetts, on January 6, 1934. He received his BA from Boston College in 1954, but it was in September of that year that his fate as a poet was determined. Walking past the Charles Street Meeting House on September 11 of that year, he was intrigued by what he overheard of a poetry reading given there by **Charles Olson**. On entering the building, he picked up copies of *Black Mountain Review*, and discovering there a radical, **experimental poetry** to which he had not previously been exposed, he enrolled in the spring of 1955 at Black Mountain College, where he studied under Olson and **Robert Duncan**. Returning to Boston in the summer of 1956, Wieners went on to produce three issues of the literary magazine *Measure*, thus bringing his Black Mountain experience back to Boston. From 1958 to 1960 he lived in San Francisco. His first published collection, *The Hotel Wentley Poems* (1958), inspired by the break-up of his relationship with boyfriend Dana, was written in San Francisco and propelled him into involvement in the Beat poetry scene that was then at its height in the city. From 1960 onward, he lived on and off in Boston and New York. After attending the Berkeley Poetry Conference in 1965, he enrolled in the graduate program in poetics at the University of New York—Buffalo, again following in Olson's footsteps. In 1967 he returned to Boston, where he worked as actor and stage manager at the Poet's Theater in Cambridge, saw three of his plays performed in New York, published what is often seen as his finest collection, *Nerves* (1970), and became a vocal and active gay rights campaigner. Wieners died on March 1, 2002.

The eight poems that make up *The Hotel Wentley Poems* represent a remarkable achievement for a first book of poems. Wieners wrote these poems at age twenty-four in San Francisco's seedy Hotel Wentley, during two weeks in the June of 1958. The hotel was notorious for being frequented by hustlers, pimps, prostitutes, and drug dealers. Unsurprisingly, *The Hotel Wentley Poems* details a life of drug deals, homosexual trafficking, and mental and bodily collapse. Yet throughout the poems in this collection there is a powerfully engaging sense of the poet's responsibility to **lyric**, to an idea of the poem in America. Repeatedly throughout this collection, Wieners speculates on the role of the poem in contemporary America. In "A poem for vipers," we are told, "The poem / does not lie to us" and "We lie under its law, alive in the glamour of this hour." Such a sense of the potency of the poem in engaging contemporary urban life suffuses Wieners's work. But if Wieners provides, as Kevin Killian has noted, "the ultimate spectacle of American abjection," this is not because his poetry makes a spectacle of his own suffering selfhood, but because it demonstrates how the idea of the American poem itself is part of a structure of abjection that runs through American ideology. This can be seen in Wieners's next collection, *Ace of Pentacles* (1964). These poems employ more traditional poetic forms that throw the personal sufferings of the Beat outsider figure they describe into sharp relief. "The Acts of Youth" is central to this collection and is one of Wieners's major poems. The power of this poem and of this collection more broadly is the hope the work invests in the ultimately redemptive power of poetry. If the poem describes "what wrecks of the mind await me," it can also assert, "And we rise again in the dawn."

The poems that Wieners wrote during his time at Buffalo, collected in *Pressed Wafer* (1967), reflect further on the redemptive power of poetry. The book's title refers to the Christian Eucharist, and many of these poems employ occult and tarot imagery to describe poetry as a mysterious power: "Without vision, we see only this world." Two subsequent volumes *Asylum Poems (For my Father)* (1969) and *Nerves* (1970) are Wieners's most desperate and dark works. These collections draw on Wieners's experiences as an inmate of a Boston mental institution in the spring of 1969. *Nerves* (which includes all eighteen of the *Asylum Poems*) represents Wieners's greatest accomplishment. The poems in this collection are tensely and finely balanced, and they demonstrate most clearly that what Wieners has learned from the wide range of his poetic influences is to go on his nerves. Painful and poignant as these poems are, they still see poetry as a saving grace. "Supplication" declares "O poetry, visit this house often, / imbue my life with success."

If the success of Wieners's poetic career is marvelously evident in *Nerves*, it is everywhere gestured toward, though never fully achieved, in the hugely sprawling poetic notebook of *Behind the State Capitol, Or Cincinnati Pike* (1975). These poems attest to the urgent demands of life in a post-industrial, media-saturated culture. Though disjunctive and disturbing, they still see the poem as the source of a distinctly American vision. In "Children of the Working Class," Wieners states that he doesn't share "Whitman's vision, but instead the / poorhouses, the mad city asylums and re- / lief worklines." Here, as throughout his career, Wieners traces a lyric trajectory through poverty, suffering, and madness that strikes to the abject heart of contemporary America.

Further Reading. ***Selected Primary Sources:*** Wieners, John, *707 Scott Street* (Los Angeles: Sun & Moon Press, 1996); ———, *Ace of Pentacles* (New York: James F. Carr & Robert A. Wilson, 1964); ———, *Asylum Poems (For My Father)* (New York: Angel Hair, 1969); ———, *Behind the State Capitol, Or Cincinnati Pike* (Boston: Good Gay Poets, 1975); ———, *Cultural Affairs in Boston: Poetry and Prose, 1956–1985* (Santa Rosa, CA: Black Sparrow Press, 1988); ———, *The Hotel Wentley Poems* (1958; rev. ed. San Francisco: Dave Haselwood, 1965); ———, *Nerves* (London and New York: Cape Golliard Press, 1970); ———, *Pressed Wafer* (Buffalo, NY: Gallery Upstairs Press, 1967); ———, *Selected Poems, 1958–1984* (Santa Barbara, CA: Black Sparrow Press, 1986). ***Selected Secondary Sources:*** Killian, Kevin, "The Only Story: The Poetic Obsessions of John Wieners" (*Alsop Review* [Spring 2002], http://www.alsopreview.com/columns/foley/ jfkevinkillian.html); Petro, Pamela, "The Hipster of Joy Street: An Introduction to the Life and Work of John Wieners" (*Jacket* 21 [February 2003], http://jacketmagazine.com/21/wien-petro.html); Wilkinson, John, "Too-Close Reading: Poetry and Schizophrenia," in *Assembling Alternatives: Reading Postmodern Poetries Transnationally*, ed. Romana Huk (Middletown, CT: Wesleyan University Press, 2003, 364–374).

Nick Selby

WIGGLESWORTH, MICHAEL (1631–1705)

Michael Wigglesworth, remembered today chiefly for *The Day of Doom* (1662), a description of the Last Judgment rendered into ballad stanzas, was Puritan New England's most popular poet. Although Wigglesworth's critical reputation has long since been eclipsed by **Anne Bradstreet**, who preceded him by a generation, and by his slightly younger contemporary **Edward Taylor**, much of Bradstreet's verse was too learned and allusive for popular consumption and Taylor took no interest in publishing his poetry during his lifetime. Wigglesworth, by contrast, conceived of poetry as a highly public medium, and owing to his considerable skill in conveying complex doctrinal positions in highly accessible form, his poems achieved popular status in seventeenth-century New England as verse catechisms directed toward the widest possible readership. *The Day of Doom*, which sold out its 1,800 first-run copies within a year, went through at least six British and American editions before the poet's death. Indeed, the poem outlived the theology that fueled it: Five more editions, full or abridged, appeared during the eighteenth century, and it was reported that many people still living at the time of the American Revolution had memorized the poem as children. *Meat Out of the Eater* (1670), a second volume of verse that placed greater emphasis on the consolatory aspects of Puritan belief, went through four editions during the poet's lifetime and reached a sixth just prior to the Revolution. Wigglesworth's gifts as a popular poet were recognized and praised even by highly educated contemporaries. Taylor reported that his first wife recited the "Doomsday Verses" frequently, and **Jonathan Mitchell**, Wigglesworth's tutor at Harvard, called him the exemplary "Christian Poet" singing in the "vast Woods" of the New World. A succinct explanation for Wigglesworth's fame appears in his funeral sermon, wherein **Cotton Mather**, a voracious reader of the classics and an admirer of Milton, commended the old poet for providing "the Edification of such Readers, as are for Truths dressed up in a *Plaine Meeter*."

Wigglesworth's family emigrated from Yorkshire, England, to New Haven, Connecticut, when the future poet was seven. After his early education with famed schoolmaster Ezekiel Cheever in New Haven was interrupted because he had to help his ill father on the family farm, Wigglesworth entered Harvard College to study medicine. While there he underwent a powerful religious conversion and began training for the ministry. Immersing himself in the Greek and Latin classics as well as in the Bible, he proved an excellent student and was given the honor of delivering one of the commencement addresses; appropriate to his future as preacher and poet, he spoke on the power of eloquence. After graduating in 1651, he stayed on at Harvard as a tutor and soon began preaching at nearby Malden. In 1656, after several years of indecision, he accepted the call of the Malden congregation and was ordained as their minister, a post he held for the rest of his life.

Wigglesworth, who also served as the town physician, was plagued by three decades of chronic ill health and was able to perform his clerical duties only sporadically. Early in this period, he turned to poetry as a substitute for preaching and applied to his verse a minister's concern with clearly defined messages and the poetic equivalent of the "plain" style central to Puritan homiletics. Of his three marriages, the second, to his much younger housekeeper Martha Mudge, provoked some scandal. Wigglesworth recovered from the gossip chiefly because his mysterious illness ended in the mid-1680s, and he spent his last two decades in vigorous service to the Malden congregation. Owing to his saintly reputation and the wide dissemination of his poetry, he became a revered figure throughout New England. When he died in 1705 at the age of seventy-four, Mather praised him as the very model of the "faithful man."

Although Wigglesworth's contemporaries saw him as an exemplary believer and citizen, later critics saw him as the very stereotype of the gloomy Puritan. This view was reinforced by the diary that he kept while tutoring at Harvard, which reveals a young man wracked with the anguish and guilt that are commonly associated with the Puritan psyche. Troubled that his students were treating him with disrespect, Wigglesworth remorsefully contemplated the pain that his own "vain thoughts," "detestable pride," and "unnatural filthy lust" were causing for Christ, "who loves me infinitely more than I do them" (3). Although it is easy, from a modern perspective, to read this statement as evidence of an unusually disturbed mind, it is important to remember that within Puritan culture, such thoughts were considered to be therapeutic: Because grace could not come without an intense awareness of one's sinful nature, remorse was itself a hopeful sign of salvation. In keeping with this experiential paradigm, the diary also confirmed the consolatory side of Puritan belief. Such episodes of a "want of dear affection" toward Christ, Wigglesworth wrote, increased his desire for Christ and salvation: "and this gives me hope" (3).

The Puritan belief that conviction in sin was the necessary first step toward repentance is also important to keep in mind when assessing Wigglesworth's achievement as a poet. The salvific efficacy of remorse is especially central to a historically sensitive appreciation of his sweeping description of Judgment Day. In 224 stanzas of ballad meter, *The Day of Doom* depicts the proceedings of the judgment through an extended debate between Christ and various categories of sinners. Within the poem's tight stanzas, Wigglesworth manages to set forth the central tenets of Puritan theology, a remarkable feat of clarity and compression for so complex a belief system. As a result, New Englanders prized the poem as *vade mecum* of experiential theology, reading it aloud in families and committing it to memory as a compact but vivid guide to the intricacies of the faith. Its dramatic confrontations between Christ and the sinners, its unflattering portrayal of human nature, its relentless rhythms, and its heavy dependence on scripture (complete with marginal Bible references) made the poem an ideal vehicle for teaching the faith to the young and uninitiated as well as for rekindling it in the hearts of more experienced believers.

Wigglesworth studded the poem with biblical phrases and allusions, thereby enhancing the poem's credibility and underscoring the homiletic role of his speaker. In so doing, he enacted the typical Puritan adaptation of the traditional view of the poet as a "seer" to a neobiblical recapitulation of the encouragements and correctives issued by the Old Testament prophets. Wigglesworth makes it clear that his intent is not to frighten or upset readers, but to issue what he saw as a legitimate warning from scripture itself—a warning that he offers, as a prefatory poem states, "in Love": He urges his audience to read the doomsday poem "for thy good, / There's nothing in't can do thee hurt, / If rightly understood." That he directed the prophetic warning to all, whether educated or illiterate, is reflected in his choice of eight-line ballad stanzas with a doubled *abcb* rhyme scheme. The galloping rhythms and driving rhymes created a brisk pace by which a great deal of theological content could be conveyed with a minimum of tedium. The relentless pace of the poem also reinforced the urgency of repentance; the rapid succession of arguments and responses must have felt like an onslaught of divinely rendered justice.

The poem's dramatic appeal will perhaps be most apparent to the modern reader in the opening and closing scenes that frame the debate. The unruffled calm of the opening lines, for instance, embodies the false sense of security harbored by sinners unprepared for Christ's coming:

Still was the night, Serene and Bright,
　　When all Men sleeping lay;
Calm was the season, and carnal reason
　　Thought so 'twould last for ay.

This calm is interrupted by a "hideous cry" and a "Light, / which turn'd the night to day," and the ordinary world quickly unravels. The saints, "their countenance full of pleasance," find themselves standing at Christ's right hand; at his left stand "the Goats," who wait to plead their cases before him. After the "Blessed Ones" hear that their sins are pardoned and are invited to sit on "Thrones, / Judging the World with me," the debate that makes up the core of the poem begins.

Given the dramatic potential of vivid depictions of sinners getting their just deserts, *The Day of Doom* gives surprisingly little space to the horrors of hell. The punishment of the damned occupies only a few stanzas, and even here, the poet does not go beyond what his scriptural sources seemed to warrant. A minister's pastoral concern with the practical needs of his hearers also emerges in the types of sin that receive the most attention. Blatant sins involving violence or sexual depravity—sins that might have generated a prurient curiosity at cross-purposes with Wigglesworth's aims—do not figure prominently. Indeed, Wigglesworth dismisses the most overt evildoers—apostates, idolaters, profaners, scoffers, adulterers, the covetous, vicious parents and children, murderers, witches, and Sabbath polluters—rather quickly, and they do not in fact speak for themselves in the debate (17–19). The poet's deeper concern lies with secret sins of mind and heart, with those categories of error that actual readers would most likely commit: hypocrisy, presumption, pride, spiritual laziness, and the like. Collectively, the sinners condemn themselves by articulating their own self-sufficiency. What Christ tells the "Civil honest Men" holds true for each rank of the damned:

Your argument shews your intent,

in all that you have done:
You thought to scale Heav'ns lofty Wall
by Ladders of your own.

As generic representatives of such pride, the ranks of sinners are not depicted with any individuality—indeed, their collective speeches are more like a series of Greek choruses. Although their defenses occasionally have a credible human ring, they display theological rather than psychological verisimilitude; prior to their final sentence, for instance, they show no real remorse for their sins, but "grudge, / and grind their teeth" in envy of the elect.

From a modern perspective, the one-sidedness of the debate robs the poem of any potential suspense: Surely the damned could have defended themselves more effectively. But such a response overlooks the theological framework in which Wigglesworth was working. To show the futility of the sinners' arguments was, of course, a theological mandate: To fail to demonstrate that Christ's "Reasons are the stronger" on Judgment Day would have been unthinkable. By having unregenerate souls voice their errors in so obvious a manner, Wigglesworth was enacting the Puritan belief that at doomsday the damned would convict themselves through their own deeds and words.

Christ's monotonous rightness at doomsday is central to what modern readers often find most repugnant in the poem: Wigglesworth's characterization of a Christ who dismisses rank after rank of the damned with a remorselessness that seems to border on glee. Most striking, perhaps, is his dismissal of the unregenerate infants, who complain that they have committed no sin beyond the stain that accrued to them through Adam:

Not we, but he, ate of the Tree,
Whose fruit was interdicted:
Yet on us all of his sad Fall,
The punishment's inflicted.

Christ's famous reply, a curious mix of sarcasm and compassion, turns the infants' argument around: If Adam had *not* fallen, would they have renounced benefits of grace that came from no actions of their own? Insisting that "every sin's a crime," including original sin, Christ nonetheless concedes that their fault "is much less":

A crime it is, therefore in bliss
you may not hope to dwell;
But unto you I shall allow
the easiest room in Hell.

In a poem whose major purpose was to confirm that "grace transcends mens thought," merely human notions of fairness did not apply. This is why Wigglesworth's portrayal of an unforgiving Christ does not reflect a lack of artistic control; if anything, it reflects artistic over-control resulting from the poet's thematic adherence to the Puritan belief that Judgment Day would signal the end of all redemptive opportunity. For the unregenerate, doomsday would mark an irreversible shift from divine mercy to divine judgment: To show Christ waffling would have blurred the very distinction between grace and sin that the poem was written to reinforce.

A more balanced view of the theology emerges not so much from the poem itself as from its experiential dynamic. Puritan theology insisted that this was precisely how Christ would appear to the damned—and it was a Christ whom Wigglesworth's readers hoped never to confront. For the elect, Christ was not judge but advocate, and the pitiless Christ *in* the poem was mitigated by the merciful Christ *outside* the poem, to whom readers were being encouraged to turn. For all its harshness, *The Day of Doom* reminded its readers that the advocate was still available to them if they sincerely repented—and that the "blessed state of the Renate," as Wigglesworth made clear near the poem's end, was well worth the effort: "O wondrous Happiness, / To which they're brought, beyond what thought / can reach, or words express!" If readers found themselves frightened by the doomsday judge, the present advocate of redemptive opportunity stood ready to offer comfort and support. This reading dynamic is reiterated in a "Postscript," where the poet makes his purposes clear: "Nor speak I this, good Reader, to torment thee / Before the time, but rather to prevent thee / From running headlong to thine own decay."

We can only presume that Wigglesworth's strategies succeeded. The popularity of *The Day of Doom* provides striking evidence that literary satisfactions can vary radically in different times, places, and cultures. Puritan readers, obsessed with religion and the Bible, must have found Wigglesworth's doomsday epic entertaining as well as instructive, a response that might be compared to our enjoyment of a Gothic novel or a disaster film. The bulk of their enjoyment clearly derived from the hope and encouragement that the poem extended by making Christian doctrine and experience seem more accessible. Hopelessly unrepentant sinners, of course, would not have been among Wigglesworth's audience—but for those in between, those "poor doubting souls" who fervently sought salvation but were plagued with uncertainties, the poem offered an opportunity to realign their thinking in accordance with the expected patterns of salvation. Part of their comfort would have derived from a theme that pervades *The Day of Doom*: Mere human logic and reason, unchecked by biblical verities, would inevitably lead to the dangerous self-reliance by which sinners felt no need for redemption. Readers who confronted chilling echoes of their own thoughts in the arguments of the damned and thus *did* feel the need for a savior could take heart from the poem's clear warning against self-sufficiency.

"God's Controversy with New-England" (1662), a much shorter poem that was written the year that *The Day of Doom* appeared but that was not published until the nineteenth century, applied the cosmic framework of the doomsday **epic** to specific problems that New Englanders were facing at the time, including a widespread fear among the ministers that the Puritan mission was in danger. Most of the founding settlers had died; New England was rapidly becoming a more secular and diverse society; Puritan rule in Old England had collapsed with the Restoration of the monarchy; and a severe drought had struck the New England colonies. Such omens seemed to signal God's disfavor, and like Jeremiah weeping for the sins of Israel, many ministers railed against New England's lukewarm zeal. These sermons, commonly called "jeremiads" for their replication of Jeremiah's prophecies against an unvigilant and backsliding Israel, became so common a homiletic genre that they came to epitomize Puritan preaching generally. The salvific benefits of harsh sermons came directly out of homiletic tradition. Preaching manuals such as William Perkins's *The Art of Prophesying* (1612) taught that sermons should take two basic forms, depending on the attitude of the hearers. Ministers were to preach to hard-hearted sinners like "sons of thunder," frightening them into remorse and repentance. By contrast, preachers were to address the already penitent like "sons of the dove," comforting them and urging them toward greater confidence in their faith. In its compressed sequence of conviction and consolation, the jeremiad sermon offered an especially clear illustration of the two sides of Puritan preaching.

"God's Controversy" offered a jeremiad in verse form, and in its lucid embodiment of the progression from conviction to consolation central to Puritan homiletics, it exhibits Wigglesworth's poetic and rhetorical skill in a small compass. However harsh the dehortative message, most jeremiads ended on a hopeful note, and "God's Controversy" is no exception. If readers sincerely repented, divine wrath could be stayed and the Puritan mission could recover its initial purpose and glory. In conveying this message, Wigglesworth adopts the preacher's role as an instrument of the biblical word, a rhetorical stance invoked at the poem's beginning: "Nor is it I that thee reproove / Let God himself be heard." Reprising Christ's role in *The Day of Doom*, Wigglesworth's God speaks in a "Dreadful-threatening voice" as divine justice personified, reminding readers that New England's former glory has been sullied by the people's decline into a "stubborn Race." Nor does the poet place himself above the sin that has prompted the decline: He blames "not thee to spare my self: / But first at home begin." Wigglesworth also underscores his inclusion among New England's sinners through the pervasive "we" of the poem.

Recasting New England's settlement as a latter-day exodus from Egypt, "God's Controversy" traces a downward spiral in faithfulness by which New Englanders have become a "Generation even ripe for Vengeance stroke"—a far cry indeed from the godly elders who had settled a land where "We, only we, enjoyd such peace / As none enjoyd before." God, who can scarcely recognize his saints, repeatedly asks, "Are these the men?" "Are these the folk?" "Are these the people?" In keeping with the Puritan sequence of remorse, repentance, and recovery, the readers' identification with the fallen generation made possible their performative realignment with New England's mission. By the poem's conclusion, Wigglesworth's readers have been redefined as those "praying saints" who issue remorseful "plaints" in both "deed and word." Such readers, transformed by the poem's directives from "Backsliders" into "sweet souls," were assured that despite their culpability in prompting New England's "controversy," it was not too late to assuage God's anger.

To read *The Day of Doom* and "God's Controversy with New-England" was to reconfirm one's sense of belonging to God's people, and in encouraging this recommitment, Wigglesworth did not neglect the consolatory dimensions of Puritan subjectivity. The gentler side of his personality, fully evident in Richard Crowder's sympathetic biography, emerges with greater clarity in the lengthy *Meat Out of the Eater* (1670). Although the more directly consolatory poems in this volume are no more pleasing to modern tastes than the calls to repent issued in *The Day of Doom* and "God's Controversy with New-England," they go far to explain Wigglesworth's popularity among those who read not for what we would see as aesthetic appreciation but to answer the great question of Puritan spiritual and literary experience: "What must I do to be saved?" (Acts 16:30). In contrast to the communal thrust of Wigglesworth's better-known verse, this second book spoke more directly to the afflictions and rewards of the individual soul.

Meat Out of the Eater includes the title poem, which encompasses "Tolle Crucem," a ten-meditation sequence and a "conclusion Hortatory" that extols the imitation of Christ by taking up the Cross of afflictions; "Riddles Unriddled," an extended treatment of a series of "Christian Paradoxes" inseparable from belief; and a small group of occasional poems. "Meat Out of the Eater," whose title refers to Samson's riddle in which honey comes from the carcass of a lion (Judges 14), introduces the overarching theme of the entire volume: the value of worldly suffering as a prelude to heavenly joy. As the poet states in the opening meditation of "Tolle Crucem," the believer is not "alway dandled" on Christ's knee: "Nor must we think to ride to Heaven / Upon a Feather-bed."

"Riddles Unriddled" holds particular interest because of the light it sheds on Puritan interiority. At the heart of the experience of Puritanism, the poet insists, lies a recognition of the extra-logical basis of true belief. Wigglesworth pursues this theme by exploring various paradoxes central to Christian faith: "Light in Darkness, / Sick mens Health, / Strength in Weakness, / Poor mens Wealth." The poet's consolatory aims are clear from the start. He asserts that in contrast to hypocrites unaware of their spiritual peril, such as the doomsday sinners, there is "a child of Light / whose state is very good, / Yet walks in sadness, in the night, / Till this be understood."

The poems gathered in *Meat Out of the Eater* encouraged such tender believers to be bolder in their faith and to take greater confidence in the salvific efficacy of their spiritual struggles. The paradoxes that Wigglesworth explores had a cumulative effect of encouraging readers to rely more heavily on the comfort that Christ extended to them. Because the mysteries of salvation lay beyond their ability to conceive or understand, Wigglesworth's underlying message, as in *The Day of Doom*, was that all such paradoxes found their resolution not through human logic but through simple, heartfelt belief. Although his rhetorical purposes were chiefly didactic rather than introspective, "Riddles Unriddled" reveals a poet fully engaged with the psychological processes, spiritual paradoxes, and experiential ambiguities that also mark Bradstreet's and Taylor's verse. Although the experiential underpinnings of Puritan belief find autobiographical expression in those poets' more private lyrics, in Wigglesworth Puritan belief receives more general treatment by a poet seeking to provide a pastoral balm to troubled souls.

Though the relative impersonality of Wigglesworth's voice clearly reflects his artistic aims, the poet did not submerge himself completely into the homiletic role. As Ronald Bosco observes, Wigglesworth offered himself to readers as "subject or example" (xxiii), as a witness to Bradstreet's lesson that each true believer is a "weary pilgrim" traveling through what Taylor calls a "Vale of tears, not mount of joyes." This is especially evident in *Meat Out of the Eater*, wherein the poet's empathy with his "Co-partners" and "Fellow-sufferers" prompts him to include several autobiographical allusions. At one point, for example, he relates "[t]he horrour of that Lonesomness, / (And state of Widowhood)" by which he felt "estranged farre" from God; elsewhere he describes the "weakness Bodily" and debilitating "feebleness" that kept him out of the pulpit for so many years. Still, such allusions are rare. Individual self-expression ranked low in his purposes, and if the resulting emphasis on generalized religious experience gives his verse less interest for modern readers, his voice embodied the selflessness that was a Puritan ideal. Written from a desire to "abase / My self unto the dust" (181), Wigglesworth's poetry enacted one of the paradoxes that he treated in his verse: "we are never stronger, / Then when we are most weak."

It is difficult for modern readers to appreciate a popular artist fully in tune with a culture that held radically different expectations from ours regarding what a poem should be and do. Wigglesworth's critical standing has been further diminished by the strikingly different poetry of Anne Bradstreet and Edward Taylor, whose psychological and linguistic complexity underscore Wigglesworth's far narrower scope. Yet contemporary criticism, which has become more receptive to popular art and to the view that poetry is a powerful agent of cultural work, may be in a better position to assess Wigglesworth's achievement than was a previous generation of critics weaned on expressivist and formalist aesthetic assumptions. Contemporary critics may also be more sympathetic toward the democratization of art that was central to Puritan literary theory in general and to Wigglesworth's work in particular. Functioning as a bridge between New England's educated elite and its lower classes, many of whom were illiterate, Wigglesworth deliberately pursued the classical dictum of *ars celare artem*: True art conceals art. He owned a copy of Horace, and even if few modern readers will discern the Horatian mix of *utile et dulce* in his poetry, Jonathan Mitchell had no trouble finding it in his former pupil's ability to roll "Truth in Sugar" so that it "may taste the sweeter."

Within cultural limits as well as populist goals that he set for himself, Wigglesworth's verse reveals an impressive control over thematic unity in **long poems**, a plain diction and even plainer prosody well suited to his intended readers (many of whom would have been *hearers* of the poems being read aloud), and occasional lines of memorable vividness and force that transcend his immediate aims. His poetry is most valuable today, however, precisely because the bulk of it does *not* transcend those aims. It is Wigglesworth, not Taylor or Bradstreet, who best exemplifies poetry as most early New Englanders experienced it, and accordingly, his work sheds valuable light on Puritan popular art and culture. Wigglesworth reminds us of the historical and aesthetic otherness of Puritan art even as he reveals his own time and place with special clarity. By forcing modern readers to confront assumptions, artistic as well as religious, that are not our own, he reminds us that the past can indeed seem like another country—and that literary history presents us with voices that are alien as well as those that seem familiar. *See also* **Puritan Poetry**; **Poetics, Seventeenth- and Eighteenth-Century**; **Religion and Poetry**; **Devotional Poetry**; **Bible and American Poetry**.

Further Reading. ***Selected Primary Sources:*** Wigglesworth, Michael, *The Diary of Michael Wigglesworth, 1653–1657: The Conscience of a Puritan*, ed. Edmund S. Morgan (New York: Harper & Row, 1965); ———, *The Poems of Michael Wigglesworth*, ed. Ronald A. Bosco (Lanham, MD: University Press of America, 1989). ***Selected Secondary Sources:*** Bosco, Ronald A., "Introduction," in *The Poems of Michael Wigglesworth*, ed. Ronald A. Bosco (Lanham, MD: University Press of America, 1989, ix–xliii); Crowder, Richard, *No Featherbed to Heaven: A Biography of Michael Wigglesworth* (East Lansing: Michigan State University Press, 1962); Daly, Robert, *God's Altar: The World and the Flesh in Puritan Poetry* (Berkeley: University of California Press, 1978); Hammond, Jeffrey, *Sinful Self, Saintly Self: The Puritan Experience of Poetry* (Athens: University of Georgia Press, 1993); Pope, Alan H., "Petrus Ramus and Michael Wigglesworth: The Logic of Poetic Structure," in *Puritan Poets and Poetics: Seventeenth-Century American Poetry in Theory and Practice*, ed. Peter White (University Park: Pennsylvania State University Press, 1985, 210–226).

Jeffrey Hammond

WILBUR, RICHARD (1921–)

Richard Wilbur is something of an anomaly in later–twentieth-century poetry. Like most of his generation educated during the academic primacy of the **New Criticism**, Wilbur began writing formal verse in intricate stanzaic structures; unlike most of his peers, he never abandoned these forms for **free verse**, even temporarily. He was first drawn to writing poetry from his experiences in World War II, but he could not be considered a war poet in the manner of such poets as **Louis Simpson**, **Anthony Hecht**, or **James Dickey.** In a time when opacity was considered a virtue by many, Wilbur stressed clarity. His poetry is also generally optimistic with a pervasive though never dogmatic Christianity, definitely out of step with the poetical fashion of the times. These and other factors often have brought Wilbur suspicion from some quarters of critical opinion and outright disregard from others. Gradually, however, as his collections appeared over the decades and he became more and more regarded as an elder statesman of the literary scene, Wilbur's accomplishment began to be more widely seen as a significant, even vital, force in American poetry of the latter half of the twentieth century.

Richard Wilbur was born in 1921 in New York City but grew up in rural New Jersey. His upbringing evidences itself in much of Wilbur's nature poetry, which always displays a thorough knowledge of wood lore. His father was a painter—much later, Wilbur himself illustrated three of his own children's books. Wilbur entered Amherst in 1938; during two summer vacations he toured the country, riding the rails with hoboes. He married Charlotte ("Charlee") Ward, a student at nearby Smith College, upon his graduation in 1942. Wilbur joined the U.S. Army, hoping to be a cryptographer. But a security check found him to be politically suspect because of his left-wing views, and he was abruptly transferred to the infantry and shipped directly into combat. He took part in three years of intensive fighting in Italy and France. The later poet of the civilized life early on saw the disaster of civilization run amok. Returning to civilian life, Wilbur earned his MA from Harvard in 1947; during this time he became friends with **Robert Frost,** a relationship eased into being by the fact that Wilbur's wife's grandfather was the first editor to publish a Frost poem. After Harvard, Wilbur taught next at Wellesley and then for many years at Wesleyan University. He finished his academic career as writer-in-residence at Smith, thus coming full circle to where he met his wife forty years previously. In 1987 Wilbur was named the second U.S. Poet Laureate. He has every award open to American poets over the years, including the Pulitzer Prize twice. The Wilburs established homes in both Massachusetts and Florida, and their three children include fiction writer Ellen Wilbur.

Wilbur's first collection, *The Beautiful Changes,* was published in 1947, the year **Robert Lowell** won the Pulitzer for *Lord Weary's Castle.* Lowell and Wilbur were fated to be compared for the next three decades as poetic opposites, Lowell representing the "raw" and Wilbur the "cooked" approach to poetry, a comparison that did an injustice to both poets. The poems in Wilbur's first collection were highly achieved, but *The Beautiful Changes*, as its title indicates, was most definitely not a volume of war poetry, despite the fact that Wilbur has frequently mentioned that it was his combat experiences that first motivated him to write poetry. In fact, the weaker poems in the book are mostly those concerned with the war. For example, in "Mined Country" the line "Cows in mid-mulch go splattered over the sky" has an almost humorous aspect to it. "On the Eyes of an SS Officer" displays anger that doesn't quite register: "I ask my makeshift God of this / My opulent bric-a-brac earth to damn his eyes." Over the years, Wilbur has shown his range to be broad, but anger is not a common ingredient. Two war poems that are effective, "Potato" and "First Snow in Alsace," have an element of celebration to them; "Potato," for example, concludes by praising the vegetable's commonness: "Awkward and milky and beautiful only to hunger." Otherwise, this first collection is unusually achieved. "Objects" is an example of the poems of ideas at which Wilbur has excelled from the beginning. The collection concludes with "Praise in Summer" and the title poem, two memorable **lyrics** of celebration and of love for this world and acceptance of its dynamic and subtle changes.

Three years later, in 1950, *Ceremony and Other Poems* appeared. This volume also included several translations by Wilbur, a feature of each of his collections to follow. This book was also very well received critically, though there were rumblings in some quarters that Wilbur's grace might come at the cost of his range. *Ceremony* established the mature Wilbur's concerns: poems about or from art and literature, poems showing both an eye practiced in its observation of nature and a penchant for ideas and argumentation. Wilbur also demonstrates his ability for sustaining unusual, almost Metaphysical imagery. "Pity" portrays a murderer who returns to the scene of the crime to free his victim's canary, thus ironically enacting pity as both gesture and poem. "The Puritans" compares the reluctant dredging up of guilt to the practice of firing cannons from a boat to raise bodies from the river bottom. "A Glance from the Bridge" describes the breaking up of ice in a city river by stating, "As if an ancient whore undid her gown / And showed a body almost like a girl's," and "A Simile for Her Smile" uses a scene of traffic waiting at a drawbridge to evoke an image of his love's "smiling, or the hope, the thought of it." One particularly fine poem, "Year's-End," works through an entire montage of images to deal with time's passage, from a New Year's celebration to leaves frozen in ice to fossils to mastodons to Pompeii and back to the party that began the reverie. And in "The Sirens" Wilbur establishes a tone unique among serious poets of this era—the Sirens are not singers of death but are simply tempters to quit the road for the view, but the speaker "listen[s] going on, / The richer for regret."

It must have seemed to his contemporaries in 1950 that Wilbur would be a highly prolific poet in future years since he had published two books before his thirtieth birthday. However, the rest of his career, as other interests such as **translation** and scholarship took more of his time, saw a diminution in amount of poetry, though not in quality. It was six years before Wilbur's next volume appeared, but *Things of This World* became his most acclaimed individual collection and won a Pulitzer Prize for the thirty-five-year-old poet. The majority of original poems in the book have been anthologized, and three of the poems—"Love Calls Us to the Things of This World," "A Baroque Wall-Fountain in the Villa Sciarra," and "For the New Railway Station in Rome"—are considered among the very best poems of the Wilbur oeuvre. The first of these is perhaps Wilbur's most popular poem and a prime example of the poet's affirmation of this world. The title is a quote from St. Augustine. The poem begins with yet another Metaphysical image: The laundry on the lines is compared to angels. These images are accompanied by puns, a tool Wilbur uses, for the most part, quite subtly. Here the "morning air is all awash with angels" and the "soul shrinks." After a brief dream of escapism, the persona accepts the mundane realm of physical reality, the reality that the laundry must come down as "clean linen for the backs of thieves," and even the "heaviest nuns" live "keeping their difficult balance" between the physical and the spiritual. Wilbur rarely treats these two realms as opposites; rather, one informs the other. We know the eternal through the temporal, the sensibility through the senses.

Another five years elapsed before the appearance of Wilbur's next collection, *Advice to a Prophet and Other Poems*, in which Wilbur begins to expand his range of voices to the natural world; in the volume, the poet lends voices to a milkweed, a stone, an aspen, and a stream. He also uses more human personae than before, partly because of his work for the stage. He begins to experiment with more forms; "Junk" is particularly interesting in its use of the Old English accentual line. Although the book does not contain nearly as many Wilbur standards as *Things of This World*, *Advice* is an achieved book, albeit not as sustained in inspiration as its predecessor. As in his previous collections, the book ends with a poem of affirmation; however, in this case "A Christmas Hymn" is the most overtly Christian poem Wilbur had collected to date. But it ends with the typical note of affirmation: Christ's birth means that the "worlds are reconciled." To much critical taste, this seemed too easy after the appearance of Robert Lowell's acclaimed *Life Studies*, which abjured affirmation of the inner life and the possibility of belief.

The 1960s were a difficult time for the traditionalist in most any area of the public sphere, far from least the arts. Wilbur seemed out-of-step to many of his generation and even more so to the young; his liberal politics seemed as dated as verse that rhymed and used meter. It was not until 1969, eight years after *Advice*, that Wilbur published his next collection, *Walking to Sleep: New Poems and Translations*. There was little evidence of overt political statement in the volume; the most direct, "A Miltonic Sonnet for Mr. Johnson on His Refusal of Peter Hurd's Official Portrait," while castigating Johnson for his Vietnam policy—"small nations dread / The imposition of our cattle-brand"—by its very title separates itself from the protest poetry of its day. But *Walking to Sleep* is a more sustained effort than its predecessor. "On the Marginal Way" is a rumination by the seaside that considers both natural and human violence but concludes with a sense of joy in being alive and the forces that make life possible. Youth, parenthood, and middle age are united in the sequence "Running." But the highlight of the volume is the title poem. "Walking to Sleep" explores what was becoming a recurrent theme in Wilbur's work, the states of consciousness, especially when the unconscious and the conscious mind have their boundaries blurred. The poem was Wilbur's longest collected verse at that date and is a sustained panoply of Metaphysical images stepping off into the surreal realms of the mind. It was in many ways a breakthrough poem for Wilbur.

Regardless, it was another seven years before his next collection arrived, but *The Mind-Reader* ranks close to *Things of This World* as the essential Wilbur collection. "The Writer," a study both of his affection for his daughter and her creative struggles and of the effort to find a metaphor adequate to experience, is one of Wilbur's most anthologized poems. His "Piccola Commedia," a remembrance of his youthful days wandering the country, is a marvelously understated vignette. Another memory is recalled in "Cottage Street, 1953," marking the occasion on which he met the young **Sylvia Plath**, more Wilbur's polar opposite than Lowell ever was, before she went on to "state at last her brilliant negative / In poems free and helpless and unjust." The boundaries between waking and sleeping, so well engaged in "Walking to Sleep," are revisited on a more personal level in "In Limbo." "Children of Darkness" is one of the poet's most minute considerations of nature as he examines fungi, concluding with the simple declaration "They are good." And the title poem of *The Mind-Reader* is once more a sustained effort that breaks new turf. Although the poem is of necessity concerned with the more suspicious areas of the mind by the choice of subject, it is the most accomplished dramatic monologue Wilbur has written. Once more, the intricacies of the mind are explored, but here is also a fully rounded character worthy of comparison with Browning's creations. Speaking in a human voice not the poet's own is something Wilbur attempted before, but never with the fullness and subtlety of "The Mind-Reader."

As the twenty-first century began, *The Mind-Reader* was Wilbur's last full-length collection; *Mayflies*, published in 2000, contains some good poems but is closer to a chapbook in length. In 1987 Wilbur's *New and Collected Poems* was published and won him his second Pulitzer, largely as a reward for a distinguished career. But there are a few new poems of considerable significance for the Wilbur canon that appear here for the first time. "The Ride" is again the stuff of dreams, a mare of the night that is not a nightmare but a (mythic?) deliverance. Another fine poem of ideas, "Lying," is included as well, and the skillful use yet again of the unexpected simile ends "Transit," wherein the motions of a woman transfix the poet, "Leaving the stations of her body there / As a whip maps the countries of the air." But probably the most important new poem is "Hamlen Brook." The persona, hot from working in the woods, leans to take a drink from the brook and sees the life within the stream as well as the reflection of the life outside it. Most of the scene is described in a long sentence meandering between several verses emphasizing the wonders illuminated for the speaker, which then is followed by the short question "How shall I drink all this?" The surface simplicity and the awe at creation are a constant in much of Wilbur's work, and there is no better example than "Hamlen Brook."

Mayflies is a short collection, about half of which is composed of translations, including a brilliant rendering of Canto XXV of *The Inferno*, but new poems such as "A Barred Owl," one of Wilbur's darker efforts; a love poem for his wife, "For C."; and "This Pleasing Anxious Being," dealing with mind, memory, and mortality, should form a lasting contribution to Wilbur's poetry. Finally, 2004 saw the edition of *Collected Poems 1943–2004,* which is Wilbur's monument. A few new poems begin the collection, the most important of which is "The Reader," describing Wilbur's wife returning in her old age to stories read a long time back in her life, knowing how they will end but still able to marvel in the "blind delight of being, ready still / To enter life on life and see them through." This would probably serve as a motto for the poet as well. A further advantage to the *Collected Poems* is the appendix featuring his children's books and light verse, *Opposites*, *More Opposites*, *A Few Differences*, *The Disappearing Alphabet*, and *The Pig in the Spigot.*

It is for his poetry that Wilbur's legacy will be most firmly established, but he is also famed for his translations, which include poems translated from French, Spanish, Italian, Hungarian, and Russian. He also wrote lyrics for Leonard Bernstein's musical production of *Candide.* But the translations that he will most likely be remembered for are his superb verse translations of the plays of Molière and Racine. Wilbur's career is one of the remarkable features of post–World War II American literature.

Further Reading. ***Selected Primary Sources:*** Wilbur, Richard, *Collected Poems 1943-2004* (Orlando, FL: Harcourt, 2004); ———, *The Catbird's Song: Prose Pieces 1963–1995* (New York: Harcourt, 1997); ———, *Responses: Prose Pieces 1953–1976* (New York: Harcourt, 1976). ***Selected Secondary Sources:*** Bixler, Frances, *Richard Wilbur: A Reference Guide* (Boston: G.K. Hall, 1991); Cummins, Paul, *Richard Wilbur* (Grand Rapids, MI: Eerdmans, 1971); Edgecombe, Rodney Stenning, *A Reader's Guide to the Poetry of Richard Wilbur* (Tuscaloosa: University of Alabama Press, 1995); Hill, Donald L., *Richard Wilbur* (New York: Twayne, 1967); Michelson, Bruce, *Wilbur's Poetry: Music in a Scattering Time* (Amherst: University of Massachusetts Press, 1991); Salinger, Wendy, ed., *Richard Wilbur's Creation* (Ann Arbor: University of Michigan Press, 1983).

Robert Darling

WILCOX, CARLOS (1794–1827)

Neglected by posterity, Carlos Wilcox was an early Vermont voice whose individuality stands out among the poets of the 1820s. Carlos Wilcox was born in 1794 in Newport, New Hampshire, the son of middle-class parents. Why he was given the Spanish-sounding name Carlos is unknown; perhaps it was intended to represent the Italian "Carlo," since Italian given names had found their way into the American population (e.g., the Methodist revivalist Lorenzo Dow). The Wilcoxes moved to Orwell, Vermont, when Carlos was about four or five. Orwell, in Addison County, was founded by John Charter, a maverick from Scotland by way of Quebec, and was a small, pastoral community. Life in Orwell certainly helped occasion or amplify the note of serenity amid rural beauty that suffuses Wilcox's poetry. A childhood injury, though, contributed to a weak constitution throughout Wilcox's life.

Wilcox attended the recently founded Middlebury College, beginning his studies there in 1809 and graduating in 1813. Wilcox's classmates at Middlebury included future New York Governor Silas Wright and future Supreme Court Justice Samuel Nelson. Vermont, never a hotbed of Calvinism like the other New England states because of its late and heterogeneous settlement, by this time had turned to less predestination-based versions of Calvinism, and Wilcox's poetry and opinions did not quite jell with those of orthodox Congregationalism, which hindered him in his later searches for pastoral positions. He went to Andover Theological Seminary from 1814 to 1817, and Wilcox then embarked on a long odyssey in search of a preaching position. His major works, "The Religion of Taste" (1824; originally delivered at Yale under the auspices of Phi Beta Kappa) and *The Age of Benevolence* (1824), were published during those years, though the commercial success of the latter did nothing to secure Wilcox a ministerial post. Wilcox finally found a position in Hartford, Connecticut, in 1824 and served there, despite increasing ill health, until 1826, when he took up a brief tenure at a church in Danbury, Connecticut, where he died in 1827. *The Age of Benevolence* consisted of four books, but only the first two are complete, though indicative fragments exist of the latter two. The first book is about benevolence in heaven, the second about benevolence manifested on earth, and the third about why earth is in need of benevolence (it is plagued by political burdens such as American slavery and the tyranny of Napoleon). Book Four, on the rewards of benevolence in heaven, displays a surprisingly embodied quality to the empyrean realm.

The biggest mistake in reading Wilcox' poetry is to see his borrowings from English eighteenth-century **pastoral** poets such as Cowper, Dyer, and Thomson as imitative and retrograde and therefore to neglect his poetic vision and his idiosyncrasies. Wilcox uses the earlier conventions strategically and, sometimes, disjunctively. His aim is not to divide and regiment landscape, as can perhaps be said of Thomson's verse; rather, Wilcox's aim is to let landscape's many elements mix together in an ecstasy, so that the plenitude of the mixed elements' vigor will evoke the divine in the poem's frame. This is especially true in Wilcox's adoption of benevolence as the theme of his major work. This is not a case of being merely ceremonial or officious. Benevolence is explored as theodicy, as justification of the divine order, and as an attribute of human society. Because Wilcox is not being merely rhetorical when he speaks of the potential effects of benevolence and because he, as a partial outsider to society, recognizes the potential defects of benevolence and passionately pleads for its recognition and redress, his language has a felt force behind its every word. The theme of benevolence permits Wilcox to explore **epic** territory covered by John Milton in the same gesture as he covers territory usually associated with John Locke, **Thomas Paine**, and other social thinkers. In fact, Wilcox espoused a visionary altruism not seem again in American poetry until the very different avatar of **Walt Whitman**. The trajectory of *The Age of Benevolence* goes from heaven to earth and back to heaven again. This inverts, for instance, the sequence of Dante's *Commedia*, which, tacitly, brings the pilgrim back to earth after he has been to heaven. It is heaven, not earth, that is transfigured by the poem. Wilcox's is a prophetic, low-Protestant viewpoint, and the poem, though enunciated in eloquent heroic couplets, has a Blakean cast to it. Wilcox's responsiveness to nature is exceptional; for him nature is always in transition, between day and night and between spring and autumn, and it is always crackling with motion and quickened, catalyzed spirit.

The best-known piece of Wilcox's work today, the excerpt from Book II of *Benevolence* that is included in the *Library of America* book *American Poetry: The Nineteenth Century*, shows this quality as poplar leaves "pendant hung / By stems elastic, quiver at a breath, / rest in the general calm." Even stillness is in some kind of alert motion. "The Religion of Taste," in Spenserian stanzas that have a more Romantic and organic cast to them than the stately classicism of *The Age of Benevolence*, also is a more complicated poem than a literal-minded reading might conclude. The poem seems to repudiate the religion of taste—closely resembling what we would today call the religion of art—for the purer love of the holy. Yet not only do the poem's early portions sketch out the beauties of taste so appealingly—especially in Wilcox's description of the Garden of Eden—that even a doctrinal reprimand cannot dispel them from the reader's mind, but also the superiority of religion is asserted by virtue of the sublimity of the White Mountains of New Hampshire, an image that, like Wordsworth's Snowdon, may stand for a wonder beyond itself, but also stands quite immovably for itself. As a sickly poet who died young, Wilcox suited all the Romantic stereotypes of the poet, but his reputation has yet to capitalize on that fact. Though neglected after his early death, Wilcox was seen as Vermont's own poet, the most notable literary voice the then-fledgling fourteenth state had yet produced. Vermont local-history interest has kept his reputation alive to the point that he can now be studied and appreciated as the singular poet that he was.

Further Reading. ***Selected Secondary Sources:*** Bearse, Ray, ed., *Vermont: A Guide to the Green Mountain State*, 2nd ed. (Boston: Houghton Mifflin, 1966); Hazen, James, "Carlos Wilcox," in *Companion to Encyclopedia of American Poetry: The Nineteenth Century* (Chicago and London: Fitzroy Dearborn, 1998, 487–489); Williamson, Chilton, *Vermont In Quandary: 1763–1825* (Barre: Vermont Historical Society, 1949).

Nicholas Birns

WILCOX, ELLA WHEELER (1850–1919)

In forty prolific years, Ella Wheeler Wilcox was published regularly by the *Atlantic Monthly*, *Harper's*, *Century*, *Galaxy*, *Demorest's Magazine*, *Peterson's Magazine*, the *New York Journal*, and the *Chicago American*. She was one of America's most beloved and best-selling poets. Wilcox's biographer Jenny Ballou writes in her preface, "Somewhere within the undefinable area which unites the sacred and the profane, she emerges firm in her heart for **Walt Whitman**'s 'divine average.'" Her verse appealed to a readership that valued emotional content as the chief indicator of a poem's value.

Ella Wheeler was born in 1850 near Madison, Wisconsin. Her father could trace his ancestry to American patriot Ethan Allen, and Ella would claim she was descended, on her mother's side, from the American Indian heroine Pocahontas. The family was not wealthy, and Ella began at an early age to try to improve their condition by writing, and she eventually attended the University of Wisconsin. She sold a poem called "Life" to the Frank Leslie Publishing House when she was fifteen years old, for six dollars. In 1881 she married Robert J. Wilcox, a Connecticut businessman, after a courtship by letter. Despite their meeting personally only three times before their wedding, the marriage was apparently a happy one. After her husband's death, Wilcox delved into spiritualism and made her experiments public, an enterprise that in the main only added to her popularity with her admirers. She was syndicated in Hearst newspapers, and she turned her ouija board and séance experiences into fodder for columns. Her autobiography, *The Worlds and I* (1918), appeared first in *Cosmopolitan*. She died at her home in Short Beach, Connecticut, after a long illness thought to have been brought on by the strain of her work for the war effort; she had toured extensively with the Red Cross in France, lecturing soldiers on sexual conduct.

Wilcox was one of a contingent of poets invited to Queen Victoria's funeral to observe and to mark the monarch's passing with verse. She was present not as a member of the press but as an invited guest. Even a poem such as "The Queen's Last Ride" (1901) has a moment of feeling: "for widowed no more, / She is crowned with the love that has gone before, / In the hidden depths of each mourner's mind."

Wilcox's poems continue to delight readers after a century and enjoy some popularity on the Internet home pages of her admirers. Although it is commonplace to focus on the emotional content of her work, it is important to note that her popularity probably has more to do with her craft. She could put words together, not in the complex and many-layered manner of a great poet, but with the deftness, energy, succinctness, and accessibility of a masterful lyricist, as in these lines from "Solitude" (1888): "Laugh and the world laughs with you, / Weep and you weep alone."

Wheeler, well aware that her poetry had failed to please critics as much as it had pleased thousands of readers, wrote in "Art and Heart" (1888), "It is not art, but heart, / which wins the wide world over."

Further Reading. ***Selected Primary Sources:*** Wilcox, Ella Wheeler, *The Best of Ella Wheeler Wilcox*, ed. Lady L'Endell Lalique (London: Arlington Books, 1971); ———, *Drops of Water: Poems, by Ella Wheeler* (New York: National Temperance Society and Publication House, 1872); ———, *Men, Women and Emotions* (Chicago: W.B. Conkey, 1896); ———, *Poems of Passion by Ella Wheeler* (Chicago: Belford, Clarke, 1883); ———, *Poems of Pleasure* (New York: Belford, Clarke, 1888); ———, *Whatever Is, Is Best: A Collection of Poems by Ella Wheeler Wilcox* (Boulder, CO: Blue Mountain Arts, 1975). ***Selected Secondary Sources:*** Ballou, Jenny, *Period Piece: Ella Wheeler Wilcox and Her Times* (Boston: Houghton Mifflin, 1940); Gaylor, Annie Laurie, ed., *Women Without Superstition: "No Gods—No Masters": The Collected Writings of Women Freethinkers of the Nineteenth and Twentieth Centuries* (Madison, WI: Freedom from Religion Foundation, 1997); Ifkovic, Edward, *Ella Moon: A Novel Based on the Life of Ella Wheeler Wilcox* (Oregon, WI: Waubesa Press, 2001).

Gail Shivel

WILLIAMS, C.K. (1936–)

C.K. Williams shares his beginning as a writer of politically charged lyrics with many other poets whose first publications appeared in the late 1960s and early 1970s. From there, however, the poet has taken a highly idiosyncratic path, evolving the long, unrhymed line reminiscent of **Walt Whitman** that became both the hallmark of his poetry and a principal innovation within the development of post–World War II and **postmodernist** American poetry. As much concerned with matters of aesthetics and forms as with ethical and political concerns, yet in opposition to **Language poetry**'s tendency to distinguish one from the other, Williams has produced a body of poetry and a poetics that strongly resist traditional categorizations and address fundamental questions of human existence in a post-nuclear and post-Holocaust age as matters of individual consciousness.

Born in Newark, New Jersey, and of Jewish background, Charles Kenneth Williams received his BA at the University of Pennsylvania. He began his career as a poet in the early 1960s, claiming not a poet, though, but the architect Louis Kahn as his first model of "being a poet" ("Beginnings"), while pointing to William Butler Yeats and Rainer Marie Rilke as the figures who were most prominent on his mind when he was beginning to compose poetry. As his career progressed, Williams began dividing his life between the United States and Europe, teaching in American creative writing programs at George Mason University in Fairfax before moving to Princeton University, and living part of the year in Paris. Resisting the idea of being an expatriate, he considers both the immersion in and the distance from United States culture necessary for his work, which deeply engages the texture and substance of American life.

His work includes *Poetry and Consciousness* (1998), a volume of critical prose, as well as numerous collections of poetry, among them *Lies* (1969), *With Ignorance* (1977), *Tar* (1983), *A Dream of Mind* (1992), and *The Vigil* (1999). Williams won the National Book Critics Award for *Flesh and Blood* (1987), the 2000 Pulitzer Prize for *Repair* (1999), and the National Book Award for *The Singing* (2003). He also published **translations**, including *Women of Trachis*, by Sophocles (with Gregory Dickerson [1978]), *The Bacchae of Euripides* (1990), *Canvas*, by Adam Zagajewski (with Renata Gorczynski and Benjamin Ivry [1991]), and *Selected Poems of Francis Ponge* (1994). In addition, Williams composed a song cycle as well as the play *The Jew*, set in nineteenth-century Germany; collaborated as script consultant with David Lynch; and served as contributing editor for the *American Poetry Review*, where he also published some of his drawings.

Retrospectively, Williams sees his first poetry evolving from a dialectical confrontation with the Holocaust and African American history. From an experience of combating ethical attitudes—and the futile attempt to measure different degrees of suffering—evolved, as Williams recalls, his poem "A Day for Anne Frank." "I learned to write poetry," he claims in "Beginnings," "when I was working on 'A Day for Anne Frank'" (*Poetry and Consciousness*). With its predominantly short, often disjunctive lines, and ten-part division, this poem is entirely different, though, in aesthetics and form as well as thematic scope, from Williams's later work. Cutting across time and space, juxtaposing and thus interrelating present experience with memory of the Holocaust, and aligning contemporaneous street scenes with the terrors of war, both Vietnam and World War II, the poem at the same time separates its different first-person speakers from "them," the others, while addressing Anne Frank as "little sister" and recovering her as a "you," a significant other. The poem became the last poem of Williams's first volume *Lies* (1969), published with support of **Anne Sexton**. **Modernist** in its aesthetics, the overall tenor of the collection, which voices a horror vis-à-vis the destructive powers of humankind, is clearly that of post–World War II American poetry. Even if only implicitly, the trauma of both the Holocaust and Hiroshima sets the scene for much of Williams's poetry, including more humorous pieces such as "The Last Deaths" (*With Ignorance*). The inclusive manner exercised in "A Day for Anne Frank," the dream of survival and triumph in the face of human tragedies, large or small, and the resistance to romantic modes and solutions remain characteristic of Williams's later work even if transformed into a different aesthetics.

In the late 1960s and early 1970s, Williams became known primarily for his urgent anti-war and political **lyrics**. The collection *I Am the Bitter Name* (1972), in particular, directly engages immediate political events. Its title poem, for instance, transforms the fury and guilt many Americans felt about Vietnam and the killing, for American conceptions of freedom and liberty, of "little generals" by little "little soldiers" into short sentences and staccato phrasing, reducing punctuation to a minimum of two question marks. Likewise, "The Beginning of April" interrogates the discomfort experienced by those whose compassion for the "kid" in Biafra, "starving on television," remains comfortably couched in a safe geopolitical distance and class difference. Throughout, the effects of guilt on the perception and consciousness of survivors as well as of well-off middle-class individuals in general, make for a significant dimension of Williams's poetics. Echoing **T.S. Eliot**'s opening line from "The Burial of the Dead," the first part of *The Waste Land* (1922)—"April is the cruellest month"—"The Beginning of April" at the same time foregrounds the fundamental shift from modern to postmodern conditions, aesthetics, and consciousness.

Drained by the high emotional amplitude and urgency of this kind of writing, Williams briefly resigned from authorship before making a radical shift in the form and tone of his poetics in the mid-1970s. In the volume *With Ignorance* (1977), he begins adopting as a crucial stylistic device the bold long line that the width of a page cannot accommodate and that, according to some of Williams's critics, functions analogous to color-field painting. Still Williams kept working on short-line lyrics, writing many of the texts that were inspired by the work of the Japanese poet Issa and collected under the title *The Lark. The Thrush. The Starling (Poems from Issa)* (1983). Though formally and visually recalling **Imagist** poetry, these poems were meant to be neither haiku in the English language nor translations of Issa's work. Instead, Williams's attempt was to transform particular moments of Issa's poetry into American poems, adding to their visual dimension by employing one of his own drawings as cover design.

In the collections that followed during the 1980s and 1990s—*Tar* (1983), *Flesh and Blood* (1987), and *Dream of Mind* (1992), with the exception of the volume motivated by Issa—Williams developed the scope of the long line and the new voice it allowed to project into eight-line vignettes *(Flesh and Blood)* as well as into longer poems that unfold personal memories and dialogic meditations. For all this work, and for *Tar* in particular, Williams claims that the work of **Elisabeth Bishop**—with her vision, use of rhetorical figures, and precision of detail—has been a significant impact. Composing in longer lines, Williams, like Bishop, turned away from a modernist poetics of deletion and ellipses that requires the reader to engage in acts of decoding and instead entered an area of signification and narration seemingly limited to prose, yet appropriated for an extension of the poetic registers of his work. Allowing the poet to deal with larger units of meaning, the long line also made for longer poems that veered away from the earlier preoccupations with certain sites or issues. Instead, Williams's texts began to take off from seemingly accidental observations, casual experiences, or apparently insignificant anecdotes related in prosaic diction and common speech, thereby frequently producing a sense of immediacy and directness. "The long line," Charles Altieri writes, "allows a naturalness of conversation folded into the intimacy of internal dialogue, so that lyric speech even at its most expansive seems entirely rooted in momentary observations and reflections on the implication of those observations" (230). These observations on the contingencies of human existence constitute the ground from which Williams's poems evolve larger political, ethical, and philosophical questions concerning the source of violence, the potential of transcendence, the pains of loss, and the powers of love.

The shift toward narration allowed Williams to design poems that accommodate multiple perspectives as narratives and thus to evolve poems which are socially or politically engaged in new ways. In the title poem of the collection *Tar*, for instance, Williams uses this device in order to interrelate two scenes that are spatially separate but synchronic and that are both being witnessed by the poem's lyrical "I": the experience of the media coverage of a major environmental accident ("the first morning of Three Mile Island: those first disquieting, uncertain, mystifying hours") and the arrival of the roofers that had been expected all winter long ("All morning a crew of workmen have been tearing the old decrepit roof of our building"). By interweaving these incidents and outbalancing the uncertainties of the environmental accident by the matter-of-fact concerns of one's immediate environment, the poem resists building metaphorical analogies between personal and political matters, between immediate and sustainable concerns. Admitting that "my roofers stay so clear to me" while "the terror of that time . . . dims so," the poem's speaker at the same time evolves a final, partly self-referential image—the leftover tar used by kids to "scribble" over "every sidewalk on the block"—that makes his protective boundaries of perception, emotion, and consciousness crumble.

Throughout Williams's work, the materiality of bodies and the urgency, if not uncontrollability, of physical desires are inextricably entwined with the dream worlds unfolding in the human mind. Subdivided like classic drama into five parts, the collection *A Dream of Mind* (1992) repeatedly capitalizes on the human body and its desires, lacks, and longings and on intimacy, loneliness, love, and sexual encounters. Exploring the psychic make-up of these universally human experiences, the anxieties and the complexities as well as the banalities that build and undo human relations, the poems grapple with the difficulty of both perceiving and voicing what it means to be human. Accordingly, the texts explore processes of communication as well as miscommunication, the inability to listen to others just as to understand one's own emotions. In this context, "Politics" and "Ethics" ironically function as titles for poems concerned with the rhetoric of seduction and the resistance to temptation and adulterous affairs.

Due to its narrative mode, Williams's writing has frequently been labeled **narrative poetry**. The poet himself, though, finds the term misleading because it undercuts both the fundamentally lyrical quality of his work and the significance of perception and thus subjectivity for his poetics. According to Altieri, Williams's long line "at once takes up and extends an ambition . . . fundamental to much of the best contemporary American poetry. . . . This ambition is to make the 'really now' of the lyric voice also a 'really now' for the personal energies of the poet," for a subjective agency (231). In this respect, Altieri finds Williams closer to the direct speech in **Adrienne Rich**, closer to **Tess Gallagher**'s narratives, closer to **John Ashbery**'s fluid conversation, and closer to the tonal controls of part of **Robert Hass**'s work than to "**William Carlos Williams**'s emphasis on a spoken American diction, [than to] from the cult of breath urgencies in **Charles Olson** and **Robert Creeley**, [and than to] **Allen Ginsberg**'s irrepressible theatricality" (230).

In his prize-winning volume *Repair*, Williams occasionally abandons the longer line and includes poems that appear highly stylized and formal. In this way his more recent work, like that of Rich, indirectly reengages its modernist "beginnings," while also addressing questions of aging, as Williams does in his collection *The Singing* (2003).

Further Reading. ***Selected Primary Sources:*** Williams, C.K., *A Dream of Mind* (New York: Farrar, Straus and Giroux, 1992); ———, *Flesh and Blood* (New York: Farrar, Straus and Giroux, 1987); ———, *I Am the Bitter Name* (Boston: Houghton Mifflin, 1972); ———, *The Lark. The Thrush. The Starling (Poems from Issa)* (Providence, RI: Burning Deck, 1983); ———, *Lies* (Boston: Houghton Mifflin, 1969); ———, *Misgivings: My Mother, My Father, Myself* (York: Farrar, Straus and Giroux, 2000); ———, *Poems 1963–1983* (Newcastle upon Tyne, England: Bloodaxe Books, 1983; New York: Farrar, Straus and Giroux, 1988); ———, *Poetry and Consciousness* (Ann Arbor: University of Michigan Press, 1998); ———, *Repair* (New York: Farrar, Straus and Giroux, 1999); ———, *Selected Poems* (New York: Farrar, Straus and Giroux, 1994); ———, *The Singing* (New York: Farrar, Straus and Giroux, 2003); ———, *Tar* (New York: Knopf, 1983); ———, *The Vigil* (New York: Farrar, Straus and Giroux, 1997); ———, *With Ignorance* (Boston: Houghton Mifflin, 1977). ***Selected Secondary Sources:*** Altieri, Charles, "Contemporary Poetry as Philosophy: Subjective Agency in John Ashbery and C.K. Williams" (*Contemporary Literature* 33 [1992]: 214–242); Gubar, Susan, "Poets of Testimony: C.K. Williams and Jacqueline Osherow as Proxy Witnesses of the Shoah," in *Mapping the Ethical Turn: A Reader in Ethics, Culture, and Literary Theory*, ed. Todd F. Davis and Kenneth Womack (Charlottesville: University of Virginia Press, 2001, 165–191); Keller, Lynn, "An Interview with C.K. Williams" (*Contemporary Literature* 29.2 [1988]: 157–176).

Sabine Sielke

WILLIAMS, JONATHAN (1929–)

Though a fine poet himself, Jonathan Williams's greatest contribution to American poetry was his founding and subsequent stewardship of Jargon Press, a publishing house first set in motion as a journal, which set the standard for **small press** publishing in the latter half of the twentieth century. Jargon discovered and promoted once overlooked influential poets and, in doing so, furthered a particular **avant-garde poetry** that experimented with and outlined the connections between the visual and the literary arts and the associations between the spiritual and physical worlds. These attributes have come to define the movements of the **San Francisco Renaissance** and the **Black Mountain** and **New York schools** of poetry as well as to mark Williams's own verse.

Williams was born in Asheville, North Carolina, and educated at St. Alban's School in Washington, and he entered Princeton University in 1947. At Princeton, Williams became familiar with the emerging **Beat** movement and was attracted to the earthy, rebellious, and musical style of poets such as **Kenneth Rexroth** and **Kenneth Patchen**, both of whom Williams engaged in correspondence. Rexroth and Williams conversed on the relationship between the visual and the written word, and as an indirect result, Williams's interest in the visual arts grew.

Williams left Princeton in his sophomore year to return to Washington's Phillips Gallery to study painting with the American modernist Karl Knaths. Following a sojourn to William Hayter's Atelier 17 in Greenwich Village to study etching, engraving, and printmaking, Williams later enrolled in the Chicago Institute of Design to study photography, where photographer Harry Callahan convinced him to attend Black Mountain College.

At Black Mountain, Williams met **Charles Olson**, whose budding theories on poetics found fertile ground for development in the minds and actions of his students. It was with Olson's encouragement, including the sanctioning of use of the school's printing press, that Williams established Jargon in 1951 and began writing serious poetry.

Jargon published what has come to be known as significant books of poetry, including Olson's first volume of *The Maximus Poems* and **Robert Creeley**'s *The Immoral Proposition*, setting the stage for Jargon's future in developing or reviving the work of writers such as **Louis Zukofsky**, **Denise Levertov**, **Robert Duncan**, and **Mina Loy**.

Williams's own poetry reflects the American Romantic and **modernist** traditions in which he was reared and subsequent contemporary influences that he propagated as publisher. His collection *The Language They Speak Is Things to Eat* (1994) is a convincing account. In it he betrays his Romantic heritage in his frequent use of nature as stage to center the persona's vision and give voice to his or her thoughts. Like **Walt Whitman**, Williams's personae luxuriate in the landscape, as evidenced in his poem "Aunt Dory Ellis, of Penland, Remembers When She Fell in Her Garden at the Home Place and Broke Her Hip in 19 and 56" (1994): "I lay / a hour in that petunia patch." And as Whitman "yawps" barbarically, Williams's personae too have "hollered." His use of the vernacular echoes both Whitman and **William Carlos Williams**; in "My Quaker-Atheist Friend, Who Has Come to This Meeting-House since 1913, Smokes & Looks Out over the Rawthey to Holme Fell" (1994), the vernacular, "solid, common, *vulgar* words / the ones you can touch," takes primacy. As he portrays common folk, what Williams finds, unlike Whitman, are folk who are "out of whack."

Much as Sherwood Anderson in *Winesburg, Ohio* does in the milieu of the Midwest, Williams's focus on individuals of Appalachia exposes the extremes inherent in the human condition and the unique complexities of America. Characters such as Aunt Dory Ellis, Daddy Bostain, and Miss Lucy Morgan reveal both the potential of Appalachia and a culture with seeming limitations, where Appalachia "represents the best / that the people were able to do" ("My Quaker Atheist-Friend"). These are the circumstances that give ground for Williams to demonstrate a biting irreverence in the more contemporary vein of a poet like Rexroth, as a dead neighbor becomes, in "Daddy Bostain, the Moses of the Wing community Moonshiners, Laments from His Deathbed the Spiritual Estate of One of His Soul-Saving Neighbors" (1994), "good kindlin wood / fer Hell." Yet it is also a culture that possesses a quiet and resolute resiliency, as in "Miss Lucy Morgan Shows Me a Photograph of Mrs. Mary Grindstaff Spinning Wool on the High Wheel" (1994): "the charred heart does not break in Appalachia, they / have not let it."

As with language and character, Williams seems intent on using form to evoke the entirety of perspective, showing the fullness of his field of vision. Taking cues from the modernists' interest in expression of the concise image, Williams's poems may be considered tightly constructed. One may recall William Carlos Williams or **Ezra Pound** in this excerpt from "An Aubade from Verlaine's Day" (1994): "berries / from the / dogwood / makes these two / clouds / one, one eye / open." Here Williams reflects his tutelage as artist and writer, exhibiting an interest in balancing pure, pictorial design with recognizable subject matter. Williams, an adept photographer himself, combines the photographer's wish to see "not with / but *thru*" the eye (quoted in Gray, 284) with Charles Olson's **projectivism**, conveying both the totality of form and the energy of the poetic to reach form through the human experience of objects.

In effect, Williams's display of a variety and range of distinctly American influences might just make him the quintessential representative of the twentieth-century American poet.

Further Reading. ***Selected Primary Sources:*** Williams, Jonathan, *An Ear in Bartram's Tree: Selected Poems, 1957–1967* (Chapel Hill: University of North Carolina Press, 1969); ———, *The Language They Speak Is Things to Eat* (Chapel Hill: University of North Carolina Press, 1994). ***Selected Secondary Sources:*** Gray, Richard, "Beats, Prophets and Aesthetes," in *American Poetry of the Twentieth Century* (London: Longman, 1990); Jaffe, James S., comp., *Jonathan Williams: A Bibliographical Checklist of His Writings, 1950–1988* (Haverford, PA: James S. Jaffe Rare Books, 1989).

John R. Woznicki

WILLIAMS, ROGER (ca. 1603–1683)

Roger Williams was a Puritan clergyman chiefly remembered for establishing Rhode Island as a haven for religious toleration and for helping to establish the first Baptist church in America. Williams's one known attempt at writing poetry appeared in his first book, *A Key into the Language of America* (1643), in which appeared several verses that lightly satirize "civilized" (and purported Christian) Englishmen by contrast with Native American customs, beliefs, and practices.

Born in London to a family of merchants and traders, Williams began to embrace the Puritan cause, to his father's dislike, in his adolescence and matriculated at Cambridge under the tutelage of Sir Edward Coke (for whom he had performed shorthand services), receiving his bachelor's degree in 1627. Despite further study at Cambridge, he never attained his MA. By 1629 he had become family chaplain for Sir William Masham, which afforded entrée to various Puritan leaders; in December, he married Mary Bernard, and the following year, they departed for New England, where he was swiftly invited to join **John Wilson** as a fellow minister in the Boston church. But Williams rejected the invitation, on the grounds that the congregation was still "unseparated." He then resided briefly at Salem before moving to Plymouth, where he penned a treatise (not extant) challenging the settlers' property rights on various grounds, including the grounds that "Kinge Iames . . . tould a solemne publicke lye" for claiming to be "the first Christian Prince that had discovered this land." The document did not come to public light until Williams had moved back to Salem, at which time the General Court demanded a retraction; he complied. He likely influenced John Endecott's controversial decision to shear the red cross from the British ensign. Salem invited him to be their minister in 1634, but the General Court disapproved and exerted pressure on the town. Williams began a letter-writing campaign to rouse sympathy for his cause; the General Court responded in 1635 with a sentence of banishment, but he was allowed to remain until the following spring on condition of his silence. When Williams violated this agreement, the General Court moved to arrest him, but he had been tipped off and fled; even so, Williams maintained a correspondence with Governor John Winthrop and, later, with Winthrop's son.

After a brief attempt to settle on the Seekonk River, Williams and a small group of followers moved to Narragansett Bay and established Providence. Williams provided able assistance to Narragansetts and English during the Pequot War. At Providence Williams established cordial relations with the Narrangasetts and also welcomed people concerned for the sake of conscience. In 1643 Williams returned to England as an agent on behalf of several settlements in Narragansett Bay to secure possession against Massachusetts Bay encroachment, an effort in which he succeeded. While there, Williams launched his publishing career with *A Key* and two works that attacked Massachusetts intolerance, especially as articulated by **John Cotton**, thus initiating a running print debate with the latter. Despite returning with a patent in 1644, internal conflict persisted, and Williams returned to England in 1651 with John Clarke; while in England, he made contact with Oliver Cromwell and John Milton, but the effort was not a complete success. He returned to Providence in 1654 to find it torn with strife and conflict. In 1663 Clarke obtained a royal charter guaranteeing "soul liberty," but Williams had increasingly withdrawn from political activity to his trading post. Despite his commitment to toleration, Williams was disturbed by Quakers in the area and publicly debated them in 1672, which led to his final book. He was also greatly disturbed by the outbreak of King Philip's War in 1675 because he was unable to stop it. In 1676 his house was burned to the ground; Williams then joined a Providence militia. He died, apparently of natural causes, in 1683.

A Key contains a set of verses to conclude each of its thirty-two chapters (Harold S. Jantz also counts a couplet in the middle of one chapter); as John Teunissen and Evelyn J. Hinz argue, they are structurally integrated with Williams's conception of each chapter. With five exceptions, the poems are all in three quatrains of common measure; additionally, they are untitled except under the heading of "more particular" (with some variants). The poems figure as part of the long subtitle's description of the book's "Spiritual Observations . . . of chiefe and speciall use . . . to all the English Inhabitants" in New England as well as to all people. In general the poems ironically upbraid English Christians for their arrogance and supposed superiority over Native Americans; instead, Williams sees both Native Americans and false English Christians as reprobate. The Native Americans, without benefit of revelation or institution, have nonetheless through nature alone attained virtuous behavior equal, and sometimes superior, to that of false but arrogant Christians. One example comes from the chapter on clothing: "Boast not proud *English*, of thy birth & blood, / Thy brother *Indian* is by birth as Good. / Of one blood God made Him, and Thee & All, / As wise, as faire, as strong, as personall." In the chapter on timekeeping, Williams notes that Indians "overprize" the sun, but the English, with "artificall helps" like clocks and watches, "unthankfully despise" the same, so he can point toward a common but fallen humanity equally in need of God and gospel. Even so, the English, with their benefits, tend to come off worse because of their access to Christian revelation, as noted in Williams's remarks that "The best clad *English-man*, / Not cloth'd with Christ, more naked is: / Then naked Indian."

Further Reading. ***Selected Primary Sources:*** Williams, Roger, *The Complete Writings of Roger Williams*, 7 vols. (New York: Russell & Russell, 1963); ———, *A Key into the Language of America*, ed. John J. Teunissen and Evelyn J. Hinz (1643; Detroit, MI: Wayne State University Press, 1973). ***Selected Secondary Source:*** Gaustad, Edwin S., *Liberty of Conscience: Roger Williams in America* (Grand Rapids, MI: Eerdmans, 1991).

Michael G. Ditmore

WILLIAMS, WILLIAM CARLOS (1883–1963)

William Carlos Williams spent his life in the small town where he was born, Rutherford, New Jersey, practicing medicine full-time for a middle- and working-class population: He estimated that he delivered two thousand babies. In the midst of this, he produced hundreds of poems and a major book-length poem; four novels and numerous short stories; an innovative history of America; an autobiography; five plays; many conventional essays and a number of prose experiments; and numerous reviews and a prolific correspondence. From unprepossessing beginnings (his first book, self-published and then disavowed, was quite bad), his work and literary activism gradually came to be increasingly respected and finally became a central presence for generations of American poets. By the end of his career, his reputation was unassailable; and in the decades after his death, his influence has become profound. There are few poets of the latter half of the twentieth century, innovative or conservative, whose work has not been affected by his example. He was a pioneering American modernist, a senior presence among the **Objectivists**, and a primary poetic source for many subsequent schools of poetry—**projective verse**, the **Beats**, the **New York School**, the **confessional poets**, the **Language poets**—as well as a model for many unaffiliated poets working in the mode of **free-verse** meditation on the everyday. None of these tendencies completely captures the import of his work, though it's safe to say that innovation was basic to it. From the vantage of the twenty-first century, his democratic **modernism**, aesthetically unlegislatable, looks to remain central to American poetry.

Williams's father, a British citizen, met his mother in her native Puerto Rico, where they married before moving to Rutherford. Williams studied medicine at the University of Pennsylvania (1902–1906), where he met the first and most lasting of his poetic influences, **Ezra Pound**, as well as **H.D.** (then Hilda Doolittle). After a year in Germany studying pediatrics (1909), he settled in his hometown, marrying Florence (Flossie) Herman in 1912, practicing medicine, and raising two sons. In 1924 he traveled to Europe for six months, but after that mostly stayed put in Rutherford, outside of a few vacation trips and reading tours. In 1948 his exceptional vitality suffered its first shock, a heart attack, followed over the next decade by a series of strokes that slowed his writing considerably. In 1952 he was nominated as Consultant in Poetry for the Library of Congress, but red-baiting prevented him from being appointed: though he had never been close to being a member of the Communist Party, this was during the height of McCarthyism, and he had written poems such as "A Morning Imagination of Russia" (1932). This setback, along with his declining health, triggered an episode of severe depression, for which he was hospitalized for several months. He recovered and continued writing throughout the 1950s despite his increasing physical impairment. He died at home in 1963.

Williams's life as a doctor provided him thorough knowledge of his local small-town community, and his literary activities made him familiar with some of the most sophisticated poets and painters in New York City and Europe. Thus, though the content of his writing might seem provincial compared with the writings Pound and **T.S. Eliot**, he was always sophisticated in his poetic methods and ambitions. The impression of his provincialism was sometimes exacerbated by his public pronouncements, generally off the cuff, often contentious. Whatever the level of tact, his attacks were aimed at causes and symptoms of poetic conservatism: the university, sonnet form and iambic pentameter, and Eliot's ubiquitous influence.

Williams interacted with a great many historically significant artists of the first half of the twentieth century, from his early appearance in Pound's initial **Imagist** anthology, *Des Imagistes* (1914), to his inclusion of letters from the young **Allen Ginsberg** in *Paterson* (1946–1958) and of a large chunk of **Charles Olson**'s "Projective Verse" essay in his autobiography (1949). In between, he was in close contact with writers (H.D., **Mina Loy**, **Marianne Moore**, **Wallace Stevens**, Robert McAlmon, **Elsa von Freytag-Loringhoven**, Nathaniel West, **Louis Zukofsky**), painters (Charles Sheeler, Charles Demuth, Marsden Hartley), and photographers (Edward Stieglitz, Man Ray) and was knowledgeably enthusiastic about Cézanne, Cubism, **Dada**, and Duchamp. In old age, he was a crucial poetic mentor for Ginsberg, **Robert Creeley**, and **Frank O'Hara**, who named Williams, **Crane**, and **Whitman** the only American poets who were "better than the movies."

Such a list only begins to suggest the range of Williams's contacts, which extended into wide and varied circles of lesser-known artists. But on the other hand, it wouldn't be inaccurate to say that his poetic career was given significant shape by two literary relationships: his lifelong, sometimes friendly emulation of Pound (whom he knew very well) and his unnuanced enmity toward Eliot (whom he only met a few times). From their meeting as teenagers at Penn, Pound, younger, confident, and knowledgeable, assumed the role of Williams's teacher, constantly giving him lists of books to read, a pattern which was to continue for half a century. (In Books III and IV of *Paterson* [1949; 1951], Williams quotes pedagogic letters that he was still receiving from Pound: "Read *all* the Gk tragedies in / Loeb.—plus Frobenius, plus Gesell.") Throughout his life Williams made irregular progress toward emancipating himself from this student position, declaring in one of his last poems, "To My Friend Ezra Pound" (1956), "Your English / is not specific enough / As a writer of poems you show yourself to be inept not to say / usurious"—the last word a knowing thrust that named the cardinal sin in Pound's poetic theology. Such moments of confident equality are not the rule, however. For the most part Pound and Eliot embodied for Williams the erudition he lacked and the European cultural finesse that he missed by staying in the United States.

Williams's attitude toward theUnited States was riven with contradictions. On the one hand, he insisted that the American poet reject the etiolated tradition of English iambic pentameter and create a new poetry based on the American language. One of his often-cited poetic coinages, "the **variable foot**," was meant to describe a method of capturing the irregular beat of American speech. At the same time, however, he railed against the triteness of America: "The pure products of America / go crazy—"; or he would make a show of accepting it bitterly: "I am a beginner. I am an American. A United Stateser. Yes, it's ugly. . . . I hate you [Europe], I hate your orchestras, your libraries, your sciences, your yearly salons, your finely tuned intelligences of all sorts."

Success came slowly to Williams, and his first small taste of it came via Pound, who was instrumental in getting *The Tempers* (1913) published in "finely tuned" London. Most of its poems are written under the influence of Pound's early pre-Raphaelite diction ("Thou art my Lady") and imagery ("Let there be gold of tarnished masonry") and are quite forgettable. Only occasionally do hints of the vivid complexity of Williams's later work appear—for instance, at the end of "The Birth of Venus," which ends with this invitation from lorelei figures: "We revel in the sea's green! / Come play: / It is forbidden!" This is a far lesser poem than Eliot's "Love Song of J. Alfred Prufrock," but the (coincidental) contrast between its ending and the mermaids at the end of "Prufrock" is striking.

In his next books, *Al Que Quiere!* (1917) and *Sour Grapes* (1921), Williams moved toward his mature style. He no longer capitalized the initial letter of each line (a significant change for him at the time), and he used everyday language and presented everyday images without comment (e.g., the sixth section of "January Suite" reads in its entirety, "—and a semicircle of dirt-colored men / about a fire bursting from an old / ash can"). He also began to conceive of the poem as an event in its own right, free from any requirement for verisimilitude. The opening lines of "Portrait of a Lady" mix sarcastic imagery, distanced but genuine eroticism, and an aggressive appropriation of art history: "Your thighs are appletrees / whose blossoms touch the sky . . . where Watteau hung a lady's / slipper." A few lines later, Williams is playing with the conceits he has invented: "Ah, yes—below / the knees, since the tune / drops that way, it is / one of those white summer days." Such a passage, neither description nor interior monologue, illustrates a point Williams would make later: "the poet thinks with his poem."

During the 1920s William began publishing substantial amounts of prose, with *In the American Grain* (1925) garnering the most contemporary attention. It is a highly personal account of American history, focusing on an irregular archipelago of representative figures: Columbus, De Soto, **Cotton Mather**, Daniel Boone, Washington, and **Poe** among others. Making no attempt at an objective history, Williams writes from a quasi-identificatory position, continually telling the same story: the unfinished creation of an American culture, a process involving the falling away of European norms under the shock of physical contact with the unknown New World. This was a scenario that applied closely to Williams's own attempts to fashion a modernist poetic idiom in America while resisting European sophistication. Poe was the exemplar: "It is NOT culture to *oppress* a novel environment with the stale, if symmetrical, castoffs of another battle. . . . Poe could look at France, Spain, Greece and NOT be impelled to copy." One could read "Williams" for "Poe" there without much distortion of meaning. There's a kind of biographical justice that *Grain* was published the year after Williams's 1924 trip to Europe, a trip in which he met Joyce, Brancusi, and the critic Valery Larbaud among others but returned to American with the strong sense that he was a very junior partner in the enterprise of modernism. From a European (cultured) perspective, he was a small fry; in America, he was as good as anyone else.

Williams's more experimental prose pieces and **prose poetry** combinations of the period, *Kora in Hell: Improvisations* (1920), *Spring and All* (1923), *The Great American Novel* (1923) and *The Descent of Winter* (1928), have widely been considered, since their re-publication in a single volume in 1970, some of his most significant and generative writing. But when they were first published, they had little impact: They were published in tiny editions (with most copies of *Spring* lost in shipment to America) and were formally iconoclastic without displaying the daunting mass of labor and literary erudition that contributed to the reputations of *The Waste Land* or *Ulysses*. Williams's experiments easily revealed the spontaneity of their composition. As the collection's title makes clear, the pieces in *Kora* were improvised. The book was the result of a year-long series of daily prose pieces, scribbled at odd hours in the midst of his medical practice: for example, "Awake early to the white blare of a sun flooding in sideways. Strip and bathe in it. Ha, but an ache tearing at your throat—and a vague cinema lifting its black moon blot all out. . . . There's no dancing save in the head's dark." To these pieces Williams added explanation, some a propos and some deliberately irrelevant. About the previous excerpt, Williams comments in part, "In the mind there is a continual play of obscure images which coming between the eyes and their prey seem pictures on a screen at the movies. . . . The wish would be to see not floating visions of unknown purport but the imaginative qualities of the actual things."

Given Williams's later involvement with the Objectivists and his best-known poetic slogan, "No ideas but in things," it is easy to think of him as rejecting everything save physical description. However, though he almost always rejected the vague interiority of "the head's dark," it was never the pure exteriority of "actual things" that his poems aimed to reveal; rather, it was the middle term that he valued, a conjunction of poetic form and perception, "the imaginative qualities" of what he perceived. In the broken and often chaotic prose that accompanies the poems of *Spring*, a constantly occurring word is "imagination," which could provide "an escape from crude symbolism, the annihilation of strained associations, complicated ritualistic forms designed to separate the work from 'reality'—such as rhyme, meter. . . . The work will be in the realm of the imagination as plain as the sky to a fisherman—A very clouded sentence. The word must be put down for itself." The prose of *Spring* is almost always "very clouded": Williams never settles on a clear definition of what he means by imagination; but the poems, in their variousness, give a sense of its capaciousness. There is his best-known poem, "The Red Wheelbarrow," which begins, "so much depends / upon / a red wheel / barrow." Its **minimalist** focus on the physical can obscure its form (three-word and one-word stanzas), its verbal dexterity (breaking "wheelbarrow" into its two constituent nouns or, later in the poem, decomposing rain into process, "rain," and material, "water"), and its ambitiously Emersonian claims for perception ("so much depends upon"). Other poems in *Spring* are very different. "The Agonized Spires," something of a portrait of nearby New York, shows Williams to have been intrigued by Cubism and Dada: "Crustaceous / wedge / of sweaty kitchens / on rock." "Shoot it Jimmy!" lineates American speech: "Our orchestra / is the cat's nuts— / . . . / That sheet stuff / 's a lot a cheese." "To Elsie" is a complex poem that, despite Williams's anti-Eliot stance, is something of an American equivalent to *The Waste Land*. Williams can be as unhappy with modernity as is Eliot; Elsie, who surfaces in the middle of poem, is no more impressive a personage than Lil or the young man carbuncular in Eliot's poem. But whereas Eliot uses scorn to distance himself (and his readers), Williams allows Elsie to be emblematic of the present that includes poet and reader: Elsie "express[es] with broken / brain the truth about us." The end of *The Waste Land* gestures, however ironically, toward some transcendent conclusion to history ("Shantih shantih shantih"), but "To Elsie" leaves us in an open-ended present, in a moving car careening toward an unknown future: "No one / to witness / and adjust, no one to drive the car."

The 1930s presented demands that struck athwart the optimism of modernist poetics. In the 1920s and the previous decade, it was easy for modernists of all stripes (Williams, Eliot, **Stein**) to imagine that their writing could function as a blueprint for remaking society. In the 1930s the Depression and the rise of fascism made such confidence obsolete. In the 1920s one can see Williams collaging different social perspectives in poems; in the 1930s he more often writes poems relevant to the current time of writing. Emblematic social figures appear—in "Proletarian Portrait," for instance, which presents a "big bareheaded woman / in an apron"; but Williams is careful to avoid the heroism of contemporaneous proletarian poetry as this woman merely takes off her shoe and "pulls out the paper insole / to find the nail / That has been hurting her." In "A Foot-Note" Williams rejects tendentious poetics: you will pretty soon have / neither food, clothing, nor / even Communism itself, / Comrades. Read good poetry!" Such a poem, however, cannot believably lay claim to being itself much of a "necessary mechanism." In "The Yachts," one of his major poems of the period, Williams maintains the tension between the exquisite calibrations of fine art and the unnuanced basic human needs. At first the yachts "appear youthful, rare / as the light of a happy eye"; but in the latter half of the poem, the yacht race becomes a "horror" and our attention is turned away from the triumphal elegance of the yachts toward the supporting medium, the water, which is seen as "an entanglement of watery bodies / lost to the world bearing what they cannot hold." Incidentally, here is another example of Williams aiming to register "imaginative qualities," rather than simply "things."

In the introduction to *The Wedge* (1944) Williams gave his notion of a poem as a made thing rather than a personal expression its most memorable form in the slogan "a poem is a machine made of words." However, "machine" shouldn't be taken as implying standardization, which Williams dismisses: "all sonnets say the same thing of no importance." Although many of his best poems of the 1940s, such as "The Clouds" and "Burning the Christmas Greens," don't conform closely to this idea and in fact are discursive, Williams often makes his poems meditations on what a new poetics might require: "Let the snake wait under / his weed / and the writing / be of words, slow and quick, sharp / to strike, quiet to wait, / sleepless."

Williams's **long poem** *Paterson* had been germinating from the mid-1920s. His 1938 *Complete Collected Poems* contained a number of short poems designated "From 'Paterson,'" as well as a longer poem, "Paterson: Episode 17," which was incorporated into Book III of the finished poem. "Paterson: The Falls" (*The Wedge*) is an anticipatory synopsis. Book I appeared in 1946 and was reviewed quite favorably. It marked a turning point in Williams's career; after this, he was considered a significant American poet and was no longer easy to omit from accounts of modernist poetry. Williams planned for *Paterson* to have four books; but by the time the next three appeared (1948, 1949, and 1951), the poem had outgrown its original conception: Williams produced a fifth book in 1958, and a few notes toward a sixth were found among his papers at his death.

Paterson resists summary, though Williams did present a number of simple schemes for it in his notes, contradicting a basic practice of his writing, which was predicated on discovery rather than fleshing out of prior thinking. For his subject he rejected New York ("too big, too much a congeries of the entire world's facets"), instead choosing Paterson as being "nearer home, something knowable," having historical associations with the American Revolution and containing "a central feature, the Passaic Falls . . . the lucky burden of what [he] wanted to say." *Paterson*'s four books were to follow the course of the Passaic: "the river above the Falls, the catastrophe of the Falls itself, the river below the Falls and the entrance at the end to the great sea." The roar of the Falls seemed "a language which we were and are seeking." Another primary theme is announced in Book I: "A man like a city and a woman like a flower / —who are in love. Two women. Three women. Innumerable women, each like a flower. / But / only one man—like a city."

Williams did not stick closely to such plans or themes, although gestures toward them do occur in a number of places. Each of the five books contains three sections, some of which are focused around specific locales or narratives. The first section of Book II, entitled "Sunday in the Park," is organized around the protagonist, sometimes referred to as "Paterson," walking amid Sunday picnickers; a large part of the second section is given over to the futile, enthusiastic harangues of a Salvation Army preacher. Section Two of Book III focuses on the fire that destroyed the Paterson library; the opening section of Book IV, subtitled "An Idyl," narrates, in jumpy, intercut fashion, the relations between three figures: It follows a New York socialite (rather mockingly called "Corydon") with lesbian longings toward her working-class masseuse ("Phyllis"), who does not reciprocate but who does appear to be having a sporadic affair with a doctor ("Paterson"). However, such capsule summaries miss the coruscating line-by-line, page-by-page texture of the poem. Any page might contain lines or short stanzas referring to other material in the poem; the verse is constantly interrupted by chunks of miscellaneous prose: passages from histories of nineteenth-century histories of Paterson, local weather reports, flyers, letters from literary and non-literary contemporaries. At times, the prose is thematically related, as when in the midst of the "Beautiful Thing" passage (Book III), a fraught, lyrical meditation on an African American prostitute who has been beaten up at a party, Williams interposes a savagely unfeeling colonial account of French explorers torturing Native Americans. But many times, Williams inserts prose with no obvious relevance to the local context. One of the most notable and controversial uses of external sources occurs in Book II, where Williams inserts many passages, only lightly edited, from the letters of a struggling aspiring poet, Marcia Nardi, who had sought him out for literary advice. He had mentioned the possibility of his using the letters to her, but they had fallen out of touch by the time Book II was going to press, so she only learned of the presence of her words in Williams's poem when she ran across a copy in a bookstore. This use of her letters raises complex ethical issues: Is Williams exploiting Nardi? Is he giving her a public platform for her eloquent and sometimes obsessive complaints about the difficulties of getting support for writing when one is a woman? The letters also raise aesthetic issues, since Book II increasingly becomes as much Nardi's and Williams's. The last five pages, densely printed in a smaller font, are given over to her. Williams makes a literary gesture by changing her signature to "La votre C," a reference to Cressida's letters to Troilus in Chaucer's poem; but Nardi can hardly be said to have betrayed Williams, as Cressida does Troilus, and the very real material difficulties Nardi details have nothing to do with Chaucer's imagined Ilium. Typical of the aesthetic issues that Williams's writing often raises, there is no easy dismissal of either side of these arguments. Mike Weaver, one of the first critics to take Williams's relation to the chaotic American cultural environment seriously, takes a judicious approach when he writes that Nardi and other figures are portrayed as human beings whose dreams are deferred or thwarted; hense they are very much in the American grain.

Pound's ongoing *Cantos* were a primary model, and the extensive collaged quotations in *Paterson* would have been unthinkable without Pound's example. But as always, Williams needed to reinvent genres for an American context: The poem was to be "a reply to Greek and Latin with the bare hands" as its opening proem has it, challenging Pound's and Eliot's conservative erudition. Whereas Eliot esteems the literature he alludes to and Pound cites material he wants the reader to seek out and learn from, the documentary material that Williams uses in *Paterson* has a decidedly parochial flavor. Two Paterson stories concern Sam Patch, a town drunk who died in a public attempt to dive from the top of the Falls, and Sarah Cummings, a minister's wife who accidentally fell from there. These are not figures of world-historical scale, to say the least. In another moment of local history, the discovery of a large pearl led to widespread frantic harvesting of local shellfish and ended with the discovery of an even larger pearl, which was ruined in the process of boiling the oysters open. Williams uses such stories to exemplify the failure of Paterson's inhabitants to meet the untamed locality on equal terms. But at the same time, he is insisting that American poets must build a culture using the imperfect local materials at hand.

Throughout Book I, the roar of the Falls is apostrophized as a source of genuine language that cannot be harnessed: "no words. / They may look at the torrent in / their minds / and it is foreign to them." Occasionally the description is physical: He writes of the air above the water, "parallel but never mingling, one that whirls / backward at the brink and curls invisibly / upward, fills the hollow, whirling, / an accompaniment—but apart"; but more often, the Falls is a pervading metaphoric backdrop, as in the following, where Williams applies imagery of falling water to both the hair of two young girls and the air surrounding them: "the pouring / waters of their hair" and proceeds, "one— / a willow twig pulled from a low / leafless bush in full bud in her hand, / . . . / holds it, the gathered spray, / upright in the air, the pouring air. . . .Ain't they beautiful!"

The last phrase of this excerpt, where the unsophisticated aesthetic enthusiasm of the girls can be read in a positive light as a critique of the possibly excessive lyricism of the previous lines, points to a recurrent tension in the poem. On the one hand, Williams constantly laments the failure of language in general terms: "They do not know the words / or have not / the courage to use them"; yet when he quotes the actual speech he hears in Paterson, it is unpretentious and lively, a source of poetic energy rather than a symptom of failure: "Hi, open up a dozen, make / it two dozen! Easy girl! / You wanna blow a fuse?" In his *Autobiography* he is explicit about this, boasting that he got his language "out of the mouths of Polish mothers." The tacit polemic here is directed against the refinement of Pound's language and the traditionalism of Eliot's. Incidentally, many of his short stories are unvarnished reportage of his interactions with the "Polish mothers" and other immigrants who made up the majority of his patients.

Paterson does not come to anything like a neat conclusion. In fact, near the end of Book IV, Williams disparages coherence as a goal for the poem: "Waken from a dream, this dream of / the whole poem." As it progresses, *Paterson* opens up more and more to its present context; the first section of Book V contains a letter from the young Allen Ginsberg that comments on the preceding parts of *Paterson*; the second section ends with an excerpt from an interview in which the journalist Mike Wallace grills Williams on the apparent eccentricities of modern poetry. The poem becomes something of a bulletin board for younger generations to post their observations on the continuities and changes of modernist poetics.

Some of Williams's most celebrated poems were written in the latter part of his career. "The Desert Music" (1951) is something of an *ars poetica*, containing a mix of modes typical of Williams. Vulgarity—"an old whore in / a cheap Mexican joint in Juárez, her bare / can waggling crazily"—appears side by side with eloquent gratitude for the human capacity for writing: "And I could not help thinking / of the wonders of the brain that / hears that music and of our / skill sometimes to record it." "Asphodel, That Greeny Flower" (1953) is Williams's longest poem—excepting *Paterson* of course—and one of his best known, primarily due to lines that articulate a most persuasive modernist credo: "If is difficult / to get the news from poems / yet men die miserably every day / for lack / of what is found there." Originally conceived as belonging to Book V of *Paterson*, "Asphodel" mixes direct address to the poet's wife, Flossie, with a wide-ranging series of meditations on the power of poetry to confront the newly unleashed might of the atomic bomb. Williams's dealings with Flossie in the poem have received a mixed reception. On the one hand, it is touching to read what is essentially love poetry written by a frail old man to his wife of fifty years. But "Asphodel" is also a confession to Flossie of Williams's many affairs (and in this aspect is the immediate ancestor of the confessional poetry that was to become ubiquitous in the 1960s), and for many readers Williams's apology shades into an almost boastful attitude: "Imagine you saw / a field made up of women / all silver-white. / What should you do / but love them?" Eroticism, sublimated to widely varying degrees, remained basic to Williams's poetry throughout his career; his commitment to **open form** (and in this he could almost be said to be a co-founder with Charles Olson of projective verse) made his work quite candid. The result of these two facts is that Williams wrote about women constantly, often in ways that contemporary readers, including feminist critic **Rachel DuPlessis**, find problematic. But there are also many poems and passages that could be called proto-feminist, a more surprising fact supported by feminist poet **Adrienne Rich**'s using a line from "Asphodel" for the title of a collection of essays, *What Is Found There*. Here as elsewhere, Williams's work resists categorization.

Almost a century after Williams began writing, his critical reception was still in its formative stage. One early critical landmark was Wallace Stevens's introduction to Williams's *Collected Poems 1921—1931*, in which, to Williams's chagrin, Stevens labeled him "anti-poetic." Another landmark was **Randall Jarrell**'s rave review of *Paterson* Book I (1946), the first praise Williams received from an academic critic. But the next decades were not totally propitious for readings of Williams's work. The Eliotic, **New Critical** 1950s would consider Williams's messiness, lack of easily identifiable theme, and formal jaggedness signs of lesser poetry. The turn to Pound with Hugh Kenner's *The Pound Era* (1970) served Williams better; but *The Cantos* seemed more ambitious and radical than *Paterson*, and compared with Pound's criticism, Williams's seemed impressionistic. British critic Mike Weaver authored a pioneering study that would be called cultural criticism; Joseph Riddel read him as a deconstructivist. Until fairly recently, however, much academic criticism read Williams thematically. The best readers of Williams, starting with Hart Crane and Louis Zukofsky in the 1920s, have been the subsequent generations of poets, for whom his writing remains centrally instructive.

Further Reading. ***Selected Primary Sources:*** Williams, William Carlos, *The Autobiography of William Carlos Williams* (New York: New Directions, 1967); ———, *The Build-Up* (New York: New Directions, 1952); ———, *The Collected Poems: Vol. 1, 1909–1939*, ed. A. Walton Litz and Christopher MacGowan (New York: New Directions, 1986); ———, *The Collected Poems: Vol. 2, 1939–1962*, ed. Christopher MacGowan (New York: New Directions, 1988); ———, *The Farmers' Daughters* (New York: New Directions, 1957); ———, *Imaginations*, ed. Walter Schott (New York: New Directions, 1970); ———, *In the American Grain* (New York: New Directions, 1956); ———, *In the Money* (New York: New Directions, 1940); ———, *Paterson*, rev. ed. prep. Christopher MacGowan (New York: New Directions, 1992); ———, *A Recognizable Image: William Carlos Williams on Art and Artists*, ed. Bram Dijkstra (New York: New Directions, 1978); ———, *Selected Essays* (New York: New Directions, 1954); ———, *Selected Letters*, ed. John Thirlwall (New York: New Directions, 1957); ———, *White Mule* (New York: New Directions, 1937). ***Selected Secondary Sources:*** Bernstein, Michael André, *The Tale of the Tribe: Ezra Pound and the Modern Verse Epic* (Princeton, NJ: Princeton University Press, 1982); Bloom, Harold, ed., *William Carlos Williams* (New York: Chelsea Press, 1986); Breslin, James E., *William Carlos Williams: An American Artist* (New York: Oxford University Press, 1970); Dijkstra, Bram, *Cubism, Stieglitz, and the Early Poetry of William Carlos Williams* (Princeton, NJ: Princeton University Press, 1969); Mariani, Paul, *William Carlos Williams: A New World Naked*

(New York: McGraw-Hill, 1981); Riddel, Joseph F., *The Inverted Bell: Modernism and the Counterpoetics of William Carlos Williams* (Baton Rouge: Louisiana State University Press, 1974); Terrell, Carroll F., ed., *William Carlos Williams: Man and Poet* (Orono, ME: National Poetry Foundation, 1983); Weaver, Mike, *William Carlos Williams: The American Background* (Cambridge, UK: Cambridge University Press, 1969).

Bob Perelman

WILLIS, NATHANIEL PARKER (1806–1867)

Nathaniel Parker Willis is perhaps best regarded as **Edgar Allen Poe**'s great champion. Willis secured his place in American letters as the editor who first published many of Poe's greatest poems, including "The Raven" and "Ulalume: A Ballad." After Poe's death, Willis fought in print against the slanderous insinuations that Poe's own executor, the Reverend Rufus Griswold, then published. His efforts kept Poe's work in the popular literary imagination and provided another perspective of the poet's dramatic personal life. Among his other literary friendships were ones with **Oliver Wendell Holmes**, **Henry Wadsworth Longfellow**, and **James Russell Lowell**.

A career editor, Willis was born in Portland, Maine, into the printing profession, which dated back through his family four generations. As a student at Yale University, he published several poems, under the pen name "Roy," in a paper that his father published. A few years after graduation, he founded the *American Monthly Magazine*, only to see it go weekly when it folded into the society rag the *New York Mirror.* Working for the Mirror, Willis first met George Morris, with whom he would work for the rest of his life.

As foreign correspondent to the *Mirror,* Willis toured much of Europe from 1931 to 1937. There he married Mary Stace. On returning to the United States, Willis and his new wife moved to upstate New York, settling in Oswego. In 1842, when the *Mirror* folded, Willis and Morris published the *New Mirror*, which later became the very successful and influential *Home Journal*, in which many of Poe's poems first appeared and which earned Willis a highly visible seat in the literary world. He returned to England following the death of his wife. In 1846 he married again and moved to Cornwall-on-the-Hudson, where he lived until his death.

As noted in the "Memoir of the Author" in the posthumous collection of his poetry, Willis was "certainly never either a very strong or a very profound writer; but he was what is here much more rare, at once a humorous and a tasteful one." Willis's best-known work continues to be his prose, particular *Pencillingss by the Way*, after Washington Irving's *Sketch Book.* In much of Willis's poetry, the influence of Poe is fairly pronounced, as suggested by lines from Willis's "The Wife's Appeal," "A book with silver clasps, / All gorgeous with illuminated lines / Of gold and crimson, lay upon a frame" and from "January1, 1829," "The year / Gives back the spirits of its dead, and time / Whispers the history of its vanished hours."

The esoteric and the ancient occasion several of his poems in which alchemists work over their crucibles or biblical figures are reconsidered, which is not surprising given that his earliest poems had been described as "Scripture Sketches" (*Memoir of the Author*).

Also as in Poe, the weight of memory can overtake the present, lending life a memorial burden, as evidenced in poems such as "The Confessional," with its repeated first line of "I've thought of thee—I've thought of thee." "I thought of thee" ends each stanza, save the last, which gives the poet at least one chance to unburden the present by asking, "Oh, dearest! hast thou thought of me?"

His **lyrics**, particularly "Unseen Spirits," "Absalom," and "The Belfry Pigeon," were well received at their publication and were reprinted in several anthologies of the day. Of particular note, for its humor, is Willis's "City Lyrics" (in octets directed to New York City), which offers a playful note before its overstated end:

> Oh, pity the love that must utter
> While goes a swift omnibus by!
> (Though sweet is I scream when the flutter
> Of fans shows thermometers high) –
> But if what I bawl, or I mutter,
> Falls into your ear but to die;
> Oh, the dew that falls into the gutter
> Is not more unhappy than I!

Further Reading. ***Selected Primary Sources:*** Willis, Nathaniel Parker, *Fugitive Poetry* (Boston: Pierce and Williams, 1829); ———, *Pencillings by the Way: Written During Some Years of Residence and Travel in France, Italy, Greece, Asia Minor, Turkey and England* (New York: Morris & Willis, 1844); ———, *Poems of Nathaniel Parker Willis, with a Memoir of the Author* (New York: AMS Press, 1970). ***Selected Secondary Sources:*** Auser, Cortland A., *Nathaniel Parker Willis* (New York: Twayne Press, 1969); Baker, Thomas Nelson, *Sentiment and Celebrity: Nathaniel Parker Willis and the Trials of Literary Fame* (New York: Oxford University Press, 1999); Beers, Henry A., *Nathaniel Parker Willis* (Boston: Houghton Mifflin, 1885).

Anthony Lacavaro

WILSON, JOHN (ca. 1591–1667)

John Wilson was pastoral minister of the Boston, Massachusetts, church for thirty-eight years. Unlike many of his New England colleagues, his prose output was slight, amounting to his last sermon, published ten years after his death, and perhaps one of the Eliot "Praying Indian" tracts of the 1650s. He published one volume of poems before his immigration to New England, after which his output was confined mainly to occasional poems in prefaces to books by other authors. However, in typically wordy exaggeration, **Cotton Mather** characterized him as "that New-English divine, who had so nimble a faculty of putting his devout thoughts into verse, that he signalized himself by the greatest *frequency*, perhaps, that ever man used, of sending *poems* to all persons, in all places, on all occasions"; similarly, Wilson's son claimed him to have been "another sweet singer of Israel" whose collected poems "would questionless make a large Folio." But the quantity of Wilson's extant poetic output is meager indeed. However, Wilson's anagrams exemplify a poetic device favored among New England Puritans.

Born in Windsor, England, Wilson was the son of a clergyman and related to Archbishop Edmund Grindal (whom his father had once served). He went to King's College, Cambridge, in 1605 and came under the influence of Puritans such as Richard Rogers (especially for his influential *Seven Treatises* [1604]) and William Ames. Despite the friction created by his turn to nonconformity (if not quite Puritanism), he received his BA in 1610 and moved to London to study at the Inns of Court, but he then returned to Emmanuel College for his MA. (1613). He first served as a private chaplain, and by 1618 he had become a lecturer at Sudbury, Suffolk. After some brushes with religious authorities, in which he was suspended for nonconformity, he decided in 1630 to go to New England, where he became, first, the teacher in the Boston church and, later, the pastor. Mather characterized him as liberal in sharing both his resources with others in need and his occasional prophetic abilities (he was remembered as once having counseled a soldier to shoot a fleeing America Indian with the admonition, "God will direct the bullet!"). He was joined by **John Cotton** as the teaching minister in 1633, and they served together until the latter's death, after which Wilson served with Cotton's successor, John Norton. However, Wilson's position was severely threatened by the Antinomian Controversy of 1637–1638 (his theology seems to have been especially targeted), but he managed to retain control. In later years, he upheld the legitimacy of synods, opposed Quakers (and other "opinionists"), and supported the Halfway Covenant.

A Song of Deliverance for the Lasting Remembrance of Gods Wonderful Works Never to be Forgotten (1626; rpt. in Boston, 1680) is a collection of poems dominated by the title poem and intended for children. Using Deuteronomy 31 (in which God directs Moses to make a song for Israel despite foreknowledge of their apostasy) as a template, Wilson recounts in easy-to-read-and-memorize fourteeners of 1,220 lines selected events in recent English history: the defeat of the Spanish Armada in 1588; the plague outbreak of 1603; the Gunpowder Plot of 1605; the disastrous collapse of a London gallery during a Roman Catholic meeting in 1623; and another outbreak of plague in 1625. Wilson borrowed heavily from contemporary prose accounts of these events; the recurrent theme is that the English, like ancient Israel, continually neglect God despite his special covenantal deliverances on their behalf. The remaining poems in the volume touch on the same historical events. There are three poems in Latin (with accompanying translations), including one by Theodore Beza.

The fifteen extant poems from Wilson's New England career are occasional poems about or addressed to specific individuals. Most were published in prefaces to books by other authors, such as four poems concerning Thomas Shepard that were prefatory to the latter's *The Church-Membership of Children* (1663); others were left in manuscript (one as an inscription in a book). Wilson's method, for which he was renowned, was to begin by ingeniously anagrammatizing the subject's name, with considerable leeway for letter substitution and variant spelling, followed by a pious character sketch in verse. The satirist Nathaniel Ward once wrote that "Mr John Wilson / the great Epigrammatist / Can let out an Anagram / even as he list." These anagrams in turn often inspire the opening line and conceit of the poem. For example, his verses "upon the Death of Mrs Abigaill Tompson" begin with an anagram on her name, "i am gon to all bliss," followed by the opening couplet: "The blessed news i send to the is this: / That i am goon from the unto all bliss." Wilson also anagrammatized into Latin; in fact, the two attempts at anagrammatizing his own name were in Latin: "Johannes Wilsonus" went to "In uno Jesu, nos Salvi" or "Non in uno Jesus Salus?" His subjects included John Harvard, Joseph Brisco, Claudius Gilbert, Thomas Shepard, John Norton, and the death of a granddaughter.

Further Reading. ***Selected Primary Sources:*** Meserole, Harrison T., *American Poetry of the Seventeenth Century* (University Park: Pennsylvania State University Press, 1985); Murdock, Kenneth B., *Handkerchiefs from Paul* (Cambridge, MA: Harvard University Press, 1927). ***Selected Secondary Sources:*** Jantz, Harold S., "*The First Century of New England*" (*Verse. Proceedings of the American Antiquarian Society* 53 [October 1943]: 219–508; reprint. New York: Russell & Russell, 1962); Mather, Cotton, *Magnalia Christi Americana* (1702).

Michael G. Ditmore

WINTERS, YVOR (ARTHUR) (1900–1968)

Yvor Winters is far better known as a critic than as a poet, and in the decades following his death in 1968, his reputation as both poet and critic (but especially the latter) underwent a rapid series of reversals, from rejection and dismissal to an unusual kind of acceptance. By the turn of the twenty-first century, most of the articles to be found on him were likely to begin with some variation of "In defense of." Moreover, even his defenders rarely defend his rigid, anti-modernist stance and his rigid adherence to a self-proclaimed dogma. Instead, Winters has become remembered as a man with the courage (and arrogance) to stand up for his convictions in the face of virtually the entire literary world.

Winters was born on October 17, 1900, in Chicago, Illinois. He began his education at the University of Chicago, where he became friends with *Poetry* founder **Harriet Monroe.** Tuberculosis forced him to relocate in 1921 to the Southwest, where he was a patient at Sunmount Sanatorium in Santa Fe, New Mexico. He later taught in nearby coal mining camp towns (ironic for a tuberculosis sufferer) and then at the University of Idaho in Moscow. He received his bachelor's and master's degrees at the University of Colorado in 1925–1926 and then went on in 1928 to Stanford University, where he would remain on the faculty until his death, earning his Ph.D. in 1934. In 1926, he married poet Janet Lewis, whom he had met at the sanatorium. He died of throat cancer on January 25, 1968, in Palo Alto, California.

He published five books of poetry: *The Immobile Wind* (1921), *The Proof* (1930), *Before Disaster* (1934), *Poems* (1940), and *To the Holy Spirit* (1947). As criticism and his own critical theories became more important to him, he grew away from the writing of poetry, but collected editions of his work were published, and the 1960 edition of his *Collected Poems* won the Bollingen Prize. His most important book of criticism, *In Defense of Reason* (1947), is a compilation of three earlier published studies. Later critical works included *The Function of Criticism: Problems and Exercises* (1957), *On Modern Poets: Stevens, Eliot, Ransom, Crane, Hopkins, Frost* (1959), and *Forms of Discovery* (1967). Posthumous collections of essays and letters have been published, as have several critical studies, including Thomas Parkinson's *Hart Crane and Yvor Winters: Their Literary Correspondence* (1978), which contains **Crane**'s letters to Winters, though the latter's replies have been lost.

In addition to the Bollingen, Winters won *Poetry* magazine's Oscar Blumenthal Prize in 1945, the National Institute of Arts and Letters Award in 1952, the University of Chicago's Harriet Monroe Award for 1960–1961, and the Brandeis University Creative Arts Award for Poetry in 1963. He was the recipient of Guggenheim (1961–1962) and National Endowment for the Arts (1967) grants.

He is also remembered for his contribution to teaching. During his tenure, Stanford University became one of the first important centers for the study of creative writing. In his early years at Stanford, he faced considerable resistance from the traditionalists who ran the English department, traditionalists who went so far as to denounce him as a disgrace to the program. In later years, he became a champion of academic scholarship against the "pure inspiration" arguments of the **Beats** and others. His students included **J.V. Cunningham**, **Robert Pinsky**, **Philip Levine**, **Thom Gunn**, **Donald Justice** (who went to Stanford to study with Winters and never actually took a course with him, but still felt his influence), and **Donald Hall**.

Winters's earliest work, mostly written at the Sunmount Sanatorium, is in the **Imagist** style that was popular during the era. Like fellow Santa Fe transplant **Witter Bynner**, his Imagist work was strongly influenced by Oriental and **Native American poetry**. The young Winters was a powerful champion of **free verse**, declaring that it could do anything that rhymed verse could do. His relationship to literature during this period was very much that of an autodidact. He had spent most of what would have been his college years in the isolation of his illness.

But as enthusiastic a supporter of the trends of the day as Winters was, he rapidly became the trends' most intense antagonist. By the end of the 1920s, he had recoiled from Imagism, free verse, and everything to do with **modernism**. Although he was hardly the only poet of his generation to write formal verse, he was that rare exception to the trend, a poet who began in free verse and then renounced it completely for formalism.

As Winters's work was reissued in collected form, and readers and critics had a chance to examine the earlier and later work side by side, his early poems found their champions. **James Dickey** compared them favorably to the best of **William Carlos Williams**. But his turnabout was swift, savage, and complete. What Dickey and others admired in his free verse—movement, energy, questioning—were no longer part of his aesthetic. Instead, in both his poetry and criticism, he championed precision, order, and moral certainty. He rejected his own early work, in his essay "The Poet and the University," as "little impressionistic notes on landscapes."

As both poet and critic, Winters rejected the modern, which is not in itself unusual. What was striking about Winters's rejection was the breadth of its inclusiveness. He did not stop with his contemporaries or their predecessors. He rejected not only the twentieth century, but also the nineteenth and much of the eighteenth, choosing for his model the "plain style" of the sixteenth and seventeenth centuries—the style associated with Sir Walter Raleigh, Ben Jonson, and one of Winters's literary heroes, Barnabe Googe, as opposed to the more ornate style of Edmund Spenser and Sir Philip Sidney. One of his own most celebrated poems is his retelling of the medieval masterpiece "Sir Gawaine and the Green Knight." He wrote in careful and precise metrics, preferring simple whole rhymes and received forms.

Winters's poetry, including his later poetry, retained its admirers, including **Allen Tate**, who thought him one of the major poets. Winters, with his characteristic thorniness, rejected praise and criticism alike, telling *Contemporary Authors* (Permanent Series, vols. 10–11, 693), "in general my admirers have read me as carelessly as my detractors."

But he is more remembered for his criticism, opinionated, powerful, dogmatic, and frequently standing as an army of one against the twentieth, nineteenth, and eighteenth centuries. Winters demanded a moral inflexibility of poetry, and his demands were absolute. Atop his list of pernicious influences on American poetry were **Ralph Waldo Emerson** and **Walt Whitman**.

Winters stated his critical doctrine most forcefully in his 1947 book, *In Defense of Reason.* He argued for a closely guarded canon, with entry granted on the basis of not simply moral instruction, but moral absolutism. To Winters, one ethically sloppy phrase was reason enough to reject a poet.

One of his first famous salvos came at the expense of Hart Crane. In 1927 he had been one of Crane's early champions, praising *White Buildings* as a masterpiece of modernism. He and Crane were, if not close friends, at least collegial, exchanging letters and expressing respect and admiration for each other. But by 1930, having completely rejected modernism, Winters had reversed his opinion on everything he had admired in Crane, and he wrote a scathing review of *The Bridge* for *Poetry*, in which he laid out the foundation of his quarrel not only with modernism, but with the modern world—Crane, the Romantics, the Transcendentalists, and any writer who privileged emotion over reason and individual sensibility over moral rigor: "If we enter the mind of a Crane, a Whitman or an Emerson with our emotional facilities activated and our reason in abeyance, these writers may possess us as surely as demons were once supposed to possess the unwary."

In general, Winters held three critical principles. First, the purpose of literature is to instruct, not to express emotion; in fact, emotion is the enemy of instruction. Second, a poem must have a "governing theme" that is moral in nature and must never stray from that theme (he rejected **Marianne Moore**, for example, on the grounds that though her poems had governing themes, she was too easily seduced away from them). And third, control must then be the artist's principal tool, which means it must also be the artist's cardinal virtue. "Spiritual control in a poem is simply a manifestation of the spiritual control within the poet." This made it easy for Winters to dismiss many poets, harder for him in the case of a few. He could not understand how Williams, "eminently virtuous" and a devoted family man, could still fall under the insidious influence of Romanticism.

Winters's challenging, dogmatic, and contrarian pronouncements about literary figures remain his most widely known legacy. As **Hayden Carruth** said, he "is able to prove . . . irrefutably . . .that our favorite poets were idiots, and in the process show just why we like them so much." Carruth's summary, loving and respectful but almost totally dismissive, perfectly captures the judgment of succeeding generations on Winters. It is virtually impossible not to relish the sting of his rapier on our major poets, but it is equally difficult to agree with them. In *Forms of Discovery*, in which Winters summarized a lifetime of opinion, he said of Pound, "One would call the style verbose, except that by definition verbosity is the use of words in the excess of the occasion, and here there is no occasion . . . all save a little of the writing is insufferably dull; there is something pathetic about Pound's slogan: 'Make it new'"(317); and he wrote of Whitman (via Crane), "The ideas which destroyed Crane's talent were the same ideas which one can find in Whitman, but they seem less destructive in Whitman . . . because Whitman is utterly lacking in literary talent, so that the effect of the ideas never becomes clear" (315).

Equally odd, today, is his list of major poets, which includes—in addition to mainstream figures like **Edward Arlington Robinson** and **Emily Dickinson**—Googe, Robert Bridges, T. Sturge Moore, **F.G. Tuckerman**, **Jones Very**, **Adelaide Crapsey**, and Elizabeth Daryush. Many of the writers Winters champions, interestingly, were either recluses or invalids. A number of them, including Crapsey and Winters's own wife, Janet Lewis, were tubercular.

Of his own influence, Winters said, in reference to an early essay, "The 16th Century Lyric in England," "[i]t has influenced a good many books and articles which have given it at most but passing acknowledgement (*Forms of Discovery*, 314)." This self-assessment may well be the best summation of this unique figure in American letters.

Further Reading. ***Selected Primary Sources:*** Winters, Yvor, *Before Disaster* (Tryon, NC: The Tryon Pamphlets, 1934); ———, *Collected Poems* (Denver, CO: Swallow Press, 1952); ———, *Edward Arlington Robinson* (Norfolk, CT: New Directions Books, 1946); ———, *The Function of Criticism: Problems and Exercises* (Denver, CO: Swallow Press, 1957); ———, *Forms of Discovery* (Denver, CO: Swallow Press, 1967); ———, *The Immobile Wind* (Evanston, IL: Monroe Wheeler, 1921); ———, *In Defense of Reason* (Denver, CO: Swallow Press, 1947); ———, *On Modern Poets: Stevens, Eliot, Ransom, Crane, Hopkins, Frost* (New York: Meridian Books, 1959); ———, *Poems* (Los Altos, CA: Gyroscope Press, 1940); ———, *The Proof* (New York: Coward-McCann, 1930); ———, *The Uncollected Essays and Reviews* (Chicago: Swallow Press, 1957). ***Selected Secondary Sources:*** Comito, Terry, *In Defense of Winters: The Poetry and Prose of Yvor Winters* (Madison: University of Wisconsin Press, 1986); Dickey, James, "Yvor Winters," in *Babel to Byzantium* (New York:

Farrar, Straus and Giroux, 1962, 182–186); Hall, Donald, "Rocks and Whirlpools: Archibald MacLeish and Yvor Winters" (*Paris Review* 33.121 [1991]: 211–248); Hyman, Stanley Edgar, "Yvor Winters and Evaluation in Criticism," in *The Armed Vision: A Study in the Methods of Modern Literary Criticism* (New York: Alfred A. Knopf, 1947, 23–53); Kirsch, Adam, "Winters's Curse" (*New Criterion* 21.8 [2003]: 32–37); Schwartz, Delmore, "On Critics: 'Primitivism and Decadence' by Yvor Winters," in *Selected Essays of Delmore Schwartz*, ed. Donald Dike and David H. Zucker (Chicago: University of Chicago Press, 1970, 332–350); Yezzi, David, "The Seriousness of Yvor Winters" (*New Criterion* 15.10 [1997]: 26–34).

Tad Richards

WOLCOTT, ROGER (1679–1767)

The work of Roger Wolcott, one of the significant colonial American poets of the early eighteenth century, signals a transition to a more secular poetry. Although his subject matter has strong theological inflections, his presentation shows the strong influence of epic narrative forms.

A native of Windsor, Connecticut, Roger Wolcott was the youngest of nine children and was eventually apprenticed to a clothier. According to his *Autobiography* (written 1755; published 1881), he began his own clothing business at age twenty and resettled to South Windsor, where he also farmed. By 1707 he was a selectman from Windsor; in 1709 he became a deputy to Connecticut's General Assembly; in 1721 he became a justice of the peace; and in 1741 he became deputy governor. In the 1730s and 1740s he represented Connecticut in the Mohegan Land Controversy. His political career culminated in service as governor of Connecticut (1750–1754). Wolcott's political rise was aided, not unusually for the time, by a career of military service: from commissary of the Connecticut stores in 1711 to militia captain in 1722 and regiment colonel in 1739. By 1745 he was a major-general, and he participated in the successful expedition against Louisbourg, during which he kept a journal published in 1887.

Among his writings are his *Autobiography*; a short draft of a history of Connecticut (from 1630 to 1758); and several situational essays, published as open letters, on political and ecclesiastical matters. His known prose works were all written between 1745 and his death in 1767.

Wolcott's known poetical works all appear in the 1725 *Poetical Meditations, Being the Improvement of some Vacant Hours*, a collection of seven poems. Six relatively short religious meditations offer reflections on Adam's fall and selected scriptural passages (from Proverbs, Psalms, and Matthew). The long final poem, entitled "A Brief Account of the Agency of the Honourable **John Winthrop**, Esq; in the Court of King Charles the Second, Anno Dom. 1662. When he Obtained for the Colony of Connecticut His Majesty's Gracious Charter," envisions Winthrop narrating a selective history of Connecticut to Charles II, detailing the Puritan quest for religious freedom and the gradual establishment of order in the perilous New World. However, the Pequot Massacre of 1636 is the clear focus of Wolcott's work, and the centrality of this epic historical narration is confirmed by the *Meditations*' fifty-six-page preface by Rev. John Bulkley, itself focused on legal and moral conflicts between settlers and Native Americans. In this context, even the scriptural elaborations refer to political conflicts, with the reflections on Adam's "bold Insulting Disposition" governing "some rough uncultivated Land," anticipating the rationales for dispossessing the Pequots in "A Brief Account." The historical poem includes theological claims—the 1630 journey of the Puritans to New England is possible only through divine intervention—but is as heavy in secular allusions and tropes. The arriving colonists' first encounter with New England's shores are "as when the Wounded Amorous doth spy / His smiling Fortune in his Ladys Eye, / O how his Veins and Breast swell with a Flood / Of pleasing Raptures that revive his Blood." In the battle between the English and the Pequots, additionally, the military leader John Mason is compared to Hercules, with the Pequots being cast as the many-headed Hydra. Mason's speech rallying his countrymen is an early-modern variation on a familiar epic trope, and with corresponding Native American speeches, it suggests the influence of Milton's "Paradise Lost." The poem concludes on yet a different note, with Charles II granting a verse charter to Connecticut's "Men of Estates and Men of Influence" and warning them of a dangerous tendency, "taught in Satan's first Erected School," to resist "every Act of Order or Restraint."

Wolcott's multifaceted career allows us to situate his poetical works. His pursuit of poetry coincided with his entry into politics, but with his increased public prominence, he turned exclusively to prose productions that in many respects rewrite his earlier poetical work. In this trajectory, we find not so much a stark secularization of poetry but a gradual translation and relocation of Puritan tropes within provincial politics. The history of the colony before the charter is cast poetically; the later political development of Connecticut finds expression in prose. If, for early New England poets, religious poetry was a sphere for personal meditation and the restatement of broad cultural principles, Wolcott's work signals a narrower deployment of religious discourse in a poetry of political advocacy—a tendency that would later flourish in Connecticut with the Hartford Wits.

Further Reading. ***Selected Primary Source:*** Wolcott, Roger, *Poetical Meditations, Being the Improvement of Some Vacant Hours* (New London, CT: T. Green, 1725).

Selected Secondary Sources: Bates, Albert C., ed., *The Wolcott Papers: Correspondence and Documents During Roger Wolcott's Governorship of the Colony of Connecticut, 1750–1754* (Hartford: Connecticut Historical Society, 1916); Tyler, Moses Coit, *A History of American Literature* (New York: G.P. Putnam's Sons, 1879).

Ed White

WOOD, WILLIAM (*fl.* 1629–1635)

William Wood's sole claim to fame is his successful, well-regarded colonial promotional tract, *New England's Prospect* (1634). His descriptive prose, detailing the natural phenomena of New England, is punctuated throughout by verses enumerating the abundance and variety of interesting plants and animals in New England.

Little is known about the life of William Wood, and most details of his biography center around the publication of *New England's Prospect.* Wood himself makes a few statements in the tract about himself; others details are conjectures based mostly on colonial records. It seems he came to Massachusetts in 1629, probably on the same boat that brought John Endecott and other early settlers. He may have settled in Lynn, Massachusetts, becoming a freeman in 1631. He returned in 1633 to England, where, a year later, his book was published. That same year, Wood was one of several "benefactors" officially thanked by letter from the General Court of Massachusetts, presumably in anticipation of the favor and assistance that the publication of *New England's Prospect* would bring to the fledgling colony. Although Wood expressed an intention to return to New England, it is uncertain whether he ever did. Records of various men named William Wood, many of whom are certainly not the author, appear throughout New England from 1636 through 1671. More is not known. Alden T. Vaughan conjectures that Wood was a man of some formal education and that the addition of the title "Mr." indicates that his status within the Puritan community rose upon publication of the book.

The title page of Wood's *New England's Prospect* describes the promotional tract as "a true, lively, and experimentall description of that part of *America*, commonly called NEW ENGLAND." Dividing his tract into two parts—one of which describes geography, climate, plant, and animals and the other of which describes local Native American tribes and their culture—Wood employs straightforward (sometimes even lighthearted) prose based on largely firsthand observation (hence "experimentall"). Vaughan notes that the popularity of Wood's subject drew not only upon the inherent interest aroused by natural wonders but also upon the practicality of such knowledge for the economic venture of colonialism and upon "the excitement of finding a land that bore some resemblance to the homeland as well as some remarkable differences" (7). With iambic pentameter couplets throughout, the verses include basic description ("Sky-towering pines, and chestnuts coated rough, / The lasting cedar, with the walnut tough") and practical information ("Within this Indian orchard fruits be some, / The ruddy cherry and the jetty plumb, / Snake-murthering hazel, with sweet saxifrage, / Whose spurs in beer allays hot fever's rage"), as well as passages that seem primarily intended to delight with poetic turns and conventions ("The horn-bound tree that to be cloven scorns, / Which from the tender vine oft take his spouse, / Who twinds embracing arms about his boughs") and even the occasional commentary ("And tortoise sought by the Indian's squaw, / Which to the flats dance many a winter jig, / To dive for cockles, and to dig for clams, / Whereby her lazy husband's guts she crams").

Some scholars, such as Robert Daly, count Wood as a Puritan poet. Vaughan remains uncertain on this point, stressing that though Wood must be counted an early New Englander, he is not necessarily a Puritan (4–5). All agree that Wood's greatest poetic inspiration was the incredible variety and abundance of the New World's natural wonders, but the significance of this inspiration might be different if Wood was a Puritan and therefore presumably suspicious of the joys of the phenomenal world. Daly uses Wood as one of several examples of Puritan poets who demonstrate that religious persuasion and aesthetic appreciation of the natural world are not incompatible. Daly argues that Wood in particular

> was so stricken by the beauty and abundance of the new World that these, and apparently little else, inspired his poetry. His poems are explosions of images drawn from the natural world and appreciated for their intrinsic beauty and limitless variety. . . . Wood's poems were intended, of course, to promote colonization; but Wood achieved that end by portraying the new world, not as a place where the Gnostic Christian would find rest from distractions of the sensible world, but as a beautiful world worth seeking and enjoying." (10)

Michael J. Colacurcio, who does not take a position one way or another on Wood's putative Puritanism, puts the verse catalogues in the context of rhapsodic prose descriptions of natural features by Christopher Columbus and others, positing a certain inevitability of conventional poetic response in promotional literature and suggesting that "again and again, at the site of discovery and praise of New World resources, poetry happens."

Although little scholarship has been devoted to the verse sections of Wood's promotional tract, the critical consensus is that his verse-cataloguing expresses a genuine and irrepressible response to the novelty and abundance of the natural world of New England.

Further Reading. ***Selected Primary Sources:*** Meserole, Harrison T., ed., *American Poetry of the Seventeenth Century* (University Park: Pennsylvania State University Press, 1985); Wood, William, *New England's Prospect*, ed. Alden T. Vaughan (Amherst: University of Massachusetts Press, 1993). ***Selected Secondary Sources:*** Colacurcio, Michael J., "A Costly Canaan: Bradford, Morton and the Margins of American Literature," in *Godly Letters: The Literature of the American Puritans* (Notre Dame, IN: University of Notre Dame Press, 2005); Daly, Robert, *God's Altar: The World and the Flesh in Puritan Poetry* (Berkeley: University of California Press, 1978); Lindholdt, Paul J., "The Significance of the Colonial Promotional Tract," in *Early American Literature and Culture: Essays Honoring Harrison T. Meserole*, ed. Kathryn Zabelle Derounian-Stodola (Newark: University of Delaware Press, 1992, 57–72).

Meredith Neuman

WOODWORTH, SAMUEL (1785–1842)

A poet, song lyricist, playwright, journalist, and editor, Samuel Woodworth is best remembered for his popular ballads "The Old Oaken Bucket" and "The Hunters of Kentucky." These lyrics, along with his most popular and successful play, "The Forest Rose," headline Woodworth's significant contribution to popular literature and culture in America during his lifetime. "The Hunters of Kentucky," about Andrew Jackson's 1814 defeat of the British in the Battle of New Orleans, became a beloved campaign song that contributed to Jackson's successful Presidential campaign in 1828.

Samuel Woodworth was born January 13, 1785, in Scituate, Massachusetts, to Benjamin and Abigail Bryant Woodworth. Benjamin, a farmer and carpenter, fought in the American Revolution. Because the family was poor, Samuel received little education and suffered poor health in his youth. After demonstrating some talent for writing verse, the Reverend Nehemiah Thomas taught Samuel English grammar and the classics. At the age of fifteen, Samuel moved to Boston to apprentice with the editor of the *Columbian Centinel*, Benjamin Russell. In 1809, after living and working in Boston, New Haven, and Baltimore, Samuel moved to New York City, and in 1810 married Lydia Reeder, with whom he had ten children.

Beginning in New Haven in 1808 with *The Belles-Lettres Repository* (March 1808–April 1808), Woodworth began, published, or edited a number of periodicals, including the *New York War* (June 1812–September 1814), the *Halcyon Luminary and Theological Repository* (January 1812–December 1813), the *New York Republican Chronicle* (December 1817–July 1818), the *New York Ladies' Literary Cabinet* (May 1819–August 1820), the *Literary Casket and Pocket Magazine* (April–November 1821), and the *New-Jerusalem Missionary and Intellectual Repository* (May 1823–April 1824). His work with each of these publications did not last long for various reasons, and this caused him financial hardship (Gray); for example, Woodworth edited the *New York Republican Chronicle* for a little over six months before the newspaper failed. Along with **George Pope Morris**, Woodworth founded the *New York Mirror and Ladies' Literary Gazette* in August 1823. Woodworth left after one year, but Morris stayed with the magazine, which eventually became the successful *New York Mirror*.

During all the years in which he moved from periodical to periodical, Woodworth wrote and published poetry, fiction, and drama. His novel, *The Champions of Freedom; or, The Mysterious Chief, a Romance of the Nineteenth Century, Founded on the Events of the War, Between the United States and Great Britain, Which Terminated in March, 1815*, was published in 1816. His third full-length theatrical production, *The Forest Rose; or American Farmers*, premiered October 6, 1825, in New York City at the Chatham Theatre and was "the first hit show of the American theater" (Gorman). *The Forest Rose; or, American Farmers* eventually played in cities such as Philadelphia, New Orleans, St. Louis, California, and London. Like much of Woodworth's poetry, the "**pastoral** opera" celebrates rural life and America. The final journal Woodworth edited was the *New York Parthenon, or, Literary and Scientific Museum* (August 1827–December 1827). He gave up his literary career because of its financial uncertainty and worked from 1835 to 1836 in the Boston Navy Yard. Woodworth lived as an invalid for the final years of his life after he had a stroke in 1837. He died in New York City on December 9, 1842.

Woodworth's poetry is conventional, patriotic, **religious**, and often **sentimental**. His most-loved and best-known poem, "The Bucket" (later known as "The Old Oaken Bucket"), was first published in the *New York Republican Chronicle* on June 3, 1818. The poem, which was often anthologized for at least 100 years after his death, is included in his *Melodies, Duets, Trios, Songs and Ballads*, published in 1826 and revised in 1831 in a collection entitled *Melodies, Duets, Trios, Songs, and Ballads, Pastoral, Amatory, Sentimental, Patriotic, Religious, and Miscellaneous Together with Metrical Epistles, Tales, and Recitations.* A note above the poem states it is to be sung to the tune of "Air-The Flower of Dumblane." The poem is a sentimental and nostalgic reflection about his childhood, beginning with the line, "How dear to this heart are the scenes of my childhood," and recalling such scenes as "the orchard, the meadow, the deep-tangled wild-wood, / And every loved spot which my infancy knew!" As the title of his collection suggests, the third edition covers everything, from lyrics he wrote for his stage productions to recitations for special occasions. For example, a poem titled "Address" is included with a note stating that it was written "for the opening of the new Park

Theatre—Spoken by Mrs. Barnes, in character of Melpomene."

Examples of lyrics he wrote for his stage productions include such titles as "Sweet Seclusion," "The Village Clock," and "My Father's Farm," which he wrote for *The Forest Rose.* Included were notes about tunes by which to sing the lyrics or notes about who wrote the music. For example, the music for "My Father's Farm" is by Davies. Some lines from "My Father's Farm" illustrate Woodworth's support of rural America: "For lords of the soil, and fed by out toil, / American farmers are blest." The "Amatory and Sentimental" section of the book includes titles such as "Music the Language of Love" (with music arranged by E. Riley) and "To My Wife," a poem to be sung as "Air-Loudon's bonny woods and braes." The poet writes, "Fortune must be blind indeed, / We mistake her powers, Lydia / Else could love unheeded plead?" and he suggests that they—he and his wife, Lydia—should "without murmer, or complaining, / Or the will of Heaven arrainging, / Fix our hopes above, Lydia." Included in the "Patriotic" section is "Freedom's Jublilee," celebrating the "immortal Washington" who "led Columbia's patriots on, / Till the glorious prize was won, / Peace and Liberty." Woodworth's second most-known and -loved lyric, "The Hunters of Kentucky," also appears in the collection under a section titled "Miscellaneous." The note above the lyrics states that the words are to be sung to the tune of "Miss Bailey." The song was so popular that is mentioned in James Fenimore Cooper's 1827 novel *The Prairie.* The "Religious, Moral, and Elegiac" section of Woodworth's collection includes "A Dirge, On the Deaths of John Adams and Thomas Jefferson. July 4, 1826." The poet writes that "millions are dissolved in tears" as "a nation famed for matchless deeds, / Weeps for a father and a chief."

In 1861 Frederick A. Woodworth edited a collection entitled *Poetical Works of Samuel Woodworth*, which was published by Scribner. Woodworth's contribution to poetry, music, theater, and magazine publishing played a significant role in shaping the popular culture of early-nineteenth-century America.

Further Reading. ***Selected Primary Source:*** Woodworth, Samuel, *Melodies, Duets, Trios, Songs, and Ballads, Pastoral, Amatory, Sentimental, Patriotic, Religious, and Miscellaneous Together with Metrical Epistles, Tales, and Recitations* (New York: Elliot & Palmer, 1831, www.hti.umich.edu/cgi/b/bib/bibperm?q1=abk3644). ***Selected Secondary Sources:*** Gorman, Anita G., "Samuel Woodworth," in *Dictionary of Literary Biography, Volume 250: Antebellum Writers in New York, Second Series*, ed. Kent P. Ljungquist (Detroit, MI: Gale Group, 2002); Gray, Janet, "Popular Poetry," in *Encyclopedia of American Poetry, The Nineteenth Century*, ed. Eric L. Haralson (Chicago: Fitzroy Dearborn, 1998).

Deborah Brown

WOOLSEY, SARAH CHAUNCEY (ALSO CHAUNCY) (1835–1905)

Sarah Chauncey Woolsey, who wrote under the pseudonym "Susan Coolidge," produced a substantial body of work in a variety of literary forms. She is best remembered for a series of loosely autobiographical children's books featuring a character named Katy Carr. The series ultimately culminated in five volumes. Several books remain in print, and they are still read in parts of the British Commonwealth, where they have also been adapted to other media. Woolsey published a volume of children's verse, *Rhymes and Ballads for Girls and Boys*, in 1892. Her other poetry was collected in three volumes—*Verses* (1880), *A Few More Verses* (1889), and the posthumously published *Last Verses* (1906)—suggesting perhaps a more discrete division from her other output than she would have otherwise encouraged. Many of her books feature original verse in a number of mediating roles.

Indeed, on one level, her works can be understood as exercises in cultural mediation, chiefly within the broader contours of the transatlantic exchange, but also in ways that have significant implications for understanding nineteenth-century feminism; American Romanticism; the moral formation and imaginative life of children; the rhetorical shift from a public, civic style to a plain and homely discourse; and the development of a domesticated Protestant piety.

Woolsey was born in Cleveland, Ohio, on January 29, 1835, into a family with distinguished New England connections. Among her ancestors were John Winthrop and Jonathan Edwards. She counted three presidents of Yale among her family relations. In 1855 her father, a land agent, retired, and the family moved to New Haven, Connecticut, where her uncle, Theodore Dwight Woolsey, presided at Yale. There she met and befriended **Helen Hunt Jackson**. After the outbreak of the Civil War, the two women worked in a hospital in New Hampshire. Woolsey later became an assistant superintendent at Lowell General Hospital in Rhode Island. After the war, she and her family vacationed in Newport, Rhode Island, where she continued her friendship with Jackson.

Upon her father's death in 1870, Woolsey and her family took an extensive tour of Europe. Upon her return in 1872, she traveled west with Jackson on the recently completed transcontinental railroad. Such an undertaking was still a novelty and, by the standards of the day, quite costly. She published an account of the journey for *Scribner's* magazine. It was perhaps on this occasion that the Colorado landscape formed a deep impression on her mind. One can get a sense of it by contrasting her idealized depiction of Western life in, for example, *In the High Valley* (1890) with the depiction by Jackson, who set *Ramona* (1884) in a similar locale with altogether different results.

Around this time, Woolsey's family built a residence in Newport that was to be her principal residence for her remaining years. She formed an amiable relationship with the publishing house Roberts Brothers in Boston, who were to publish her work until the company's demise in 1898. (The chief editor, Thomas Niles, had shepherded Louisa May Alcott to success with *Little Women* in 1869.) Woolsey found a receptive audience for the first two books in her series, *What Katy Did* (1872) and *What Katy Did in School* (1873). Critics and readers alike have counted these among the best of her works.

She also acted as a consulting editor at Roberts Brothers for many years. In 1880 she published a revised and edited volume of *The Diary and Letters of Frances Burney, Madame d'Arblay*, and she presented a selected edition of *The Letters of Jane Austen* in 1892. She translated Théophile Gautier's *My Household of Pets* in 1882. She is credited with having influenced Helen Hunt Jackson to change publishing houses and to contract with Roberts Brothers, a decision that reportedly had a salutary effect on the firm's fortunes. She produced numerous stories for children, many making their first appearance in *St. Nicholas*, then edited by **Mary Mapes Dodge**. She also wrote for adults, publishing poems, stories, and travel pieces in *Outlook* and *Scribner's*, among other periodicals. She died on April 9, 1905.

Like many women in the Edwards family, she was tall, and she clearly possessed a strong intellect. She was well educated by contemporary standards. She never married and bore no children. She thereby avoided the usual lot of women, and she seems not to have endured the wearying confinement of the domestic sphere. On the other hand, she did not experience the bonds of connubial or maternal attachment, which may account for her less successful forays into adult fiction. Having access to only the sketchiest details of her life, one is hard-pressed to discern fully her motivation for writing, especially in attempting to understand what role, if any, financial need played. What little attention her work has received tends to be focused on her writing for children, chiefly the early volumes in the Katy Carr series. To date, no critical edition of her poetry has appeared; thus, it is not certain that the volumes published through 1906 gather all of her work. One observer has noted that her poems are not among those of the first rank. This view, in light of a general critical neglect, may imply a wider, unarticulated consensus.

And yet her verse does possess attractive, indeed intriguing, features. One is immediately struck by the private context of the work's production, noting that it was only after her father's death that Woolsey embarked on a prolific and successful career as a woman of letters. Furthermore, one sees a persistent emphasis on associations—familial and comradely, of sensibility and intellect—which constitute a genial, harmonious community. The verse also reflects a perceptive and responsive familiarity with the Romanticist poetry of both sides of the Atlantic. Indeed, it bears signs of a broad and fruitful understanding of the general line of the development of Western literature. And one can detect, however faintly, a distinctively American tone in the occasional glimmerings of her forebear's religious affections suffusing the work. Despite its perceived limitations, her poetry speaks of a singular and authentic sensibility.

Woolsey's poem "Helen" was collected in *An American Anthology, 1787–1900*, edited by Edmund Clarence Stedman. Presumably addressed to her friend Helen Hunt Jackson, who died in 1885, its elegiac, autumnal setting evokes Milton and his classical **pastoral** influences. Because it is addressed to an auditor, here absent, it also brings to mind the conversation poems of Coleridge. She discloses a keen eye for natural details almost as charming and skillful as John Clare's. The poem, however, resonant as it is with these pleasing echoes, is not simply the work of a slavish epigone. Woolsey displays this best, perhaps, in her determination to avoid the dialectical or tutelary impulses of Wordsworth's most popular nature poetry. Rather, she aims to affirm an accord reached through a mutual interchange of companions and peers in mortal years, an accord the speaker envisions deepening and flourishing in the after life: "And some day, glad, but wondering not, / We two shall meet, and, face to face, / In still, far fields unseen as yet,

John Bartlett excerpted the poem's opening lines, as well as passages from three additional poems, in the tenth edition of *Familiar Quotations*.

The claims of her verse are slight but persistent. Her poetry often gives voice to the concerns, but not the pathologies, of her generation. At its best it exhibits a felicity and sweetness of tone that speaks to earnest and aspiring sensibility. In its less distinguished form, it resists engagement. But it rarely, if ever, evidences affectation, pretense, or moral indifference. What it lacks in sublimity or obscurity, it sufficiently restores with a calm and knowing gentility. It is a body of work that would doubtless reward greater scrutiny.

Further Reading. ***Selected Primary Sources:*** Coolidge, Susan (pseud. of Sarah Chauncey Woolsey), *A Few More Verses* (Boston: Roberts Brothers, 1889); ———, *Last Verses* (Boston: Little, Brown, 1906); ———, *Rhymes and Ballads for Girls and Boys* (Boston: Roberts Brothers, 1892); ———, *Verses* (Boston: Roberts Brothers, 1880). ***Selected Secondary Sources:*** Foster, Shirley, and Judy Simons, *What Katy Read: Feminist Re-readings of "Classic" Stories for Girls* (Iowa City: University of Iowa Press, 1995); Gray, Janet, ed., *She Wields a Pen: American Women Poets of the Nineteenth Centrury* (Iowa City: University of Iowa Press, 1997); MacDonald, Ruth K., "Sarah Chauncy Woolsey (Susan Coolidge)," in *Dictionary of Literary Biography*, vol. 42 (Detroit, MI: Gale Research, 1985, 397–400); Vallone, Lynne, *Disciplines of Virtue:*

Girls' Culture in the Eighteenth and Nineteenth Centuries (New Haven, CT: Yale University Press, 1995).

John P. Koontz

WOOLSON, CONSTANCE FENIMORE (1840–1894)

In Constance Fenimore Woolson's posthumously published poem "Alas," the "wise" advise the "timid poet" to let "all the beauty / Of thy inmost altar-fires / Sing in glowing, cadenced verse; / To the world's hot eager ear / All thy deepest love rehearse." The sad and frustrated poet responds, "But my heart I cannot / Share with the world, Alas! Alas!" It is tempting to read this poem autobiographically as a possible indication of why Woolson turned away from writing poetry after 1880. Perhaps she found poetry too revealing, or, as critics have suggested, perhaps she realized her talent was better served writing fiction. Indeed, scholars today regard Woolson more widely as a novelist and short-story writer, associating her with the development of realism. Nevertheless, early in her career, Woolson wrote just as much poetry as prose. Published regularly in leading magazines, Woolson's poetry shows the author addressing many of the themes she would continue to explore in her later writing, including regionalism, nature, love, and art.

Woolson was born on March 5, 1840, in Claremont, New Hampshire. Within weeks of her birth, three of her five sisters died of scarlet fever, devastating her family. Soon after, the family moved to Cleveland, Ohio. Constance attended school there and in New York, graduating at the top of her class in 1858. Her literary career began after her father's death in 1869, when she began publishing sketches and stories. By 1877 most of the sixty or so poems she would write had appeared in prestigious magazines, including the *Atlantic Monthly*, *Galaxy*, and *Appleton's Journal*. Ultimately, she would also write four volumes of short stories, a novella, four novels, and a travel book. Although she always considered herself a New Englander, Woolson traveled throughout the country, including Virginia, the Carolinas, Tennessee, and especially Florida, where she spent many winters. After her mother's death in 1879, she traveled to Europe, living and working in England and Italy, where her close friends included Edmund Clarence Stedman and Henry James. Struggling with depression, health problems, and increased hearing loss, Woolson died in Venice on January 24, 1894, possibly by suicide.

A large number of Woolson's poems concern the specific places she visited and knew well, prefiguring the regional writing featured in her fiction and travel writing. Especially noteworthy are those verses on the American South, including two landscape poems, both published in 1874. In "The Florida Beach," the poet recreates a remote and seemingly magical place where time and space operate by different rules. Standing by the shore, the speaker explains, "The world seems far away, / The tide comes in, the birds fly low, / As if to catch our speech. / Ah destiny! Why must we ever go / Away from the Florida Beach?" Similarly, "Pine-Barrens" concludes, "How little seem earth's sorrows, how far off the lost to-morrows, / How broad and free the Barrens lie, how very near to God!" In these works and in others like "Corn Fields" (1872) and "Lake Erie in September" (1872), nature serves as a pathway to the divine. In other poems, like "March" (1873) and "The Heart of June" (1872), nature's presence is decidedly more sensual, connected with human eros and emotion.

Most often, though, Woolson presents love and emotion as distant, delayed, or frustrated—unattainable in the present. In "I Too!" (1877) the despondent speaker wonders why she cannot share in the joy she sees all around her. "Love Unexpressed" (1872) imagines that true feelings will only be acknowledged in the next world: "The only difference of the love in heaven / From love on earth below / Is: Here we love and know not how to tell it, / And there we all shall know." Similarly, poems like "Memory" (1873) and "The Haunting Face" (1873) address lost or forsaken love. Though readers might assume these poems are autobiographical, the speakers are ambiguous and are never clearly defined as male or female.

When Woolson does explore characters and their emotions more directly, she often does so through dramatic monologue. It is here, also, that her poems sometimes take on a political tone, albeit subdued. In "At the Smithy" (1874) an elderly Southern blacksmith explains the tragedies of his life—including losing all four of his sons in the war—to a Northerner passing through. The poem ends with a rather ambiguous endorsement of the Reconstruction, as the speaker shoes the horse of a newly elected black judge and explains, "'Eh, what's that you say? / He's colored? Of course; we're used to that here.'" Similarly, in "Only the Brakesman" (1876) a mother breaks down on hearing the news that her son has died in a train accident, acknowledging that for the company, such losses are rather routine and insignificant. Other, more conventional works like "On the Border" (1876) and "Fire in the Forest" (1875) are adventure pieces featuring daring escapes from perilous situations. Especially interesting is *Two Women, 1862* (1877), a **long poem** on the meeting of a young, pious, country maiden and a wealthy, worldly widow who love the same wounded soldier. Reversing traditional assumptions, the passionate older woman emerges as the truer lover, and her rival seems close-minded and naive.

The chief challenge for those who wish to study Woolson's poetry is accessibility. Although Clare Benedict, her niece, includes a number of the poems in her biography, many poems have not been reprinted since they first appeared in periodical form. Nevertheless, for those willing to track the poems down, Woolson's verses offer glimpses into her early views on region, nature, artistry, and love, providing even more context for this increasingly important nineteenth-century American writer.

Further Reading. ***Selected Primary Source:*** Benedict, Clare, ed., *Five Generations: 1785–1923* (London: Ellis, 1930). ***Selected Secondary Sources:*** Brehm, Victoria, ed., *Constance Fenimore Woolson's Nineteenth-Century: Essays* (Detroit, MI: Wayne State University Press, 2001); Kern, John D., *Constance Fenimore Woolson: Literary Pioneer* (Philadelphia: University of Pennsylvania Press, 1934); Tornsey, Cheryl B., *Constance Fenimore Woolson: The Grief of Artistry* (Athens: University of Georgia Press, 1989).

Heidi M. Hanrahan

WORK, HENRY CLAY (1832–1884)

Henry Clay Work's songs and poetry were very popular during his lifetime, yet he is not widely known to most literary scholars in the twentieth and twenty-first centuries for a variety of reasons: Work's poems reflected popular nineteenth-century American sentiments during the pre–Civil War era, sentiments that may not be shared by many Americans today; in addition, many modern readers may find his diction and perspective antiquated. Work's poems and songs also reveal how many Americans in the mid- to late nineteenth century held covert (if not overt) racial stereotypes about African Americans. This, along with naive attitudes about America's moral landscape and the evils of warfare, simply make Work's poems hard for most twenty-first–century Americans to appreciate.

Work was primarily known for his patriotic Civil War songs and poems, and many of his most popular poems glorified war. However, America was a very different country before the Civil War than it was after the war, and America's loss of innocence after the Civil War is arguably the reason Work's poems seem irrelevant today. Despite their seeming irrelevance, the moral attitudes embedded in Work's poetry, along with the many biblical references, continue to resonate with readers today.

The son of a famous abolitionist, Henry Clay Work was born in Middleton (now Middletown), Connecticut, on October 1, 1832. His father was imprisoned for twelve years for helping slaves escape, and this undoubtedly influenced his son's view of slavery and his belief about America's responsibility to eliminate the institution of slavery. Henry Clay worked first as a printer in Chicago, but he always wrote poems and songs for himself. It was only after a song producer encouraged him to produce some songs that his career took off. Work eventually wrote over seventy-five songs and poems, with several selling nearly one million copies. He became extremely wealthy, although he lost most of his money in a poor investment in the fruit business. Work died on June 8, 1884, at the age of fifty-one.

In his poem "Kingdom Coming," Work celebrates the liberation of African American slaves by the hands of Northern soldiers, yet his stereotypical dialect of the "darkies" makes his attitude toward slavery seem ambiguous at best. The question is whether Work is genuinely celebrating the slaves' freedom or simply reinscribing traditional racist stereotypes that depict African Americans as unschooled, ignorant, and lazy. In part because of the efforts of Alan Work, his father, as a devout abolitionist who helped thousands of slaves escape the institution of slavery before his imprisonment, most scholars believe that Henry Clay Work was simply using the accepted, conventional language of his day.

Another problematic poem, "Babylon Is Fallen," also contains statements that seem to re-inscribe racial stereotypes. For example, Work states that the black Civil War soldiers are "darkies" wearing uniforms and carrying guns. Work uses biblical allusions throughout the poem, but the most obvious is the connection between the Southern slave states and "Babylon." In the final stanza of the poem, Work states that the slaves "will be the Massa, he (the white slave master) will be the servant." This inversion of roles signifies the importance Americans accorded post-slavery possibilities.

In the poem "Wake Nicodemus," the dominant Christian theme of salvation and redemption is alluded to, connecting America within the Christian perspective that there is a heaven and hell. Indeed, Work's poetry describes America as heaven-on-earth rather literally. In the poem, the year of Jubilee—the fiftieth year in the Hebrew scriptures, which state that all debts (and slaves) were to be released upon that date—is quite literally connected to America's liberation of its slaves after the Civil War. This idea that America was "God's nation" is repeated throughout many of Work's poems, but it is most notable in "Song of a Thousand Years." In this poem Work connects America with Heaven in the opening stanza: "Lift up your eyes desponding freemen! / Fling to the winds your needless fears! / He who unfurl'd your beauteous banner, / Says it shall wave a thousand years!" America is defined as the land of freedom, and Work implies that the slave states were holding America back from its heavenly calling. To Work (and many nineteenth-century Americans), America had a Christian destiny that was being compromised by the institution of slavery. Similarly, in Work's poem "Ring the Bell, Watchman!" the abolition of slavery is interpreted within a spiritual context that viewed the Civil War as "some great deed." This "good news" is the spiritual connection made throughout many of Work's poems.

Another theme that runs throughout many of Work's poems is the romantic nature of warfare. Work's poems seem to glorify war, especially his poem "Marching Through Georgia." The opening stanza states, "Bring the good old bugle, boys! We'll sing another song— / Sing it with a spirit that will start the world along— / Sing it as we used to sing it fifty thousand strong, / While we were marching through Georgia." The good old days of battles in the Civil War are described by Work as both spiritual and heroic. Certainly many Americans interpreted their involvement in the Civil War as necessary and right, yet the glorification of war in Work's discussion may seem harsh to modern readers. Ironically, it is for this very reason that Work's poems were so popular in his day: They captured the popular sentiments of the American people at the end of the nineteenth century. Americans were patriotic and viewed themselves within a spiritual context that may no longer be familiar to American society in the twenty-first century, making Work's poems seem old-fashioned and outdated.

Further Reading. ***Selected Secondary Sources:*** Hollander, John ed., *American Poetry: The Nineteenth Century* (New York: Viking Press, 1993); Kelley, Bruce C., and Mark A. Snell, eds., *Bugle Resounding: Music and Musicians of the Civil War Era* (Columbia: University of Missouri Press, 2004).

Tad Wakefield

WRIGHT, C.D. (1949–)

The poetry of C.D. Wright merges an interest in precise observation, regional- and class-consciousness, experimental form, and cross-genre collaborations. In her work, Arkansas Southern poetry meets the experimental techniques associated with **Language poetry** and poetics. These dual tendencies are noted in "Our Dust," an early poem from *String Light* (1991), where Wright notes the presence of both the "simple music" of her work and the "side B of me." In later books, the experimental "side B" has emerged as the dominant force in her poetry, but the social concerns of Wright's "simple music" continue as the subjects of her literary maps of Arkansas and Rhode Island and of her collaborations with photographer Deborah Luster.

Wright was born in Mountain Home, Arkansas, to a judge father and a court stenographer mother. She was educated at Memphis State College and the University of Arkansas, where she received her MFA in 1976 and where she met the poet Frank Stanford, an important early influence on her work. In 1979 she moved to San Francisco, where she worked at the San Francisco Poetry Center and taught at San Francisco State University. In 1983 she started teaching at Brown University in Providence, Rhode Island, where she became Israel J. Kapstein Professor of English. She is married to the poet **Forrest Gander**, with whom she edits Lost Roads Publishers; they have one son. Wright has received numerous grants and awards, including fellowships from the National Endowment for the Arts, the Guggenheim Foundation, and the Lannan Literary Foundation. In 2004 Wright was named the recipient of a fellowship from the John D. and Catherine T. MacArthur Foundation.

Wright's early work shows a strong interest in **narrative**; many of the poems in *Translations of the Gospel Back into Tongues* (1982) tell brief stories of people at the edge of events. In "Obedience of the Corpse," a midwife attending a baby whose mother has died in childbirth "hopes the mother's milk is good awhile longer, / the woman up the road is still nursing." In "Tours," "A girl on the stairs listens to her father / beat up her mother." Hints of her poetry's recurrent interest in sexuality are present in "Blazes," a poem in which the girl narrator swoons over a visitor to the house: "It was a school night. I held my pillow to my chest / and said Kiss me Frankie." To the extent that these early poems are autobiographical, their stories are frequently intertwined with the lives of others: The lovestruck girl in "Blazes" could be the aging spinster in "Vanish."

In *Further Adventures with You* (1986) and *String Light*, Wright starts to develop a more pronounced interest in experiment and in establishing dialogues with other genres. Some poems, such as "Elements of Night" from *Further Adventures* and "Remarks on Color" from *String Light*, amount to lists and start to display the influence of Language poetry's experiments with parataxis. In "Why Ralph Refuses to Dance," from *String Light*, the odd-numbered lines answer the question of the title while the even-numbered lines tell a narrative leading to the moment that prompts the poem; the total effect is more than the sum of these parts. These combined narrative and associative impulses are also present in the twin poems "What No One Could Have Told Them" and "Detail from *What No One Could Have Told Them*." The former is an associative poem of parenting; the latter takes a single image from "What No One Could Have Told Them" and reworks it into a comic musical moment: "He pees into a paper plate a plate the guest set down / into a plate of white paper the guest set down He pees."

Wright's poetry obtains a new level of experimental drive in *Just Whistle* (1993), a book-length poem including photographs by Deborah Luster, with whom Wright would collaborate on several more books. The image of "the body" is the persistent focus of the book, though without the single-mindedness of **Deep Image** poetry; rather, individual parts circle around the image with a varying insistence reminiscent of **Leslie Scalapino**. A variety of forms attend these poems, from prose paragraphs to lyric moments to a set of short poems ("They Sleep") employing the same five words.

Just Whistle was followed by *Tremble* (1996), a book of short lyrics that continue Wright's search for new forms and subjects. The poem "And It Came to Pass," set on the anniversary of Frank Stanford's death, seeks to move beyond Stanford's influence and shadow and into an independent mode, wondering, "What will my new instrument be." The answer came quickly with *Deepstep Come Shining* (1998), another book-length poem, wherein the "instrument" is the American road itself and the technique represents a full flowering of Wright's experimental voice. *Deepstep Come Shining* continues a long tradition of American road literature, from **Walt Whitman**'s "Song of the Open Road" to **Jack Kerouac**'s *On the Road.* The title of the work comes in part from Deepstep, Georgia, one of the towns visited on the road; indeed, Wright's work fascination with regional names goes back at least to "The Ozark Odes," from *String Light,* where one section, entitled "Arkansas Towns," is an alphabetical list of quirky town names such as "Greasy Corner" and "Monkey Town."

In *Deepstep Come Shining,* Wright's regional interests and her experimental form find their most sustained connection, with the influence of Language poets such as **Ron Silliman**, for whose work Wright has proclaimed admiration, absorbed and transmuted. The trope of the road trip gives the book its immediacy and its contact with real events and people, and the looseness of the form allows Wright to return to particular memories and fragments of the trip, including not only town names but also loose scraps of conversation, recitals of bathroom graffiti, verses from the Bible and Shakespeare, and quotes from filmmakers, assembling them into a kind of narrative-driven collage. As a result, the Language poet's obsession with textual effects is grounded in quotidian experience: The line "God is Louise. Is that what it says" suggests a vandalized variation on a fundamentalist roadside sign but also a feminist theological text as well as a whole history of a region's dominance by a single religion and indigenous resistance to that dominance.

Wright's subsequent books include *Steal Away: Selected and New Poems* (2002) and *Cooling Time* (2004), an assemblage of prose from various occasions into something of a literary manifesto. In that book, Wright notes that her poetry "careens along two vectors that do not always parallel, intersect, or coalesce." It is, she says, "compatibly tendentious and personal." Thus, her collaborations with Deborah Luster, *The Lost Roads Project* (1994) and *One Big Self* (2003), suggest both a love of region and human frailty and, in the latter book, a provocative assertion of the social damage that has been done to the South by its insistence on incarceration. In *Steal Away,* Wright includes a series of "Retablos" published in both English and Spanish (the retablo is a genre of Mexican folk iconography). Like the "Girl Friend Poems" also collected in *Steal Away,* the retablo sequences are essentially short lyrics of intimately charged friendship. They assert the persistence of the local in the face of Wright's ambitious experimental forms.

Further Reading. ***Selected Primary Sources:*** Wright, C.D., *Cooling Time: An American Poetry Vigil* (Port Townsend, WA: Copper Canyon Press, 2004); ———, *Deepstep Come Shining* (Port Townsend, WA: Copper Canyon Press, 1998); ———, *Just Whistle: A Valentine,* photog. Deborah Luster (Berkeley, CA: Kelsey St. Press, 1993); ———, *The Lost Roads Project: A Walk-in Book of Arkansas,* photog. Deborah Luster (Fayetteville: University of Arkansas Press, 1994); ———, *One Big Self: Prisoners of Louisiana,* photog. Deborah Luster (Santa Fe, NM: Twin Palms, 2003); ———, *Steal Away: Selected and New Poems* (Port Townsend, WA: Copper Canyon Press, 2002); ———, *Tremble* (New York: Ecco, 1996). ***Selected Secondary Sources:*** Burt, Stephen, "'I Came to Talk You into Physical Splendor': On the Poetry of C.D. Wright" (*Boston Review* 22.6 [1997]: 31–33); Colburn, Nadia Herman, "About C.D. Wright" (*Ploughshares* 28.4 [2002]: 204–209); Kirsch, Adam, "Discourtesies" (*New Republic* [21 October 2002]: 32–36).

David Kellogg

WRIGHT, CHARLES (1935–)

Charles Wright has distinguished himself as the leading contemporary writer interested in the idea of poetry as spiritual autobiography. Consistently placing himself between two landscapes, "One that's eternal and divine, / and one that's just the back yard" (*Negative Blue*), Wright has revitalized this older form, making his failure to pass straightforwardly from one landscape to the other the grounds for a powerfully original, nonnarrative, meditative art. Description, reminiscence, and sometimes elaborate associational structures combine in his work to produce moving accounts of yearning or loss or vision that are free of the tight focus on personal details that sometimes limits the work of his contemporaries who share his interests. In this, he is much like **Emily Dickinson** and **Wallace Stevens**, his two greatest models.

Wright is the author of thirteen books of poetry, the first eleven collected into three trilogies: *Country Music: Selected Early Poems* (1982) and *The World of the Ten Thousand Things: Poems 1980–1990* (1990), which display a three-part structure but are actually composed of material from four books, and *Negative Blue: Selected Later Poems* (2000). He was born in Pickwick Dam, Tennessee, in 1935 and grew up in Kingsport, and these landscapes are evident in his poetry. After graduating from Davidson College, he joined the U.S. Army and was sent to Verona, Italy, where, under the influence of the striking landscape and the poetry of **Ezra Pound**, he began developing a lyric investigation of landscape that he has deepened and extended throughout his career. After the army, he attended the Iowa Writers' Workshop from

1961 to 1963 and then spent two years in Italy on a Fulbright. He began teaching at the University of California–Irvine in 1966 and moved to the University of Virginia in 1983, where he became the Souder Family Professor of English.

One of Wright's favorite artists is the Italian painter Girogio Morandi, and Wright's comments about Morandi's drawings in which bottles and dishes, marked by only a few fragmentary lines, seem to dissolve before our eyes, serve as a clear account of his own intentions as a writer. The bottles, he writes, seem to "becom[e] larger the more they dissemble. It's almost as though they are drawn on the air, that masterly, and in that instant starting to be borne away" (*Halflife*). It is as if the bottles reside in some other realm—Wright calls it "the invisible"—and the artist had tried and failed to approximate a glimpse of their invisible presence, the few lines recorded testifying to something quite beyond their reach, even now slipping free of them. Those partial lines draw the eye and imagination to what's not there, a white space whose power we sense as it retreats from our approximations, refusing to be handled. Wright calls this "the power and domination of what's not there, the energy of absence" (*Quarter Notes*). It is an effect of "retreating radiance" (*Quarter Notes*), built on the realization that "what's missing is what appears / Most visible to the eye" (*Ten Thousand Things*).

Wright gets that same effect in landscape descriptions, often at twilight or with sun or birds or clouds slipping out of sight. His quick, improvised observations seem all he's managed to salvage from failed, yet still-luminous encounters with "the secret landscape behind the landscape we look at here" (*Negative Blue*). So, too, failed attempts to remember the lost worlds of Tennessee or Italy or California become, at the same time, radiant, dissolving testimony to "an otherness inside us / We never touch" called the past (*Ten Thousand Things*). In a similar manner, individual words, lines, journal entries, weather reports, and bits of theological reflection—all of these—are caught just before they are overwhelmed and abandoned, are "negative shapes sketched in / And luminous here and there" (*Negative Blue*). Wright's is a poetry in which "each word / Is a failure" and "each object / We name and place / leads us another step away from the light" (*Negative Blue*), but in that failure what will not be named and placed is powerfully encountered.

Wright's career has been a long investigation of ways of presenting and deepening this vision. Each of his trilogies follows a similar movement while also unfolding a distinctive stylistic pattern. A number of critics and even Wright himself have noted that that movement—roughly, a statement of the problem of the separation between timeless and infinite realms in the first book; an analysis of the charged, fragmentary nature of the various attempts to speak for that wordless realm in the second; and an attempt to follow those dissolving attempts back toward the unknowable realm in the third—bears a marked resemblance to the movement in Dante's *Divine Comedy* from the Inferno to Purgatory to Paradise. Wright's, of course, is a more skeptical and casual version of that pattern. His shift in styles from trilogy to trilogy has to do with compression and expansion, most notably in his use of the image and the **line**—his primary means of encountering and being erased by what remains stubbornly outside his reach.

In the first trilogy, *Country Music*, the problem of separation between realms is often spoken of in terms of memory. "Dog Creek Mainline," from *Hard Freight* (1973), remembers the smells and sounds of a childhood landscape ("Spindrift and windfall; woodrot"), but associates that now-vanished landscape with the poet's seemingly atrophied senses. His ear, "cold cave, is an absence, / Tapping its own thin wires." His heart, accordingly, is an unreadable hieroglyphic, its deepest feelings at some unreachable distance. If Dog Creek is on a railroad line, it is "hard freight" to ever reach it, located as it is up a series of metaphorically long steep hauls, off on an unused spur. The writing here, as throughout the first trilogy, is imagistic—with argument and investigation being carried out primarily by the juxtaposition of images. *Bloodlines* (1975), the second book of the trilogy, is notable primarily for two extended sequences, "Tattoos" and "Skins," which link a series of short image-centered poems focusing memory (car wreck, death of parents, and so on) and poetic themes (beauty, truth, magic), respectively. One might think of these individual imagistic poems as stars in an unfixed constellation or candles floating on a dark ocean. They never quite form a complete argument; each image seems adrift in what Wright calls "the river of heaven" or on something that "does not appear." The images glimmer and wink out; they come and go.

In *China Trace* (1977), with eyes on the images and bits of order that, like car lights in a canyon far below, drop "like match flames through the great void / Under our feet / . . . burning and disappearing," Wright's speaker allows himself to feel and respond to that tug toward an other realm. His images for this are striking and mark a significant turn in his work. Sunrise becomes "The bright nail of the east I usher my body toward." He is a wafer on the tongue of "nothingness," a figure staring out "a window into Away-From-Here," a bit of dust, one of innumerable "things in a fall in a world of fall." These images are powerful statements of yearning—attempts, the speaker notes, "to untie myself, to do penance and disappear / Through the upper-right hand corner of things, to say grace." And yet, as the book continues, it becomes clear that no such release is fully forthcoming; the poems are increasingly marked by a sense of waiting or melancholy, a fear that "Like a bead of clear oil the Healer revolves through the night wind, / Part eye, part tear, unwilling to recognize us."

Wright's second trilogy, *The World of the Ten Thousand Things*, is marked by a lengthening of Wright's line and, often, an extension of his poems. Things in the world, memories, flashes of insight—all of these are handled and turned one way and then another, rather than being fixed in a moment of imagistic precision. Still, the poet's drive is much the same: to try to make visible some portion of a realm just out of reach and to suffer, and make use of, the failure to do so. *The Southern Cross* (1981) once again establishes the problem. It is dominated by two longer poems. "Homage to Paul Cézanne" begins with an image of pieces of paper in a field in the moonlight; they look to the poet like "the dead," wearing white shirts and "nudg[ing] / Close to the surface of things." They seem about to speak, asking to be remembered, reaching a hand from one realm to the next. Wright compares the long, layered lines of this poem, working with their voices in a series of linked images, to Cézanne's "broad blocks and planes": "We layer them stroke by stroke / In steps and ascending mass, in verticals raised from the earth." And yet, there is no true movement between realms. The dead finally drift away, caring nothing for the poem's "fringe of words" or "the honk and flash of a new style." "The Southern Cross," an even longer sequence, catalogues a series of memories, all linked to water—Venice, lakes and rivers in Tennessee and Italy, streams in Montana, the Mediterranean. His lines—juxtaposing scenes, touching then moving on—once again mimic the process of trying to reach back and arrive at coherence: "Overlay after overlay tumbled and brought back." What dominates, however, is the melancholy sense that one can never remember enough and that such remembered scenes are at best "the edges around what really happened." What "defines us," he acknowledges, is still waiting "to be rediscovered." It is a lost city—inaccessible inside us or, like towns in Tennessee lost to the dams, swallowed up by the waters of time.

In *The Other Side of the River* (1984), middle book of the second trilogy, Wright's long line, sometimes broken in the middle under the weight it is attempting to carry, reaches full maturity. That line stays constant in his work from this point forward. The poems are a sometimes exuberant cataloguing of memories and landscapes. Their world, shaped by the poet's sense that what eludes him is partially visible in the things around us, is a representation of Wright's dominant vision. It is "synaptical"—filled with gaps, energy incompletely arcing from line to line, memory to memory—and "rearranged." Countering Wright's sense that "each tactile thing / repeats the untouchable / In its own way" is the acknowledgment that "something infinite behind everything appears, / and then disappears." No one, he concludes, will ever reach over or answer back from the other side. Still, he slyly remarks, he has learned something: "I'd like to think I know how to conjugate / 'Can you hear me?' and 'What?'"

The final book in Wright's second trilogy, *Zone Journals* (1988), is perhaps Wright's greatest accomplishment as a poet. As in the other final books, the poet's eye is constantly drawn beyond the buzzing, vanishing, "unspooling" outlines of landscape and memory to what waits beyond, eluding those approximations of memory and landscape. "Somewhere out there," he writes, "an image is biding its time, / . . . Waiting to take me in and complete my equation." He introduces the journal form in this volume, making poems out of sequences set off by dashes and dates. What this does is bring the notion of working in time to the forefront of the poet's and reader's attention. Not only is the poet's world spatially rearranged to reflect his sense that things are fragmentary outlines of something beyond them, but in these poems it is temporally rearranged as well. "I keep coming back, like a tongue to a broken tooth," to a specific slant of light, one journal entry begins, the speaker convinced that in that play of light something is "Opening, closing beyond any alphabet's / Recall to witness and isolate." "I look for it constantly," another entry insists. What this leads to is a more charged poetic surface. At times, in Wright, one grows almost hypnotized as glints of meaning appear and then are drawn back in, in an almost constant rhythm. Foregrounding the notion of time foregrounds the notion of struggle. We sense the poet actively reentering the dark, groping for connections, trying to reformulate a dominant problem, and we are forced as readers to work in the same sort of way. In fact, in the strongest poem of the book, the yearlong "A Journal of the Year of the Ox," the call to "concentrate, listen hard" dominates the poem. If the poem's vision is of a "great river of language that circles the universe, / [in which] everything comes together," poetry's "true work" is simply to "sit very still, and listen hard." Poetry never fully enters that river; it only catches bits of its murmur, testifying to its presence as it modifies and discards entry after entry.

Wright's final trilogy, *Negative Blue*, might be said to consolidate the work of the first two trilogies. It turns from the longer, spreading forms of *The Ten Thousand Things* back to the predominantly one- and two-page poems of *Country Music*, yet it retains the sense of thinking in time by having each poem unfold a single, clearly marked moment: "Warm day, early March," "Shank of the afternoon, wan weight-light," and so forth. It is as if the journal entries of the previous volume had become more concentrated and shaped—retaining their potential connections with other entries across a synaptical gap while also quite deliberately trying (and failing) to reach, as it were, across the river. Each attempt is a focused, whole-hearted attempt to speak the unspoken; there is no holding back. Perhaps because of that whole-hearted commitment, Wright's linguistic resources seem to open up in this trilogy as well. Added to the precise, ever-straining imagistic thinking of the first trilogy and the circling, ever-revising layering of the second trilogy is a reflective, evaluative tone. It is as if, with this final trilogy, the poet is trying to describe how far his project had been able to take him.

Chickamauga (1995), first book of this final trilogy, defines the problem engaging the poet as not only the distance between landscape and a true, absent landscape or the distance between memory and an unfathomable, internalized past, but the distance between words and something ever beyond them. Much as in **T.S. Eliot**, but with a more skeptical inflection, this is a distinction between words and the Word, worked out, poem by poem, as the poet grapples with "these words" taking shape before him. "Each word / is a failure," the poems suggest, "lead[ing] us another step away from the light." Just as in remembering and reading the landscape, writing leads only to the splintering of glints and sparks: "We who would see beyond seeing / see only language, that burning field." And yet, asserts *Black Zodiac* (1997), second book in the trilogy, there is much to treasure in one's history with the word, just as there was in one's sacred landscapes or inescapable memories. Looking back over decades of writing, one takes a certain satisfaction in its failures, knowing that those failures are a sort of indirect testimony. "How else would we keep in touch," the poet says to the absolute, save for "tracing our words upon the air?" It is, after all, "Journal and landscape / —Discredited form, discredited subject matter—," "writ[ing] in order to erase again," which have reconfigured his suspended life as a quest. It is language's "fall through the two worlds— / . . . [which] sanctions our going up and our going down, our days / And the lives we infold inside them."

In *Appalachia* (1998), last of the concluding books, one senses a slow movement from the desire expressed in its first poem—"Lift up that far corner of landscape, / there, toward the west. / Let some of the deep light in, the arterial kind"—to the dawning recognition in its final poem: "All my life I've looked for this slow light, this smallish light / starting to seep, coppery blue, / out of the upper right-hand corner of things." That light, one assumes, is what his fragile poems and journal entries have consistently spoken and misspoken. As their "syllables [have been] scatter[ed] across the new grass, in search of their words," bringing the poet to "an end to language / . . . an end to handing out the names of things," he has entered a state in which his words have no real weight. To be "wordless is what the soul wants, the one thing that I keep in mind." And if he is only waiting, still, he comforts himself, "Surely some splendor's set to come forth, / Some last equation solved, declued and reclarified." Certainly the three trilogies have accomplished that—if not an awakening to splendor, a clarifying (and perhaps a solving) of the terrible equation separating weightless splendor from time, the body, and language.

It's perhaps a little too early to confidently describe the new directions Wright's work has taken since completing the trilogy in 2000. Two books have followed—*A Short History of the Shadow* (2002) and *Buffalo Yoga* (2004). Many aspects of his earlier work have been carried over. "I sit where I always sit," the first poem in *A Short History* insists—which is to say, the Charlottesville study and backyard, the Montana cabin. Long lines continue to flare and drop away as the poet continues to work his way back or down to the secret landscape behind each poem's specific landscape. There are, however, two new directions that one might take special note of, aside from the quite marked insistence by Wright's speaker that he is gathering himself for something like a final push.

The first new direction is fairly easy to spot. In both books, after a first series of I-centered poems, the speaker more and more frequently adopts a plural point of view. "*Our* dreams are luminous," he writes, "a cast fire upon the world." "If it stays hidden, it's *we* also who hide." "*We* can see nothing, or take in nothing, it is so still." At times, the speaker begins from his position as a single observer, but the majority of the poems close with this plural voice. One thinks of **Whitman**, dissolving into the landscape at the end of "Song of Myself." In a similar way, Wright's voice, like his favorite twilight time of day, seems to even out and disperse. His struggle is everyone's struggle, bound as we all are to the wheel of time.

The second new direction has to do with the way each book is focused. A vast majority of the meditations in *A Short History of the Shadow* take place at evening or in the dark, ending up there even if they don't begin there. *Dark, darkness, twilight, dusk light, half light, last light, night light, night mouth, nightstone*—the reader begins to anticipate such words in each poem. In *Buffalo Yoga*, over and against a few references to sunset, last light, and night, one hears a steady series of references to light. The poems unfold in the sun, in a glare, in the morning. One hears of a "Sun-sliding morning" or "sun-soured Montana daydreams"; one listens to "the light, / Inveterate stutterer"; one's eyes are drawn to "The slow seep and sad shine of sunlight." The covers of the two volumes—panels or swatches of color and no color against dark backgrounds by Mark Rothko and Milton Avery—when contrasted, for example, with Morandi's disappearing line, also on a Wright cover, suggest that Wright has begun thinking about the problem of two worlds in broader terms. Rather than charting one bright arc of a bird's flight as it breaks away from sight and is absorbed back into the gathering twilight, *A Short History* paints an entire world in shadow, insisting we see all the world *as if* in "half-light, half-dark, / when everything starts to shine out," each object a spark, "Arising out of the emptiness" and being drawn back in. Similarly, *Buffalo Yoga* forces our eyes to adjust to a world whose edges are everywhere touched with fire, yet "mute and glittering" in their refusal to speak. The world is "luminous, transubstantiated," and yet, though its doors stand open and we are "Twice-blessed by their golden handles, / We try them both, but they don't open, not yet, they don't open." That is to say, Wright's themes and deep uncertainties seem much the same, even as there seems no real end to his restless drive to refashion the world so that its full weight stirs and shakes us.

Further Reading. ***Selected Primary Sources:*** Wright, Charles, *Country Music: Selected Early Poems* (Middletown, CT: Wesleyan University Press, 1982); ———, *Halflife: Improvisations and Interviews, 1977–1987* (Ann Arbor: University of Michigan Press, 1988); ———, *Negative Blue: Selected Later Poems* (New York: Farrar, Straus and Giroux, 2000); ———, *Quarter Notes: Improvisations and Interviews* (Ann Arbor: University of Michigan Press, 1995); ———, *The World of the Ten Thousand Things: Poems 1980–1990* (New York: Farrar, Straus and Giroux, 1990). ***Selected Secondary Sources:*** Andrews, Tom, ed., *The Point Where All Things Meet: Essays on Charles Wright* (Oberlin, OH: Oberlin College Press, 1995); Costello, Bonnie, "Charles Wright, Giorgio Morandi and the Metaphysics of the Line" (*Mosaic* 35.1 [March 2002]: 149–171); Gardner, Thomas, "Restructured and Restrung: Charles Wright's *Zone Journals* and Emily Dickinson" (*Kenyon Review* 26.2 [Spring 2004]: 149–175); Suarez, Ernest, *Southbound: Interviews with Southern Writers* (Columbia: University of Missouri Press, 1999).

Thomas Gardner

WRIGHT, JAMES (1927–1980)

James Wright was instrumental in the refinement and advancement of a new style of American poetry in the 1960s and 1970s. Feeling stifled by meter and rhyme early in their careers, Wright and other **Deep Imagist** poets turned to **free verse**, emphasizing abstract or surrealist imagery as a means to trigger the subconscious. The sharp transformation one sees in Wright's poetry is one of the clearest single examples of a general trend among many American poets of his generation. He applied the attributes of many European poetries to descriptions of the vacant prairies, grimy industrial landscapes, and beleaguered characters of the American Midwest. Wright was an active translator of several languages, an incisive critic, and a tireless correspondent with other poets. Given his relatively short life, he had a remarkably influential role in remaking what would become a dominant mode of American poetry.

James Arlington Wright was born on December 13, 1927 in Martin's Ferry, Ohio, the second of three sons. His father, Dudley Wright, worked as a die-setter at the Hazel-Atlas Glass Company across the Ohio River in Wheeling, West Virginia. Neither of his parents was educated past the eighth grade. Wright wrote his first poems at age fifteen. At sixteen, he suffered the first of several nervous breakdowns and missed a year of high school. He joined the U.S. Army upon graduating in 1946 and served as clerk and typist in Japan for a little over a year. Shortly after he was discharged, determined to avoid a life of plant labor like that of his father, Wright enrolled at Kenyon University and studied under the poet **John Crowe Ransom**. In a letter to his friend, the poet **Donald Hall**, he explained this decision as one between "the Ohio Valley (i.e. death, real death to the soul) on the one side and life (escape to my own life . . .) on the other" (Hall, xxv). Life, for Wright, meant a life in poetry. He excelled at Kenyon, and in 1951 Ransom published two of his poems, "Lonely" and "Father," in the prestigious *Kenyon Review*.

After graduating in 1952, Wright married Liberty Kardules, a high school classmate from Martin's Ferry, and was awarded a Fulbright scholarship to study at the University of Vienna. There he translated the work of German poet George Trakl. The couple's first son, Franz Wright (who later became a poet), was born there. Their second son, Marshall, followed in 1958. Wright later earned a Ph.D. in literature at the University of Washington under **Theodore Roethke**, another mentor. Wright's first book, *The Green Wall* (1957), was published in the Yale Series of Younger Poets, selected by **W.H. Auden**. It was widely acclaimed, as was *Saint Judas* (1959). Wright rapidly began to publish both poetry and reviews in virtually all of the important magazines of the day, including the *Sewanee Review*, the *Hudson Review*, and the *New Yorker*.

A pivotal shift occurred after Wright found a selection of Trakl's poems in a magazine called the *Fifties* and wrote to its editor, **Robert Bly**. He was invited to visit Bly on his farm in Minnesota. Bly and his fierce convictions about the failings of American poetry and its necessary new directions became a major influence on Wright. The two would become allies in the advancement of a new mode of poetry. Wright made several visits to the farm throughout the 1960s, befriending other poets there like Donald Hall, **Louis Simpson**, and **Thomas McGrath.** Awakened to new possibilities, he withdrew a forthcoming collection titled *Amenities of Stone* from his publisher and began to refashion the poems. He then published *The Branch Will Not Break* (1963), a book in a decidedly different direction.

But as Wright reinvented himself poetically, his depression continued and was worsened by drinking. After many separations, Wright and Liberty divorced in

1962. He held two short-term professorships at midwestern universities. (He was denied tenure at the University of Minnesota primarily for missing classes and drinking.) In 1966 he took a job at New York City's Hunter College, where he would stay until his death. In 1967 he married Edith Anne Runk (Annie), and *Shall We Gather at the River* (1968) soon appeared. The couple traveled in Europe often throughout the next decade, mainly to France and Italy, thanks to several fellowships and grants Wright received for his books. He won the Pulitzer Prize and an Academy of American Poets fellowship for his *Collected Poems* (1971), and he next published *Two Citizens* (1973), whose title refers to his and Annie's making their way across Europe.

His marriage to Annie alleviated but did not completely erase Wright's periods of depression. After the deaths of his parents in 1973 and 1974, he suffered another nervous breakdown and later joined Alcoholics Anonymous. He published *To a Blossoming Pear Tree* in 1977 and first showed signs of cancer of the tongue while in France in 1979. He was able to attend a gathering of poets at the White House in January 1980, but was hospitalized soon after. James Wright died on March 25, 1980, in the Bronx at Calvary Hospital. *This Journey* (1982), a manuscript he had completed, was published posthumously.

Both Martin's Ferry and the Hazel-Atlas Glass Plant turn up in many of Wright's poems, as both autobiographical details and emblems of what he viewed as the dispiriting industrial landscape and lifestyle of the Midwest. Throughout his career, he wrote poems about or in the voices of people he viewed as marginalized or forgotten. One of the more peculiar examples of this is found in "The Assignation" (1957). The long monologue is spoken by the ghost of a woman who searches for a lover who had promised to meet her in the afterlife. Every year at the appointed time, in the appointed orchard, she rises to look for him and is disappointed. Written in eight-line stanzas of effortless blank verse, "The Assignation" also announced Wright's technical deftness.

The most famous piece of Wright's early, formal work is the title poem from his second collection, "Saint Judas." Here again, Wright shows a fascination with the dispossessed. Like "The Assignation," the poem "Saint Judas" (1959) is a dramatic monologue. (Wright wrote dramatic monologues often, mimicking two of his favorite American poets, **Edward Arlington Robinson** and **Robert Frost**.) Judas, after his betrayal of Christ, describes stopping to help a beaten and abandoned man on the side of the road. In the brief framework of a Petrarchan sonnet, Wright attempts to humanize even Judas, whom he considered the essential betrayer, and turn him into—if not a saint—at least a moral man with whom we can sympathize. The poet who would spend much of his career writing about social outsiders tackled the definitive social outsider early in his career. Many critics, particularly Peter Stitt, latched on to Wright's decision to canonize Judas, as it were, as a reflection of his belief that compassion is man's greatest virtue in a tragic, imperfect world.

Equally illuminating of Wright's worldview is the poem "At The Executed Murderer's Grave" (1959), also in *Saint Judas.* The **long poem**, again in blank verse, shows Wright taking stock of his own humanity—his imperfections and virtues—while speaking to the grave of executed Ohio serial killer, George Doty, another infamous outsider. Wright stresses the similarities of all men—their equal potential for good and evil—insisting that he and the murderer are not easily distinguishable. "We are nothing but a man," he wrote.

In retrospect, Wright's self-reproach in "At the Executed Murderer's Grave" can be viewed as the beginning of his massive, stylistic transformation. In 1958 **James Dickey** published a scathing review of an anthology in which Wright was featured, *New Poets of England and America* (1957). Appraising young, formal poets such as Wright, **Anthony Hecht**, and **Thom Gunn**, Dickey found them likable but absolutely irrelevant. Though angered at the time, Wright soon came to agree with Dickey. In a letter to Donald Hall (one of many throughout his life in which he pledged to quit writing poetry for good), Wright accused himself of "betraying whatever was true and courageous" in himself and of having become "one of the slickest, cleverest, most 'charming' concocters of the do-it-yourself *New Yorker* verse" (Hall, xxix). Wright was revising "At the Executed Murderer's Grave" during this time and now began changing it dramatically. He dampened what he viewed as dishonest artifice, making the poem more personal and direct. It was at around this time that Wright met Robert Bly and was influenced by his vehement belief in free verse and Deep-Image-laden poetry. Critics initially called the style "surrealist," though its practitioners rejected the term. Bly's influence on Wright's poetry was to accelerate and intensify changes that were already under way.

Wright next published *The Branch Will Not Break*, now widely regarded as one of the most influential collections of the decade. Critical reactions to the book were mixed, however. Many rued Wright's abandonment of rhyme and meter, a seemingly abrupt shift, as Wright had withdrawn from publication his intermediary step, *Amenities of Stone. The Branch Will Not Break*, however, contained one of Wright's most famous poems and by far the single most widely debated and quoted line of his oeuvre: the concluding line of "Lying in a Hammock at William Duffy's Farm in Pine Island, Minnesota." (The unadorned, utilitarian title signifies Wright's new goal of directness.) The thirteen-line free-verse poem describes, in straightforward diction, the scene around the speaker: a butterfly, leaves, horse manure, and so on. Without drawing any explicit connection, it concludes with the line "I have wasted my life." The sudden and unqualified leap from external imagery to inner feeling or epiphany is emblematic of deep imagist poetry—using imagery to sidestep the rational mind and get at the subconscious. It was, in short, everything Bly thought poetry should be. "A Blessing," another memorable poem from the book, operates in a similar way.

The Branch Will Not Break contained one other of Wright's best-known poems, and the most famous by far about his hometown, "Autumn Begins in Martin's Ferry Ohio" (1963). After brief descriptions of weary, working-class men and women, Wright turns to a high school football game where the sons of these people "grow suicidally beautiful" and smash their bodies into one another. This poem, perhaps more than any other, betrays Wright's fear of entrapment by the brutal economic realities of Martin's Ferry—the very fear that propelled him into a life in letters.

Few single poems from 1968's *Shall We Gather at the River* are as often quoted or anthologized as those mentioned above. In retrospect, the collection seems uneven and a harbinger of the less-stimulating work that followed—the selection of new poems included with Wright's *Collected Poems* and *Two Citizens.* During the next decade, Wright also wrote many **prose poems** and continued to translate from several languages. Wright's subjects during this period, however, did not dramatically change. In "The Minneapolis Poem" (1968) he again explores the lives of outsiders—here African Americans, Native Americans, homosexuals, and the urban poor of Minneapolis, specifically—while juxtaposing them with hints of the compassion and hopefulness in all men, including himself. "A Centenary Ode: Inscribed to Little Crow, Leader of the Sioux Rebellion in Minnesota, 1862" (1971) also reflects this theme.

To a Blossoming Pear Tree was a far more successful volume. Wright steered his free-verse style ahead in innovative ways, while beginning to integrate stray hints of the "first" James Wright. Donald Hall points out in the introduction to Wright's posthumous *Above the River: The Complete Poems* (1990) that one poem in *To a Blossoming Pear Tree*, in particular, "The First Days" (1977) represents such a synthesis. After rescuing a bee from drowning in an overripe pear, Wright quotes Virgil: "The best days are the first / to flee." The poem is set in Virgil's hometown of Mantua, where the looming industrial gasworks remind Wright of Martin's Ferry. He has synergized the poet he yearned to be (the romantic image of Virgil and of Italy) and the blue-collar Ohioan son he feared becoming.

During the final year of his life, while the Wrights continued to travel in Europe, James Wright wrote poems vigorously. When he became ill, he made certain his final collection would be published posthumously. In *This Journey*, the stylistic progress and the equanimity shining through in *To a Blossoming Pear Tree* are even more profound. "Your Name in Arezzo," (1977) for example, even returns to the rhymed iambic pentameter of his first collections while maintaining the directness of the free-verse work.

Despite his bouts with alcoholism and depression, James Wright is remembered by friends and fellow poets as a vivacious and humorous man, a lover of good jokes, apt to burst into poetry recitations on the spur of the moment. In poetry, he found a way to escape what he saw as his bleak, decidedly un-poetic roots in Martin's Ferry—and eventually, a way of poeticizing them.

Further Reading. ***Selected Primary Sources:*** Wright, James, *Above the River: The Complete Poems*, intro. Donald Hall (New York: Farrar Straus and Giroux, 1990); ———, *Collected Prose*, ed. Anne Wright (Ann Arbor: University of Michigan Press, 1982); Wright, James, and Leslie Marmon Silko, *The Delicacy and Strength of Lace*, ed. Anne Wright (St. Paul, MN: Graywolf Press, 1986). ***Selected Secondary Sources:*** Graziano, Frank, and Peter Stitt, eds., *James Wright: A Profile* (Durango: Longbridge-Rhodes, 1988); ———, eds., *James Wright: The Heart of the Light* (Ann Arbor: University of Michigan Press, 1990); Smith, Dave, ed., *The Pure Clear Word: Essays on the Poetry of James Wright* (Urbana: University of Illinois Press, 1982).

Jon Mooallem

WRIGHT, JAY (1934–)

Jay Wright is among the most ambitious poets in American history. Among American poets, only Ezra Pound has comparable range; among African American writers, only Ralph Ellison set his sights so high. Deeply spiritual, but too heterodox to be called a Christian poet, Wright is much in the tradition of the Gnostics, syncretistic, learned, and esoteric. In fact, the American poet he resembles most might be **H.D.**; they both see the poet as a priestly physician, whose task is to heal the world. Learned and admittedly "bookish," Wright writes an English all his own, often interwoven with other languages, especially Spanish but also Scots, Yoruba, and Nahuatl—languages that stand for different dimensions of the poet's history.

As yet, there is no biography of Wright. Despite some confusion among scholars, it appears that Jay Wright's birth certificate shows that he was born on May 25, 1934. His father is listed as George Wright, his mother as Leona Dailey. Jay was George's first child; he was Leona's eighth. Complicating matters, George Wright's given name was George Murphy, and he let it be known that Jay Wright was therefore also Jay Murphy; George also preferred a 1935 birthdate for his son. It is no wonder the poet is obsessed with doubles and twins: Born twice, with two names, he was also raised in two households. Leona Dailey seems to have had her hands full with her other children, and Jay went back to his father at age three, who left him with Frankie Faucett, immortalized in Wright's early poem, "The Hunting Trip Cook," and his deeply religious wife, Daisy, who introduced her young charge to the ways of the black Baptist Church. The passion and yearning of that church has cast a long shadow over Wright's poetry, for his favored stance is an earnest seeker after God, an initiate into the mysteries.

Wright was thirteen or fourteen when his father brought him to live in San Pedro, a fishing town south of Los Angeles, where the elder Wright, now known as Mercer, having found good work during the wartime boom, was living with and possibly married to Billie Bowden. Young Jay had shown promise as a baseball player, and his father kept him out of the shipyards and canneries to preserve him for a future in the slowly integrating sport. In fact, Jay Wright was soon rated one of the top young catching prospects in California. Major league baseball would not reach the West Coast until 1957; but Wright worked out with the then-PCL San Diego Padres and was assigned to Class C Fresno. Later, he would play for Mexicali in the Mexican League. Conversation with Wright suggests that racism, not lack of talent, made him tire of professional baseball.

In 1954 Wright enlisted in the U.S. Army. He served for three years as a medic, stationed in Germany. During this period he read voraciously and starred on regimental baseball teams. Wright was discharged from the army in 1957, and he was determined to get an education, thinking he might study chemistry. After a semester at the University of New Mexico, he transferred to the University of California–Berkeley, at first to pursue his scientific studies, but soon as a self-designed major, to study comparative literature. By this time, Wright had become an accomplished jazz-bassist and played around the Bay Area, sometimes accompanying the young Pharaoh Sanders. In 1961, with Berkeley BA in hand, Wright landed a Rockefeller scholarship that would enable him to study theology at Union Theological Seminary in New York, though he left after only one term because he wanted to continue his work as a comparativist. Wright talked his way into the new program at Rutgers University and moved to New Brunswick, New Jersey, in 1962, staying until 1964. It was there he met the poet **Henry Dumas**; and through him, several years later, he met his future wife, Lois Silber. In 1964, having finished all doctorate work but his dissertation, he embraced his calling to be a poet and moved to Guadalajara to teach in a small school and write. He returned to New York in 1965 and moved to Harlem. **Langston Hughes** lived nearby and offered friendship and encouragement as Wright continued writing the poems that would become his chapbook, *Death as History* (1967). Deciding against writing a dissertation, Wright also took his MA from Rutgers that year. The chapbook may have helped Wright land an NEA grant that enabled him to return to Guadalajara in February 1968. Lois joined him there in September, and they were married. They soon moved across Mexico to Xalapa, the capital of Vera Cruz; its name occurs frequently in Wright's work. In 1970 Francis Fergusson arranged for Wright to receive a Hodder fellowship from Princeton for the fall semester of 1970. After a brief return to Xalapa, the couple decided in September 1971 to move to Scotland, which they had heard was cheap and poet-friendly. After giving a reading at the University of Dundee, Wright was offered the Joseph Compton fellowship by the University. Though he would only use the fellowship for a year, Wright stayed in Scotland until 1973, living in Penicuik, just south of Edinburgh. The couple then returned to the United States, living for many years in New Hampshire before settling in Vermont. Since finding his way, Wright has never been interested in being anything but a poet. Though he has taught occasionally and has accepted limited residencies, Wright has refused the security of a full-time university position, preferring to pursue his muse.

Wright's immersion in Scottish literature and the example of the Scottish nationalist poet Hugh MacDiarmid gave him a more sophisticated model for writing in a subaltern literature than that promulgated by Wright's contemporaries in Harlem, Leroi Jones (better known as **Amiri Baraka**) and Larry Neal. His reading in African philosophy (J.B. Danquah, Wole Soyinka, and Ogotemmêli via French cultural anthropology) at this time, melding with his formal training in comparative literature, gave him a cultural range broader than any other living American poet. Wright juxtaposed a statement from theologian Karl Barth and a remark from John Coltrane to Sonny Rollins as epigraphic moments in the same poem. He linked Greek muse and Egyptian goddess, St. Augustine and Dogon ritual; a wholly characteristic title is "Zapata and the Egúngún Mask."

As a practiced musician, Wright's knowledge of **jazz** is reflected in the "scoring" of certain poems, most notably "MacIntyre, the Captain and the Saints," where the different voices of Hugh MacDiarmid, David Hume, R.S. Rattray, and Wright himself are made legible by their distance from the left margin, sometimes merging, sometimes playing solos. Likewise, call-and-response and improvisation, two standard features of black music and African American writing, can be found throughout his work. The improvisation is evident in his "playing the changes" on the work of other writers, through quotation, allusion, and translation. See, for example, his highly successful revision of "Poem for Willie Best" called "Variations on a Theme by Leroi Jones"; note his quotations from the Nigerian poet Christopher Okigbo in "Beginning Again" and most obviously his multiple quotations in "MacIntyre, the Captain and the Saints." In *Boleros*, Wright deploys the *Egyptian Book of the Dead* and a Mexican saints' calendar as armatures for poetic meditations in ways analogous to John Coltrane's transformation of the show tune "My Favorite Things." An extended quotation from the pianist Art Tatum in "Bolero #19" makes the method clear: After audience members—"cats"—complain that they want to hear an original tune, he "lay[s] two notes in the bar ahead, / diminish[es] a major, / tunnel[s] trough the dark / of the brightest minor, / and come[s] out on the right side of the song"; he "picks the composer's pocket." So does Wright in his transformations of a variety of literatures and cultural influences.

It is useful to think of the body of Wright's eight books of poetry, now collected in *Transfigurations,* as a curriculum, not unlike **Ezra Pound's** *Cantos.* Wright's wide range of reference make him hard to characterize, though his interest in African philosophy, mythology, and pedagogy make him in many ways an "Afrocentric" writer, the term coined by Molefi Kete Asante as a contrast to Eurocentricity: "literally, placing African ideals at the center of any analysis of African culture or behavior." Wright's frequent recourse to African concepts—such as the Akan, Odomankoma (roughly, wisdom), or Wole Soyinka's African theory of tragedy—suggests, in Isadore Okpewho's words, "Wright's progressive acceptance of a guiding African(ist) sensibility, an ever-tightening embrace of a cultural something that he felt he needed as a dependable beacon in his continuing explorations through cultural history." An ineffable, "cultural something" is certainly one object of the poet's quest, but he is also in quest of a divine something—Wright usually calls it a "name." This word reverberates throughout Wright's work.

If Wright is African, he is also Celtic, as his Murphy heritage and his many Scottish poems show. Intellectually, this poetic space is dominated by the spirit of Hugh MacDiarmid (Christopher Grieve), the Scottish cultural nationalist poet whose *The Drunk Man Looks at a Thistle* (1926) taught Wright what a truly ambitious cultural nationalist literature could be like. Scots literature has a relationship to English literature not unlike African American to American literature; both have been marginalized as minor literatures deemed written in a semiliterate dialect. MacDarmid's invention of a synthetic "Lallans" Scots as the language of a new Scottish nation inspired Wright's invention of a culturally synthetic poetic speech.

Wright is most obviously an American of the Southwest, which is for him a broad imaginative territory that includes not only Wright's home state of New Mexico, but also southern California and Mexico itself, and the Spanish and Nahuatl languages. Another dimension for Wright is the Caribbean and Brazil—"creolized" spaces that have been deeply influenced by the African diaspora to the new world, but that are, in their vibrant mix of African, European, Asian, and Amerindian cultures, something new altogether, as Caribbean writers from Wilson Harris to **Derek Walcott** and V.S. Naipal have been insisting. Harris has had a deep impact on Wright, both in his way of thinking and in his way of writing; both men are interested in "transfigurative bridges," the "chasm," the inchoate spaces between cultures, which await transformation and transfiguration via the poet. Pursuing the same idea in a different key, Vera Kutzinski, the critic who has taken the deepest measure of Wright, has called him a "New World writer," coupling him with **William Carlos Williams** and the Cuban poet Nicolas Guillen as writers whose work overflows artificially maintained English and Hispanic borders.

Wright's books are integrated with each other in complex ways. Most of his initial chapbook, *Death in History* (1967) was incorporated into his first volume, *The Homecoming Singer* (1971). This is a work triumphantly within the main current of African American writing and, indeed, of American poetry of its time. Autobiographical, lyrical, and obsessed with family matters, the volume also explores Wright's complex legacy of Protestant fundamentalism and his concerns with literary politics—here Wright's ambivalence to the **Black Arts Movement**. *Soothsayers and Omens* (1976), is "roots work," a review of "sources" of various kinds, including the eighteenth-century American polymath Benjamin Banneker. The book ends with the first fruit of the poet's engagement with Africa, "Second Conversations with Ogotemmelli." The poems in *Explications/Interpretations* (1984) reveal Wright's Celtic dimension, authorized by his partly Irish ancestry and composed primarily during his pivotal time in Scotland from 1970 to 1973.

The next two books are Wright's most difficult; both are deeply "Afrocentric" texts. *Dimensions of History* (1976) was published with useful notes to help illuminate its recondite allusions; it addresses the Caribbean, Brazilian, and Mexican dimensions of Wright's project, and this is the prime example of Kutzinski's "New World writing." *The Double Invention of Komo* (1980) is a ritual autobiography that revisits the primal scene of writing in the excision and circumcision of the poet and initiate, and the "trace" of primal writing via Bambara initiation rites, with which Wright became familiar by reading Germaine Dieterlen and Tata Cisse's *Les fondements de la societe d'initiation de Komo* (1972). *Elaine's Book* (1980) explores the dimension of the feminine, putting the poetry in "confrontation" with female testimony, including unattributed quotations from various women, among them poet **Phillis Wheatley**, the philosopher Suzanne Langer, and Dr. Cecilia Payne-Gaposhkin, an astronomer, who Kutzinski points out was the first female full professor at Harvard. Here, the very anonymity of these voices helps Wright make a point about oppression and silence. *Boleros* (1991) is one of Wright's most accessible books and for many years was the only one in print, except for his *Selected Poems* (1987). Here, among other things, the poet explores the relationship between "Africa" (Egypt) and "Europe" (Greece) by refracting autobiographical poems through the lenses of the Egyptian *Book of the Dead*, the Greek muses, and a Mexican saints' calendar. The later book, *Transformations*, is not printed separately, but is bound together in *Transfigurations: The Collected Poems* (2000). *Transformations* is remarkable for its complex rhymed poems, playing the changes on *abba*—the rhymes coupling with and swallowing each other. There is an intense conversation with English poetry at work here. One hears Blake, Yeats, and **Emily Dickinson**. The book is dominated by a major poem "The Anti-Fabliau of Saturnino Orestes 'Minnie' Minoso." The great Afro-Cuban outfielder's name is the kind of palimpsest Wright especially enjoys, and this tale of the young poet and ballplayer's initiation into mysteries requires serious critical scrutiny.

There are good reasons to see *Transfigurations* as a single work in eight phases or movements; together the volume makes up an octave and also reflects the importance of the number eight in the West African cosmologies that fascinate the poet. In her excellent summary of Wright presented in the reference work, *African-American Writers*, Kutzinsky has noticed a shift in Wright's work from books obsessed with the search for the father and a recovery of a usable history to an approach to the feminine and even the goddess in the later books. *Elaine's Book* is so named because it was originally written in a blank book given to Wright by his sister-in-law, and *Boleros* is dedicated and addressed to Lois Wright. *Transformations,* the final section of *Transfigurations*, is situated mostly in Mexico, yet, as mentioned, it plays complex prosodic homage to the English language poetic tradition.

In addition to his poetry, Wright has written numerous plays—about fifty—few of which have seen print. Just as Emily Dickinson's letters tend to merge with her poetry, so Wright's published plays merge with his poems. Like the poetry, they are liturgical and ritualistic. Human characters shade off into cosmic types, as in "Love's Equations" (1983), which features an epigraph by Derrida: The woman, Sassy, is revealed as the Goddess; she "means more than you can understand." Wright's plays have the bare-bones feel of Beckett, but the religious dimension one finds not in Western theater but in aboriginal ritual. The plays potentially could make splendid theater, but only from a very dedicated company steeped in an "African" sensibility.

Wright's few published essays show the same erudition as his poetry. In keeping with their stylistic affinity to the writing of Wilson Harris, they are dense and abstract, a form of not-quite-Western philosophy. They also betray a deep interest in abstruse literary theory. As early as 1972, in his (unpublished) "Feeling and Some Related Problems Concerning Poetry," given at the University of Dundee, Wright was thinking in terms and frames provided by Ernst Cassirer, Suzanne Langer, Kenneth Burke, and the American semiotician A.B. Johnson. Wright's superb education at Berkeley and Rutgers and his own research make him dense and formidable; his range of diction, from jive to erudite—not unlike Cornell West or Ishmael Reed—and the astonishing range of reference familiar from the poetry make his essays both challenging and worthwhile. Unfortunately, his scattered prose has yet to be collected in a single place.

Since *Transfigurations*, Wright has published little but written much. As of 2005, Wright had completed four new books of poetry as well as ten new plays, and he was working on two further poetical projects on the Bambara "guide-signs," presumably those in *Dimensions of History*.

Critics have been slow to meet the challenge presented by Wright's work. *Calalloo* gave Wright a special issue in 1983, featuring a rare interview, which is especially illuminating about *Explications/Interpretations*. Several short, sympathetic essays of an introductory nature by Rowell himself, Robert Stepto, Gerald Barrax, and Vera Kutzinski, perhaps Wright's best and deepest critic, are included. Most welcome is Isadore Opekwho's "From a Goat Path in Africa: An Approach to the Poetry of Jay Wright," a full-scale reading of Wright's most difficult volume, *The Double Invention of Komo*. Some of these have been included in Harold Bloom's book on the poet, *Jay Wright* (2004). In *Writing America Black: Race Rhetoric in the Public Sphere* (1998), C.K. Doreski spends an important chapter on a reading of *Soothsayers and Omens* as, in part, a dissident contribution to the bicentennial of the United States. Doreski's reading of *Soothsayers and Omens* is very much in the Yale-influenced tradition, for it assumes Wright's theory of history is deconstructive, when it is visionary, if not openly prophetic, as his title suggests. Blake, not Benjamin, is an apt model for Wright's way of thinking, but his deeper masters lie outside the West altogether.

Despite this work, one is left with the feeling that with the exception of Kutzinski and the earnest support of the idiosyncratic Bloom, critics have largely failed Wright. Too erudite and esoteric to fit the black populist aesthetic of Black Arts poetics, Wright does not appear to have attracted a black readership. Awards from the "white" establishment have earned Wright the envy of his black peers. Finally, the narrow notions of Afro-America that determine African American literature courses have found Wright hard to assimilate. Mythic rather than political, religious rather than Christian, and learned, not "street smart," Wright remains largely unexplored. To be fair, Wright has not helped himself; he refuses to attach himself to a creative writing program or a university faculty except as a visitor, and he shuns interviews.

In sum, Wright's linguistic ambition and cultural eclecticism have meant relative neglect by contemporary criticism—even by critics who are known to respect his work. Aldon Neilsen names but does not discuss Jay Wright in his recent study *Black Chant: Languages of African-American Postmodernism* (1997)—and perhaps one could argue that this is because Wright's spiritual questing means that he is not properly **postmodern**. Lorenzo Thomas, in an even newer book that would seem to speak more directly to Wright's deep concern with Africa—its philosophy, sign systems, and rituals—*Extraordinary Measures: Afrocentric Modernism and Twentieth Century American Poetry* (2000), does not even mention Wright. Indeed, Wright is not easily pigeonholed. Ideological critics are understandably worried about Wright's cultural politics because he appears mandarin and his politics seem transcendental—not sufficiently material and populist on the one hand, and neither comfortably "black" nor uncritically "Afrikan" on the other. A comparison with the work of his one-time Harlem acquaintances, the black nationalist Amiri Baraka and the Afrocentric Askia Touré, shows Wright's political differences—and the other poets' ideological limitations—very clearly. Wright is perhaps too truly multicultural and too visionary to be politically definable and therefore aesthetically acceptable by the canons of present-day Afro-American literary criticism.

Despite this, Wright has won numerous prestigious awards, including a Guggenheim. The publication of *Transfigurations* netted him the 2000 Lannan Award for Poetry, and in 1986 he received a five-year MacArthur "genius" award. He was honored by the American Academy of Poets in 2001, and he is a member of the American Academy of Arts and Sciences.

Further Reading. ***Selected Primary Sources:*** Wright, Jay, *Selected Poems* (Princeton, NJ: Princeton University Press, 1987); ———, *Transfigurations. Collected Poems* (Baton Rouge: Louisiana State University Press, 2000). ***Selected Secondary Sources:*** Bloom, Harold, ed., *Jay Wright* (New York: Chelsea House, 2004); Doreski, C.K., *Writing America Black: Race Rhetoric in the Public Sphere* (Cambridge, UK: Cambridge University Press, 1998); "Jay Wright: A Special Issue" (*Calalloo* 19.6 [Autumn 1983]); Kutzinski, Vera, *Against the American Grain* (Baltimore, MD: Johns Hopkins University Press, 1987); ———, "Jay Wright," in *African-American Writers*, ed. Valerie Smith (New York: Scribner's, 2001).

Alec Marsh

WRIGHT, SUSANNA (1697–1784)

Susanna Wright's achievement as a poet is significant, yet difficult to assess. She published none of her poetry, and the poems discovered thus far suggest that her best work may be lost or undiscovered. However, Wright is of undeniable importance as a crucial figure of the colonial and early republican period in North America.

Susanna Wright lived most of her adult life at the border of European civilization, on the banks of the Susquehanna River, near present-day Columbia, Pennsylvania. The Wrights were Quakers, and James Logan, one of the most prominent Quakers in Philadelphia, desired a Quaker settlement in Lancaster County, a land dominated by Germans and Scots-Irish. Here Wright became that exemplary Enlightenment figure, the polymath. She raised prize-winning silk worms and wove silk that Benjamin Franklin presented to the English royal family; researched the medicinal uses of herbs; studied law, politics, and medicine; corresponded widely; and entertained travelers such as Franklin and physician Benjamin Rush. It is no surprise that Rush wrote in his journal about meeting "the famous Suzey Wright" and that others referred to her as "the Susquehanna Muse."

As was the case for many writers of both sexes, but especially for poets and women, Wright circulated her poetry in manuscript form. We know most about her correspondence with a small group of Quaker women that included **Hannah Griffitts**, **Elizabeth Fergusson**, Elizabeth Norris, and **Milcah Martha Moore**. Students of American poetry owe a great debt to Moore for recording so many poems by Wright and Griffitts in her third **commonplace** book. Many literate folk in the eighteenth century kept these books, in which they transcribed poetry and prose of particular importance.

Moore transcribed twenty-four Wright poems. Only a half dozen more have been discovered. Because the commonplace book entered a library collection in 1966 and was published for the first time in 1997, readers now have access to a significantly enlarged Wright oeuvre. Two scholars in particular have led this revival of interest in and access to Wright. Karin Wulf and Catherine La Courreye Blecki are responsible for the publication of Moore's commonplace book and have done outstanding recent scholarship on Wright and her circle of correspondents.

Wright's poetry rarely strays from conventional poetic forms, and her subject matter, especially in Moore's commonplace book, was treated by many poets of her day. The Wright of the commonplace book has more value as an exemplar of literate eighteenth-century society than as a poet. In these poems she is a fascinating woman who happened to use verse as a creative medium. Virtually every poem is written in heroic couplets, yet Wright at times seems overwhelmed by these expectations of rhyme and metrical regularity with variations of significance. In places the rhymes become leaden or the use of meter too regular, as in "On Friendship," contained in the *Milcah Martha Moore Book*:

But if a Friend, we're suffer'd to possess,
It colours all our Days with Happiness;
Improves the Relish of neglected Joys.
And every potent Ill of Life destroys

In the commonplace-book poems she writes on equally conventional themes, such as friendship, convalescence, infant mortality, the virtue of hard work, anxiety about her skill as a poet, and, most of all, her spiritual life. Wright's twenty-first century reader may be surprised to find such traditional religious beliefs from a woman of such impressive intellectual accomplishment, as in "A Meditation," also in the *Milcah Martha Moore Book*:

Would Heaven all wise, all Merciful & just
Have chang'd this intellectual Soul to Dust
If she no State of Pre existance [sic] knew?
If all these Ills were not her righteous Due?

Acknowledgements of depravity, assertions of faith, and prayers that yearn for heaven would not have disappointed Wright's Quaker correspondents or most eighteenth-century readers. Wright was not an urban intellectual in the style of Voltaire or Paine; intellectual inquiry and sincere piety could easily coexist.

Wright also wrote at least three poems that suggest a more innovative poet and daring thinker. "To Eliza Norris—at Fairhill" was written to an unmarried Quaker friend in Philadelphia. Though here Wright still uses heroic couplets, her message is far from conventional. Men and women are of equal value: "No right has man his equal to control, / Since, all agree, there is no sex in soul." Norris's celibacy is celebrated: "Then bless that choice which led your bloom of youth / From forms & shadows to enlight'ning truth." This poem, like many others by Wright, ends in heaven. But she imagines a celestial accounting for men's "darling vice of sway": "When strip'd of power, & placed in equal light, / Angels shall judge who had the better right." Karin Wulf calls this "possibly the most powerful piece of poetry produced by an eighteenth-century American woman."

"Anna Boylens Letter to King Henry the 8th" (*Milcah Martha*, 3) was written in a venerable, though now forgotten, form: the verse epistle to a historical or legendary person. Boylen was Henry VIII's second wife and the mother of Elizabeth I. She was accused of adultery and beheaded. The artifice of the epistle form appears to free Wright from her usual sense of propriety, and she employs striking gothic imagery to imagine a conjugal scene between Henry and his new wife, Jane Seymour: "When Lamps burn blue & guilty Tapers fade, / As by your bridal Bed I glide a ghastly Shade."

Wright's longest and most ambitious poem has only recently come to light. "The Grove" was not written for Wright's usual female circle; instead, it was part of her correspondence with James Logan, the learned and politically powerful Quaker who allocated to Wright's family the Susquehanna property. Wright writes from a detached third-person perspective and contemplates the destruction of an idealized pastoral grove complete with a philosopher who "sought to try the utmost Stretch of Humane thought." Thought Wright concludes with a conventional religious assertion, much of the poem contemplates the loss of nature, human frailty, and the limits of poetry with remarkable insight and detail.

The Wright we glimpse in these three poems suggests a poet who need not be considered merely a "woman poet" or a "Quaker poet." Her best work compares favorably not only with that of her female contemporaries **Phillis Wheatley**, **Mercy Otis Warren**, and **Annis Boudinot Stockton**, but also with that of American men like **Timothy Dwight** and **Joel Barlow**. We can only hope that more work by the innovative Wright is yet to be found.

Further Reading. ***Selected Primary Source:*** Bleecki, Cartherine la Courreye, and Karin Wulf, eds., *Milcah Martha Moore's Book* (University Park: University of Pennsylvania Press, 1997). ***Selected Secondary Sources:*** Blecki, Catherine la Courreye, and Lorett Treese, "Susanna Wright's 'The Grove'" (*Early American Literature* 38 [2003]); Blecki, Catherine la Courreye, and Karin Wulf, essays in *Milcah Martha Moore's Book* (University Park: University of Pennsylvania Press, 1997); Cowell, Patti, *Woman Poets in Pre-Revolutionary America* (Albany, NY: Whitston, 1981).

Robert Battistini

WYLIE, ELINOR (1885–1928)

Although she published four books of poetry, three from reputable publishers, as well as several novels, the jury is still out on whether Elinor Hoyt Wylie's legacy is that of a poet or poetaster, a person who loved to write or one who merely loved being a writer. Those who praise her poetry are most often friends, family, or lovers, and one driving force in her life was her desire to become a famous literary personality. Even Thomas A. Gray, contracted to write the Twayne volume on her poetry, has difficulty finding positive qualities in her verse. He points out that her first American poetry volume, *Nets to Catch the Wind*, seems the work of a fledgling imagist, yet her later volumes do not seem to develop in any particular aesthetic direction. He even finds that her last poems—many of which were not published until the posthumous issue of her *Collected Poems* in 1932 and *Last Poems* in 1943—seem to regress to the mannered earliest verse.

Wylie was born in 1885 in Somerville, New Jersey, to a family that became increasingly more wealthy, culminating in her father's appointment as Solicitor General of the United States in Theodore Roosevelt's administration. While Wylie was still a girl, the family often summered in Maine, and in 1903 she took the grand tour of Europe with her grandfather. In 1905 she married Philip Hichborn, a Harvard graduate and the son of an American admiral, but five short years later, she left Hichborn, who was rumored to be abusive, and her three-year-old son to begin living with Horace Wylie, a married Washington lawyer who had courted her for some time. This action caused scandal among members of her social class and necessitated a move to England, where the couple began life under assumed names. When World War I started, they moved back to America, and they married in 1916, when their divorces were final.

Though she never was educated beyond a private secondary school, Wylie was well read and aspired from a young age to write literature. While in England, she arranged for a private, anonymous printing of her first book of poems, *Incidental Numbers*, in London and then, upon her return to the states, made several literary acquaintances. Among her fellow writer friends were Sinclair Lewis, Edmund Wilson, Carl Van Vechten, and William Rose Benet. Under the latter's auspices, Wylie quickly became part of the New York literary scene. Her first American book of poetry, *Nets to Catch the Wind*, was published in 1921.

This publication catapulted Wylie into the center of the New York literati of the 1920s. Demanding her place in this society, she became a fixture at the MacDowell Colony in Petersborough, New Hampshire; the poetry editor of *Vanity Fair*, and later, an editor of the *Literary Guild of New York*. During the early 1920s, she also divorced Wylie and married William Rose Benet, who managed to help her secure a literary reputation. Between 1923 and 1929, she published three more books of poetry, *Black Armour* (1923), *Trivial Breath* (1928), and *Angels and Earthly Creatures* (its sonnet sequence was published separately in 1928, and the complete book of poems appeared posthumously in 1929).

Throughout her life, Wylie was both fragile and dynamic. Friends were quick to support and praise both her natural beauty and her writing because any criticism caused her to lapse into hysterics and cut off relationships immediately. Part of this volatility may have been due to her poor health, which plagued her for most of her life and caused an early death. She suffered an accident that broke her back, an injury from which she never fully recovered, aggravated as it was by Bright's disease. Always troubled by headaches caused by uncontrolled high blood pressure, Wylie suffered a stroke and died on December 16, 1928, at the age of forty-three.

The major feature of her poetry is her ability to describe an image in picturesque terms—crystalline and perfect. As her sister Nancy Hoyt notes in her biography, Wylie liked things that were small and precise. Poems such as "Silver Filigree" illustrate this quality. In four short, equally metrical stanzas, she captures a picture of melting icicles. The familiar picture is enhanced by unusual but descriptive imagery; they are "made of the moon" and "transparent as paper." In the third stanza they "pass into crystal" and fall to the ground like "brittle / And delicate glass." Like this one, many of her poems appear to capture in verse the principle that **Archibald MacLeish** declares in his poem "Ars Poetica": "A poem should not mean / But be." This quality of palpability and presence beyond language seems consonant with the goals of the poetic school of **Imagism**, in which critics often place Wylie, but her direct focus and careful wordplay with the "thing," though they capture the object with crystal clarity, seem to be all there is to most poems. Wylie herself said she had "the skills of a miniaturist," emphasizing this technique as the sole focus of her poetry.

Most of Wylie's poems seem without theme or message at best and full of non sequiturs at worst. She seems at times so attentive to the word picture that she is creating that any meaning beyond description is obscure or even nonexistent. Reading her poems consecutively at one sitting, the reader is at once captivated by the beauty of a word picture and stymied by the lack of any meaning-making activity in the poem. Additionally, most poems wander from vague idea to vague idea. "Sleeping Beauty," for example, alludes to the fairy tale by beginning with a picture of "Beauty" imprisoned, comparing her to the presence in a block of marble that a sculptor might unearth. In the second stanza, the poem reads, "For me the obdurate stone is shut; / How shall I wake her from her sleep?" Thus far, the poem appears to make an interesting connection between Wylie's own creative abilities and those of a sculptor. But in the third stanza, the poem lapses into a series of disconnected nature images that have nothing to do with the analogy the earlier poem has created. This meandering quality into obscurity occurs in more poems than not and violates the Imagist tenet that all words in a poem should contribute to the **objective correlative** it presents.

Because of such anomalies in her style, critics have found it difficult to pinpoint what school Wylie belongs to or who her influences were. Many of her poems, particularly in *Trivial Breath*, carry the same womanly cynicism as those of her contemporaries **Edna St. Vincent Millay** and **Dorothy Parker**. Gray, in the Twayne volume, also attributes her style to her knowledge of the poetry of the 1890s, which lionized art for art's sake, such as that of Algernon Charles Swinburne. Her stylized cynicism is most often born out of a conflict between the persona of the poem and her world, although such conflicts remain static rather than developed to their denouement. Sometimes, the persona leaves the conflict behind in mid-poem to describe apparently unrelated objects in an ideal world to which she has retreated. Wylie also shares the attention to nature and natural detail of the female lyrist poets of the early twentieth century, such as **Adelaide Crapsey** and **Sara Teasdale,** who address themes of loss and death, as Wylie does often, most prominently in "Breastplate," the first section of *Black Armour.* Gray also finds much paraphrase and even borrowed phrasings from a great number of poetic sources, illustrating Wylie's prolific knowledge of the history of English poetry. One example of a poem that is full of literary allusions, most with no apparent logical connection to one another, is "Demon Lovers" from *Black Armour.*

Wylie also claimed to be enthralled with the work of Romantic poet Percy Bysshe Shelley, who appears most lucidly in her novel *The Orphan Angel* (1926), where he is the model for the character Shiloh. The poem "A Red Carpet for Shelley" in *Trivial Breath* compares what Wylie perceives as her poetic gift unfavorably to his, exclaiming about her own "ragged syllables." She knew all his poems by heart, and considered him—despite the differences in their talents—her poetic soulmate, another individual who was troubled by the real world and thus opted to create an alternate idealized reality in words.

Nets to Catch the Wind contains mostly obscure verbal vignettes, although two of her better, more lyrical poems that are often anthologized, "Velvet Shoes" and "Wild Peaches," create pleasing word pictures in the reader's mind. Both feature her favored austere landscapes, the former in winter and the latter—contemplating her move back to the United States—depicting all seasons in New England.

Black Armour contains several small sections that move from ballad-like poems about medieval subjects to poems that are more personal. Toward the end, she once again shows off her knowledge of history with three songs from the Gaelic, the Icelandic, and the Breton, respectively. The style remains Wylie's, however; it is clear they are not translations.

In *Trivial Breath*, Wylie includes some poems about love, death, and ghosts that anticipate the sonnet sequence in her final published volume. Although most of these are personal lyrics, she also includes a strange, almost Faulkneresque **narrative poem** called "Miranda's Supper," set in postbellum Virginia. Miranda lives on a ruined plantation; she dresses up and pretends that the men she knows are back from the Civil War.

The sequence of nineteen sonnets that begins *Angels and Earthly Creatures* seems much better than anything else Wylie wrote. Titled "One Person," it chronicles a couple living together as they face death. Her sonnets are perfect, with a consistent rhyme scheme. Some allusions, however, seem somewhat over the top, such as the lines from Sonnet XII, in which she dreams that her lover is her child: "I dreamt I was the mother of a son / Who had deserved a manger for a crib." Later in the poem, she also pictures her lover as Adam, whose rib has been torn from him and fashioned into her. Some critics believe that the persona's lover in this sequence is Shelley, although many of the poems seem vivid enough to be autobiographical. This vividness continues into the second part of the volume, "Elements and Angels," where poems seem to be about a love affair that needs to be ended.

One of her better poems, "Pretty Words," from the "Hitherto Uncollected Poems" section in the posthumous *Collected Poems*, sums up her poetic philosophy: "Poets make pets of pretty, docile words: / I love smooth words, like gold-enamelled fish." The poem continues to express her love of words that are tender, shy, playful, bright, luminous, lazy, cool, and pearly. Each type of word is described in colorful nature imagery, most often of animals. The better poems, such as "Wild Peaches," illustrate this philosophy in their rhythmic creation of beautiful pictures that show more of a love affair with words than any deeper meaning or wisdom about life. Wylie clearly treasured playing with language and sounds, and she valued this capability over the creation of verse that would resonate with deeper truth or meaning.

Further Reading. ***Selected Primary Sources:*** Wylie, Elinor, *Angels and Earthly Creatures* (New York: Knopf, 1929); ———, *Black Armour* (New York: George H. Doran, 1923); ———, *Collected Poems of Elinor Wylie* (New York: Knopf, 1932); ———, *Last Poems of Elinor Wylie*, transcr. Jane D. Wise (New York: Knopf, 1943); ———, *Nets to Catch the Wind* (New York: Harcourt, Brace, 1921); ———, *Trivial Breath* (New York: Knopf, 1928). ***Selected Secondary Sources:*** Farr, Judith, *The Life and Art of Elinor Wylie* (Baton Rouge: Louisiana State University Press, 1983); Gray, Thomas A., *Elinor Wylie* (New York: Twayne, 1969); Hively, Evelyn Helmick, *A Private Madness: The Genius of Elinor Wylie* (Kent, OH: Kent State University Press, 2003); Hoyt, Nancy, *Elinor Wylie: The Portrait of an Unknown* (New York: Bobbs Merrill, 1935); Olson, Stanley, *Elinor Wylie: A Life Apart* (New York: Dial Press, 1979).

Rosemary Fithian Guruswamy

Y

YAU, JOHN (1950–)

With more than a dozen books of poetry, John Yau is also a widely published art critic, fiction writer, essayist, and editor; his straddling of genres sometimes makes readers wonder whether the writing is prose or verse, fiction or nonfiction. And despite his Chinese heritage, his work's relationship to **Asian American** literature is often ambivalent, so much so in his early career that critics could accuse him of veiling ethnicity. Indeed, it is as difficult to squeeze Yau into the camp of ethnic writing as into that of the **Language poets** or the **New York School**, both of which he has affinities with. Regarding the latter association, while never denying **John Ashbery**'s influence on him, Yau refuses to identify with what he calls the "gabby" and "social" poetics of the New York School. Also appropriating surrealism, deconstruction, popular culture, and art history in writing, Yau considers himself "a poet too post-modern for the modernists and too post-modern for the modernists" (40 [1994]).

John Yau was born on June 5, 1950, in Lynn, Massachusetts, shortly after his parents settled in the United States. His mother was from an influential Shanghai family; his father was the child of a Chinese man and an Englishwoman who met in England during World War I. His family later moved to Beacon Hill in Boston and then to Brookline, where they lived from the time that Yau was in sixth grade through his junior high years. Yau went to Boston University for two years from 1967 to 1969, and then moved to Annandale-on-Hudson in upstate New York, where he received his BA from Bard College in 1972. Before long he decided to move to New York City. He studied with John Ashbery, and in 1978 earned his MFA from Brooklyn College.

Yau had two chapbooks published while still pursuing his MFA under Ashbery: *Crossing Canal Street* (1976) and *The Reading of an Ever-Changing Tale* (1977). Many of his earliest poems, influenced by **Ezra Pound**, are imitative of haiku and the "pictographic" Chinese style. *The Reading* moves to a more cynical tone that would characterize much of Yau's later work. Some poems from *The Reading* appear also in his next, more accomplished volume, *Sometimes: Poems* (1979). In *Sometimes* Yau takes up **narrative poetry**, as in the second section, titled "Marco Polo." By this time, Yau had also begun his experiments with using words as physical things, a conscious reaction against his earlier dependency on imagery, so that he could have another way to "make sense," as the poem "Ten Songs" indicates: "Finding the saying of something weighing the sense / of it trying." In such passages, sense is generated more by means of sound than by imagery or exposition. Following *Sometimes,* Yau published the genre-mixing *The Sleepless Night of Eugene Delacroix* (1980); a collaboration with the artist Jake Berthot titled

Notarikon (1981); and a collection of poetry: *Broken Off By The Music* (1981), whose middle section, "Late Night Movies," prefigures in theme and style his later "Genghis Chan: Private Eye" series.

Though Yau was already a widely published author, it was his seventh book, *Corpse and Mirror* (1983), a collage of poetry and prose, that established his national reputation when it was selected by John Ashbery for the National Poetry Series. The title is derived both from Jasper Johns' crosshatch diptych *Corpse and Mirror* and from its inspiration, the surrealist game called *cadavre exquis* (exquisite corpse), in which a phrase is passed from person to person, undergoing distortion in the process, and thus exploiting the mystique of accident. Yau also borrows the technique of diptych from Johns, a technique that enables the double sides of story to "mirror" each other inaccurately. For example, "Carp and Goldfish" is constructed like two panels of a diptych: The first tells the story of a little prince in ancient China watching the carp in his royal garden pond, unaware of the coming fall of his kingdom; the second tells of a contemporary boy adding salt to a fishbowl, not knowing it will kill the goldfish. Just as the prince in Ancient China is related to the Chinese American boy, the goldfish and carps are kin, in that goldfish were bred from carp centuries ago in China. The transmutation suggests not only that salt water proves fatal to goldfish but also that China proves "alien and indifferent" to Chinese Americans.

Over the next ten years, Yau began to teach art and writing in various universities, but he continued to write and publish poetry. His three collections of poems of this period are *Dragon's Blood* (1989), *Radiant Silhouette: New and Selected Work, 1974–1988* (1989), and *Edificio Sayonara* (1992). Yau's "Genghis Chan: Private Eye" series—one of his most important and most frequently discussed sequences—first appeared in *Dragon Blood*, was reprinted in *Radiant Silhouette*, and continued in *Edificio Sayonara*. During this time, Yau also published poetry in nine collaborative books with paintings or photographs by other artists.

Hawaiian Cowboys (1995) registers Yau's return to prose. In effect, like two other, later books—*Symptoms* (1998) and *My Heart Is That Eternal Rose Tattoo* (2001)—it contains no verse. *Hawaiian Cowboys* is a collection of thirteen short stories blending fiction and biography, with a young man of Asian descent as the chief narrator in each story. None of the narrators' identities are explicit (they may or may not be the same person), and the vagueness of individual identity contributes to the sense of a surrealistic world filled with lonely and often perverted people. In general, critics consider Yau's prose pieces more straightforward and autobiographical than his poetry. However, to turn to the autobiographical is not, for Yau, to turn **confessional** or even personal. He struggles to find a way to deal with autobiographical material that neither narrates a life nor reduces the subject to language.

In his two later volumes of poetry, *Forbidden Entries* (1996) and *Borrowed Love Poems* (2002), Yau continues his experimentation with language, his exploration of identity, and his inquiries into the relations between the two. Yau constructs, in each book, a sensual and painfully comic world, in a language that absorbs film, music, and painting. The dense **prose poetry** of the more linguistic *Forbidden Entries* includes anagrammatic permutations of "Mona Lisa": "Maison Al / Oils Amna," "Mia Salon / Omni Alas," and others. *Borrowed Love Poems*, by contrast, is more lyric-prone, offering at times the simplicity of the earliest Yau: "What can I do, I have dreamed of you so much / What can I do, lost as I am in the sky." Along with new poems, these two volumes continue earlier series, including the parodic "Genghis Chan: Private Eye." The title "Genghis Chan" presents the hybrid of two stereotypes: "Genghis Khan," the Mongol conqueror, and Charlie Chan, the "Chinese" detective of early Hollywood films, played by a white actor. By the time he published *Borrowed Love Poems*, Yau had written thirty "Genghis Chan" poems, addressing a range of related themes about Asian American identity.

Unlike the earlier poems of the "Genghis Chan" series, centering on parodic scenes designed to unsettle the identities of the "I", those in *Forbidden Entries* and *Borrowed Love Poems* often have no first-person narrator. They are also syntactically and grammatically more unconventional, dependent on word-play, as in the poem "Genghis Chan: Private Eyes XXIV" in *Forbidden Entries*: "Grab some / Grub sum /" and "On floor / all fours." Puns and images refer to Chinese *topoi* and stereotypes, such as dim sum and chow mein. Meanwhile, sound and spelling approximations between *grab* and *grub*, *sum* and *some*, characteristic of the way racist literature portrayed Oriental language, become counter-mockery of the mockery of Charlie Chan's pidgin English. Rather than rejecting characters like Charlie Chan and protesting against such stereotyping, Yau chooses to exaggerate what is already exaggerated in normative terms, thus undermining the notions of the normative through double parody.

Further Reading. ***Selected Primary Sources:*** Yau, John, "Between the Forest and Its Trees" (*Amerasia Journal* 20.3 [1994]: 31–50); ———, *Borrowed Love Poems* (London: Penguin Poets, 2002); ———, *Broken Off by the Music* (Providence, RI: Burning Deck, 1981); ———, *Corpse and Mirror* (New York: Holt, Rinehart & Winston, 1983); ———, *Forbidden Entries* (Santa Rosa, CA: Black Sparrow Press, 1996); ———, *Hawaiian Cowboys* (Santa Rosa, CA: Black Sparrow Press, 1995); ———, "Interview by Edward Foster" (*Talisman* 5 [Fall 1990]); ———, *Sometimes: Poems* (New York: Sheep Meadow

Press, 1979). ***Selected Secondary Sources:*** Yu, Timothy, "Form and Identity in Language Poetry and Asian American Poetry" (*Contemporary Literature* 41.3 [Fall 2000]: 422–461); Wang, Dorothy J., "Undercover Asian: John Yau and the Politics of Ethnic Self-Identification," in *Asian American Literature in the International Context*, ed. Rocio G. Davis and Sami Ludwig (Hamburg: LIT, 2002, 135–153); Zhou, Xiaojing, "Postmodernism and Subversive Parody: John Yau's 'Genghis Chan: Private Eye' Series" (*College Literature* 31.1 [Winter 2004]: 73–102).

Jun Lei

YIDDISH POETRY

Historically, Yiddish, the native language of Eastern European Jews, was used to create an inclusive yet distinct culture among its speakers. Yiddish is a unique language because it carries connotations of the religion and culture, of a select group of people. The values and experiences associated with Yiddish have influenced generations of American poets.

When Yiddish writers arrived in the United States during the 1880s, Jewish literature had not yet become a part of the **canon**. Yiddish writers soon realized that their immigrant experience gave them a new perspective on the possibility of a better life. Although crossing the borders of an insular Europe to an assimilated society brought freedom, it also carried with it the constant threat of alienation and marginalization. Yiddish immigrants arriving in large American cities such as New York and Chicago felt this threat all too well and wasted little time in creating and solidifying a distinctive poetic voice.

American poetry does not owe its seminal Yiddish influence to Yiddish poets alone. Prose writers such as Abraham Cahan (1860–1951) and Sholem Aleichem (1859–1960) had already produced a body of work in their native Europe. When they arrived in the United States, they found that Yiddish had little influence on American literature and had not established even a footing in the culture. Later arrivals such as Isaac Bashevis Singer (1904–1991), one of the best-known and most prolific Jewish American writers, regarded this deficiency as a potential threat to their Eastern European spirit and culture. They sought, in turn, to create stories that preserved the values of the old world while living in the new one. As Howe and Greenberg point out, the body of work of Yiddish writers in America "bears the imprint of the American Jewish Immigrant" (1). The displacement and feeling of detachment that many newly arriving immigrants experienced in their new home became a dominant theme at the heart of early Yiddish verse throughout the twentieth century. Away from the comfort and security of the insular shtetl, Yiddish immigrant poets were now vulnerable to the **modernism** developing in the United States.

To some degree, Yiddish literature propagated a continuity of values. At the heart of Yiddish language and culture are the Bible and other religious doctrines, but the culture's literary themes include heritage, cultural identity, preservation of language and old world values, the conflict between realist and idealist perspectives, and the Jewish Diaspora.

The first group of Yiddish poets in the United States were the sweatshop poets. Also referred to as labor poets, this group of writers during the last two decades of the nineteenth century included educated and skilled men. As their name suggests, the sweatshop poets lived under difficult conditions but with hope: the promise of a better life through hard work and by assimilation into American culture and society. Among these poets was Morris Winchevsky (1856–1932) (affectionately known as "*der zayde*" or "the grandfather"), who brought from Europe a rich Jewish culture. Winchevsky attempted to bridge the gap between *haskalah* (Jewish enlightenment) and Jewish socialism. In America Winchevsky's work employed complicated rhyme schemes and the occasional use of satire. Compared to his contemporary David Edelstadt (1866–1892), Winchevsky's poetry lacks a distinctive American Jewish voice. Edelstadt, in contrast, sought to provide a more poignant, idealistic account of the immigrant experience. The most popular of the sweatshop poets was Morris Rosenfeld (1862–1923). A worker in the sweatshops, Rosenfeld experienced firsthand the hard labor that his fellow immigrants endured on a daily basis. His lyrics, naturally, resonate with the sufferings of the Jewish immigrant, the new proletariat of the large American city. His opening stanza to "The Sweatshop" (*Shriftn* [1910]) articulates this: "Scoundrels sit below, and all day long they souse. / On the floor above them, Jews sob out their prayer."

Throughout his life Rosenfeld was committed to portraying accurately the life of the immigrant, however harsh or unpleasant. In his later years, he would shift interests from socialism to Jewish nationalism, all the while attempting to struggle with the collective experience of the Jewish immigrant. Joseph Bovshover (1873–1915), another sweatshop poet, composed his early poems at a young age. Like Edelstadt, Bovshover developed a revolutionary style, but in his late twenties he developed emotional problems that would result in a short-lived career.

The sweatshop poets endured for almost two decades, but they were displaced by a more progressive group of poets, Di Yunge. If the sweatshop poets bridged the gap between the old home in Europe and their new one in America, Di Yunge ("The Young Ones") completed the transition. Formed in New York around 1907, and named after the members' periodical *Yugend* (Youth), Di Yunge was a group of immigrants who felt a sharp isolation from their old world roots. Unlike their sweatshop predecessors, Di Yunge poets strove to achieve an aesthetic autonomy in their lyrics. What at first was a term given almost resentfully by older Yiddish writers, "Di Yunge" was soon welcomed by the younger group as indicative of their demarcation from the socialist and nationalistic leanings of their predecessors. Not unlike **T.S. Eliot** and the **New Critics**, who were forming their own aesthetic philosophy at the time, Di Yunge eliminated from their poetics any external agency, producing lyrics that had an organic whole and an aesthetic sensibility.

The most celebrated figure of Di Yunge was **Mani Leib** (also spelled Leyb) (1883–1953). Unlike his predecessors and many of his Di Yunge contemporaries, Leib fashioned for himself a distinct poetic persona, as illustrated in the opening lines to "I am" (*Lidur un Baladn*): "I am Mani Leyb, whose name is sung— / In Brownsville, Yehupets, and farther, they know it." His lyrics show signs of influence from folk songs and folklore, consistent with the aesthetic simplicity he admired in poetry. These characteristics can be seen in "Hush" (*Shriftn* [1914]), for example, wherein Leib evokes a parody of the fervid messianic belief commonplace among the sweatshop poets: "Out of the dark night will he / Riding on a snow-white steed / To our house come quietly."

Other members of Di Yunge carved their own literary path and produced a new mode of expression. The originality of the verse of Moishe Leib Halpern (1886–1932), for example, with lyrics of loneliness and self-loathing ("So I wait for a bolt from above / And I live like a zombie who moves"), left a profound impact on the poetic oeuvre of Di Yunge. H. Leivick (1888–1962), another influential figure who gave new dimension to the emotional and physical sufferings of his fellow American Jews, is credited with being a poet deeply tethered to the burden of the Jew in exile. Other members of Di Yunge included Zisha Landau (1889–1937), Reuben Iceland (1884–1955), and Joseph Rolnick (1879–1955).

Di Yunge not only established a new aesthetic for American poetry in general but also opened doors for those who were otherwise excluded from participating in the male-dominated poetry landscape early in the twentieth century. Contemporary women writers such as Anna Margolin (1887–1952) and Celia Dropkin (1888–1956), for example, found an outlet for their literary voices in the Di Yunge publications.

The end of World War I saw the development of another group of Yiddish American writers, this time in direct opposition to the formal characteristics seen in the poetry by Di Yunge. By 1920 the *In Zich* (Introspectivists) represented the creation of a truly modern voice by Yiddish writers. Jacob Glatstein (1896–1971), Aaron Glanz-Leyeles (1889–1966), and N.B. Minkoff (1893–1958) were some of the leading figures who shared a common goal: to portray life as it really was. Glatstein himself criticized Di Yunge for being "too poetic," the result of which was a distortion of the real Jewish immigrant experience in America. Consistent with their realist philosophy, the *In Zich* poets defined themselves as experimental; their lyrics are written in **free verse**, are devoid of common literary conventions, and lack strict metrical forms. But as Howe and Greenberg write, "it is in their work that the impress of American poetry first makes itself felt" (41).

In New York during 1931, a short-lived movement referred to as **Objectivist poetry** identified an even more experimental poetic form influenced by the Yiddish immigrant culture. **Louis Zukofsky** (1904–1978), its leading figure, published a groundbreaking essay titled, "Sincerity and Objectification: With Special Reference to Works of Charles Reznikoff." In his essay Zukofsky sought to explain the works of **Charles Reznikoff** (1894–1976), a poet whose verse exhibited clear and concise language with the rich details of city life. With respect to Reznikoff's work, Zukofsky admired the elder poet's eye for historical details. In his article, Zukofsky defined "sincerity" in a poem as having "care for detail," in contrast to objectification, which was regarded as having structural unity. Zukofsky's argument was that sincere language is tied to the sound and movement of the lyric. While his thesis was not widely adopted or understood, Zukofsky's coinage of the term "Objectivists" nevertheless launched *An "Objectivists" Anthology*, a collection of works by key contemporary American poets, including **William Carlos Williams**. Included in the volume were **Robert Creeley** and **Robert Duncan**, younger poets of the next generation who had been influenced by Zukofsky's work. Zukofsky's influence would later also extend to experimental poets during the 1970s and 1980s.

The modern influence of Yiddish is seen in the poetry of **Muriel Rukeyser** (1913–1980), whose work portrays her stuggles with her multiple roles as woman, mother, and Jew. Other modern influences include **Sylvia Plath** (1932–1963), whose poem "Daddy" (1962) voices the rejection of familial and religious ties ("Daddy, I have had to kill you. / You died before I had time") in the hopes of becoming an independent self. Much like their Yiddish predecessors from Eastern Europe, the works of these modern poets wrestle with marginalization, self-expression, and Jewish identity. Another American female writer bearing the influence of Yiddish is **Adrienne Rich** (1929–). In poems such as "Tattered Kaddish" (*An Atlas of the Difficult World: Poems 1988–1991*), for example, Rich challenges literary conventions but also questions her Jewish identity by establishing a connection with her father: "Split at the root, neither gentile nor jew / yankee nor rebel." Rich's exploration of both her Jewish identity and her communal ties is just one of the many motifs in her emotionally charged lyrics.

World War II gave way to an insurgence of spirited American poets who challenged the motives of their political leaders and the norms of mainstream society. One of the most outspoken and visible poets of this generation was **Allen Ginsberg** (1926–1997), a prominent figure among the **Beat** writers, a group of artists with a common set of social attitudes. Ginsberg's emphasis on self-expression and anti-establishmentarianism is reminiscent of the early Di Yunge poets. His strong vocal reactions to war and to the restraints on artists of his generation brought a new self-consciousness to American poetry, most visibly seen in his celebrated poem, "Howl" (1956) (*Howl and Other Poems*): "I saw the best minds of my generation destroyed by madness, starving hysterical naked." Other traces of Yiddish influence in Ginsberg are seen in "Kaddish" (1961) (*Kaddish and Other Poems, 1958–1960*). In the poem, an **elegy** to Ginsberg's mother, the poet revisits his Jewish roots. Ginsberg's focus on family is evocative of the writings of early Yiddish writers and their attempt to preserve an ethnic and religious identity in a new culture.

The remnants of Yiddish remain a steady influence on contemporary poets. **Jerome Rothenberg** (1931–) and **Irena Klepfisz** (1941–), for example, explore themes of identity in their experimental bilingual verse. Although some writers and critics continue to place Yiddish in its appropriate context within the canon, others point out that Yiddish will always retain its distance from American poetry because of its unique link to a history underscored with moral and religious inflections. In Cynthia Ozick's "Envy; or, Yiddish in America," the writer laments that "the language was lost, murdered. The language—a museum. Of what other language can it be said that it died a sudden and definite death." Although Ozick's sentiment about Yiddish is valid, Yiddish language and culture nevertheless have had a lasting impact on American poetics.

Further Reading. ***Selected Secondary Sources:*** Bluestein, Gene, *Anglish/Yinglish: Yiddish in American Life and Literature*, 2nd ed. (Lincoln: University of Nebraska Press, 1998); Howe, Irving, and Eliezer Greenberg, eds., *A Treasury of Yiddish Stories* (New York: Holt, Rinehart and Winston, 1969); Howe, Irving, Ruth R. Wisse, and Khone Shmeruk, eds., *The Penguin Book of Modern Yiddish Verse* (New York: Viking, 1987); Roback, A.A., *The Story of Yiddish Literature* (New York: Yiddish Scientific Institute, 1940); Shreiber, Maeera Y., "Jewish American Poetry," in *The Cambridge Companion to Jewish American Literature*, ed. Michael P. Kramer and Hana With-Nesher (Cambridge: Cambridge University Press, 2003); Wisse, Ruth, *The Modern Jewish Canon* (New York: Farrar, Straus and Giroux, 1984).

Jeffrey Gruenglas

YOUNG BEAR, RAY (1951–)

The trajectory of Ray Young Bear's poetry parallels the development and active presence of Native American political activism and the outpouring of Native American literary criticism, figuring most prominently in the late 1960s and continuing to the present day. Young Bear's poetry engages historical and contemporary political issues and employs dream sequences within which he is able to explore the ephemeral boundaries between reality and dreams, between the past and present, and between ancestors and progeny. The liminality of Young Bear's poetic dreams serves as antidote to social and historical trauma, but it also carves out an artistic space that is distinctly by and for Mesquakie people. Written in both English and Mesquakie, Young Bear's poems posit a Mesquakie epistemological rendering of historical and existential tensions and their attendant relationships to internal and external forces.

Ray Young Bear was born on the Mesquakie (Red Earth) Indian Settlement in 1951, near Tama, Iowa. He attended Pomona College, University of Iowa, Grinnell College, Northern Iowa University, and Iowa State University. Raised by his grandmother, he has continued in adulthood to live near his birthplace on the Mesquakie settlement. He received a creative writing grant from the National Endowment for the Arts and an honorary Doctorate in Letters from Luther College in 1993, and he cofounded the Woodland Song and Dance Troupe of Arts in 1983. His first publication, *Waiting to Be Fed*, was published in 1975 and was limited to 225 hand-signed copies. He then went on to publish *Winter of the Salamander: The Keeper of Importance* (1980), *The Invisible Magician* (1990), and *The Rock Island Hiking Club* (2001). He received the 1998 Ruth Suckow Award for his novel, *Remnants of the First Earth* (1998). Young Bear's poems have been anthologized and critically engaged by Elizabeth Cook-Lynn, Gretchen Bataille, and Katherine Shanley, among others.

Young Bear's poems contrast dream-states with visceral, embodied reality. The heightened effect of this contrast and the development of a liminal space create an aesthetic framework within which the function of apocalyptic prophecy, malignancy and healing, the paradoxical juxtaposition of popular culture and tribal tradition, and the role of veterans in the Mesquakie community are thematically developed. His first widely distributed collection of poems, *Winter of the Salamander* (1980), uses no capitalization, a technique that changed as Young Bear's poetry developed. In "part: my grandfathers walked speaking 1970" from *Winter of the Salamander* (1980), it is within the space of a dream that words give shape to creation through an enactment, both past and present, of a Mesquakie ritual. The "i" in the poem stands for both Young Bear's grandfathers and himself, creating continuity between past and present, creation and progeny. The poem's investment in these artistic and ritualistic enactments of creation is undercut by Young Bear's diction, which denotes threats of death. The tensions between cycles of life and the threat of death and paralysis are also found in "A Drive to Lone Ranger" from *The Invisible Magician* (1990). In his "Notes" at the end of *The Invisible Musician*, Young Bear discusses a Mesquakie prophecy whereby when the Northern Lights reach the Southern horizon, there will be an "end to all life" (98). Likewise, in "A Drive to Lone Ranger" (1980), the earth is beginning to rebel against mining and nuclear attack by a "force" that "cannot be trusted." Young Bear maps out the unnatural effects of this Euro-American "force" on the lands and bodies of the Mesquakie people. The prophetic threat of illness and the unnatural is highlighted by Young Bear's reference to the Northern Lights: a reminder to Mesquakie people of impending apocalyptic disaster.

Young Bear locates threats to his community not simply as external forces but also as rivalry, greed, and political disparities within the Mesquakie community. In "winter of the salamander" from *Winter of the Salamander* (1980), Young Bear depicts a peyote ritual in response to how "the dead grow" and the "mouths . . . darken blue." As part of the ritual, they "sit before a body the size of [their] hand" and those present refuse to claim responsibility. Alongside his depiction of this small death, Young Bear discusses the internal community tensions between mixed-blood and full-blood tribal members, seeming to suggest that it is this type of interior digression that contributes to a series of symbolic deaths. The poem calls for a "covenant" with the badger and the presence and nourishment of ancestors as a healing antidote to this metonymic death. Likewise, in "Laramie's Peripheral Vision" from *The Rock Island Hiking Club* (2001), Young Bear illustrates the tensions over casino culture, the detrimental shift in ownership and rights of property and homes, and the epistemological changes these shifts entail. The family, depicted at the end of the poem, serves as healer to the threat suggested: evacuated cultural and tribal meaning at the hands of casino culture.

Young Bear positions Vietnam veterans as key figures in many of his poems. In "poem for viet nam" from *Winter of the Salamander* (1980), Young Bear suggests the mediation of visceral, bodily violence by dreams of home and family and explores the tenuous and precarious balance between the natural and unnatural in war. In "American Flag Dress" from *The Rock Island Hiking Club* (2001), Young Bear celebrates the bravery and community of veterans who have shared the horrors of "burning fields, twisted armor, and death," yet still "smiled with arms interlocked." However, these two poems do not present conventional descriptions of national patriotism: What they do denote is the "warrior" link between these men that locates patriotism in the Mesquakie community against a "common Teutonic threat."

Young Bear's poems, especially "Gift of the Star Medicine," from *Black Eagle Child* (1992), interlock images of U.S. popular culture and traditional Mesquakie practice, suggesting the inclusion of contemporary U.S. popular culture alongside, but not in replacement of, what Young Bears describes as the "self-prescribed, self-imposed geographic isolation" that protects Mesquakie people's relations to self and community. Young Bear's poetry reveals an artistically sovereign space that reflects an equally sovereign community.

Further Reading. ***Selected Primary Sources:*** Young Bear, Ray, *Black Eagle Child* (Iowa City: University of Iowa Press, 1992); ———, *The Invisible Musician* (Duluth, MN: Holy Cow! Press, 1990); ———, *Remnants of the First Earth* (New York: Grove Press, 1996); ———, *The Rock Island Hiking Club* (Iowa City: University of Iowa Press, 2001); ———, *Waiting to Be Fed* (St. Paul, MN: Greywolf Press, 1975); ———, *Winter of the Salamander* (San Francisco: Harper & Row, 1980). ***Selected Secondary Sources:*** Highwater, Jamake, ed., *Words in the Blood: Contemporary Indian Writers of North and South America* (New York: New American Library, 1984); Krupat, Arnold, ed., *New Voices in Native American Literary Criticism* (Washington, DC: Smithsonian Institution Press, 1993); Rich, Adrienne, and Alden Turner, eds., *The Best American Poetry 1996* (New York: Scribner's, 1996).

Patricia Ploesch

YOUNG, DAVID (1936–)

As a result of living in and writing about Ohio for many decades, David Young has come to be regarded as a bio-regionalist poet, but this label is far too limiting. Young's poems are often set in a midwestern landscape; but when he writes, Young is powerfully engaged in a meditation that transcends both his locale and his era. In his moving book *Earthshine*, he writes of his first wife's illness and death and of his own grief and recovery. Describing himself as a well with two buckets, "one for grief and one for love," he says "Sometimes the daylight has bewildered me" (55). In his poetry he looks for the right way to live with life's strangely mixed offerings, and though he may consult the landscape, Young is just as likely to look to science, mythology, the work of other poets (as interestingly varied as Miroslav Holub and Petrarch), or even "The Gospel Lighthouse Church's lemon-yellow bus," which "says 'Heaven Bound' up front" for answers. Young's poetry reflects patience, depth, and a resilient aptitude both for delight and for gazing into the void. These qualities, coupled with his editorial contributions and his artful **translations** of poets like Rilke, Eich, the T'ang Dynasty poets,

Montale, and others, have earned him a wide and appreciative audience.

David Young was born in 1936 in Davenport, Iowa. He went to high school in Omaha, Nebraska. After attending Carleton College, he earned an MA and a Ph.D. from Yale University. He returned to the Midwest to teach at Oberlin College, where he was a professor of English and creative writing for over forty years and where he and his wife, Georgia Newman, a physician, established their home. The undergraduate writing program he developed there in conjunction with **Stuart Friebert** and others continues to be one of the most successful in the country, producing many fine writers, including Franz Wright, **Thylias Moss**, Linda Gregorson, Bruce Beasley, Bruce Weigl, and Robin Behn. Although Young retired from the Oberlin faculty in 2003, he continues his editorial work for Oberlin College Press's FIELD Translation Series, FIELD Editions, and FIELD Poetry Series and remains an editor of FIELD, a "Journal of Poetry and Poetics."

Young's first book, *Sweating Out the Winter*, opens with these lines: "Nearly a year since word of death / Broke off the summer." Although mid-poem he admits, "I swore I'd write no letters to the dead," there is something prescient in this early reference to death's power and a writer's need to address it. Young has produced a body of elegiac work, most notably *Earthshine* and the later volume *At the White Window*. The latter book contains poems with titles like "Landscape with Disappearing Poet" (for Miroslav Holub), "Landscape with Grief Train" (in memory of Tom Linehan), "My Father at Ninety-four," and "Elegy Lacking in Grace" (for Andrew Bongiorno). Even so, it would be as much of a mistake to assume that Young's work is based only in grief as it would be to think it grounded only in the Ohio landscape. His books also include poems sparked by his interest in cooking, by the thoughts of Chairman Mao, by "The Beautiful Names of the Months," by heavy machinery, and even by the timing of Tarzan's swing.

It is the extent of Young's interest in the world that underscores the fascinating complexity of his work. A look at the "Notes" for poems in *At the White Window* provides insight into the variety of influences that Young braids into a single poem. For "Landscape with Bees" he notes, "The ideas about bees' abilities to sense quarks and magnetic fields referred to in this poem are discussed by Adam Frank in an article in *Discover*, November 1997. . . . a *borgo* is an Italian medieval community within a fortified hilltop castle" (75). In the notes for his "Cloudstown Lightfall: Prelude and Ten Sonnets," he mentions Dionysis a line he quotes from an honors thesis on Nabokov; the Tang Dynasty poet Yu Xuanji, and a line adapted from a student's prose poem (76).

In addition to this breadth of interest and depth of feeling, Young brings to his work enviable skill with form, both experimental and long-established. As early as 1977, Cleveland State University Press brought out his *Work Lights: Thirty-Two Prose Poems*. On the back cover Young notes, "Most people think of the **prose poem** as perverse, an excuse for laziness on the part of the poet." He goes on to say that though he had once shared that view, he found it more worthwhile to consider prose poems' "interesting possibilities." The results of his investigation are prose poems that at first reading seem to be built on a comic sense of fun (e.g., "Four About the Letter P," which asks the reader to "swear on this stone you will not steal yams," or "Four About Heavy Machinery," which tells the reader "We have strong feelings about bulldozers"). An appealing thing about these prose poems is that however playful the initial impulse, the reader soon finds herself drawn in, considering seriously the poem's claim that "The bulldozer thinks of itself as a lover."

In an even earlier book, *Boxcars*, Young has a poem in an even less traditional form. "A Project for Freight Trains" reads like a grant application for a moving art installation. Young begins by invoking a sight common at railroad crossings—words on the railroad cars. He speaks directly, proposing to "capitalize" on the existence of this movable text system. Then the poem takes a surprising turn as Young calls out words ("cloud," "star," "meadow," etc.) and certain colors ("burnt orange," "peagreen," rose-red," etc.) as the building blocks of his created system of "random train poems" and outlines ways that combinations can be read for luck ("The 5-6 combination, which makes AIRPORT, is to be considered a lucky omen"). This poem borders on concept art and is an example of Young's willingness to experiment.

Young is also a veteran of traditional forms—the sonnet and the ghazal, for example. In his Cloudstown sonnet series (*At the White Window*), the naturalness of the language and the appearance of ease in the rhymes and in the shifts between Petrarchan sonnet and English sonnet forms demonstrate a mastery that allows Young to explore his subject matter fluidly, moving from the upstairs bedroom of a young poet in Ohio to a conversation with a Chinese poet who died a thousand years ago and then to a place where "a fox / lifts her head sniffing by the creek."

Young's contribution to American letters extends beyond this body of work. He has translated Rilke, Miroslav Holub, Pablo Neruda, Yu Xuanji, Petrarch, and Eugenio Montale, among others, with new Montale translations published in 2005.

Further Reading. ***Selected Primary Sources:*** Young David, *At the White Window* (Columbus: Ohio State University Press, 2000); ———, *Boxcars* (New York: Ecco Press, 1969); ———, *Earthshine* (Middletown, CT: Wesleyan University Press, 1988); ———, *Foraging*

(Middletown, CT: Wesleyan University Press, 1986); ———, *The Names of the Hare in English* (Pittsburgh, PA: University of Pittsburgh Press, 1979); ———, *Night Thoughts and Henry Vaughn* (Columbus: Ohio State University Press, 1994); ———, *The Planet on the Desk, Selected and New Poems 1960–1990* (Hanover, NH: Wesleyan University Press, 1991); ———, *Sweating Out the Winter* (Pittsburgh, PA: University of Pittsburgh Press, 1969); ———, *Work Lights: Thirty-Two Prose Poems* (Cleveland, OH: Cleveland State University Press, 1977). ***Selected Secondary Sources:*** Academy of American Poets, Biography of David Young, www.poets.org/poet.php/prmPID/327; Tittle, Diana, "David Young Poet," Cleveland Arts Prize website, www.clevelandartsprize.org/lit_99.htm.

Deborah Bogen

Z

ZUKOFSKY, LOUIS (1904–1978)

One of the foremost poets of the twentieth century, Louis Zukofsky is an **Objectivist** who formulated a poetic ethos based on structure and form related to the way in which objects construct meaning out of connections that resonate sound. In the foreword to *A Test of Poetry* (1948), Zukofsky says his concept of art is a manifestation of "sight, sound and sense, and how each has to do with the other, and how words themselves form a company—all gave me an immediate locus, a place where I might put my own experience in reading, hearing, seeing" (viii). Speaking of *Anew* (1946), **Williams Carlos Williams** enthusiastically endorsed Zukofsky's work and felt that his postwar material might revitalize the world, revolutionize the line, and create a new way of thinking about poetry that would "potentially penetrate the very bases of knowledge and open up fields that might be exploited for a century" (quoted in Comens, 132).

Zukofsky appeared on the literary scene in 1931 when **Ezra Pound** suggested to the editor of *Poetry* magazine, **Harriett Monroe**, that he edit a special issue of *Poetry* that would feature those writers who believed that the poem as an object should emphasize precision, intellectual rigor, and emotional sincerity in conjunction with innovations in structure and sound. **Charles Reznikoff**, **George Oppen**, **Carl Rakoski**, and Zukofsky himself, as well as Basil Bunting of Britain and Zukofsky's friend and correspondent, **Lorine Niedecker**, comprised the group known as Objectivists. Zukofsky subsequently edited *An Objectivist Anthology* in 1932. Along with Reznikoff and Oppen, Zukovsky formed the Objectivist Press to publish their own and William Carlos Williams's books. Jennifer Carnig, in the *University of Chicago Chronicle* (4 November 2004) writes that "the Objectivists initially received attention because of the rapid growth of the American left after the 1929 stock market crash." She quotes Robert von Hallberg, the University of Chicago's Helen A. Regenstein Professor in English Language and Literature, as saying that "it wasn't just that [the Objectivists] were merely leftists, it was the fact that nobody had seen leftist **avant-gardist** poets before. Ezra Pound and **T.S. Eliot** were on the right."

Zukofsky ushered in this new Objectivist movement, but it was short-lived, in part because the poetry practiced by the Objectivists was too dense and difficult, and by 1978, the year of Zukofsky's death, he had not received the recognition or canonical status of Ezra Pound, T.S. Eliot, and William Carlos Williams. It was not until the 1960s and 1970s that Zukofsky's work began to receive attention and major awards: the Longview Foundation Award (1963); the Union League Civic and Arts Foundation Prize from *Poetry* magazine (1964); the Oscar Blumenthal Prize, also from *Poetry* (1966); a

National Endowment for the Arts grant (1967 and 1968); a National Institute of Arts and Letters grant (1976); and an honorary doctorate from Bard College (1977). In the 1970s, Zukovsky's work attracted the attention of the **Language poets** because of its emphasis on and concern with **sound**. In 2004 both the University of Chicago and Columbia College–Bernard College organized conferences around the work of Zukofsky, and scholars are beginning to devote texts to elucidating his material, ranking him alongside Williams and Pound.

Louis Zufovsky was born on January 23, 1904, on the Lower East Side of Manhattan. His parents, Pinchos Zukofsky (ca. 1860–1954) and Chana Pruss Zukofsky (ca. 1862–1927) were Russian Jewish immigrants from what is now Lithuania. Pinchos Zukofsky came to the United States in 1898 and worked as a night watchman and pants-presser in the garment district of New York. His wife, Chana, their daughters, and their son, Morris, joined him in 1903. Louis was the only child born in the United States, but he spoke Yiddish until he began public school. Zukofsky's *Autobiography* (1970) describes visits to Yiddish theaters where, by the age of nine, he had seen productions of Ibsen, Strindberg, Tolstoy, and Shakespeare, whose plays he had read in English by the time he was eleven.

Zukofsky's parents sent him to Columbia University, where he majored in English and philosophy, became a member of the school's literary society, and began to publish his poetry. He failed to graduate because he never took the required physical education course. He did, however, attend graduate school and received his MA degree in 1924. He later developed his master's thesis on Henry Adams into *Henry Adams: A Criticism in Autobiography* (1929). Zukofsky subsequently taught at the University of Wisconsin in 1930–1931; was a visiting assistant professor at Colgate University in 1947; taught at the Polytechnic Institute of Brooklyn, New York, in 1947–1966; and served as poet-in-residence at San Francisco State College in 1958.

Zukofsky's canvas is a composition writ large: music and history; politics, literature, and philosophy; a symphony made up of objects in anafractuous alignment; everything from A to "the"; family, friends, and calculus. Anything that attracted his attention—the dictionary, sonnets, sestinas, indeed language itself—served as his material. Mark Scroggins aptly called his study *Louis Zukofsky and the Poetry of Knowledge* (1998) and says that Zukofsky is "perhaps the greatest American poet born in this century—perhaps even the greatest American English-language poet *of* the century" (4). Although Zukofsky's reputation largely rests on his contribution to American poetry and **poetics**, his writings include fiction, criticism, and plays. The collection of Zukofsky materials housed at the Harry Ransom Humanities Research Center at the University of Texas–Austin is a rich resource for those interested in studying his work.

Zukofsky's *magnum opus*, *"A,"* serves as a frame through which a reader can examine the themes of the poet's works. Zukofsky worked on *"A"* intermittently from 1928, when "A-1" was written, until 1968, when he wrote the final movement, "A-24." The University of California Press published the poem for the first time in its entirety in 1978. Movements 7, 9, 11, and 12 of *"A"* are said to be masterpieces of twentieth-century American poetry.

Barry Ahern, in a critical book titled *Zukofsky's "A,"* says that the poem "grew directly out of "Poem Beginning The," a response to T.S. Eliot's "The Waste Land," published by Ezra Pound in his periodical, *Exile*, in 1928. "A-1" elucidates Zukofsky's claim that

> the order of all poetry is to approach a state of music wherein the ideas present themselves sensuously and intelligently and are of no predatory intention. A hard job, as poets have round reconciling contrasting principles of facts. In poetry the poet is continually encountering the facts which in the making seem to want to disturb the music and yet the movement cannot exist without the facts, without its facts. ("An Objective," *Prepositions*, 18)

Pound had written in "Vers Libre and Arnold Dolmetish" (1918) that

> poetry is a composition set to music. Most other definitions of it are indefensible, or metaphysical. The proportion of quality of the music may, and does, vary; but poetry withers and "dries out" when it leaves music, or at least an imagined music, too far behind it. The horror of modern "readings of poetry" [is] due to oratorical recitation. Poetry must be read as music and not as oratory. (*Literary Essays*, 437)

"A-1" opens with the poet's commentary on a concert performance of Bach's *St. Matthew Passion* in New York on April 5, 1928. This performance is conjoined with that of Ossip Gabrilowitsch's Easter 1928 "bare arms, black dresses" concert and the 1728 Leipzig rendering of Bach. Time is conflated, suggesting a comparison between differing places and times. What goes on in the mind of the poet need not adhere to reality, such as the fact that Johann Sebastian Bach had not fathered twenty-two children by 1929. What is going on when "desire [longs] for perfection"? Zukofsky says there are "perhaps a few things to remember," and he points out that "there are different techniques," and "we really are and never quite live" (4).

It is Passover, and "the blood's tide like music" is "a round of fiddles playing." Zukofsky, in a contributor's note in the 1931 Objectivist issue of *Poetry*, writes:

> "A"—in process—includes two themes: I—desire for the potentially perfect finding its direction inextricably the direction of historic and contemporary particulars; and II—approximate attainment of this perfection in the feeling of the contrapuntal design of the [fugue] transferred to poetry; both themes related to the text of Bach's *St. Matthew Passion,* (quoted in Scroggins, 201)

The fugue adheres to Zukofsky's interest in form, and provides Zukofsky a structural mechanism that allows him to include whatever he desires in rendering the *wor[l]d* (emphasis added) according to his dictates.

"A-2" continues a debate with a character named "Kay" on the subject of poetics that is of central concern to Zukofsky. In this movement of the poem, music and nature are conjoined. "Listen Kay," the poet writes. "The music is in the flower, / Leaf around leaf ranged around the center" (7). The poem and nature are one. All things are one in poetry. "A-2" concludes with the poet's assumption of other voices—those of Christ and Walt Whitman. "I walked on Easter Sunday," Zukofsky writes and, echoing Mark 14:22–24, adds, "This is my face / This is my form" (8). The poet is the conduit for "the song out of the voices." "A-3" is an **elegy** for a character named Ricky, who died young. Life and death, like music and nature, argues for a unification of all things. Death and resurrection implicit in the Passion are figured in Zukofsky's positioning himself as "Joseph of Arimathea to Ricky's Christ." Ricky is at once "lion-heart, my dove, / Pansy over the heart, dicky-bird" (11).

"A-4" harkens back to Zukofsky's origins and to his Jewish parentage, to the "father's precursors / Set masts in dinghies, chanted the Speech" (15), and examines the necessity of rendering multiple voices. The voices of the young that assail their elders with the words "religious, snarling monsters" (13) mouth the jargon of the time. What Zukofsky implies is a question of how the past and what comes after it are to be reconciled.

"A-5" begins an odyssey in and through which "sailors" come to know the press of convergent voices: "'As you say.' / 'Your people?' 'All people'" (17) together manifesting their "strange speech" (18), "words ranging forms" (20).

"A-6," in which the fugue is specifically mentioned for the first time, serves as a retrospective on the previous movements. It addresses the difficulty of saying when speech, mere jargon, is rendered sterile. Ahern calls this movement "a catalogue of slides toward the void" in which "traditions, imperialism, popular taste, contemporary morality—all seem to be going downhill fast" (54).

The first six movements of *"A,"* Scroggins says, "form something of an overture to the work as a whole, a finding out and testing of 'what will suffice,' what aesthetics and poetics will serve in writing an **epic**-length poem in twentieth-century America" (*Knowledge,* 200). "A-6" is a turning-point. The language of the poem from movements "A-1" through "A-5" constitutes a "singing" that shifts to the stammering and silence mentioned in "A-2." Zukofsky asks, "With all this material / To what distinction—" (42), for, as Zukofsky has pointed out, "saying. It's a hard world anyway / Not many of us will get out of it alive" (22).

"A-7," written from 1928 to 1930, comprises seven Shakespearian sonnets, in which the poet contemplates a set of "street closed" "wooden-sawhorses" that he transforms into imaginary "horses" and puts through incredible paces. One object or thing that is itself becomes, at the same time, another. It is a matter of words: "Trot, trot—? No horse is here, no horse is there?" Well, then, "we'll make / Wood horse, and recognize it with our words" (39). The movement's intent, however, is to examine the art of poetry in decline, and this is the only segment that Zukofsky included in the Objectivist issue of *Poetry.* If *"A"* is, at least in part, the means by which desire finds realization in an inclusive object, Zukofsky's statement in *Objectivists Anthology* is definitive of what he hopes poetry in the 1930s might become:

> The desire for what is objectively perfect, inextricably the direction of historic and contemporary particulars—a desire to place everything—everything aptly, perfectly, belonging within, one with, a context—A poem. The context based on a world—idle metaphor—a lime base—a fibre—not merely a charged vacuum tube—an aerie of personation—The desire for an inclusive object. (15)

Is this no more, then, than all words "spoke: words, words, we are words, horses, manes, / words (42)? *"A"* shows how a poem—over eight hundred pages of it—objectifies Zukofsky's life along with the other lives, real and presented, that he had come to know in actuality or through the medium of quoted or invented words. An overview of *"A"* provides a grounding in the canon of Zukofsky's work—particularly the collections of critical essays *A Test of Poetry* (1948) and *Prepositions+* (1967).

Ahern says that between "A-7" and "A-8," Zukofsky "fortified himself with book-learning: economic, social, political" that resulted in numerous references and quotations. The fugal movement of "A-8" was written between 1935 and 1937. On November 9, 1935, Zukofsky wrote his friend, Lorine Niedecker, with whom he exchanged letters and manuscripts from 1931 to the time of her death in 1970, that the work is a "music of statements, but not explanation ever, that's why I seem to leave out—but the reader will have to learn to read statement, juxtaposed constructs as music," as well as reckon with the eight themes, which, according to Ahern, are "labor, Bach, economics, science, nominalism, personal history, literature and art, and the Adamses," Henry, John Quincy, and Brooks (77).

I's Pronounced "Eyes" (1963) grew out of the correspondence between Zukofsky and Niedecker that discussed the importance of visual perception and its place in the craft of writing poetry. Correspondence with Niedecker that references writing is incorporated into Zukofsky's thoughts on the importance of personal tradition in "A-12": "Each writer writes / one long work."

Niedecker published a review of Zukofsky's *A Test of Poetry* in the *Capital Times* on December 18, 1948, describing it as "distilled excellence" but noting that the "comparison and considerations" (poetic comments on such poets as Homer, Virgil, Ovid, Catullus, Chaucer, Shakespeare, Samuel Johnson, Shelly, Hopkins, and a host of others) might be an unrewarding challenge for a general reader. "A-8" is the longest of the first eight movements of *"A,"* and, in general, it answers the question of whether or not the design of the fugue can be transferred to poetry. Significant in "A-8" is the way binary structures intertwine with ways of seeing, producing stereoscopical thinking. "Light-wave and quantum, we have good proof both exist: / Our preset effort is to see how this is" in order to "effect the composition of a two-point view" (49). Zukofsky finished "A-8" in 1937, rendering the most fully realized section up to this point of the "poem of a life" (Scroggins, *Knowledge*, 161).

The first half of "A-9," a **translation** of Cavalcanti's canzone "Donna mi priegha," serves as an example Zukofsky's amazing poetic virtuosity. Pound had said that the translation of this canzone was impossible. Nevertheless, Zukofsky did it while preserving the elaborate rhyme of the original by means of adapting phrases of Karl Marx's *Capital* and discussing the economics involved in "use-value" and "exchange value." A letter by Zukofsky to Neidecker suggests how Marx and Spinoza fit together in the two halves of "A-9." Zukofsky tells her to read the second stanza of the first half. "The Marx is in Spinny," he says. Zukofsky's aim is to show that reason has power over the emotions.

"A-10," an inverted mass on the fall of Paris to the Nazis in 1940, was written in between the construction of the two halves of "A-8" and "A-9." "A-11" and "A-12" provide insights into the Zukofsky family; Celia Thaew, a composer whom Zukofsky married in 1933; Paul, a concert violinist; and Zukofsky himself. Experience is seen less as history or politics, and more in terms of the poet's domestic situation.

"A-12" comprises twelve years' work. A lengthy work in itself, it serves as the center of the work as a whole. Scroggins calls it "the heart of Zukofsky's work" (*Knowledge*, 12). It may be seen that *Bottom: On Shakespeare* (1963) serves as a corollary to "A-12," for Zukofsky set *"A"* aside to work on it from 1947 to 1960. Zukofsky says that he spent twenty years on whatever it is that *Bottom* is—a treatise on Shakespeare, an intertwining of the physical eye and the erring brain, a musical rendition, a "score," or Zukofsky's placement of the bottom on top? Zukofsky "on top" of Shakespeare? **Bob Perelman,** in his foreword to *Bottom: On Shakespeare*, writes, "*Bottom* uses Shakespeare's *Works* to stage a visionary poetics, pursuing literalism to a pitch where writing and world would be co-extensive and where the divisions of history would be bridged by a more capacious, unchanging perspective" (xiii). Shakespeare's words, Perelman says, are "objects that Zukofsky, all eyes, hears as music. This uses the sensory epistemology of Nick Bottom: the eye of man hears Shakespeare" (xi).

Between 1950 and 1968, when Zikofsky wrote "A-12" through "A-24," he also published the completed manuscripts of *Some Time / Short Poems* (1956); *5 Statements for Poetry* (1958); *Barely and Widely* (1958); *It Was* (1961); *I's Pronounced "Eyes"* (1963); *Found Objects 1962–1926* (1964); *After I's* (1964); *An Unearthing: A Poem* (1865); *Iyyob* (1965); *I Sent Thee Late* (1965); *Finally A Valentine* (1965); *All: The Collected Short Poems, 1923–1958* (1966); *All: The Collected Short Poems, 1956–1964* (1967); *Little, a fragment* (1967); *Prepositions: Collected Critical Essays of Louis Zukofsky* (1968); *From Thanks to the Dictionary* (1968); and *Ferdinand, Including It Was* (1968).

Such prodigious activity may be responsible for what Steven Helming calls the "difficulty and obscurity of the second half of *'A'*" and for Zukofsky's "apparent unconcern with his audience [which] can be attributed to his Objectivist poetic and to his immanentist, Spinozistic sense of the self in the world, but it has its springs also in his alienation from the literary scene and his bitterness at the indifference and worse that had greeted his work" (431). Zukofsky has been referred to as a poet's poet or as a poet's poet's poet because of the "disconnect" between his work and his audience. Asked about the reception of his poetry, he told George Oppen that "it doesn't matter, they don't care if they understand you or not" (quoted in Helmling, 431).

The difficulty of later Zukofsky, Scroggins says, "is much more than a matter of hidden references or withheld knowledge" (235). "A-13," titled "partita," a dance form, asks—although there is no question mark—"What do you want to know / What do you want to do" (262). The reader may not know what is wanted in terms of knowing when the wo[r]ld is slippery, when it is and is not Zukfsky's, when it is music. The sounds of words in Zukofsky's lexicon are often as important as the meaning of the words. Poetry is music; music is poetry; language is "liquid." It is all linked with seeing. In *Prepositions+*, he says: "What I am talking about—well, actually I'm talking about *sight, and* sound, *and then the third word has always bothered me but I've ended up with* intellection" (171). The conclusion of *Prepositions+* sums up Zukofsky: It is what Zukofsky's work is about, if only the reader could hear the line's music, twiddle the note "a," master the sonnet, sestina, syllabics, and accentual verse, all the while playing the violin. Zukofsky explains:

> Under the aspect of eternity, where all things exist equally with the same force as when they began to exist, nothing of the mutual need of course be *said*; thought is only conflation of extension, and extension of thought, until the bass-string of humility is suddenly aware of the presumption of having said something about the holiness of the treble. And then without reference to an all's equal, external existence art exists in agitation and activity where no human sense is cut off from another and netted in is whatever *Ethics* such an organism as Spinoza can produce, or be increased or diminished by, "in so far as it is understood by his nature." (172)

"Well, maybe that explains it," Zukofsky says. "They'll tell me it's difficult" (*Prepositions+*, 172). The "poem of life" brings poetry to life. Zukofsky's work rewards a diligent reader. It likewise teaches poets what they would know about craft as it represents singing, the capacity to hear and to see.

Further Reading. ***Selected Primary Sources:*** Zukofsky, Louis, *"A"* (Berkeley: University of California Press, 1978.); ———, *Anew: Poems* (Prairie City, IL: Decker, 1941); ———, *Bottom: On Shakespeare* (Austin: University of Texas Press, 1963); ———, *I's Pronounced "Eyes"* (New York: Trobar Press, 1963); ———, *Prepositions: Collected Critical Essays of Louis Zukofsky* (1967; New York: Horizon Press, 1968); ———, *A Test of Poetry* (New York: Objectivist Press, 1948). ***Selected Secondary Sources:*** Ahearn, Barry, *Zukofsky's "A": An Introduction* (Berkeley: University of California Press, 1983); Comens, Bruce, *Apocalypse and After: Modern Strategy and Postmodern Tactics in Pound, Williams, and Zukofsky* (Tuscaloosa: University of Alabama Press, 1995); Helmling, Steven, "Louis Zukofsky," in *Dictionary of Literary Biography, Volume 5: American Poets Since World War II* (Detriot: Gale, 1980); Scroggins, Mark, ed., *Upper Limit Music: The Writing of Louis Zukofsky* (Tuscaloosa: University of Alabama Press, 1997); ———, *Louis Zukofsky and the Poetry of Knowledge* (Tuscaloosa: University of Alabama Press, 1998).

Sue Brannan Walker

Bibliography

Anthologies of Poetry

Allen, Donald, ed. *The New American Poetry, 1945–1960.* New York: Grove, 1960.

Axelrod, Steven, Camille Roman, and Thomas Travisano, eds. *The New Anthology of American Poetry.* Vol. 1, *Traditions and Revolutions, Beginnings to 1900.* New Brunswick, NJ: Rutgers University Press, 2003.

———, eds. *The New Anthology of American Poetry.* Vol. 2, *Modernisms, 1900–1950.* New Brunswick, NJ: Rutgers University Press, 2005.

Bennett, Paula, ed. *Nineteenth-Century American Women Poets.* Oxford: Blackwell, 1997.

Berg, Stephen, and Robert Mezey, eds. *Naked Poetry: Recent American Poetry in Open Forms.* Indianapolis: Bobbs-Merrill, 1969.

Bierhorst, John, ed. *In the Trail of the Wind: American Indian Poems and Ritual Orations.* New York: Farrar, Straus and Giroux, 1971.

Hall, Donald, and Robert Pack, eds. *New Poets of England and America.* New York: Meridian, 1957.

Hollander, John, ed. *American Poetry: The Nineteenth Century.* Vol. 1, *Philip Freneau to Walt Whitman.* New York: Library of America, 1993.

———, ed. American Poetry: The Nineteenth Century. Vol. 2, Herman Melville to Trumbull Stickney; American Indian Poetry; Folk Songs and Spirituals. New York: Library of America, 1993.

Honey, Maureen, ed. *Shadowed Dreams: Women's Poetry of the Harlem Renaissance.* New Brunswick, NJ: Rutgers University Press, 1989.

Hoover, Paul, ed. *Postmodern American Poetry: A Norton Anthology.* New York: Norton, 1994.

Jarman, Mark, and David Mason, eds. *Rebel Angels: 25 Poets of the New Formalism.* Brownsville, OR: Story Line, 1996.

Lehman, David, ed. *The Best American Poetry.* Annual series, 17 vols. to date. New York: Scribners, 1988–.

Mandelbaum, Allan, and Robert Richardson, eds. *Three Centuries of American Poetry, 1620–1923.* New York: Bantam, 1999.

McClatchy, J.D., ed. *The Vintage Book of Contemporary American Poetry.* New York: Vintage, 1990.

Messerli, Douglas, ed. *The Language Poetries: An Anthology.* New York: New Directions, 1987.

———, ed. *From the Other Side of the Century: A New American Poetry 1960–1990.* Los Angeles: Sun and Moon, 1994.

Nelson, Cary, ed. *Anthology of Modern American Poetry.* New York: Oxford University Press, 2000.

Niatum, Duane, ed. *Harper's Anthology of Twentieth-Century Native American Poetry.* San Francisco: Harpers, 1988.

Parini, Jay, ed. *The Columbia Anthology of American Poetry.* New York: Columbia University Press, 1995.

Poulin, A., ed. *Contemporary American Poetry.* 5th ed. Boston: Houghton Mifflin, 1991.

Ramazani, Jahan, et al., eds. *The Norton Anthology of Modern and Contemporary Poetry.* New York: Norton, 2004.

Robinson, William Henry, ed. *Early Black American Poets.* Dubuque, IA: Wm. C. Brown Company, 1969.

Rothenberg, Jerome, ed. *Revolution of the Word: A New Gathering of American Avant Garde Poetry, 1914–1945.* New York: Seabury, 1974.

———, ed. *Shaking the Pumpkin: Traditional Poetry of the Indian North Americas.* New York: Alfred van der Marck, 1986.

Schwartz, Leonard, Joseph Donahue, and Edward Foster, eds. *Primary Trouble: An Anthology of Contemporary American Poetry.* Jersey City: Talisman House, 1996.

Silliman, Ron, ed. *In the American Tree.* Orono, ME: National Poetry Foundation, 1986.

Sloan, Mary Margaret, ed. *Moving Borders: Three Decades of Innovative Writing by Women.* Jersey City: Talisman House, 1998.

Swann, Brian, ed. *Native American Songs and Poems: An Anthology.* Mineola, NY: Dover, 1996.

Untermeyer, Louis, ed. *Early American Poets.* Lincoln, NE: iUniverse, 2001.

Vendler, Helen, ed. *Contemporary American Poetry.* Cambridge, MA: Harvard University Press, 1985.

Wegelin, O, ed. *Early American Poetry: 1650–1799.* Peter Smith, 1988.

Weinberger, Eliot, ed. *American Poetry Since 1950: Innovators and Outsiders.* New York: Marsilio, 1993.

Wood, Marcus, ed. *The Poetry of Slavery: An Anglo-American Anthology, 1764–1865.* New York: Oxford University Press, 2004.

Anthologies of Essays by Poets on Poetry

Allen, Donald, and Warren Tallman, eds. *The Poetics of the New American Poetry.* New York: Grove, 1973.

Bellamy, Joe David, ed. *American Poetry Observed: Poets on Their Work.* Urbana: University of Illinois Press, 1984.

Finch, Annie, ed. *After New Formalism: Poets on Form, Narrative and Tradition.* Ashland, OR: Story Line, 1999.

Friebert, Stuart, and David Young, eds. *A Field Guide to Contemporary Poetry and Poetics* (New York: Longman, 1980)

McCorkle, James, ed. *Conversant Essays: Contemporary Poets on Poetry.* Detroit: Wayne State University Press, 1990.

Critical Studies

Altieri, Charles. *Enlarging the Temple: New Directions in Contemporary American Poetry.* Lewisburg, PA: Bucknell University Press, 1979.

———. *Self and Sensibility in Contemporary American Poetry.* New York: Cambridge University Press, 1984.

Anderson, Elliot, and Mary Kinzie, eds. *The Little Magazine in America: A Modern Documentary History.* Yonkers, NY: Pushcart, 1978.

Baker Dorothy Z., ed. *Poetics in the Poem: Critical Essays on American Self-Reflexive Poetry.* New York: Peter Lang, 1997.

Beach, Christopher. *The ABC of Influence: Ezra Pound and the Remaking of American Poetic Tradition.* Berkeley: University of California Press, 1992.

Bennett, Paula Bernat. *Poets in the Public Sphere: The Emancipatory Project of American Women's Poetry, 1800–1900*

Bernstein, Charles. *Content's Dream: Essays 1975–1984.* Los Angeles: Sun and Moon Press, 1986.

———, ed. *Close Listening: Poetry and the Performed Word.* New York: Oxford University Press, 1998.

Bigelow, Gordon. *Rhetoric and American Poetry of the Early National Period.* University of Florida monographs, Humanities. Gainesville: University of Florida Press, 1960.

Blasing, Mutlu K. *American Poetry: The Rhetoric of Its Forms.* New Haven, CT: Yale University Press, 1987.

Bly, Robert. *American Poetry: Wildness and Domesticity.* New York: Harper & Row, 1990.

Bogan, Louise. *Achievement in American Poetry.* Chicago: Gateway Editions, 1951.

Bolden, Tony. *Afro-Blue: Improvisations in African American Poetry and Culture.* Urbana: University of Illinois Press, 2003.

Bove, Paul A. *Destructive Poetics: Heidegger and Modern American Poetry.* New York: Columbia, 1980.

Breslin, James. *From Modern to Contemporary: American Poetry, 1945–1965.* Chicago: University of Chicago Press, 1985.

Brooks, Cleanth. *The Well Wrought Urn: Studies in the Structure of Poetry.* New York: Harvest/HBJ, 1956.

———. *Modern Poetry and the Tradition.* Chapel Hill: University of North Carolina Press, 1939. Revised edition, New York: Oxford University Press, 1965.

Brown, Fahamisha P. *Performing the Word: African American Poetry as Vernacular Culture.* New Brunswick, NJ: Rutgers University Press, 1999.

Bush, Andrew. *The Routes of Modernity: Spanish American Poetry from the Early Eighteenth to the Mid-Nineteenth Century.* Bucknell Studies in Latin American Literature and Theory. Lewisburg, PA: Bucknell University Press, 2002.

Byers, Thomas. *What I Cannot Say: Self, Word, and World in Whitman, Stevens, and Merwin.* Urbana: University of Illinois Press, 1989.

Cambon, Glauco. *The Inclusive Flame: Studies in Modern American Poetry.* Bloomington: Indiana University Press, 1965.

Comens, Bruce. *Apocalypse and After: Modern Strategy and Postmodern Tactics in Pound, Williams, and Zukofsky.* Tuscaloosa: University of Alabama Press, 1995.

Conte, Joseph. *Unending Design: The Forms of Postmodern Poetry.* Ithaca, NY: Cornell University Press, 1991.

Costello, Bonnie. *Shifting Ground: Reinventing Landscape in Modern American Poetry.* Cambridge, MA: Harvard University Press, 2003.

Cushman, Stephen. *Fictions of Form in American Poetry.* Princeton, NJ: Princeton University Press, 1993.

Daniels, Jim, ed. *Letters to America: Contemporary American Poetry on Race.* Detroit: Wayne State University Press, 1995.

Davidson, Michael. *The San Francisco Renaissance: Poetics and Community at Mid-Century.* New York: Cambridge University Press, 1989.

———. Ghostlier Demarcations: Modern Poetry and the Material Word. Berkeley: University of California Press, 1997.

Davis, Alex, and Lee M. Jenkins. *Locations of Literary Modernism: Region and Nation in British and American Modernist Poetry.* New York: Cambridge University Press, 2000.

Davison, Peter. *The Fading Smile: Poets in Boston, from Robert Frost to Robert Lowell to Sylvia Plath.* New York: Knopf, 1994.

Diehl, Joanne. *Women Poets and the American Sublime.* Bloomington: Indiana University Press, 1990.

Diggory, Terrence, and Stephen Paul Miller, eds. *The Scene of My Selves: New Work on New York School Poets.* Orono, ME: National Poetry Foundation, 2001.

Duke, Charles R., and Sall A. Jacobsen, eds. *Poets' Perspectives: Reading, Writing, and Teaching Poetry.* Portsmouth, NH: Boynton/Cook, 1992.

DuPlessis, Rachel Blau, Albert Gelpi, and Ross Posnock, eds. *Genders, Races, and Religious Cultures in Modern American Poetry, 1908–1934.* Cambridge Studies in American Literature and Culture. New York: Cambridge University Press, 2001.

Edelberg, Cynthia D., ed. *Scars: American Poetry in the Face of Violence.* Tuscaloosa: University of Alabama Press, 1995.

Erkkila, Betsy, and Jay Grossman, eds. *Breaking Bounds: Whitman and American Cultural Studies*. New York: Oxford University Press, 1996.

Evers, Larry, and Felipe S. Molina. *Yaqui Deer Songs, Maso Bwikam: A Native American Poetry*. Tucson: Sun Tracks with University of Arizona Press, 1987.

Ferguson, Suzanne. *Jarrell, Bishop, Lowell, & Co.: Middle Generation Poets in Context*. Knoxville: University of Tennessee Press, 2003.

Fink, Thomas. *'A Different Sense of Power': Problems of Community in Late-Twentieth-Century U.S. Poetry*. Madison, NJ: Fairleigh Dickinson University Press, 2001.

Finkelstein, Norman. *The Utopian Moment in Contemporary American Poetry*. Lewisburg, PA: Bucknell University Press, 1993.

Fletcher, Angus. *A New Theory for American Poetry: Democracy, the Environment, and the Future of Imagination*. Cambridge, MA: Harvard University Press, 2004.

Foster, Jeanne. *A Music of Grace: The Sacred in Contemporary American Poetry*. New York: Peter Lang, 1995.

Fraser, Kathleen. *Translating the Unspeakable: Poetry and the Innovative Necessity*. Tuscaloosa: Alabama University Press, 2000.

Fredman, Stephen. *Poets' Prose: The Crisis in American Verse*. Cambridge: Cambridge University Press, 1990.

French, William P. *Afro-American Poetry, 1760–1975*. Detroit: Gale, 1979.

Fussell, Edwin. *Lucifer in Harness: American Meter, Metaphor, and Diction*. Princeton, NJ: Princeton University Press, 1973.

Gage, John. *In the Arresting Eye: The Rhetoric of Imagism*. Baton Rouge: Louisiana State University Press, 1981.

Gelpi, Albert. *A Coherent Splendor: The American Poetic Renaissance 1910–1950*. Cambridge: Cambridge University Press, 1990.

———. The Tenth Muse: The Psyche of the American Poet. Cambridge: Cambridge University Press, 1991.

Gelpi, Albert, Elisa New, and Ross Posnock, eds. *The Regenerate Lyric: Theology and Innovation in American Poetry*. Cambridge Studies in American Literature and Culture. Cambridge: Cambridge University Press, 1993.

Gelpi, Albert, Jeffrey Hammond, and Ross Posnock, eds. *The American Puritan Elegy: A Literary and Cultural Study*. Cambridge Studies in American Literature and Culture. Cambridge: Cambridge University Press, 2000.

Gelpi, Albert, Ross Posnock, and John P. McWilliams, Jr., eds. *The American Epic: Transforming a Genre, 1770–1860. Cambridge Studies in American Literature and Culture*. Cambridge: Cambridge University Press, 1989.

Gilbert, Sandra. *Shakespeare's Sisters: Feminist Essays on Women Poets*. Bloomington: Indiana University Press, 1981.

Golding, Alan. *From Outlaw to Classic: Canons in American Poetry*. Madison: University of Wisconsin Press, 1995.

Gray, Jeffrey. *Mastery's End: Travel and Postwar American Poetry*. Athens: University of Georgia Press, 2005.

Gregory, Elizabeth. *Quotation and Modern American Poetry: "Imaginary Gardens with Real Toads."*

Hambrick-Stowe, Charles E., ed. *Early New England Meditative Poetry: Anne Bradstreet and Edward Taylor*. Sources of American Spirituality, No. 15. New York: Paulist Press, 1989.

Hammond, Jeffrey A. *Sinful Self, Saintly Self: The Puritan Experience of Poetry*. Athens: University of Georgia Press, 1993.

Hartman, Charles O. *Free Verse: An Essay on Prosody*. Princeton, NJ: Princeton University Press, 1980.

———. *Jazz Text: Voice and Improvisation in Poetry, Jazz and Song*. Princeton, NJ: Princeton University Press, 1991.

Hinton, Laura, and Cynthia Hogue (eds.). *We Who Love to Be Astonished: Experimental Women's Writing and Performance Poetics*. Tuscaloosa: University Alabama Press, 2002

Holden, Jonathan. *Style and Authenticity in Postmodern Poetry*. Columbia: University of Missouri Press, 1986.

———. *The Fate of American Poetry*. Athens: University of Georgia Press, 1991.

Howard, Richard. *Alone with America: Essays on the Art of Poetry in the United States since 1950*. New York: Atheneum, 1980.

Huk, Romana, ed. *Assembling Alternatives: Reading Postmodern Poetries Transnationally*. Middletown, CT: Wesleyan University Press 2003.

Kalaidjian, Walter. *Languages of Liberation: The Social Text in Contemporary American Poetry*. New York: Columbia, 1989.

Kalstone, David. *Five Temperaments: Elizabeth Bishop, Robert Lowell, James Merrill, Adrienne Rich, John Ashbery*. New York: Oxford University Press, 1977.

———. *Becoming a Poet: Elizabeth Bishop with Marianne Moore and Robert Lowell*. New York: Farrar, Straus, Giroux, 1989.

Keller, Lynn. *Forms of Expansion: Recent Long Poems by Women*. Chicago: University of Chicago Press, 1997.

Keller, Lynn and Cristanne Miller, eds. *Feminist Measures: Soundings in Poetry and Theory*. Ann Arbor: University of Michigan Press, 1994.

Kinzie, Mary. *The Cure of Poetry in an Age of Prose: Moral Essays on the Poet's Calling*. Chicago: University of Chicago Press, 1993.

Kramer, Aaron. *The Prophetic Tradition in American Poetry, 1835–1900*. Rutherford, NJ: Fairleigh Dickinson University Press, 1968.

Lazer, Hank. *Opposing Poetries*. Vol. 1, *Issues and Institutions*. Evanston, IL: Northwestern University Press, 1996.

———. *Opposing Poetries*. Vol. 2, *Readings*. Evanston, IL: Northwestern University Press, 1996.

Lee, A. Robert, ed. *Nineteenth-Century American Poetry*. Totowa, NJ: Barnes & Noble, 1985.

Lentricchia, Frank. *Modernist Quartet*. Cambridge: Cambridge University Press, 1994.

Leo, John R., and James Ruppert. *Guide to American Poetry Explication*. Boston, MA: G.K. Hall, 1989.

Libby, Anthony. *Mythologies of Nothing: Mystical Death in American Poetry, 1940-1970*. Urbana: University of Illinois Press, 1984.

Loeffelholz, Mary. *From School to Salon: Reading Nineteenth-Century American Women's Poetry*.

Longenbach, James. *Modernist Poetics of History: Pound, Eliot, and a Sense of the Past*. Princeton, NJ: Princeton, University Press, 1987.

———. *Modern Poetry After Modernism*. New York: Oxford University Press, 1997.

———. *The Resistance to Poetry.* Chicago: Chicago University Press, 2004.

Mackey, Nathaniel. *Discrepant Engagements: Dissonance, Cross-Culturality, and Experimental Writing.* New York: Cambridge University Press, 1994.

Martin, Robert K. *The Homosexual Tradition in American Poetry.* Austin: University of Texas Press, 1979.

McClatchy, J.D. *White Paper: On Contemporary American Poetry.* New York: Columbia University Press, 1989

———. *Twenty Questions.* New York: Columbia University Press, 1998.

McCorkle, James. *The Still Performance: Writing, Self, and Interconnection in Five Postmodern American Poets.* Charlottesville: University Press Virginia, 1989.

Meserole, Harrison T., ed. *Seventeenth-Century American Poetry.* New York: New York University Press, 1968.

Miller, J. Hillis. *Poets of Reality.* New York: Belknap, 1965.

———. *The Linguistic Moment: From Wordsworth to Stevens.* Princeton, NJ: Princeton, University Press, 1987.

Miller, Perry. *The American Puritans: Their Prose and Poetry.* Peter Smith, 1959.

Morris, Timothy. *Becoming Canonical in American Poetry.* Urbana: University of Illinois Press, 1995.

Myers, Jack, and David Wojahn. eds. *A Profile of Twentieth-Century American Poetry.* Carbondale: Southern Illinois University Press, 1991.

Nelson, Cary. *Our Last First Poets: Vision and History in Contemporary American Poetry.* Urbana: University of Illinois Press, 1984.

———. *Repression and Recovery: Modern American Poetry and the Politics of Cultural Memory, 1910–1945.* Madison: University of Wisconsin Press, 1989.

New, Elisa. *The Regenerate Lyric: Theology and Innovation in American Poetry.* Cambridge: Cambridge University Press, 1993.

———. The Line's Eye: Poetic Experience, American Sight. Cambridge, MA: Harvard University Press, 1998.

Nielsen, Aldon Lynn. *Reading Race: White American Poets and the Racial Discourse of the Twentieth Century.* Athens: University of Georgia Press, 1988.

———. *Black Chant: Languages of African-American Postmodernism.* New York: Cambridge University Press, 1997.

———, ed. Reading Race in American Poetry: An Area of Act. Urbana: University of Illinois Press, 2000.

Oser, Lee. *T.S. Eliot and American Poetry.* Columbia: University of Missouri Press, 1998.

Ostriker, Alice. *Stealing the Language: The Emergence of Women's Poetry in America.* Boston: Beacon Press, 1986. [CE—OK—JG]

Parini, Jay, ed. *Columbia History of American Poetry: From the Puritans to Our Time.* New York: MJF, 1998.

Paul, Sherman. *Olson's Push: Origin, Black Mountain, and Recent American Poetry.* Baton Rouge: Louisiana State University Press, 1978.

Pearce, Roy Harvey. *The Continuity of American Poetry.* Princeton, NJ: Princeton University Press, 1961. Revised edition, Middletown, CT: Wesleyan University Press, 1987.

Perelman, Bob. *The Marginalization of Poetry: Language, Writing, and Literary History.* Princeton, NJ: Princeton University Press 1996.

Perkins, David. *A History of Modern Poetry: From the 1890's to the High Modernist Mode.* New York: Belknap, 1976.

———. *A History of Modern Poetry: Modernism and After.* New York: Belknap, 1989.

Perloff, Marjorie. *The Dance of the Intellect: Studies in the Poetry of the Pound Tradition.* New York: Cambridge University Press, 1985.

———. *Poetic License: Essays on Modernist and Postmodernist Lyric.* Evanston, IL: Northwestern University Press, 1990.

———. *Radical Artifice: Writing Poetry in the Age of Media.* Chicago: University of Chicago Press, 1991.

———. *Wittgenstein's Ladder: Poetic Language and the Strangeness of the Ordinary.* Chicago: University of Chicago Press, 1996.

———. *The Poetics of Indeterminacy: Rimbaud to Cage.* Evanston, IL: Northwestern University Press, 2000.

———. *21st-Century Modernism: The "New" Poetics.* Malden, MA: Blackwell, 2002.

Phillips, Robert. *The Confessional Poets.* Carbondale: Southern Illinois University Press, 1973.

Pinsky, Robert. *The Situation of Poetry.* Princeton, NJ: Princeton University Press, 1976.

———. *Poetry and the World.* New York: Ecco, 1988.

Poirier, Richard. *Poetry and Pragmatism.* Cambridge, MA: Harvard University Press 1992.

Quartermain, Peter. *Disjunctive Poetics: From Gertrude Stein and Louis Zukofsky to Susan Howe.* New York: Cambridge University Press, 1992.

Ramazani, Jahan. *Poetry of Mourning: The Modern Elegy from Hardy to Heaney.* Chicago: University of Chicago Press, 1994.

Rasula, Jed. *The American Poetry Wax Museum: Reality Effects, 1940–1990.* Urbana: National Council of Teachers of English, 1996.

Redmond, Eugene. *Drumvoices: The Mission of Afro-American Poetry: A Critical History.* Garden City, NY: Anchor Press, 1976.

Reinfeld, Linda. *Language Poetry: Writing as Rescue.* Baton Rouge: Louisiana State University Press, 1992.

Revell, Peter. *Quest in Modern American Poetry.* London: Vision Press, 1981.

Rieke, Alison. *The Senses of Nonsense.* Iowa City: University of Iowa Press, 1992.

Rifkin, Libbie. *Career Moves: Olson, Creeley, Zukofsky, Berrigan, and the American Avant-Garde.* Madison: University of Wisconsin Press, 2000.

Rosenthal, M.L. *The New Poets.* New York: Oxford University Press, 1967.

Scheick, William J., and JoElla Doggett. *Seventeenth-Century American Poetry: A Reference Guide.* Boston: G.K. Hall, 1977. Ross, Andrew. The Failure of Modernism: Symptoms of American Poetry. New York: Columbia University Press, 1986.

Schwartz, Sanford. *The Matrix of Modernism: Pound, Eliot, and Early Twentieth-Century Thought.* Princeton, NJ: Princeton University Press, 1988.

Schweitzer, Ivy. *The Work of Self-Representation: Lyric Poetry in Colonial New England.* Chapel Hill: University of North Carolina Press 1991.

Selinger, Eric M. *What Is It Then between Us? Traditions of Love in American Poetry.* Ithaca, NY: Cornell University Press, 1998.

Shetley, Vernon. *After the Death of Poetry: Poet and Audience in Contemporary America.* Durham, NC: Duke University Press, 1993.

Shucard, Alan, William J. Sullivan, and Fred S. Moramarco. *Modern American Poetry, 1865–1950.* Boston: Twayne, 1989.

Shields, David S. *Oracles of Empire: Poetry, Politics, and Commerce in British America, 1690–1750.* Chicago: University of Chicago Press, 1990.

Silverman, Kenneth, ed. *Colonial American Poetry.* New York: Hafner, 1968.

Simpson, Megan. *Poetic Epistemologies: Gender and Knowing in Women's Language-Oriented Writing.* Albany: State University of New York Press, 2000.

Smethurst, James E. *The New Red Negro: The Literary Left and African American Poetry, 1930–1946.* New York: Oxford University Press, 1999.

Spiegelman, Willard. *The Didactic Muse: Scenes of Instruction in Contemporary American Poetry.* Princeton, NJ: Princeton University Press, 1989.

———. *How Poets See the World: The Art of Description in Contemporary Poetry.* New York: Oxford University Press, 2005.

Stauffer, Donald B. *A Short History of American Poetry.* New York: Dutton, 1974.

Steinman, Lisa. *Made in America: Science, Technology, and American Modernist Poets.* New Haven, CT: Yale University Press, 1987.

Stetson, Erlene. *Black Sister: Poetry by Black American Women, 1746–1980.* Bloomington: Indiana University Press, 1981.

Sweet, Timothy. *American Georgics: Economy and Environment in Early American Literature.* Philadelphia: University of Pennsylvania Press, 2002.

Taggart, John. *Songs of Degrees: Essays on Contemporary Poetry and Poetics.* Tuscaloosa: University of Alabama Press, 1994.

Travisano, Thomas. *Midcentury Quartet: Bishop, Lowell, Jarrell, Berryman and the Making of a Postmodern Aesthetic.* Charlottesville: University Press Virginia, 1999.

Turco, Lewis P. *Visions and Revisions of American Poetry.* Fayetteville: University of Arkansas Press, 1986.

Vendler, Helen. *Part of Nature, Part of Us: Modern American Poets.* Cambridge, MA: Harvard University Press, 1980.

———. *The Music of What Happens: Poems, Poets, Critics.* Cambridge, MA: Harvard University Press, 1988.

———. *The Given and the Made: Strategies of Poetic Redefinition.* Cambridge, MA: Harvard University Press, 1995.

Vincent, John Emil. *Queer Lyrics: Difficulty and Closure in American Poetry.* New York: Palgrave Macmillan, 2002.

Von Hallberg, Robert. *American Poetry and Culture, 1945–1980.* Cambridge, MA: Harvard University Press, 1985.

Waggoner, Hyatt H. *American Visionary Poetry.* Baton Rouge: Louisiana State University Press, 1982.

Walker, Cheryl. *Masks Outrageous and Austere: Culture, Psyche, and Persona in Modern Women Poets.* Bloomington: Indiana University Press, 1991.

Ward, Geoffrey. *Statutes of Liberty: The New York School of Poets.* New York: St. Martin's Press, 1988. Second edition, New York: Palgrave, 2001.

Watten, Barrett. *Total Syntax.* Carbondale: Southern Illinois University Press, 1984.

White, Peter, ed. *Puritan Poets and Poetics: Seventeenth-Century American Poetry in Theory and Practice.* University Park: Pennsylvania State University Press, 1985.

Williams, Anne. *Prophetic Strain: The Greater Lyric in the Eighteenth Century.* Chicago: University of Chicago Press, 1984.

Williams, Miller. *Patterns of Poetry.* Baton Rouge: Louisiana State University Press, 1986.

Woods, Tim. *The Poetics of the Limit: Ethics and Politics in Modern and Contemporary American Poetry.* New York: Palgrave Macmillan, 2002.

Wilson, Rob. *American Sublime: The Genealogy of a Poetic Genre.* Madison: University of Wisconsin Press, 1991.

Zillman, Lawrence J. *The Art and Craft of Poetry.* New York: Macmillan, 1966.

Reference Works

Chapman, Dorothy. *Index to Black Poetry.* Boston: G.K. Hall, 1974.

Conte, Joseph, ed. *Dictionary of Literary Biography.* Vol. 165, *American Poets Since World War II, Fourth Series.* Detroit: Gale Research, 1996.

———, ed. *Dictionary of Literary Biography.* Vol. 169, *American Poets Since World War II, Fifth Series.* Detroit: Gale Research, 1996.

A Directory of American Poets and Fiction Writers. New York: Poets & Writers, distributed by Pushcart/W.W. Norton, 1997.

Ellmann, Richard, ed. *The New Oxford Book of American Verse.* New York: Oxford University Press, 1976.

Haerens, Margaret, and Christine Slovey, eds. *Poetry Criticism.* Vols. 1–16. Detroit: Gale Research, 1991–1997.

Hazen, Edith P., ed. *The Columbia Granger's Index to Poetry.* 10th ed. New York: Columbia University Press, 1994.

Katz, William, and Linda Sternberg Katz, eds. *The Columbia Granger's Index to Poetry Anthologies.* 2nd ed. New York: Columbia University Press, 1994.

Katz, William, Linda Sternberg Katz, and Ester Crain, eds. *The Columbia Granger's Guide to Poetry Anthologies.* New York: Columbia University Press, 1994.

Leo, John R., and James Ruppert. *Guide to American Poetry Explication.* Vols. 1 and 2 Boston: G.K. Hall, 1989.

Pater, Alan F., ed. *Anthology of Magazine Verse and Yearbook of American Poetry 1997.* Palm Springs: Monitor Book, 1997.

Preminger, Alex, and T.V.F. Brogen, eds. *The New Princeton Encyclopedia of Poetry & Poetics.* Princeton, NJ: Princeton University Press, 1993.

Quartermain, Peter, ed. *Dictionary of Literary Biography.* Vol. 54, *American Poets, 1880–1945, Third Series* Detroit: Gale Research, 1987

Websites

Academy of American Poets, http://www.poets.org/
The American Verse Project, http://www.hti.umich.edu/a/amverse/
Electronic Poetry Center, SUNY–Buffalo, http://www.epc.buffalo.edu
The Internet Poetry Archive, http://www.ibiblio.org/ipa/
The Library of Congress Poetry and Literature Center, http://www.loc.gov/poetry/
Modern American Poetry, http://www.english.uiuc.edu/maps/index.htm
Project Bartleby, http://www.bartleby.com
Twentieth-Century Poetry in English, http://www.lit.kobe-u.ac.jp/~hishika/20c_poet.htm

Index

About the Editors and Contributors

Editors:

JEFFREY GRAY is Associate Professor of English at Seton Hall University, New Jersey, where he teaches courses in American poetry, postcolonial literature, and literary theory. A two-time Fulbright Award recipient, he is author of *Mastery's End: Travel and Postwar American Poetry* (University of Georgia Press, 2005) and contributor to numerous journals, including *Callaloo, Contemporary Literature, Papers on Language and Literature,* and *Profession.* A Seattle native, he has lived and taught in Latin America, the South Pacific, Asia, and Europe.

JAMES MCCORKLE, Adjunct Professor at Hobart and William Smith Colleges, is a poet and essayist. His collection of poems, *Evidences,* received the *American Poetry Review*/Honickman Award in 2003; he has also received fellowships from the National Endowment for the Arts and the Ingram Merrill Foundation, as well as the first Campbell Corner Poetry Award from Sarah Lawrence College. With an MFA and Ph.D. from the University of Iowa, he is the editor of *Conversant Essays: Contemporary Poets on Poetry* and the author of *Still Performance,* a study of five postmodern poets, as well as numerous articles on contemporary poets, poetics, and the visual arts.

MARY MCALEER BALKUN is Associate Professor of English and Chairperson of the English Department at Seton Hall University, New Jersey. Her research interests include material culture, gender issues, and constructions of identity in early American literature. She has published articles on Phillis Wheatley, Sarah Kemble Knight, Walt Whitman, F. Scott Fitzgerald, and William Faulkner. Her book *The American Counterfeit: Studies in Authenticity, Identity, and Material Culture* is forthcoming from University of Alabama Press.

Contributors:

ANTONY ADOLF is an independent scholar and creative writer working in Chicago. He has published numerous essays on modern and contemporary poetry and poetics, multilingualism, the long poem, and philosophy, and he is the recipient of Marjorie Holmes Award for literary research and the Van Kuren Award in English Studies. In 2004 he was nominated for a Pushcart Prize for his creative work. His long poem *The Corpus Hermeticum: A Neo-Vorticist Trans-Substantiation* was published in 2005.

JOE AHEARN is a writer living in Dallas, Texas. His most recent books of poetry include *Five Fictions* (Sulphur River Review Press, 2003) and *synthetik* (Firewheel Editions, 2002). In 2001 he was named a Distinguished Poet by the City of Dallas.

ELISABETH C. AIKEN is Visiting Instructor at Western Carolina University. Her research interests include nineteenth-century American literature, women's literature, and composition and rhetoric studies. She divides her time between the classroom and various writing projects.

HÉLÈNE AJI is Associate Professor of American Poetry at the Université de Paris–Sorbonne. She is the author of *Ezra Pound et William Carlos Williams: pour une poétique américaine* (2001) and *William Carlos Williams: un plan d'action* (2004), and the editor of *Ezra Pound and Referentiality* (2003).

DAN ALBERGOTTI is Assistant Professor of English at Coastal Carolina University. His poems have appeared in *Meridian, Mid-American Review,* the *Virginia Quarterly Review,* and other journals. He has held scholarships at the Sewanee and Bread Loaf writers' conferences and a fellowship at the Virginia Center for the Creative Arts.

KAREN ALEXANDER is a Ph.D. candidate and the Fourth-Year Fellow in the English Department at University College, London. Her Ph.D. thesis is titled "Minimalism in Twentieth-Century American Writing." Her research interests include modernism, contemporary American literature, experimental fiction and poetry, relations between the visual arts and literature, and philosophy of literature.

SIMONE A. JAMES ALEXANDER is Assistant Professor in the Department of African American Studies at Seton Hall University, New Jersey, where she teaches courses in African, African American and Caribbean literatures. She is the author of *Mother Imagery in the Novels of Afro-Caribbean Women* (University of Missouri Press, 2001), and "Walking on Thin Ice: The Il/legitimacy of Race and Racial Issues in the Classroom" in *The Teacher's Body: Embodiment, Identity, and Authority in the Academy* (SUNY Press, 2003). Her articles have appeared in such journals as *African Literature Association Bulletin, Langston Hughes Colloquy, Middle Atlantic Writers Association Review*, and *Revista Interamericana.*

MAUREEN ANDERSON is currently completing her Ph.D. in Comparative Literature and Linguistics at Illinois State University. She has published extensively on American literature, feminist literature, and the rhetoric of oppressive language. In 2002 she earned Best Thesis in Arts and Sciences for her thesis, *Poetic Resistance: Mercy Otis Warren's Poetry of the American Revolution.* The title of her dissertation is *"Witch" as Metaphor.*

MICHAEL ANDERSON is currently an Adjunct at New Jersey City University. Since completing his magister artium at Eberhard-Karls-Universität Tübingen, he has specialized in fin de siècle literature of America and the Continent, the Great Depression, and sociopolitical approaches to art.

STEVE ANDERSON is Professor of English at the University of Arkansas at Little Rock. His research interests are in the film and literature of the Vietnam War. He has also published fiction. In 2004 he received the university-wide award for teaching excellence.

ROBERT ARCHAMBEAU is Associate Professor of English at Lake Forest College. A poet and critic, his books include *Home and Variations* (2004), *Vectors* (2001), *Citation Suite* (1999), and *Word Play Place: Essays on the Poetry of John Matthias* (1998).

JULIE BUCKNER ARMSTRONG is Assistant Professor of English at University of South Florida–St. Petersburg. She is co-editor of *Teaching the American Civil Rights Movement: Freedom's Bittersweet Song* (Routledge, 2002) and is currently working on a book titled *Mary Turner and the Rhetoric of Lynching.*

ROBYN ART is Adjunct Professor of English and Creative Writing at Jersey City University and Felician College. She's the author of the poetry chapbooks *Degrees of Being There* (Boneworld Press 2003) and *No Longer a Blonde* (forthcoming Boneworld 2005.) She has received four Pushcart Prize nominations, and was a finalist in 2003.

JUSTIN ASKINS is Professor of English at Radford University. He has published many poems, essays, articles, book reviews, and photographs in a variety of newspapers and magazines. His writings focus mainly on the natural world and issues concerning its survival.

RISE B. AXELROD is Professor of English and Director of Composition at the University of California, Riverside. Her books include *The St. Martin's Guide to Writing* (7th edition, 2004), *Reading Critically, Writing Well* (7th edition, 2005), and the *Thomson Guide to Poetry* (forthcoming 2007).

STEVEN GOULD AXELROD is Professor of English at the University of California, Riverside. He is the author of *Robert Lowell: Life and Art* (Princeton University Press 1978) and *Sylvia Plath: The Wound and the Cure of Words* (Johns Hopkins University Press, 1990). He is co-editor (with Camille Roman and Thomas Travisano) of *The New Anthology of American Poetry, Volumes 1 and 2* (Rutgers University Press, 2003, 2005).

DAVID BAKER holds the Thomas B. Fordham Chair of English at Denison University and is also poetry editor of the *Kenyon Review.* His most recent books are *Changeable Thunder* (poems, 2001) and *Heresy and the Ideal: On Contemporary Poetry* (criticism, 2000).

MARY MCALEER BALKUN is Associate Professor of English and Chairperson of the English Department at Seton Hall University, New Jersey. Her research interests include material culture, gender issues, and constructions of identity in early American literature. She has published articles on Phillis Wheatley, Sarah Kemble Knight, Walt Whitman, F. Scott Fitzgerald, and William Faulkner. Her book, *The American Counterfeit: Studies in Authenticity, Identity, and Material Culture,* is forthcoming from University of Alabama Press.

SUSAN BARBA is a doctoral candidate in Comparative Literature at Harvard University. She is completing a dissertation on Russian, Armenian, English, and American poetry of the 1930s. In 2002 she won the Bowdoin Prize at Harvard for distinguished graduate student essays in English.

RACHEL BARENBLAT is Executive Director of Inkberry, a literary arts center in North Adams, Massachusetts. She has written for the *Oxford Encyclopedia of American Literature* and the *Companion to 20th-Century American Poetry.* She is author of two poetry chapbooks, most recently *What Stays* (Bennington Writing Seminars Alumni Chapbook Series, 2002).

JONATHAN N. BARRON is Associate Professor of English at the University of Southern Mississippi. He has written extensively on American poetry and Jewish American poetry and is the editor of the *Robert Frost Review.* In addition, he has edited *Jewish American Poetry: Poems, Commentary and Reflections* (2000), *Roads Not Taken: Rereading Robert Frost* (2000), and *New Formalist Poets* (DLB Vol. 282, 2003).

PATRICK BARRON is Assistant Professor of English at the University of Massachusetts, Boston. His publications include *Circle of Teeth: 55 Poems* (2000) and *Italian Environmental Literature: An Anthology* (2003). He is currently working on *The Selected Poetry and Prose of Andrea Zanzotto,* forthcoming from the University of Chicago Press in 2005.

DOUGLAS BASFORD, Lecturer in the writing seminars at Johns Hopkins University, has published essays on poetry and photography in *Chain, Multi-Ethnic Literature of the United States,* and *MLA Approaches to Teaching;* his poems have appeared in *can we have our ball back?, 32 Poems, 580 Split,* the *Sewanee Theological Review,* and elsewhere.

MICHAEL BASINSKI is Curator of the Poetry Collection of the University Libraries, the State University of New York at Buffalo. He has published more than thirty little books of poetry, and he frequently writes on Charles Bukowski, Gerald Locklin, and other underground poets.

ROBERT BATTISTINI is Assistant Professor of American Literature at Franklin & Marshall College in Lancaster, Pennsylvania.

IAN A. BETHELL BENNETT is Associate Professor in the Department of English at the University of Puerto Rico Rio Piedras campus. His work focuses on social history and literature in the French-, English-, and Spanish-speaking Caribbean.

PAULA BENNETT is Professor of English, Emerita, at Southern Illinois University at Carbondale. She has published widely in the field of nineteenth-century American women's poetry. Her latest book is *Poets in the Public Sphere: The Emancipatory Project of American Women's Poetry, 1800–1900* (Princeton, 2004). With Karen L. Kilcup, she has edited *Options for Teaching Nineteenth-Century American Poetry* for the MLA Options series (forthcoming).

CHARLES BERGER is Professor of English at Southern Illinois University. He is the author of *Forms of Farewell: The Late Poetry of Wallace Stevens* and many articles and reviews on modern and contemporary American poetry.

JASPER BERNES is Visiting Assistant Professor of English and Creative Writing at Hobart and William Smith Colleges. A selection of his poems appears in *The Iowa Anthology of New American Poetries* (2004).

ROBERT J. BERTHOLF is Charles D. Abbott Scholar of Poetry and the Arts in the Poetry Collection, the State University of New York at Buffalo. He has written on modern American and British poetry, is the co-editor of *The Letters of Robert Duncan and Denise Levertov*, and is editing an edition of the collected works of Robert Duncan.

JENNIFER BILLINGSLEY is Associate Dean of Continuing Education at MacMurray College in Jacksonville, Illinois. She directs a college program for the Illinois Department of Corrections while working toward a doctorate at Illinois State University.

CARMEN BIRKLE is Associate Professor of American Studies at the Johannes Gutenberg-Universität Mainz. She has taught as a guest professor at the University of Vienna and at Columbia University in New York City. She is the author of *Women's Stories of the Looking Glass* (1996) and *Migration – Miscegenation – Transculturation* (2003), and co-editor of *(Trans)Formations of Cultural Identity in the English-Speaking World* (1998), *Frauen auf der Spur* (2001), and *Sites of Ethnicity* (2004).

NICHOLAS BIRNS is Lecturer in English at New School University in New York. He is editor of *Antipodes* and has contributed to *Science Fiction Studies*, the *Hollins Critic*, and *Arizona Quarterly*. He is the author of *Understanding Anthony Powell* (University of South Carolina Press, 2004.).

S. BETH BISHOP is a poet and Adjunct Instructor of Writing at the University of Memphis and Memphis College of Art. Her work has appeared in *Crab Orchard Review, Greensboro Review, Quarterly West*, and other print journals, as well as in online literary publications such as *Exquisite Corpse* and *the Pedestal.* She received an AWP Intro Journals Award in 2001 for the poem "Self Portrait with Monkeys," and her poetry manuscript, *Shouldering Zero*, has been listed as a semifinalist for the Kathryn A. Morton/Sarabande Books Prize and other first-book awards.

CHANTAL BIZZINI lives in Paris, where she teaches Latin, Greek, and French for the Education Nationale and Comparative Literature for American University programs; she defended a doctoral dissertation in Comparative Literature on Ezra Pound and Hart Crane. Her forthcoming projects include Hart Crane's complete poetical works translated into French and an essay about Adrienne Rich's poetry.

LENORA P. BLOUIN, a bibliographer/librarian and former Head of Reference at the San Jose (CA) Main Library, has written books and articles on May Sarton including the bibliographic essay "The Stern Growth of a Lyric Poet" and "A Poet's Life." Her most recent book is *May Sarton: A Bibliography* (2000). She is a member of the National Coalition of Independent Scholars.

JUNE D. BOBB is Director of the Africana Studies Program and Associate Professor of English at Queens College (CUNY). The author of *Beating a Restless Drum: The Poetics of Kamau Brathwaite and Derek Walcott*, she is currently working on a study of strategies of resistance in the works of contemporary Caribbean women poets.

DEBORAH BOGEN is a writer whose poetry and reviews have appeared in numerous publications. Her chapbook, *Living by the Children's Cemetery*, was chosen by Edward Hirsch as the 2002 ByLine Press Competition winner.

COLLEEN GLENNEY BOGGS is Assistant Professor of English and Women and Gender Studies at Dartmouth College. She is currently finishing a book manuscript, *American Translation and the Transatlantic Nation, 1773–1892.* Her most recent article, "Margaret Fuller's American Translation," appeared in *American Literature.*

WILLARD BOHN is Distinguished Professor of French and Comparative Literature at Illinois State University. He has published extensively on Dada and surrealism and is the author of *The Rise of Surrealism* (2002). His numerous writings on visual poetry include *The Aesthetics of Visual Poetry, 1914–1928* (1986, 1993) and *Modern Visual Poetry* (2001).

ENIKŐ BOLLOBÁS is Associate Professor of American Studies at Eötvös Loránd University, Budapest. She has written books and essays on American literature, especially modern and postmodern poetry, women writers, and canon theory. Her latest book is the comprehensive *History of American Literature* (2005), written in Hungarian.

MELBA JOYCE BOYD, Professor of African American Studies at Wayne State University, is the author of six books of poetry, two biographies, a documentary film, and thirty-three essays. She is a Fulbright Scholar (Germany, 1983–1984), and her poetry has been engraved in the Wright Museum of African American History in Detroit.

ELIZABETH BRADFIELD is a poet whose work has appeared or is forthcoming in the *Atlantic Monthly, Field, Epoch,* and other publications. She lives in Anchorage, Alaska, and works as a teacher, web designer, and naturalist.

BECKY BRADWAY is the author of a collection of creative nonfiction essays, *Pink Houses and Family Taverns* (Indiana University Press, 2002). She also edited *In the Middle of the Middle West: Literary Non-Fiction from the Heartland* (Indiana University Press, 2003), which was a finalist for the Great Lakes Booksellers Association Award. *Fishing for Polyester*, a creative nonfiction book, was a finalist for the Great Lakes American

Studies Association/Ohio University Press award in 2004. Her creative nonfiction anthology/textbook, *Creating Non-Fiction*, will be published by Bedford/St. Martins in 2006. Her fiction and nonfiction has been published in many magazines and anthologies.

MATTHEW C. BRENNAN, Professor of English at Indiana State University, is a poet and critic. In addition to two books of poems, he has published *Wordsworth, Turner, and Romantic Landscape* (1987) and *The Gothic Psyche* (1997). His work has appeared in *Sewanee Review*, *Georgia Review*, *Southern Quarterly*, and *South Dakota Review*.

DEBORAH BROWN is an Associate Professor of English and Program Coordinator for English Education at the University of Central Oklahoma in Edmond, Oklahoma. She teaches methods courses for prospective secondary English teachers and courses in young adult literature, advanced composition, and composition theory and research. Her publications include a chapter in *Censored Books II* (Ed. Nicholas J. Karolides) and articles in journals such as *the Journal of Adolescent and Adult Literacy*, *Research in the Teaching of English*, and *the Ohio Journal of the English Language Arts*.

ANN M. BRUNJES is Associate Professor of English at Bridgewater State College in Bridgewater, Massachusetts. She has written and presented papers on writers of the early American republic. Her current research is on Timothy Dwight's *Travels in New England and New York*.

KRISTIN BRUNNEMER is Lecturer in English and Film and Visual Culture at the University of California, Riverside. Her interests include media studies, minority discourses and twentieth-century American literature. She is currently writing her dissertation about the road trip in American film and literature.

GERALD BRUNS is the William P. and Hazel B. White Professor of English at the University of Notre Dame. His most recent book is *The Material of Poetry: Sketches for a Philosophical Poetics* (University of Georgia Press, 2005).

VIOLET HARRINGTON BRYAN, Ph.D., is Professor of English at Xavier University in Louisiana, where she teaches classes in African American literature, world literature, literature of black women writers, and New Orleans literature. Her book *The Myth of New Orleans Literature: Dialogues of Race and Gender* was published by the University of Tennessee Press in 1993.

CHRISTOPHER BUCKLEY is the author of thirteen books of poetry, most recently *SKY* from the Sheep Meadow Press, 2004. He is the editor of many anthologies on contemporary poetry, including *A Condition of the Spirit: On the Life & Work of Larry Levis* (2005). He teaches in the Creative Writing Department at the University of California Riverside.

ALYSON R. BUCKMAN is Assistant Professor in the Humanities and Religious Studies Department at California State University, Sacramento. Her degrees are in American studies, and her field of specialization is contemporary American literature. She enjoys working with minority literatures and popular culture, as well as gender studies. She has been published in *FEMSPEC*, the *Journal of American Culture*, and *Modern Fiction Studies (MFS)*.

MARK BUNDY is completing his dissertation at the University of California, Riverside, as a Chancellor's Distinguished Fellow. His most recent publications are *Reading Six Feet Under* (I.B. Tauris, 2005) and *Reading Sex and the City* (I.B. Tauris, 2004), with articles forthcoming in *EntreMundos/Among Worlds: New Perspectives on Gloria Anzaldua* and *Reading the L Word*.

SANDRA BURR is Assistant Professor of American Literature at Northern Michigan University. She co-edited, with Adam Potkay, the anthology *Black Atlantic Writers of the Eighteenth Century* (1995). Her research interests include eighteenth- and nineteenth-century Anglo-American children's books, African-American literature, and women writers.

MARGARET BURTON is Adjunct Lecturer in Literature at Kansas State University, Manhattan, Kansas. Her research interests include late nineteenth-century American literature, and the relation between narrativity and historiography in Holocaust literature.

LOUIS CABRI is a Ph.D. candidate at the University of Pennsylvania. He writes on U.S. and Canadian modern, postmodern, and contemporary poetry and poetics. His poetry book, *The Mood Embosser* (Coach House), won a 2003 book award from the Small Press Traffic Literary Arts Center, San Francisco.

EDWARD CAHILL is Assistant Professor of English at Fordham University. His work focuses on early American literature and intellectual history. His articles have appeared in such journals as *American Literature* and *Early American Literature*.

STEPHEN CAIN is a Contract Professor at Wilfrid Laurier University in Waterloo, Ontario, where he teaches poetry and Canadian literature. He is the author of *dyslexicon* (Coach House, 1999) and *Torontology* (ECW, 2001). Recent critical work has appeared in the collection *Sound as Sense* (Peter Lang, 2003), and in the journals *Studies in Canadian Literature* and *Open Letter*.

ALLAN CAMPO, an independent scholar, has pursued his interest in William Eversonís work since the late 1950s. In addition to his published essays on Everson, Campo has been an editor for *William Everson: A Descriptive Bibliography*, *Prodigious Thrust* (Eversonís autobiography), and the three volumes of Eversoní*Collected Poems*.S

MARK CANTRELL recently earned a Ph.D. in English from the University of Wisconsin, Madison. His dissertation is titled "Poetical Investigations: Philosophical Thought as Enactive Process in Twentieth-Century American Experimental Poetry." He currently teaches in the English Department at the University of Miami in Coral Gables, Florida.

PAUL R. CAPPUCCI is Assistant Professor of English at Georgian Court University in Lakewood, New Jersey. He has published journal articles on Dickinson, Whitman, and Frank O'Hara. He also published a book with Edwin Mellen Press titled *William Carlos Williams' Poetic Response to the 1913 Paterson Silk Strike* (2002).

SUSAN CASTILLO is John Nichol Professor of American Literature at Glasgow University. She has published extensively on colonial writing of the Americas and on Native American women writers, and is Associate Editor of *Journal of American Studies*. Her publications include *The Literature of Colonial Amer-*

ica (co-edited with Ivy Schweitzer), *Notes from the Periphery*, *Engendering Identities*, and *Pos-Colonialismo e Identidade.*

KRISTINA CHEW is Assistant Professor of Classics at Saint Peter's College, Jersey City, New Jersey. She is the author of a translation of Virgil's *Georgics* (2002) and has written on classics and multiculturalism. She is currently writing on the development of the soul in ancient medical and philosophical texts, and on autism and poetry.

EDWARD CLARKE teaches nineteenth- and twentieth-century literature at Oxford University. His most recent work is about Wallace Stevens in "creative conversation" with post-Milton English and American poets. An article, *Writing the Character of Wise Men: Stevens and Emerson in Creative Conversation*, is forthcoming.

BRIAN CLIFF is a Brittain Post-Doctoral Fellow at the Georgia Institute of Technology. He has published on Frank McGuinness, Paul Muldoon, and the Irish Literary Theatre, and co-edited *Representing the Troubles: Texts and Images, 1970–2000* (2004). His current book project examines forms and representations of community in contemporary Irish literature

MICHAEL CODY is Assistant Professor in the Department of English at East Tennessee State University, where he teaches courses ranging from early American literature to contemporary Native American literature. He is the author of *Charles Brockden Brown and the Literary Magazine: Cultural Journalism in the Early American Republic* (2004).

J. ROBIN COFFELT is Adjunct Instructor in English at the University of North Texas and DeVry University. Her research interests include twentieth-century North American literature, especially women's literature, Southern fiction, and the prose and poetry of Margaret Atwood.

PHILIP COLEMAN is Lecturer in the School of English at Trinity College, Dublin, where he teaches American, British, and Anglo-Irish poetry and fiction. A Fulbright Scholar at the University of Minnesota in 1998, he has published several essays on John Berryman, as well as articles on Carl Rakosi, Muriel Rukeyser, and Donald Davie.

FLOYD COLLINS's critical study, *Seamus Heaney: The Crisis of Identity*, was published by the University of Delaware in 2003. His books of poetry are *Scarecrow* (1980), *The Wedding Guest* (1987), and *Forecast* (1993). He teaches composition and literature at Gordon College.

BRIAN CONNIFF is Professor of English and Department Chair at the University of Dayton. He is the author of *The Lyric and Modern Poetry: Olson, Creeley, Bunting* (1988) and recent essays on a wide range of authors, including Gabriel García Márquez, W.H. Auden, Robert Hayden, and contemporary American prison writers.

Dr. LIAM CORLEY is Assistant Professor of English at California State Polytechnic University, Pomona. His research interests include travel writing and nineteenth-century American poetry. He is at work on a literary biography of Bayard Taylor titled *Determined Dreamer: Bayard Taylor and the Millstone of Culture.*

ANGELO COSTANZO, Professor Emeritus of English, Shippensburg University, Pennsylvania, does research in African American literature, concentrating on black autobiography. He has published numerous essays and a study of early slave writing titled *Surprizing Narrative: Olaudah Equiano and the Beginnings of Black Autobiography* (1987). In 2001 he edited Equiano's 1789 classic life story.

JAMES FINN COTTER, Professor of English at Mount Saint Mary College, Newburgh, New York, is the author of *Inscape: The Christology and Poetry of Gerard Manley Hopkins* (1972) and has written articles on Hopkins, Chaucer, Sidney, Salinger, and modern poetry. He has published poetry in *America*, *Commonweal*, the *Hudson Review*, the *Nation*, the *New York Times*, *Spirit*, *Thought*, and elsewhere, and has translated *The Divine Comedy* (Stony Brook, 2000). He is President of the International Hopkins Association.

PATTIE COWELL is Professor of English and University Distinguished Teaching Scholar at Colorado State University. She has written extensively on colonial North American poets and is the author of *Women Poets in Pre-Revolutionary America* (1981) and co-editor of *Critical Essays On Anne Bradstreet* (1983).

RAYMOND CRAIG is Associate Professor of English at Kent State University. He has published on early American poetics, textual studies (including *A Concordance to the Complete Works of Anne Bradstreet* in 2000), and teaches literature as well as rhetoric and theories of writing and representation.

KATHLEEN CROWN teaches at Princeton University, where she is the Director of Studies at Mathey College. She has written extensively on modern and contemporary poetry.

CATHERINE CUCINELLA teaches at Oakland University, Rochester, Michigan. Besides publishing articles on Elizabeth Bishop in several journals, she also is the editor of *Contemporary American Women Poets: An A-to-Z Guide* (Greenwood, 2002).

JOHN CUSATIS earned a Ph.D. in English from the University of South Carolina in 2003. He has published articles and presented conference papers on numerous twentieth-century American writers. His other scholarly interests include music and linguistics. He teaches English and journalism at the School of the Arts, Charleston, South Carolina.

JOHN D'AGATA is the author of *Halls of Fame* and editor of *The Next American Essay*, the first in a projected trilogy of anthologies on the history of experimental nonfiction. He currently edits lyric essays for *Seneca Review* and teaches creative writing at the University of Iowa.

YVONNE DALEY is Associate Professor of Journalism at San Francisco State University and Director of the Green Mountain Writers Conference. The author of more than five thousand news, feature, and investigative articles, her books include *Vermont Writers: A State of Mind* and *An Independent Man,* the biography of Vermont Senator James M. Jeffords.

ROBERT DARLING is Professor of English at Keuka College. He is the author of *A.D. Hope* (Twayne) and a collection of poetry, *So Far,* as well as three chapbooks of poems.

FRANK DAVEY holds the Carl F. Klinck Chair in Canadian Literature at the University of Western Ontario. He has published numerous books on Canadian writing, literary institutions, and culture, as well as more than twenty collections of poetry. He was co-founder of *SwiftCurrent* (1985–1990), the first online literary magazine.

ROCÍO G. DAVIS has degrees from the Ateneo de Manila University and the University of Navarre (Spain), where she is currently Associate Professor of American and Postcolonial Literatures. She has published *Transcultural Reinventions: Asian American and Asian Canadian Short Story Cycles* (TSAR, 2001) and numerous articles on Asian American writing.

JACQUELINE DE ANGELIS has her MFA from Bennington College. Her writing has appeared in *Another City, Writing from Los Angeles, Paterson Review, International Quarterly,* and *Agni* magazine. She has won the Crossing Boundaries Award for innovative and experimental writing and was a finalist in both the Allen Ginsberg and Emily Dickinson awards

HELEN DEESE is Lecturer at the University of California, Riverside. She has published, with Steven Gould Axelrod, on modern American poets, including *Critical Essays on William Carlos Williams* (1995), *Critical Essays on Wallace Stevens* (1989), *Robert Lowell: New Essays on the Poetry* (1986), and *Robert Lowell: A Reference Guide* (1982).

MICHEL DELVILLE is a writer and musician living in Liège, Belgium. He is the author of several books, including *J.G. Ballard* (1998) and *The American Prose Poem,* which won the *1998 SAMLA Studies Book Award.* He recently co-edited three volumes of essays on postwar U.S .poetry and has just completed two new volumes, *Hamlet et ses héritiers* (with Pierre Michel) and *Frank Zappa, Captain Beefheart, and the Secret History of Maximalism* (with Andrew Norris). His new poetry collection, *Le troisième corps,* has just been published by the Editions Le Fram and is currently being translated into English by Gian Lombardo. He teaches English and American literatures, as well as Comparative Literatures, at the University of Liège, where he directs the Interdisciplinary Center for Applied Poetics. He has been playing and composing music since the mid-eighties.

RICHARD DENNER, writer and artist, is the impresario of dPress chapbooks. He lives in Sebastopol, California, and is a member of California Poets in the Schools. In 2004 he participated in the Jack Straw Writers Program. His *Collected Poems: 1961–2000* has been published by Comrades Press.

FELIPE DE ORTEGO Y GASCA is Professor Emeritus of English Language and Literature, Texas State University SystemSul Ross. Recipient of the 2005 Rudolfo and Patricia Anaya Critica Nueva Award for literary criticism from the University of New Mexico, he is currently Visiting Scholar and Lecturer in English at Texas A&M University—Kingsville.

THOMAS DEPIETRO is a book critic and independent scholar in Eastchester, New York. He has contributed to numerous scholarly and literary journals (*CLIO,* the *Centennial Review,* the *Georgia Review,* and the *Sewanee Review,* among others) and has reviewed books for the *New York Times Book Review,* the *Nation, Commonweal,* and other publications. A contributor to *The Oxford Companion to Twentieth-Century Poetry* (ed., Ian Hamilton, 1994), he wrote and edited the poetry review section of *Kirkus Reviews* for three years. He has also edited *Conversations with Don DeLillo* (University Press of Mississippi, 2005).

THOMAS DEVANEY is Lecturer in Creative Writing at the University of Pennsylvania, where he is coordinator of the Kelly Writers House. He is the author of *Letters to Ernesto Neto* (Germ Folios, 2004) and *The American Pragmatist Fell in Love* (Banshee Press, 1999).

TERENCE DIGGORY is Professor of English at Skidmore College, Saratoga Springs, New York. His research on interartistic collaboration in the New York School has contributed to publications and art exhibitions. With Stephen Paul Miller, he co-edited *The Scene of My Selves: New Work on New York School Poets* (2001).

MICHAEL G. DITMORE is Associate Professor of Early American Literature and Great Books at Pepperdine University, Malibu, California. His current research interests include William Bradford, John Winthrop, Jonathan Edwards, and the Declaration of Independence.

ANDREW DUBOIS is Assistant Professor of English at the University of Toronto at Scarborough. He is the co-editor of *Close Reading: The Reader* (Duke) and has published work in *American Literary History, Explosive, Harvard Review, South Atlantic Quarterly,* and the *Lights Are Out.* His book *Ashbery's Forms of Attention* is forthcoming from the University of Alabama Press.

PATRICK F. DURGIN is a poet and critic whose books include *Sorter* (Duration Press) and *The Route* (written with Jen Hofer and published by Never Die Books). He is a Jacob K. Javits Fellow in English at the Poetics Program of SUNY Buffalo.

CRAIG DWORKIN is Associate Professor of English at the University of Utah. He is the author of *Reading the Illegible* (2003) and the editor of two online archives, Eclipse, and the UbuWeb Anthology of Conceptual Writing.

ERICA JOAN DYMOND is a Ph.D. candidate and teaching fellow in the English Department at Lehigh University, Bethlehem, Pennsylvania. She has published a short article on Margaret Atwood's *The Handmaid's Tale* in the academic journal *the Explicator.*

JACOB EDMOND is Lecturer in Modern and Contemporary Poetry at the University of Otago, New Zealand. He has published articles on modern and contemporary American, Chinese, and Russian poetry, including "'A Meaning Alliance': Arkadii Dragomoshchenko and Lyn Hejinian's Poetics of Translation" in *Slavic and East European Journal.*

JAMES EGAN is Associate Professor of English at Brown University. His focus in scholarly work is colonial British American writing.

KEVIN ELSTOB is Associate Professor of French at California State University, Sacramento. In addition to writing about French and Québécois theatre, he is engaged in documenting the evolution of relations between France and North America. His current research and teaching investigate contacts between American Indians and the French.

LORI EMERSON is a doctoral candidate at the State University of New York at Buffalo in the English Department. She has written on Leonard Cohen, bpNichol, and digital poets John Cayley and Kenneth Goldsmith.

JENNIFER ENGLERT is Visiting Instructor of English at Western Carolina University. Her research interests include postcolonial literature, with an emphasis on India, as well as literature of the American South.

PATRICK M. ERBEN is Assistant Professor of English at the University of West Georgia and 2004–2006 NEH/Institute Fellow at the Omohundro Institute of Early American History and Culture in Williamsburg, Virginia. He is completing a monograph on German and English literary constructions of spiritual community in colonial Pennsylvania.

BRUCE A. ERICKSON is Graduate Teaching Assistant and Writing Program Technical Liaison at Illinois State University, Normal. He expects to complete his doctoral degree in English studies in 2006.

LOGAN ESDALE is Assistant Professor of American Literature and Poetry at Chapman University, in Orange, California. An essay of his appeared in *Ronald Johnson: Life & Works* (2004), and he is currently writing a book on epistolary poetics in the modernist period.

JOHN O. ESPINOZA is a Chicano poet with an MFA from Arizona State University. He teaches English literature and composition at the National Hispanic University in San Jose, California.

BARBARA L. ESTRIN is Professor of English at Stonehill College. Her books include *The Raven and the Lark: Lost Children in Literature of the English Renaissance* (Bucknell, 1985), *Laura: Uncovering Gender and Genre in Wyatt, Donne and Marvell* (Duke, 1994), and *The American Love Lyric after Auschwitz and Hiroshima* (Palgrave, 2001).

STEVE EVANS is Associate Professor of English at the University of Maine, where he teaches modern and contemporary American poetry, critical theory, and poetics. His critical and scholarly work on American poetry has appeared in numerous venues, including Qui Parle, differences, Jacket, and his own Third Factory website (www.thirdfactory.net).

Scholar and author, DINA RIPSMAN EYLON has a Ph.D. from the University of Toronto. She has taught various undergraduate courses at Carleton University and the University of Toronto. Ripsman Eylon has written extensively on literary theory, feminism, and religion. She publishes and edits *Women in Judaism: A Multidisciplinary Journal.*

SAMUEL JASON EZELL is a Humanities Specialist librarian at the Memphis Public Library. He is a former English teacher with a particular interest in contemporary American queer and experimental poetries. He has published his own poetry in *gestalten* and *River City* and has been nominated for a Pushcart Prize.

SIDRA EZRAHI is Professor of Comparative Jewish Literature at the Hebrew University of Jerusalem. She has written extensively on literary representations of the Holocaust and on the cultures of diaspora and homecoming. Her most recent publication, *Booking Passage: Exile and Homecoming in the Modern Jewish Imagination,* was a finalist for the Koret Jewish Book Award (2001). She interviewed Grace Paley for the video archive project "Words and Images."

MELISSA GABOT FABROS is a doctoral candidate in the English Department at the University of California at Berkeley. She publishes and presents widely on topics in twentieth-century American literature as well as on allied interests in postcolonial and Asian American literature.

JANE E. FALK is Instructor in English Composition at the University of Akron, Akron, Ohio. Her research interests include writers associated with the Beat Generation and Zen and American culture.

JEFFREY B. FALLA is Lecturer in the Department of Cultural Studies and Comparative Literature at the University of Minnesota.

PATRICK FARRELL is a Ph.D. candidate in English at Temple University. He is engaged in research on twentieth-century American poetry.

ROBIN RILEY FAST is Associate Professor of Literature at Emerson College in Boston. Her publications include many articles on Native American and other American poetry; *Approaches to Teaching Dickinson's Poetry* (1989), co-edited with Christine Mack Gordon; and *The Heart as a Drum: Continuance and Resistance in American Indian Poetry* (1999).

D.W. FENZA is Executive Director of the Association of Writers and Writing Programs. He is the author of a book-length poem, *The Interlude* (1989). In 1955, he received a fellowship in poetry from the National Endowment for the Arts for Latin from *Manhattan,* a novel in verse.

NICOLÁS FERNÁNDEZ-MEDINA is a dual Ph.D. candidate in the Department of Spanish and Portuguese and the Department of Humanities at Stanford University. He has published various articles on Spanish and Latin American literature that have appeared in *Ajiaco, Torre de Papel, BoletínRAMON, Abel Martín,* and *El Pasajero,* among others.

ELIZABETH FERSZT is adjunct faculty at a community college in Southeastern Michigan; she is also a doctoral candidate in Early American Literature at Wayne State University in Detroit. She has won a 1985 Hopwood writing award and the 2002 American Academy of Poets John Clare First Prize. She is a contributing scholar and member of the Society of Early Americanists. Her dissertation is titled "Rejecting a New English Aesthetic: The Early Poems of Anne Bradstreet."

JULIA FIEDORCZUK-GLINECK is Assistant Professor at the Institute of English Studies, Warsaw University. She specializes in modern American poetry and literary theory. She has published numerous articles as well as two award-winning books of poetry. She also translates American poetry into Polish.

EDWARD FIELD received a Lambda Award for *Counting Myself Lucky, Selected Poems, 1963–1992* (1992). The documentary "To Be Alive," for which he wrote the narration, won an Academy Award. Forthcoming is *The Man Who Would Marry Susan Sontag, and Other Intimate Literary Portraits,* from the University of Wisconsin Press.

ROLAND FINGER is a post-doctoral Lecturer in English at the University of California, Davis. He specializes in colonial discourse analysis, American literature, and gender studies. He is currently completing a book that examines intersections between female and familial fetishisms and American imperialism.

STEPHANIE FISCHETTI has an MA in English Literature from the University of North Carolina in Greensboro. She currently teaches English at the University of South Florida in Tampa, and works as a freelance book editor in her spare time. She has taught at Greensboro College, Bennett College and

North Carolina Agricultural and Technical State University in the past. In 2006 she plans to pursue a Ph.D. in English literature.

JIRI FLAJSAR is Assistant Professor of English and American Literature at Palacky University, Olomouc, Czech Republic. He has received several research grants and fellowships. He is the author of *Epiphany in American Poetry* (Palacky University Press, 2003) and numerous articles on American, British, and Czech poetry and fiction.

REBECCA FLANNAGAN is an Associate Professor of American Literature at Francis Marion University in Florence, South Carolina where she also co-directs the Swamp Fox Writing Project. She has written numerous reviews on contemporary authors. In 2004 she won the Francis Marion University award for teaching excellence.

JAMES FLEMING is a master's candidate at the University of Florida. His areas of research include English Romantic and modern American poetry, late-Victorian fiction, and critical theory. He is the 2004–2006 recipient of the Kirkland Fellowship from the University of Florida.

ED FOLSOM is Carver Professor of English at the University of Iowa, where he edits the *Walt Whitman Quarterly Review*, co-directs the Whitman Archive (www.whitmanarchive.org), and edits the Whitman Series at the University of Iowa Press. He is the author or editor of numerous books and essays on Whitman and other American writers.

LINDA LUSSY FRASER is Lecturer in Business Communication at California State University, Fullerton. She has written on the use of the visual arts, especially the cinema, in the poetry of Sylvia Plath.

GLENN J. FREEMAN Assistant Professor of English at Cornell College in Iowa. He has received an MFA from Vermont College, two Minnesota State Arts Board Fellowships, and a Loft-McKnight Award. His poetry has been published in such journals as *Poetry*, the *Cimarron Review*, and the *Birmingham Poetry Review*.

KORNELIA FREITAG holds the chair of American Studies at Ruhr-Universty Bochum, Germany. She has written on ethnic literature and American poetry. Her study on cultural criticism in contemporary women's experimental writing is forthcoming in 2005.

DARREN PAUL FREY is an adjunct professor and a writer at Emerson College with interests in religious and philosophical poetry, and whose educational background is in both disciplines.

GABRIEL FRIED currently teaches at Baruch College (C.U.N.Y.) and is poetry editor at Persea Books. His poems have appeared in a number of journals, including the *American Scholar* and the *Gettysburg Review*.

BENJAMIN FRIEDLANDER is Assistant Professor of English at the University of Maine. He is the author of *Simulcast: Four Experiments in Criticism* (2004) and co-editor of *The Collected Prose of Charles Olson*.

DAN FRIEDMAN is the Head of English at Schechter Regional High School (Teaneck, NJ) and a founding editor of *Zeek* (http://www.zeek.net). He has a Ph.D. in Comparative Literature from Yale University, writing and performing credits with Stimmt (an art-performance group), and co-authored *Da Gospel According to Ali G*.

NORMAN FRIEDMAN is former Professor of English at Queens College, CUNY. He has published books on e.e. cummings, poetry and composition, and fiction theory, as well as two volumes of poetry. He is the recipient of numerous honors and awards, including the All Nations Poetry Contest and the *North American Mentor* annual poetry award. His research interests include Victorian and modern literature, literature and psychology, and literary theory.

DAVID FRITZ, an English teacher at Harrison High School in New York, holds a Ph.D. from Indiana University of Pennsylvania. As a recipient of the Albert Shanker National Conference Scholarship, he chaired a panel at the Society of Early Americanists conference in Alexandria, Virginia.

CAROL FROST is Writer-in-Residence and Professor of English at Hartwick College, where she directs the Catskill Poetry Workshop. She is the author of nine volumes of poetry, including *Loave and Scorn* and *I Will Say Beauty*. She has won two NEA fellowships in poetry and has edited poetry for the Pushcart Prize Anthology.

KIT FRYATT is Arts Faculty Teaching Fellow in Anglo-Irish Literature at University College, Dublin. Her research interests are in Irish, British, and American Poetry, and she is presently completing a study of allegory in twentieth-century Irish poetry.

CHRISTOPHER FUNKHOUSER, poet, multimedia artist, editor, and critic, joined the faculty of the Humanities Department at New Jersey Institute of Technology in 1997. His work has appeared in *Callaloo, Hambone, African American Review*, the critical anthology *Telling It Slant: Avant-Garde Poetics of the 1990s*, and in many other publications.

AMANDA GAILEY is a doctoral candidate in nineteenth-century American literature and digital text editing at the University of Nebraska, where she is an editorial assistant for the *Walt Whitman Archive*. She has articles forthcoming in the *Emily Dickinson Journal* and Blackwell's *A Companion to Whitman*.

JEFFREY GALBRAITH is a Ph.D. candidate specializing in eighteenth-century British literature at Indiana University, Bloomington. He holds an MA in creative writing from Boston University.

Dr. KATE GALE is Managing Editor of Red Hen Press, Editor of the *Los Angeles Review* and President of PEN USA. She has five books of poetry, a novel, and a bilingual children's book. She is the author of the libretto *Rio De Sangre* with composer Don Davis.

WENDY GALGAN is an Adjunct in English and Philosophy at St. Francis College in Brooklyn, and is a doctoral candidate in English at the CUNY Graduate Center. She has published poetry and articles on science fiction literature. Her current research interests include philosophy, film, and contemporary American women's poetry.

GENEVA M. GANO is a graduate student in English at the University of California, Los Angeles. She has written on nationalism and imperial expansion in nineteenth- and twentieth-century American literature, and is writing a dissertation on modernism and regionalism in the American West.

THOMAS GARDNER is Clifford Cutchins Professor of English at Virginia Tech. His most recent books are the edited collection *Jorie Graham: Essays on the Poetry* (Wisconsin) and *Emily Dickinson and Contemporary Writers* (forthcoming from Oxford). He has been the recipient of Guggenheim, NEA, and Fulbright fellowships.

MELISSA GIRARD is a Ph.D. candidate in the Department of English at the University of Illinois at Urbana-Champaign. She is currently completing a dissertation on modern American poetry and the politics of middle class from between 1890 and 1950.

LOSS PEQUEÑO GLAZIER is a poet, Professor of Media Study, and Director of the Electronic Poetry Center (http://epc.buffalo.edu), Department of Media Study, SUNY Buffalo. He is the author of *Anatman, Pumpkin Seed, Algorithm* (Salt), and *Digital Poetics: The Making of E-Poetries* (Alabama). His selected digital poems are available on his EPC author page (http://epc.buffalo.edu/authors/glazier).

ELIZABETH GOLDBERG, Ph.D. is Assistant Professor of English at Babson College, Wellesley, MA. She specializes in postcolonial literatures and human rights, and has published in the areas of human rights, postcolonial literature and film, and multicultural pedagogy. She has just completed a manuscript titled *Beyond Terror: Gender, Narrative, Human Rights.*

JOY GONSALVES earned an MFA from the University of Florida. A Cave Canem fellow, she is a contributor to the forthcoming *Quotes Community: Notes for Black Poets*, edited by Thomas Sayers Ellis, and has been published in *Limestone, Verse,* and *Sable.*

ANDREW GOODSPEED was educated in the United States, United Kingdom, and Republic of Ireland. He lectures for Santis Educational Services, Ulaan Baatar, Mongolia.

STEPHANIE GORDON received her Ph.D. in American Literature and Creative Writing from the University of Georgia. She is currently an instructor of English at Auburn University and has published articles on N. Scott Momaday, Sherman Alexie, Elias Boudinot, Beverly Lowry, and Judith Ortiz Cofer.

JEFFREY GRAY is Associate Professor of English at Seton Hall University, New Jersey, where he teaches courses in American poetry, postcolonial literature, and literary theory. A two-time Fulbright Award recipient, he is author of *Mastery's End: Travel and Postwar American Poetry* (University of Georgia Press, 2005) and contributor to numerous journals, including *Callaloo, Contemporary Literature, Papers on Language and Literature,* and *Profession.* A Seattle native, he has lived and taught in Latin America, the South Pacific, Asia, and Europe.

AMY GLYNN GREACEN is an independent writer working in San Francisco. Poetic form, particularly in twentieth century poetry has been a major area of research interest for her. Her poems have appeared in a number of journals in the United States and the UK., and she is currently completing her first novel.

AMY GROSHEK teaches writing at Alaska Pacific University. Her poems have appeared in *Ice Floe, Alaska Quarterly Review,* and *Bloom.*

JEFFREY GRUENGLAS is Instructor of English and College Composition at Touro College, New York. His chief area of interest is cultural linguistics. His most recent work, "What I'm Crying About: Discourse and Dialogism in the Works of Raymond Carver," was published in the Proceedings of the XI International Bakhtin Conference (2003).

ERIC GUDAS is a doctoral student in English at UCLA. His poems, interviews, and literary criticism have appeared in such publications as the *American Poetry Review, Crazyhorse,* the *Iowa Review,* the *Southern Review,* and *Poetry Flash.* His chapbook of poems, *Beautiful Monster,* was published by Swan Scythe Press in 2003.

ARLENE GUERRERO-WATANABE is Assistant Professor of Spanish at Assumption College. She specializes in the literature of the Caribbean and of Latino writers in the United States. Her most recent publications focus on bilingual aesthetics in contemporary literature. She recently received a Mayoral Citation from the city of Worcester for mentoring inner-city high school students.

KATIE ROSE GUEST is a doctoral student in English at the University of North Carolina at Greensboro. She earned her master's degree in creative writing from the Writing Seminars at Johns Hopkins University. Her research interests include rhetoric and American literature.

ROSEMARY FITHIAN GURUSWAMY is Professor and Chairperson of English at Radford University in Virginia. Her academic areas include early American literature and African American literature. She is the author of *The Poems of Edward Taylor* (Greenwood Press, 2003).

PAVLÍNA HÁCOVÁ is Assistant Professor of English and American Literature at Palacky University, Olomouc, Czech Republic. She is the author of *The Bridge and the Eclipse: Metaphor in the Poetry of Samuel Taylor Coleridge* (Palacky University Press, 2004). She has published extensively on British and American poetry and fiction.

GORDON HADFIELD is a poet, translator, and Ph.D. candidate in poetics at SUNY Buffalo. He co-edits the journal *Kiosk: A Journal of Poetry, Poetics, and Experimental Prose* and is the author of *Correspondence* (Handwritten Press 2004), a collaborative book of poems.

STEPHEN HAHN is Professor of English and Associate Provost at the William Paterson University of New Jersey. He is the author of books on Thoreau and Jacques Derrida and essays on American and British writers, as well as co-editor of two volumes on approaches to teaching the works of William Faulkner.

ERIC ASHLEY HAIRSTON is an English faculty member at North Carolina State University. His interests include American, African American, and classical literature. From 2001 to 2003 he was the Honors Program Fellow at Sweet Briar College. From 1998 to 2000 he was an undergraduate academic dean and assistant to the dean at the University of Virginia.

JUDY HALDEN-SULLIVAN is Associate Professor of English at Millersville University of Pennsylvania, where she teaches composition studies, rhetoric, and experimental writing. In addition to writing poetry, she has published a hermeneutic phenomenological interpretation of Charles Olson's prose texts and is currently preparing two studies on Gadamer's poetics.

JOAN WYLIE HALL is Instructor of English at the University of Mississippi. Editor of the interview-collection *Conversations with Audre Lorde* (2004) and author of *Shirley Jackson: A Study of the Short Fiction* (1993), she is currently writing a book about the Southern local colorist Ruth McEnery Stuart.

DEBORAH HALLETT is a doctoral student at the University of California, Riverside. She completed her master's degree in American literature at San Diego State University in 2005. Her interests include feminist and cultural studies, and she recently published a thesis titled *Contemporary Women's Literature and the Beauty Myth* (2005).

JEFFREY HAMMOND is George B. and Willma Reeves Distinguished Professor in the Liberal Arts at St. Mary's College of Maryland. His most recent books include *The American Puritan Elegy: A Literary and Cultural Study* (Cambridge University Press, 2000) and *Ohio States: A Twentieth-Century Midwestern* (Kent State University Press, 2002).

HEIDI M. HANRAHAN is a doctoral candidate specializing in nineteenth-century American literature at the University of North Carolina at Greensboro. Her dissertation is titled "Competing for the Reader: The Writer/Editor Relationship in Nineteenth-Century American Literature."

BENJAMIN HARDER works in poetry and modernism. He received his Ph.D. in 1994 from the University of California, Riverside, where he now lectures in the English Department. His current project is a study of unreliable narrators in twentieth-century poetry.

VICTORIA FRENKEL HARRIS is Professor of English at Illinois State University. Author of *The Incorporative Consciousness of Robert Bly* (1991), she has published extensively on the work of Bly, Denise Levertov, Adrienne Rich, and Carole Maso, among others. Her current book examines language, ethics, and agency in the poetry of Jorie Graham and Lyn Hejinian.

Dr. S.L. HARRISON, Associate Professor, University of Miami, is editor of *Menckeniana*, a quarterly journal, and author of *a.k.a. H. L. Mencken*; *Cavalcade of Journalists, 1900–2000*; *H. L. Mencken Revisited: Author, Editor & Newspaperman*; *The Editorial Art of Edmund Duffy*, and other books.

CHRISTOPHER HARTER is the owner and editor of Pathwise Press in Erie, Pennsylvania. His research interests include twentieth-century American little magazines and small presses. He is currently compiling an author index for little magazines published during the "mimeograph revolution" of the 1960s and 1970s.

CHARLES O. HARTMAN is Poet-in-Residence and Professor of English at Connecticut College. He has published six collections of poems and three critical studies (*Free Verse, Jazz Text,* and *Virtual Muse*).

TAMARA HARVEY is Assistant Professor of English at George Mason University. Her research focuses on early American women writers, and she has published several articles on seventeenth-century poets Anne Bradstreet and Sor Juana Inés de la Cruz. She has also co-edited a volume titled *George Washington's South.*

BURT HATLEN is Professor of English at the University of Maine and Director of the National Poetry Foundation. He has published many articles on Shakespeare, Renaissance poetry, literary theory, and modern fantasy, along with articles on such modern and postmodern poets as Pound, Williams, H.D., Zukofsky, Oppen, Olson, Duncan, and Spicer.

THOMAS HAWKS is completing a doctoral degree in English and creative writing at the University of Utah. His research interests include English prosody and American modernist poetry. His poems have appeared in the *Seneca Review*, the *Antioch Review*, the *Western Humanities Review*, and the *Literary Review.*

ROBERT W. HAYNES is Associate Professor of English at Texas A&M International University in Laredo, Texas, where he teaches medieval and Renaissance courses. He is also interested in classical literature and the literature of the American South.

ELOISE KLEIN HEALY, Founding Chair of the Antioch University MFA in Creative Writing Program, has published five books of poetry. Both *Passing* and *Artemis In Echo Park* were finalists for the Lambda Book Award. Healy taught in the Feminist Studio Workshop at the Woman's Building in Los Angeles and is the co-founder of Eco-Arts, an ecotourism/arts venture.

SYLVIA HENNEBERG is Associate Professor of English at Morehead State University. She has written extensively on American women poets. In 2002 she was awarded a postdoctoral fellowship from the American Association of University Women (AAUW) to conduct research on American women poets and aging.

THOMAS L. HERAKOVICH is a Ph.D. candidate at Illinois State University. He is currently working on his dissertation on sentimentality and the American novel, with particular focus on women novelists and their relationship with the public sphere, power, and change.

TERRY HERTZLER is a Southern California poet, writer, and teacher. His poetry and short stories have appeared in a variety of publications, including *Stand Up Poetry: An Expanded Anthology* (University of Iowa Press, 2002). His most recent book of poetry is *Second Skin* (Caernarvon Press, 2004).

SEAN HEUSTON is Assistant Professor of English at The Citadel: The Military College of South Carolina. He has published essays and reviews on Southern literature, American and Irish poetry, film, and sports in American society. He is currently completing a book manuscript that includes a chapter on Robert Penn Warren.

JANE HIKEL coordinates the writing center and teaches writing and American literature at Central Connecticut State University. Her scholarly interests lie in the early American novel and conduct books.

ERNEST HILBERT's poetry has appeared in the *New Republic*, the *Boston Review*, *LIT*, *Pleiades*, *McSweeney's*, the *New Formalist*, the *American Scholar*, *Verse*, *Fence*, and *Volt.* He is the editor of *NC*, an annual journal of new writing, and is the managing editor of the *Contemporary Poetry Review.* He is a regular reviewer for the *New York Sun* and *American Poet.* He will appear in the anthology *And Gentlemen: Younger American Male Poets* from Stride Books in the UK in 2005. Hilbert received his doctorate in English literature from Oxford University, where he earlier completed a master's degree and founded the *Oxford*

Quarterly. He is an agent at Bauman Rare Books, the largest antiquarian and first edition book dealer in North America.

MELVIN G. HILL is a Ph.D. student and a Ronald McNair Scholar at Illinois State University, Normal. His research interests include African American literature and culture, and racial identity representations in American literature and history, particularly antebellum and Reconstruction era. His current project includes an exploration of the significance of Sutton E. Griggs and the inclusion of his literary works in the African American canon.

RICHARD HISHMEH is a Ph.D. candidate at the University of California, Riverside. He is currently concluding his dissertation on representations of American genius. His primary areas of research are American literature, poetry, and film and visual culture

GEOFFREY HLIBCHUK is a Ph.D. candidate at the State University of New York at Buffalo. He is currently writing his dissertation on Canadian avant-garde poetry.

MATTHEW HOFER is Assistant Professor of American and British Modernist Literature at the University of New Mexico.

TYLER HOFFMAN is Associate Professor and Director of Graduate Studies in the Department of English at Rutgers University, Camden. His book *Robert Frost and the Politics of Poetry* received the South Atlantic Modern Language Association Studies Book Award for the best scholarly book of 2001. He has published essays on a range of modern American poets, including Whitman, Dickinson, Vachel Lindsay, Frost, Snyder, Bishop, Gunn, and performers in the contemporary rap-meets-poetry scene. He is currently working on a book about American public poetry and the performance of culture, and he is editor of the electronic American studies journal the *Mickle Street Review* and associate editor of the *Robert Frost Review.*

SUSAN HOLBROOK is an Assistant Professor at the University of Windsor, where she teaches North American literatures and creative writing. She works primarily on feminist experimental writers such as Nicole Brossard and Gertrude Stein. Her first book of poetry is titled *misled* (Red Deer Press, 1999), her second *Good Egg Bad Seed* (Nomados, 2004).

DONNA KROLIK HOLLENBERG is Professor of English at the University of Connecticut. She has published three books on H.D. including, most recently, *H.D. and Poets After* (2000), as well as many essays on other writers. She is currently writing a biography of Denise Levertov.

PETER C. HOLLORAN is Assistant Professor of History at Worcester State College and the author of *Historical Dictionary of New England*.

JOHN HOPPENTHALER is a writer whose first book of poetry, *Lives of Water,* was published by Carnegie Mellon University Press in 2003. Poetry Editor of *Kestrel,* he regulary teaches creative writing at various universities, colleges, and conferences. Among his honors are an Individual Artist Grant from the West Virginia Commission on the Arts and a Foreign Travel Grant from West Virginia University.

ELIZABETH B. HOUSE is Professor of English at Augusta State University in Augusta, Georgia. She has written extensively on various women authors, and her scholarly articles have appeared in *American Literature, Studies in American Fiction, Modern Fiction Studies, Dictionary of Literary Biography, Approaches to Teaching Toni Morrison's Novels,* and *Journal of Advanced Composition.*

MICHAEL HOUSEHOLDER is Assistant Professor of English at Southern Methodist University. He works in early American literature to 1860, with an emphasis on transatlantic literature of exploration and discovery from the sixteenth and seventeenth centuries, and early American encounter narratives.

WILLIAM R. HOWE received his Ph.D. in the Poetics Program at the State University of New York at Buffalo. He is a poet and a publisher, as well as a critic and a scholar. Currently, he is a Visiting Assistant Professor and Poet at Miami University of Ohio. He is working on a book about concrete and visual poetries.

MELANIE HUBBARD is Assistant Professor of English at University of Tampa in Tampa, Florida. She has published essays on Emily Dickinson's manuscripts; an essay on Dickinson's relation to early photographic technologies is forthcoming in *Mosaic.* She's writing a book about Dickinson, representation, and nineteenth-century popular and intellectual culture.

EDWARD HUFFSTETLER is Professor of English and American Literature at Bridgewater College. He received his Ph.D. from the University of Iowa (1988) and has published a collection of Native American stories, *Tales of Native America* (Michael Friedman Publishing, 1996) as well as articles in various areas of American literature.

COLEMAN HUTCHISON, a Ph.D. candidate in the Department of English at Northwestern University, teaches and writes about American literature and culture to 1900. Hutchison's dissertation, "Revision, Reunion, and the American Civil War Text," theorizes the cultural work of literary revision during and immediately after the American Civil War.

SUSAN CLAIR IMBARRATO is Associate Professor of English at Minnesota State University Moorhead. Her teaching and research areas include early American literature, travel narratives, women's letters and diaries, and frontier literature. She is the author of *Declarations of Independency in Eighteenth-Century American Autobiography* (1998).

IGNACIO INFANTE is currently a Ph.D. student in Comparative Literature at Rutgers University and a Fulbright Fellow. A graduate of Trinity College, Dublin, his primary academic interests are translation theory and the twentieth century poetry of Europe and the Americas. In 2003 he translated into Spanish John Ashbery's collection *A Wave* for Random House Mondadori.

MARK IRWIN is the author of *Bright Hunger* (BOA, 2004), four other collections of poetry, and two volumes of translations. He divides his time between Colorado and Los Angeles, where he teaches in the graduate writing program at the University of Southern California.

MICHAEL IVES is a writer and musician living in the Hudson Valley. His work with the language/performance trio *F'loom* was featured on National Public Radio, on the CBC, and in the anthology of international sound poetry, *Homo Sonorus.* He is the author of *The External Combustion Engine,* a collection of short prose pieces. His poetry and prose have appeared in numerous magazines and journals both in the United States and abroad. He teaches at Bard College.

GEUN YOUNG JANG is Lecturer of Modern British and American Poetry at Inchon University, Korea. She has recently published articles on Korean American women poets and female modernisms in 1920s Korea within a comparative frame. She is currently working on generational conflicts of Korean American poets.

MARIAN JANSSEN is Director of External Relations at Radboud University Nijmegen, the Netherlands. She has written on literary magazines and contemporary poets and is the author of *The Kenyon Review (1939–1970): A Critical History* (1990). She is at work on a biography of Isabella Gardner.

KRIS JENSEN, Associate Instructor and doctoral candidate in American literature at University of California, Davis, graduated with honors in literature and anthropology from University of California, Santa Cruz. His interests include protest literature and Native American and African American literature, and he is a published poet.

CARLE JOHNSON is a poet who created and organized the 1985 weeklong Stanley Kunitz Poetry Festival for the Worcester County Poetry Association's celebration of Kunitz's eightieth birthday. As treasurer of the WCPA he coordinated the 2005 Stanley Kunitz Conference and Poetry Festival at Clark University and other Worcester colleges and universities. He is a past president and present treasurer of the WCPA. He was the feature poet in the Spring/Summer 2001 issue of *Sahara, A Journal of New England Poetry.*

CHERI JOHNSON is Instructor of English at the University of Minnesota in Minneapolis. She writes fiction and poetry as well as criticism, and has had work included in magazines such as *Clare*, the *Rio Grande Review*, and the *Hollins Critic.*

DANIEL MORLEY JOHNSON received his MA from McGill University (Canada) in 2005, where he now works in the Faculty of Arts. He is a graduate of the Aboriginal studies program at the University of Toronto. His research interests include literary theory and indigenous studies.

DAVID JONES is Assistant Professor of English and Women's Studies at the University of Wisconsin, Eau Claire. His writing examines social movements and popular culture using tools from critical race studies. His essay on Lorraine Hansberry and sexuality in the civil rights movement is collected in *Growing Up Postmodern* (2002).

SHARON L. JONES is Assistant Professor of English at Wright State University in Dayton, Ohio. Her research interests include American literature and African American literature. She is the author of *Rereading the Harlem Renaissance: Race, Class, and Gender in the Fiction of Jessie Fauset, Zora Neale Hurston, and Dorothy West* (Greenwood Press, 2002). She is also co-editor of *The Prentice Hall Anthology of African American Literature* (Prentice Hall, 2000).

SIOBHAN KANE is a graduate student at St. Bonaventure University who is currently working on her MA in English literature as a part of the Teaching and Learning Fellowship Program. She received her BA in English from St. Bonaventure University and graduated summa cum laude in 2004.

HOLLY KARAPETKOVA is currently pursuing her Ph.D. at the University of Cincinnati. Her poems and translations have appeared in a number of literary journals, including the *Crab Orchard Review*, the *Formalist*, and *Calyx*.

JAMES KARMAN, Professor Emeritus of English and Religious Studies at California State University, Chico, is the author of *Robinson Jeffers: Poet of California* (1987, 1995) and the editor of *Critical Essays on Robinson Jeffers* (1990), *Of Una Jeffers* (1998), and *Stones of the Sur* (2001).

MARY ROSE KASRAIE, Ph.D., has been Lecturer in the Department of English at Georgia State University, Atlanta, Georgia, and is presently Adjunct Professor, English, at Strayer University, Atlanta, Georgia. Her interests are early American literature and eighteenth-century British literature, as well as composition and rhetoric.

JEREMY KAYE is a graduate student in English at University of California, Riverside. His research interests include contemporary American literatures, cultural studies, and Jewish studies. His current research project investigates the "male conduct book" in contemporary American culture, focusing on its influence in constructions of masculinity and in modes of masculine self-fashioning.

DOUGLAS KEARNEY is a writer from Altadena, California. His first book of poetry, *Fear, some*, will be published by Red Hen Press in the winter of 2005/2006. He teaches at the California Institute of the Arts and is a Cave Canem Fellow.

M. BETH KEEFAUVER is Visiting Instructor in English at Western Carolina University. Her research interests include Gothic literature and Romanticism; nineteenth- and twentieth-century women's literature; and feminist, postcolonial, and ecocritical theory. She has received several awards for excellence in teaching and research and has published in the area of Native American literature.

ANNE KEEFE is a doctoral student focusing on modern and contemporary poetry at Rutgers University, New Brunswick, New Jersey. She has taught creative writing in her community and academic writing at Rutgers and at the University of Maryland, where she received her MFA in poetry. Her poems have appeared in several literary journals, including *Prairie Schooner.*

PRATIBHA KELAPURE is a multilingual poet and writer. As an independent scholar, she has presented a paper on Hindi poet Mahadevi Verma at SALA, an MLA-affiliated organization for South Asian literature. She has written articles for *Writing African American Women: An Encyclopedia of Literature by and about Women of Color*, forthcoming from Greenwood Press in 2006.

ALLISON KELLAR is currently obtaining a Master of Arts in literature at Clemson University. Recently, she published "James Dickey: An Exploration of 'Exchanges'" in the *South Carolina Review.* She is also a contributor to the Oxford University Press's *African American National Biography.*

DAVID KELLOGG is Assistant Professor of English and Director of Advanced Writing in the Disciplines at Northeastern University. He has published on contemporary American and

Irish poetry and poetics in journals such as *Diacritics*, *SAQ*, *Cultural Critique*, and *Fence*.

ALAN KELLY is Associate Professor of English at Millersville University of Pennsylvania where he teaches modern American poetry, fiction, and drama. He has published and presented conference papers on modern American poetry, especially on the topic of estrangement between men and women in the works of several modern American poets.

ROBIN KEMP teaches English at Kennesaw State University near Atlanta, Georgia. She holds a Master of Fine Arts from the University of New Orleans. Her work appears in *Texas Review* and *Able Muse*. A Hambidge Fellow and West Chester regular, she was voted Best Poet in New Orleans for 2000.

JENNIFER KILGORE teaches English as *maître de conférences* at the University of Caen. She is interested in issues of memory, identity, testimony, literature, and belief. Her articles about Geoffrey Hill, as well as "The Geoffrey Hill Server" (a website begun in 2002), have appeared in English and in French.

BURT KIMMELMAN is Associate Professor of English at New Jersey Institute of Technology. He is the author of two book-length literary studies: *The "Winter Mind": William Bronk and American Letters* (1998) and *The Poetics of Authorship in the Later Middle Ages: The Emergence of the Modern Literary Persona* (1996, paperback 1999), and he is the editor of *The Facts on File Companion to 20th-Century American Poetry* (2004). He is also the author of four collections of poetry: *Somehow* (2005), *The Pond at Cape May Point* (2002), *First Life* (1999), and *Musaics* (1992). He is currently developing a book on modern science and the mid-twentieth-century American avant-garde.

VALERIE FELITA KINLOCH is Assistant Professor of English Education at Teachers College, Columbia University. She has written on the politicalization of race, identity, language, and literacy practices of diverse learners. Her recent co-edited book is titled *Still Seeking an Attitude: Critical Reflections on the Work of June Jordan* (2004).

GREG KINZER is a doctoral candidate in the poetics program at the University at Buffalo, New York. His research interests center around interdisciplinary poetics and the intersections of poetry and science.

DENISE D. KNIGHT is Professor of English at the State University of New York, Cortland. She has published widely on Charlotte Perkins Gilman. In 2002 Knight received SUNY Chancellor's Awards for Excellence in Teaching and Excellence in Scholarship; in 2004 she won a Distinguished Alumni Award from the University of Albany.

DENISE KOHN is Associate Professor of English at Greensboro College in North Carolina, where she teaches American literature, adolescent literature, and writing. Her research and publications focus on eighteenth- and nineteenth-century American women writers.

JOHN P. KOONTZ is an independent scholar living in New Jersey.

STEVE KOWIT, Professor of English at Southwestern College, is the recipient of a National Endowment for the Arts Fellowship in poetry and two Pushcart Prizes. He is the author of *In the Palm of Your Hand: The Poet's Portable Workshop (1995)* and several collections of poetry.

CHRISTOPHER M. KUIPERS is Assistant Professor of English and member of the graduate faculty in literature and criticism at Indiana University of Pennsylvania. A comparatist, he has also taught at the University of California at Irvine, the California State Universities at San Luis Obispo and at Fullerton, and Eastern Illinois University.

STEPHEN KUUSISTO is Assistant Professor in the Department of English at the Ohio State University in Columbus. He teaches poetry and nonfiction in the graduate creative writing program. He is the author of a memoir, *Planet of the Blind*, and a collection of poems from Copper Canyon Press titled *Only Bread, Only Light.*

ANTHONY LACAVARO is a writer and contributing editor to Open City Books and Magazine. His work has appeared in *New Republic*, the *Yale Review*, the *Paris Review* and other journals and magazines.

KIMBERLY LAMM is completing her Ph.D. in English at the University of Washington. Her dissertation examines literary and visual portraiture in American culture, and she has written extensively on contemporary American poetry and theories of feminism.

ERIC D. LAMORE is a Ph.D. candidate at Illinois State University. His interests include early American literature, Comparative Literature, and the teaching of writing.

DAVID LANDREY spent thirty-five years teaching literature at Buffalo State College. He studied briefly with Charles Olson at SUNY Buffalo and feels blessed to have met and worked with so many exciting poets, known and unknown. He told his late son, who wanted to be an architect, "Terrific; poets and architects may save the world."

DIETER LANGE was former Professor of Art History at the University of Applied Sciences and Arts in Hannover, Germany. He has written on the history of architecture and design. Since 2002 he has lived in California and has changed the subject of his research to literary German Americans of the nineteenth century.

LINDA LEAVELL, Associate Professor of American Literature at Oklahoma State University, won the SCMLA book award for *Marianne Moore and the Visual Arts: Prismatic Color* (1995). She is co-editor of a forthcoming collection of essays about Moore and is currently writing a biography of Moore.

MICHAEL LEBLANC is working on his Ph.D. in English at the University of California, Riverside. He has had work published in *Camera Obscura* and is currently writing his dissertation titled *The Art of Confidence.*

JUN LEI has published articles on Nathaniel Hawthorne, Kate Chopin, and Zora Neale Hurston. Her current research interests include Asian American literature and culture, multiethnic American literature, and twentieth-century American women's literature. She received her MA in English from Wuhan University, China, and is currently a graduate student in Asian Studies at Seton Hall University.

GARY LEISING is a poet who has taught at the University of South Carolina, the University of Cincinnati, and Northern Kentucky University. In 2005 he began as Assistant Professor of English at Utica College. His poems have appeared in *River Styx*, *Quarterly West*, *Margie*, *Cortland Review*, and elsewhere.

MICHAL M. LEMBERGER was until recently Lecturer in the Department of English at the University of California, Los Angeles, where she received her Ph.D. in 2001 with a specialty in twentieth-century American poetry. Currently working as a freelance writer and editor, she writes about books and politics for various journals.

AMY LEMMON is Assistant Professor of English at the Fashion Institute of Technology in New York. She holds a Ph.D. from the University of Cincinnati and has published poems, translations, and interviews in *Verse*, *Prairie Schooner*, *Barrow Street*, *Rattapallax*, *Crab Orchard Review*, and other magazines.

JAMES S. LEONARD is Professor and English Department Head at the Citadel. He is co-editor of Prentice Hall's *Anthology of American Literature* (8th edition, 2003), editor of *Making Mark Twain Work in the Classroom* (1999), coeditor of *Satire or Evasion?* (1992), and co-author of *The Fluent Mundo* (1988).

VALERIE LEVY is Assistant Professor of English at Montclair State University, where she teaches American literature, world literature, and multicultural literature. Her publications and conference presentations include a book chapter on Zora Neale Hurston and pieces on Alice Walker, Judith Cofer, and abolitionists Lydia Maria Child, Maria Weston Chapman, and Frances Ellen Watkins Harper.

ERNESTO LIVON-GROSMAN is Assistant Professor of Romance Languages and Literatures at Boston College. He is the translator of *Charles Olson: Poemas* (Tres Haches, 1997) and the editor of *The XUL Reader: An Anthology of Argentine Poetry* (Roof Books, 1997). His most recent book is *José Lezama Lima: Selections* (California, 2005).

MARK C. LONG is Associate Professor and Chair in the Department of English at Keene State College. He has published essays, book chapters, and reviews on a range of American poets and writers, and is a co-editor of *Teaching North American Environmental Literature,* forthcoming from the Modern Language Association.

JOSÉ R. LÓPEZ MORÍN is Assistant Professor of Chicana/o Studies at California State University, Domínguez Hills. He is the author of the book titled *Américo Paredes: A Man from the Border* (2006), which will be published by Texas A&M University Press. His interests are in folklore, history, literature, and music.

SUZANNE LUMMIS is the Founding Director of the Los Angeles Poetry Festival. Her poems appear in the anthologies *California Poetry from the Gold Rush to the Present* (Heyday), *Poems of the American West* (Knoph), *Poetry Daily* (Sourcebooks), and her most recent book, *In Danger*, was part of the California Poetry Series (Roundhouse Press).

SARA LUNDQUIST teaches modern and contemporary American literature at the University of Toledo. She has published on the American poets Ashbery, Guest, Williams, Jeffers, Graham, and Schuyler. She has a particular interest in aesthetics and in ekphrastic poetry. She is completing a book, titled *Implacable Poet*, about the New York School poet Barbara Guest.

MARIT J. MACARTHUR received a Ph.D. in English from the University of California, Davis in 2005. Her dissertation is titled "Abandoning the House: Landscape Meditation in Twentieth Century Poetry." She has published articles on the poetry of Thomas Hardy, Robert Frost, and Elizabeth Bishop.

GLEN MACLEOD is Professor of English at the University of Connecticut, Waterbury. He is the author of *Wallace Stevens and Company* (1983) and *Wallace Stevens and Modern Art* (1993). His research interests are in American literature and the visual arts.

MICHAEL JAMES MAHIN is a Ph.D. candidate at the Claremont Graduate University with interests in contemporary American literature, American studies, and postmodernism. In addition to being the recipient of a Pew Younger Scholars fellowship and a Durfee Foundation grant, he is also a developing screenwriter and children's book author.

DEVONA MALLORY is a Ph.D. candidate in English Studies at Illinois State University, Normal. Her research areas are magical realism, women's literature, and Comparative Literature. Her work has been featured in *American National Biography* and *African American Lives.*

MANIJEH MANNANI has a Ph.D. in Comparative Literature. She teaches Comparative Literature at the University of Alberta, Edmonton, and English and world literature at Grant MacEwan Community College, Edmonton. Her writings have appeared in various journals and encyclopedias, including the *Canadian Review of Comparative Literature* and *Beacham's Encyclopedia of Popular Fiction.*

H.J. MANZARI is Assistant Professor of Spanish and International Studies at Worcester Polytechnic Institute. He has written extensively on postmodernism, race, and identity in the contemporary Caribbean narrative and the Caribbean diaspora and U.S. Latino literatures. He is co-editor (with Edward H. Friedman and Donald Miller) of *A Society on Stage: Essays on Spanish Golden Age Drama* (1998).

STEPHEN MARINO teaches at Saint Francis College in Brooklyn, New York. His work on Arthur Miller has appeared in *Modern Drama*, the *Journal of Imagism*, and *South Atlantic Review.* He is the editor of "*The Salesman Has a Birthday": Essays Celebrating the Fiftieth Anniversary of Arthur Miller's Death of a Salesman* (2000). He is the author of *A Language Study of Arthur Miller's Plays: The Poetic in the Colloquial* (2002).

ALEC MARSH is an Associate of English at Muhlenberg College. He is the author of *Money & Modernity: Pound, Williams and the Spirit of Jefferson.* He writes frequently on Pound and other modern poets.

JOHN EDWARD MARTIN is a Visiting Lecturer in American Literature at Wake Forest University. He specializes in the study of nineteenth-century American Romanticism, the gothic, and religion and literature. He has done recent work on Edgar Allan Poe, Emily Dickinson, and confessional poetry, and is a published poet.

DAVID MASON's books of poems include *The Buried Houses*, *The Country I Remember*, and *Arrivals.* His book of essays, *The Poetry of Life and the Life of Poetry*, appeared in 2000, and he is also the co-editor of four anthologies. He teaches at the Colorado College.

JACK MATTHEWS is Distinguished Professor of English Emeritus at Ohio University in Athens. He has published twenty-three books of fiction, nonfiction, plays, and poetry. His most recent is a Czech translation of his novel, *Schopenhauer's Will*. Last year the Theatre Studio in New York produced three of his one-act plays.

ASIMA FX SAAD MAURA is Assistant Professor of Spanish at Temple University, Philadelphia. She primarily teaches transatlantic studies in Spanish Golden Age and colonial Latin American literatures and cultures. She has published in the *Hispanic Review* (2002) and the *Journal of the Southeastern Council of Latin American Studies* (2003).

SUSAN MCCABE is Associate Professor of English at University of Southern California, Los Angeles. Her books include *Elizabeth Bishop: Her Poetics of Loss* (Penn State, 1994), *Swirl* (Red Hen Press, 2003), and *Cinematic Modernism: Modern Poetry and Film* (2005).

JANET MCCANN is Professor of English at Texas A&M University, where she has taught since 1969. Her most recent critical book is *Wallace Stevens Revisited: The Celestial Possible* (1995) and her newest poetry collection is *Looking For Buddha in the Barbed-Wire Garden* (1996).

JAMES MCCORKLE, Adjunct Professor at Hobart and William Smith Colleges, is a poet and essayist. His collection of poems, *Evidences*, received the *American Poetry Review*/Honickman Award in 2003; he has also received fellowships from the National Endowment for the Arts and the Ingram Merrill Foundation, as well as the first Campbell Corner Poetry Award from Sarah Lawrence College. With an MFA and Ph.D. from the University of Iowa, he is the editor of *Conversant Essays: Contemporary Poets on Poetry* and the author of *Still Performance*, a study of five postmodern poets, as well as numerous articles on contemporary poets, poetics, and the visual arts.

JEANNE MCNETT, Associate Professor of Management, Assumption College, Worcester, MA, teaches international management. Her research centers on globalization and the role of liberal arts in management education. Her writing won the 2004 Best Paper award from the *Journal of Management Education*. Recent work includes *The Blackwell Handbook of Global Management: A Guide to Managing Complexity*.

DOUGLAS MESSERLI is the author of numerous books of poetry, fiction, and drama, most recently *First Words* (Green Integer, 2004). He is also a noted editor, well known for his series of international anthologies, *The Pip Anthologies of World Poetry of the 20th Century*) and publisher of Green Integer.

PHILIP METRES is Assistant Professor of English at John Carroll University. He has published numerous articles on war resistance poetry, two books of poetry translations–*Catalogue of Comedic Novelties: Selected Poems of Lev Rubinstein* and *A Kindred Orphanhood: Selected Poems of Sergey Gandlevsky*–and a chapbook, *Primer for Non-Native Speakers*.

JESSICA METZLER is currently a doctoral candidate in American literature at Cornell University.

BRUCE MEYER is Professor of English in the Laurentian University BA Program at Georgian College and Instructor in Literature in the St. Michael's College Continuing Education Program at the University of Toronto. He is author of twenty-three books, including *The Golden Thread: A Reader's Journey Through the Great Books*. His internationally acclaimed broadcasts on *The Great Books* are the CBC's bestselling audiocassette series. He has won numerous awards for his teaching and writing.

CAROL N. MOE earned her Ph.D. in English from the University of California, Riverside in 2004. She

specializes in contemporary ethnic American novels and poetry.

ASHLEY NICOLE MONTJOY received her MA in creative writing from Florida State University in April 2005. She is an editorial associate at the *Apalachee Review* and *Southeast Review*. Her poems and reviews have appeared or are forthcoming in *Circle Magazine*, *Slipstream*, and the *Apalachee Review*.

As Associate Editor of the *Hudson Review*, JON MOOALLEM co-edited the audio anthology *Along These Lines: Fifty-Five Years of "Hudson Review" Poetry*. His own poems, essays, and reviews have appeared in *Poetry*, the *Dark Horse* (Scotland), the *Threepenny Review*, *Rattapallax*, the *San Francisco Chronicle*, and the *Believer*.

MICHAEL P. MORENO is a Ph.D. candidate in English at the University of California, Riverside. His areas of discipline include twentieth-century American literature, Latino literature, spatial theory, and urban/suburban studies. He has published in these areas.

PATRICK MOSELEY is a graduate student at Illinois State University.

A. MARY MURPHY teaches English at Alberta College of Art and Design and the University of Calgary. Her scholarly publications are primarily focused on both the theory and practice of life writing, particularly literary lives and biographical film. She also publishes extensively as a poet.

Ms. EVELYN NAVARRE is a doctoral student in the American Studies Department at SUNY Buffalo. Her two master's degrees, in English and women's studies, respectively, are from the University of Cincinnati. Prior to returning to graduate school, she was the Academic Director of the Women's Center at the University of Cincinnati Clermont College.

CARY NELSON is Jubilee Professor of Liberal Arts and Sciences and Professor of English at the University of Illinois at Urbana-Champaign. His books include *Repression and Recovery: Modern American Poetry and the Politics of Cultural Memory* (1989) and *Revolutionary Memory: Recovering the Poetry of the American Left* (2001).

MEREDITH NEUMAN is Assistant Professor of Early American Literature at Clark University and is currently developing a book on theories of the seventeenth-century Puritan sermon.

KEITH NEWLIN is Professor of English at the University of North Carolina at Wilmington. He is the editor of *A Theodore Dreiser Encyclopedia* (2003) and co-editor of *The Collected Plays of Theodore Dreiser* (2000) and *Selected Letters of Hamlin Garland* (1998).

WALT NOTT is Instructor of English at Kutztown University in Pennsylvania. His research interests include early American literature, Melville, and literary theory and the teaching of writing. He has published on American poet Phillis Wheatley and is currently at work on a project concerning discourse communities and Melville's magazine fiction.

PETER O'LEARY is an instructor in the liberal arts program at the School of the Art Institute of Chicago. His books include *Watchfulness* (2001) and *Gnostic Contagion: Robert Duncan & the Poetry of Illness* (2002). He has edited two collections of Ronald Johnson's poetry: *To Do as Adam Did: Selected Poems* (2000) and *The Shrubberies* (2001).

DIEDERIK OOSTDIJK is Assistant Professor of English Literature at the Vrije Universiteit in Amsterdam in the Netherlands. He has published various articles on twentieth-century American poets, including James Dickey, Randall Jarrell, and Karl Shapiro as well as on *Poetry: A Magazine of Verse.* A recipient of two Fulbright scholarships, he is now working on a book about American poetry and World War II.

BEA OPENGART is Field Service Assistant Professor of English and Creative Writing at the University of Cincinnati. Her poems have appeared in numerous journals, most recently *Folio, The Madison Review, Sou'wester,* and *Tiferet.* Her book, *Erotica,* was published by Owl Creek Press.

HEATHER OSTMAN is Assistant Professor and Writing Program Coordinator at the Manhattan Metropolitan Center of Empire State College of the State University of New York. She has written articles on women writers and activists, including Elizabeth Cary, Jane Addams, and Emma Goldman.

JOHN OUGHTON teaches English at Centennial College, Toronto. He studied literature at York University and Naropa Institute in Boulder, Colorado. He has published four books of poetry, most recently *Counting Out the Millennium* (Pecan Grove Press), and over three hundred freelance articles, and he and edited the online edition of *Poetry Markets for Canadians.*

SHIN YU PAI was Artist-in-Residence in the University of Texas at Dallas' South Side on Lamar Studio Program from October 2004 until October 2005. Her publications include *Equivalence* (2003) and *Ten Thousand Miles of Mountains and Rivers* (1998).

MIKEL PARENT is a doctoral student at Brandeis University. He is currently at work on a dissertation project on twentieth-century American epic long poems and Cold War ideology. He specializes in twentieth-century American literature, film, and philosophy.

JAMES PARINS is Associate Director of the Sequoyah Research Center and Professor of English at the University of Arkansas at Little Rock. He has published extensively on American Indian literature and history, having written *John Rollin Ridge: His Life and Works, Elias Cornelius Boudinot: A Life on the Cherokee Border,* and guides to Native newspapers and periodicals. He has also edited several editions of the works of Native American writers.

JOSEPHINE PARK is Assistant Professor of English and Asian American Studies at the University of Pennsylvania. She is at work on a book-length project on modernism, Asia, and Asian American poetry titled *Apparitions of Asia.*

BOB PERELMAN is Professor of English at the University of Pennsylvania. He has published sixteen books of poetry, including *Ten to One (Selected Poems), Playing Bodies,* and *The Future of Memory,* and two critical books on modernism and contemporary poetry, *The Trouble with Genius* and *The Marginalization of Poetry.*

MARJORIE PERLOFF is Sadie Dernham Patek Professor Emerita of Humanities at Stanford University and currently Scholar-in-Residence at the University of Southern California. She is the author of twelve books on poetry and poetics as well as the visual arts, including *The Poetics of Indeterminacy: Rimbaud to Cage, The Futurist Moment, Wittgenstein's Ladder,* and, most recently, a memoir titled *The Vienna Paradox* and *Differentials, Poetry, Poetics, Pedagogy,* which won the 2005 Warren-Brooks Prize for literary criticism. In 2006 she will be President of the Modern Language Association.

JEANNE PERREAULT is a Professor in the Department of English, University of Calgary, Calgary, Alberta, Canada. She has co-edited an anthology of Western Canadian Native women writers, *Writing the Circle,* and has written a number of articles on First Nations writers. Her primary research is on women's life writing and she has co-edited a collection of critical essays, *Tracing the Autobiographical* (forthcoming). She has published on whiteness and feminism, chain gangs, and propaganda.

JENNIFER PERRINE is a poet and doctoral student in English at Florida State University. Her poetry has appeared in numerous literary journals, and she was awarded the 2004 Poetry Fellowship from Writers at Work. Her critical writing has been included most recently in *The Holocaust Film Sourcebook* (2004).

BECKY PETERSON is currently working on a Ph.D. in English at the University of Minnesota.

KATIE PETERSON is a graduate student in English and American literature at Harvard University. She has written on Walt Whitman, Emily Dickinson, and other American poets. She has also published poetry in a number of national publications and has been nominated for a Pushcart Prize in Poetry.

ZACHARY S. PETREA is a graduate student at Illinois State University and an independent scholar in early American literature.

RHONDA PETTIT is Associate Professor of English and Women's Studies at University of Cincinnati Raymond Walters College. She is the author of *A Gendered Collision: Sentimentalism and Modernism in Dorothy Parker's Poetry and Fiction* (2000) and the editor of the first collection of critical essays about Parker's work, *The Critical Waltz* (2005).

PATRICK PHILLIPS is a MacCracken Fellow in English Renaissance Literature at New York University. His first book of poems, *Chattahoochee,* received a 2003 "Discovery"/*The Nation* Award from the Unterberg Poetry Center and was published by the University of Arkansas Press in 2004.

STACY PIES is Master Teacher at the Gallatin School of New York University. Her work on Allen Grossman appears in *Poetry's Poet: Essays on the Poetry, Pedagogy, and Poetics of Allen Grossman,* edited by Daniel Morris, She has also published on Stéphane Mallarmé in *French Forum.*

PATRICIA PLOESCH is a Ph.D. candidate at the University of California, Riverside. Her work investigates indigenous film and visual culture, and ethnology and gynecology in American literature.

AIMEE L. POZORSKI is Visiting Assistant Professor of English at Central Connecticut State University. She writes on trauma in contemporary American literature with a special focus on Ernest Hemingway, Philip Roth, and Toni Morrison. She is currently revising her book project, *Figures of Infanticide: Traumatic Modernity and the Inaudible Cry.*

ANNA PRIDDY is an instructor of English at Louisiana State University.

SINA QUEYRAS is a writer. She teaches creative writing at Rutgers, New Brunswick, New Jersey. She is the author of two collections of poetry, and she recently edited *Open Field: 30 Contemporary Canadian Poets* (Persea, 2005).

JESSICA G. RABIN is Assistant Professor of English at Anne Arundel Community College in Arnold, Maryland. She has extensively published and presented on Willa Cather and is the author of *Surviving the Crossing: (Im)migration, Ethnicity, and Gender in Willa Cather, Gertrude Stein, and Nella Larsen* (2004).

BEN RAILTON is Assistant Professor of American and Ethnic Literature at Fitchburg State College. He has written on William Faulkner, Margaret Mitchell, postbellum Southern poetry, and the African-American historical novel, and is currently finishing a manuscript titled *Contesting the Past: History and Dialogue in American Literature, 1876–1893.*

JAHAN RAMAZANI is Kenan Professor of English at the University of Virginia. Co-editor of *The Norton Anthology of Modern and Contemporary Poetry* (2003), he wrote *The Hybrid Muse* (2001), *Poetry of Mourning* (1994), and *Yeats and the Poetry of Death* (1990). He has received Guggenheim and NEH fellowships.

LAURI RAMEY is Associate Professor of Creative Writing and English at California State University, Los Angeles. She is the co-editor of *Black British Writing* (2004) and *Every Goodbye Ain't Gone* (2006).

CAROLE REALFF is completing a DPhil at the University of Sussex, UK, titled *Studies in the Poetry of Richard Realf 1850–1900.* She has a passionate interest in the culture of abolition in North America and recently delivered *An Englishman in Kansas: Richard Realf, Free State Poet and Soldier* at the 2004 Bleeding Kansas lecture series at Constitution Hall State Historic Site, Lecompton, Kansas. She contributed the biography and poetic selections on Realf in *The Poetry of Slavery an Anglo American Anthology*, edited by Marcus Wood (Oxford University Press, 2003).

J. C. REILLY is a doctoral candidate in creative writing with a specialization in women's studies at the University of Nebraska–Lincoln. Her work has appeared in or is forthcoming from *the Louisville Review, Blackwidow's Web of Poetry, Rive Gauche*, and other journals, and she has been nominated for AWP Intro awards.

DEBORAH ADAMS RENVILLE is Professor of English at Kankakee Community College in Kankakee, Illinois. She also is a Ph.D. candidate in English studies at Illinois State University, where she is specializing in American and Canadian literature.

JEFFREY H. RICHARDS is Professor of English at Old Dominion University. He has written extensively on American drama and theater, including two pieces on Samuel Davies. His article "Samuel Davies and the Transatlantic Campaign for Slave Literacy in Virginia" won the Rachal Prize (2004) from the Virginia Historical Society.

PAGE RICHARDS is Assistant Professor at the University of Hong Kong, publishing in American literature, poetry, and drama. She has a Ph.D. from Harvard University and an MA in creative writing from Boston University.

TAD RICHARDS is a poet, independent scholar, and artistic director of Opus 40 in Saugerties, New York. He is the author of over thirty books, including a poetry collection, *My Night with the Language Thieves*; a novel in verse, *Situations*; and *The New Country Music Encyclopedia.*

KELLY L. RICHARDSON is Assistant Professor of English at Winthrop University, where she teaches American Literature. Her research interests include investigating spirituality and gender in nineteenth-century literature. She is currently the Book Review Editor of *Studies in American Humor.*

EUGENE RICHIE is Director of Writing, at Pace University in New York. His poetry collections include *Moiré* (1989), *Island Light* (1998), and, with Rosanne Wasserman, *Place du Carousel* (2001). He has edited John Ashbery's *Selected Prose* (2004), translates Jaime Manrique (Colombia) and Matilde Daviu (Venezuela), and is founding editor of Groundwater Press.

AMY MOORMAN ROBBINS is an independent scholar interested in American poetry, particularly the Language movement and postmodern poetics. She has given papers or published articles on Amy Gerstler, Fanny Howe, Alice Notley, Anne Sexton, and Sterling Brown. She completed her Ph.D. in American literature at the University of California, Riverside.

TARA L. ROBBINS is a Teaching Fellow at the University of North Carolina at Chapel Hill. Her work on *Amos Bronson Alcott* comes from a larger project, titled *Sympathy and Self-Reliance: Transcendentalism's Emergence from the Culture of Sentiment.*

SUSAN L. ROCKWELL is Instructor of English at Rio Salado College and Chair of the Department of English at St. Mary's High School in Phoenix, Arizona. She has written extensively about Native American authors and autobiography. The recipient of two teaching awards in 2004, she is devoted to classroom diversity.

ZINA RODRÍGUEZ is a graduate student studying at the University of California, Riverside. Her areas of expertise include Latina/o Discourse and Theater, Nuyorican literature, twentieth-century American literature, and Film/Visual Culture.

CE ROSENOW is Visiting Assistant Professor of Literature in the Robert D. Clark Honors College at the University of Oregon. Her current research explores the Japanese influence on American modernist poetry.

NICOLE ROUSSOS holds an MA in English from Boston College and is currently a student in the Ph.D. program in English at the University of Minnesota. She has conducted prior biographical research on Rev. Benjamin B. Wisner and Sarah Josepha Hale.

KATHY RUGOFF is Associate Professor of English at the University of North Carolina at Wilmington. Her publications in modern and contemporary American poetry include articles on music and Walt Whitman, William Carlos Williams, and

W. H. Auden. American music and literature is also a teaching interest.

RICHARD RANKIN RUSSELL is Assistant Professor of English at Baylor University. His current project examines the work of the significant Northern Irish writers that emerged from the Belfast Group in the early 1960s and explores their contribution to a regional literature that helped effect reconciliation in the province.

LINDA RUSSO is a graduate of the Poetics Program at the University at Buffalo. Her essays are published in *Girls Who Wore Black: Women Writing the Beat Generation* (Rutgers, 2002) and *Don't Ever Get Famous: Essays on New York Writing Beyond the 'New York School'* (Dalkey Archive, forthcoming). She is currently a lecturer at the University of Oklahoma.

RUSSELL RUTTER is Professor of English at Illinois State University, Normal, where for thirty years he has taught early modern literature and technical communication. He has published on several medieval and early modern authors, and on early printing, medieval literature of prophecy, and technical communication in England and America.

ANGELA M. SALAS is Associate Professor of English at Clarke College, in Dubuque, Iowa. Salas has published on Edith Wharton, Willa Cather, Yusef Komunyakaa, and the Vietnam Veterans Memorial. Her book, *Flashback Through the Heart: the Poetry of Yusef Komunyakaa* (2004), is an examination of Komunyakaa's work and place in American poetry.

MARK A. SANDERS is Associate Professor in the English Department at Emory University.

INGRID SATELMAJER is Lecturer in the English Department at the University of Maryland, College Park. She has published articles on nineteenth-century periodicals and poetry culture in *Book History* and *American Periodicals.* Her dissertation was "Remapping Dickinson and Periodical Studies."

JUDITH P. SAUNDERS is Professor of English at Marist College in New York State. Her published commentary addresses a wide range of literary figures and topics, including contemporary poets and poetics. She is the author of *The Poetry of Charles Tomlinson: Borderlines* (Fairleigh Dickinson University Press, 2003).

CHRISTOPHER SAWYER-LAUÇANNO is the long-time Writer-in-Residence at MIT. His books include *E.E. Cummings: A Biography* (2004), *An Invisible Spectator: A Biography of Paul Bowles* (1989), and *The Continual Pilgrimage: American Writers in Paris, 1944–1960* (1991). He is also a translator and poet.

STANDARD SCHAEFER is a writer living in San Francisco. He has written extensively on contemporary poetry and has two volumes of his own: *Nova* (Sun & Moon Press, 2001), which was selected for the National Poetry Series in 1999, and *Water & Power* (Agincourt Books, 2004). He is also an editor for the *New Review of Literature.*

The J.R. Millikan Centennial Professor at the University of Texas at Austin, WILLIAM J. SCHEICK has published many books, including *Design in Puritan American Literature* (1992), *Paine, Scripture, and Authority: The Age of Reason as Religious and Political Idea* (1994), and *Authority and Female Authorship in Colonial America* (1998).

KYLE SCHLESINGER is completing his doctorate in the Poetics Program at SUNY Buffalo. He is the proprietor of the literary fine press Cuneiform, and co-editor of *Kiosk: A Journal of Poetry, Poetics & Prose.* Recent book-works include *Reading in Bed, Moonlighting, A Book of Closings,* and *Mantle* in collaboration with Thom Donovan.

AMY NEWLOVE SCHROEDER's poems and reviews have appeared in *Denver Quarterly, American Poetry Review, Colorado Review,* and *Georgia Review.* A doctoral fellow at the University of Southern California, she is a founding editor of the Los Angeles poetry magazine *Pool.*

KATHY LOU SCHULTZ's collections of poetry and experimental fiction include *Some Vague Wife* (Atelos Press, 2002), Genealogy (a+bend press, 1999) and *Re dress* (San Francisco State University, 1994), winner of the Michael Rubin Award. She is completing her doctoral dissertation on African American modernist poetry at the University of Pennsylvania.

SUSAN M. SCHULTZ is Professor of English at the University of Hawai'i in Honolulu. She is a widely published poet and literary critic. She runs Tinfish Press out of her home in Kane'ohe.

ROXANNE Y. SCHWAB is Instructor in English/Literature at Saint Louis University, St. Louis, Missouri. She has written extensively on drama, film, business and professional writing, and rhetoric. In 2004 she was nominated for the Lucien Fournier Excellence in Teaching Award and the Rev. Walter J. Ong Excellence in Academic Research Award.

JO SCOTT-COE currently teaches creative writing at the University of California, Riverside. Her poetry and essays have appeared in publications such as the *Chariton Review, Pearl, KB Journal,* and the *Los Angeles Times.*

LAURA SCURIATTI is Assistant Professor of Literature at the European College of Liberal Arts, Berlin (Germany). She has published articles on H.G. Wells, Ford Madox Ford, and Mina Loy, and edited an anthology of contemporary German literature. Her current research focuses on modernist literature and feminist avant-garde writers.

SAMUEL R. SEE is a graduate student in English at the University of California, Los Angeles, where he studies twentieth-century literature, poetry, and queer studies. He has a paper forthcoming in the *Journal of Bisexuality* and has won awards from UCLA for his poetry.

NICK SELBY is Lecturer at the University of Glasgow. He has written widely on American literature and poetry and is the author of *From Modernism to Fascism: Poetics of Loss in the Cantos of Ezra Pound.* He is Associate Director of the Andrew Hook Centre for American Studies in Glasgow.

LISA SEWELL is Associate Professor of English and Creative Writing at Villanova University. She the author of two books of poetry, *The Way Out* (Alice James) and *Name Withheld* (Four Way Books), and co-editor of *American Poets in the 21st Century: The New Poetics* (Wesleyan University Press). She has published essays on Ted Hughes, Brenda Hillman, Frank Bidart, and Louise Gluck.

RAVI SHANKAR is Poet-in-Residence at Central Connecticut State University and the founding editor of the online journal of the arts, www.drunkenboat.com. His book of poems, *Instru-*

mentality, was published by Cherry Grove in 2004. He has published poems and reviews in numerous publications, including the *Paris Review, Time Out New York,* and *Poets and Writers.*

JOHN C. SHIELDS is Professor of American, African American, and Comparative Literatures at Illinois State University. He has published on these literary fields and is editor of *The Collected Works of Phillis Wheatley* (1988), and advisory editor of and contributor to *The Oxford Companion to African American Literature* (1997) and *The American National Biography* (1999). In 2001 he published *The American Aeneas: Classical Origins of the American Self* (pb 2004), which has won *Choice*'s Outstanding Academic Book for 2002 and Honorable Mention for the Harry Levin Prize (2000–2003) sponsored by the American Comparative Literature Association.

GAIL SHIVEL (Ph.D., University of Miami) is associate editor of *Menckeniana* and book review editor (North America) for *SHARP News*. Her *New Yorker Profiles 1925–1992: A Bibliography* was published in 2000. She lectures part-time at the University of Miami and Florida International University.

EVIE SHOCKLEY is Assistant Professor of English at Rutgers University. Her poetry and scholarship appear in her collection *The Gorgon Goddess* (2001) and numerous journals and anthologies. A Cave Canem fellow, she is working on a study of race and innovation in African American poetry.

SABINE SIELKE is Chair of North American Literature and Culture and Director of the North American Studies Program and the German-Canadian Centre at the University of Bonn. Her publications include *Reading Rape* (2002), *Fashioning the Female Subject* (1997), and editions on (post)modernism, 9/11, cultural theory, and gender matters.

RICHARD SILBERG is Associate Editor of *Poetry Flash.* Among his publications are *Reading the Sphere,* essays on poetry (Berkeley Hills Books, 2002), and four books of poems, most recently *Doubleness* (Heyday Books, 2000). A new collection, *Deconstruction of the Blues,* will be published by Red Hen Press in 2005.

MARK SILVERBERG is Assistant Professor of American Literature at the University College of Cape Breton, Nova Scotia. His publications on twentieth-century poetry, theory, and culture have appeared in journals such as *Arizona Quarterly, English Studies in Canada,* the *Dalhousie Review, Essays on Canadian Writing,* and *Contemporary Literature.*

KENNETH SILVERMAN is Professor Emeritus of English at New York University. A fellow of the American Academy of Arts and Sciences, he has published biographies of Cotton Mather, Edgar Allen Poe, Houdini, and Samuel F. B. Morse, and has been awarded the Bancroft Prize and the Pulitzer Prize for Biography.

SEAN SINGER's first book, *Discography,* won the 2001 Yale Series of Younger Poets Prize, selected by W.S. Merwin, and the Norma Farber First Book Award from the Poetry Society of America. He also won a grant from the Massachusetts Cultural Council and a Fellowship from the National Endowment for the Arts. He lives in New York City.

JAMES SMETHURST is Assistant Professor in the W.E.B. DuBois Department of Afro-American Studies at the University of Massachusetts–Amherst. He is the author of *The New Red Negro: The Literary Left and African American Poetry, 1930–1946* (1999) and *The Black Arts Movement: Literary Nationalism in the 1960s and 1970s* (2005), and the co-editor with Bill V. Mullen of *Left of the Color Line: Race, Radicalism and Twentieth-Century Literature of the United States* (2003).

DORSÍA SMITH SILVA is a Ph.D. student in Caribbean literature at the University of Puerto Rico, Río Piedras. She also teaches English and has several forthcoming articles in *La Torre.*

ERNEST SMITH, Associate Professor of English, University of Central Florida, is the author of *The Imaged Word: The Infrastructure of Hart Crane's White Buildings,* as well as numerous articles. Recently published essays examine the father elegies of Sylvia Plath and John Berryman, and socially oriented poems by Alfred Corn and Adrienne Rich.

JAMES M. SMITH, JR. is Associate Editor of *Southern Poetry Review* and Associate Professor of English at Armstrong Atlantic State University in Savannah, Georgia. His poems have appeared in *Agni* (online), *Atlanta Review, Connecticut Review, Nebraska Review, Passages North,* and *Quarterly West.* His fiction has appeared in *American Short Fiction.*

JOYCE C. SMITH is Assistant Professor of English at the University of Tennessee at Chattanooga. She teaches American literature, Latino literature, and Children's literature. She has written on Stephen Crane and Erskine Caldwell, and she is currently working on a juvenile edition of Crane's poetry.

JULES SMITH is a freelance writer living in Kingston upon Hull, United Kingdom. He is the author of *"Art, Survival and So Forth": The Poetry of Charles Bukowski* (2000), and is a regular reviewer for the *Times Literary Supplement* (London). He has contributed extensively to the British Council's contemporary writers website and to several reference books, including *The Good Fiction Guide* (2001) and *The New Oxford Dictionary of National Biography* (2004).

ALISA M. SMITH-RIEL is a Learning/Teaching Fellow at St. Bonaventure University pursuing graduate work in American and modern British literature, with subfields in the novel and William Faulkner. She recently served as Senior Editor of *Encyclopedia of Celebrities from Western New York and Pennsylvania.*

STEFANIE E. SOBELLE is a Ph.D. candidate in English and Comparative Literature at Columbia University. She works primarily on experimental literature and has taught modern and postmodern poetry and fiction at Sarah Lawrence College, Cooper Union, and Columbia.

REBECCA SOPPE is a doctoral student at Florida State University. She received an MFA from the University of Florida, and she writes short fiction.

ANGELA SORBY is Assistant Professor of English at Marquette University, where she teaches American literature and creative writing. She is the author of *Schoolroom Poets: Childhood, Performance, and the Place of American Poetry* (2005), and she has also published a volume of poetry, *Distance Learning* (1998).

JULIANA SPAHR is Assistant Professor at Mills College. Among her books are *This Connection of Everyone with Lungs* (University of California Press, 2005), *Fuck You-Aloha-I Love You* (Wesleyan University Press, 2001), and *Everybody's*

Autonomy: Connective Reading and Collective Identity (University of Alabama Press, 2001).

JASON SPANGLER is a Ph.D. candidate in English at the University of California, Riverside. He is currently completing his dissertation, tentatively titled *From the Great Depression to the Grateful Dead.* In 2004 he was made a fellow of the National Writing Project.

ROBERT SQUILLACE is a Master Teacher of Cultural Foundations in the General Studies Program of New York University. He has written on the poet Tony Harrison and extensively on Arnold Bennett, including *Modernism, Modernity and Arnold Bennett* (1997) and "Arnold Bennett's Other Selves" in *Marketing the Author* (2004).

JONATHAN STALLING is a doctoral candidate in English literature at SUNY Buffalo, where he is a Lecturer in Asian Studies and holds a fellowship in ethnopoetics. His research interests include American modernism, East-West studies, and comparative poetics.

CRYSTAL STALLMAN is Regular Part-Time Instructor of Writing at Hawkeye Community College, Waterloo, Iowa, and Adjunct Instructor of Writing at Hamilton College, Cedar Falls, Iowa. She has written an article on Indian captivity narratives for the *Dictionary of Midwestern Literature.* She also writes poetry, fiction, and creative nonfiction.

JEFFREY STEELE, Sally Mead Hands Professor of English at the University of Wisconsin–Madison, is the author of *The Representation of the Self in the American Renaissance, The Essential Margaret Fuller,* and *Transfiguring America: Myth, Ideology, and Mourning in Margaret Fuller's Writing,* as well as numerous articles on nineteenth-century literature.

SASHA STEENSEN is the author of *A Magic Book* (Fence Books), which received the 2004 Alberta Prize for poetry. She co-edits the journal *Kiosk: A Journal of Poetry, Poetics, and Experimental Prose* and is currently completing a Ph.D. in poetics at the State University of New York at Buffalo.

MATTHEW STEFON has taught English at Middlesex Community and Worcester State Colleges. He will resume graduate study at Boston University. Interested in the intersection of religious belief and literary art, he is currently researching Dwight Goddard, whose writings on Buddhism were a foundational influence on Jack Kerouac.

PAUL STEPHENS is a semi-independent scholar living in New York City. He recently earned his Ph.D. in English from Columbia University.

DAVID STERRITT, Ph.D., is Professor of Theater and Film at Long Island University, Adjunct Arts Professor at Columbia University, co-chair of the Columbia University Seminar on Cinema and Interdisciplinary Interpretation, film critic for the *Christian Science Monitor,* and author of several books and essays on the Beat Generation.

CRAIG SVONKIN is A.B.D. at the University of California, Riverside. He writes on American literature, focusing on poetry, Jewish American writers, and children's literature. His publications include "Melville and the Bible: *Moby-Dick; or the Whale,* Multivocalism, and Plurality" and *New Directions in American Literary Scholarship: 1980–2002,* co-written with Emory Elliott.

DEBORAH TALL is Professor of English and Comparative Literature at Hobart and William Smith Colleges, Geneva, New York. She is the author of four books of poetry, most recently *Summons,* which won the Katherine A. Morton Prize, and two books of creative nonfiction. She is also editor of *Seneca Review.*

NANETTE C. TAMER is Associate Professor of English at Villa Julie College in Maryland. Her prior publications concern the use of Greek and Roman genres in English and American literature.

JAYANTI TAMM is a Professor of English at Ocean County College, New Jersey. She is a poet, playwright, and novelist whose works have been published nationally and internationally. In 2000 she was nominated for a Pushcart Prize.

PAUL TAYYAR is Lecturer in English at Golden West College in Huntington Beach, California. His poetry has been published in a variety of literary journals, and he is working on his Ph.D. in American literature from the University of California, Riverside.

MARK TEMELKO is a poet currently completing his first book. He holds a BA from Northeastern University and an MFA from the University of Alaska, Anchorage. He has taught as an adjunct instructor at the University of Alaska Anchorage and Alaska Pacific University.

ALICE TEMPLETON teaches English at the Art Institute of California–San Francisco. She has published poetry in the *American Voice, Poetry, 88,* and elsewhere, and is the author of a critical study of Adrienne Rich's poetics, *The Dream and the Dialogue* (University of Tennessee Press, 1994).

WILLIAM B. THESING is Professor of English at the University of South Carolina, Columbia. He is currently the editor of the *James Dickey Newsletter.* He has written or edited fifteen books, including *The London Muse, Critical Essays on Edna St. Vincent Millay,* and *Robinson Jeffers and a Galaxy of Writers.* In 2003 he won several teaching and mentoring awards.

JOSEPH T. THOMAS, JR. is Assistant Professor at California State University, Northridge, where he teaches contemporary poetry and children's literature. Co-editor and co-founder of the zine *Formerly Known as l'Bourgeoizine,* Thomas's critical work has appeared, among other places, in *Children's Literature, Children's Literature Association Quarterly,* and *Style.*

LORENZO THOMAS, before his death in 2005, was Professor of English at University of Houston–Downtown. He authored several volumes of poetry and the critical study *Extraordinary Measures: Afrocentric Modernism and Twentieth-Century American Poetry* (2000), winner of a Choice Outstanding Academic Book award.

STEVEN THOMAS is a graduate student in the English department at Pennsylvania State University, University Park. His dissertation is about liberty and mercantilism in colonial American literature.

WAYNE THOMAS is a Ph.D. candidate in creative and critical writing at the University of Wales, Cardiff. His dissertation comprises a collection of short stories and a critical essay largely focused on the role of Anglo-Welsh working-class humor in his fiction.

J. C. TODD is a Writing for College program instructor at Bryn Mawr College. Publications include *Nightshade* (2000) and poems and translations in the *Paris Review* and other journals. Selected awards include Leeway Awards (2001, 2003) and fellowships from the Pennsylvania Council on the Arts (1998) and Baltic Centre for Writers and Translators (2004).

CATHERINE TUFARIELLO is Instructor of English at Valparaiso University. Her collection of poems, *Keeping My Name*, won the Walt McDonald First-Book Award in Poetry and was published by Texas Tech University Press in 2004. Her poetry criticism has appeared recently in the *Dictionary of Literary Biography*.

MARK TURSI is Instructor of Creative Writing, Literature, and Rhetoric at the University of Denver. He is also one of the founders and editors of the online literary magazine *Double Room: A Journal of Prose Poetry and Flash Fiction*.

JEFFREY TWITCHELL-WAAS is Academic Dean at OFS College in Singapore. His recent publications on modern poets include articles on Robert Creeley, Louis Zukofsky, H.D., and Yang Lian, as well as translations of contemporary Chinese poetry.

MADONA GRACE TYLER is a graduate student in education at the University of California, Riverside. Through her studies, she is currently exploring issues of gender, hybridity, technology, and globalization in the postmodern world.

PAT TYRER is Assistant Professor of English at West Texas A&M University, Canyon. She has written extensively on the work of American modernist Evelyn Scott and has published both scholarly and creative pieces. In 2004 she won the George Nixon Creative Writing Award with her co-writer, Pat Nickell.

GEORGE UBA, Ph.D., is Professor and Chair of the Department of English at California State University, Northridge. He has published extensively on Asian American poetry. His own book of poetry, *Disorient Ballroom*, was published by Turning Point Books in 2004.

PHILLIP JOHN USHER received his BA in French literature from London University (UK) and his AM and Ph.D. in Romance languages from Harvard University.

KATHRYN VANSPANCKEREN, Professor of English at the University of Tampa, writes poetry and scholarship, including *Outline History of American Literature* (1998), maintained on the Web. Her articles on Schwerner have appeared in *American Poetry Review* and *Dialectical Anthropology*.

EDITH M. VASQUEZ, Ph.D., is Visiting Assistant Professor of Ethnic Studies at the University of California, Riverside and Adjunct Instructor of Chicano and Latino Studies at California State University, Long Beach.

ANGELA VIETTO is Associate Professor of English at Eastern Illinois University. Her book *Women and Authorship in Revolutionary America* is forthcoming from Ashgate Press. She has also been associate editor of the anthology *Early American Writings* (Oxford, 2002).

STEPHEN VOYCE is a doctoral student at York University, Toronto, Canada. His main area of research focuses on contemporary poetry and poetics.

TAD WAKEFIELD teaches literature and composition at Riverside Community College in Riverside, California. His research interests include American poetry, drama, and short stories. Currently, Tad is working on a critical reader's companion to the plays of August Wilson.

CHERYL WALKER is Richard Armour Professor of Modern Languages at Scripps College. She is the author of several books about American women poets, including most recently *God and Elizabeth Bishop: Meditations on Religion and Poetry* (Palgrave Macmillan, 2005).

SUE BRANNAN WALKER, University of South Alabama Professor of English, Poet Laureate of Alabama and Publisher/Negative Capability Press, specializes in poetry, environmental, and Southern literature, such as James Dickey, Carson McCullers, Flannery O'Connor, and Marge Piercy. Recent books include *In the Realm of Rivers* and *It's Good Weather for Fudge*.

KRISTA WALTER is Associate Professor of English at Pasadena City College. She specializes in early American literature and literary theory. She has written on literary abolitionism and the literature of U.S. slavery.

DIANE MARIE WARD is Principal Poetry Cataloger for the SUNY Buffalo Poetry Collection. She is an adjunct faculty member of the SUNY Buffalo School of Informatics and has given presentations on the small press poets at local and national conferences. She has contributed a chapter on a new critical study of Gerald Locklin.

JOHN P. WARGACKI is Assistant Professor of English at Seton Hall University, South Orange, New Jersey, where he specializes in American poetry. In addition to editing "College English Notes," the official publication of the New Jersey College English Association, his scholarly pursuits focus on Hart Crane, Wallace Stevens, and Emily Dickinson.

DIANE WARNER (Ph.D. English, Texas Tech, 2001) is Associate Librarian at the Southwest Collection/Special Collections Library of Texas Tech University, Lubbock, Texas.

AIDAN WASLEY teaches modern poetry at the University of Georgia. Recent essays on W.H. Auden, John Ashbery, Adrienne Rich, and John Hollander have appeared in *Raritan*, *Contemporary Literature*, *Symbiosis*, and elsewhere. He recently spent a year as Writer-in-Residence at the James Merrill House in Stonington, Connecticut, and is currently at work on a book on Auden and American poetry.

ROSANNE WASSERMAN has published several poetry collections, and her work has appeared in many journals and anthologies, including *Best American Poetry*. Currently a professor at the United States Merchant Marine Academy, she has directed the Groundwater Press, a nonprofit poetry publisher in New York, with Eugene Richie for thirty years.

WILLIAM WATKIN is Lecturer in Literature at Brunel University, West London, where he specializes in contemporary poetry and literary theory. He is the author of *In the Process of Poetry: The New York School and the Avant-Garde* (2001) and *On Mourning: Theories of Loss in Modern Literature* (2004).

VIRGINIA WEIGAND received her MA in English from the University of California, Davis (2002), where she studied under Sandra McPherson, Sandra Gilbert, and Alan Williamson. She served as an editorial board member of the Swan

Scythe Press and co-translated Victor Manuel Mendiola's *Flight 294* (Swan Scythe Press, 2002).

ANGELA JANE WEISL is Associate Professor of English at Seton Hall University. She is the author of *The Persistence of Medievalism* (2003), *Conquering the Reign of Femeny: Gender and Genre in Chaucer's Romance* (1995), and many articles on medieval subjects. She is the editor, with Cindy Carlson, of *Constructions of Widowhood and Virginity in the Middle Ages* (1999).

DOUG WERDEN is Assistant Professor of English at West Texas A&M University. He teaches American literature and autobiography and researches the intersection between literature and rural life. Currently he is collecting and writing about unpublished narratives of women homesteaders.

RACHEL WETZSTEON is the author of two books of poems, *The Other Stars* and *Home and Away.* She has received an Ingram Merrill grant and the 2001 Witter Bynner Prize for Poetry from the American Academy of Arts and Letters, and is currently Assistant Professor of English at William Paterson University.

LORNA WHEELER is a professor at the University of Colorado at Boulder. Her scholarly interests include Harlem Renaissance women writers and a pervading impulse to queer the archive.

ED WHITE is Assistant Professor of Early American Literature at Louisiana State University.

DAVID WIDUP is a poet and information technologist. He has written two books of poetry: *Over to You!* (with Stellasue Lee) and *In Country* (with Michael Andrews) both published by Bombshelter Press in Los Angeles. David has also published poetry and literary criticism in many literary journals and publications. He lives with his wife in the Santa Cruz Mountains.

ANDRIA WILLIAMS is a fiction writer who received her bachelor's degree in English at the University of California, Berkeley, and her Master of Fine Arts in Creative Writing at the University of Minnesota.

MELISSA J. WILLIAMS is a Ph.D. student in British literature at Claremont Graduate University. Her research interests include feminist studies and discourse. She teaches composition and literature at Southwestern College in Chula Vista, California.

TYRONE WILLIAMS teaches literature and literary theory at Xavier University in Cincinnati, Ohio. His first book of poems, *c.c.*, was published in 2002 by Krupskaya Books. A chapbook, *Convalescence,* was published in 1987 by Ridgeway Press. Two more chapbooks, *AAB* and *Futures, Elections,* will appear in 2004.

STEVE WILSON is Professor of English at Texas State University–San Marcos, where he regularly teaches undergraduate and graduate courses on poetry and creative writing. A published poet, among his scholarly interest are Beat literature and Irish literature. Wilson has served as Senior Fulbright Lecturer in Romania and Slovenia.

CHRISTINA WOLAK is a writer whose research interests include pre–twentieth-century American women writers. She received her BA from Loyola University–Chicago and her MA from the University of Nebraska, Lincoln and has taught at the University of Nevada, Reno and the University of North Carolina, Charlotte.

CECILIA WOLOCH is the author of *Sacrifice* (Cahuenga Press, 1997), *Tsigan: The Gypsy Poem* (Cahuenga Press 2002), and *Late* (BOA Editions, 2003). She is the director of Summer Poetry in Idyllwild and serves on the faculty of the MFA Program in Professional Writing at Western Connecticut State University.

JOHN R. WOZNICKI is Assistant Professor of English and Communications at Georgian Court University. He is the author of *Ideological Content and Political Significance in Twentieth-Century American Poetry* (2001), as well as articles on Wallace Stevens, the language poets, and Stephen King.

DAVID N. WRIGHT is Assistant Professor of Modernism at Concordia University, Montreal. He has written about F.T. Marinetti, Ezra Pound, Charles Olson, and Marshall McLuhan, particularly in terms of their relationship to cultural and media studies.

LESLEE WRIGHT is a Ph.D. candidate in at the University of Nebraska in Lincoln, Nebraska, where she studies twentieth-century American literature. She holds an MFA in poetry from Bowling Green State University.

RAYMOND YANEK is an independent scholar living in Streator, Illinois.

EARL YARINGTON received his doctorate from Indiana University of Pennsylvania and is currently Assistant Professor of English at Neumann College. His interests include the nineteenth-century novel and nineteenth-century women writers. He has been awarded the Modern Language Association's Bibliography Fellowship for 2003–2006.

DAVID YOUNG is Longman Professor of English and Creative Writing Emeritus at Oberlin College. He is a poet, translator, critic, editor, and teacher. His most recent books are *The Poetry of Petrarch, Six Modernist Moments in Poetry, At the White Window,* and *Seasoning: A Poet's Year.*

ELIZABETH MARIE YOUNG is a translator, poet, and Ph.D. candidate in the Comparative Literature program at U.C. Berkeley, where she works on ancient Greek, Roman, and twentieth-century American poetry. She has published poems in *Aufgabe,* the *Poker,* and many other journals. She is currently in the midst of a dissertation that examines the impact of translation on the development of the Catullan corpus in late Republican Rome and the twentieth-century United States.

JENNIFER YOUNG is a Ph.D. candidate in creative and critical writing at Cardiff University. Her poetry has appeared in *Ore* and *Hypertext.* She has published book reviews in the *British Journal of Canadian Studies* and *BMa: The Sonia Sanchez Literary Review* and an essay in *BMa: The Sonia Sanchez Literary Review.*

ROBERT ZAMSKY is Visiting Assistant Professor in the English Department at DePaul University. His published and forthcoming work addresses the role of music in modern and contemporary American poetry. In 2004 he was a National Endowment for the Humanities Research Fellow in the Department of Music at Princeton University.

JIM ZEIGLER received a Ph.D. in English literature from the University of California, Irvine in 2004. He currently teaches courses in the history and politics of immigration for the Expository Writing Program at the University of Oklahoma.

About the Advisory Board

STEVEN GOULD AXELROD is Professor of English at the University of California, Riverside. He is the author of *Robert Lowell: Life and Art* (Princeton University Press, 1978) and *Sylvia Plath: The Wound and the Cure of Words* (Johns Hopkins University Press, 1990). He is co-editor (with Camille Roman and Thomas Travisano) of *The New Anthology of American Poetry, Volumes 1 and 2* (Rutgers University Press, 2003, 2005).

PAULA BENNETT is Professor of English, Emerita, at Southern Illinois University at Carbondale. She has published widely in the field of nineteenth-century American women's poetry. Her latest book is *Poets in the Public Sphere: The Emancipatory Project of American Women's Poetry, 1800–1900* (Princeton, 2004). With Karen L. Kilcup, she has edited *Options for Teaching Nineteenth-Century American Poetry* for the MLA Options series (forthcoming).

CHARLES BERNSTEIN is Regan Professor of English at the University of Pennsylvania. His books include *My Way: Speeches and Poems* and *With Strings*, from the University of Chicago Press

PATTIE COWELL is Professor of English and University Distinguished Teaching Scholar at Colorado State University. She has written extensively on colonial North American poets and is the author of *Women Poets in Pre-Revolutionary America* (1981) and co-editor of *Critical Essays on Anne Bradstreet* (1983).

HENRY LOUIS GATES, JR., is W.E.B. DuBois Professor of the Humanities at Harvard University. He is the author of numerous works of literary history and criticism, including most recently *African American Lives* (2004), edited with Evelyn Brooks Higginbotham. With K. Anthony Appiah, he is the editor of *Africana: The Encyclopedia of the African and African American Experience.*

DONALD G. MARSHALL is Fletcher Jones Chair of Great Books at Pepperdine University, Malibu. He has also taught at UCLA, the University of Iowa, and the University of Illinois at Chicago. He has published on Wordsworth and on literary theory, rhetoric, and their history.

MARJORIE PERLOFF is Sadie Dernham Patek Professor Emerita of Humanities at Stanford University and currently Scholar-in-Residence at the University of Southern California. She is the author of twelve books on poetry and poetics as well as the visual arts, including *The Poetics of Indeterminacy: Rimbaud to Cage*, *The Futurist Moment*, *Wittgenstein's Ladder*, and, most recently, a memoir titled *The Vienna Paradox* and *Differentials, Poetry, Poetics, Pedagogy*, which won the 2005 Warren-Brooks Prize for literary criticism. In 2006 she will be President of the Modern Language Association.

JOHN C. SHIELDS is Professor of American, African American, and Comparative Literatures at Illinois State University. He has published on these literary fields and is editor of *The Collected Works of Phillis Wheatley* (1988) and advisory editor of and contributor to *The Oxford Companion to African American Literature* (1997) and *The American National Biography* (1999). In 2001 he published *The American Aeneas: Classical Origins of the American Self*, which won *Choice*'s Outstanding Academic Book for 2002 and Honorable Mention for the Harry Levin Prize (2000–2003) sponsored by the American Comparative Literature Association.

LORENZO THOMAS, before his death in 2005, was Professor of English at University of Houston–Downtown. He authored several volumes of poetry and the critical study *Extraordinary Measures: Afrocentric Modernism and Twentieth-Century American Poetry* (2000), winner of a Choice Outstanding Academic Book award.

ROBERT VON HALLBERG is Helen A. Regenstein Professor in English and Comparative Literature at the University of Chicago. He is the author of *Poetry, Politics, Intellectuals*, which is part of volume 8 of the new *Cambridge History of American Literature* (1996).

CHERYL WALKER is Richard Armour Professor of Modern Languages at Scripps College. She is the author of several books about American women poets, including most recently *God and Elizabeth Bishop: Meditations on Religion and Poetry* (Palgrave Macmillan, 2005).